Praise for

The House That George Built

"A delightful, delovely homage to the composers and lyricists who 'tripled the world's supply of singable tunes.' With songs lodged 'in every hole and corner' of his memory, She ed, a fine critic and novelist, has found a topic in tune with his tastes."   —*The Philadelphia Inquirer*

"[A] big, appreciative history of the golden age of American popular music . . . It captures the spirit, the mood, the exuberance, the peak and the bittersweet decline of a great American art form."

—Cleveland *Plain Dealer*

"Sheed's writing voice, which I've been reading for years, has always struck me as some sort of lovely musical instrument, even as he addresses sobering personal or politically historic moments in this knowledgeable and accurate book about the true citizens of music, the creators of what has come to be known as the American Songbook. Sheed covers the turf as eloquently as anyone who has ever tried. He brings to the table a true love for the guys who wrote the songs. The book sings, and so will you."

—JONATHAN SCHWARTZ

who wrote it. At turns witty social history, aphoristic biography, and perfectly tuned analysis, this book echoes and revives all the joys of its subject."
—ADAM GOPNIK

"What you want from a book like this is an elegance to match its subject and intelligence that will bring fresh insights to the music and lyrics. *The House That George Built* offers all that in spades."
—*The Palm Beach Post*

THE HOUSE THAT GEORGE BUILT

The House That George Built

With a Little Help from Irving,
Cole, and a Crew of About Fifty

WILFRID SHEED

RANDOM HOUSE TRADE PAPERBACKS

NEW YORK

2008 Random House Trade Paperback Edition

Copyright © 2008 by Wilfrid Sheed

Published in the United States by Random House Trade Paperbacks,
an imprint of The Random House Publishing Group,
a division of Random House, Inc., New York.

RANDOM HOUSE TRADE PAPERBACKS and colophon are trademarks
of Random House, Inc.

Originally published in hardcover in the United States by Random House,
an imprint of The Random House Publishing Group,
a division of Random House, Inc., in 2007.

Portions of this work appeared in slightly different form
in *The Atlantic, GQ,* and *The New Yorker.*

All photographs courtesy of ASCAP except for piano (page 3), iStock.com;
Richard Whiting (page 179), courtesy of Margaret Whiting; Jimmy Van Heusen
(page 225) by George Brich, courtesy of Brook Babcock/Van Heusen Music;
and Arthur Schwartz (page 301), courtesy of Jonathan Schwartz.

LIBRARY OF CONGRESS CATALOGING-IN-PUBLICATION DATA

Sheed, Wilfrid.
The house that George built: with a little help from Irving, Cole,
and a crew of about fifty / Wilfrid Sheed.
p. cm.
Includes index.
ISBN: 978-0-8129-7018-0
1. Composers—United States.   2. Lyricists—United States.
3. Popular music—United States—History and criticism.   I. Title.
ML385.S582 2007   782.42164'0973—dc22   2006051030

Printed in the United States of America

www.atrandom.com

2 4 6 8 9 7 5 3 1

Book design by Dana Leigh Blanchette

To the memory of
Harry Warren

CONTENTS

Part Three
The Stage—Broadway Swings

Part Four
Hollywood—The Sugar Daddy

Part Five
Survival on Broadway—
The Curtain That Won't Stay Down

A NOTE ON SOURCES

What follows is a labor of love, not a work of scholarship, which means that I have been researching it for most of my life without knowing it—starting at the family piano, singing and memorizing Irving Berlin's ragtime spin-offs, and ending with the last phone conversation with the last fellow addict fifteen minutes ago.

Although I've read every single word I could get my hands on, I'll spare you the list of out-of-date books, articles, and quotations that this represents in favor of a short list of people I've talked to, and in some cases sung with. The proper medium for studying the American song is, after all, neither the lecture nor the library but the sing-along and the rap session, or as it used to be called, the bull session, with its overtones of the tall story and the overconfident assertion.

In this offbeat branch of learning, the best research comes from the best bulls, and I have talked to some of the finest, including a handful who actually wrote some of the songs, one of whom tends to lead to another. In the late half of the 1960s, for instance, I lucked into the same building as the great lyricist Yip Harburg, and became, as one must with Yip, his devoted friend and fan.

Yip was never content just to leave the building and go on about his business. He invariably lingered in the lobby or in the open elevator

doorway, pulling bits of paper out of his pockets, on which he'd jotted
some verses about the day's news, and reading them with glee, or else
telling me how his friend Harold Arlen was coping with his recent depressive breakdown. Mostly, though, he just liked to talk politics, so I was
grateful that his other great pal and partner, Burton Lane, was also happy
to talk about songs as long as I wanted, especially if the topic was Judy
Garland, whom he discovered, or the Gershwins, who discovered him.

And it was there I also met a (recovered) Harold Arlen, quoted herein,
and Arthur Schwartz, who told me how his partner Howard Dietz had
greeted some life crisis or other with the repeated phrase "What is life
but dancing in the dark?" "So," he said, "I dashed off the tune in twenty
minutes." And I thought of the unusual soliloquy in the middle of that
song ("What though love is old, what though song is old?" etc.) and I
asked if *that* only took twenty minutes, and Arthur conceded that it actually took three weeks. (Songwriters' estimates of these things seem
mostly designed to make a point. Irving Caesar's whole career couldn't
have taken more than about an hour and a half, to hear him tell of it.)

Other great-talking writers were the lyricist-librettists Betty Comden
and Adolph Green, whose work on *Singin' in the Rain* had made them
both scholars of early screen musicals, and the lyricist Ed Eliscu, who had
actually gone out there in the old days and lived the songwriting life.

The multiply gifted Stephen Sondheim told me over drinks what was
wrong with Ira Gershwin, while Jerry Lieber, the rock poet, told me,
over other drinks, what was good about him. And I agreed with both of
them.

Another great source of information and atmosphere were a handful of
songwriters' grown children, including Mary Ellin Barrett, whom I first
knew as the excellent book reviewer at *Cosmopolitan* and only later as Irving Berlin's daughter and the author of an invaluable book about him;
and Shana Alexander, the highly successful writer and daughter of Milton
"Happy Days Are Here Again" Ager, who had happy memories of her various "uncles," Jerry (Kern), Harold (Arlen), and Harry (Warren). Shana
also introduced me to her charming father, who told me that Ira Gershwin
was upset about something I'd written (funny how he kept coming up).
The singer Margaret Whiting didn't remember as much as I'd hoped

about her father, Richard, but more than made up for it with her picture of Johnny Mercer, who virtually adopted her after Richard's early death. And I also met Mary Rodgers, Ellen Donaldson, and Irving Berlin's two other daughters, Linda and Elizabeth, who proved if nothing else that songwriters went in for girl children, and charming ones too. Over and against this, Hoagy Carmichael Jr. was also charming, and helpful and co-operative. But Hoagy had written two rich memoirs himself, *The Stardust Road* and *Sometimes I Wonder,* and I didn't want to make the whole book about him. So—I still owe Hoagy Jr. a phone call.

Another son I met was Dorothy Fields's only one, David Lahm, who became a first-rate cocktail pianist and gave me my jolliest evening ever by playing every song I could think of at a friend's birthday party, thus providing me the only chance I've ever had to sing some of those old lyrics that we all memorized automatically back then. And Michael Feinstein, who had served as an archivist to both the Gershwins and Harry Warren before he himself became a star, provided some great evenings too, playing and chatting and incidentally helping me to imagine Warren as if he'd been a relative of mine. Uncle Harry, indeed. Michael can also stand in for the gallant army of cabaret artists who crisscross the land like religious missionaries on a great crusade. All the ones I've talked to have doubled as scholars of the great songs and enthusiasts for their cause, spectacularly so in the case of Mary Cleere Haran.

And finally there are my two talkers-in-chief, Jonathan Schwartz and Jim Lowe, a couple of professionals who both jockeyed the classic discs for years at the legendary radio station WNEW, and have continued ever since to serve the old-time religion of great American songs every way they know how. Jonathan has compared our very first conversation (about songs, of course) to the longest baseball game ever played, a record we've broken a couple of times since, and Jim, as a neighbor, has hosted some of the best bull sessions of the twenty-first century—with himself at the piano, needing only a jug of moonshine on top of it to round out the honky-tonk scene. (In fact, I can't swear I didn't see one.)

I like to think of the book that follows as my contribution to the great bull session in the sky. So feel free to scribble in the margin in agreement or raucous disagreement.

If this great session ever settles anything, it has failed. But there's no chance of that. New verdicts are never more than just a song away. And the next song is no further away than your memory.

I must have sung a couple of hundred songs to myself in writing this book, and I hope it's contagious. And to invoke the mighty Irving Berlin for a moment, if the resulting book, or any part of it, "starts you tapping your feet, I'm happy" beyond words.

I Could Write a Book
if They Asked Me

The line has been stolen so often that I might as well steal it again. "This book," as somebody once said, "was not finished, it was abandoned"—and abandoned not just once in this case, but several times.

My most serious prior assault on this subject was to be a collaboration with the late Alec Wilder, who had himself just written the greatest of all books ever on the American song. Still, Alec was entirely in favor of helping a friend write another one. Our original scheme was simplicity itself, simply to assemble Johnny Mercer, and build the whole thing around him, in a series of conversations with fellow songwriters that would tell the whole story, from Irving Berlin to Burt Bacharach, and from ragtime to R & B and wherever we were that year.

Our scheming turned out to be quite Byzantine, because to begin with, Berlin was no great friend of Mercer, who had probably slammed him with one boozy insult too many over the years, but he was a close phone pal of Harold Arlen, who was himself going through a reclusive phase just then, but might be smoked out by my own friend Yip Harburg. In short, Alec and I were having a high old time of it gossiping away while the clock ticked down and down and suddenly out.

"John is quite ill." I can still see Alec climbing onto our porch in the twilight to pass on this bleak bulletin. It seems that Mercer had suffered

a stroke while riding a London bus, and might conceivably never be quite the same. And then, after a period of holding our breath, the call came. "John died today." In Alec's world, only two men were called by their baptismal names, John, and Francis Sinatra, which gave his voice a positively religious inflection as it spoke these last words.

And with that, Alec's heart seemed to leave the room for good. Although, theoretically, there were still lots of ways to do our damn book, Alec was not a theorist but an artist, and his vision had gone to black on the whole subject. If John could die, so could he, and he had better start work on his own testament while there was still time. And a curious testament it would turn out to be, including some imaginary letters to Francis, his other first-name friend, and a quirky account of his own personality. My friend Alec was indeed an anomaly: a proud man with a low opinion of himself.

Which left me with just the bare notion of rounding up some writers and talking to them. Big deal! And I was almost relieved to learn that someone else had just done this anyway, wonderfully well, thus supplying the only other essential book that I'm aware of on this subject. In fact, Max Wilk's *They're Playing Our Song* makes the perfect complement to Wilder's masterpiece, *American Popular Song: The Great Innovators, 1900–1950*, because it takes all the follow-up questions, such as, Who were these guys, and what precisely did they think they were doing?

This is obviously indispensable material, and when I met Mr. Wilk sometime later, I warned him with, no doubt, grating jocularity that I planned to rob him blind someday in my own book, to which he answered wistfully that I might as well do that since everybody else had. But fortunately the American song proved big enough for both of us and I haven't needed to pick on Wilk that much, except for a few priceless references to Jerome Kern and some aperçus of Johnny Mercer's, and perhaps some other bits and pieces. In the one case of Jule Styne, I felt that Wilk had done such a splendid job that there was no point in doing another one.

But was there really any point in doing another book either? And if not, what do you do with yourself next when you're all dressed up and have nothing to write? In my case, what you do first is sleep on it. In Sammy Cahn's favorite phrase, the words and music can always wait. "First comes the phone call."

And to my surprise it came, out of the blue. It seems that once upon a time some Italians had visited our apartment in New York and had later reported their surprise to find that Americans seemed to have a quaint custom of singing after dinner each night. And now their guide and translator of that evening, an old pal and editor, Alice Mayhew, was calling to talk about a possible book I might like to do on the great American songs. And I said yes, of course. I'd gotten the phone call, hadn't I? That was the hard part. So now just write the book. It will come to you as you go along.

And so it did, for years and years and years. It was as if I'd asked the Pacific Ocean over for tea one afternoon and couldn't get rid of it, and what's more didn't want to. But wasn't I getting tired of songs by now? No, I felt fresh as a daisy. Wouldn't I like to write about something else for a change? No, it's all in here, everything I want to say. How about an honest-to-God, full-court memoir while there's still time?

It dawned on me that that was exactly what I had been doing. Songs had lodged themselves in every hole and corner of my memory, reminding me of where I'd been that summer and what it felt like in the salty air or the misty light, and also what Hitler was up to just then and how far the Allied Forces had advanced in North Africa—from Tobruk to Benghazi, "From Natchez to Mobile, from Memphis to St. Joe." It was like finding a suitcase full of old letters and forgotten headlines: "Silk Stockings Disappear from Market" . . . "Nylon Needed for Parachutes" . . . "Women Take to Painting Their Legs." But "I walk alone." So who cares? So tightly are the tunes and the news intertwined that they recall each other; for example, in 1941 the baseball star Hank Greenberg was drafted prematurely to prepare the public for a war that hadn't started yet, and soon enough the hit came out that I, then aged ten, diverted to suit the occasion. "Somebody else is taking my place" went the song; "Somebody else is playing first base," I added, and still add, every time I hear it. And in fact I even remember being driven crazy by it on a hot Philadelphia night, but enough memory is enough.

Songs are circumstantial in ways that headlines can never be. I can remember perfectly things like the tree I sat in as I sang my first Latin American number, "The Breeze and I" it was called, and I can still feel the pebbles underfoot as my sister and I took turns with "I've got spurs that jingle jangle jingle" on the banks of the Delaware River, and can almost

hear the piously empty streets of Wildwood, New Jersey, and hear myself muttering Porter's "Under stars chilled by the winter / Under an August moon . . ." (hey, that's a great line), and I realize that I wouldn't have remembered that tree or those pebbles and empty streets at all without the illumination of melody, which still turns on like a bedside reading lamp when I feel like remembering something.

The standards were not just about my private history, but about the whole country, concerning which they provide maybe the most trustworthy record we have. Americans are notoriously impatient with the past, and Hollywood epics used to be an international joke, so packed with anachronisms that at any moment you expected the ship's phone to ring and Columbus to say "What's buzzin', cuzzin" to his gorgeous sponsor, the queen of Spain. But then *sometimes* at the right moment, the band would strike up with a "Yankee Doodle Dandy" or "Battle Hymn of the Republic" and suddenly we were hearing the truth, as honestly as the arranger wanted to make it, but at least some kind of truth. And I still believe ardently in the "moonlight on the Wabash" and "Moonlight Bay," if not the moonshine in the scripts. In fact, if you combine a Mathew Brady photograph with, let us say, "Dixie," you are almost there, so long as you don't play it nostalgically. Once upon a time these songs were the latest thing, and that's what's so sad about them now. In this respect, the songwriter can be as crucial as the embedded photographer or reporter, and almost as precise in that, when you hear a George Gershwin tune, you are hearing not only the 1920s, exactly as they were, but the atmospheric difference between, let's say, 1924 ("Somebody Loves Me") and 1926 ("Someone to Watch over Me").

Somewhere along here, I bumped absentmindedly into my next question. "Who wrote 'Dixie,' anyway? And why don't I know?" There is surely no more atmospheric song than this one, but we've always been content to leave it there, up in the air. The whole South wrote it, that's who. But then, why do we know so much about the guy who wrote "My Old Kentucky Home" and "O, Susanna"? Probably the public didn't want to know about him either, at first. The minstrel shows that staged such songs were themselves the soul of anonymity, featuring both white actors and black ones disguised in identical blackface and singing the same allegedly black songs.

But Stephen Foster had found himself in a modern quandary that re-

quired a modern positively futuristic solution, which he only half came up with—or stumbled upon. As an upper-middle-class youth, he could hardly double as a blackface song-and-dance man. Not only was the stage the devil's playground, but there was no money in it by the Fosters' standards, and there wouldn't be so long as it stayed anonymous. So Foster's daddy became perhaps the first of many in here to say no to his son's ambitions and tell him that songwriting was a low-life waste of time. And Stephen became the first to prove his old man at least half-wrong, by making a truly huge amount of money for *someone,* if only his publishers, and a giddy, unprecedented reputation for himself out of selling his songs to the devil, and inadvertently selling his legend as well. How did a white boy from the Pittsburgh area know what it felt like to be an "old black Joe" on the plantation? The more his songs drifted loose from their minstrel ambience the more singular they seemed. The possibility that his darkies might have been just the usual stage darkies faded from mind.

Once the public has learned a new name, whether it be Stephen Foster or Sigmund Freud, we like to think of the subject as completely original, and not just as a working stiff punching a time clock. And incidentally, we also want him to have written everything, so we don't have to learn any other names.

But even the great Stephen Foster had to go through channels. Minstrel shows *were* popular music, the hot center or Motown of the horse-and-buggy era, and you either wrote for them or wrote more sedately for grown-ups and prayed that sheet-music sales would pick up.

You might almost say that Foster had to wear blackface himself to reach his maximum audience. And the role of his subject, the stage darkie, was simply to let it all hang out, to go to the furthest extreme of laughter and tears and especially of nostalgia, which goes so well with music. The audiences that laughed and cried in response were not predominantly black but white men who had brought their libidos along for an airing, before locking them up again in church the next day. And Foster's songs were so wholesome that you didn't have to confess them but could take them home to the family. His songs became so familiar to all audiences that his outline seemed to appear in them. There's a man in here! Tell me about him.

From that day to this, people have told and retold the short poignant

life story of Stephen Foster in the form of books and movies and, just the other night, a TV special. Not that there is anything intrinsically interesting about a talented man drinking himself to death, but we do love to hear those songs again as much as we like to hear Christmas carols again every year.

So now if I could just find a few more Fosters, I might also find the answer to a question I'd been keeping at bay, namely, what is that interesting about *any* kind of writer? Okay, maybe if they ran with the bulls or danced in the Plaza Hotel fountain, like Papa Hemingway or Scott Fitzgerald. But if they just sat at a piano or desk with a pencil? Luckily some magazine editors, knowing of my interest in the subject, helped me out by asking me to write some review essays about the likes of Cole Porter, George Gershwin, and Hoagy Carmichael—but why? Weren't these names ancient history by now? And why not ask a trained musician about them?

Never mind. You don't ask editors such questions; they ask you these questions, usually just before hanging up. So I shut up myself and wrote the pieces and got the most mail I'd had in years. And I deduced from this small success that if you named a few familiar songs, these would form a kind of background music that would heighten the interest in everything you put in front of them. So the editors had found my Stephen Fosters for me, but there weren't that many of them, as I found when I tried out some other names on them. In this game, it seems you are either an immortal or a nobody.

And for a while after Foster, it seemed as if the nobodies had won. The nineteenth century went on about its business, attracting more and more songs out of more and more songwriters, but no more superstars, which led me to the curious conclusion, later confirmed by the movies, that the entrepreneurs were happy to exploit your fame once you had some, but were not going to raise a finger until then. Because for them the ideal audience wants Bing Crosby to create his own tunes and Bob Hope his own jokes as if they'd just that moment thought of them. Which meant, and still does, that the best road to the stars is to become one yourself and perform your own music, like George M. Cohan, or pretend it's your own, like some musicians today.

But in those days, before talkies and really good records, international

entertainment was still pretty hit-or-miss, and Cohan's type of all-American songs did not come with a visa. (I'd never heard of them in England.) Foster's songs alone were contagious enough and so evocative of *something* in everybody to cross oceans and mountains, in the way that only music can, smuggled by absentminded whistlers and the kind of susceptible musicians who pick up everything lying around. As a small boy in England in the 1930s, I knew just two American songsmiths by name, Stephen Foster and Irving Berlin—who had apparently exploded some half century after Foster to write ten times as many hit songs and to live ten times as long, while creating and maintaining a more edifying kind of legend and becoming a kind of finger-snapping Benjamin Franklin for immigrants.

We surely wouldn't see anything like *that* again. And in fact we didn't quite. But we came close as, in fairly quick succession, America actually would hatch out two more names that everyone who was interested in anything had heard of at least vaguely, Berlin's occasional disciple, George Gershwin, and his most surprising one, Cole Porter, who proved that rich kids could make it too in this fabulous country; and also with a slight stretch of the rules, two more, the illustrious Jerome Kern, who'd been around a while but would assume a new kind of fame in Berlin's wake, and Irving's last rival, Richard Rodgers, although Rodgers would come in two parts, Rodgers and Hart and Rodgers and Hammerstein, one of whom you probably like much better than the other, but both of whom qualify in terms of quantity.

Which doesn't mean it had suddenly become easier. Looking more closely at the entrance requirements for this musical Mount Rushmore: Besides the quaint condition that each of them must have checked in on the public bulletin board by the end of the 1920s, with Cole Porter just making it and Berlin overlapping comfortably at both ends, there was also the nearly impossible criterion that each of them, except maybe Kern (who wrote some great, but quiet, theater songs too), had published more than fifty standards, by which I mean in this case more than fifty tunes that are still popular enough over fifty years later for most cocktail lounge pianists to have a rough idea of them, and for their copyrights still to be worth fighting for.

This is an astonishing achievement that would more than double or triple the world's total supply of singable tunes. Yet even more astonishingly,

most Americans seem barely to have noticed it then or since. Although collectively it constitutes far and away our greatest contribution to the world's art supply in the so-called American Century, what the hell, they're still only songs, and this I'll admit is a limitation, because, apart from anything else, they're always over so quickly. During the time it takes to watch just one full-length stage play, you can have sung your way through the whole lifework of at least one major songwriter, and two for a Eugene O'Neill play. Elsewhere, these songs have been referred to as America's classical music, but if so, they are like a literature consisting entirely of epigrams and haiku, or at most sonnets.

So you're going to be hungry again in half an hour. And that's the limitation. Yet listening by chance to Vernon Duke's "Autumn in New York" last night, I thought, what would it *do* with more space? Oscar Wilde's one-liners are better than his plays. And what's wrong with being hungry again?

The more pressing question for the writers was, How did anyone get a chance to publish that much, and what did he live on while he was doing so? Clearly there must have been a happy moment when Murphy's Law was suspended and replaced by McGonnigle's Exception, whereby everything that can go *right* does so, beginning this time with the favoring winds and timetables that brought families called Baline and Gershowitz all the way from Russia to Ellis Island, as if in answer to some great casting call.

And then there was America's part in the Great War in 1917–18, a well-disguised blessing, which came along at just the right moment to pull the nation together and introduce us to each other, and for a giddy moment to the outside world as well.

"How you gonna keep them down on the farm after they've seen Paree," Americans sang nostalgically when they had to come home again. The farm was probably a lost cause by then anyhow, but maybe we could at least keep them in New York and make it a bit more like Paree, if only by filling it with foreigners and Midwesterners. Every great artistic movement needs a great city, and New York was more than ready, with both of its relevant thoroughfares, Tin Pan Alley and Broadway, already up and blazing, with kids like Jacob Gershowitz, aka George Gershwin, plugging songs, to kids like Frederick Austerlitz, aka Fred Astaire, of Nebraska, on

the Alley. And with over five hundred theaters on the Great White Way providing all the publishing opportunities a genius could ask for, plus enough newspapers to hammer his name into the public consciousness, so that even if people didn't read the names on the sheet music, they read them in the gossip columns. And there was no better way to plug your latest hit than by showing up at the Algonquin (bringing along some funny lines by your press agent as well). Meanwhile sheet music for your latest darling might sometimes run to the same kinds of numbers as the hottest CD today, and theater, in the form of touring companies and sundry vaudeville spin-offs, circled the United States ceaselessly, distributing New York produce in bushel baskets, and naming the writers too, which counts at least a little on sheet music and a lot on playbills, but was about to count much less, as pop culture turned the next corner into the new technologies, which would be truly mixed blessings, making the writers richer than Croesus and more anonymous than the Unknown Soldier.

On the plus side, three of the hottest new developments, to wit, radio, microphoned records, and talking pictures, all addressed themselves squarely to the public's ears, and needed all the new music they could get their hands on just to strut their stuff. What they didn't need was the authors' names, unless, as noted, those names had already become famous. The phrase "Irving Berlin's latest" might actually sell a few tickets or records—not like "Bing Crosby's latest," but it was perhaps worth mentioning, while "Joe Schmo's latest" definitely wasn't. To take a sublime example among many, RKO bought Cole Porter's show *The Gay Divorce* largely on the strength of his name, then threw out all but one of his songs, the big hit "Night and Day," and actually went on to win the first songwriting Oscar with one of its own called "The Continental" by Con Conrad and Herb Magidson, whose names remain unknown even to trivia buffs who know what street Cole Porter was born on.

With the arrival of talking pictures, movie stars had quickly become, without much struggle, the only fixed celebrities in the American sky, sharing their space on a strictly temporary basis with such shooting stars as presidents, champion athletes, and the various Joey Buttafuocos of their day. Fortunately, complete cultural change never happens quite that fast, even today, and people with even the faintest interest continue to learn a few names, such as Harold Arlen, who had sort of "made it" in

New York and hence theoretically made it everywhere; and Frank Loesser, also of New York, and a few more who had had the wisdom or luck to appear on-screen themselves, such as Hoagy Carmichael, or to sing songs on radio and records, like Johnny Mercer. Duke Ellington played movie bits as a bandleader to help register his name on the national blackboard as something or other, so that his songs could move on to the next stage of recognition. In those days, the paleo-disc-jockeys just played songs without attribution until they came to one by a celebrity; then it became George Gershwin's "Soon" or Irving Berlin's "Always" or Duke Ellington's "I'm Beginning to See the Light."

What the mass media took away, or harshly rationed, in terms of fame, the songwriters of the period more than made up for in opportunity and money (thanks to their amazing union, ASCAP). Movies positively ate up new songs, not just in its deluxe Gold Diggers and Broadway Melody series but in odd items of the "Shirley Temple Goes to College" genre and nonmusicals like *Casablanca,* which needed *something* for Sam to play again, or like *Laura,* which just needed background music but wound up with a great title song as well.

Radio ate songs too, usually as provided by various big bands broadcasting from hotel ballrooms around the country, and by such shows as Bing Crosby's *Kraft Music Hall* and even by George Gershwin's own radio show, and Hoagy Carmichael's too, and who knows who else's radio shows. I can still remember a fifteen-minute slot that Dinah Shore had in the 1940s that seemed to feature a brand-new bad song every single day.

Thus, from the birth of radio circa 1922 until its death by TV and reruns in the mid-1940s, there was almost enough work for all the talent in a ballooning country, and all bets were off concerning the incidence of genius. "Who wrote that, George Gershwin or Cole Porter?" the crowd asks the piano player. But even if he's played an immortal song, the odds are that it won't be by either of them. Along with the great writers who get chapters to themselves in this book, I've dashed off a list of some fifty who have published at least two standards (see the Appendix), and I expect to hear of fifty more that I've overlooked. As with Elizabethan England and Periclean Athens, if someone will provide the stage and the cash, the genius will take care of itself.

There's musical genius and then there's verbal genius. To match the

explosion in melody came a river of light verse that turned up everywhere, from the largest magazines to the smallest local papers, and it seeped into the most minor songs, guaranteeing some wonderfully literate and accomplished lyrics.

But—and here some readers and I may split—the tunes were still the big news. "Didn't they write great lyrics back then?" is a common question I've heard, to which I have two *Yes, but* . . . answers, one being *Yes, but* it's my impression that they still do. From Broadway to the Grand Ole Opry to the *Prairie Home Companion,* you still find good lyrics, and you will keep on finding them. So long as there are ears to hear, there will be tongues to wag and wit to flail.

But how long has it been since you heard a really good *new* tune—one, that is, that made your hair stand up? Compared with the dictionary, the keyboard is tiny, and a new tune is like a Sudoku puzzle that must be not only original but somehow comely. This rare achievement, however, seemed quite commonplace in the "Stardust" years.

My second answer is *Yes,* they wrote some great lyrics, *but* they also wrote some lousy ones. The standards didn't care. There have seldom been dumber words to anything than those of the young Ira Gershwin's "Lady Be Good" and "The Man I Love," while the Ellington-Strayhorn gem "Take the 'A' Train" barely *has* a lyric, only an address you wish would change from time to time.

On the other hand, there has never been a standard without a great tune—not even a great *funny* standard. Surf the Cole Porter songbook and you will undoubtedly find some great comic poems still waiting for the right tune to drive them off and make them rich and famous. But although Cole could have dashed off another two hundred choruses of "You're the Top," he couldn't have written a second tune to save his life. And without those magic tunes, his light verse was as unsalable as most poetry.

This doesn't mean the right lyric can't make all the difference. A lyricist is a musician too, one who arranges tunes for the human voice so that you can "hear" them for the first time. But once the lyrics have done that, and made you laugh or cry two or three times at most, they fade in importance. Again and again, people will request a favorite song while knowing only its tune.

To resort to a few more inches of memoir, at age eleven or so I liked the movie title song "It Could Happen to You" so much that I went right out and bought the sheet music just to have around, though I couldn't play a note of it. A few years later, I traipsed all over New York looking for a record, any record, of "There's a Small Hotel." Both songs have first-class lyrics, but I wouldn't have crossed the street just for those words. After all, I'd heard them once, hadn't I? And between songs, I'd swear I'd located the gold standard for words, though it was in a realm outside of music. Without making no-win comparisons, I felt that the poems of Keats and Byron, like the songs of Van Heusen and Rodgers, were a call to *do* something, if it was only to get out of my chair and maybe give a small whoop of delight. The world was a slightly better place now, and there was more where that came from.

Thus the tunes became for me and others of my age an entry-level art form. And with so many standards still pouring out, or being re-recorded, we became gluttons for melody and, within our limits, connoisseurs of it. When I read Alec Wilder's great book, I nearly always agreed with him, or at least I got to know in particular what he would *not* like, and why. So if I still didn't make it as an expert, I did have the makings of a snob.

Anyway, this book is no technical study. A life of Keats or Robert Frost doesn't depend on metrics. This is also a book about a time and place, America 1900–1950, in between the horse and buggy and the jet plane, and the men who wrote music that would still sound good on "Jupiter and Mars," and wherever we decide to fly to next.

Part One

The Piano Era

The Road to Berlin

*T*here are several ways of defining and measuring an era, but an excellent place to start is by checking out the media of the day and what they could or could not do at the moment. For example, when sound recording first came along, the singers belted into it as if performing to an empty stadium. The name that springs to mind is Caruso, the world's biggest voice. But with the coming of microphones in the 1920s, singing became more personal, and the name became Bing Crosby, the world's friendliest voice. So songs became brisker and less operatic, to suit not only the mike but the piano rack and the record cabinet. In short, the familiar thirty-two-bar

song, which now seems to have been fixed in the stars, was actually fixed by the practicalities of sheet-music publishing and confirmed by the limitations of ten-inch records.

Or one might define an era in terms of women's fashions and the consequent rise of impulse dancing on improvised dance floors. You can't really jitterbug in a hoopskirt or bustle. Swing follows costume, and the big news was that by the 1910s skirts had become just loose enough and short enough to liberate the wearer from the tyranny of twirling through eternal waltzes in ballrooms as big as basketball courts, and freed her to do fox-trots and anything else that could be done in short, quick steps on, if necessary, living room floors with rugs rolled up. So that's what the boys wrote for next. By the 1920s, the whole lower leg could swing out in Charlestons and other abandoned exercises. Songwriters celebrated that with a decade of fast-rhythm numbers. This has always been a dancing country, and never more so than in the Depression, when people trucked their blues away in marathons, or in seedy dance halls. "Ten Cents a Dance" was better than no income at all. And the Lindy Hop was as good as a gym class too.

And so on, through the arrival of women's slacks in the late 1930s and their increased popularity in World War II for both work and play—Rosie the Riveter could jitterbug on her lunch break without leaving the floor. All she needed was a beat. Which brings us with a final bump and a grinding halt to rock and roll and the totally free-form dancing of today, which can be done with no clothes at all to a beat in your own head while you're watching something else on television.

The huge, nonnegotiable gap between then and now is that in the past, music and dancing had always been disciplined by *something* or other. There had always been rules for doing it right, and even the wildest flights of swing and swing dancing had rested on a bed of piano lessons and dance lessons, and dress codes as well. Cab Calloway in a zoot suit was still a dressy man, a dandy; Cab Calloway in jeans or shorts over his knees would not have been dressed at all in the old sense. Going out dancing used to be an event, like going to church. Today all that remains are the rituals of prom night, which must seem weirder every year.

The era might also be measured in demographics or political cycles or even weather patterns. But the brilliant strand of music that, running

through Irving Berlin and George Gershwin, has become *the* music of the standards began with a bang—with pianos being hoisted into tenements, a magnificent and noisy event, and it ended with guitars being schlepped quietly, almost parenthetically, into ranch houses and split-levels to herald the arrival of the great non-event that has been with us ever since.

But first the bang, then the whimper. There was no way of receiving such an impressive object as a piano quietly in such close quarters. Whether it bounced up the staircase or jangled its way over the fire escape and in through the window, the neighbors knew about it all right, and would be reminded again every time Junior hit the keys and shook the building. Short of a Rolls-Royce or carriage and horses, there was never such a status symbol, with the consequence that although "all the families around us were poor," said Harry Ruby, "they all had pianos." For such important matters, time-payments were born.

So the parents went into hock and found room for the damn thing someplace, and artistic Darwinism did the rest. You buy a piano for Ira Gershwin, and George is the one who plays it, although sometimes you had to live through a week of hell to learn this. As anyone knows who has ever housed a child and a piano, every tot who walks through the door will bang the bejesus out of the new toy for a few minutes, get bored, and come back, and back again, and bang some more, but then successively less and less until the dust starts to move in and claim it. . . . Unless the child finds something interesting in the magic box, a familiar tune that stammers to life under his fingers, or a promising and unfamiliar one; a chord that sounds good, and rolls out into a respectable arpeggio as well, with, saints be praised, a bass line that actually works for a bar or two—after which a gifted kid with an instrument is like a teenager with his first car and a tank full of gas. Where to, James: Charleston, Chattanooga, or Kalamazoo? Two-steps, or concertos, or parts unknown?

"Well, he'll probably settle down eventually," hoped the parents who had only bought the thing for the sake of respectability and maybe for some civilized graces around here. It speaks wonders for those parents in that era that they knew that being a famous lawyer or doctor wasn't enough in life. If you weren't a person of cultivation, you were still a bum.

But some of the kids insisted on being bums anyway, and sometimes

the piano only made them worse. There were low-life uses for the instrument as well as high, and all the classical music lessons the parents could shout for weren't always enough to keep Junior out of the gutter, especially once ragtime had come along, in Frank Loesser's phrase, "to fill the gutters in gold." Talk about subversive—not even Elvis Presley rolling his hips had as many parents and preachers up and howling and sending for the exorcism unit as ragtime did. After all, not too many kids have hips like Elvis's, but anyone who could play "Chopsticks" or whistle "The Star-Spangled Banner" could syncopate, and in no time, as Irving Berlin bragged in two of his hits, "Everybody's doing it" in one form or another, from "Italian opera singers" learning to snap their fingers, to "dukes and lords and Russian czars," who settled for throwing their shoulders in the air and no doubt rolling their eyes. And there was no place to hide from it, even in an ivory tower. In fact, it would become a staple of B-movie musicals to show a professor at first frowning mightily as he hears the kids jazzing up a well-known classic, only to furtively wind up, beneath the gown or the desk, tapping his own foot too, as if the body snatchers had seized that much of him. And if the "professoriate" and the "long hairiate" couldn't stand up to it, the kid at the keyboard wasn't even going to try. Because this is where ragtime belonged, its birthplace, its office and its home, and the great Scott Joplin was still making tunes out of it, which maybe they could use in place of Czerny's finger exercises while no one was listening.

"What's that you're playing? That's not what you're supposed to be playing." Someone was always listening, and one imagines a thousand fights a day over this as George or Harold or Fats would stray once more from his scales and his Bach-made-easy and start to vamp the music of his pulse, the music of the streets.

Well, just because everybody was doing it didn't make it right. But remember: There was no other living music around except the music of the streets; there were no radios or records, or even talking pictures. Unless your parents took you to the theater, like Jerome Kern's, or to concerts, like no one I can think of, "good" music only existed in the form of hieroglyphs on a page, which meant that in effect it was a dead language, and a growing child could not survive on dead languages alone. So they listened instead to the sounds that seeped out of the vaudeville house rear

windows and under the doors of taverns, and to the riffs of the barrel or-gans and ice cream trucks playing "Nola" and "The Whistler and His Dog," and from the upstairs windows of the tenements themselves, where seditious neighbors had actually acquired the latest sheet music and couldn't wait to bang it out on their new pianos, for the rest of the com-munity to swing to and curse.

But perhaps the most effective medium for spreading the new music around were the average absentminded whistlers and hummers whose names were legion in those days, and still semi-legion when I was grow-ing up in the 1940s and '50s. In fact, I have a vague feeling I was one my-self. Anyway, you had little choice about it. If you knew the music, you whistled it, as if all the backed-up melody in your head was forcing its way out through your mouth like steam from a kettle. And this medium was no respecter of class or location either. As late as the 1950s, you could still hear respectable bankers and businessmen in stark colors and homburg hats whistling their way to work like newsboys or Walt Disney's dwarves. The very last time I heard a recognizable tune being whistled all the way through, it turned out to be coming from a natty distinguished senior in the next booth of a men's room who was whistling while he whatever. By that point in time, this man's whistling had become the only sound in a quiet building, like a trumpet blowing "Taps" over an empty battlefield, but imagine how that whistle sounded for the first time, back in the days when the natty old man was still a scruffy old boy adding his two cents' worth to the noise of the whistling businessmen and the cheerful whine of the calliopes and the soughs of violins being scraped on street corners.

And then imagine how it all sounded to that other small boy trying to get serious at the piano, but tempted like sin by the sounds of freedom outside, all of which, from the barrel organ to the guy on the corner trying to make a buck from his fiddle or harmonica, was at that moment synco-pated. And it all went into Junior's ears and hands and came out again, jumbled perhaps with Mr. Mozart's music or whoever was on the rack that day for him to torture, and maybe with some verbal help from the wise guy next door, the result might be a song that someday might sell like hotcakes and cross the ocean too, until the whole world was playing and whistling it and some of the bums whose parents had despaired of them became

very rich indeed, and the parents frowned and learned to tap their feet too, and moved uptown, where, thanks to their one very shrewd investment in a musical black box, they'd never have to work again. The piano lessons might have been wasted, but the hooky lessons were pure gold.

Or were the piano lessons really wasted? One of the proudest claims made for the American standards is that they were good music written by real musicians, however they got there, whether by studying at the best schools, like Kern and Rodgers, or by just listening, like Irving Berlin. Berlin never did learn the piano, but could spot a wrong note on the next block.

The school of "just listening" received an endorsement from the arrival of jazz in those years. The best jazz musicians created intricate harmonies without benefit of pencil or paper—disciplines that could take years to master at school. Classical lessons were still useful because they taught good from bad and what was good about good.

But playing hooky was vital—not just at the piano, playing Chopin and Brahms in ragtime, but playing hooky *from* the piano, just walking around and listening to the music of the city itself, which was experiencing a creative transformation right under these players' ears.

The same wave of good luck that had brought so many eastern European Jews to New York had also brought enough Southern blacks to mount a Harlem renaissance, and just like that, two of the principal ingredients had arrived. The standards have actually been referred to as a Jewish response to black music, but this definition is a loaded compliment that neither party has rushed to claim. With such praise, Jews never know whether to take a bow or duck. In a safe house like this book, it is the highest compliment I can think of. But in the mouth of a WASP supremacist like Henry Ford, "Jewish" meant un-American and subversive, so don't wave that compliment around or it might explode; and for blacks it just meant more of the minstrel-show syndrome. There go those darkies, making music again, haven't they got a great sense of rhythm? As outsiders, both Jews and blacks had been positively expected to entertain, but when they did so, it automatically became a second-class thing to do. Show biz in general was the ultimate club that accepted Groucho Marx and invited his scorn.

Music is not produced by whole groups, but by one genius at a time,

and it may be significant that the two families that gave us Irving Berlin and George Gershwin both fled Russia on the same great wave of czarist pogroms, only to find American black people not only singing about a similar experience, but using the Hebrew Bible as their text.

Blacks too had been to heaven and back. They had found the promised land in the form of emancipation, and for a few giddy years the taste of freedom had been all the milk and honey they needed. But when they (and the white man) woke up, they realized nothing much had changed. The slaves had been moved to another part of the ledger. They would still be working for the boss, the pharaoh, but they would have to look for their own food and lodging now and pay for it out of their still-empty pockets. And somehow the boss seemed to have multiplied to include any white man who wanted a shoe shine or simply a glass of water. Just say the word "boy" to any African American, even today, and he'll remember.

Slavery had at least been a great cause that had bound them like brothers. "Let my people go," they had sung; but now they were only a people on special occasions, such as when sociologists wanted to talk about them. Otherwise, they were on their own and had to cut their own deals with the All-Mighty as well as with the Man (and the woman). So they invented the blues, which could reasonably be called spirituals with a hangover, secular spirituals to match the shabbiness and sour taste of Reconstruction. Resisting slavery had been a noble cause worthy of noble songs, but what could you sing about sharecropping except that your feet hurt and the roof leaked and your woman had just left for a cat with more bread, or your man had split for a fox with a fancy wig and a lying heart?

But was that always so bad? "I'll be glad when you're gone, you rascal you." From the first, there was as much irony as heartbreak in the blues, and by the time you got to Bessie Smith, these were funny songs. And the famous song "Basin Street Blues" is actually about losing the blues and celebrating with a blues beat.

In other words, black music was losing its specific folk content and meeting the white man halfway—or getting taken over, if you prefer. (In a lawsuit over cultural rights, the Jews could always demand their Bible back.) The five-minute promised land of emancipation would be stretched indefinitely into the fixed smile of Dixieland, which became Tin Pan Alley's image of everybody's Great Good Place where you arrived by

choo-choo train, not cattle car, and the magnolias blossomed 'round *everybody's* door. The signature entertainer of the Dixieland years was a Jew wearing blackface, and there was no insult involved. It was one showman imitating another, and I've always wondered about the true color of Al Jolson's Mammy. By the time Bing Crosby began imitating Jolson, the blackface was understood and no longer had to be painted on—on Bing, or later on Elvis.

One striking bond between Berlin and Gershwin was their over-the-top love of their new country. "God Bless America," wrote Irving, with all his heart. And George, who thrived between the wars when patriotism was quieter, nevertheless said, "My place is America and my time is now" because it was clearly important to him, a statement of intent. Other new Americans, such as Italians and Irish, still sang the old songs, or new songs (like "Galway Bay") that pretended to be old songs.

But after enough pogroms, you haven't all that much to sing about. It's time to start over, as insiders this time, and in the first country that has ever asked you in. It has been suggested to me by someone who listened closely that Gershwin actually sounds more Russian than Jewish. But George wasn't familiar with either genre from his nonmusical household. He was only trying to write American as it sounded to a new arrival in a city of foreigners.

The result was American music through a distorting lens like El Greco's. To get there, George had rounded out his classical lessons by vamping regular American pop on Tin Pan Alley and finally by going to Harlem and hearing some real American music from such great jazz pianists as James P. Johnson and Willie "the Lion" Smith, whom he would later invite back to his apartment for informal concerts—a gutsy thing to do back then. But he owed them that much.

Gershwin was the last link in the chain that led to the standards, which were almost all written from 1925 to 1950. But to get to George you have to pass through Irving, who walked the streets first and founded the unofficial New York School of Song, which would eventually stretch to California without losing its accent, and would pretty much commandeer the word "standards" for its own.

And if this school had a motto and a golden rule, Duke Ellington

phrased it early on: "It don't mean a thing if it ain't got that swing." All the standards harkened back to the kid kibitzing at the piano, although all those pianos were not delivered to the Lower East Side, whose reputation in fact rests largely on the one that was *not* delivered to Irving Berlin himself. And several fine standard writers, such as Victor Young and Matty Malneck, actually began swinging on violins.

But the piano remained the instrument of choice and favored home companion. Incredibly, syncopation remained the preferred means of rebellion and escape right through the Depression, which prolonged the Jazz Age by the sheer force of house-to-house inertia. People wanted at least one chance to live like Fred Astaire before they switched to something new. And then World War II gave swing, its latest name, a couple more great years, because you can't change music in midstream. After which, nostalgia held back at least some of the tide until the great writers had time to empty their trunks, leaving us the incredible body of work called the standards.

It is perhaps worth adding that even at their peak the standards never quite had the national stage to themselves. Jule Styne told Max Wilk of hearing a whole different Hit Parade as he drove west in the Golden Age, but even in New York some great Broadway songs, like "My Funny Valentine," didn't make the Hit Parade at the time, while other nondescripts, like "Three Little Fishes" and "Deep in the Heart of Texas," did.

Time, and records, and great musicians have all been kind to the standards, which live on in cabarets as sheer entertainment. Because they still have "that thing." The English critic Benny Green deplores the phrase "jazz song" on the grounds that jazz is a process, something you do *to* music, not the music itself.

True enough. But some songs are friendlier to jazz than others—as witnessed by two songs by Victor Herbert: "Ah, Sweet Mystery of Life," which just sounds silly if syncopated, and "Indian Summer," which Jimmy Dorsey and his band could swing into a national success.

Is there a word for this kind of innate swingability? The pianist Dick Hyman refers to a "built-in syncopation," which even he couldn't locate, but which even you and I can't miss. Louis Armstrong famously said of jazz, "If you have to ask what it is, you'll never know." So much for defini-

tions. "Jazz song" is just a quick way of saying what can't be said anyway, and I've used it loosely throughout, wincing slightly on behalf of Mr. Green every single time.

To sum all this up in one sentence or so: Jazz songs were the pop music of the Jazz Age, and talented kids wrote them as naturally and spontaneously as they would later write rock songs. And when the songs lost "that thing"—or acquired a different thing—the era ended. The old piano left the building, taking its music with it.

Irving Berlin:
The Little Pianist Who Couldn't

IRVING BERLIN

*I*f one picture is worth a thousand words, what price a great bar of music? Or a pointed facial expression?

Fortunately, the cost of such items is not fixed. And while some pictures actually are priceless, some expressions truly are blank. Perhaps the most talkative picture I've ever come across is a small snapshot of a child that I had the good luck to glimpse one day—without a caption. Who *was* this? I had just time to ask myself, but the answer was already waiting. This picture of a young Irving Berlin was not just *worth* a thousand words, but it

told you exactly what they were, to wit: Genius. Music. Russia, or one of those places. (Hungary? That was the other place.) Violin? Probably, because that's what they played around there, although a piano is possible. And, of course, his music would be classical. Just look at all that hair.

Well, that's one facet that has changed. Long-haired music is not what it used to be. But this kid is no mop-top either. That extra hair is there expressly to run one's fingers through while thinking about classical music.

But suppose, for the sake of argument, that this kid never heard any classical music and isn't about to. . . . What might become of him then? Mathematics? Perhaps, but only if it is set to music. To save him from that, one more question. What kind of music *does* this little boy hear? It turns out that he hears some synagogue chanting from his father, who is a cantor, but Papa dies when little Isidore Baline is just eight, and after that he hears nothing but street junk. Is there hope?

Since this is New York, that musical junk was at least the junk of all nations, and all corners of this one: Manhattan folk music contained a bit of everything, and all of it came with words. So could he combine this with Jewish music?

The one thing that Izzy Baline knew about music was that he'd better start making money out of it at once or move on to something else. Immigrant life was hard enough even while the breadwinner was still winning. With their father dead, the eight Balines were so broke, even by Lower East Side standards, that they couldn't even afford a piano. Indeed, they couldn't even afford Isidore, who could barely squeeze himself in at night and out again in the morning with that head of his so full of music and money—a combination that would never leave him, no matter how much it might later hurt his reputation. The critics could consider him a hack, but talk is cheap, and a "cheque" (as we say in England) is worth more than a compliment any day—it costs more and is more sincere. For Irving, honor would begin with paying his own way in life, and he never committed the basic dishonesty of claiming to write for art. He told his friend Cole Porter, "Never apologize for a song that sells a million copies." Like other children who have had to work to survive, part of his young mind became a little old man, who saw nothing at all funny about money.

So he hit the streets and began, of course, to run errands and sell newspapers—was there any famous American who didn't hawk papers

back then? And he would also sing songs to anyone who would hold still for him, either in friendly cafés or on street corners while his audience waited for the cars and horses to go by. Raised on street music, he was now returning the favor, busking for a while with an old minstrel memorably called Blind Sol, who also played the city by ear and who perhaps afforded Izzy some protection in saloons, where it was probably bad luck to throw out blind people. After that, Izzy acquired his master's degree in the school of hard knocks and sweet music by working for Harry Von Tilzer, the legendary writing publisher. Plugging Harry's latest in theater balconies, Irving learned the arts of self-promotion and rights of use.

Thus, before he had written any songs at all, he knew everything about how to sell them. Soon he was old enough to work the city's fancier joints, and street-smart enough to know which ones they were. His next port of call was as a singing waiter at a fashionable Chinese place called, jarringly, Nigger Mike's, where he did what the job said, he sang and he waited, though not for long. Pretty soon the perfect fish swam into view: one Prince Louis of Battenburg, who would soon become a Mountbatten when the German image turned ugly in 1914. He gave Izzy an uninflated five-dollar tip for his combined services. This in turn gave Baline a heaven-sent chance to turn it down on the grounds that serving such a noble fellow was its own reward. Nearby, an ambitious young reporter called Herbert Bayard Swope took it all down, giving both himself and Irving a leg up with a piece in the next day's paper describing the episode—thus a new generation of hustlers was born.

All Irving needed now was some published songs of his own, preferably both words and music, because as a lyricist he would only have been a minor legend at best. Although it was obviously quite a feat for an unschooled immigrant kid to write good lyrics in what amounted to a second language, it happened so often you have to notice certain advantages as well. The syntax and vocabulary of pop songs were pretty close to those of the streets anyway, but were so far from the kind taught or even allowed in the classroom that maybe the less classroom the better. And as for Izzy's understanding of American life, he wouldn't need much of it to write his first hit lyric (the title of which is "My Wife's Gone to the Country, Hurrah, Hurrah"). Most lyrics are simply verbal clichés about emotional clichés, so once again maybe the less you know the better. And it is not

surprising that several of the wittiest lyricists, such as Gus Kahn (Germany), Al Dubin (Switzerland), and Lew Brown (Odessa), were all born into foreign-speaking families in foreign-speaking lands. And purely as lyricists, each of them was, I believe, as good or even better than Irving.

As for the other point of the story, that he'd been discovered as a singing waiter in a Chinese saloon—where better? There was no "normal" way to bring on these epiphanies, but Nigger Mike's was at least close to the heart of the Lower East Side school of music. The real miracle would have been to start in a place like Peru, Indiana, like Cole Porter, or be sent to Poland on a violin scholarship at age ten like Victor "I Don't Stand a Ghost of a Chance with You" Young. And while a name like Nigger Mike's might cause a sharp intake of breath now, Irving Berlin's own song "Cohen Owes Me Ninety-Seven Dollars" would be *breathtakingly* anti-Semitic coming from someone else. (The singer is dying, but he doesn't want to let his debtors off the hook that easily.) But Irving was just proving himself a good sport, the highest accolade an immigrant could hope for. New York in the early twentieth century was not so much a melting pot as a chafing dish, and if Irving could seem abrasive in later years, it's worth remembering that he was rubbed raw himself at an impressionable age.

Berlin's first commercial hit set to his own music was called "Dorando" and was written in crass Italian dialect that consisted mostly of adding an A to everything, as in "the sonna of a gunna no runna." The news item that had inspired it concerned a quite gallant marathon runner who had recently collapsed while entering the Olympic stadium and been carried across the finish line by his fans. But in Irving's version, a sniveling Dorando comes up with a ridiculous excuse for this: He has been tricked into eating Irish stew instead of "da spaghetts." ("And dats why he no winna.") The tune is second-drawer Berlin, which is to say facile and professional and lacking any trace of genius until you put them all together. Soon he would be able to produce such songs on demand and in his sleep, which made it a useful second drawer to have.

By 1911, Irving earned his MBA in music by acquiring a publisher-cum-partner to facilitate the flow, and with that he exploded onto a new level. The triggering device was "Alexander's Ragtime Band," a song that he himself didn't appreciate immediately, but which caught on so thoroughly wherever it was played that it seemed like a standard before its

time. It is called a rag because the title says it is, but it is in fact a hybrid with a syncopated verse and a marching chorus. With that in the bank, he then set out to write some regular rags. Suddenly, one hit seemed to run into another, just as they did on Henry Ford's assembly line. In his erudite book on Berlin's first songs, Charles Hamm shows how thoroughly the young man had absorbed all the pop formulas. It was like someone learning to dance with a booklet in his hand telling him where to put his feet. But this is where the miracle kicks in, for the novice suddenly begins to dance like Fred Astaire. And if everyone else has the same instructions, why is he the only one doing it? What has he added to the lesson?

Irving never really found out, but he kept on making music, better and better, while apparently becoming more and more convinced that, like some fairy-tale character with a magical gift, he might lose the knack if he asked too many questions. In this, he was fortified by his superbly well-trained contemporary Victor Herbert, who also advised him not to learn any more about music. He never did.

And in all the years since, no one else has been able to say whether he made the right decision, or even exactly what he was doing so very right on his own. After a bar-by-bar search, Alec Wilder swears that he can find no personal musical mannerisms in Berlin, and yet I'm certainly not alone in being able to spot an Irving Berlin tune every time. The same goes for his lyrics—which seem not so much brilliant as inevitable. They simply come with the notes. "Everybody's doing it," but of course they are. It says so in the tune.

At first, observers may have supposed that Irving's genius was entirely wrapped up in the latest thing, ragtime, in which case he would probably grow out of it. At his most introspective, he would never call his gift anything but a knack, and knacks never know what they can do next until they've already done it.

Irving himself may have wondered too. But before time could tell anything, Berlin's life took another turn that launched him willy-nilly into a second legend. Later on, Irving would acquire a reputation for fierce publicity-seeking, and no doubt he always knew the value of the stuff. But at this stage, he began to demonstrate another law of American life, which says that just as money makes more money in a capitalist society, so do legends beget legends.

In fact, Irving decidedly did not want the next bit of attention he got. In 1913, he had married a young lady called Dorothy Goetz, who promptly died after contracting typhoid fever right after their Cuban honeymoon. Irving was heartbroken and wrote his first successful ballad in mourning, which would indicate a life beginning after ragtime. But because legend calls for a *great* ballad, posterity has conspired to overrate this particular song. In the cold air of the morning after, "When I Lost You" has the ring of a barroom tearjerker yanked from Irving's second drawer. Few if any great songs have ever been written on demand or for an occasion. The muses prefer your undivided attention. And when they've got it, they'll probably send you a funny song, as they did several times that year to Irving. Save the sad stuff until you feel better.

Which was fine so long as the funny songs sold enough copies. Irving's actual response to grief was maybe the sanest possible one, which was to work harder than ever, on every aspect of the business, from his own publicity to the publishing of others, which kept him right in the middle of the swim as his rivals mailed him their distillations of the latest sounds. As Irving Berlin, Inc. (he shed the partner), he promoted the whole profession, not just one writer at a time—but in the form of a new craft union that protected last year's songs as well as the very latest, thus making a real, full-time profession possible. So even colleagues who found him outrageously self-centered owed him something for his crucial support of ASCAP at the creation.

But Berlin himself certainly didn't get overlooked either. And I was startled to realize that less than a year after his wife's death he went barnstorming through England as the King of Ragtime—a title that seemed easier to claim over there, but wasn't. The British public might not have known much about ragtime, but they were sufficiently weaned on the minstrel tradition to know that whoever the king was, the beat itself was black. The joke went into permanent circulation that Irving kept a little black boy in his trunk to help him out with it.

In fact, Irving kept his black friend closer than that, never went anywhere without him. Whatever he'd heard as a boy in Harlem was part of him now, although he used it more on some days than others.

Even more then than now, triumphs on either side of the Atlantic automatically reverberated to the other, so that by the time Irving came

home to write his first Broadway show, called *Watch Your Step*, he was an "international star," and not just in the sense that an airport with one flight to Canada becomes international. The name Irving Berlin seemed to have translated catchily into French and German as well, and his geopolitical timing was perfect: The world was about to enter the first of its great wars, and wars, the bigger the better, have a tendency to freeze the music of the moment and give it abnormal weight and duration. (How long would "Tipperary" have lasted in peacetime, or "When Johnny Comes Marching Home"?) "Alexander" seemed like a natural anthem, "so natural that you want to go to war" all dressed up and ready to go. But it wasn't just a matter of hits. By sheer dint of fertility, Irving Berlin had done more than anyone by then to secure the beachheads of the dance floor and the music rack for his own kind of lightly syncopated, semi-black, and faintly Jewish melodies, which may seem like nothing but housebroken jazz nowadays but constituted the light at the end of Gatsby's dock for all the fresh young geniuses waiting in the postwar world.

And what the Great War, as it was called, did for his songs it double-did for his legend. By chance, a rival sharpshooter called George M. Cohan had virtually cornered the corn market on patriotism with "You're a Grand Old Flag," and on team spirit with "Over There." So Irving went around to the back with a song about the little guy in the trench and about the particular blahs of reveille, the trumpet call that jerks you out of bed just as you are falling asleep every night.

Later on, insomnia would actually prove to be Irving's defining nightmare and his downfall, so it's nice to know that he got not only a bestselling hit out of it ("Oh, How I Hate to Get Up in the Morning"), but a touchstone song for two wonderful wars. Personally, it dawned on Irving with his first bugle call that the only way to get away from this noise was to blow his own horn even louder, and he let the army know immediately that the famous Private Berlin was available to do a benefit show for this very army that would put it on the map and raise recruitments to infinity.

"Operation Chutzpah" one is tempted to call it. But who knows how much purebred government-inspected ham lurks in the hearts of generals? Irving would get his way completely in both wars and en route become what he wanted most in the world to be: a great American citizen-songwriter who had paid his dues and would reap untold rewards, in the

form of a national Irving Berlin Day in 1919. He'd won so much glory by the end of World War II that there was suddenly nowhere to go but down, and plenty of time to get there.

But that truly is another story. Not the least legendary of Irving's feats was to live to be one hundred, by which time all guarantees can be assumed to have expired, but running the tape back to, let's say, his thirty-first birthday in 1919, one finds what should be by all rights a happy, completed man. *Yip Yip Yaphank* had just brought off the ultimate triumph in street smarts, and in the course of it Irving had quietly made the army over in his own image, by turning his whole base into a wing of Broadway, where several postwar theatrical careers would get their start and Irving would get at least one first-class client for his publishing house, namely, Harry "Three Little Words" Ruby.

Berlin had, in short, passed through World War I like a rattlesnake through a cobra, emerging intact and ready for its next adventure. Which would come, of course, immediately, when Irving was offered part ownership of a Broadway theater called the Music Box, to do what he liked with. By now it seemed that the very name "Irving Berlin" that he'd plucked from the air one day to replace Izzy Baline had become his greatest creation and was already worth its weight in old-world titles. It was plastered all over postwar New York and London: words by, music published, produced, and staged by, and even in a pinch sung by Irving Berlin. He could do everything for a song except play it properly on the piano, and even this had become a story; the kid who couldn't even afford a piano to learn the white notes on could now afford one that played only black ones.

At a later date the word for all this might have been megalomania, and he'd have been advised to drop at least a few of his stars and ribbons. But success stories were steaming hot, and since he was being compared to the likes of J. P. Morgan and the ghost of John Jacob Astor, he offered a welcome change. Speaking as a willfully unsuccessful schoolkid of the period, I can personally report the relief of finding a rich songwriter among all the steel magnates and money managers. "I'd rather lead a band," said Irving, and every time I heard it, my own prefrontal lobes and cerebral cortex would break into spontaneous applause.

A cynic might interject here that Irving had gotten over his broken heart pretty thoroughly by this time, but the fact is that he hadn't really.

So far as anybody knows, he lived a completely celibate life for over a decade, abstaining from even the showgirls who were considered virtually part of a songwriter's salary. (Like heads of state, the writers were deemed to be just dispensing favors to the little dears.) His love songs during those years tended to be anything but sexy. "A Pretty Girl Is Like a Melody" sounds wistful at best, while "All Alone" and "What'll I Do" sound downright desperate.

But then a young woman at a dinner party told him one night that she loved his song "What *Shall* I Do," and the spell was broken. Ellin Mackay's gentrification of his song title defined in one word what a different world she came from and what a perfect romantic-comedy couple they would make together. And she was drawn to him like a moth to a flame, a fan to a movie star, or a reporter to a good story, while attracting him right back insofar as convention permitted. "A man chases a girl until she catches him," he would later write, describing and obviously approving of this process that had somehow freed him from the bonds of his own past, making him again a young lover capable perhaps of writing real love songs.

The first thing to be said about Ellin Mackay and the family Mackay is that they were not an old New York family themselves or even a famous new one, but just anonymous new money from the Midwest, which made them outsiders too. And as a sometime writer for the new "in" magazine, *The New Yorker*, Ellin knew where the real balance of social power lay those days. "I was the one who was marrying up," she would say succinctly, and as far as the headlines were concerned, she was embarrassingly right. "Irving Berlin Pursues [Weds, Elopes with, whatever] Heiress." Not the Vanderbilt heiress or the Rockefeller heiress, just "the heiress," which in the new café-society aristocracy meant "the nobody," "the extra," "the pawn."

What she could not have known, because it was unprecedented, was the sheer size and force of the wave of curiosity that was about to hit her because of Irving, or how little control either of them would have over the public story.

One could define the twenties and thirties as the start of the information era, overlapping the last days of King Print. In other words, everything was out there now, but the only way to immediately hook into it was through a primitive device called the stop press, which teletyped scraps of

breaking news onto a corner of the front page. So while people might dream about wristwatch radios and such, what they still actually did was buy newspapers all day long, to follow the stock reports and the latest from Flamingo Park and Ebbets Field and to keep up with whatever stories the press had goosed up and strung out into national dramas. "Jury Is Out in Scopes Trial," "Jury Is Still Out, Foreman Sneezes" snaps the stop press while the rest of the paper struggles to come up with fresh angles and aperçus that made it all worth reading.

"Stop the presses! Get me rewrite!" Newsrooms in the movies always seemed like outpatient clinics in mental hospitals. And what in the world could be so important? Well, it was a question of whether *The Sun* could beat *The Star* by an hour to the latest fragment of trivia from today's hot news story. Like much else in the twenties—marathon dancing, flagpole sitting, and so on—journalism was both redeemingly silly and casually cruel.

"Names make news," as Henry Luce decreed when he founded the first newsmagazine in 1925. And if you happen to have a famous name like Irving Berlin, you could become a hunted man or woman overnight as reporters from all over the country lined the docks and train platforms like so many bloggers scavenging for stories, after Clarence Mackay gave them a perfect lead by refusing to give his consent to his daughter's marriage. Irving and Ellin did the rest by eloping anyway, bringing into play those great 1920s stage sets, namely, ocean liners and first-class hotels.

In fact, Clarence's opposition to a wedding between his Catholic daughter and a Jewish show business legend fifteen years older was inevitable and so reasonable that Irving himself would claim to understand it. At that point, Lutherans thought twice about marrying Methodists, while Jews and Catholics viewed even their own members with squinty-eyed suspicion (Orthodox or Reform? Rich or poor?). And since Irving had no wish to put on a public show, or an uptown version of *Abie's Irish Rose,* the press itself had to do most of the hard work.

They had plenty of clichés at the ready to help them out. The moment after Clarence unwittingly unleashed the hounds of publicity, like Buster Keaton tripping over a loose wire, the world knew everything it wanted to about him. He became the eternal fuddy-duddy and snob that every generation needs, the cartoon character with "Old Fool" practically printed

on his back. The role of an American upper class has never been that clear to most people anyway, but one of its functions has always been to be laughed at, and when the joke wears thin, to be sneered at too, in this case for anti-Semitism, which doesn't seem to have been a real issue. Anti-Semitism has always made so little sense in this nation of outsiders that it loses almost all its spice when mixed in with our real religion, Celebrity.

Anyhow, the story ended delightfully for the public when the self-made Jewish songwriter had to bail out the huffy millionaire in the Depression. ("Poor Clarence is down to his last four million," as my father overheard someone say.) And it ended well enough for Clarence too, who would cut a benign, slightly fuzzy figure as Grandpa, a role he was born to play. Ellin's scorecard was more mixed.

She had won her battle of wills with her father, but how could anyone tell when he or she had won around here? Irving took her to the Algonquin Round Table, where she found herself a nobody, Irving's *shiksa,* a gold trophy wife. And back in her world, some doors (dull ones, but still) were now closed to her. The Mackays had not advanced on any fronts at all.

But here was the press anyway, still hanging about and still hounding Irving and the wife of Irving, the unknown millionairess. And one day, while undergoing the ups and downs of early pregnancy—which hadn't much improved since the Garden of Eden—she snapped. These same implacable "just doing my job" journalists would soon turn Charles Lindbergh from a bright young man into a premature sourpuss and near traitor who loved Nazi Germany because it didn't have a free press. In a smaller way, the press broke Ellin too, removing much of her fun and youthfulness, and for the rest of her days subjecting her to a series of what she called "walking breakdowns."

And I think some of the fun went out of it for Irving too, or at least it began a slow leak, although he still cultivated lapdogs like Alexander Woollcott to write Mother Goose stories about him and his princess. But the dark side of the press had turned even darker, and the least he could do now was protect his young wife and oncoming children from any more of it. So he built a metaphysical fortress of silence around them all, a sort of Castle Irving from which he would venture forth alone within strictly controlled parameters, and in which he would eventually entomb himself in his old age, after the glare of the American dream had worn him out.

But to begin with, his uptown captivity had been anything but tomb-like. Irving was simply doing what "everybody" (who was anybody) was doing now, and the upper class was part of America too and part of his subject. So his Central Park apartment served not just as a first-class work-shop but also as a spy-hole on the rich at play. "Let's go slumming," as he wrote, "on Park Avenue." Some doors might be closed to the Berlins, but they weren't the ones he needed and there were more than enough tal-ented arrivistes behind other ones to make up the difference. Musical theater did not expect you to write about the very top people, the Cabots and the Biddles, but only about imitation top people like Fred and Ginger and occasionally Bing Crosby, two hoofers and a groaner dressed up in evening clothes to constitute a kind of take-out aristocracy of make-believe.

And not the least of Irving's studies and research tools was his own wife. The one thing that had *not* suffered from the recent unpleasantness was the marriage itself, which could probably have endured on their joint determination alone if necessary—failure was unthinkable—but their union had a couple of other good things going for it besides.

For openers, they passed the first and most crucial test of a happy mar-riage by simply enjoying each other's company, and not just in its hard-breathing aspects. They both liked to talk, and as a professional lyricist, Irving was a scavenger of talk, forever on the prowl for fresh turns of phrase and untrodden byways to get from here to there. And Ellin enjoyed the sheer game of it too. Their daughter Mary Ellin remembers growing up to a crackle of smart-chat and literal word games, some of which would undoubtedly metamorphose into song lyrics at the other end of the as-sembly line. A likely suspect pops into my mind right now, along with a matching clue to go with it. "I'm going around in circles, getting nowhere." Clue: Express futility in seven words or less. Where else but in games and songs could one hear such phrases? Ira Gershwin's " 'S Wonderful," for in-stance: Don't ever try using it in the real world.

The game is contagious, even when just describing it, and I can imag-ine Alan Jay Lerner popping his head in right here with "Why can't the Ba-lines teach the Mackays how to speak?" Later, Cole Porter would talk ironically of envying Irving's advantages, so it's nice to think of Berlin in-structing his young bride in the niceties of Lower East Side English. Mar-rying up might be called the very highest form of slumming, but it hadn't

been the couple's only wedding present to each other, because Ellin also gave him whatever it took to write real love songs, which is to say a muse, a model, and a sense of potential excitement, and real love. (By which I don't mean the famous one, "Always," that he had ostentatiously given to Ellin as a lifelong wedding gift, royalties and all, but that he had apparently written a bit earlier to help out a friend, who had a girlfriend named Amy, which has the same cadence as "always.") And this raises some instructive questions. Does "I'll be loving you, Amy" still sound like a great song, and can you simply transfer the whole *schlamozzel* to somebody else and still keep it a love song? The unmusical George S. Kaufman would point out the basic difficulty when he called it "I'll be loving you, Tuesday" instead. "Always" is a song of generalities, a kind of hymn to whatever you feel like today, almost a rental, which would happily come into its own as background music, expressing nostalgia for a fallen hero in *The Pride of the Yankees*. A somewhat more real song written around then is "You Forgot to Remember," but this also plunges us back into wistfulness and paper-thin heartbreak, and we've done that. By contrast, "How Deep Is the Ocean" seems to me his first full-throated love song written by one real person to another. It pulls out all the stops on the organ at once and plugs the air with genuine feeling. "And if I ever lost you/how much would I cry?" There is nothing paper-thin about that. The man really means it.

Doesn't he? Once again, it seems as if the muses were just having their little joke. Irving did not write "How Deep" on a great tide of emotion, but on a widening ripple of aspiration, as he strove to claw or con his way out of a composing slump, a "dry spell" that nobody else was aware of. And as far as he could judge, this particular attempt had failed as much as any of the others, and went into his trunk for an even rainier day.

So his slump went on, and on, and on, until it seemed, in Mary Ellin's account of it, to fill up the whole house, as if song creation were a palpable form of combustion that required endless tinkering with the boiler. "I'm breaking my neck, trying to find a new sound" was how he put it, and since even the best-trained writers can sound like piano tuners while creating, one boggles at the thought of the untrained Irving "breaking his neck," humming and whistling like a teakettle and batting out strange chords. Park Avenue had probably never heard the like. But seriously— what *had* gone wrong? And what did he *think* had gone wrong?

Somewhere in the vague area of 1931, Irving found himself at major war with his own self-confidence—a battle that seems all the more gripping by its invisibility and by the sheer number of songs that nevertheless kept appearing. His own typically puritan explanation of what he called his inferiority complex was that he just hadn't been working hard enough, that is, around the clock. But breast-beating aside, there was an awful lot for anyone to feel inferior about just then. From the moment George Gershwin walked into his office looking for work, Irving must have felt subject to occasional second thoughts about his own willful ignorance of music as well as his blind faith in simplicity. Should a boss really know that much less than the help, and be that much simpler? By 1925, he had pronounced that all of America was now a listening nation, rather than a performing one, which was grounds for another small twinge. After all, simplicity might be good enough to sing, whistle, and dance to, but listening might want a little something to think about as well, and to sink its teeth into, and in that same short period Richard Rodgers and Cole Porter and Harold-Arlen came blazing out, flashing new ideas with trained musicianship to burn.

What made Berlin's new sound so particularly elusive was that he neither knew exactly what it was he was looking for, nor could be sure of knowing when he found it. Like most of his colleagues, only a little more so, Irving always needed someone else to tell him when he was good. Witness the famous instance when he almost discarded that most palpable of hits "There's No Business Like Show Business" because his secretary didn't like it, and perhaps more seriously, because Richard Rodgers didn't light up when he first heard it. A more confident man might have realized that Richard Rodgers never lit up over anything and that he was hearing this new song under the worst possible conditions: Irving was playing it himself. And Irving's pianism was so primitive that Hoagy Carmichael once said that it had given him the heart to go on, on the grounds that "If the best in the business is that bad, there's hope for all of us." Because Irving's variety of ineptitude was not just manifestly self-taught, but badly self-taught, as if by a deaf person, he couldn't trust it himself until he had heard one of his famous musical secretaries play it to him and show him how good the latest Berlin tune sounded outside his own head.

Luckily, the rest of humanity had less trouble knowing it when Irving

was good. His dry spell abruptly ended when someone in his office went behind his back and offered one of his rejects, called "Say It Isn't So," to Rudy Vallee with results so spectacular that Irving agreed to reconsider an adjoining lemon, "How Deep Is the Ocean." These were no ordinary songs but A-list standards, and once all the second opinions were in, Berlin himself considered "How Deep" among his greatest ever.

Possibly it even contained that new sound he was looking for, now that someone else had heard it too. And with that taken care of, he would return to Broadway in triumph, as if he had actually been away someplace. He then fired off a volley of brand-new hits such as the haunting "Soft Lights and Sweet Music" and his nod to the Depression, "Let's Have Another Cup of Coffee," that must have been gestating in his trunk during his dry spell, which, when you throw in a couple of fine movie songs, "Puttin' On the Ritz" and "Let Me Sing and I'm Happy," must have made this either the richest or the shortest dry spell in the history of droughts. His Broadway spectacular after that took an equally long stride in the way of all-around sophistication. As Thousands Cheer was a revue arranged like a newspaper, with songs and sketches to illustrate the various sections, for example, "Heat Wave" for the weather page and "Easter Parade" for fashion. Thus, the institution of journalism that had so plagued the Berlins lately was reduced to a series of harmless entertainments with Irving getting the last word and the last laugh each time.

However, the high point of the show gets no laughs, or even applause, but takes its chances on stunned silence. The subject of it actually did not appear in the papers, or not often enough. "Suppertime" must be the first pop song ever written about a lynching, and the tone is just right, without one false note or melodramatic word. A member of the family will not be coming home this evening, or tomorrow, or in fact ever again so we'd better just get on with life. And the tune says the same thing. The song is written in that rarest of forms, an understated blues, and it sounds just African American enough to show that Irving "gets it" as much as Gershwin or any other white man can. Like his clumsily titled "How About Me," "Suppertime" shows that Irving digs the blue sound but isn't planning to horn in on it or take over à la the white man. There's a long distance between "Dorando" and "Cohen Owes Me Ninety-Seven Dollars" and the political correctness of today, but Irving Berlin's brand of irony and re-

spectfulness in "Suppertime" seems like a felicitous way station and a good place for a white songwriter to stop. Berlin had made his statement and would not be making it again.

It was a high point. Yet if Irving Berlin's career had ended right there, he would no doubt be enshrined today as an incomparable pioneer, or missing link, though not quite as a colleague, of George Gershwin or Duke Ellington in the field of the jazz song. But something radical would still happen to the know-it-alls who make these estimates, or at least to me. During my wartime layover in the United States, there had been virtually no such thing as movie revivals: Either you caught a film on its first whip-round ("Tues. to Thurs." or, if you were lucky, "Fri. to Mon.") or you caught the next one. But when I finally escaped from England in the fall of 1947, I found that New York had changed delightfully in this respect. Presumably Hollywood had begun to gird itself for its last stand against TV, and simultaneously for its new role after that as a supplier of TV, by releasing lots of its old movies for general distribution and exposure. And I spent that whole fall catching up with the Marx Brothers, and spent Christmas day itself alone in an empty movie house, catching up with Fred Astaire and Ginger Rogers, who until that year I had seen over and over in just one (excellent) movie, *Shall We Dance*. This time the film was *Top Hat* and I haven't recovered yet.

"Isn't this a lovely day to be caught in the rain"—incredible. Who wrote this again? Where has he been all my life? And what on earth is he doing with the beat now? "I just got an invitation in the mail." This couldn't be Irving Berlin because it wasn't simple enough. Before leaving London I'd already been inundated with the score of *Annie Get Your Gun* and had found it amiably regressive and a touch simpleminded. Okay, it was also perfect. That was the least you could expect from America in those days, but except for one lonely song called "Moonshine Lullaby," it completely and ominously lacked the sound that I was going back to America for.

But now here it was, that sound in all its glory, and not just a good copy of the sound but in some sense the original that all the other guys had been copying. At least a part of Irving Berlin was an intuitive jazzman who had once heard the sounds of Harlem as clearly as those of Hester Street and had, so to speak, finally hatched out the embryonic sounds of his

early rags into the swinging majesty of "Cheek to Cheek." "Heaven," as he puts it perfectly, "I'm in heaven."

You can say that again. Also, "I'm fancy free and free for anything fancy." The fact that it was Christmas might just be a coincidence, but I had just received an incomparable present anyway that has kept on giving from that day to this. What Norman Mailer has called the little capillaries of bonhomie began to go off everywhere like firecrackers.

Broadway itself smiled on the way out, and now every year I think the same ritual words, "I'm dreaming of a white Christmas," but with any luck I won't get it. And I'll have to settle for Fred and Ginger in the rain again, or perhaps just Fred solo celebrating Easter, Washington's birthday, and July the Fourth.

Fred Astaire was of course a phenomenon unto himself. Every writer did his best work for Fred, because, among other reasons, he asked for it. But *Top Hat* is somehow always the first that comes to mind, the prototype. It's as if Astaire's sense of the sounds he wanted and Berlin's sense of Fred's essence, his image, added up to a third personality, a city boy harnessed to a country boy in the cause of that magnificent anomaly, American sophistication. And wonderfully, inexplicably, their songs still sounded simple, although they were anything but. For instance, the bridge of "I'm Putting All My Eggs in One Basket" seems to drop into an abyss when you try singing it, and you'd better know where he put the branch that you'll have to hang on to; and the second B section of "Let's Face the Music and Dance" makes a small move that can leave egg on your face time after time. And so on. "I Used to Be Color Blind" actually goes on what the Australian aborigines call walkabout. It's as if the singer were deciding where to put his feet down next.

Under cover of Astaire's dancing and his flexible, throwaway singing, Irving didn't need to rush to any conclusions, but could, as he said, "write anything" without fear of commercial reprisal—Astaire's feet would turn it to gold, whatever it was. And the result is the only tunes in this whole book that I've ever had trouble memorizing, most particularly the one called "You're Easy to Dance With."

On second thought, Irving had always liked to play games with the beat, and I have almost as much trouble learning his song "Everybody

Step," vintage 1921, but that one is clearly a rhythm number as opposed to a "felt" one, written for the feet and not the heart. With Astaire, everything is a rhythm number, love songs and all, so you get the whole Irving writing at once, the jester and the troubadour moving like quicksilver but in no special hurry, and with the added bonus that Fred was always in fashion. As a Broadway veteran, Astaire had worked out his own West Coast compromise so that everything he touched became the latest thing, and now Irving did likewise, whipping out a trunk song and a retread, "You're Laughing at Me" and "I've Got My Love to Keep Me Warm," and transforming them into the toast of 1937 for *On the Avenue* with Dick Powell and Alice Faye. And then there's the Astaire-type nonsense song, "My Walking Stick," sung in basic Broadway style by the other side of Berlin's brain, Ethel Merman, in the film *Alexander's Ragtime Band.*

But now it was time for another war and for another burst of two-fisted patriotism, although Irving would actually begin this one by taking a huge step backward in hepcat esteem. Even when he had first written "God Bless America" in 1919, Harry Ruby had talked him out of using it then, on the grounds that the country was already drowning in patriotism and didn't need another bucket of it from its greatest songwriter. But that's when Berlin should have published it anyway, because that's when it still sounded right. By 1939, "God Bless America" seemed strictly from squaresville and Berlin himself seemed to have gone backward in time to where perhaps he belonged, a grand old man singing grand old songs.

It suited World War II just fine, as it happened, and thus suited Irving too. The U.S. home front was in a retro frame of mind throughout, as it would prove by falling in love with the defiantly corny *Oklahoma!* (which actually uses the word "corn" in its very first song), and as homesick GIs had already proved by laughing nostalgically as Irving himself sang "Oh, How I Hate to Get Up in the Morning" for his show *This Is the Army* in a quavering voice that sounded as old as their collective grandfathers. *This Is the Army* remains, note for note, a splendid historic artifact, beginning with its title song and running on through a twinkling trove of second-drawer tunes that have all been scrupulously updated. "How About a Cheer for the Navy" actually names the current secretaries of the army and the navy while Berlin's politically dubious "That's What the Well-

Dressed Man in Harlem Will Wear" features the "Brown Bomber," Joe Louis himself dressed up in ODs (olive drabs) "with a tin hat for overseas." Irving might not walk the streets in person anymore, but he was still a singing journalist and those were exactly the sounds I remember from *my* streets.

Afterward, a war commonly grants its heroes a few years of momentum and grace on the house, so that an Audie Murphy can capsize gently from a great soldier to a third-class actor, and an Irving Berlin can evolve from a great American into a great *old* one. In fact, the saga of his first postwar show, *Annie Get Your Gun*, could almost be called a ceremony of grand old men, because Jerome Kern had agreed to write it first with his grand old partner Dorothy Fields, but had died just before he could, and grand old producers Rodgers and Hammerstein were producing it, but couldn't very well write it themselves because Ms. Fields had already agreed to combine with her brother Herbert on the book and lyrics, and Dick hadn't been married to Oscar long enough to cheat on him with Dorothy.

But Irving by himself took precedence over everyone, and besides, he suited Rodgers's retro game plan by even being the right age. The original "Alexander's Ragtime Band" had actually been written around the same year that the original Oklahoma had become a state. And Rodgers and Hammerstein's show of that name had established a style that might also appeal to the fogy in Irving, the part of him that wrote "God Bless America," that is, no sophistication or street smarts. (Try a little country-lane smarts—stop "Puttin' On the Ritz" and try "Doin' What Comes Natur'lly.") And try to avoid syncopation, if possible—that stuff's fer city folk.

And best of all, Irving really needed no advice at all as to which way the wind was blowing. The growing popularity of country music was in itself a welcome invitation to come home to simplicity, and fill out his musical portrait of America. So he proceeded to build *Annie's* love story, which is to say the heart of the matter, on a simple waltz, "The Girl That I Marry." He surrounded it with such a simple, down-home score that he out-Hammersteined Oscar himself, as he had once tried to out–Porter Cole himself with Fred Astaire. The results haven't come down yet, but still circle the globe eternally alongside *Oklahoma!* and *Kiss Me, Kate* and the

other classic postwar musicals. It had been one more stupendous triumph of the will for Irving's mantelpiece, and can only have left the cranky Richard Rodgers with the most exquisitely mixed feelings in history.

Berlin had once unforgivably upstaged Rodgers by writing a song of his own for Flo Ziegfeld to insert into an early Rodgers and Hart show. It had been insurance for Flo's investment, and to please his star singer, one Belle Baker, who had worked well with Irving before. The song turned out to be the immortal "Blue Skies," which stole the show and the reviews, leaving a nasty cold sore on Rodgers's wintry soul that probably still cried out for some balm of vengeance.

As good luck would have it, though, Rodgers was also a snob, a practicing gentleman, who understood the uses of sportsmanship, if not the point of it, and being the producer of a major musical must have provided its own kind of balm as well. In his bland memoir, *Musical Stages,* he would get a chance to pay his superficial respects to Irving and sound like a hell of an all-around good chap in doing so. So there were no losers. Irving had played right into Richard's hand by giving him such a great score. So hooray for all of us! A hit show heals all wounds, at least, as I say, superficially.

For a moment, the total triumph of *Annie* shot Irving back to the top. But at his age, no one expected him to stay there long. So he bent his talent to at least one more surprise, and with the help of good old reliable Ethel Merman, he came up with another only slightly smaller smash Broadway hit, *Call Me Madam,* which, with its contrapuntal hit song, "You're Just in Love," forms, in my mind anyway, a memorable bookend around the primest part of his prime with "Play a Simple Melody," written more than thirty years earlier. Outside of Gershwin's elegant "Mine," I can't think of another song by anyone that accomplishes this tricky piece of musical calisthenics. So perhaps the old boy was just trying to show he could still do it. After that, he wrote another great movie with his other prewar alter ego, Fred Astaire, called *Easter Parade,* featuring one of his most passionate, most exuberant, no-holds-barred songs, "It Only Happens When I Dance with You." "A Couple of Swells" featured Irving slumming again, and getting Fred and Judy to slum with him, under a gross of greasepaint and some slept-in evening clothes. It only goes to show, as Irving's own career had, that class will always tell.

So okay, the guy was immortal, and you don't bet against the gods. As

long as postwar America stayed mostly in the past, Irving seemed safe. But rock and roll could not be kept at bay forever, after which a case can be made for him, as for the others included in this book, that the music began to leave him and not the other way around. At least I have heard a couple of unpublished songs of Berlin's that might have gone somewhere, if anyone else had been going that way too anymore. And conceivably, if he'd been younger, he might have learned to play a guitar at this point, at least as well as he played the piano, and dashed off some rock and roll to top things off—the kid in that early photograph I was talking about seemed capable of anything short of hip-hop. But so few creative musicians have lived as long as this that there were no precedents to guide either him or us. How much can you or he ask of an eighty-year-old man, anyway? And then what about when he turns ninety?

All we can say for sure is that he died not long after his 101st birthday, before the question could come around again. But long before that, he had retired all the way into his own castle on the Upper East Side, just a couple of hard-earned miles away from where it had all begun, but with enough space now to house, with a little notice, all the Balines in Russia and most of the tea in China. And here, in a just world, he should have been free to cash his last chips and live happily ever after. But in the doleful phrase of the great Satchel Paige, something had "been gaining on him" for a while now and perhaps it was just an inherent melancholia (a sister committed suicide in the 1920s) or perhaps it was not having enough work to do, or, most likely, it was mainly the sleeping pills he'd been popping for years to keep his own personal buglers out of range. As a mythical character, Irving was inevitably promoted to drug addict, but this is much too melodramatic; lots of respectable folk took the same pills, including a couple of others in this book. So maybe the rule should be that if the doctor prescribes it, he's the one with the problem.

Meanwhile, Irving seems to have kept up a telephone friendship with one of his fellow pill poppers, Harold Arlen, during several years of mutual distress. By the late 1960s, the songwriters of their era no longer needed Nembutal to feel sorry for themselves. It was now official that musical fashion had turned its back on them for good, and they all needed someone to cry with as their collective lifeworks inched toward the brink of extinction.

Although Berlin and Arlen might seem like two basically different breeds of cat, Berlin tended to regard all kinds of other songwriters as family, and in return they tended to see him as a father or uncle. After all, these songwriters had each grown up with Berlin and knew where he belonged in their own development. And I believe most would have agreed that if there had been no Irving Berlin, there would have been nothing, for instance, quite like Harold Arlen either, or Jimmy Van Heusen, or even Cole Porter in quite the same form. So in those latter days, at the very least they owed him a phone call. And of course, he'd already written a song about his end of the deal. "All Alone (by the Telephone)" had been written in his mother's last years, but it remains the last word on old age and loneliness and perhaps on his own fears as well.

But if so, he needn't have worried. For a famous recluse, he stayed surprisingly talkative. If only telephones could talk, Berlin's telephone would have become his best, last biographer. At least one phone call has survived in full that tells as much about his last days as that old snapshot does of his beginnings. Irving had just read Alec Wilder's great book on songwriters. Naturally, he was calling to complain. Typically it seems that he had either missed the purple profusion of compliments that Wilder had heaped on him or else had read them but wasn't interested. Instead he had fastened on one extra-mild demurral of Wilder's where he said the song " 'Always' is frankly not a favorite of mine." At this, Irving went wild. What does he mean "not a favorite"? Who the hell did Wilder think he was?

Luckily for us, the phone was answered not by Alec himself but by his literary partner, James T. Maher, who captured the whole thing, including the growls. And it leaves us with a core question. Allowing that "Always" was certainly a burningly sensitive subject, because it was an official part of his love story, who exactly did Irving *want* Alec Wilder to be? Whose authority would he have accepted? One senses how fragile the whole edifice had become. Irving had always had a chip on his shoulder about critics. Songs were written for people, damn it, not experts. The man in the street and the woman in the kitchen—these were his people, his judges. And also, a check representing a million copies sold was the only prize worth having.

But now, if he so much as opened the window or turned on the radio, there were his judges, the real people, all dancing to "baby, baby, baby," or

words to that effect, and the prizewinners with the gold platters knew even less about music than he had. It wasn't a listening nation anymore, but a shaking, rattling, and rolling one, and frankly, who cared what the man in the street thought anymore? Public taste was not, as he supposed, the last word, but is only as good in each generation as the music it gets to feed on. And the current diet was enough to drive a man into the arms of the nitpicking connoisseurs. But not if they were going to dump on "Always" and "God Bless America" and "A Pretty Girl Is Like a Melody." Good songs are forever and he didn't care to trade his old ones in for the new models.

Boy wonders may be obliged to pay a steep price for growing older. As Irving Berlin's songs had become more sophisticated, as the 1930s went on, so had his audiences, so that when he seemed to change his mind about this in the 1940s, the whippersnappers who sneered at him actually had to stand on his shoulders to do so. He had taught the whole world too well.

But were we ever right to sneer, even from the vantage point of his shoulders? Right after the terrorists struck at the very heart of Irving's own city on the 9/11 that lives in infamy, nobody's words or tunes rang the bell more resonantly or accurately than good old "God Bless America." So if you allow for ups and downs, perhaps Berlin's songs *are* forever.

Opinions remain mixed about Irving, though—more so for him than for just about anyone else—partly because he was so mixed himself, with a bright side and a dark one almost agreeing to take turns. It is hard to read the mind of a hermit, but especially when he seems to expect both the worst and the best at the same time. For instance, he had thought when it came along that this new gizmo, radio, would ruin the song business by overexposure, and that the movies would ruin it too, by moving the publishing business to Hollywood. And yet toward the end of his life, when Steven Spielberg asked permission to build his next movie around "Always," Irving said that he had "other plans" for it, which suggests that his boyish optimism was still giddier than ever.

So Spielberg used Jerome Kern's "Smoke Gets in Your Eyes" instead, which means that Irving's decision likely altered the balance of power and popularity slightly for a moment, as would other decisions he made restricting the use of his tunes. For instance, I can't remember hearing a

single Berlin tune in a commercial, for what that's worth, or—except for "Always" in *The Pride of the Yankees*—as background music in a movie. In general, it would seem to me that for any of these men or their estates to play hard to get was futile verging on crazy. But having scrambled for pennies once in his life, and having ended up in a palace, Irving Berlin was not in the market for professional advice. Since he'd practically invented the business, there was no point telling him about it now. You didn't lecture this man—you took notes.

Perhaps the darkest sequence in Irving's telephone life came when his long conversation with Fred Astaire finally ended. It is impossible, but tantalizing, to imagine how such a great musical friendship might have translated into chitchat. But so long as the conversation lasted, one could still imagine Irving writing another completely original song for Fred at a moment's request, and another and another.

In such a relationship, it seemed almost a dirty trick for either man to die first. But everyone in the music game had died before Irving, leaving him a bit lonelier each time, to the point of infinity, and the death of Astaire must have seemed like a final amputation. "It's over," as he'd once written in an achingly sad song. "All over . . . but how about me?"

It doesn't answer his question, but perhaps it serves poetic justice to note that at least Irving Berlin's reputation seems to be doing nicely again, after its own dry spell. He himself might never be able to get quite past those early death struggles with money, but he had raised three generous-minded daughters, who could now do so for him, and they, plus whoever else the estate consists of these days, have made his songs more available than they've ever been—and now there's not a damn thing Irving can do to stop them.

Also, I'm afraid that his ghost may have to settle for a connoisseur audience now, which seems, incidentally, to be getting younger every year. In such bull sessions as I've had lately, he goes straight into the top five before the argument even starts, along with Gershwin, Kern, Rodgers, and Porter, plus usually one more per player—Harold Arlen in Wilder's book and Arlen's best friend Harry Warren in mine, and of course whoever you like in yours.

One always feels one needs to add one more word about Berlin. Something to sum up his sheer scale and importance. Cornerstone? Fountain-

head? His colleagues seemed to use the word "genius" about him more than about anyone else except George Gershwin—and perhaps more significantly, Igor Stravinsky also used that word to describe Berlin. Stravinsky was a great musical theorist with a special curiosity about the nature of melody, which after all Igor's theorizing still seems so elusive that maybe Irving was right after all—it actually helps if you don't know what you're doing.

What matters most to this particular story is that perhaps our most gifted original musician gave his whole life and whole gift entirely to popular songs, and that he overlapped so closely with another genius, who could add classical training to the mix. Many other types of song have been written in America, and there are many varieties within this type too. But parts one and two of the standard jazz song trace back to the man who wrote "I can do anything better than you" and to the man (or men, if Ira Gershwin counts) who answered "It Ain't Necessarily So."

Of Thee I Sing, Gershwin

GEORGE GERSHWIN

*L*ike many artistic happenings in this hurry-up land of ours, the jazz song boom seems in retrospect like a movement that didn't know it was a movement. Harold Arlen, that most introspective of second-wave writers, did know that he and his buddies were doing something special all right, and even that they were in some sense all in it together. But if so, they were in it like a jazz band, not a chorus line, which is to say that they wanted the other guys to be good so that they could be better. The greatest solos come from the greatest ensembles, and the biggest sales occur when the whole market is bullish. So the lore of the trade is amazingly full of encouraging words and deeds, from Berlin to Porter, and Kern to Arlen,

and from Gershwin to everybody—a level of uncomplicated niceness unique among the arts.

But a movement? Come on—they didn't like each other *that* much. And besides, "movement" was just the kind of word that these refugees from piano lessons and respectability had signed on to get away from. The whole essence and point of syncopation is to kid formal music and kick the stuffing out of it. If the maestro says the tempo should go thus and so, let's surprise him with this and that. And let's do it with a gorgeous new chord that has never seen pen nor paper—a chord straight from heaven itself. You don't find such in movements.

But even if they didn't know they were a movement, there was no doubt who their leader was. Evidence suggests that every writer of the time who met George Gershwin (and nearly all did) was mightily proud of his friendship. Those who missed him looked up to him anyway, as the closest thing to a role model that this happy-go-lucky profession would allow itself.

George even passed the most acid of tests for great leadership by remaining a presence to his followers even after he'd left the planet. Ann "Willow Weep for Me" Ronell told me some half century after his death that she still "saw" Gershwin regularly in the crowds of the Upper West Side, looking as if he'd just walked out the door. And on that same day, Burton "How About You" Lane testified to an even more precise epiphany. Lane had recently been to a concert of Gershwin's newly refurbished piano rolls being played on a baby grand pianola in a pool of spotlight. And as the notes began to go mechanically down and up, "There was George for a moment," he exclaimed, "playing away. I almost passed out."

Both Ronell and Lane had good reason for their memories. And since their memories were all about the excitement of meeting George Gershwin and getting to know him, they might as well serve the same purpose here. Because George the man, the phenomenon, is at least as important to our story as George the writer, which is to say absolutely central.

Ms. Ronell, a cheerful, pocket-size individual, was particularly cheerful the day I met her, because Clint Eastwood had just played her song, her lifework, "Willow Weep for Me," in his latest movie. And with minimal coaxing, she proceeded to hand me a list of the ninety-some recordings that had been made of "Willow," featuring everybody you could ever

want to have record you: a Hall of Fame and who's who of great bands and soloists.

So I jumped into the conversation with a go-fish type of question about this. Why had she dedicated her masterpiece to George Gershwin? And at this, she lit up as if I'd accidentally turned on all the lights of the Rockefeller Center Christmas tree. Although Ms. Ronell had obviously told her tale many times before, she hadn't lost an ounce of her delight in it. Imagine a little girl from the Midwest meeting a great man like George Gershwin! And this is how it happened.

Way back when, Ms. Ronell, née Rosenblatt, had gone from Omaha to Radcliffe with her eye on a career in music, which she decided could be advanced by interviewing as many musical eminencies as she could for the Radcliffe student paper.

But it turned out she wouldn't need more than one, because after maneuvering her way past Ira, who tried to keep his brother's bulging guest list within reason, she found that "in five minutes, George was interviewing *me*," and auditioning her too, to see if she could dance or sing or anything else he might be able to help her with. And when he learned about her writing dreams, George didn't just give her the usual vague advice, and the usual list of names to call ("Who the hell are you?" is what they say if you make those calls), but followed up by personally introducing her to the names himself, as if he were an agent and she his star client. So not only was Ronell spared the usual hours of waiting in a publisher's office, vainly hoping to catch a glimpse of the back of the boss's head as he went out to lunch, but she had also been represented by the most distinguished and irresistible salesman in the business. "Your songs don't have verses," snapped the great Max Dreyfus. "They don't need verses," snapped back Gershwin. And that settled it, at least as long as George was around. Later, she would find herself waiting in offices again, but she did get her classic song published, thanks to George.

Nor was this just an isolated case involving a pretty girl who'd caught his eye. George might have done the same, or something like it, for anyone who got past Ira and walked through his door, as witness the very next person whose door I walked through that day, namely, my old friend the aforementioned Burton Lane, who, like Ronell, continued to live on the Upper West Side in the heart of the Gershwin country.

Since I already knew Burton's basic Gershwin story, I didn't ask him to repeat it, just to embellish it a little if he felt like it. But I'll repeat it here in the short form. Young Burton, né Burton Levy, age sixteen, had been dutifully practicing the piano and hoping to find a song in there at a New Jersey resort that his Realtor father favored, when he heard a booming Russian-sounding voice that could only be coming from someone as important as Catherine the Great. "You play just like my son George," said the woman's voice, and before he knew what hit him, Burton, like Ronell, found himself swept into the Gershwin family circle for what amounted to the next two years. Under Mama's formidable wing, he would, of course, have no trouble getting past Ira, but he did sometimes have a little difficulty getting past the court jester, Oscar Levant, who used to intercept him and insist on a game of Ping-Pong before letting him in.

It was a small, amusing price to pay for entering the enchanted Kingdom of George. Half of New York always seemed to be there—the exciting half, the young artists and writers who were going places—and at the center sat the king on his throne, his piano bench, with a different consort at his side each time, dispensing magic music from his enchanted piano.

Or so it seemed to a teenager. And no doubt a squinty-eyed psychobiographer would fit this into the standard legend of George, the sublime egomaniac, who obviously recruited acolytes like Ronell and Lane just so they could join the crowd at his feet. "There was nothing small about George Gershwin," said Jerome Kern, but the same cannot be said for some of the people who have written about him. What would be missing from their picture this time would be that no matter how well Gershwin played, (1) some of the worshippers apparently never stopped talking themselves, which didn't seem to bother the king at all: George could have composed music on the floor of the New York Stock Exchange at high noon, and (2) what Lane and Ronell talked to me about was not George's spectacular playing, which soon became part of the background, but his attentiveness between times to them and their particularities, to the things that made them different. Burton recalled with particular wonderment how George had personally set up an appointment for him with Walter Damrosch, the panjandrum of the New York Philharmonic, in case Lane had classical possibilities like his own. If Lane just wanted to join

him downtown in the Alley, great! But if Lane had uptown potential as well, okay, he'd help with that too. For an egomaniac, George Gershwin took an astonishing interest in other people.

The third thing wrong with the picture of George as an egomaniac is that, of course, he didn't have to send out for acolytes; he had only to leave the door open. Perhaps the longest and strangest pilgrimage to Gershwin's court was made by one Vladimir Dukelsky, a White Russian on the run not from the czars, like Gershwin's other friends, but from the czar's enemies, Lenin, Trotsky, and the whole unwashed revolutionary rabble, as seen from the top of the ivory tower where families like the Dukelskys lived.

Any generalizations about Gershwin's benefactions must surely pause at this one because Dukelsky was not only *not* a pretty girl, but he was not helpless or, by God, inferior to anyone on the planet. Born into the Cossack class, Vladimir had been trained as a music prodigy from the age of four, and had predictably grown up to be, at least at first and by most accounts, a fairly insufferable adult, whose basic relationship unit with the outside world seems to have been the feud. Perhaps if one splits the difference between Dukelsky's fellow White Russians George Sanders and Vladimir Nabokov one can at least imagine the capacity to annoy, and be annoyed, of such a creature.

At that, Dukelsky's hauteur might have passed unnoticed if he had simply proceeded on his appointed way to classical music, where snobbish wunderkinds disappear in the crowd. But meanwhile, a funny thing happened to Vladimir on the way out of Russia. During a stopover in Istanbul, where he supported his family playing the piano (no doubt with his nose in the air) in cafés, he heard a record of Gershwin's "Swanee" and was transfixed. Suddenly he too wanted to write like that, and began on the spot dashing off Gershwin and Irving Berlin imitations, made in Istanbul, with lyrics painfully winnowed out of an English dictionary. And unlike most classicists slumming on Tin Pan Alley, Vladimir kept doing it for the rest of his life, even when his pop songs decisively flopped at first and his classical compositions showed signs of taking off, with Diaghilev signing him up to write some ballets. It isn't often that you find pop music lined up on the side of art versus commerce. But for a while it seems as if Dukelsky actually wrote ballets for money and jazz songs for love.

So obviously the next step was to meet George Gershwin himself, and the next act finds him in a setting where he was really out of place, the Gershwin apartment on Riverside Drive, where he got hooked in earnest, this time by George's piano playing and the man's endless, breathtaking improvisations. (He noted with surprise that George never varied his tempo—a holdover from his job of making piano rolls, perhaps.) Dukelsky also got hooked on George himself, with his bubbling curiosity and the sense he gave of infinite possibility. So his visitor wrote songs too? Great! Gershwin liked a couple of "Duky's" art songs and the one-man Gershwin promotion machine rumbled into gear. How about changing the name Dukelsky to, say, Vernon Duke? And how about meeting my publisher? And when that didn't work out right away, George lent him some money, and some more after that, without ever making it seem like a big deal or a wall between them.

What followed is as much a history of the new-born Vernon Duke, who deserves one for himself anyway, as it was a history of Gershwin, because Duke became one of our best, most distinctive songwriters and more gradually turned, according to Bobby Short, into a genuinely nice and helpful guy, easily outstripping his classical twin Vladimir the Oaf in both respects.

So perhaps Gershwin's generosity was as contagious as his music, and maybe that was part of his service. At any rate, the Vernon Duke saga makes such a picture-book example of George in action and of the ripple effect of his influence that it's worth dwelling on just one moment longer. To repeat, Duke was not some hard-luck case with a small talent, the kind great men love to patronize, but a major potential rival with extraordinary musical gifts and self-confidence that needed bolstering from no one. Never mind. Gershwin would later lend moral support to Harold Arlen, too, who would eventually threaten almost to eclipse him. It was as if George wanted all those great songs to be written by *somebody,* preferably by himself, of course, but not exclusively. And in this cause, he studied other people's music so closely and empathetically that Duke was startled one day to hear Gershwin break off from his usual piano soliloquy to imitate Duke's own piano playing perfectly.

Since George listened so closely, he must also have noted that Duke actually played the piano better than he did, which a lesser man might

have considered another good reason to get rid of him. But George, as usual, was fascinated and Duke became part of the set at Riverside Drive, whatever the rest of the set may have made of him. (Oscar Levant once said, "Since you're destined for oblivion anyway, why do you need two names?" which shows what *he* thought of Vladimir, anyway, but Duke found Levant to be a nerve-racking neurotic, so they were even.)

Joining Gershwin's set was like hooking into a powerhouse that consisted of more than just George. Within a few years, Duke found himself writing songs with Ira's old classmate Yip Harburg, who would never have worked with a guy like Duke in any other circumstances. As the most dedicated left-winger in the business, Harburg disapproved on principle of Duke's foppish, foreign-sounding harmonies, and after each of their first two standards together, "April in Paris" and "I Like the Likes of You," failed to take off right away, Yip really yapped and hollered nasty words like "European" and "decadent" and "Never again!" But perhaps what had happened was that Duke had brought out Harburg's own inner fop, and Yip never wrote better. Then later when Duke found himself stuck with a tune that literally couldn't get started in the marketplace, Ira himself would chime in with a title and lyric based on that very phrase. "I Can't Get Started" became Duke's biggest hit.

So knowing George could be a total experience, and Duke's decision to drop in on him that first day would produce, in effect, a whole great songwriter that might not have happened otherwise. And as a truly far-out bonus, a most charming and surprising memoir from Duke called *Passport to Paris* brings Gershwin back to life as well as anything we have.

Beyond the creative windfall, it was quite an extraordinary case of what might be called social lion-taming. The stiff-necked Duke must have seemed like quite hopeless disciple material, but he responded to George with a total loyalty to both the man and his music, happily putting his own reputation on the line by defending both against his highbrow buddies like Prokofiev and Diaghilev, and even taking the trouble to complete his old friend's unfinished songs and arrangements for Gershwin's posthumous movie, *The Goldwyn Follies,* of 1938. And for good measure, he would defend both Ira and his prickly wife, Leonore, against charges of callousness toward George in his last days.

This is to introduce yet another large aspect of the Gershwin phenom-

enon. To love George was at least to try to love his relatives. George became famous for ostentatiously not getting married, but he was also a great family man who made sure no one ever got left behind; not Ira, whose lyrics he began to use perhaps before they were strictly ready (some of Ira's early attempts are plain awful); nor his sister, Frances, whose singing career he watched over as vigilantly as he watched over her honor (like other lotharios, he was terrified that she might run into someone like him); nor even his parents, who were just the kind of rough-edged immigrants that arrivistes commonly try to hide but whom George seemed to relish and expect other people to relish too. Gershwin obviously saw the world not just through rose-colored glasses but through magnifying ones, so that Papa Gershwin became, in his son's versions, one of the great characters of all time, while Momma Gershwin got promoted to the equivalent in mothers. So who wouldn't want to meet such giants? Anyway, there was no question of leaving them behind. So anyone coming to see Gershwin, however grand, might find himself desperately trying to decipher one Russian accent or the other from the parent in residence that day instead.

George would probably have laughed. Perhaps he could afford to feel so detached about his family because he actually owed them so little. In fact, since both senior Gershwins were completely unmusical, and George had been making his own living since age twelve or so, his debt was about as small as a child's can be. But he probably did owe them something, and was all too happy to acknowledge and exaggerate it. From his mother, George may possibly have inherited his powerful drive to "be somebody," although her own version of how you did this was as crude as any peasant's. All that young Rose Gershowitz had learned about the great ladies of Russia was that they glittered and shone: So one imagines many quixotic trips to the beauty parlor and the dressmaker. Females new to America have always been easy to make fun of for their optimistic do's and dyes and their death-or-glory stabs at makeup. But Rose also raised some very functional children in an alien world who would, partly thanks to her, have plenty of time and money to get those things right, and it's entirely possible that George appreciated that.

A couple of other clues to the Gershwins can perhaps be deduced from two disconnected remarks of Levant's, one being that they were an

"even more undemonstrative" family than his own. Back in Russia, Rose had probably also observed that great ladies tend to act standoffish, or, as the word then was, hoity-toity, toward the outside world. Both Lane and Ronell would testify that Rose actually treated them quite warmly once they were safely inside the circle, but she did believe in style, as she understood it, and she presumably passed this on to George, leaving it up to him to translate the concept into American.

Most immigrant parents could only transmit the vague yet powerful ambition that brought them here; the children usually had to do most of their own steering. But Momma did do George one favor that would make up for any mistakes. Although she could see (it's hard to miss it) that money was the one indispensable component of Being Someone in this country, she also knew, or sensed, that classiness mattered too. So while all she basically wanted was for her gifted son to write a lot of hits like Mr. Berlin and make the family rich, some impulse (of snobbery? ancestral memory?) also told her to make sure that he got the best classical training that the Gershwin treasury could spring for. Which makes her one of the great unconscious benefactors of all time, a patron of the American arts second to none.

Levant's second comment was that George seemed to have a "natural aristocracy" about him, which sounds like the same thing Kern was talking about, but doesn't sound like Rose at all. Whatever her virtues, Rose was anything but a "natural" at anything, and when she got what she wanted, namely, a successful and classy son, her instincts told her absolutely nothing about how to handle it. So George's fame went to Momma's head a lot more than it went to his, and it ultimately rendered her, from all accounts, rather pointlessly aloof and difficult and not particularly happy about it. If, as his music suggests, George had his own streak of melancholy beneath all the bubbles, this at least may be due to Momma, who at any rate makes a better suspect for the blues than Papa the clown.

But it's hard to tell about Papa. As in many bios of the period, the father seems to be almost missing from George's formative years. And maybe Morris was—sister Frances says he was missing from hers. But even a remote father can leave traces, if only sometimes in his observed style. "The way he wears his hat," as Ira would say, "the way he sips his

tea." These are the kinds of things you remember, especially about someone who doesn't talk much.

So, since Morris undoubtedly wore his share of hats in that hat-wearing age, and probably sipped a barrel of tea as well, during his beloved pinochle games, it is probably among these small touches that something as elusive and hard to pin down as "natural aristocracy" is to be found. At any rate, it may be worth nothing here that, George's own opinion to the contrary, Morris Gershwin was the parent George reminded people of, not Rose. In fact, Papa Gershwin's response to fame seemed to have mirrored his son's precisely in that he was pleased as punch about it ("I'm *Judge* Gershwin's father," as it sounded like to the traffic cop, a misunderstanding that caused the cop to promptly wave him through—was this a great country or what?), but oddly bemused and detached. Morris knew more than most people about the ups and downs of life. And though he is mostly remembered now, when he is, for his malapropisms and off-the-wall observations, it should be noted that he passed the sternest of all Lower East Side tests with flying colors: He always had some money.

"The Gershwins were not poor," confirmed Yip Harburg. But why weren't they? Rose and Morris had no natural advantages over here, no grubstake or rich relatives, and Morris's only professional training was in a trade (shoe-cutting) that apparently bored him, so instead he plunged, broken vowels and all, into the restaurant business and the Turkish bath business and any other business he could take by the scruff and manage for. And this did his son George the unwitting favor of introducing him to the whole city, as the family moved from one address to another, picking up new sights, sounds, and neighbors, and giving him the day-to-day panorama that would make the "Rhapsody in Blue" such a unique evocation of a modern city. Yet even regarding this particular masterpiece, Morris affected only boredom. "Again? The 'Rhapsody'?" he would say each time it was played.

But that's about all the hard news we're going to get about Papa Gershwin. One of the sturdiest barriers between that era and this is the hedge of wisecracks and funny anecdotes that automatically brewed up around celebrities and near celebrities, sometimes hiding their true selves completely. For instance, the young Gershwins used to bandy the name of one "cousin Botkin the painter" around so facetiously that I was surprised to

find years later that there really was such a person and that he was a most distinguished painter.

And at a second glance, one wonders further whether George and Ira might not have invented Morris altogether, along with Cousin Botkin, for their own professional purposes as counters in the endless game of Can You Top This? played at the Algonquin Round Table and in the gossip columns. Never has the humor of broken English been quite so over-worked, and Papa Gershwin could have been inserted into Georgie Jessel's menagerie of goofy relatives without anyone noticing.

So too Morris, who must in real life have worked very hard and una-musingly to support his family, comes down to us now entirely in the form of a few funny stories. All his real work has gone the way of Rose's washing and ironing and floor-mopping, to be replaced by a kind of lordly insou-ciance. Viz, one day, when George was showing off his art deco apartment to some upscale visitors, Papa Gershwin tiptoed up and, in his most win-ning manner, said, "Tell me, ladies, whatever became of 'oh fudge'?"

With a slight change in circumstance, one can easily imagine some daffy peer of the realm or lord of the manor saying this, but one can't imagine Rose doing so. She would have boasted; Morris had reached the next stage in evolution, where you don't need to boast—you know it. In his book, the ladies wouldn't have come to the apartment at all if the Gershwins hadn't been very important people, so that was taken care of, and he could concentrate on being a perfect host. Most of the jobs he'd taken had required certain PR qualities and some natural charm, so it's safe to assume that George got some version of these from his old man. But did Morris even know that he was funny? Well, he knew that people laughed and that they came back for more, and we know that the Gersh-wins always had some money. So it is safe to guess that much of his charm had a commercial basis, and that, when he wasn't promoting ei-ther his son or his business, he became again one of the "undemonstra-tive" Gershwins.

But that really is it for both Papa and Momma, because George didn't hang around the house like Ira, absorbing influences, but was out the door every chance he got, absorbing something his own size, namely, the city itself.

Juggle the chromosomes as one will, and squeeze every nuance out of

the anecdotes, and one can still find nothing in Gershwin's immediate background to account either for his musical genius or the extraordinary aura and the magnanimity that seemed almost to flow out of the music, in the direction of other songwriters. "He was very warm and very encouraging," said Arthur Schwartz, who as an unknown youth had just brazened his way into George's apartment and been asked immediately to play some of his tunes. "And he gave me the feeling that perhaps I did have some talent and to persevere." Or, as George said to young Harold Arlen, "Hey, kid, that new song of yours is a pip."

"I had the thrilling feeling he meant it," added Arlen, who, like Schwartz, would go on to give Gershwin some of his stiffest competition, without ever losing his friendship.

Gershwin's extended family of songwriters was never just some private club consisting of fellow New Yorkers and/or fellow Jews. One day, the Boston Irishman Jimmy "Don't Blame Me" McHugh ran into George on the street and confessed under friendly questioning that as a matter of fact he had just been wiped out by the stock market crash and could use a new piano. So naturally he found that very thing waiting for him when he got back to his apartment, courtesy of George.

Once again, one is struck, as Lane and Ronell would be, by the particularity of George's thoughtfulness. All a celebrity strictly needs to do to be considered a great guy is to strew a little money around vaguely or, if that's too painful for him, to dispense smiles, warm handshakes, and unspecific words of encouragement. But George took the trouble to find out precisely what was needed, even if it took time as well as money—or even if all it took was thoughtfulness. For instance, when the young Anglo-Scots Midwesterner Hoagy Carmichael decided to get married in New York, it was George who coaxed Hoagy's mother to play the piano at the wedding. Although Mrs. Carmichael had once played ragtime at a local movie house, no one else had apparently learned this or thought to ask her. But she jumped at the request and played up a storm that day—"much better than that Gershwin fellow," according to her dour husband.

Gershwin's embrace of other songwriters was, in short, universal, reaching back into the past and forward into the future. Someone who once made the mistake of questioning Irving Berlin's musicianship in George's presence was met with an answering volley of felicitous exam-

ples that the junior of the two geniuses had obviously memorized. And even after serious people had begun asking George serious questions about his own concert works, he'd passed up the invitation to show off with lists of impressive classical influences and would continue to cite Berlin and Kern instead, not out of coyness, but out of loyalty and his usual disconcerting honesty. He had been influenced by the older songwriters and was still being influenced by younger ones and wanted the world to know it. Mozart didn't need his help now. Ronell and others did.

"He listened to all of us," Arlen told me—after, of course, they'd listened to his latest first, an agreeable condition that they would probably have set themselves if the roles had been reversed. And again, "We were always together in one bunch trying to help each other," as Arlen added another time. Curiously, I found this second quote cited in a book that otherwise tends to slight Gershwin's songs in favor of his concert work, as most of the writing about George has tended to do, even if it has to fly in the teeth of its own evidence.

But suppose we follow George's own lead for once, and think of him first and last as a songwriter instead—how did even that happen? There was no music of any kind in the Gershwins' various houses, even if he'd stuck around to listen, and the chief sound he heard outside was the non-stop clatter of his own roller skates. He didn't even know he liked music until age eleven or so, at which point it must have hit him all in a body—classical and pop alike. Where Berlin had grown up with and assimilated the melody of the streets, Gershwin found his ears flooded simultaneously with both Berlin and Beethoven, the latest and the oldest. And no sooner had he started serious tutoring under the esteemed Charles Hambitzer than he went to work plugging songs and making piano rolls and steeping himself in that as well. So, theoretically, he had a choice of directions. But when his adventurous piano playing began to wander into composition, there was no contest. Songs were the currency around there. Even young Mozart would have had to start with pop if he'd been born on the Lower East Side. And if pop music wasn't ready for Gershwin yet, he'd have to make it ready.

If he could, that is. Even Gershwin's preternatural optimism seems to have paused at this. The songs he must have been plugging and piano-rolling circa 1910 were catchy but trite beyond measure and could all be

vamped on exactly the same chords, like some of the rock hits of the 1960s. And who was to say that the folks who bought the sheet music and sang it round the piano could ever be wooed into wanting anything better? None of the places George's fingers chose to roam seemed to lead in the direction of sing-alongs. So what was a teenage prodigy to do?

In the lingo of Horatio Alger, it was Ragged Dick's darkest hour, and it is in this context that Gershwin's reverence for Berlin and Kern should be viewed. Their timing in his life was perfect, as if they'd been waiting in the next room. Although both men had been writing quietly for several years, Berlin didn't really find his voice (or his copyrights) until about 1911, when George was twelve or so, at which point Irving rolled out a sufficient sample of ragtime songs to show how much room there was for more. Where earlier songs in this mode seem mostly to call attention to their own syncopation, practically tapping your foot for you, Berlin syncopates or not as it suits him, burying it in the verse of "Alexander's Ragtime Band" and sliding it in and out of songs like "I Love a Piano." "Over the keys/the ivories" is like a miniature sleigh ride placed in the middle to reward you for getting this far. Irving is at play in the fields of ragtime, and Gershwin never needed two invitations to a party like that.

And then while he was still playing around with that, along came part two of the course, Jerome Kern's show tunes and especially "They Didn't Believe Me" (1914), to show how the new jaunty, loose-gaited American style could be transferred to truly distinguished music and could be marched right up the hill to the most distinguished addresses on Broadway, which must have towered like Mount Fuji above George's various workshops.

Now if only George could write like that himself . . . but of course he could, magically soon, and so well that both his idols welcomed him to the fraternity as an equal while he was still young enough to savor just meeting them. In fact, no songwriter ever wasted less time reaching his prime and coming into his own. For once, it happened almost the way it did in the movie. Al Jolson, the hottest entertainer of the day, comes around to George's place of business, looking for new material, and falls in love with "Swanee," the selfsame song that would captivate Vladimir Dukelsky a little later, presumably in Jolson's very own version. "How I love ya, how I love ya." Thus Gershwin had answered the main question about himself

with his very first hit. He would not need to write two different kinds of music to win two different kinds of audience. Jolson, the blackface minstrel, and Duke, the White Russian fussbudget, were brothers under the skin. Of course, in the normal course of events, Gershwin's lowbrow career had to come first, in the form of regular assignments on the tits-and-ass end of Broadway, where the follies and scandals, the gags and the gals, labored to divert the tired businessmen. No matter how crummy the milieu, Gershwin's music turned it just as classy, and before he knew it, he'd caught the approving attention of Kern and Berlin.

After that, nothing could harm or deflect him. There are no idols like your first ones, and although Gershwin would soon have other targets and more highbrow models, he would never forget that it was by aiming at Berlin and Kern that he had arrived at wherever he was now. And besides, his heroes hadn't precisely handed the baton over to him, but clung teasingly to it themselves, and kept right on running. "You're pretty good, son. Now try to catch me," and the three of them were still chasing each other's tails, unofficially of course, as they disappeared one by one over the horizon.

So, in this book anyhow, Gershwin is first and last a songwriter—which doesn't mean we have to throw a drop cloth over his classical work. The two sides of George were exquisitely mixed and played into each other constantly. But classically minded writers on the subject have tended to assume that their kind of music in some sense "won" because they consider it better music and more worthy of George's ambitions, but this was never true. Every great concert work of his would be followed by a volley of new and better songs, clearly based on the same inspiration that gave him the longer work. The year before George died, he went to Hollywood, not just to make up for the money he'd lost while working on *Porgy and Bess,* but, by Levant's firsthand account, to catch up with Cole Porter and Richard Rodgers, who'd sneaked past him as songwriters while he was plodding through his masterpiece.

Guesses as to what he would have done had he lived longer outnumber our conjectures about Jack Kennedy—who, like George, said different things to different people, depending on the arc of his enthusiasms—but what Gershwin did do was write songs, right up to the final day, when half of his brain was occupied with a tumor.

So songs literally did come first and they came last, and in between he brought out a book of his best ones that spells out what they meant to him. In contrast to most sheet music, which was always as simple as the publisher could make it, Gershwin's arrangements look like Jackson Pollock paintings and can only be played properly by expert pianists. And in his introduction, he makes the illuminating argument that it is precisely the improvement in the nation's piano playing that had made possible the great leap forward in American songs in the 1920s. And if this leap can, by any stretch, be called a movement, this one-page introduction was surely its manifesto, because unlike the Gershwin of legend, he wasn't just talking about himself or his songs. Gershwin's vanity was never small enough to settle for mere preeminence in his field; he wanted the field itself to be preeminent, and he watched the competition like a hawk for signs of excellence, noting, for instance, that the musical phrase in the first measure of Arlen's "Stormy Weather" is never repeated, and expressing envy over the bridge of Ellington's "Sophisticated Lady." He needed these men to be good if only for the sake of his own place in music, which, as he may have sensed, depended squarely on the "genus of the American song" and its final stock price. If Jerome Kern sank without a trace, Gershwin might wind up clinging to a footnote himself.

At any rate, the highbrow critics of his own day had no trouble remembering that he was a songwriter, and never missed a chance to hold it against him. To them, Tin Pan Alley was a critical disability, a chain around his leg, and every time they seemed on the verge of saying something nice about him, they would remember the magic phrase and hit him over the head with it instead. And despite the changes along that street, the name Tin Pan Alley never sounded any better to the critics, but remained the same old dead-end street between Skid Row and Featherbed Lane that could always be used to put George back in his place, perhaps even after one had grudgingly admitted his God-given, thoroughly wasted gift.

On these terms, the serious reviewers were predictably kinder to Gershwin's early work than they would be to his later, because it made no uppity claims. According to George, they actually overpraised *Blue Monday*, which was a fragment of opera, or song-plus. George was a surprisingly cool self-critic. And "Rhapsody in Blue" got off lightly too, perhaps because it was part of a pseudo-jazz concert in which, if nothing else, it

outshone the competition. (Elsewhere in the program, there was even something by Victor Herbert, and the mere phrase "Jazz by Victor Herbert" is enough to put anyone in a good mood, so the critics felt free to throw out the rulebook, praise the composer's vitality, and in one or two cases even to enjoy themselves, on the understanding that tapping one's foot is not what music is really about.)

One critic mysteriously found "Rhapsody" "lifeless [and] derivative"— of what he didn't say—but the derivative charge would be leveled again, more plausibly, some years later, from George's own side of the tracks, by his friend and fellow songwriter Hoagy Carmichael, who thought "Rhapsody" was made up mostly of familiar bits and pieces of jazz, and that George "was not a real jazzman" anyway, but merely a "Tin Pan Alley genius," concerning which type Hoagy had interestingly mixed feelings.

With this we're back where we belong. Inasmuch as Carmichael was a jazzman himself, he was predisposed to despise commercial music as much as any highbrow, and the above criticism shows him defending his turf every bit as stubbornly as his counterparts on the musical right. Jazz didn't want to let George in at first any more than Carnegie Hall did, though both sides were quite happy to concede him Tin Pan Alley. But the catch for Carmichael was that he had just written the most commercial song in history himself, and hoped to write some more, and there was no denying that the success of his "Stardust" owed at least something to George's enlargement of the form.

So if George wasn't precisely a jazzman, he'd opened the door to jazzmen, and was someone you could talk to on the Alley. (Hoagy's two memoirs reveal no other friends in the songwriting business at all, except his collaborators.) Better yet, Gershwin was someone you could play tennis with as well.

It's symbolic of the great Gershwin misunderstanding that everyone seems to know about his tennis games with the famous atonalist Arnold Schoenberg, but no one seems to know that he also played it with the likes of Hoagy Carmichael, an equally piquant pairing in its own world— or indeed, that he would play it with anyone who'd give him a match. The *thunk* of tennis balls and *plink* of Ping-Pong balls, and whatever the sound is that golf balls make, followed George everywhere, like background music that's too insistent to ignore. How a man spends half his

waking hours surely belongs in the text, not the footnotes, of his life. It seems that whenever George wasn't playing the piano, he was playing something else (he has even been called a sexual athlete), and at the piano itself, he was playing as much as working, in the compulsive style of America in the 1920s, when you played until you dropped. No one ever got more sheer physical exercise out of a keyboard, so perhaps it isn't too Hollywood-fanciful to flash back again to the beginning, to our hyperactive hero's boyhood, at the point where he has just gotten hooked by Dvořák's "Humoresque" and Rubinstein's "Melody in F" and can put off music no longer. And one pictures him hitting the piano with the force he usually devoted to hitting balls or occasional faces, and deciding on the spot that this is a great game too, because, like a character in a dream, he could play it superbly almost on sight and could have this same dream anytime he wanted.

Everyone talks about the childlike awe with which Gershwin discussed his own music, and about his famous sprints to the piano at other people's parties, as if to show off this new trick he's just learned. But seldom has a vice been easier to understand. Imagine a great, somewhat tongue-tied athlete who is actually encouraged to play his sport in the living room and who, by doing so, is guaranteed to outshine the brightest company in London, Paris, and New York. Who could ask for anything more?

It really was a new trick too, every single time, and not just a worn-out party piece. "What comes out of that piano frightens me," he's alleged to have said, and it was this sheer unpredictability as much as his technique that drew people. Who knew what great song might be born tonight and merely live forever? George seemed as excited to find out as anyone.

"George at the piano was George happy," said Rouben Mamoulian, which means that he must have been happy an awful lot of the time, although witnesses report bursts of operatic gloom when George was at rest—all the more reason to keep playing. Relief was never more than a keyboard away. (Speaking of gloom, though, Joan Peyser passes on the important news that George first smelled burning rubber as early as 1934, which means his fatal tumor might have set up shop three years before his death, which would explain the gloomy episodes I've heard of.)

"He was the only man I knew who could make a piano laugh," said

Abram Chasins, and numerous photographs show the piano apparently returning the favor, with George fiendishly grinning over the instrument's latest joke. Also, he had a cheerful way of attracting pretty girls to come sit next to him at the piano bench, a knack Vernon Duke says he was never able to master himself, although he too was a handsome fellow and a dazzling pianist.

Yet Gershwin's hyperactivity was too laid-back and self-possessed to be mistaken for simple nervousness, or escapism, or the other pop-psychology staples that his less physical critics might be tempted to reach for. But it wasn't all hyperactivity; he also enjoyed goofing off and kidding around. Levant records the two of them actually lolling about, talking football and girls like college roommates. And Carmichael reports that one day after he and George had wrapped up their business on the court, they swore a mighty oath never to write a piece of music set for the ukulele. One picks up the immortal sounds of the locker room and of athletes winding down with wisecracks and jocose rituals of friendship. This side of George is missing from the conventional biography—George the jock, the sports-man, a type so alien to writers on the arts that they've tended to circle this robust figure cautiously, as if it were a Hottentot or noble savage, reading whatever they like into him. (One analyst has even suggested Gershwin had low self-esteem, a diagnosis that would have had his friends roaring for days.)

Expeditions to Gershwin's dark side have a way of foundering on his boisterous physicality, which seems to call for a different kind of analysis. This was not some introvert discovering his body aesthetically, but a macho little street brawler hitting the arts like a cyclone and realizing they're not just for sissies after all, but can fit perfectly into his daily round of ball bashing as it ascends from roller-skate hockey to tennis to the top of the hill—golf, which he found kind of slow, and played occasionally at the speed of Charlie Chaplin, but played expertly too; and in the same spirit, he would, as time went on, add such indoor sports as oil painting, interior decorating, and ballroom dancing (at which he was a whiz) to his frantic schedule.

When George hit upon anything new, be it art deco or Joseph Schil-linger's mathematical theory of composition, he was, says Vernon Duke, like a kid with a new toy, as if mental activity were to be prized for its

gamelike quality. (Gershwin's interest in Schillinger was picked up by Oscar Levant, who studied with him to no avail. The one positive result I know of from Schillinger's theories was, of all things, Glenn Miller's theme song, "Moonlight Serenade." Go figure.) Luckily for all concerned, Gershwin was no superstar at his various games (his tennis was only fair), so he brought his athletic temperament to bear on music instead, where it seemed as strange as an artistic temperament would seem in a baseball dugout.

One doesn't want to exaggerate this. George might have seemed a little strange in a dugout too. Yet a sportswriter might note that at least some of Gershwin's puzzling quirks are commonplace in the sports world, including his slightly comical "I am the greatest" swagger, his stoicism under fire—criticism rolled off him like jabs off Muhammad Ali—and the curious blend of generosity and competitiveness that characterized his dealings with colleagues. Only in sports can people be such wholehearted enemies and friends at the same time, and only in sports does a man actually feel let down if the opposition isn't good enough and he wins too easily. Thus, when George declared his envy of "Sophisticated Lady," it is not far-fetched to picture a tennis player jumping over the net to congratulate an opponent. "Well played—I'll get you next time."

Ellington had just raised the stakes, and forced George to play better too. Yet perhaps only a man who also gets to play both music and tennis with the likes of Arnold Schoenberg could manage to be quite as sporty and breezily good-humored as George. Gershwin's classical alter ego may have had a bumpy ride at times, but at least Gershwin had an alter ego, to absorb life's shocks: Most songwriters had no alter egos at all. And tellingly, one of the few who did, our old friend Vladimir Dukelsky, actually received worse reviews for his classical work than George ever did, but behaved as if he came from a superior species anyhow, just for having written it.

Gershwin was certainly pleased with himself too, but his sporting impulse was to share the wealth, and his magnanimity undoubtedly helped usher in an era of goodwill along Tin Pan Alley, which a battle-scarred veteran like Kern might have particularly appreciated. Earlier in the century, a songwriter "with nothing small about" him would have been as lost as Gulliver. Veterans like George M. Cohan and Irving Berlin had to fight so

many small fights with small people—over copyrights, royalties, credits, survival—that they remained slightly crouched and suspicious for the rest of their days. But by the twenties, ASCAP was in place and the new technology of radio and records was about to open up a musical superhighway like unto a yellow brick road for composers to stroll down arm in arm. So it was high time for a large free spirit like Gershwin to come bouncing along, and his name went up on the national marquee almost immediately and stays there still alongside Babe Ruth's and Scott Fitzgerald's as a symbol of that Roman candle of an era.

With all this established and certified in neon by the midtwenties, it may not have required all that much stoicism for George to shrug off the scattering of sneers that greeted his concert works. If Schoenberg fortified one for Ellington, he also equally fortified one for Virgil Thomson and the other highbrows. Still, it must have taken the detachment of Morris Gershwin himself to withstand the gale force advice that blew in from all sides after his Concerto in F in 1925. It seemed that everyone was telling George how to use his, unfortunately undeniable, talent. Since, among other things, he would eventually write a perfect pastiche of Wozzeck for "Of Thee I Sing" and an authentic madrigal for A Damsel in Distress, it seems odd that Gershwin couldn't have taken the few simple steps it required to placate the New York critics—whose own brilliance should not be exaggerated—and remove the curse of Tin Pan Alley forever.

If he'd wanted to. This was the heart of the matter: George did not consider Tin Pan Alley a curse at all, but a gold mine into which one could probably invest all one's time and talent, including one's classical talent, in hopes of finding a genuine new American art. So he went his serene way, alternately writing songs and concert pieces that ran together into a single sound that could be played in a pinch by a jazz band or a symphony orchestra, or by some fusion of both that didn't yet exist.

But while everyone noticed, and mostly deplored, the effect of this process on classical music, only a few initiates like Arlen and the envious Vincent Youmans seemed to take in the simultaneous effect it was having on songs. While the critics were guarding all the entrances to make sure Gershwin didn't smuggle any of his dirty Tin Pan Alley tricks into the classical shrine, George was busy smuggling the sophistication and resourcefulness of "good music" out the exits and into Broadway musicals, and

thence onto the street. Alec Wilder, who was oddly allergic to Gershwin, blurs the importance of this development by comparing George's 1920s songs with other people's more evolved 1930s ones that had built on them. But if you go back to the very beginning, to the piano piece "Rialto Ripples" (1917) or the song "Some Wonderful Sort of Someone" (1918), you can already hear something completely fresh and different, something not quite jazz and not quite classical, but a newborn sound that would influence American songs for the next and best quarter century.

Fortunately, a book has been written that illustrates roughly how the traffic worked. Although Deena Rosenberg's *Fascinating Rhythm* doesn't undertake to trace Gershwin's influence through the whole American songbook, her X-rays of a few of his songs are enough to establish a continuum between his classical work and his popular, and to suggest another continuum between his songs and other people's. Clearly, one of the games he most liked to play at the piano was to see how many songs he could winkle out of a single musical phrase, the most spectacular examples being the three he got from simply reciting his beloved pentatonic scale— the reflective "Maybe," the noisy "Clap Yo' Hands," and the comic "They All Laughed"—and three others he "found," with a little help from Ira's words and a few grace notes of his own, lurking in the "Good Evening Friends" sequence in "Rhapsody in Blue." And I have no doubt Rosenberg could have discovered as many in the Concerto in F if she'd gotten around to it: the song "Soon," for instance, which illustrates beautifully how a song runs one way and an orchestral piece another. Gershwin never stopped shuffling his themes until, or after, he'd found the perfect setting of rhythm and emphasis. "Maybe" is a gorgeous song, "Clap Yo' Hands" sounds too busy, and while that theme from the "Rhapsody" may have sounded cliché to Carmichael, it seemed breathtakingly original to everyone else once George had disguised it lightly as "The Man I Love."

In fact, Rosenberg considers that particular song such a breakthrough that it cleared the way not only to George's own best, but to other people's best too, like "My Funny Valentine" and "Night and Day"—in short, to the best of Rodgers and Porter as well—thus locating a single pipeline between Carnegie Hall and Broadway. And whether it was one song that did the trick or many, "The Man I Love" makes a plausible landmark because in 1925, the year after George wrote it and started putting it into shows

and taking it out again (it holds some kind of record for this), three break-out songs by other writers appeared among the usual welter of "Yes Sir, That's My Baby." Rodgers's first hit, "Manhattan," Carmichael's first, "Riverboat Shuffle," and Kern's far and away hippest to date, "Who," which signified respectively that a classical music student, a "jazz baby" (as Carmichael described himself), and a master of American operetta had all found homes on the new Tin Pan Alley, as at least partly redesigned by Gershwin.

After which, the deluge. Over the next five years, Youmans went from "I Want to Be Happy" to "More Than You Know." Berlin, following his brief ego-shaking crisis of confidence, would go from "Always" to "How Deep Is the Ocean," and Donaldson from, indeed, "Yes Sir, That's My Baby" to "Little White Lies" . . . and so on all along the street. Gershwin had proved with one song or several that sophistication sells, and had shown his comrades at least one way to write it, and the bell curve, the boom within the boom, began to rise sharply, with Gershwin sitting on top of it all the way until his death a decade later.

And it was in that same epic year of 1925 that the serious New York critics began seriously to give up on George, like philanthropists who've tried everything for some child of the streets and found the kid just hope-less. His most ambitious work, the Concerto in F, orchestrated after some laborious self-instruction, had debuted, and all it proved to them was that you can't take the Alley out of the boy, especially when the Alley has turned into a boulevard. To Gershwin's ear, the kind of American music that the critics themselves thought they wanted *had* to contain elements of pop (as they didn't yet call it), partly because Berlin and Kern happened to be the most interesting composers in the country just then, and partly because in his brief, kaleidoscopic apprenticeship, the two kinds of music had, as we've seen, arrived simultaneously and virtually intertwined. There was no stage at which George could have organically evolved from one to the other, because he was too busy evolving back and forth be-tween the two of them in a dizzy dialectic, studying the classics at one moment with a teacher who was already urging him to higher things, just like a critic, and at the next making his ragtime piano rolls and plugging schlock. But perhaps the most annoying thing about the Concerto was that Gershwin hadn't even needed to get pushy about it—a vandal crash-

ing the temple and writing graffiti—but was in the concert hall by invitation again and always would be. The grim fact was that the serious people needed him there to attract their own customers, their own highbrow fans. It was humiliating, so the least they could do was insult him for it.

If the critics were not going to like his concert stuff any way that he did it, maybe he should skip all that for now and try doing it all with songs, which, incidentally, had recently become a family business—always a factor with George. In fact, the late 1920s might be called the years of apprenticeship for Ira as well, as he edged his way up from the simpleminded *Lady, Be Good* (1924) to his own sound in " 'S Wonderful" (1927), and then the Pulitzer-winning lyrics of the political satire *Of Thee I Sing*. "All the sexes from Maine to Texas" is more than confident: It also hits the notes just right, and makes the whole song work better. "Who cares what banks fail in Yonkers?" The brothers could do their own banking now.

A trip abroad that same epic year of 1925 might also have been an occasion for Gershwin to concentrate just on his songs. Europeans had their own kind of snobbery, and it was almost the opposite of ours. For at least two centuries, they had been sneering at pale American imitations of their own forms, but they could be awestruck, and reluctantly impressed, by our vulgarity. Americans could study their hearts out in Paris, but our grand master was Walt Disney, our Mona Lisa was Donald Duck. And what the Europeans liked about our music was that they couldn't do it themselves.

To American critics, Gershwin sounded exactly like what they wanted to get away from. It was the essence of their own time and place represented musically, just as James Joyce had verbally rendered Dublin in *Ulysses*. This kind of rendering absolutely had to include the time and place's vulgarity, its flash and its hustle, and what can only be called its gorgeous ugliness. Two years earlier, G. K. Chesterton had pointed out how beautiful Times Square must look to someone who couldn't read, and here was that same thought set to music. If Gershwin's music had been any purer or more correct, it wouldn't have been New York.

And the rest of the world probably wouldn't have liked it so much either. After all, Europeans couldn't read Times Square themselves, and the phrase "Tin Pan Alley" probably sounded both Dada and wonderfully American.

If the Old World wanted anything from us at all it was modernity, and Gershwin was as modern as a skyscraper. And, as it so often is, the curse of commercialism and cheap popularity was softened in translation. Call a song an aria, or a show an opera, and it steps up in class. Call Gershwin's music "le jazz hot" and it takes on artistic pretensions. Thus every popular musician—from Chopin to the Beatles—needs to be heard by fresh ears against a fresh background. At home, it usually takes forever for pop music to become folk music, let alone classical music, but foreigners don't have to wait that long, and Gershwin's reception in Europe in that same overflowing year of 1925 was less grudging and embarrassed than it was here. He would thenceforth return from each of his few trips abroad fortified and bubbling with ideas and optimism. Levant says that Gershwin was particularly taken to learn that the last movement of his Concerto in F had been reprised by audience demand at the Venice International Festival of Contemporary Music, something that had happened only once before in history, "In 1894," as he told people reverently.

With this in his pocket, or about to be, the American critics probably looked as small to him as he did to them. After all, they had their own troubles in the twenties, trying to lay down the law in the world of the New and post-New, and they must have been relieved to find someone they could condescend to so confidently. If Stravinsky wrote something in jazz, he could make up his own rules. But if Gershwin did the same, he was judged by the strictest European standards. Gershwin was a kid from the neighborhood, trying to improve himself. And not trying hard enough.

Because no matter how serious he tried to be he wouldn't stop writing songs, as if concert music couldn't scratch his itch by using up enough of the tunes in his head. Thus it came to pass that even while he was studiously orchestrating the last movement of his make-or-break Concerto, he was dashing off songs for his next musical, *Tip-Toes*. And by the time he had brought the finished concerto to New York (a phrase that sounds show-bizzy itself), he was actually shepherding two musicals through rehearsal. He was like a man cheating on his wedding night. No wonder some critics—not all—railed at him like schoolmasters. They knew impertinence when they saw it. Gershwin was in effect saying that Broadway songs were just as important as what they did, and this was intolerable.

Anyhow, there's no need to caricature Gershwin's critics here or any-

where else. George could be maddeningly cavalier about his musical ABC's, and you didn't have to be a provincial American to construe this in terms of his haste to make lots of money doing something else.

The Europeans probably assumed the same thing (he was an American, wasn't he?), but were less annoyed and more impressed. In a wonderfully useful anecdote, Vernon Duke describes taking his expatriate pals Prokofiev and Diaghilev to hear an execrable French translation of the concerto played in Paris, and all three were variously disappointed; Duke by the French musicians; Diaghilev because it was "good jazz and bad Liszt" (if you wrote rhapsodies, you had to sound like Liszt); and Prokofiev by the same thing that bothered the American critics, Gershwin's failure to build adequate bridges between his themes.

The big difference was that Prokofiev, being less familiar with the cheap American materials in Gershwin's work, was better able to hear the completely new thing he'd made of them; and whatever he heard was enough to make him immediately want to meet Gershwin. Accordingly, George showed up the next morning at Sergey's hotel and proceeded to "play his head off," after which the Russian was pleased to pronounce that his guest would go far "if he left dollars and dinners alone."

Like everyone else, Prokofiev assumed that Gershwin wrote songs only for dollars and had to drop his real work to do them. Yet the chances are that for at least some of the morning, he'd been listening to George's songs and enjoying them just as much as the "serious" parts. But if he'd known the songs better, he might have realized, as Duke did, that Gershwin just wrote Gershwin, and the dollars he made only helped him to write more Gershwin. And the same went for "dinners" in his honor and other attentions, all of which he seems to have regarded as so many more invitations to play the piano and impress new people with new ideas. American geniuses as a breed are known to have notoriously weak hearts for flattery— one compliment wipes out some of them—but George could take any amount of it because it played to his strength, and he emerged like a giant refreshed from an orgy of recognition in Paris and elsewhere, recognition much noisier and more palpable than the amount that so poleaxed Ernest Hemingway. The curious detachment that George had inherited from his father must have told him that some of the attention was chic and silly— Gershwin's blue notes were "in" this year like Papa's fractured sentences—

but he loved the attention anyhow; and at least some of it was the real thing. After all, Prokofiev *had* wanted to meet him, and so would Alban Berg in Vienna, and other serious musicians everywhere he went. There seems to have been a consensus, as firm as it was vague, that Gershwin was on to something and that he mattered, whether or not any particular pieces of his music did. And there the matter rests to this day, with Arnold Schoenberg's heartfelt eulogy summing up the unresolved consensus at the time of Gershwin's death. "George Gershwin was one of this rare kind of musician to whom music is not a matter of more or less ability. Music to him was the air he breathed, the food that nourished him, [etc.]. There is no doubt that he was a great composer." But was he a good one also? Never mind. Gershwin was of this rare breed that doesn't have to be.

Primed with such ambiguous approval ("Why be a second-rate Ravel when you can be a first-rate Gershwin?" as another prospective teacher told him), Gershwin returned from Europe apparently less anxious to prove himself in the traditional forms of serious music—why be a second-rate Mozart? And right then "being a Gershwin" could be satisfied by immediately writing some new songs. However important his concert music had ever been to him (and you couldn't be a great composer without it, could you?), he could wait for the critical acclaim. In the meantime, one particular song, "I Got Rhythm," sounded as much like "being Gershwin" as anything else he ever did.

His mad sprints to the piano were prompted not just by vanity, but by deadlines, as he hustled to finish his new show and the one after. Musicals were perfect because they required new songs immediately, never mind polishing the old ones. It is often overlooked that for all of their harmonic brilliance, some of his early songs had the same slapdash quality as his concert pieces. Just as Vernon Duke notes how unadventurous Gershwin could be in matters of tempo, relying on the same old beat that had seen him through his piano-roll days, Alec Wilder comments on the conventionality of Gershwin's song forms, even when he was writing for the theater, where you could use any form you liked. Thirty-two bars divided four ways, A A B A—who had time for anything more? Although he could chop up the beat with the best of them, as in "Fascinating Rhythm," and would write his last great song, "Our Love Is Here to Stay," in the slightly

more demanding (and I think rewarding) A B A B + form, in general he stuck to the fastest kind of delivery he knew.

In other respects, his songs began to sound markedly better and more thoughtful as the twenties went on, and his orchestral pieces more slap-dash, as if they were now the thing that was being done to meet his con-tractual obligations while the songs were his real self. "He Loves and She Loves," "Someone to Watch over Me," "Embraceable You"—the addi-tional warmth of these songs hark back to that second trip to Europe in 1928, which may have prompted him not just to write like Gershwin but to find out what a Gershwin was.

With this in mind, he even allowed his disciple-cum-girlfriend Kay Swift to talk him into a fling with the latest rage, psychoanalysis, but with-out his magic piano he seemed to have found himself not particularly in-teresting. What came out of the piano might frighten him, but what came off the couch probably just bored him and made him want to go out and play something, either a game or a piano.

Without his instrument, he wasn't really George Gershwin anyway, so he took to exploring himself in ever more varied musical settings instead. Each of his next, and last, three orchestral works could have been a jour-nal entry chronicling his response to some new experience. *An American in Paris* starts with a tourist's description of the city he's just arrived in (with a tip of his cap to one of his early heroes, Debussy), then switches to the visitor's sense that he doesn't really belong there and wants to go home, before proceeding to a joyous reconciliation as the American hears a way to have it all, his own city and this one, a richer version of himself. What Gershwin couldn't know was that he had also contributed to a form that didn't exist yet, that might be called a travelogue-ballet, complete with animated postcards from the Louvre. "They did right by George," I said to my father when the eponymous movie ended. "Yes," he thought-fully answered, "they did right by George."

After that, the second "Rhapsody," which was originally called "Rhap-sody in Rivets," returns the American to New York with a bang and with a slight sense of alienation—what's happening to this place? By the late twenties, Manhattan was right in the middle of the frantic building boom that would give it most of its famous skyline, with scaffolding indeed

seeming to scrape the sky, and hammers pounding down from there like thunder, and this is what it sounded like to George—the aural equivalent of Fritz Lang's jarring film *Metropolis*. Fittingly, though, George's piece was originally written as a species of special effects for the movies, yet already one feels he'd rather say it in a song or two, and perhaps he finally did in the sunny number "Slap That Bass," which shows the American no longer in awe of technology, but airily familiar with it as he dances along with the ship's pistons. And the "Cuban Overture" would probably have worked itself out as songs too, had Gershwin lived a few months longer. By the midthirties, Latin rhythms had insinuated their way into Tin Pan Alley and Hollywood, and his Broadway rival Youmans had already written a samba and a tango for the film *Flying Down to Rio* in acknowledgment. But as it stands, Gershwin's "What I Did on My Vacation" homage to the Caribbean sounds perfunctory, like a bread-and-butter letter, as if he hadn't really started to think in this form yet, and perhaps never would. "Just be yourself" was mischievous advice to give to this man of a thousand whims living in the land of perpetual change, but Broadway musicals had recently become coherent and more hospitable to the kind of social and political satire that the times suddenly seemed to call for, so he had to try one or two of those. *Strike Up the Band. Let 'Em Eat Cake*. Gershwin didn't do politics, he did moods. And as usual, he was up-to-the-minute.

Surely no American has ever done so much work so well *after* being the toast of Paris. But now as Broadway itself began to slow down in the early 1930s, Gershwin too decided to settle down with his true love, a little novel he'd read sometime before called *Porgy*, which really was worth taking his time over, and losing some chances to make money over. He had always been fascinated by black music and must have brought just about every black pianist in Harlem home to his apartment at one time or another, and to hell with the landlord's opinion. But this would give him a chance to go back a step further to the beginning and write black choral music as well, which is where it all began.

He'd often had to work hard, but in the Broadway sense of blitzkrieging projects through marathon sessions (he'd even scored his concerto that way). But now he had to slow down and work *really* hard, like a bank clerk or intricate craftsman, laboriously cranking out pages and pages by

hand of the kind of music that gets you unbrilliantly from here to there, the equivalent of Yeats's "numb" lines of poetry. Unfortunately, Gershwin's vision did not reach all the way into production. And by the time *Porgy*, with "Bess" added to the name, opened for the first time on Broadway, his hard work had disappeared, leaving behind the usual malcontents in the press box and a dysfunctional hybrid on the stage: a Broadway musical slowed down by gobbits of opera, but not by enough of them to attract *that* audience either. The show dribbled along for one hundred-odd performances and died—to everyone's dissatisfaction. Later, other souls learned to get *Porgy and Bess* just right, and some brilliant words have been written about this.

So George wouldn't live to see it and at this point in time he didn't even have time for a broken heart. "I'd be very upset by this if I wasn't so busy right now," he's reported to have said after a busted romance— although really the words could have applied to any of his life's tragedies up to and almost including death itself.

Levant's book suggests a mood of enormous postpartum buoyancy after *Porgy*, marked by much stepped-up portrait painting and interior design and rumors of marriage. Gershwin had just written a masterpiece and knew it, and he had also had a ball with the black actors in *Porgy*. He now had a blank slate and a head full of melodies, so where to next? Certainly not to Broadway, where so many theaters had turned into movie houses that even a Gershwin had to line up for the next one, and where his songs would be expected to make some kind of sense in terms of a play that he hadn't even seen yet. In contrast you could go to Hollywood in a boom year like 1936 with a suitcase full of hits and dump them anywhere, regardless of subject matter. Love could "Walk Right In" absolutely any place it wanted and land on any singer of either sex who happened to be on the set that day, and anyone from Mickey Mouse to Zasu Pitts could remember the way anyone else "sipped his (or her) tea" or "danced till three."

So Gershwin signed on with Fred Astaire at RKO, the closest thing to a safe house for Broadway writers in Hollywood. But even Astaire couldn't guarantee his old friend the basic Broadway privilege of seeing his own songs through production—or even prevent Ginger Rogers from singing a couple of them. Actually, George didn't think that highly of Fred's singing either, perhaps wanting a bigger, richer instrument. Still, Fred would turn

out to be not just his most effective interpreter then, but has remained so ever since, as he continues to audition Gershwin's last great songs for one generation after another. Astaire had already gone from being the least likely suspect as a movie star to the closest thing to a guaranteed immortal in film musical history.

Also, as Irving would say, Fred could sing just about anything you gave him, including whatever you had in your trunk. And George undoubtedly gave him at least one from there, "They Can't Take That Away from Me." But in general George never used an old song when a brand-new one would do, and he seemed to be in a particularly hyperactive phase at the moment, painting some great portraits, conducting some major concerts in L.A., chasing Paulette Goddard and Simone Simon around the backs of limousines, and playing golf and tennis at the same time, as if he didn't have a moment to lose.

In the circumstances, and with his fatal brain tumor pounding in, Gershwin's last days in Hollywood and on earth seemed downright epic, but also a bit confusing because the tumor seems to have struck so erratically. At one moment, we find George cast into deep gloom by Sam Goldwyn's command (for his next and last film assignment) to "write me some hits like Irving Berlin," which is where he'd come in some twenty years earlier. But at another, he's chuckling, perhaps for his last time, at hearing Sam and George Balanchine hotly arguing in broken Russian, the language of his youth. To judge from Levant's resolutely sunny—and indispensable— account in *A Smattering of Ignorance,* George barely seems to have had time for a tumor. So one deduces that its jabs remained intermittent, though increasingly ferocious, till very near the end, and it seems certain that George stayed at his post as long as he humanly could. If trouble really was coming, where better to be than at the piano?

Besides, there was work to be done. The competition had caught up with him amazingly fast, and what Rosenberg says about Gershwin's late songs applies equally to everyone else's as well, circa 1936, "George's music . . . is on the whole less given to the repetition of melodic fragments against shifting harmonies" (as in, to take a quintessential non-Gershwin example, Donaldson's "Carolina in the Morning"). Now he (and everyone else) preferred to use "a style of longer melodic lines and phrases . . . the harmonies, while still complex, sound even smoother

and more fluid" and they contain what she quotes Dick Hyman as calling the "built-in syncopation," which was by now their defining ingredient of the whole jazz song movement. His Astaire movies gave him a chance to fool around with a form of music specific to film, which might be called the background cartoon or illustration. In *Shall We Dance*, Astaire and Rogers get into a unique love-hate walking-the-dog contest that you just have to see for yourself, and Gershwin's sublime music for it just has to be heard as well: It goes perfectly with Gershwin's two great preludes as a sublime concert substitute. In this case I am also reminded of a *New Yorker* one-liner set to jazz. Then the whole score of *A Damsel in Distress* seems to help the movie in telling its story, as if he has thrown away his trunk and is actually thinking of music for Joan Fontaine to sort of dance to, and for George Burns and Gracie Allen to be funny to. He even writes a madrigal to fit the English castle in the background.

It's too bad George didn't keep a diary—although its entries would probably have surprised *him* every day as much as anyone. What's missing in that last year or so is his next big plan. The problem was that modernist music took him away from his people, his audience. He'd managed to get away with a brilliant pastiche of Wozzeck in "Of Thee I Sing," and maybe he could score a whole movie in the style of "Walking the Dog," but ominously the "Second Rhapsody" and the "Cuban Overture" were the only things he ever wrote that you couldn't whistle on your way out of the concert hall.

It might be unfair to blame this on the modernism he'd picked up abroad. Still, for now, Porter and Rodgers were more stimulating targets than Shostakovich or Sibelius. The game seemed to be to see how much he could say in songs—from the laid-back country style of "I'm Biding My Time" to the wisecracking buoyancy of "Let's Call the Whole Thing Off" ("you say either, I say either"—what kind of song is that?), to the somber satisfaction of "A Foggy Day," which could be called "An American in London" to complete the trilogy and incidentally show how far he had come himself. Since "A Foggy Day" also comes so near the end of his life, it provides an elegiac moment to pause and consider George's own evolution from wide-eyed young genius to grand master.

Just as Gershwin had previously captured the screaming clangor of New York and the good-natured squeaks of Paris, he and his brother now

set to work on the defining sounds of London, which they apparently (and quite correctly) took to be a compound of bells, and of people talking about the weather. Anyone lucky enough to have heard the carillon at Riverside Church in one of its exuberant flights of fancy toward the end of World War II will recognize how brilliantly "A Foggy Day" plays with the possibility of bells, from the verse's stentorian opening, on through the American's jazzy interjections, to the mock-solemn chimes that greet the final dispersal of the fog, like a winking Te Deum. The Age of Miracles hasn't passed. The sun has come out in London!

The other notable thing about "A Foggy Day" is that for once the lyrics make a real difference to the effect, so that George can now say almost as much in a song as he ever had in his concert works. Unlike George's earlier tunes, which had seemed like moving targets for Ira to throw lyrics at if he could ("I got rhythm . . . music . . . my man" . . . time's up), the long lines of his last songs finally gave his lyricist some room to breathe and work in, and the brothers began to click as never before.

It may come as a shock at this point to realize that George and Ira were still a shade younger when George died than Harpo and Chico were before the *first* Marx Brothers movie. Both were still in the middle of maturing. Already it's hard to imagine any of George's last batch of tunes (all of which even the Gershwin-phobic Alec Wilder praises to the utmost, except for "Slap That Bass") being composed in his early rattly-bang, race-you-to-the-barn piano style, and equally hard to imagine the author of "He'll be big and strong, the man I love" being up to matching them. But as far as the team was concerned, this was just the beginning.

George's death at that excruciating moment would give all his last songs a weight of association that is for once altogether worthy of them. Songwriters regularly used to put more power into musical comedy songs than the settings strictly justified, in the hopes that some great singer or band would come along later and yank them out of the boy-meets-girl context and drive them at full speed. But in this case the mere passage of time has done the trick. The throwaway title song of the film *Shall We Dance,* for instance, now echoes across the years like music over water, conveying the jaunty, sad sound of a whole society that won't let the band go to bed, because tomorrow is going to be so awful: "The Long Weekend"

between the wars was almost over, Gershwin music and all. And the brothers' last song together, "Our Love Is Here to Stay," has since been rescued from the trackless waste of *The Goldwyn Follies* of 1938 to become an anthem to friendship—a final hand-clasp of the Gershwins as the ship goes down, an ode to immortality in four-quarter time.

"The Rockies may crumble, Gibraltar may tumble" said the song, which George had just written with the half of his brain that hadn't been eaten yet by his tumor, and which he was still working on the day before he died. It was like a man planting a flag in the future, and giving rivals and partners in the Great American Jam Session something else to shoot for after he'd gone. In fact, like all his work in that dazzling Indian summer of creation, the song could have been expressly designed to stay here itself, and when I heard it again a decade later in Vincente Minnelli's gorgeous production of *An American in Paris,* I found myself thinking that this song simply gets better every year.

His dramatic death right after that would ensure not only that all his songs were here to stay but that everything about Gershwin was here to stay as well, including questions about the nature and inevitability of his death, which scientists have been arguing about ever since, but not in here they don't. Here, the big story is the shuddering impact of his death on his own gang, particularly on the two great rivals who had been most obsessed by him.

"I'm so upset at the moment I can hardly think," wrote the usually phlegmatic Richard Rodgers to his wife. "I just can't believe he's gone. . . . The whole town [Hollywood] is in a daze and nobody talks about anything but George's death." And Rodgers's fellow Gershwin-envier Vincent Youmans showed comparable shock in his own particular way by grabbing a bottle of scotch and playing Gershwin tunes on the piano till dawn the next day. An obsessive needs his subject (what would Ahab have done with himself the next day if he had ever actually killed his whale?), and trying to keep up with George had given not only the disheveled Youmans but the whole fraternity a target to aim at for the next quarter century or so, when this kind of music began to peter out on its own.

But perhaps the strongest evidence we have of George's sheer charisma is the annihilating effect of its absence on his brother. For the

next two years or so, Ira seemed simply paralyzed with regret, as if his spirit had been unplugged. By nightmarish chance, just weeks before he died, George had actually received something like a clean bill of health from the Cedars of Lebanon Hospital, which had ruled out a tumor but had suggested he might have psychological problems (though George's former shrink knew better and had actually advised him to see a regular doctor). Ira's fussy wife, Leonore, had suggested that George take his erratic, tumor-related behavior elsewhere for a little while until he got over it.

So Ira's ruefulness was apparently compounded with guilt and he had no inner fire to fight it with, or strength of his own. He needed help, so naturally he eventually got some from his brother in the form of the sub-lime record that Astaire would make with Johnny Green of the brothers' last songs together. Ira listened and suddenly felt as if George were "back in the room" and power had been restored. Soon after that, his friend Kurt Weill suggested that the two of them do a show together, and Ira batted out some surprisingly high-spirited numbers for *Lady in the Dark,* and a few after that for *Cover Girl* for Jerome Kern, until he'd run through a quite satisfactory second minicareer, using all the skills he'd just begun to master when George died. So Ira had become half a songwriter and a very good one after all, fully worthy of his own place in here. But he was not a natural, and one pictures him in the ASCAP group picture squirming and tugging at his collar like the late Rodney Dangerfield. Tunesmiths could be shy because their talent talked for itself, but lyricists had to make themselves heard like gag writers over the noise of their talented rivals, so an heir to the throne like Ira never quite fit. The equally shy Burton Lane had once confessed to taking a sedative before he could face a business lunch with Ira, and Ira had confessed right back that he had to take one too. And perhaps the strain of going it alone began to tell, and he let out a desolate howl of a song called "The Man That Got Away," with Harold Arlen, and quit soon afterward. "The road gets rougher, it's lonelier and tougher." Ira wasn't really writing about himself, but coming from the au-thor of "Do, Do, Do" and " 'S Wonderful," the voice is unrecognizable and would not be heard again in a musical score.

As if to keep an eye on George and make sure he never left the room again, Ira retired in earnest this time, to become the full-time keeper of

the flame, reviving unpublished songs, giving countless interviews, and in general living the kind of scholarly, word-playing, arm-chair-dwelling life that nature had probably designed him for in the first place. If there had been no George, the odds seem good that Ira would have become an English teacher with a sideline in light verse and an unassuming wife to match.

What he got, unfortunately for both of them, was the stage-villainous but somewhat maligned Leonore, who may have been the worst victim of George's absence of anyone, and with whom you don't have to be a feminist to sympathize a little. As a bright young woman from a brilliant family, Leonore Strunsky had once had every reason to look forward to an exciting lifetime spent within Gershwin's glamorous, unpredictable ambience. And now she was stuck with this placid lump, living out his and her endless days on their own personal Sunset Boulevard, scarcely able to move, it seems. A friend of mine once called Ira and was startled to hear the old boy wheezing heavily into the phone. Had Ira's house caught fire? Had someone, by some miracle, persuaded the chap to jog or something? "No," panted Ira, "I'm just breaking in a new pair of shoes." So a trip to Europe was probably out.

By the time young Michael Feinstein moved in to lend Ira a hand with his archives, he found himself obliged willy-nilly to play kindergarten mind games with his hostess as well, who would treat him some days like her best friend on earth, and on others like a trespasser with bad breath. In a word, it seems safe to guess that the lady had become bored out of her mind. On one of her friendly days, she told Feinstein that she'd really wanted to marry George all along, but one suspects she told a lot of people this. It didn't really matter. None of the several other accounts I've read of other people's visits to Ira's even bothered to mention her.

A glum household indeed. But people's old selves shouldn't be held against their young ones. And even as Feinstein describes them, one has only to imagine, as Ira probably did again and again, young George bounding into the room and perching at the piano, for the whole scene to be transformed. George was the whole point of these people, and one pictures them coming to life like waxworks in a dream, and the lights going on all over the house to greet him.

Having myself witnessed old Burton Lane and Ann Ronnell lighting up at the mere mention of his name—and having also heard his own light, quicksilver voice on tape—I have no doubt about George's electricity, or about how far it reached or how long it lasted. "Oh, yes, my father really loved George Gershwin"—I have heard some variant of this from the daughters of Richard Whiting, Walter Donaldson, Milton Ager, and Irving Berlin, and I'm sure I'd have heard it from more daughters if I'd known any more.

If Gershwin's contributions had stopped at cheerleading, they would still have been major, because his judgment was so sure both musically and professionally. His song playing had been a crucial part of his education, teaching him not just about songs but also about public taste as it was that very afternoon at four P.M., and his own songs can still be used as a diary of the twentieth century: "Swanee," "Do It Again," "Somebody Loves Me," the latest song was great, but get a load of this next one! George was never content with last year's revolution, so no one else was allowed to rest either. Irving Berlin's epic late-1920s malaise and his sense that he was "losing it" spoke for a whole profession. After hearing a particularly snazzy new arrangement of something or other, Vincent Youmans groaned apocryphally, "It's no use. I can't keep up with these new guys," only to be told, "But, Vincent, you wrote that yourself."

And it wasn't just the writers now who had to keep moving at the speed of Gershwin, but the audience. While Irving had called this "a listening nation," George was teaching it how to listen better and more adventurously, to the benefit of all the writers, but of two general types in particular: those raised mostly on the classics, like Vernon Duke and Johnny Green and Jule Styne, and those who had grown up with jazz, like the three who come next, each of whom collided with George one way or another, without necessarily being influenced directly.

And here I must resist a show-bizzy temptation to exaggerate Gershwin's legacy. By no means did he invent the jazz song by himself, or any of its aspects. In the end, nobody else wrote quite like George, but perhaps a few of them wrote better because of George; in particular, the brilliant cohort of stage writers who followed in his wake—Rodgers, Porter, and Arthur Schwartz, and by degrees a couple of holdouts, the aforemen-

tioned Youmans and, kicking and screaming, the great Jerome Kern himself, who started the ball rolling with the proto-jazz number "They Didn't Believe Me," but then left the game until Gershwin and the others had made it worthy of him.

So I'll limit George's claim to this: You can subtract any other great name from the story, and it would be basically the same story. Without Gershwin, or his godfather, Irving Berlin, it would be unrecognizably different. And you probably wouldn't be reading books about it, and people like me wouldn't be writing them.

Part Two

Consequences—The Great Jazz Songwriters

Harold Arlen:
The Songwriter's Songwriter

HAROLD ARLEN

While working on—or maybe the phrase should be "wallowing in"—this book, a remark I heard again and again was, "Do you know who my real favorite is?" Well, yes, after a while I did, because it was always Harold Arlen. Whatever the essence of this music is, Harold Arlen had the most of it.

And perhaps it's a coincidence—but perhaps not—that unlike Gershwin and the rest, Arlen really knew Jewish music, and unlike the other white writers, he had actually worked professionally with some of the best black musicians from quite an early age. His father, Samuel Arluck, was

an active cantor with a good ear who had also picked up some other sounds in his own travels from Louisville to Buffalo and incorporated them into his own work, so that when he first heard Louis Armstrong, he could honestly say in effect that "he's doing some of the same things I do." Which means that his son Hyman must have heard them too.

Thus began what seems like one of the most important father and son partnerships in music, at least since the Bach family. To be sure, Papa Arluck did eventually try to talk his son out of becoming a professional jazz musician once he saw what was happening, but by that time he had already filled Hyman's head with enough music, both sacred and profane (opera mostly), and worse still had allowed the devil's latest instrument, a Victrola, into the house, that it was too late. And when he did try to dissuade his son, his spokesman was Jack Yellen, an Orthodox Jew, but also a successful songwriter himself, who a few years later would wind up asking Harold to do a show with him. So it's hard to believe that Arluck Senior wasn't just going through the motions and was, at least subconsciously, pleased to have a son who could chaperone him in this strange, sinfully attractive pagan world.

If this story, or legend, were entirely about music, it would have been a relatively happy one, beginning with young Hyman jazzing up some of his father's holy music on the family piano, and ending with Cantor Arluck introducing bits of his son's hits such as "Stormy Weather" and "Blues in the Night" into his temple singing. But Cantor Arluck couldn't really be all that happy about his son's tendency to swing absolutely everything he touched. And any hipness the two shared would end sharply at the piano's edge. The cantor's ears might be Liberal, but his heart was Orthodox, and Harold would have to pick up the other elements he needed, Americanness and black-American-ness, by rebelling at least a little bit and striking out into a world diametrically different from his old man's.

Nature had never intended him to be a rebel; it was a triumph of vocation. When I met Harold Arlen in person years later, I could only wonder, as many people must have, how such a mild, unimposing little man could have produced such powerful and turbulent music. Since appearances are seldom completely deceptive and all witnesses agree that Arlen really was mild in most respects—a man who would go to great lengths to *not* talk things out—the force of his vocation must indeed have been nuclear,

and might be enough to account for the power of the music itself, as well as for the unhappiness which would blight his later years.

Then again, his father also tended to be an evasive and nonconfrontational man. Perhaps it didn't take that much chutzpah for Harold just to walk out the door and find someone else to play with. He certainly didn't have to go far. World War I had done its appointed work of stirring the music and excitement about the music around, and Arlen's biographer, Edward Jablonski, reports an estimated number of sixty thousand dance bands at large in the land, playing everything from the sweetest sweet to the hottest hot. And by the time Harold accidentally found himself writing songs in his early twenties, this sheltered youth had lived the life of a minor league ball player or a vaudeville hustler, banging around the Northeast in buses and picking up the usual dents and scratches along the way, along with a sense of middle America that Gershwin and the New Yorkers were not yet privy to.

"Hear that lonesome whistle blowing/'cross the trestle" John Mercer would write to Arlen's music, and suddenly Tin Pan Alley seemed to contain railway yards and bus depots that hadn't been there before. "It's quarter to three/there's no one in the place except you and me," writes Mercer also, and Arlen's music conveys all the solitude of a roadhouse in the outback, as far from Johnny's Savannah social register as it is from the Arluck parlor. Both Mercer and Arlen saw this other America as clearly as the half-British Raymond Chandler saw Los Angeles, with the freshness and sharpness of outsiders, and their songs constitute priceless social documents. "I've been in some big towns/and heard me some big talk." But the most important place either of them had visited was the black section, where Harold had apprenticed with, among others, the incomparable black pianist, bandleader, and composer Fletcher Henderson, whose arrangements would go on to make Benny Goodman the alleged "King of Swing"; and Arlen would come of age by writing some of his greatest songs for the famous Cotton Club in Harlem while the Duke Ellington and later the Cab Calloway bands were in residence.

Perhaps there really was a natural affinity between black and Jewish sensibilities across the board, or perhaps it was specific to certain east European musicians. (There's no trace of it in the west European Kern and not much in the part-Alsatian Richard Rodgers.) But insofar as black sub-

ject matter is contained in the blues, Arlen not only wrote it but sang it more authentically than any white person, Jewish or otherwise, has a right to. Like Hoagy Carmichael, Arlen was a singing pianist, but in his case, it is the voice that seems like the primary instrument, the mirror of his soul. Unlike Hoagy, whose singing can be extremely artful and sly, Arlen's is shatteringly direct, and what it sounds like is something close to clinical depression warring with a stoical vitality and at times a curious impishness. "Can't go on" say the words. "Everything I have is gone." But the tune seems to add, like Samuel Beckett himself, "I'll go on."

Arlen's sad songs bend to the wind, but they don't break. Yet Arlen could never quite get out of the wind either. Even when he swings into a snappy number like "Happy As the Day Is Long," he still sounds, at best, like a melancholic trying to look on the bright side, while his version of "Accentuate the Positive" is as far from the gleeful cackle of Johnny Mercer's recording of it as you can get. As sung by Arlen "Accentuate the Positive" could almost be funeral music.

Still, it is a funny song, and Arlen himself could be a funny man at times. The bass line of gloom that runs through his art and his life couldn't keep him from being a great laugher as well, and an occasional practical joker. An artist doesn't need to feel the emotions he's expressing at the moment he's expressing them, only to have them somewhere in his system. "Stormy Weather" was, as he told me, a throwaway. He wrote it first, and found out why years later.

In retrospect, Arlen's manic side may have been almost as necessary to his compositions as his gloomy one, simply because it gave him the heart to write in the first place. In other words, he had to feel that good to tell you how bad he felt; if he felt any worse, he couldn't have written at all, even sadly. And when, for reasons beyond his control, he couldn't write any more anyway, the depression that had been waiting to happen became quite suicidal. As described earlier, another old partner of Arlen's, Yip Harburg, happened to be my upstairs neighbor for several of Harold's worst years, and he described his friend as living in catatonic gloom and solitude as if the lousy weather he'd been reporting on for thirty years had all landed on him at once.

But just because I entered Arlen's life at the end is no reason to do so now. In fact, Arlen's first major hit song was a happy one that he wrote

without even knowing he was doing it. Arlen had recently signed on as a rehearsal pianist for Vincent Youmans's *Hit the Deck* and was just fooling around with some chords he liked for the dancers to rehearse to. Someone else heard a song in these chords, and the composer Harry Warren not only heard the song but found a lyricist for it and a publisher. Just like that, the young singing pianist learned that he was a songwriter as well.

By a curious chance, Arlen's boss of the moment, Youmans, was also a manic-depressive, the occupational disease of songwriters, who was famous for his get-happy-damn-you music. So Arlen's lyricist gave the song a Youmanizing title, namely, "Get Happy," which neatly suits its role in history. Youmans had blazed brilliantly in the early 1920s, but was already looking back to see where the next fire was coming from, and when I asked Arlen in the early 1970s if any of the great songwriters had been jealous of one another, he said, "Yes, Vincent Youmans. Every time he heard a new Gershwin song, he said, 'So the son of the bitch thought of it.'" And here, in his very own employ, was another son of a bitch in the making, thinking of things that would carry this kind of music even further beyond his reach.

Certainly young Arlen had begun writing very close to the top, so much so that even his contemporary and fellow boy wonder Richard Rodgers wasn't sure he could keep up with his intricate harmonies. Rodgers probably had better formal training than Arlen, but like Carmichael, what Harold had was the extra training you get from improvising jazz and hearing it improvised all night every night for a few years. Later on, the fussbudget Alec Wilder would be enthralled by Arlen's pure musicianship, but the rough-and-ready give-and-take of the bandstand had been his finishing school, and the Cotton Club was the name on his diploma, not the Juilliard or the Sorbonne.

To top off this brief run of luck, the lyricist his friend Warren had chosen for him proved to be just right too. Ted Koehler was one of the many word-men who might still be famous if they'd just made a little more noise about themselves. Then again, he was the man who also wrote about ill winds and stormy days, and he seems to have understood his partner's moods so well that when Harold finally wanted to work with somebody else, but, typically, didn't want to tell Koehler—he understood that as well. (Koehler's response seems to have been, "You'd be a fool not to try it.")

Of Arlen's three principal partners, one might sweepingly say that Yip Harburg was the most literary, Mercer was the flashiest and most "with it," but Koehler wrote closest to the gut, to the essence of Arlen.

And on the scoreboard now, a few of the early songs Koehler wrote with Arlen have stood the test of time, better than Harburg's and almost as well as Mercer's: "Stormy Weather," of course, but also the exuberant "I've Got the World on a String," "Between the Devil and the Deep Blue Sea," and perhaps the sweetest of all Arlen melodies, "Let's Fall in Love," which, if not quite his and Koehler's swan song together, was part of their swan medley. And Arlen had been inspired to write it on their first and last train ride together to that most sundering of places, Hollywood, the home of divorce, where business partners break up even quicker than married ones and where even Siamese twins are likely to wind up just good friends.

To carry the image one sentence further, Arlen had actually begun to play around before leaving New York, and the primary agent of change in his life had been not the movies but that other mighty institution, the Gershwins. As far as I can tell, no song ever got written in New York without George hearing and judging it immediately, and "Get Happy" was no exception. So before he knew it, Harold found himself another Gershwin acolyte at large, receiving visits and verdicts from the master in a manner that sounds more French than American. If Arlen didn't appreciate "Stormy Weather," Papa Gershwin would tell him exactly what was so good about it. And if he needed professional connections, "My empire is your empire." Meeting the Gershwins was a total experience somewhere between a social debut and a Baptist baptism. And it usually meant meeting Broadway too, which must have seemed like practically an extension of the Gershwins, part of the family estate. So to put it all together, Arlen soon found himself writing a Broadway show with virtually a member of the family, Ira's old schoolmate Yip Harburg, and another with both Yip and Ira himself as lyricists.

In fact, Harold would soon have needed to make a move anyhow, because with the end of Prohibition in sight, glorified speakeasies like the Cotton Club would soon be closing their doors, and their employees would find themselves mingling on the street with refugees from vaude-ville, almost all of whom would end up in Hollywood but who right now

did not know what to do with themselves. So an invitation to Broadway inscribed by the Gershwins was a handy thing to have, and Harold would make the most of it. In the end, his stage work would occupy a comparatively small place in his catalogue, but a vital one, because it is just different enough to show how different he could be. Counterintuitively, songs like "Down with Love" and "Let's Take a Walk Around the Block" were lighter and frothier than his nightclub work and would place him at the moment in a middle class of one in the musical celebrity register, which is to say just below the big five and Arthur Schwartz and just above Vernon Duke and all the Broadway writers you've never heard of. And it gave him a useful credential to wave at the moguls when he inevitably went to Hollywood next.

Writing with Harburg had solved one problem but would create another. Like Oscar Hammerstein, Yip was first and last a Broadway man who had helped Arlen pick up a Broadway sound, but what Arlen needed right then was a Hollywood sound, with cash registers thrumming softly in the background. And he was not going to get much of this from Yip, who loathed every inch of Hollywood and seems to have spent his spare time out there becoming even more radical than when he started.

The Harburg years would be characterized by some of Arlen's most interesting and entertaining songs, for example, Groucho's "Lydia the Tattooed Lady," but a rather modest list of standards or radio songs. In New York, the two of them had written "It's Only a Paper Moon," which still flourishes, but in Hollywood—besides "Over the Rainbow"—they wrote only the gorgeous but difficult "Last Night When We Were Young," which is sort of a standard after the fact and against the odds. In fact it was based on an old tune of Arlen's that even Gershwin had advised him to forget about because it couldn't possibly be a hit. No doubt George hadn't reckoned on the coming of Frank Sinatra and his capacity for making a hit out of any song he loved so much, and his record of this one is so beautiful that it virtually forces its way into your heart. But even if George had reckoned on it, so what, these guys were not writing for posterity. A hit song in twenty years' time would have seemed cold comfort on the brink of World War II.

But if Arlen wanted a hit any sooner than that, he'd better find himself another partner, because Yip Harburg was simply not lotus land material.

First, though, in a burst of inspiration, luck, and homesickness, the two friends had returned to New York for one goodbye show that still shines brightly in both of their dossiers. Timing is everything with Method plays, and a show about a young woman who insists on wearing bloomers instead of hoopskirts turned out to be just right for 1944, when the issue was skirts versus slacks in the workplace and when independent women were about to be let off the leash for the next few years. And the setting of *Bloomer Girl* in the middle of the American nineteenth century would give Arlen a great chance to widen his own vocabulary with, among other things, the nostalgically choral "Evelina" and the faux primitive "The Eagle and Me," a sound that he would return to a couple of times after the war.

In the post–Pearl Harbor era, morale became the magic word—morale for everybody: for soldiers, workers, mothers, and infants, and Harold and Yip reported back to Hollywood to align themselves as entertainingly as possible for the duration. And Harold at least would have the time of his life. For one thing, he was one of the few songwriters on record who actually liked Hollywood. And unlike his old friend Harry Warren, Arlen had never really spent enough time there to feel trapped or seriously bored. On his first trip out he had been caught up in the gaiety and sadness of Gershwin's last month, and can still be seen smiling shyly and happily in George's home-away-from-home-movies. So they returned to Broadway—and got their major-motion-picture break and ticket back from there.

MGM had been casting around for a Broadway-like score to go with its latest hot property, *The Wizard of Oz*. This meant thinking not in terms of hit songs that would turn up over and over again on radio, but of total scores specific to that one story and meaningless outside it. Unsurprisingly, Harburg actually argued against using the one out-and-out standard in *Oz*. "Over the Rainbow" is emphatically not a Broadway song, but one of those rich, heavy, and vague numbers that radio loved and Harburg hated. And yet he wrote a great lyric for it anyway. That was a paradox about Yip: He neither cared nor possibly even realized that having your songs on the Hit Parade sold tickets and was good for your movie regardless of whether it belonged there. And yet he wrote some wonderful Hit Parade songs in spite of himself.

As if by magic, they had been whisked from the black-and-white breadline city to the Technicolor of MGM Studios to take the white-hot

Wizard of Oz assignment. And the magic didn't end there. It was implicit in Harold's unwritten contract with life itself that if the music ever stopped, he would go back to black and white immediately, like Dorothy translated back to Kansas. But out here in Oz, everything looked good. "They brought us money on bicycles," Arlen explained at our meeting: And the image of a kid tossing a check onto your porch as casually as an evening newspaper must have packed a positively Norman Rockwell enchantment to eyes used to Depression New York.

Before those West Coast bicycle messengers had lost their charm, Arlen joined forces with a new West Coast partner, Johnny Mercer, who in some ways perfectly combined the best of both coasts. In New York, Johnny had sung with Harold's brother, Jerry, as members of Paul Whiteman's Rhythm Boys, part two. But since then he had been in Hollywood long enough to learn movies the way Harburg knew plays, and particularly what he could get away with in movies. A song like "Blues in the Night," for instance, was much too long for sheet music and just a little too abstract for Broadway: It tells no story and illuminates no character. It doesn't go with anything, except with a bunch of images that you could easily render for yourself if the camera didn't feel like it. And Arlen loved it on sight. "Did you ever write a song that you knew was good before anyone else said so?" I asked him. "Yes, thank God," he answered. " 'Blues in the Night,' because Harry Warren saw it lying around the house and said, 'That middle section has to go. It'll never work.' "

Warren was hearing it as a songwriter, with a songwriter's sense of limits. But Mercer and Arlen had already heard it as fellow jazzmen under the skin who knew that a riff has to run its course and to hell with the sheet-music publishers and their three skimpy pages or the record companies with their piddly ten inches of wax, or even the film producers with their tiny attention spans.

So Arlen not only got to keep his middle section but succeeded so well with it that he felt free to launch into another rambling masterpiece called "That Old Black Magic," which had been granted some extra slack anyway to accommodate a ballet of sorts for George Balanchine's special friend, Vera Zorina. Playing this for the umpteenth time in my head one day, I realized that these extra-long riffs are most likely to occur when Mercer is the lyricist, and when he is, he is most likely addressing himself to the

space requirements of jazz licks, to wit: Ziggy Elman's great trumpet solo that became "And the Angels Sing," Rube Bloom's "Day In, Day Out," and the super suspension bridge of Hoagy Carmichael's "Skylark." At a first, superficial listen (to "Magic" in particular), it sounds as if it's the words that are taking their time, and that the melodist is just supplying notes to accommodate Mercer's long-winded poem. But if you separate the elements, you'll see that Johnny is the one who's vamping, virtually ad-libbing extra lines, and the tunesmith is the one writing the poem and providing the continuity and momentum. Meanwhile, Mercer really puts the imaginary narrator through his paces, at one moment as a man in an elevator and at the next as a leaf caught in the tide, right after which, so help me, he seems to be on fire and needs help putting himself out.

Stop the elevator. I feel like flying for a while.

But meanwhile you realize that the melodist has told his own story in all its complexity and that Mercer's words have helped at every turn. "Darling, down and down I go/Round and round I go"—I defy anyone to forget these lines of music any more than one can forget "From Natchez to Mobile, from Memphis to St. Joe." (You may forget the order the towns come in, but the general idea is embedded deeper than forgetfulness.)

Probably the best-known and defining moment in the partnership came when Arlen looked at Mercer's notes for "Blues in the Night" and moved a line—"My mama done told me"—from the bottom of the page to the top. He never presumed to write lyrics himself but he knew what he wanted them to do, and Mercer was delighted to oblige. As two gentlemen of two old schools, the rabbi's son and the son of the South seemed to have accommodated each other at every turn. Indeed, in that sublime little hitch in the tune of "My Shining Hour" ("Like the lights of home before me/Or an angel watching o'er me"), which made the hair stand up on the back of Alec Wilder's neck, the words and music actually seemed to be holding the door open for each other. It doesn't get any better than that.

In the five years of 1941 to 1946, between, let's say, "This Time the Dream's on Me" (which I can't even mention without humming the whole thing through) and, let's say, "Out of This World," the names Arlen and Mercer seemed to be fixed in the stars like Roosevelt the president and Joe Louis the champ. But then the whistle blew, after which it proved to be just another wartime marriage, intense, doomed, and slightly puzzling.

In the bonus year of 1946, which combined the best of the wartime boom and the safety of peace, the team extended its holdings from the West Coast to Broadway with the show *St. Louis Woman,* and once more they did what they did so well—they produced a great album of songs that played wonderfully well on its own, and one powerful standard, "Come Rain or Come Shine." But the show itself closed quickly, and suddenly everything about it seemed wrong. In the orgy of finger-pointing that followed, there is no conclusive reason to single out Mercer's lyrics, which still sound swell on records. According to witnesses, Pearl Bailey's unremitting orneriness might have sunk any show ever devised. But Mercer was just starting on a lifelong losing streak in theater, which would make him a more likely suspect with each failure. And Broadway doesn't give you much time to prove your innocence. A bum rap is usually forever, and our two fixed stars would only try one other musical together, and that only when Harold was desperate.

Okay, no big deal. *Louis* was just a flop, not a portent. Before the war, Harold had learned his lesson about Harburg and movies, and now he had learned it about Mercer and plays. But Broadway was still booming, and there was always Hollywood, wasn't there? In 1946, everything seemed possible, and it is almost tempting to end the story right here. But the air went out of Harold's dreams so quickly that it is possible to tell quickly too. In the short version, Arlen did get to do some more films, but only one innocuous one with Mercer. And there would be a few more Broadway shows, but only two with Harburg. All in all, the high points in postwar Hollywood boiled down to no more than about two. First, a silly movie with a great score called *Casbah* (1948), which Arlen wrote with the chronically underrated Leo Robin, and which contained the standards "Hooray for Love" and the near-standards "Written in the Stars" and "What's Good About Goodbye." And, second, his last filmed hoorah, if not quite his last film, *A Star Is Born* (1954), which includes "The Man That Got Away." This Judy Garland weepie features a strong lyric by Ira Gershwin and, to my ear, an unsurprising tune that fits the story almost too perfectly. (Every critic has his deaf spots, and this is one of mine.) It seems poignant to the point of corny to find this fading song, getting older and colder in the midst of this age-old tale of rising and falling stars. But that was the Hollywood studios just then, cashing in their old assets, selling

their old feature films to TV and immortalizing them as quickly as possible, all the while canceling contracts and keeping wonderful songs around purely for background music.

So Broadway was suddenly the only place to be, but this time preferably with an old pro like Harburg, who knew the stage and who knew the street. Yip had already had a huge postwar success there with their mutual friend Burton Lane. What Harold needed now was for Yip to respect this and do another *Finian's Rainbow,* but with him this time.

But something had gone wrong here too, it seemed. Besides its great songs, *Finian's Rainbow* had contained some quite clumsy analogies to American politics, which had been okay in 1946–47, but were highly suspect in 1948–55 or so. In no time, Yip would find himself on the omnivorous blacklist, which of course Broadway was free to ignore if it wanted to, but only if it wanted to very much. Harburg was on the wrong side of the divide. In the harsh 1930s, his left-wing radicalism had seemed close enough to the mainstream to get pretty much lost in the crowd, but by the fat 1950s, he stood alone—a menace to conservatives and a bore to liberals, who had heard that song before. In fact, even his fellow West Side Democrat, Lane, eventually got tired of old Yip's insistence on message musicals and even more tired of having them turned down, while his other old partner, Arlen, wasn't a liberal to begin with.

So by the time Harold and Yip finally got around to doing another show together, ten years had passed and the national mood had changed completely in the subtle but imperious way of these things. McCarthyism had largely faded away, not for any specific reason, but because it didn't interest people anymore, and Yip could now send all the messages he wanted, so long as they were entertaining. And Arlen, for his part, found himself faced with sounds that wouldn't have been possible in his prime, such as steel bands and bongos and calypsos, which he found melodically dreary. (Fortunately, perhaps, he didn't live to hear rap.)

It was enough to make a man feel his age. The show, called *Jamaica,* was a success anyway, because David Merrick insisted on it, but it was Merrick's show more than Arlen's or Yip's. By the time I talked with Harold, it was clear that the last musical he had really enjoyed and was still proud of had come three years earlier. *House of Flowers,* as it was called, represents his last sustained attempt to "keep up," and give the

world one more new Arlen. And perhaps if he'd done it with Merrick, it might have worked. As it was, *House of Flowers* flopped, and in a small way, this broke Harold's heart. The end had begun.

Thanks to the one incontrovertibly good invention of modern times, namely, sound-recording, one can at least hear the remains of this last good moment. To get to *House of Flowers,* Arlen agreed to the most improbable partnership in this, or any other, book. Truman Capote at that stage was entirely famous for his self-promotion and for flaunting his teeth-grinding cuteness and his Southern childhood to any audience that would have him. And now he and Arlen were about to undertake a show in an idiom completely new to both of them, West Indian folk.

Fortunately, Capote turned out to be a serious and very good writer under the act, to whom Arlen responded both artistically and personally. And Capote returned the compliment by understanding Harold and his demons as well as anyone had. On the one hand, Truman felt that Arlen was "obsessed with a tragic view of life," but on the other, Arlen also genuinely loved to laugh, and did a lot of it, with a signature laugh you could spot anywhere. And somewhere between the laughter, which Capote induced even more by passing on outrageous gossip, and the tears in both of their hearts, they found a remarkable score, unlike anything else in Arlen's repertory, and unlike anything else a mass audience could assimilate. So Arlen now showed wonderful promise as an avant-garde, serious composer, but none at all as a commercial one. And he might have had trouble even with the avant-garde. *House* flopped off-Broadway too, and the end came a little closer.

To sum it all up, Arlen could do no wrong in the 1930s and nothing right in the 1950s, even when he took no chances. The one card he still held that was money in the bank was the score of *St. Louis Woman,* which people kept on praising right through the disasters, so he and Mercer put it together once again in the form of an opera and threw in "Blues in the Night" and "That Old Black Magic" just for good measure, and sent it on a world tour that was meant to eventually culminate on Broadway. But it fell sick in Amsterdam, and died in Paris. And this time, that was really that. One last show with Mercer, called *Saratoga,* was hailed as "another *Show-Boat,*" which has always been the kiss of death. Arlen's Broadway career was over.

With work petering out, Arlen's defenses against depression had gradually begun to come down too. Up to now, his rule of thumb toward real life had been to ignore it and hope it would iron itself out. Thus he knew he had been courting his parents' rage when he first lived with and then married a beautiful gentile girl—but maybe they would get used to her, especially if he kept her out of sight; and maybe this girl, a model-cum-showgirl named Anya Iaranda of Russian Orthodox origin, was lonely herself in his long absences. But maybe she could make some friends on her own and perhaps acquire some hobbies or something; and even when he knew for sure that this wasn't working and that Anya was becoming tense to the point of insanity, he thought that maybe she would still be okay if she lived in a nice sanitarium for a while. By all accounts, he really did love her, but apparently in the manner of a love song, and not in the more workable manner of a long-running soap opera.

And meanwhile, he tended to see a bit of Marlene Dietrich when she was in New York—and why not? She was, after all, a musical soul mate and inspiration. One always assumes sex with Dietrich—it was her version of a handshake. The gossip columns never tell you what people actually do when they "see" each other; presumably Harold and Marlene did whatever people do. But as creative artists go, Harold Arlen was not at all the monster that the above makes him sound. Even nice artists have to do what it takes to keep their work flowing. And Arlen's work depended on his not slipping below a certain level of euphoria and unreality. "Forget your troubles, come on get happy" was no whim with Arlen, but an order: Ignore your troubles and keep on working.

But as every manic-depressive artist (and is there any other kind?) knows, the whole machine has to operate together. The work has to deliver its share of euphoria too, or else one has to find some substitute for it. And the most popular one is that ultimate depressive, tranquilizers, which, of course, make things worse. These now entered Harold's life, and soon those troubles he'd been forgetting came pounding back like Hieronymus Bosch goblins. His parents' disapproval, for instance, had never really gone away at all, but had become a habit that would last until they died reproachfully, or so it must have seemed to their son. So long as the music kept coming, he had never needed to grow up at all and face things head-on. But now he found himself transferred back to adult black

and white, and shipwrecked on the blank reefs of real life, which he'd hitherto written about but sailed safely around. And to his infinite credit, he did his best with it, living with Anya full-time in New York, and right through the 1960s working grimly on individual songs with younger partners who just might lead him back to the promised land. And because, by his own admission, he was almost terminally depressed, these songs had to serve as his shrink and his confessor.

But a song that nobody else listens to can't bear that much freight, and meanwhile Anya was getting worse and worse, twitching, making faces, and throwing tantrums until a brain tumor similar to George Gershwin's was finally discovered behind it all—too late to be removed completely. She died, leaving Harold to feel like a bad son, a failed husband, and a burned-out songwriter all in one go.

According to Harburg, the truly suicidal depression that rounded out the sixties was caused by Harold's relief that Anya had died, combined with his guilt over this relief. By Yip's no doubt accurate account, I picture Arlen locking himself in his room like a teenager until he'd figured things out. But from Jablonski's biography, I would also learn that there were enough pills in there with him to account for his depression all by themselves.

Whatever the cause, by the time I met him in 1972, two years after Anya's death, Harold seemed more or less himself again, guardedly cheerful and even willing to be interviewed at some later date. (Max Wilk finally got the interview, and it was amazingly loquacious.) Perhaps the most surprising thing he said to me was that "Stormy Weather" was "a song I could have mailed Monday or Tuesday. It wasn't anything special." After that, of course, real life walked him through it again, slowly and painfully, the shrink to end all shrinks. "Keeps raining all the time." Yes, indeed.

But he was out on the other side of that too, and if it wasn't exactly the other end of the rainbow, it would do. Instructively enough, the last time he and Anya had been happy together had been on a trip to Europe with Harry Warren and his wife in the early fifties. Harry was a down-to-earth, non-show-bizzy kind of guy, and Anya felt comfortable and blessedly sane around him. And the secret of Warren's equilibrium was his nonstop grumbling, beginning with his own anonymity—which was a dirty, rotten shame—but branching out in all directions. And now that all the old

songwriters were slipping out of the spotlight in a body, Warrenism, or grumble-therapy, began to catch on throughout this particular retirement community, and it's my confident guess that Arlen's lengthy phone calls to Irving Berlin must have been in the Warren vein: What's happened to the damn music, anyway? And will the public ever return to its senses? Or will we, like Bertolt Brecht's dictator, simply have to order up a new public?

Misery loves company, and this company was of the finest, even though these two men had actually been forgotten a lot less than most of their colleagues. Berlin was still a monument, although not so many people went to that part of the park anymore, and Arlen, who hadn't been all that well known in his prime, seems to be at least as well known now. Tributes are still paid to him on TV just often enough to keep his name in play, and his fans still seem to find one another like Maltese dog owners. No composer has a better ratio of recognition-to-adulation. And there's always just enough Arlen music in the air to keep the converts trickling in, and the reservoir remains at the same medium level. Arlen may not be our best songwriter, whatever that means, but in one sense he is our most necessary one, because he is the one you have to hear if you want to know exactly what the vague but necessary phrase "jazz song" meant, and where the Gershwin wing of it went next, and where it wound up.

•

Hoagy Carmichael:
The Jazz Song Goes West

HOAGY CARMICHAEL

*I*f Harold Arlen is the special favorite of jazz song connoisseurs, Hoagy Carmichael probably comes first with just about everyone else, regardless of time, place, or musical persuasion—partly because of his early-American image at the piano and his collector's item of a voice, but even more so because of at least two songs he wrote that still speak to Americans all over. The first is "Stardust," with which he first announced his presence and which went on to become the most recorded song in its era, and the second is "Georgia on My Mind," which on my occasional travels

seems to take turns with "Route 66" as our real national anthem. And what makes these numbers central to our story is that they both *are* and *are not* New York jazz songs, and because of this they give the category a much-needed infusion of outside, all-American blood.

If jazz songs hoped to maintain their sway over the ever-widening country, they had to start recruiting a bit farther out than Buffalo. This was easier said than done.

Once upon a time, a guy I knew from Pittsburgh tried to sell some songs and found in effect that you simply couldn't do it from there because (1) you couldn't mail your stuff without receiving it back immediately unopened, and (2) you couldn't call up anyone in the business unless you already knew someone in the business, and how were you going to do that in Pittsburgh? Songs were harder to fence than diamonds. And in both cases, the other guy wouldn't even look you in the eye as he said no.

So my friend did the only other thing he could think of. He marched onto a local stage and demanded an audition with a well-known band that was passing through. By that point, all he *thought* he wanted was a hearing and a verdict, and in a sense he got both, plus a lesson as to why all those precautions were necessary. In fact, the bandleader liked his best tune so much that the next time he came to town, he was still playing it as part of his own repertory, and my friend found that there wasn't a damn thing he could do about it.

There was of course one more option that might have given said friend at least a chance in hell of making it, and that was to take his songs in person to the cold heart of the city, New York, or the frigid one of Chicago, and try to massage himself into the system as a song-plugger or rehearsal pianist—which by the 1940s must have been like trying to get your kid into Harvard or West Point, though sometimes it happened. Tommy Dorsey held some talent hunts and came up with a striving young singer from the West Coast named Matt "Angel Eyes" Dennis. And before that a coal miner from Ohio named Isham "It Had to Be You" Jones had parlayed his own band into a songwriting career.

But as radios and phonographs fanned out farther across the country, it was easy to imagine that a lot of local talent just couldn't be bothered with the old cultural center. Moving house was a big deal in those days,

and besides, Horace Greeley hadn't said, "Go west, young man—and then come back again." The current ran the other way, if it ran anywhere, and the natural thing was to work with local stations and under local labels to produce increasingly local music. As Jule Styne told Max Wilk, there was a whole different Hit Parade in the Southwest on the cusp of the 1940s, but the one man he might have heard on either program was Hoagy— a geographical anomaly who just seemed to write generic American that sounded just right regardless of where you were—even in New York.

Hoagy Carmichael was, like many Americans, a divided soul, part no- mad and part homebody, who seemed a little bit at home everywhere, but was probably more so someplace else, if he could just find it. In fact, you'll still see him on Greyhound buses, either hoping to change his luck in the next county or heading back after failing to.

What had dislocated him the most was the arrival of jazz, which had sneaked into rock-ribbed Indiana by way of the great music river, the Mis- sissippi, and which would hit young Hoagland with the force of a religious conversion. When he came to his senses the next day, he was puzzled to see that the lawns and the houses hadn't actually changed. Life went on. But there was a force at large now that could take him a million miles away anytime it wanted to, while—and this was the curious part—leaving him back home when it was done.

Thus, in his early teens, Hoagy became one of the first "jazz babies" (his phrase) in the land of Square; but part of him would stubbornly re- main a square in the world of Hip, and some thirty years later, we would find him actually squaring off, in the other sense, with Humphrey Bogart over a matter of politics, an Indiana Republican versus a Hollywood lib- eral, "Put up your dukes." (Fortunately, their womenfolk easily restrained the two bantamweights.)

Even in the matter of deciding whether to become a professional mu- sician, Carmichael stayed in two minds as long as he decently could, solemnly studying the law and working a cement mixer for a living by day, and bopping the piano by night, alongside Bix Beiderbecke and other nonacademic specimens; also, recording his first song, "Riverboat Shuf- fle," with Paul Whiteman in 1926 (aged twenty-seven by now) and being called to the bar as an attorney that same year.

How long he could have kept going in opposite directions like this as a

jazz lawyer was suddenly resolved for him by a deus ex machina, aka a check in the mail, or the promise of one. On the strength of that one Whiteman record, Irving Mills, the new apostle to the outback, offered Hoagy a contract to write more songs; and just like that, the Great Divide or man-made chasm that kept New York safe from outside talent had been cleared and all Hoagy had to do now was write the songs.

This turned out to be the easy part. As Sammy Cahn would famously say, every song begins with a phone call, and no sooner did Hoagy have his contract in hand than he also received a private epiphany which would confirm his gift once and for all, at least in his own mind. Rolling home drunk and early one Sunday morning from an all-night jam session, he "found" a tune in his own head that resolved every last doubt—if he could just find a piano to play it on. There followed a minidrama as he began searching the Indiana campus for an open door with a piano behind it before the tune could escape and turn him back into a lawyer for good.

Fortunately for him and posterity, the door of the college lab opened in time and Hoagy's masterpiece somehow survived the night. That one tune told that he was a songwriter for a life, but he had to wait another few years before he was able to convince anyone else. This bought him precious time to polish his art and find his voice before the outside world caught sight of him and began asking him to repeat himself. That one incredible song was like an insurance policy that only he knew about. After a brief, disdainful look at Hollywood, where absolutely everyone told him he was uncommercial ("We'll just see about that!"), he hitched a ride to New York, where, among other things, he would join and jam with some other out-of-towners, such as his old friend Bix Beiderbecke and such other names as Dorsey, Goodman, and Crosby, who were also trying to insert as much jazz as they could into their commercial work. As America continued to homogenize itself into one Great Picture Show, it seemed that the old distinction between hot bands and sweet bands was about to melt away, and that whatever they wound up doing would be a compromise. But sometimes the public surprises you. And one famous night when Goodman was playing California's Palomar Ballroom, the audience made it clear that it would rather listen than dance. This was the best news that the jazz babies could have hoped for, and it would make the jazz song the official sound of Amer-

ica right through World War II—after which, fashion would blow these same men off center stage with unexpected violence.

As for Hoagy, he arrived in New York certain that the jazz he had worshipped as a kid was already dead. But then one night he heard Duke Ellington play, among other things, "Mood Indigo" at the Cotton Club, and he realized that he might barely have to compromise at all. Because "Mood Indigo" was the real thing and all that Duke had actually done to it was remove the sense of danger, and replace what Hoagy calls the "switchblade" from jazz with something more peaceful. He had changed a nightmare into a beautiful dream—but wasn't this exactly what would happen to the tune in his pocket, which he had named provisionally "Stardust"?

By then "Stardust" had already failed fair and square as a hard-driving jazz song, but now it was in the same hands that had guided "Mood Indigo," and Irving Mills was about to make the same suggestion to Hoagy as to Duke, that they slow their tunes down and get Irving's house lyricist, Mitchell Parish, to write some dreamy lucrative words. And just like that "Stardust" would prove that Hoagy could actually make money being himself, keep his integrity, and eat his cake too. With one song, Hoagy became both our most and least commercial composer. And meanwhile, he had become too set in his ways to sell out, even if he'd wanted to. Before he had a hit, he had a style.

Which doesn't mean that success had done the impossible and put Hoagy completely together. One moment, he was still a Hoosier poet on Tin Pan Alley, dealing in such down-home matters as washboards and rocking chairs, lazy rivers, and little old ladies passing by; the next he was a licensed lawyer and snappy dresser whose best friends were still his clever college chums and whose favorite nonmusical pastimes were new acquisitions like golf and tennis, neither of which was played much on the Alley, at least below the level of George Gershwin.

In the circumstances, it probably struck him as the most logical thing in the world to dash off a heartbreaking hymn to a completely different place, where he'd never been at all. In his second memoir, *Sometimes I Wonder*, Hoagy describes how his father would get a faraway look in his eye, and then the family would light out hopefully for parts unknown—

only to find that this wasn't the right place either, and return to Indiana puzzled. So when Hoagy got that look, he didn't bother going anywhere. He stayed home and wrote a song instead—in this case about Georgia, which was on his mind if not his itinerary, and later about New Orleans, Memphis in June, old Hong Kong, and even Indiana. Few writers have ever traveled less than Hoagy in ratio to the number of miles he logged in his dreams.

So naturally, his next real-life port of call had to be Hollywood, the dream capital, where *everybody* was a misfit. Yet even there, Hoagy managed to seem like an odd man out. "He wasn't one of the (songwriting) gang," said Shana Alexander. This may have been because he felt, deep down, that the real composers were the guys who played and improvised the music in the first place, the pipers, strummers, and troubadours of jazz. And these would always be his musical gang of choice as they blew in and out of town, and he would not so much hang out with them as sit in, a lonely prospector eternally prospecting for gold at the piano while his companions let the gold dust slip through their fingers.

Then as now, the one way to be truly different in Hollywood was genuine, off-camera domesticity, and Hoagy now flung himself into this with enough thoroughness and intelligence to help raise two loving and flourishing sons (not adopted) who are still around at this writing to sing his praises when called upon. And he also invested enough imagination into family life to extract some of the few first-rate songs that we have relating to this condition, including "Small Fry" ("My my, put down that cigarette/You ain't a grown-up high and mighty yet"), "Two Sleepy People" ("Do you remember the reason/why we married in the fall?/to rent this little nest and get a bit of rest"), and "We're the Couple of the Castle," a little-known title that speaks for itself. All three were written with a fellow bourgeois named Frank Loesser, who, like Hoagy's other lyricists, managed to sound exactly like him so long as they worked together. (Carmichael wrote some lyrics entirely by himself, but obviously had a voice in all of them, which may be why he wrote so disappointingly little with Mercer. Two stubborn men with a taste for strong waters might have trouble agreeing, and I believe there was at least one actual fistfight with no wives to break it up.)

Thus, following his own eccentric star, Hoagy picked up enough bits and pieces to become eventually "the great American songwriter"—if

there is such a creature. To my mind, he clinched that mythical title once and for all (in peaceable cahoots with Mercer) in the epic "The Cool, Cool, Cool of the Evening" ("In the shank of the night/When the doings are right/you can tell them I'll be there"). Different words may be used to describe different details now, but the whole laid-back essence of this country can still be found in the multiple cool of this song.

Hoagy didn't just write the nation's songs, but unusually for his day, he sang them himself in a voice that sounded as if it had actually been grown in American soil and aged in a cracker barrel or a keg of hard cider. And this voice would be the tiebreaker between the two faces of Hoagy—the one he preferred himself, that of a dandy who looked so good in a dinner jacket that Ian Fleming originally described James Bond as looking just like him, and the face of the roustabout at the piano with his hat tilted back and features that looked like a road map of the United States. The great director Howard Hawks captured that look one day when Hoagy came in from the yard dressed, for once, in old work clothes and looking comparatively disheveled. "That's it," piped Hawks, or words to that effect. He'd been casting around for some birds of passage to populate a saloon in the film *To Have and Have Not,* and he'd just hit his fourth home run in a row, Bogart, Lauren Bacall, Walter Brennan, and now the man who would, for many of us, steal the movie out from all of them.

So that, like it or not, was the official Hoagy Carmichael from then on, the one we all know so well and that he would proceed to embed in the world's consciousness with several similar screen and TV appearances, with songs to match. "Baltimore Oriole" in particular takes lonely barfly songs to a new level. This guy has been there—as well as everywhere else, of course.

So was this the real Hoagy Carmichael? Probably yes and no, as usual. San Francisco's beatniks would make him a mascot in the late 1950s. He liked the way the beats were trying to keep jazz alive, and was amused by the rest. Unlike most of the old-timers, he was interested in the twists and turns of modern jazz and did not feel displaced by it. And nobody who had hung out with Beiderbecke and the others was likely to be shocked by anything the beats could come up with in the way of bad behavior. After all, he had once been a wild young man himself—half the time. You can't pin the whole of a dreamer like Hoagy down at one moment. In the gorgeous song

"Skylark," his alter ego jogs down some of the territory Carmichael's music and Mercer's words fly over, including "a meadow in the mist . . . a valley green with spring . . . [and] a blossom-covered lane." And that was just one trip.

So he finally settled in Palm Springs, which is somewhere you go when you don't know where to go, and he did his damnedest to write some more songs. Failing that, he would play a bunch of golf and drink a bunch of booze. And one hopes that some of his dreams were still beautiful, even if they didn't come with tunes anymore. But there was undoubtedly some sadness too because that was part of his greatness. Listen to "Memphis in June," with the clock a-ticking in the kitchen and the chairs a-rocking on the verandah, and it's gorgeous all right, but unbearably sad.

Anyway, whatever the mixture of joy and sadness, the only regret he ever voiced was his wish that he'd "tried harder" when the tunes were still coming. Well, then, there might have been *more* songs, but it's hard to believe they would have been *better* ones. Songs don't get any better.

In fact, Hoagy's best songs are literally incomparable. The moment you move into, say, "I Get Along Without You Very Well," you realize that no one has ever been down this road before, or anywhere near it. And I can imagine a lesser man than Hoagy saying, "So what the hell am I doing here?" And perhaps after the next bar adding, "Hey, this isn't a song at all. I'm getting out of here."

But Hoagy had lived through the epic night of the "found song" and still had the "Stardust" memory to prove it. So he trusted his stars all the way, as he would again when he came to the respective bridges of "Skylark" and "How Little We Know" (not to be confused with a later namesake, which simply isn't as good). Once again, our imaginary hack would see at once that both these bridges are way too long, and would probably desert halfway across, but Hoagy keeps on marching like Alec Guinness, crossing the River Kwai, trusting the song itself to tell him when it is finished. Meantime, he allows his number-two themes full equality to grow to their natural limits, and to hell with the rules. Let the bird sing his whole song if it takes all day.

Thus with these two adventures at least, as well as with the verse that was later added to "Stardust," you feel as if you've escaped completely from the drawing board and the music paper, with all its lines and boxes,

and into the open air, and the result can be almost dizzying. Once upon a time, a friend of mine was driving out West when he came, without warning, upon a choir, arrayed up the side of a hill, singing Hoagy's gorgeous song "One Morning in May."

Naturally, my friend thought he'd died and gone to heaven. But as it doesn't quite say in the movie, it wasn't really heaven, it was only Indiana, which, in one of my own dreams, Hoagy never really left at all but where part of him still sits on the porch flirting like Tom Sawyer with his Aunt Polly, or he's off down the river, like Huck Finn and his black companion, looking for the one thing that Mr. Twain had failed to report on, the music of the river.

But with one major difference. The black man is not a slave in this version, or even a former slave, but, so long as they are on this mission, a master and a model. Although the square side of Carmichael would never completely quit but would continue to think that even so modest a step as interracial dancing was in bad taste, the swinging side of Hoagy had known the score from the start, and immediately after his teenage rebirth, had gone straight to a local black musician for instruction in his new religion. Later he would find no better or more simpatico interpreters of his work than Ray Charles for "Georgia" or Louis Armstrong for "Old Rockin' Chair's Got Me" and everything else.

It seems at least arguable that what had happened here was that he, like his pal Mercer, had been wantonly and fatally seduced by black music and was fighting for his honor, his identity, in other ways. Their first great song together, "Lazy Bones," seems to make fun of the laid-back black boy "sleeping in the sun," but they had to be that boy themselves to do their best work and be their best selves. So Hoagy had lost his all-white musical identity, and everyone is the richer for it. The excitement that greeted him in London after World War II tells the story. If Mark Twain was the first completely original American sound to reach foreign ears, and ragtime was the second, Hoagy added a vibrant variation to both: laid-back at one moment but moving with the speed and sureness of a cat in his fast-patter songs like "Billy-a-Dick" and "No More Toujours L'Amour." A few years later, Norman Mailer would foresee the arrival of a white Negro, but here we already had one—up to a point. This least likely suspect had, to my ears anyway, combined white and black perfectly.

Duke Ellington: Royalty

DUKE ELLINGTON

*D*uke Ellington undoubtedly wrote some of our greatest songs, if, that is, they really were songs and if he actually did write them. Alec Wilder couldn't decide whether Ellington strictly belonged in a book of American songs at all—but there was no question of leaving him out either.

And there is no question of *not* talking about him, perhaps more than any other American composer of any kind, because he did first-rate work in several fields at once, from classical to spiritual to pure jazz, stretching each of their boundaries while challenging the genre itself. Many younger Americans now believe that categories don't count, and the Duke surely had a hand in this.

For instance, what exactly is a song, anyway? Is it just a bunch of words

and music timed to go off together, or are there fixed rules—and why? And to what extent can anyone be said to create one as opposed to the recurrent phenomenon of finding it? The air is so full of sounds (and clichés to go with them), and yet the tonal range is so small that the problem is not just that the sounds get stolen, but that even the most original writers keep bumping into one another in their pursuit. Richard Rodgers's "This Can't Be Love," for instance, swipes a couple of crucial bars from Bach's "Peasant Cantata" while Berlin's "Cheek to Cheek" seems to recall some riffs from Chopin. "We only steal from the best," George Gershwin said to Milton Ager optimistically, and in the same vein Arthur Schwartz would deliver the last word on the subject when someone asked him whether an agreement he'd just made to write a song a week for radio wouldn't "take a lot out of" him, and he said, "Not as much as it will take out of Bach, Beethoven, and Brahms."

That's who he would poach from on his good days, anyhow. On others, you might catch him stealing even more from Tom, Dick, and Harry without even knowing it. Since you need so few notes to establish a tune, anybody from one to a hundred can do that part, and the composer is simply the guy who can see the possibilities and know what to do next. For instance, suppose for the hell of it some little kid at a piano decides to drive everyone crazy by playing D and B over and over, until he finally bores even himself and moves on to a repetition of E and C: He will by then have written over half of "Carolina in the Morning," which might seem like grounds for a lawsuit. (But could the babysitter claim the rights to it, under the ancient right of finders keepers?)

Far-fetched, no doubt, but far-fetched in the right direction. If Duke Ellington was not exactly a babysitter, he was the next best thing, a jazz bandleader (which sounds like a contradiction in terms: Jazz cannot be led). As such, he was immersed day and night in the unpredictable sounds of jam sessions, all begging to be noticed and turned into songs, and we'll never know how many were. Frankie Carle's "Sunrise Serenade" and Glenn Miller's "Moonlight Serenade" were just two bandleaders' songs that might have been arrived at by just following the logic of someone else's catchy phrase; or if the leader was also part of the band, like Duke at the piano, he might introduce an idea of his own into the mêlée and let them fight it out. Whatever Ellington's methods, the results sound as if they all came

from the same man, but who was that? To be on the safe side, Duke signed everything "By Duke Ellington and His Band," allowing for an enormous spread and endless questions. Was the band being a full partner today or just a brilliant instrument?

Either way, it was not unheard of for the leader of a jazz band to slap his own name on the final product, on the Walt Disney principle that people weren't going to remember more than one name anyway and it might as well belong to the guy who signed the contracts and paychecks, Mister Big, Il Duce, the Leader himself. And this system must have had an enormous appeal to minority geniuses. In the 1920s, there weren't that many distinguished careers open to African Americans, and Edward Kennedy Ellington was born and raised to be distinguished, by a father who exuded style and a mother who got down to brass tacks and made sure he learned not just to play music, but to speak and think like a gentleman. Indeed, a snobbish boyhood friend christened him Duke simply because he wanted him to be one. And Ellington was definitely duke material, if he could just find the right duchy.

So it was his lifelong good luck to be a genius in the one field where blackness did not count against you, but might even be made to serve. A decade earlier, before World War I had done its extremely modest bit to bring Americans together, Irving Berlin's famous black alter ego would not have needed to stay in a closet. In the same way that women had been conceded to be quite good novelists long before they were allowed to vote, so too African Americans were understood to be pretty good at this kind of music, inferior though this kind of music might be, and besides, whoever knew who actually wrote the songs? The minstrel show tradition of anonymity behind painted faces had left the matter conveniently vague. Stephen Foster wrote some of them, and "I Don't Know" wrote the rest. And now they were either by another white man, Irving Berlin (with a black one in the closet), or by no one in particular.

Since nobody cared, nobody had to hide, and it's not surprising that maybe the first of the really great jazz songs, "Some of These Days," was both written and performed loud and clear by a black vaudeville pianist called Shelton Brooks, an aristocratic-looking Canadian who would follow it up later with the politically incorrect classic "Darktown Strutters' Ball." Singing and playing one's own material would remain far and away

the surest way for blacks to get their stuff known and paid for, and it's possible that they actually possessed a small advantage along this route. The central irony of the entertainment wing of segregation was that an African American who tried to buy a theater ticket would likely find himself sent right up to the stage.

Obviously, he'd come to the right place, he belonged here, but the closest thing to a servants' quarters was the dressing rooms, and in 1917 the great piano man Eubie Blake would take full advantage of this dispensation by filling all the dressing rooms with fellow blacks and writing the music for an all-black show, that is, a minstrel show called *Shuffle Along* that used real black faces. It also included Blake's first standard, "(I'm Just) Wild About Harry." And some fourteen years later his signature song, "Memories of You," would turn up in another such show. There was a limit to how many all-black shows the traffic would bear, and waiting for the next one was no way to build a full-time Irving Berlin–type career.

A better bet for that would still be to lead one's own band and wait for the right white entrepreneur or agent to come along and do the introductions and paperwork. Ellington didn't have long to wait. Irving Mills, the unsung songwriters' helper of the early twenties, who had spotted Carmichael as well, snatched Ellington up at once, not specifically for songwriting, which might or might not come along, but for the sheer sound of his band, which Mills could start selling right away to the two color-blind young media, radio and records, which were just then hitting their full strides and were reaching out blindly for any kind of music that could be squeezed into three minutes or so, the exact length of a song.

Ellington ruled the music, while Mills did the paperwork. Napoléon meets Napoléon. Fortunately, Mills thought big too, and long, and not just in terms of immediate hits. And he knew that the first thing to do for his client was to make sure he had the best possible band to work with, his very own Stradivarius of a band, primarily just to play on, but also to compose on if he could. So he bankrolled Ellington a couple more members to dispose of as he saw fit. Probably not even the Duke could have put into words exactly what he wanted, because it was a complete impossibility; namely, the best of both worlds, a band that could improvise like a jazz band but also follow his instructions perfectly. In other words, he wanted a musical instrument made up entirely of human beings, who could prac-

tice free will and obedience at the same time. It was a godlike wish that, to put it temperately, would take a little time, as he handpicked the players and broke them in to their unique chores. And I was not surprised to learn that Frank Sinatra some twenty years later would find the latest edition of Ellington's band exasperating to sing with, because, unlike Count Basie's disciplined outfit, they consisted entirely of prima donnas. And their mandate apparently did not include accompanying singers, or possibly even playing songs as such. In their ideal world, you just played music and saw what happened.

So, presto, Mills would provide them with a place where they could do just that, the perfect lab in which to learn what they were doing. In other words, Mills signed Ellington up for a gig at the Cotton Club in the booming community of Harlem, which was already witnessing an artistic renaissance of which Ellington was about to become a crucial part. The Cotton Club was at that stage a distillation of America's zany racial patterns and might sardonically be called an example of segregation at its finest. The cast and the neighborhood looked and was black through and through, but the audience was equally white. And while the music sounded black, whatever that meant, some of it was written by white men like Harold Arlen and Jimmy McHugh, who immediately became honorary blacks, if honorary is the right word, while the rest of the music was by blacks like Cab Calloway or Ellington, who could, in this ambiguous setting, be completely himself and incidentally produce his greatest songs—not jazz songs, but jazz compositions, which, if time had stood still, is what they would have remained.

There are some things that publishers know quicker than anyone, and what Irving Mills knew best was that by the time Ellington had begun to unpack his melodic gift, jazz as such had already lost its novelty for the larger public, so he might as well start chopping up his music into songs right now. By 1925, the human voice had finally started to sound like itself on records, under the unofficial leadership of Bing Crosby, who was a great jazz singer capable of keeping things going in the right direction for a while. (If Bing ever stopped swinging, it would all be over.) Anyway, so long as you gave your music some words and called it a song, maybe you could just go on doing your own thing.

So what kind of lyrics went best with Ellington? Obviously, you wanted

lots and lots of mood. Establish, for instance, the dark, dark blue of the singer's mind right now. This is indigo, man. You could never go back to mere blue after this. Or mere "Solitude" after you've heard that one. "I sit and I stare" de-dum-de-dum-dum. The song text has already been riveted into the melody, and people will just think you're saying something.

A few key words are quite enough if the listeners only want to have a particular mood reinforced while they drive their car or try to sleep or fall in love. Later on, they'll think that the words were perfectly swell too. But real singers want a little more than that: not just words that make sense occasionally, but some connection with the melody. The great saxophone player Lester Young used to talk about "playing the lyrics," as if this was the best way to read the composer's mind. But this is to assume a real connection between the elements. At some point the tunesmith looks at a bunch of words and says, "By George, you've got it! I couldn't have put it better myself." After which, all he needs is for the right performer to come along to dig them both, and you have magic à la Astaire and Berlin or Ethel Merman and Cole Porter.

Since both Berlin and Porter wrote their own songs all the way, coordination could go no further. These are our two best pure songwriters, and singers still love them both. Contrariwise, for the furthest you can go in the other direction, I can't think of a less inviting lyric to step up to than that of "Sophisticated Lady," for which Mills had allowed his hayseed hit man Mitchell Parish to apply a country boy's reading of the word "sophisticated," thereby turning an enigmatic *chanson* about a city at night into a cautionary tale about what happens to nice girls when they leave home. This is not "down in the depths on the ninetieth floor," as in Cole Porter, but down in the depths in the diner, with the mascara running and the roots showing and the lipstick smears piling up in the ashtray. It seems that this poor lamb not only drinks but smokes and (the line that always brings down the house) dines "with some man in a restaurant." Gasp!

It sounds more like an army training film ("one minute with Venus can mean a lifetime with Mercury") than a great ballad, and for once Ellington was heard to murmur that it wasn't quite what he'd had in mind. So why had he let it happen? Well, Parish wrote the hits around here, and he seemed to have a good thing going with the American outback. And clever lyrics can be quite distracting.

More seriously, the Duke had already delivered his own version, all he had to say, with his band. Jazz was not in its heart a singing medium, and if the public insisted on words anyway, Louis Armstrong's response was instinctively right—to sing nonsense, sing scat. Use the human voice purely as an instrument, and make clear that that's what you're doing. Jazz tells its own stories. It doesn't need words, and scat is simply jazz's way of saying, "Get lost."

Yet Ellington's music doesn't seem to scat all that well either. In his own arrangements of numbers like "Mood Indigo" and "Prelude to a Kiss," there don't seem to be any parts for singers at all that wouldn't sound better played on something else. And singers can take a hint. Once the master has spoken, you'd feel like a fool answering back with your own interpretation, so his songs just don't seem to get sung as much as other people's. "Prelude to a Kiss" carries a serviceable lyric, but unlike most such, I've never found myself memorizing it automatically the way my generation used to, or even been fully aware of it. The bare chords as played on the piano are so gorgeous that for once I can imagine why bobby-soxers used to squeal over Frank Sinatra and tribes used to beat their tom-toms: Some music demands a response, if it's only a low growl, and I would instantly vote this the most beautiful song ever written, except for this one problem of the words. By contrast "All the Things You Are," its nearest rival, is a singer's song in the most fundamental sense; you want to start singing it immediately. And although it's a great piece of music in its own right, I've never heard a purely instrumental version of it. Although the words boil down to the usual grandiose piffle, you are quite likely to find yourself singing them with real feeling.

"Prelude" came out in 1938, and one senses that Ellington, or whatever constitutes Ellington, was thinking a bit more about songs as such by then. The two matching tunes "I Let a Song Go Out of My Heart" and "Don't Get Around Much Anymore" go perfectly together, as if they were written that way, but they also break down into most singable songs, while "I Got It Bad (and That Ain't Good)" is so songlike that it's even got a humpty-dumpty bridge that is manifestly just there to carry singers across. Perhaps Ellington's most successful and least debatable song in the 1940s was "I'm Beginning to See the Light," but "Do Nothin' Till You Hear from Me" also passes the automatic memorization test and the compulsive

sing-along test too, as does "Satin Doll," with some help from Johnny
Mercer's lyrics. And finally there are several others, like "Jump for Joy"
and that pleasant surprise "Just A-Sittin' and A-Rockin'," that may not be
conventional songs but that still require singing if you're going to do them
at all.

The list goes on. Out of the huge mixed bag that the Duke has left us,
you can certainly extract at least one genuine songwriter—but possibly
one with another black man or two in his closet. This time, the gossip
can't be avoided altogether, because for Ellington's great early instrumen-
tals the suspects were usually Barney Bigard and Johnny Hodges, while
for the songwriter years, the tragic young Billy Strayhorn appeared in the
picture, and his name has since replaced the boss's in first place on
Ellington's jazzy lead-in "Take the 'A' Train" and probably should at least
share full credit on "Satin Doll" and others.

Yet one hears no sharp breaks or strange voices in the music. It is still
the same Duke Ellington talking—not three different men taking turns at
it, but one man in different moods and phases trying different things. As
my son, Frank, pointed out when George Harrison died, each of the Beatles wrote his best only as a Beatle, as a member of a band. The Duke was
a master not just of music but of human interaction.

Just from reading about him, one senses that the man was a presence,
a focal point, the producer and director of his own scenes. His father,
James, had been at various times a butler and chauffeur to the Washington, D.C., elite, both positions that could teach one an awful lot about
irony and the way the world works, and perhaps James imparted some of
this outlook to his son. Indeed, by the end of just one meal or one week's
driving, a servant would probably know more about most kinds of people,
white and black, than they would ever know about him.

Wherever he got it, Ellington always entered the room with enormous
confidence in the cards he was holding for today's game. Photos from the
late 1930s show him jamming happily with white musicians like Tommy
Dorsey and Eddie Condon and joshing with politicians as if he was born
to do so. Like Joe Louis, Ellington didn't "beat down doors," he walked
through them. And if some people didn't like it, well, this might be a white
world, but the music was black right now and he was royalty.

Irving Mills knew it. Usually, when a white name and a black one are

linked like theirs were, it is automatically assumed that the white one must have exploited the black one. But no one ever exploited Ellington unless there was something in it for him; a fair exchange of exploitations. And both he and Mills profited enormously from their association.

As an aristocrat of the servant class, his daddy must have learned the one profound secret, namely, how much more his employers needed him than he needed them. Rich people tend to be disproportionately helpless, and never more so than in their endless, wistful search for good servants. William Ellington knew that he could always get another boss, but where were they going to find a great butler? He was a luxury item, like a yacht or an extra house, by virtue of his style and smarts and whatever mysterious quality makes a man seem like officer material and makes Fred Astaire's clothes look better than anyone else's. Whatever indeed it was, father William seems to have passed it on to his son by precept, example, and simple inheritance.

Now Ellington was a boss himself, an aristocrat in his own right, and as such he knew how much he now depended on other people, and how to get what he needed from them, not by confrontation, which would have cut him off from half the country—including the half that jazz came from—but by an instinct for the possible. For instance, when he *did* take his band down South, he didn't fight the railroad, he simply acquired his own railway carriage so that his men could travel first-class.

This kind of thing would come to seem far too roundabout for the radicals of the 1960s, who considered Duke inauthentic and irrelevant. For them, black experience had to be harsh and bitter, or else it didn't count, and black power was supposed to come from the barrel of a gun, not from a smile or a handshake. The Pullman porter image of the grinning darkie with the natural sense of rhythm had put a curse on simple politeness, and even Martin Luther King Jr. was considered a borderline Uncle Tom. Yet even by then, such totally hip geniuses as Charlie Parker and Miles Davis had once again demonstrated that artistic originality and authentic black style have an awkward way of coming from the middle class, and indeed that there *was* a black middle class. In fact, there was a chapter missing from the Black Panther cosmology, and it would take Bill Cosby several years to help publish it.

Meanwhile, though, Ellington was quite insistent about his own black heritage, considering it intrinsic to his music, and virtually his subject matter. The distinction was that, to him, black did not mean primitive but referred to something like a great lost civilization that was right now in the vibrant process of rediscovery. And he was happy in the best black American tradition to accept that great African book, the Bible, as his guide to the promised land.

Not altogether surprisingly, his theology seems to have caused him to take a sharp turn against his friend Gershwin's *Porgy and Bess*. At first I assumed that his problem with it was the usual possessiveness all groups feel when their idioms are commandeered. Foreigners writing American slang usually get it wrong, but how dare they anyhow?

Ellington's chief grievance, though, concerned just the one song "It Ain't Necessarily So," which, in the voice of a scapegrace character, pokes fun at the Good Book. Ellington felt that Gershwin was risking hellfire with this one, and that maybe his surprise brain tumor was retribution for it.

It must have come as a jolt back then to find a sophisticated man like Ellington throwing the Book at a sinner like this. The reading public had been sufficiently conditioned by H. L. Mencken's sneers at fundamentalism to sneer at it themselves, but obviously the Duke lived in a different world part of the time, and at least there can be no more question about his authenticity in it.

Sometimes the best part of a story doesn't come at the end, and for a true believer death isn't the end anyhow, and within a year of George's fatal tumor Ellington had authorized his "Prelude to a Kiss" to carry a friendly reference to him. There were no hard feelings. A much more typical story is the one about the new band member who nervously asked Ellington what he should start out with. "Just play 'I Got Rhythm,'" said the great man, "and we'll think of something."

It was one thing for white musicians to accept their own "inner blacks," quite another for African American musicians to accept *them* as brothers. To some extent, Duke's attitudes were dictated by the practicalities of band leading. During their most creative years, Ellington and his men still had to double as a regular band playing other people's songs, including the early proto-black ones of such great white contemporaries as

Arlen and Jimmy McHugh written for the Cotton Club. Resentment would have thrown a spoke in his own wheels. And pray, who did Edward Kennedy Ellington have reason to envy?

Perhaps, though, there was a little something else at work between him and Gershwin. If jazz songs really were a Jewish meditation on black music, these two would be the prototypes, the best black musician and the most brilliant and thoroughly converted Jew. Fortunately, George's admiration for Ellington was not only profound but irresistible, and the friendship held. But perhaps when George took the logical last step into *Porgy and Bess,* the Duke let out a yelp. "What the hell are you doing *here?*" One man's homage is another man's encroachment. But there was something almost biologically inevitable about this. Gershwin had needed to work this closely to the black ethos in order to produce the baby, but you probably can't get this close without falling in love.

George's love was not, I believe, unrequited. *Porgy* may not be Ellington's version of black life, or anyone else's, but it has acquired by now a kind of artistic validity, and the proof is that only black actors can play it. *Guys and Dolls, Kiss Me, Kate,* even *Oklahoma!* could be performed by anybody, but "Bess, You Is My Woman Now" just doesn't sound white and never will. Gershwin had been there and sung with the choir, even taking part in the famous shouts.

After an awkward pause, Gershwin's homage, his gift, was accepted and adopted, and something had changed. Although whites had been imitating blacks from the moment they'd clapped eyes on them a century earlier, they had always done so in quotation marks and disguise. But *Porgy* is as real as it gets on a stage, and Catfish Row is his real address too, the first Southern one we've ever really visited in a song, and a triumphant landmark on one of our most satisfactory national journeys.

After World War II, foreigners would likely have voted popular music to be both the best and the most American thing about us. A good reason for this was that it fed from both our major streams at once. Everything else about us might be segregated, and even this was as segregated as we could make it; for example, as late as 1938, Benny Goodman would make the headlines scream when he took Lionel Hampton onstage with his white band. And that was in Chicago, not down South in Little Rock. But the essential truth here is that Lionel Hampton fit in perfectly from the

first note, and with their eyes shut, the audience wouldn't have noticed a thing.

Music is, of course, incorrigibly promiscuous, and its devotees are constantly fraternizing. But it forms its own mainstreams anyhow in response to time and circumstance. In our own technically unsegregated, if not totally integrated, world, a white kid may, if he likes, sing rap, or even soul, but at first it will sound like a pure imitation and his "street" and "hood" will seem as phony and made-up as the tin pan land of Dixie: But maybe, after a while, it will be called white rap.

So why didn't it happen that way with jazz? The hardest part may have been to find enough white musicians who could keep up with the black ones, and to this day there are snobs of both races who insist that we never did find them. (This argument flares up and subsides on a regular basis, and probably nothing can be done about it except to apply the famous Roy Eldridge test on a case-by-case basis, that is, play some obscure jazz passages, and ask the listener to name the race of the musicians. Be warned: This test may cause nervous breakdowns.) As one who spent some formative years ricocheting around Fifty-second Street between the white School of Chicago Jazz and the black Sons of New Orleans, I have my own opinions. But whatever the final answer as regards live performance, performance at the composing desk is another matter, and there is no serious doubt on either side that certain geniuses like Gershwin and Arlen truly were able to *think* in jazz and make immortal music with black virtuosos like Louis Armstrong and Billy Eckstine and Sarah Vaughan.

But if the white folk could do it at all, the odds were that they would soon take it over completely, not through racism but through the inevitable arrival of an old-boy network, and they would wind up bleaching it out and making way for things like rock and roll and rhythm and blues and other things they could bleach out too—all of which did happen, but not quickly, and not before we'd had enough time for a good long Golden Age. And this is where Ellington becomes one of the two or three essential figures, the one who kept the music honest, and ensured that the proper jazz levels were maintained, even if he had to overdo it at times. By writing some songs that really weren't quite songs and others that were, he defined the concept of jazz songs as well as it could be defined, and I am willing to rest my own case right here.

Part Three

The Stage—Broadway Swings

Jerome Kern:
Jazz Comes to Broadway... Slowly

JEROME KERN

*I*n any bull session on the general subject of songs, everyone inevitably praises Harold Arlen, but it's also foreseeable that at some point someone leans forward with eyes glittery and says, "Of course, Jerome Kern was the best." In fact, it's almost a part of his definition, that his music makes you want to say something nice about him and immediately declare your allegiance. Even that professional crab and Gershwin-champion, Oscar Levant, proposed that a taste for Kern's music should actually be made a requirement for citizenship, as if it were a test of moral character and simple decency.

Like George Gershwin, Jerome Kern projected an aura, but one made entirely of music. Gershwin at least had a face; Kern was pure sound. If Gershwin was Times Square at midnight, and skyscrapers and jackhammers by day, Kern was more like a cathedral at high noon for worshippers to gaze at and dream about. Kern's music leaves one feeling not just good but noble. The world must be a superior place to produce such music and such peace (and such a good building too, because simply as music, his songs are sturdy as well as beautiful, and you can move right in).

Not surprisingly, Kern's real self, insofar as one can find it now, did not entirely live up to this. Anecdotal history gives the impression that the words heard most often to describe him at his funeral, officially and otherwise, were alternately "pixieish" and "overbearing," which not only don't seem to fit his songs, but don't even fit each other. P. G. Wodehouse, who met Kern early in both their lives, skips both images and describes "Jerry" as something else again, a ball of energy who looked on sight as if he could get things done, a look I find it difficult to conjure. But Wodehouse also makes a useful distinction between a young Kern, who sounds like fun to work with if you could keep up with him, and an older one, slightly overwhelmed by his own magnificence.

Or so Wodehouse had heard. And that's the problem. There has always been more hearsay than fact about the private Kern. When I asked Harold Arlen why there were so few anecdotes, he said, "Maybe because he was such a son of a bitch that nobody wants to talk about him." Whether or not Kern himself was impressed by his magnificence, other people certainly were. Nobody, it seems, who had ever heard "Smoke Gets in Your Eyes" or the music from *Show Boat* could ever view him as just another human. So all it took was an occasional growl from him to terrorize practically everybody, including such potential new lyricists as Leo Robin and Johnny Mercer and the incorrigibly underconfident Ira Gershwin. And Kern wasn't above giving the legend a nudge by browbeating waiters and such in the manner of a bratty European maestro, or by imposing his favorite party games on visitors and playing them pedantically and indigestibly.

Yet while poring over Kern lore in all its vagueness and unreliability, one notes another sentence recurring its way into a pattern. "He was much nicer than I expected." So perhaps there really can be such a thing

as an overbearing pixie. Shana Alexander, who had a child's-eye view of Kern, considered "Uncle Jerry" the most fun and the kindliest of any grown-ups she knew, an opinion pretty much endorsed by another song-writer's daughter, Margaret Whiting. Like his disciple, Richard Rodgers, Kern got his best reviews from women of all ages, including the one he worked with the most, Dorothy Fields, the lyricist. But unlike Rodgers, he also got occasional raves from men too, most notably from the cantanker-ous Harry Warren, who found Kern's lordliness funny—a word seldom used about Rodgers. The truth seems to be that Kern liked to keep people guessing.

But who was he? Ancestrally, the Kerns had the cachet of having ar-rived in this country before the Civil War. But they were also some dis-tance from the "Our Crowd" of great Jewish families. Jerry's mother, Fannie Kakeles, might conceivably have made the very outside edges of that world, courtesy of her father, who was a popular sexton at a fashion-able temple, but Henry Kern remains such a shadowy figure that one might almost suspect a con man. Even after Jerry spent some time in Ger-many himself, neither he nor his brothers could ever name a single rela-tive or ancestor over there, or even state for sure whereabouts the old man came from in that country. And to top it off, his biographer Gerald Bord-man couldn't even find a record of his marriage to Fannie over here either.

Shadowy or no, Henry did manage to succeed almost immediately, first as a stabler of horses in Manhattan when that was hot, and later as a merchant in neighboring Newark. Maybe it was his mobility that made him so untraceable, but the main thing was that, while Henry Kern was obviously not too keen on supporting a songwriter, Jerry always had some kind of money in back of him, which in itself raised him several tiers above his colleagues in song.

To reinforce his status as a rich kid, he had most likely also been spoiled fairly rotten, which can be as good as a title in terms of self-confidence. The clue here is that of Fannie Kern's seven sons, four died in infancy, a monstrous toll by the late 1800s. But then, toward the tail of this woe, along came number six, a fragile little genius who seemed to have blessedly inherited all her own musical tastes and gifts, only more so, and who seemed to be almost ready to use them at birth, as born musi-cians so often are. So just like that, she had someone else to play with and

a stake in the future, a child who might make the Kerns a truly great family someday. And to complete *her* happiness anyway, he even looked like Fannie. So what was not to spoil?

Unfortunately, Fannie is a bit shadowy too—maybe it went with the Henry Kern territory—so we don't know how she acquired her own musical education, only that the results suggest a terrific one, and we do know that she enjoyed playing eight-handed concerts with her three surviving boys while Jerry was still a tot. Since he was far and away the youngest, he must, as he unwrapped his own gifts, have practically begun his life feeling giddy with accomplishment and ready to take on the world—so long as the game was music.

His strong suit was indeed strong, maybe the best one that a kid can have outside of a gift for humor or football. Unlike baby physicists or mathematicians, musical prodigies can usually entertain their way out of trouble. And all the scant records and memories of Kern's school days show him perched at the piano, playing songs and writing them for his life. From now on, music would be his shield and his sword and his calling card; to be on the safe side, it would be show music. For his tenth birthday, his mother took Jerry to the theater, and whether or not it was lifelong love at first sound, as it would be with Richard Rodgers, this kind of music was obviously a game he could play at school as well. Classical music wars with community life, by yanking away the kid for hours at a time of solitary practice, but show music fits right in. In fact, songwriters and comedians may be the only kinds of artists who learn anything really useful in school, and Kern is not the only subject in this book to have taken full advantage of this.

By the time Kern graduated from high school, his vocation had become not just obvious but imperious. And after botching his first business assignment (by famously ordering up two hundred pianos instead of two), his doting parents left him to pursue his own musical apprenticeship in his own way, studying here and making a buck there. A certified genius now, both at home and at school, he hit the ground purring, with a coating of self-satisfaction that nothing could dent, and the aristocratic gift of not needing to be liked or understood, just a bow or a curtsy would do. So he has probably been misunderstood a lot, not least by me.

Kern could take care of himself in anybody's world, with charm and with iron and workable dialogue, and perhaps a touch of guile too, inherited from who-knows-exactly-where. What we do know is that in the course of a too-short life he had a way of getting involved in high-profile lawsuits, and would be accused of plagiarism a suspicious number of times, even for this coincidence-plagued profession ("We only had twelve notes between us," as Arthur Sullivan explained), all of which suggests the type of guy who, despite his almost sacred-sounding music, definitely bore watching—which may have suited the role-playing Kern just fine.

Now back to business. Since Kern seemed to be locked into some kind of theater music, by both fate and inclination, the question now was, what kind? French or Austrian? Strauss or Offenbach? Perhaps Sir Arthur Sullivan? As the twentieth century loomed, what was then called the civilized world, and now just the Western one, was seized with a millennial frenzy. Art was about to be stood on its head by Picasso, ditto the novel, by Joyce and Proust, and music by Stravinsky, and ditto everything else by someone or other. So maybe we could actually try an American musical? Well, it was just a thought.

There have been three generally acknowledged (though seldom by the same people at the same time) revolutions in the American musical theater, but since two of these involved Oscar Hammerstein, one might expect those ones anyway to have rolled backward. Oscar loved the past like a trendy taxidermist who is happy to use the latest techniques to bring it back to life. And since two of these revolutionary moments also involved Kern, you can bet that the music was beautiful but not radical.

Uprising number one is sometimes named after the Princess Theater, a cozy off-Broadway-size house where the trio of Kern, Guy Bolton, and P. G. Wodehouse undertook to sabotage the two reigning styles of American musical. The first of those was the Transylvanian operetta, in which the queen of Ruritania, disguised as a chambermaid, is wooed by the crowned prince of Bratislava, disguised as a busboy, to the strains in both senses of imported music, or quasi-imported music. The other would be the revue, aka follies, scandals, and so on, made up of bits of business—here a comedian, there a tenor, everywhere a chorus girl—in short, vaudeville to the nth degree, dazzling at times, but innately frustrating because it is in

the nature of audiences to want to know what happens next to these people, to the tenor and his victims, and what kind of songs they will all wind
up singing about it.

So the game plan of revolution one (and incidentally of revolutions two
and three as well) was simply to integrate the songs with the dialogue and
the dialogue with the songs in order to combine the best (or worst) of
opera with the ditto of theater. It was a great but obvious idea, and the
only wonder was that no one had thought of it sooner—if indeed no one
had.

The one element nobody else could have thought up sooner was Kern's
music, which, if not yet precisely 100 percent American was at least
Anglo-American, which means several pounds lighter. Kern has sometimes been called the greatest Austrian composer ever born in the United
States. But despite a year spent studying in the Heidelberg vicinity, Kern's
overseas training was overwhelmingly pursued in English theaters and
music halls, and his very first hit—"How'd You Like to Spoon with
Me?"— shows just how much of London's street sounds he had absorbed
into his style. Kern's personal haughtiness, combined with the aristocratic
distinction of his music, has persistently led people to assume that he was
basically a highbrow slumming with musicals. But, as noted, his affair
with stage musicals went back to childhood, particularly his affair with
English ones, and much of his professional apprenticeship was spent
running musical- or vaudeville-level songs back and forth between the
two countries. "How'd You Like to Spoon with Me?" was precisely that—
an "English-type" song interpolated into the American production of an
English show, with nothing Viennese or semiclassical about it.

So when World War I came along, making England our friend and
Transylvania our enemy, Jerome Kern was sitting particularly pretty. Although the war was officially being fought to avenge the death of an Austrian archduke, which sounds like our kind of cause, a mind-blowing
maze of alliances left us on the side of the Serbian assassin and his friends
instead, and thus fighting for English humor and French pastry and
against German and Austrian heaviness and turgidity, and by extension
against the Chocolate Soldier himself.

Jerome Kern may have seen it coming. At any rate, he had begun by
then to pool his talents with those of the young Englishman Guy Bolton

in the creation of some genuine transatlantic musicals, in which Vienna and the Wilhelmstrasse might magically emerge as Mayfair and Park Avenue, and in which the busboys really were busboys and the chambermaids generally turned out to be the daughters of self-made millionaires from Kansas, who, when they appeared in the last scene, sounded suspiciously like Englishmen with dictionaries of Yankee slang in their pockets. A further Englishing would occur a couple of shows later when the team of Bolton and Kern became a trio with the piping on board of Wodehouse, soon to be the great humorist and right now about to be the best lyricist on Broadway.

But since Kern and Wodehouse had already worked together successfully in London back in 1905, it's possible to say that the first great American musicals were actually born in England—but they were never quite English, because just as Kern was less highbrow than people thought, he was also considerably more American. Before he had gone to England as a young man, and shortly after Irving Berlin and the boys had popularized the ragtime song, Jerry worked as a song-plugger at Wanamaker's department store in New York. And Kern wrote at least one rag too, as if to prove he could. But in the best circles, ragtime was still considered a vulgar, low-life-and-rent fad, and it would be another twenty years or so before Fred Astaire induced the great Kern to topple off his throne and really swing. In the meantime, he forged ahead with his own sound of a well-brought-up American who had lived abroad a bit and missed the jazz epidemic altogether except to write, as if with his left hand, one song in the "new" American mode, which would prove to be perhaps the most influential song in this book.

"They Didn't Believe Me" shines out brilliantly and eccentrically in the history of American musical theater. In the year it was written, circa 1914, syncopated songs could usually still be identified by a certain facetious jocularity, and frequently by the word "rag" in the title as well. No one had begun writing real songs in this style yet—until suddenly here it was: a perfect loosey-goosey, syncopate-me-if-you-care, a relaxed and smiling American asterisk-jazz song.

But by the time most people were aware of it, Kern had gone on about his regular business, leaving the next step to a couple of other and younger geniuses who would hear it and decide on the strength of it

precisely what they wanted to do for the rest of their lives. George Gershwin, who was already plugging rags on the Alley and studying for Carnegie Hall on the side, found in "They Didn't" the answer to a prayer: distinguished theater music that actually swung—or could be made to ("And when I told them [syncopate? It's up to you] how beautiful you are [ditto], they didn't believe me," and so on). It was sassy but high-class, commercial but not cheap; and young Richard Rodgers coming the other way, from uptown to down, felt the same. "They Didn't Believe Me" was a gentleman's rag, without paw prints or coffee stains. As Alec Wilder would say, it didn't smell of cheap-cigar smoke.

After Kern fired the starting pistol, he seems to have lost interest in the chase, and would later have to run to catch up with his own disciples. The Princess show scores were not particularly syncopated or emphatically American. In fact, for the U.S. upper class and its camp followers, who included Kern, Rodgers, and haute Broadway in general, British was probably as close as they wanted to get, because anything more American might contain the dreaded jazz virus.

If you had an ounce of the snob in you, or the smallest stake in the system, jazz was the enemy, and perhaps it seemed even more frightening because so many other parts of the sky were falling at that same time. Modern art had gone crazy and turned ugly, the buildings didn't know when to stop and neither did the flappers, and jazz was just the music to make it all sound dangerous and uncontrollable. Also, it was terribly rude. As civilization strove to pull itself together from the recent bloodbath in France, denouncing jazz provided a field day for fogies.

In the wake of World War I, Kern now *was* the establishment, but outside of avoiding any jazzy arrangements (or indeed any arrangements other than his own) of his songs, Kern doesn't seem to have had any fixed ideas about librettos. He stuck with his English partners until the inevitable rift (over money), after which he seems to have looked around for the least jazzy American collaborators he could find, which would bring him straight to that reactionary revolutionary, Oscar Hammerstein.

Whether Kern knew it or not, he was now on course for revolution number two, an even more integrated musical, telling a *real* story about *real* people. Wodehouse once wrote a funny piece about starting on a script for a singer who couldn't dance and winding it up with a dancer

who couldn't sing. It was hard to create real characters out of such a fluid labor pool. But for Kern, there was now no turning back from integrated musicals, if only because they made the composer a much bigger player than revues ever had, virtually the author in fact; revues could use a dozen songs by as many different writers, who would all remain equally anonymous. But in a book musical, the composer's voice had the chance to sound off in all its various modes, and perhaps more crucially, his name had a chance to dominate the Broadway playbill, the famous poop-sheet that stares up from your lap during intermissions, and it was a hundred times more likely to make you famous than five times as many movie screenplays. "A musical by Jerome Kern" became as plausible a description of a whole evening as "An opera by Richard Wagner."

But what story would Kern tell? There is no reason to suppose that he had anything particularly striking in mind as the roaring twenties began. Formally speaking, his partnering with Hammerstein would suggest that for now he was willing to go backward into the fusty world of operettas and to heck with revolutions. Hammerstein, along with his mentor and partner Otto Harbach, was already on record as wanting to bring operettas back to New York even before they had completely left. So undertaking anything new with either of them would be like driving with the brakes on.

However, their effort together yielded *Sunny,* an old-world type of American show that included the great bridge song between the old Kern and the new, "Who?" (which for some reason sounds like a French café song to me—that is, it swings, but not quite Americanly).

Any revolution with this cast of characters would only go so far and no further. If all they wanted to do was move Viennese shows to various parts of the globe, why not go back to England again? The country would continue to tempt Kern, partly because of his mastery of both musical languages, and partly because of whatever it was that also persuaded him to marry and stay married to an English wife. But while *Sunny* was technically transatlantic, anyone really keen on writing English dialect would probably not turn to Hammerstein for it.

Hammerstein's role in two of these so-called revolutions was never more than what the AA people would call an enabler. In the case of the great *Show Boat,* it was Kern who first read the book and insisted on its

musical possibilities. And with the groundbreaking *Oklahoma!* the equally strong-willed Richard Rodgers not only found it but had also tried the story on his old partner, Larry Hart, before springing it on Hammerstein. So it looks as if both men chose Oscar Hammerstein partly because he was so obliging and adaptable.

With such authors, it is not surprising that *Show Boat* now seems a lot more like, yes, an operetta set in America than like the totally new kind of musical that has been advertised ever since. By later standards of authenticity, the plot and dialogue now seem as stagy and artificial as if they had been set in a German beer hall. The novelist Edna Ferber of the Algonquin had only just heard about showboats herself when she wrote the book, and yet both Jerry and Oscar were quite content to take her word for them and for the Old Man River they sailed on, and did not bother to go out and see or hear for themselves whether any of it rang true. And indeed most of its incomparable songs are not particularly any kind of American, except in the sense that everything Kern wrote sounded a little American. "Make Believe" had an unspecific kind of beauty—American? Okay, if you say so. And the same goes for "Why Do I Love You?" While "You Are Love" could almost pass for downright Viennese with just the slightest trace of Kern's Yankee accent. Only the stylized "Can't Help Lovin' Dat Man" makes any concession to the new American sound either in lyrics or tune. But then as the authors might answer, why should it? You could probably hear all kinds of sounds on the old riverboats, who really knew for sure?

The point about *Show Boat,* as it would be about *Oklahoma!,* is that the writers were both at least temporarily on the run from jazz and had found properties dealing with a couple of imaginary Americas—imaginary to them, anyway—that predated the Jazz Age, or lived outside it, or both. And they used these Americas as canvases on which to paint their own feelings and impressions, using Hammerstein's all-purpose slang and universal emotions. And each is handsomely justified by the work of the composer, the actual dreamer who dreamed the dream and wrote the tunes. Kern's score in particular is so good and indeed noble that *Show Boat* has been overrated ever since. *Show Boat* without music would be laughed off the stage, not to mention jeered off.

Yet nobody seems to have doubted *Show Boat*'s absolute greatness the night it came out, or its nobility of heart. The only question might be whether the public was quite ready for it or worthy of it. Although the critics agreed unanimously that on this night of nights the American musical had finally come of age, impresarios like Flo Ziegfeld and the Shuberts could not necessarily see what was supposed to be so hot about this. (Call me when the audience comes of age too.) From where they sat, the tired businessman and the buyer from out of town were still the demographic that counted for long-running musicals, and these simple fellows didn't really care where the girls came from or why, or what kind of folk costume the comic was making fun of. So for all *Show Boat*'s acclaim, it would be almost a decade before a writer with equal clout to Kern's would be able to get even a streamlined version of *Porgy* into a Broadway theater (where, as we've read, by Gershwin's standards it flopped badly the first time).

Revolution two would in fact have to wait for revolution three for its final ratification. By the time *Oklahoma!* came along in 1943, Americana had become a thousand points of pride as well as curiosity; as the choral stunts and special effects became ever more expert, it became clear that what was winning the war was all those clambakes and cattle drives. As a youngster myself, perched in the back of the theater, watching *Oklahoma!*, I can still feel the surge and glow that rose through the house with the title song. Yessir! If we could tame this great crazy bronco of a country, I reckon we can patch up this funny old world any time we put our minds to it. And the simple fact that I was there should have told me something too, namely, that all the grown-ups were missing, of the male persuasion that is, except for the very occasional serviceman and for the odd businessman, who really did look tired by now and didn't care if the showgirls wore bloomers and didn't kick, anyway. However, all over the place were the ladies from Scarsdale, probably calling the new tunes as much as anyone.

Whoever we were, we were worlds away from the audiences that Kern had first written for—not only a world of war and depression, of course, but also the world of Busby Berkeley and Walt Disney and of technological hijinks that had left Broadway flickering in last year's gaslight. No

sooner had *Show Boat* advanced the stage musical a couple of daring moves on the old checkerboard than talking pictures transferred the whole game to another dimension and began to co-opt the very word "entertainment" for itself. Was there anything that the stage could still do better? As if to settle the question, Hollywood quickly purchased Broadway's crown jewel, *Show Boat* itself, and reached a whole continent with its own excellent version.

Show Boat was not so much the start of something as the summation of everything, like a gorgeous firecracker on display celebrating the grand climax of the Jazz Age, when the stage was still king and could, for one last breathless minute, still do anything better than you could. And there was Jerome Kern perched by acclamation on top of the old ship *Showbiz,* virtually an institution himself now, and just the tiniest bit stuck up there.

At any rate, even he could never do *Show Boat* again, although he was constantly expected to. Because, with the coming of hard times in the 1930s, it seemed like just what the doctor ordered, but it wasn't. And Broadway instinctively began to specialize in the things that it *could* do better than Hollywood, notably sophistication, the in-humor of the small audience that could still afford an evening out, as opposed to the large audience that just grabbed a movie and some budget-busting popcorn.

The next surprise would be that sophistication would be what moviegoers wanted as well. But that's a joke for another chapter. The headline for now is that Cole Porter and the young team of Rodgers and Hart were and remain the names that best conjure up the Depression in Manhattan, while Kern spent much of the decade in Hollywood, like a king in exile. His partner in revolution, Hammerstein, went into a bicoastal slump on both stage and screen, one that could only be snapped by the war and the rather special atmosphere of the postwar, with its curious blend of piety and optimism.

As if history wanted to draw a diagram, any chance that Kern's prestige and musical charm might have been able to hold their own against both the talkies and the gals an' gags preferences of the butter-and-egg men was scotched once and for all by the market crash of October 1929. Up to that very day, Kern and Hammerstein's follow-up show, another integrated slice of Americana called *Sweet Adeline,* had been doing a brisk business. But upon hearing the grim news, the box office immediately plunged alongside

the millionaires. Maybe it was bad luck at this particular moment to have a hit song called "Why Was I Born?" Not that most people foresaw a whole Depression, but Broadway was always primarily about what do we want to do tonight. And so with the first sign of discouragement, the great American musical went on indefinite hold, while Harbach and Hammerstein took advantage of the confusion to return the American musical to Europe and to opera and operetta-land, taking Kern, at least temporarily, with them.

Kern's next two shows—*The Cat and the Fiddle* with Harbach and *Music in the Air* with Hammerstein—were not really operettas but light comedies about operetta. While World War I had been harsh on Transylvania, it had been kind to England and France, and the years that followed would be even more so as ships began to cross the Atlantic faster and faster until every man, woman, and child who wanted to had "seen Paris," and probably taken in a Broadway show before leaving. By then the transatlantic musical did not need any actual foreigners in the cast, but simply reasonable facsimiles who could play either Englishmen or Americans and in a pinch do French or Italian accents convincingly enough to fool Anglo-American audiences with a will to believe. Theatrically speaking, London and New York had become twin cities, connected by an unbroken stream of ocean liners that took turns exchanging road companies. So the faster you could get your show over there or here and reassembled without fuss or undue expense, the better.

Thus Gershwin's *Oh, Kay!* is set in a Long Island mansion that could easily pass for an English mansion and starred Gertrude Lawrence (English, but it doesn't matter), while Cole Porter's *Gay Divorce* requires one hotel room, one ballroom, and Fred Astaire.

At this name, one pauses, because with Astaire the form had found its archetype, its ideal expression, and it is tempting to say that all that any transatlantic musical needed was this man, in one of his familiar settings, to wit, somewhere between a first-class stateroom and a hotel lobby, because by then the ships themselves had become standard locations, and hotels were where you went when you got off.

Kern's next Broadway show was based on a book called *Gowns by Roberta,* which was made to measure, featuring Americans in Paris singing costume-music without the old starch or upholstery. All the same, under Kern's personal direction, *Roberta* played so heavy that the leg-

endary Max Gordon removed the starch in Philadelphia, and insisted on adding a slice of pungent vaudeville ham—young Bob Hope—to modernize and Americanize the show. And when *Roberta* went to Hollywood, it still creaked a little, because the movies didn't yet trust Fred Astaire to carry the show. In a prestige match against Kern, Astaire was still number two and he was consigned to a variant of the Bob Hope role as the kibitzer from the world of swing, crashing the old-world garden party. So all Fred could do was commence the two-stage reconstruction of Jerry. By amazingly good chance, Fred himself had already heard just the song he needed in a Kern show that had never made it out of London.

It could be said without too much exaggeration that this song, "I Won't Dance," deftly inserted into *Roberta,* would do as much as any one thing to drag Kern, kicking and screaming, out of the old realm of Prince Rudolph of What's-His-Name and into the modern world as then constituted. By the time Astaire was through with this song, it had introduced the public, and perhaps Jerry himself, to a new flavor of Kern, of which it would soon be wanting more. And incidentally, it would introduce Kern to the perfect lyrical partner to lead him around in this new language.

Dorothy Fields had already written (with Jimmy McHugh) such swingaroos as "Diga Diga Doo" and "Doin' the New Low-Down." You could get no hipper or hepper than that. Despite her credentials, Ms. Fields was as terrified of the ferocious Kern legend as anybody. For the film *Roberta,* she'd written some lyrics for a brand-new Kern tune called "Lovely to Look At," which had gone into production before he'd had a chance to hear them, so she thought she had plenty to be afraid of. She needn't have worried. Kern loved her lyrics, and loved her, and they were up and running together, hand in hand through the lower depths, or as close to them as Kern ever allowed himself to get.

So "Lovely to Look At" is pivotal too, and like *Roberta* is itself something of a hybrid, halfway between the grandeur of the old Kern and the friskiness of the new; at a stretch, it might have been at home back in *Show Boat,* but it also sounds like a Fred Astaire song. Either way, I have always found this song absolutely hypnotic and it was the first Kern number to jerk those time-honored words out of me. "He's the best, you know, the very best."

The bar was so high by the early 1930s that *Roberta's* score had to be great to be good, so Kern responded with a marvelous one that included perhaps his best song yet, although he may not have known he had written it.

The origins of "Smoke Gets in Your Eyes" are sublime evidence of just how subtly the music in the air goes about the work of getting itself written, and of how subconscious and sneaky the pressure of the New could be. Because the tune of this classic had actually begun its majestic life as virtually a throwaway, a piece of "material" for the dancers to tap to while the scenery was being changed, and although Kern himself always denied this, that's all it might have remained if someone else hadn't spotted its potential. "Try playing it slowly," said the director. And voilà, the same angel dust that had turned Carmichael's "Stardust" to gold a couple of years earlier sprinkled itself on Kern's jingle, immortalizing it on the spot and renewing Kern's lease on the crown too, for another millennium or so.

To admit that perhaps his greatest song ever was partly an accident was too much to ask of a control freak, or perhaps of anyone. "I may not have thought of it," as Hoagy famously said of "Stardust," "but I'm the one who found it." But Kern hadn't even precisely done that. Finding music where others have failed was and is just as good as finding it in your head, and Kern had gladly shared credit for "I've Told Every Little Star" with a bird who had obligingly whistled the bridge for him outside his window. But all he could honestly have said about this one was what he said elsewhere about songs in general, that you may feel twenty tugs on your line and only one of them will turn out to be a fish worth keeping, and it might sometimes take a while to know which one.

Kern had by no means converted to the new music full-time, and his decision to go to Hollywood and stay there might actually have been made in a reactionary mood, because if there was any place left where he could still write the old songs the old way and get anyone to listen, it was Hollywood, where Jeanette MacDonald and Nelson Eddy might have been warming up expressly for him. And then there was the money, which he intermittently seemed to need very badly indeed. Benny Green has written disdainfully of Kern's apparently insatiable avarice, but he leaves out the crucial fact that Kern was also a lifelong gambler of a kind that is

sometimes called degenerate, with an insatiable need for quick fixes of cash. In his biography of Alexander Woollcott, Samuel Hopkins Adams says that Kern was one of the high rollers who ultimately drove the Algonquin Round Table's poker playing branch out of business by raising the stakes too high.

Hollywood was where the big money was now, and Kern's decision to camp out there was presumably sweetened by the prospect of finding someone to play with again. But first of all, he needed a grubstake himself. Shortly before the Crash, Kern had sold a huge rare book collection that he'd been quietly compiling for years for an impressive sum of ready cash, but instead of betting the proceeds, like a sensible man, on a horse or a greyhound, he bet it all on the stock market in its last few minutes of life. And overnight, he found himself as broke as a Whitney.

Far be it from Kern to complain, or indeed to acknowledge the Depression in any way at all; but not far be it to think about money as he wrote his Hollywood songs. "Stay uncommercial," as he once advised a young disciple, "there's a lot of money in it."

Or so he hoped, at any rate. The first film he agreed to make with MGM was to be an original operetta so uncommercial that it should have made a fortune. But this would be Kern's introduction to the caprices of the industry and its apparent compulsion in those days to give its new arrivals their comeuppance. Because, despite his status as a living classic, Kern's first musical was simply dumped, after he'd already written three songs for it, and was replaced in toto by Rudolf Friml's clanking *Rose-Marie*. Baptism by insult.

Kern prided himself on being a good businessman, and after that he began to stick to one film contract at a time with smaller studios like RKO, over which he might hope to exert some shadow of his old Broadway mastery in exchange for slightly less expensive-looking movies.

Once again, as in the early twenties, Kern began to get his own way right and left without quite knowing what his own way was. He made all of two movies about the humanizing of opera singers, Lily Pons and Grace Moore, respectively, and the one you still see occasionally, *I Dream Too Much* with Pons, is truly charming, especially the title song, and a number called "The Jockey on the Carousel." But there is something small and "niche-y" about the film—Jerome Kern under glass.

He was still royalty, and advertised as such, but there was a lot of minor royalty in Hollywood—crowned heads of obsolete powers known for their postage stamps. If he was a master, he was an old one now, vintage Victor Herbert, and spelled in smaller type (this year) than Cole Porter and (next year) who knows?

The problem was, Hollywood tended to make two kinds of movies in the midthirties, big bad ones and good small ones, and the big musicals tended to be overstuffed turkeys like *Rosalie,* for which MGM would pay Cole Porter zillions of dollars.

Fortunately, though, a school of good small movies emerged that would rescue Kern and three more of the Big Five writers (all but Richard Rodgers). In one sense, Fred Astaire movies, with their goofy, airheaded plots and their cornball sophistication, must have struck Kern as a step backward to the frothy musicals he had cooked up with P. G. Wodehouse way back when. Whatever he did with Astaire would not only be a far cry from *Show Boat* but, worse still, an ominous stride toward the jazz he abominated.

Or did he still abominate it? Like Rodgers and Youmans and everyone else in here, he had heard the music in the air, and like the professor in the movies, he was unconsciously beginning to tap his foot. And if he wanted to be a headline-size master again, perhaps he shouldn't resist too much this time.

Swing Time was an interesting site for a baptism because for once Fred was not playing an American dancer in the Old World, but a small-town gambler very much at home in America. Frederick Austerlitz of Nebraska would be touching base at last in a thoroughly relaxed and finger-snapping ambience. And the professor could start tapping his foot for real.

Unlike *Roberta,* which is Kern's creation all the way, *Swing Time* is Astaire's turf. Fred had uniquely mastered the art of swinging tastefully, without entirely tipping over into the down and dirty. He could be hot and cool at the same time. So if Kern was ever going to get hot himself, clearly this was the man to do it with. Whether anyone else could ever have persuaded Kern to make the crossing into jazz songs, we'll never know, because the fact is that nobody else ever did, until world politics turned the screws once again and assigned him to write some songs for *someone* in uniform, preferably not a four-star general, as the name "Kern" might sug-

gest. In wartime, even national monuments were expected to take a cream pie in the chops occasionally to show solidarity. So Kern would swing one more time with Gene Kelly in *Cover Girl,* to which, incidentally, the awed Kelly contributed a quite classy performance himself, to go with Kern's quietly swinging score.

But it was Astaire who really gave us the best of the new Kern, including the songs that people ask the cocktail pianists to play most often, particularly "The Way You Look Tonight," but also "I'm Old-Fashioned" and "A Fine Romance." And it was Astaire alone who really got Kern to swing all the way to the outer limits in "Bojangles of Harlem."

The story of how this number came about provides one of the epic moments in pop history. Fred had seen Kern's original score and pronounced it undanceable. "No syncopation at all." So he and Dorothy Fields went up to the master's suite at the Beverly Wilshire and undertook his education, which Astaire apparently tapped out for him all over the furniture in what must have been one of his most inspired routines. By the end of it, Kern had learned, if nothing else, how to "let himself go" with the kind of classy abandon that was Fred's stock-in-trade.

What is easily missed in the blinding light of Kern's conversion to swing is how far *Jerry* took *Fred* out to where *he* wanted to go. "Bojangles" and Kern's other great dance number, "Never Gonna Dance," were as close to gutbucket as anything written for Fred so far. And he responded with some of his most intense dancing yet. He had challenged Jerry, and Jerry had answered in kind, in a dignified version of the old "call and response" of black music. And what makes *Swing Time* so curiously happy a movie is the sense of not one but three kids let out of school and chasing one another around the playground, as Fred and Ginger enjoy the American air and freedom from hotel rooms and ship decks, and in the unlikely company of our greatest European songwriter.

But that was as far as Kern could go in that direction without vandalizing his image, and he certainly wasn't planning to go there again with anyone else. The next few years would find his libido safely back on its throne. After the humanizing of his second opera singer, Kern continued to march backward by working with his old partner, Oscar Hammerstein, who was so out of it himself at this point that he could scarcely get work on either

coast. (An act of kindness on Kern's part? It's not the sort of legend that suited him, but Oscar was at Jerry's bedside when he died and gave him the most moving funeral oration he could have gotten from anyone.)

Kern's health had actually become part of the story as early as 1937, when he received a killer warning shot in the form of a heart attack, combined with a mild stroke. In those days, as I've often been reminded in my recent reading, the first heart attack usually meant "you're out," unless you were lucky indeed. So any sense Kern had while growing up of living a charmed but precarious life must have been reinforced in spades by this episode, and one imagines his remaining years being passed in its shadow.

Nevertheless, he emerged smiling, and for his next movie he wrote a positively bouncy song called "You Couldn't Be Cuter," smacking of his English music hall days, and dedicated it to the baby in Dorothy Fields's womb, or so the story goes. Actually, the baby himself, who is now named David Lahm and is a terrific café pianist, tells me that he would have to have been in utero for about five years for that to be the case. But with legends, it's the thought that counts.

Actually, this story fits in well with other people's Kern memories, as if he truly were a European prima donna, heckling writers and making bad puns in English. In fact, Jerry kept a little bust of that most unlikely role model, Richard Wagner, which he turned to the wall when he was having a bad morning. "Mr. Wagner is not pleased today."

But would Wagner have been pleased with "You Couldn't Be Cuter"? There were two Kerns by then, numbered after his two revolutions, and after he'd made his Wodehouse-type movie with Astaire, he wrote a song in his number-two mode with Hammerstein. "The Folks Who Live on the Hill" is a warm ball of fluff about reg'lar folk doin' a heap of livin'. Oscar had found his rich vein of calendar poetry, and was back at war for Jerry's soul. One could only wonder what Wagner would have thought about that one.

But it would take an ugly war to make Oscar's version look like good sense to Americans. And meanwhile, the rhythms of show business and of regular history suggested another film with Astaire—this time set in Cuba, now that Europe had pulled down its shutters so sharply. And once again, Jerry's ghost owes a debt to Fred's ghost, if only for the title song, "You Were Never Lovelier," which does honor to the word "lovely," as well

as to the lilt in Fred's voice. And Jerry's ghost also owes for the great song "I'm Old-Fashioned," which is one of Kern's finest cathedrals, a regal song that sounds wonderful even as sung by Rita Hayworth's voice-over.

As if to prove that composers don't know best, Kern's own favorite in the film, "Dearly Beloved," sounds more like a suburban wedding with too many flowers on the altar, while his other song, "The Shorty George," is a war-effort song that performs its function. It's the kind of song that proves Kern was a good sport, while the hit from his next film, *Cover Girl,* "Long Ago and Far Away," for all its majesty, has a cut-rate sound to it that could have come from a pool of World War II songwriters. It's the only Kern song (good or bad) that doesn't bear his signature.

About that same midwar time, another signal went out. The smashing success of *Oklahoma!* proved that it was already time for Hammerstein—time for regular Americans to start boasting in an unpretentious sort of way about our own sheer variety and colorful ordinariness.

As the other author of *Show Boat,* Jerome Kern saw his destiny and jumped to it, with two America-the-wonderful movies. *Can't Help Singing,* which is Hollywood's answer to *Oklahoma!,* and a ponderous clunker called *Centennial Summer,* which belonged more in the Smithsonian than the Roxy. Kern couldn't have enjoyed the latter much, to judge from the way he's said to have growled at his word-man, Leo Robin, who was paralyzed with awe, and who consequently wrote slowly and indifferently. Presumably, neither was in the mood for Philadelphia in 1876, and like everyone else, wanted to get it all over with and find out what the postwar world would be like.

The first order of business would be, of course, a revival of *Show Boat,* which had just reached its prime as an American monument. Every second review of *Oklahoma!* had said something like "not since *Show Boat,*" and Jerry was already primed and cocked to give them the real thing. In fact, Kern's absorption in this work during his last years almost suggests a man making out his last will. And as his clock struck sixty, it must have sounded quite deafening.

So he went to New York on *Show Boat* business and also to discuss a project suggested by the new production team of Rodgers and Hammerstein to musicalize the story of Annie Oakley, the great sharpshooter. It's a tantalizing note to end on; but one show can only answer so many ques-

tions. And *Annie Get Your Gun* is such a thorough progress report on Irving Berlin that it couldn't have done that much more for Kern as well.

"Whom the gods love die young." By the time Kern collapsed definitively on a New York sidewalk in 1945, he was not that young by the standards of his time, but he was still young enough to leave the world wondering what he might have written next, whether more jazz songs in his own refined sense of the form, or more operettas. There are hints both ways.

Although almost all his jazz-worthy songs so far had been written for movies, *Annie Oakley* had been written by Herbert Fields, who worked as a team with his sister Dorothy as lyricist. She was an expert swinger and starch remover onstage as well as on-screen, as she would prove a few years later with the toe-tapping *Up in Central Park* with the ponderous Sigmund Romberg, who was a much stodgier proposition than Kern.

Also, it's possible that Kern may have noticed that every time he got down from his high horse, he wrote hits, and when he got up again, as in "The Longest Hour" and those folks on the hill, he sounded like a second-drawer Richard Rodgers. So it was a choice between stage and film, and between Oscar and Dorothy. Uptown or downtown?

Meanwhile, in a riveting parenthesis, Kern had left Hollywood briefly in 1939 to write his greatest song in this swinging mode, and everybody else's greatest as well, for the Broadway flop *Very Warm for May*. And he wrote it with Oscar Hammerstein. The only hitch was that the song, "All the Things You Are," was almost too good and is so musically sophisticated that Kern almost yanked it from the show because the public wouldn't get it. And speaking strictly as a failed pianist and lifelong beginner (the word "amateur" is much too pretentious), I can testify that its sheet music is the most formidable I've seen so far, outside of Gershwin's own arrangements. Listening to it, I can only marvel at how it gets from here to there.

The closest parallel I can think of to its uncanny progressions is a mountain-climbing fable called "Mallory's Pipe." It seems that after a hard day's workout on a rock face, the greatest of all climbers, George Mallory, said, "Whoops" [or "Damn" or "Egad"], I seem to have left my "damned [dashed, bloody]" pipe behind. And with that, took off in the deep twilight up what must have been the wrong side of the rock, the one

without the footholds, returning a few minutes later serenely puffing on the still-warm pipe.

Just so, "All the Things You Are" finds footholds no one else had ever noticed before, or anyone has used again, and in no time it went straight onto the Hit Parade. This was surely a great moment in our history and perhaps the public's finest hour. Kern, who swung one foot on the stage with "They Didn't Believe Me," finally swung out the other with this greatest of American songs. And the rich kid wound up part of the gang anyway, second only to the *really* rich kids in the next chapter.

Cole Porter:
From Peru to Paree to Broadway

COLE PORTER

Of all the friendships in this business, the one between Cole Porter and Irving Berlin seems the most superficially improbable. Respectively rich and poor, WASP and Jew, Yale and sidewalk—maybe it was one of those rare cases when opposites actually do attract; or maybe they were not quite as different as they seemed. At a minimum, they were both self-generated legends with outrageously enlarged glands of showmanship and a love of it. And in Cole's case, the show he put on himself is still running, a reassuring fixture on the American scene like *42nd Street* or *The Nutcracker*.

New celebrities whiz by so quickly these days that even the real ones seem to last only fifteen minutes. Yet all the while, Cole Porter still sits up there high and dry on the ninetieth floor, untouched by time or fashion, like a cast-iron statue of a basic joke. Whatever else the culture may be up to this year, there always seems to be room for Cole at the top. His wit still clicks, his tunes lilt, and the mere mention of his name makes people smile in both anticipation and memory.

Most surprising of all, sociobiologically speaking, Cole's love songs still work. Evolution doesn't know much about music, and still less about interior rhymes, but it does like to keep those babies coming, and a Porter song can still jump-start the process as well as anyone's—from Jerome Kern to Elton John to whatever is hot this minute. Whether you're in the market for a "let's get married" song or a "let's not wait to get married" one, you can't do better than a Cole tape playing in the back of the canoe, the limousine, or even the pickup truck.

Yet the other curious thing about Cole Porter is that when people talk about him, they often leave out the music altogether, concentrating instead on the funny lyrics or the funny fellow who wrote them, who sounds as if he wouldn't have been caught dead in the back of a pickup truck, let alone endangering his crease with a mad embrace. In short, a cool chap who free-associates roughly as follows: Adjectives—dry; brittle; serve slightly chilled. Setting—parties (pause) great big parties; fancy dress preferred. Working clothes—smoking jacket, velvet. Principal product—wit. Hobbies—writing songs. Real occupation—giving parties, and so forth; also traveling abroad; first-class all the way, with an option to pose in grass skirts, war paint, and so on. Phobias—boredom; fresh air; Behaving himself. Orientation—well, not the kind to keep those babies coming.

The logo "Cole Porter" represents a brand image so imperious that it gets stamped on certain songs whether he wrote them or not, for example, "You Go to My Head" by J. Fred Coots and Haven Gillespie *must* be by Cole, because who else writes about champagne? But think of "You've Got That Thing," "Let's Do It," and "Most Gentlemen Don't Like Love." You can't miss a real Porter song. It must have been lonely at the top of Cole's skyscraper.

In each of his scores, though, you will find at least one song, secreted among the singing commercials for penthouses on the Lido, that seems to

come from somewhere else completely, if not several places. For practical purposes, Cole Porter can be boiled down to at least three different song-writers: one, a smarty-pants like for those songs above; two, a passionate writer of jazz songs; and three, a sentimental country boy who can tug on your heartstrings without any tricks at all.

Turning next to the Hot and Bothered file in search of missing pieces, one finds something even less like the mannequin with the cigarette holder—to wit, a devastating lack of coolness and protective irony. Cole's noble little masterpiece "After You, Who?" (catch it any way you can) must be, words and music, one of the most naked songs ever written, a wild cry from the heart, and it sounds a note that recurs again and again.

"For without you there, what could I do?" Note that nothing has even happened yet in the song, but the singer can't wait to be abandoned: He's heartbroken by the mere possibility. Anyone as vulnerable as that obviously needs a good carapace, be it a smoking jacket or a clown's costume, just to hide his hide from the world's laughter and curiosity—not to mention its rejection of his songs at the ticket window. To this day, many people have trouble swallowing love songs from gays, but fortunately, in Cole's own day the general public didn't know a homosexual from the Father of the Bride, and he was able to hide his gay self inside an even gayer persona, and wrap it all up in an acceptable marriage and pass the whole rigamarole off as a facsimile of Cary Grant, who played him in the hilarious movie *Night and Day* (and there couldn't be anything odd about Cary, could there?).

Insofar as Cole's brand image had PR value, Cole's third kind of song-writer was a real menace, and word leaked down from the Porter camp that songs like "Don't Fence Me In" and "Rosalie" were not the real Cole at all, but were written purely for money—as if, for the right price, our hero was even willing to be corny.

Concealment by exaggeration—well, it worked at the time. But now that everyone knows everything, and can explain it too, there's no place left to hide the fact that those love songs were indeed written by not just a gay man, but by an off-the-wall, over-the-top gay man. His latest biographer, William McBrien, documented this exhaustively, almost Kenneth Starr-ly, listing enough names and dates to suggest that Cole could be serially monogamous and serially polygamous at the same time, depending on which kind of song he needed.

It was the monogamous streak that put him over the top. Cole was never just an itchy man writing for itchy people. Great ballads also have to prove themselves on quiet, shadowy porches, and it is here that Cole actually scored best, partly because, like Cyrano de Bergerac and other odd-looking lovers, he was a great seducer by other means. He had the formula down cold for alchemizing lust into romance, and for selling the customer on a lifetime of bliss in exchange for a few trifling minutes of hoop-di-do; but mainly because, like the greatest seducers, he meant what he was saying. More than anyone, he craved the happy ending he was selling, and was even more heartbroken when he didn't get it. For the time being, anyway.

Even at its most agitated, as in "I've Got You Under My Skin," Cole's fever typically wars with, and finally gives way to, something quite thrillingly tranquil, if only in the form of eggs and bacon or a seat by the fire. And even when the words don't find this kind of peace, as in "Get Out of Town," the melody goes ahead and makes a separate one anyhow. "The thrill when we meet is so bittersweet that, darling, it's getting me down." The words solve nothing, but the notes could be wedding bells. And it is these musical phrases, just as much as his lyrics, that most clearly identify a song as Cole Porter's. All his tunes at least have happy endings: The mood they arouse is satisfied and everyone drives, or rows, home happy, regardless of gender.

It is these same chronically undervalued tunes that make it perfectly safe to ask the man at the piano to "play some Cole Porter," knowing that whether he picks a funny one or a sad one, and whether he sings the words or not, it will do. And it will do not just for you, but for most of the barflies in most of the bars in the English-speaking world, obliging one to wonder whether gay love might be closer to straight than either team cares to recognize. Whatever the answer to that, Cole's gay lifestyle seems to have given him an awful lot of practice at falling in love, and he kept on doing it as assiduously as a research student and as ardently as a teenager long after most married men have finally conquered the habit, and after even his famous electric eels and moths in rugs had packed it in. And each new lover seems to have been an occasion of song, as he "concentrated" on this one, and kept "his eye on" that, and experienced yet again the torment of breaking up and the joy of starting over almost with the speed of a swinging door. In fact, it seems that Cole sometimes wrote his

lyrics and love letters in the same giddy, boozy rush, which is why the love in the songs seems so real. And if his lyrics couldn't name who he loved, or even precisely what, they certainly could show how much, and he doubled up on this part, expressing his passion with a gusto that simply blows away such pantywaist contemporaries as Ira Gershwin and Oscar Hammerstein. "Only make believe" coos Oscar, and "Come to papa, come to papa do," twitters Ira, and a couple of powerful tunes are slightly weakened, but "the look in your eyes when you surrender" writes Cole, and the tune picks up enough steam to drive home triumphantly.

But where is the fop in the smoking jacket amid this blur of activity? Probably hanging in the closet next to Fred Astaire's top hat and tails. Neither of these Midwestern masters of sophistication was born that way—and in fact Fred could only play the part onstage and on-screen. Between gigs, he remained a lifelong hayseed, as did an important part of Cole.

Geniuses don't let anything go, they just add stuff. As a mythical neighbor from Peru (pronounced Pea-ru), Indiana, might put it, different folks have different ways of coping with the Big City. Cole's fellow Hoosier, Hoagland Carmichael, for instance, was a university man, a licensed lawyer, and a snappy dresser, but elected to go the good-old-boy route, becoming more down-home than he'd ever been back in Bloomington. Cole preferred to beat the slickers at their own game, literally outwitting them by being more Yalie than Dink Stover, more New York than Eustace Tilly, and more Parisian than Ernest Hemingway and Gertrude Stein rolled into one.

Talk about different strokes . . . but both boys loved their mothers and wrote good American music and kept their own tough kind of integrity. When Cole died, it seemed perfectly fitting for him and his globe-trotting wife, Linda, to be buried together, torment over at last, in Peru, Indiana; and when Hoosiers still get together to celebrate Cole as a native son, that probably rings true too, hauntingly so, in fact.

"Don't Fence Me In" was absolutely genuine.

ROLLING IT ALL BACK to the beginning, one finds a suspiciously typical gay childhood, with an overpowering mother force-feeding her son the arts, and a shadowy, withdrawn father. But the wrinkle in this case is that

it was actually Cole's father, Sam, who had the real artistic interests, in-cluding a passion for romantic poetry and an indeterminate skill at the guitar, and his withdrawal seems to have been as much social and eco-nomic as personal. For instance, the affable Sam left the matter of his son's education entirely up to his wife, Kate, not necessarily from indif-ference but because it was really a question of deciding what schools his rich, cantankerous father-in-law, J. O. Cole, could be talked into paying for. Sam had no say in this, or in anything else that mattered. So although the genes that he'd already passed on to Cole would eventu-ally prove infinitely more valuable than J.O.'s provincial real estate for-tune, this was not clear at the time and Sam had to content himself with his local pharmacy, which he grittily expanded, and the consola-tions of poetry.

Kate's bequest, on the other hand, became clear immediately. Like her father, Mrs. Porter had nothing much to offer genetically save a blind drive to succeed, and if music was the way for Cole to get there, she would see to it that the kid had music coming out of his ears, with piano and violin lessons and practice sessions scheduled round the clock—which she ex-pected Sam to enforce with the approved growls and spankings of the pre-Spock era. So Daddy was pain and Mommy was encouragement, and the war for the boy's love was presumably over if it had ever begun.

The exhibitionism he seems to have provided himself. By the age of eight, Cole had already bounced onto a real stage at the local (silent) the-ater, played the wrong music on the piano, and been bounced off again. And not long after that, we find him being chased off one of the lake boats and into the water for sitting at the steamboat's piano, this time in a wet bathing suit, and pounding away as the boat set off.

A gift like his is a great liberator, and by the time Cole left Peru for school at the age of twelve, he was a welcome regular at both the movie house and the steamboat, with a lifetime visa stamped on his brain enti-tling him to go anywhere in the world he liked that contained a piano and an audience.

In view of which, Kate's eagerness to have Cole's first song published by age eleven seems less pushy and more like an attempt to catch a ride on a whirlwind. "Take me with you," she started saying early, and some-times he would and sometimes he wouldn't.

Away from the piano, Cole seems to have been a spasmodically shy but immensely curious and sociable little boy, just as interested in words as he was in music. His curiosity led him repeatedly to the local circus, where he learned all about clowns and their strategies, and possibly of the mating habits of "chimpanzees" and "bears in pits," among other things. His sociability introduced him to friendship, which he would swiftly make into an art form, a beautiful alternative to life. Before he'd left knee pants, his prototypes were in place: a boy and a girl, and himself in the middle as best friend of both.

Desdemona Bearss was the girl he would have fallen in love with if he possibly could have, and thus in a sense she was his true love, the one his heart could go "all the way" with without fear of being hurt. Since friendships with women were guaranteed never to become too hot not to cool down, he could indulge in the pleasures of constancy, and when Desdemona died unseasonably young, Cole was as shattered as he later would be by the deaths of his mother and his wife, Linda. When male lovers left, he presumably died a little, but when women checked out for good, it was like a crack in the universe. Even permanence let one down eventually.

At what exact point Porter also discovered that men were fickle and began to "kick it around" himself, is a secret he proceeded now to bury in the best of all possible hiding places, a couple of all-male establishments, Worcester Academy and Yale University (both in the sinful Northeast—Kate won that fight with J.O.). Through these places, a certain number of inmates perennially pass through under a question mark—it's no big deal. In stag societies, all the parts have to be played by males anyway, and Cole's natural roles of mascot and court jester, Puck and Yorick, are traditionally ambiguous—all sexes and none—and often musical too. (See Michael Jackson.)

In later years, Cole would allegedly say that he wished he'd had his friend Irving Berlin's "advantages," which is funny because, in his own odd way, he kind of did. As a rule, the old prep schools produced few artistic geniuses, because the well-rounded curricula they favored were no match for the monomania and total immersion available to dropouts like Berlin, who was off plugging songs for Harry Von Tilzer, or ad-libbing his own lyrics as a singing waiter, at an age when Cole was still supposed to be bounding over playing fields, parsing Greek verbs, and taking in sermons about clean minds and clean bodies.

Fortunately, though, Cole's own monomania was already full-blown and now asked only the basics of life, and once he'd gotten a piano installed (immediately) in his room, the second basic took care of itself: A whole school was out there waiting to be wooed and amused to the best of his adolescent ability, and it's fair to deduce that he used, as usual, everything he had in the cause, from his father's love of poetry to the classics he was devouring at school to the slight hypochondria instilled by his mother, which kept him indoors and added a welcome lick to his new persona. Cole might not be plugging songs for a living like Irving, but he had just as much riding on them, because he was putting his whole self over, and creating that self as he went, while in general making the world a safe and hilarious place for a Cole Porter to be.

His songs had to be, above all, likeable, or he would have instantly reverted to a noxious young outsider from the boondocks. And maybe he still felt like that anyway. At any rate, his best friend at Worcester seems to have been the headmaster, and teenage boys don't dig teacher's pets, so the art of friendship would be put on hold until Yale, which he would love with the grateful devotion of someone who hasn't really cared for school that much but has used it well and is ready.

Yale must have seemed like the big leagues of schoolboy entertainment. All the envious little creeps and the slow-witted ones who don't get the joke magically disappear into the gully between the twelfth and thirteenth grades, and he could be precocious now forever. And better still, Yale was close to New York and had a "special" relationship with Broadway. Age for age, Cole had probably matched young Irving song for song, and the only advantage he even half-seriously envied was Berlin's setting. New York's Lower East Side happened at that moment to be the Vienna of the American song, and you had only to keep your ears open there to advance your education daily. Cole, meanwhile, was stuck with the quaint sounds of young WASPs at play, which had in no time entered his own throat for good, driving out any trace of the Midwest and forever cementing him into the role of urban dandy.

On the surviving recordings of his own singing, Porter's voice comes across as not merely campy but so preppy that Henry Higgins could probably identify the exact schools and the years attended. Funny travel photos notwithstanding, Cole would never really be just a dilettante passing

through places, but a natural enthusiast who sucked up the air and steeped himself in the sound and style of wherever he happened to be. So, probably nobody ever got more out of either Worcester Academy or Yale than he did, or wound up sounding, vowel for vowel, less like a Broadway songwriter.

Yet he used Yale as a professional school, a songwriting school where work and play were the same things. In those happy-go-lucky pre–World War I days, the game at most Ivy League colleges was still to see who could have the most fun this year, this term, this second, and since Cole's talent fit this agenda perfectly, it was child's play to string the clubs and private parties together into a species of upscale borscht belt where Porter could work nonstop at making up doggerel about the guests and about Yale and Shakespeare and bulldogs and whatever anyone hollered for. Just how far he still was from nearby New York he would later learn when he took a batch of his material to the equally unreal world of Broadway and got clobbered, or worse, ignored: His collegiate-style comedy *See America First* sank without a trace and Cole either had to start work devising a bridge between the two cultures or content himself with playing the prep school circuit forever.

But any conjectures about Cole's professional plans and dreams run onto a blank tape at this point, because Old Ivy had placed yet another layer of reticence upon his bubbling soul. A gentleman, it seems, should never appear to want anything very much, unless it's something quite trivial—a rare stamp, a perfect boiled egg—let alone be seen working at it. And one wasn't even allowed to send messages from this prison of style, because letters to friends had to be kept light, shallow, and slightly off the point.

So to the naked eye, Cole's only care at this time, no deeper than a Wodehouse plot, was to flimflam his grandfather into thinking that he was a solid citizen who thoroughly deserved every penny of the old boy's fortune, and this basically boiled down to not getting thrown out of Yale, which from his grandfather's distance presumably looked like a serious place. And even after he had graduated, then gotten thrown, or nudged, out of Harvard Law School in the direction of the music school, all he had to do was pretend it hadn't happened and the charade could continue.

Or so he may have supposed. In fact, J. O. Cole dispossessed him anyway, perhaps because he was watching more closely than supposed, or be-

cause that was simply what Coles did to Porters, and left all the money to his daughter—who split it with Cole, thus becoming a fuller partner in his life than perhaps either had planned. Grandfather Cole departed the planet totally oblivious to what he'd wrought or to the kind of story he'd just taken part in. Too bad: If he'd lived long enough—say another fifty years or so—he might have realized that his grandson was basically a chip off the old block in gorgeous disguise, a J. O. Cole with talent. "Frankly," as Alec Wilder would put it in his book *American Popular Song,* "I find it extraordinary any time a wealthy person manages to create anything besides more wealth," let 'alone such a huge body of painstaking work as Porter's. Yet so much heavy labor also went into Cole's pretense of *not working* that for most of the 1920s he was able to pass for the worst kind of rich brat, succumbing to every temptation that a well-heeled young Yale man at large in the world's great cities could find to succumb to.

College lifestyles of Cole's particular type did not necessarily end with graduation in those days, but were known to gather hurricane strength as the Whiffenpoofs and Old Crimsons, lions and tigers, transferred their frat house shenanigans to a larger stage with more opportunities and fewer rules. And Cole would stay their troubadour, their living legend, paying dues to both the jolly side of that life by tomcatting around town with his old pal Monty Woolley until he was almost too old to walk, and to the dull parts, by leaving his door open to Yalies of all kinds, bores included. Because Yalies never bored him, and neither did Peruvians, with whom he kept in touch too, in the spare time of his spare time by going home every chance he got to talk local talk to local people, as if his art commanded him to keep in touch with ordinary citizens just as much as clever ones.

Although Cole's horror of boredom was a running gag in his usual set, the word actually seems to have meant something more like depression, a blankness and coldness that startled visitors who caught him between laughs and shows. So long as he was "up," Cole was interested in just about everything, as one might guess from his lyrics. So his life may be viewed as an endless campaign to stay up, unbored and undepressed.

The difference between Cole and such musical fellow-depressives as Berlin, Rodgers, and Harold Arlen was that most of the time he was able to chase the blues with sheer hyperactivity, starting with a bang in World

War I, which he seems to have treated as his private fancy-dress and coming-out party. Monty Woolley claimed that Cole showed up at the fashionable cafés in a different uniform every night, as he bounded from group to group, looking for ones that would keep him in Paris a bit longer. He had found a subject and he had found a style in this incomparable city, and was not about to budge.

And if he could change his uniform, why not his whole identity? It was there, amid the forged passports and phony résumés of war that Cole hit his stride as a fabulist and self-creator. If he could pretend to be straight, why not fake the French Foreign Legion as well? And would a Croix de Guerre be going too far?

Porter's actual war record is, in fact, so impenetrable that some of his less playful commentators have dismissed the whole farrago as a neurotic evasion, but the subject was having much too much fun for that, trying on different faces for the real party that was to follow. Paris was filling up with brilliant refugees from the Russian Revolution, and these would soon be joined by their Western counterparts on the run from Prohibition. Cole would be there waiting, like a maestro watching a new audience, the perfect audience, file into the hall.

Although it's hard to date the actual writing of some of Porter's early songs, one can almost hear the hum of the party in the funny ones and picture Cole smiling at the keyboard, as he knocks the smart set dead, night after night. The eternal preppie has seen Paree now, and knows all about gigolos and cocottes, and serenades them in a cosmopolitan style closer to Noël Coward's than Irving Berlin's.

Surely at this pinnacle, a million miles from Peru and with the laughter of princes real and imaginary braying in his ears, a less driven man would have come to rest and wallowed. For the average American genius in Paris, the big news would be simply that he hadn't cracked up yet, because Porter seemed to drink enough to crack up anyone, and his love life constantly threatened to spin out of control as well. Paris had also filled up with brilliant homosexuals. Cole experienced a grand passion with one of Diaghilev's dancers and was very probably tempted by the whole troupe.

Yet in a surprising but wise move, he kicked off the twenties by marrying a woman with an equal genius for appearances. Bernard Berenson

claimed that Linda Porter had perfect taste in absolutely everything, and in his memoir, *Musical Stages,* Richard Rodgers suggests that she was somehow perfect in herself too, both to look at and to talk to, an art object worth collecting in her own right.

Cole proceeded to use his wife as a safety brake on his wantonness by insisting on the Jane Austen–like condition that all his lovers must first make friends with her before proceeding. But it would be a mistake to assume the cliché that Linda was his mother all over again, because the evidence suggests that Cole preferred to worship his real mother, an unreconstructed hick, at a slight distance, while he relished Linda's company.

So the truer parallel would surely be with Desdemona Bearss, his inseparable pal and dream girl, who had magically returned to him all grown up now, as if to specifications, to play the part of Zelda Fitzgerald better than the original ever could and to pose for happy endings as needed. Regally cool and lovely, Linda could henceforth serve as Cole's indispensable muse of eggs and bacon and everything else that might be nice for his songs and himself to "come home to" and cool off with after the fiery tortures of love. He, for his part, would be true to her "in his fashion."

After having fled from her own previous brutal marriage, Linda could now easily play the lighter role of providing a beard, not just for her new husband's sexuality, but for his ferocious work habit. By the time Cole's songs had made him unmistakably famous, legend had already decided that it must be his wife who was dragging him home from the party and making him do it—as if a Cole needed help getting to work. In fact, what Linda wanted was for Cole to become a serious composer, not a famous one, and he cheerfully went along with this detour by studying advanced composition and harmony at the elite Schola Cantorum and even scoring a ballet that earned respectful notices in Paris.

But no matter how hard he pretended to look the other way, Cole apparently never for a moment took his eye off Broadway. Both his ear and his curiosity must have told him that his natural rivals there, men like George Gershwin and Jerome Kern, were classically trained musicians too and that the harmony he was learning at the Schola Cantorum might be jazzed up à la Gershwin into the Broadway sound he was looking for.

Thus, under cover of the high life, Cole patiently polished his songs to

the familiar gleam, and quietly sent them off to New York and London, where they began to catch on a bit, then suddenly a lot. By the end of the decade, Cole Porter had been most thoroughly discovered overnight as a mysteriously accomplished Broadway professional, who also happened to be a well-known around-the-clock playboy in exile.

During his long apprenticeship, Cole also worked so hard at the self-promotion end of the business that his famous image had actually arrived in New York and London several years before his songs. By cultivating such dedicated exhibitionists as Elsa Maxwell, the fabulous society-hostess-cum-reporter, and Elsie de Wolfe (later Lady Mendl), the far-out decorator, Cole saw to it that his name got into the papers before he'd done anything at all, except make the Riviera the place to be in winter, and Venice the place to throw parties. (You mean he writes songs too? Wow!)

Later, of course, he immortalized his promoters in song, as round and round the publicity machine went: café society between the wars consisted largely of people like Cole and the Elsa girls, all hard at work in the cause of play, and scratching one another's backs to beat the band, in a daisy chain that stretched from the Algonquin Hotel to the Lido, or wherever the Porters happened to be at that moment.

In 1926, Cole's worlds of work and play collided with a small bang when Noël Coward, who epitomized the whole arrangement, introduced him to his future rival, Richard Rodgers. Since these two men would later be contesting or sharing the title of King of Broadway for over two decades, it seemed only right that Cole would take the occasion to announce his wish to write "Jewish songs" from now on, which was the next best thing to throwing his hat into the ring. The year before, George Gershwin had blown through Paris, playing pianos everywhere he went, and had either told Cole in so many words or shown him by example the element Cole had been missing in the Broadway sound. Later, Rodgers acknowledged that Porter wound up writing "the most enduring Jewish music" of anyone.

"I want to write little Jewish songs" became Cole's mantra. There was absolutely nothing condescending about it because the more "Jewish" he got, the better his music. By adding the mystery ingredients of jazzness and bluesness, he reached a new depth in himself that hadn't been previously accessible to the public. It was a turning point for both him and his

art, and if this book were a musical, the chorus would burst into a shout-song here, like "Oklahoma!" or "Happy Days Are Here Again." The movement that wasn't quite a movement had made its most important convert, and Cole really meant it too. As just another "American Gilbert and Sullivan," he probably could have gone just so far and no further; there are limits built into the very phrase. Instead, Porter stayed in Paris another three years, looking for the sound he wanted among the minor keys and innate melancholy of so-called Jewish music.

He had probably known all along that the tunes would be the hard part, but they were also the part he wanted most. In a defining anecdote, Michael Feinstein reports that Cole and George were once asked at a party to write a song together, and Cole retorted that he preferred the hard labor of devising his own melodies. Writing lyrics was by implication the easy part and much closer to a real party game, in which you are allowed to use a thesaurus or a rhyming dictionary and anything else you can get your ears on. I believe that the phrase "A trip to the moon on gossamer wings" came from an ad for mattresses or bedsprings or some such, while the words "It's delightful, it's delicious, it's de-lovely" were originally intoned by Monty Woolley on a tropical night while they were off cruising someplace. As every comic knows, you can't beat the right cliché in the right place, in which spirit let's just say that, in lyric writing, anything goes. Well, did you ever?

But there was only one right tune, and Cole would sit at his desk with the dedication of a monk, abstaining from even the comforts of the piano until he had written out the gist of it. His words might have made it to Broadway at any time, but not by themselves, and it would take him the best part of a decade to get the tunes he wanted, that's to say tunes that could "touch your heart" or tickle your funny bone. Two songs may serve to measure his progress. In 1924, "I'm in Love Again" was his first genuine hit and probably the first one that you might find yourself humming without remembering anything else about it. And then "What Is This Thing Called Love" in 1929, which sounds exactly like what he was looking for.

But once he had turned this key, all of Broadway fell open to him at once: He wasn't just allowed onto the street, he owned it. And just like that, Cole Porter became synonymous with Broadway to an extent that

not even Kern could claim. You were definitely not in Peoria tonight. Or were you?

On a closer look, even Cole's slyest lyrics could have been written with at least half of his other eye on Peoria. The fact is, Americans of all kinds seemed then, as they do now, to enjoy hearing lists of celebrities read, especially if you threw in references to cellophane and Mickey Mouse then (or to e-mail and Britney Spears now). And there is nothing especially arcane about the thought of "electric eels" and "lazy jellyfish" doing it. This is sophistication for the masses, well within the reach of a bright traveling salesman. As an old Peruvian himself, he knew that at least half the people in the outback would rather be someplace else anyway, and were planning to go there sometime. So why not take them there right now and give them an evening in Paree, or the Rainbow Room, or the South Pacific?

And clinching it was something else that Cole knew about Peru, and Peoria, and Podunk too. The West had *already* been melodically won by Irving Berlin and his little Jewish songs. When Jerome Kern said that Berlin *was* American music, he wasn't just referring to Broadway or the Brill Building. And now, by putting all his own various know-hows together, Cole Porter could start to "be" American music too.

In fact, for years he scored first on a list of America's tip-top favorite songs with five entries—which, since he wrote both words and music, made him the champ, one-two with Irving Berlin himself.

Grounds for envy, one might suppose—but not in this profession, or with these two men. Berlin and Porter really were too completely unalike to hate each other, and besides, each had something the other wanted. Before they even met, Irving was looking for fresh talent to stuff into his own little theater, the Music Box, and Porter was looking for a ticket to Broadway: and voilà! They were partners for a season with an interest in each other's immediate success.

And in a more general way, Berlin wanted to go more uptown with his music, while Porter wished to delve further into the little Jewish song, which Irving was still writing better than anyone. And then of course there was the inevitable Fred Astaire on hand to serve as an interested party and test site. The stagy number "Let's Face the Music and Dance" is widely considered Berlin's most direct response to Porter. But both men met in that amorphous concept known as the typical Fred Astaire song.

And another curious bond these three men shared was that they all had rich wives who were utterly out of place in Hollywood and culturally much too good for it, which made them a useful trio of muses for the work the men did together.

Berlin would tip his cap to the Cole connection by naming his second daughter after Linda Porter, while Cole would say thanks to Irving the best way he knew how, by comparing a Berlin ballad to a Waldorf salad and placing it at the top.

Linda had to be a muse in absentia for a while. Although she had been the perfect companion for an American in Europe, a Henry James character with an exquisite sense of style and nuance who had helped him to be a positively superb expatriate, Cole had done Europe now and was ready to go home to America—with all its slang and its swing, its intoxicating vulgarity and self-satisfied lack of nuance. More prosaically, as the twenties began to wind down, Cole must have seen that he couldn't very well conduct a Broadway career completely from Europe, and he returned to New York sans Linda. Possibly, she hoped he would just get his silly business over with—he didn't need the money—and he would then return to his senses and Europe quite soon. With still-fresh memories of a dreadful first marriage in America, Linda had no wish to return for a second. But artistic repatriation cannot be done overnight, and Cole had some catching up to do with the intangibles—the small changes of phrase and attitude that you can't hear from abroad, and such far-out developments as Ethel Merman or the nose of the great Durante.

From this vantage, his early shows, such as *Gay Divorce* and *Nymph Errant,* were like halfway houses, and could easily have been written in Paris or Venice. But his big one, *Anything Goes* (1934), was unmistakably American. "You're the Top," "I Get a Kick Out of You," "Anything Goes." I'm back! And ready to start a brand-new chapter, with new scripts and new stories. And the whole point of the Astaire figure is that he blends high style with a certain street authenticity. In a prototypical role, his real name is Pete Peters of Pittsburgh, P-A, but he is posing as the great Petrov, the ballet master, and he will finally turn out somehow to be both, an American gentleman whose innate classiness is worth any number of fancy titles. And here was a role waiting for Cole too, as that other plot device, the rich snob becoming a regular guy, with a touch of the great

Petrov too, the serious artist tapping his foot. But there didn't seem to be a part for Linda, at least so long as she remained an expatriate dilettante who wasn't about to budge.

Linda must have seen that the jig was up, and she agreed to come over, at least as far as New York, which must have seemed like a halfway house in itself, a kind of Europe West, which was not without its subtleties or its Europeans either, many of whom never got beyond it. And Linda could always decorate the Porters' suite at the Waldorf like Versailles and pretend. In short, the Porters as an entity still made some kind of remembered sense in New York. In Hollywood, Cole's next port of call, they would make none at all.

Before testing these next and perhaps final roles together, the Porters took off together on an epic around-the-world cruise in 1935 with Cole's old pal Woolley and his new working partner, Moss Hart, which would prove to be a Last Hurrah and Goodbye to All That to the beautiful life, and out of which would come not only the musical *Jubilee*, but also Cole's slap-happiest song, "It's De-Lovely," and his most rhythmically adventurous one, "Begin the Beguine." The chief musical gift the non-Caucasian world had to offer back then was a variety of exotic beats, and Cole would use these as a semisecret weapon to provide the kicker in his songs, in the form of vivid bass lines that worked like pistons under the melody.

But now back to America at its corniest, namely, Hollywood, which in that pre–Las Vegas dawn was still the undisputed world capital of vulgarity. Linda's love of appearances, both social and aesthetic, must have been affronted by every sight and sound of it. Cole, on the other hand, thought it was the funniest joke ever, a sublime parody of the land he loved, and to hell with sophistication. He ordered up a jacket made up of every sample in the store ("be a clown," the song says, not "be a fop") and got set to run amuck.

After all the tasteful years abroad, Cole gulped up this crazy new atmosphere as he had once gulped up Yale and Paris. And if promiscuity was what they did here, he would be the best at that too, vying with George Cukor to conduct the most star-studded gay salon in the West. Everyone in Hollywood was beautiful and everyone was tied up at the moment, so romances lasted no longer than shooting schedules. Now Cole even dispensed with the charade of introducing his lovers to Linda, leaving her to

keep up grim appearances by herself, a game she continued to play so conscientiously that to this day people don't know if she had any sex life herself at all, and if so what kind.

It was startlingly cruel, and Cole probably knew it. The fickleness that so terrified and tormented him had always been first and last his own, and his dealings with Linda would be for a while a heartbreaking mixture of icy detachment and unflagging solicitousness, interspersed, since Cole never threw away anything, with flashes of the old feelings as well. Linda was still "nice to come home to" occasionally and "love" in one's fashion.

Finally, Linda could take no more. She offered to put Cole out of their mutual misery or else further into it, by telling him to choose between Hollywood and her. It was a dramatic peak. "How'm I riding?" he wrote around then. "I'm riding high." And he was. At his crest in 1936, he received two diplomas proving it, the more obvious being a lush three-year contract at MGM, the other a spontaneous compliment from a producer called Sam Katz. "That song is beautiful. Why, it's Jewish."

"Mission accomplished," although not in a flight jacket but a velvet smoking one. As we've seen, Oscar Levant says that Gershwin had gone West that very same year to snatch back his crown from Rodgers and Porter, and now, with his own death just a year away, he would get a chance to square off against one of these young pretenders. "I've got you under my skin," wrote Porter. "They can't take that away from me," wrote Gershwin, as if in answer. American popular songs never got better than that.

Maybe at that peak of fame and confidence Cole might have faced down his fears of abandonment once and for all by saying goodbye to a woman friend.

But before Cole could make his decision, a real horse, on which one day he was literally riding high, decided the question for him by first throwing him and then rolling over both his legs (like a hitman making sure).

Linda paused in the doorway. If she hoped that this would sober Cole up or even slow him down much, she was in for a nasty surprise. But at least she had a role again, if not her old one. Henceforth, she really could be his mother—she looked old enough at this point—and her first decision as such would be that Cole's leg *not* be amputated, for the sake of his

pride—a choice that has since been debated almost as hotly as George Gershwin's brain tumor.

What we do know is that from now on, pain would be the invisible presence in every Cole Porter anecdote, and in every assessment of his character too. Some days it seemed that the postaccident Cole could be unbelievably bitchy (even Noël Coward found him hard to take), but on others, more frequent ones, he was preternaturally thoughtful and kind. And then sometimes a streak of snobbery flared up, although he despised it in others. The only constant was restlessness.

Whatever has been said about Cole in his later years—selfishness or altruism, lust or love—is undoubtedly true. But always there was pain too, coming or going or in full possession, and nearly always there was defiance. Cole's preferred attitude is best summed up in the report he broadcast himself as fast as he could get it out, that as he lay under the horse, he worked on the lyrics to "At Long Last Love." Maybe he did. But then again, maybe he had once served in the French Foreign Legion. All he owed the public was a good story.

And the big story now was that this thing had not gotten him down for a minute! At least to judge from the songs that never stopped coming, more ebulliently than ever. "If they ever put a bullet through your brain, I'll complain," "If you're ever . . . sawed in half, I won't laugh" he wrote in 1939, a time when extreme measures must have passed through his mind quite a lot. So he'd make fun of them and of everything else besides. "Astrology, mythology . . . stupidity, solidity, frigidity" he wrote for Danny Kaye, in one of his giddiest list songs.

In the years right after his accident, Cole wildly overindulged in his two favorite pain medicines: work, and play. If World War I had been a party for Cole, he saw to it that World War II would be a downright orgy, certainly proving that the greatest of all wars can be won with gays in the military. Or perhaps his handsome companions were just queens for a day, beguiled by a chance to sit with a celebrity around his pool in Hollywood or at the men's bar of the Waldorf-Astoria in New York, as he snatched at pleasure in mind-numbing quantities.

"Happy people don't need to have fun" as the late Jean Stafford would intone on bad mornings, by which gauge Cole must have been truly desperate. At around that time, Cole seems to have thought about Catholic

instruction too, for a different kind of relief. His friend Lawrason Riggs, with whom he'd written *See America First,* had since fetched up as the Catholic chaplain at Yale, and he might have made an understanding guide for Cole through the barbed wire of moral theology. (My father, who knew and liked Mgsr. Riggs, found him a bit "perfumy" himself.) But Riggs's sudden death by heart failure in 1943 blocked off that particular exit for good. So, on with the orgy!

But all the pleasure in the world still left plenty of time for Cole to work, and he dashed off a couple of unsuccessful musicals. Just like that, the vultures were on him. Obviously, the old boy was beginning to lose it. Although he was still batting out gems like "I Love You (Hums the April Breeze)" and "Ev'ry Time We Say Goodbye," he was in his midfifties now, an age when the waiter looks over every few minutes to see if you've left yet. The war was almost over and the music was changing and a crowd of new customers was straining the rope to get in.

But this time the joke was on the vultures. Cole's alleged burnout proved to be a superb theatrical buildup to an astonishing comeback. *Kiss Me, Kate* was like a salesman's sample case, containing a choice bit of everything he did. Since the plot concerns some Americans putting on a Shakespeare play, Porter seizes the opportunity to divide the songs into two, giving the cast some jazzy, beat-driven ones ("Too Darn Hot," "Why Can't You Behave") to sing on its own time, and some traditional singer-driven ones ("Where Is the Life That Late I Led?") to insert into the play, plus subdivisions of both categories, before wrapping the whole adventure up in a swirl of timeless but curiously Shakespearean-sounding joy. Now I shall ever be, now I shall ever be, mi-ine, thi-ine: as if the composer himself was laughing in triumph at pulling off this caper. With this one score, Porter accomplished all he could reasonably have dreamed of, as a boy on a ferryboat, and a student of Shakespeare at Yale, and as a student of both jazz and classical composition in the bistros and classrooms of Paris. And Robert Browning, Irving Berlin, and both his mother and his father could all have felt equally proud.

After such an explosion, everything else had to seem a slight anticli-max, although two more of his shows, *Can-Can* and *Silk Stockings,* and one more movie, *High Society,* contained more good music than anything done by the postwar popinjays who had once challenged him. In each of

these emanations, Porter would play the unlikely role of custodian to the great "Jewish" songs whose run on Broadway and elsewhere was now drawing to a close.

It's hard to keep the faith when the sounds in the air change, but Cole had worked too hard to write that way, and loved it too much to give it up now, and such later numbers as "It's All Right with Me" and "You're Sensational" sound as if the 1930s had never ended—which they hadn't yet if you didn't want them to. How long he could have kept this going against hard rock, acid rock, rap, we'll never know, because by then, "Miss Otis" had sent her last regrets. After a last round of pleasure trips that might best be described as "brisk and bracing"—the buses ran on time and you'd better be on them, and all the sights were seen and you'd better be prepared to discuss them—his legs finally gave out for keeps, both literally and metaphorically. The fun ended. The surgeons of the day, who seemingly never got anything quite right, but who never gave up on it either (e.g., Thurber's twenty-plus eye operations), decided after thirty or so in Cole's case that the right leg really had to go this time. Since by then Linda was no longer around to give them an argument, they went ahead and inevitably botched it, or so one assumes from the screaming, uncontrollable pain they left him in, and the mind-fogging painkillers that they thus condemned him to.

But perhaps the process had really begun a few years earlier with the deaths of both Linda and his mother in the early 1950s. If every goodbye really caused him to "die a little," these two long goodbyes must have caused an unearthly loneliness, as if all his bleakest lyrics had come true. "Don't you know, little fool, you never can win?"

So this, combined with martinis and painkillers, finally did what wild horses had failed to do. If it didn't crush his spirit, it did sap his will and his capacity to express it. Accounts from Cole's last years suggest a stoic down to his last hair shirt, keeping up appearances, sort of, and trying to take an interest, and still freakishly craving sex. But no more songs or jokes now. Most of the time the host just mutely stares at his dinner guests, of which he never invites more than two at a time. Any bright conversation has to come from them.

In that last sad silence, which one imagines broken by the scraping of chairs as his manservant tries to hoist him from the table while no one's

looking, one gets a chance to consider what we've lost. Cole had lived every moment of his life till now as fully and entertainingly as a life can be lived. This, after the myths have been enjoyed and put away for the night, may be the reason his songs still work. They have a pulse, as if someone is still in there, a real pining lover in the serious ones, eating out a real heart; and in the funny ones, a kid showing off as merrily as ever, conquering Peru and Yale, Paris and Broadway, forever and ever, amen.

In a strange, throwaway ending, it seems that, although Cole had insisted on no religion or fuss at his graveside, he made two exceptions. He wanted the Lord's Prayer recited and he wanted the verse that states Christianity's central proposition to be read: "I am the resurrection, and the life; he that believeth in me, though he were dead, yet shall he live."

What was that again? Cole Porter with an inner life? It was the perfect curtain.

Richard Rodgers:
Dr. Jekyll and Mr. Rodgers

RICHARD RODGERS

*I*n drastic contrast to Irving Berlin and Cole Porter, Richard Rodgers generated practically no gossip and left behind no legend. Judging from his amazing output, maybe he was simply too busy writing music to have an outsize reputation, let alone invent one. Or maybe he was smart enough to let his music do the talking for him. But the fact is that his identity is quite hard to pin down in his music too. If personal style is what one falls back on when one runs out of new things to say, Rodgers had either no style or perhaps too many styles to count—a different one for every scene

of every show, in fact. So although his music is, by some accounts, the most often played of any composer in history, such was its sheer variety, melodic inventiveness, and lack of musical ego that his work keeps disappearing into the crowd of great American songs, like a huge anonymous donation, taking himself with it.

So to learn that he actually wrote a memoir called *Musical Stages* is rather like discovering that the Sphinx kept a diary: One turns to it eagerly, if not skeptically. How much can you trust a sphinx? Well, maybe if you read between the lines, and wait for someone else's book to compare it with . . .

His memoir immediately puts one on guard by lashing out at his family, telling us how impossible they were to live with—a charge that rings strangely down the years, because in an introduction to a later edition of this book, his daughter, Mary, levels exactly the same charge against him: not that he was a bad man exactly (he could be startlingly generous), just an impossible one. It seems the one gift this gifted family lacked through two generations was the smallest one: the kind of amiable in-house chitchat that happy families run on. The first sounds that young Dick's sensitive ears picked up in the family's city quarters were his grandmother's sarcastic tirades and his grandfather's defiant growls, broken only by his mother's occasional wistful piano playing between bouts—which may have given Dick his first, fatal taste for comfort music. His father, Dr. William Rodgers, preferred to spend his family time in lofty, apparently disapproving, silence. Although allegedly Dr. Rodgers showed quite a bit of charm with his patients, he wasn't wasting it on his family.

If words wounded, music healed. In no time at all, Dick Rodgers struck the piano himself, finding with almost the first chord that it could solve practically everything, bringing peace even to his grandmother. It also enormously enhanced his own status—if he could just get to the instrument before his envious brother, Mort, broke his fingers or set fire to the piano. In *Musical Stages,* Rodgers introduces the piano first. With time, it became his imaginary friend and alter ego, through which he could say everything he wanted and explore his own outer limits of tenderness and wit, while his impossible family looked on in admiring silence—or, at any rate, in silence.

The next lesson he learned from the instrument was that if humans *must* open their mouths, the best you could hope for was a song. His parents had a cheerful hobby of bringing sheet music home from new musicals and singing together at the piano while his mother played. And the apartment was transformed into a cloud-cuckoo-land. And Rodgers had found himself a lifelong model of perfect happiness. Harmony at home, love on the stage, music everywhere.

The piano never taught Richard Rodgers a better way to cope with domestic situations than just to play something, or shut up like his father, or turn truculent like his grandfather. Any finer points, such as manners or conversation, he would have to learn from the Broadway stage, which would become his spiritual home and family court from the moment he entered one at the age of twelve or so. From then on, his parents would magically cease to matter until they later showed up in the orchestra seats, warmly applauding their son—nice people, after all, in that context, who, rare among artists' parents, thoroughly approved of his chosen life: a life that he, perhaps in return, proceeded to keep as outwardly square as he possibly could, dressing and comporting himself like a banker, hiding any private sins in the best Ivy League manner, and eventually courting at full length a most suitable and ladylike young woman named Dorothy Feiner, to whom he tried vociferously to be faithful, for a while.

Meanwhile, back in his real life, he met the two most important elements in his coming career: the music of Jerome Kern, which combined for the first time the concepts "American," "classy," and "popular"— Eureka! And the indispensable Larry Hart, with whom Rodgers, at sixteen, would start almost immediately to unwrap his extraordinary gift for melody.

At first, *Musical Stages* seems to be completely candid about Larry Hart too, quite thrillingly so because this time the candor is 100 percent favorable. In brief, Rodgers was poleaxed by his new friend and galvanized to the point where you could almost see his own young life start to change as you read. And these few pages should be underlined and returned to, because the ebullient mood doesn't last long, but soon gives way to a viperish tone of condescending exasperation that can only give aid and comfort to the conventional portrayal of Hart as a funny-looking little guy

who writes exquisite love songs and who cannot find love himself, so naturally drinks himself to death. In the silly movie *Words and Music* (1948), Mickey Rooney hammered this image home by playing Hart as a lovelorn dwarf, so perhaps it's worth noting that offscreen Rooney himself married the likes of Ava Gardner and Martha Vickers, proving if nothing else that dwarfs and near-dwarfs don't *have* to be lovelorn. And Larry Hart might have married just as well if he'd really wanted to. Witnesses attest that he could look positively handsome with a wave of his wit and charm. Like Cole Porter, Hart was a homosexual who genuinely loved women. However, unlike Cole, Hart desired them only to step out with and paint and repaint the town over and over—not to come home to and love.

The one thing that dwarfs really can't do is drink as much as the Jolly Green Giant, and Hart's attempts to do so would lead to most of the grief that followed. In the cramped world of psychohistory, nobody has ever gotten drunk just for fun, but only to escape from some problem he or she can't face. So the possibility that Hart might have had an inspired and highly productive capacity for enjoying himself is simply squeezed into a box marked "manic-depressive," from which nothing good or beautiful has ever emerged.

So it's worth repeating that *Musical Stages* gives absolutely no impression that the reader is about to meet a basket case when Rodgers first walks into the Hart apartment. On the contrary, Rodgers proceeds to find that Hart has easily the richest, most entertaining mind he has encountered in his sixteen years, a mind stuffed to the brim with both high culture and low—from the German operettas that Hart had recently translated (he was also distantly related to Heinrich Heine) to the latest word from the street (and below the street). Better still, here was a mind stuffed with ideas about both songs and musicals, which echoed and clarified Rodgers's own. In later years Rodgers would privately talk about "the statute of limitations on gratitude," but in this case it shouldn't be invoked for at least a thousand years, because in a crucial sense, he was born that day. The Rodgers-in-the-piano had finally met his match and his counterpart—not only a friend he could talk to, but one who could talk back, and who, while loving Rodgers unconditionally, would meet the first threat of Rodgers's disabling musical sentimentality with the cold eye and sour tongue of a perpetual hangover, and would interject a derisive lyric like a stop sign.

So Rodgers was forced to dig down beyond his natural facility into parts unknown. Alter egos have inner lives too. And the Rodgers-in-the-piano proved to be as subtle and witty and even likable as anyone in American music—so long as Hart was waiting next to the piano to guide and keep him company. In her introduction to *Musical Stages,* Mary Rodgers talks of loving her father's songs, and of that being enough. But if so, it was also enough to make one love Larry Hart. Because Larry, along with his gemütlich mother and his disreputable father, taught Rodgers that you could belong to a technically higher social class than his own without being the least bit respectable, thus (for a while) loosening the grip of Rodgers's nastiest attribute, his innate snobbery.

Unfortunately, the lesson and the likableness would last only as long as Hart did, and nature invariably sees to it that the greatest of partnerships—whether of George and Ira, or John and Paul, or Gilbert and Sullivan—never last quite long enough. But something else seems to have let them know that they'd better get moving right away, and by the time Richard Rodgers had reached a ripe seventeen, he and Hart had already written an establishing song to prove that indeed they could do it. "Any Old Place with You," with its immortal thought "I'd go to hell for ya, or Philadelphia."

Okay, you're songwriters, now grow up, on the double. Over the next few years, Dick would attend Columbia briefly and the Juilliard School (as it's now called) of music while intermittently writing varsity shows for both. After which, these two really poured it on for the next fifteen years, until they had piled up an oeuvre that a couple of centenarians could be proud of.

It's still a pleasure just to recite the titles and start the tunes spinning in one's head, beginning anywhere on the list and ending up anywhere else. "Where or When," "My Funny Valentine," "Little Girl Blue," "The Lady Is a Tramp," "With a Song in My Heart." A friend of mine recently gave a party just to celebrate the day when he and his brother and I had all discovered and first played and sung the Rodgers and Hart book. So that statute of limitations on gratitude still has a ways yet to go—at least for some of us.

"I can pee melody," Rodgers is alleged to have said, which also suggests a compulsion: When you've got to go, you've got to go, and at a certain

point their assembly-line production turned out to be the pace that kills. Perhaps you can't keep revving up a manic-depressive like Hart without tearing something within. And soon Hart's alcoholism galloped toward the finish line in the manner of a Dylan Thomas and Brendan Behan.

But this was Dick's own schedule, and his whip was never far from Larry's back. By the midthirties, Hart responded by regularly disappearing for days on end (which I might have done too, if I had had to work with Rodgers) and scribbling his lyrics on envelopes and cocktail napkins and fraying any enchantment his increasingly prickly partner had ever felt for him, until probably the only thing keeping them together was the imperturbably high quality of these lyrics. "Bewitched" and "Falling in Love with Love"—the scores of *Pal Joey* and *The Boys from Syracuse*—were dashed off during these nightmare years, as if disappearing for days on end was just what Hart's craftsmanship called for, and as if to prove that the artist within him was ultimately just as serious and indomitable as the one inside Richard Rodgers.

Perhaps it was. But the facts on the ground said otherwise, and after writing a prophetic song called "I Didn't Know What Time It Was," it was all over. Hart died after literally lying in a gutter, in circumstances that truly deserve the name of classic tragedy. Dick felt as innocent of causing this death as Oedipus, but he may also have been just as cursed by it too. To sum it up quickly, Rodgers had wanted to write up a namby-pamby story called *Green Grow the Lilacs,* and Hart had not. So Dick wrote it with Hammerstein instead—nothing wrong with that so far, just a one-shot deal and then back to Hart for a revised version of their first great hit, *A Connecticut Yankee,* with sparkling new words from Larry that would include one of his coolest, driest lines yet: "I admire the moon as a moon, just a moon."

Away from the desk, though, or an envelope or an old menu to write on, Hart became a confused soul. The score Rodgers wrote with Hammerstein for the namby-pamby play, renamed *Oklahoma!,* seemed to explode with relief, as if Richard Rodgers had been simply dying to cut loose from Hart. The critics prattled on about breakthroughs and new beginnings—presumably involving Rodgers and Hammerstein. And against this—what?—a revival with Hart of a 1920s show? In 1943, Hart went to see both shows—his revival and Oscar's bombshell—and apparently liked them both, but he also talked loudly and drunkenly during them, to the

point where Dick ordered their respective box offices not to let him in. So Larry went outside to lie down in his gutter, acquiring pneumonia from which he never recovered.

What else could Rodgers have done? Perhaps there's no good answer. But Dick never got that close to anyone else again. Instead the scene changes sharply from a 1930s tableau of kids putting on shows together to one of those slick 1950s offices from which Mr. Big, now Rodgers, emerges in time for the 5:25 to Greenwich every day and a cocktail on the lawn in his Bermuda shorts.

Of course, songwriters need to stay in tune with their times, but this was ridiculous. And even the family Rodgers returned to at night was a perfect period piece: happy on the outside, rotten on the inside. Its tasteful suburban façade proved to be an arena in which the latest ailments and prescription drugs slugged it out in human disguise, while the children, who assume that the whole thing is really about them, can start work on their own *Mommie Dearests*. In one corner, we find Dorothy Rodgers (anorexic, constipated), who turns into a raging, capricious monster—who wouldn't? And in the other, her husband (boozed, tranquilized), who seems permanently depressed and half-stoned. He comes to life one show at a time—just long enough to romance a new heroine, alienate the writer and the director forever, and kiss the whole chorus line goodbye before returning home to keep up appearances for the neighbors, as his father had once kept them up for his patients.

Needless to say, none of these ghoulish phenomena can be found in Dick's memoir, which doesn't tell any significant truths from Larry's death on. After a long and no doubt agonizing wait, his daughters finally commissioned that other book we've been waiting for—Meryle Secrest's *Somewhere for Me: A Biography of Richard Rodgers*—which contains the gist of their combined *Mommie Dearests*, which time has not mellowed perhaps as much as they had hoped for. The first question it answers is the one we began with, to wit, why did Rodgers seem so invisible?

Like each of the other four classic songwriters that everyone has still heard of—Jerome Kern, Irving Berlin, Cole Porter, and George Gershwin—Rodgers first made his mark in New York in the high noon and early sunset of the golden age of newspaper publicity, when there were allegedly a million stories in Manhattan, with reporters trying to cover all of

them. And each of the others had learned how to be good copy and fun to read about, particularly if the reporter was lucky enough to catch Kern at the track or Porter in his gondola. But where would you catch Rodgers? And why would you bother? He appeared to possess no characteristics whatever, and worked with a lyricist who possessed enough color for two and a lifetime. The hyperactive Larry Hart could not only talk enough to fill whole newspapers at a sitting but could also carouse so conspicuously between times that keeping his name *out* of the papers became the issue. Rodgers came of age playing the sobering part of sometime guardian and straight man to one of New York's major characters.

So who, outside of Agatha Christie, would ever suspect *him* of anything? Since Hart was going to get the story anyway, who would notice if Rodgers had gotten a little squiffy as well, and appeared to be with a different chorus girl tonight? And one night led to another until by the time Hart had died and been replaced by the much milder Oscar Hammerstein, Rodgers was doing so much carousing that covering up for himself had become a necessity. Suddenly with Oscar, one had a sense of two straight men working together with no top banana in sight.

Did Hammerstein also have something to hide? Gossip should not be multiplied unnecessarily, although it has been. But let's leave it in here that Rodgers's name in particular never seemed to go out by itself anymore, but invariably became RodgersandHammerstein at work and DickandDorothy at play; in sum, he seemed to be the most dedicated partner and thoroughly married man in show business—a perfect ornament of the Eisenhower years.

Signing up with Hammerstein in the first place had been the artistic equivalent of moving to the suburbs, and Rodgers's literal move to the burbs would prove to be the perfect postwar blend of hypocrisy and wish fulfillment. On the one hand, his bilocation permitted his double life to go into overdrive between evening clothes and Bermuda shorts—but, as I learned from a friend of mine who knew him, Dick Rodgers also wasted several of his most celebrated years vainly trying to talk his way into a local country club that didn't take Jews or theater people or whatever. So even in his Connecticut castle, he could never just relax and be himself. You can't keep a good snob down forever, and without

Larry Hart to cauterize it, his snobbery apparently ballooned to Macy's Parade proportions.

Which leaves us with the unanswerable question: Why, with genuine royalty virtually at his feet, did Rodgers bother with the provincial nonentities at this snooty country club? Well, his father would have understood. By 1902, when Dick was born, Dr. William Rodgers had reached what might be called the awkward stage of assimilation. Professionally, he was almost too respectable. But he sent his two sons mixed signals by raising the family in the home of his much richer and cruder in-laws, who embodied all the harshness, noise, and sense of overcrowding of an earlier time.

Anyhow, maybe this contrast nudged Dick's imagination on the eventual road to quiet lawns and empty rooms, toward PTAs and country clubs. At any rate, that is where his Second Act found him, growing ever more remote and regal in his suburban casuals and even, like a regular mogul, writing a memoir to hide behind forever. Later, Joe Fox, his editor on that book, would confide his frustration at having to beg for a straight answer to the simplest personal question: "Was Larry Hart really a homosexual?" "I never noticed," said Rodgers.

Gentlemen may not notice things like that, but Rodgers most certainly had, and now that his family has also delivered on the second half of its one-two punch to Daddy's pretensions, we can also pick up his own tone in his breezy, sometimes bitchy, and always articulate published letters to his late wife. And one realizes, among other things, that his secret drinking had rubbed his own nerves raw years before and that his impatience with Larry had become almost as neurotic as the latter's response to it. "That little fag," he wrote several times, referring to the man whose orientation he hadn't noticed.

Like many tragedies, Richard Rodgers, Part Two, is basically a soap opera with the stakes raised—the stakes in this case being nothing less than the future of the American musical. And the tragedy, if that's the right word, is that in the end Rodgers's lifelong attempt to merge music, words, dance, and even scenery into something like great art would be deemed kitsch, and hardly art at all. His climactic masterpiece, *The Sound of Music*, has survived into this century as a festival of high camp.

As it was, he was stunned enough to find that later generations preferred his earlier work with Hart. Wasn't Hammerstein supposed to be the revolutionary around here?

But Hammerstein, as Rodgers might have known, if his literary taste had kept up with his music, wasn't even facing in the right direction. Back in the 1920s, while Rodgers and Hart were already talking about a new kind of American musical, Hammerstein was still cheerfully dabbling in old-fashioned operettas like *Rose-Marie* and *The Desert Song*. He obviously loved the form in all its artifice and sentimentality, and this antiquated taste would sabotage every later attempt to add realism. Are we meant to be in Iowa this time or Oklahoma, or possibly Connecticut? "Durned if I know." The effects are gorgeously inauthentic, and the judgment of the sixties would be cruel.

Yet one can seldom be absolutely sure that a genius doesn't know what he's doing. Since Rodgers wasn't going to find another Hart to jam with anyway, why not try something different? Instead of concocting tunes for the lyricist to chase, why not let him go first, as Hammerstein manifestly preferred, and see where that led? Any artist who wants to last as long as Rodgers did had better change his style at least once to keep the flow going; Hammerstein's proudly corny words tapped not only a new vein of ideas but also a new aspect of his talent. Even the fertile Jule Styne expressed amazement at the speed and sureness of Rodgers's response to other people's words. Just say something like "Bali Ha'i" or "Oh, what a beautiful morning," and out would pop the musical equivalent of these words, the perfect tune.

But not the perfect jazz tune. Hammerstein had turned his back on the Jazz Age from the first downbeat onward, and jazz returned the favor to him in the Big Band Era by cutting him off. Now in the postwar years of inventory, as America began to count its blessings and bask in old glories, he had once again become the man who wrote *Show Boat*, and even perhaps the man who would write the *next Show Boat* too. One could hardly become classier than that.

To be specific, Oscar's gentility seems to have leaned toward voices over instruments and leaned away from brass instruments altogether and the syncopation that went with them. Well, okay, compromising on tempo was no deal breaker for Dick, as it would have been for Cole Porter. His

only trademark in this respect was a taste for unobtrusive, all-purpose waltzes, from the intense "Lover (When We're Dancing)" for Hart to the dreamy "Out of My Dreams" for Oscar, and the perky "Oh, What a Beautiful Mornin'."

Since he was now basically writing settings for Hammerstein's poetry, it made perfect sense to drop "that thing" and give Oscar the extra space for his lush emotions and warm humor that would take the place of Larry's irony and wit, to the delight of amateurs with big voices and to the massed yawns of interpreters like Sinatra and Sarah Vaughan, who instead kept finding more and more gems in the old Hart songbook, and erecting a monument of discs in their joint name that towers over Rodgers's oeuvre with Hammerstein. But perhaps genius still knew best in that Dick was at least still able to work with Oscar and the tunes did at least keep coming, as they would not with anyone else. And some of the tunes were beauties too, with or without "that thing." *Oklahoma!*, which was written under Hart's influence, and indeed when he himself was still above ground, is a perfect specimen of show-tune writing, with a song to cap every mood and occasion, all the while disguising its basic silliness. And even as Rodgers drifted farther from the jazz song, and from the scope of this book, he kept adding to the pool of melody for jazzmen to make into fresh jam, up to and including the elegant "My Favorite Things," which John Coltrane would redeem from its Austro-Hungarian trappings and transfer back to pure jazz.

After Oscar Hammerstein's death, Dick's first instinct was to write his own lyrics—maybe to prove he could, and maybe because he knew how impossible he was to work with. Anyone he had or ever would try it with would become part of an unhappy family of two; this had been the only model Rodgers knew. Hart had run away, while Hammerstein had worked in his own splendid isolation—I go first, you go second. There is no image of real teamwork even in this most famous of teams.

So Dick went solo on a show called (ironically?) *No Strings*. But although *No Strings* was a success, modest by his standards and colossal by anyone else's, perhaps he found something flat about it, or perhaps *he* didn't like working with himself either, for he never again tried a one-man turn. Instead, he proceeded to strike out with the likes of Alan Jay Lerner and Stephen Sondheim, merely the best in the business. And maybe even

worse from his point of view, he began to acquire the equivalent of a po-lice dossier in gossip. If his drinking up till then had been a family secret, it was all over Broadway now, and the street version was, if anything, even worse than the family one.

Bad drunks leave bad memories, and we currently know much more about the years when Rodgers was slipping than about his heights. Which has left him with an irony that would have pained him beyond endurance. Larry Hart, like Scott Fitzgerald, had gone down in flames early and has been unequivocally admired ever since. Rodgers, like Hemingway, lived longer and crashed slower and harder, and there seems no rush to dig up either of them from the rubble. Each of them had made the further boozy mistake of condescending to their more likable partners, using phrases like "poor Scott" and "the little fag," for which they would end up paying again and again. When vengeance and justice arrive at the same verdict, it can be irresistible, but finally can any fellow human really be so easily and decisively judged?

Well, maybe if the judge is on a tight deadline. But the longer this essay sits on my desk, the more questions arise from it. For one thing, I met Dick's well-balanced and good-humored daughter, Mary, and cannot easily imagine anyone so manifestly functional emerging from not one but two such monsters as her parents have been described. I've also met a cousin who passes along an ancestral memory of Dick Rodgers and Larry Hart actually playing together in the backyard around an old tree house during what was supposed to be the peak of their alienation. And I quite recently met a doctor from Sloan-Kettering cancer hospital who remem-bers Dick as a positively inspiring patient, which in hospital lingo means cheerful, cheerful, and more cheerful—not an easy mood to sustain when you suddenly need to have your jaw removed and replaced, as Dick did in 1955, seemingly at the height of his success. This leads to a final clue in Rodgers's memoir itself, which might be called the dog that didn't bark, or rather the cure that didn't work.

Faced at a certain point in his own story with the undeniable, he sud-denly admits that, yes, he did indeed drink too much once upon a time and succumbed to angst and existential aphasia and everything else that has been said about him. But he sweeps the whole syndrome into a few

manageable months in 1957, some of which were spent in the Payne Whitney Psychiatric Clinic, where the shrinks would proceed to clear the whole thing up forever—a happy ending that has since been endorsed by absolutely nobody, perhaps because it is flatly impossible.

Once more, the last laugh is on him, because as everyone knows now but practically nobody knew back then, psychiatry can't do anything for addiction-depression unless the sufferer agrees to go on the wagon and stay on it—and not just the booze wagon but the pill wagon or whatever-else-you're-on wagon as well. Rodgers would unconsciously bear this out by feeling "cured" at Payne Whitney, just as he had felt so well at Sloan-Kettering. "Cured" not, as he now supposed, because of the world-famous head-shrinkage that was the main event at Payne, but because of the sideshow—temporary abstinence—that made him into a positive "doctor's helper," as he shyly and self-mockingly boasted of becoming while there.

This phenomenon is known to former drunks as the pink cloud, and is as insubstantial as it sounds. Just laying off the downers you've been taking makes you feel preternaturally buoyant at first, but if you sit on the cloud, you go right through it. So in no time Rodgers was back to stay on his booze and painkillers, a victim and perpetrator of not a crime but a sloppy cover-up of the pharmaceutical anarchy that raged in America after World War II.

So for the most part the man Mary Rodgers describes in her introduction sounds drearily familiar: a man without friends or hobbies or any life at all. Yet the malaise had not altogether consumed the Rodgers in the piano, who continued to fight his own private wars with the Death Wish and the Life Principle. On various occasions, Mary has talked of the piano as a hub of activity, and of it lugubriously falling silent for long periods, as the instrument waited for a great script to enter the room and activate it once more. In a devastating sentence that pares the situation to the bone, she says that her father actually had no interest in music as such, no matter how challenging, but only in telling stories, no matter how banal. It was his belief that all music was basically descriptive, whether it knew it or not. Three of his own best pieces were pure descriptions of, respectively, a *Slaughter on Tenth Avenue,* a *Victory at Sea,* and a Carousel Waltz,

in the show of the same name. So now, in his solitude, why didn't he take one further step into abstraction by boiling down the basic formula—the boy, the girl, and the eye candy—and rendering *them* as pure music too?

The technical problem toward the end was getting him from his chair to the piano, and it never happened. But perhaps the last word should go to the demiurge in the music box, taken from the one occasion when it chose to speak to itself in *No Strings*. Two lines in particular seem to have survived the years since, one of them because it seems so acutely true, and the other because it doesn't. "The kindest words I'll ever know are waiting to be said." They are still waiting, as far as I know, but "the sweetest sounds I'll ever hear are still inside my head" seems far-fetched. The sweetest songs *I've* ever heard—perhaps not the best or most interesting, but definitely the sweetest—are safe and sound in the Rodgers and Hart songbook.

Yet Rodgers was speaking a songwriter's truth that I've heard echoed at least twice by other practitioners—by Gershwin, who said that he had more songs in his head than he could write down in a hundred years, and just the other night by my friend Cy Coleman, who confirmed that he, too, had more in there than he could count, so perhaps songwriting can best be defined as the wonderful ability to go in there and get them.

Part four

Hollywood—The Sugar Daddy

Hooray for Hollywood (Sometimes)

RICHARD WHITING

"*H*ow is your book on the great *show* songs coming?" Although I had never actually called them that, the translation was instantaneous and unanimous, because one of the sturdiest prejudices in this field insists that all the great songs began on Broadway. Nothing *that* good could have come out of Tin Pan Alley, let alone the crass movie business. From the moment that Hollywood opened its mouth to talk and sing, it seemed that you were either in thrall to the results or you despised them with all your soul. And while you were most likely to outgrow the first mistake, the second one, the unconditional contempt, could be a life sentence, as in the case of Alec

Wilder, who forever maintained that theater songs were better than movie songs . . . because they had to be. That's just the way it was.

Based on the stage writers' autonomy versus the movie guys' servitude, Wilder makes a plausible case too. For the most part, the best stage writers were free to score their own stuff, and decide on things like length and shape and musical arrangement. Trained musicians like Gershwin and Kern valued this freedom and made the most of it. But, significantly, a lot of others, such as Richard Rodgers, didn't—because, as Cy Coleman explained to me, while you were home arranging your songs, the producer and director were quite likely removing the scenes your songs were in and hence the songs too. And to completely counter Wilder's argument, one need only play one other card, which is that by his own reckoning each of the above-mentioned songwriters wrote some of his very greatest songs for movies, while as for length and shape, Harold Arlen's "Blues in the Night" and Rube Bloom's "Day In, Day Out" ramble on at interminable length and are as free-form as anything ever produced on Broadway.

In movies, the longer your song lasts, the more time the studio gets to show off its scenery and choreography, and how much better it can make a number like "Begin and Beguine" look than all the stage carpenters and small-as-life dancers of Broadway put together. Movie songs have another huge built-in advantage. Stage songs generally have to be part of a story or else they seem intrusive, but movie songs can play quietly in the background, establishing a mood, behind our backs as it were, and selling us on the tune before we're even aware of having heard it. It is a truism of the stage that even professionals can't always spot a hit the first time they hear it, while as for critics, there is a long honor roll of great songs that didn't make it into first-night reviews, for example, the mutt who found Kern's score for *Roberta* "sweetly forgettable." Yeah, right, so much for "Smoke Gets in Your Eyes."

In contrast, I recommend that you take a look at the great Bing Crosby and W. C. Fields movie *Mississippi*. Listen for the Richard Rodgers song "It's Easy to Remember." Notice how often it is played before Bing officially introduces it. By the time he does, it's like an old friend.

All the tunes used to be replayed so often that even the background music could be turned into songs, as in the case of David Raksin's "Laura," which wound up with a lyric by Johnny Mercer (and with the

rare encomium of being the song Cole Porter would most have liked to have written himself). With bandleaders and singers and Hollywood itself beating the bushes for new material, no good tune went unheard. Eddie Cantor's archetypal film *Kid Millions* ends with a perfect metaphor for the situation: an ice cream factory stretching to infinity, with different shades of ice cream bursting from every pore while an infinity of kids pour through to become presumably, infinitely sick. By the time you left the movie house on a Saturday afternoon, the entertainment was coming out of your ears, but you knew all the songs too.

There's no need to catalogue all the usual horror stories about Hollywood, which were undoubtedly just as true, of talent ignored or manhandled. Two specimens cover most of this ground: Saul Chaplin had already passed the first and most important requirement for movie glory; he had "made it" in New York with a couple of hits, "Please Be Kind" and the immortal (i.e., Sinatra liked it) "Until the Real Thing Comes Along," plus another hit that he had by the tail, "Bei Mir Bist du Schoen," a song that he and his partner Sammy Cahn hadn't precisely written but had rearranged and signed.

Unfortunately, though, Saul never learned how to play politics in New York because Cahn played it for both of them from morning to night. This would be Chaplin's downfall because Hollywood was such a politician's delight that Sammy kept right on playing it until he had played himself into a whole new partnership with the red-hot Jule Styne. Saul didn't know what to do next, or what the first step was in this dance, so he finally retired upward into management, where he happily worked alongside such fellow drop-ups as Johnny "Body and Soul" Green at MGM and Victor "Stella by Starlight" Young at Paramount to help turn out the last great crops of musicals, in the forties and fifties, that Hollywood would ever produce. Finally, this is what makes it so hard to stay mad at Hollywood; even the losers got ice cream.

But even the winners had to play politics. And sometimes they lost and had to eat humble pie with their ice cream. As we have seen, even Berlin, Kern, and Gershwin got hazed at least once by the philistines before winding up in glory. The only one who was too proud to take it was Richard Rodgers. His brief film career proves a useful parable and recap of the songwriter's role out there. It reminds one, among other things, of how

quickly the scene kept changing, of how much screen history might be crammed into a few years, so that "the good old days" could refer to any time up to last night, and the end of the world might have begun already.

When Rodgers and Hart arrived in late 1931, the first wave of musicals had just passed and Hollywood didn't know what to do next. For writers, it was like finding all the doors of the palace unlocked. The boys moved right in and, with the help of the adventurous director Rouben Mamoulian, produced a film, *Love Me Tonight*, that still seems avant-garde. For openers, the sequence of scenes that accompanies the hit song "Isn't It Romantic" is like a zoom lens that takes us from the big picture, of poilus fighting for France, to a smaller one of regular Parisians going about their business, to one street, and then to one shop and one man whistling, all done in the newsreel style that would later be used in *Duck Soup* ("Fredonia Goes to War") and makes a sublime overture to the operetta courtship that ensues between Maurice Chevalier and Jeanette MacDonald, which in turn is a study in felicitous high-comedy song placement. And the songs themselves, such as "Mimi," "Lover," "Isn't It Romantic," are so good that Rodgers and Hart went straight to the top of the class without quite knowing what was so unique about this movie that got them there. So after a routine musical with George M. Cohan flopped, the pair resumed the same general method of integrating songs and pictures with Al Jolson in *Hallelujah, I'm a Bum!*, which was a step backward, because Jolson was a step backward. Maurice Chevalier was a one-on-one entertainer, a confider of songs, perfect for the movies, while Jolson and Cohan preferred to work the whole crowd, which usually just looks silly in movies. Still, *Hallelujah* succeeded, just enough anyway to prompt MGM to sign up Rodgers and Hart with a flourish and a big banquet in their honor.

And then that same year *42nd Street* was released and with that, comic impressionism gave way to sexy sentimentalism and technological narcissism, and a moment later Rodgers and Hart found themselves out of style and almost out of work, taking stabs at projects that were soon abandoned, and wasting precious time rewriting, among other things, maybe the greatest song that never made it into a movie. Hart had written one set of words to it to suit one kind of movie, and then another set, and finally gave up and just wrote some words that could have been a parody and called it "Blue Moon."

At this point, it was too soon in musical comedy history to know just how long the latest trend would last. All Rodgers needed to do now was get out of town, and either do another stage show or go around the world. Then he could return to another banquet in his honor. Hollywood was always celebrating new arrivals, however often they'd been there before, and if you timed it right, like Gershwin and Porter in 1936, you might even become the latest trend yourself.

The year 1932 was not a good time to be anywhere. The Depression had finally sunk in all the way and musicals seemed to be dying on Broadway as well. For the hyperactive Rodgers, it was a taste of hell. Because he and Hart had apparently lost the war on both coasts to just the kind of tired businessman leg-waving that they'd been trying to drive off Broadway. What else was *42nd Street* and its gold-digger children than bits and pieces of the old Ziegfeld Follies photographed from the ceiling and wrapped in a flimsy backstage romance?

Fortunately, Broadway was resilient too and was just about to come back from the dead, as is its wont. Rodgers returned, a grumpier but wiser man, to make a huge New York splash with Billy Rose's *Jumbo,* and then a whole string of splashes which would eventually prove that if you sold enough Broadway musicals to Hollywood, you could make the same millions, revolutionize the stage musical to your heart's content, and never again have to go to the dreaded West Coast. And any second thoughts Rodgers might have had about leaving were erased in advance when he went around to say goodbye to the big MGM pooh-bah Irving Thalberg, who had originally begged to sign him, and now Thalberg didn't even recognize him.

That was how it went in Hollywood—feast or famine, a banquet or a stale ham sandwich. As Rodgers read it, in their hearts, movie people didn't really like Broadway people, beyond their publicity value, which was good for roughly one film and a half, after which the hacks with the connections resumed their sway. (For the hacks' point of view, see my chapter on Harry Warren.) So after one last, moderately humiliating trip back to make *Mississippi* for W. C. Fields, and at the last minute Bing Crosby, Rodgers swore never to return for anything. If the studio wanted his big Broadway successes, or even the original *State Fair,* they would have to come and get 'em.

A reasonable condition, one might have supposed, and one that most New York writers might well have imposed a few years earlier. The arrival of talkies in 1927 had coincided with the greatest year in Broadway musical history, with Youmans, Gershwin, Rodgers, and Kern all hitting their peaks at once. It must have seemed like the ultimate sellers' market for songwriters. Hollywood would need all the pretty sounds it could get, on the double, and it needed New York authentication for its artistic pretensions. From the start, the studios saw great profit in glorifying the Great White Way and keeping it alive through the Depression, so they could advertise their latest movies as coming hot from Broadway, all of which suggests that they wanted the composers to stay at their pianos and get on with it.

The balance of arrogance must have seemed to run even more in the writers' favor after everyone had seen Al Jolson's performance in *The Jazz Singer*. Al seemed so much smaller on the screen, as if his famous charisma had been left out in the theater lobby. If this was the "world's greatest entertainer," as he billed himself, spare us the minor ones. "Valentino Talks." Big deal. The Bearded Lady sings. The possibility that someday Fred Astaire might loom over both Jolson and Valentino as a film presence was not how people were thinking yet. (Could less *really* be more? The idea was in the air, but people always need more proof.)

Whatever you thought of the songs in *The Jazz Singer*, no one had to leave New York to provide them. The city was still coming into its own as a match for Paris and London as a great world capital. And as new buildings raced one another to the sky, in a joint leap of faith and vote of confidence down below, the legitimate theaters were multiplying like rabbits. And, as always, talent was flooding into town on every bus and train. Could you really tell them all to go back out West? Meanwhile, a sturdy little Broadway-based film colony had been growing up on Long Island to provide day jobs for all the new talent. And how much sunlight did you need for movies, anyway? They made them in Germany, didn't they? And wasn't it more important to be where the life was and where the culture was coming from? If you *have* a city like New York, for heaven's sake, use it.

That was the view from 1927, a most misleading year. Flash forward just a few years more: The market has crashed, and there is Gershwin all right, on his Hollywood estate taking home movies of himself with friends

and starlets in the latest beachwear. George is definitely visiting royalty, but not city-style royalty. As with Kern and Rodgers before him, his West Coast lifestyle foreshadows the suburbanization of haute Broadway, with tennis and golf replacing booze and breakdowns.

That was one end of town, anyway. But if you could look simultaneously into the bar of Hollywood's Roosevelt Hotel, you would find that the lowlifes of Tin Pan Alley had actually re-created their own New York as if for a movie scene, drink for drink, gag for gag, and also bet for bet. For them, the one blessing of the West was the multiplicity of racetracks, where, if spotted, you could always claim to be trying to find Bing Crosby, or later Bob Hope, for your next movie.

But you couldn't have found these types on day one in 1927. No one was there yet. No one who was anybody, that is. There were, as always in Hollywood, at least a couple of nonentities-in-waiting ready to form an aristocracy, and while Nacio Herb Brown looked more like the gentleman's tailor that he was than Gene Kelly, and Arthur Freed, the one time I saw him, seemed like the last man in the world to "Make [Anybody] Laugh" like Donald O'Connor, these two did share the one indispensable gift that *Singin' in the Rain* is based on: *being* there when the bell rang and being ready for it as if they'd been preparing for it all their lives.

Young Nacio (or Ignacio) Brown had the unusual songwriters' distinction of being born in New Mexico, but his father had since moved on to become the sheriff of Los Angeles, so that his son had pretty much grown up with the film colony while it was still in its small-town phase. The VIPs hadn't yet hedged themselves off in their castles for tourists to dream about, but still walked the streets and talked to normal folk, so it was the easiest thing in the world for Brown to set himself up as a haberdasher to the stars, trading suits for connections, or later for song plugs. And it was equally easy for him to spread himself, like everyone else, into real estate so that in a pinch he could say, "If you don't need a suit today, how about a house?" Short of becoming a celebrity hairdresser or a bartender at the Brown Derby, it's hard to imagine what more the man could have done to position himself to catch the latest buzz and meet the biggest buzzards, which would include in the course of time Irving Thalberg, the boy wonder at MGM.

And after dark, Brown played the piano in a local bistro, on the

strength of which he hooked up with a hustler from all over called Arthur Freed, who on the side wrote lyrics. Unlike Brown with his Southwestern roots, Arthur Freed seemed to have touched base with all four corners of America and several corners of show biz. Born in Charleston, he had somehow managed to be raised in Seattle, and educated at Phillips Exeter, although presumably not for the life he proceeded to live, which ran from plugging songs and producing shows for the army to running a music shop and even doing a stint onstage with the young Marx Brothers, who were the last word in discombobulation. Perhaps Freed's most prophetic achievement of all was the assemblage of the enduring standard "I Cried for You," which may be the only song ever written by two bandleaders and one jack-of-all-trades. Clearly this man knew how to put packages together and make his own opportunities. Combining him with Brown was almost unfair. Not until Rodgers joined Hammerstein, or as J.F.K. might put it, not since Irving Berlin dined alone, would songwriting see such concentrated business acumen in one room.

So, what with Freed writing the lyrics, and Brown playing all his tunes in every bistro for miles around, chances were that by the time *The Jazz Singer* came out, Thalberg and the others had already heard all the songs for MGM's answer to it, the first *Broadway Melody* of 1929, and for the film after that as well.

The Broadway stick-in-the-muds finally got the message, some faster than others, that Hollywood worked too quickly and spasmodically to wait for you to mail in your songs. The highly successful and commercial team of Brown, Henderson, and DeSylva was out there in a flash and wrote one of the first anthems, "You Ought to Be in Pictures." DeSylva, the most businesslike of the three, proceeded into management, as would Freed himself. If every writer in the world was coming out here, why tie yourself down to one? Lyric writers as such are hustlers by calling and are also frequently subject to the question, "But what do you *really* do for a living?" By 1960 or so, Freed had developed a particularly satisfactory answer, namely, that he had saved the American musical forever, or at least for a few precious decades, by producing masterworks including *Meet Me in St. Louis, Easter Parade,* and *An American in Paris,* which have so far proved immortal.

One last benefaction of Freed's second career was to the studio that had housed him for so long and had bankrolled that whole gorgeous sunset

of the great musicals. If one had nothing to go on but the two *That's Enter-tainment* movies, one might suppose that MGM had been the undisputed king of the genre all along. But this is winner's history; by continuing to bet big bucks while the other players folded and left the table, MGM had picked up an Astaire here and a Crosby there, and then with a series of film bios, all the songs of Porter, Kern, and Rodgers and the team of Kalmar and Ruby, until finally, it had almost the whole deck in its hands. This was no great scandal or even a secret. Hollywood history works like that. You can buy all the rights to history itself, if you can afford it.

Yet from the writers' point of view, and ours, the multiplicity of studios may be the single most important fact in this chapter. If any one person ever really owned history, it would immediately stop moving at whatever phase the owner liked best. To put it dialectically, the czar of MGM, Louis B. Mayer, loved what he considered classiness, while the genius, Thalberg, believed that spectacle was the essence of movies, so the ideal for both of them was something like operetta with its massed choirs of braided uniforms and bobbing Adam's apples, playing a real palace. But at Paramount, Maurice Chevalier could do this same scene with a leer and a wink that changed everything, while at Warner Bros. the spectacle would be Americanized by Busby Berkeley into something flashier and less classy but more truly cinematic. And when all these cards had been played, a pair of Broadway hoofers at RKO named Astaire and Rogers would trump any number of MGM's epaulets and evening gowns and Warner Bros.'s leg shows too, with sheer gracefulness and art deco, and Bing Crosby would make things even simpler at Paramount in the role of a classy common man. All these changes and many more called for new songwriters, until every American who could carry a tune seemed to be under contract to some Hollywood muckety-muck or other. But once again, I'll choose just two representatives who played a modified form of leapfrog with each other at Paramount, which was incidentally the edgi-est of the studios and perhaps the best candidate to put together a *That's Entertainment* of its own.

From day one, or at the latest day two, of the talkie era, Paramount began stockpiling writers, one of these being Richard Whiting, a jewel of the Chicago wing of Tin Pan Alley and a most unlikely man to find in Hol-lywood at all.

In fact, Whiting's presence at or near the creation of talkies was a great deal chancier than Nacio Brown's was, so much so that he even wrote a song about it, or the lyric of one anyway—he refused to take credit for the tune, although his fingerprints are all over it. "She's Funny That Way" is apparently a hymn to a wife's willingness to adapt to her husband's capriciousness, but the real life wrinkle is that it was actually Mrs. Whiting's caprice that got Richard out to Hollywood to try his luck in the Great Sound Rush, so that *he* was the one who had to be "funny that way."

Left to his own devices, it is questionable whether Whiting would ever have gone anywhere at all. A Midwesterner by birth and conviction, young Richard used up his whole supply of wanderlust early in life by attending a military school in California. After that, just getting him from Detroit to Chicago was almost more trouble than it was worth, while he didn't get as far as New York until the 1920s were almost over. Yet during that decade, he wrote some of the nation's hippest songs from right where he was. Although the Chicago wing housed only three names that anyone still remembers, all three were, as Spencer Tracy put it, "cherse": Gus Kahn, who came closest to being the official Alley lyricist to the decade without abandoning his base; Isham Jones, a taciturn coal miner turned bandleader, who wrote, among other hits, the trailblazing tune for "It Had to Be You," which Johnny Mercer considered the perfect song; and Whiting himself, who kicked off the twenties with such with-it numbers as "Japanese Sandman" (words: Raymond B. Egan) and "Ain't We Got Fun" (Gus Kahn and Ray Egan) and went on to such period excellences as "Sleepy Time Gal" and "Breezing Along with the Breeze." So who needed New York?

But Hollywood in the 1930s was something else. Even homebodies like Kahn and Whiting had to get out there and play their songs in person, during what must have seemed like a perpetual casting call from contract to contract and job to job. Perhaps the studios felt that if the writers ever got comfortable, they'd all fall asleep. So even after they wangled that first precious two-year contract, the boss knew how to keep everyone sweating, most notoriously by assigning the same picture to all of them at once or else by gutting the latest Broadway scores of everything but the hits and handing the carcasses over to the studio's geniuses for embalming.

Yet the force of inertia is awfully strong out there. Its racetracks and

golf courses tended to be full of musical talent all the time. By establishing himself so early out there, Richard Whiting was the closest thing to Old Hollywood, and it was only half a joke that Johnny Mercer talked about him almost as if he were the resident golf pro. Since golf was also the pastime of the elite writers, the Jerome Kerns and the Harold Arlens as opposed to the barflies of Tin Pan Alley, Whiting's social set was partly determined for him by his sheer skill at the game. And what could be more appropriate than that he end up playing it and writing songs as well with Johnny Mercer of the Savannah Mercers?

But before getting to Johnny, Whiting had already written his identifying songs with the *other* nicest guy in the business, Leo Robin, who was very much a Broadway lyricist in his heart, and who would later achieve his dream of actually being one with Nice Guy Number Three, Jule Styne, for the score of *Gentlemen Prefer Blondes*. Since Robin would prove to be Whiting's best other half, platonically speaking, he deserves a few words on his own.

Leo is probably best remembered now for a few unforgettable lines, "It's then that those louses go back to their spouses." From *Gentlemen,* "Strictly between us/you're cuter than Venus/and what's more you've got arms" from the movie song "Love Is Just Around the Corner," and "Thanks for the Memory" from one thousand years of Bob Hope.

Robin's other specialty, which he shared with Whiting, was writing great theme songs that fit the singers they were aimed at so well that he or she would need no other. With Whiting, for instance, Robin wrote "Louise" for Maurice Chevalier, which forced its way straight to the top of Chevalier's mostly French repertoire, and also for Maurice, "One Hour with You," which *he* didn't adopt, but which Eddie Cantor did for his long-running radio show; and for Jeanette MacDonald a quintessential number that could almost serve as a career résumé. When "Beyond the Blue Horizon" is played as it was in the movie with an express-train accompaniment, it conveys all the melodramatic, high-octane optimism that would eat poor Nelson Eddy alive in film after film and would, with a little help from Eddy's wimpishness, turn a pleasant light comedy actress into a dragon to reckon with.

The key to such songs is obviously empathy and interest in other people, and in this respect, Whiting's and Robin's legendary niceness may ac-

tually have helped them professionally. "I haven't seen it yet," Jonathan Schwartz reports Robin saying about some show or other, "but I'll bet it's good." Robin and Whiting both *wanted* people and things to be good, and anything they could do to help was gladly done. Thus, without each other, Whiting also wrote "On the Good Ship Lollipop" for Shirley Temple, and Robin, with Ralph Rainger, batted out "Please" and "Love in Bloom" for Bing Crosby—although the latter was grabbed by Jack Benny for his radio show—and of course for Hope, "Thanks for the Memory."

One other song Whiting wrote for Chevalier insists on being mentioned, if only because it was his own special favorite, "My Ideal." This song would also make my own top ten, for what that's worth, if simply for the second A section, which like that of Rodgers's "A Ship Without a Sail," takes you at least one step further into the unknown than you thought possible, and unleashes a terrible beauty.

With that one, Whiting touched greatness, yet Paramount kept signing up more songwriters anyway, including the aforesaid Rodgers, who worked with Chevalier, whom Dick might have considered his own personal property. As the oldest settler, Whiting was also one of the first to illustrate another great law of Hollywood life, namely, that the longer you stayed in one place, the less respect you got. In fact, Whiting might have lost any of the remaining clout he still possessed had Chevalier carried out his threat to go home to France before his novelty wore off, and be completely replaced by the new house star, Bing Crosby. Crosby, in his acting style at least, was no respecter of persons of any kind. It was his first order of business to lower the tone of any joint he was in, and the tone of the songs as well, which would now need to contain more jazz and more schmaltz to service the famous throb of his own voice, a sound more Tin Pan Alley than Broadway.

Although I don't know the particulars of Whiting's decision, I do know that he jumped ship to Fox for a short while for one contract, while Bing and his boyos settled into Paramount. The Crosby gang was made up of various combinations of Arthur "Pennies from Heaven" Johnston and Jimmy "You Made Me Love You" Monaco on the tunes, and increasingly Crosby's New York pal Johnny Burke on the words, which combination was starting to give Paramount a blue collar bull pen all the way until the

arrival of a new compromise candidate named Ralph Rainger, who while not Broadway in the highest sense was not quite Tin Pan Alley either. Like Carmichael and Schwartz, Rainger had gone the same law school route for the same reasons—to play the piano a bit longer—and he was now manifestly acceptable to the uptown crowd. He would even supply the music for a Dorothy Parker lyric, the haunting "I Wished on the Moon," which is typical of both her and him.

Above all, Rainger was preeminently what you had to be in Hollywood: intuitive and adaptable. Without realizing it, he had discovered that he was a songwriter by composing the perfect piece of material for the singer Libby Holman, for whose latest show he had been working as a rehearsal pianist. "Moaning Low" was one of those "found" songs like "Smoke Gets in Your Eyes." It suited Holman so well that it probably saved her young career from crashing before takeoff, and it seems likely he got the idea for it from just being around her.

So what might being around Bing Crosby produce for him? Rainger didn't have to wait long to find out, because his first song for Bing was an enduring hit, and worked as a magical calling card for himself at Paramount. "Please," as Leo Robin's plaintive lyrics add, "lend your little ear to my pleas." The tune whines in the plaintive style of the young Crosby, but it whines classily, if that's possible. And for Rainger's next go-round with Bing in *The Big Broadcast of 1936*, the hit "June in January" seemed to keep step with Crosby's own evolution from a groaner to the streamlined crooning machine that people remember today. Rainger was right there with him.

Perhaps Rainger was almost too much in tune with his own times and what was happening for him to last into ours. It is hard to believe what huge stature he once had in the Hollywood music game—even people outside of Hollywood had heard of him—and how small a figure he cuts in history. Never underestimate the journalistic value of a catchy name, of course; but unfortunately Ralph was also a master of the A-minus and B-plus song that doesn't quite make it into the future. See the funny movie *Moon over Miami* sometime (it's still around, thanks to Betty Grable) and you'll hear a charming score without a single standard in it except for the title song, which wasn't written by Rainger. And before Ralph

could pick up the accelerated beat and inspirational charge of wartime (Write a song for your Uncle Sam!), he died in one of the epidemic plane crashes of the day.

In his interview with Max Wilk, Harry Warren, the King Crab in Hollywood, complained that you had to have a Broadway reputation to get treated right in Hollywood, but he admits in another connection that the work never stopped coming for him. And as we have seen, the work did stop coming for Warren's fellow sourpuss, Richard Rodgers of Broadway.

Anyhow, as we have also seen, musicals were hurting all over by the end of 1931, and with even Chevalier threatening to return to France, Whiting jumped ship and signed on with Fox. And within a few months Warren and Dubin's *42nd Street* had saved musicals all over, and Bing Crosby had saved Paramount, so what, Whiting may have wondered, had been the point of moving?

Whether one's Hollywood moves worked or not, one kept on making them—anything else was a sin against optimism, but Whiting's last one was a beauty, a rendezvous with Mercer at yet another studio, Warner Bros. At age forty-five, Whiting was by then a grand old man, in pop music time, and Johnny Mercer had had lots of time to venerate him. And Johnny was unbelievably hot just then, and happy to share his heat with Whiting in a spray of new songs, two of which are probably now played more often than the rest of his work put together. "Too Marvelous for Words" was produced in a style worthy of a going-away present to himself. Looking at it today, one would swear it was choreographed by Busby Berkeley, since it was tapped out by a group of chorus girls on the keys of a kind of giant piano that at one time only Busby could have thought of, but that anyone could imitate now, and which eventually no one would be able to afford anyway. In this case, as in so many, Whiting's tune is immortal because Mercer's words are too. Even lyrical-amnesiacs can always come up with "that old standby amorous" and "Webster's dick-shun-ary," and once you have those, you have the whole song. In the matter of teamwork, both men had met their match and would meet it once more before parting.

"Hooray for Hollywood" has remained an anthem because both men were equally plugged in not only to each other but to their peculiar time and place, Hollywood in 1937, where "every barmaid can be a star made,"

or alternatively you could always "go out and try your luck, you could be Donald Duck." And with that you can see it all: the orange juice stands and the jalopies covered in funny sayings ("Aw faw down go boom"), and filled with good-looking or funny-looking kids who had gone out there to make it. It has often been said that Hollywood never made a real movie about the Depression, and yet if you saw it in person, apparently the whole place seemed to be about the Depression and its dreams.

In the early black days of the slump, one dreamed about impossibilities like ocean liners and dancing with Fred Astaire. "If I Had a Million"? Yeah, sure. But by Roosevelt's second term, things really did seem to be looking up, as the Gershwin song assured us, and some serious daydreaming seemed to be in order, not about Ruritania anymore, which Hitler seemed to be sealing off right then, but about yourself making it right here in the U.S.A., and specifically in Hollywood, where Lana Turner had just been discovered on a drugstore stool, thus changing a whole nation's consciousness. So perhaps Fred Astaire was still out of reach, but Mickey Rooney? Come on! Or possibly Shirley Temple? You bet that your daughter could look just as cute if they could do something about her teeth. From 1938 on, the musicals increasingly started to use real surfaces for their fantasies. Even at the old house of fantasy, MGM, the first thing they showed visitors now was Andy Hardy's hometown, and the master daydream in this real land of Oz was of having your car waved through the gates. "Good morning, Mr. Gable. Mr. Mayer is expecting you."

Mercer and Whiting were right next door at Warners in the cusp year 1937, capturing the whole sense of possibility in both music and words. Never mind whether "the dreams that you dared to dream" ever actually came true, because by then you'd be dreaming something else. In Tinseltown, the dream itself was the message, as Marshall McLuhan would say. The real story might end in the bitter confusion of Nathanael West's worst day of the locust, but it began with hooray for Hollywood. When I found myself there in 1950, they still seemed to be dreaming it. Every waitress and bellhop was good-looking and every one of them had a style and a shtick, if you'd just give them a moment.

It was a great note for Richard Whiting to end on. He was not out of it, after all, but had again become the latest thing. So he had his own dream to ride out on when his death came suddenly in February 1938.

"Richard Whiting was an original," said Mercer, and one reflects again on how many of these people were original, although they were consigned for the most part to the same thirty-two-bar choruses and identical tempo and other conventions. There is no mistaking a Whiting song for a Walter Donaldson or an Arthur Schwartz for a Burton Lane. Richard Whiting might be thought to have brought something new from the Midwest, as Hoagy had, but with everyone now primed on the same movies, records, and radio shows, regionalism quietly dropped out of this kind of music to burrow further into "country" and the less familiar "Western." Otherwise, whether you came from Texas or New Jersey was hardly worth mentioning. Once the jazz song cut its guide ropes to New York City, it became just plain American—perfect for World War II, but less so afterward. Meanwhile, back at Paramount, Ralph Rainger's timing and luck might have seemed better than Whiting's, but they weren't really, because he never could become the sole proprietor to Bing Crosby, which was the name of the game in the thirties. So when his contract came up for renewal in 1938, it apparently struck him as a good time to leave. He had struck gold once with the new boy on the lot, Bob Hope, but the sequel to "Thanks for the Memory" was assigned to the team of Hoagy Carmichael and Frank Loesser. Besides, Hope was becoming more exclusively a comedian and was just using whoever his partner Crosby liked at that moment, which usually meant whoever Bing's friend Johnny Burke liked, and that wasn't Rainger's professional set.

So Rainger jumped to Twentieth Century, which Darryl Zanuck was already turning into a haven for musicals. There he ran into a buzz saw called Harry Warren, who could, and very nearly did, write all the studio's musicals himself. And then Rainger's story suddenly ended with that plane crash. Even in retrospect one would hesitate to give advice to any of these men, because everyone else was moving around out there too. New people were entering, and no doubt, had Whiting and Rainger lived, they would have bumped into each other again, at least once.

Those two were a pair of stay-at-homes next to the ultimate politician, Jimmy McHugh, who, if not for music, might have wound up running a political machine in his native Boston and earning his own last hurrah that way. As it was, McHugh graduated from a job at the Boston Opera House to a composing one at the Cotton Club, and thence to the movies,

revealing along the way a pure musical gift to match his calculating heart. For all his undoubted excellence, which included some of the most pleasantly surprising bridges I know of, and some of the cleverest tunes, such as "Don't Blame Me" and "Say It (Over and Over Again)," McHugh is best remembered for a couple of rumors about him, and the damning fact that these rumors are still believed by many.

Everyone in town knew that young Fats Waller would sometimes try to peddle his latest tunes around the Brill Building in exchange for all their worth in gin. But since there was nothing to keep him from selling the same song to someone else on the next floor, he didn't find many takers, and the only actual songs to emerge from the rumor mill were "On the Sunny Side of the Street" and "I Can't Give You Anything but Love," both ostensibly by McHugh and his partner, Dorothy Fields. The only reason I don't believe these rumors myself is Fields, who was a lady, and would also give Wilk a most circumstantial account of hearing the words "I can't give you anything but love," whispered by a swain to his sweetie just outside of Tiffany's.

Besides which, Dorothy Fields had no reason to front for Jimmy McHugh, who had once bummed a few bucks off her himself by demanding a piece of her lyric royalties to Kern's *Roberta*. This was big league caddishness, and when Wilk asked her to assess working with McHugh, she answered with the faintest praise applicable. "Professional," she said. And that he was, down to the smallest detail, such as (again, according to legend) hanging out with the portly Louella Parsons, whose gossip columns were law in Hollywood.

As a married Catholic, McHugh was assumed to be making the most of the Spencer Tracy privilege, which entitled one to unlimited whoopee so long as one is truly sorry for it at least once a year, and thus it was inevitable that the rumors bubbled up about him and Dorothy Fields, which there was no particular reason to believe. What is not fair to assume in a case like McHugh's is that all his (many) good deeds were pure hypocrisy. Like Richard Rodgers and so many others, McHugh lived his whole life theatrically, bordering on operatically, with his outsize virtues and vices slugging it out on a scale of overgrown contraltos and bassi, with his own soul going alternately to heaven and hell, sometimes in the course of a single evening. Thank God I am not called upon to judge any of them.

Where McHugh's professionalism did spring a leak was in his tendency to be in the wrong place when the good movies were handed out, as you'll see his name on a raft of clunkers. Still, as Mercer tells us, anyone could get lucky out there, and McHugh would also find himself in line, with the excellent lyric writer Harold Adamson, to write the songs for Frank Sinatra's first movie, *Higher and Higher.* Luck followed him to the keyboard on that one, where he wrote the superefficient "I Couldn't Sleep a Wink Last Night," which sticks in your head like flypaper on contact, and the gorgeous "A Lovely Way to Spend an Evening," which has a bridge that reminds me of one of those small real ones occasionally found in gardens, a splendid little artifact.

Whiting and Rainger and McHugh were just three of the writers throwing the dice year after year and film after film. To throw a final bone to Hollywood, everyone wanted these writers to get lucky, and even conspired toward it. Unlike the witless owners of baseball teams, the studio heads had the sense to realize that they were partners as well as rivals and that their joint goal was just to get people to the movies, *all* the movies, and get them to buy all the songs on the way out as well. Anyone who learns one lyric will learn two, or twelve. Studios were in the habit-forming business, and every little bit helped.

With this in mind, these greedy, unscrupulous cartoons would actually lend each other their contract writers as they lent their actors for particular projects, making the best exchange they could get for them on the spur of the moment, and even allowing the writers a say in the transaction, to wit and as follows: Jule Styne, who had begun life as a classical prodigy and gone West as a voice coach, had apparently come to a dead end at Republic Pictures writing songs for cowboy movies, presumably to be sung to the horses. But when they asked him who he'd like for a partner and he said Frank Loesser, they actually borrowed Loesser for him from Paramount in its unofficial rent-a-writer program. Just like that, Jule became a real songwriter, simply by handing over his best tune and having a third-rate poem but absolutely first-rate lyric stamped on it. The result, "I Don't Want to Walk Without You," also helped Loesser, who, after fobbing off Republic with some real horse music, smuggled this gem back to Paramount, where it enhanced his standing enormously. Nobody complained—that was how the game was played.

With which, I rest my case. With so many talented people scheming between golf shots to place their material, and receiving so many chances to do so, something good had to happen—as well, of course, as something bad. To throw a last bone to the naysayers, a film called *That's* Not *Entertainment* could probably fill a few hours too.

But perhaps not so very many. Hollywood was so rich back then that, like the government, it could afford to pay writers *not* to produce, or at least not to publish. Warren talks of writing eighteen tunes for one movie, and of publishing maybe four of them—nice odds, although not foolproof. If even one of these songs became a standard, thank Hollywood for spending like a drunken sailor on these lunatic investments. The Great American Songbook would not be the same without them.

Harry Warren: The King of the Unknowns
and His Quiet Reign in Hollywood

HARRY WARREN

*I*nsofar as Harry Warren is famous for anything at all, it's for not being famous—so much so that I've never heard him discussed without that subject dominating the conversation.

A lot of things had to go wrong to produce such majestic anonymity as Harry's. Had his father, Antonio Guaragna, just stayed put in his native Calabria, our subject, born Salvatore Guaragno, might have succeeded his idol, Puccini, as the last of the classic Italian opera writers; or if Antonio had stopped at his next port of call, Argentina, the title "King of the Tango" might have been Salvatore's for the taking.

But Antonio kept moving until he settled down in Brooklyn Heights,

New York, which pop-musically speaking placed his boy practically in the middle of the cattle call. Yet even that might have worked out if he hadn't also decided to Americanize the family name into the most forgettable one in the whole show biz register. A young man named Salvatore Guaragna might have stood out even in the crowd on Tin Pan Alley. Or he might have stood out under any name at all if he'd had the time and opportunity to write a few really big Broadway shows. But the Depression came along shortly before he could do that and, as Harry Warren, he decamped for Hollywood—where his luck got both better and worse. Warren became such a prodigious success out there that he could never quite afford to leave "just yet." And by the time he could finally afford to, he'd been hopelessly typecast in the trade as a movie writer and was by definition not classy enough for Broadway.

So Antonio Guaragna's son disappeared into Warner Bros.'s studio, and was never heard of again—until, that is, he eventually became an archivist's delight as the king of the unknowns and the prototype to the point of caricature of all the New Yorkers who went West in the 1930s, kicking and screaming, and stayed there moaning and groaning, and vanishing one by one from public view, like a pack of Cheshire cats, leaving behind not smiles but forgettable movies and unforgettable music.

In his role as King Anonymous, Warren illustrates to profuse perfection how Hollywood could immortalize a song like nobody's business, while deep-sixing its creators beyond recall. To be fair, Tinseltown handsomely delivered on both ends of the deal, and still does in some cases. For instance, quite recently, Warren's flagship "I Only Have Eyes for You" could be heard in the background of three new movies in the same year, making it one of those rare songs like Rodgers's "Blue Moon" and Carmichael's "Georgia" that seems to roll over into the next generation and the next and just keep on rolling. And by selling its old films to TV, Hollywood has conspired to keep several other Warren standards around in the half-light of the nation's subconscious. Is there, for instance, anyone in America who hasn't heard "Chattanooga Choo Choo" or "(I've Got a Gal in) Kalamazoo" at least once? Or some scrap of music from the *42nd Street* cycle ("Shuffle Off to Buffalo," anyone? Or "You're Getting to Be a Habit with Me"?) Or, failing that, one or both of his swan songs, sacred and profane—the

haunting theme music of the Grant-Kerr edition of *An Affair to Remember* or our subject's last tip of the cap to his own origins, the droll "That's Amore," which parodies Italian pop so well that it's become part of it?

Then there are the TV commercials that keep so many old songs in subliminal circulation, but most recently Warren's "At Last," "The Gold Diggers' Song (We're in the Money)," and "About a Quarter to Nine," all of which I've heard peddling products, and I'm not even a serious couch potato. TV has also dished out numerous Warren classics in its retrospectives of other people that he helped to make famous, most particularly Busby Berkeley, who seems to be being celebrated every time I turn on the set, but also of Betty Grable, Ruby Keeler, and the Glenn Miller Orchestra, among others. Although Warren was never sure that Busby even liked music as such, Buzz was obviously the right scene-designer-cum-drill-sergeant at the right time in movie history, so his name is now the only one on the old musicals (as in Busby Berkeley's *Gold Diggers of 1933*) while Warren, whose songs old Buzz depended and insisted on, left his name on nothing.

In fact, as a kind of postmortem pie in the face, two main studios, Warner Bros. and Twentieth Century–Fox, even managed to leave Harry's name out of their own self-congratulatory retrospectives toward the end of the last century. They were both (quite justly) as pleased as punch over their great musicals, and about such performers as Keeler and Alice Faye and the Nicholas Brothers, but modest to a fault about the songwriter they'd hired to supply the music. And Twentieth Century really rubbed the whipped cream into Harry's headstone when it showed a clip of Irving Berlin instead, sitting by his obligatory pool. Although Irving had indeed batted out a couple of those famous musicals for Fox, he was better remembered for his work at RKO and Paramount, and was not in the least central to the Fox story.

So okay—they weren't really all out to get Harry. Popular history goes with the names everyone knows, and you don't clutter people's minds with new names at this late date. But it wouldn't have fooled our subject for a moment because the studio had retroactively played right into the great Harry Warren–Irving Berlin joke—a mock-epic feud between the two men, which, as Burton Lane assured me, really was a joke—up to a point.

The best way to picture Harry Warren is, I gather, to imagine a sensitive little guy with a Roman nose and the conversational style of an old-fashioned New York cabbie, which meant that he always sounded annoyed about something or other, but how annoyed was he really this time? Since the complaints never stopped coming, they served as a perfect cover for the speaker's real feelings. One never knew for sure whether the cabdriver really hated the mayor, or whether Warren hated Berlin. Over the years, Harry played every kind of riff on his major gripe, namely, his world-famous anonymity, about which he could be genuinely humorous, à la mode de Rodney Dangerfield, or unmistakably bitter, when his lifelong rash got the occasional better of him.

But as with the old cabbie, the overall impression Warren made was of a man with a basically good nature, and he wound up one of the most popular guys in what remained of Hollywood. And, after all, he did have something to grumble about. During the years they were competing, Warren actually had more songs on the Hit Parade than Irving Berlin, but you'd never have guessed it from the papers or the fan magazines or even from the conversations of quite knowledgeable people, many of whom have still never heard of him. If Irving Berlin was a King Midas who didn't even have to touch things to turn them to gold, Warren was the Invisible Man. He could make a fortune too, but he couldn't show up to claim it—almost literally on one occasion. When he turned up at the Academy to pick up his Oscar, at first he wasn't allowed in. He didn't look the part.

Harry got the joke and knew it was funny, but it was also maddening, and it had gone on too long. Still, friends like Burton Lane and Harold Arlen took advantage of this competition with Berlin, fanning the feud every chance they got, one time going so far as to print up a playbill proclaiming "Irving Berlin's new production of *42nd Street*" in the hopes of hearing a gratifying growl out of Warren, and perhaps a funny line, such as his most, and only, famous one in World War II, "They bombed the wrong Berlin."

But even this apparent score over Irving wound up being just another joke on Warren himself, because (1) the line became famous immediately but Harry didn't and the crack about him soon became "His name could vanish from the page while you were looking at it," and (2) life would eventually imitate jest by producing some *actual* playbills that read "David

Merrick's *42nd Street,"* omitting Harry's name yet again for the whole ten years that show first ran on Broadway and replacing his name with that of a *real* megalomaniac.

And although he has picked up some random champions over the years, including Michael Feinstein and a guy I heard from in the Kalamazoo area who persuaded Mayor Giuliani to name a Brooklyn block after Harry, his luck never seems to turn enough to stay turned. As I write this, *42nd Street* is back where it belongs and occasionally honors his name. But the name refuses to stick or really register. In a recent uncomprehending biography of Irving Berlin, the author doesn't seem to know much about Warren except for his obvious credits, and "the joke," but he adds gratuitously that he doesn't know if Warren was anti-Semitic.

Seldom would evidence have been easier to find if he'd felt Warren was worth looking into. Just about everyone who counted in Warren's life was Jewish, most particularly his closest friend, Harold Arlen, with whom he toured Europe in the 1950s, and his beloved partners, Al Dubin and Mack Gordon, as well as his living hero, Jerome Kern—who was not only Jewish but almost as famous as Irving Berlin (fame in general was not a problem for Warren, just Berlin's fame). This was the gang Harry chose to run with in Hollywood, as opposed to, let's say, the Walter Donaldsons or the Jimmy McHughs. And before that he had kept the same sort of company in New York, working with and enjoying among others his soon-to-be lifelong friend Ira Gershwin and the nerve-racking Billy Rose, who took big bows and major money for just supplying the title to Warren's early hit "I Found a Million Dollar Baby (in a Five and Ten Cent Store)." Rose was widely resented by other writers for just such tricks, but not by Warren, who admired Billy for having precisely what he lacked himself, the gift for promotion. He felt Rose's salesmanship, which would later run to aquacades and live elephants, was worth his cut anytime.

But perhaps the real reason he liked Billy so much was that the little man's vitality, inventiveness, and mind-boggling audacity reminded Warren of New York, and Harry loved to be reminded of New York. Which brings us to Warren's defining crotchet number two—giving Irving Berlin a rest. ("Let the bum get his own chapter.") By the midthirties, Al Dubin must presumably have had at least two earfuls of his partner's homesick-

ness and decided to give the old boy a present in the form of a lyric that expressed the problem perfectly. Although the words of "Lullaby of Broadway" probably described Al Dubin's nightlife a lot better than Harry's, the sounds are all Warren's and all New York, with its rumbling subways and rattling taxis and its inimitable phrases. "The daffydils who entertain at Angelo's and Maxie's"—where else would you hear them called "daffydils," or did Dubin make that up himself? New Yorkers were always doing this to you—coining new words, or borrowing them from other countries or parts of this one. Times Square alone was and is a great clearinghouse for words, and Harry with his great ear must have missed them a lot more than he missed Angelo's or Maxie's. So if you're lucky enough to hear Warren sing "Lullaby" himself (a rare tape exists of this), you're probably as close to his essence, his soul, as one could get. This is Harry's signature song and his signature voice too—light, breezy, and smart—and you realize that perhaps his accent and his attitude were themselves mementos of New York, lovingly preserved in brine and marinated in the toxic air of Los Angeles. When his young friend and disciple Michael Feinstein asked him one day about his somewhat stylized grouchiness, Harry was at something of a loss to explain it. But perhaps it's obvious: He grumbled because New Yorkers grumbled; it was the first sound you heard in those days. Even the daffodils grumbled between numbers. And everyone in L.A. was so damn upbeat and positive, someone had to complain around here.

And while I'm reading his mind, I'd guess that much of the fuss with Berlin dates back to "Lullaby" too, which beat out Irving's entry, "Cheek to Cheek," for the 1935 Oscar, to the reported annoyance of Berlin. But "Lullaby" had as many associations for Warren as "Always" had for Berlin and was definitely the wrong song to pick on. And no doubt Harry thought, doesn't Irving have enough awards already? Aren't I allowed to win at least once around here?

Berlin was only a symbol of Warren's anonymity, and incidentally Harry wasn't the only songwriter to jeer at Irving for hogging all the fame. In his usual self-mocking mode, Harry might have pointed out that he had never had a chance anyway, Berlin or no Berlin, because he'd been born on Christmas Day, which meant that he'd been upstaged from day one. By

which reading, God undoubtedly summoned up the Great Depression just to annoy Harry Warren, and invented Hollywood too, in the same malicious let's-get-Harry spirit.

But on more serious inspection, Harry's bad luck looks much like everyone else's bad luck, except that he had more of it. When people hear a tune, apparently it's not in their nature to ask, who wrote that? But in New York, they tell you anyway, loud and clear. In movies, they told you once quietly, and it didn't stick. You were lucky, in fact, to keep the reputation you came in with.

It's a toss-up. Different names stick in different heads. Sammy Fain is an easy one, because it sounds like Tin Pan Alley. Likewise, the team of DeSylva, Brown, and Henderson stayed familiar for a while after its heyday in the 1920s, but only in that form. You had to be a real fanatic to know which one wrote the tune, or even what all their first names were. And when DeSylva quit, Brown and Henderson sounded completely unfamiliar. Better to be called Tin Pan Alley–sounding Sammy Fain, or Ray Noble, which arrestingly changes the subject, or just about anything but Harry Warren, who had a further handicap: He wrote so many hits that they began to sound like typical movie songs, straight off the assembly line.

The idea of a one-man assembly line turning out quality products might spell genius on Broadway, but was just more mass production in Hollywood, where the more hits he wrote the more of a hack he was assumed to be. If only he'd made his mark earlier, like Rodgers or Porter, or even been born later like Jerry Herman and Stephen Sondheim—when Broadway was un-Depressed and there was no Hollywood left to get lost in. So Harry's worst luck was simply having had all his best years during the great movie blackout, and what made it hurt so much is that they were such very good years. If you enjoy the sight of jaws dropping, read a list of Warren's movie titles and stand back. Of course, by now these don't sound particularly commercial, any more than Gershwin's movie songs do.

Yet in another sense, he wasn't unlucky. If one takes fame off the scale for a moment and measures his actual life next to those of the other superstars, his life looks pretty darn good, starting with his birth into a congenial family in a gorgeous part of New York and ending with his peaceful death in Hollywood some eighty-eight years later surrounded to the end by all the

creature comforts a rich man could want, and always by enough friends and admirers never to feel abandoned or insignificant. "Isn't it ridiculous that Harry isn't famous?" Everyone felt exactly as he did about it.

Like his fellow Brooklynite, George Gershwin, Harry Warren's talent appears to have come to him from out of the blue, genetically speaking. His family was of the cheerful Italian persuasion that, if you wanted to listen to some music today, you sang it yourself. And presumably, if you wanted to turn it off, you yelled, "Shut up!"

So, if that was how you did it, Harry would just do more of it. He would later describe his gift in terms of pure appetite, not necessarily for composition but simply for music itself. And in this spirit, he joined the local church choir—and here his luck ran very good indeed, because Brooklyn Heights boasted one of the rare Catholic churches in America to concentrate on the classical masses of Bach and Palestrina, which plunged Harry into both polyphony and plainchant faster and better than any music teacher could have. And Harry would always be preeminently a composer for the voice first, and for the ensemble of voices and instruments second.

So far, Harry's luck had begun okay and would continue so for a while when he got a job in a store that sounds too good to be true—a barbershop that sold musical instruments on the side. Naturally, in his greed, he learned all of them at once. And it is pleasant to picture, in a movie-biography sort of way, an unusually small kid in knickers feeling his way with a trombone slide as the full Glenn Miller Orchestra begins tentatively to play "Serenade in Blue" or another of Harry's grown-up songs on the soundtrack. Henceforth, all the odd jobs in Harry's life centered on music, one way or another, whether it was serving stints as the world's shyest song-plugger, or strumming piano chords to go with silent movies, and learning incidentally how to fit them around the contours of the storytelling. Long before talkies, accompanists were learning how to heighten movie themes with just the right music, or the right silence.

Songs have so many facets that every different job seemed to teach him something else about them, and Harry's occasional gigs playing home-style piano at parties perhaps also instructed him as to what people liked to dance to all night and what contrariwise would bring them around the piano attempting to sing.

The actual call to write his own songs came to him on his one ostensibly nonmusical beat as a humble employee of the U.S. Navy stationed
peacefully and dreamily at Montauk, Long Island, during World War I.
Once again, Harry got lucky in a small way. Stateside service can be a
great incubator of talent, and as the closest thing to an entertainer at that
particular camp, he got lots of chances to play for a captive and most contemporary audience.

One of the most surprising things to learn about this great writer of,
among other things, love songs, is that he himself got married in 1917 in
his twenty-second year, before he'd even been published, and he stayed a
homebody all his life, later claiming that he had never been to a single
Hollywood party, at least in the grand sense of the phrase, and that he
couldn't make even a short public appearance without getting slightly lit
beforehand. (I've heard a tape of him slurring an acceptance speech and
can attest that he sounds like a most amiable drunk, when he had to be.)
Harry loved people, but not in bulk, and he liked to talk, but he wasn't a
word-man, and one senses that his grumbling was partly a resort to verbal
formulas that seemed to amuse people.

The obvious question is, Why on earth should such a quiet soul love
New York so ardently, and hate Los Angeles so? Give or take a swimming
pool, what difference did it make? The answer, as always, is music, and
the pleasure of learning step by step that he could create it himself, and
that he loved the other people making it, and best of all, that he could
hear it all over town, leaking out of theaters and drumming through publishing offices and at the parties he did go to in those days, in the only way
he felt comfortable, as a musician. To those of us who don't have the call,
the total confidence this shy man felt at the piano is the astonishing part,
because truth to tell, he wasn't all that good at it. ("I play better than
Berlin, though," he told Max Wilk defensively. "And Jerry Kern too.") But
the thing was, Harry was at home in music, and felt easy and unembar-
rassed as he slopped around his musical home.

Warren's songwriting career got off to a stuttering start, as if he didn't
really believe it yet. His first minor hit, "Rose of the Rio Grande" (1922),
was followed by nothing much—a light patter of forgotten titles—until he
suddenly broke out in 1925 with a really big one, the utterly 1920s-
sounding "I Love My Baby (My Baby Loves Me)," which encouraged him

to step up production to something like full-time. But the dam hadn't yet broken by any means. Around the same time, he wrote a funny little immigrant song called "Where Do You Work-a, John?" that the school kids were still singing when I came to the States a generation later. Then in another two years one more, "Nagasaki," and that was it until after the market crash—a pleasant trickle of minor titles that left Harry serenely jogging in the middle of the Broadway pack as the good times ended. On a happiness graph, he'd had a wonderful decade, and it would seem a bit more wonderful every year he moved further from it. But there was precious little about his track record or his personality to suggest anything like greatness or even a wish for it. He wasn't built on that scale and apparently didn't want to be. "One of the boys" is a nice thing to be too, and his lack of recognition should have made it easy to remain one for the rest of his days.

A teaspoon of ambition sooner might have saved him a lot of groaning later. Because things really began to happen in 1930. There were some hungry lyricists and entrepreneurs wheeling around Broadway that year, as if they knew the end was coming, and Harry began to get enough assignments to qualify for the law I've named after him, that if you get to bat often enough, both your game and your chances improve exponentially, and the hits come. At any rate, that year he wrote his best song so far, with Billy Rose and an ex-vaudevillian, Mort Dixon, called "Would You Like to Take a Walk?" and a charming number with the already famous Ira Gershwin, "Cheerful Little Earful," a step up in itself, and then as a harbinger of things to come, his first song for the movies.

Hollywood had just bought the Rodgers and Hart show *Spring Is Here,* and as usual, gutted it, and was looking around for parts. Harry took his first trip West—and hated it on sight. After contributing an ephemeral hit called "Absence Makes the Heart Grow Fonder (For Somebody Else)" he hightailed it back East, no doubt complaining all the way. He had seen the future, and it was awful. "It looked like a small town in South Dakota" was how he described his first impression of Hollywood to Terry-Thomas, or "like being on an Indian reservation." I can verify that as late as 1950, when Warren's best years were behind him, Los Angeles still seemed like a cow town to eastern eyes, with a defiantly antiquated-looking trolley clanking its way from a vestigial downtown to a string of minimalist

beaches without a dune or an honest-to-God wave to be seen. The water moved just enough to prove it wasn't a lake, and it didn't so much invite you in as put up with you when you got there—if, that is, you were one of those eastern nerve-cases keen on swimming. For everyone else, the beach was just another place to have one's picture taken and to be discovered by a famous producer.

It was almost enough to make a man miss Coney Island on a steamy Fourth of July weekend, and Harry raced back to New York as fast as a three-day train ride could carry him. This so-called Depression couldn't last forever, could it? In the years 1929 through 1931, the whole nation was holding its breath about this, and Broadway buzzed with nervous energy and spasms of wild optimism. Harry wrote two more megahits, "I Found a Million Dollar Baby" and "You're My Everything," which might have attracted more attention if Cole Porter and his first songs hadn't hit town around the same time. Still, they got just enough notice to place Warren on the brink of fame, if Broadway would just hang on a little bit longer.

It seems in retrospect as if Broadway might well have weathered the Depression just fine if that had been its only problem, as the London West End would survive World War II. Theater thrives on hard times. As Londoners later testified, the London Blitz actually made theater-going more exciting. There's nothing like the sound of bombs falling outside and the sight of ushers sealing up doors and windows to keep all the light inside to bring Shakespeare to total life.

But what Broadway could not so easily compete with was the news of good times happening somewhere else in the country. And as the Depression dug itself in, the combination of high movie salaries for the actors, cheap movie tickets for the public, and the sheer novelty of a new art form that made the stage seem obsolete, began to strip Broadway of both talent and customers—not all of either, fortunately: Broadway survived the thirties and had some glorious moments too, but they were partly subsidized by Hollywood and there were never enough to go around or to provide a reliable living for more than a few people. So Arthur Schwartz made it on Broadway, but was unlucky in Hollywood. It was still the wrong way to bet, and by 1931, just about everyone you'd ever heard of, including all

the famous songwriters, had been to Hollywood at least once; and while most hated it every bit as much as Harry did, they would all be back.

Well, at least Harry liked train rides. He also got some great songs out of them and the places they went, like Buffalo and Chattanooga, and even out of the train lines themselves, like the famous Atchison, Topeka, and Santa Fe Railway. By 1931, it must have been clear that while his star might be rising in the East, the light itself was failing in that area. Like it or not, he had better go West again at least for a while. (Nobody ever went yet for more than a while.)

By chance, Warner Bros. had reached the same conclusion. While his relatively hot streak lasted, they wanted Warren out there immediately to write the music for a new musical called *42nd Street*. It was a fateful moment, because after the first flourish of movie musicals, the form had started dying almost immediately. The studios would never fathom the fact that musicals are always dying, or else being reborn, or both at once; they need constant resuscitation by new talents and styles, from, for instance, Maurice Chevalier to Bing Crosby to Dean Martin and Jerry Lewis to the end of that particular line.

Anyhow, the Warner execs dramatically decided to terrify the bankers with one all-or-nothing roll of the dice. Since movie musicals always died of the same thing, namely, costing too much, the studio chose to fight fire with fire by spending twice as much as ever for this next one, and as proof of intent, they signed up Busby Berkeley, the boy wonder and budget-buster extraordinaire. A modest success would get them nowhere. The musical *42nd Street* had to be a smash, or it would serve as the last great meal the movie musical would have before its execution.

Harry Warren was ready for the pressure, and ready also to go from two hit songs a year tops to sometimes two or more hits a movie, starting with this most crucial one. The title song itself has an epic quality to it, as if to say "I now declare this era open." The movie *42nd Street* gives you not just New York, even better to my mind than "Lullaby of Broadway" does, but almost the exact year in New York, something Harry had never come close to while he was still living there. Like Thomas Wolfe in London and James Joyce in Zurich and Trieste, it seemed he needed to step this far back from his subject to see it properly. But like Wolfe's Asheville and

Joyce's Dublin, the Warren version of New York would remain stubbornly in the past. Later in life, when he might easily have gone back there to stay, it wasn't there anymore. So he stayed in the land he hated, for keeps.

But it was too soon to worry about that now. In 1931 (and in 1932 and 1933 and 1934) Harry still planned to take the money and run back to God's country (and Gershwin's), where he belonged, not realizing yet that, as S. J. Perelman put it, they paid you in magic money out there that vanished as you flew over the Rockies. Right now Harry was hot, and his title song for *42nd Street* was joined by two other gems: "Shuffle Off to Buffalo" and one of Sinatra's hardy perennials, "You're Getting to Be a Habit with Me," which makes as good a place as any to introduce Harry's new partner, the one made in heaven for him, who had just helped Warren as he had never been helped before. Harry had already worked briefly with Al Dubin in New York, but that didn't count because that was when he was working with everybody. The Hollywood contract system allowed for no such promiscuity. The studios couldn't afford to sign up an alley full of guys and wait for them to find each other. If you didn't have a partner, they matched you up with someone from the office pool and hoped for the best.

Sometimes arranged marriages work out better than love matches, and besides, these two guys had something important in common. Each had been groping his way through the transition from the mostly funny song to the great ballad takeover. Dubin had already scored a major hit in between modes with "Tiptoe Through the Tulips" (music: Joe Burke), which was such a prime example of a funny-tender compromise with whimsy and sentiment that he too had received an RSVP from Warner Bros. that coincided with Harry's. So *42nd Street* was crucial for Al too, and blessedly the script was right up his street, because it was about the world they had both just come from, and it seemed to be set in the year before last, their best year, so there was nothing stopping them from homing in on the territory of Arthur Freed and Nacio Brown and getting it right this time. Where *The Broadway Melody* had presented an elegant fantasy of Broadway made in Hollywood, *42nd Street* was the real thing and one knew it right away.

Away they went, in a cloud of song titles, which in no time had become pretty much transferable from one silly story to another. The speed of this

is worth stressing because Warren's best shot at recognition had probably already come and gone with *42nd Street*. At that point, he had just helped to bring movie musicals back to life and thus incidentally kept the business open for countless entertainers and colleagues who now had no place else to go—no vaudeville and not much Broadway. But if he expected a round of applause for this, he didn't know Hollywood. Certainly none of the other concerned parties were talking about him. The actors had their own places in the sun to worry about, and were fully occupied just trying to keep Busby Berkeley from absorbing all the rays himself—a contest that the studios viewed benignly. May they both win! But the writers—what writers? Movie songs were just there, don't worry about it. Go back to your nice dream.

The time was never riper, but if Warren wanted fame, he had to get it himself, preferably by doing something completely irrelevant, like suing the studio, or joining the Abraham Lincoln Brigade or setting fire to his contract—anything but writing. The one way he could never get it was simply by writing more great songs.

Unfortunately, that was the only way he wanted to get it. The second best-known story about Warren tells of how he once hired a press agent, and fired the man almost immediately for getting his name in the paper— probably for being sighted at a screening, or some other incendiary event. Like many people who have had to work all their lives, Warren knew the value of a dollar. Reading about where he'd been last night was not it.

So his lifelong attitude began to form: of resignation, anger, irony, and perhaps maddening, indestructible hope—dashed again and again—that this time would be different, and that one more hit might win him his elusive fame.

But if such a song or show existed, he had already written it with *42nd Street,* or if not that one, with his next, *Gold Diggers of 1933,* which also stands out from the pack because at that primal stage, its formula of showgirls "making it" still seemed fresh, even to moviemakers, and the Depression itself seemed relatively fresh, a scary but perhaps manageable blip on the business cycle that would be ironed out any day now by sheer high spirits and optimism. Anyhow, Hollywood did its bit, and here was its latest pitch: that for every old-timer moping around cadging dimes, there was a kid out there who was "in the money," having found shiny new op-

portunities in the debris and most particularly in show biz, a miracle industry that seemed to be laying on new workers almost as fast as the other businesses were laying them off. So might it not be possible for show business to turn this whole thing around single-handed? "Old Man Depression, you are through, you've done us wrong."

Those first Warren-Berkeley movies have an additional poignancy because they ignore the extent to which Hollywood had already killed off so many other forms of show business. In those early days of talking pictures, it still seemed possible to think of Broadway as the Great White Way to fame and fortune, because in a way it still was—but not in the old way.

Although *Singin' in the Rain* exaggerated the problem of turning silent actors into talking ones, it was a real problem, and the studios still hadn't figured a better way to find and groom the latter than to grab them ready-made off the New York stage. So it was very much in Hollywood's interest to glorify Broadway and exaggerate its importance. "You're going to come back a star," says the producer. But in real life his next words would have been, "So I'll see you in Hollywood," as he waved his own ticket. Ginger Rogers, who first sang "The Gold Diggers' Song (We're in the Money)," nicely illustrated the way things really worked. After just one leading role on the stage, Ginger proceeded to a long career in movies, with an immortality bonus that the theater no longer guaranteed. Stars might be born on Broadway, but they grew and bloomed forever in Hollywood.

Not so with songwriters. They had to be big indeed on arrival to retain any size at all out there. Otherwise they shrank to the size of screen credits, and were almost as invisible as screenwriters and photographers.

What happened in between vestigial recognition and none at all could be summed up in a single phrase: "double features." In what looks from here like in no time flat, the talkies mutated from special events that you dressed up for to the stuff of habit and blue jeans. Distributors took to treating them that way by piling people's plates high twice a week with the audiovisual equivalent of junk food, mostly based on tiny variations on the exact same theme: different cartoon but same characters and setup—cat chases mouse, gets clobbered. Fade to newsreel—different beauty contest, same old Joe Louis; to travelogue—different island, same contrast of rich and poor, old and new, same regret upon leaving; to coming attrac-

tions, adventure serial, funny subject, and what have we here? The new Charlie Chan? Or the last Mr. Moto held over?

It was the second feature that clinched the incoherence, because even the voice over the telephone, supposing you could reach one, could no longer tell you within the nearest hour precisely when the main movie came on. And after a while, it seemed pretentious to ask. So you just "went to the movies" like everyone else, and enjoyed the total experience, buying popcorn during the credits, shushing new arrivals at big moments, and trying to remember when you came in yourself. ("Didn't we see this already?" "No, I think that was last week.") Also, you had to decide if you really wanted another set of dishes.

It was all highly exhilarating and American and vague, and a pop quiz afterward would have yielded a lot less information than the most ama- teur film buff knows today. "So what was the name of the second movie, anyway?" "I'm not sure, but I know the music was by Al Dubin and Harry Warren."

Fat chance. What you did remember in descending order of vividness was (1) the clumsy hippo who stepped on your foot, (2) the lady with the Carmen Miranda hat that she wouldn't, or perhaps couldn't, take off, and (3) the names of the stars, which in a couple of years the studios had learned how to mass-produce in daunting numbers. MGM boasted that it actually housed more stars than the sky itself, and would sporadically prove it with regimental photos covering every inch of the *Life* magazine centerfolds. And kids who couldn't even find World War II on a map had no trouble identifying every one of them. In a word, they were gods; and gods don't need writers.

That's where Harry's fame went, somewhere between "Coming soon to this theater" and "That's all, folks." It was almost enough to make a man move to Europe, where Harry had become famous almost immediately because the natives watched one movie at a time and the credits were part of the show, so you might as well enjoy them. Okay, it was only Eu- rope, and he only learned about it twenty years later when he finally went there. But at least Hollywood had paid Harry handsomely for his anonymity, in terms not only of cash but with assignments, and all the times at bat he could handle. Two sets of double features a week adds up

to an awful lot of films to fill with music, quite enough to exhaust a thin
talent or, in Warren's case, to reveal a major one. To the puzzlement and
admiration of old friends like the Gershwins, Warren got better as he
went along, until even he must have wondered whether Hollywood might
in some strange way be good for him. After all, no one in his New York
days had ever compared him to Irving Berlin, but that was because back
then he really, by sheer weight of numbers, wasn't in the same league.
Now he was, and the people who counted knew it. And if he didn't have
fame, he won the two next best things—grounds for endless complaint
and a suspiciously good life.

There were a lot worse ways to pass the Depression than playing golf
every afternoon with one's fellow writers—one's favorite game in one's favorite company—or, if you were Warren's partner Dubin, drinking and
eating your heart out at the Brown Derby, and if you were either of them,
cooling off as needed in the world's snazziest swimming pools.

And then there were the studios, which dotted the landscape like
shopping malls or fortified medieval towns, and which collectively were
Hollywood, the closest thing to a city you could find out there. And what
the commissaries lacked as restaurants, they made up for in the quality of
their customers, who constituted everybody who was anybody, and in
their gossip, which was of the very latest and dirtiest.

All these people knew who Harry Warren was and how good he was,
except, apparently, one lady who turned up in a typical Burton Lane anecdote that I wish I remembered better. It seems that Harry was also the
spitting image of the MGM studio doctor, so this lady ran up to him in
distress one day to tell him that his latest prescription had brought on all
kinds of horrible side effects, such as palpitations, itches, and God knew
what all, and he answered, "If I were you, I'd stop taking it immediately,"
before disappearing through the nearest door. Lane was in high spirits
himself as he told the story, but Warren didn't sound like an unhappy
man. And certainly when he and Dubin wrote their defining hymn to hard
times, "Remember My Forgotten Man," nobody supposed they were talking about themselves, affluent songwriters who couldn't get their names
in the paper. Well, boo-hoo.

So Warren joined the crowd and complained about the boss instead (at
Warner Bros.), and when the boss turned out to be okay (at Fox), he com-

plained about the boss's lawyers, and finally, when there was no boss left, what was happening to the nation's music. The arc of Harry's gripes tells the tale. In the first gold-digging days of talkies, amateurs such as producers and even the moguls themselves thought that they knew all about music, and you were lucky if they didn't think their nephews did too. So Harry resorted to playing one of these geniuses off another. "You don't like this one? That's funny, Jack Warner does."

Gradually, the real experts took over, but it still helped to play politics. Comparing Harry's groans with those of the East Coast champion, Richard Rodgers, one finds that the latter got a ceremonial welcome out of Louis B. Mayer, but no work to speak of. Meanwhile, Harry "got no respect," but more job offers than even he could cope with. So naturally he railed against the Broadway hotshot like Rodgers who got all the glory, while Rodgers himself whined about the studio hacks who got all the plum assignments.

Time in Hollywood starts and stops and starts again, but the one thing it has never done is just keep rolling peacefully along for a few years. While it may have looked for a moment as if there'd be no end to the Busby Berkeley cycle, suddenly it was over. And Warner Bros. hired the new rage, Johnny Mercer, with a view perhaps to replacing Dubin, who could take a hint and moved to New York, where he more or less imploded, from too much of everything you can have too much of, although the food alone would probably have done it. Three hundred pounds must have seemed even bigger in those days, and as he wrote in one of his last songs with Harry, "Just a little filthy lucre buys a lot of things." So he hit New York again to see how far his Hollywood lucre would go. After all, Harry had only written the tunes; the daffodils and Broadway babies were Dubin's ideas. And he would die of an excess of everything before the lucre ran out.

Thus ended the first phase of Harry's career, with all guns firing. "Lulu's Back in Town," "She's a Latin from Manhattan," "September in the Rain," and a lot of filthy lucre in *his* pockets too. Also already present, a legendary hatred of Hollywood that he could dine out on forever.

So why didn't Harry go back to New York too? Perhaps he liked Hollywood better than he pretended—or perhaps his wife did, or his children. They counted too. Harry's life was far from a typical show biz one, full of flashy career moves and caprice. And something else happened the year

Dubin left. Harry would always call himself a good family man, but he didn't say anything about being a happy one, and from 1938 on, he almost certainly wasn't one, because that spring the Warrens' nineteen-year-old and only son, Harry Jr., died of pneumonia, and it seems that it was possible to blame Harry for not getting him to the hospital in time. In the best accounts of what happened next, his wife never quite forgave him; and in the worst, she had no more to do with him at all.

There are always huge blanks in any marriage, and there may have been some good days even at the Warrens'. But it seems like thin pickings for a family man, even if you throw in a lovely daughter and a couple of grandchildren; and a contemporary reader has to wonder why Harry didn't just listen to his own songs and swing a little, like his fellow Catholics Jimmy McHugh and Bing Crosby, who, at least intermittently, made out like bandits under cover of Catholicism. This was Hollywood, after all, which was an occasion of sin in itself. So make a good confession, my son, give lots of money, and try to be a good example when you have a moment and somebody's watching.

Yet, allowing again for blanks, the answer seems to have been probably nix on the swinging. Since Harry had sung in all those good choirs as a kid, chances were he'd learned something about the Church as well, and knew that the Spencer Tracy Exception, as we'll call it, was just a little too good to be true. Spencer would fry for it someday, or at least do some serious time in purgatory. Instead, Harry most likely joined that small legion of "Graham Greene" Catholics who believed that being true to a bad marriage was the heart of the matter.

Of such types, and there were a lot of them, I can say from fuzzy, youthful memory that they did not necessarily act particularly gloomy, but seemed to draw genuine strength from their faith, along with a serene conviction, rare in anyone, that they were somehow on the right track and that their lives meant something.

The other thing about them, which fits Harry too, is that they tended to fill the empty spaces in life with sheer hard work. The Warrens' marriage may have died in 1938, but his talent rose from the ashes soon afterward, and kept on rising. "You'll find your life will begin/the very moment you're in Argentina" is not a song line you'd normally associate with a broken heart, nor is "Chattanooga Choo Choo" two years later. By then,

World War II was breaking up non-Catholic marriages as well, quite brutally, and smiling through the tears and soldiering on were much in vogue, so that perhaps it's no coincidence that novelist Graham Greene and his fellow Catholics harped on it so much in wartime and right afterward. But I should stress here that I'm just guessing about Harry, as I am periodically about all these guys. Harry definitely belongs to the school of Catholics that does not carry on about it, and I'll gladly follow his lead on this.

So Warren, equipped now with a sad home life, acquired an unpromising partner at work, lyricist Mack Gordon. Frank Loesser describes Mack as ranting on about something or other at an ASCAP meeting while the audience slept, and while Johnny Mercer actually read a newspaper, and a friend once told me a firsthand, slightly slanderous anecdote concerning Gordon's unrequited love of a chorus girl, all of which adds up to a bore by day and a strikeout at night.

Luckily, Gordon's lyrics were, in Mark Twain's phrase, quite a bit better than they sounded. To begin with, Gordon offers an advanced lesson in why good song lyrics don't have to be great poetry. For a reputed windbag, he had a wonderful ear for the regular phrases people were using that year. "I'm going to send a wire, 'hopping on a flyer,' leaving today." Only in 1941! And an even better ear for fitting them on the right notes, for example, the innocuous phrase "how long can a guy go on dreaming," which attached to Harry's tune "I Had the Craziest Dream," still brings back World War II as vividly as any line I can think of, with the possible exception of Frank Loesser's "Why'd you have to turn off all that sunshine?" The scene I picture in both cases is someplace like Penn Station, piled high with duffel bags and lined from wall to wall with gobs and GIs waiting, waiting, waiting . . .

It wasn't literary, and singers with a taste for good writing tend to shy away from Gordon's lyrics. "The More I See You," for instance, has a wonderful singer's melody—but who wants to get his chops around "I know the only one for me could only be you"? If, as Samuel Taylor Coleridge says, a poem is like a palace that must also be a good house, this lyric is like a Quonset hut that hasn't been lived in yet. And the lyrics of "At Last" or even of Harry's biggest hit, "You'll Never Know," are not much better. The words of the ballads are consistently undistinguished second-class

verse saved by the music. No wonder Gordon's own love life was not an unbroken success. Admittedly, he picked up nicely for half-funny novelty songs such as "Chattanooga Choo Choo" and wonderfully for the handful of Brazilian imitations he and Harry concocted for the Portuguese bomb-shell Carmen Miranda ("Boom-chicka-boom"). But when it came to the million ways of saying "I love you," he returned to the back of the line. But oh, those tunes. At least Gordon obeyed the first rule of the lyricist's code, "at least do no harm"—and is it possible that just in terms of sound he might have done something to help?

For an answer, one turns to Warren's most beautiful song of all, "There Will Never Be Another You." There one finds, amid the clumsiness and the clichés, four ordinary little words that turn a good number into a great one, "There will be other songs to sing (pause) Another fall, another spring." Not beautiful perhaps, but beautifully efficient, and Warren him-self put his finger on how this worked when he said, "He had an innate sense of song."

Apparently Gordon needed to hear each new tune over and over again like a musical illiterate, but when he got it, he got the whole thing from the punchy first line to the well-articulated caboose. "When I hear that serenade in blue," sounds in performance much more powerful than the words deserve. The trick for the listener is to turn off the switch that tells you what words mean. Forget you know English altogether if you can and just listen, for instance, to the pounding of that bridge, "It seems like only yesterday a small café, a crowded floor . . ." That goes double for "I Know Why." You'll find yourself listening closely to the first line and you'll re-member it forever, "Why do robins sing in December?" But your attention veers off from there. Who really cares why the little so-and-so's sing then, if they even do? This is the standard song about a guy falling in love and hallucinating, right? Enough said.

Like most teams, Warren and Gordon arrived at these blends of great music and mesmeric words along the following conventional lines: The lyricist comes up with a theme and a title, which the composer tries to translate into music before handing it back to the other guy for further decoration, or "songing." And the main question is, do we have to fit this into a story of some kind or can we just concentrate on selling the mother? Clearly, the proof of this latter kind of writing was on the Hit Parade, and

Gordon did so well on it that you could almost suppose that he had crammed for it like for an examination, as if his life depended upon it.

By this time, Warren had become a very big man indeed on campus, if nowhere else, and helping him onto the Hit Parade seemed like the minimum requirement for working with him at all. Otherwise there were several hundred perennial lyricists out there forever ready to pounce, who made their living from pouncing, in fact—and maybe the best of them, Leo Robin, would write a warning wartime hit with Warren right under Gordon's nose. "No Love, No Nothin'" was not just pretty but was clever enough to be on Broadway, maybe even taking Harry with it someday.

But in the suspended animation of wartime, the Hit Parade was still the accepted stock exchange. Nobody was about to argue with it until at least V-E Day. So Gordon concentrated on making Warren's sounds as catchy as they could be, and the hits kept coming and have astonishingly been enjoyed to this day by all the world, as if they really were great, words and all.

After which, Harry changed studios, and Mack was out on the street—not because he had done anything worse than usual, or even because Warren was trying to get rid of him. Warren was as loyal to individuals as he was vindictive about institutions. He seemed to have been genuinely sorry to lose any partner to the system. But his vendetta against Fox's lawyers remained the first order of peacetime business. It seems these shysters had once taken him off salary while he sweated out an inconvenient attack of pneumonia, and although he was no Tony Soprano, some scores must be settled. And it might be worth recalling that his own son had died of pneumonia just a couple of years earlier. Getting it himself may have been an unusually intense experience for Harry.

On the other side of the fence, Arthur Freed had his own list of favorite lyricists, very much including himself. Even before Warren technically left Fox, he found himself collaborating with his future employer on the beautiful "This Heart of Mine," for use when he got to MGM. Thus began what Harry Warren always swore were the happiest days of his life.

Warren's insistence on the absolute wonderfulness of his MGM years gives rise to several thoughts and guesses, because professionally speaking, only one of these years was really good, while the rest were so-so verging on ominous. If Harry had simply wanted what we all want—less work

for more money—after the grind of Warner Bros. and Fox, okay. But that is one of those dreams you have to be careful about, because by the time he had left his utopia a half decade or so later, he was down to almost no work at all.

Still, he held tight to his memory of unalloyed happiness throughout, and there's no reason not to let him have it, if only in comparison with most other writers who were getting no work at all. Nevertheless, only his first year was really good by his own standards.

Every serious grumbler needs to have something ideal to point to just to prove that he knows the difference. Being hard to please is fine, but being impossible to please is just annoying. So attention should be paid to Harry's good year, and bits of the others. To begin with, the chances of any kind of happiness at MGM hung entirely on the whim of Louis B. Mayer, a guy famous for making life a living hell for people he didn't like—for example, the Marx Brothers. However, Louis B. could also make life pleasant indeed for those he fancied. And whatever his personal feelings toward Warren (if he had any—he could be vague about the identities of underlings), he decided just then that he loved musicals, classy ones, that is, and would make the whole operation positively heavenly—for a while. Through Freed, he would grant Warren his own bungalow, or home away from home, and the run of the Versailles of movie studios in its last gorgeous flush. And on the professional side, Harry also had the run, via Freed, of Louis B. Mayer's wallet. So what lyricist would Harry like today, besides myself, of course? And what actors and directors?

The result was one of the last great original musicals to come out of anywhere. *The Harvey Girls* had words by Johnny Mercer, and starred Judy Garland and Ray Bolger, all at their very best. Warren's score too shows him not just shining but incandescent, courtesy of all the overwork he'd recently been getting at his previous sweatshops. Warner Bros. and Fox might have worked him like a dog, but they bred a champion, and to borrow a phrase ballplayers use during the World Series, he would have all winter to rest.

Starting almost immediately. It was still only 1946 when *The Harvey Girls* came out—still wartime, culturally speaking, but without the rationing. But already TV was rumbling in the distance, and Hollywood would soon be hauling out its biggest guns to counter it, such as the best

of the Gershwins for *An American in Paris*, Arthur Schwartz for *The Band Wagon*, and Rodgers, Kern, and Porter for what were laughingly called biographies but were more like music racks. And Freed found a few minor names that could be turned into big guns too, for at least one movie. What separated the great writers from the good ones was sometimes merely their sheer volume, and if you could make, let's say, five or more great films out of Gershwin, maybe you could eke out at least one (*Three Little Words*) from the great vaudeville team of Bert Kalmar and Harry Ruby, and another from Arthur Freed himself and his buddy Nacio Brown. Arthur was not the least shy about invoking his own droit du seigneur, or boss's privilege, and he asked the great writing team of Comden and Green to "make me a star," or at least immortalize my songs, and oh my, did they ever! *Singin' in the Rain* would turn out to be the biggest gun ever—the joke being that I possibly saw it just once in a movie house, and at least a dozen times since on dreaded TV, that medium the movies never managed to kill.

In the face of this gaudy barrage of masterpieces, even the best original musicals inevitably began to seem quite pale. Using a simple memory test, I find such average scores as Warren's *The Barkleys of Broadway* and his *Summer Stock* have faded almost completely while several others are now completely unfamiliar, maybe because they didn't last long enough or get distributed widely enough to be generally seen. Suddenly the odds against them were too high. Even the original *42nd Street* or the miraculous early Astaires had never coughed up more than four or five great songs, but Freed's all-star teams routinely carried nine or ten. Even Harry couldn't compete with MGM's whole inventory, which now contained everything Freed wanted. So if my cast-iron prejudice is the least correct, that musicals are basically only as good as their songs, the jig was almost up with new musicals even before TV had completed its conquest.

Hollywood had cut its own throat in anticipation but, incidentally, left a few necks like Warren's hanging by threads in the process. After all the modified, "writer-cized" hoopla surrounding Harry's arrival at MGM, the enthusiasm for him proved to be as ephemeral as most Hollywood enthusiasms. By the time his contract with MGM was over, circa 1952, he was happy to accept a one-shot call from Bing Crosby at Paramount (hit song, "Zing a Little Zong," words by Leo Robin) and others from Jerry Lewis,

who needed songs for his still relatively shy partner, Dean Martin, and who would get almost more than he could have bargained for. It was as if Harry, fully aware of his mortality by now, killed two birds with one song. Not only would Warren give Martin the best, most characteristic piece of work in Dino's career, but Warren also proved that he himself was as good and unbelievably versatile as ever. Although upon first thought "That's Amore" (words: Jack Brooks) might seem like the exact opposite of a great song, at that time and in that situation it took a great craftsman to write it.

It's hard to believe, but we've still only reached 1953, because by then the writing was all over the wall for Warren. Arthur Freed even contemplated a drastic reduction of his *own* schedule. So much history had come and gone that World War II seemed like ancient times; Stalin's death, the rise and fall of Joe McCarthy, and the beginning and end of a whole new war in Korea, with its own little postwar. It was time for the music to move along as well, and for the revival houses to give up or turn into TV studios, and for the writers to go into their final grumbles.

The endless natural war between musicals and inflation was well and truly over if the musical itself wasn't that popular anymore. Within not much more than a year, the remaining writers in Hollywood found themselves down to their last gimmick—title songs. Or at least so the Oscars say. In 1953, Sammy Fain won the top prize with a traditional and quite characteristic jazz song, "Secret Love," which might have won in any year, but he then came back in 1955 to win it again with a piece of featureless mush called "Love Is a Many-Splendored Thing" that might have been written by anybody. In between, Jule Styne played hooky from Broadway, where he was still safe, long enough to win the 1954 Oscar with "Three Coins in the Fountain"—mush to end all mush! Without being told, you *know* it's a film title. And here the bull session aspect of this book must take over for a moment, as one recalls the novelty of seeing bits of the movie run before the credits, and then run right in back of them—wow, typescript and music and action all at once—and the novelty of hearing title songs that were literally about the movie. *High Noon* kicked off a bunch of those—"He made a vow while in state's prison."

Any way you sliced it, it came down to just one song per movie, and even that made a weak reed for a whole profession to lean on because it was only as sturdy as the gimmick itself. Perhaps that was only there to

keep ASCAP happy until the studios were safely out of the music-publishing business altogether, and could let it sink quietly back in the East.

Since theme music was virtually the last game left, it seemed only fair that Warren should take twice as much time as usual to provide maybe the best ever piece of it before going down with the whole ship himself. The Charles Boyer classic *Love Affair* was about to be handed over to the new king, Cary Grant, and by the time everyone had calmed down and finished the coronation, Harry had worked longer on the title song, "An Affair to Remember," than he had usually been allowed for whole movies. He had turned it into haunting background music as well, and a successful pop song in its own right.

He had not planned for it to be his swan song, and in a strict sense it was not. But for all that history cared, it could have been—unless, that is, history discovers something new. For instance, my own scorecard gives Warren five more years, courtesy of a beautiful Latin mass that Michael Feinstein sent me part of recently, which Harry had finished in 1962, the year Catholics went off the Latin standard. But the Church has been known to change its mind over the centuries, and maybe Harry will be revived in vestments someday as a good Catholic boy. He earned it.

And who knows what else Michael might come up with? Right after serving hard time at the Gershwins, Feinstein went to work on Harry's files and found him a much more congenial host. And perhaps the arrival on the scene of such a brilliant archivist-musician might in itself be considered a mark of fortune's favor, as if history had finally decided to give Harry a break—long after he'd left the room, that is. In fact, his life had already ended on a typically mixed note.

On the plus side, the rapacious David Merrick undertook the first stage version of *42nd Street,* which would balloon into the best anthology a writer ever had, giving Harry Warren the longest hearing he could ask for—almost ten years that first time, and four years the next, and who knows what the future may bring?

On the minus side, the thought of all that ink going to someone like Warren might have been too much for Merrick. In the cloud of acrimony that followed this man wherever he went, Merrick yanked Harry's name off his creation and confirmed the legend of triumphant songs and an un-

known, unknowable writer. Period. He had finally gotten Warren onto his beloved Broadway, but left off the name.

When Harry died, it only seemed to confirm his anonymity for eternity.

Or so it seemed at first, as I and other diehards gloomily continued to ask our reasonably knowledgeable friends if they'd yet heard of him. But with its return in 2001, with his name attached, the show began to reveal an unearthly streak of stubbornness. The musical *42nd Street* may just not leave Broadway until *somebody* learns where it came from.

There the matter rests. The pantheon of great writers has been fixed in the stars for a long time now, and Harry's name is a tough sell in any circumstance. Every now and then, I sense a crack in the amnesia. And who knows what another millennium may bring? If Harry Warren miraculously lost his anonymity, he'd also lose his chief claim to fame. Meanwhile, I can't help wishing they could find a way simply to change the guy's name back to the more ear-catching Salvatore Guaragna and do the "Who?" era over.

Jimmy Van Heusen:
On the Radio with Bing and Frank

JIMMY VAN HEUSEN

$\mathcal{C}$ompared with writers like Harry Warren—but perhaps only compared with them—Jimmy Van Heusen was practically a household word for a while, partly because of an eye-catching last name. Could Jimmy possibly be related to the shirts of that name? And partly because he wrote a lot for Frank Sinatra, who was punctilious about naming names and attaching compliments to them, as in "a wonderful song by Jimmy Van Heusen brought to you by the wonderful band of Count Basie."

But Van Heusen was more famous for his less formal relationship with Sinatra, which consisted of hanging out with him after the music stopped, when the band and the serious people had gone home, leaving the scene to the parasites of night, the gossip-writers and paparazzi, to whom Van Heusen was basically the other guy in the picture and the unidentified witness to the latest Sinatra scene. In her interminable hatchet job on Frank, Kitty Kelley mentions Van Heusen several times while barely mentioning his profession. This probably suited Jimmy almost as much as it would have disgusted Harry Warren. As the younger of the two, Van Heusen had grown up to see the gap widening between celebrity and actual accomplishment, and it may even have tickled him to be good at one thing and famous for another.

"Broads, booze, songs, and Sinatra" was how he preferred to list his interests, thus slurring over one of the last truly classy catalogues, as well as one of the great musical friendships, in the whole archive of pop. In his own way, Van Heusen worked just as hard as Cole Porter at the gentlemanly convention of hiding both his work and his feelings, so that the only proof we have of either of them has to be found in the songs themselves. "Here's That Rainy Day," for instance, has a melody so sad it squeezed tears out of the stoical Johnny Carson on his last broadcast, but nobody ever caught Jimmy having a rainy day himself, unless you count hangovers. "But Beautiful" is such a moving tribute to love that it verges on a hymn, yet Van Heusen's own love life was anything but holy. His little black book was said to be the envy of Hollywood, which is like being praised for your cooking in Paris.

"Van Heusen never got past the age of nineteen," says Jonathan Schwartz, who knew him well. And the first thought that occurs is that nineteen was also exactly the age of his target audience and thus a good place to stop. Almost all great love songs are written either for nineteen-year-olds or for, as in "Rainy Day," people who remember nineteen all too well and only wish they could do it over again.

"Maybe I should have saved those leftover dreams," says the song— but why save them in the first place?—was Jimmy's philosophy. Why not spend them right now and dream some new ones, then spend those too? If one accepts the Cole Porter principle that falling in love is the Research

Department of songwriting, then Jimmy becomes one of the most consci-
entious craftsmen in the business.

And so too with Sinatra, whose singing seemed to get wiser as his life
got sillier and more childish. To hear Frank pour his soul into Cahn and
Van Heusen's stark little tribute to monogamy, "All the Way" ("Through
the good or lean years . . . come what may"), you could swear this was a
grown-up singing a grown-up song. Yet perhaps later that night, two of the
song's perpetrators might have been observed winging their way across the
continent to wake up Sinatra's pal Jilly in New York for some drinks and
laughs that couldn't be found right that minute in Vegas or Palm Springs,
and then maybe picking up some chicks they'd overlooked last time. The
true signature song of their friendship was not one of their grown-up ones
but a celebration of the great game of hooky, "Come Fly with Me," which
was written and sung in their preferred mode of one nineteen-year-old to
another. Another obvious reason Van Heusen was indispensable to Frank
in his rodent phase was his pilot's license, and his willingness to use it at
any hour of the day or night, drunk or sober. Van Heusen could usually
drink Old Blue Eyes under the carpet and still fly a plane perfectly, at a
point when Frank could barely have mounted a bicycle, which gave
Jimmy another good reason for staying nineteen: He was so good at it, particularly in comparison to Frank and his little band of middle-aged amateurs. (Peter Lawford? Are you kidding?) The saying in Hollywood was
that "Sinatra would have been Van Heusen, but he flunked the physical."
Yet if Jimmy ever took any exercise at all, it was another of his secrets.

In his ego-soaked memoir *I Should Care,* lyricist Sammy Cahn, who
also flunked the physical, reveals a glint of some hard metal in Jimmy's
character, when he reports that Van Heusen couldn't stand being around
sloppy drunks. Surely, this had to include Sinatra once or twice. Jimmy
further qualified his taste for Chairman Frank in his own words: "He was
a bastard when I met him forty years ago, and he's still a bastard."

He was kidding, of course, as show biz guys usually are when they talk
about or to each other, but the tone of this crack establishes that here was
no camp follower talking. By staying up so late, Jimmy had seen many
sides to his friend, from the sublime to the stomach-turning, and he
didn't have to like all of them all of the time. Just one. The secret that

even Kitty Kelley couldn't tell, because it wasn't in her language, was that every session between these two was a potential working session, even one well disguised as an orgy. Booze and broads provided not just their own reward but also an excellent cover for an endless if choppy professional dialogue between the two reprobates. Music hovered just above Frank's head like a comic-strip bubble. An evening with him could lead practically anywhere, from the local police station to a celestial new song.

So in a sense, Sinatra was Van Heusen's work, the way Dr. Johnson was James Boswell's. Tonight you might get a great epigram, tomorrow a not particularly funny insult. But this was the guy he was writing both for and about, his model and canvas, so the time wasn't wasted for either of them. Sinatra could always find lots of other people to play with, but how many of them could he trust to pause in middrink and give him priceless advice about what to use on his next album? The sober truth is that Van Heusen and Sinatra were artistic soul mates who needed each other equally. And in this aspect, they had no choice but to "go all the way" together, "through the good or lean years," and the bright, fat ones as well, because no one else could go with them.

"If you had the only voice in the world and I wrote the only songs." These two characters were about all that was left in the garrison after Elvis and his hordes swept through. And they had unwittingly spent their lives preparing for it. Both exploded onto their respective scenes about the same time, the golden cusp of the 1930s and '40s, and this coincidence became more crucial as the music around them changed, and the ranks of survivors thinned. Like a blind man and a deaf one in the wilderness, Sinatra and Van Heusen kept each other on track with the Tradition, so long as they stayed together. And although they both would probably have done ever better work if the national style hadn't changed so much, the fact that they did any work at all in the alien air of the late fifties and early sixties was a triumph of—and I'm glad they're not reading this—character.

Sinatra and Van Heusen actually began working and talking music together way back in 1940, when Frank's record of Jimmy's "Imagination" was a major hit for both of them. But before they could become full-fledged partners, both had appointments to keep, Sinatra's with his young bobby socks fans, who screamed so loud you could barely hear the

songs—"I'll never smile again—" "Frank-y-y!" All he needed was a great first line and the rest could be taken on faith. And Van Heusen had Bing Crosby.

Like Richard Rodgers, Van Heusen comes in two distinct parts. The parts weren't just divided by different lyricists but by singers as well. The songs Jimmy and his first word-man, Johnny Burke, tailored for Bing Crosby were as different from the ones he and lyricist two, Sammy Cahn, wrote for Sinatra as the two singers were from each other.

Which is to say, *very* different by the standards of their day, but not so different from this end of the telescope—not as different as, say, Pavarotti and Guns N' Roses. Bing and Frank had one crucial thing in common besides their allegedly happy-go-lucky personas, which made them just right for Van Heusen. They were both primarily microphone singers who, if anything, sounded better on radio than in person. Van Heusen belonged to the first wave of songwriters to grow up almost exclusively on radio music, with its mixture of coolness and intimacy. You didn't have to raise or project your voice on radio, or seduce more than one person. And you didn't have to come from a big city.

With the fascinating exception of Cole Porter, who later made up for it by becoming the most urbane of them all, all the first-wave geniuses of the Jazz Age were city guys writing primarily for city people. But as radio got big in the late 1920s, the Lower East Side suddenly reached to infinity and the progenitors could come from any place and beam their stuff at anybody. Where a Gershwin song had once said "Made in New York—Place in a crowded theater immediately," a Van Heusen song said "Made in the U.S.A.—Sounds best in a lonely bar or an empty apartment where the owner is experiencing sleeping problems due to heartbreak."

And another note might be added in large type, "Safe to use in a moving vehicle." With the coming of car radios came a need for songs to drive by at all hours, songs not too soporific for the late shift, or too stimulating to hold still for, sung by voices that were first and last good company, perfect passengers who could turn into whoever you wanted, the guy overseas or the girl next door.

And if there must be other talk as well, please try to keep it short and smooth so as not to break the spell, by either waking the driver or putting him all the way to sleep. Thus was born the disc jockey and thus died the

average songwriter's last chance of name recognition, because even when
the obligatory names like Gershwin and Porter were spoken, they had to
be spoken often indeed to sink in and suspend the human Will to Dream.
"It never occurred to me that the songs were written by different people,"
as Cy Coleman put it. "They were all just The Radio." And he actually
cited the box itself as his first major influence.

So Van Heusen and Sinatra shared a generational secret that remains
the key to performing this type of music. Pre-radio singers like Al Jolson
and writers like Irving Berlin and George M. Cohan needed you to register their names—their livelihoods depended on it. Much, much later, of
course, when video took over, the singing songwriters of rock would need
to show off even more to sell the whole package.

But in the quiet years between, when the only sound was the song itself, music alone was center stage, and the experience of the music, as
brought to you by whichever name you had heard before the hypnosis
began, be it Bing Crosby or Connie Boswell, Glenn Miller or Harry James.
These performers proceeded quietly but insistently to stamp their styles
on each song, and make it theirs, a typical Peggy Lee or a vintage Tommy
Dorsey. The composer became a ghostwriter indeed, without even the
equivalent of a screen credit. I suspect in many cases that even the disc
jockeys hadn't heard of them.

If it was Harry Warren's comic fate to serve his apprenticeship in the
Boom and cash his chips in the Depression, Van Heusen had no such
problem. By the time he hit New York in the thirties the issue was not between fame and obscurity, but between working and not working. You
could eat anonymously with Mr. Big and the Company, or you could
starve anonymously with the Okies and grape pickers.

And anyway, Jimmy had been majoring in anonymity since the age of fifteen, when he applied for a job at what must have been one of the first radio
stations in the Syracuse area, thus moving right into the epicenter of
anonymity. "Abandon self-promotion all ye who enter here" might have
been the station's motto. The first glimpse we have of small-fry Van Heusen
finds him actually listening to other people's latest songs on the radio, with
a view to stealing them by copying them down in shorthand and singing
them himself on his channel as if he had just thought of them. "The Best

Things in Life Are Free" might have been the radio station's other motto. When memory failed him, he probably wrote a few bars himself.

Van Heusen even got his name from the radio, in a roundabout sense. Unlike most stage names chosen for their all-American, that is, Englishy, sound, Jimmy leaned for his an inch or two in the other direction. There is such a thing as sounding *too* English, and the station manager made it clear right away that the new kid couldn't go on the air or stay there with a name like Edward Chester Babcock, which was the name real life had thrown Jimmy's way. He changed it on the spot to another one that he just happened to see on a truck sitting outside the window. Or so the story goes. Presumably, if some store in Syracuse hadn't ordered a consignment of Van Heusen shirts that day, we might know him now as—well, what? Johnny Kleenex? Herbert Hoover? Elmer Street?

Anyway, an alias suited Jimmy fine because he didn't particularly want the powers that be at his current school, or in his own house, to know that he was moonlighting as a premature disc jockey. And perhaps he was already used to the idea that writers don't have names on radio.

Middle-class families tell no tales, and the rest of Jimmy's childhood and adolescence tends to get summarized under the rubric "kicked out of school again," a phrase that occurs suspiciously often in celebrity bios. It adds a raffish touch and no one ever checks on it. What one does know is that boys with names like Chester Babcock usually wind up graduating— it's a yearbook kind of name. And this particular one would eventually wind up in the Syracuse University Hall of Fame.

More to the point, we also know that his father, Arthur, was an amateur cornet player and that his mother, Ida Mae, claimed descent from the ultimate layabout, Stephen Foster. So they must at least have appreciated his piano playing, which would later be called the best for party purposes in Hollywood. His family must also have realized that in this family, being a black sheep obsessed with pop music wasn't the worst thing that could happen. And, more seriously, I just discovered one last trace of his family, which would otherwise disappear obligingly from the scene. (They were nice people, but not part of the story, the legend, and tempermentally speaking, they needed attention even less than he did.) It seems that Jimmy had a schizophrenic brother, on the strength of whom

he decided never to marry and have children himself. So perhaps the eternal nineteen-year-old did know something after all about shadows and rainy days.

The next step for any songwriter then was to head for New York and simply start mixing, and in no time Jimmy would find a fellow out-of-towner to write some words with him, namely, Harold Arlen's brother, Jerry, who lived in the anteroom of Tin Pan Alley all his life, singing with young Johnny Mercer in the second generation of Paul Whiteman's Rhythm Boys, and writing words for anyone who would have him. It must have been a delightful life for all concerned, and Van Heusen lingered in it for a bit, not breaking through like a boy wonder, but singing here, writing there, and haunting publishers' offices, so that when he did start publishing he was already at his best. His first big hit carried a disclaimer testifying to his eclectic modus vivendi in the person of a Johnny Mercer lyric. "I Thought About You" finds him bursting from the gate at the height of his powers and already blending perfectly with Mercer. Although I've never actually heard Mercer sing it, I can't imagine anyone doing it better, and it is tantalizing to think of all the other songs Van Heusen and Mercer might have given us. But Johnny was already famous and had begun trading his services farther up the food chain, most especially with Harold Arlen, the one you got for first prize. Jimmy and Johnny had to settle for this one collaborative masterpiece.

That song plus a couple or three others he wrote first off the bat would actually outlive most of the stuff he wrote later, which suggests that in work as in life, it suited him to jump from one partner to another, thus avoiding a rut. For instance, another of those first standards, "Darn That Dream," was written with the expert handyman Eddie "Moonglow" DeLange for Louis Armstrong to swing the life out of in a crazy, swinging, all-black version of Shakespeare called *Swingin' the Dream.* You can't get much more promiscuous than that. It is probably the jazziest thing Jimmy ever wrote. Jazz groups still seem to think so anyway, and again it suggests how far Van Heusen might have gone in that direction if his career and his personality had taken the same kind of turn as, say, Duke Ellington's and he had found himself composing jazz through the medium of other musicians.

But Jimmy preferred working *around* jazz, dropping in and out of the neighborhood rather as the swing bands did, thus catching the sound of

that era better than anyone. He definitely did not have the job profile of a bandleader, or of any other kind of responsible citizen. Eventually World War II would blow his cover and reveal him retroactively to have been capable of enormous self-discipline all along. Of all his concealments, this was his most thorough. Without breaking stride, he continued his whole life to project the air of a borderline delinquent rescued—but only just— from becoming a total deadbeat by music, the way inner-city kids are saved by boxing. If worse came to worst, perhaps he could make it as a soldier of fortune. But he was definitely not a leader of men.

Yet he seems to have worked wonderfully well with all his lyricists, as you might actually guess by looking at a photograph of him, and it's a pet theory of mine that he may even have let the bridge of "Darn That Dream" go slightly astray to accommodate DeLange's lyrics. But when I mentioned this to Sammy Cahn, he said that Van Heusen had never done that much for him.

In the few photos I have seen, Van Heusen looks something like Senator John McCain, which is to say a comfortable, good-natured fellow, somewhat prematurely bald in a friendly sort of way, as if hair were pretentious. And he always seemed happy to sit in the corners of other people's pictures. Working with him seems to have been anything but a clash of egos. A Babcock doesn't need to prove anything, except that he is not a creep.

In the cutthroat era that gave us Kern and Berlin, egomania was a necessary tool of the trade, and Kern in particular would not have changed a note for Shakespeare himself. "Write another soliloquy, we've got time." A generation later, Gershwin would at least have shelved the tune for him or written another one, but Van Heusen, I suspect, would have let Bing Crosby change it on the spot. Cahn describes him as a what-the-hell kind of guy, from the moment he rolled out of bed around midday, yawning and scratching, and doing his chores at the piano, until the moment he sensed he had caught his fish for the day and could really start living. Writing hits was nothing to lose sleep over, an attitude that sounds more like Bing Crosby than Bing himself did in real life, just as Van Heusen's daily hangovers, real or feigned, would also make him the perfect partner for Frank Sinatra.

Van Heusen's empathy for such happy-go-lucky types might, I sup-

pose, have been feigned sometimes too, but if so it was certainly not something he had to work on very hard. His lethargy, real or posed, would almost immediately make him the perfect tailor or court-composer for Crosby, but fortunately he was not confined to that exclusively. During the tantalizingly short while it lasted, the entertainment fever of World War II kept Jimmy bombarded with a fury of assignments from all over, and four of my own all-time favorites would be written for such a tatterdemalion cast as Harry Babbitt, "Humpty Dumpty Heart"; Ginger Rogers, "Suddenly It's Spring"; Fred MacMurray, of all people, "It Could Happen to You"; and Dinah Shore, "Like Someone in Love"—in other words, whoever the studio rotation made available that month.

The one constraint on his freedom was that he was handcuffed to lyricist Johnny Burke, which was no constraint at all. They had been a dream team from the start, and two of the three first hits they wrote have almost outlived anything either did later. Only the first, "Oh, You Crazy Moon," may have slipped even slightly, and significantly this is the only one that sounds like a "typical" Van Heusen tune in that it never really takes off but plays beguiling and ingenious games on the runway, a formula he fell back on quite a lot in his later songs with Cahn and Sinatra. But the other two songs took off like rockets. Since "Imagination" was number one on the Hit Parade the week I arrived in this country, it still sounds to me like the whole American continent. In contrast, their next, "Polka Dots and Moonbeams," seems more specific and is set not far away from wherever you are in the cardboard village of Tin Pan Alley on the Wabash, where it begins with a garden party and ends in a cottage for two, a million miles away from Caesars Palace and the ring-a-ding world of Frank Sinatra that Van Heusen and Sammy Cahn dealt with later.

With these two songs, Johnny Burke and Van Heusen made a Siamese connection, sounding like one writer, not two. Even better, they were on a roll and had a contract. Johnny Burke had been a Paramount writer for some time and had become the perfect mouthpiece for Bing's supposedly lighter side, with lyrics like in "Pennies from Heaven" and in such cornpone soufflés as "Sweet Potato Piper" and "That Sly Old Gentleman from Featherbed Lane"—which might not have gone too well with Jimmy's hangovers. (Burke's hangovers were bad enough.) But fortunately, by 1940 the chief order of business for the new team would be the *Road* pic-

tures with Bob Hope, in which the cold, dark side of Crosby was finally given a hilarious airing for the world to see and laugh at. Perhaps not since the plays of Ben Jonson has comedy gotten any blacker than it does in this running saga of betrayal and double-crossing between friends.

The good news for Burke and Van Heusen was that they did not have to sound pixieish for the new Bing. Although Crosby was still supposed, incredibly, to be Mr. Relaxation without a care in the world, this didn't have to be a virtue anymore. The breezy songs the boys wrote for him, like "Ain't Got a Dime to My Name" and "My Heart Is a Hobo," could also be consonant with total irresponsibility and cynicism; this was not necessarily a nice guy, just a supremely lazy and selfish one who would later be consigned by Father "Bing" O'Malley himself to his famous menagerie of delinquents. ("Would you rather be a fish . . . or a pig?") Van Heusen had no better training for the *Road* pictures than getting kicked out of school regularly.

And the boys quit kidding occasionally and got to write some great love songs that sounded particularly good on Crosby, like "Moonlight Becomes You," "It's Always You," and "But Beautiful" as well as some fine edgy duets for Hope and Crosby, like "Put Her There, Pal," and the title song of the *Road to Morocco* that nicely captures the Friar's Club Roast aspect of their friendship while setting the table for the feast of amorality to follow. The *Road to Morocco* theme song actually reminds me of a Greek chorus on its day off saying what it really thinks. In their courtly way, they even concocted a perfect showcase for the generally underscripted Miss Lamour, a song titled "Personality," "What did Romeo see in Juliet/or Pierrot in Pierrette/or Jupiter in Juno?/(pause) you know."

This one was from *Road to Utopia* (1946), a funny movie with a great score that included, by way of contrast, the lush "Welcome to My Dreams" and the beautifully understated "It's Anybody's Spring," and as the trailers never got tired of saying, much, much more; but it was also, in retrospect, a film with the hint of a death rattle. Bing and Bob were now manifestly middle-aged men, still acting like college boys but *old* college boys, paunchy and sly and on the verge of being out of wind. The next *Road*, one senses, would be Sunset Boulevard itself for all of them.

In this, the *Road* pictures symbolized the life span of a whole profession. The Hollywood songwriters had entered the war a short while before

as fresh and bouncy as the annual New Year baby, and they were already leaving it as old men and has-beens, their best work behind them.

Like the army itself, the great original musicals and their providers took their time demobilizing, and the songwriters didn't all get kicked out on the same day. Burke and Van Heusen stayed on at Paramount several more years, but there was increasingly less to do except hang around the club and check the mail. Their glory days were over and, ready or not, so were their primes—which in Hollywood are allotted to you by a Higher Power, aka the marketplace. In the great postwar drought that hasn't ended yet, Hoagy Carmichael was surely not the only writer to regret not having tried harder when the going was good, most specifically during the war itself. It is a law of life in this business that whether you're an old-timer like Jimmy Monaco, whose big hit "You Made Me Love You" had actually been written in 1912, or a new kid on the block like Gene "I'll Remember April" DePaul, who began during the war itself, you'd better be at your best when the gold rush is announced. Forget your biological clock or the arc of your creative development; the market will tell you when your prime occurs—or else tell you, "Whoops, you missed it. Better luck in the next life."

Compared with those extremes, Burke and Van Heusen were among the lucky ones, but they could have been luckier. Their careers stood at high noon as the war arrived, and by the time it was over they had enjoyed a very good war. But it could have been better, if it hadn't been for Van Heusen's other war work, which virtually no one knew about at the time and which perhaps tells more about his character than all his salacious press clips put together. As he told it later, and without heroics, to David Ewen, Jimmy's 1942 through '44 schedule went roughly like this: Four days in a row, up at four A.M. to test-fly new Lockheed warplanes until noon, under the name of Chester Babcock; then off to Paramount to write songs for the rest of the day as his other self, Jimmy Van Heusen; then, a two-and-a-half-day break, during which he only had to get up whenever the studio did, to write songs all day this time. Then back to Go, and you can sleep as long as you like when the war is over, buddy.

Okay, things were tough all over. Testing airplanes was always danger-ous, especially when they'd been built at breakneck speed by overworked, undertrained amateurs, and which may well have embodied technical

breakthroughs each time, but at least he didn't have to do it under enemy fire, so Jimmy wouldn't have assigned himself to the World War II Hall of Fame.

What twenty-first-century sensibilities might find harder to grasp is not the deed but the cover-up. Imagine the glory at the Lockheed base if he ever so much as let one colleague know that he had recently written that song they were all humming, "Sunday, Monday, or Always"; and imagine the megaglory of tipping off Louella Parsons, the gossip queen, that you were not just another Hollywood draft dodger, the kind people hooted and whistled at in the street, but a hero on two fronts, the entertainment one as well as the real one, in which he was entrusting his life again and again to the skills of Rosie the Riveter between songs. Ronald Reagan would have told Ms. Parsons even if he *hadn't* done it, as an inspirational story. But the hell with it. Jimmy was not the inspirational type, and besides, he was only a great songwriter, not a minor movie star, so he mightn't even have inspired anyone that much. And finally, of course, there was his job at Paramount to worry about. No doubt his bosses would have crooned his praises in public—but who wants to make movies with a guy who might go down in flames any minute, and hold up your next picture? Who did this guy think he was anyway? Joan of Arc?

In retrospect, the myriad changes of sensibility that occur in this country seem like earthquakes that no one notices at the moment they occur. In the 1920s, a writer could genuinely think of himself, and be thought of, as a star. In the thirties and forties, he was just a working stiff to all concerned. From the 1990s until today, a guy with Van Heusen's war record would undoubtedly have sold the book and movie rights and established his own website as the Singing Test Pilot or the FlyingTroubador.com. In the 1940s the worst thing that you could be was a hotshot or a big deal. "What are you?" as the kids used to say. "A wise guy or Boy Scout?" To this, there was no correct answer except to put up your dukes and pray.

Further proof of Jimmy's character would be considerably less spectacular. To put it briefly, he survived in a dying business. Most didn't. Anyone can be a hero, but getting out of bed every day takes real character, and resisting the noonday devil, aka the third dry martini, and taking jobs he wouldn't even have looked at a few years before. Peacetime can really take it out of you after a while, because it is at once pointless and unpre-

dictable. During the war, everything that could be stabilized had been, even fame, so that if you didn't go down in flames, you stayed up there forever. No celebrity ever faded away in those days, although several, like Al Jolson, came back to life.

So the hardest work a writer had to do back then was hitch his wagon to a fixed star and watch the money roll in. And, as Jonathan Schwartz pointed out to me, Jimmy's smartest career move had simply been to buy a house in Palm Springs, which would place him with one stroke of the pen in the same playground as first Crosby, and then Sinatra, a one-two punch that should have been good for a lifetime—and was, in a way, although probably not as good as it looked at the time.

Van Heusen indeed needed them both, because in the acceleration of peacetime, they were suddenly the only games in town—when, that is, they were available, and so long as they were able to keep surviving themselves. In the new Hollywood, no star was that fixed anymore, and Jimmy was in for a bumpy ride indeed, as both Bing and Frank fought to redefine and resell themselves in the brave new world. The second half of Van Heusen's career would be defined by these bumps—a tale of two singers taking their own lumps every time fashion hit a curve, then passing them on to Jimmy. None of this was clear at first. As peace arrived, Bing at least looked like money in the bank. As Bob Hope would later learn and go to exhaustive lengths to prove, an audience of soldiers can serve as the closest thing we have to a fountain of youth for both a man and his work for several lifetimes, and as an embalming fluid after that. Crosby splashed deep and well and emerged from the war as perhaps the nation's ultimate entertainer, or, as Alec Wilder would put it, the first guy you would send for if your theater was on fire and you wanted everyone to keep calm.

At this point, Sinatra's position was considerably trickier and uniquely modern. Like Superman, Francis Albert came in two distinct aspects. At one moment, he was the skinny little kid that half the country made fun of, and at the next, he was the greatest sound ever to come out of a radio. This side of him was simply called the Voice, a spectral figure who had somehow leaped over the technology in a single bound to broadcast from inside your own head, not just singing to you but at certain points becoming you and singing to the girl, or the whole sex, that you loved. It sounds impossible and was presumably never that clear-cut, but it still certainly

is possible to love listening to him without having any particular personal feelings about him, one way or the other.

If the army had ordered him to specifications, they couldn't have come up with anything better. As a voice in the dark and as everybody's closest friend, Sinatra offered the last word in specialization: a buddy with all the bugs removed, and 100 percent guaranteed not to get on your nerves or die at your side. In other words, he was perfect company for men over-seas—so long as they stayed there.

As for so many, the problem would be peacetime, which means day-light. Daylight wakes you from the good dreams as well as from bad ones. So even if the real live Sinatra turned out to be perfect, he would have been disappointing, if only because, let's face it, he was another male, a biological rival, and as such a stranger. The part he'd been playing doesn't exist in real life and would soon be blown away completely as the faucets and fire hoses of gossip turned on again. But before this could happen, Sinatra signed up with one of the great protection syndicates, which would prolong his cover for a bit longer. If you worked for MGM, you au-tomatically became whatever they wanted. And what Louis B. Mayer wanted was for Frank to go on with the fan-magazine version at its most simpleminded. Although Old Blue Eyes is now widely remembered as a cross between Don Corleone and Francis of Assisi, a thug whose good deeds held world records, he came across in the 1940s more as an Ital-ianate Andy Hardy, everybody's kid brother who had, as the GIs might un-fortunately recall now, stayed home with the girls while the grown-ups were off fighting and dying. But that was all right, I guess, because he was obviously still a kid, still called "Frankie," not "Frank," let alone the "Chair-man of the Board."

As if to ram this home, Sinatra also contrived to have one of those chil-dren's book marriages in which the tender smile and the melting glance are the hottest units of exchange and which didn't count at all against your juvenile status. Any babies born to such babies were invariably bun-dles of joy brought by a friendly stork directly from the angel factory. A grim little slice of sociology packaged in a song called "I'll Buy That Dream" spells out the peacetime promise of such marriages with ghoulish touches like "Imagine . . . you thanking Dad for my dowry" and "Someone like you in the nursery." "I'll Buy That Dream" quotes a slaphappy GI be-

fore he has even had a good chance to look at the contract, not realizing that this may be the last love song he will ever be allowed to sing, unless he has a cheating heart and a first-rate lawyer.

Somebody would have to pay for this someday, and that somebody might be Frank if he ever broke the rules. But meanwhile, in the limbo of the late 1940s, Sinatra stumbled upon another way to be two people at once. On-screen he remained the perfect middle-class boy-man, fetched out in a cute little sailor suit to prove it, while on radio and records he was still the Voice who had so recently brought love to life for thousands of grateful adults, in direct and day-to-day contrast with death. But then for a moment, the Voice itself seemed to split, as Sinatra busted a gut trying to figure out how to keep up with the current taste.

The cusp of the 1950s marked the only period when Frank's voice was ever untrue to itself, as he struggled to get his chops around the latest baby boomer novelty numbers. The day on which he recorded "Mama Will Bark" for the Mephistopheles of pop, Mitch Miller, seems in retrospect like a total eclipse of the sun. After that, even so gifted a singer as Frank would have to give up and find a new style, a singing self that suited the times, but did not belong to them. "Songs," as he might say, "for swinging grown-ups."

The kid brother persona wasn't working that well either, on the screen or at the box office. The real big brothers were back, so who needed kid ones? The only catch was that Franky couldn't seem to stop playing one anyhow, whether to Gene Kelly or Marlon Brando, to Bing Crosby or even Keenan Wynn. Never mind how tough he wanted to be now, it wouldn't project that way. As a frail kid in a tough world, and as a lifelong mama's boy to a powerful and socially ambitious mother, he had developed a style he could never quite shake. With time, his cuteness would wear off (there are few cute middle-aged men) but the boyishness remained like a tattoo to narrow his movie possibilities in an unusual way, that is, it was always easy enough to find parts and movies for him, but hard to make him the star, the hero.

So Franky did the next best thing; he dropped the *y* from his name and learned how to act. For one thing, kid brothers can suffer, can't they? They could become drug addicts (for *The Man with the Golden Arm*), and they could sing about going "All the Way" (for *The Joker Is Wild*). And best of

all, they could become obnoxious bums. And here real life would help him out with one of the best-disguised blessings in history by turning him into Public Enemy No. 1.

It is hard to convey now, and even harder to believe, the atmosphere in America just a couple of years after World War II. But imagine it this way: The public celebration is over and people have finally run out of excuses, but some of the crowd hasn't gone home yet, and is now spoiling for a fight with someone, anyone, before they have to disperse back into privacy. "Too much laughing turns to crying," as my grandmother used to warn, and somebody usually has to pay for getting you so drunk last night. So who can we still get mad at in the name of the U.S.A.? Although we didn't have enough outright traitors to keep the bonfires going, we did have communists, real and suspected, and comsymps and fellow travelers, and the ruckus we were able to make over these should have been enough vengeance for anyone. But puritans can be hard to satisfy, and there were a few other folk out there who had let us down badly, weren't there? And while we still had this length of rope anyway . . . And thus one arrived at perhaps the two most unlikely war criminals of all time: Ingrid Bergman for sinning against her role in *Casablanca* and running off with a foreign (ugh) film director, and Frank Sinatra for betraying his own publicity and doing what practically every man in America at least wanted to do—cheating on his wife and chasing after Ava Gardner.

Now wait a damn minute—isn't this the guy who sold us that dream? One of those guys, anyway. About thanking Dad for her dowry? Not that every postwar marriage in America had gone bad quite yet, but all of them had proved hard work, and precious few were like songs. And here was a guy who could actually afford babysitters and all the vacations he wanted, giving up on an allegedly perfect marriage. And Frank only got himself in deeper by singing a gorgeous Van Heusen love song to one "Nancy," which had in fact been written for somebody else's newborn baby, but which also happened to be his own picture-perfect wife's name, and that settled it. "Don't bother to explain. Never do we want to hear another note from this bum," who didn't sound that good anymore, anyhow.

Thus, one small footnote to history and one huge kick in the head for Burke and Van Heusen, who would thereby lose the use of half of their nest egg for another few prime years, and the full use of it forever, because

when Sinatra did fight his way back into acceptance it was as a straight, nonmusical actor on-screen and largely as a singer of already-written standards on wax. And before things got even a little bit better, Burke was gone.

Which left the team with Bing Crosby and nothing but Bing Crosby— when he wasn't too busy. The trouble with Bing was that there wasn't enough of him to go around. Ominously, none of the occasional new singers that Hollywood was now trying to make into stars, from Howard Keel to Mario Lanza, was of a kind to share Crosby's workload. Which meant that although Bing might be overworked at the moment, he probably wouldn't be for long because his work was out of date; and when he closed up shop, that shop would not open again. The casual, unspectacular, original musical would be no more.

Thus, in bits and pieces, and in a deceptive fever of activity, Death began to make its presence clear to the old Hollywood. The Marx Brothers, for instance, made a new movie. For a second, it seemed like a comeback, but it was just a chance for them to take a last bow. And "Gable's back and Garson's got him" screamed the ads, but not for long. An old man returning to an old lady was really nothing to get excited about, or at least so it seemed to those all-important kids, of which, incidentally, I was one myself. And when Fred and Ginger put on their taps once again, they seemed older than time itself, even to young me, their keenest fan of my age in America. There's a limit to how much you can doubt your own eyes. Even half-blind with idolatry, I found myself wishing that Ginger at least would retire for good and Fred could just stick to dancing from now on and leave the romance, which was a bore anyway, to the kids—a heresy that I would take back after his next movie and never commit again.

By keeping his continuity in our eyes right through the war, Crosby did not yet seem so moribund, but the clock was ticking on him too. The remaining songwriters all wanted to grab at least one more ride on the old Bingo Shuttle, until there was hardly room for Van Heusen himself on his own life raft.

Meanwhile, Emerson's famous "Imp of the Perverse" entered the picture. In 1943, Bing with justified misgivings made the mistake of playing a priest on-screen in *Going My Way*, and now the Catholic hierarchy was holding him to it, not just in terms of future roles, but in terms of his off-

camera behavior and image. Once a good example, always a good example, and suddenly Bing's natural tendency to keep his sins under his hat anyhow found itself reinforced by clerical mandates. As Gary Giddins showed in his excellent biography, Bing's sins became worse as his image got better, and apparently his sins worsened with every screen appearance. Burke and Van Heusen were stuck with the image, and a truly exasperating problem—Sinatra too sinful to get any part at all and Bing so virtuous his writers had to work the sunshine shift and write just the kind of "smile, damn you" songs they'd managed to avoid before.

Considering the extent to which it ran against their collective grain, the score Burke and Van Heusen concocted for *Going My Way* was astoundingly good, in the same way that *Oklahoma!* was in that same year—which might suggest that a sophisticated man can get away with one corny show, but he'd better not make it a habit. Because naturally they were asked immediately to do *Going My Way* again in the form of another priest movie called *The Bells of St. Mary's*. And this score would seem eerily professional—just right for a thoroughly second-rate occasion, but totally unlike themselves.

Okay—no sweat, just some time wasted and perhaps some sweat to come. Perhaps an expert on postwar booms could have seen what was coming. But *The Bells* exemplified the next problem around the corner: how to keep busy while protecting your talent, by absorbing the musical changes around you into your style so that you seem to have thought of them first. So that if you're suddenly asked to write, say, a mambo, it will be a Van Heusen mambo and not just an exercise in mambo writing. But suppose the public wants a mambo at one moment and a Charleston the next? The first years of peace could be called the years of cultural indigestion, as Americans wanted to try everything they had been missing, all at the same time, through a background ringing with salesmen and driveways honking with new cars as the austerity of wartime began to fill up like a Christmas pudding.

So what kind of music would you like to go with all this? Well, everything ever written would be nice. Thus in some suburban ranch houses and split-levels you might hear the latest LPs playing in one room while kids harmonized to "Moonlight Bay" in the next, or attempted to learn the

rumba. And meanwhile, in the kitchen there was this guy demonstrating pressure cookers or ice cream makers, while in at least one of the five rooms, new radios blared selections from the world's million greatest hits.

That's what it seemed like, anyway, to a kid returning from England in 1947—or half of what it seemed like. The other half, the bestseller list and the Hit Parade, seemed to show no variety at all. One day, for instance, it seemed as if the whole city of New York had conspired to play the exact same record out of every door and window I passed, a dental drill of a song called "Near You" that apparently had the power to keep itself playing indefinitely. "There's just one place for me—near you." Couldn't there be at least two places for me? And was America really down to just one record?

One at a time, it seemed, until you got it home and looked at the mail-order catalogues. Later that same day, I visited an old friend's apartment and found a trove of great records that had just become available for the first time in years and featured enough old songs that I had never heard before to seem like a whole new movement. Thus a sturdy little betwixt-and-between generation was born that fell in love with the standards just as they slowed to a trickle, and then stopped altogether.

It was, as it always is, the best of times and the worst of times, but the good parts tended to be more and more private and the bad parts inescapable. It seemed that by 1945, the kids had seized control of all the jukeboxes and radios and wouldn't let go for a moment. And just like that, the magical coincidence of quality and popularity was over, the music in the public square was nowhere near the best music anymore. Listening to a program recently of the top pop hits from 1940 to 1955, I was startled all over again at how sharp the break was at the end of World War II, as if the bad stuff had been waiting for its cue. And perhaps it had, because several of the new hits seemed to depend on the latest gimmickry and special effects, to celebrate technology more than music. The kid at the piano syncopating everything had died in the war and been replaced by his country cousin.

As far as the number-one hits were concerned, the great Broadway shows had never happened, couldn't have happened. To cut a short story shorter, we lived in two musical worlds then, and the jazz world was losing. And Arthur Freed's great compilations of songs by Gershwin and

Kern, and so forth, were indeed "classical" now in the sense that the kids didn't listen to them much. Without new babies, the greatest nation perishes. And the mass audience was not willing to pay good money for any more new jazz babies.

So here was Van Heusen, still trying to churn them out on the piano as though nothing had happened. And his best bet was still to churn the songs through Bing Crosby, who seemed to enjoy some kind of immunity and could probably have made a gold record out of "Alice Blue Gown" or "After the Ball" in that peculiar time.

But the sunlight had begun to get in its licks on Bing the movie star too, if not Bing the singer. I remember wondering as early as his *Mr. Music* in 1950 whether "The Groaner" might be just a little too old to be courting this particular girl. It was a rigidly conventional time in our national history, as I recall, meaning that an actor only proceeds on such an unwholesome course if the lady insists on it.

As the English say, "Time, gentlemen, please." Or almost time. From roughly now on, Crosby would be down to playing married men or, God forbid, more priests, neither of which groups tended to march to the same drum as Jimmy Van Heusen, so perhaps it's not too surprising that Bing's only two Oscar nominations in the early fifties were both written by older, married men, which, on second thought, describes all the other songwriters left in Hollywood: "In the Cool, Cool, Cool of the Evening," by Mercer and Carmichael, and "Zing a Little Zong," by Robin and Warren.

Well, married men probably don't sing that much anyway, except to themselves (though Kathryn Crosby says that Bing never stopped singing around the house). By the time Sinatra came back in favor as a straight actor, Bing was heading the same way from the other direction, playing parts that had either no songs at all or that had just an occasional one or two to prove that he, like Frank, could still do it, as with the gorgeous Van Heusen and Cahn "Second Time Around" for Bing and their "High Hopes" for Frank. It was a starvation diet after the banquets of wartime. Jimmy eked it out as best he could with such crumbs from the commissary table as movie title songs to accompany the latest fad—protracted screen credits for films like *Indiscreet* and *The Tender Trap,* and occasional odd-job songs to cram into musicals like *Anything Goes* and *Star,* which needed a whiff of new stuff to go with the old stuff that was already in

there, or genre songs like his virtually last "Thoroughly Modern Millie" to remind viewers of a particular time and place.

A diet consisting almost entirely of snacks is inevitably a thin one, but it was still better than anyone else's for reasons of his sheer consistency, and perhaps of studio politics, as played by his second and last new partner, Sammy Cahn. Van Heusen kept on getting assignments long after everyone else but Henry Mancini had packed in their music sheets.

Once again Van Heusen's technique for advancing himself had begun with simply making the right connection and letting nature take its course. The exact story of how Jimmy came finally to split up with Burke and proceed with the braggadocious Sammy Cahn has been somewhat muddied by Cahn's own inevitable boasting and everyone else's reticence. In Sammy's version, Frank Sinatra was always so eager to have Sammy write his songs that he personally engineered the partnership, in the manner of a Godfather, or the capo de capo to the stars that Frank liked to come on as.

But an equally plausible counterversion has the boozy but ferociously disciplined Bing Crosby ordering Burke to quit drinking, or else. Johnny, who might well have been bored and frustrated by postwar Hollywood by then anyway, shrugged and pushed off to the more congenial climate of New York—not exactly Siberia—where he and Van Heusen would actually write their last masterpiece together, "Here's That Rainy Day." Drunk or sober, Burke would also write maybe his own best-known words of all after that to go with Erroll Garner's classic "Misty." As with his fellow lyrical lushes Dorothy Fields and Larry Hart, Johnny Burke's real or imagined drinking never showed in his work.

Van Heusen himself never said why Burke quit. But Sammy Cahn made obvious sense as a replacement. To survive in a shrinking business, it was no longer enough to have talent or even character. What you needed most was hustle. And Jimmy, like many gifted people, was always happy to have other people do his hustling, as well as help give him a new sound and a new subject matter in lyrics. In short, being born again was suddenly the only way to go for him *or* Johnny.

In contrast, nothing had ever come easy to Sammy Cahn, and he wasn't geared to quit, now or ever. In the midthirties, when Sammy had come along, the country was falling down with would-be songwriters, and

he was just another funny-looking kid from the Bronx trying to get noticed by someone. And he tried so hard that he would become kind of a joke in the business, as in "You're pulling a Cahn on me" or "Quit Cahning around." Like other hustlers, he never grasped the fact that at a certain point it's safe to stop boasting and let someone else do it for you. In his heart he seemed to feel that the only thing standing between himself and complete extinction was his own tongue. Of course, if Cahn hadn't had that particular temperament, we might well have never heard of him. And it's possible that we might not have heard quite so much of Jule Styne or Jimmy Van Heusen either.

What is particularly funny and touching about Sammy is that once he began writing for Sinatra again, he also wanted to be recognized as a member of the Rat Pack in full swing. Thus, he may actually have underplayed his real service to Sinatra, which was *not* to swing with him but simply to get himself to bed every night and to get Van Heusen out of bed the next morning to write the songs that made Frank seem what he no longer was, up-to-date.

But Sammy insisted on being a swinger, and in his memoir, *I Should Care,* he wastes no chance to assure us that he too had plenty of broads, thus paradoxically reminding us of the most repulsive side of Sinatra too—the celebrity arrogance that mistakes broads for real women and one-night stands for romantic conquests.

One now sees a cultural disconnect between what the Pack thought it was doing and the public's actual perception of it. In the original *Ocean's Eleven* film, for instance, Frank and the boys posed as their dream selves—combat veterans, which none of them was, who wanted to recapture the happy-go-lucky spirit of World War II with one last operation, a coordinated scam in Las Vegas that required more planning than Normandy itself. No doubt some cashiers and other small fry would lose their jobs, of course, but ho, ho, ho!

But no "over thirty" person can really fool a young one in any decade, let alone the sixties. We knew who they really were—a bunch of middle-aged 4-F millionaires on an endless spree, who are happy-go-lucky mainly because they have chauffeurs to drive them home later and lawyers to clean up the mess. They could never become what they thought they were, the advance guard of an edgy counter-counterculture that brought

the generations up to par. They reminded hippies too much of their own daddies, and they probably even had trouble keeping up with Hugh Hefner and his Playboy mansion, where the real swingers lived on carrot juice and marijuana, and where Sinatra's Jack Daniel's bottle would have seemed like an antique.

There was one respect in which Frank Sinatra did remain up to speed—his music, which had a leanness and a sharpness that fit the changing times better than his smug, out-of-shape persona did. Singing, Sinatra could pass the Van Heusen physical, and the Mick Jagger test too. And it gave him some credibility with the young fans who ultimately determine who lives and who dies these days. Lots of fossilized entertainers were living out their days in the dry air of the desert, not changing a thing and knocking them dead at the Sands or Caesars Palace until both they and the audience were carried out for good. But Sinatra continued to be a presence to the whole nation's youth, and he owed an awful lot of it to the team of Cahn and Van Heusen.

Both of them. To hear Sammy tell it in his last years (as I did a couple of times, at exhausting lengths), he wrote the songs virtually by himself. But Sammy's self-promotion set up a critical counterforce. And some fans, myself included, have been tempted to go the other way and give him no credit at all. Since the songs Van Heusen wrote with Burke were on the whole unarguably better than the later ones with Cahn, Sammy must be to blame, no?

Yet with both men, Van Heusen's tune came first, and after much listening, I can't imagine how Sammy could have caught those particular notes better. His lyrics were every bit as right for Frank and his times as carrying moonbeams home in a jar had been right for Bing and his. It's just that polka dots and moonbeams were out and blowing your own horn and going all the way were in. By the same token, Jimmy's old tunes might have sounded almost too pretty to be true in an age of hard rock and heavy metal. Charm was out now, and machismo was in. Even a truly tender song like "All the Way" sounded, if you didn't listen too closely, like an ad for Viagra or whatever snake oil they were using back then. So Cahn did precisely what he had signed on to do: He found them both a way to change their styles without losing them.

But it isn't just sweetness that Van Heusen's later tunes lost, but also some freshness and unexpectedness. This was not the fault of either man. Sammy's songs with young Jule Styne sounded fresher too. As the last practitioners of a dying form, it was all they could do to avoid catching the plague that was killing all the other music. The one-shot deals that Van Heusen and Cahn were getting now, all those title songs and that "special material," were a far cry from the bonanzas of yesteryear, for which a studio writer like Warren might empty his desk drawer over the studio's head and be sure of one or two hits tumbling out. The creative law of averages that roughly regulates the ratio of hits to misses and of rosebuds to lemons had just been nullified. There was simply no time for all the misfires and wrong turns from which greatness unpredictably emerges. Where Jerome Kern had once said, "I don't do auditions," now each individual song had to audition and sound at least moderately good to some not-particularly-musical executives at first hearing, if the songwriter wanted to keep the shrinking field of other writers from beating him to the next assignment. To the highest batting average went the spoils, so Van Heusen began, perhaps unconsciously, perhaps not, to concentrate on that, and to depend more and more on formulas of which he was a master, just to get on base, never mind the home runs anymore. Henry Mancini later expressed his enormous admiration for Van Heusen's "logic," which was indeed extraordinary. Jimmy once showed Jonathan Schwartz precisely how to write a hit song from A to B and back—"Here, you take it. You write the rest of it, kid!" But, of course, neither Jonathan nor anyone else could write the rest of it without Chester Babcock guiding his fingers.

Van Heusen's formulas were instantly recognizable after you'd heard them, but nobody else could make them work because there was always at least one original twist among the theorems and equations that made the formulas jump to life. Jimmy probably held the lead in the "Why didn't I think of that idea?" stakes, and began piling up the Oscar nominations, but the best young talent was now in rock and roll, which is neither flexible nor modulated enough for the average movie's agenda. You can't play rock and roll in the background. And the other old-timers and would-be old-timers seemed to be cut off not only from the music in the air, but from their own life supports. You can't receive all your inspiration from lis-

tening to old records; it's like receiving your fresh air in cans. With all the skill in the world, a writer in the 1970s can only write an imitation of a 1930s song, not a real one.

Yet the new music had cut the old-timers off too. For a large part of the twentieth century, writers like Warren and Walter Donaldson had brilliantly adapted to changes of fashion in the jazz song. Several like Sammy Fain and Rube Bloom had made a fairly good fist of it with the bland, unaccented music of the fifties, with such margarine items as "Dear Hearts and Gentle People." Van Heusen and Cahn's first hit together, "Love and Marriage," demonstrated an equal willingness to play ball, within reason.

But rock was thundering and disorienting—not just a change of fashion, but total nudity, or something equally drastic. And the older songwriters couldn't really stand it, which didn't help. You had to think differently to write a rock song. Yet once your ears filled up on the stuff, it was hard to write anything else. "Selective deafness" was Cy Coleman's answer to this, shutting off the music in the air and on the jukebox and improvising on his memories. It may have worked for him, but for most people, listening only to the voices of the past is like living full-time in a museum. The best you can hope to produce is museum pieces—not collectors' items either, because great artworks have at least been out in the fresh air once.

And it is against this background that the later work of Van Heusen must be judged. Never mind how it compares with his best earlier stuff or how, incidentally, Cahn's lyrics compare with Johnny Burke's, but how does it stack up against Green Day's "American Idiot" or Christina Aguilera's "Beautiful"? Immortality can wait.

Van Heusen still had Sinatra, who needed him almost as badly. The class of 1940 was down to its last trick, and Sinatra had to decide year by year whether to stop running and become a monument, living on as a great but slightly out of it celebrator of last year's roses, or to wade into the latest catalogues, searching vainly for a few bars of music worthy of his golden but aging chops. The Greeks or someone must have had a myth about all this, of an old king and a receding tide, but by the end, Sinatra's incomparable technique was too subtly nuanced for the new songs, and one sometimes got the feeling that he was only singing them under protest and as badly as he could. Then a surprise like Kander and Ebbs's anthem "New York, New York" burst out, reminding one that Frank would

never be completely out of it so long as there were still writers around who had been influenced by him. And one senses an answering spurt of youthfulness and gratitude on his part as he rises to meet, say, George Harrison's "Something" (in the way she moves).

There was still the team of Sammy, Jimmy, and Blue Eyes, until one day there wasn't. Although Jimmy lasted several years longer than almost anyone, he also walked away more briskly than most—and probably much more so than his feisty partner Cahn, who in a sense never quite walked away at all. Cahn went on like Yip Harburg and others, writing light verse for his own amusement and for anyone else he could find to listen, and to supply Sinatra with fourth and fifth choruses as long as Frank stayed open. As noted earlier, lyricists can go on adapting for at least as long as the average lifetime. But there does come a time when even a Sammy Cahn's phone falls silent.

Offstage, both Van Heusen and Frank finally wound down a bit too. Sinatra made a respectable marriage for himself outside of show business, and as far from another Ava Gardner fiasco as he could get. Van Heusen stunned his crowd by getting married too, not to some tomato, chick, or broad, but to an old girlfriend of Crosby's. Jimmy's friendship with Bing had been quieter than his lifelong spree with Frank (Bing was less ring-a-ding-ding than buh-buh-buh-buh), but it was every bit as steady, and amiably boozy too. So—the party was over, and as if to underline it, Bing's second wife, Kathryn, told me that Frank wrote a note to her husband not long before he died, expressing concern over Jimmy's drinking. "I know," she said with a smile, "I know." Any one of them could have written the note about any of the others.

Sinatra's records sound better than ever, Crosby has just been revived, and no doubt will be again, and to my ear Van Heusen's songs lasted the best of all—in the friendly hands not only of his buddies but of generations of jazz musicians who recognize that he had simply taken this kind of music a step further than anyone else had, except possibly Harold Arlen. Good music can now be brought back to life within seconds (as can bad music, of course). But some music comes back to life sounding old, and some young. Van Heusen's songs sound as though they were written this morning.

Johnny Mercer:
The All-American Voice

JOHNNY MERCER

"You have to start with John," Alec Wilder said to me one night. We sat on the porch, talking about that book we never got around to writing. Alec didn't need to say who John was. As mentioned earlier, in his pantheon there were just two first names, two saints, if you will: John (Mercer) and Frank (Sinatra). Everyone else had to grub along with two names.

"All roads lead through John," he added, and for a while that must have seemed true—not just the road to the writers but the road that ran between the past and the future. In the 1930s, Mercer's lyrics had done more than anyone's to split the difference between Tin Pan Alley and the Great

American Outback, between Broadway and Hollywood, thus widening the vocabulary and subject matter of the New York–based standards to embrace a new generation of audiences from all over. As the thirties moved along, Hollywood ceased to be New York West. Old vaudevillians like Bob Hope had been absorbed and reconstituted as Californians, other constituencies began to be heard from in the form of dancers like Buddy Ebsen and comics like Judy Canova, who would have looked just plain peculiar in evening clothes. And seriously—considering the number of kids who went to the movies now—wouldn't Gene Autry, the singing cowboy, really make a more suitable role model than Scarface?

The wave of primness that swept in as Prohibition swept out heavily favored country values over city ones. Jazz songs were speakeasy music—music to get drunk to, and worse. In fact, they were just right for 1940s film noir, which was all about cities and sin. There might be nothing positively sinful about this Gershwin fellow, but he undoubtedly wrote city music and indeed speakeasy music. Now that Daddy was out of the saloon at last, couldn't we try some family music for a change?

Although it seems far-fetched, the cycle actually would play itself out after World War II. Music lost its edge under Perry Como, and sin came thundering back in the new guise of Elvis Presley. But in the late thirties, there were still a couple of breakwaters against wholesomeness—the swing band movement, and the continued presence of the great songwriters. With Cole Porter in full spate and Mr. Kern just learning to swing, the jazz song was still mainstream enough. And if the words of the new songs said "From Natchez to Mobile, from Memphis to St. Joe," and celebrated the Atchison, Topeka, and Santa Fe Railway and "the visiting firemen from Kansas City," who cared where the tunes came from?

For once, the tyranny of lyrics came in handy—these were Mercer's songs and no one else's. And mind you, this wasn't just some city slicker with a road map of Dixie talking, but a regular good old boy. If Johnny Mercer wrote it or sang it, it automatically became country and western, and north and south too. So a couple of years later, in the forties, when America was called upon to perform its occasional miracle of seeming like one country, instead of fifty or a hundred, it needed a sound that could immediately remind kids from Brooklyn, Texas, Alabama, and the Pacific Northwest equally of

home. Who better to turn to than Johnny Mercer? His voice was probably not quite the sound of your own neighborhood, but it definitely came from *a* neighborhood, a real one, a very American one, and one very much worth fighting for. So what if it also reminded you that America was very big? "My Mama Done Tol' Me" and "Accentuate the Positive" belonged to all of us, as did their author. As an average ten-something of the period, I can still remember Johnny as one of the Big Faces, next to people like Harry James, Der Bingle (Crosby), and the Andrews girls, with only two other songwriters in sight—Irving Berlin, who was left over from the last war, and Johnny's old partner, Hoagy Carmichael, who significantly also performed his own songs.

In reality, most of the lyrics our boys marched off singing were not by Mercer at all, but were merely of the "school of Mercer." Like Cole Porter, Johnny so dominated his corner of the musical universe that by December 1941 all songs of a certain kind were reflectively attributed to him, from Frank Loesser's "Small Fry" to Mack Gordon's "Chattanooga Choo Choo" to Tom Adair's "Let's Get Away from It All." Gossip, which is the research department of the obituary page, also prefers one superstar to several neb-ulae, and once established, Johnny's fame was self-perpetuating because his name was mentioned on radio, and other songwriters' weren't.

It was a vicious cycle to those who weren't in it, because Mercer's singing not only made his own songs famous, and vice versa, but it also put a lien on everything it touched. Johnny Burke's "Personality," for in-stance, is always assumed to be Mercer's because Mercer made the hit record of it. And Mack Gordon's "I've Got a Gal in Kalamazoo" goes to Mercer too, because Tex Beneke made the record and Beneke had a twang kind of like Mercer's, and besides has a name that takes at least twenty seconds to memorize, and who has the time?

To clinch his monopoly, Johnny looked and sounded exactly like peo-ple wanted him to: with a Huck Finn face, a gap-toothed grin, and an old shoe of a voice that reminded bandleader Paul Whiteman of a man singing in his sleep. Most of the great songwriters, as we've seen, looked like something else, but Mercer could have won an open casting call for the part of himself. When an artist resembles his work (as did Picasso, Gershwin, Hemingway), he seems twice as much of a genius, and fre-quently picks up all the marbles for his generation.

Yet although Mercer's reputation is by now almost as padded as

Dorothy Parker's with other people's creations, one finds little or no trace of serious resentment among his contemporaries. The consensus seems to be that (1) Mercer was simply too nice a guy for even a writer to resent, and (2) like Parker, he deserved his reputation, because he simply wrote better "Mercer" songs than anyone else. In terms not only of versification but also of sheer effectiveness (i.e., hits), Mercer's words were never just clever but extremely functional: "Bye bye baby/Time to hit the road to dreamland/You're my baby/ Dig you in the land of nod" caps its notes perfectly, punctuating them on the nose and making them sound as good as they possibly could.

Mercer may or may not have been the best poet among the lyricists, but he was one of the most musical, and he wrote enough "just right" tunes of his own to prove it. "I Wanna Be Around (to Pick Up the Pieces)" and "Something's Gotta Give" could not be improved melodically by Richard Rodgers himself, because Mercer—like Berlin, Porter, Loesser, and other complete songwriters—knew exactly what went where in a song and could always make up in aptness for what he lacked in musical brilliance. Mercer's special gift was to feel as at home with other people's tunes as with his own. If a hit could be found in a piece of material, Johnny would find it, or else he might put it there by changing a note or two. So the high road to Mercer Junction jostled with tinkers bringing their pots and pans, sharps and flats, to the old alchemist in hopes of a gold record.

But the roads Alec Wilder was talking about were also packed with old friends coming back for more. Anyone lucky enough to have caught Mercer's classic evening at the Ninety-second Street Y in New York in March 1971, or even to have heard a recording of it, can attest to the astonishing pleasure of his company. Mercer wasn't only entertaining but curiously authentic: Courtesy wasn't second nature to him; it was his essence. He didn't need to turn on the charm; he just had to be himself.

Above all, he didn't have one face for the public and another for friends. Everyone got the same Mercer, and as if to prove it, he warbled special greetings that night to some real pals in attendance—his old partner Harold Arlen; his teacher Yip Harburg; and Burton Lane, who just wrote songs—which warmed the whole audience the way great entertainers do. The entertainer whispers a private message, and a million people swear it's for them.

Like Frank Sinatra, Mercer never seemed to be addressing more than one person at a time—a person of immense importance to him. So if he was by chance addressing you, with the jokes and the compliments specially tailored for you, you would presumably walk through fire to keep in touch. And that's pretty much what you had to do, except that the fire usually came on your way out because Mercer also happened to be the meanest, cruelest of drunks this side of James Thurber.

As Wilder described it to me, when the bottle reached a certain level—he pointed to a spot two inches or so from the bottom—Johnny switched from friend to enemy in the course of a single sentence, flaying you alive with the nastiest crack he could think of. (He allegedly told Irving Berlin he had no talent for writing lyrics.)

Fortunately, Wilder, who had once suffered from the same malignancy himself, also knew the antidote: You sang a certain tune (he told me the name once, but I forgot it, and when I asked again, he'd forgotten it too), and Johnny would immediately burst into tears and forget what he was mad at. As every bartender knows, sadism and sentimentality are so closely wired in the human psyche that they constantly trip over each other in a drunk's head. But apparently only this one song would do it for Mercer, and if you didn't know it, you simply had to sing everything you knew while enduring the Jekyll-and-Hyde transformation and wait patiently for Johnny's flowers of remorse and the funny note that came with them the next day. Since Johnny could seldom remember whom he'd insulted, there must have been a lot of unexplained gifts. All his friends knew exactly what singer Jo Stafford meant when she said, "Please don't send me flowers tomorrow, Johnny."

Why a man drinks until his heart turns so black that he even hates the cat is a mystery understood only by the one doing it, and only while he's doing it. But one reason Johnny didn't quit is that it seems to have cost him no friends that he couldn't win back the next day. Nobody took it personally, for long at any rate. Whoever this foul-mouthed demon might be, he clearly wasn't the real Johnny Mercer.

So where *was* this unreal voice coming from? Drunken blather is a maddeningly opaque source, but one might find an echo someplace in the shadows and echoes of Savannah, Georgia, Johnny's hometown. He certainly came from pugnacious stock. An ancestor no more than four or five

generations earlier had gone down fighting in the Battle of Princeton during the Revolutionary War, while his great-grandfather Brigadier General
Hugh Weedon Mercer seems to have left the Confederate Army under a
cloud after the Civil War, brought on by his trial for the murder of two de-
serters. Perhaps old Hugh was doomed to roam the earth and pour his un-
used rage through the mellifluous pipes of his amiable descendant.

Such unearthly goings-on seem entirely possible as you wander the
moonlit squares of old Savannah, where the haunting of houses and of
people is like a plain fact of life. A young poet growing up here might find
it almost too rich, too overwhelming. What on earth could one write to
equal it? But at least Johnny was spared the handicap of living in a great
house or coming from a top family. The Mercer residence was and is a no-
big-deal affair on the outskirts of town. And, socially speaking, the Mercers were virtually arrivistes.

So Johnny grew up with an artist's double vision of Savannah, part
F. Scott Fitzgerald peering through the rich folks' windows, and part in-
sider, much too proud to be bowled over by what he saw. From a certain
point of view, he was in a rare position to look down on the town if he felt
like it. The Mercers were originally a great Virginia family, and when his
violent great-grandfather, General Weedon Mercer, married into Savannah in the 1840s, he had graduated from West Point and probably thought
he was doing Savannah a favor. Weedon Mercer would leave behind a decidedly mixed inheritance. On the upside, he built one of the greatest of
all great houses, thereby implanting the family name like a memorial in
the heart of the town, but then he saw to it by his army disgrace that no
Mercer would ever live in the Mercer house. His own last days were spent
out of gossip range in Baden-Baden, Germany. Meanwhile, he'd sown the
seed that would end up inside a man who could someday write "Any place
I hang my hat is home," which is either a very democratic thing to say or
a very arrogant one, depending on how you say it.

An artist never completely lets go of anything, but on a conscious and
working level, Mercer's drunken nonsense really did come from a phan-
tom of sorts, namely, the self he might have been if he hadn't been subverted by American popular music from the age of six months, when he
hummed his first tune. Although his parents sent him to a posh Virginia
prep school called the Woodberry Forest School, he had already received

his basic education from the Victrola in the parlor, to which he listened with a child's ravenous capacity to learn, memorizing everything he heard and singing along with it.

Listening to those old Victrolas was an intense experience. The machines constantly needed cranking and the cylinders or records had to be changed every few minutes, and you'd better be paying attention. For the three minutes or so it lasted, the song was your whole universe, subsuming everything around it. To this day, I can remember the furniture around me as I sat listening to Mercer's early hit "I'm an Old Cowhand" as a tot in England.

If he'd heard anything but songs on the Victrola, he didn't bother to mention it. Basically, music for him would always be something that came with words. You might call the notes do-re-me or B-sharp and E-flat, or you might call them "I'm an old cowhand"—they answered to a thousand names, depending on the context, and matching them up became an early hobby. (He wrote his first complete song at age fifteen.) The only instrument he ever mastered was the human voice, which had to serve him as pianos serve other writers, as his lab, workshop, and rumpus room.

While still in his garbage-can years, absorbing everything, he picked up maybe his only non-American influence: W. S. Gilbert, who would become a crucial part of the mix. In most respects, Mercer might have come from a different planet than did Ira Gershwin and Yip Harburg, yet all three learned their ABC's from this same teacher, a Victorian English wit working in a language as remote from Southern vernacular as it was from that of the Lower East Side. No one trained in this school could ever be tempted by a rhyming-dictionary rhyme or a stale thought or a shabby word. Although Mercer would continue to use the dialect of his region, and everyone else's, he did it with the snap and the literacy of a Gilbert and Sullivan patter song. "But who was in the pantry a-laughin' and scratchin'/The waiter and the porter and the upstairs maid" (words and music: J. Mercer) isn't Broadway, but it isn't Tin Pan Alley either. It's what might be called "the Mercer compromise," a mishmash of high and low idioms that's both slangy and classy, an American *Upstairs, Downstairs* set to a jazz beat, and a quaint fragment of Mercer's autobiography, if you translate it a little.

Nothing sharpens the ear or the tongue like going from one social class to another, and that's pretty much what Johnny had to do, slipping out of the stuffy front rooms of Savannah society and into the pantry to find his voice and his material. At some unknown early date, he took to crossing over regularly to the black side of town, where he immersed himself so deeply in jazz and blues that he would one day receive a citation from a black social group calling him "our favorite colored singer." As Hoagy Carmichael, his partner in jazz, would say, "Johnny knew." For all his adaptability, there was a black-jazz base in everything Mercer wrote.

But the parlors of Savannah had their own siren song, and he never fully gave up his citizenship there either. In the sixties, when the writer Budd Schulberg asked Johnny if he could bring the great black pianist Hazel Scott to a party Johnny was giving, Johnny said, in effect, "I don't think it's that kind of party." The waiters and porters and upstairs maids might be his superiors in some ways, but he wouldn't know what to say to them if he found them in the parlor. In an old clip of Mercer appearing on the Nat King Cole TV show, Johnny looks friendly enough (he's there, isn't he?), but for once utterly tongue-tied, sheepish, and unsure of himself. He undoubtedly venerated black musicians: He led the singing of "Happy Birthday" on Louis Armstrong's fiftieth birthday at the Newport Jazz Festival in Rhode Island, and there's a picture of him in Bob Bach and Ginger Mercer's book *Our Huckleberry Friend* posed manfully cheek to cheek with Lena Horne. No one ever accused him of faking these overtures. It's just that in all his trips to the black side of Savannah, there is no record of his ever talking to anyone or making any friends. His manner with Nat King Cole is not that of an arrogant racist, but of a small boy who has never gotten over his shyness and slight fear. It may be that he crossed the tracks too early, before he could cope socially, but he had to be that young to get the gold, the beat.

Luckily for his peace of mind, Johnny's break with the upstairs life of Savannah was rendered infinitely easier by the Depression, which emptied a lot of parlors like his and removed yards of stuffing from American society. The real estate business of his father, George Mercer, went belly-up, and any thoughts the son might have had of writing for the Whiffenpoofs of Yale or the Triangle Club of Princeton went out the window.

Johnny had already been to New York, his dream city—the first time with a local stage company and the second time as a ship's stowaway—and he'd played a few bit parts in legitimate theater.

But then suddenly the sky was the limit. Survivors like John Cheever and Walter Kerr have testified to the giddy freedom young people felt during the Great Depression. "Goodbye, family business" was the song they were singing. "Farewell, old school tie." You were free at least to wait tables and wash dishes to your heart's content, and write songs and "dream, dream, dream," as Mercer's own song says.

The closest Johnny would come to washing dishes was serving as a Wall Street runner. But for once in history, songwriting proved a more solid profession than brokering. (People were doing a lot more singing than banking.) And in no time, Johnny was placing lyrics in shows and edging his way into the fraternity. His first sale, a bouncy number called "Out of Breath (and Scared to Death)" appeared in the Garrick Gaieties revue alongside an early effort by his next great friend, Yip Harburg, while a singing job with Paul Whiteman got John into a trio with Harold Arlen's ubiquitous brother, Jerry, who, as we've seen, would soon be writing lyrics with another future partner, Jimmy Van Heusen. So it went, like some hilarious frat party, as a brilliant new generation pulled into town, all set to take over from fuddy-duddys like Jerome Kern, Sigmund Romberg, and Vincent Youmans.

New York lived up to Johnny's dream so well that he remained somewhat starry-eyed about it until the day he died. By all accounts, the city has never been more charming than when it was dead broke and down at the heels, and there was no better place to watch it from than Paul Whiteman's bandstand, which seemed to be situated in the eye of the party. Everyone in music seemed to pass either through it or by it, and the gleeful Johnny met not only his heroes, the great songwriters who had raised him, but half the guys he would be working with in the coming years, including Whiteman's trombonist-singer, Jack Teagarden, his ex–Rhythm Boy Bing Crosby, and his violinist-arranger, Matty Malneck, with whom Johnny wrote "Goody Goody" and other goodies. Even Hoagy Carmichael, who would coauthor Johnny's first big hit, "Lazy Bones," had cut his first record of his first song with Paul Whiteman, the talent scout of the era.

In these circumstances, there was nothing to do but go ahead and be-

come a songwriter. The choice may seem like a foregone conclusion in retrospect, but Mercer apparently couldn't believe his luck at first and was convinced only by his extraordinary success and the huge amount of work the boss gave him to do. Whiteman hosted a weekly radio show, and feeding special material to this monster is probably what made Mercer finally feel like the professional he'd been all along. Early hits like "P.S. I Love You" (music: Gordon Jenkins) suggest he was born professional, but it took a while for the country boy to stop scuffing his feet and calling people "sir" and "ma'am" and come into his estate.

He made the break with Savannah's rules official by marrying a New York showgirl named Ginger Meehan. Notarizing the split in his personality, so to speak, he marched off with the rest of the gang to Hollywood, which, as the Depression deepened, seemed like the last room in the house with the lights on. In 1935, Mercer signed on briefly as a writer and singing actor at RKO, but after two crummy movies, no one ever called him an actor again. As Mercer's name continued to penetrate the great American vagueness with songs he could sing himself, like "The Old Music Master" with Carmichael and "Bob White" (music: Bernie Hanighen), it didn't matter how hard the studios tried to bury his name between the art director's and the costume designer's; he was a star. "If you were a composer," says Margaret Whiting, "you tried to get Johnny Mercer or Frank Loesser, or else it didn't matter." And even Loesser felt Mercer was getting all the best assignments. Johnny reigned alone, in the public mind and in fact.

Thus, by his late twenties, the only question left to answer in that slaphappy community was: Who was lazier, he or Ira Gershwin? With Johnny and, I suspect, with Ira too, it was largely a matter of style. Although Mercer got through a prodigious amount of work, he appeared to do it all, like his singing, in his sleep. His preferred modus operandi was to lie on his back with his eyes closed like a psychiatric patient, as if he could dream songs into existence. But when Harry Warren tested this by saying, "How's Ginger?" on his way out to lunch one day, Mercer said, "She's fine," when Harry got back.

These naps must have been hives of activity as Mercer first mastered the tune, amazingly fast, and then laid various versions on it. Sometimes he opened his eyes with a complete lyric, and sometimes he came up empty. This kind of creation went in fits and starts. One particular assign-

ment took him so long that Carmichael couldn't remember having written the tune when he finally received the finished song, "Skylark." But fast or slow, Mercer's style suited the image of casualness and added a finishing touch to his public persona. Movie people of the 1930s didn't have lives at all in the New York sense; they had anecdotes. And Mercer's laziness took care of all his duties in that department.

The shallowness of the legend can be gauged by a story Margaret Whiting tells. It seems that when Warner Bros. offered him the use of either Harry Warren or Margaret's father, Richard Whiting, as a partner, he said, "I guess I'll have to go with Dick—I think he can help me with my golf game." What Johnny remembered saying in his own, more sober, version was, "I'd rather work with Dick Whiting than with anybody," because he hero-worshipped Whiting for his work in the twenties even more than he hero-worshipped Warren. In the end, he managed to write with both of them: "Jeepers Creepers" with Warren and "Too Marvelous for Words" with Whiting. His golf game was never heard from again.

Likewise, the real Johnny probably closed his eyes not to relax but to "get in tune with the infinite," as he told his father. But he wasn't brought up to talk like that in public, or to talk about himself at all for more than a few minutes. So we'll never know. "I could tell you a lot/But it's not/in a gentleman's code" is how the lines originally read—and that went double for Johnny.

"Hooray for Hollywood," he wrote ironically (along with Richard Whiting), but artistically speaking, crazy old Hollywood gave him a lot to cheer about. The luck of the studio draw may have kept him from writing with Carmichael as much as nature had intended, but it gave him Harold Arlen instead, an even better partner in some ways. Mercer and Carmichael were so much alike, it might have been one man writing; with Arlen it was definitely two, each with an infinite capacity to surprise the other. "Blues in the Night," "One for My Baby," "That Old Black Magic," "My Shining Hour." What will he think of next? one imagines each of them thinking as he plunged in for more. And the system also gave him one dance with Jerome Kern, of which Johnny made the most. The persnickety Kern was so tickled by the lyrics to "I'm Old-Fashioned" that he summoned his wife to come listen—not an everyday occurrence in the Kern household. Mercer wrote just as well with Rube Bloom ("Fools Rush In") and Victor

Schertzinger ("Tangerine") as with the masters. Johnny Mercer was in the middle of a lifelong roll, and he wrote (and sang) like a happy man. Founding and helping run Capitol Records would be fun too for a while, giving him a chance to launch his spiritual daughter, Dick Whiting's orphan Margaret, on her great career and to give us the best of Jo Stafford. His records with Bing Crosby sound like a gas, as those two tightly coiled men vied with each other in feats of relaxation. "Allegretto, Mr. Crosby?" "Alligator, Mr. M." Singing with Crosby felt like family, as singing with Bobby Darin later would. It was the only style he knew.

Today his real family remains as private as ever, by unanimous consent. His marriage was perfect on the surface, as marriages were in those days, although people tend to roll their eyes when you mention Ginger, indicating perhaps that she was, or had become, a handful. His children, Amanda and John Jeff, were perfect too, as of course were Bing Crosby's and Joan Crawford's, but the real difference was that no one has ever wanted to write anything bad about Mercer, nor has anyone ever wanted to read it. Even the prodigious gossip mill has managed to cough up only one rumored affair, with Judy Garland. In movies, Garland never made a convincing romantic lead, but Johnny might have responded to the great singer and interpreter within.

Foraging for clues in the texts, one notes that he wrote not one but two mouthwatering songs of vengeance, "Goody Goody" and "I Wanna Be Around" ("And that's when I'll discover that revenge is sweet/As I sit there applauding from a front-row seat"), as well as some of the most roundabout love songs to come out of a most roundabout period. Like most American males, Johnny had a devil of a time with "I Love You," which the cheek-to-cheek dancing of the thirties and forties demanded a lot of, and he frequently resorted to far-out metaphors. The narrator of "Day In, Day Out" (music: Rube Bloom), for instance, feels a pounding in his heart whenever he even thinks of his loved one, which escalates abruptly into an ocean's roar and a thousand drums beating, the moment he makes contact. Clearly, this chap is inches away from cardiac arrest and must never kiss anyone again—or try to sing either.

But you don't take in the prose of the matter as you dance and hum across the floor, just sense a surge of primal feeling that seems to come from the music. And that's all that a love song strictly requires. Mercer

piles the gorgeous sounds up to the roof, and if you wind up thinking, as I did for years, that this song is set in the tropics, so much the better. Johnny plants these travel-guide images subliminally enough for lovers to miss, with a dab here and a dab there, going (in "And the Angels Sing") from "water and moonlight beaming" to "long winter nights with the candles gleaming" and home again, like Dorothy returning from Oz, and you leave the floor thinking you've just had a wonderful dream.

Johnny's ballads are not great or even fairly good poetry, but they're superb musical poetry because everything fits. In his interview with Max Wilk, Mercer doesn't even mention poetry but talks about tunes, and the value of having a feel for them, of recognizing them, as Michelangelo allegedly recognized King David in a block of stone. Then, in the words of his colleague Oscar Hammerstein, "never let her go," and almost any old lyric will do. Mercer's own favorite song of all time, "It Had to Be You" (music: Isham Jones; words: Gus Kahn), bears a lyric of no distinction whatever, except that you remember it forever, after one hearing, because everything fits.

In short, Mercer was 100 percent professional, revealing next to nothing about himself in his work while seeming to reveal everything. A later partner, Bobby Dolan, used words like "listened," "learned," "absorbed," "transformed" to describe Mercer's trade secrets. His rumored laziness was long forgotten in his later period. Johnny was all business.

But there's always a little something besides professionalism in a Mercer song. Hacks walk away untouched when the job is done, but real artists go deeper, leaving behind bits of themselves. You'd swear there was a drop of Mercer's own blood in the gallon the man is bleeding as he sits at the bar, wailing about his code and his baby, although they may not be bleeding over the same thing. "When my life is through . . . then I shall tell them I remember you." Again, one doesn't have to take this literally: "You's" and "baby's" come and go, but the emotion in the sobbing is genuine if you listen to the subtext, which is the same in all Mercer's songs. "Isn't this a goddamn beautiful tune?" is what they're saying so passionately. "Can you hear what I hear? Please love it as much as I do."

Mercer was a man of more than one Rosebud, and if the Victrola in the parlor was his first true love, a second comes through almost as strongly. Without a doubt, what he liked best about Hollywood was that to get

there and back you had to take a train: the only form of transportation ever devised capable of breaking a man's heart. Mercer seems to have dreamed about locomotives before he ever took one, and he remained a lifelong addict. "I took a trip on the train," he wrote for Jimmy Van Heusen, "and I thought about you." But I'll bet what he really thought about was more trains—not cardboard choo-choos leaving for Chattanooga and Alabam', whisking babies hither and yon, but real ones, blowing lonesome whistles across trestles on the way out of Philadelphia. Trains were worlds unto themselves, everywhere and nowhere, with parlors and pantries, uppers and lowers, chugging along together to a solid beat; and they were full of America and its talk, like rolling dictionaries of slang. No wonder Mercer's lyrics traveled so well. They were all written in the *lingo de club car,* not to mention of mothers whispering to infants and Pullman porters cajoling drunks into upper berths. "Time to hit the road."

So Mercer must have felt that things were truly winding down when both the songs and the trains seemed to stop running in the midfifties. But his mild bitterness about this did not consume him, as it did so many of his colleagues, or consign him to his memories. He revised his slang every year, popping in a "switcheroonie" in the fifties and using verbs like "bug" and "split" in the sixties and seventies. He kept going. As that great song with Carmichael says, "You can tell 'em I'll be there." This was a determined man, and while there was still a tune left out there unattended by an English lyric, he'd sing tenor or countertenor, and forget he'd ever heard of jazz if he had to, just to be there, giving his all. As the years went by, he laid words on top of French tunes such as "Autumn Leaves" and "When the World Was Young" and a swell German one called "Summer Wind" and a little something by Rimsky-Korsakov ("Song of India"). He did the best he could with Henry Mancini's maudlin "Moon River" and better than that with "Days of Wine and Roses," winning Oscars for both in a by-now-empty field. If he had slowed down, it wasn't because his creative powers were failing.

Even his one big disappointment was of a kind to keep a man trying. He couldn't seem to buy a hit show on Broadway, with the half exception of *L'il Abner.* Mercer's songs were private worlds, complete unto themselves, and they never seemed comfortable as parts of plays. So for all the ingenuity he poured into shows like *Texas Li'l Darlin', Saratoga,* and *Foxy,*

he achieved only one Broadway standard, "Come Rain or Come Shine" (music: Arlen), from *St. Louis Woman*. Ah, well. He didn't much care for that mode of song-plugging anyhow, as he explained to us at the Y that night. Someone might steal your ideas while you dawdled through tryouts and cast changes. Still, if you had a good story for him . . .

Meanwhile, offstage, he kept on going around, like the whirling dervish he wrote about, doing people "real good turns" in the private sector. He secretly paid off his father's Depression-related real estate debts, only to have the press get hold of the story, which a cynic might say was the best of all possible outcomes. He cofounded the Songwriters Hall of Fame, apparently to cheer up an old friend called Abe Olman, who had found life a touch stale after co-writing the hit "Oh Johnny, Oh Johnny, Oh!" in 1917. And he did more small acts of kindness than he ever wanted people to know about.

In my mind, his last days will always be entwined with Alec Wilder. One late-summer evening in 1975, when Johnny Mercer was ill, I remember Alec mentioning in passing that he couldn't for the life of him remember that song that neutralized John's drunken rages. Not that it mattered anymore. When I next heard from Wilder, he said, "Did you hear that John died?"

A stroke, a tumor, life support—Johnny loathed and avoided hospitals, so there's no reason to hang around one now, and even less reason to end his story there. After dying on June 25, 1976, Johnny resumed official residence in Savannah, where his body now lies alongside his wife's and parents' in Bonaventure Cemetery, of which it is said locally that it is almost as good to be dead there as alive anywhere else. Typically, his grave does not have pride of place, which belongs by protocol to his father's first wife. His is the next one over and bears the simple legend "And the Angels Sing." Ginger's headstone says "You Must Have Been a Beautiful Baby." Amen and amen.

Whatever ambiguity Brigadier General Weedon Mercer may have left behind has been long since cleared up. Johnny owns the town now, with a boulevard and a theater named after him and with his own personal sign in the cemetery pointing to his grave. And maybe he has brought Savannah some good luck in return by helping to inspire John Berendt's evocative book *Midnight in the Garden of Good and Evil*, which has filled the

town with the kind of tourists who don't want to change anything, a rare and valuable breed.

But one can't imagine Johnny staying put year round. Johnny may have been an Episcopalian choirboy once upon a time, but his spirit was always pure pantheist and can still be found in woods and streams and blossom-covered lanes—not to mention railroad depots, late-night saloons, and any town in America that has a funny name. All you have to do is whistle. Or, if you can still find one, hop a train going anywhere, and listen.

Part Five

Survival on Broadway—
The Curtain That Won't Stay Down

Frank Loesser's
Great New York Musical

FRANK LOESSER

Simply in terms of keeping up with the Joneses—the Romes and the Parises—both world wars were quite good for New York. At the end of World War I, New York emerged fully armed as a great world city, as if it had been rehearsing and designing sets all along, and here it was, complete with its own Left Bank (Greenwich Village) and Rue de Rivoli (Fifth Avenue) and London's West End (Broadway), only with lights.

But then suddenly at the end of the real world war, New York was the *only* great world city. But it wasn't quite the same New York, and two musicals tell the story. *On the Town,* by the team of Comden and Green and Leonard Bernstein, is about New York as seen from the outside by its first

postwar tourists, the U.S. military. Every time you turned around in 1945, the fleet seemed to be in town and fracturing New Yorkers' most venerable rule by actually looking up at the buildings. (Did they think they were in Kansas City?)

Naturally, Broadway was on the tour. But to get there you had to wade through, or bypass, the district called Hell's Kitchen, where a quite different New York was in the works. *West Side Story* is all about that world, and as always with this city, it is full of strangers, but their foreign accents have changed and they dance to a very different drummer. And as the Jets and Sharks act out their blood feud, it's hard to believe that just a few years and blocks away, the Algonquin wits zinged each other with one-liners and left it at that. So it was perhaps appropriate that the scores to both these guidebooks were written by Bernstein, a New Yorker with a deep feel for the city but with a Carnegie Hall accent and point of view, capable of turning out brand-new folk songs without a trace of Tin Pan Alley about them.

However, there was still life in the old Alley. It was trickling out of Hollywood and taking up full residence in the Brill Building. It was less like an alley now and more like the United Nations building, with Alexander Borodin's music being placed in Baghdad for the show *Kismet,* and the Austrian Fritz Loewe contributing scores set in Paris, London, and Scotland. Or, as Cole Porter put it, "We open in Venice." And we next play Bali Hai and the palace in Siam.

Amid this smorgasbord of styles and places, the Alley struck in 1950 with its most authentic and welcome gift: nothing less than the great *New York* musical and the most brilliant evocation ever of the city where the songs and shows and so many of the writers came from. It dawned on me, as I reach for my pencil, that the last act of *Guys and Dolls* is still being written at this very moment, because right outside my window the streets of Manhattan are undergoing a transformation that will permanently move the setting of this glorious story beyond the reach of living memory. Thus, I decided to write this last-minute salute to a part of the New York imagination that would never be imagined quite so well again. Unless we somehow get lucky.

Walt Disney, meet Damon Runyon: It's a New Yorker's worst nightmare. So ever since the Disney company announced its plans to renovate

the *Guys and Dolls* country, aka Times Square, old-timers have had visions of theme parks full of wax figures dialing imaginary bookies, while Harry the Horse quietly turns into Horace Horsecollar, Louie the Lip splits into Huey, Dewey, and Louie, and Mindy's Bar and Grill changes its name to Minnie's Ice Cream Emporium. No Smoking Anywhere, of course.

Say it ain't so, Nathan. And so far, it ain't . . . quite. But the Disney people seem bent on making the formerly seedy Times Square area wholesome, a shining suburb on the hill, full of empty space and clean air. A Runyon character might experience difficulty breathing in such an atmosphere. If he were still around, that is. Luckily for Disney, most of Runyon's originals left town years ago, sometime between the death of the nickel phone call and the arrival of offtrack betting. No doubt Harry the Horse is now on the Internet, wondering why Big Louie insists on the Mac, while Bennie Southgate mows the lawn in his Bermuda shorts. Meanwhile, their old hunting ground had become an urban wasteland like any other, where telephones dangled from broken hooks and first-night audiences showed up in blue jeans, the way they do it in Moscow.

So maybe the best Disney could do was clean it up and start over. No doubt, the dirt will be back. Either way, history doesn't care, because by good chance the old place has been preserved forever in maybe the most authentic folk-musical we have. As we've seen, you could move Rodgers and Hammerstein's *State Fair* from Iowa to Oklahoma, or the South Pacific or the Austrian Tirol, and it would still be the same old place: Broadway, in the Scarsdale years.

But in the same period, a couple of real New York guys had put their heads together and managed to replicate this time and place with pitch-perfect fidelity, down to the last pari-mutuel ticket floating in the gutter outside Sardi's. And they locked it into a script so evocative that *Guys and Dolls* may also be our most cast-proof musical. Give it to any group of actors you like, from Englishmen to inner city African Americans to surfing high school students from Malibu, they'll all wind up reminding you of New Yawk.

And the aforementioned two guys accomplished all this in spite of Damon Runyon. All that Mr. Runyon of Florida and Colorado actually did was take one strand of New York speech—the occasionally eloquent pedantry of self-taught street guys on their best behavior—and reduce it to a formula as easy to imitate as Jimmy Cagney reciting Ernest Hemingway.

So Frank Loesser kept Runyon's three-page plot and his characters' names and wrote some songs in his own language, and Abe Burrows wrote some dialogue in *his* own language around the songs, and Loesser wrote some more songs around the dialogue, and Presto!—Times Square as it was and always will be. "Sidown, you're rockin' the boat," "I got the horse right here"—the phrases come straight off the street, as if the actors had just rushed them into the theater, as they do in "Waiting for Lefty."

Only more so, because they are set to equally red-hot, street-smart tunes, which is where the genius comes in. Ask anyone what he remembers best about the show and it's a probable, twelve to seven, he'll shoot back with a song title or phrase: "Take back your mink / To from whence it came," "It's a cinch that the bum/is under the thumb/of some little broad."

Once upon a time, New Yorkers really did talk like that, and a few still do, but Henry and Julia Loesser most decidedly had not raised their little boy Frank to do so. What he was supposed to talk was German, and the songs he was supposed to write, between symphonies, were presumably German lieder. The Loessers were Prussian immigrants fresh off the boat and for all of their high-minded lives they carried a torch, a blowtorch in fact, for high culture.

So Frank, one of nature's lowbrows, had his work cut out for him from the cradle. Since his old man was a well-known classical piano teacher, Frank's wayward genius warned him to avoid piano lessons at all costs— although he apparently could play the instrument anyhow, by instinct. And since his mother was a snob at large, he naturally took to talking like a Dead End kid or stage-gangster, apprenticing himself to the culture that came in through the window, the music of the street, as thoroughly as a Juilliard student learning his Bach and Mozart.

Yet Frank also loved his parents, and at the age of sixteen would wander the streets desolately himself after his father suddenly up and died. Although Henry is best remembered for the screaming rages that terrorized his students, and although Julia would remain, according to her granddaughter, Susan, cold and unapproachable to the end of her days, young Frank emerged from this menacing household bubbling with confidence, as if he'd just had the happiest childhood in history. So the Loessers presumably loved each other, whatever they thought of the rest of us, and they especially loved Frank, whose preternatural charm and

good humor show up even in his baby photos and would serve him as a talisman against malice all his life. No one could ever stay mad at Frank for long, either as a child or as an adult.

Which is just as well, because he grew up to be a Loesser himself, in an upside-down sort of way, with a ferocious, perfectionist temper just like his daddy's. Eyewitnesses swear that they saw both his feet leave the ground together midtantrum. And on one famous occasion, he actually slugged the singer Isabel Bigley for messing up at a rehearsal. But his rage was so theatrical and kind of funny, and over so quickly, that it left no serious trace on anyone. (Except on Frank Sinatra, who never forgave Loesser for telling him how to play Nathan Detroit. The nerve of some people.)

The other thing Frank got from his family was a sufficiently thick skin to survive on Broadway, in Hollywood, or in Hell itself. The Loessers flung criticism around like cream pies in a silent comedy, and even after Frank became rich and fairly famous, his half-brother, Arthur, would write a lordly put-down of all pop music as being ephemeral "merchandise" which was rammed "down the ears of an abject public." (He admitted that his brother, Frank, did it quite well—but so what?)

Arthur Loesser had by then become Cleveland's arbiter of taste, and his condescension borders on the comical, not to say the maddening. Yet the two men apparently rejoiced in each other's company. And icy old Julia stayed close too, in the curious family style of loving the man and hating his music. "Baby, It's Cold Outside" simply doesn't sound like an art song, even in German, and neither does "Bloop Bleep," Frank's meditation on leaky faucets. By the end, Frank's royalties had swept Julia up from genteel poverty to the top of the hog, but neither she nor Arthur could ever face the possibility that the author of "Bloop Bleep" might be the real musical genius of the family and themselves the stooges and straight men in his life story.

Frank seems to have had trouble facing it himself. When he first edged into songwriting in the early thirties, it was strictly as a lyricist, not a tune guy. By then the Depression was raging and no form of making money was to be sneezed at, even by the Loessers, who hit bottom right after Henry's death in 1926. So Frank wrote some material for vaudeville and such while his mother waited for him to find a real profession. As Richard "*Damn Yankees*" Adler describes him a few years later, this should not have

been a problem, even in the worst of times, since he was also a "skilled astronomer, a master carpenter and cabinet maker, a terrific cartoonist." So why go on with a career his family despised?

Well, astronomy didn't pay that well, and there wasn't much call for cabinets, and one song led to another . . . until thirty years had gone by in a twinkling, with his mother still waiting for him to find a profession. By the time Frank hit Hollywood in 1937, his new partner, Hoagy Carmichael, would find him "so packed with ideas, he was overloaded." But they were still ideas for words only. It took another five years or so for anyone to find out that Loesser could write tunes too.

So he settled for being the best or second best lyricist in Hollywood in the late thirties and early forties, depending on how you rate Johnny Mercer. As with Mercer, his double gift gave him an almost unfair advantage in the race for hits, because his words were not just clever but musical. They made the tunes they went with sound their absolute best. Songs like Burton Lane's "The Lady's in Love with You," Victor Schertzinger's "Sand in My Shoes," and almost everything he wrote with Jimmy McHugh— "Let's Get Lost" and "Say It (Over and Over Again)"—are good songs that sound like great ones because of Loesser's touch.

"Don't get a clever rhymer," he said to Jule Styne, after the two of them had together written "I Don't Want to Walk Without You" and gone back to their separate studios. When a genius gives advice, he's usually talking about himself and it's a sure sign of a Loesser song that afterward you can't be absolutely sure whether it rhymed or not. A Loesser lyric is a poem that you forget is a poem because there's so much else going on. Not even Mercer could sound so natural while being so literary. "I've got spurs that jingle jangle jingle." Who else on Tin Pan Alley ever wrote a song about his spurs or packed so much music into a verbal phrase?

The other thing the Hollywood years revealed was that Loesser didn't turn his ears off when he crossed the Hudson. He continued to pick up phrases from all over, including places he'd never been. "Small Fry" (music: Carmichael) is so all-American that people assume it must be one of Mercer's, and "Murder, He Says" (music: McHugh) remains the best guide we have to the slang the kids were using in World War II. And then there's "I get the rumble seat ride," which conveys not just the sound of middle-American life, but the whole texture of it. "When there's a com-

pany weekend/I get the couch in the hall" (McHugh again). As a boy, Loesser had somehow managed to get thrown out of both school and college, but this was obviously because they couldn't keep up with him; no one could teach as fast and as well as he could learn on his own.

Finally, his gift of melody came squirming out, not cocky like everything else about him, but as a last resort. In 1941, America needed a patriotic song right away to match the suddenness of Pearl Harbor. In no time, lyricist Loesser found just the phrase he wanted, "Praise the Lord and Pass the Ammunition." A real chaplain had said it, never guessing it was just what the nation needed: something jaunty but not irreverent, as if to say, "We're a God-fearing nation, but we're not pantywaists, by golly."

The only trouble was that no one could come up with a tune fast enough that caught this mood as well as Frank's own dummy version did, so out it came at last, a rollicking hymn that perfectly launched Tin Pan Alley's war effort, with a wink at God and a growl of determination and a subtext that said "This war is going to be a riot."

But one song does not a great songwriter make, and Loesser's next wartime classic, "They're Either Too Young or Too Old," would find him back safe and sound in the studio system, writing words to Arthur Schwartz's tune. And so it might have continued if it hadn't been for the war itself and its manic demand for entertainment. In the fall of 1942, Frank decided at his own whim to become a private in the U.S. Army— perhaps the only private ever to have all his uniforms tailored.

He was eventually stationed by a prescient War Department in a hotel just off Times Square, where his only duty was to manufacture entertainment on the double, any way he knew how. This meant that if he thought up a lyric, he had better provide his own tune, and stand by to sing it too, in a voice he once compared to that of an auctioneer, and in an accent somewhere to the right of William Bendix. Thus, under the lash of military discipline (he was once reprimanded for sleeping when he should have been meeting the general), his knack for matching the tune to the circumstance surfaced once again and earned him the title of "the GIs' own songwriter." "What do you do in the infantry? You march, you march, you march" captures the essence of war, namely, the drudgery and grumbling; the song makes your feet hurt just to listen to it. So the brass rejected it and the infantry marched to it anyway.

Loesser's own war doesn't sound that drudging—three suites at the Navarro Hotel is a long ways from a pup tent or a foxhole—but he'd already known for several bad years in Hollywood what it was like to dine on a can of beans for two, so now he captured the stoicism and frustration of the real grunts to their total satisfaction. "Ain't I never gonna get a girl in my arms?" was his other big army hit, and the tune self-mockingly whines to set the precise mood. The U.S. was winning the war, and that was great, of course, but it wasn't happening quickly enough for the singer to get started with the fräuleins and mademoiselles, and he was having a high old time feeling sorry for himself about this.

Clearly, Loesser's songs now belonged in stage musicals, where the music helped the story, or was the story. However, he returned to Hollywood, where the songs had nothing to do with the story, but were instead dotted around like comfort stations among the clichés. The big difference now was that the dam had broken. Frank wrote some tunes himself, including the gorgeous standard "Spring Will Be a Little Late This Year" and the semistandard "I Wish I Didn't Love You So."

And by the late forties, when television ended the party and Hollywood had kicked most of its songwriters out, or at least off the payroll, half of ASCAP was milling up and down Broadway looking for work. Frank found himself back on the Broadway job line with the likes of Ralph Blane and Burton Lane and Sammy Fain, watching the aristocrats Berlin, Rodgers, and Porter sweep by in their limos.

For once, though, luck was a lady to Frank. He agreed to write the lyrics for the kind of show that usually closes after one horrible night in Philadelphia—a musical based on the Victorian farce Charley's Aunt. At the late minute, the composer Harold Arlen's house burned down and Frank was asked to write music as well as words for this dog. He seized the moment, dashing off some Englishy-sounding songs (as he would later write Danishy-sounding ones for the film Hans Christian Andersen) that, with the strenuous help of Ray Bolger, made Where's Charley? the surprise hit of the Golden Age of Musicals.

Broadway success comes fast or not at all. With one show behind him, Frank was on a collision course with immortality. He'd proved he could write all the types of songs you need for a musical, from ballads ("Once in Love with Amy") to comedy ("Make a Miracle") to bits of business. His

neo-Californian soul ached for New York, and these were the two chief prerequisites for the masterpiece he was about to write. All he needed was a fellow spirit to help with the libretto, and this he already had, though it took him a minute to realize it, and a couple of more minutes to nail his man down.

Frank first met Abe Burrows at a party in 1943, where Abe, as was his wont, was making up and singing a funny song called "I'm Strolling Down Memory Lane Without a Single Thing to Remember." Frank liked it so much he wrote it down, which was a good thing, because Burrows claims in his book *Honest, Abe*, the next day, he, the composer, had forgotten the song completely.

It was friendship at first sight, and it rapidly ripened at the omnipresent pianos of the period, where the two self-taught musicians took turns improvising new songs, or improvising them together, until it was hard to tell who wrote what. But one that they definitely did concoct together suggests they'd started work on *Guys and Dolls* long before they knew it. "Leave us face it/we're in love" could have been inspired by either Nathan Detroit or Miss Adelaide. "Leave us not blush with no shame/if people bandage our name." By George, they'd got it. Even before they needed it.

Abe Burrows was a New Yorker through and through, born and raised in, respectively, Manhattan, the Bronx, and Brooklyn (like many New Yorkers, he found Queens unnecessary), but not exactly in the streets. The Burrows family was as respectable as you can be on a shoestring, and Abe's own earliest ambition was to be a Latin teacher. But the streets crept in, and Burrows grew up sounding, in his own words, "the way Jersey City residents think Brooklynites talk and the way Brooklynites think people from Jersey City talk." Which, if you split the difference between the two locations, lands you somewhere near Times Square.

Abe's second ambition had been to be a businessman like the only successful adults he knew, but once again the Depression took over, drastically downsizing Wall Street and reducing Abe to selling all he had: his wit. A customer where he worked thought he was funny, introduced him to a gag-writer, and away he went.

By the time Frank Loesser met Abe, he was the head writer of the immortal radio program that began with the words "Hello, this is Duffy's

Tavern, where the elite meet to eat—Archie the manager speakin', Duffy ain't here . . . oh hello Duffy," which is vintage Burrows right there, half-Virgil, half-Brooklyn. You can't write good slang if you don't have a poet's heart and a solid beat, and it's no accident that one of Burrows's throw-away lines of dialogue for *G&D*—"the oldest established permanent float-ing crap game in New York"—sounded like a song to Loesser the moment he heard it.

In his five years at Duffy's Tavern, Abe blazed whole new trails in bad English. Characters like Clifton Finnegan, Clancy the cop, and Two Top Gruskin did not require that a person stand on ceremony, and before his time was up, Burrows even received a diploma in bad English from the master himself, Mr. Runyon, who wrote him a note praising the show's dialogue and admitting that his own was a fake.

After the war, Abe performed solo for a few years in cabarets, radio, and TV, for which he did a show called *Breakfast with Burrows* that aired at nine P.M. ("I sleep late"), which produced yet more songs and song ti-tles in the Loesser-Burrows vein, which now ran straight through both of them. After *G&D*, Frank would write an homage to their partnership in the form of a song in *The Most Happy Fella* called "Likewise, I'm Sure," which was actually one of Miss Duffy's taglines, but could have been writ-ten by either one of them. As Pogo might have put it, they had met two-headed Gruskin—and he was them.

So when they at last put their heads together for *G&D*, their heads didn't have far to go. And it's nice to imagine the moment of recognition "You?" "Yes. You too?" and then firing lines at each other, like jazzmen ex-changing riffs, competing and collaborating in one breath and hitting the gong again and again. "Marry the man today and train him/sub-sequently," "You'll know at a glance/by the two pair of pants," "What's playin' at the Roxy?" "What's inna *Daily News*?" There should be a picture of this mo-mentous cataclysm in the National Gallery.

"They were just a couple of mugs," Abe's son Jimmy says fondly, and it's a tribute to how thoroughly Loesser had willed himself into this role that Jimmy assumed he had worked his way up from the gutter, not down to it. "If you heard his voice in the next room," says lyricist Richard Adler, sharpening the point, "you'd swear he was a street-corner bookie," except

that Loesser's version came with both words and music. "And just a minute boys/I got the feedbox noise," "The name is Epitaph/he wins it by a half"—even the horse players in the audience must have relaxed as this song rang out, starting *Guys and Dolls* on its run to infinity. This was clearly a show in which a person could repose his confidence without fear of being sold a bill of goods by parties ignorant whereof they spoke.

But *Guys and Dolls* is more than just the sum of its great lines. It is also a superb piece of theatrical construction, with a great opening and a dandy close and maybe the best first-act curtain in musical history: Sky Masterson has just sung the loveliest song in the show, "My Time of Day," and won the girl, when the mission house door flings open and the gamblers fly out in all directions, pursued by a red-faced Lieutenant Brannigan.

The show is also one of the minute number of musicals without a single weak tune. So these were the respective directions the two men would take off in afterward: Burrows into construction work as a play doctor and director, and Loesser into ever more ambitious tunesmanship. When you're born to do a particular masterpiece, you're not going to do anything else quite so well, but neither would rest on his laurels. (Loesser could barely sit still.) Burrows's fingerprints can be found all over the Broadway history of the fifties, while Loesser's scores for *The Most Happy Fella* and *Greenwillow* show him out of the closet all the way, as a serious composer by even his family's standards.

Having proved these points, the two mugs joined forces one more time for the admirable show *How to Succeed in Business Without Really Trying*, giving Abe a chance to thumb his nose at the career he never had, and Loesser to celebrate one he did have—because it goes without saying that he was a crackerjack businessman too, in his spare nanoseconds. As the founder and proprietor of Frank Music Corp. music publishers, he was, among other things, "a better copyright lawyer than the lawyers who worked for him" (Adler), not to mention, no doubt, a better typist than his secretary and a better accountant than the computer. Loesser's weakness, if you can call it that, was too much talent and too many ideas. He spent a frustrating five years after *How To* concocting elaborate plots for musicals that went nowhere. Maybe they were just *too* clever, or maybe luck

had decided to get back on the shelf and blow on some other guy's dice for a change. More to the point, the Age of Aquarius was just around the corner and Frank liked nothing about it, starting with its music. So when the five years or so were up, he quit, at least for a while, absentmindedly closing an era on the way out. In the catalogue of revivals, *How to Succeed in Business* now figures to be the last of the great post–World War II musicals born of the Depression, war, and jazz, and everything since simply has to be called something else.

So, as fan magazines say, what was he really like? Exactly the same as you thought he was. His peculiar family kept him from ever getting seriously stuck on himself, and the first and last word everyone I talked to used about him was not "brilliant" but "nice"—nice to everyone, that is, not just to cronies but to such unpromising groups as strangers, lawyers, and other people's children. Jimmy Burrows, who knew him from infancy (and who, incidentally, would grow up to direct the splendid TV equivalent of *Duffy's Tavern,* to wit, *Cheers*), even manages to glow over the telephone as he speaks of Frank.

But the best of all character references comes from that sternest of judges, one of Loesser's children. Susan's loving, sparkling book, *A Most Remarkable Fella,* hides no warts, neither his nor anyone else's. She reveals that her father had a terrifying temper, at least to a child, and that when he turned it on her for the first time, swear words and all, "It was annihilation. . . . I felt sure I was being blown to bits." His perfectionism was scary too, albeit exhilarating, because his appreciation was as extravagant as his rage, and everyone wanted a piece of it. But his disappointment could be towering too, and it took him much too long to realize that his laid-back son, John, had a right *not* to be a genius if he didn't want to be. Also, Loesser smoked too much.

And there the warts end, to be drowned in the howls of laughter one imagines echoing through the Loesser household whenever Frank was around, or whenever one of his letters arrived from someplace else. Better than nice, he was funny, and unlike most pros, he took at least as much trouble entertaining his family as he did the paying customers, with a stream of cartoons, comic verses, and thoughtful gifts. The man was alive every minute of his life, expending enough energy to light up a baseball stadium or small city, not to mention a living room.

Perhaps it was too much. There are hints in Susan's book that Loesser's gregarious vitality simply overwhelmed his first marriage, to her mother, Lynn. Many of Susan's early memories take place in a daze of Hollywood parties and a wash of alcohol, which he burned up like so much fuel for his high-combustion brain. He could even start his workday with a predawn dry martini, like a Rabelaisian giant downing a barrel of mead before battle. (Susan denies this, but my source is good enough to suggest that maybe, sometimes, anyway, a man tends to get the legends that suit him.)

Loesser's wife Lynn, being merely human, seems to have fallen apart somewhat trying to keep up, and became known, inevitably, as "the evil of the two Loessers." No one in that set escaped without a wisecrack, and this one followed poor Lynn, who had once been the life of the party, to the grave and beyond.

But nobody, including Lynn, seems to have gotten really angry at Frank when the marriage finally broke up and he married, instead, the genial young singer Jo Sullivan from the cast of *The Most Happy Fella.* His talisman still worked, because as usual he behaved as decently as circumstances allowed—but also because, if you got angry, you might miss the next joke.

In the end, Susan holds only one thing against her father, and that is the maniacal smoking that eventually killed him in 1969, the year his beloved New York Mets won the World Series. (To repeat, he was interested in everything.) And even on this she can imagine him giving her an argument, in a loud voice in her head. "It was my life, kid." Dramatically speaking, this ghost has a point. Frank wasn't about to write rock and roll, and one can't imagine him hanging around as a museum piece, writing oldies for the old folk. He'd had a perfect life of its kind—why spoil it with a sour old age? He'd accomplished his main mission here on earth, which was obviously to write *Guys and Dolls.* That show, and the world it celebrates, will be around long after George Steinbrenner has turned Times Square into a skating rink and moved it to Englewood, New Jersey, with Donald Duck in hot pursuit.

Frank Loesser, as his daughter stresses, wrote entirely for the moment, not for immortality. And the odds can go on forever against your ever seeing this particular parlay occur more than once in a person's lifetime. After that, quick curtain, and out.

Gershwin's Last Heir:
Burton Lane

BURTON LANE

*A*nd then there were none.

Of the handful of musical geniuses who lit up the smog of Hollywood in the golden thirties and the off-pink haze over Broadway in the plutonium forties and fifties, Burton Lane was the last to leave this planet in January 1997, turning off the lights as he left.

Not that the composer of *Finian's Rainbow* and *On a Clear Day You Can See Forever,* and a peck of fine individual songs to boot, had ever seemed like the end of anything to his friends. When I last heard him a couple of

years before he died, he was pounding the piano as vigorously as ever and singing, if anything, slightly better. Lane had been the youngest member of the club for so long that youthfulness seemed part of his character. But technically speaking, he was indeed the last of the great theater writers in the jazz song mode, and one of the least known. For reasons of temperament as much as history, Lane has apparently been consigned forever to the limbo between the immortals and the trivia questions—where, the evidence suggests, you can live a lot longer and a bit happier than the neighbors both upstairs and down. Some artists have obscurity thrust upon them, early and often, but Lane won his mild variety of it fair and square by going to Hollywood before he was famous on Broadway, and as Warren and several others proved, you can't get here from there: No one ever made a name writing anything in Hollywood, and if his great friend Harry Warren couldn't dent the public awareness with his record of forty-four songs on the Hit Parade, there was no point bothering it with less.

And besides, Burton wasn't the type to bother. It was a good life out there, and he was quite content to jog his way through the thirties, raising the occasional divot by day, in the eternal songwriter's golf game, and playing the best party piano in the county by night. There were worse ways to pass the Great Depression. Lane had taken the precaution of hitting town with a masterpiece, "Everything I Have Is Yours," written, I believe, before he was twenty-one, so he had a wobbly sort of tenure out there and was free to indulge his occasional hobby of rising to challenges, even if he had to invent them himself.

For instance, Burton set himself right away the task of writing "the perfect" Fred Astaire song just in case he should ever need one. Eighteen years later, Fred danced on the ceiling to this very song in *Royal Wedding*: "You're All the World to Me." (Talk about being upstaged; no one has ever heard the song to this day.) And later, at studio request this time, he would also write the perfect Bob Hope song, to round out the great trilogy, "Thanks for the Memory" (music: Ralph Rainger), "Two Sleepy People" (music: Hoagy Carmichael), and Lane's entry, "The Lady's in Love with You," which sounds more like Bob Hope than Bob Hope did, but is typically the least known of the three.

Another challenge Lane seized upon or created was a chance to work his patron's name into a song, and this he did with a bang. The only line

of lyric he ever wrote for himself must be one of the best-known in Tin Pan Alley history—"I like a Gershwin tune," from "How About You." Gershwin was his biggest challenge, so naturally Lane wrote him into his best song. Yet thereby hangs not just a tale, but a whole biography.

"You play just like my son George." I've already told this story in relation to Gershwin, and George hardly needs another story. So imagine this time how it must have felt to a kid who'd been practicing and fooling around at a summer hotel piano when he heard a Russian lady say these words. For perhaps a split second Burton Levy, as he was then called, must have wondered "Who's George?" before doing a double take that lasted the rest of his life.

Mama Gershwin didn't talk like that to just anybody. So it is fair to assume that Burton in his teens was already better than good. As a veteran at sixteen now, he'd long since made the crucial discovery that his mistakes at the piano were more interesting than his right notes. But if his mistakes were anything near as interesting as George Gershwin's (to repeat, Mama's compliments didn't grow on trees), he might need to hire a Brink's truck just to transport them to the publisher, and his future suddenly lay serene before him. The only question that remained was whether to take his golden egg upmarket to the investment house of Carnegie Hall or down to the ATMs of Tin Pan Alley, two opposite worlds less than five minutes apart on the subway. Either way, his first stop had to be the Gershwin townhouse on West One Hundred-third Street, where by chance "my son George" was wrestling with the same problem, dashing off orchestrations for his Concerto in F with one hand and great middle-period songs like "Soon" and "How Long Has This Been Going On?" with the other.

For the next two years or so, Burton apprenticed, or more precisely listened, under this divided soul, the rough equivalent of receiving private revolution lessons from Lenin in the years 1915 through 1917. Not that Gershwin ever made that kind of difference on the classical scene, which was one big revolution already—another bomb-thrower here or there couldn't blow it any higher; still, his effect on the American popular song was positively seismic. And Burton Lane was there, sitting at the master's pedals, the last, truest heir to the family fortune.

To make doubly sure that his new protégé knew exactly what he wanted, Chairman George set the kid up with an appointment to meet

Walter Damrosch of the New York Philharmonic. If Lane had a symphony up his sleeve, now was the time to roll it out. But Burton had already made the same choice as Irving Berlin to avoid technical instruction: He didn't know where the music came from, and he didn't want to know—although fifty years later he still wasn't sure that this was the right decision. Anyhow, all the trains were running downtown that year, and Burton had the fever, the thing that "It Don't Mean a Thing" if it ain't got, and all that rolled out were more and more songs, a half-century's worth if you count the unpublished ones he kept writing after the bell sounded and the tide turned against him. Yet to the end, you can still find a potential classical composer in there someplace who announces his fleeting presence in the middle of songs with harmonic notions just too rare and sly for one hearing, which is usually the only hearing that songs can ever count on. So there's much snobbish pleasure to be had discovering all the Lane songs that were simply too good to be standards, like "Something Sort of Grand-ish," which may be the best, and is certainly the least-known, song from *Finian's Rainbow.* Lane's instinctive sophistication did him no harm at all in 1930s Hollywood, because that was the decade when sophistication went public. But it did him no particular good after World War II because sophistication was now *out* all over America—look where it got you. And then there was TV, which had already robbed the studios of enough mad money to pay for new songs on spec. The musical class system had returned to stay, with the good songs heading henceforth to Broadway and the rest heading in the general direction of "The Doggie in the Window."

So Burton Lane rounded up, or was rounded up by, a fellow member of the Manhattan diaspora named Yip Harburg, and together they batted out *Finian's Rainbow* while they were still in California. Not surprisingly the result was a very New York show. Although Harburg loved the idea of Ireland, his lyrics never really got out of the harbor, or all that far from McSorley's Wonderful Saloon either. This suited Broadway fine in its postwar phase of rediscovering the outside world only to find that, once you got past the funny phrases and costumes, it was just like the good old U.S.A. And the show passed the other more serious post–Rodgers and Hammerstein test of perfectly matching the melodies to the scenes, so that the tune sounds as if the scene had written *it.* This was quite an achievement for a Hollywood trainee who'd been raised on the unspoken

division of labor out there, whereby you just shut up and write your nice songs and leave the rest to us. On Broadway, contrariwise, the more you could do for yourself the better, from picking the project and finding a like-minded producer whose casting of it would not be too ridiculous, to placing the songs and protecting them just by hanging around rehearsals and making a pest of yourself. Like Frank Loesser, that prince of pests.

Just to recite the requirements is to picture Yip Harburg, a charming but persistent fellow, who had actually gotten his nickname from his terrier-like qualities, and who had employed them to squeeze in a successful business career just in time for the Crash in 1929 and a new career in songwriting. Now Yip was back on his home ground and one imagines him fairly exploding onto Broadway. Anything MGM could do musically he could do better on his own, and just as he had helped his old friend Harold Arlen to write his most successful show, *Bloomer Girl,* he now helped his other friend Burton Lane to write his, leaving him even more stranded afterward.

In a more reasonable world, *Finian* would have constituted a flying start, but immediately afterward, Lane went back and stood on line with all the other composers to compete for an ever-shrinking number of theaters. It was as if the dream factory of Hollywood had been replaced overnight by a small cottage industry that kept losing cottages because the same real estate costs that were squeezing the Brooklyn Dodgers and New York Giants out of the city were driving up theater rents beyond endurance. In those same 1950s, John Osborne called the British royals a gold tooth in a mouthful of decay, but he could have said it even more accurately about the Great White Way, which only became even a gold tooth as long as the curtain was up on the latest million-dollar investment. Between epiphanies, it reverted to a small number of shabby buildings set among future massage parlors—or, from another angle, a handful of clean theaters overlooking fleabag streets.

So Burton needed the right partner more than ever, and Harburg's obsession with politics, which had been an inconvenience to Arlen but not a fatal one, tied Burton in knots. It seems that those years in Hollywood had accentuated a tendency in Burton to sit on the tracks and wait for someone, Mama Gershwin or Louis B. Mayer, to tap him on the shoulder and tell him what to do next. And since good partners were hard to find

and Yip was still right there, Burton wasted valuable prime time before giving up on him, and even more time looking for Mr. Right in the next generation. In the forty-plus years remaining to him, he would in fact find only one—and it would be magic, like the village of Brigadoon, for five minutes or so.

Alan Jay Lerner was perfect while he lasted, incredibly venturesome with a rich kid's knack for getting what he wanted. He had virtually begun his career with the hit show *Brigadoon,* and with an Oscar for screenwriting the movie *An American in Paris,* before proceeding to the daunting task of rewriting George Bernard Shaw and reimagining his great play *Pygmalion* into the great un-American musical *My Fair Lady.* The only catch was, of course, that for most of his firecracker prime, he had been tied to Fritz Loewe. Burton would only get Lerner for one perfect screen score—*Royal Wedding,* which exploded with pent-up talent in such gems as "Too Late Now" and "I Left My Hat in Haiti"—and one sublime Broadway musical featuring a batch of songs so vivacious and inventive that they seemed to announce the high noon of a career and certainly not the twilight. It is typical of Lane that he was at once passive enough to wait a Rip Van Winkle–like twenty-eight years between stage appearances and sharp enough to be at his absolute best. "What Did I Have That I Don't Have," "Come Back to Me," and most particularly the title song of the show, "On a Clear Day," may be his most adventurous ever. Unlike certain rock composers, who seem stunned by the first musical phrase they come to and repeat it with mounting excitement until the tape runs out, Lane gave us a lot of tune each time. In fact, the A section of "On a Clear Day" seems itself like a mere suggestion, a launching pad from which he and his co-pilot, Alan Jay Lerner, take off to the wild blue yonder in a series of breathtaking maneuvers, as if they expect to stay up there forever.

But forever proved even shorter than usual, Broadway time, and within the next year or so, all of the old songwriters had been grounded and an era had ended, just like that, like a record spinning to a close. It was the midsixties by then and the noise outside the theater couldn't be kept out much longer. Shows like *Grease, Tommy,* and, God help us, *Jesus Christ Superstar* were more like it, not because the public demanded it—the average theatergoer was still as square as ever, and any revival of anything was warmly welcomed—but in response to supply-side imperatives. The creative spirits

of any era will always want to express their own world and their own moment in time, and starting with the midsixties, this became hard to do if you weren't young. The peace movement and the civil rights marches, combined with all the phrases and attitudes of the hippie revolt and the free speech movement and the drug culture, flung down a barrier between the generations that reached from coast to coast like our own Great Wall of China. By chance, I was present on a night when even Yip Harburg found his visa being rejected, although I'm not sure he ever realized it.

Since the hippies simply loved the word "political" and applied it to everything from brushing your teeth to refusing to brush your teeth, Yip assumed that they were fellow spirits and going his way. So, in a spirit of gemütlich solidarity, worthy of the Popular Front in the 1930s, he threw a party to welcome Dan Berrigan, the Jesuit peacenik, home from a short stretch at the aptly named Danbury State Prison. And the generational battle lines were drawn immediately with a cartoon sharpness and sublime unconsciousness. On the one side, in straight chairs, sat old Yip and his Old Left friends, who could have passed collectively for a meeting of a Garment Workers local, and on the other, crouched or sprawled on the floor, Dan and his Hippies for Jesus, wondering no doubt what the hell they were doing here with all these old people. The session kicked off with a few condescending words from the trendy lawyer William Kunstler, who talked to the old-timers as if they were pale-faced middle-class types in need of reassurance ("I don't blame you for feeling scared"), and ended on the high and low note of the evening, when our host got up and sang his own masterpiece "Brother, Can You Spare a Dime?" with wattles fluttering and Adam's apple going up and down like a grain elevator. "Once in khaki suits, gee, we looked swell. . . ." I myself would have gladly slogged "through hell," as the song says, for this man, but from a cool corner of my eye I noted some of Dan's disciples actually still chattering and even tittering among themselves. And I thought, Never trust a song over thirty minutes old, I suppose. Now if someone had just grabbed a guitar and started riffing on Danbury Dan in the Danbury Can, well, all right.

But the old songs were the worst thing they could be just then, inauthentic and unspontaneous and definitely on the wrong side of the Great Wall. Any new jazz songs that made it now would have to follow the

famous advice of Gertrude Stein to Ernest Hemingway—"Do it over," and "Make it new." Lane's *On a Clear Day* and Loesser's *How to Succeed* were perfect shows about fifties themes, psychiatry and office work, that were no longer in the worldview or on the national screen. Yet mysteriously another, even older, theme showed up around then and did just fine. The plot of *Cabaret* had actually run on Broadway in the 1950s without music and under a different name. But the young team of Kander and Ebb had made it new, musically speaking, by plugging in its nostalgia and making it jump and live for at least fifty years, especially as accompanied by the staccato and erotic irony of Bob Fosse's choreography.

Being, and staying, "with it" does not necessarily require constant changes, maybe just one or two in a lifetime. But Burton had missed the big one and watched its ship sail away.

So Mr. Van Winkle returned to his couch and slept right through the Age of Aquarius, woke up long enough to try one more musical with Lerner (*Carmelina* in 1977), only to realize that the jig seemed to be up with Lerner as well. Even before *On a Clear Day*, Alan Jay had proved much too slow and erratic for the fussy Richard Rodgers, but now, under the rumored influence of certain drugs, he was almost too much for the patient Lane. Talking a few years later with the last Mrs. Lerner, I found her presuming that Burton must have been an awful man—until, that is, she met him. So obviously, bad blood had begun to flow on both sides before they quit.

Burton returned to his piano and waited for posterity to come to its senses, while meanwhile "Who do you like for mayor next time?" was what you were most likely to hear if you called up the Lanes. Lynn Lane took a particularly ferocious interest in Upper West Side politics, but when I last saw Burton at a meeting some years back, his dreamy smile suggested he might possibly be humming under his breath. Happy the man with a good tune in his head, especially a tune that might be a hit in the next century or so.

And this time, Lane's limited times at bat (compared with Berlin's and Porter's) may have cost him a piece of his rightful glory. In a prolonged burst of muddleheadedness the sages at the Kennedy Center managed to overlook him to the end, which was plain embarrassing, like the Oscar that Cary Grant didn't get. Not that it ever seemed to bother Burton. If it took even a pinch of self-promotion to attract that kind of attention,

Burton couldn't be bothered with it. By show biz standards, the man had a serious showing-off disorder, a most un-Gershwinian ego deficiency brought about, he explained, by that unsung specimen, a "stage father." Repeated doses of the line "You must listen to my son play" had sent Burton into permanent reverse early in life, and as I know from experience, he could waste whole interviews talking about other people.

Although he seemed, like a sports announcer might say, very tall for a songwriter, he even looked self-effacing in a distinguished sort of way—so much so that Louis B. Mayer went to his grave convinced that his ace composer was actually Judy Garland's rehearsal pianist. If ever a man was handed an innocent chance to shine, Burton's discovery of Garland should have been it. Judy was still a mere Gumm sister when he spotted her, one childish voice out of three, although admittedly the dominant one from the get-go. But Lane was so sure of her greatness and of his own judgment that he marched the tot round to MGM himself and insisted she be auditioned—not the act of a milquetoast. Yet when it came to taking a bow for himself, he got stuck.

So you can imagine how many bows he took for his own work. As far as Burton was concerned, no award or applause for past achievements could provide anything like the kick of putting on a new show or even just playing a new tune for a friend, of which I believe he had enough to fill at least an off-Broadway theater. But his friends weren't the kind of hustlers who would help him get back in the game. I don't believe he really liked such people. And perhaps the game itself had lost some of its flavor. He kept writing songs because that's what songwriters do.

Whatever an artist may think he thinks, his heart decides at some point whether he really wants to stay in the swim that much or is content just to be remembered. And all I can say is that Burton was remembered and seemed happy about it. One time I found him bristling because he was having trouble getting paid for a commercial that was using "How About You," but it was a major commercial so he had cause, and he wasn't bristling that hard.

"I hear music/Mighty fine music." If you had to reduce Lane's oeuvre to one song for the space capsule, how about this? The opening is a solemn tease, deadpan music that might go anywhere—and then it magically springs to life, and for a moment you feel as if you've moved

into an actual music box with melody coming from everywhere. This was Burton Lane's regular neighborhood, and its physical counterpart was, as nature intended, the Upper West Side, which provided the real-life doors and windows through which the music streamed. All the inspiration Burton ever needed could be found someplace between Riverside Drive, next to which he once played Ping-Pong with Oscar Levant and the piano with George Gershwin, and Central Park West, on which he lived and worked nonstop for his last forty years or so. If the great modern jazz songs began life on the Lower East Side, they wasted no time moving to more spacious quarters, many of them in the upper left corner of the city, where Richard Rodgers was born and raised, and George Gershwin of Brooklyn held court: the uptown school of American music of which Burton Lane was for years the dean, crown jewel, and Grand Old Man in residence.

The last amiable proof that he must have been doing something good on this planet, Burton Lane was one of those blessed souls who look better as they age. Just a few minutes of conversation usually revealed his secret. As soon as the talk turned to music, the man lit up like a stained-glass window. And if you could maneuver him toward the piano stool, by, say, dropping a hat, you could watch the years slide away and, on a clear day, maybe even see Mama Gershwin, that somewhat different fairy godmother standing just behind him. Anything might happen at the piano, which served Lane over the years as best friend, cash cow, and fountain of youth. There is no love like that of a composer for his instrument; Hemingway and his typewriter, Salk and his test tube, and Hershey and his chocolate bar all finish far down the track.

"I Love a Piano," wrote the great Irving Berlin, and he could barely play the damn thing. When you played as elegantly as Burton Lane did, you had the makings of a grand passion to which no earthly honor could add much of anything. In a profession in which depression seems to expand in ratio to success (e.g., Berlin, Rodgers, and Arlen), Lane struck a salubrious balance: enough success, a major talent, a happy man.

Or at least he was the last time I saw him, because he was doing a two-man concert with the indispensable Michael Feinstein. This metamorphosed into some excellent tapes that will undoubtedly soon become collector's items. And, as I say, Lane sounded better than ever.

Cy Coleman and the Future

CY COLEMAN

This book is lightly suffused throughout by the presence of Cy Coleman, whom I met toward the start of the project and who died, to my shock and sorrow, just as I began to wind it down. In between, I would see enough of him—laughing his gleeful chuckle and, above all, always working on a new show—to get a sense of the writing life as it is and has been for living memory. These guys were *always* working on new shows. The great songs began life as by-products, although they might wind up living forever while main products—the new shows themselves—probably would not.

So why not just skip the show and write songs for their own sake? Because the biology of the business seems to insist on shows. Around the time I met Cy, I had (unknowingly) said my last goodbye to Burton Lane, and

had already sensed the frustration of a showman without a show, trying to write songs in a vacuum without something to hang them on or put them in. In contrast to Lane, Cy Coleman presented the bustle and optimism of a man at work. He didn't just have to think up new songs, he also had to bring down curtains and introduce characters. And the hits would come—or, if not, maybe the show itself would be a big hit and cover for them.

Cy Coleman was of special interest to me because he had apparently kept the faith with the old songs and gotten away with it. He was of interest also to Walter Isaacson at *Time* magazine because he had just scored the old-fashioned, Richard Rodgers–style double of two hit shows on Broadway at the same time. So *Time* asked me to write about Cy.

Fortunately, Coleman lived just down the street, a mere two Hamptons away as the gossip flies, and quite close enough to go from a journalism subject to a friend in no time flat. He was a comfortable man. Some musicians may be inarticulate, but songwriters work with words, and usually like to talk, and they know how to do it.

We dived right in. In the interest of my book—*Time* could wait—I wanted to know whether a form of music like the jazz song could still be said to be alive if nobody wrote it anymore. I can't remember who were that particular year's hot contemporary concert artists, but whoever they were, where were their matching songwriters? If a young modern-day writer suddenly wants to write like Gershwin, what does he do next? How does the machinery work these days?

Back in those days, Cy said, you knew you'd written a hit and were on your way "when Tony Bennett made the record." But, he supposed, starting off today he would have to establish his own record company and make his own records (maybe even playing the piano himself—I can't hear him singing). And, by the way, to hell with the sound synthesizers, he added, which he considered the great Satan and the enemy of all human creation. "I would always write music," he added so decisively that I can still hear him.

And what kind of music would he "always write"? I didn't have to ask, but did anyway. It seems he had fallen in lifelong love with the music that came out of the radio in the late 1930s and early 1940s, and that was the sort of thing he still wrote: great old radio songs. Although, as he said, one never knows how they will come out. For example, when the great Brazilian

stylist Antonio Carlos Jobim wrote "The Girl from Ipanema," he was convinced that he was writing regular American jazz. Cy said the main thing was to avoid imitations ("pastiche is for kids"), write what comes naturally, and hope some of the year's fresh air will sneak in and blow the dust off.

His master strategy for somehow staying both hip and out of date became clear to me a few days later when I visited his Manhattan office on Fifty-seventh Street and realized that the occupant had taken full advantage of our greatest modern convenience: the freedom to live in the tense of one's choice, if not in several of them. At first glance, his office was the model of an old-show biz shop, spilling over with playbills and fading photographs, plus an upright piano and a rolltop desk big enough to hold an escaped convict.

Yet Cy himself did not seem like an anachronism or a museum keeper. Although it was then too soon for most people to own computers, I'm sure he later snapped one up as fast as you can say George Gershwin (who always bought the latest of everything). And even then, Cy's musty rolltop probably contained at least one possible show script set in the twenty-fifth century.

In fact, of his two hit shows running just then, one, *City of Angels,* was set in a futuristic Los Angeles, and contained a streamlined score written with an up-to-the-minute lyricist, David Zippel, of the Richard Rodgers family. The other, *The Will Rogers Follies,* was set comfortably back in the 1920s and '30s, with my old friends Betty Comden and Adolph Green on the lyrics.

In order to find new things in himself and maybe find new song ideas in the script, Cy told me that he liked to work with new lyricists each time out. And he volunteered two examples of songs dictated by the needs and limitations of particular productions and helped into life by a like-minded words person.

His show *Wildcat* required a signature song for Lucille Ball, who had begun her career as a chorus girl, but had since developed incipient stage fright at the prospect of singing in front of living people. So Cy ordered up from his subconscious a song for everywoman, or at least for everycelebrity. He came up with "Hey Look Me Over," a brassy but simple barroom ballad that even Minnie Mouse could belt out, or seem to

belt out, right through to its triumphal ending. "So, look out world—here I come!" Take that, you amateurs!

Similarly, *Little Me* needed a showstopper for yet another television casualty, Sid Caesar, a comedian not famous for his singing. For him, Cy dashed off a bathtub waltz called "Real Live Girl," which practically sings itself and barely even needs a real live singer. And once again, one imagines the real-life ambience of the great songs, the influence of performers like Sophie Tucker and Bob Hope and Frank Sinatra on their histories.

In both of Cy's examples, the words seem to understand the tune like a perfect marriage. It figures, because the partnership between Cy and his fellow Bronxite Carolyn Leigh was artistically if not humanly perfect. Besides (or because of) being brilliant, Carolyn Leigh seems to have been a (thoroughly justified) perfectionist. She demanded the same from her writing partner in what may have struck the so-far single Cy as a shrill married sort of voice. Apparently, she brought out the screamer in him, too—along with some of his best, jazziest work. Like Irving Berlin, Cy was never happier than when chopping up his rhythms and injecting a surprise kick to them. And Leigh could ride his choppiest beats like a bronco buster in such typical numbers as "Witchcraft" and "I've Got Your Number." Carolyn even insisted on writing a lyric for one of Cy's more demanding warm-up finger exercises. "The Best Is Yet to Come" became a hit when Frank Sinatra made the record, although Cy said it couldn't be done right up until the point when it was.

However fruitful, such a comic-strip professional marriage could not endure. Perhaps no writing partnership ever should come that close to a marriage. Cy could be excessively complimentary about Carolyn, although their rows were not just audible, they were actually legendary, so I didn't need to pry and could just imagine. As Cy elsewhere described the act of composition, it sounded almost mystical and, hence, solitary. So, to return from his efforts and find someone waiting with a rolling pin—and find himself raging back—may have ultimately been just too much.

To picture Cy in memory is to remember him smiling. His natural means of expression was the chortle, not the insult, the celebration rather than the postmortem. His last partner, Ira Gasman, even went so far as to say that songs came from him "like gurgles from a baby."

Not that there was anything infantile about Cy. But he had found a locus of pure joy in music dating back to the days when his carpenter father used to nail the piano shut to get a little peace around there. Luckily, "as a carpenter's son, I knew how to un-nail it." And the family milkman, hearing the same sounds, declared that whoever was making them was a genius, which led somehow or another (who knows how grown-ups arrived at these things?) to lessons and a spell as a child prodigy with a special gift for Beethoven. Years later, Jule Styne, another prodigy, would say to him at ASCAP meetings, "You and I are the only real pianists here." And Cy never stopped playing the classics, but gave excellent mixed concerts right to the end.

As a teenaged maestro in World War II, he found immediate work entertaining the troops, who seldom requested Beethoven. Thus, he stayed in touch with radio, until his musical bones hardened. And his first big hit afterward strikes a note of iron resolve. "Why Try to Change Me Now?" could be a declaration of musical intent, although the actual words were written by Joseph A. McCarthy.

Nevertheless, the world *would* try to change him, as it changes everybody. So my second question at our first meeting concerned this issue: How in the world had he managed to keep out "the music in the air" all this time while letting in any fresh air at all?

"Selective deafness," he said quickly, with his biggest smile, as if there really were no way to change him now. Rock and roll had come and mostly gone, in all its mutations, and *nouvelle* folk music, and then New Age, or dentists' music, until at last melody itself seemed to be on the run from rap and heavy machinery. Cy Coleman still found all he needed by listening to the classical radio stations and to jazz in all *its* permutations. When these weren't available, he tuned in to the orchestra playing in his own head, which he could strike up when the going got dull over cocktails or dinner. I don't know if I ever talked to him at such a moment, but if so, the Coleman grin covered every possibility in the wide world. He carried it off perfectly.

Meanwhile, back at the office. Cy didn't leave Ms. Leigh (or hadn't been left by her) for just some nobody. His next partner, Dorothy Fields, was a step up from practically everyone. Sublimely peaceable, she'd withstood the thunderbolts of Jerome Kern, and even coaxed an all-American

score from Transylvanian Sigmund Romberg. (*Up in Central Park* must be the best musical never revived, and its big hit "Close as Pages in a Book" the best song never played.)

Blessedly, Fields had one more great show in her arsenal, and it would turn out to be Cy Coleman's greatest claim on the future. Listening to *Sweet Charity* today—with its great bordello numbers, "Big Spender" and "If My Friends Could See Me Now"—it's hard to believe that the words came from one of Broadway's great ladies on her next-to-last assignment. Before Dorothy died, the pair did manage one more quickie, the unpromising and unsuccessful *Seesaw,* thus ending a professional marriage made in heaven (like all of Dorothy Fields's marriages—which is not to say that they lasted, just that they were heavenly).

Working with Dorothy Fields must have seemed as close to graduation as it gets in this field. From then on, Cy was the old master, and a gracious one he was, enjoying both the role and the work, which kept coming in bushel baskets. I remember that he was particularly tickled at having won (on his scorecard anyhow) an exchange of insults in the London press with Andrew Lloyd Webber. He also expressed a lordly disapproval of Bob Fosse for building a recent show out of old songs instead of commissioning some new ones. (He and Fosse still owed each other plenty for *Sweet Charity,* so there were no real hard feelings.) Above all, Cy found time in those later mellow years to make a most serene and satisfactory marriage to a most unshrewish young lady. She was tactful enough to tell me that she read my *Time* piece on Cy at the right moment, and so she accepted a date. And she made me feel like Cupid every time we met.

As noted, Cy was kept young and busy by the endless small chores of the theater, punctuated by the flow of downright rebirths and do-overs as new shows blew into town to play musical chairs (or musical theaters) with old ones. And the old-timers returned too, like Harold Prince or the late George Abbott, gliding in as if on pink clouds, as good as new with each revival.

Although there are fashions on Broadway, as everywhere, they are not binding. Every show is its own small world, free to set up its own styles or to borrow one from the ever-present past. Kander and Ebb's *Chicago* is a splendid rendering of the American twenties, and so is Jerry Herman's *Mack & Mabel,* but they are completely different interpretations. And who would ever try to typecast Stephen Sondheim, a man of a thousand styles?

To answer my first question, the jazz song still lives on Broadway: on stage, in the wings, or on somebody's drawing board. It's always changing, as if to reassert that it's still alive, but its very roots are never more than just one or two degrees away from Irving or Cole themselves. And though Burton Lane and Ann Ronell are no longer around to "see" George Gershwin on his daily rounds, he lives on in the musicians' heads and on the boards of Broadway.

Cy Coleman gave me a sense of this undying brotherhood of song. I was amazed, though I shouldn't have been, to realize that he must have been seventy-six years old at our last meeting. His age made no difference in his plans or his life. If he grew old in one decade, he could always move into another one and keep right on going. And if you heard him play, say, George Gershwin, it was not an old man playing old music, but an immortal taking a dip in the fountain of youth.

Until further notice, these songs live and breathe on Broadway, as well as on the mini-Broadways of the cabaret circuit. Together these two live venues replicate two former musical workshops: the Vaudeville tour and the speakeasy. For the speakeasy effect, nowadays you have to imagine the illegal part, with the sirens and the Keystone Kops, but that very real tingle is still very much available. One night, the fine entertainer Baby Jane Dexter said, "I feel as though something very exciting is going to happen tonight." And I felt it too. Mary Cleere Haran was, as I recall, about to interpret Irving Berlin in the twenties as he had never been interpreted before.

And I understood why the English won't leave Shakespeare alone, why the Austrians fiddle with Mozart. Not that I'm making great claims to artistic purity, only placing these songs in the American story and in the girders of our cities, the memory of our railroads and our Ford V-8's. At one important moment in history, these songs represented America to the world, and they represented us well. As Hoagy Carmichael said to me in 1947 at the London Stage Door, "You and me got to be good ambassadors for America, son," and he certainly was, along with the rest of the musical diplomatic corps represented in this book.

As noted earlier, George Gershwin said, "My place is America and my time is now." That still goes. And if Cy throws in a medley of his own music, you needn't adjust your watch or your calendar. These songs are here to stay.

Coda: Three More Majors
(for Good Measure)

ARTHUR SCHWARTZ

*B*y its nature, any book on this subject will try to become an encyclopedia, if you let it. So just to prove this isn't, I'll end with some loose ends—three representative names from the top of the class, each of whom is a byword to fans but rings only the most distant of bells, if any, with the Unwashed. (The word is not pejorative. I am myself unwashed in many areas, including the latest rock music, and indeed the exact significance of the word "rock" by now—I am unwashed and unbowed.) Although millions of people have heard the song "Makin' Whoopee" and perhaps seen the film *The Band Wagon,* the authors' names have not been indelibly attached to either of them. Walter Donaldson and Arthur Schwartz remain

head-scratchers. "Hmm, the name sounds familiar. Give me a clue." The drive to amnesia is mighty strong, and even Vincent Youmans, whose name seems close to unforgettable, remains shrouded in fog. " 'No, No, Nanette'? 'Tea for Two'? 'The Curse of the Bambino'?" There is an underlying financial connection. Harry Frazee, the iniquitous chap who sold Babe Ruth from the Red Sox to the Yankees, is said to have used the proceeds of the sale to fund *No, No, Nanette,* and it is by this thread that the composer Vincent Youmans's name recognition now hangs.

So where did Walter Donaldson, Arthur Schwartz, and Vincent Youmans—and all the other near misses—go wrong? Walter Donaldson had actually gotten off to a fine start by being a protégé of Irving Berlin as World War I ended and Prohibition opened up a brand-new market for saloon songs. In fact, Donaldson seemed the closest thing to an heir apparent to the very throne of Tin Pan Alley. Admittedly, that was while people still thought of Irving as mortal, and before all the other heirs had checked in. But so long as the Alley remained in New York, Donaldson at least reigned supreme in their speakeasies and on what might be called lowercase Broadway—the several hundred theaters that did not run operettas like *Naughty Marietta,* or anything like it. But songs like "My Buddy," "My Blue Heaven," and "Yes Sir, That's My Baby" sold an awful lot of sheet music with Donaldson's name on it, and physically speaking the man was quite a familiar figure around town, especially if you fancied the racetrack. And in the later twenties, he would establish perhaps his best claim on immortality with the songs that became the repertoire of Ruth Etting. (She's the saloon singer with the sad, sad story told so well in the great Doris Day movie *Love Me or Leave Me.* As long as that film remains in stock, so does Donaldson.)

But then came sound, and Tin Pan Alley moved to Hollywood, where Walter gradually evolved into just another studio writer. MGM gave him one last chance to shine by making a Busby Berkeley spectacular out of his Broadway show *Makin' Whoopee,* to which Donaldson added the standard "My Baby Just Cares for Me." And he made the most of smaller openings too, with the Broadway style barn burner "You" and the song that Cary Grant mauled unforgettably, "Did I Remember?" But on the whole, Walter Donaldson was just another misplaced New Yorker.

Hollywood was simply not his kind of town, or any kind of town at all, and one imagines his personal map of it consisting of a few good racetracks connected by some trolley tracks and various watering places or safe houses where he might find some other Gotham exiles. In those same years, his own map would change too, from that of a sensitive, almost ethereal young poet to a middle-aged voluptuary along the lines of Sydney Greenstreet. Johnny Mercer, who met him halfway through the thirties, found him wonderful company and still brimming with talent. But he had lost his place in line to the latest carpetbaggers. And since the studio paid you whether you worked or not, Donaldson preferred playing the horses to playing studio politics. He wasn't fixated on personal immortality, and so he didn't quite get it, although his daughter, Ellen, who barely had time to meet him (she was seven years old when he died, but remembers him as a warm and loving man), seems to be ambitious enough for two and keeps his name in the well-earned running.

Arthur Schwartz also has a relative, the super-disc-jockey and old friend of mine Jonathan Schwartz, who has also served his old man well by keeping *all* the boats afloat, Arthur's very much among them, and letting them speak for themselves. "Dancing in the Dark," "Alone Together," "You and the Night and the Music"—there is a classic quality to Schwartz's best tunes that separates them from the crowd and seems to qualify him for his own statue and his own book. "Something to Remember You By" is a song my grandmother used to sing, and that one, along with her other favorites, Berlin's "What'll I Do" and Romberg's "When I Grow Too Old to Dream," form their own little timeless repertoire in my head dating back to the Garden of Infancy, when all the songs were young.

Of Arthur Schwartz as much as anyone, it could be said that in any less crowded time and place, he would surely have been deemed a grand master, but that in any such normal circumstances, he might not have become a songwriter at all—certainly not if his father, Solomon, had had anything to say about it. I have seldom heard of such implacable opposition to anything as Solomon's was to music. He went to the root of the matter by forbidding all music instruction in the home. And after that Daddy Schwartz insisted that Arthur become a real lawyer (like himself)

rather than a piano-playing graduate student. Arthur set a songwriter's record with four years of actual legal practice.

But the music in the air prevailed. There was simply so much demand for more of it and so many young men (and even a few women) looking for ways to provide it that they finally outnumbered Solomon. A kid with a head full of melodies was money in the bank, and Sol had made the fatal mistake of not getting his kid out of town immediately. Worse, he let him go to Columbia University, where three great, hungry lyricists—Hart, Hammerstein, and Howard Dietz—prowled the halls of learning in search of musical kids like Schwartz (since there just wasn't enough of Richard Rodgers to go around).

Probably, Arthur didn't need all that much temptation. In his quiet way, he was as willful as his old man—but the mix of talent and opportunity gave him the most useful of gifts in a sticky situation: early success. Arthur had actually already written a standard as a camp counselor with Larry Hart, of all unlikely camp counselors. But Hart's lyric for it was so unstandardlike and, in fact, so summer-camp-like ("I Love to Lie Awake in Bed," for Pete's sake) that Arthur retired it to the back of his head for better times, which were just around the corner.

It is typical of the King Midas–like hot streak that was about to pass through Schwartz that his next partner, the third man in the Columbia triumvirate, Howard Dietz, would quickly turn that same tune into the ever-popular "I Guess I'll Have to Change My Plan." Arthur had found the best possible partner for him. And to make things even better, the one-two punch of talking pictures and the financial depression that had reduced the Great White Way to off-Broadway size made it just right for this year's crop of geniuses—that is, if they already knew all the angles. Like Dietz and like Schwartz, they needed at least a valise full of unforgettable tunes ready to go. The (East) Coast was clear, because at least half the A-list writers had gone to Hollywood, while at the same time the local streets still swarmed with song-and-dance refugees from the closed vaudeville houses, who hadn't gone west yet themselves. So the young men joined forces in the kind of graduate school revue one now associates with the *Harvard Lampoon,* called *The Band Wagon,* and it took Broadway by storm in 1931. Besides packing enough hit songs to guarantee success in any era, it starred, for the last time on any stage or in any form, the great

brother-and-sister team of Fred and Adele Astaire, as much a big-ticket item then as it would be now.

Even the audiences were just right for them then, because they were too hip for the movies but hell-bent on escape. In Schwartz and Dietz's golden years that followed, roughly 1931–36, all the businessmen were tired—or in the polite phrase, "between jobs"—and were in no mood for the emotional travails of a *Show Boat* or the integrated musical in general. Gags, gals, and tunes you could whistle on the way out and take home in sheets were more like it. And the hit shows from the freshmen class bore names like Harold Arlen's *Life Begins at 8:40,* Vernon Duke's *Ziegfeld Follies of 1934* (and also *of 1936*), and Schwartz's own *Flying Colors.*

And it wasn't just the freshmen at play, lowering the tone and bond rating of Broadway. Some of the best people also catered to the short attention spans of those straitened years. Irving Berlin scored with a great one called *As Thousands Cheer,* and the world's oldest sophomore, Cole Porter, whipped off *Red, Hot and Blue!* starring Ethel Merman, Jimmy Durante, and Broadway's hottest young hoofer, Bob Hope. Next stop, Hollywood, for all concerned: 1936 would witness the greatest emigration of musical talent since the outbreak of sound almost a decade earlier and, incidentally, see the end of Arthur's one and only real run of luck.

The arrival of Cole Porter that same year would symbolize the end of Schwartz's winning streak. For some time now Howard Dietz had doubled as publicity director for MGM, inventing both the company lion and the fancy motto, *Ars Gratia Artis,* as a sort of hobby supporting a hobby; but the stakes had never been so high before, and the dabbling days were done. By 1936, it was no longer enough to mail in one's work. Louis B. Mayer had to *see* you working.

That year, MGM signed up Cole Porter for the most money ever paid to any composer to do anything, and you can't make such a rich omelet without breaking a few eggs like Schwartz and Dietz. So Arthur was on his own. To make a long story short, he never again captured the same magic with anyone else, or even with Dietz himself when they rejoined forces a few years later. Instead, he used his all-around intelligence to become a successful film producer and, during World War II and afterward, to develop a rare knack for writing funny songs, the secret of which, he claimed, was to start with the most romantic tune he could think of.

Sometimes I can hear it and sometimes I can't. "What do they do on a rainy night in Rio?" could be romantic, I guess. "They're either too young or too old" merely sounds kind of wistful, and "Rhode Island is famous for you" is too well hidden behind its whimsical wall of words. "Pencils come from Pennsylvania." Oh my.

But why, hearing what he heard, didn't he turn his romantic themes to love songs anymore? Perhaps he was prescient. A TV set cannot whisper "I love you" the way a radio can. With the box, one is aware of technicians in between. With radio, it was just Frank Sinatra (or Peggy Lee) and you. Besides which, the baby boom had just started and a large part of the audience wanted to know the price of "The Doggie in the Window" more than how much some grown-up singer out there loved them.

But just before the standards stopped coming altogether, Hollywood made up for at least some of its damages by reviving Schwartz's lucky title "The Band Wagon," and placing it in a movie that expertly celebrated the six glorious years in which Schwartz and Dietz poured out hits as if there were no tomorrow—as indeed there wasn't on that scale. For the occasion, Fred Astaire himself was on hand, appropriately older and wiser. "I'll go my way by myself," he sang, now that he'd lost Adele for sure, and Ginger too; Fred was ready to take his old bandwagon on its last ride. Schwartz and Dietz also rose to the occasion, as if it were still routine to do so, with one of those anthem songs built to last forever. Like Berlin's "There's No Business Like Show Business" or Cole Porter's "Another Opening Another Show," so too Schwartz and Dietz's "That's Entertainment" will probably stick around in some kind of digitalized form as long as MGM's ghost has anything to say about it and listeners can still carry a tune, or still want to.

So perhaps not quite the immortality that Arthur Schwartz deserved, but his musical legacy is solid, and can still make you laugh, or fall in love, as the case may be. Which is more than can be said about most dead lawyers, including, rest his soul, Solomon Schwartz. As I give Arthur's work one last hum-through, I am struck by the fact that while he obviously could write good songs with anyone, they only sounded like genuine Schwartz songs if they had genuine Dietz lyrics. And the rapport cut both ways. Dietz was a firm believer that how the words sounded was more important than what they meant.

For a similar attitude among composers, one turns to Vincent You-mans, the ultimate lothario of lyrics, who never stopped playing the field among wordmen, partly, like Cy Coleman, to find something new in him-self but mainly to find hits—and perhaps because nobody else wanted to work with him more than once.

The saintly Oscar Hammerstein even went so far as to call Youmans the only man he didn't like. But that was probably, in Gatsby's words, "just personal." The usual problem was Vincent's work habits, which didn't go into effect until the last speakeasy in New York had closed, at which point he'd totter home and start strumming chords and whistling tunes and calling for lyrics as if they were another drink. As his last part-ner, Ed Eliscu, told me, "It helped if you'd been napping at his place waiting for developments."

As it was, perhaps his most famous song was rounded off by a partner who'd already gone home and had to hear the chords over the telephone. "Oh, tea for two," said Irving Caesar, I assume sarcastically, "and me for you, et cetera, et cetera," and call me in the morning for the real lyric. All he needed right at that moment was a dummy, a beat to hang his real words on.

What is also both typical and strange is that the resulting song, dummy lyrics and all, would end up expressing the 1920s—1925 to be exact—so perfectly because, according to Eliscu, Youmans got everything wrong in real life, from the wrong clothes and haircut to the wrong things to say for every occasion—from which one might deduce that either he or Eliscu was slightly displaced. Conversely, my next interlocutor, Margaret Whit-ing, met Youmans as a child in Hollywood and thought he looked like the most glamorous thing she'd ever seen even in that community. And in the 1920s, the newspaper gossip rated him one-two with George Gershwin as "the most eligible." Scott Fitzgerald also used Youmans's persona in one of his novels.

Larchmont, where Youmans grew up, was a million miles from Tin Pan Alley, which may explain why he seemed so glamorous and out of synch. The Youmanses could fairly be described as a rich WASP family on their way down, just at the point where things start to degenerate. Vincent's father had already succumbed all too zestfully to the glamour of the White Way, not to mention its chorus girls and what are now called adult beverages.

So his stern, but blessedly musical mother seems to have taken the cartoon-WASP course of keeping the old man home, high and dry, but then not talking to him. And she adopted the rare child-raising technique of buying a pair of grand pianos for her son and daughter to serve as babysitter and tutor. Vincent spent his early years listening to more music than dialogue and learning how to express his feelings and to hide them on the keyboard. So perhaps it's not surprising that he wrote the tune for his impossibly happy hit "Hallelujah!" while still a teenager serving a hitch in the navy and relishing his freedom.

Soon after which, Zelda Fitzgerald claimed, he pretty much took over New York, in the early 1920s pouring out the songs that you heard everywhere, or at least everywhere Zelda went. Youmans was spurred by desire to keep up not just with the times but with George Gershwin, his virtual twin in life and a pacesetter, or mechanical rabbit, to a whole generation. "So the son of a bitch thought of it," he'd say after each Gershwin tune. But through the whole decade he kept up nicely with George, writing some great songs in the new bluesy, jazz mode, such as "Time on My Hands" and "More Than You Know," and then actually beating him to a gorgeous slice of the new Latin American territory with the swinging samba "The Carioca," and the best tango ever penned by a gringo, "Orchids in the Moonlight." "That's a lot of song," a friend of mine who is a singing pianist herself claimed as she formed the chords. And it's a good thing, because with the great score of *Flying Down to Rio,* which contains these gems, Youmans stopped. Not quite literally, because he still tried to write. But a double dose of alcohol and TB seem to have affected his judgment, and he thought he should advance in the classical front now and write a ballet—in short, still keep up with the Gershwins, who were currently taking time off to write an opera. Perhaps, as with Donaldson, the Hollywood assembly line had also taken away some of the fun. "Don't you wish it was still 1927?" he wrote to his friendly enemy, but Gershwin was always too busy to look back. And George was still setting the pace on his deathbed in 1937.

Gershwin's death may have taken whatever wind was left out of Vincent's sails, and although Youmans would remain a name to contend with until his own death in 1946, there was an expiration date on him now. As

if to make doubly sure, he had actually turned down an offer to make a film out of his life, on the grounds that he wasn't good enough.

Ed Eliscu was right: The man was truly a raging misfit in show business. (Not good enough? The guy must be nuts.) Still, it's always a good time to revive *No, No, Nanette*, which remains incurably young and fresh, or to play Frank Sinatra's version of "Without a Song" and hear two great musical intelligences jamming along the lane together for all eternity.

"Those whom the gods love die young," said the Greeks, although fate had a funny way of proving it to Youmans. But at least his short career has kept his music forever young. It has also left him with the highest batting average—or ratio of hits to misses—in the business. So it's a pleasure to rediscover him and get a sense of how his music exploded into the 1920s, matching the brilliance of the Lower East Side with the best of the Silk Stocking district.

I have already paid tribute to the black and Jewish contributions to these songs, but there was a third, sturdy stream proceeding from the British Isles and emanating in the stomps and reels of the hill country and the tavern singing of New England. "Songs that smile," as the advertisers would call it: "There Is a Tavern in the Town," "Turkey in the Straw," "Too Many Rings Around Rosie." Vincent Youmans, the eternal American misfit, forms a link with the nineteenth-century American songbook, and his rivalry with Gershwin would carry their same sound to the 1950s. To someone like Scott Fitzgerald, Youmans was a classmate who could introduce him to the new thing that was happening. And for anyone unfamiliar with this music, he remains a charming and irresistible starting point.

APPENDIX

Some Names That
(Almost) Got Away

For years I have lulled myself to sleep conjuring names of songwriters who have written two standards or more. What follows is the product of this labor—nothing definitive about it. It's a list of occasional or full-time swingers from the top of my head on this particular day. Other heads and other days would no doubt yield other lists. Since it usually takes two to make a songwriter, I have appended (in parentheses) the names of lyricists where they seem part of a whole.

RICHARD ADLER AND JERRY ROSS: "Hey There," "Whatever Lola Wants." In a heroic span of just two or three years, this team—who apparently wrote words and music interchangeably—worked in the shadow of Mr. Ross's medical death sentence to finish two classical musicals, *The Pajama Game* and *Damn Yankees*. Mr. Ross died at the age of twenty-nine.

MILTON AGER (Jack Yellen): "I'm Nobody's Baby," "Ain't She Sweet?" "Hard-Hearted Hannah."

FRED AHLERT (Roy Turk): "I'll Get By," "Mean to Me," "Walkin' My Baby Back Home."

HARRY AKST: "Am I Blue," "Dinah," "Baby Face."

LOUIS ALTER: "Do You Know What It Means to Miss New Orleans," "You Turned the Tables on Me," "Manhattan Serenade." Alter studied at the

Boston Conservatory, and was always more a swinging musician than a song-writer proper.

HARRY BARRIS: "Wrap Your Troubles in Dreams," "I Surrender, Dear," "Mississippi Mud." One of the Rhythm Boys, with Bing Crosby and Al Rinker, who probably deserve credits too.

EUBIE BLAKE (Noble Sissle): "I'm Just Wild About Harry," "Memories of You." A long-lived black pianist-entertainer, Blake's a transitional figure who wrote shows called *Shuffle Along, Chocolate Dandies,* and *Blackbirds of 1930*— "Look at me, I'm black" titles that lived on, like occasional blackface itself, right up till World War II. Eubie triumphantly outlived both trends.

RUBE BLOOM: "Day In, Day Out," "Fools Rush In," "Don't Worry 'Bout Me." Bloom was a great jazz pianist and a modest man. "I didn't know that Ruby wrote songs too," said Ellen Donaldson. Yes, indeed. And not just any songs: great ones.

JERRY BOCK: "Too Close for Comfort," "She Loves Me," and a lot of fine songs from *Fiorello!* and *Fiddler on the Roof* that don't quite count.

BROOKS BOWMAN: "East of the Sun (West of the Moon)." Here I break my own (two-standard) rule, but with a note from teacher. Brooks wrote the above classic for Princeton's Triangle Club, signed up with Warner Bros., and promptly died in a car crash after a Princeton-Yale game. I'm willing to put my money where Warners once did, betting on this man's enormous promise. But for tragedy, there had to be more music (and at least one more standard).

SHELTON BROOKS: "Some of These Days," "Darktown Strutters' Ball." See Duke Ellington chapter.

NACIO HERB BROWN (Arthur Freed): *Singin' in the Rain* in toto. Also, "You Stepped out of a Dream." See Hollywood chapter.

JOE BURKE: "Moon Over Miami," "Tiptoe Through the Tulips," "Shoe Shine Boy."

SAUL CHAPLIN: "Please Be Kind," "Until the Real Thing Comes Along."

CON CONRAD: "Margie," "Barney Google," "The Continental." The titles perfectly illustrate the difference between vaudeville, where Conrad began, and movies, where he won his Oscar.

J. FRED COOTS: "You Go to My Head," "For All We Know," "Santa Claus Is Comin' to Town." A gentleman about town and a habitué of the New York Athletic Club. By chance, we shared the same doctor, though years apart. In his final days, he once asked our doctor if he could possibly hurry up, and the doc answered, "I'm dancing as fast as I can." To which J. Fred replied, "Well, I'm dancing with tears in my eyes," thus going down in a volley of song titles.

MATT DENNIS (Tom Adair): "Let's Get Away from It All," "Everything Happens to Me," "Angel Eyes." A protégé of Tommy Dorsey, Dennis was still playing the clubs some fifty years later.

GENE DePAUL: "I'll Remember April," "Teach Me Tonight," "You Don't Know What Love Is." A latecomer, DePaul began with wartime novelties like "Mr. Five by Five" and "Milkman, Keep Those Bottles Quiet," before going on to the above postmodern beauties.

WALTER DONALDSON: "My Blue Heaven," "Yes Sir, That's My Baby," "Love Me or Leave Me," "Those Little White Lies," and "My Baby Just Cares for Me." See the Coda for more on Donaldson.

VERNON DUKE: "April in Paris," "Autumn in New York," "Taking a Chance on Love." See Gershwin chapter.

SAMMY FAIN: "That Old Feeling," "I'll Be Seeing You," "Secret Love." Not only his name sounds like Tin Pan Alley, so does his work, which is schmaltzy, prolific, versatile—everything but major. In fact, Sammy flopped badly on Broadway, though he could write his own ticket in Hollywood.

FRED FISHER: "Chicago (That Toddling Town)," "Peg o' My Heart," "Your Feet's Too Big."

JOHNNY GREEN: "Body and Soul," "I Cover the Waterfront," "I Wanna Be Loved." A rich kid classically trained, he had graduated from Horace Mann and Harvard by the age of twenty with a major in economics, yet Green wrote with as much soul and gut emotion as anyone on the street. After a meteoric career, he continued to serve music for several years as the musical director at MGM and conductor of the studio orchestra.

MARÍA GREVER: "What a Difference a Day Made," "Magic Is the Moonlight." Ms. Grever was a Mexican, Americanized after the fact by Stanley Adams and I can still hear the Mexican street bands in the background.

RAY HENDERSON: "Bye Bye Blackbird," "The Birth of the Blues," "The Best Things in Life Are Free" (Lew Brown and Buddy DeSylva). The third title is a tough choice because Henderson was one of the great prolifics, and it's hard to turn off the faucet. "Button Up Your Overcoat," "Alabamy Bound," "Life Is Just a Bowl of Cherries." Is this all really the same guy? Yet for all his variety, Alec Wilder's book does not even pay Henderson the compliment of a put-down; it does not mention him once. To an aesthete maturing in the 1920s, Henderson must have personified commercialism. But the pop song is an impure form, and commercialism by itself need not be fatal.

ARTHUR JOHNSTON (Johnny Burke): "Pennies from Heaven," "Just One More Chance," "Moon Song." One of Irving Berlin's brilliant musical secretaries. Johnston's "Moon Song" is a sublime composition for jazz piano.

ISHAM JONES: "It Had to Be You," "I'll See You in My Dreams," "On the Alamo." A Midwestern coal miner with a Welsh gift of harmony, Jones led one of the great "sweet" bands, which somehow metamorphosed into Woody Herman's Herd, a postmodern swing band and a joy of my youth.

JERRY LIVINGSTON (not to be confused with Jay "Mona Lisa" "Que Sera, Sera" Livingston): "Blue and Sentimental," "It's the Talk of the Town," and "Under a Blanket of Blue," which opens with the most exquisite series of chords since "Prelude to a Kiss."

MATTY MALNECK: "Goody Goody," "I'm Through with Love," "Stairway to the Stars." A violinist and arranger for Paul Whiteman, and hence an early friend of Crosby and Mercer, which placed him at the heart of a movement-within-a-movement, where he thrived.

GERALD MARKS: "All of Me," "Is It True What They Say About Dixie?"

HUGH MARTIN (Ralph Blane): "Buckle Down, Winsocki," "The Girl Next Door," "Have Yourself a Merry Little Christmas," one of the few defensible Christmas pop songs.

JIMMY McHUGH: "I Can't Give You Anything but Love, Baby," "Don't Blame Me," "A Lovely Way to Spend an Evening." "Professional" is the one word his partner Dorothy Fields used to describe McHugh, and I daresay her successors Frank Loesser and Harold Adamson would have nodded. The son of a plumber, boy Jimmy became what the Brits call a "dogsbody" at the Boston Opera House, improvising on the arias in his spare time and later becoming with Ms. Fields the first writers for Duke Ellington at the Cotton Club, then

with Adamson the first writers for Sinatra at the movies. My McHugh kick
comes from guessing how the bridge will jump. He's a resourceful chap, and I
somehow have a hunch his old man was a good plumber too.

KERRY MILLS: "Meet Me in St. Louis," "At a Georgia Camp Meeting," which is
played in old movies but never sung because the old tune celebrates the great
black contribution to American minstrels while its words inevitably sound pa-
tronizing. Interracial laughter was still up the road.

JIMMY MONACO: "You Made Me Love You," "I've Got a Pocketful of
Dreams," "I'm Making Believe." Born in Italy, Monaco wrote the first of these
way back in 1912, and had to wait a generation for Harry James and Judy Garland to catch up. Luckily, he had the time, and was still writing hits at Paramount thirty years later.

RAY NOBLE: "The Very Thought of You," "I Hadn't Anyone till You," "Chero-
kee." An Englishman who "got" the Yank sound perfectly while playing a Brit
twit on-screen and radio. He led an all-star band originally handpicked by
Glenn Miller before Glenn got a band of his own.

RALPH RAINGER (Leo Robin): "Thanks for the Memory," "Love in Bloom,"
"June in January." See Hollywood chapter.

HARRY REVEL (Mack Gordon): "Did You Ever See a Dream Walking?" "Stay As
Sweet As You Are," "Goodnight, My Love." Another Brit, Revel may hold the
record for most songs published that *weren't* standards. He was always good,
but seldom memorable.

HARRY RUBY AND BERT KALMAR: See the movie *Three Little Words.*

VICTOR SCHERTZINGER: "I Remember You," "Sand in My Shoes," "Tangerine."
A violin prodigy from Pennsylvania who evolved into a movie-producer-cum-
songwriter and was still evolving when he died at age fifty-one before his last
film, *The Fleet's In,* premiered and introduced two of the above standards to
the outside world.

ARTHUR SCHWARTZ: "Alone Together," "You and the Night and the Music,"
"Louisiana Hayride." See Coda, which discusses Schwartz.

STEPHEN SONDHEIM: "Comedy Tonight," "Everybody Ought to Have a Maid,"
"Send in the Clowns." Sondheim loves the old songs, and I wish he would
write more of them.

SAM STEPT: "All My Life," "That's My Weakness Now," "Please Don't Talk About Me When I'm Gone." Stept also joined another native of Odessa, Lew Brown, and one American, George Tobias, to write the great home-front anthem of World War II, "Don't Sit Under the Apple Tree (with Anyone Else but Me)."

AXEL STORDAHL AND PAUL WESTON: "I Should Care," "Day by Day." Young Frank Sinatra's favorite arranger, Stordahl, and Jo Stafford's husband, the bandleader Weston, dashed these off to see how the other half lived. Too bad they didn't do it more often.

JULE STYNE: "I Don't Want to Walk Without You," "Time After Time," "The Party's Over." The only writer to master the stage completely *after* he'd been a star writer for films, Styne was so prolific sitting at the piano that Sondheim would tell him to back up: Jule had just played through a whole new tune without noticing. By all accounts, Jule was the nicest guy in the business, and one of the few men to finish a show while simultaneously on dialysis *and* handicapping the horses.

KAY SWIFT: "Can't We Be Friends?" "Fine and Dandy." George Gershwin's legendary girlfriend ("There goes the future Kay Swift!") and musical soul mate. Odds are that the two never would have married, but would still be friends.

BOBBY TROUP: "Daddy," "(Get Your Kicks on) Route 66." Troup wrote the former, a hymn to the profit system, while still at the Wharton School of business, but his own best years were unselfishly devoted to helping rehabilitate his wife Julie London from addiction problems and to making her incomparable records of standards as good as they could get. On the other hand, the only kick I could find on Route 66 came from imitating Ezio Pinza at the top of my lungs on what was, back when Troup wrote about it, the loneliest road in Christendom.

ALBERT (GUMM) VON TILZER: "I'll Be with You in Apple Blossom Time," "Oh, by Jingo," "I Used to Love You, but It's All Over Now." His older brother, music publisher Harry (Gumm) von Tilzer, was the famous one, but Albert was the swinger—partly thanks to the Odessan genius Lew Brown, who divined the mythic hold of apples on the American soul and the latent swing in catchwords like "gosh" and "dolly," and indeed "by jingo." I believe the Gumm brothers were related to the Gumm sisters, i.e., to Judy Garland.

FATS WALLER (Andy Razaf): "Ain't Misbehavin'," "Honeysuckle Rose," although I prefer his jazz vamps like "Alligator Crawl" and "The Minor Drag."

Misbehaving was exactly what Fats did, jiving behind the teacher's back and swinging into a Bach cantata for appearances. As a kid in charge of the record player, I found Waller my best compromise with the highbrows who came calling. Fats knew their language—good music—and he spoke to the devil in every man.

MABEL WAYNE: "Ramona," "It Happened in Monterey," "In a Little Spanish Town." Born in Brooklyn, she had private music lessons in Switzerland and became a singer, pianist, and dancer in vaudeville. Clearly, like many women, Ms. Wayne deserves to be much better known.

SPENCER WILLIAMS: "I Ain't Got Nobody," "Basin Street Blues." Along with many black jazz musicians, Williams "made it" in Europe between the wars, writing and adapting jazz classics for Josephine Baker at the Folies-Bergère in Paris, where he was probably more celebrated than Henry Ford and Calvin Coolidge put together.

HARRY WOODS: "When the Red, Red Robin Comes Bob, Bob, Bobbin' Along," "Try a Little Tenderness," "What a Little Moonlight Can Do." Famous for his ferocious temper and his artificial hand, legend has it that someone once saw Woods pounding some poor chap with the latter and said, "So that's the guy that wrote about *tenderness*?"

ALLIE WRUBEL: "Zip-a-Dee-Doo-Dah," "Music, Maestro, Please," "Gone with the Wind." As with the part of Scarlett O'Hara, there was much competition for the use of the famous book title for a song. Mr. Wrubel's excellent entry won, and his son was one of the celebrators at a copyright party I attended more than fifty years later. Once again, the standards had been good to children and grandchildren yet unborn.

VINCENT YOUMANS: "I Want to Be Happy," "Sometimes I'm Happy," "Hallelujah," "Great Day." Could anyone *really* be that happy? See the Coda for more on Youmans.

VICTOR YOUNG: "Stella by Starlight," "Street of Dreams," "I Don't Stand a Ghost of a Chance with You." One more violin prodigy and later a great arranger for Paramount and others, and one of the most musically sophisticated composers ever to embrace this particular form. Incidentally, Young's "Street of Dreams" was allegedly Manhattan's Fifty-second Street, where the jazz jumped and the drugs flowed and the dreams, while they lasted, were the best ever dreamed in America.

INDEX

WILFRID SHEED is the author of six novels, two of which, *Office Politics* and *People Will Always Be Kind,* were nominated for National Book awards. He has written three collections of criticism, one of which was nominated by the National Book Critics Circle. Among his other books is a notable memoir of Clare Boothe Luce, who told him that Irving Berlin was the vainest man she had ever met and George Gershwin one of the most basically modest. He lives with his wife, Miriam Ungerer, in North Haven, New York.

A NEW PRACTICAL, COMPARATIVE CONCORDANCE

TO THE

OLD AND NEW TESTAMENTS

Arranged in a simplified form for easy reference. It embraces the salient and ready-working features of the larger Concordances. In its Comparative feature it notes the word-changes made in the Revised Version, wherever such are of moment. Words omitted in the Revised Version are indicated by a —— (dash). The Subject Words are set in **BLACK FACE CAPITALS**, and those derived from them are shown in *italic* type. Plural Nouns are referred to under their singulars. Past tenses of Verbs and their Participles, as a rule, follow their present tenses.

A

ABASE, make low, &c.
Job 40. 11. every one proud *a.*
Isa. 31. 4. lion will not *a.* himself
Ezek. 21. 26. exalt him that is low and *a.* him that is high
Dan. 4. 37. those that walk in pride he is able to *a.*
Matt. 23. 12. whosoever shall exalt himself shall be *abased*
Phil. 4. 12. how to be *a.* and how to
2 Cor. 11. 7. offence in *abasing* myself
R. V. Matt. 23. 12; Luke 14. 11; 18. 14. humbled

ABATED, waters were, Gen. 8. 3.
Gen. 8. 11. so Noah knew that the waters were *a.*
Lev. 27. 18. it shall be *a.* from thy
Deut. 34. 7. his eye was not dim, nor his natural force *a.*
Judg. 8. 3. then their anger was *a.*
R. V. Gen. 8. 3. decreased

ABBA, *father*, Mark 14. 36. Rom. 8. 15. Gal. 4. 6.

ABHOR, greatly hate and loathe
Lev. 26. 11. my soul shall not *a.* you
15. if your soul *a.* my judgments
30. my soul shall *a.* you
Deut. 7. 26. utterly *a.* it
1 Sam. 27. 12. made his people to *a.* him
Job 30. 10. they *a.* me, they flee
42. 6. I *a.* myself and repent
Ps. 5. 6. Lord will *a.* the bloody
119. 163. I hate and *a.* lying
Jer. 14. 21. do not *a.* us for thy name's sake
Amos 5. 10. they *a.* him that speak.
6. 8. I *a.* the excellency of Jacob
Mic. 3. 9. ye that *a.* judgment
Rom. 12. 9. *a.* that which is evil
Ex. 5. 21. made our savour *abhorred*
Lev. 26. 43. their soul *a.* my statutes
Deut. 32. 19. when the Lord saw it he *a.*
1 Sam. 2. 17. men *a.* the offering of
Job 19. 19. all my inward friends *a.*
Ps. 22. 24. nor *a.* affliction of afflict.
78. 59. wroth and greatly *a.* Israel
89. 38. hath cast off and *a.* anoint.
106. 40. he *a.* his own inheritance
Prov. 22. 14. *a.* of the Lord shall fall
Lam. 2. 7. Lord hath *a.* his sanctuary
Ezek. 16. 25. made thy beauty to be *a.*
Rom. 2. 22. thou that *abhorrest* idols

Zech. 11. 8. their soul *abhorreth* me
Job 33. 20. his life *a.* bread
Ps. 10. 3. covetous whom the Lord *a.*
107. 18. their soul *a.* all manner of
Isa. 49. 7. him whom the nation *a.*
66. 24. be an *abhorring* to all flesh
R. V. Ps. 89. 38. rejected; Ezek. 16. 25. an abomination

ABIDE, continue, bear
Ex. 16. 29. *a.* ye every man in his
Num. 35. 25. *a.* in it unto the death
2 Sam. 11. 11. ark and Israel *a.* in tents
Ps. 15. 1. who shall *a.* in thy tabernacle
7. he shall *a.* before God for ever
Prov. 7. 11. her feet *a.* not in her house
Hos. 3. 3. shall *a.* for me many days
4. Israel shall *a.* without a king
Joel 2. 11. day of the Lord is great and very terrible; who can *a.* it
Mal. 3. 2. who may *a.* the day of his coming
Matt. 10. 11. there *a.* till ye go thence
Luke 19. 5. to-day I must *a.* at thy
John 12. 46. should not *a.* in dark.
15. 4. *a.* in me and I in you, 7.
Acts 20. 23. afflictions *a.* me.
1 Cor. 3. 14. if any man's work *a.*
7. 8. it is good for them if they *a.* even as I
20. let every man *a.* in the same calling wherein he was called
24. is called therein *a.* with God
Phil. 1. 24. to *a.* in the flesh is needful
25. know that I shall *a.* with you
1 John 2. 24. let that therefore *a.* in you
27, 28. ye shall *a.* in him
Ps. 49. 12. man in honor *abideth* not
Eccl. 1. 4. the earth *a.* for ever
John 3. 36. wrath of God *a.* on him
8. 35. servant *a.* not but the Son *a.* ever
12. 24. except it die it *a.* alone
1 Cor. 13. 13. now *a.* faith, hope
2 Tim. 2. 13. yet *a.* faithful
1 Pet. 1. 23. word of God *a.* for ever
1 John 3. 6. whoso *a.* in him sinneth not
24. hereby we know he *a.* in us
John 5. 38. not his word *abiding* in you
1 John 3. 15. no murderer hath eternal life *a.*

John 14. 23. make our *abode* with him
R. V. Ps. 15. 1. sojourn; Hos. 11. 6. fall upon; Rom. 11. 23. continue

ABILITY, in strength, wealth, &c.
Lev. 27. 8. Ezra 2. 69. Neh. 5. 8. Dan. 1. 4.
Matt. 25. 15. to every man according to his *a.*, Acts 11. 29.
1 Pet. 4. 11. as of the *a.* God giveth
R. V. 1 Pet. 4. 11. strength

ABJECTS, *base men*, Ps. 35. 15.

ABLE men, such as fear God, Ex. 18. 21.
Lev. 14. 22. such as he is *a.* to get
Deut. 16. 17. every man give as he is *a.*
2 Chron. 20. 6. none is *a.* to withstand
Prov. 27. 4. who is *a.* to stand
Ezek. 46. 11. as he is *a.* to give
Dan. 3. 17. our God is *a.* to deliver
4. 37. walk in pride he is *a.* to abase
Matt. 3. 9. God is *a.* of these stones to raise up children, Luke 3. 8.
9. 28. believe ye that I am *a.* to
20. 22. are ye *a.* to drink of cup
Mark 4. 33. as they were *a.* to hear
John 10. 29. no man *a.* to pluck
Rom. 4. 21. promised he was *a.* to perform
14. 4. God is *a.* to make him stand
1 Cor. 3. 2. neither yet now are ye *a*
10. 13. tempted above that ye *a.*
2 Cor. 9. 8. *a.* to make all grace abound
Eph. 3. 20. *a.* to do exceeding
2 Tim. 1. 12. *a.* to keep that committed
Heb. 2. 18. *a.* to succor the tempt.
5. 7. *a.* to save him from death
7. 25. *a.* to save to the uttermost
James 1. 21. *a.* to save your souls
4. 12. *a.* to save and to destroy
Jude 24. *a.* to keep you from fall.
R. V. Lev. 25. 26. waxen rich; Josh. 23. 9 ——; Acts 25. 5. are of power; 2 Cor. 3. 6. sufficient as; Eph. 3. 18. strong.

ABOLISHED, made to cease
Isa. 2. 18. idols he shall utterly *abolish*
Ezek. 6. 6. your works may be *a.*
2 Cor. 3. 13. to the end of that *a.*
2 Tim. 1. 10. Jesus Christ who hath *a.* death
R. V. Isa. 2. 18. pass away; 2 Cor. 3. 13. passing away.

Published by Barbour Publishing, Inc. Printed in the United States of America.

ABOMINABLE, very hateful.
Lev. 7. 21. & 11. 43. & 18. 30. Isa.
14. 19. & 65. 4. Jer. 16. 18.
1 Chron. 21. 6. king's word was *a.*
to Joab
Ps. 14. 1. have done *a.* works, 53. 1.
Jer. 44. 4. do not this *a.* thing
Ezek.16 52. has committed more|*a.*
Tit. 1. 16. in works deny him being *a.*
1 Pet. 4. 3. walked in *a.* idolatries
Rev. 21. 8. unbelieving and *a.* shall

ABOMINATION, what is very
filthy, hateful, and loathsome as
sin, Isa. 66. 3. idols, Ex. 8. 26.
Prov. 6. 16. seven things are an *a.*
11. 1. a false balance is *a.* to the
Lord.   [Lord
12. 22. lying lips are *a.* to the
15. 8. the sacrifice of the wicked
is an *a.*   [the Lord, 3. 32.
16. 5. proud in heart is an *a.* to
20. 23. divers weights are an *a* to
the Lord.
Isa. 1. 13. incense is an *a.* to me.
Dan. 11. 31. *a.* that maketh desolate.   [of desolation
12. 11. Matt. 24. 15. Mark 13. 14. *a.*
Luke 16. 15. is *a.* in the sight of
God   [*a.*
Rev. 21. 27, whatsoever worketh
2 Kings 21. 2. *abominations* of the
Ezra 9. 14. join with the people of
these *a.*
Prov. 26. 25. seven *a.* in his heart
Jer.7.10.delivered to do all these *a.*
Ezek. 16. 2. cause Jerusalem to
know her *a.* 20. 4. & 23. 36.
18. 13. hath done all these *a.* shall
Dan. 9. 27. for the overspreading
of *a.*
Rev. 17.5. mother of harlots and *a.*

ABOUND, become very full,
large, Prov. 8. 24. Rom. 3. 7.
Prov. 28. 20. the faithful shall *a.*
Matt. 24. 12. iniquity shall *a*
Rom. 5. 20. offence might *a.* but
where sin *a.* grace did much
more *a.*
2 Cor. 9. 8. able to make all gr. *a.*
Phil. 1. 9. that love may *a.* more
4. 12. I know how *a.*   [count
17. fruit that may *a.* to your ac-
18. I have all and *a.*
1 Thes. 3. 12. the Lord make you *a.*
2 Pet. 1. 8. if these things be in
you and *a.*   [us
Eph. 1. 8. hath *abounded* toward
1 Cor. 15. 58, always *abounding*
Col. 2. 7. *a.* with thanksgiving
R. V. Matt. 24. 12. multiplied.

ABOVE, higher, heaven,Ex.20.4.
John 3. 31. cometh from *a.* is *a.* all
19. 11. power given thee from *a.*
Gal. 4. 26. Jerusalem, which is *a.* is
Eph. 4. 6. one God who is *a.* all
Col. 3. 1. seek things which are *a.*
James 1. 17. every perfect gift is
from *a.*

ABSENT one from another, Gen.
31. 49. 2 Cor. 10. 1.   [ent
1 Cor. 5. 3. as *a.* in body but pres-
2 Cor. 5. 6. in body we are *a.* from
the Lord
10. 1. being *a.* am bold toward you
Col. 2. 5. though I be *a.* in the flesh

ABSTAIN from idols, Acts 15. 20.
1 Thess. 4. 3. *a.* from fornication.
5.22.*a.* from all appearance of evil
1 Pet. 2. 11. *a.* from fleshly lusts
Abstinence from meat, Acts 27. 21.

ABUNDANCE, great fulness,
and plenty. Job 22. 11. & 38. 24.
Deut. 33.19. 1 Chron. 22. 3, 4, 14, 15.
Deut. 28. 47. for the *a.* of all things
Eccl. 5. 10. he that loveth *a.* with
12. *a.* of the rich will not suffer
him to sleep

Isa. 66. 11. delighted with *a.* of her
glory
Matt. 12. 34, out of *a.* of the heart
the mouth speaketh, Luke 6. 45.
13. 12. shall have more *a.* 25. 29.
Mark 12. 44. they did cast in of
their *a.*   [*a.*
Luke 12. 15. life consisteth not in
2 Cor. 8.2.*a.* of their joy abounded
12. 7. through *a.* of revelations
R. V. 2 Cor. 8. 20 bounty

ABUNDANT in goodness and
truth, Ex. 34. 6. 2 Cor. 4. 15. & 9. 12.
2 Cor. 11. 23, in labors more *a.*
1 Tim. 1. 14. grace of Lord ex-
ceeding *a.*
Job 12.6. God bringeth *abundantly*
Ps. 36. 8. shall be *a.* satisfied with
fatness
S. of S. 5.1. yea drink *a.* O beloved
Isa. 55. 7. he will *a.* pardon   [*a.*
John 10. 10. might have life more
Eph. 3. 20. able to do exceeding *a.*
Tit. 3. 6. shed on us *a.*thro. Jesus
2 Pet. 1. 11. entrance shall be min-
istered unto you more *a.*
R. V. 2 Cor. 4. 15. multiplied ; 1
Pet. 1. 3. great

ABUSE not my power, 1 Cor. 9.
18. 1 Cor. 7. 31. use the world as
not *abusing* it   [full
R.V.1 Cor. 9.18. not to us to the

ACCEPT, receive kindly in favor, Gen. 32. 20. Acts 24. 3 .
Lev. 26. 41. *a.* punishment of iniquity, 43.
Deut. 33. 11. *a.* work of his hands
2 Sam. 24. 23. Lord thy God *a.* thee
Job 13. 8. will ye *a.* his person, 10.
32. 21. let me not *a.* any man's
person
42. 8. servant Job, him will I *a.*
Ps. 119. 108. *a.* free-will-off. of my
mouth
Ezek. 43. 27. I will *a.* you
Mal. 1. 13. should I *a.* this of your
hand
Gen. 4.7.shalt thou not be *accepted*
Lev. 1. 4, shall be *a.* for atone-
ment
Luke 4. 24. no prophet *a.* in his
own country   [is *a.*
Acts 10. 35. worketh righteousness
2 Cor. 5. 9. we may be *a.* of him
Eph. 1.6.made us *a.*in the beloved
Luke 20. 21. neither *acceptest* the
person
Job 34. 19. him that *accepteth* not
the persons of princes
Eccl. 9. 7. God now *a.* thy works
Hos. 8. 13. Lord *a.* them not
Gal. 2. 6. God *a.* no man's person
Heb. 11. 35. not *accepting* deliver-
ance   [58. 5.
Acceptable day of the Lord, Isa.
Ps. 19. 14. let the meditation of
my heart be *a.*
Eccl. 12. 10. sought out *a.* words
Dan. 4. 27. let my counsel be *a.*
Rom. 12. 1. sacrifice holy *a.* to God
2. know good and *a.* will of God
Eph. 5. 10. proving what is *a.*unto
the Lord   [ing.
Phil. 4. 18. sacrifice *a.* well-pleas-
Heb. 12. 28. serve God *acceptably*
with fear
1 Tim. 1. 15. worthy of all *accepta-
tion*   [respect
R. V. Job 13. 10 ; 32. 21 ; Ps. 82. 2.

ACCESS, admission through
Christ, Rom. 5. 2. Eph. 2. 18.
and 3. 12.

ACCOMPLISH, perform fully,
finish, Lev. 22. 21. Job 14. 6.
Ps. 64, 6. *a.* a diligent search
Isa. 55. 11. it shall *a.* that I please
Ezek. 6. 12. thus will I *a.* my fury
Dan. 9. 2. would *a.* seventy years

Luke 9. 31. decease he should *a.* at
Jerusalem
2 Chron. 36. 22. word might be *ac-
complished*
Prov. 13. 19. desire *a.* is sweet to
soul
Isa. 40. 2. her warfare is *a.* her sin
Luke 12. 50. how am I straitened
till it be *a.*
John 19. 28. all things were now *a.*
Heb. 9. 6. *accomplishing* service of
God.
R. V. Jer. 25. 34. fully come ; 44. 25.
establish ; Luke 1. 23 ; 2. 6, 21, 22.
fulfilled

ACCORD, hearty agreement, Acts
1. 14. & 2. 1, 46. & 4. 24. & 15. 25.
Phil. 2. 2. of one *a.* of one mind
R. V. Lev. 25. 5. itself ; Acts 2. **L**
together

ACCOUNT, reckoning, esteem
Job 33. 13. giv. not *a.* of his matters
Ps. 144. 3. that thou mak. *a* of him
Eccl. 7. 27. one by one to find out
the *a.*
Matt. 12. 36. give *a.* in the day of
judgment
Luke 16. 2. give *a.* of thy steward-
ship
Rom. 14. 12. give *a.* of him. to God
Heb. 13. 17. as they that must
give *a.*
1 Pet. 4. 5. shall give *a.* to him that
is ready to judge the quick and
Ps. 22. 30. *accounted* to the Lord for
a generation
Isa. 2. 22. wherein is he to be *a.* of
Luke 20. 35. shall be *a.* worthy to
obtain that world
21. 36. *a.* worthy to escape
22. 24. which should be *a.* greatest
Gal. 3. 6. *a.* to him for righteousness
Heb. 11. 19. *a.* God able to raise
R. V. 2 Chr. 26. 11 ; Matt. 18. 23.
reckoning

ACCURSED, devoted to ruin
Deut. 21. 23. hanged is *a.* of God
Josh. 6. 18. keep yourselves from
the *a.* thing
Isa. 65. 20. sinner a hundred years
old shall be *a.*
Rom. 9. 3. wish myself *a.* from
Christ
1 Cor. 12. 3. no man by Spirit calls
Jesus *a.*
Gal. 1. 8, 9. preach other gospel
be *a.*
R. V. 1 Chr. 2. 7. devoted thing ;
Rom. 9. 3 ; 1 Cor. 12. 3 ; Gal. 1. 8.
anathema.

ACCUSATION, Ezra 4. 6. Matt.
27. 37. Luke 6. 7. & 19. 8. John 18.
29. Acts 25. 18.
1 Tim. 5. 19. against an elder receive not an *a.*
2 Pet. 2. 11. bring not railing *a.*
Jude 9.
R. V. 2 Pet. 2. 11 ; Jude 9. judgment

ACCUSE, charge with crimes
Prov. 30. 10. *a.*not servant tomaster
Luke 3. 14. neither *a.* any falsely
John 5. 45. that I will *a.* you to the
Father
1 Pet. 3. 16. that falsely *a.* your
good conversation in Christ
Tit. 1. 6. not *accused* of riot
Rev. 12. 10. *a.* them before our God
Accuser of brethren is cast down
Acts 25. 16. have *a.* face to face
2 Tim. 3. 3. false *a.,* Tit. 2. 3.
John 5.45. there is one that *accuseth*
Rom. 2. 15. thoughts *accusing* or
excusing
R. V. Prov. 30. 10. slander

ACCUSTOMED, Jer. 13. 23.

ACKNOWLEDGE, own, confess
Deut. 33. 9. neither did he *a.* his
brethren
Ps. 51. 3. I *a.* my transgression
Prov. 3. 6. in all thy ways *a.* him
Isa. 33. 13. ye that are near *a.* my
might
Jer. 3. 13. only *a.* thine iniquity

Hos. 5. 15. until they *a.* their offence
1 Cor. 16. 18. *a.* them that are such
Ps. 32. 5. I *a.* my sin
1 John 2. 23. that *acknowledgeth* the Son
2 Tim. 2. 25. *acknowledging* the truth
Tit. 1. 1. *a.* of the truth which is after godliness
Col. 2. 2. to the *acknowledgment* of the mystery of God
R. V. 1 John 2. 23. confesseth

ACQUAINT thyself with him, Job 22. 21.
Ps. 139. 3. *acquainted* with my ways
Isa. 53. 3. *a.* with grief
Acquaintance, familiar friends or companions, Job 19. 13. & 42. 11.
Ps. 31. 11. & 55. 13. & 88. 8, 18.
R. V. Acts 24. 23. friends

ACQUIT, hold innocent, Job 10. 14.
Nah. 1. 3. will not at all *a.* the wicked

ACTS of the Lord, Deut. 11. 3, 7.
Judg. 5. 11. rehearse righteous *a.*
1 Sam. 12. 7. reason of all righteous *a.* of the Lord
Ps. 106. 2. utter mighty *a.* of Lord
145. 6. speak of thy mighty *a.,* 4.
150. 2. praise him for his mighty *a.*
Isa. 28. 21. his *a.* his strange *a.*
John 8. 4. taken in adultery in very *a.*
ACTIONS weighed, 1 Sam. 2. 3.
ACTIVITY, men of, Gen. 47. 6.
ADAMANT, Ezek. 3. 9. Zech. 7. 12.
ADD fifth part, Lev. 5. 16. & 6. 5. & 27. 13, 15, 19, 27, 31.
Deut. 4. 2. shall not *a.* unto the word
1 Kings 12. 11. I will *a.* to your yoke
Ps. 69. 27. *a.* iniquity to their iniquity
Isa. 30. 1. that they may *a.* sin to sin
Matt. 6. 27. can *a.* one cubit, Luke 12. 25.
Phil. 1. 16. to *a.* affliction to my
2 Pet. 1. 5. *a.* to your faith, virtue
Rev. 22. 18. if any man *a.* unto these things, God shall *a.* unto him
Deut. 5. 22. he *added* no more
Jer. 36. 32. were *a.* many like words
Matt. 6. 33. all these things shall be *a.* unto you, Luke 12. 31.
Acts 2. 41. same day were *a.* about three thousand souls
47. Lord *a.* to the church such
5. 14. believers were the more *a.* to
11. 24. much people was *a.* to the Lord
Prov. 10. 22. *addeth* no sorrow with
ADDER, poisonous serpent, Gen. 49. 17. Ps. 58. 4. & 91. 13. & 140. 3.
Prov. 23. 32. Isa. 14. 29.
ADDICTED, gave up, 1 Cor. 16. 15.
R. V. 1 Cor. 16. 15. set.
ADJURE, to charge under pain of God's curse, 1 Kings 22. 16. 2 Chron. 18. 15. Matt. 26. 63. Mark 5. 7. Acts 19. 13. Josh. 6. 26. 1 Sam. 14. 24.
ADMINISTRATION, 1 Cor. 12. 5.
2 Cor. 9. 12. & 8. 19, 20. *administered*
ADMIRATION, high esteem, Jude 16. or wonder and amazement, Rev. 17. 6.
2 Thes. 1. 10. *admired* in them that believe
R. V. Rev. 17. 6. wonder; Jude 16. respect of persons.
ADMONISH, warn, reprove
Rom. 15. 14. able to *a.* one another
2 Thes. 3. 15. *a.* him as a brother
Eccl. 12. 12. by these be *admonished*
Jer. 42. 19. know that I have *a.* you
Acts 27. 9. Paul *a.* them
Heb. 8. 5. as Moses was *a.* of God
Col. 3. 16. *admonishing* one another in psalms and hymns
1 Cor. 10. 11. are written for our *admonition*
Tit. 3. 10. after first and second *a.* reject
R. V. Jer. 42. 19. testified unto;
Heb. 8. 5. warned.

ADOPTION, putting among God's children, Jer. 3. 19. 2 Cor. 6. 18.
Rom. 8. 15. received spirit of *a.*
23. *a.* redemption of our body
Gal. 4. 5. might receive *a.* of sons
Eph. 1. 5. unto *a.* of children
ADORN, deck out, Isa. 61. 10. Jer. 31. 4.
Tit. 2. 10. *a.* the doctrine of God
Jer. 31. 4. *adorned* with thy tabrets
Luke 21. 5. *a.* with goodly stones
1 Pet. 3. 5. holy women *a.* themselves
Rev. 21. 2. as a bride *a.* for her
Isa. 61. 10. as a bride *adorneth* herself
1 Pet. 3. 3. whose *adorning* let it not
1 Tim. 2. 9. women *a.* themselves in modest apparel
ADULTERER, put to death, Lev. 20. 10.
Job 24. 15. eye of *a.* waits for twilight
Isa. 57. 3. seed of *a.* and whore
Jer. 23. 10. land is full of *adulterers*
9. 2. Hos. 7. 4. be all *a.*
Mal. 3. 5. I will be a swift witness against *a.*
1 Cor. 6. 9. neither *a.* shall inherit the kingdom of God
Heb. 13. 4. whoremongers and *a.* God will judge
James 4. 4. ye *a.* and *adulteresses*
Prov. 6. 26. *adulteress* will hunt for
32. committeth *adultery* lacks
Matt. 5. 28. committeth *a.* in his heart
2 Pet. 2. 14. having eyes full of *a.*
Matt. 15. 19. out of the heart proceed *adulteries,* fornications, Mark 7. 21.
Prov. 30. 20. way of *adulterous* woman
Matt. 12. 39. *a.* generation seeketh a sign, 16. 4. Mark 8. 38.
ADVANTAGE hath Jew, Rom. 3. 1.
2 Cor. 2. 11. lest Satan get an *a.*
Luke 9. 25. what is a man *advantaged*
R. V. Luke 9. 25. profited
ADVERSARY, opposer, enemy Ex. 23. 22. I will be *a.* to thy *a.*
1 Kings 5. 4. is neither *a.* nor evil
Job 31. 35. my *a.* had written a book
Matt. 5. 25. agree with thine *a.*
Luke 18. 3. avenge me of mine *a.*
1 Pet. 5. 8. your *a.* the devil as a
1 Sam. 2. 10. *adversaries* of the Lord
Lam. 1. 5. her *a.* are the chief
Luke 21. 15. all your *a.* not be able
1 Cor. 16. 9. and there are many *a.*
Heb. 10. 27. shall devour the *a.*
R. V. enemy, in most O. T. texts
ADVERSITY, affliction, misery
2 Sam. 4. 9. redeem my soul from all *a.*
Ps. 10. 6. I shall never be in *a.*
35. 15. in my *a.* they rejoiced
94. 13. give rest from days of *a.*
Prov. 17. 17. brother is born for *a.*
Eccl. 7. 14. in the day of *a.* consider
Isa. 30. 20. give you the bread of *a.*
1 Sam. 10. 19. saved you out of all *a.*
ADVICE, Judg. 19. 30. 1 Sam. 25. 33.
2 Sam. 19. 43. Prov. 20. 18.
ADVOCATE with Father, 1 John 2. 1.
AFAR off, Gen. 22. 4. & 37. 18. Ps. 65. 5.
138. 6. proud he knoweth *a.*
Ps. 139. 2. understandest my thoughts *a.* off
Acts 2. 39. promise is to all *a.* and
Eph. 2. 17. preached peace to you *a.*
2 Pet. 1. 9. blind and cannot see *a.*
AFFAIRS, Ps. 112. 5. 2 Tim. 2. 4.
AFFECT, incline, move
Gal. 4. 17. they zealously *a.* you
18. good to be zealously *affected*
Lam. 3. 51. mine eye *affecteth* my heart
Rom. 1. 31. natural *affection*
Col. 3. 5. mortify inordinate *a.*

Rom. 1. 26. them up to vile *affections*
Gal. 5. 24. crucify flesh with *a.*
Rom. 12. 10. be kindly *affectioned*
1 Thes. 2. 8. *affectionately* desirous
R. V. Col. 3. 2. mind; Rom. 1. 26;
Gal. 5. 24. passions
AFFINITY, relation by marriage, 1 Kings 3. 1. 2 Chron. 18. 1. Ezra 9. 14.
AFFLICT, grieve, trouble, Gen. 15. 13. Ex. 1. 11. & 22. 22.
Ezra 8. 21. that we might *a.* ourselves
Lev. 16. 29, 31. shall *a.* your souls 23. 27, 32. Num. 29. 7. & 30. 13.
Isa. 58. 5. day for a man to *a.* his soul
Lam. 3. 33. doth not *a.* willingly
2 Sam. 22. 28. *afflicted* people thou wilt save, Ps. 18. 27.
Job 6. 14. to *a.* pity should be
34. 28. heareth the cry of the *a.*
Ps. 18. 27. wilt save the *a.* people
71. it is good that I have been *a.*
107. I am *a.* very much
140. 12. wilt maintain cause of *a.*
Prov. 15. 15. all days of *a.* are evil
Isa. 49. 13. he will have mercy on *a.*
53. 4. smitten of God and *a.*
Mic. 4. 6. gather her I have *a.*
James 5. 13. is any *a.* let him pray
Ex. 3. 7. seen *affliction* of people
2 Kings 14. 26. Lord saw *a.* of
Job 5. 6. *a.* cometh not forth of
Ps. 25. 18. look on my *a.* and pain
107. 10. bound in *a.* and iron
39. brought low through *a.*
119. 50. this is my comfort in *a.*
Isa. 48. 10. chosen thee in the furnace of *a.*
63. 9. in all their *a.* he was
Hos. 5. 15. in their *a.* they will seek
Obad. 13. not have looked on their *a.*
Zech. 1. 15. helped forward the *a.*
2 Cor. 4. 17. our light *a.* which is
Phil. 4. 14. communicate with my *a.*
1 Thes. 1. 6. received word in much *a.*
James 1. 27. to visit fatherless in their *a.*
Ps. 34. 19. many are the *afflictions* of the righteous
132. 1. remember David and all his *a.*
Acts 7. 10. delivered him out of all *a.*
Col. 1. 24. which is behind of *a.* of Christ
1 Thes. 3. 3. no man moved by these *a.*
2 Tim. 1. 8. partaker of *a.* of gospel
Heb. 10. 32. endured great fight of *a.*
1 Pet. 5. 9. the same *a.* accomplished
R. V. Ez. 8. 21. humble; Ps. 55. *'*3. answer; Job 6. 14. ready to faint;
James 5. 13. suffering
AFRAID, Lev. 26. 6. Num. 12. 8.
Job 13. 21. Ps. 56. 3. & 119. 120.
Not be *afraid,* Ps. 56. 11. & 112. 7.
Isa. 12. 2. Matt. 14. 27. Mark 5. 36.
Luke 12. 4. 1 Pet. 3. 6, 14. Heb. 11. 23.
AFRESH, crucify Son of God, Heb. 6. 6.
AGE is as nothing before thee, Ps. 39. 5.
Job 5. 26. come to grave in full *a.*
Heb. 5. 14. strong meat to those of full *a.*
11. 11. Sarah when she was past *a.*
Tit. 2. 2, 3. *aged* men be sober
Ages Eph. 2. 7. & 3. 5, 21.
Col. 1. 26. mystery hid from *a.*
R. V. Josh. 23. 1, 2. years; Job. 11. 17. life; Job 12. 20. elders
AGONY, Christ's, in the garden, Matt. 27. 36; Luke 22. 44, &c.
AGREE, Acts 5. 9.
Matt. 5. 25. *a.* with thine adversary
1 John 5. 8. these three *a.* in one
Amos 3. 3. walk together except *agreed*
Isa. 28. 15. with hell at *agreement*

2 Cor. 6. 16. what *a.* has temple of God
R. V. 2 Kings 18. 31; Isa. 36. 16. your peace
AIR, 1 Cor. 9. 26. & 14. 9. Eph. 2. 2.
1 Thes. 4. 17. Rev. 9. 2. & 16. 17.
R. V. In Gos. and Acts, heaven
ALARM, how sounded, Num. 10. 5.
ALIEN, stranger, Ex. 18. 3. Job 19. 15.
Ps. 69. 8. heathens, Deut. 14. 21. Isa. 61. 5. Lam. 5. 2. Heb. 11. 34.
Eph. 2. 12. *a.* from commonwealth
4. 18. *alienated* from life of God
Col. 1. 21. were sometimes *a.*
R. V. Ex. 18. 3. sojourner; Deut. 14. 21. foreigner.
ALIVE, Gen. 12. 12. Num. 22. 23.
Rom. 6. 11. *a.* to God through Jesus
1 Sam. 2. 6. killeth and maketh *a.*
15. 8. he took Agag *a.*
Luke 15. 24. son was dead and is *a.*
Rom. 6. 13. as those *a.* from the dead
7. 9. I was *a.* without the law once
1 Cor. 15. 22. in Christ shall all be made *a.*
1 Thes. 4. 15, 17. we who are *a.*
Rev. 1. 18. I am *a.* for evermore
2. 8. was dead and is *a.*
R. V. Gen. 7. 23; Lev. 10. 16; 26. 36——; Num. 21. 35. remaining
ALLEGING, Acts 17. 3.
ALLEGORY, Gal. 4. 24.
ALLOW deeds of fathers, Luke 11. 48.
Acts 24. 15. which themselves *a.*
Rom. 7. 15. that which I do I *a.* not
14. 22. in that which he *alloweth.*
1 Thes. 2. 4. as we were *allowed* of God
R. V. Luke 11. 48. consent unto;
Acts 24. 15. look for; Rom. 7. 15. know; Rom. 14. 22. approveth; 1 Thes. 2. 4. approved.
ALLURE, Hos. 2. 14. 2 Pet. 2. 18.
R. V. 2 Pet. 2. 18. entice.
ALL THINGS lawful, but not expedient, 1 Cor. 6. 12.
ALMIGHTY GOD, Gen. 17. 1. & 28. 3. & 35. 11. & 43. 14. & 48. 3. Ex. 6. 3. 2 Cor. 6. 18. Rev. 4. 8. & 15. 3. & 16. 14. & 19. 15. & 21. 22.
Job 21. 15. what is the Almighty that we serve
26. shall have delight in Almighty
Ps. 91. 1. under shadow of Alm.
Rev. 1. 8. is to come, the Almighty
ALMOST all things, Heb. 9. 22.
Ex. 17. 4. *a.* ready to stone me
Ps. 73. 2. my feet were *a.* gone
Prov. 5. 14. was *a.* in all evil in cong.
Acts 26. 28. *a.* persuadest me to
R. V. Ps. 94. 17. soon; Prov. 5. 14. well nigh; Acts 26. 28. with but little
ALMS, Acts 3. 2, 3. & 24. 17.
Matt. 6. 1. do not your *a.* before men
Luke 11. 41. give *a.* of such things
12. 33. sell that ye have, give *a.*
Acts 10. 2. gave much *a.* to people
4. thine *a.* are come up for memorial
9. 36. Dorcas full of *a.* deeds
R. V. Matt. 6. 1. righteousness
ALONE, Gen. 32. 24.
Gen. 2. 18. not good for man to be *a.*
Num. 23. 9. peopled well *a.*, Deut. 33. 28.
Deut. 32. 12. Lord *a.* did lead him
Ps. 136. 4. who *a.* doth great wonders
Isa. 5. 8. that they may be placed *a.*
63. 3. I have trodden wine-press *a.*
John 8. 16. I am not *a.*, 16. 32.
17. 20. neither pray I for these *a.*
Ex. 32. 10. *let me a.* that my wrath
Hos. 4. 17. Ephraim is joined to idols, let him *a.*
Matt. 15. 14. let them *a.*
R. V. Mark 4. 34. privately

ALTAR, Deut. 7. 5. & 12. 3.
altar to Lord, Gen. 8. 20. & 12. 7. & 22. 9. & 35. 1, 3. Ex. 30. 27. & 40. 10.
Judg. 6. 25. throw down *a.* of Baal
1 Kings 13. 2. cried against *a.* O *a. a.*
24. leave there thy gift before the *a.*
Acts 17. 23. found *a.* with inscription
Heb. 13. 10. we have an *a.* whereof
Rev. 6. 9. saw under the *a.* souls of
8. 3. & 9. 13. the golden *a.*
R. V. Isa. 65. 3.
ALWAY, Deut. 5. 29. Job 7. ...
Gen. 6. 3. my Spirit not *a.* strive
Deut. 14. 23. learn to fear the Lord *a.*
1 Chron. 16. 15. be mindful *a.* of covenant.
Job 27. 10. will he *a.* call on God
32. 9. great men are not *a.* wise
Ps. 9. 18. needy not *a.* be forgotten
16. 8. I set the Lord *a.* before me
103. 9. he will not *a.* chide
Prov. 5. 19. ravished *a.* with her love
28. 14. happy is the man that feareth *a.*
Isa. 57. 16. neither will I be *a.* wroth
Matt. 26. 11. have poor *a.* with you
28. 20. I am with you *a.* to the end
John 8. 29. I do *a.* things that please
Acts 10. 2. Cornelius prayed God *a.*
2 Cor. 6. 10. yet *a.* rejoicing
Eph. 6. 18. praying *a.* with all prayer
Phil. 4. 4. rejoice in the Lord *a.*
Col. 4. 6. your speech be *a.* with
I AM that I AM, Ex. 3. 14. Rev. 1. 8.
Ambassador, Prov. 13. 17. Isa. 33. 7.
2 Cor. 5. 20. Eph. 6. 20.
R. V. Job 32. 9.
AMBITION reproved, Matt. 18. 1. 20. 25. & 23. 8. Luke 22. 24.
punishment of, Prov. 17. 19. Isa. 14. 12. Ezek. 31. 10.
of Babel, Gen. 11. 4.
of Aaron and Miriam, Num. 12. 10.
Korah, Dathan, and Abiram, Num. 16. 3.
Absalom, 2 Sam. 18. 9.
Adonijah, 1 Kings 1. 5.
Babylon, Jer. 51. 53.
James and John, Matt. 20. 21.
Man of sin, 2 Thes. 2. 4.
Diotrephes, 3 John 9.
AMBUSH, Josh. 8. 4; Judg. 20. 29; 2 Chron. 13. 13; 20. 22.
AMEN, so come Lord Jesus, Rev. 22. 20.
2 Cor. 1. 20. promises in him *a.*
Rev. 3. 14. these things saith the *a.*
R. V. *a.* is omitted in Matt. 6. 13; 28. 20. and many other places in N. T.
AMEND your ways, Jer. 7. 3, 5. & 26. 13. your doings, 35. 15.
R. V. Restitution
AMIABLE thy tabernacles, Ps. 84. 1.
AMISS, 2 Chron. 6. 37. Dan. 3. 29. Luke 23. 41. James 4. 3.
ANCHOR, Acts 27. 30. Heb. 6. 19.
ANCIENT, wisdom is with, Job 12. 12.
Dan. 7. 9. the *a.* of days did sit
Ps. 119. 100. I understand more than *a.*
ANGEL, who redeemed me, Gen. 48. 16.
24. 7. send his *a.* before me
Ex. 23. 23. my *a.* shall go before thee
Angel of the Lord, Ps. 34. 7. Zech. 12. 8. Acts 5. 19. & 12. 7, 23.

Isa. 63. 9. *a.* of his presence saved.
John 5. 4. *a.* went down at *a*
Acts 6. 15. saw as face of an *a.*
23. 8. Sadducees say neither *a.* nor
Dan. 3. 28. sent his *a.* and delivered
6. 22. sent his *a.* and shut lions' mouths
Ps. 8. 5. a little lower than *a.*
68. 17. chariots of God thousands *a.*
78. 25. man did eat *a.* food
Matt. 4. 11. *a.* came and ministered
13. 39. reapers are the *a.*
18. 10. their *a.* always behold
36. no, not the *a.* of heaven
Mark 12. 25. are as *a.* in heaven, 13. 32.
Luke 20. 36. equal to the *a.*
Acts 7. 53. the law by disposition of *a.*
1 Cor. 6. 3. we shall judge *a.*
Col. 2. 18. beguile worshipping of *a.*
2 Thes. 1. 7. with his mighty *a.*
1 Tim. 3. 16. seen of *a.* preached unto
Heb. 2. 16. took not the nature of *a.*
12. 22. an innumerable company of *a.*
13. 2. entertained *a.* unawares
2 Pet. 2. 4. God spared not *a.* that
11. *a.* greater in power and might
Jude 6. *a.* who kept not their first
Rev. 1. 20. *a.* of seven churches
Angel of God, Gen. 28. 12. & 32. 1.
Matt. 22. 30. Luke 12. 8. & 15. 10.
John 1. 51.
R. V. Rev. 8. 13. eagle; Rev. 8. 7; 16. 3, 4, 8, 10, 12, 17.
ANGER of the Lord wax hot, Ex. 32. 22.
Deut. 29. 24. meaneth heat of this *a.*
Josh. 7. 26. from fierceness of *a.*
Job 9. 13. if God will not withdraw *a.*
Ps. 27. 9. put not away servant in *a.*
30. 5. his *a.* endureth but *a*
77. 9. hath he in *a.* shut up
78. 38. turned he his *a.* away
50. he made a way to his *a.*
90. 7. we are consumed by thine *a.*
11. who knoweth power of thine *a.*
Eccl. 7. 9. *a.* resteth in the bosom of fools
Isa. 5. 25. for all this his *a.* is not turned away, 9. 12, 17, 21. & 10. 4.
Hos. 11. 9. not execute fierceness of *a.*
Mic. 7. 18. retaineth not *a.* for ever
Nah. 1. 6. who can abide fierceness of *a.*
Eph. 4. 31. let all *a.* be put away
Col. 3. 8. put off all these; *a.* wrath
Slow to anger, Neh. 9. 17. Ps. 103. 8.
Joel 2. 13. Jonah 4. 2. Nah. 1. 3.
James 1. 19.
Ps. 106. 32. they *angered* him at
Gen. 18. 30. let not Lord be *angry*
Deut. 1. 37. Lord was *a.* with me
9. 20. Lord was *a.* with Aaron
1 Kings 11. 9. the Lord was *a.* with Solomon
7. 11. God is *a.* with the wicked
76. 7. who may stand when thou art *a.*
Prov. 14. 17. that is soon *a.* dealeth
22. 24. no friendship with an *a.* man
Eccl. 7. 9. be not hasty to be *a.*
S. of S. 1. 6. mother's chil. were *a.*
Isa. 12. 1. though thou wast *a.* with
Jonah 4. 9. I do well to be *a.* even
Matt. 5. 22. whoso is *a.* with brother
Eph. 4. 26. be *a.* and sin not
Tit. 1. 7. bishop must not be soon *a.*
R. V. Ps. 38. 3; 85. 4. indignation;
Prov. 22. 8. wrath; Isa. 1. 4.
ANGUISH, excessive pain
Gen. 42. 21. saw the *a.* of his soul
Ex. 6. 9. hearkened not for *a.* of spirit
Ps. 119. 143. trouble and *a.* take hold
John 16. 21. remember not *a.* for joy
Rom. 2. 9. tribulation and *a.* upon
R. V. Gen. 42. 21. distress

ANOINT, rub with oil, appoint, to qualify for office of king, priest, or prophet, Ex. 28. 41.
Dan. 9. 24. to *a*. the most holy
Amos 6. 6. *a*. with chief ointments
Matt. 6. 17. when fastest *a*. thy head
Rev. 3. 18. *a*. eyes with eye salve
1 Sam. 24. 6. *anointed* of the Lord
Ps. 45. 7. *a*. thee with oil of gladness
Zech. 4. 14. two *a*. ones before the Lord
Acts 4. 27. Jesus whom thou hast *a*.
10.38.how God *a*.Jesus of Nazareth
2 Cor. 1. 21. who hath *a*. us is God
Ps. 2. 2. Lord and his *a*.,18. 50. 2 Sam. 22. 51. 1 Sam. 2. 10. Ps. 20, 6. & 28. 8.
1 Chron. 16. 22. touch not my *a*., Ps. 105. 15. & 132. 17.
Ps. 23. 5. *anointest* my head with oil
Isa. 10. 27. because of *anointing*
1 John 2. 27. the *a*. teacheth you of all
Jas. 5. 14. *a*. him with oil
ANSWER, Gen. 41. 16. Deut. 20. 11.
Prov. 15. 1. soft *a*. turneth away
16.1. *a*. of tongue is from the Lord
Job 19. 16. he gave me no *a*.
S. of S. 5. 6. he gave me no *a*.
Mic. 3. 7. there is no *answering* of God
Rom. 11. 4. what saith the *a*. of God
2 Tim. 4. 16. at my first *a*. no man
1 Pet. 3. 15. ready to give an *a*. to
21. the *a*. of a good conscience
Job 40. 4. what shall I *a*. thee
Ps. 102. 2. *a*. me speedily
143. 1. in thy faithfulness *a*. me
Prov. 26. 4, 5. *a*. fool according to
Isa. 50. 2. I called was none to *a*.
58. 9. shalt call and Lord shall *a*.
66. 4. when I called none did *a*.
Dan. 3. 16. not careful to *a*. thee
Matt 25. 37. then shall righteous *a*. Lord
Luke 12. 11. what thing ye shall *a*.
13. 25. he shall *a*. I know you not
21. 14. meditate not what to *a*.
2 Cor. 5. 12. have somewhat to *a*.
Col. 4. 6. know how to *a*. every man
Job 14. 15. thou shalt call and I will *a*. & 13. 22. Ps. 91. 15. Isa. 65. 24. Jer. 33. 3. Ezek. 14. 4, 7.
Ps. 18. 41. to Lord but he *answered* not
81. 7. I *a*. thee in secret place
99. 6. called on the Lord and he *a*.
Prov. 18. 23. rich *answereth* roughly
13. he that *a*. matter before hear
27. 19. as in water face *a*. to face
Eccl. 10. 19. money *a*. all things
Gal. 4. 25. *a*. to Jerusalem that now
Tit. 2. 9. not *answering* again
R. V. Acts 25. 16. to make defence; 2 Tim. 4. 16. defence; 1 Pet. 3. 21. interrogation.
ANT, Prov. 6. 6. & 30. 25.
ANTICHRIST, 1 John 2. 18, 22. & 4. 3. 2 John 7.
APART, Ps. 4. 3. Zech. 12. 12. Jas. 1. 21.
R. V. Jas. 1. 21. away
APOSTATES, Deut. 13. 13; Matt. 24. 10; Luke 8. 13; John 6. 66; Heb. 3. 12; 6. 4; 2 Pet. 3. 17; 1 John 2.
their doom, Zeph. 1. 4; 2 Thes. 2. 8; 1 Tim. 4. 1; Heb. 10. 25; 2 Pet. 2. 17.
APOSTLE, minister sent by God, or Christ, infallibly to preach the gospel, and found churches, Rom. 1. 1. 1 Cor. 1. 1. & 12. 28.
Rom. 11. 13. I am *a*. of Gentiles.
1 Cor. 9. 1. am I not a free *a*.
2 Cor. 12. 12. signs of *a*. wrought
Matt. 10. 2. names of the twelve
Luke 11. 49. I will send proph. and *a*.
1 Cor. 4. 9. God hath sent forth us *a*.
15. 9. I am the least of the *a*.
2 Cor. 11. 13. such are false *a*.
Rev. 2. 2. say they are *a*. and
18. 20. holy *a*. and prophets, Eph. 3. 5.
21. 14. names of twelve *a*. of the
Acts 1. 25. part of this *apostleship*

Rom. 1. 5. received grace and *a*.
1 Cor. 9. 2. seal of my *a*. are ye
Gal. 2. 8. to *a*. of circumcision
R. V. Acts 5. 34. men
APPAREL, Isa. 63. 1. Zeph. 1. 8.
1 Tim. 2. 9. 1 Pet. 3. 3. Jas. 2. 2.
R. V. Isa. 3. 22——; Jas. 2. 2. clothing
APPEAR, Gen. 1. 9. Heb. 11. 3.
Ex. 23. 15. none shall *a*. before me empty, 34. 20. Deut. 16. 16.
2 Chron. 1. 7. did God *a*. to Solomon
Ps. 42. 2. when shall I *a*. before God
90. 16. let work *a*. to servants
Isa. 1. 12. when ye *a*. before me who
66. 5. shall *a*. to your joy, but they
Matt. 6. 16. may *a*. to men to fast
Luke 19. 11. kingdom of God immediately *a*.
Rom. 7. 13. sin that it might *a*. sin
2 Cor. 5. 10. we must all *a*. before the
Col. 3. 4. when Christ shall *a*. ye also *a*.
1 Tim. 4. 15. thy profiting *a*. to all
28. *a*. second time without sin to salvation
1 Pet. 5. 4. when the chief shepherd shall *a*.
1 John 3. 2. not yet *a*. what we shall
1 Sam. 16. 7. man looks—*appearance*
John 7. 24. judge not according to *a*.
1 Thes. 5. 22. abstain from all *a*. of
2 Tim. 1. 10. manifest by *a*. of Jesus
4. 1. judge quick and dead at his *a*.
8. all them that love his *a*.
Tit. 2. 13. look for glorious *a*. of
1 Pet. 1. 7. unto praise at *a*. of Jesus
Tit. 2. 11. grace hath *a*. to all men
Heb. 9. 26. he *a*. to put away sin
R. V. 1 Sam. 2. 27. reveal myself;
S. of S. 4. 1; 6. 5. lie along the side;
Acts 22. 30. come together; Rom. 7. 13. shewn to be; 2 Cor. 5. 10; 7. 12; Col. 3. 4; 1 Pet. 5. 4; 1 John 2. 28. manifested; 2 Cor. 10. 7. that are before your face; 1 Thes. 5. 22. every form; 1 Pet. 1. 7. revelation
APPETITE, Prov. 23. 2. Isa. 29. 8.
APPLE of eye, Deut. 32. 10. Ps. 17. 8.
Prov. 7. 2. Lam. 2. 18. Zech. 2. 8.
Apple-trees, S. of S. 2. 3. & 8. 5.
Apples, Prov. 25. 11. S. of S. 2. 5 7. 8.
APPOINT, Gen. 30. 28.
Isa. 61. 3. *a*. to them that mourn in Zion
26. 1. salvation will God *a*. for walls
Matt. 24. 51. *a*. him portion with the hypocrites
Luke 22. 29. I *a*. unto you a kingdom
Job 7. 1. is there not an *appointed* time
14. 14. all the days of my *a*. time
30. 23. to house *a*. for all living
Ps. 79. 11. preserve those *a*. to die
Jer. 5. 24. reserve *a*. weeks for harvest
Mic. 6. 9. hear rod and him who *a*. it
Hab. 2. 3. vision is for an *a*. time
Heb. 9. 27. *a*. to men once to die
1 Pet. 2. 8. whereunto they were *a*.
R. V. Num. 35. 6. give; 2 Sam. 15. 15. choose; Ezek. 21. 22. set; 1 Sam. 19. 20. as head; 2 Chr. 34. 22. commanded; Acts 1. 23. put forward
APPLY heart to wisdom, &c. Ps. 90. 12. Prov. 2. 2. & 22. 17. & 23. 12.
Eccl. 7. 25. & 8. 9, 16. Has. 7. 6.
R. V. Eccl. 7. 25. heart was set
APPREHENDED, take fast hold of, Phil. 3. 12, 13. Acts 12. 4. 2 Cor. 11. 32.
R. V. Acts 12. 4. taken; 2 Cor. 11. 32. take
APPROACH, come near to, marry
Lev. 18. 6. *a*. to any near of kin, 20. 16.
Ps. 65. 4. blessed whom thou causest to *a*.
Jer. 30. 21. engageth heart to *a*. to
1 Tim. 6. 16. light to which none can *a*.

Isa. 58. 2. delight in *approaching* to God
Heb. 10. 25. as ye see the day *a*.
R. V. Ezek. 42. 13; 43. 19. are near
APPROVE, like, commend
Ps. 49. 13. posterity *a*. their sayings
Phil. 1. 10. may *a*. things excellent
Acts 2. 22. man *approved* of God
Rom. 14. 18. *acceptable* to God, *a*. of
16. 10. Apelles *a*. in Christ
2 Tim. 2. 15. show thyself *a*. to God
Rom. 2. 18. *approvest* things excellent
Lam. 3. 36. to subvert Lord *approveth* not
2 Cor. 6. 4. in all things *approving* ourselves
APT to teach, 1 Tim. 3. 2. 2 Tim. 2. 24.
ARE, seven years, Gen. 41. 26, 27.
1 Cor. 1. 28. bring to nought things that *a*.
30. of him *a*. ye in Christ Jesus
8. 6. of whom *a*. all things
Heb. 2. 10. for and by whom *a*. all
Rev. 1. 19. write things that *a*.
20. *a*. angels; *a*. seven churches
ARGUE, Job 6. 25. & 23. 4.
ARIGHT, set not their hearts, Ps. 78. 8.
50. 23. ordereth conversation *a*.
Prov. 15. 2. useth knowledge *a*.
Jer. 8. 6. they spake not *a*.
R. V. Prov. 23. 31. smoothly
ARISE for our help, Ps. 44. 26.
1 Chron. 22. 16. *a*. be doing
Amos 7. 2. by whom shall Jacob *a*. 5.
Mic. 7. 8. when I fall I shall *a*.
Mal. 4. 2. Son of righteousness *a*.
Ps. 112. 4. to the upright *ariseth* light
Matt. 13. 21. persecution *a*. because
ARM of flesh with him, 2 Chron. 32. 8.
Job 40. 9. hast thou an *a*. like God
Ps. 44. 3. own *a*. did not save them
Isa. 33. 2. be thou their *a*. every
51. 5. mine *a*. shall judge; on my *a*.
9. put on strength, O *a*. of Lord
52. 10. Lord made bare his holy *a*.
53. 1. *a*. of Lord revealed, John 12. 38.
63. 12. led them by his glorious *a*.
1 Pet. 4. 1. *a*. yourselves with same
Ihs arm, Ps. 98. 1. Isa. 40. 10, 11. & 59. 16. Jer. 17. 5. Ezek. 31. 17. Zech. 11. 17. Luke 1. 51.
Stretched-out arm, Ex. 6. 6. Deut. 4. 34. & 5. 15. & 7. 19. & 11. 2. & 26. 8. 2 Chron. 6. 32. Ps. 136. 12. Jer. 27. 5. & 32. 17, 21. Ezek. 20. 33, 34.
Gen. 49. 24. *arms* of his hands made strong
Deut. 33. 27. underneath everlast.
Luke 11. 21. strong man *armed* keep
R. V. Job 31. 22. shoulder
ARMIES of living God, 1 Sam. 17. 2.
Job 25. 3. any number of his *a*.
Ps. 44. 9. goest not forth with our, 60. 10. & 108. 11.
S. of S. 6. 13. company of two *a*.
Rev. 19. 14. *army* in heaven followed
R. V. Gen. 26. 26; 1 Chr. 27. 34. host; Rev. 9. 16. armies.
ARMOR of light, Rom. 13. 12.
2 Cor. 6. 7. by *a*. of righteousness
Eph. 6. 7. put on whole *a*. of God
R. V. 1 Sam. 17. 38, 39. apparel
ARRAY, in order of battle, 2 Sam. 10. 9. Job 6. 4. Jer. 50. 14.
Array, to clothe, Esth. 6. 9. Job 40. 10. Jer. 43. 12. Matt. 6. 29. 1 Tim. 2.
9. Rev. 7. 13. & 17. 4. & 19. 8.
R. V. 1 Tim. 2. 9. raiment
ARROGANCY, presumptuous self-conceit, 1 Sam. 2. 3. Prov. 8. 13. Isa. 13. 11.
ARROWS of the Almighty, Job 6. 4.
Ps. 91. 5. nor for *a*. that flieth by day
Deut. 32. 23. I will spend my *a*. upon
Ps. 38. 2. thine *a*. stick fast in me
45. 5. thine *a*. are sharp in heart
Lam. 3. 12. set me as a mark for *a*.
R. V. Lam. 3. 13. shafts

ARTIFICER, Tubal-Cain the first, Gen. 4. 22.

ASCEND into hill of Lord, Ps. 24. 3.
Ps. 139. 8. if I a. to heaven, Rom. 10. 6.
John 20. 17. I a. to my Father
Ps. 68. 18. hast *ascended* on high
Prov. 30. 4. who hath a. into heaven
John 3. 13. no man hath a. up to
Rev. 8. 4. smoke of incense a. before God
Gen. 28. 12. angels *ascending* and descending, John 1. 51. upon Son of man

ASCRIBE greatness to God, Deut. 32. 3.
Job. 36. 3. I will a. righteousness to
Ps. 68. 34. a. strength unto God

ASHAMED and blush to lift, Ezra 9. 6.
Gen. 2. 25. man and wife naked not a.
Ezek. 16. 61. remember ways and be a.
Mark 8. 38. shall be a. of me
Rom. 1. 16. I am not a. of gospel
5. 5. hope maketh not a. because
Not be ashamed, Ps. 25. 2. & 119. 6, 80.
Isa. 49. 23. Rom. 9. 33. 2 Tim. 2. 15.
R. V. Job 6. 20. confounded; Luke 13. 17; Rom. 9. 33; 10. 11; 2 Cor. 7. 14; 9. 4; 10. 8; Phil. 1. 20; Heb. 11. 16; 1 Pet. 3. 16. put to shame

ASHES, Gen. 18. 27. Job 2. 8. & 13. 12. & 30. 19. & 42. 6. Ps. 102. 9. Isa. 44. 20. & 61. 3. Jer. 6. 26. Ezek. 28. 18. Mal. 4. 3.
R. V. 1 Kings 20. 38, 41. his headband

ASK the way to Zion, Jer. 50. 5.
Matt. 7. 7. a. and it shall be given
20. 22. ye know not what ye a.
Luke 12. 48. of him they will a. more
John 14. 13, 14. whatsoever ye a. in my name, & 15. 16. & 16. 23.
16. 24. a. and ye shall receive—*asked*
Eph. 3. 20. above all we can a. or
Jas. 1. 5. wisdom let him a. of God
6. let him a. in faith, not wavering
4. 2, 3. a. not; a. receive not; a. amiss
Isa. 65. 1. sought of—*asked* not for me
Jer. 6. 16. a. for good old paths
Matt. 7. 8. every one that *asketh* receiveth

ASLEEP, 1 Cor. 15. 16. 1 Thes. 4. 13.

ASP, poisonous serpent, Deut. 32. 33. Job 20. 14, 16. Isa. 11. 8. Rom. 3. 13.

ASS knows master's crib, Isa. 1. 3. Zech. 9. 9. riding upon an ass, Matt. 21. 5. John 12. 15.

ASSEMBLY of wicked, Ps. 22. 16. 89. 7. God feared in a. of his saints
Heb. 12. 23. general a. of first-born
Eccl. 12. 11. nails fastened by masters of a.
Isa. 4. 5. create on her a. a cloud
Heb. 10. 25. forsake not *assembling*
R. V. Lev. 8. 4; Num. 8. 9; 10. 2, 3; 16. 2; 2 Chr. 30. 23. congregation; Ps. 89. 7; 111. 1; Ezek. 13. 9. council; Jas. 2. 2. synagogue

ASSUAGE, Gen. 8. 1. Job 16. 5, 6.

ASSURANCE, firm persuasion
Isa. 32. 17. effect of righteousness a.
1 Thes. 1. 5. gospel came in much a.
Heb. 6. 11. to full a. of hope unto end
10. 22. in full a. of faith
1 John 3. 19. *assure* our hearts before
R. V. Heb. 6. 11; 22. 10. fulness

ASTRAY, Ps. 119. 176. Isa. 53. 6. Matt. 18. 12. Luke 15. 4. 1 Pet. 2. 25.

ATHIRST, sore, and called, Judg. 15. 18.
Rev. 21. 6. give to him a. of fountain
22. 17. him that is a. come take of

ATONEMENT, pacifying, satisfaction for sin, Lev. 16. 11. & 24.
2 Sam. 21. 3. wherewith shall I make a.

Rom. 5. 11. by whom we received a. R. V. Rom. 5. 11. reconciliation

ATTAIN to wise counsels, Prov. 1. 5.
Ezek. 46. 7. according as hand shall a.
Phil. 3. 11, 12. a. to resurrection not already *attained*
R. V. Acts 27. 12. could reach

ATTEND to my cry, Ps. 55. 2. & 61. 1. & 66. 19. & 86. 6. & 142. 6.
Prov. 4. 1. a. to know understand.
20. a. to my words, 7. 24.
Acts 16. 14. she *attended* to—spoken
Attendance, 1 Kings 10. 5. 1 Tim. 4. 13. Heb. 7. 13. Rom. 13. 6.
Attentive, 1 Chron. 6. 40. & 7. 15. Neh. 1. 6. & 8. 3. Ps. 130. 2. Luke 19. 48.
R. V. Ps. 86.- 6. hearken; Acts 16. 14. to give heed

AUTHOR of confusion, 1 Cor. 14. 33.
Heb. 5. 9. a. of eternal salvation
12. 2. Jesus a. and finisher of our
R. V. Rom. 16. 17. turn away from;
2 Tim. 2. 23. refuse; Tit. 3. 9. shun

AUTHORITY, power to govern
Matt. 7. 29. taught as one having a.
John 5. 27. given him a. to execute
Luke 15. 24. down all a. and power
1 Tim. 2. 2. prayer for all in a.
1 Pet. 3. 22. angels and a. subject
Rev. 13. 2. dragon gave him a.
R. V. 1 Tim. 2. 2. high place; 2. 12. have dominion

AVAILETH, Esth. 5. 13. Gal. 5. 6. & 6. 15. Jas. 5. 16.

AVENGE not, nor grudge, Lev. 19. 18.
Lev. 26. 25. shall a. quarrel of covenant
Deut. 32. 43. he will a. blood of
Isa. 1. 24. I will a. me of mine enemies
Luke 18. 7. shall not God a. his
Luke 18. 8. he will a. them speed.
Rom. 12. 19. a. not yourselves
Rev. 6. 10. dost thou not a. our blood
Rev. 18. 20. God hath a. you on her
Avenger, Num. 35. 12. Ps. 8. 2. & 44. 16. 1 Thes. 4. 6.
2 Sam. 22. 48. God that *avengeth* me
Judg. 5. 2. praise Lord for *avenging* Israel.
R. V. Lev. 19. 18. take vengeance; 26. 25. execute; Rev. 18. 20. judged your judgment.

AVOUCHED, Deut. 26. 17, 18.

AVOID it, pass not by it, Prov. 4. 15.
Rom. 16. 17. cause divisions, a.

AWAKE for thee, Job 8. 6.
Ps. 35. 23. a. to my judgment
139. 18. when I a. I am still with
1 Cor. 15. 34. a. to righteousness
Eph. 5. 14. a. thou that sleepest
Ps. 78. 65. Lord *awaked* out of sleep
73. 20. when thou *awakest* thou

AWE, stand in a. sin not, Ps. 4. 4.
Ps. 33. 8. would stand in a. of him
119. 161. heart stands in a. of word

AXE, Deut. 19. 5. 1 Kings 6. 7. & 2 Kings 6. 5. Isa. 10. 15. Jer. 51. 20.
Axes, 2 Sam. 12. 31. Ps. 74. 3, 6. Jer. 46. 22.
R. V. Ps. 74. 6. hatchet.

B

BABBLER, Eccl. 10. 11. Acts 17. 18.
1 Tim. 6. 20. avoid vain *babblings,* 2 Tim. 2. 16. Prov. 23. 29.
R. V. Eccl. 10. 11. charmer.

BABE leaped in womb, Luke 1. 41.
Heb. 5. 13. unskil. in words is a b.
Ps. 8. 2. out of mouth of *babes*
Isa. 3. 4. b. shall rule over them
1 Cor. 3. 1. as unto b. in Christ
1 Pet. 2. 2. as new-born b. desire

BACK to go from Samuel, 1 Sam. 10. 9.
1 Kings 14. 9. cast me behind b.
Prov. 26. 3. rod for the fool's b.
Isa. 38. 17. cast my sins behind thy b.
50. 6. gave my b. to smiters
Jer. 2. 27. turned their b. 32. 33.
18. 17. I will shew them b. not face
Ps. 19. 13. keep b. thy servant from
53. b. when God bringeth b. captivity
Acts 20. 20. kept b. nothing profit.
Neh. 9. 26. cast law behind *backs*
Backbiters, haters of God, Rom. 1. 30.
Ps. 15. 3. *backbiteth* not with his
Prov. 25. 23. *backbiting* tongue
2 Cor. 12. 20. strifes, *backbitings*
Backslider in heart, Prov. 14. 14.
Jer. 2. 19. thy *backslidings* reprove thee
3. 6, 12. return thou b. Israel, 14. 7. & 31. 22. & 49. 4.
14. 7. b. are many, we have sinned
Hos. 11. 7. my people are bent to b.
14. 4. I will heal their b.
Isa. 1. 4. they are gone away b.
59. 14. judgment is turned away b.
John 18. 6. went b. and fell to the ground

BAG, sack, or pouch, Deut. 25. 13.
Job 14. 17. Prov. 16. 11. Mic. 6. 11.
Hag. 1. 6. Luke 12. 33. John 13. 29.
R. V. Luke 12. 33. purses

BALANCE, Job 31. 6. & 6. 2. Ps. 62. 9. Isa. 40. 12, 15. & 46. 6. Dan. 5. 27.
16. 11. just weight and b. are
Mic. 6. 11. count pure with wick. b.

BALD, 2 Kings 2. 23. Jer. 16. 6. & 48. 37. Ezek. 27. 31. Mic. 1. 16.
Baldness, Lev. 21. 5. Deut. 14. 1. Isa. 3. 24. & 15. 2. & 22. 12. Ezek. 7. 18.

BALM, Gen. 37. 25. & 43. 11.
Jer. 8. 22. is there no b. in Gilead
46. 11. & 51. 8. Ezek. 27. 17.

BANNER, Isa. 13. 2. Ps. 20. 5.
Ps. 60. 4. b. to them that fear thee
S. of S. 2. 4. his b. over me was love
6. 4. terrible as an army with *banners*
R. V. Isa. 13. 2. ensign

BAPTISM of water, Matt. 3. 7.
Baptism of John, Matt. 21. 25. Mark 11. 30. Luke 7. 29. & 12. 50. Acts 1. 22. & 10. 37. & 18. 25. & 19. 3, 4.
Baptism of repentance, Mark 1. 4. Acts 13. 24. & 19. 4.
Baptism of suffering, Matt. 20. 22,23. Mark 10. 38, 39. Luke 12. 50.
Rom. 6. 4. buried with him by *baptism,* Col. 2. 12.
Eph. 4. 5. one faith, one b.
1 Pet. 3. 21. b. doth now save us
Heb. 6. 2. doctrine of *baptisms*

BAPTIZE with water, with the Holy Ghost, Matt. 3. 11. Mark 1. 8. Luke 3. 16. Acts 1. 5. John 1. 26, 28, 31, 33.
Mark 1. 4. John did b. in wilder.
5. were all *baptized* of him, 8.
Mark 16. 16. believeth and is b.
Luke 3. 7. came to be b. 12.
7. 29, 30. publicans b. lawyers not b.
John 4. 1. Jesus b. more disciples
2. though Jesus himself b. not
Acts 2. 38. repent and be b. every one
8. 13. Simon believed and was b.
10. 47. that these should not be b.
48. Peter command. them to be b.
18. 8. believed and were b.
Rom. 6. 3. as many as were b. were
1 Cor. 1. 13. were ye b. in name of
15. none—b. in own name
10. 2. were all b. unto Moses
Gal. 3. 27. as have been b. into Christ
Matt. 28. 19. *baptizing* in name

BARE you on eagles' wings, Ex. 19. 4.
Isa. 53. 12. he b. the sins of many

Matt. 8. 17. himself *b.* our sicknesses
1 Pet. 2. 24. *b.* our sins in his own
BARN, Matt. 13. 30. Prov. 3. 10.
Matt. 6. 26. Luke 12. 18, 24.
R. V. Job 39. 12; 2 Kings 6. 27.
threshing-floor
BARREL of meal, 1 Kings 17. 14.
BARREN, Gen. 11. 30. & 25. 21. &
29. 31. Judg. 13. 2. Luke 1. 7.
Ex. 23. 26. nothing shall be *b.*
1 Sam. 2. 5. *b.* hath borne seven
S. of S. 4. 2. none is *b.* among, 6. 6.
Luke 23. 29. blessed are *b.* wombs
2 Pet. 1. 8. neither *b.* nor unfruitful
R. V. 2 Kings 2. 19. miscarrieth;
Job 39. 6. salt; S. of S. 4. 2; 6. 6.
bereaved; 2 Pet. 1. 8. idle
BASE in my own sight, 2 Sam. 6. 22.
1 Cor. 1. 28. *b.* things of this world
2 Cor. 10. 1. who in presence am *b.*
Ezek. 29. 14, 15. *basest* of kingdoms
BASTARD not enter, Deut. 23. 2.
Zech. 9. 6. *b.* shall dwell in Ashdod
Heb. 12. 8. without chastisement
are *bastards*
BATTLE not to strong, Eccl. 9. 11.
Jer. 8. 6. as horse rusheth into *b.*
Ps. 140. 7. covered head in day of *b.*
R. V. Num. 31. 14; Josh. 22. 33;
2 Sam. 21. 18, 19, 20; 1 Cor. 14. 8;
Rev. 9. 7, 9; 28. 8. war
BEAM out of timber, Hab. 2. 11.
Matt. 7. 3. considered not *b.* in own
eye
8. of 8. 1, 1, 17. *b.* of our house are
BEAR, Gen. 49. 15. Deut. 1. 9, 31.
Prov. 9. 12. & 30. 21. Lam. 3. 27.
Gen. 4. 13. punishment greater
than I can *b.*
Num. 11. 14. not able to *b.* all this
people
Prov. 18. 14. wounded spirit who
can *b.*
Amos 7. 10. land not able to *b.* words
Luke 14. 27. whoso doth not *b.* his
18. 7. though he *b.* long with them
John 16. 12. ye cannot *b.* them now
Rom. 15. 1. strong *b.* the infirmities
1 Cor. 3. 2. hitherto not able to *b.* it
10. 13. that may be able to *b.* it
Gal. 6. 2. *b.* ye one another's burdens
5. every man *b.* his own
17. I *b.* in my body the marks
Heb. 9. 28. offered to *b.* sins of many
Rev. 2. 2. canst not *b.* which are
evil
Bear fruit, Ezek. 17. 8. Hos. 9. 16.
Joel 2. 22. Matt. 13. 23. Luke 13. 9.
John 15. 2, 4, 8.
Ps. 106. 4. favor thou *bearest* to
Rom. 11. 18. *b.* not root but
13. 4. *beareth* not sword in vain
1 Cor. 13. 7. charity *b.* all things
Ps. 126. 6. *bearing* precious seed
Heb. 13. 13. *b.* his reproach
BEASTS, animals without reason,
Gen. 1. 24, 25. & 3. 1. — for ministers, Rev. 4. 6, 7, 8, 9. & 5. 6, 14. &
6. 1, 3. & 7. 11. & 14. 3. & 15. 7. & 19.
4. — for antichrist, Dan. 7. 11. Rev.
11. 7. & 13. 1. & 15. 2. & 16. 13. &
17. 8. & 19. 19. & 20. 10.
Prov. 9. 2. wisdom killed her *b.*
Dan. 7. 17. four *b.* are four kings
1 Cor. 15. 32. I fought with *b.* at
Ephesus
R. V. Ex. 11. 5; Num. 20. 8; Isa.
63. 14. cattle; in Rev. generally,
living creatures
BEAT, Prov. 23. 14. Isa. 3. 15. Luke
12. 47, 48. 1 Cor. 9. 26.
R. V. Judg. 8. 17; 2 Kings 13. 25.
smite; Mat. 7. 27. smote.
BEAUTY, Ex. 28. 2.
1 Chron. 16. 29. in the *b.* of holiness
Ps. 27. 4. to behold *b.* of the Lord
39. 11. makest his *b.* to consume
45. 11. king greatly desire thy *b.*
Prov. 20. 29. *b.* of old men gray head
31. 30. favor deceitful *b.* is vain
Isa. 3. 24. be burning instead of *b.*
33. 17. see the king in his *b.* and

Isa. 61. 3. give them *b.* for ashes
Zech. 11. 7. two staves, one called *b.*
Beautify, Ps. 149. 4. Isa. 60. 13
Beautiful, Eccl. 3. 11. S. of S. 6. 4. &
7. 1.
Isa. 52. 1, 7. & 64. 11. Jer. 13. 20. Ezek.
16. 12, 13. Matt. 23. 27. Acts 3. 2.
Rom. 10. 15.
R. V. 2 Sam. 1. 19. glory; Job 40. 10;
Lam. 1. 6. majesty; Isa. 61. 3. garland
BED, set for him, 2 Kings 4. 10.
Ps. 41. 3. make all his *b.* in sickness
S. of S. 3. 1. by night on my *b.* I
Isa. 28. 20. the *b.* is shorter than
Heb. 13. 4. marriage *b.* undefiled
Rev. 2. 22. I will cast her into a *b.*
Isa. 57. 2. rest in their *beds*
Amos 6. 4. lie on *b.* of ivory
R. V. many places in O. T., couch
BEFORE, in sight, Gen. 20. 15. & 43.
14. Ex. 22. 9. 1 Kings 17. 1. & 18. 15.
2 Kings 3. 14. — (in time or place)
Gen. 31. 2. Job 3. 24. Josh. 8. 10.
Luke 22. 47.
2 Chron. 13. 14. — (in dignity) 2
Sam. 6. 21. John 1. 15, 27.
Phil. 3. 13. those things which are *b.*
Col. 1. 17. he is *b.* all things and
R. V. Rev. 13. 12; 19. 20. in his sight
BEG, Ps. 109. 10. & 37. 25. Prov. 20. 4.
Luke 16. 3. & 23. 52. John 9. 8.
Beggar, 1 Sam. 2. 8. Luke 16. 20, 22.
Beggarly elements, Gal. 4. 9.
R. V. Matt. 27. 58; Luke 23. 52. asked
for
BEGIN at my sanctuary, Ezek. 9. 6.
Ex. 12. 2. the *beginning* of months
Gen. 49. 3. *b.* of strength, Deut. 21. 17.
Ps. 111. 10. fear of Lord is the *b.* of
wisdom, Prov. 1. 7. & 9. 10.
Heb. 7. 3. neither *b.* of days nor end
2 Pet. 2. 20. latter end is worse
than *b.*
Rev. 1. 8. I am Alpha and Omega,
b. and the ending, 21. 6. & 22. 13.
3. 14. saith the *b.* of creation of
R. V. 1 Chr. 17. 9; Acts 26. 5; 2 Pet.
2. 20. first
BEGOTTEN drops of dew, Job
38. 28.
Ps. 2. 7. this day have I *b.* thee,
Acts 13. 33. Heb. 1. 5, 6.
John 1. 14. only *b.* of the Father, 18.
3. 16. sent his only *b.* Son, 18.
1 Pet. 1. 3. *b.* us again to a lively
1 John 4. 9. sent his only *b.* Son
Rev. 1. 5. first *b.* of the dead
BEGUILE, Col. 2. 4, 18. Gen. 3. 13.
2 Cor. 11. 3. 2 Pet. 2. 14.
R. V. Col. 2. 4. delude; 2. 18. rob;
2 Pet. 2. 14. enticing
BEGUN to fall, Esth. 6. 13.
Gal. 3. 3. having *b.* in the spirit
Phil. 1. 6. hath *b.* a good work in
BEHAVE myself wisely, Ps. 101. 2.
Ps. 131. 2. I *b.* myself as a child
1 Tim. 3. 2. bishop of good *behavior*
Tit. 2. 3. in *b.* as becometh holiness
R. V. 1 Tim. 3. 2. orderly; Tit. 2.
3. reverent in demeanor.
BEHELD not iniquity in Jacob,
Num. 23. 21.
Luke 10. 18. I *b.* Satan fall
John 1. 14. we *b.* his glory
Rev. 11. 12. their enemies *b.* them
BEHIND, Lev. 25. 51. Judg. 20. 40.
Ex. 10. 26. not an hoof left *b.*
Ps. 139. 5. beset me *b.* and before
Isa. 38. 17. cast all my sins *b.* thy
1 Cor. 1. 7. ye come *b.* in no gift
Col. 1. 24. fill up that is *b.* of afflict.
R. V. Col. 1. 24. lacking
BEHOLD with thine eyes, Deut.
3. 27.
Job 19. 27. my eyes shall *b.* and not
Ps. 11. 4. his eyes *b.* his eyelids try
7. countenance; *b.* upright
17. 15. I will *b.* thy face in right.
27. 4. desired to *b.* beauty of Lord
37. 37. *b.* the upright man
113. 6. humbles himself to *b.*
Hab. 1. 13. of purer eyes than to *b.*
Matt. 18. 10. their angels *b.* face of

John 17. 24. they may *b.* my glory
19. 5. *b.* the man, 14. *b.* your king
26. *b.* thy son, 27. *b.* thy mother
1 Pet. 3. 2. *b.* your chaste conver.
Ps. 33. 13. Lord *beholdeth* all the
Jas. 1. 24. he *b.* himself and go.
Prov. 15. 3. *beholding* evil and good
Ps. 119. 37. turn eyes from *b.* vanity
Eccl. 5. 11. save *b.* of them with
Col. 2. 5. joying and *b.* your order
Jas. 1. 23. like man *b.* natural
BEING, Num. 104. 33. & 146. 2. Acts
17. 28.
BELIAL, devil, furious and obstinate in wickedness, Deut. 13. 13.
Judg. 19. 22. & 20. 13. 1 Sam. 1.
16. & 2. 12. & 10. 27. & 25. 17, 25. &
30. 22. 2 Sam. 16. 7. & 20. 1. & 23. 6.
1 Kings 21. 10, 13. 2 Chron. 13. 7.
2 Cor. 6. 15.
BELIEVE, credit as testimony,
Ex. 4. 1. Num. 14. 11. & 20. 12.
Deut. 1. 32. ye did not *b.* the Lord
2 Chron. 20. 20. *b.* Lord, *b.* prophets
Isa. 7. 9. will not *b.* surely not
Matt. 9. 28. *b.* ye that I am able
Mark 1. 15. repent and *b.* the gos.
24. Lord I *b.* help my unbelief
11. 24. *b.* that ye receive them
Luke 8. 13. for a while *b.* and
24. 25. slow of heart to *b.* all
John 1. 12. even to them that *b.*
6. 29. ye *b.* on him whom he sent
69. we *b.* and are sure thou art
7. 39. they that *b.* him should
8. 24. if ye *b.* not I am he ye shall
11. 42. may *b.* thou hast sent me
13. 19. ye may *b.* that I am he
14. 1. ye *b.* in God, *b.* also in me
17. 20. pray for them who shall *b.*
20. 31. written that ye might *b.*
Acts 8. 37. I *b.* Jesus Christ is the
13. 39. all that *b.* are justified
16. 31. *b.* on the Lord Jesus and
thou shalt be saved
Rom. 3. 22. on all them that *b.*
10. 9. shalt *b.* in thine heart
14. how shall they *b.* on him
2 Cor. 4. 13. we *b.* and therefore
Phil. 1. 29. not only to *b.* but suffer
1 Tim. 4. 10. especially those that *b.*
Heb. 10. 39. *b.* to saving of the soul
11. 6. cometh to God must *b.* that
he is
Jas. 2. 19. devils also *b.* and
1 Pet. 2. 7. to you who *b.* he is prec.
1 John 3. 23. his command that we
b. on Jesus Christ
Believe not, Isa. 7. 9. John 4. 48. &
8. 24. & 10. 26. & 12. 39. & 16. 9, 20,
25. Rom. 3. 3. 2 Cor. 4. 4. 2 Tim. 2.
13. 1 John 4. 1.
Gen. 15. 6. *believed* in Lord and he
counted, Rom. 4. 3. Gal. 3. 6.
Jas. 2. 23.
Ps. 27. 13. fainted unless I had *b.*
119. 66. I *b.* thy commandments
Isa. 53. 1. who hath *b.* our report,
John 12. 38. Rom. 10. 16.
Dan. 6. 23. because he *b.* in his God
Jonah 3. 5. people of Nineveh *b.*
Matt. 8. 13. as thou hast *b.* so be it
21. 32. publicans and harlots *b.*
John 4. 53. himself *b.* and his house
17. 8. have *b.* thou didst send me
20. 29. blessed—not seen and yet *b.*
Acts 4. 32. that *b.* were of one heart
8. 13. Simon *b.* and was baptized
11. 21. great number *b.* and turned
48. as many as were ordained to
eternal life *b.*
Rom. 4. 18. against hope *b.* in hope
Eph. 1. 13. after ye *b.* ye were
1 Tim. 3. 16. God was *b.* on in the
2 Tim. 1. 12. know whom I have *b.*
Believed not, Ps. 78. 22, 32. & 106. 24.
Luke 24. 41. Acts 9. 26. Rom. 10. 14.
2 Thes. 2. 12. Heb. 3. 18. Jude 5.
Believers, Acts 5. 14. 1 Tim. 4. 12.
Believest, Luke 1. 20. John 1. 50. &
11. 26. & 14. 10. Jas. 2. 19.
Acts 8. 37. if thou *b.* with all thy
26. 27. *b.* thou prophets — thou *b.*
Believeth, Job 15. 22. & 39. 24.

Prov. 14. 15. simple *b.* every word
Isa. 28. 16. that *b.* — not make haste
Mark 9. 23.all things possible to—*b.*
  16. 16. he that *b.* shall be saved, he
    that *b.* not shall be damned
John 3. 15, 16. *b.* in him should not
  18. he that *b.* is not condemned
  5. 24. *b.* on him that sent me
  6. 35. *b.* on me shall never thirst
  40. seeth the Son and *b.* may
  11. 25. *b.* in me though he were d.
  26. he that *b.* in me shall never d.
  12. 44. *b.* on me, *b.* not on me, but
  46. *b.* on me shall not abide in
Acts 10. 43. *b.* in him — receive remission
Rom. 1. 16. power of God—to every
  one that *b.*
  3. 26. justifier of him that *b.* in
  4. 5. worketh not, but *b.* on him
  9. 33. *b.* on him — not ashamed, 10.
  11.
  10. for with the heart man *b.* unto
  righteousness
1 Cor. 7. 12. wife that *b.* not
  13. husband that *b.* not
  13. 7. charity *b.* all things
  14. 24. come in one that *b.* not
2 Cor. 6. 15. he that *b.* with infidel
1 Pet. 2. 6. *b.* on him shall not be
  confounded
1 John 5. 1. whoso *b.* that Jesus is
  5. overcom. world, but he that *b.*
  10. he that *b.* on Son of God hath
  —*b.* not God hath made him a
  liar because he *b.* not record that
Matt. 21. 22. ask in prayer, *believing*
John 20. 27. be not faithless, but *b.*
  31. that *b.* ye might have life
Acts 16. 34. *b.* in God with all his
Rom. 15. 13. all joy and peace in *b.*
1 Pet. 1. 8. yet *b.* ye rejoice with joy
2 Thes. 2. 13. *belief* of the truth
R. V. Acts 19. 9; Heb. 3. 18. disobedient

BELLOWS are burnt, Jer. 6. 29.
BELLY, on *b.* shalt go, Gen. 3. 14.
  Num. 5. 21. *b.* to swell and thigh
  25. 8. thrust them through the *b.*
Job 3. 11. when I came out of *b.*
  15. 2. fill his *b.* with east wind
  35. their *b.* prepareth deceit
  20. 15. God cast them out of his *b.*
  20. not feel quietness in his *b.*
Ps. 17. 14. whose *b.* thou fillest with
  22. 10. art my God from mother's *b.*
Prov. 20. 27. search inw. parts of *b.*
Isa. 46. 3. borne by me from the *b.*
Jonah 1. 17. in the *b.* of the fish,
  Matt. 12. 40.
  2. 1. prayed to God out of fish's *b.*
  2. out of the *b.* of hell cried I
Luke 15. 16. fill his *b.* with husks
John 7. 38. out of his belly shall
  Rom. 16. 18. serve their own *b.*
Phil. 3. 19. whose God is their *b.*
Rev. 10. 9. make thy *b.* bitter
Tit. 1. 12. Cretians slow *bellies*
R. V. Job 20. 20. within him; 31. 9.
  body; S. of S. 5. 14. body; Jer. 51.
  34. maw; Tit. 1. 12. gluttons
BELONG, Lev. 27. 24. Luke 23. 7.
  Gen. 40. 8. interpretations *b.* to
  Deut. 29. 29. secret things *b.* to
  Lord, things revealed *b.* to us and
  to our children
Ps. 47. 9. shields of earth *b.* to God
  68. 20. to God *b.* issues from death
Dan. 9. 9. to the Lord *b.* mercies
Mark 9. 41. because ye *b.* in Christ
Luke 19. 42. things that *b.* to thy
Deut. 32. 35. to me *b.* vengeance
  Ps. 94. 1. Heb. 10. 30. Rom. 12. 19.
Ezra 19. 4. this matter *belongeth* to
Ps. 3. 8. salvation *b.* to the Lord
  62. 11. power *b.* to God, 12. *b.* mercy
Dan. 9. 7. righteousness *b.* to thee
Heb. 5. 14. strong meat *b.* to them
BELOVED—other hated, Deut.
  21. 15.
Deut. 33. 12. *b.* of Lord shall dwell
Neh. 13. 26. Solomon *b.* of his God
Ps. 60. 5. thy *b.* may be delivered
  127. 2. Lord giveth his *b.* sleep

S. of S. 1. 14. *my beloved*, 2. 3, 9, 16, 17.
  & 4. 16. & 5. 2, 6, 10, 16. & 6. 2, 3. &
  7. 10, 13. Isa. 5. 1.
S. of S. 5. 9. thy *b.* more than another *b.*
Dan. 10. 11, 19. O man, greatly *b.*
  9. 23.
Matt. 3. 17. my *b.* Son, 17. 5.
Rom. 9. 25. *b.* which was not *b.*
  11. 28. *b.* for the Father's sake
  16. 8. Amplias *b.* in the Lord
Eph. 1. 6. accepted in the *b.*
2 Pet. 3. 15. *b.* brother Paul
Rev. 20. 9. compassed *b.* city
R. V. Luke 9. 35. my chosen ; Phile.
  2. sister
BEMOAN, Jer. 15. 5. & 16. 5. & 22.
  10. & 31. 18. & 48. 18.
BEND bow, Ps. 11. 2. & 64. 3. & 58. 7.
  & 7. 12. & 37. 1. Lam. 2. 4. & 3. 12.
  Isa. 5. 28.
  Jer. 9. 3. *b.* their tongues like a bow
Isa. 60. 14. afflicted thee shall come
  bending unto thee
Hos. 11. 7. people *bent* to backslid.
Zech. 9. 13. I have *b.* Judah for me
R. V. Ps. 58. 7. aimeth
BENEATH, Prov. 15. 24. John 8. 23.
BENEFACTORS, Luke 22. 25.
BENEFITS, loaded us with, Ps.
  68. 19.
Ps. 103. 2. forget not all his *b.*
  116. 12. render to the Lord for all
  his *b.*
R. V. Phile. 14. goodness
BENEVOLENCE, due, 1 Cor. 7. 3.
  R. V. 1 Cor. 7. 3. her due
BEREAVE soul of good, Eccl. 4. 8.
  Jer. 15. 7. *b.* them of children, 18. 21.
  Gen. 42. 36. & 43. 14. Ezek. 5. 17. &
  36. 12, 13, 14. Lam. 1. 20. Hos. 9. 12.
  & 13. 8.
R. V. Jer. 18. 21. childless
BESEECH God to be gracious,
  Mal. 1. 9.
  2 Cor. 5. 20. as though God did *b.*
  R. V. In O. T. mostly changed to
  pray; Phil. 4. 2; 1 Thes. 4. 10;
  Heb. 13. 22. exhort
BESET me behind and before, Ps.
  139. 5.
  Hos. 7. 2. own doings have *b.* them
Heb. 12. 1. sin which doth easily
  b. us
BESIDE waters, Ps. 23. 2. Isa. 32. 20.
  S. of S. 1. 8. feed kids *b.* shepherd's
  Isa. 56. 8. others *b.* I have gathered
  R. V. Judg. 20. 36. against ; Mat. 25.
  20 — ; Acts 26. 24. mad ; 2 Pet. 1.
  5. for this very cause
BESIDE SELF, Mark. 3. 21. Acts
  26. 24. 2 Cor. 5. 13.
BESOM of destruction, Isa. 14. 23.
BESOUGHT the Lord, Deut. 3. 23.
  2 Sam. 12. 16. 1 Kings 13. 6. 2 Kings
  13. 4. 2 Chron. 33. 12. Ezra 8. 23.
  2 Cor. 12. 8.
BEST estate is vanity, Ps. 39. 5.
  Mic. 7. 4. *b.* of them is as a brier
Luke 15. 22. bring forth *b.* robe
1 Cor. 12. 31. covet earnestly *b.* gifts
  R. V. 1 Cor. 12. 31. greater
BESTEAD, hardly, Isa. 8. 21.
BESTOW a blessing, Ex. 32. 29.
Luke 12. 17. room to *b.* my fruits
  13. 3. *b.* all my goods to feed the
John 4. 38. *bestowed* no labor
1 Cor. 15. 10. his grace *b.* on me
2 Cor. 1. 11. gift *b.* on us by means
  8. 1. grace of God *b.* on churches
Gal. 4. 11. lest *b.* labor in vain
1 John 3. 1. love the Father hath
  b. on us
R. V. 2 Cor. 8. 1. which hath been
  given in ; John 4. 38. ye have not
  labored
BETIMES, 2 Chron. 36. 15. Job 8.
  5. & 24. 5. Prov. 13. 24. Gen. 26. 31.
  R. V. 2 Chron. 36. 15. early ; Job
  8. 5 ; 24. 5. diligently
BETRAY, Matt. 24. 10. & 26. 21.
  Mark 13. 12. & 14. 18.
  R. V. In N. T. mostly, delivered
  up

BETROTH, Deut. 28. 30. Hos. 2.
  19. 20.
BETTER than ten sons, 1 Sam. 1. 8.
  Judg. 8. 2. gleanings *b.* than vintage
1 Kings 19. 4. I am not *b.* than
Prov. 15. 16. *b.* is little with the fear
  17. *b.* is a dinner of herbs with love
  16. 8. *b.* is a little with righteous.
  16. how much *b.* to get wisdom
  27. 10. *b.* is a neighbor near that
Eccl. 4. 9. two are *b.* than one
  13. *b.* is a poor and wise child than
  7. 1. *b.* is a good name than precious
  2. *b.* to go to the house of mourning
  3. *b.* is sorrow than laughter
  5. *b.* to hear rebuke of the wise
  9. 16. wisdom is *b.* than strength
  18. wisdom is *b.* than weapons of
S. of S. 4. 10. how much *b.* is thy
  love than wine
Matt. 6. 26. are ye not much *b.* than
1 Cor. 9. 15. were *b.* for me to die
Phil. 1. 23. with Christ is far *b.*
  2. 3. esteem others *b.* than them.
Heb. 1. 4. made so much *b.* than
  the angels.
  6. 9. persuaded *b.* things of you
  22. Jesus made surety of a *b.* testament
  10. 34. a *b.* enduring substance
  35. obtain a *b.* resurrection
  40. provided some *b.* things
  12. 24. blood speaketh *b.* than Abel
2 Pet. 2. 21. *b.* not to have known
  R. V. Mat. 12. 12. of more value ;
  Mark 9. 43 ; Luke 5. 39 ; 1 Cor. 9. 15.
  good
BETWEEN thy seed and her, Gen.
  3. 15.
1 Kings 3. 9. discern *b.* good and
  18. 21. how long halt ye *b.* two
Ezek. 22. 26. no difference *b.* holy
  and profane, 44. 23. & 34. 17. Lev.
  10. 10.
Phil. 1. 23. in a strait *b.* two having
1 Tim. 2. 5. one mediator *b.* God
BEWARE of men, Matt. 10. 17.
  Matt. 7. 15. *b.* of false prophets
  16. 6. *b.* of leaven of Pharisees, 11.
  Mark 8. 15.
Luke 12. 15. *b.* of covetousness
Col. 2. 8. *b.* lest any man spoil you
  R. V. Ex. 23. 21 ; Col. 2. 8. take heed ;
  Luke 12. 15. keep yourselves from
BEYOND or defraud, 1 Thes. 4. 6.
  R. V. 1 Thes. 4. 6. transgress
BIBBER, Prov. 23. 20. Matt. 11. 19.
BID, Matt. 22. 9. & 23. 3. Luke 14. 10,
  24. 2 John 10, 11.
BIDE, not in unbelief, Rom. 11. 23.
BILL, Deut. 24. 1, 3. Isa. 50. 1. Jer.
  3. 8. Mark 10. 4. Luke 16. 6, 7.
  R. V. Luke 16. 6. bond
BILLOWS, Ps. 42. 7. Jonah 2. 3.
BIND sweet influences, Job 38. 31.
  Job 31. 36. I would *b.* it as a crown
Ps. 105. 22. to *b.* his princes at
  118. 27. *b.* the sacrifice with cords
Prov. 3. 3. *b.* them about thy neck
  Isa. 8. 16. *b.* up testimony, seal law
Matt. 12. 29. first *b.* strong man and
  13. 30. *b.* them in bundles to burn
  16. 19. thou shalt *b.* on earth, 18. 18.
  22. 13. *b.* him hand and foot, and
  Bindeth up, Job 5. 18. Ps. 147. 3.
BIRD hasteth to snare, Prov. 7. 23.
  Ps. 124. 7. escaped as a *b.* out of the
  Eccl. 10. 20. *b.* of air tell the matter
Isa. 46. 11. ravenous *b.* from the east
Jer. 12. 9. heritage as a speckled *b.*
  Birds, Gen. 15. 10. & 40. 17. Lev. 14. 4.
  2 Sam. 21. 10. Ps. 104. 17. Eccl. 9. 12.
  S. of S. 2. 12. Isa. 31. 5. Jer. 5. 27.
  & 12. 4, 9. Matt. 8. 20.
BIRTH, 2 Kings 19. 3. Eccl. 7. 1.
  Isa. 66. 9. Ezek. 16. 3. Gal. 4. 19.
  Birthday, Gen. 40. 20. Matt. 14. 6.
  Firthright, Gen. 25. 31, 32, 33. & 27.
  36. & 43. 33. 1 Chron. 5. 1. Heb. 12. 16.
BISHOP, 1 Tim. 3. 1, 2. Tit. 1. 7.
  1 Pet. 2. 25. return to *b.* of souls
Phil. 1. 1. with *bishops* and deacons
BITE, Num. 21. 6, 8, 9. Eccl. 10. 8,
  11. Jer. 8. 17. Amos 9. 3. Hab. 2. 7.

Mic. 3. 5. prophets b. with their
Gal. 5. 15. if ye b. and devour one
  another
Prov. 23. 32. at the last it b. like a
BITTER made their lives, Ex. 1. 14.
Ex. 12. 8. with b. herbs eat it, Num.
  9. 11.
Deut. 32. 24. devoured with b. de-
  struction
  32. their grapes of gall, clusters
  are b.
2 Kings 14. 26. affliction was very b.
Job 3. 20. why is life given to the
  b. in soul
Ps. 64. 3. their arrows even b. words
Prov. 27. 7. every b. thing is sweet
Isa. 5. 20. woe to them put b. for
Jer. 2. 19. evil thing and b. that
Col. 3. 19. wives be not b. against
Rev. 10. 9. it shall make thy belly b.
Judg. 5. 23. curse *bitterly* inhabit.
Ruth 1. 20. Almighty dealt b. with
Isa. 22. 4. I will weep b., 33. 7.
Hos. 12. 14. provoked him most b.
Matt. 26. 75. wept b., Luke 22. 62.
Bitterness of soul, 1 Sam. 1. 10.
1 Sam. 15. 32. b. of death is past
2 Sam. 2. 26. it will be b. in end
Prov. 14. 10. heart knows its own b.
Zech. 12. 10. in b. for first-born
Acts 8. 23. in gall of b. and bond of
Rom. 3. 14. mouth full of cursing
  and b.
Heb. 12. 15. root of b. springing up
R. V. Job 23. 2. rebellious
BITTERN, Isa. 14. 23. & 34. 11.
BLACK, 1 Kings 18. 45. Matt. 5. 36.
S. of S. 1. 5. I a n b. but comely, 6.
Blackness of darkness, Heb. 12. 18
  Jude 13.
R. V. S. of S. 1. 6. swarthy
BLAME, Gen. 43. 9. & 44. 32. 2 Cor.
  8. 20. Eph. 1. 4.
Blamed, 2 Cor. 6. 3. Gal. 2. 11.
Blameless, Gen. 44. 10. Josh. 2. 17.
  Judg. 15. 3. Matt. 12. 5. Phil. 3. 6.
  1 Tim. 5. 7.
Luke 1. 6. in all the ordinances of
  the Lord b.
1 Cor. 1. 8. be b. in the day of our
1 Thes. 5. 23. be preserved b.
1 Tim. 3. 2. bishop must be b.
Tit. 1. 6, 7, 10. office of deacon
  found b.
2 Pet. 3. 14. without spot and b.
R. V. Eph. 1. 4. blemish; Matt. 12.
  5. guiltless; 1 Tim. 3. 2; 5. 7. with-
  out reproach
BLASPHEME, revile God, &c.
Ps. 74. 10. enemy b. thy name
Mark 3. 29. b. against Holy Ghost
Acts 26. 11. compelled them to b.
1 Tim. 1. 20. may learn not to b.
Lev. 24. 11. *blasphemed* the name
  of the Lord
2 Kings 19. 6. servants b. me, Isa.
  37. 6.
Isa. 52. 5. my name continually is b.
Rom, 2. 24. the name of God is b.
Tit. 2. 5. word of God be not b.
Rev. 16. 9, 11, 21. b. the God of
Lev. 24. 16. *blasphemeth* put to death
Matt. 9. 3. said this man b.
Luke 12. 10. to him that b. against
  the Holy Ghost
Blasphemer, 1 Tim. 1. 13. & 2 Tim.
  3. 2.
Blasphemy, 2 Kings 19. 3. Isa 37. 3.
  Matt. 12. 31. Mark 7. 22. Col. 3. 8.
  Rev. 2. 9.
R. V. 2 Tim. 3. 2. railers; 2 Kings
  19. 3; Isa. 37. 3. contumely; Mark
  7. 22; Col. 3. 8. railing
BLAST, Ex. 15. 8. 2 Sam. 22. 16.
  2 Kings 19. 7. Job 4. 9. Isa. 25. 4.
Blasting, Deut. 28. 22. 1 Kings 8. 37.
BLEMISH, without, Ex. 12. 5. & 29.
  1. Lev. 1. 3, 10. & 4. 23.
Dan. 1. 4. children and no b.
Eph. 5. 27. church holy, and with-
  out b.
1 Pet. 1. 19. as a lamb without b.
BLESS them that b. thee, Gen. 12. 3.
Gen. 22. 17. in blessing I will b. thee

Gen. 32. 26. not let thee go except
  thou b. me
Ex. 23. 25. b. thy bread and water
Num. 6. 24. Lord b. and keep thee
Ps. 5. 12. wilt b. the righteous
  29. 11. will b. his people with peace
  67. 1. be merciful to us and b. us
  115. 13. he will b. them that fear
Matt. 5. 44. b. them that curse you
Rom. 12. 14. b. them that persecute
Acts 3. 26. sent him to b. you in
  turning many
1 Cor. 4. 12. being reviled we b.
Bless the Lord, Deut. 8. 10. Judg.
  5. 9. Ps. 16. 7. & 34. 1. & 103. 1, 21,
  22. & 104. 1, 35. & 26. 12.
Bless thee, Ps. 63. 4. & 145. 2, 10.
Gen. 1. 22. God *blessed* them and
  2. 3. God b. the seventh day
Ex. 20. 11. the Lord b. the sabbath
Ps. 33. 12, 13. b. whose God is the
Prov. 10. 7. memory of the just is b.
Matt. 13. 16. b. are eyes, they see,
  Luke 10. 23.
  24. 46. b. is that servant when his
  43. Lord cometh, Luke 12. 37, 38.
Mark 10. 16. took them in his arms
  and b. them
Luke 1. 28, 42. b. art thou among
  48. all generations shall call me b.
Acts 20. 35. more b. to give than to
Rom. 1. 25. Creator b. for ever, 9. 5.
2 Cor. 11. 31. Eph. 1. 3. 1 Pet. 1. 3.
1 Tim. 1. 11. glorious gospel of b.
Ps. 119. 1. b. are the undefiled in
  84. 4. b. *are they* that dwell in thy
  106. 3. b. — that keep judgment
Prov. 8. 32. b. — that keep my ways
Isa. 30. 18. b. — that wait for him
Matt. 5. 3—11. b. — the poor in spirit
  — mourn — meek — hunger and
  thirst — merciful — pure in heart
  — peacemakers, persecuted —
  when men revile you, Luke 6.
  21, 22.
Luke 11. 28. b. — that hear the word
  and do it
John 20. 29. b. — that have not seen,
  and yet have believed
Rom. 4. 7. b. — whose iniquities
  are forgiven
Rev. 19. 9. b. — called to the marriage supper
  22. 14. b. — that do his command.
Num. 24. 9. b. is he that blesseth
Ps. 32. 1. b. — whose transgression
  is forgiven
  41. 1. b. — that considereth the
Dan. 12. 12. b. — that waiteth and
  cometh
Matt. 11. 6. b. — who shall not be off
  21. 9. b. — cometh in the name of
  the Lord, 23. 39. Mark 11. 19.
  Luke 13. 35.
Rev. 1. 3. b. — that readeth this
  16. 15. b. — that watcheth and keep.
  20. 6. b. — that hath part in the first
  resurrection
  22. 7. b. — that keepeth the sayings
  of this book
Ps. 1. 1. b. *is the man* that walketh
  not in the counsel of the ungodly
  34. 8. b. — that trusteth in him,
  84. 12.
  65. 4. b. — whom thou choosest
  84. 5. b. — whose strength is in
  thee
  112. 1. b. — that feareth the Lord
Prov. 8. 34. b. — that heareth me
Isa. 56. 2. b. — that doeth this, and
Ps. 49. 18. he *blesseth* his soul
Blessedness, Rom. 4. 6, 9. Gal. 4. 15.
Gen. 12. 2. thou shalt be a *blessing*
  27. 36. he hath taken away my b.
  28. 4. give thee b. of Abraham
Deut. 11. 26. set before you a b. and
  a curse, 30. 19. Jas. 3. 9, 10.
  23. 5. turned curse into b., Neh.
  13. 2.
Neh. 9. 5. exalted above all b.
Job 29. 13. b. of him ready to perish
Ps. 3. 8. thy b. is upon thy people
129. 8. the b. of Lord be upon you
Isa. 65. 8. destroy it not for a b. is

Joel 2. 14. leaveth a b. behind him
1 Cor. 10. 16. the cup of b. which
Gal. 3. 14. b. of Abraham might
Blessings, Gen. 49. 25, 26. Josh. 8.
  34. Ps. 21. 3. Prov. 10. 6. & 28. 20.
BLIND, Ex. 4. 11. Lev. 21. 18.
Job 29. 15. I was eyes to the b.
Ps. 146. 8. openeth the eyes of the b.
Isa. 42. 7. to open the b. eyes, 18.
  19. who is b. but my servant?
  43. 8. bring the b. people that have
  56. 10. his watchmen are b.
Matt. 11. 5. the b. receive sight,
  Luke 7. 21.
  23. 16. woe to you, b. guides, 24.
Luke 4. 18. recovery of sight to b.
Rev. 3. 17. thou art b. and naked
John 12. 40. *blinded* their eyes
Rom. 11. 7. the rest were b.
2 Cor. 3. 14. their minds were b.
  4. 4. the God of this world hath
  b. the minds
1 John 2. 11. darkness hath b. his
R. V. Rom. 11. 7; 2 Cor. 3. 14.
  hardened
BLOOD of grapes, Gen. 49. 11.
Job. 16. 18. cover not thou my b.
Ps. 9. 12. maketh inquisition for b.
  72. 14. precious their b. in his
Isa. 26. 21. the earth shall disclose
  her b.
Ezek. 3. 18. his b. will I require
  9. 9. the land is full of b.
  16. 6. polluted in thine own b.
Hos. 4. 2. they break out, and b.
Mic. 3. 10. they build up Zion with b.
Matt. 26. 28. b. of New Testament
Mark 14. 24. Luke 22. 20. 1 Cor. 11.
  25. & 27. 8. field of b., Acts 1. 19.
  25. his b. be on us and on our child.
Luke 13. 1. whose b. Pilate had
  22. 44. as it were great drops of b.
John 1. 13. born not of b. nor of flesh
  6. 54, 56. whoso drink. my b. hath
  55. my b. is drink indeed
  19. 34. out of his side came b. and
Acts 17. 26. made of one b. all
  18. 6. your b. be upon your own
Rom. 3. 25. through faith in his b.
  5. 9. being justified by his b.
1 Cor. 11. 27. guilty of body and b.
  of Christ
Col. 1. 20. made peace through the
  b. of the cross
Heb. 9. 20. this is the b. of the test.
  22. without shedding of b. no
  10. 19. into the holiest by the b. of
  12. 4. ye have not yet resisted
  unto b.
  24. b. of sprinkling that speaketh
1 Pet. 1. 2. sprinkling of the b. of
  19. with precious b. of Christ
1 John 1. 7. his b. cleanseth from
  5. 6. came by water and b.
Rev. 1. 5. washed us in his own b.
  6. 10. dost thou not avenge our b.
  7. 14. made white in the b. of the
  8. 7. hail and fire mingled with b.
  12. 11. overcame by the b. of the
  16. 6. shed b. — given them b. to
  17. 6. drunken with the b. of saints
Blood-guiltiness, Ps. 51. 14.
Bloody, Ex. 4. 25, 26. Ps. 5. 6. & 55.
  23.
R. V. Ps. 5. 6; 55. 23; 59. 2; 139.
  19. bloodthirsty; Acts 28. 8. dysen-
  tery
BLOSSOM, man's rod shall, Num.
  17. 5.
Isa. 5. 24. their b. shall go up as
  dust
  27. 6. Israel shall b. and bud
  35. 1. the desert shall b. as the
Hab. 3. 17. the fig-tree shall not b.
Ezek. 7. 10. rod hath *blossomed*
  pride
R. V. Num. 17. 5. *bud*.
BLOT, Job 31. 7. Prov. 9. 7.
Ex. 32. 32, 33. b. me out of thy book,
  Num. 5. 23. Ps. 69. 28. Rev. 3. 5.
Blot out their *name* or *remem*.
  Deut. 9. 14. & 25. 19. & 29. 20. 2 Kings
  14. 27. Ps. 109. 13.
Blot out sin, transgression, ini-

9

quity, Neh. 4. 5. Ps. 51. 1, 9. &
109. 14.
Isa. 43. 25. & 44. 22. Jer. 18. 23. Acts
3. 19.
Col. 2. 14. *blotting* out the hand-
writing
R. V. Job. 31. 7. spot.
BLOW on my garden, S. of S. 4. 16.
Hag. 1. 9. I did *b.* upon it
John 3. 8. wind *bloweth* where it is
BLUSH to lift up my face, Ezra
9. 6.
Jer. 6. 15. neither could they *b.*
8. 12.
BOAST, Ps. 10. 3. & 34. 2. & 49. 6.
& 52. 1.
Prov. 20. 14. & 25. 14. Jas. 3. 5.
Ps. 44. 8. in God we *b.* all the day
Prov. 27. 1. *b.* not of to-morrow
Boasting, Acts 5. 36. Rom. 3. 27.
Jas. 4. 16. now ye rejoice in your *b.*
Rom. 1. 30. proud *boasters*, 2 Tim.
3. 2.
R. V. Rom. 11. 18; 2 Cor. 9. 2; 10.
8. glory.
BODY of heaven, Ex. 24. 10.
Job 19. 26. though worms destroy
this *b.*
Matt. 6. 22. *b.* full of light, Luke
11. 34.
10. 28. them that kill the *b.*, Luke
12. 4.
Matt. 26. 26. this is my *b.*, 1 Cor.
11. 24.
Rom. 6. 6. the *b.* of sin be destroyed
7. 4. dead to the law by the *b.* of
24. deliver me from the *b.* of this
8. 10. *b.* is dead because of sin
13. do mortify deeds of the *b.*
23. the redemption of our *b.*
1 Cor. 6. 13. *b.* is not for fornication,
for the Lord; and the Lord for
the *b.*
18. every sin a man doeth is without the *b.*
19. your *b.* is the temple of the
Holy Ghost
7. 4. wife hath not power of her
own *b.*
9. 27. I keep under my *b.* and
10. 16. communion of *b.* of Christ
11. 27. guilty of *b.* and blood of the
29. not discerning the Lord's *b.*
12. 14. the *b.* is not one member
27. ye are the *b.* of Christ
15. 35. with what *b.* do they come?
44. sown a natural *b.* raised a
spiritual *b.*
Eph. 3. 6. fellow heirs of the same *b.*
5. 23. he is the Saviour of the *b.*
Phil. 3. 21. who shall change our
vile *b.*
Col. 1. 18. he is the head of the *b.*
the church
2. 11. putting off the *b.* of sins of
17. shadow — but the *b.* is of Christ
23. neglecting of the *b.*
1 Thes. 5. 23. spirit, soul, and *b.* be
Jas. 3. 6. able to bridle the
whole *b.*
Jude 9. disputed about the *b.* of
John 2. 21. his own *b.*, 1 Cor. 6. 18.
1 Pet. 2. 24.
1 Cor. 5. 3. in the *b.*, 2 Cor. 5. 6, 10.
& 12. 2. Phil. 1. 20. Heb. 13. 3.
Deut. 28. 11, 18, 53. fruit of the *b.*,
30. 9. Ps. 132. 11. Mic. 6. 7.
Rom. 8. 11. quicken your mortal
bodies
12. 1. present your *b.* a living sacri.
1 Cor. 6. 15. your *b.* are members of
Eph. 5. 28. husbands love your
wives as your own *b.*
Luke 3. 22. Holy Ghost descended
in a *bodily* shape
2 Cor. 10. 10. his *b.* presence is
Col. 2. 9. dwelleth the fulness of
the godhead *b.*
1 Tim. 4. 8. *b.* exercise profiteth
R. V. Isa. 51. 23. back; Matt. 14. 12;
15. 45. corpse
BOLD as a lion, Prov. 28. 1.
2 Cor. 10. 1. being absent am *b.*
11. 21. if any is *b.* I am *b.* also

Phil. 1. 14. are much more *b.* to
Mark 15. 43. went *boldly* unto Pilate
Heb. 4. 16. come *b.* to the throne of
2 Cor. 7. 4. great is my *boldness* of
Heb. 10. 19. *b.* to enter into the
1 John 4. 17. *b.* in the day of judg.
R. V. 2 Cor. 10. 1. good courage; 7.
26. openly; Eph. 6. 19 ——; Heb.
13. 6. with good courage; Eccl. 8.
1. hardness
BOND of the covenant, Ezek. 20.
37.
Acts 8. 23. in gall and *b.* of iniquity
1 Cor. 12. 13. *bond and free*, Gal. 3. 28.
Eph. 6. 8. Col. 3. 11. Rev. 6. 15. &
13. 16. & 19. 18.
Ps. 116. 16. has loosed my *bonds*
Job. 12. 18. he looseth *b.* of kings
Acts 20. 23. *b.* and afflictions abide
23. 29. worthy of death or of *b.*
26. 29. such as I am except these *b.*
Eph. 6. 20. I am an ambassador in *b.*
Phil. 1. 16. to add affliction to my *b.*
2 Tim. 2. 9. suffer trouble even
unto *b.*
Phile. 10. whom I have begotten
in my *b.*
Heb. 10. 34. compassion in my *b.*
13. 3. remember them that are in *b.*
Ex. 13. 3. house of *bondage*, 20. 2.
1. 14. lives bitter with hard *b.*
2. 23. sighed by reason of the *b.*
Rom. 8. 15. received again the
spirit of *b.*
1 Cor. 7. 15. brother or sister is not
in *b.*
Gal. 4. 24. Sinai which gendereth
to *b.*
5. 1. entangled with the yoke of *b.*
Bondwoman, Gen. 21. 10. Gal. 4.
23, 30.
BONDMAID, laws concerning,
Lev. 19. 20. & 25. 44.
BONDMAN, laws concerning,
Lev. 25. 39. Deut. 15. 12.
R. V. Ex. 1. 14; Isa. 14. 3. serve;
Deut. 7. 8; Jer. 34. 13. bondage;
1 Kings 9. 22 `ondservants; Gal.
4. 23, 39, 31. handmaid
BONE of my bone and flesh of my,
Gen. 2. 23. & 29. 14. Judg. 9. 2. 2 Sam.
5. 1. & 19. 13. 1 Chron. 11. 11.
Ex. 12. 46. not break a *b.* of it
John 19. 36. *b.* of him shall not be
Ps. 51. 8. *b.* thou hast broken may
Eccl. 11. 5. how the *b.* grow in the
Matt. 23. 27. full of dead men's *b.*
His bones, Ps. 34. 20. Eph. 5. 30.
Job 20. 11. Ezek. 32. 27. Prov. 12. 4.
Ps. 6. 2. my *bones* are vexed
22. 14. all — are out of joint
31. 10. — are consumed
38. 3. there is no rest —
102. 3. — are burnt as an hearth
5 — cleave to my skin
BONNETS, of the priests, direc-
tions for making, Ex. 28. 40. & 29.
9. & 39. 28. Ezek. 44. 18. *See* MITRE.
BOOK, Gen. 5. 1. Esth. 6. 1.
Ex. 32. 32. blot me out of thy *b.*
Job 19. 23. O that they were print-
ed in a *b.*
31. 35. mine adversary had written a *b.*
Ps. 40. 7. in the volume of the *b.*,
Heb. 10. 7.
Book of life, Phil. 4. 3. Rev. 3. 5. &
13. 8. & 17. 8. & 20. 12, 15. & 21. 27.
& 22. 19.
Books, Eccl. 12. 12. Dan. 7. 10. & 9.
2. John 21. 25. 2 Tim. 4. 13. Rev.
20. 12.
R. V. 1 Chr. 29. 29; 2 Chron. 9. 29; 12.
15; 20. 34. history; Jer. 32. 12.
BOOTHS, Lev. 23. 42, 43. Neh. 8. 14.
BORDER of his garment, Mar
6. 56.
BORING of the ear, Ex. 21. 6.
BORN to trouble, man is, Job 5. 7.
Job 14. 1. *b.* of a woman, 15. 14. &
25. 4. Matt. 11. 11. Luke 7. 28.
Ps. 58. 3. the wicked go astray as
soon as they are *b.*

Ps. 87. 5. this and that man was *b.* in
her
Prov. 17. 17. a brother is *b.* for
Eccl. 3. 2. a time to be *b.* and a
time to die
Isa. 9. 6. unto us a child is *b.* a son
66. 8. shall a nation be *b.* at once
Jer. 15. 10. *borne* me a man of strife
Matt. 11. 11. among them that are
b. of women
John 3. 4. can a man be *b.* when
5. *b.* of water and of the Spirit
Rom. 9. 11. children being not yet *b.*
1 Cor. 15. 8. one *b.* out of due time
Gal. 4. 23. *b.* after the flesh, 29.
1 Pet. 2. 2. as new *b.* babes desire
sincere milk of
John 3. 3, 5, 7. *b.* again
John 1. 13. *born of God*, 1 John 3.
9. & 4. 7. & 5. 1, 4, 18.
BORROW, Deut. 15. 6. & 28. 12.
Ex. 22. 14. *b.* aught of his neighbor,
3. 22. & 11. 2. & 12. 35.
Matt. 5. 42. would *b.* of thee turn
Ps. 37. 21. the wicked *borroweth* and
payeth not
Prov. 22. 7. *borrower* is servant to
Isa. 24. 2. as with the lender so
with *b.*
R. V. Ex. 3. 22; 11. 2; 12. 35. ask
BOSOM, Gen. 16. 5. Ex. 4. 6.
Num. 11. 12. carry them in *b.* as a
Deut. 13. 6. wife of thy *b.*, 28. 54, 56.
Ps. 35. 13. prayer returned into my
own *b.*
Prov. 5. 20. why embrace the *b.* of a
6. 27. take fire in his *b.* and not be
17. 23. gift out of *b.* to pervert, 21.
14.
19. 24. hideth his hands in his *b.*
26. 15.
Isa. 40. 11. carry them in his *b.*
65. 6, 7. recompense into their *b.*
Ps. 79. 12. Jer. 32. 18.
Mic. 7. 5. her that lieth in thy *b.*
Luke 6. 38. shall men give into
your *b.*
16. 22. carried into Abraham's *b.*,
23.
John 1. 18. who is in the *b.* of the
Father, 13. 23. leaning on Jesus' *b.*
R. V. Prov. 19. 24; 26. 15. dish
BOTH, Gen. 2. 25. & 3. 7. & 19. 36.
Zech. 6. 13. counsel of peace be-
tween *b.*
Eph. 2. 14. our peace made *b.* one
18. we *b.* have access by one spirit
BOTTLE, Gen. 21. 14, 15, 19.
Ps. 56. 8. put my tears into thy *b.*
Jer. 13. 12. every *b.* filled with wine
Job 38. 37. who can stay *bottles* of
Matt. 9. 17. new wine into old *b.*
Mark 2. 22. new wine into new *b.*
Matt. 9. 17.
R. V. generally, skins or wine
skins
BOTTOMLESS pit, Rev. 9. 1. & 11.
7. & 17. 8.
Satan bound there, Rev. 20. 1, 2.
BOUGHT, Gen. 17. 12, 13. & 33. 19.
Deut. 32. 6. he thy father that *b.*
Matt. 13. 46. sold all and *b.* it
1 Cor. 6. 20. *b.* with a price, 7. 23.
2 Pet. 2. 1. denying the Lord that
b. them
BOUND Isaac, Gen. 22. 9.
Job 36. 8. if they be *b.* in fetters
Ps. 107. 10. being *b.* in affliction
Prov. 22. 15. foolishness *b.* in heart
Matt. 16. 19. whatsoever ye bind on
earth shall be *b.* in heaven, 18. 18.
Acts 20. 22. I go *b.* in the spirit
21. 13. ready not to be *b.* only, but
Rom. 7. 2. wife is *b.* to her hus-
band, 1 Cor. 7. 39.
1 Cor. 7. 27. art thou *b.* to a wife,
seek
2 Tim. 2. 9. the word of God is
not *b.*
Heb. 13. 3. in bonds as *b.* with them
Isa. 1. 6. closed nor *bound up*
Ezek. 30. 21. not — to be healed
34. 4. neither have ye *b.* the broken
Hos. 13. 12. iniquity of Ephraim is

BOUNTY, 1 Kings 10. 13. 2 Cor. 9. 5.

Prov. 22. 9. *bountiful* eye be blessed

Ps. 13. 6. dealt *bountifully* with me, 116. 7. & 119. 17. & 142. 7.

2 Cor. 9. 6. he that sows *b.* shall reap *b.*

BOW in the clouds, Gen. 9. 13, 14, 16.

Gen. 49. 24. his *b.* abode in strength

Josh. 24. 12. not with sword nor *b.*

2 Sam. 1. 18. teach children use of *b.*

Ps. 7. 12. he hath bent his *b.*

44. 6. I will not trust in my *b.*

78. 57. turned aside like a deceit. *b.*

Jer. 9. 3. bend tongue like a *b.* for

Lam. 2. 4. bent his *b.* like an enemy

Lam. 3. 12. bent his *b.* and set me

Hos. 1. 5. break their *b.*

17. I will not save them by *b.*

7. 16. turned like a deceitful *b.*

1 Sam. 2. 4. Ps. 37. 15. *bows*, & 64. 3. & 78. 9. Jer. 51. 56.

Bow down thine ear, 2 Kings 19. 16.

Ps. 31. 2. & 86. 1. Prov. 22. 17.

Job 31. 10. let others — upon her

Ps. 95. 6. let us — and worship

Gen. 23. 12. Abraham *bowed down* himself before the people, 27. 29.

Judg. 7. 5, 6. — on their knees to

Ps. 38. 6. I am—greatly, I go mourning all the day long

Isa. 2. 11. haughtiness of men —, 17.

BOWELS did yearn, Gen. 43. 30.

1 Kings 3. 26. 2 Chron. 21. 15, 18.

Ps. 71. 6. took me out of my mother's *b.*

Isa. 63. 15. where is the sounding of thy *b.*

Jer. 4. 19. my *b.* my *b.* I am pained

31. 20. my *b.* are troubled for him, Lam. 1. 20. & 2. 11. S. of S. 5. 4.

Acts 1. 18. all his *b.* gushed out

2 Cor. 6. 12. straitened in your *b.*

Phil. 1. 8. I long after you in the *b.* of Christ

2. 1. if any comfort, if any *b.* and

Col. 3. 12. put on *b.* of mercies

1 John 3. 17. shutteth up *b.* of

R. V. Ps. 109. 18. inward parts; 2 Cor. 6. 12. affections; Phil. 1. 8; 2. 1. tender mercies; Col. 3. 12; Phile. 7. 20. heart

BOWL, Num. 7. 85. Eccl. 12. 6. Zech. 4. 2, 3. & 9. 15. & 14. 20.

R. V. Ex. 25. 31, 33, 34 ; 37. 17, 19, 20; 1 Kings 7. 50; 2 Kings 12. 13. cups; 2 Kings 25. 15; 1 Chr. 28. 17; Jer. 52. 18. basons

BOYS, Gen. 25. 27. Zech. 8. 5.

BRAKE the tables, Ex. 32. 19. & 34. 1. Deut. 9. 17. & 10. 2.

Judg. 16. 12. Samson *b.* the new

1 Sam. 4. 18. Eli *b.* his neck and

1 Kings 19. 11. wind *b.* in pieces the

2 Kings 11. 18. *b.* Baal's image, 10. 27.

18. 4. *b.* the images and brazen ser.

23. 14. *b.* in pieces the images, 2 Chron. 31. 1.

Job 29. 17. *b.* the jaws of the wick.

Ps. 76. 3. *b.* the arrows of the bow

105. 16. *b.* the whole staff of bread

Jer. 31. 32. my covenant they *b.*, Ezek. 17. 16.

Dan. 2. 34. his sleep *b.* from him

6. 24. *b.* all their bones to pieces

Matt. 14. 19. blessed, and *b.* and gave, 15. 36. & 26. 26. Mark 6. 41. & 8. 6. & 14. 22. Luke 9. 16. & 22. 19. & 24. 30. 1 Cor. 11. 24.

Mark 14. 3. *b.* box and poured the

Brake down images—altars of Baal, 2 Kings 10. 27. & 11. 18. 2 Chron. 14. 3. & 23. 17. & 34. 4. — wall of Jerusalem, 2 Kings 14. 13. & 25. 10.

2 Chron. 25. 23. & 36. 19. Jer. 39. 8. & 52. 14. — houses of Sodomites — high places — altars — altar of Bethel, 2 Kings 23. 7, 8, 12, 15.

BRAMBLE, Judg. 9. 14. Luke 6. 44.

R. V. Isa. 34. 13. thistles

BRANCH, with clusters of grapes, Num. 13. 23. Isa. 17. 9. & 18. 5.

Job 15. 32. his *b.* shall not be green

Ps. 80. 15. *b.* thou madest strong

Prov. 11. 28. the right. flourish as a *b.*

Isa. 4. 2. of the Lord be beautiful

9. 14. cut off *b.* and root, 19. 15.

14. 19. cast out like an abomi. *b.*

25. 5. *b.* of terrible ones be brought

Jer. 23. 5. unto David a righteous *b.*

Ezek. 8. 17. they put *b.* to their nose

Zech. 3. 8. bring forth my servant *b.*

6. 12. behold man whose name is *b*

Mal. 4. 1. leave neither root nor *b.*

Matt. 24. 32. when his *b.* is yet ten.

John 15. 2. every *b.* in me that bear

4. *b.* cannot bear fruit of itself

Lev. 23. 40. take *branches* of palmtrees, Neh. 8. 15. John 12. 13.

Job 15. 30. flame shall dry up his *b.*

Ps. 80. 11. sent her *b.* unto the river

104. 12. fowls sing among the *b.*

Isa. 16. 8. her *b.* are stretched out

Jer. 11. 16. the *b.* of it are broken, Ezek. 17. 6, 7. & 19. 10, 14.

Dan. 4. 14. hewn down tree, cut off *b.*

Hos. 14. 6. his *b.* shall spread as

Zech. 4. 12. what be these two olive *b.*

John 15. 5. I am the vine, ye are the *b.*

Rom. 11. 6. if root be holy, so are *b.*

17. if some of the *b.* be broken off

21. God spared not natural *b.*, 24.

BRAND, Judg. 15. 5. Zech. 3. 2.

BRASS, Gen. 4. 22. Dan. 5. 4.

Num. 21. 9. made serpent of *b.*

Deut. 8. 9. out of whose hills may est dig *b.*

28. 23. heaven over thy head shall *b.*

Job 6. 12. is my strength of *b.*—flesh

41. 27. he esteemeth *b.* as rotten

Isa. 48. 4. thy neck iron, and brow *b.*

60. 17. for wood I will bring *b.*

Dan. 2. 32. belly and thighs of *b.*

Zech. 6. 1. were mountains of *b.*

1 Cor. 13. 1. become as sounding *b.*

Rev. 1. 15. feet like fine *b.*, 2. 18.

Brazen, Num. 16. 39. 2 Kings 18. 4. & 25. 13. 2 Chron. 6. 13. Jer. 1. 18. & 15. 20. & 52. 20. Mark 7. 4.

BRAWLER, 1 Tim. 3. 3. Tit. 3. 2.

Prov. 21. 9. & 25. 24. *brawling* woman

R. V. 1 Tim. 3. 3. contentious

BRAY, Job 6. 5. Prov. 27. 22.

BREACH, be upon thee, Gen. 38. 29.

Num. 14. 34. know my *b.* of promise

Judg. 21. 15. Lord made *b.* in tribes

2 Sam. 6. 8. Lord made *b.* on Uzza, 1 Chron. 13. 11. & 15. 13.

Job 16. 14. break. me with *b.* upon *b.*

Ps. 106. 23. Moses stood in the *b.*

Isa. 30. 13. this iniq. shall be as *b.*

Lam. 2. 13. thy *b.* is great like sea

Ps. 60. 2. heal *breaches* thereof

R. V. Num. 14. 34. alienation ; Judg. 5. 17. creeks ; Isa. 30. 26. hurt

BREAD shall be fat, Gen. 49. 20.

Ex. 16. 4. I will rain *b.* from heaven

Lev. 21. 6. *b.* of their God they offer

Num. 14. 9. they are *b.* for us

21. 5. soul loatheth this light *b.*

Deut. 8. 3. not live by *b.* only, Matt. 4. 4.

Ruth 1. 6. visited his people giving *b.*

1 Sam. 2. 5. hired themselves for *b.*

1 Kings 18. 4. fed them with *b.* and

Neh. 5. 14. not eaten of *b.* of gover., 18

9. 15. gavest them *b.* from heaven

Ps. 37. 25. nor his seed begging *b.*

78. 20. can he give *b.* also

80. 5. feedest them with *b.* of tears

102. 9. I have eaten ashes like *b.*

132. 15. satisfy her poor with *b.*

Prov. 9. 17. *b.* eaten in secret

31. 27. she eateth not *b.* of idleness

Eccl. 9. 11. nor yet *b.* to the wise

11. 1. cast thy *b.* upon the waters

Isa. 3. 1. whole stay of *b.*, 7.

30. 20. Lord give you *b.* of adversi.

55. 2. spend money for that is not *b.*

10. give seed to sower, *b.* to eater

Lam. 4. 4. the young children ask *b.*

Ezek. 18. 7. hath given *b.* to hun.

Hos. 2. 5. give me my *b.* and water

Amos 4. 6. want of *b.* in all your

Mal. 1. 7. ye offer polluted *b.* on

Matt. 4. 3. these stones be made *b.*

4. not live by *b.* alone, Luke 4. 4.

6. 11. this day our daily *b.*, Luke 11. 11.

7. 9. son ask *b.* will he give a stone

26. 26. meet to take the children's *b.*

26. 26. took *b.* and blessed it

Mark 8. 4. satisfy these men with *b.*

Luke 7. 33. neither eating *b.* nor

15. 17. servants have *b.* enough

24. 35. known in breaking of *b.*

John 6. 32. Moses gave you not that *b.*

33. the *b.* of God is he that cometh

34. evermore give us this *b.*

35. I am *b.* of life, 48. true *b.* 32.

41. I am the *b.* which came down

50. this is the *b.* that cometh down

13. 18. he that eateth *b.* with me

Acts 2. 42. breaking *b.* and in pray.

20. 7. came together to break *b.*

27. 35. he took *b.* and gave thanks

1 Cor. 10. 16. *b.* we break is it not

11. 23. night he was betrayed took *b.*

26. as often as ye eat this *b.*, 27.

Deut. 16. 3. *bread of affliction*, 1 Kings 22. 27. 2 Chron. 18. 26. Isa. 30. 20.

Gen. 3. 19. *shall eat bread*, 28. 20. Ps. 14. 4. & 127. 2. Prov. 25. 21. Eccl. 9. 7. Mark 7. 5. Luke 14. 15. 1 Cor. 11. 26. 2 Thes. 3. 12.

1 Sam. 2. 36. *piece of bread*, Prov. 6. 26. & 28. 21. Jer. 37. 21. Ezek. 13. 19.

Lev. 26. 26. *break staff of bread*, Ps. 105. 16. Ezek. 4. 16. & 5. 16. & 14. 13.

Gen. 19. 3. *unleavened bread*, Ex. 12. 8, 15. & 18. 20. & 13. 6, 7. Mark 14. 12. Luke 22. 7. Acts 12. 3. & 20. 6. 1 Cor. 5. 8.

BREAK, Gen. 19. 9. Ex. 34. 13.

Judg. 7. 19. *b.* the pitchers that were 9. 53. and all to *b.* his skull

Ezra 9. 14. should we again *b.* thy

Ps. 2. 3. let us *b.* their bands asunder

9. shalt *b.* them with a rod of iron

58. 6. *b.* their teeth in their mouth

89. 31. if they *b.* my statutes

141. 5. oil which shall not *b.* head

S. of S. 2. 17. till the day *b.* and the shadows, 4. 6.

Isa. 42. 3. bruised reed not *b.*, Matt. 12. 20.

58. 6. that ye *b.* every yoke

Jer. 14. 21. *b.* not covenant with us

15. 12. shall iron *b.* northern iron

Ezek. 4. 16. *b.* the staff of bread, 5. 16. & 14. 13. Hos. 2. 18.

17. 15. shall he *b.* covenant and be

Hos. 1. 5. *b.* the bow of Israel, 2. 18.

Zech. 11. 10. might *b.* my covenant

14. might *b.* the brotherhood

Matt. 5. 19. *b.* one of these least

Acts 21. 13. mean ye to *b.* my heart

1 Cor. 10. 16. bread which we *b.*

Ex. 23. 24. *break down*, Deut. 7. 5. Ps. 74. 6. Eccl. 3. 3. Jer. 31. 28. & 45. 4. Hos. 10. 2.

Ex. 19. 22, 24. *break forth*, Isa. 55. 8. Jer. 1. 14. Gal. 4. 27.

Isa. 14. 7. *break forth into singing*, 44. 23. & 49. 13. & 54. 1. & 55. 12. & 52. 9.

Dan. 4. 27. *break off thy sins by right*.

Ex. 22. 6. *break out*, Isa. 35. 6. Hos. 4. 2. Amos 5. 6.

Job 19. 2. *break in pieces*, 34. 24. Ps. 72. 4. & 94. 5. Isa. 45. 2. Jer. 51. 20, 21, 22. Dan. 2. 40, 44. & 7. 23.

Ex. 19. 21, 24. *break through*, and Matt. 6. 19, 20. where thieves — and

Jer. 4. 3. *break up* your *fellow* ground, Hos. 10. 10.

Ps. 74. 13, 14. *breasts* heads of dra.
Gen. 32. 26. let me go, for the day
   breaketh
Job 9. 17. he *b.* me with a tempest
16. 14. he *b.* me with breach
Ps. 29. 5. voice of the Lord *b.* the
119. 20. my soul *b.* for the longing
Prov. 25. 15. a soft tongue *b.* the
Eccl. 10. 8. whoso *b.* a hedge, a ser-
   pent shalt bite them
Jer. 19. 11. as one *b.* a potter's vessel
23. 29. like a hammer that *b.* rocks
Hos. 13. 13. a place of *breaking* forth
   of children, 1 Chron. 14. 11.
Luke 24. 35. known of them in *b.*
Acts 2. 42. *b.* of bread, 46.
Rom. 2. 23. through *b.* the law dis-
   honorest thou
R. V. Gen. 27. 40. shake; Ex. 34. 13;
   Deut. 7. 5; 12. 3. dash in pieces;
   Job 13. 25. harass; 39. 15. trample;
   S. of S. 2. 17; 4. 5. be cool; Isa. 54.
   3.spread; Ezek. 23.34.gnaw; Matt.
   9. 17. burst; Rom. 2. 25. transgres-
   sors; Job 41. 25. consternation;
   Rom. 2. 23. thy transgression of
BREASTS, Gen. 49. 25. Job 3. 12.
Job 21. 24. his *b.* are full of milk
Ps. 22. 9. I was upon my mother's *b.*
Prov. 5. 19. let her *b.* satisfy thee at
S. of S. 1. 13. shall lie all night be-
   tween my *b.*
4. 5. thy *b.* are like two roes, 7. 3.
7. 7. thy *b.* to clusters of grapes, 8.
8. 1. sucked the *b.* of my mother
10. I am a wall and my *b.* like
Isa.59.16. suck the *b.* of kings, 49. 23.
60. 16. suck the *b.* of kings, 49. 23.
Ezek. 16. 7. thy *b.* are fashioned
8. bruised the *b.* of her virginity
Hos. 2. 2. adulteries from between
   her *b.*
Joel 2. 16. gather those that suck *b.*
Luke 23. 48. smote *b.* and returned
Rev. 15. 6. their *b.* girded with
Ex. 28. 4. *breastplate,* Rev. 9. 9, 17.
Isa.59.17. put on righteousness as *b.*
Eph. 6. 14. *b.* of righteousness
1 Thes. 5. 8. *b.* of faith and love
BREATH of life, Gen. 2. 7. & 6. 17.
   & 7. 15, 22. Isa. 2. 22. Hab. 2. 19.
Job 12. 10. in whose hands is *b.* of all
19. 17. my *b.* is strange to my wife
Ps. 33. 6. made by *b.* of his mouth
104. 29. thou takest away their *b.*
150. 6. all that hath *b.* praise Lord
Eccl. 3. 19. they have all one *b.*
Isa. 2. 22. whose *b.* is in his nostrils
11. 4. with *b.* of his lips shall slay
Lam. 4. 20. the *b.* of our nostrils
Dan. 5. 23. in whose hand thy *b.* is
Acts 17. 25. giveth life and *b.* and all
Ps. 27. 12. breathe out cruelty
Ezek. 37. 9. come *b.* upon these slain
John 20. 22. he *breathed* on them
Acts 9. 1. *breathing* out slaughter
R. V. Job 4. 9. blast; 17. 1. spirit
BRETHREN, we be, Gen. 13. 8.
Gen. 49. 29. him that was separate
   from his *b.*, Deut. 33. 16.
Deut.17.20. be not lifted up above *b.*
33. 9. neither did he acknowledge
   his *b.*
24. let him be acceptable to his *b.*
1 Chron. 4. 9. more honorable than
   his *b.*
Job 6. 15. my *b.* have dealt deceit.
19. 13. put my *b.* far from me
Ps. 22. 22. declare thy name unto
   my *b.*
69. 8. I am become a stranger to
   my *b.*
Hos. 13. 15. fruitful among his *b.*
Matt. 23. 8. all ye are *b.*, Acts 7. 26.
12. 48. who are my *b.*
25. 40. the least of these my *b.*
28. 10. go tell my *b.* that they go
Mark 10. 29. left house of *b.*, Luke
   18. 29.
John 7. 5. neither did his *b.* believe
20. 17. go to my *b.* and say, I ascend
Acts 11. 29. send relief to the *b.*
Rom.8.29.firstborn among many *b.*
9.3.accursed from Christ for my *b.*

1 Cor. 6. 5. to judge between his *b.*
15. 6. seen of above 500 *b.* at once.
Gal. 2. 4. false *b.* unawares brought
1 Tim. 4. 6. put *b.* in remembrance
Heb. 2. 11. not ashamed to call
   them *b.*
1 Pet. 1. 22. unfeigned love of the *b.*
1 John 3. 14. because we love the *b.*
16. to lay down our lives for the *b.*
3 John 10. neither doth he receive *b.*
Gen. 27. 29. *thy brethren,* 48. 22. &
49. 8. Deut. 15. 7. & 18. 15. 1 Sam.
17. 18. Matt. 12.47. Mark 3. 32. Luke
8. 20. & 14. 12. & 22. 32.
Jer. 12. 6.—have dealt treacherous.
Rev. 19. 10. I am of —, 22. 9.
1 Kings 12. 24. *your brethren,* 2
Chron. 30. 7, 9. & 35. 6.
Neh. 4. 14. fight for—your sons and
Isa. 66. 5.—that hated you
Acts 3. 22. raise up of—prophet
   like unto me, 7. 37. Deut. 18. 15.
Matt. 5. 47. if you salute—only
R. V.Acts 20, 32; Rom. 15. 15; 1 Cor.
   11. 2—; 1 John 2. 7. beloved
BRIBES, 1 Sam. 3. 8. Amos 5. 12.
1 Sam. 12. 3. have I received any *b.*
Ps. 26. 10. right hand full of *b.*
Isa. 33. 15. hands from holding *b.*
Isa. 45. 34. tabernacles of *bribery*
R. V. 1 Sam. 12. 3. ransom
BRICK, Gen. 11. 3. Ex. 1. 14. & 5. 7,
8, 14, 16, 19. Isa. 65. 3. & 9. 10.
2 Sam. 12. 31. *brick-kiln,* Jer. 43. 9.
Nah. 3. 14.
BRIDE, doth clothe with an orna.,
   Isa. 49. 18.
Isa. 61. 10. as a *b.* adorneth herself
Jer. 2. 32. can a *b.* forget her attire
Joel 2. 16. *b.* go out of her closet
John 3. 29. that hath *b.* is bridegr.
Rev. 21. 2. as a *b.* adorned for her
9. I will shew thee *b.* Lamb's wife
22. 17. spirit and *b.* say, come
Matt. 9. 15. *bride-chamber,* Mark 2.
19. Luke 5. 34.
BRIDEGROOM, Joel 2. 16. John
   2. 9.
Ps. 19. 5. as a *b.* coming out of
Isa. 61. 10. as a *b.* decketh himself
62. 5. as a *b.* rejoiceth over the
Jer. 7. 34. cease the voice of *b.* and
   bride, 16. 9. & 25. 10. & 33. 11. Rev.
   18. 23.
Matt. 9. 15. as long as the *b.* is—
   them, Mark 2. 19, 20. Luke 5. 34.
Matt. 25. 1. went forth to meet *b. b.*
BRIDLE for the ass, Prov. 26. 3.
Ps. 32. 9. mouth held with *b.*
Isa. 37. 29. put my *b.* in thy lips, 30.
28. 2 Kings 19. 28. Rev. 14. 20.
Jas. 3. 2. able to *b.* the whole body
1. 26. *bridleth* not his tongue
BRIERS, Judg. 8. 7, 16. Isa. 7. 23,
24, 25. & 32. 13. Heb. 6. 8. Mic. 7. 4.
Isa. 5. 6. come up *b.* and thorns
9. 18. wickedness, shall devour *b.*,
10. 17.
27. 4. set *b.* against me in battle
Ezek. 2. 6. though *b.* and thorns be
28. 24. no more a pricking *b.* unto
R. V. Heb. 6. 8. thistles
BRIGHTNESS, 2 Sam. 22. 13.
Ezek. 1. 4, 27, 28. & 8. 2. & 28. 7, 17.
Job 31. 26. beheld moon walking
   in *b.*
Ezek. 10. 4. full of the *b.* of Lord's
Dan. 12. 3. wise shall shine as the
   b. of the firmament
Amos 5. 20. very dark and no *b.*
   in it.
Hab. 3. 4. his *b.* was as the light
Acts 26. 13. a light above *b.* of sun
2 Thes. 2. 8. Lord destroy with *b.*
Heb. 1. 3. being the *b.* of his glory
R. V. Heb. 1. 3. effulgence
BRIMSTONE, Gen. 19. 24. Deut.
29. 23. Job 18. 15. Ps. 11. 6. Isa. 30.
33. & 34. 9. Ezek. 38. 22. Luke 17.
29. Rev. 14. 10. & 19. 20. & 21. 8.
BRING a flood, Gen. 6. 17.
Josh. 23. 15. *b.* upon you all the evil
1 Kings 8. 32. to *b.* his way upon

Job 14. 4. who can *b.* a clean thing
Ps. 60. 9. who *b.* me into strong, 72.
10. Isa. 60. 9. & 66. 20.
72. 3. mountains *b.* peace to people
Eccl. 11. 9. God will *b.* thee into
   judgment, 12. 14. Job 14. 4. & 30.
   23.
S. of S. 8. 2. *b.* thee to my mother's
Isa. 1. 13. *b.* no more vain oblations
43. 5. I will *b.* thy seed from east
46. 13. I *b.* near my righteousness
66. 9. shall I *b.* to the birth and
Hos. 2. 14. allure and *b.* her into
Zeph. 3. 5. every morning *b.* his
Luke 2. 10. I *b.* you good tidings
John 14. 26. *b.* all things to remem.
5. 28. intend to *b.* this man's
   blood
1 Cor. 1. 28. *b.* to nought things
1 Thes. 4. 14. God will *b.* with him
1 Pet. 3. 18. that he might *b.* us to
Gen. 1. 11, 20, 24. *bring forth,* 3. 16.
Matt. 1. 21. Job 39. 1. Ex. 3. 10
2 Kings 19. 3. there is not strength
   to—
Job 15. 35. conceive mischief and
   —vanity
Ps. 37. 6. he shall—thy righteous.
92. 14. still—fruit in old age
Prov. 27. 1. what a day may—
Isa. 41. 21.—your strong reasons
42. 1.—judgment to the Gentiles,4.
66. 8. made to—in one day
Zeph. 2. 2. before the decree—
Mark 4. 20.—fruit some thirty fold
Luke 3. 8.—fruits worthy of re-
   pentance
8. 15.—fruit with patience
John 15. 2. that it may—more fruit
Ps. 1. 3. *bringeth forth* fruit in its
Hos. 10. 1.—fruit to himself
Matt. 3. 10. *b.* not forth good fruit,
7. 19. & 12. 35. Luke 6. 43.
John 12. 24. if it die it—much fruit
Jas. 1. 15.—sin—death
BROAD, Num. 16. 38, 39. Nah. 2. 4.
Matt. 23. 5.
Job 36. 16. out of strait into *b.* place
Isa. 33. 21. Lord a place of *b.* rivers
Matt. 7. 13. *b.* is way to destruction
R. V. Num. 16. 38. beaten
BROIDERED work, Ezek. 16. 10.
BROKEN my covenant, Gen. 17.
14. Ps. 55. 20. Isa. 24. 5. & 33. 8. &
36. 6. Jer. 11. 10. & 33. 21.
Ps. 34. 18. nigh to them of *b.* heart
44. 19. sore *b.* us in place of drag.
17. *b.* spirit, *b.* and contrite heart
147. 3. healeth the *b.* in heart
Isa. 61. 1. to bind up the *b.* hearted
Jer. 2. 13. hewed out *b.* cisterns
Dan. 2. 42. strong and partly *b.*
Hos. 5. 11. Ephraim is *b.* in judg-
   ment
Matt. 21. 44. shall fall on stone, shall
   be *b.*
John 10. 35. Scripture cannot be *b.*
Ps. 110. 7. drink of the *b.* in the way
Job 20. 17. the *b.* of honey and
Isa. 19. 6. *b.* of defence shall be
R. V. Num. 21. 14, 15. valleys
BROTHER, born for adversity,
   Prov. 17. 17.
Prov. 18. 19. a *b.* offended is harder
24. is a friend that sticketh closer
   than a *b.*
27. 10. neighbor near, than *b.* far
Jer. 9. 4. trust not in any *b.* for
   every *b.*
Matt. 10. 21. *b.* shall deliver up *b.*
   to death, Mark 13. 12. Mic. 7, 2.
1 Cor. 5. 11. *b.* be a fornicator
6. 6. but *b.* goeth to law with *b.*
7. 15. *b.* or sister is not in bondage
2 Thes. 3. 15. admonish him as a *b.*
Jas. 1. 9. let *b.* of low degree
Ps. 35. 14. *my brother,* S. of S. 8. 1.
Matt. 12. 50. & 18. 21. 1 Cor. 8. 13.
Ps. 50. 20. *thy brother,* Matt. 5. 23,
24. & 18. 15. Rom. 14. 10, 15.
Gen. 45. 4. *your brother,* Rev. 1. 9.
Zech. 11. 14. *brotherhood,* 1 Pet. 2.
17.

Amos 1. 9. remember not *brotherly* covenant
Rom. 12. 10. kindly affectioned with *b.*
Heb. 13. 1. let *b.* love continue
2 Pet. 1. 7. to godliness *b.* kindness
R. V. Luke 6. 16; Acts 1. 13. son
BROUGHT me hitherto, 2 Sam. 7. 18.
Neh. 4. 15. God *b.* their counsel to
Ps. 45. 14. be *b.* unto the king in
79. 8. we are *b.* very low
107. 39. *b.* low through oppression
116. 6. I was *b.* low and he helped
Isa. 1. 2. nourished and *b.* up child.
Matt. 10. 18. *b.* before governors, Mark 13. 9. Luke 12. 12.
1 Cor. 6. 12. not be *b.* under power
Gal. 2. 4. false brethren, unawares *b.* in
1 Tim. 6. 7. *b.* nothing into this world
Ps. 107. 12. *brought down,* Matt. 11. 23.
Deut. 33. 14. *brought forth,* Ps. 18. 19.
BRUISE thy head—his heel, Gen. 3. 15.
Isa. 53. 10. it pleased Lord to *b.* him
Isa. 42. 3. *bruised* reed not break, Matt. 12. 20.
53. 5. he was *b.* for our iniquities
Ezek. 23. 3, 21. *b.* breasts, *b.* teats
R. V. Jer. 30. 12; Nah. 3. 19. hurt; Dan. 2. 40. crush; Isa. 28. 28. ground
BRUIT, report, Jer. 10. 22. Nah. 3. 19.
BRUTISH man knows not, Ps. 92. 6.
Ps. 94. 8. understand, ye *b.* among
Jer. 10. 14. man is *b.* in his knowledge, 51. 17.
BUCKLER to all that trust, Ps. 18. 30.
Ps. 18. 2. my *b.* and horn of my
91. 4. his truth shall be thy *b.*
Prov. 2. 7. a *b.* to them that walk
R. V. 2 Sam. 22. 31; Ps. 18. 2; Prov. 2. 7. shield; 1 Chron. 12. 8. spear
BUDDING of Aaron's rod, Num. 17.
BUFFETED, 2 Cor. 12. 7. Matt. 26. 67. 1 Cor. 4. 11. 1 Pet. 2. 20.
BUILD walls of Jerusalem, Ps. 51. 18.
Ps. 102. 16. Lord shall *b.* up Zion
Eccl. 3. 3. a time to *b.* up
Mic. 3. 10. *b.* up Zion with blood
Acts 20. 32. able to *b.* you up
Job 22. 23. if thou return shalt be *built* up
Ps. 89. 2. mercy shall be *b.* up for
Matt. 7. 24. *b.* his house on a rock
Eph. 2. 20. ye are *b.* on foundation
Col. 2. 7. rooted and *b.* up in him
Heb. 3. 4. he that *b.* all things is
1 Pet. 2. 5. *b.* up a spiritual house
Heb. 11. 10. *builder* and maker is
Ps. 118. 22. stone which the *b.* refused, Matt. 21. 42. Mark 12. 10. Luke 20. 17. Acts 4. 11. 1 Pet. 2. 7.
1 Cor. 3. 10. *master builder*
Josh. 6. 26. cursed that *buildeth*
Jer. 22. 13. woe to him that *b.* house
Amos 9. 6. *b.* his stories in heaven
Hab. 2. 12. *b.* a town with blood
1 Cor. 3. 10. another *b.* thereon
9. ye are God's *building*
2 Cor. 5. 1. we have a *b.* of God
Heb. 9. 11. tabernacle*s* not of this *b.*
Jude 20. *b.* up yourselves in faith
BULLS compassed me, Ps. 22. 12.
Ps. 50. 13. will I eat the flesh of *b.*
Heb. 9. 13. if blood of *b.* and goats
Ps. 69. 31. than *bullock* with horns
Jer. 31. 18. as a *b.* unaccustomed to
Ps. 51. 19. offer *b.* on thy altar
Isa. 1. 11. delight not in blood of *b.*
R. V. Isa. 51. 20. antelope; Lev. 4. 10; 9. 18; Deut. 17. 1. ox; Jer. 31. 18. calf; Jer. 50. 11. strong horses

BULRUSHES, Ex. 2. 3. Isa. 18. 2. & 58. 5.
R. V. Isa. 58. 5. rush; 18. 2. papyrus
BULWARKS, Ps. 48. 13. Isa. 26. 1.
R. V. 2 Chr. 26. 15. battlements
BUNDLE, Gen. 42. 35. Acts 28. 3.
1 Sam. 25. 29. bound in the *b.* of
S. of S. 1. 13. *b.* of myrrh is my
Matt. 13. 30. bind tares in *bundles* to burn
BURDEN, 2 Kings 5. 17. & 8. 9.
Ex. 18. 22. shall bear the *b.* with thee, Num. 11. 17.
23. 5. ass lying under his *b.*
Deut. 1. 12. how can I bear your *b.*
2 Sam. 15. 33. thou shalt be a *b.*
2 Kings 5. 17. two mules *b.* of earth
2 Chron. 35. 3. not be *b.* on should.
Neh. 13. 19. shall be no *b.* brought in on Sabbath day, Jer. 17. 21. & 22. 24, 27.
Job 7. 20. I am a *b.* to myself
Ps. 38. 4. a *b.* too heavy for me
55. 22. cast thy *b.* upon the Lord
Eccl. 12. 5. grasshopper shall be a *b.*
Isa. 9. 4. broken the yoke of his *b.*
10. 27. *b.* taken from thy shoulder
Zeph. 3. 18. reproach of it was a *b.*
Zech. 12. 3. all that *b.* themselves
Matt. 11. 30. my yoke is easy, my *b.*
20. 12. borne the *b.* and heat of day
Acts 15. 28. no greater *b.* than nec.
2 Cor. 12. 16. I did not *b.* you
Gal. 6. 5. every man bear his own *b.*
Rev. 2. 24. put on you no other *b.*
Isa. 13. 1. *b.* threatening of heavy judgments, 14. 28. & 15. 1. & 17. 1. & 19. 1. & 21. 1, 11. & 22. 1. & 23. 1.
Ezek. 12. 10. Nah. 1. 1. Hab. 1. 1. Zech. 9. 1. & 12. 1.
Mal. 1. 1. *b.* of the word
2 Cor. 5. 4. we groan bein*g burdened*
Gen. 49. 14. *burdens,* Ex. 1. 11. & 2. 11. & 5. 4.
Isa. 58. 6. to undo the heavy *b.*
Lam. 2. 14. seen for thee false *b.*
Matt. 23. 4. bind heavy *b.,* Luke 11. 46.
Gal. 6. 2. bear one another's *b.*
Zech. 12. 3. *burdensome,* 2 Cor. 11. 9. & 12. 13, 14. 1 Thes. 2. 6.
R. V. Gen. 49. 14. sheepfolds ; Amos 5. 11. exactions ; 2 Cor. 8. 13. distressed
BURN upon altar, Ex. 29. 13, 18, 25.
Lev. 1. 9, 15. & 2. 2. & 3. 5, 11, 16. & 5. 12. & 6. 15. & 9. 17.
Gen. 44. 18. let not thine anger *b.*
Deut. 32. 22. shall *b.* to lowest hell
Isa. 27. 4. go through them and *b.*
Mal. 4. 1. day cometh shall *b.* as an
Luke 3. 17. chaff he will *b.* with unquenchable fire
Luke 24. 32. did not our heart *b.*
1 Cor. 7. 9. it is better to marry than *b.*
Rev. 17. 6. eat her flesh and *b.* her
Ex. 3. 2. the bush *burned* with fire
Deut. 9. 15. and mount *b.* with fire
Ps. 39. 3. while I was musing fire *b.*
1 Cor. 3. 15. if any man's work shall be *b.*
13. 3. though I give my body to *b.*
Heb. 6. 8. whose end is to be *b.*
Ps. 46. 9. *burneth* the chariot in fire
97. 3. *b.* up his enemies round
Isa. 9. 18. wickedness *b.* as the fire
Rev. 21. 8. lake which *b.* with fire
Gen. 15. 17. *burning* lamp that passed between those pieces
Jer. 20. 9. his word was as *b.* fire
Hab. 3. 5. *b.* coals went forth at his
Luke 12. 35. loins girded and your lights *b.*
John 5. 35. a *b.* and a shining light
Ex. 21. 25. *b.* for *b.* wound for wou.
Deut. 28. 22. smite thee with extreme *b.*
Isa. 3. 24. *b.* instead of beauty
4. 4. by the spirit of judgment and *b.*
Amos 4. 11. firebrand plucked out of the *b.*
Isa. 33. 14. dwell with everlasting *b.*

Gen. 8. 20. *burnt-offerings,* Deut. 12. 6. 1 Sam. 15. 22. Ps. 50. 8. Isa. 1. 11. & 56. 7. Jer. 6. 20. & 7. 21, 22.
Hos. 6. 6. knowledge of God more than—
Mark 12. 33. more than all whole—
Heb. 10. 6. in—for sin and sacrifices
Ps. 74. 8. *burnt* up all synagogues
Isa. 64. 11. our beautiful house is—
Matt. 22. 7. destroyed and—their city
2 Pet. 3. 10. works that are therein be—
BURST thy bands, Jer. 2. 20.
Prov. 3. 10. presses *b.* out with new
Mark 2. 22. new wine doth *b.* the bottles, Luke 5. 37. Job 32. 19.
Acts 1. 18. *b.* asunder in the midst
R. V. Prov. 3. 10. overflow ; Isa. 30. 14. pieces
BURY my dead out of my sight, Gen. 23. 4.
Gen. 49. 29. *b.* me with my fathers
Ps. 79. 3. there was none to *b.* them
Matt. 8. 21. first to go and *b.* my
Rom. 6. 4. *buried* with him by baptism into death, Col. 2. 12.
1 Cor. 15. 4. he was *b.* and rose again
Gen. 23. 4. a possession of a *burying*
47. 30. *b.* me in the *b.* place
Mark 14. 8. anoint my body to the *b.*
John 12. 7. against the day of my *b.*
2 Chron. 26. 23. *burial,* Acts 8. 2.
Eccl. 6. 3. that he have no *b.*
Isa. 14. 20. not joined with them in*b.*
Jer. 22. 19. buried with *b.* of an ass
Matt. 26. 12. she did it for my *b.*
BUSH is not burnt, Ex. 3. 2, 3, 4.
Acts 7. 30. Mark 12. 26.
Deut. 33. 16. good will of him that dwelt in *b.*
R. V. Isa. 7. 19. pastures
BUSHEL, Matt. 5. 15. Luke 11. 33.
BUSHY and black, S. of S. 5. 11.
BUSINESS, Gen. 39. 11. Rom. 16. 2.
Ps. 107. 23. do *b.* in great waters
Prov. 22. 29. seest a man diligent in *b.*
Luke 2. 49. must be about Father's *b.*
Acts 6. 3. we may appoint over this *b.*
Rom. 12. 11. not slothful in *b.*
1 Thes. 4. 11. study to do your own *b.*
BUSY-BODIES censured, Prov. 20. 3. & 26. 17. 1 Thes. 4. 11. 2 Thes. 3. 11. 1 Tim. 5. 13. 1 Pet. 4. 15.
BUTTER and milk, Gen. 18. 8.
Deut. 32. 14. Judg. 5. 25. 2 Sam. 17. 29. Prov. 30. 33.
Job 20. 17. brooks of honey and *b.*
Ps. 55. 21. words were smoother than *b.*
Isa. 7. 15. *b.* and honey shall he eat, 22.
BUY the truth, Prov. 23. 23.
Isa. 55. 1. *b.* and eat, yea, *b.* wine
1 Cor. 7. 30. they that *b.* as possessed
Jas. 4. 13. *b.* and sell, and get gain
Rev. 3. 18. I counsel thee *b.* gold
Prov. 20. 14. it is nought saith *buyer*
Isa. 24. 2. as with *b.* so with seller
Ezek. 7. 12. let no *b.* rejoice
Prov. 31. 16. considereth a field and *buyeth* it
Matt. 13. 44. selleth all and *b.* field
Rev. 18. 11. no man *b.* her merchan.
BY and by, Matt. 13. 21. Mark 6. 25. Luke 17. 7. & 21. 9.
By-word among all nations, Deut. 28. 37.
1 Kings 9. 7. Israel shall be a—
2 Chron. 7. 20. make this house a—
Job 17. 6. made a—of the people
30. 9. I am their song and their—
Ps. 44. 14. makest us a—among the heathen

C

CAGE, Jer. 5. 27. Rev. 18. 2.
R. V. Rev. 18. 2. hold
CAIN and Abel, Gen. 4. 1-17. Heb. 11. 4. & 12. 24. Jude 11.

CAKE of bread tumbled into host, Judg. 7. 13.
1 Kings 17. 12. I have not a *c.* but
Hos. 7. 8. Ephraim is a *c.* not turned
Cakes, Gen. 18. 6. Judg. 6. 19.
Jer. 7. 18. make *c.* to queen of
44. 19. made *c.* to worship her
R. V. 1 Chr. 23. 29. wafers
CALAMITY at hand, Deut. 32. 35.
Job 6. 2. my *c.* laid in the balance
Ps. 18. 18. prevented me in the day of my *c.*
Prov. 1. 26. I will laugh at your *c.*
6. 15. his *c.* shall come suddenly
Jer. 18. 17. the face in day of their *c.*
46. 21. day of thy *c.* is come, 48. 16. & 49. 8, 32. Ezek. 35. 5. Obad. 13.
Ps. 57. 1. till these *calamities* be overpast
Prov. 17. 5. that is glad at *c.* shall
24. 22. their *c.* shall rise suddenly
R. V. Ps. 141. 5. wickedness
CALDRON, 1 Sam. 2. 14. Job 41. 20. Ezek. 11. 3, 7, 11. Mic. 3. 3. Jer. 52. 18.
R. V. Job 41. 20. burning rushes; Jer. 52. 18, 19. pots
CALEB and Joshua, Num. 13. 30. & 14. 6, 24, 38. & 26. 65. & 32. 12.
CALF, Gen. 18. 7. Job 21. 10. Ps. 29. 6. Isa. 27. 10. Rev. 4. 7.
Ex. 32. 4. made a molten *c.,* 20. Deut. 9. 16. Neh. 9. 18. Ps. 106. 19.
Isa. 11. 6. *c.* and young lion lie
Hos. 8. 5. thy *c.* O Samaria, hath
8. 6. the *c.* of Samaria shall be
Luke 15. 23. bring hither the fatted *c.*
27. thou hast killed the fatted *c.* 30.
CALL them what he would, Gen. 2. 19.
Gen. 24. 57. we will *c.* the damsel
30. 13. daughters will *c.* me bless.
Deut. 4. 7. all that we *c.* upon him
1 Sam. 3. 6. here am I, for thou didst *c.* me
1 Kings 8. 52. in all they *c.* to thee
17. 18. to *c.* my sin to remembrance
1 Chron. 16. 8. *c.* upon his name
13. 22. *c.* thou and I will answer
27. 10. will he always *c.* upon God
Ps. 4. 1. hear me when I *c.* O God
49. 11. *c.* lands after their names
72. 17. all nations shall *c.* him
80. 18. we will *c.* on thy name
86. 5. plenteous in mercy to all that *c.*
145. 18. nigh to all them that *c.* upon
Prov. 31. 28. children rise and *c.* her
Isa. 5. 20. woe to them that *c.* evil
55. 6. *c.* upon him while he is near
65. 24. before they *c.* I will answer
Jer. 25. 29. I will *c.* for a sword upon all
Joel 2. 32. remnant whom the Lord shall *c.*
Jonah 1. 6. sleeper arise, *c.* upon
Zech. 13. 9. they shall *c.* upon my
Mal. 3. 12. all nations shall *c.* you
Matt. 9. 13. I came not to *c.* right.
but sinners, Mark 2. 17.
22. 3. to *c.* them that were bidden
Luke 1. 48. all generations shall *c.*
6. 46. why *c.* ye me Lord, Lord?
John 4. 16. *c.* thy husband and
13. 13. ye *c.* me master and Lord
Acts 2. 39. as many as Lord shall *c.*
10. 15. God hath cleansed *c.* not
Rom. 9. 25. I will *c.* them my people
10. 12. rich in mercy to all that *c.* on
2 Cor. 1. 23. I *c.* God for a record
Heb. 2. 11. not ashamed to *c.* them
Jas. 5. 14. *c.* for the elders of the
1 Pet. 1. 17. if ye *c.* on the Father
Call on the name of the Lord, Gen. 4. 26. & 12. 8. & 13. 4. & 21. 33. & 26. 25. 1 Kings 18. 24. 2 Kings 5. 11. Ps. 116. 4, 13, 17. Joel 2. 32. Zeph. 3. 9. Acts 2. 21. Rom. 10. 13. 1 Cor. 1. 2.
I will call unto, or, *on the Lord,* 1 Sam. 12. 17. 2 Sam. 22. 4. Ps. 18. 3. & 55. 16. & 86. 7.
Call upon me, Ps. 50. 15. & 91. 15. Prov. 1. 28. Jer. 29. 12.

Gen. 21. 17. angel of God *called* to Hagar
22. 11. the angel of the Lord *c.* to Abraham out of heaven, 15.
Ex. 3. 4. God *c.* unto him out of the
19. 3. Lord *c.* unto him out of the
Judg. 15. 18. was athirst, and *c.* on
2 Kings 8. 1. Lord hath *c.* for a
1 Chron. 4. 10. Jabesh *c.* on God of
21. 26. David *c.* on the Lord and he
Ps. 17. 6. I have *c.* upon thee, 31. 17.
18. 6. in my distress I *c.* upon Lord
79. 6. not *c.* on thy name, Jer. 10. 25.
88. 9. I have *c.* daily upon thee
118. 5. I *c.* upon the Lord in my dis.
Prov. 1. 24. I have *c.* and ye refused
S. of S. 5. 6. I *c.* him, he gave me
Isa. 41. 2. who *c.* him to his foot
42. 6. I the Lord *c.* thee in right.
43. 1. I have *c.* thee by thy name
22. thou hast not *c.* upon me
48. 1. *c.* by the name of Israel, 44. 5.
49. 1. Lord *c.* me from the womb
50. 2. when I *c.* was none to answer
51. 2. I *c.* him alone, and blessed
61. 3. be *c.* trees of righteousness
62. 4. thou shalt be *c.* Hephzibah
Lam. 1. 19. I *c.* for my lovers they
3. 55. I *c.* upon thy name, O Lord
Hos. 11. 1. I *c.* my son out of Egypt
Amos 7. 4. Lord *c.* to contend by
Hag. 1. 11. I *c.* for a drought on
Matt. 20. 16. many be *c.* but few chosen, 22. 14.
Mark 14. 72. Peter *c.* to mind word of the Lord
Luke 15. 19. not worthy to be *c.* thy
John 1. 48. before that Philip *c.* thee
10. 35. if he *c.* them gods to whom
15. 15. I have *c.* you friends
Acts 9. 41. when he had *c.* saints
21. destroy them that *c.* on this
10. 23, 24. *c.* in — *c.* together his kinsmen
Acts 11. 26. disciples were *c.* Christians
13. 2. for work whereto I *c.* them
19. 40. we are in danger to be *c.* in question, 23. 6. & 24. 21.
20. 1. Paul *c.* to him the disciples
Rom. 1. 1. *c.* to be an apos. 1 Cor. 1. 1.
6. *c.* of Jesus Christ, 7. *c.* to be
2. 17. thou that art *c.* a Jew
8. 28. *c.* according to his purpose
30. predestinate, them he also *c.*
9. 24. whom he hath *c.* Jews also
1 Cor. 1. 9. faithful by whom ye were *c.*
26. not many wise, — noble are *c.*
5. 11. if any man *c.* a brother be
7. 18. *c.* being circumcised
21, 22. *c.* servant
24. every man wherein he is *c.*
15. 9. I am not meet to be *c.* an
Gal. 1. 6. *c.* you into the grace of
15. God who *c.* me by his grace
Eph. 2. 11. who are *c.* uncircum.
4. are *c.* in one hope of your calling
Col. 3. 15. to which ye are *c.* in one
1 Thes. 2. 12. *c.* you unto his king.
4. 7. God hath not *c.* us to unclean
2 Thes. 2. 4. above all that is *c.* God
1 Tim. 6. 12. whereunto thou art *c.*
2 Tim. 1. 9. *c.* us with a holy calling
Heb. 3. 13. exhort while it is *c.* to.
5. 4. *c.* of God, as was Aaron
10. *c.* of God a high priest
9. 15. that they who are *c.* may
11. 16. not ashamed to be *c.* their
24. refusing to be *c.* the son of Pharaoh's daughter
Jas. 2. 7. name by which ye are *c.*
1 Pet. 1. 15. as he that *c.* you is holy
21. hereunto were ye *c.*
2 Pet. 1. 3. *c.* us to glory and virtue
1 John 3. 1. we should be *c.* sons of
Jude 1. preserved in Christ Jesus and *c.*
Rev. 17. 14. with him *c.* and chosen
19. 9. are *c.* unto marriage supper
2 Chron. 7. 14. *called by my name,* Isa. 43. 7. & 65. 1. Jer. 7. 10, 11, 14, 30. & 25. 29. & 32. 34. & 34. 15. Amos 9. 12.

1 Kings 8. 43. *called by thy name,* 2 Chron. 6, 33. Isa. 4. 1. & 43. 1. & 45. 4. & 63. 19. Jer. 14. 9. & 15. 16. Dan. 9. 18, 19.
2 Kings 8. 43. to all that the stranger *calleth* for, 2 Chron. 6. 33.
Job 12. 4. who *c.* on God and he ans.
Ps. 42. 7. deep *c.* unto deep at noise
Isa. 59. 4. none *c.* for justice nor for
Hos. 7. 7. none among them that *c.*
Amos 5. 8. that *c.* for waters of sea
Luke 15. 6. *c.* together his friends, 9.
John 10. 3. he *c.* his own sheep by
Rom. 4. 17. *c.* those things which be
Gal. 5. 8. persuasion not of him that *c.*
1 Thes. 5. 24. faithful is he that *c.*
Rom. 11. 29. gifts and *calling* of God
1 Cor. 1. 26. ye see your *c.* brethren
7. 20. let every man abide in same *c.*
Eph. 1. 18. what is the hope of his *c.*
4. 4. called in one hope of your *c.*
Phil. 3. 14. prize of high *c.* of God
2 Thes. 1. 11. count you worthy of this *c.*
2 Tim. 1. 9. called with a holy *c.*
Heb. 3. 1. partakers of heavenly *c.*
2 Pet. 1. 10. make your *c.* and elect.
Isa. 41. 4. *c.* the generation from the beginning
Matt. 11. 16. sitting and *c.* their
Mark 11. 21. Peter *c.* to remembrance
Acts 7. 59. stoned Stephen *c.* upon
22. 16. *c.* upon the name of Lord
1 Pet. 3. 6. obeyed Abraham, *c.* him
CALM, Ps. 107. 29. Jonah 1. 11, 12.
Matt. 8. 26. Mark 4. 39. Luke 8. 24.
CALVE (cow), Job 21. 10. (hinds) 39. 1. Ps. 29. 9. Jer. 14. 5.
1 Kings 12. 28. made two *calves* of
Hos. 14. 2. we will render *c.* of our
Mic. 6. 6. come with *c.* of a year old
Heb. 9. 12. blood of goats and *c.,* 19.
CAME, Ps. 18. 6. & 88. 17. Matt. 1. 18. & 9. 14. John 1. 7, 11. & 8. 14, 42. & 18. 37. Rom. 5. 18 & 9. 5. 1 Tim. 1. 15. 1 John 5. 6.
Came down, 2 Kings 1. 10, 12, 14. 2 Chron. 7. 1, 3. Lam. 1. 9. John 3. 13. & 6. 38, 41, 51, 58. Rev. 20. 9.
Came forth, Num. 11. 20. Judg. 14. 14. Eccl. 5. 15. Zech. 10. 4.
John 16. 28. I — from the Father
CAMEL, Gen. 24. 19. Lev. 11. 4.
Matt. 3. 4. raiment of *c.*'s hair, Mark 1. 6.
19. 24. easier for a *c.* to go through
23. 24. strain at a gnat, and swallow *c.*
CAMP, Ex. 32. 17. & 36. 6.
Ex. 14. 19. angel went before the *c.*
16. 13. quails came and covered *c.*
Num. 11. 26. they prophesied in *c.*
31. let the quails fall by the *c.*
Deut. 23. 14. Lord walketh in midst of *c.* therefore shall thy *c.* be holy
Judg. 13. 25. began to move him in *c.*
2 Kings 19. 35. smote in the *c.* of the Assyrians
Heb. 13. 13. go unto him without *c.*
Rev. 20. 9. compassed *c.* of saints
CAN we find such a one, Gen. 41. 38.
Deut. 1. 12. how *c.* I myself alone
32. 38. neither is there any *c.* deliver
2 Sam. 7. 20. what *c.* David say more
2 Chron. 1. 10. who *c.* judge this
Esth. 8. 6. how *c.* I endure to see the destruction of my people
Job 8. 11. *c.* the rush grow without
25. 4. how *c.* man be justified with
Ps. 40. 5. more than *c.* be number.
Ps. 49. 7. none *c.* redeem his brother
89. 6. who *c.* be likened unto Lord
Eccl. 4. 11. how *c.* one be warm
Isa. 49. 15. *c.* a woman forget her
Jer. 2. 32. *c.* a maid forget her orna.
Ezek. 22. 14. *c.* thy heart endure
37. 3. *c.* these dry bones live
Amos 3. 3. *c.* two walk together
Matt. 12. 34. how *c.* ye speak good
19. 25. who then *c.* be saved

Mark 2. 7. who *c.* forgive sins but
19. *c.* children of bride-chamber
10. 38. *c.* ye drink of the cup that I
John 3. 4. how *c.* man be born again
9. how *c.* these things be, Luke 1. 34.
5. 19. Son *c.* do nothing of him., 30.
6. 44. no man *c.* come to me except
9. 4. night, when no man *c.* work
15. 4. no more *c.* ye except ye abide
1 Cor. 12. 3. no man *c.* say that Jesus
2 Cor. 13. 8. *c.* do nothing against
1 Tim. 6. 7. we *c.* carry nothing out
Heb. 10. 11. *c.* never take away sins
Jas. 2. 14. *c.* faith save him
Rev. 3. 8. open door and no man *c.*
Gen. 32. 12. which *cannot* be numbered for multitude, 1 Kings 3. 8.
Hos. 1. 10.
Num. 23. 20. he hath blessed; and I *c.* reverse it
Josh. 24. 19. ye *c.* serve the Lord
1 Sam. 12. 21. vain things which *c.*
1 Kings 8. 27. heaven of heavens *c.* contain thee, 2 Chron. 6. 18.
Ezra 9. 15. we *c.* stand before thee
Job 9. 3. he *c.* answer for one of a 23. 8, 9. I *c.* perceive him—*c.* behold
28. 15. it *c.* be gotten for gold
36. 18. a great ransom *c.* deliver
Ps. 40. 5. they *c.* be reckoned up in 77. I am so troubled that I *c.* speak
93. 1. world establish. that it *c.* be
139. 6. too high, I *c.* attain unto it
Isa. 38. 18. the grave *c.* praise thee
44. 18. they *c.* see; they *c.* under.
20. he *c.* deliver his soul
50. 2. hand shortened that it *c.* redeem
56. 11. shepherds that *c.* understand
Jer. 4. 19. I *c.* hold my peace
6. 10. are uncircumcised, they *c.*
7. 8. ye trust in lying words that *c.*
14. 9. as a mighty man *c.* save
18. 6. *c.* I do with you as this potter
29. 17. like the vile figs that *c.* be
33. 22. the host of heaven *c.* be
Lam. 3. 7. hath hedged me, that I *c.* get
Matt. 6. 24. ye *c.* serve God and mammon, Luke 16. 13.
7. 18. a good tree *c.* bring forth evil 27. 42. himself he *c.* save, Mark 15. 31.
Luke 14. 26. *c.* be my disciple, 27. 33.
16. 26. would pass from hence to you *c.*
John 3. 3. *c.* see the kingdom of 5. he *c.* enter into the kingdom of
8. 43. because ye *c.* hear my word
10. 35. the Scripture *c.* be broken
14. 17. whom the world *c.* receive
15. 4. branch *c.* bear fruit of itself
Acts 4. 20. we *c.* but speak the things 5. 39. if it be of God ye *c.* overthrow
27. 31. except these abide in the ship, ye *c.* be saved
Rom. 8. 8. that are in flesh *c.* please God
26. groanings which *c.* be uttered
Cor. 7. 9. if they *c.* contain, let
10. 21. ye *c.* drink cup of the Lord
15. 50. flesh and blood *c.* inherit the kingdom of God
2 Cor. 12. 2. in body or out, I *c.* tell
Gal. 5. 17. ye *c.* do the things that
2 Tim. 2. 13. he *c.* deny himself
Tit. 1. 2. God who *c.* lie hath
2. 8. sound speech *c.* be condemned
Heb. 4. 15. high priest which *c.* be
9. 5. we *c.* now speak particularly
12. 27. those things which *c.* be
28. kingdom that *c.* be moved
Jas. 1. 13. God *c.* be tempted with
1 John 3. 9. he *c.* sin because born
Ex. 33. 20. *canst* not see my face
Deut. 28. 27. *c.* not be healed
Job 11. 7. *c.* thou by searching find
22. darkness that thou *c.* not see
Matt. 8. 2. if thou wilt, thou *c.*
Mark 9. 22. if *c.* do any thing have

John 3. 8. *c.* not tell whence it
13. 36. thou *c.* not follow me now
CANDLE shall be put out, Job 18. 6. & 21. 17. Prov. 24. 20.
Job 29. 3. when his *c.* shined on
Ps. 18. 28. the Lord will light my *c.*
Prov. 20. 27. spirit of man is *c.* of
31. 18. her *c.* goeth not out by
Matt. 5. 15. do men light a *c.* and— it, Mark 4. 21. Luke 8. 16. & 11. 33.
Luke 11. 36. shining of *c.* doth give
15. 8. light a *c.* and sweep house
Rev. 18. 23. light of *c.* shine no more at all, Jer. 25. 10.
Rev. 22. 5. they need no *c.* neither
Zeph. 1. 22. search Jerusalem with *candles*
Ex. 25. 31. *candlestick*, & 37. 17, 20.
Lev. 24. 4. Num. 8. 2. 2 Kings 4. 10.
Dan. 5. 5.
Zech. 4. 2. behold a *c.* all of gold
Matt. 5. 15. but on a *c.* and it giveth light to all, Mark 4. 21. Luke 11. 33.
Rev. 1. 20. seven *c.* are the seven 2. 5. I will remove thy *c.* out of his
R. V. Matt. 5. 15; Mark 4. 21; Luke 8. 16. stand
CANKER, 2 Tim. 2. 17. Jas. 5. 3.
CAPTAIN, Num. 2. 3. & 14. 4.
Josh. 5. 14, 15. *c.* of the Lord's host
2 Chron. 13. 12. God himself is our *c.*
Heb. 2. 10. *c.* of their salva. perfect
R. V. 1 Sam. 9. 16; 10. 1; 13. 4. prince;
Jer. 51. 23, 28, 57; Dan. 3. 2, 3, 27; 6. 7. governors
CAPTIVE, Gen. 14. 14. & 34. 2.
Judg. 5. 12. lead thy captivity *c.*
Isa. 49. 24. shall the lawful *c.* be
Jer. 22. 12. die whither they led him *c.*
Amos 7. 11. Israel shall be led away *c.*
2 Tim. 2. 26. taken *c.* by him at his
Deut. 30. 3. I will turn thy *captivity*
Job 42. 10. the Lord turned the *c.*
Ps. 14. 7. Lord bringeth back the *c.*
68. 18. lead *c.* captive, Eph. 4. 8.
85. 1. brought back the *c.* of Jacob
126. 1. turned again the *c.* of Zion
Jer. 15. 2. such as are for *c.* to *c.*
29. 14. I will turn away your *c.*
30. 3. bring again *c.* of my people
Hos. 6. 11. when I returned *c.* of
Zeph. 2. 7. Lord shall turn away their *c.*
Rom. 7. 23. bringing me into *c.* of
2 Cor. 10. 5. bringing into *c.* every
Rev. 13. 10. lead into *c.* shall go into *c.*
R. V. Isa. 20. 4; 45. 13; 49. 21. exile
CARCASS, Matt. 24. 28. Luke 17. 37.
R. V. Lev. 11. 26; Judg. 14. 8. body
CARE, Luke 10. 40. 1 Cor. 7. 21.
Matt. 13. 22. *c.* of this world choke, Mark 4. 19. Luke 8. 14.
1 Cor. 9. 9. doth God take *c.* for
12. 25. have the same *c.* one for
2 Cor. 11. 28. *c.* of all the churches
1 Tim. 3. 5. how shall he take *c.* of
1 Pet. 5. 7. casting all your *c.* on
Ps. 142. 4. no man *cared* for my
John 12. 6. not that he *c.* for the
Acts 18. 17. Gallio *c.* for none of these things
Matt. 22. 16. *carest*, Mark 4. 38.
Deut. 11. 12. land thy God *careth*
John 10. 13. hireling *c.* not for
1 Cor. 7. 32, 33, 34. unmarried *c.* for things of Lord, married *c.* for things of the world
1 Pet. 5. 7. for he *c.* for you
2 Kings 4. 13. been *careful* for us
Jer. 17. 8. not be *c.* in the year of
Dan. 3. 16. not *c.* to answer thee
Luke 10. 41. art *c.* and troubled about many things
Phil. 4. 6. be *c.* for nothing; but
10. were *c.* but ye lacked opportunity
Tit. 3. 8. be *c.* to maintain good

Ezek. 12. 18, 19. *carefulness*, 1 Cor. 7. 32. 2 Cor. 7. 11.
Isa. 32. 9. *careless* daughters, 10. 11.
R. V. Ezek. 4. 16. carefulness; 1 Pet. 5. 7. anxiety; Phil. 4. 19. did take thought; Deut. 15. 5; Phil. 2. 28; Heb. 12. 17. diligently; Mic. 1. 12. anxiously; 1 Cor. 7. 32. be free from cares; 2 Cor. 7. 11. earnest care; Judg. 18. 7. in security; Ezek. 39. 6. securely
CARNAL, sold under sin, Rom. 7. 14.
Rom. 8. 7. *c.* mind is enmity against God
15. 27. minister to them in *c.*
1 Cor. 3. 1. not speak but as to *c.*
3. ye are yet *c.*—are ye not *c.*
9. 11. if we reap your *c.* things
2 Cor. 10. 4. our weapons are not *c.*
Heb. 7. 16. law of a *c.* commandment
Rom. 8. 6. to be *c.* minded is death
R. V. 1 Cor. 3. 4. men; 2 Cor. 10. 4. of the flesh; Rom. 8. 6, 7. mind of the flesh
CARPENTER, 2 Sam. 5. 11. Isa. 41. 7. Jer. 24. 1. Zech. 1. 20.
Matt. 13. 55. *carpenter's son*, Mark 6. 3.
R. V. Jer. 24. 1; 29. 2. craftsmen; Zech. 1. 20. smiths
CARRY us not up hence, Ex. 33. 15.
Num. 11. 12. *c.* them in thy bosom
Eccl. 10. 20. bird of air shall *c.*
Isa. 40. 11. *c.* lambs in his bosom
Luke 10. 4. *c.* neither purse nor scrip
1 Tim. 6. 7. can *c.* nothing out
Luke 16. 22. *carried* by angels into Abraham's bosom
Eph. 4. 14. *c.* about with every
Heb. 13. 9. *c.* about with divers
Rev. 17. 3. *c.* me away in spirit, 21. 10.
CART is pressed full, Amos 2. 13.
Isa. 5. 18. as it were with a *c.* rope
CASE, Ex. 5. 19. Ps. 144. 15.
R. V. Deut. 22. 1; 24. 13. surely
CAST law behind their backs, Neh. 9. 26.
Ps. 22. 10. *c.* upon thee from the
55. 22. *c.* thy burden on the Lord
Prov. 1. 14. *c.* in thy lot among us
Eccl. 11. 1. *c.* thy bread upon
Isa. 2. 20. a man shall *c.* his idols
Ezek. 23. 35. *c.* me behind thy back
Dan. 3. 20. *c.* them into the fiery
6. 24. *c.* them into the den of lions
Jonah 2. 4. I am *c.* out of thy sight
Mic. 7. 19. *c.* all their sins into the
Mal. 3. 11. vine shall not *c.* her fruit
Matt. 3. 10. hewn down and *c.* into the fire, 7. 19. Luke 3. 9.
5. 25. thou be *c.* into prison
7. 6. neither *c.* pearls before swine
15. 26. children's bread, and *c.* it to
22. 13. *c.* him into outer darkness
29. 30. *c.* it from—*c.* into hell, 18. 8, 9.
Mark 11. 23. be thou *c.* into the sea
12. 44. she *c.* in all, Luke 21. 4.
Luke 1. 29. she *c.* in her mind what
58. lest the officer *c.* thee into prison
John 8. 7. let him first *c.* a stone at
Acts 16. 23. they *c.* them into prison
Rev. 2. 10. devil shall *c.* some of you into prison
20. 3. *c.* him into the bottomless
Lev. 26. 44. I will not *cast away*
2 Sam. 1. 21. shield is vilely—
Job 8. 20. God will not—perfect man
Ps. 2. 3. let us—their cords from us
51. 11. *c.* me not away from thy
Isa. 41. 9. I will not *c.* thee away
Ezek. 18. 31. *c.* away your transgress.
Rom. 11. 1. hath God—his people, 2.
Heb. 10. 35. *c.* not away your confid.
1 Cor. 9. 27. myself be a—
2 Chron. 25. 8. God hath power to *cast down*

Job 22. 29. when men are — then
Ps. 37. 24. though he fall he shall
  not be —
  42. 5. why art thou —, 11. & 43. 5.
Ps. 102. 10. lifted me and again — again
2 Cor. 4. 9. — but not destroyed
Ps. 44. 9. thou hast *cast off* and put
  23. *c.* us not off for ever
71. 9. *c.* me not off in time of old
94. 14. Lord will not — his people
Jer. 31. 37. I will —all seed of Israel
Lam. 3. 31. Lord will not—for ever
Hos. 8. 3. Israel hath—thing is good
Rom. 13. 12. let us —the works of
1 Tim. 5. 12. they — their first love
Gen. 21. 10. *cast out* this bond woman and her son, Gal. 4. 30.
Ex. 34. 24. I will — the nations
Lev. 18. 24. which I — before thee
Deut. 7. 1. — many nations before
Ps. 78. 55. he—heathen before them
Prov. 22. 10.—the scorner, and contention
Isa. 14. 9. thou art—of thy grave
26. 19. the earth shall — the dead
66. 5. *c.* you out for my name's sake
Jer. 7. 15. I will *c.* out of my sight
15. 1. *c.* them out of my sight
Matt. 7. 5. *c.* beam out of thine eye
8. 12. children of kingdom shall
  be—
12. 24. doth not—devils but by
  Beelzebub
21. 12. — them that sold and
Mark 9. 28. why could not we *c.* out
16. 9. he had — seven devils
17. in my name shall they—devils
Luke 6. 22. — your name as evil
John 6. 37. that cometh will in no
  wise—
Rev. 12. 9. the dragon was—
Ps. 73. 18. thou *castedst* them down
Job 15. 4. thou *castest* off fear
Ps. 50. 17. *c.* my words behind thee
Job 21. 10. cow *casteth* not her calf
Ps. 147. 6. *c.* the wicked to ground
Jer. 6. 7. he *c.* out her wicked.
Matt. 9. 34. he *c.* out devils through
  Beelzebub, Mark 3. 22. Luke 11.
  15.
1 John 4. 18. perfect love *c.* out fear
3 John 10. *c.* them out of the
Job 6. 21. ye see my *casting* down
Rom. 11. 15. if *c.* away of them
2 Cor. 10. 5. *c.* down imaginations
1 Pet. 5. 7. *c.* all your care on him
CASTOR and Pollux, Acts 28. 11.
CATCH every man his wife, Judg.
  21. 21.
Ps. 10. 9. he lieth in wait to *c.* poor
Jer. 5. 26. they set a trap, they *c.*
  men
Mark 12. 13. they *c.* him in his
Luke 5. 10. henceforth thou shalt
  c. men
R. V. Matt. 13. 19; John 10. 12.
  snatcheth
CATTLE on a thousand hills are
  mine, Ps. 50. 10.
104. 14. he causeth grass to grow
  for *c.*
Ezek. 34. 17. I judge between *c.*
  and *c.*
John 4. 12. drank thereof and his *c.*
R. V. Gen. 30. 40-43. flock
CAUGHT him and kissed him,
  Prov. 7. 13.
John 21. 3. that night they *c.* noth.
Acts 8. 39. Spirit of the Lord *c.*
  away Philip
2 Cor. 12. 4. he was *c.* up into para.
16. being crafty I *c.* you with guile
1 Thes. 4. 17. *c.* up together with
Rev. 12. 5. her child was *c.* up to
CAUL, Isa. 3. 18. Hos. 13. 8.
CAUSE come before judges, Ex.
  22. 9.
Ex. 23. 2. not speak in a *c.* to
6. nor wrest judgment of poor in *c.*
Deut. 1. 17. *c.* that is too hard for
1 Kings 8. 45. maintained their *c.*,
  49.
Job 5. 8. to God would I commit
  my *c.*

Ps. 9. 4. maintain my right and
  my *c.*
Prov. 18. 17. that is first in his own *c.*
Eccl. 7. 10. what is *c.* that former
Isa. 51. 22. pleadeth *c.* of his people
Jer. 5. 28. judge not *c.* of fatherless,
  22. 16.
11. 20. to thee I revealed my *c.*, 20.
  12.
Lam. 3. 36. to subvert a man in his *c.*
Matt. 19. 3. put away his wife for
  every *c.*
2 Cor. 4. 16. for which *c.* we faint
5. 13. if we be sober it is for your *c.*
Ex. 9. 16. *for this cause*, Matt. 19. 5.
  Ex. 5. 31. John 12. 27. & 18. 37. Rom.
  1. 13. & 13. 6. 1 Cor. 11. 30.
1 Tim. 1. 16. — I obtained mercy
Ps. 119. 161. *without cause*, Prov. 23.
  29. Matt. 5. 22. John 15. 25.
Ps. 4. 4. *c.* me to understand
Ps. 10. 17. wilt *c.* thine ear to hear
67. 1. *c.* his face to shine, 80. 3, 7,
  19.
143. 8. *c.* me to know the way
Isa. 3. 12. lead thee, *c.* thee to err,
  9. 16.
58. 14. I will *c.* thee to ride on
66. 9. and not *c.* to bring forth
Jer. 3. 12. not *c.* my anger to fall
7. 3. *c.* you to dwell in his place, 7.
15. 4. *c.* them to be removed
11. *c.* the enemy to treat thee
44. *c.* their captivity to return,
  33. 7. & 34. 22. & 42. 12.
32. 37. *c.* them to dwell safely
Lam. 3. 32. though he *c.* grief, yet
Ezek. 36. 27. *c.* you to walk in my
  statutes
Dan. 9. 17. *c.* thy face to shine on
  sanctuary
Rom. 16. 17. mark them which *c.*
  division
Prov. 7. 21. fair speech *caused* him
Prov. 10. 5. a son *causeth*, 17. 2. &
  19. 26.
Matt. 5. 32. *c.* her to commit adultery
2 Cor. 2. 14. always *c.* us to triumph
Prov. 26. 2. curse *causeless* shall not
R. V. 2 Chron. 19. 10. controversy;
  Prov. 31. 9. judgment; John 18.
  37. to this end; Matt. 5. 32; Rev.
  13.12. maketh; 2 Cor. 9. 11. worketh
CAVE, Adam's alone lay on it,
  John 11. 41.
Gen. 19. 30. Lot dwelt in a *c.* he and
23. 19. buried Sarah his wife in *c.*
25. 9. buried him in the *c.*
49. 29. bury me with my fathers
  in *c.*
Josh. 10. 16. hid themselves in a *c.*
1 Kings 18. 4. hid them by 50 in a *c.*
Isa. 2. 19. go into *caves* for fear of
Ezek. 33. 27. that be in the *c.* shall
  die
Heb. 11. 38. wandered in *c.* of the
R. V. Job 30. 6; Heb. 11. 38. holes
CEASE not day nor night, Gen. 8.
  22.
Deut. 15. 11. poor shall never *c.* out
  of
Neh. 6. 3. why should the work *c.*
Job 3. 17. there the wicked *c.*
Ps. 37. 8. *c.* from anger and wrath
46. 9. he maketh wars to *c.* unto
Prov. 19. 27. *c.* to hear instruction
23. 4. *c.* from thine own wisdom
Isa. 1. 16. *c.* to do evil, learn to do
1. 22. *c.* ye from man whose breath
Acts 13. 10. wilt thou not *c.* to per.
1 Cor. 13. 8. there be tongues, they *c.*
Eph. 1. 16. *c.* not to give thanks for
Col. 1. 9. *c.* not to pray for you
2 Pet. 2. 14. that cannot *c.* from sin
Ps. 12. 1. the godly man *ceaseth*
Prov. 26. 20. no talebearer, strife *c.*
1 Thes. 5. 17. pray without *ceasing*,
  2. 13. 1 Sam. 12. 23. Acts 12. 5. Rom.
  1. 9. 2 Tim. 1. 3.
R. V. Rom. 1. 9; 2 Tim. 1. 3. unceasingly; Acts 12. 5. earnestly
CEDAR, Lev. 14. 4. Jer. 22. 14, 15.
2 Sam. 7. 2. I dwell in a house of *c.*

2 Kings 14. 9. thistle sent to *c.* in
Ps. 29. 5. voice of Lord breaketh *c.*
92. 12. grow like a *c.* in Lebanon
S. of S. 1. 17. the beams of our
  house are *c.*
Isa. 9. 10. we will change them
  into *c.*
Ezek. 17. 22. of the high *c.*
23. goodly *c.*
Amos 2. 9. like the height of the *c.*
CELEBRATE, death cannot, Isa.
  38. 18.
R. V. Lev. 23. 32. keep
CELESTIAL, 1 Cor. 15. 40.
CHAFF, wicked as, Job 21. 18. Ps.
  1. 4. & 35. 5. Isa. 5. 24. & 17. 13. & 29.
  5. & 41. 15. Dan. 2. 35. Hos. 13. 3.
  Luke 3. 17.
Isa. 33. 11. ye shall conceive *c.* ye
Jer. 23. 28. what is the *c.* to the
Zeph. 2. 2. before the day pass as
  the *c.*
Matt. 3. 12. burn up *c.* in unquench.
R. V. Isa. 5. 24. dry grass; Jer. 23.
  28. straw
CHAIN, Gen. 41. 42. Dan. 5. 7. Ezek.
  19. 4, 9. Mark 5. 3, 4.
Ps. 73. 6. pride compasseth them
  as a *c.*
S. of S. 4. 9. with one *c.* of thy neck
Acts 28. 20. I am bound with this *c.*
2 Tim. 1. 16. was not ashamed of
  my *c.*
Ps. 149. 8. bind their kings with
  chains
Prov. 1. 9. shall be a *c.* about neck
2 Pet. 2. 4. delivered into *c.* of dark.
Jude 6. reserved in everlasting *c.*
R. V. Num. 31. 50. ankle chains;
  S. of S. 1. 10. strings; Isa. 3. 19.
  pendants; Jer. 39. 7; 52. 11. fetters
  Ezek. 19. 4. hooks; Jude 6. bonds
CHALDEANS, Job. 1. 17. Isa. 43
  14. & 48. 20. Jer. 38. 2. & 39. 8. & 40
  9. & 50. 35. Ezek. 23. 14. Dan. 1. 4
  & 9. 1.
CHAMBER, Ps. 19. 5. Joel 2. 16.
Job 9. 9. maketh the *chambers* of
  the
Ps. 104. 3. beams of *c.* in the waters
Prov. 7. 27. going down to the *c.* of
S. of S. 1. 4. king brought me into
  his *c.*
Isa. 26. 20. enter into *c.* and shut thy
Matt. 24. 26. he is in the secret *c.*
Rom. 13. 13. not in *chambering* and
  wantonness
R. V. 1 Kings 6. 6. story; Ezek. 40.
  7. lodge
CHANCE, happens, 1 Sam. 6. 9.
  Eccl. 9. 11. 2 Sam. 1. 6. Luke 10. 31.
CHANGE of raiment, Judg. 14. 12,
  13. Zech. 3. 4. Isa. 3. 22.
Job 14. 14. patiently wait till my *c.*
  come
Heb. 7. 12. made of necessity a *c.*
  of law
Job 17. 12. they *c.* the night into
Ps. 102. 26. as a vesture shalt thou *c.*
Jer. 13. 23. can Ethiopian *c.* his skin
Mal. 3. 6. I am the Lord, I *c.* not
Phil. 3. 21. who shall *c.* our vile
1 Sam. 21. 13. *changed* his behavior
Ps. 102. 26. and they shall be *c.*
Jer. 2. 11. hath a nation *c.* their gods
Rom. 1. 23. *c.* the glory of God
1 Cor. 15. 51. shall all be *c.*, 52.
2 Cor. 3. 18. *c.* into the same image
Job 10. 17. *changes* and war are
  against
Ps. 55. 19. they have no *c.* therefore
15. 4. sweareth and *changeth* not
Dan. 2. 21. he *c.* the times and seas.
Mark 11. 15. *money changers*, Matt.
  21. 12. John 2. 14, 15.
R. V. Job 30. 18. disfigured
CHANT to sound of viol, Amos 6. 5.
CHAPEL, the king's, Amos 7. 13.
CHARGE, Gen. 26. 5. & 28. 6.
Ps. 91. 11. give his angels *c.* over
Acts 7. 60. lay not this sin to their *c.*
Rom. 8. 33. any thing to the *c.* of
S. of S. 2. 7. I *c.* you, O daughters
  of Jerusalem, 3. 5. & 5. 8. & 8. 4.

1 Tim. 6. 17.. *c.* them that are rich
Job 1. 22. nor *charged* God foolishly
1 Thes. 2. 11. *c.* every one as a father
2 Cor. 11. 5. *chargeable*, 1 Thes. 2. 9.
   2 Thes. 3. 8.
R. V. 1 Thes. 2. 9; 2 Thes. 3. 8.
   burden

CHARIOT, Gen. 41. 43. & 46. 29.
Ex. 14. 25. took off their *c.* wheels
2 Kings 2. 11. appeared a *c.* of fire
S. of S. 3. 9. Solomon made himself *c.*
Mic. l. 13. bind the *c.* to swift beasts
Acts 8. 29. join thyself to this *c.*
Ps. 20. 7. some trust in *chariots*
68. 17. *c.* of God are 20,000
S. of S. 6. 12. made me like the *c.*
Hab. 3. 8. ride upon thy *c.* of salva.
R. V. S. of S. 3. 9. palanquin; Isa.
   21. 7, 9. troop; 2 Sam. 8. 4 —

CHARITY edifieth, 1 Cor. 8. 1.
13. 1. if I have not *c.* I am nothing,
   2, 3.
4. *c.* suffereth long, 8. *c.* never fail.
13. now abideth faith, hope, *c.*
Col. 3. 14. above all things put on *c.*
1 Thes. 3. 6. tidings of your faith
   and *c.*
1 Tim. 1. 5. end of the commandment is *c.*
2. 15. if they continue in faith and *c.*
2 Tim. 2. 22. follow righteousness,
   faith, *c.*
2 Tim. 3. 10. know my doctrine,
   faith, *c.*
Tit. 2. 2. sound in faith, in *c.*, in
   patience
3 John 6. borne witness of thy *c.*
1 Pet. 4. 8. have fervent *c.* among
   yourselves
5. 14. greet one another with a
   kiss of *c.*
2 Pet. 1. 7. add to brotherly kindness, *c.*
Jude 12. spots in your feasts of *c.*
Rom. 14. 15. walketh not *charitably*

CHARMED, Jer. 8. 17.
Deut. 18. 11. *charmers*, Ps. 58. 5.
Isa. 19. 3.

CHASTE virgin, 2 Cor. 11. 2.
Tit. 2. 5. to be discreet, *c.*, good
1 Pet. 3. 2. your *c.* conversa., with
R. V. 2 Cor. 11. 2. pure

CHASTEN with rod of men, 2
   Sam. 7. 14.
Ps. 6. 1. neither *c.* me in thy, 38. 1.
Prov. 19. 18. *c.* thy son while there is
Dan. 10. 12. to *c.* thyself before thy
Rev. 3. 19. as many as I love, I *c.*
Ps. 69. 10. *chastened* my soul with
1 Cor. 11. 32. we are *c.* of the Lord
Heb. 12. 10. for a few days *c.* us
Ps. 94. 12. blessed is the man whom
   thou *chastenest*
Deut. 8. 5. as a man *c.* his son
Prov. 13. 24. loveth him *chasteneth*
   him betimes
Heb. 12. 6. whom Lord loveth he *c.*
Job 5. 17. despise not thou *chastening* of the Lord, Prov. 3. 11.
   Heb. 12. 5.
Isa. 26. 16. when thy *c.* was upon
   11. no *c.* for present is joyous
R. V. Dan. 10. 12. humble

CHASTISE you seven times, Lev.
   26. 28.
Deut. 22. 18. elders shall *c.* him
1 Kings 12. 11. I will *c.* with scorpions, 14.
Hos. 7. 12. *c.* them as their congre.
Luke 23. 16. *c.* and release him, 22.
1 Chron. 10. 11, 14. father *chastised*
   with whips
Ps. 94. 10. *c.* the heathen
Deut. 11. 2. not seen *chastisement*
   of the
Isa. 53. 5. *c.* of our peace was upon
Jer. 30. 14. with the *c.* of a cruel one
Heb. 12. 8. if ye be without *c.* then
R. V. Heb. 12. 8. chastening

CHATTER like a crane, Isa. 38. 14.

CHEEK, 1 Kings 22. 24. Job 16. 10.
Isa. 50. 6. Lam. 1. 30. Mic. 5. 1.
Matt. 5. 39. Luke 6. 29. Deut. 18. 3.

S. of S. 1. 10. thy *cheeks* are comely
5. 13. his *c.* are as a bed of spices
R. V. Joel 1. 6. jaw

CHEER be of good, Matt. 9. 2. & 14.
   27. Mark 6. 50. John 16. 33. Acts
   23. 11. & 27. 22, 25.
Prov. 15. 13. *cheerful*, Zech. 9. 17.
2 Cor. 9. 6. *cheerfulness*, Rom. 12. 8.
Acts 24. 10. *cheerfully* answer for
   my.
R. V. Zech. 9. 17. flourish

CHERISH, Eph. 5. 29. 1 Thes. 2. 7.
CHERUBIMS, between, 1 Sam.
   4. 4. 2 Sam. 6. 2. 2 Kings 19. 15.
1 Chron. 13. 6. Ps. 80. 1. & 99. 1. Isa.
   37. 16.
R. V. cherubim

CHICKENS, hen gathereth, Matt.
   23. 37.

CHIDE, not always, Ps. 103. 9.
R. V. Ex. 17. 2. strive, strove.

CHIEF, Ezra 9. 2. Neh. 11. 3.
Matt. 20. 27. that will be *c.* among
Luke 22. 26. that is *c.* as he that ser.
Eph. 2. 20. Jesus Christ himself
   being *c.*
1 Tim. 1. 15. sinners, — of whom I
   am *c.*
S. of S. 5. 10. *chiefest* among 10,000
Rom. 3. 2. *chiefly*, Phil. 4. 22. 2 Pet.
   2. 10.
R. V. In O. T. frequently, prince,
   head, captain; Matt. 20. 27. first;
   Luke 11. 15. prince; 14. 1. rulers;
   Acts 18. 8–17 —; Luke 19. 47;
   Acts 25. 2. principal men; Mark
   10. 44. first; Rom. 3. 2. first of all;
   Phil. 4. 22. especially

CHILD, Gen. 37. 30. 1 Cor. 13. 11.
Ex. 2. 2. saw he was a goodly *c.*
2 Sam. 12. 16. David besought God
   for the *c.*
Ps. 131. 2. quieted myself as a *c.*
   weaned
Prov. 29. 15. *c.* left to himself bring.
Eccl. 4. 8. hath neither *c.* nor
   brother
Isa. 3. 5. *c.* behave himself proudly
   9. 6. unto us a *c.* is born
11. 6. a little *c.* shall lead them
Jer. 1. 6. cannot speak for I am a *c.*
31. 20. dear son is he a pleasant *c.*
Hos. 11. 1. when Israel was a *c.* I
   loved
Matt. 18. 2. Jesus called a little *c.*
Mark 9. 36. took a *c.* and set him in
   10. 15. receive kingdom of God as
   little *c.*
2. 43. *c.* Jesus tarried behind in
   Jerusalem
Acts 4. 27. against thy holy *c.* Jesus
13. 10. thou *c.* of the devil, thou
1 Cor. 13. 11. when I was a *c.*
Gal. 4. 1. as long as a *c.* differs noth.
2 Tim. 3. 15. from a *c.* hast known
Rev. 12. 4. to devour her *c.* as soon
   5. her *c.* was caught up to God
1 Tim. 2. 15. to be saved in *childbearing*
Eccl. 11. 10. *childhood* and youth
   are
1 Cor. 13. 11. put away *childish*
   things
Gen. 15. 2. *childless*, Jer. 22. 30.
25. 22. *children* struggled together
30. 1. give me *c.* or else I die
Ps. 17. 14. they are full of *c.* and
Prov. 17. 6. the glory of *c.* are their
   fathers
S. of S. 1. 6. mother's *c.* were angry
Isa. 1. 2. I brought up *c.* and they
3. 12. *c.* are their oppressors
30. 9. lying *c.* — *c.* that will not hear
Mal. 4. 6. turn hearts of fathers to *c.*
Matt. 3. 9. of these stones to raise
   up *c.*
15. 26. not meet to take *c.*'s bread
16. 8. *c.* of this world wiser than *c.*
Acts 3. 25. ye are *c.* of the prophets
Rom. 8. 17. if *c.* then heirs, heirs of
1 Cor. 7. 14. else were your *c.* unclean
14. 20. be not *c.* in understanding
Eph. 2. 3. are by nature *c.* of wrath

Eph. 5. 6. cometh the wrath of God
   upon the *c.* of disobedience. Col.
   3. 6.
6. 1. *c.* obey your parents, Col.
   3. 20.
Heb. 12. 5. speaketh unto you as *c.*
1 Pet. 1. 14. as obedient *c.* not fashioning
Rev. 2. 23. kill her *c.* with death
Ex. 34. 7. *children's children*, Jer.
   2. 9. Ps. 103. 17. & 128. 6. Prov. 13. 22.
Prov. 17. 6. — are crown of old
   men
Matt. 5. 9. *children of God*, Luke
   20. 36. John 11. 52. Rom. 8. 21. &
   9. 8, 26. Gal. 3. 26. 1 John 3. 10. &
   5. 2.
Ps. 89. 30. *his children*, 103. 13.
Luke 16. 8. *children of light*, John
   12. 36. Eph. 5. 8. 1 Thes. 5. 5.
Matt. 18. 3. *little children*, 19. 14.
   Mark 10. 14. Luke 18. 16. John 13.
   33. Gal. 4. 19. 1 John 2. 1, 12, 13. &
   4. 4.
Rom. 9. 8. *children of promise*,
   Gal. 4. 28.
Ps. 128. 3, 6. *thy children*, 147. 13.
   Isa. 54. 13. Matt. 23. 37. Luke 13.
   34. 2 John 4.
Ps. 115. 14. *your children*, Matt. 7.
   11. Luke 11. 13. Acts 2. 39.
Job 19. 18. *young children*, Lam. 4.
   4. Nah. 3. 10. Mark 10. 13.
CHOKE, Matt. 13. 7, 22. Mark 4. 7,
   19. & 5. 13. Luke 8. 14, 33.
CHOOSE life, Deut. 30. 19.
Josh. 24. 15. *c.* you whom ye will
2 Sam. 24. 12. *c.* thee one of them
Ps. 25. 12. teach in the way that he
   shall *c.*
47. 4. *c.* our inheritance for us
Prov. 1. 29. did not *c.* the fear of
Isa. 7. 15. *c.* good and refuse evil,
   16.
Phil. 1. 22. what I shall *c.* I wot not
Ps. 65. 4. man whom thou *choosest*
Heb. 11. 25. *choosing* rather to suf.
Josh. 24. 22. ye have *chosen* the
   Lord
1 Chron. 16. 13. children of Jacob
   his *c.*
Ps. 33. 12. *c.* for his own inheritance
105. 6. children of Jacob his *c.*, 43.
Prov. 16. 16. rather to be *c.* than
22. 1. a good name is rather to be
   c. than
Isa. 66. 3. have *c.* their own ways
Jer. 8. 3. death shall be *c.* rather
Matt. 20. 16. many are called, but
   few *c.*, 22. 14.
Mark 13. 20. elect's sake whom he
   hath *c.*
Luke 10. 42. Mary hath *c.* that good
John 15. 16. ye have not *c.* me
Acts 9. 15. he is a *c.* vessel to me
22. 14. God hath *c.* thee that thou
1 Cor. 1. 27. God hath *c.* the foolish
Eph. 1. 4. hath *c.* us in him before
2 Thes. 2. 13. from beginning *c.* you
1 Pet. 2. 4. *c.* of God and precious
9. ye are a *c.* generation
Rev. 17. 14. are called, and *c.* and
Isa. 41. 9. *I have chosen*, 43. 10. &
   58. 6. Matt. 12. 18.
Ps. 119. 30. — the way of truth
   173. — thy precepts
Isa. 44. 1, 2. Israel — Jeshurun
   48. 10. — thee in the furnace of affli
John 13. 18. I know whom —
   15. 16, 19. — you out of the world
R. V. Acts 22. 14; 2 Cor. 8. 19. appointed

CHRIST should be born, Matt.
   2. 4.
16. 16. thou art *C.* son of the living
23. 8. one is your master even *C.*, 10.
Mark 9. 41. because ye belong to *C.*
Luke 24. 26. ought not *C.* to have
   suffered
46. it behooved *C.* to suffer and
John 4. 25. Messias which is call.
13. 34. that *C.* abideth for ever

Acts 8. 5. preached C. to them
Rom. 5. 6. C. died for the ungodly
8. while yet sinners C. died for us
10. if C. be in you the body is dead
10. 4. C. is the end of the law for
15. 3. C. pleased not himself
1 Cor. 1. 24. C. the power of God
3. 23. ye are C.'s and C. is God's
Gal. 2. 20. crucified with C. C. liveth
3. 13. C. hath redeemed us from
5. 24. that are C's have crucified
Eph. 2. 12. ye were without C. being alienated
4. 20. ye have not so learned C.
5. 14. C. shall give thee light
23. as C. is the head of the church
6. 5. in singleness of heart as
unto C.
Phil. 1. 21. to me to live is C.
23. I desire to dep., and be with
3. 8. that I may win C.
4. 13. can do all things through C.
Col. 1. 27. C. in you hope of glory
3. 4. when C. who is our life shall
Rom. 8. 1. to them in *Christ Jesus*
2. law of the spirit of life in —
1 Cor. 1. 30. of him are ye in —
2. 2. save — and him crucified
2 Cor. 13. 5. how that — is in you
Gal. 3. 28. ye are all one in —, 6.
Eph. 1. 1. saints and to faithful
in —
2. 10. created in — unto works, 1. 1.
Phil. 2. 11. confess that — is Lord
3. 3. rejoice in — and have no
confidence
12. for which I am apprehended
of —
Col. 2. 6. received — the Lord, 3.
24.
1 Tim. 1. 15. that — that came into
1 Tim. 2. 5. one mediator, the
man —
Heb. 13. 8. — the same yesterday
Rom. 12. 5. one body *in Christ*
16. 3, 7. were — before me, 10.
1 Cor. 15. 18. fallen asleep — are
perished
19. in this life only have hope —
2 Cor. 5. 17. if any man be — he is a
19. God was — reconciling world
Gal. 1. 22. churches which were —
Phil. 1. 13. my bonds — are manifest
2. 1. if there be any consolation —
Col. 1. 2. saints and faithful breth.
1 Thes. 4. 16. the dead — shall rise
John 1. 25. *that Christ,* 6. 69.
Matt. 16. 20. *the Christ,* 26. 63. Mark
8. 29. & 14. 61. Luke 3. 15. & 9. 20.
& 22. 67. John 1. 20, 41. & 3. 28. &
4. 29, 42. & 7. 41. & 10. 24. & 11. 27.
& 20. 31. 1 John 2. 22. & 5. 1.
Rom. 6. 8. if we be dead *with*
Christ
8. 17. heirs of God and joint
heirs —
Gal. 2. 20. I am crucified —
Eph. 2. 5. quickened us together —
Col. 2. 20. if ye be dead — from the
Rev. 20. 4. reigned — 1000 years
Acts 26. 28. persuadest me to be a
Christian
1 Pet. 4. 15. suffer as a C. let him
not be
Acts 11. 26. first called *Christians*
at Antioch
CHURCH, Acts 14. 27. & 15. 3. 1
Cor. 4. 17. & 14. 4, 23. 3 John 9.
Matt. 16. 18. on this rock will I
build my c.
18. 17. tell it to the c. neglect to
hear the c.
Acts 2. 47. Lord added to c. daily
8. 1. great persecution against c.
11. 26. assembled themselves
with c.
14. 23. ordained elders in every c.
1 Cor. 14. 4, 5. that c. may receive
edifying
Eph. 1. 22. head over all things
to c.
3. 10. known by c. the wisdom of

Eph. 5. 25. as Christ loved the c.
and gave
32. concerning Christ and the c.
4. 15. no c. communic. with me
Col. 1. 18. head of the body, the c.
1 Tim. 5. 16. let not c. be charged
Heb. 12. 23. assembly and c. of
first-born
3 John 6. witness of charity before c.
Acts 7. 38. *in the church,* 13. 1. 1 Cor.
6. 4. & 11. 18. & 12. 28. & 14. 19, 28,
35. Eph. 3. 21. Col. 4. 16.
Acts 20. 28. *the church of God,* 1 Cor.
1. 2. & 10. 32. & 15. 9. 2 Cor. 1. 1.
Gal. 1. 13. 1 Tim. 3. 5.
9. 31. then had *churches* rest
15. 41. confirming the c.
16. 5. so were the c. established
in
Rom. 16. 16. c. of Christ salute you
1 Cor. 7. 17. and so ordain I in all c.
14. 33. as in all c. of saints
34. women keep silence in the c.
1 Thes. 2. 14. became followers
of c.
2 Thes. 1. 4. glory in you in the c.
Rev. 1. 4. seven c. in Asia, 11.
20. angels of the seven c. and
2. 7. hear what the Spirit saith to
the c., 11, 17, 29. & 3. 6, 13, 22.
2. 23. and all the c. shall know I
22. 16. testify these things in the c.
CHURL, Isa. 32. 5, 7. *Churlish,*
1 Sam. 25. 3.
CIRCUIT, 1 Sam. 7. 16. Job 22. 14.
Ps. 19. 6. Eccl. 1. 6.
CIRCUMCISE the flesh, Gen. 17.
11.
Deut. 10. 16. c. the foreskin of your
Josh. 5. 2. c. again Israel
4. Joshua did c.
Jer. 4. 4. c. yourselves to the Lord
Gen. 17. 10. every male shall be
circumcised, 14. 23, 26. Phil. 3. 5.
21. 4. Abraham c. his son Isaac
Josh. 5. 3. c. the children of Israel
Acts 15. 1. except ye be c. ye cannot be
Acts 16. 3. c. him because of the
Gal. 2. 3. neither was compelled
to be c.
John 7. 22. Moses gave unto you
circumcision
Acts 7. 8. God gave him the cove-
nant of c.
Rom. 2. 25. c. profiteth if thou
29. c. is that of the heart in the
3. 1. what profit is there of c.
30. which shall justify c. by faith
4. 9. comes this blessedness on
the c. only
11. he received the sign of c.
15. 8. Christ was minister of the c.
1 Cor. 7. 19. c. is nothing but keep.
Gal. 2. 7. gospel of the c. was unto
Phil. 3. 3. we are the c. which
Col. 2. 11. circumcised with c.
Tit. 1. 10. especially they of the c.
CIRCUMSPECT, Ex. 23. 13.
Eph. 5. 15. that ye walk *circum-*
spectly
R. V. take ye heed
CISTERN, Prov. 5. 15. Eccl. 12. 6.
Jer. 2. 13. hewed them out *cisterns*
CITY, Cain builded a, Gen. 4. 17.
Ps. 107. 4. found no c. to dwell in
7. might go to c. of habitation
127. 1. except the Lord keep the c.
S. of S. 3. 2. I will go out about
the c. in
Isa. 1. 21. the faithful c. is become
33. 20. the c. of our solemnities
Jer. 3. 14. take one of a c. two of a
Amos 3. 6. shall there be evil in a c.
Zeph. 2. 15. this is the rejoicing c.
Zech. 8. 3. shall be called c. of truth
Matt. 5. 14. a c. set on a hill
Luke 10. 8. into whatsoever c. ye
19. 41. he beheld c. and wept over
Heb. 11. 10. he looked for a c.
12. 22. to the c. of the living God
Rev. 3. 12. name of the c. of my
Neh. 11. 1, 18, *holy city,* Isa. 48. 2.

Isa. 52. 1. Dan. 9. 24. Matt. 4. 5. & 27.
53. Rev. 11. 2. & 21. 2. & 22. 19.
Num. 35. 6. *cities of refuge,* Josh.
21. 13, 21, 27, 32, 38.
Amos 4. 8. two or three *cities* wan-
dered unto one city
Luke 19. 17. have thou authority
over ten c.
Acts 26. 11. persecuted unto
strange c.
Rev. 16. 19. the c. of the nations
Luke 15. 15. *citizen,* & 19. 14.
Eph. 2. 19. fellow *citizens* with
saints
CLAMOR, Eph. 4. 31. Prov. 9. 13.
CLAY, Job 27. 16. & 38. 14.
4. 19. them that dwell in houses
of c.
10. 9. thou hast made me as the c.
Isa. 64. 8. we are the c. thou our
potter, 45. 9. Jer. 18. 6.
Ps. 40. 2. brought me out of miry c.
Dan. 2. 33. part of iron, part of c.
Hab. 2. 6. that ladeth himself with
thick c.
CLEAN beasts, Gen. 7. 2. & 8. 20.
Lev. 10. 10. between unclean and
c., 11. 47. Ezek. 22. 26. & 44. 23.
Job 14. 4. who bring c. thing out
15. 14. what is man that he should
be c.
Ps. 19. 9. the fear of the Lord is c.
enduring for ever
Prov. 16. 2. ways of man are c. in
Isa. 1. 16. wash ye, make you c. put
Jer. 13. 27. wilt thou not be made c.
Ezek. 36. 25. sprinkle c. water, ye
shall be c.
Matt. 8. 3. I will, be thou c., Luke
5. 13.
23. 25. make c. outside of, Luke 11.
39.
Luke 11. 41. all things are c. to you
John 13. 11. ye are c. but not all
Rev. 19. 8. fine linen, c. and white
Job 17. 9. *clean hands,* Ps. 24. 4.
Ps. 51. 10. *clean heart,* 73. 1.
18. 24. according to the *cleanness*
Amos 4. 6. given you c. of teeth in
all cities
Ps. 19. 12. *cleanse* me from secret
119. 9. shall a young man c. his way
Jer. 33. 8. I will c. them fr. all sin
Ezek. 36. 25. from your idols will I
c. you
Matt. 10. 8. heal sick, c. the lepers
2 Cor. 7. 1. let us c. ourselves from
Eph. 5. 26. c. it with the washing of
Jas. 4. 8. c. your hands, ye sinners
1 John 1. 9. c. us from all unright.
2 Chron. 30. 19. though not *cleansed*
according
Ps. 73. 13. I have c. my heart in vain
Ezek. 36. 33. c. you from all iniqui.
Matt. 11. 5. the lepers are c.
Luke 17. 17. were there not ten c., 9.
Acts 10. 15. what God hath c., 11. 9.
1 John 1. 7. blood of Jesus Christ c.
R. V. Matt. 23. 25; Luke 11. 39.
cleanse; Neh. 13. 22. purify; Ps.
19. 12. clear
CLEAR the guilty, Ex. 34. 7.
Ps. 51. 4. be c. when thou judgest
Zech. 14. 6. light shall not be c. nor
R. V. Zech. 14. 6. with brightness;
2 Cor. 7. 11; Rev. 21. 18. pure; 22.
1. bright; Job 33. 3. sincerely
CLEAVE to his wife, Gen. 2. 24.
Matt. 19. 5. Mark 10. 7. Eph. 5. 31.
Deut. 4. 4. ye did c. to the Lord, 10.
20. & 11. 22. & 13. 4. & 30. 20. Josh.
22. 5. & 23. 8.
Ps. 22. 15. tongue *cleaveth* to my
119. 25. my soul c. unto the dust
137. 6. my tongue c. to the roof
Rom. 12. 9. c. to that which is good
CLIMB, Jer. 4. 29. Joel 2. 7, 9.
Amos 9. 2. though they c. up to
John 10. 1. *climbeth* some other way
CLOAK, Matt. 5. 40. Luke 6. 29.
Isa. 59. 17. clad with zeal as with c.
John 15. 22. have no c. for their sin
1 Thes. 2. 5. nor used c. of covetous.
1 Pet. 2. 16. liberty for c. of malic

CLOSET, Joel 2. 16.   Matt. 6. 6.
R. V. Luke 12. 3. inner chamber
CLOTHE, Matt. 6. 30.   Luke 12. 28.
Job 10. 11. *clothed* me with skin and
Ps. 35. 26. be *c.* with shame, 132. 18.
109. 18. he *c.* himself with cursing
132.16.*c.*her priests with salvation
Ezek. 16. 10. I *c.* thee with broid.
Zeph. 1. 8. *c.* with strange apparel
Matt. 11. 8. *c.* in soft raiment
25. 36. naked, and ye *c.* me
43. *c.* me not
2 Cor. 5. 2. desiring to be *c.* upon
1 Pet. 5. 5. be *c.* with humility
Rev. 3. 5. be *c.* with white raiment
11. 3. prophecy *c.* in sackcloth and
12. 1. a woman *c.* with the sun
19. 14. *c.* in fine linen, clean and
white
Job 22. 6. *clothing,* 24. 27.   Mark 12.
38. Acts 10. 30. Jas. 2. 3.
Ps. 45. 13. her *c.* is of wrought gold
Isa. 59. 17. garment of vengeance
for *c.*
Matt. 7. 15. come in sheep's *c.*
11. 8. that wear soft *c.* are in
CLOUD, Gen. 9. 13. Isa. 18. 4.
Isa. 44. 22. blotted out as a *c.* and
1 Cor.10.1.our fathers were under *c.*
2. baptized unto Moses in the *c.*
Heb. 12. 1. so great a *c.* of witness.
Rev. 11.12. ascended to heaven in *c.*
Hos. 6. 4. *morning cloud,* 13. 3.
Judg. 5. 4. *clouds* dropped water
2 Sam.23.4.as a morning without *c.*
Ps. 36. 5. faithfulness reacheth to *c.*
57. 10. thy truth unto the *c.,* 108. 4.
104. 3. who maketh *c.* his chariot
Matt. 24. 30. coming in the *c.* of
heaven, 26. 64. Mark 13. 26. & 14. 62.
1 Thes. 4. 17. caught up in *c.* to
meet
2 Pet. 2. 17. *c.* carried with a temp.
Jude 12. *c.* without water, carried
Rev. 1. 7. he cometh with *c.*
R. V. In Job and Ps. mostly skies
CLOVEN tongues, Acts 2. 3.
R. V. Acts 2. 3. parting asunder
COAL, 2 Sam. 14. 7. Isa. 47. 14. & 6.
6. Lam. 4. 8. Ps. 18. 8, 12. & 120. 4.
& 140. 10.
Prov. 6. 28. can one go on hot *coals*
25. 22. heap *c.* of fire on head,
Rom. 12. 20.
26. 21. as *c.* are to burning
S. of S. 8. 6. *c.* thereof are *c.* of fire
R. V. Prov. 26. 21. embers; S. of S.
8. 6. flashes; Hab. 3. 5. bolts
COAT, Gen. 3. 21. & 37. 3. Ex. 28. 4.
S. of S.5.3. put off my *c.* how put
Matt. 5. 40. if any man take away
thy *c.*
R. V. 1 Sam. 2. 19. robe; Dan. 3.
21, 27. hosen
COLD, Gen. 8. 22. Job 24. 7. & 37. 9.
Matt. 24. 12. the love of many wax *c.*
Rev. 3. 15. neither *c.* nor hot, 16.
R. V. Prov. 20. 4. winter
COLLECTION, 1 Cor. 16. 1.
R. V. 2 Chron. 24. 6, 9. tax.
COME not into my secret, Gen.49.6.
Ex. 20. 24. I will *c.* and bless thee
1 Sam. 17. 45. I *c.* to thee in name
1 Chron. 29. 14. all things *c.* of thee,
12.
Job 22. 21. good shall *c.* unto thee
Ps. 22. 31. they shall *c.* and shall
40. 7. lo I *c.,* Heb. 10. 9.
Eccl. 9. 2. all things *c.* alike to all
S. of S. 4. 16. awake north wind, *c.*
thou south
Isa. 26. 20. *c.* my people enter into
35. 4. God will *c.* and save you
Ezek. 33. 31. *c.* to thee as the people cometh
Mic. 6. 6. wherewith shall I *c.* before the Lord
Mal. 3. 1. Lord shall suddenly *c.* to
4. 6. lest I *c.* and smite the earth
Matt. 8. 11. many shall *c.* from the
east and west, Luke 7. 19, 20.
11. 28. *c.* unto me all ye that labor
16. 24. if any man will *c.* after me
Luke 7. 8. I say *c.* and he cometh

Luke 14. 20. **I have married a wife,**
I cannot *c.*
John 1. 39. *c.* and see, 46. & 4. 29.
Rev. 6. 1, 3, 5, 7. & 17. 1. & 21. 9.
John 5. 40. ye will not *c.* to me to
6. 44. no man can *c.* to me, except
7. 37. if any man thirst, let him *c.*
Acts 16. 9. *c.* over, and help us
1 Cor. 11. 26. show the Lord's death
till he *c.*
2 Cor. 6. 17. *c.* out from among them
7. 25. save them that *c.* to God by
10. 37. he that shall *c.* will *c.*
Rev. 18. 4. *c.* out of her, my people
22. 7. *c.* quickly, 12. 20.
17. Spirit and the bride say, *c.*
athirst *c.*
20. amen, even so *c.* Lord Jesus
Ps. 118. 26. that *cometh* in the name
Eccl. 11. 8. all that *c.* is vanity
Matt. 3. 11. he that *c.* after me, is
mightier
Luke 6. 47. whosoever *c.* to me and
John 3. 31. he that *c.* from above,
is above all
6.37.*c.*to me, I will in no wise cast
45. hath learned of Father, *c.* unto
me
14. 6. no man *c.* to Father, but
Heb. 11. 6. that *c.* to God must
Jas. 1. 17. gift *c.* down from Father
Heb. 10. 1. make the *comers* perfect
Ps. 19. 5. as a bridegroom *coming*
121. 8. Lord shall preserve thy *c.* in
Mal. 3. 2. who may abide the day of
his *c.*
4. 5. before the *c.* of the great day
Matt. 24. 3. what shall be sign of
thy *c.*
27. so shall the *c.* of Son of man
48. my Lord delayeth his *c.,* Luke
12. 45,
John 1. 27. *c.* after me is preferred
before
1 Cor. 1. 7. waiting for the *c.* of our
1 Cor. 15. 23. that are Christ's at
his *c.*
1 Pet. 2. 4. to whom *c.* as to a living
2 Pet. 1. 16. the power and *c.* of God
3. 12. hasting unto *c.* of day of God
1 Thes. 4. 15. *coming of the Lord,*
2 Thes. 2. 1. Jas. 5. 7, 8.
COMELY, 1 Sam. 16. 18. Job 41. 12.
Ps. 33. 1. praise is *c.* for the upright, 147. 1.
Prov. 30. 29. yea, four are *c.* in go.
S. of S. 1. 5. I am black but *c.*
10. thy cheeks are *c.* with rows
2. 14. thy countenance is *c.*
6. 4. thou art *c.* as Jerusalem
1 Cor. 7. 35. for that which is *c.*
Isa. 53. 2. no form nor *comeliness*
Ezek. 16. 14. perfect through my *c.*
R. V. Prov. 30. 29. stately; 1 Cor.
7. 35; 11. 13. seemly; Ezek. 16. 14.
majesty
COMFORT in my affliction, Ps.
119. 50.
Matt. 9. 22. be of good *c.,* Mark 10.
49. Luke 8. 48. 2 Cor. 13. 11.
Acts 9. 31. walking in *c.* of the
Rom. 15. 4. patience and *c.* of the
1 Cor. 14. 3. to exhortation and *c.*
2 Cor. 7. 4. I am filled with *c.*
Col. 4. 11. have been a *c.* to me
Job 7. 13. my bed shall *c.* me
Ps. 23. 4. thy rod and staff they *c.*
119. 82. when wilt thou *c.* me
S. of S. 2. 5. *c.* me with apples, for
Isa. 40. 1. *c.* ye *c.* my people
51. 3. Lord shall *c.* Zion, Zech. 1. 17.
61. 2. to *c.* all that mourn
Jer. 31. 13. I will *c.* and make them
Lam. 1. 2. none to *c.* her, 21.
2 Cor. 1. 4. be able to *c.* them — by *c.*
Eph. 6. 22. might *c.* your hearts
1 Thes. 4. 18. *c.* one another with
5.14. *c.*the feeble minded, support
2 Thes. 2. 17. *c.* your heart and
Isa. 40. 2. *comfortably,* Hos. 2. 14.
2 Sam. 19. 7. 2 Chron. 30. 22. & 32. 6.
Gen. 24. 67. *comforted,* 37. 35.
Ps. 77. 2. my soul refused to be *c.*
119. 52. I have *c.* myself

Isa. 49. 13. God hath *c.* his people
Matt. 5. 4. that mourn, they shall
be *c.*
Luke 16. 25. now is he *c.* and thou
Rom. 1. 12. I may be *c.* together
1 Cor. 14. 31. learn and all may be *c.*
2 Cor. 1. 4. wherewith we our-
selves are *c.*
Col. 2. 2. that their hearts might
be *c.*
1 Thes. 3. 7. were *c.* over you in all
John 14. 16, 26. *comforter,* 15. 26. &
16. 7.
Job 16. 2. *comforter,* Ps. 69. 20.
Isa. 51. 12. I am he that *comforteth*
2 Cor. 1. 4. *c.* us in all our tribula.
John 14. 18. *comfortless*
Ps. 94. 19. *comforts,* Isa. 57. 18.
R. V. Mal. 9. 22; Mark 10. 49. cheer;
1 Cor. 14. 3; Phil. 2. 1. consolation; 1 Thes. 2. 11. encouraging;
5. 11. exhort one another
COMMAND, Ex. 8. 27. & 18. 23.
Gen. 18. 19. he will *c.* his children
Lev. 25. 21. I will *c.* my blessing
Deut. 28. 8. Lord shall *c.* the bless.
Ps. 42. 8. Lord will *c.* his loving
kindness
44. 4. *c.* deliverance for Jacob
Isa. 45. 11. work of my hands, *c.* ye
Matt. 4. 3. *c.* that these stones be
John 15. 14. if ye do whatsoever I *c.*
1 Cor. 7. 10. unto the unmarried I *c.*
2 Thes. 3. 4. do things which we *c.*
1 Tim. 4. 11. these things *c.* and
Ps. 68. 28. God hath *commanded* thy
strength
111. 9. he hath *c.* his covenant
133. 3. *c.* blessing, even life for
Matt. 28. 20. whatsoever I have *c.*
you
Heb. 12. 20. could not endure that
was *c.*
Lam. 3. 37. when Lord *commandeth*
Acts 17. 30. now *c.* all men every.
Gen. 49. 33. end of *commanding* his
1 Tim. 4. 3. *c.* to abstain from meats
Num. 23. 20. receive *commandment*
to bless
Ps. 119. 96. thy *c.* is exceed. broad
Prov. 6. 23. the *c.* is a lamp
Hos. 5. 11. willingly walked after *c.*
Matt. 22. 38. is the first and great *c.*
John 10. 18. this *c.* I received of
12. 49. the Father gave me a *c.*
50. his *c.* is life everlasting
13. 34. a new *c.* give I unto you
15. 12. this is my *c.* that ye love
Rom. 7. 8. sin taking occasion by *c.*
1 Tim. 1. 5. end of the *c.* is charity
Heb. 7. 16. law of a carnal *c.*
2 Pet. 2. 21. turn from the holy *c.*
1 John 2. 7. an old *c.* which ye had
Ex. 34. 28. wrote ten *command-*
ments, Deut. 4. 13. & 10. 4.
Ps. 111. 7. all his *c.* are sure
112. 1. delight greatly in his *c.*
119. 6. I have respect unto all thy *c.*
19. let me not wander from thy *c.*
19. hide not thy *c.* from me
21. which do not err from thy *c.*
35. make me to go in path of thy *c.*
47. I will delight myself in thy *c.*
48. thy *c.* which I have loved
66. I have believed thy *c.*
86. all thy *c.* are faithful
98. thy *c.* hath made me wiser
127. I love thy *c.*
131. longed for *c.*
143. thy *c.* are my delights
151. all thy *c.* are truth
166. I have done thy *c.*
172. all thy *c.* are righteousness
176. I do not forget thy *c.*
Matt. 15. 9. for doctrines *c.* of men
Matt. 22. 40. on these two *c.* hang
all
Mark 10. 19. knowest the *c.,* Luke
18. 20.
Luke 1. 6. walking in all the *c.* of
Col. 2. 22. after the *c.* of men
1 John 3. 24. keepeth his *c.* dwelleth
2 John 6. love that walk after his *c.*
Num. 15. 40. *do all, — these, — my*

— *his c.,* Deut. 6. 25. & 15. 5. & 28.
1, 15. & 19. 9. & 27. 10. & 30. 8.
1 Chron. 28. 7. Neh. 10. 29. Ps. 103.
18, 20. & 111. 10. Rev. 22. 14.
R. V. very frequently, especially
in N. T., charged or enjoined.
Frequently, word, decree, precept, charge, statute.
COMMEND, Gen. 12. 15. Rom. 16.
1. 2 Cor. 3. 1. & 5. 12. & 10. 12.
Luke 23. 46. into thy hands I *c.*
Acts 20. 32. I *c.* you to God and to
14. 13. *commended* them to Lord
Luke 16. 8. Lord *c.* unjust steward
Rom. 5. 8. God *commendeth* his love
1 Cor. 8. 8. meat *c.* us not to God
2 Cor. 4. 2. *commending* ourselves
to every man's conscience
6. 4. *c.* ourselves as ministers of
2 Cor. 3. 1. epistles of *commendation*
Ezra 8. 36. *commission,* Acts 26. 12.
COMMIT adultery, thou shalt not,
Ex. 20. 14. Deut. 5. 18. Matt. 5. 27.
& 19. 18. Rom. 13. 9. Lev. 5. 17.
Luke 18. 20.
Gen. 39. 8. Lord *c.* or to *give in charge*
Job 5. 8. to God would I *c.* my cause
Ps. 31. 5. into thy hands I *c.* my
37. 5. *c.* thy way unto the Lord
Prov. 16. 3. *c.* thy works unto Lord
Luke 12. 48. *c.* things worthy of
John 2. 24. did not *c.* himself to
Rom. 1. 32. *c.* such things worthy
1 Tim. 1. 18. this charge I *c.* unto
Jer. 2. 13. *committed* two evils
Luke 12. 48. men have *c.* much
1 Tim. 1. 11. gospel *c.* to my trust,
1 Cor. 9. 17. 2 Cor. 5. 19. Tit. 1. 3.
Gal. 2. 7.
6. 20. keep that which is *c.* to thee
2 Tim. 1. 12. which I have *c.* to him
1 Pet. 2. 23. *c.* himself to him that
judgeth righteously
Jude 15. which they have un-
godly *c.*
Ps. 10. 14. poor *committeth* himself
John 8. 34. who *c.* sin is the servant
1 John 3. 8. who *c.* sin is of the devil
COMMON, Num. 16. 29. 1 Sam. 21.
4, 5. Eccl. 6. 1. Ezek. 23. 42.
Acts 2. 44. had all things *c.,* 4, 32.
1 Cor. 10. 13. temptation *c.* to man
Tit. 1. 4. son after the *c.* faith
Jude 3. write of the *c.* salvation
Eph. 2. 12. *commonwealth* of Israel
Matt. 28. 15. *commonly,* 1 Cor. 5. 1.
R. V. Eccl. 6. 1. heavy upon; Jer.
31. 5. enjoy the fruits thereof;
Acts 5. 18. public; 1 Cor. 10. 13.
can bear; Matt. 28. 15. was spread
abroad; 1 Cor. 5. 1. actually
COMMUNE with your own heart,
Ps. 4. 4. & 77. 6. Eccl. 1. 16.
R. V. Gen. 42. 24; 43. 19; Judg. 9.
1; 1 Sam. 25. 39. spake; Zech. 1.
14. talked
COMMUNICATE to him that
teacheth in all good things, Gal.
6. 6.
Phil. 4. 14. *c.* with my affliction
1 Tim. 6. 18. distribute, willing to *c.*
Heb. 13. 16. to *c.* forget not
Gal. 2. 2. *communicated* to them the
Phil. 4. 15. no church *c.* with me in
2 Kings 9. 11. *communication*
Matt. 5. 37. let your *c.* be yea, nay
Eph. 4. 29. let no corrupt *c.* proceed
Luke 24. 17. what manner of *c.* are
1 Cor. 15. 33. evil *c.* corrupt good
10. 16. *communion* of the blood of
Christ — *c.* of the body of Christ
2 Cor. 6. 14. what *c.* hath light
13. 14. *c.* of the Holy Ghost be with
R. V. Gal. 2. 2. laid before them;
Phil. 4. 14, 15. had fellowship;
2 Kings 9. 11. talk; Matt. 5. 37;
Eph. 4. 29. speech; Col. 3. 8. speak-
ing; Phile. 6. fellowship
COMPACT, Ps. 122. 3. Eph. 4. 16.
COMPANY, Gen. 32. 8, 21.
Ps. 55. 14. to the house of God in *c.*
Prov. 29. 3. keepeth *c.* with harlots
S. of S. 6. 13. as the *c.* of two armies
Acts 4. 23. went to their own *c.*

Rom. 15. 24. first filled with your *c.*
1 Cor. 5. 11. not to keep *c.* with
2 Thes. 3. 14. have no *c.* with him
Heb. 12. 22. innumerable *c.* of
angels
Ps. 119. 63. I am a *companion* of all
Mal. 2. 14. thy *c.* and wife of cove.
Phil. 2. 25. Epaphroditus my *c.* in
Rev. 1. 9. your *c.* in tribulation
Ps. 45. 14. *companions* that follow
122. 8. for my *c.* sakes — peace be
S. of S. 1. 7. aside by flocks of
thy *c.*
Isa. 1. 23. princes *c.* of thieves
Heb. 10. 33. became *c.* of them
R. V. Num. 14. 7; 16. 16; 22. 4.
congregation; Luke 5. 29; 23. 27.
multitude; Acts 17. 5. crowd;
Heb.12.22.hosts; Job 41.6.bands of
fishermen; 1 Chron. 27. 33. friend;
Phil. 2. 25. fellow-worker; Rev.
1. 9. partaker with you
COMPARE, Isa. 40. 18. & 46. 5.
Ps. 89. 6. who in heaven can be *c.* to
Prov. 3. 15. not to be *c.* to wisdom,
8. 11.
S. of S. 1. 9. I have *c.* my love to
company
Rom. 8. 18. not worthy to be *c.*
1 Cor. 2. 13. *c.* spiritual things with
Judg. 8. 2. *comparison,* Hag. 2. 3.
Mark 4. 30.
R. V. Mark 4. 30. set it forth
COMPASS, Ex. 27. 5. & 38. 4. 2 Sam.
5. 23. 2 Kings 3. 9. Prov. 8. 27.
Ps. 5. 12. with favor *c.* him about
Isa. 50. 11. *c.* yourselves with sparks
Jer. 31. 22. a woman shall *c.* a man
Hab. 1. 4. wicked doth *c.* about the
Matt. 23. 15. ye *c.* sea and land to
Ps. 16. 4. sorrow *compassed* me,
116. 3.
Jonah 2. 3. floods *c.* me about, 5.
Heb. 12. 1. we are *c.* about with a
Ps. 73. 6. pride *compasseth* them
Hos. 11. 12. Ephraim *c.* me about
R. V. Prov. 8. 27. circle; Isa. 44. 13.
compasses; 2 Kings 3. 9; Acts 28.
13. made circuit. Frequently in
O. T., turned about
COMPASSION, 1 Kings 8. 50.
2 Chron. 30. 9. 1 John 3. 17.
Matt. 9. 36. *moved with compassion,*
14. 14. & 18. 27.
Ps. 78. 38. *full of compassion,* 86. 15.
& 111. 4. & 112. 4. & 145. 8.
Deut. 13. 17. have *compassion,* 33. 3.
2 Kings 13. 23. 2 Chron. 36. 15. Jer.
12. 15. Lam. 3. 32. Mic. 7. 19. Rom.
9. 15. Heb. 5. 2. & 10. 34. Jude 22.
Lam. 3. 22. his *compassions* fail not
R. V. Matt. 18. 33; Mark 5. 19; Jude
22. mercy; Heb. 5. 2. bear gently
with
COMPEL them to come in, Luke
14. 23.
Esth. 1. 8. drinking, none did *c.*
2 Chron. 21. 11. *compelled* Judah
Acts 26. 11. I *c.* them to blaspheme
2 Cor. 12. 11. I am a fool, ye *c.* me
Gal. 2. 3. not *c.* to be circumcised
14. why *compellest* Gentiles to live
R. V. 1 Sam. 28. 23; Luke 14. 23.
constrain
COMPLAIN, Num. 11. 11. Job 7.
11.
Lam.3. 39.why doth a living man *c.*
Num. 11. 1. *complainers* Jude 16.
Ps. 144. 14. *complaining* in streets
Job 21. 4. *complaint* 23. 2. Ps. 142. 2.
R. V. Acts 25. 7. bringing charges
COMPLETE in him, Col. 2. 10.
4. 12. stand *c.* in all the will of
God
R. V. Col. 2. 10. made full; 4. 12.
fully assured
COMPREHEND, Job 37. 5. Eph.
3. 18. Isa. 40. 12. John 1. 4. Rom.
13. 9.
R. V. John 1. 5; Eph. 3. 18. appre-
hend; Rom. 3. 9. summed up
CONCEAL his blood, Gen. 37. 26.
Job 27. 11. with Almighty I will
not *c.*

Job 41. 12. I will not *c.* parts nor
proportion
Prov. 25. 2. glory of God to *c.* a
thing
Ps. 40. 10. I have not *concealed* thy
loving kindness
Prov. 12. 23. prudent man *conceal-
eth* knowledge
R. V. Job 6. 10. denied; 4. 12. keep
silence concerning
CONCEIT, own, Prov. 18. 11. & 26.
5, 12, 16. & 28. 11. Rom. 11. 25. & 12.
16.
R. V. Prov. 18. 11. imagination
CONCEIVE, Judg. 13. 3. Luke 1. 31.
Job 15. 35. they *c.* mischief, Isa.
59. 4.
Ps. 51. 6. in sin did my mother *c.*
Isa. 7. 14. a virgin shall *c.* a son
Num. 11. 12. have I *conceived* all
this people
Ps. 7. 14. hath *c.* mischief — false-
hood
Jer. 49. 30. *c.* a purpose against you
Acts 5. 4. why hast thou *c.* in thy
heart
CONCISION, Phil. 3. 2.
CONCLUDED them all in unbe-
lief, Rom. 11. 32.
Gal. 3. 22. Scripture *c.* all under sin
Eccl. 12. 13. *conclusion* of matter
R. V. Rom. 11. 32. shut up; Acts
21. 25. given judgment
CONCUPISCENCE, sinful lust.
Rom. 7. 8. Col. 3. 5. 1 Thes. 4. 5.
R. V. Rom. 7. 8. coveting; Col. 3.
5. desire; 1 Thes. 4. 5. lust
CONDEMN wicked, Deut. 25. 1.
Job 9. 20. my own mouth shall *c.*
Ps. 37. 33. nor *c.* him when he is
judged
94. 21. they *c.* innocent blood
Isa. 50. 9. Lord will help me who
c. me
Luke 6. 37. *c.* not and ye shall not
be *c.*
John 3. 17.God sent not his Son
into the world to *c.* the world
1 John 3. 20. heart *c.* us, 21.
Matt. 12. 37. by words—*condemned*
John 3. 18. who believe is not *c.*
Rom. 8. 3. for sin *c.* sin in the flesh
1 Cor. 11. 32. not be *c.* with world
Tit. 2. 8. speech that cannot be *c.*
Prov. 17. 15. *condemneth* the just
Rom. 8. 34. who is he that *c.*
Luke 23. 40. same *condemnation*
John 3. 19. this is the *c.* that light
Rom. 8. 1. no *c.* to them in Christ
1 Tim. 3. 6. fall into *c.* of the devil
Jas. 3. 1. receive the greater *c.*
5. 12. swear not, lest ye fall into *c.*
R. V. Ps. 109. 31; John 3. 17. judge;
John 3. 19; 5. 24; 1 Cor. 11. 34; Jas.
5. 12. judgment
CONDESCEND, Rom. 12. 16. to
low
CONFESS, Lev. 5. 5. & 16. 21.
Lev. 26. 40. if they *c.* their iniquit.
Ps. 32. 5. I will *c.* my transgres.
Matt. 10. 32. shall *c.* me before men
Luke 12. 8. him will I *c.* before my
Rom. 10. 9. *c.* with thy mouth
Jas. 5. 16. *c.* your faults one to
1 John 1. 9. if we *c.* our sins, he is
faithful
4. 15. *c.* Jesus is Son of God, 2. 3.
2 John 7.
Heb. 11. 13. *confessed,* Ezra 10. 1.
Prov. 28. 13. *confesseth* and forsak.
Josh. 7. 19. *confession,* 2 Chron. 30.
22. Ezra 10. 11. Dan. 9. 4.
1 Tim. 6. 13. witnessed a good *c.*
CONFIDENCE, Job 4. 6. & 31. 24.
Ps. 65. 5. *c.* of all the ends of the
earth
118. 8. than to put *c.* in man
Prov. 3. 26. Lord shall be thy *c.*
Mic. 7. 5. put not *c.* in a guide,
Phil. 3. 3. have no *c.* in the flesh
Heb. 3. 6. if we hold fast the *c.,* 14.
10. 35. cast not away your *c.*
1 John 2. 28. appear we may have *c.*
Ps. 27. 2. *confident,* Prov. 14. 16.

R. V. Judg. 9. 26. trust; Acts 28.
31; Heb. 3. 6; 10. 35; 1 John 2. 28;
3. 21. boldness; 2 Cor. 5. 6, 8. of
good courage
CONFIRM feeble knees, Isa. 35. 3.
Dan. 9. 27. shall c. the covenant
Rom. 15. 8. to c. the promises
1 Cor. 1. 8. shall c. you to the end
Isa. 44. 26. confirmeth word of his
servant
Acts 14. 22. confirming souls of the
R. V. 2 Kings 14. 5; 1 Chron. 14. 2. es-
tablished; Dan. 9. 27. made firm;
Heb. 6. 17. interposed with
CONFLICT, Phil. 1. 30. Col. 2. 1.
CONFORMED to the image, Rom.
8. 29.
Rom. 12. 2. be not c. to this world
R. V. Rom. 12. 2. fashioned ac-
cording
CONFOUND language, Gen. 11. 7.
Jer. 1. 17. lest I c. thee before them
1 Cor. 1. 27. foolish things to c. wise
Ps. 97. 7. confounded that serve
Jer. 17. 18. let not me be c.
Ezek. 16. 52. c. and bear shame, 54.
1 Pet. 2. 6. believeth shall not be c.
Ezra 9. 7. confusion of face, Dan.
9. 7, 8.
Ps. 44. 15. my c. is continually
1 Cor. 14. 33. God is not author of c.
R. V. Jer. 1. 17. dismay; 1 Cor. 1.
27. that he might put to shame;
Ps. 66. 6. brought to dishonor; 83.
17; Ezek. 16. 54; Mic. 7. 16.
ashamed; Jer. 10. 14; 46. 24; 50. 2.
put to shame
CONGREGATION, Lev. 4. 21.
Job 15. 34. c. of hypocrites desolate
Ps. 1. 5. sinners in c. of righteous
26. 5. hated c. of evil doers
74. 19. forget not c. of thy poor
89. 5. faithfulness in c. of saints
Prov. 21. 16. remain in c. of dead
Hos. 7. 12. chastise as c. hath heard
Joel 2. 16. sanctify the c.
R. V. in O. T. generally, assembly,
meeting; cts 13. 43. synagogue
CONIES, Ps. 104. 18. Prov. 30. 26.
CONQUER, Rev. 6. 2.
Rom. 8. 37. more than conquerors
CONSCIENCE, John 8. 9. Acts
23. 1.
Acts 24. 16. a c. void of offence
Rom. 2. 15. c. bearing witness, 9. 1.
2 Cor. 1. 12. estimony of our c.
1 Tim. 3. 9. mystery of faith in
Tit. 1. 15. mind and c. is defiled
Heb. 9. 14. purge c. from dead
10. 2. worshippers no more c. of
Acts 23. 1. good conscience, 1 Tim.
1. 5. Heb. 13. 18. 1 Pet. 3. 21.
R. V. John 8. 9 —
CONSENT, with one, Ps. 83. 5.
Zeph. 3. 9. Luke 14. 18. 1 Cor. 7. 5.
Prov. 1. 10. entice thee, c. thou not
Rom. 7. 16. I c. to law that it is
Ps. 50. 18. consentedst to thief
Acts 8. 1. consenting, 22. 20.
R. V. 1 Sam. 11. 7. as one man;
Dan. 1. 14. hearkened unto
CONSIDER, Lev. 13. 13. Judg. 18.
14.
Deut. 4. 39. c. it in thy heart
32. 29. O that—c. their latter end
Ps. 8. 3. when I c. the heavens
Eccl. 5. 1. c. not that they do evil
7. 13. c. the work of God
Isa. 1. 3. my people doth not c.
5. 12. neither c. operation of hands
Hag. 1. 5, 7. Lord c. your ways, 2.
15, 18.
2 Tim. 2. 7. c. what I say and Lord
Heb. 3. 1. c. apostle and high priest
10. 24. c. one another to provoke
12. 3. c. him that endured such
Job 1. 8. hast thou considered my
Ps. 31. 7. hast c. my trouble
Mark 6. 52. c. not miracle of loaves
Rom. 4. 19. c. not his own body
Matt. 7. 3. considerest not the beam
Ps. 41. 1. blessed considereth poor
Prov. 31. 16. she c. a field and buy.
Isa. 44. 19. none c. in his heart

Heb. 13. 7. considering end of con-
versation
R. V. Jer. 23. 20; 32. 24. under-
stand; Lam. 1. 11; 2. 20; 5. 1. be-
hold; Mark 6. 52. understood
CONSIST. Col. 1. 17. Luke 12. 15.
CONSOLATION, Acts 4.36.&15.31.
Luke 2. 25. waited for c. of Israel
Rom. 15. 5. God of c. grant you be
2 Cor. 1. 5. so our c. aboundeth by
Phil. 2. 1. if any c. in Christ
2 Thes. 2. 16. given us everlasting c.
Heb. 6. 18. might have strong c.
Job 15. 11. consolations
R. V. Acts 4. 36. exhortation; Rom.
15. 5; 2 Cor. 1. 5; 7. 7; 2 Thes. 2.
16; Phile. 7. comfort; Heb. 6. 18.
encouragement
CONSPIRACY against Christ,
Matt. 26. 3; Mark 3. 6; 14. 1; Luke
22. 2; John 11. 55; 13. 18.
against Paul, Acts 23. 12.
CONSTANCY of Ruth, Ruth 1. 14.
Rom. 16. 3. of Priscilla and Aquila
CONSTRAIN, Gal. 6. 12. Acts 16.
15.
2 Cor. 5. 14. for the love of Christ
constraineth us because we
1 Pet. 5. 2. not by constraint
R. V. Gal. 6. 12. compel
CONSUME, Deut. 5. 25. & 7. 16.
Ex. 33. 3. lest I c. thee in the way
Ps. 37. 20. they shall c. into smoke
78. 33. days did he c. in vanity
Ezek. 4. 17. c. away for iniquity
2 Thes. 2. 8. Lord shall c. with spirit
Jas. 4. 3. c. it upon your lusts
Ex. 3. 2. bush was not consumed
Ps. 90. 7. we are c. by thy anger
Prov. 5. 11. thy flesh and body
are c.
Isa. 64. 7. c. us because of our
Lam. 3. 22. of Lord's mercy we are
not c.
Gal. 5. 15. be not c. one of another
Deut. 4. 24. Lord is consuming fire
Lev. 26. 16. consumption, Deut. 28.
22. Isa. 10. 22, 23. & 28. 22.
R. V. Frequently in O. T. devour;
2 Thes. 2. 8. Jesus shall slay
CONTAIN, Ezek. 23. 32. & 45. 11.
1 Kings 8. 27. heaven of heavens
cannot c. thee, 2 Chron. 2. 6. & 6.
18.
John 21. 25. world not c. the books
1 Cor. 7. 9. if they cannot c. let
R. V. 1 Cor. 7. 9. have not conti-
nency
CONTEMN, God, — wicked, Ps.
10. 13.
Ezek. 21. 13. if sword c. the rod, 10.
Ps. 15. 4. a vile person is contemned
Job 12. 21. pours contempt on prin.
Ps. 123. 3. filled with c., 4.
Dan. 12. 2. some to everlasting c.
Mal. 1. 7. the table of the Lord is
contemptible
2. 9. made you c. before all people
2 Cor. 10. 10. his speech is c.
R. V. Ps. 15. 4. despised
CONTEND, Deut. 2. 9. Job 9. 3.
Isa. 49. 25. I will c. with them that c.
Jer. 12. 5. how canst c. with horses
Amos 7. 4. Lord calleth to c. by fire
Jude 3. c. earnestly for the faith
Job 10. 2. cause why thou contendest
40. 2. that contendeth with the
mighty instruct
Hab. 1. 3. contention, Acts 15. 39. 1.
16. 1 Thes. 2. 2.
Prov. 13. 10. by pride cometh c.
Jer. 15. 10. borne me a man of c.
Prov. 18. 18, 19. contentions, 19. 13.
& 23. 29. & 27. 15. 1 Cor. 1. 11. Tit.
3. 9.
21. 19. contentious, 26. 21. & 27. 15.
Rom. 2. 8. 1 Cor. 11. 16.
R. V. Prov. 29. 9. hath controversy
CONTENT, Gen. 37. 27. Luke 3. 14.
Phil. 4. 11. state therewith to be c.
1 Tim. 6. 8. raiment let us be c.
Heb. 13. 5. be c. with such things
3 John 10. with malicious words
not c.

1 Tim. 6. 6. godliness with content-
ment
CONTINUAL, Ex. 29. 42. Num. 4.
7. Prov. 15. 15. Isa. 14. 6. Rom. 9. 2.
Gen. 6. 5. only evil continually
Ps. 34. 1. his praise c. in my
71. 3. 1 may c. resort
73. 23. yet I am c. with thee
119. 44. keep thy law c. for ever
Prov. 6. 21. bind them c. upon thy
Isa. 58. 11. Lord shall guide thee c.
Hos. 12. 6. wait on thy God c.
Acts 6. 4. give ourselves c. to prayer
Heb. 13. 15. sacrifice of praise to
God c.
Deut. 28. 59. continuance, Ps. 139.
16. Isa. 64. 5. Rom. 2. 7.
R. V. Rom.9.2.unceasing; 1 Chron.
16. 11. evermore; Ps. 44. 15. all day
long; 58. 7. apace; 109. 10—; Ps.
139. 16. day by day; Isa. 64. 5. them
have we been of long time; Rom.
2. 7. patience
CONTINUE, Ex. 21. 21. Lev. 12. 4.
1 Sam. 12. 14. c. following the Lord
1 Kings 2. 4. Lord may c. his word
Ps. 36. 10. c. thy loving-kindness
John 8. 31. if ye c. in my word
15. 9. c. ye in my love, 10.
Acts 13. 43. to c. in grace of God
14. 22. to c. in the faith
Rom. 6. 1. shall we c. in sin that
11. 22. if thou c. in his goodness
Col. 1. 23. if ye c. in faith and not
4. 2. c. in prayer and watch
1 Tim. 2. 15. if they c. in faith
4. 16. doctrine c. in them
2 Tim. 3. 14. c. in things learned
Heb. 13. 1. let brotherly love c.
Rev. 13. 5. to c. forty-two months
Gen. 40. 4. continued, Neh. 5. 16.
Luke 6. 12. c. all night in prayer
22. 28. c. with me in temptations
Acts 1. 14. c. with one accord in
Heb. 8. 9. c. not in my covenant
1 John 2. 19. would have c. with
us
Job 14. 2. shadow and continueth
not
Gal. 3. 10. that c. not in all things
1 Tim. 5. 5. c. in supplication
Jas. 1. 25. looketh into the law
and c.
Jer. 30. 22. continuing, Rom. 12. 12.
Acts 2. 46. Heb. 13. 14.
R. V. John 2. 12; 8. 31; 15. 9. abide,
abode; Acts 15. 35. tarried; 18. 11.
dwelt; 20. 7. prolonged; in O. T.
frequent changes to; abide
CONTRADICT-ING-ION, Acts
13. 45. Heb. 7. 7. & 12. 3.
R. V. Heb. 7. 7. any dispute; 12. 3.
gainsaying
CONTRARY, Esth. 9. 1. Matt. 14.
24.
Lev.26. 21. walk c. to, 23. 27,28,40,41.
Acts 18. 13. c. to the law, 23. 3.
26. 9. many things c. to the name
Rom. 11. 24. grafted c. to nature
1 Thes. 2. 15. are c. to all men
1 Tim. 1. 10. is c. to sound doctrine
CONTRIBUTION, Rom. 15. 26.
CONTRITE heart, or spirit, Ps.
34. 18. & 51. 17. Isa. 57. 15, 16. & 66. 2.
CONTROVERSY, Deut. 17. 8. &
21. 5. & 25. 1. 2 Chron. 19. 8. Ezek.
44. 24.
Jer. 25. 31. Lord hath a c., Isa. 34. 8.
Hos. 4. 1. & 12. 2. Mic. 6. 2.
1 Tim. 3. 16. without c. great is the
R. V. 2 Sam. 15. 2. suit
CONVENIENT, Jer. 40. 4, 5. Acts
24. 25.
Prov. 30. 8. feed with food c. for me
Rom. 1. 28. to do things — not c.
Phile. 8. to enjoin thee which
is c.
R. V. Prov. 30. 8. that is needful;
Rom. 1. 28. fitting; Eph. 5. 4;
Phile. 8. befitting; 1 Cor. 16. 12.
opportunity
CONVERSATION, Gal. 1. 13.
Eph. 2. 3. & 4. 22. Heb. 13. 7.
1 Tim. 4. 12.

Ps. 37. 14. such as be of upright c.
50. 23. orders his c. aright, I will
2 Cor. 1. 12. in sincerity had our c.
Phil. 1. 27. let c. be as becometh
Heb. 13. 5. let c. be without covetousness
Jas. 3. 13. show out of good c. works
1 Pet. 1. 15. holy in all manner of c.
2 Pet. 2. 7. vexed with filthy c. of the
3. 11. in all holy c. and godliness
R. V. Ps. 37. 14. in the way; Gal. 1. 13; Phil. 1. 27; 1 Tim. 4. 12; 1 Pet. 3. 16. manner of life; 1 Pet. 2. 12; 3. 1. behavior; Heb. 13. 7; 2 Pet. 2. 7. life; 2 Pet. 3. 11. living
CONVERSION of Gentiles, Acts 15. 3.
CONVERT, and be healed, Isa. 6. 10.
Jas. 5. 19. err, and one c. him, 20.
Ps. 51. 13. sinners — *converted* to thee
Isa. 60. 5. abundance of the sea, c. to thee
Matt. 13. 15. should be c. and I heal
Luke 22. 32. when thou art c. strengthen
Acts 3. 19. repent and be c.
Ps. 19. 7. *converting* the soul
R. V. Ps. 19. 7. restoring; Isa. 60. 5. turned; Matt. 13. 15; 18. 3; Mark 4. 12; Luke 22. 32; John 12. 40; Acts 3. 19; 28. 27. turn, or turn again
CONVINCE, Tit. 1. 9. Jude 15.
Job 32. 12. *convinced*, Acts 18. 28.
1 Cor. 14. 24. Jas. 2. 9.
John 8. 46. who *convinceth* me of sin
R. V. 1 Cor. 14. 24. reproved by; Acts 18. 28. comforted; John 8. 46; Tit. 1. 9; Jas. 2. 9; Jude 15. convict
COPY of the law to be written by the king, Deut. 17. 18.
CORD, Josh. 2. 15. Mic. 2. 5.
Job 30. 11. he hath loosed my c.
Eccl. 4. 12. a threefold c. is not brok.
Isa. 54. 2. lengthen thy c. and strengthen
Job 36. 8. holden in *cords* of affliction
Ps. 2. 3. cast away their c. from us
Prov. 5. 22. holden with c. of his sins
Isa. 5. 18. draw iniquity with c. of vanity
Hos. 11. 4. drew them with c. of
R. V. Judg. 15. 13. ropes; Mic. 2. 5. the line
CORN, Gen. 41. 57. & 42. 2, 19.
Josh. 5. 11. eat of the old c. of the land, 12.
Job 5. 26. as a shock of c. cometh in
Ps. 65. 13. valleys covered with c.
72. 16. handful of c. in the earth
Prov. 11. 26. withholdeth c. people curse
Isa 62. 8. I will no more give c. to
Ezek. 36. 29. call for c. and increase
Hos. 2. 9. take away my c. in
10. 11. loveth to tread out the c.
14. 7. shall revive as c. and grow as
Zech. 9. 17. c. make young men cheer.
Matt. 12. 1. to pluck the ears of c.
John 12. 24. except c. of wheat fall
R. V. Matt. 12. 1. cornfield; John 12. 24. grain
CORNER, Prov. 7. 8, 12. Lev. 21. 5.
Prov. 21. 9. better dwell in c., 25. 24.
Isa. 30. 20. teachers removed into c.
Zech. 10. 4. out of him came forth c.
Matt. 21. 42. become head of c.
Ps. 118. 22. *corner stone*, Isa. 28. 16.
1 Pet. 2. 6. Eph. 2. 20. Matt. 21. 42.
R. V. Ex. 25. 12; 37. 3; 1 Kings 7. 30. feet; Ex. 30. 4; 37. 27. ribs; Ex. 36. 25; 2 Kings 11. 11. side; Zech. 10. 4. corner stone
CORRECT thy son and he, Prov. 29. 17.
Ps. 39. 11. with rebuke dost c. man
Jer. 2. 19. own wicked. shall c. thee

Job 5. 17. happy is man whom God c.
Prov. 3. 12. whom Lord loveth he c.
Job 37. 13. whether for *correction*
Prov. 3. 11. but be not weary of his c.
23. 13. withhold not c. from child
Jer. 2. 30. they received not c., 5. 3. & 7. 28. Zeph. 3. 2.
Hab. 1. 12. established them for c.
2 Tim. 3. 16. Scripture profitable for c.
R. V. Prov. 3. 12. reproveth; Heb. 12. 9. to chasten; Prov. 3. 11. reproof; Jer. 7. 28. instruction
CORRUPT, Job 17. 1. Ps. 38. 5.
Gen. 6. 11, 12. earth c. before God.
Ps. 14. 1. they are c., 53. 1. & 73. 8.
Mal. 1. 14. sacrificeth to the Lord a c.
Matt. 7. 17, 18. a c. tree brings —
Eph. 4. 22. old man which is c.
29. let no c. communication
1 Tim. 6. 5. c. minds, 2 Tim. 3. 8.
Matt. 6. 19. rust doth c., 20.
1 Cor. 15. 33. evil communications c.
Gen. 6. 12. all flesh had *corrupted* his
Deut. 9. 12. thy people c. themsel.
Hos. 9. 9. have deeply c. themselves
2 Cor. 7. 2. we have c. no man
1 Cor. 9. 25. *corruptible*, 15. 53. 1 Pet. 1. 18, 23.
Job 17. 14. *corruption*, Ps. 16. 10. & 49. 9. Isa. 38. 17. Dan. 10. 8. John 2. 6. Acts 2. 27, 31. & 13. 34, 37. Rom. 8. 21. 1 Cor. 15. 42, 50. Gal. 6. 8. 2 Pet. 1. 4. & 2. 12, 19.
R. V. Job 17. 4. consumed; Ps. 73. 8. scoff; Dan. 11. 32. pervert; Mal. 1. 14. blemished; Matt. 6. 19. consume; Jude 10. destroyed; Jonah 2. 6. pit; 2 Pet. 2. 12. destroying
COST, 2 Sam. 19. 42. & 24. 24. 1 Chron. 21. 24. Luke 14. 28.
R. V. John 12. 3. precious
COUNSEL, Num. 27. 21. & 31. 16.
Job 5. 13. c. of froward carried headlong
12. 13. he hath c. and understanding
21. 16. c. of the wicked far, 22. 18.
38. 2. who is this that darkeneth c. by words without knowledge, 42. 3.
Ps. 1. 1. walks not in c. of ungodly
33. 10, 11. c. of Lord stands for ever, Prov. 1 . 21. Isa. 46. 10, 11.
55. 14. we took sweet c. together
Prov. 1. 25. set at nought all my c.
8. 14. c. is mine and sound wisdom
11. 14. where no c. is people fall
20. 18. purpose established by c.
24. 6. by wise c. make war
27. 9. sweetness — by hearty c.
Isa. 11. 2. spirit of c. and might
28. 29. Lord wonderful in c. and
Jer. 32. 19. God great in c. mighty
Zech. 6. 13. c. of peace between them
Luke 7. 30. rejected c. of God against
Acts 2. 23. by determinate c., 4. 28.
20. 27. to declare all the c. of God
Eph. 1. 11. after c. of his own will
Ezra 4. 5. *counsellors*, 7. 14. Job 3. 14. & 12. 17. Dan. 3. 24.
Ps. 119. 24. thy testimonies are my c.
Prov. 11. 14. in the multitude of c. is safety, 24. 26. & 15. 22.
12. 20. to c. of peace is joy
Isa. 9. 6. Wonderful, C., the mighty
19. 11. wise c. of Pharaoh — brutish
R. V. Num. 27. 21; Prov. 11. 14; 24. 6. guidance; Isa. 19. 17. purpose; Acts 5. 33. were minded
COUNT, Ex. 12. 4. Lev. 23. 15.
Num. 23. 10. who can c. the dust of
Job 31. 4. doth not he c. all my steps
Ps. 139. 18. if I c. them — more than
22. hate thee, I c. them my ene.
Acts 20. 24. neither c. I my life dear
Phil. 3. 7, 8, 9. I c. all things loss — dung
13. I c. not myself to have apprehended

Jas. 1. 2. c. it all joy when ye fall
5. 11. we c. them happy who endure
Gen. 15. 6. *counted* to him for righteousness, Ps. 106. 31. Rom. 4. 3.
Isa. 40. 17. c. to him less than nothing
Hos. 8. 12. of law c. as a strange thing
Luke 21. 36. c. worthy to escape
Acts 5. 41. that c. worthy to suffer
2 Thes. 1. 5. c. worthy of kingdom
1 Tim. 1. 12. he c. me faithful
5. 17. c. worthy of double honor
Heb. 3. 3. c. worthy of more glory
R. V. Mark 11. 32. verily held; Rom. 2. 26; 4. 3, 5; 9. 8. reckoned
COUNTENANCE, Gen. 4. 5. & 31. 2.
Num. 6. 26. lift up his c. on thee
1 Sam. 1. 18. her c. was no more sad
16. 7. look not on his c. nor height
Neh. 2. 2. why is thy c. sad
Job 29. 24. light of thy c. they cast
Ps. 4. 6. lift up light of thy c., 80. 3, 7.
90. 8. settest secret sins in light of c.
S. of S. 2. 14. let me see thy c. comely
Matt. 6. 16. as hypocrites of a sad c.
Acts 2. 28. full of joy with thy c.
R. V. Ex. 23. 3. favor; Ps. 11. 7; 2 Cor. 3. 7. face; Ps. 21. 6. presence; S. of S. 5. 15. aspect; Matt. 28. 3. appearance
COUNTRY, far, Matt. 21. 33. & 25. 14. Mark 12. 1. Luke 15. 13. & 19. 12. & 20. 9. Prov. 25. 25.
Heb. 11. 14. declare they seek a c.
16. they desire a better c. — heavenly
2 Cor. 11. 26. *countrymen*, 1 Thes. 2. 14.
R. V. Matt. 9. 31; Acts 7. 3. land, Matt. 14. 35; Luke 3. 3; 4. 37. region; in O. T. mostly land, region, inheritance
COURAGE, Josh. 2. 11. Acts 28. 15.
Num. 13. 20. be of good c., Deut. 31. 6. & 7. 23. Josh. 1. 6, 7, 9, 18. & 10. 25. & 23. 6. 2 Sam. 10. 12. & 13. 28. 1 Chron. 22. 13. & 28. 20. Ezra 10. 4. Ps. 27. 14. & 31. 24. Isa. 41. 6.
COURSE, Acts 13. 25. & 16. 11.
Acts 20. 24. finish my c. with joy
2 Thes. 3. 1. may have free c. and
2 Tim. 4. 7. I have finished my c.
R. V. Acts 21. 7. voyage; 1 Cor. 17. 27. in turn; 2 Thes. 3. 1. run; Jas. 3. 6. wheel
COURT, Jer. 19. 14. Isa. 34. 13.
Amos 7. 13. Bethel is king's c.
Ps. 65. 4. may dwell in thy c.
84. 10. day in thy *courts* better
92. 13. flourish in c. of our God
Isa. 1. 12. who required to tread my c.
62. 9. drink it in c. of my holiness
Luke 7. 25. delicate are in king's c.
Rev. 11. 2. c. without temple leave
1 Pet. 3. 8. be pitiful, *courteous*
Acts 27. 3. *courteously*, 28. 7.
R. V. 2 Kings 20. 4. part of the city; Amos 7. 13. royal house; 1 Pet. 3. 8. humble minded; Acts 27. 3. treated kindly
COVENANT, Gen. 17. 2. & 26. 28.
Gen. 9. 12. token of the c., 13. 17.
17. 4. my c. is with thee, 7. 19.
11. a token of the c. betwixt
13. my c. shall be in the flesh
14. he hath broken my c.
Ex. 2. 24. God remembered his c.
31. 16. sabbath for a perpetual c.
34. 28. wrote words of c.
Lev. 26. 15. ye brake my c.
Judg. 2. 1. never brake c. with you
1 Chron. 16. 15. always mindful of his c., Ps. 105. 8. & 111. 5.
Neh. 9. 38. we may make a sure c.
Job 31. 1. I made a c. with mine
Ps. 25. 14. Lord will show them c.
44. 17. not dealt falsely in thy c.
55. 20. broken his c., Isa. 33. 8.
74. 20. have respect to the c.,
78. 37. not steadfast in his c., 10.

Ps. 78. 28. my *c.* shall stand fast, 34.
132. 12. children will keep my *c.*
Prov. 2. 17. forgetteth *c.* of her God
Isa. 28. 18. your *c.* with death
42. 6. given thee for *c.* of people
56. 4. take hold of my *c.*, 6.
Jer. 14. 21. break not *c.* with us
Ezek. 20. 37. bring into bond of *c.*
Dan. 9. 27. break *c.* with many
Hos. 6. 7. have transgressed the *c.*
10. 4. swearing falsely in making *c.*
Mal. 2. 14. the wife of thy *c.*
3. 1. messenger of the *c.*
Acts 3. 25. the children of the *c.*
Rom. 1. 31. *c.* breakers
Heb. 8. 6. he is the mediator of a better *c.*, 7. 9.
Gen. 9. 16. *everlasting covenant*, 17.
7, 13, 19. Lev. 24. 8. 2 Sam. 23. 5.
1 Chron. 16. 17. Ps. 105. 10. Isa. 24.
5. & 55. 3. & 61. 8. Jer. 32. 40. Ezek.
16. 60. & 37. 26. Heb. 13. 20.
Gen. 17. 9, 10. *keep, keepest, keepeth,*
covenant, Ex. 19. 5. Deut. 7. 9, 12.
& 29. 9. & 33. 9. 1 Kings 8. 23. & 11.
11. 2 Chron. 6. 14. Neh. 1. 5. & 9.
32. Ps. 25. 10. & 103. 18. & 132. 12.
Dan. 9. 4.
Gen. 15. 18. Lord *made covenant*,
Ex. 34. 27. Deut. 5. 2, 3. 2 Kings
23. 3. Job 31. 1.
Jer. 31. 31. *new covenant*, Heb. 8. 8,
13. & 12. 24.
Gen. 9. 15. *remember covenant*, Ex.
6. 5. Lev. 26. 42, 45. Ps. 105. 8. &
106. 45. Ezek. 16. 60. Amos 1. 9.
Luke 1. 72.
Lev. 2. 13. *covenant* of salt, Num.
18. 19. 2 Chron. 13. 5.
Deut. 17. 2. *transgressed the cove-*
nant, Josh. 7. 11, 15.& 23. 16. Judg.
2. 20. 2 Kings 18. 12. Jer. 34. 18.
Hos. 6. 7. & 8. 1.
Rom. 9. 4. *covenants*, Gal. 4. 24.
Eph. 2. 12. *c.* of promise
R. V. Matt. 26. 15. weighed unto
COVER, Ex. 10. 5. & 40. 3.
Ex. 21. 33. dig a pit and not *c.* it
33. 22. I will *c.* thee with my hand
Deut. 33. 12. Lord shall *c.* him all
1 Sam. 24. 3. *c.* his feet, Judg. 3. 24.
Neh. 4. 5. *c.* not their iniquity
Job 16. 18. *c.* thou not my blood
Ps. 91. 4. *c.* thee with his feathers
Isa. 58. 7. naked that thou *c.* him
11. 9. as waters *c.* sea, Hab. 2. 14.
Hos. 10. 8. say to mountains, *c.* us,
Luke 23. 30. Rev. 6. 16.
1 Cor. 11. 7. man ought not *c.* head
1 Pet. 4. 8. charity shall *c.* a multi.
Job 31. 33. if I *covered* my trans.
Ps. 32. 1. whose sin is *c.*, Rom. 4. 7.
85. 2. hast *c.* all their sin
Lam. 3. 44. *c.* thyself with a cloud
Matt. 10. 26. nothing *c.* that shall not
Ps. 104. 2. *coverest* thyself with
73. 6. violence *covereth* them as a
Prov. 10. 12. love *c.* all sins
Isa. 28. 20. *covering*, 1 Cor. 11. 15.
Isa. 4. 6. *covert*, 16. 4. & 32. 2. Ps. 61.
4. Jer. 25. 38.
R. V. Ex. 40. 21. screened ; 1 Kings
6. 35 ; Prov. 26. 23. overlaid ; 1 Cor.
11. 6. veiled ; Ex. 35. 12 ; 39. 34 ;
40. 21. screen ; Prov. 7. 16 ; 31. 22.
carpets ; Isa. 30. 22. overlaying ;
S. of S. 3. 10. seat
COVET, Ex. 20. 17. Mic. 2. 2.
1 Cor. 12. 31. *c.* earnestly best gifts
Acts 20. 33. *coveted*, 1 Tim. 6. 10.
Prov. 21. 26. *coveteth*, Hab. 2. 9.
Ps. 10. 3. wicked blesseth *covetous*
Luke 16. 14. Pharisees who were *c.*
1 Cor. 5. 10. or with the *c.*, 11.
6. 10. nor *c.* shall inherit kingdom
Eph. 5. 5. nor *c.* who is an idolater
1 Tim. 3. 3. bishop must not be *c.*
2 Pet. 2. 14. exercised with *c.* pract.
Ex. 18. 21. hating *covetousness*
Ps. 119. 36. to testimonies and not to *c.*
Ezek. 33. 31. heart goeth after their *c.*

Luke 12. 15. beware of *c.* for man's
Col. 3. 5. *c.* which is idolatry
Heb. 13. 5. conversation without *c.*
R. V. Hab. 2. 9. getteth ; 1 Cor. 12.
31. desire ; 14. 39. desire earnestly ;
1 Tim. 6. 10. reaching ; Luke 16.
14 ; 1 Tim. 3. 3 ; 2 Tim. 3. 2. lovers
of money ; Ex. 18. 21. unjust gain ;
Ezek. 33. 31 ; Hab. 2. 9. gain ; Mark
7. 22. covetings ; 2 Cor. 9. 5. extor-
tions ; Heb. 13. 5. free from love
of money
CRAFT, Dan. 8. 25. Mark 14. 1.
Acts 18. 3. & 19. 25, 27. Rev. 18. 22.
Job 5. 12. disappointeth devices of the *crafty*
15. 5. uttereth iniquity, choosest tongue of *c.*
Ps. 83. 3. taken *c.* counsel against
2 Cor. 12. 16. being *c.* I caught you with guile
Job 5. 13. *craftiness*, 1 Cor. 3. 19.
Luke 20. 23. 2 Cor. 4. 2. Eph. 4. 14.
R. V. Mark 14. 1. with subtilty ;
Acts 18. 3 ; 19. 27. trade ; 19. 25. business
CREATE, Gen. 1. 1, 21, 27. & 2. 3.
Ps. 51. 10. *c.* in me a clean heart
Isa. 4. 5. *c.* upon every dwelling-place
45. 7. I form light and *c.* darkness
57. 19. I *c.* the fruit of the lips, peace
65. 17. I *c.* new heavens and new earth
18. rejoice in what I *c.* I *c.* Jeru-salem
Ps. 104. 30. spirit they are *created*
Isa. 43. 7. I have *c.* him for my
Jer. 31. 22. *c.* a new thing in earth
Mal. 2. 10. hath not one God *c.* us
Eph. 2. 10. *c.* in Christ Jesus unto good
3. 9. *c.* all things by Jesus Christ
Col. 1. 16. all things were *c.* by him
3. 10. image of him that *c.* him
1 Tim. 4. 3. which God *c.* to be re-ceived
Rev. 4. 11. hast *c.* all—are and were *c.*
10. 6. *c.* heaven and things therein
Amos 4. 13. *createth* the wind
Mark 10. 6. *creation*, 13. 19. Rom. 1.
20. & 8. 22. Rev. 3. 14.
Rom. 1. 25. *creature* — *Creator*
Eccl. 12. 1. remember thy *C.* in days
Isa. 40. 28. *C.* of ends of earth
43. 15. Lord the *C.* of Israel, your king
1 Pet. 4. 19. as to a faithful *C.*
Gen. 1. 20. *creature*, Lev. 11. 46.
Mark 16. 15. preach the gospel to every *c.*
2 Cor. 5. 17. man in Christ a new *c.*
Gal. 6. 15. availeth but a new *c.*
Col. 1. 15. first-born of every *c.*
1 Tim. 4. 4. every *c.* of God is good
Heb. 4. 13. nor any *c.* not manifest
Isa. 13. 21. *creatures*, Jas. 1. 18.
Ezek. 1. 5, 19. *living creatures*, 3.
13. Rev. 4. 6, 9. & 5. 6, 11, 14.
R. V. Mark 16. 15. whole creation ;
Col. 1. 15. all creation
CREDITOR, parable of the, Luke
7. 41 ; of two creditors, Matt. 18. 23.
CREEP, Lev. 11. 31. Ps. 104. 20.
2 Tim. 3. 6. who *c.* into houses
Jude 4. *crept* in unawares
R. V. Gen. 8. 19 ; Lev. 11. 44. mov-ing
CRIB, Prov. 14. 4. Isa. 1. 3.
CRIME, Job 31. 11. Ezek. 7. 23.
CRIMSON, as wool, Isa. 1. 18. Jer.
4. 30. 2 Chron. 2. 7. & 3. 14.
R. V. Jer. 4. 30. scarlet
CRIPPLE healed at Lystra, Acts 14. 8.
CROOKED generation, Deut. 32. 5.
Ps. 125. 5. aside to their *c.* ways
Prov. 2. 15. whose ways are *c.* and
Eccl. 1. 15. that which is *c.* cannot
Isa. 40. 4. *c.* shall be made straight

Phil. 2. 15. in midst of *c.* generation
R. V. Job 26. 13. swift ; Isa. 45. 2. rugged
CROSS, John 19. 17–31. Luke 23. 26.
Matt. 10. 38. takes not up his *c.* and
follows, 16. 24. Luke 9. 23. & 14. 27.
1 Cor. 1. 17. lest the *c.* of Christ be made
18. preaching of *c.* is to them fool.
Gal. 5. 11. then is offence of the *c.* ceased
6. 12. suffer persecution for *c.* of Christ
14. glory save in *c.* of Lord Jesus
Phil. 2. 8. obedient to death of *c.*
3. 18. they are enemies of the *c.*
Col. 2. 14. took—nailing it to his *c.*
Heb. 12. 2. for joy — endured the *c.*
CROWN, Lev. 8. 9. Esth. 1. 11.
Job 31. 36. bind it as *c.* to me
Ps. 89. 39. hast profaned his *c.*
Prov. 12. 4. virtuous woman is a *c.*
14. 24. *c.* of wise is their riches
16. 31. hoary head is a *c.* of glory
17. 6. children's children are *c.* of
S. of S. 3. 11. behold king Solo-mon with *c.*
Isa. 28. 5. Lord of hosts for *c.* of glory
62. 3. thou shalt be a *c.* of glory
1 Cor. 9. 25. to obtain corruptible *c.*
Phil. 4. 1. my joy and *c.*, 1 Thes. 2. 19.
2 Tim. 4. 8. laid up—a *c.* of righte.
Jas. 1. 12. receive a *c.* of life
1 Pet. 5. 4. receive a *c.* of glory
Rev. 2. 10. give thee a *c.* of life
Ps. 8. 5. *crowned* with glory and honor
Prov. 14. 18. prudent are *c.* with knowledge
Ps. 65. 11. *crownest* the year with
103. 4. *crowneth* with loving-kind.
Zech. 6. 11, 14. *crowns*, Rev. 4. 4,
10. & 9. 7. & 12. 3. & 13. 1. & 19. 12.
R. V. Rev. 12. 3 ; 13. 1 ; 19. 12. dia-dems
CRUCIFY, Matt. 20. 19. & 23. 34.
Luke 23. 21. John 19. 6, 15.
Acts 2. 23. *crucified* and slain, 4. 10.
Rom. 6. 6. our old man is *c.* with him
1 Cor. 1. 13. was Paul *c.*
23. Christ *c.*
2. 2. save Jesus Christ and him *c.*
Gal. 2. 20. I am *c.* with Christ nevertheless
3. 1. Christ is set forth *c.* among
6. 14. world is *c.* to me and I to
Rev. 11. 8. where also our Lord was *c.*
CRUEL, Prov. 5. 9. & 11. 17. & 27. 4.
Gen. 49. 7. cursed wrath for it was *c.*
Job 30. 21. thou art become *c.* to me
Prov. 12. 10. tender mercies of the wicked are *c.*
S. of S. 8. 6. jealousy is *c.* as grave
Isa. 13. 9. day of Lord cometh *c.* with
Jer. 6. 23. *c.* and have no mercy, 50. 42.
Heb. 11. 36. had trial of *c.* mockings
CRUELTY condemned, Ex. 23. 5.
Ps. 27. 12. Prov. 11. 17. & 12. 10.
Ezek. 18. 18.
of Simeon and Levi, Gen. 34. 25. & 49. 5.
of Pharaoh, Ex. 1. 8.
of Adoni-bezek. Judg. 1. 7.
of Herod, Matt. 2. 16. (Judg. 9. 5. 2 Kings 3. 27. & 10. & 15. 16.)
R. V. Heb. 11. 36 —— ; Gen. 49. 5 ; Judg. 9. 24 ; Ps. 74. 20. violence ; Ezek. 34. 4. rigor
CRUMBS, Matt. 15. 27. Luke 16. 21.
CRY, Ex. 5. 8. & 3. 7, 9.
Gen. 18. 21. to the *c.* that is come
Ex. 2. 23. their *c.* came up to God
22. 23. I will surely hear their *c.*
2 Sam. 22. 7. my *c.* did enter into
Job 34. 28. he hears *c.* of afflicted
Ps. 9. 12. he forgets not the *c.* of
34. 17. his ears are open to their *c.*

Ps. 145. 19. he will hear their c.
Jer. 7. 16. neither lift up c. nor prayer for them, 11. 11, 14.
Matt. 25. 6. at midnight a c. made
Ps. 34. 15. righteous c. and Lord
Isa. 40. 6. voice said c. — what c.
42. 2. not c. nor lift up voice
58. 1. c. aloud, spare not
Ezek. 9. 4. that c. for all the abom.
Joel 1. 19. to thee will I c.
Jonah 3. 8. c. mightily to God
Matt. 12. 19. shall not strive nor c.
Luke 18. 7. c. day and night to him
Luke 19. 40. stones would c. out
Rom. 8. 15. spirit c. Abba, Father
Ps. 22. 5. *cried* and were delivered
34. 6. this poor man c. and Lord
Lam. 2. 18. their heart c. to Lord
Prov. 2. 3. thou *criest* after know.
Gen. 4. 10. brother's blood *crieth*
Prov. 1. 20. wisdom c. without
Mic. 6. 9. Lord's voice c. to the city
Prov. 19. 18. *crying*, Zech. 4. 7.
Matt. 3. 3. Heb. 5. 7. Rev. 21. 4.
R. V. Rev. 14. 18. great voice
CUBIT unto his stature, Matt. 6. 27.
CUMBER. Luke 10. 40. & 13. 7.
CUP. Gen. 40. 11. & 44. 2.
Ps. 11. 6. portion of their c.
23. 5. my c. runneth over
73. 10. waters of a full c. are wrung out
116. 13. take c. of salvation
Isa. 51. 17. c. of trembling, 22. Zech. 12. 2.
Jer. 16. 7. nor give c. of consola.
25. 15. wine c. of fury, 17. 28. Lam. 4. 21. Ezek. 23. 31, 32.
Hab. 2. 16. c. Lord's right hand, Ps. 75. 8.
Matt. 10. 42. c. of cold water only
20. 22. able to drink of the c.
26. 39. let this c. pass from me
John 18. 11. the c. which my Father hath given
1 Cor. 10. 16. c. of blessing which we
21. drink c. of the Lord and c. of devils
11. 25. this c. is new testament
26. drink this c., 27, 28. Luke 22. 20.
Rev. 16. 19. c. of his wrath, 14. 10.
CURIOUS, Ex. 35. 32. Acts 19. 19.
Ps. 139. 15. *curiously* wrought
CURSE them, Num. 5. 18, 19, 22, 24, 27.
Gen. 27. 12. bring a c. upon me
13. on me be thy c. my son
Deut. 11. 26. blessing and c., 30. 1.
23. 5. turned c. into blessing, Neh. 13. 2.
Prov. 3. 33. c. of the Lord in house of
26. 2. c. causeless shall not come
Mal. 2. 2. send a c. upon you
3. 9. ye are cursed with a c.
Isa. 65. 15. *for*, or, *to be* a c., Jer. 24. 9. & 25. 18. & 29. 18. & 42. 18. & 44. 8, 12. & 26. 6. & 49. 13.
Gen. 8. 21. I will not again c. the ground
12. 3. c. him that curseth thee
Ex. 22. 28. nor c. ruler of people
Lev. 19. 14. shall not c. the deaf
Num. 22. 6. come, c. me this people, 17.
Deut. 23. 4. hired Balaam to c., Josh. 24. 9. Neh. 13. 2.
Judg. 5. 23. c. ye Meroz, c. bitterly
Job 1. 11. he will c. thee to face, 2. 5.
2. 9. c. God and die
Ps. 109. 28. let them c. but bless
Prov. 11. 26. people shall c. him, 24. 24.
Eccl. 10. 20. c. not king in chamber
Jer. 15. 10. every one doth c. me
Mal. 2. 2. I will c. your blessings
Matt. 5. 44. bless them that c. you
Rom. 12. 14. bless and c. not
Gen. 49. 7. *cursed* be their anger
Job 3. 1. opened Job his mouth, and c. his day, 8.
5. 3. I c. his habitation, 24. 18.

Ps. 119. 21. proud are c., 37. 22.
Jer. 11. 3. c. be man that obeys not
17. 5. c. be man that trusteth in
Deut. 30. 19. *cursing*, Rom. 3. 14.
Heb. 6. 8. Ps. 10. 7. & 59. 12. & 109. 17.
R. V. Josh. 6. 18. accursed; Jer. 29. 18. execration; Deut. 7. 26; 13. 17. devoted; Job 1. 5. renounced; John 7. 49. accursed; Prov. 29. 24. adjuration
CURTAINS of the tabernacle described, Ex. 26. 36.
CUSTOM, Gen. 31. 35. Rom. 13. 7.
Luke 4. 16. 1 Cor. 11. 16. Jer. 10. 3.
R. V. Gen. 31. 35. manner; Ex. 3. 4. ordinance; Matt. 9. 9; Mark 2. 14; Luke 5. 27. place of toll; Matt. 17. 25. receive toll
CUT, Lev. 1. 6, 12. & 22. 24.
Zech. 11. 10. *cut asunder*, Matt. 24. 51. Luke 12. 46. Jer. 48. 2. & 50. 23. Ps. 129. 4.
Luke 13. 7, 9. *cut down*, Job 22. 16, 20.
Job 4. 7. *cut off*, 8. 14. Ps. 37. 9, 28. & 76. 12. & 90. 10. & 101. 5. Prov. 2. 22. Matt. 5. 30. & 18. 8. Rom. 11. 22. 2 Cor. 11. 12. Gal. 5. 12.
Acts 5. 33. *cut to heart*, 7. 54.
R. V. Isa. 38. 10. noontide
CUTTING the flesh forbidden, Lev. 19. 28; Deut. 14. 1; practised by prophets of Baal, 1 Kings 18. 28.
CYMBAL, Ezra 3. 10. Ps. 150. 5.
1 Cor. 13. 1. I am become a tinkling c.

D

DAINTY, Job 33. 20. Prov. 23. 6.
Gen. 49. 20. yield royal *dainties*
Ps. 141. 4. not eat of their d.
Prov. 23. 3. not desirous of his d.
DAMNED who believe not, Mark 16. 16. 2 Thes. 2. 12.
Rom. 14. 23. doubteth, is d. if he eat
2 Pet. 2. 1. *damnable* heresies
Matt. 23. 14. greater *damnation*
33. how can ye escape d. of hell
Mark 3. 29. in danger of eternal d.
John 5. 29. come forth to resurrection of d.
1 Cor. 11. 29. eateth and drinketh d.
R. V. Mark 16. 16; Rom. 14. 23. condemned; 2 Thes. 2. 12. judged; Matt. 23. 14 — ; 22. 33; John 5. 29; Rom. 13. 2. judgment; Mark 3. 29. sin; 12. 40; Luke 20. 47; Rom. 3. 8; 1 Tim. 5. 12. condemnation
DANCE turned to mourning, Lam. 5. 15. Ps. 30. 11. Luke 15. 25.
DANCING, as a mark of rejoicing, Ex. 15. 20. & 32. 19. Judg. 11. 34. 1 Sam. 11. 2 Sam. 6. 14. Eccl. 3. 4. of Herodias's daughter pleases Herod, Matt. 14. 6; Mark 6. 22.
DANDLED on knees, Isa. 66. 12.
DANGER of the judgment, Matt. 5. 22.
Matt. 5. 21, 22. d. of the council — hell fire
Mark 3. 39. in d. of damnation
Acts 19. 27. craft in d.
40. we in d.
R. V. Mark 3. 29. guilty
DARE, 1 Cor. 6. 1. 2 Cor. 10. 12.
Rom. 5. 7. some would d. to die
R. V. 2 Cor. 10. 12. not bold to
DARK, Gen. 15. 17. Job 18. 6. & 24. 16.
Lev. 13. 6. if plague be d., 21. 26.
Num. 12. 8. speak not in d. speech.
2 Sam. 22. 12. d. waters, Ps. 18. 11.
Ps. 49. 4. d. sayings, 78. 2.
Dan. 8. 23. understanding d. sent.
2 Pet. 1. 19. light shineth in d.
1 Cor. 13. 12. through a glass *darkly*
Ex. 10. 15. *darkened*, Eccl. 12. 2, 3.
Ps. 69. 23. let eyes be d., Rom. 11. 10.

Zech. 11. 17. his right eye utterly d.
Rom. 1. 21. foolish heart was d.
Gen. 1. 2, 5, 18. *darkness*, 15. 12.
2 Sam. 22. 29. Lord will lighten. my d.
1 Kings 8. 12. Lord dwell in thick d.
Job 34. 22. no d. where workers
Ps. 104. 20. makest d. and it is night
Isa. 5. 20. put d. for light, and light for d.
45. 7. I form light and create d.
Matt. 6. 23. whole body full of d.
8. 12. outer d., 22. 13. & 25. 30.
John 1. 5. d. comprehended it not
3. 19. men loved d. rather than lig.
Acts 26. 18. turn them from d. to
Rom. 13. 12. cast off works of d.
2 Cor. 4. 6. light to shine out of d.
6. 14. communion hath light with d.
Eph. 5. 8. were sometimes d. but
Col. 1. 13. delivered us from power of d.
1 Pet. 2. 9. called you out of d.
2 Pet. 2. 4. reserved in chains of d.
1 John 1. 5. in him is no d. at all
Jude 13. blackness of d. for ever
Deut. 28. 29. *in darkness*, 1 Sam. 2. 9. Ps. 107. 10. & 112. 4. Isa. 9. 2. & 50. 10. Matt. 4. 16. & 10. 27. John 1. 5. 1 Thes. 5. 4.
R. V. Zech. 14. 6. with gloom; Luke 23. 45. failing
DARLING, Ps. 22. 20. & 35. 17.
DARTS, fiery, of devil, Eph. 6. 16.
R. V. Job 41. 29. clubs; 2 Chron. 32. 5. weapons; Prov. 7. 23. arrow; Heb. 12. 20.
DASH, 2 Kings 8. 12. Ex. 15. 6. Isa. 13. 16, 18. Hos. 10. 14. & 13. 16. Ps. 137. 9. Jer. 13. 14.
Ps. 2. 9. d. them in pieces like a potter's vessel
91. 12. lest thou d. thy foot against a stone
DAVID, for Christ, Ps. 89. 3. Jer. 30. 9. Ezek. 34. 23, 24. & 37. 24, 25. Hos. 3. 5. Isa. 55. 3.
DAY, Gen. 1. 5. & 32. 26.
Ps. 19. 2. d. unto d. uttereth speech
84. 10. a d. in thy courts is better
118. 24. this is the d. which the Lord
Prov. 27. 1. what d. may bring forth
Amos 6. 3. put far away evil d.
Zech. 4. 10. despised the d. of small
Matt. 6. 34. sufficient to d. is the
25. 13. know neither the d. nor
John 8. 56. rejoiced to see my d.
1 Cor. 3. 13. the d. shall declare it
Phil. 1. 6. till d. of Jesus Christ
1 Thes. 5. 5. children of the d.
Matt. 10. 15. *day of judgment*, 11. 22, 24. & 12. 36. Mark 6. 11. 2 Pet. 2. 9. & 3. 7. 1 John 4. 17.
Isa. 2. 12. *day of the Lord*, 13. 6, 9. & 34. 8. Jer. 46. 10. Lam. 2. 22. Ezek. 30. 3. Joel 1. 15. & 2. 1, 31. & 3. 14. Amos 5. 18. Obad. 15. Zeph. 1. 8, 18. & 2. 2, 3. Zech. 1. 7. & 14. 1. Mal. 4. 5. 1 Cor. 5. 5. Rev. 1. 10. 2 Cor. 1. 14. 1 Thes. 5. 2. 2 Pet. 3. 10.
Ps. 20. 1. Lord hear thee in the *day of trouble*
50. 15. call on me in —, 91. 15.
59. 16. my defence and refuge in—
77. 2. in — I sought the Lord
Isa. 37. 3. it is a — and rebuke
Ezek. 7. 7. time is come, — is near
Hab. 3. 16. I might rest in —
Zeph. 1. 15. a — and distress, desolation
Job 8. 9. *days* on earth as a shadow
14. 1. of few d. and full of trouble
Ps. 90. 12. teach us to number our d.
Prov. 3. 16. length of d. is in her right
Eccl. 7. 10. former d. better than
11. 8. remember d. of darkness, many
12. 1. while evil d. come not
Jer. 2. 32. forgotten me d. without
Matt. 24. 22. except those d. be shortened

Gal. 4. 10. observe *d.* months, and
Eph. 5. 16. because the *d.* are evil
1 Pet. 3. 10. would see good *d.*
Gen. 49. 1. *last days,* Isa. 2. 2. Mic.
  4. 1. Acts 2. 17. 2 Tim. 3. 1. Heb.
  1. 2. Jas. 5. 3. 2 Pet. 3. 3.
Num. 24. 14. *latter days,* Deut. 31.
  29. Jer. 23. 20. & 30. 24. Dan. 10. 14.
  Hos. 3. 5.
Job 10. 20. *my days,* 17. 1, 11.
  7. 6. — are swifter than a shuttle
  16. I loathe it, — are vanity
  9. 25. — are swifter than a post
Ps. 39. 4. know measure of —
  5. made — as a handbreadth
Isa. 39. 8. peace and truth in —
Jer. 20. 18. — are consumed with
Ps. 61. 8. *daily* perform my vows
Prov. 8. 34. watching *d.* at my gates
Isa. 58. 2. seek me *d.* and delight in
Acts 2. 47. added to church *d.*
Heb. 3. 13. exhort one another *d.*
Job 9. 33. *day's-man,* or umpire
  38. 12. *day-spring,* Luke 1. 78.
2 Pet. 1. 19. *day-star* arise in your
  hearts
R. V. Matt. 27. 62; John 1. 29; Acts
  14. 20; 21. 8; 25. 6. on the morrow
DEACON, Phil. 1. 1. 1 Tim. 3. 8, 10,
  12, 13.
DEAD, Gen. 20. 3. & 23. 3.
Num. 16. 48. stood between *d.* and
1 Sam. 24. 14. after a *d.* dog after
Ps. 88. 10. shall *d.* praise, 115. 17.
Eccl. 9. 5. the *d.* know not any
  thing
  10. 1. *d.* flies cause the ointment
Matt. 8. 22. let the *d.* bury their *d.*
  22. 32. not God of *d.* but of living
Luke 8. 52. the maid is not *d.* but
John 5. 25. *d.* shall hear the voice
  11. 25. though he were *d.* yet
Rom. 6. 8. *d.* with Christ
  11. *d.* to sin
Gal. 2. 19. I through law am *d.* to
  law
Eph. 2. 1. who were *d.* in trespasses
Col. 2. 13. being *d.* in your sins
1 Thes. 4. 16. *d.* in Christ shall rise
2 Tim. 2. 11. *d.* with him, we shall
Heb. 11. 4. being *d.* yet speaketh
Rev. 14. 13. blessed are *d.* — in Lord
Ps. 17. 9. *deadly,* Jas. 3. 8. Rev.
  13. 3.
R. V. Rev. 13. 3, 12. death stroke
DEAF, Ex. 4. 11. Ps. 38. 13. Isa. 29.
  18. & 35. 5. Mic. 7. 16.
Lev. 19. 14. shalt not curse the *d.*
Isa. 42. 18. hear, ye *d.* and look, ye
  blind
  19. who is *d.* as my messenger
  43. 8. *d.* people that have ears
Matt. 11. 5. *d.* hear, dead are raised
DEAL, a measure, Ex. 29. 40. Lev.
  14. 10.
DEATH, Gen. 21. 16. Ex. 10. 17.
Num. 23. 10. let me die the *d.* of the
Deut. 30. 15. set before you life
  and *d.*
Ps. 6, 5. in *d.* no remembrance of
  33. 19. deliver soul from *d.,* 116. 8.
  73. 4. have no bands in their *d.*
  89. 48. liveth and shall not see *d.*
  116. 15. precious — is *d.* of saints
Prov. 2. 18. her house inclines to *d.*
  8. 36. they that hate me, love *d.*
  18. 21. *d.* and life in power of tong.
Eccl. 7. 26. more bitter than *d.* the
  8. 8. hath no power in day of *d.*
Isa. 25. 8. swallow up *d.* in victory
  28. 15. made covenant with *d.*
Jer. 8. 3. *d.* chosen rather than life
  21. 8. way of life, way of *d.*
Hos. 13. 10. O *d.* I will be thy plagues
Matt. 16. 28. not taste of *d.,* Luke 9.
  27.
  26. 38. sorrowful even unto *d.*
John 5. 24. passed from *d.* to life,
  1 John 3. 14.
John 8. 51. shall never see *d.*
  12. 33. what *d.* he should die, 21. 19.
Acts 2. 24. loosed the pains of *d.*
Rom. 5. 12. sin entered, and *d.* by
  6. 3. baptized into his *d.*

Rom. 6. 4. buried by baptism into *d.*
  5. 9. *d.* hath no more dominion
  21. end of these things is *d.*
  23. the wages of sin is *d.* but gift
    of God
  8. 2. free from law of sin and *d.*
  6. to be carnally minded is *d.*
  38. *d.* nor life shall separate from
1 Cor. 3. 22. or life, or *d.* or things
  present
  11. 26. ye show Lord's *d.* till he
    come
  15. 21. by man came *d.* by man
  54. *d.* is swallowed up in victory
  55. O *d.* where is thy sting
  56. sting of *d.* is sin, and strength
2 Cor. 1. 9. had the sentence of *d.*
  10. deliver from so great a *d.*
  2. 16. we are savour of *d.* unto *d.*
  4. 11. delivered to *d.* for Jesus'
  12. *d.* worketh in us, but life in you
Phil. 2. 8. obedient to *d.* the *d.* of
Heb. 2. 9. tasted *d.* for every man
  15. through fear of *d.* are subject
  11. 5. should not see *d.,* Luke 2. 26.
Jas. 1. 15. sin finished brings *d.*
  5. 20. save a soul from *d.* and hide
1 Pet. 3. 18. put to *d.* in the flesh
1 John 5. 16. there is a sin unto *d.*
  17. there is a sin unto *d.* I do not
Rev. 1. 18. I have the keys of hell
  and *d.*
  2. 10. be faithful unto *d.* and I will
  6. second *d.* hath no power
  21. 4. there shall be no more *d.*
R. V. Mark 14. 1; Luke 18. 33. kill
  him
DEBATE, Prov. 25. 9. Isa. 27. 8. &
  58. 4. Rom. 1. 29. 2 Cor. 12. 20.
R. V. Isa. 58. 4. contention; Rom.
  1. 29. strife; 2 Cor. 12. 20. should
  be strife; Isa. 27. 8. dost contend
DEBT, Rom. 4. 4. Matt. 6. 12, 18, 27.
  Ezek. 18. 7, 11. *debtor,* Gal. 5. 3.
  Rom. 1. 14. & 8. 12. & 15. 27. Luke
  7. 41. Matt. 6. 12.
R. V. Matt. 18. 30. which was due
DECEASE, Luke 9. 31. 2 Pet. 1. 15.
DECEIT, Jer. 5. 27. & 9. 6, 8.
Ps. 72. 14. redeem their souls
  from *d.*
  101. 7. worketh *d.* shall not dwell
Prov. 20. 17. bread of *d.* is sweet
Isa. 53. 9. any *d.* in his mouth
Jer. 8. 5. they hold fast *d.* and refuse
Col. 2. 8. spoil you through vain *d.*
Ps. 35. 20. *deceitful,* 109. 2. Prov. 11.
  18. & 14. 25. & 23. 3. & 27. 6.
Ps. 5. 6. abhor bloody and *d.* man
  78. 57. turn like a *d.* bow, Hos. 7. 16.
  120. 2. from a *d.* tongue, 52. 4. Mic.
  6. 12. Zeph. 3. 13.
Prov. 31. 30. favor is *d.* and beauty
  vain
Jer. 17. 9. heart is *d.* above all
  things
Eph. 4. 22. according to *d.* lusts
Matt. 13. 22. *deceitfulness* of riches
Ps. 24. 4. *deceitfully,* Jer. 48. 10. Job
  13. 7. 2 Cor. 4. 2.
R. V. Ps. 55. 11; 72. 14. oppression;
  Prov. 20. 17. falsehood; 1 Thes. 2.
  3. error; Prov. 27. 6. profuse; 29.
  13. oppressor; Eph. 4. 22. deceit;
  Gen. 34. 13. with guile
DECEIVE, 2 Kings 4. 28. & 18. 29.
Prov. 24. 28. *d.* not with thy lips
Matt. 24. 4. take heed that no man
  d. you
  24. if possible *d.* the very elect
1 Cor. 3. 18. let no man *d.* himself
2 Thes. 2. 10. *deceivableness*
Deut. 11. 16. heart be not *deceived*
Job 12. 16. the *d.* and the deceiver
  are
Isa. 44. 20. a *d.* heart hath turned
Jer. 20. 7. O Lord, thou hast *d.* me
Ezek. 14. 9. I the Lord have *d.*
Obad. 3. thy pride hath *d.* thee
Rom. 7. 11. *d.* me, and by it slew me
1 Tim. 2. 14. Adam was not *d.* but
2 Tim. 3. 13. *deceiving* and being *d.*
Gal. 27. 12. *deceiver,* Mal. 1. 14.
2 John 7. 2 Cor. 6. 8. Tit. 1. 10.

Prov. 26. 19. *deceiveth,* Rev. 12. 9.
Jas. 1. 26. *d.* his own heart, 22.
R. V. Matt. 24. 4, 5, 11, 24; Mark 13.
  5, 6; 1 John 3. 7. lead astray; Rom.
  16. 18; 2 Thes. 2. 3. beguile; Lev.
  6. 2. oppressed; Job 31. 9. enticed;
  Prov. 20. 1. erreth; Luke 21. 8;
  John 7. 47. led astray; Rom. 7. 11.
  1 Tim. 2. 14. beguiled; Jas. 1. 22.
  deluding
DECENTLY, 1 Cor. 14. 40.
DECLARE, Gen. 41. 24. Isa. 42. 9.
Ps. 22. 2. I will *d.* thy name unto
  38. 18. I will *d.* my iniquity and
  145. 4. shall *d.* thy mighty acts
Isa. 3. 9. they *d.* their sin as Sodom
  53. 8. who shall *d.* his generation
Mic. 3. 8. to *d.* to Jacob his transgression
Acts 17. 23. worship, him *d.* I unto
  20. 17. not shunned to *d.* all counsel
Rom. 3. 25. to *d.* his righteousness
Heb. 11. 14. say such things *d.* plain.
1 John 1. 3. seen and heard *d.* we
Rom. 1. 4. *declared* — Son of God
  with
2 Cor. 3. 3. manifestly *d.* to be the
  epistle
Amos 4. 13. *d.* to man what his
  thought
1 Cor. 2. 1. I *d.* to you test. of God
R. V. Ps. 2. 7; 73. 28; 75. 1; 78. 6. tell
  of; Eccl. 9. 1. explore; Isa. 43. 26.
  set forth thy cause; Matt. 13. 36.
  explain; Rom. 3. 25. shew; John
  17. 26; Col. 4. 7. make known;
  1 John 1. 5. announce; Acts 15. 4, 14.
  rehearsed; Rom. 9. 17. published
DECLINE, Ps. 119. 51, 157.
DECREE, Ezra 5. 13, 17. & 6. 1, 12.
Ps. 2. 7. I will declare the *d.*
Prov. 8. 15. princes *d.* justice
Isa. 10. 1. that *d.* unrighteous decr.
Zeph. 2. 2. before *d.* bring forth
Isa. 10. 22. *decreed,* 1 Cor. 7. 37.
R. V. Dan. 2. 9. law; 6. 7, 8, 9, 12,
  13, 15. interdict; Esth. 9. 32. com-
  mandment
DEDICATE, Deut. 20. 5. 2 Sam. 8.
  11. 1 Chron. 26. 20, 26, 27. Ezek. 44.
  29.
Num. 7. 84. *dedication,* Ezra 6. 16,
  17. Neh. 12. 17. John 10. 22.
R. V. 2 Kings 12. 4. hallowed; Ezek.
  44. 29. devoted
DEED, Gen. 44. 15. Judg. 19. 30.
Rom. 15. 18. obedient in word
  and *d.*
Col. 3. 17. whatsoever ye do in
  word or *d.*
Neh. 13. 14. wipe not out my good
  deeds
Ps. 28. 4. give them according to
  their *d.,* Jer. 25. 14. Rom. 2. 6. 2 Cor.
  5. 10.
John 3. 19. because their *d.* were
  evil
Rom. 3. 20. by *d.* of law no flesh
Jude 15. of all their ungodly *d.*
R. V. In N. T. mostly, works
DEEP, Gen. 1. 2. Job 38. 30.
Ps. 36. 6. thy judg. are a great *d.*
  42. 7. *d.* calleth unto *d.* at the noise
1 Cor. 2. 10. yea, *d.* things of God
2 Cor. 11. 25. I have been in the *d.*
Isa. 31. 6. *deeply* revolted
Hos. 9. 9. *d.* corrupted themselves
Mark 8. 17. sighed *d.* in spirit
R. V. Isa. 63. 13; Jonah 2. 3. depth;
  Luke 8. 31; Rom. 2. 7. abyss; Ps.
  135. 6. deeps; Ezek. 32. 14; 34. 18.
  clear
DEFAME, 1 Cor. 4. 13. Jer. 20. 10.
DEFENCE, 2 Chron. 11. 5. Isa. 19. 6.
Num. 14. 9. their *d.* is departed
Job 22. 25. Almighty shall be thy *d.*
Ps. 7. 10. my *d.* is of God who save.
Eccl. 7. 12. wisdom is a *d.* money
Isa. 4. 5. on all the glory shall be *d.*
  33. 16. place of *d.* the munitions
R. V. Job 22. 25. treasure; Ps. 7. 10;
  89. 18. shield; 59. 9, 16; 62. 2, 6;

94. 22. high tower; Isa. 4. 5. canopy;
19. 6. Egypt; Nah. 2. 5. mantelet
DEFER, Eccl. 5. 4. Isa. 48. 9. Dan.
9. 19. Prov. 13. 12. & 19. 11.
R. V. Prov. 19. 11. maketh him slow
DEFILE, Lev. 11. 44. & 15. 31.
S. of S. 5. 3. how shall I *d.* them
Dan. 1. 8. would not *d.* himself
Matt. 15. 18. they *d.* the man, 20.
1 Cor. 3. 17. if any *d.* temple of God
Mark 7. 2. eat bread with *defiled*
hands
Isa. 24. 5. earth is *d.* under inhabit.
Tit. 1. 15. are *d.* and unbelieving
Heb. 12. 15. thereby many be *d.*
Rev. 3. 4. have not *d.*their gar.
14. 4. are not *d.* with women
21. 27. any thing that *defileth*
R. V. Ex. 31. 14; Ezek. 7. 24; 28. 18.
profaned; Num. 35. 33; Isa. 24. 5;
Jer. 3. 9; 16. 18. polluted; Gen. 34.
2. humbled; Deut. 22. 9. forfeited;
Lev. 13. 14; 15. 32; Num. 5. 2; Ezek.
4. 13; Rev. 21. 27. unclean
DEFRAUD, Lev. 19. 13. Mark 10.
19. 1 Cor. 6. 7, 8. & 7. 5. 1 Thes. 4. 6.
1 Sam. 12. 3, 4. 2 Cor. 7. 2.
R. V. Lev. 19. 13. oppress; 2 Cor.
7. 2. took advantage of; 1 Thes.
6. wrong
DELAY, Ex. 22. 29. & 32. 1.
Ps. 119. 60. I *delayed* not to keep
Matt. 24. 48. my lord *delayeth* his
coming
R. V. Matt. 24. 48. tarrieth
DELICATE, Deut. 28. 56. Isa. 47. 1.
Jer. 6. 2. Mic. 1. 16. Jer. 51. 34.
1 Sam. 15. 32. *delicately,* Prov. 29. 21.
Lam. 4. 5. Luke 7. 25.
R. V. Mic. 1. 16. of . . delight
DELIGHT, Gen. 34. 19. Num. 14. 8.
Deut. 10. 15. Lord had *d.* in fathers
1 Sam. 15. 22. hath the Lord as
great *d.* in burnt offerings
Job 22. 26. have thy *d.* in Almighty
27. 10. will he *d.* himself in Almighty
Ps. 1. 2. his *d.* is in the law of God
16. 3. saints in whom is all my *d.*
37. 4. *d.* thyself in Lord, he will give
40. 8. I *d.* to do thy will, O my God
94. 19. thy comforts *d.* my soul
119. 24. thy testimonies are my *d.*,
174.
Prov. 11. 20. upright are his *d.*, 12. 22.
15. 8. prayer of upright is his *d.*
S. of S. 2. 3. under shadow with
great *d.*
Isa. 55. 2. let your soul *d.* itself in
fatness
58. 2. *d.* to know — take *d.* in approaching
13. call the sabbath a *d.* holy of
Rom. 7. 22. I *d.* in the law of God
Ps. 112. 1. *delighteth* greatly in his
commandments
Prov. 3. 12. son in whom he *d.*
Isa. 42. 1. elect in whom my soul *d.*
Mic. 7. 18. because he *d.* in mercy
Ps. 119. 92. thy law hath been my
delights, 143. Eccl. 2. 8.
Prov. 8. 31. my *d.* with sons of men
S. of S. 7. 6. how pleasant, O love,
for *d.*
Mal. 3. 12. for ye shall be a *delight-
some* land
R. V. Prov. 19. 10. delicate living
DELIVER, Ex. 3. 8. & 5. 18.
Job 5. 19. *d.* thee in six troubles and
10. 7. none can *d.* out of thy hand
Ps. 33. 19. to *d.* their souls from
death
50. 15. I will *d.* thee, and thou, 91. 15.
56. 13. wilt thou not *d.* my feet
74. 19. *d.* not the soul of thy turtle
91. 3. *d.* thee from snare of fowler
Eccl. 8. 8. shall wickedness *d.* those
Ezek. 14. 14. should *d.* but their own
Dan. 3. 17. our God is able to *d.* us
Hos. 11. 8. how shall I *d.* thee, Israel
Rom. 7. 24. who shall *d.* from body
1 Cor. 5. 5. to *d.* such a one to Satan
2 Tim. 4. 18. the Lord shall *d.* me
Heb. 2. 15. *d.* them who thro. fear

2 Pet. 2. 9. Lord knows how to *d.*
2 Kings 5. 1. *deliverance,* 13. 17.
2 Chron. 12. 7. Esth. 4. 14. Ps. 32.
7. & 44. 4. Isa. 26. 18. Joel 2. 32.
Obad. 17. Luke 4. 18. Heb. 11. 35.
Gen. 45. 7. great *deliverance,* Judg.
15. 18. 1 Chron. 11. 14. Ps. 18. 50.
Ezra 9. 13. given us such *d.* as this
Heb. 11. 35. not accepting *d.*
Prov. 11. 8. righteous is *delivered*
out of trouble, and the wicked
cometh, 9. 21.
28. 26. walketh wisely shall be *d.*
Isa. 38. 17. in love to soul, *d.* it
49. 24, 25. lawful captive — prey
be *d.*
Jer. 7. 10. *d.* to do all abominations
Ezek. 3. 19. hast *d.* thy soul, 21. &
33. 9.
Dan. 12. 1. thy people shall be *d.*
Mic. 4. 10. Babylon, there shalt
thou be *d.*
Matt. 11. 27. all things are *d.* to me
Acts 2. 23. *d.* by determinate coun.
Rom. 4. 25. who was *d.* for our
offences
7. 6. we are *d.* from the law that
8. 32. God *d.* him up for us all
2 Cor. 1. 10. who *d.* us from so great
4. 11. *d.* unto death for Jesus' sake
1 Thes. 1. 10. which *d.* us from the
1 Tim. 1. 20. whom I have *d.* to
2 Pet. 2. 7. *d.* just Lot vexed with
Jude 3. faith once *d.* to the saints
R. V. Lev. 6. 4; 2 Sam. 10. 10;
1 Chron. 19. 11. committed; Deut.
5. 22. gave; Judg. 2. 16, 18; 3. 9, 31;
8. 22; 10. 12; 12. 2, 3. saved;
2 Kings 18. 30; 19. 10; Isa. 36. 15.
given; 1 Chron. 11. 14. defended;
Ps. 55. 18; 78. 42. redeemed; 81. 6.
freed; Ezek. 6. 21; Mark 9. 31; 15.
1, 10. delivered up; Mark 14. 10. rescued; 2 Kings 5. 1; 13. 17; 1 Chron.
11. 14. victory; Joel 2. 32; Obad.
17. those that escape; Luke 4. 18.
release; Judg. 3. 9, 15. savior
DELUSION, 2 Thes. 2. 11. Isa. 66. 4.
R. V. 2 Thes. 2. 11. working of error
DEMONSTRATION, 1 Cor. 2. 4.
DEN, Judg. 6. 2. Job 37. 8. Heb.
11. 38. Rev. 6. 15. Ps. 104. 22.
Ps. 10. 9. *den of lions,* S. of S. 4. 8.
Dan. 6. 7, 24. Amos 3. 4. Nah. 2. 12.
Jer. 7. 11. *den of robbers* — of
thieves, Matt. 21. 13. Mark 11. 17.
Jer. 9. 11. *den of dragons,* 10. 22.
R. V. Jer. 9. 11; 10. 22. dwelling
place; Job 37. 8. coverts; Rev.
6. 15. caves
DENY, 1 Kings 2. 16. Job 8. 18.
Prov. 30. 9. lest I be full and *d.*
thee
Matt. 10. 33. shall *d.* me before
men
26. 34. before the cock crow thou
shalt *d.*
35. I will not *d.* thee, Mark 14. 31.
2 Tim. 2. 12. if we *d.* him he will *d.*
Tit. 1. 16. in works they *d.* him
1 Tim. 5. 8. hath *denied* the faith
Rev. 2. 13. hast not *d.* my faith
2 Tim. 3. 5. godliness *denying* the
power
Tit. 2. 12. *d.* ungodliness and
2 Pet. 2. 1. *d.* Lord that bought he.
DEPART from, Job 21. 14. & 22.
17.
28. 28. to *d.* from evil, is understanding
Ps. 34. 14. *d.* from evil, 37. 27. Prov.
3. 7. & 13. 19. & 16. 6, 17.
Hos. 9. 12. woe to me when I *d.*
from
Matt. 7. 23. *d.* from me, ye that
work
Luke 2. 29. lettest thy servant *d.* in
5. 8. *d.* from me — a sinful man,
O Lord
1 Tim. 4. 1. some shall *d.* from faith
2 Tim. 2. 19. name of Christ *d.* fr.
Ps. 18. 21. wickedly *departed* from
Prov. 14. 16. feareth and *departeth*
from evil

Isa. 59. 15. *d.* from evil makes him.
Acts 20. 29. after my *departing,*
wolves
2 Tim. 4. 6. *departure,* Ezek. 26. 18.
R. V. very largely, go, went away,
withdrew
DEPTH, Job 28. 14. & 38. 16. Prov.
8. 27. Matt. 18. 6. Mark 4. 5.
Rom. 8. 39. nor *d.* separate us
11. 33. O the *d.* of riches of wis-
dom
Eph. 3. 18. *d.* of the love of Christ
Ex. 15. 5, 8. *depths*, Ps. 68. 22. & 71.
20. & 130. 1. Prov. 3. 20. & 9. 18.
Mic. 7. 19. cast sins into *d.* of sea
Rev. 2. 24. known *d.* of Satan
R. V. Ex. 15. 5, 8; Ps. 33. 7. deeps;
Job 28. 14; 38. 16; Prov. 8. 27. deep;
Mark 4. 5. deepness
DERISION, Job 30. 1. Ps. 2. 4. &
44. 13. & 59. 8. & 119. 51. Jer. 20. 7, 8.
R. V. Jer. 20. 7. laughing stock
DESCEND, Ex. 19. 18. & 33. 9.
Ps. 49. 17. glory shall not *d.* after
Isa. 5. 14. rejoiceth shall *d.* into it
Gen. 28. 12. angels of God ascend-
ing and *descending*, John 1. 51.
Matt. 3. 16. Spirit of God *d.* like
dove, Mark 1. 10. John 1. 32, 33.
Rev. 21. 10. city *d.* out of heaven
R. V. Num. 34. 11; 1 Sam. 26. 10. go
down; Mark 15. 32; Ps. 133. 3; Acts
24. 1; Jas. 3. 15; Rev. 21. 10. come
or came down; Josh. 17. 9; 18. 13,
16, 17. went down; Heb. 7. 3, 6.
genealogy
DESERT, Ex. 3. 1. & 19. 2. Num.
20. 1. Isa. 21. 1. & 35. 1. & 40. 3. &
43. 19. & 51. 3. Jer. 25. 24. & 50. 12.
Ezek. 47. 8. Matt. 24. 26.
R. V. Ps. 102. 6. waste places; Ezek.
47. 8. Arabah; Ex. 3. 1; 5. 3; 19. 2;
23. 31; Num. 21. 1; 27. 14; 33. 16;
2 Chron. 26. 10; Isa. 21. 1; Jer. 25. 24;
Matt. 24. 26; John 6. 31. wilderness
DESIRE, Deut. 18. 6, & 21. 11.
Gen. 3. 16. thy *d.* shall be to thy
husband
4. 7. to thee shall be his *d.* and
thou
Ex. 34. 24. nor any man *d.* thy land
Deut. 18. 6. with all the *d.* of his
heart
2 Sam. 23. 5. this is all my *d.* though
2 Chron. 15. 15. with their whole *d.*
Job 14. 15. wilt have a *d.* to work
21. 14. we *d.* not knowledge of thy
Ps. 38. 9. all my *d.* is before thee
73. 25. none that I *d.* besides thee
145. 16. fulfil the *d.* of them that
Prov. 10. 24. *d.* of righteous shall
11. 23. *d.* of righteous is only good
21. 25. *d.* of slothful killeth him
Eccl. 12. 5. *d.* shall fail, because
Isa. 26. 8. *d.* of our soul is to thy
Ezek. 24. 16. take the *d.* of thy eyes
Hag. 2. 7. the *d.* of all nations shall
Luke 22. 15. with *d.* I have desired
Jas. 4. 2. *d.* to have and cannot
Rev. 9. 6. *d.* to die, and death shall
flee
Ps. 19. 10. more to be *desired* are
they
Isa. 26. 9. with my soul have I *d.*
thee
Jer. 17. 16. nor have I *d.* woeful day
Ps. 37. 4. give the *desires* of heart
Eph. 2. 3. fulfilling *d.* of the flesh
Ps. 51. 6. thou *desirest* truth in
16. thou *d.* not sacrifice, else
Job 7. 2. servant earnestly *desireth*
12. what man *d.* life and
68. 16. hill which God *d.* to dwell
Prov. 12. 12. wicked *d.* not of evil
13. 4. soul of sluggard *d.* and hath
21. 10. soul of wicked *d.* evil
R. V. Job. 31. 35. signature; 2 Cor.
7. 7; Rom. 15. 23. longing; Ps. 78.
29. lusteth after; Job 20. 20. delighteth; Ps. 27. 4; Matt. 16. 1;
Mark 15. 6; John 12. 21; Acts 3.
14; 7. 46; 9. 2; 13. 21, 28; 18. 20;
1 John 5. 15. asked; Hos. 6. 6; Mic.
7. 1. desire; Luke 9. 9; Acts 3. 7.

sought; 2 Cor. 8. 6; 12. 18. exhorted

DESOLATE, 2 Sam. 13. 20. Job 15. 28. & 16. 7. Ps. 25. 16. Isa. 49. 21. & 54. 1. Matt. 23. 38. Rev. 17. 16.
Isa. 49. 6. *desolations*, 61. 4. Jer. 25. 9, 12. Ezek. 35. 9. Dan. 9. 2, 18, 26.
R. V. Jer. 49. 13, 17. astonishment; Prov. 1. 27. storm; Lam. 3. 47. devastation; Job 30. 14; Ezra 9. 9; Ps. 74. 31. ruins

DESPAIR, 2 Cor. 4. 8. & 1. 8. Eccl. 2. 20.
1 Sam. 27. 1. *d. i. e.* to be past hope
Job 6. 20. *desperate,* Isa. 17. 11.
Jer. 17. 9. *desperately* wicked

DESPISE my statutes, Lev. 26. 15.
1 Sam. 2. 30. that *d.* me shall be lightly
Job 5. 17. *d.* not chastening of
Ps. 102. 17. will not *d.* their prayer
Prov. 23. 22. *d.* not mother when
Matt. 6. 24. hold to one and *d.* other
Rom. 14. 3. *d.* him that eateth not
Gen. 16. 4. mistress was *despised* in
2 Sam. 6. 16. she *d.* him in her
Prov. 12. 9. is *d.* and hath a serv.
S. of S. 8. 1. kiss thee I should not be *d.*
Isa. 53. 3. he is *d.* and rejected, Ps. 22. 6.
Zech. 4. 10. who *d.* the day of small
Luke 18. 9. righteous and *d.* others
Heb. 10. 28. that *d.* Moses' law died
Acts 13. 41. *despisers*, 2 Tim. 3. 3.
Rom. 2. 4. *despisest* thou riches of goodness
Job 36. 5. God *despiseth* not any
Prov. 11. 12. void of wisdom *d.* neighbor
13. 13. *d.* the word shall be destroyed
14. 21. that *d.* his neighbor sinneth
15. 32. refuseth instruction *d.* his
Isa. 33. 15. *d.* gain of oppression
49. 7. whom man *d.* nation abho.
Luke 10. 16. *d.* you, *d.* me, *d.* him
1 Thes. 4. 8. *d.* not man but God
Heb. 12. 2. *despising* the shame
10. 29. done *despite* to the Spirit of grace
R. V. Lev. 26. 15. reject; 26. 43; Num. 11. 20; 14. 31; Ps. 53. 5; Ezek. 20. 13, 16, 24; Amos 2. 4. rejected; Luke 18. 9; Heb. 10. 28. set at nought; Jas. 2. 6; 1 Cor. 4. 10. dishonor; Acts 19. 27. made of no account; Prov. 19. 16. careless of; Luke 10. 16; 1 Thes. 4. 8. rejecteth; 2 Tim. 3. 3. no lovers of

DESTROY, Gen. 18. 23. & 19. 13.
Ps. 101. 8. I will *d.* all wicked of the
Prov. 1. 32. the prosper. of fools *d.*
Matt. 5. 17. not come to *d.* but to fulfil
10. 28. able to *d.* both soul and body
John 2. 19. *d.* this temple, and I will raise
Rom. 14. 15. *d.* not him with thy
20. for meat *d.* not work of God
1 Cor. 3. 17. if defile temple, him God will *d.*
6. 13. God shall *d.* both it and them
Jas. 4. 12. able to save and to *d.*
1 John 3. 8. might *d.* works of devil
Hos. 4. 6. my people are *destroyed*
13. 9. Israel, thou hast *d.* thyself
2 Cor. 4. 9. cast down but not *d.*
Job 15. 21. *destroyer,* Ps. 17. 4. Prov. 28. 24. Jer. 4. 7. 1 Cor. 10. 10.
Esth. 4. 14. *shall be destroyed,* Ps. 37. 38. & 92. 7. Prov. 13. 13, 20. & 29. 1. Isa. 10. 27. Dan. 2. 44. Hos. 10. 8. Acts 3. 23. 1 Cor. 15. 26.
Deut. 7. 23. *destruction,* 32. 24.
Job 5. 22. at *d.* and famine shall laugh
18. 12. *d.* is ready at his side
Ps. 90. 3. thou turnest man to *d.*
91. 6. *d.* that wasteth at noonday
Prov. 10. 29. *d.* shall be to workers of

iniquity, 21. 15. Job. 21. 30. & 31. 3.
15. 11. hell and *d.* are before the Lord
16. 18. pride goeth before *d.*
18. 12. before *d.* the heart of man
Jer. 4. 20. *d.* upon *d.* is cried, for land is spoiled
Hos. 13. 14. O grave, I will be thy *d.*
Matt. 7. 13. way that leads to *d.*
1 Cor. 5. 5. for the *d.* of the flesh
2 Cor. 10. 8. not for your *d.*, 13. 10.
1 Thes. 5. 3. peace and safety; then sudden *d.* cometh upon them
2 Thes. 1. 9. punished with everlasting *d.*
2 Pet. 2. 1. bring on themselves swift *d.*
3. 16. wrest Scriptures to their *d.*
R. V. Gen. 18. 23, 24; 1 Chron. 21. 12. consume; Ex. 23. 27; Deut. 7. 23; Ps. 144. 6. discomfit; Ex. 34. 13; Num. 24. 17; Deut. 7. 5; Ps. 28. 5. break down; Deut. 7. 24; 9. 3; 28. 51; Josh. 7. 7. perish; 2 Sam. 22. 41; Ps. 18. 40; 54. 5; 69. 4; 101. 5; 1 Kings 15. 13. cut off, or down; Ps. 5. 10. hold guilty; Prov. 15. 25. root up; Acts 9. 21; Gal. 1. 23. made havoc; Rom. 14. 20. overthrow; 1 Cor. 6. 13; Heb. 2. 14; 2 Thes. 2. 8. bring to nought; Rom. 6. 6. done away; 1 Cor. 15. 26. abolished; 1 Cor. 10. 9, 10; 2 Pet. 2. 12. perish; Acts 19. 27. despised; Jer. 50. 11. that plunder; 1 Pet. 2. 11. spoiler; Ps. 17. 4. violent

DETERMINED, 2 Chron. 25. 16. Job 14. 5. Isa. 10. 23. & 28. 22. Dan. 9. 24. Acts 2. 23. & 4. 28. & 17. 26.
R. V. 2 Chron. 2. 1; Isa. 19. 17; Acts 20. 3. purposed; Dan. 9. 24. decreed; Acts 15. 37. was minded; 19. 39. settled in the regular; 15. 2. the brethren appointed

DETESTABLE, Deut. 7. 26. Jer. 16. 18. Ezek. 5. 11. & 7. 20. & 11. 18. & 37. 23. 1 Cor. 2. 7.

DEVICE, Eccl. 9. 10. Job 5. 12. Ps. 33. 10. Prov. 1. 31. & 12. 2. & 14. 17. & 19. 21. Jer. 18. 11, 12, 18. 2 Cor. 2. 11.
R. V. Ps. 33. 10. thoughts; Lam. 3. 62. imagination

DEVIL, Matt. 4. 5. & 8. 11. & 9. 32.
Matt. 4. 1. to be tempted of the *d.*
11. 18. they say he hath a *d.*
13. 39. enemy that sowed is the *d.*
25. 41. fire prepared for the *d.* and
John 6. 70. twelve, and one of you is a *d.*
7. 20. thou hast a *d.*, 8. 48.
8. 44. of your father the *d.*, 49.
13. 2. *d.* having now put it into, 27.
Acts 13. 10. thou child of the *d.*
Eph. 4. 27. neither give place to *d.*
2 Tim. 2. 26. recover out of the snare of the *d.*
Jas. 4. 7. resist *d.* and he will
1 Pet. 5. 8. your adversary the *d.* goeth
1 John 3. 8. to destroy works of *d.*
10. children of God and children of the *d.*
Jude 9. Michael contending with *d.*
Rev. 2. 10. the *d.* shall cast some
Lev. 17. 7. offer sacrifice to *devils*
Deut. 32. 17. they sacrifice to *d.*
Ps. 106. 37. sacrificed their sons to *d.*
Matt. 4. 24. possessed with *d.*, 8. 16, 28, 33. Luke 4. 41. & 8. 36.
10. 8. raise the dead, cast out *d.*
Mark 16. 9. cast out seven *d.*, Luke 8. 2.
Luke 10. 17. even *d.* are subject to
1 Cor. 10. 20. have fellowship with *d.* sacrifice to *d.*
21. cup of *d.* table of *d.*
Jas. 2. 19. *d.* believe and tremble
R. V. Lev. 17. 7; 2 Chron. 11. 15. he-goats, Deut. 32. 17; Ps. 106. 37. demons

DEVISE not evil against, Prov. 3. 29.
14. 22. do they not err that *d.* evil
16. 30. shutteth eyes to *d.* froward
Jer. 18. 18. come let us *d.* devices
Mic. 2. 1. woe to them that *d.* iniquity

DEVOTED, Lev. 27. 21, 28. Num. 18. 14.
Ps. 119. 38. servant who is *d.* to thy
Acts 17. 23. I beheld your *devotions*

DEVOUR, Gen. 49. 27. Isa. 26. 11.
Matt. 23. 14. ye *d.* widows' houses
Gal. 5. 15. if ye bite and *d.* one another
Heb. 10. 27. which shall *d.* the ad.
1 Pet. 5. 8. seeking whom he may *d.*
Isa. 1. 20. ye shall be *devoured*
Jer. 3. 24. shame hath *d.* the labor
Hos. 7. 7. *d.* judges
9. *d.* strength
Mal. 3. 11. I will rebuke *devourer*
Ex. 24. 17. *devouring fire,* Isa. 29. 6. & 30. 27, 30. & 33. 14.
Ps. 52. 4. lovest all *devouring* words
R. V. Ps. 80. 13. feed on; Isa. 42. 14. pant together; Prov. 19. 28; Hab. 1. 13. swalloweth up; Prov. 20. 25. rashly to say; Matt. 23. 14 —

DEVOUT, Luke 2. 25. Acts 2. 5. & 10. 27. & 17. 4, 17. & 22. 12.

DEW, Deut. 32. 2. & 33. 28. Deut. 32. 2.
Ps. 110. 3. hast the *d.* of thy youth
Isa. 26. 19. thy *d.* is as the *d.* of
Hos. 6. 4. goodness is as the early *d.*
Mic. 5. 7. Jacob — as *d.* from Lord
R. V. Ps. 133. 3 —

DIADEM, Job 29. 14. Isa. 28. 5. & 62. 3. Ezek. 21. 26.
R. V. Ezek. 21. 26. mitre

DIE, Gen. 5. 5. & 6. 17.
Gen. 2. 17. thou shalt surely *d.*, 3. 4. & 20. 7. 1 Sam. 14. 44. & 22. 16. 1 Kings 2. 37, 42. Jer. 26. 8. Ezek. 3. 18. & 33. 8, 14.
Num. 14. 14. if a man *d.* shall he live
Ps. 82. 7. ye shall *d.* like men
Prov. 23. 13. with rod he shall not *d.*
Eccl. 3. 2. there is a time to *d.*
Isa. 22. 13. to-morrow we shall *d.*
Ezek. 3. 19. *d.* in his iniquity, 33. 8.
18. 4. soul that sinneth shall *d.*
31. why will ye *d.* O house of
Jonah 4. 3. better for me to *d.* than
Matt. 26. 35. though I should *d.*
Luke 20. 36. neither can *d.* any more
John 8. 21. ye shall *d.* in your sins, 24.
11. 50. expedient that one *d.* for
Rom. 14. 8. we *d.* we *d.* unto Lord
1 Cor. 9. 15. better for me to *d.* than
15. 22. as in Adam all *d.* so in Christ
Phil. 1. 21. to live is Christ, to *d.* is gain
Heb. 9. 27. it is appointed for men to *d.*
Rev. 3. 2. that are ready to *d.*
14. 13. blessed are the dead who *d.*
Rom. 5. 6. Christ *died* for ungodly
8. while yet sinners, Christ *d.* for us
6. 9. being raised he *d.* no more
14. 9. to this end Christ *d.* and rose
1 Cor. 15. 3. Christ *d.* for our sins
2 Cor. 5. 15. he *d.* for all, that they
1 Thes. 5. 10. who *d.* for us that whether
Heb. 11. 13. these all *d.* in faith, not
Rom. 14. 7. no man *dieth* to himself
2 Cor. 4. 10. *dying,* 6. 9. Heb. 11. 21.

DIFFER, who makes, 1 Cor. 4. 7.
Phil. 1. 10. that *d.*, Rom. 2. 18.
Lev. 10. 10. *difference,* Ezra 22. 26. & 44. 23.
Acts 15. 9. no *d.*, Rom. 3. 22. & 10. 12.
R. V. Lev. 20. 25. separate; Acts 15. 9; Rom. 3. 22; 10. 12. distinction; Ezek. 22. 26. discern; 1 Cor. 12. 5. diversities; Jude 22. who are in doubt

DILIGENCE, 2 Tim. 4. 9, 21.
Prov. 4. 23. keep thy heart with all *d.*
Luke 12. 58. art in way give *d.* that

2 Pet. 1. 5. giving all *d.* add to faith
10. give *d.* to make calling and election
Jude 3. I gave all *d.* to write unto
Deut. 19. 18. *diligent,* Josh. 22. 5.
Prov. 10. 4. hand of *d.* maketh rich
12. 24. hand of *d.* shall bear rule
21. 5. thoughts of the *d.* tend to
22. 29. man *d.* in his business
2 Pet. 3. 14. be *d.* to be found of him
Ex. 15. 26. will *diligently* hearken to voice of, Deut. 11. 13. & 28. 1. Jer. 17. 24. Zech. 6. 15.
Deut. 4. 9. keep thy soul *d.*
6. 7. teach them *d.* unto thy children
17. *d.* keep the commandments, 11. 22.
24. 8. that thou observe *d.* and
Ps. 119. 4. to keep thy precepts *d.*
Heb. 11. 6. rewarder of them that *d.* seek
R. V. Cor. 8. 7. earnestness ; 2 Cor. 8. 22. earnest ; Tit. 3. 12 ; 2 Pet. 3. 14. give diligence
DIMINISH, Deut. 4. 2. Prov. 13. 11.
Rom. 11. 12. *diminishing* of them the riches of
R. V. Isa. 21. 17. few ; Rom. 11. 12. their loss
DIMNESS of anguish, Isa. 8. 22. & 9. 1.
DIRECT, Eccl. 10. 10. Isa. 45. 13.
Ps. 5. 3. will I *d.* my prayer to thee
Prov. 3. 6. he shall *d.* thy paths
Isa. 61. 8. I will *d.* their work in truth
Jer. 10. 23. that walks to *d.* his steps
2 Thes. 3. 5. Lord *d.* your hearts
Isa. 40. 13. who *directed* the Spirit
Ps. 119. 5. ways were *d.* to keep
Prov. 16. 9. a man's heart deviseth, Lord *directeth* his steps
R. V. Gen. 46. 28. shew ; Ps. 5. 3 ; Prov. 21. 29. order ; Ps. 119. 5. established ; Isa. 45. 13. make straight ; 61. 8. give them ; Num. 19. 4. toward front of
DISCERN, Eccl. 8. 5. 2 Sam. 14. 17. & 19. 35. 1 Kings 3. 9, 11. 1 Cor. 2. 14.
Mal. 3. 18.*d.* between righteous and
Heb. 5. 14. to *d.* both good and
4. 12. *discerner* of thoughts
1 Cor. 11. 29. not *discerning* Lord's body
12. 10. to another *d.* of spirits
R. V. Luke 12. 56. know how to interpret ; 1 Cor. 2. 14. judge
DISCHARGE, in war, Eccl. 8. 8.
R. V. 1 Kings 5. 9. broken up
DISCIPLE, John 9. 28. & 19. 38.
Matt. 10. 24. the *d.* is not above
42. in the name of a *d.*
Luke 14. 26. ye cannot be my *d.*
John 8. 31. then are ye my *d.* ind.
Acts 21. 16. an old *d.* with whom
R. V. Matt. 26. 20 ; 28. 9 ; Mark 2. 18 ; Luke 9. 11 ; John 6. 11 —— ; Acts 1. 15. brethren
DISCORD, soweth, Prov. 6. 14, 19.
DISCRETION, Ps. 112. 5. Prov. 1. 4. & 2. 11. & 3. 21. & 11. 22. & 19. 11. Isa. 28. 26. Jer. 10. 12.
R. V. Ps. 112. 5. in judgment ; Isa. 28. 26. aright
DISEASE, Ps. 38. 7. & 41. 8. Eccl. 6. 2. Matt. 4. 23. & 9. 35. & 10. 1. Ex. 15. 26. Deut. 28. 60. 2 Chron. 21. 19.
Ps. 103. 3. who healeth all thy *d.*
Ezek. 34. 4. *diseased,* have ye not, 21.
R. V. 2 Kings 1. 2 ; 8. 8, 9 ; Matt. 9. 35. sickness ; John 5. 4 —— ; Matt. 14. 35 ; Mark 1. 32 ; John 6. 2. sick
DISFIGURE bodies, Matt. 6. 16.
DISGRACE not, Jer. 14. 21.
DISGUISES resorted to, 1 Sam. 28. 8. 1 Kings 14. 2. & 20. 38. & 22. 30. 2 Chron. 18. 29. & 35. 22.
disfiguring of face for the dead forbidden, Lev. 19. 28. Deut. 14. 1.

DISHONOR, Ps. 35. 26. Prov. 6. 33.
Mic. 7. 6. son *d.* his father
Ps. 71. 13. cloth. with shame and *d.*
Rom. 1. 24. to *d.* their own bodies
1 Cor. 15. 43. it is sown in *d.* it is raised
DISOBEDIENCE, 2 Cor. 10. 6.
Eph. 2. 2. & 5. 6. Col. 3. 6.
Rom. 5. 19. by one man's *d.* many
DISOBEDIENT, 1 Kings 13. 26.
Neh. 9. 26.
Luke 1. 17. *d.* to wisdom of the just
Rom. 1. 30. *d.* to parents, 2 Tim. 3. 2.
Tit. 1. 16. abominable and *d.*
3. 3. *d.* deceived, serving divers lusts
1 Pet. 2. 7, 8. stumble being *d.*
R. V. 1 Pet. 2. 7. such as disbelieve
DISORDERLY, 2 Thes. 3. 6, 7, 11.
DISPENSATION, 1 Cor. 9. 17. Eph. 1. 10. & 3. 2. Col. 1. 25.
DISPERSED, Ps. 112. 9. Prov. 5. 16. Isa. 11. 12. Zeph. 3. 10. John 7. 35.
R. V. John 7. 35. Dispersion ; Acts 5. 37 ; 2 Cor. 9. 9. scattered
DISPLEASED, Gen. 38. 10. 2 Sam. 11. 27. 1 Chron. 21. 7. Zech. 1. 2, 15. Isa. 59. 15. Mark 10. 14. 1 Kings 1. 6. Ps. 60. 1.
Deut. 9. 19. *hot* or *sore displeasure,* Ps. 2. 5. & 6. 1. & 38. 1.
R. V. Gen. 31. 35 ; Ps. 60. 1. angry ; Gen. 38. 10. evil in sight of ; Num. 11. 1. speak evil in ears of ; Matt. 21. 15 ; Mark 10. 14, 41. moved with indignation ; Judg. 15. 3. mischief
DISPOSING is of the Lord, **Prov.** 16. 33.
Acts 7. 53. *disposition* of angels
R. V. As if ordained by
DISPUTE, Job 23. 7. Mark 9. 33. Acts 6. 9. & 9. 29. & 17. 17. & 19. 8, 9.
Rom. 14. 1. doubtful *disputations*
Phil. 2. 14. *disputings,* 1 Tim. 6. 5.
R. V. Job 23. 7. reason ; Mark 9. 33. were ye reasoning ; Acts 17. 17. reasoned ; Acts 15. 2. questioning ; Acts 19. 8, 9. reasoning ; 1 Tim. 6. 5. wranglings
DISQUIETED, Ps. 39. 6. & 42. 5, 11.
R. V. Prov. 30. 21. doth tremble
DISSEMBLE, Josh. 7. 11. Jer. 42. 20. Gal. 2. 13. Ps. 26. 4. Prov. 26. 24.
Rom. 12. 9. *dissimulation,* Gal. 2. 13.
R. V. Jer. 42. 20. dealt deceitfully ; Rom. 12. 9. hypocrisy
DISSENSION, Acts 15. 2. & 23. 7, 10.
DISSOLVED, Ps. 75. 3. Isa. 24. 19. 2 Cor. 5. 1. 2 Pet. 3. 11. Job 30. 22.
R. V. Isa. 14. 31. melted away
DISTINCTLY, read law, Neh. 8. 8.
DISTRACTED, suffer terrors, Ps. 88. 15.
1 Cor. 7. 35. *distraction* without
DISTRESS, Gen. 42. 21. Deut. 2. 9, 19. Neh. 9. 37. Luke 21. 23, 25. Gen. 35. 3. answered in day of my *d.*
2 Sam. 22. 7. in my *d.* I called on
1 Kings 1. 29. redeemed my soul out of all *d.*
2 Chron. 28. 22. in his *d.* trespassed
Ps. 4. 1. enlarged my heart in *d.*
Isa. 25. 4. strength to needy in *d.*
Zeph. 1. 15. that day is a day of *d.,* 17.
Rom. 8. 35. shall *d.* separate from Christ
1 Sam. 28. 15. *distressed,* 30. 6. 2 Sam. 1. 26.
2 Cor. 6. 4. in *distresses,* 12. 10.
Ps. 25. 17. *out of my distresses,* 107. 6, 13, 19, 28. Ezek. 30. 16. 2 Cor. 6. 4.
R. V. Ezek. 30. 16. adversaries ; 1 Kings 1. 20. adversity ; Neh. 2. 17. evil case ; Rom. 8. 35. anguish ; Deut. 2. 9, 19. vex ; 2 Cor. 4. 8. straitened
DISTRIBUTE, Luke 18. 22. 1 Tim. 6. 18. 1 Cor. 7. 17. Job 21. 17. Rom. 12. 13.

Acts 4. 35. *distribution,* 2 Cor. 9. 13.
R. V. 1 Chron. 24. 3. divided ; Rom. 12. 13. communicating ; 2 Cor. 10. 13. apportioned
DITCH, Job 9. 31. Ps. 7. 15. Prov. 23. 27. Isa. 22. 11. Matt. 15. 14. Luke 6. 39.
R. V. 2 Kings 3. 16. trenches ; Isa. 22. 11. reservoir ; Matt. 15. 14 ; Luke 6. 39. pit
DIVERSITIES, 1 Cor. 12. 4, 6, 28.
R. V. 1 Cor. 12. 3. divers kinds
DIVIDE, Gen. 1. 6, 14. Job 27. 17. 1 Kings 3. 25. *d.* living child, 26.
Ps. 55. 9. destroy—*d.* their tongues
Isa. 53. 12. I will *d.* him a portion
Luke 12. 13. to *d.* inheritance with
2 Sam. 1. 23. in death not *divided*
Dan. 2. 41. kingdom shall be *d.*
Matt. 12. 25. kingdom, house *d.* against itself shall not stand, 26.
Luke 11. 17.
12. 11. *dividing* to every man sever.
2 Tim. 2. 15. rightly *d.* the word of
Heb. 4. 12. to *d.* asunder of joints
Judg. 5. 15, 16. *divisions,* Luke 12. 51. Rom. 16. 17. 1 Cor. 1. 10. & 3. 3.
R. V. Lev. 11. 4, 7 ; Deut. 14. 7, 8. part ; Num. 33. 54. inherit ; Josh. 19. 45. distributing ; 23. 4 ; Neh. 9. 22. allot ; Matt. 25. 32. separateth ; Acts 13. 19. gave them their land for an inheritance ; 2 Tim. 2. 13. handling aright ; Dan. 7. 25. half a ; Judg. 5. 15, 16. watercourses ; 1 Cor. 3. 3 ——
DIVINE sentence, Prov. 16. 10.
Heb. 9. 1. ordinance of *d.* service
2 Pet. 1. 3. his *d.* power hath given
Mic. 3. 11. prophets *d.* for money
Num. 22. 7. *divination,* 23. 23. Deut. 18. 10. Acts 16. 16.
Deut. 18. 14. *diviners,* Isa. 44. 25.
Mic. 3. 6, 7. Zech. 10. 2. Jer. 29. 8.
DIVORCE, Jer. 3. 8. Lev. 21. 14. & 22. 13. Num. 30. 9. Matt. 5. 32.
Deut. 24. 1, 3. *divorcement,* Isa. 50. 1. Matt. 5. 31. & 19. 7. Mark 10. 4.
R. V. divorcement ; Matt. 5. 32. put away
DO, Gen. 16. 6. & 18. 25. & 31. 16.
Matt. 7. 12. men should *d.* to you, *d.*
John 15. 5. without me ye can *d.*
Rom. 7. 15. what I would that *d.* I not
Phil. 4. 13. I can *d.* all things throu.
Heb. 4. 13. with whom we have to *d.*
Rev. 19. 10. see thou *d.* it not, 22. 9.
Rom. 2. 13. the *doers* of it shall
Jas. 1. 22. be ye *d.* of word and not
1 Chron. 22. 16. *doing,* Ps. 64. 9. & 66. 5. & 118. 23. Prov. 20. 11. Isa. 1. 16. Jer. 7. 3, 5. & 18. 11. & 26. 13. & 32. 19. Zech. 1. 4. Ezek. 36. 31. Zeph. 3. 11. Mic. 2. 7.
Rom. 2. 7. *well-doing,* Gal. 6. 9. 2 Thes. 3. 13. 1 Pet. 2. 15. & 3. 17. & 4. 19.
R. V. 2 Kings 22. 5. workmen ; Ps. 101. 8. workers of iniquity ; 2 Tim. 2. 9. malefactor
DOCTOR, Acts 5. 34. Luke 2. 46. & 5. 17.
Deut. 32. 2. *doctrine* shall drop as rain
Jer. 10. 8. the stock is a *d.* of vanities
Matt. 7. 28. astonished at his *d.,* 22. 33. Mark 1. 22. & 11. 18. Luke 4. 32.
Matt. 16. 12. beware of the *d.* of
Mark 1. 27. what new *d.* is this
John 7. 17. shall know of the *d.*
Acts 2. 42. apostles' *d.* and fellowship
Rom. 6. 17. form of *d.* which was
16. 17. contrary to *d.* ye have learn.
Eph. 4. 14. with every wind of *d.*
1 Tim. 5. 17. labor in word and *d.*
2 Tim. 3. 16. profitable for *d.*
Tit. 2. 7. in *d.* showing uncorrupt
10. may adorn the *d.* of God
Heb. 6. 1. principles of *d.* of Christ
Matt. 15. 9. teaching for *d.* the
Col. 2. 22. after *doctrines* of men

Heb. 13. 9. carr. about by strange d.
R. V. in N. T. generally, teaching
DOG, Ex. 11. 7. Deut. 23. 18.
1 Sam. 17. 43. am I a d., 2 Kings 8. 13.
Prov. 26. 11. d. return to his vomit, 2 Pet. 2. 22.
Eccl. 9. 4. living d. better than
Isa. 56. 10. all dumb dogs
11. greedy d.
Matt. 7. 6. cast not that which is holy to d.
15. 27. d. eat of crumbs, Mark 7. 28.
Rev. 22. 15. without are d. and sorcerers
DOMINION, Gen. 27. 40. & 37. 8.
Num. 24. 19. he that shall have d.
Job 25. 2. d. and fear are with him
Ps. 8. 6. have d. over the works of
19. 13. not have d. over me, 119. 133.
49. 14. upright have d. over them
145. 13. thy d. endureth through
Isa. 26. 13. other lords had d. over
Dan. 4. 3. his d. is from generation
34.—an everlasting d., 7. 14.
7. 27. all d. shall serve and obey
Rom. 6. 9. death has no more d.
14. sin shall not have d. over you
Col. 1. 16. thrones or d. or principalities
Jude 8. despise d. and speak evil
25. to God d., 1 Pet. 4. 11. & 5. 11.
R. V. Judg. 14. 4. rule ; 2 Chron. 21. 8. hand ; Neh. 9. 37. power ; 2 Cor. 1. 24. lordship ; Matt. 20. 25. lord it
DOOR, Judg. 11. 31. & 16. 3.
Gen. 4. 7. sin lieth at the d.
Ps. 84. 10. d. keeper in the house
141. 3. keep d. of my lips
Prov. 26. 14. as d. turns on hinges
Hos. 2. 15. valley of Achor, d. of
John 10. 1. entereth not by the d. is
7. I am the d. of sheep
9. I am d.
Acts 14. 27. opened d. of faith
1 Cor. 16. 9. great d. and effectual
2 Cor. 2. 12. a d. was opened to me
Jas. 5. 9. judge stands before d.
Rev. 3. 8. I set before thee an open d.
20. I stand at d. and knock, if any
Ps. 24. 7. lift up ye everlasting doors
Mal. 1. 10. shut ye the d. for nought
Matt. 24. 33. near, even at the d.
R. V. Amos 9. 11. chapters ; Ezek. 41. 2, 3. entrance ; 41. 16. thresholds ; 1 Kings 14. 17. house
DOTING, 1 Tim. 6. 4. Ezek. 23. 5, 20.
DOUBLE, Ex. 22. 4. Deut. 21. 17.
2 Kings 2. 9. d. portion of thy spirit
1 Chron. 12. 33. not of a d. heart
Job 11. 6. secrets are d. to that
Ps. 12. 2. with a d. heart do they speak
Isa. 40. 2. d. for all her sins, Jer. 16. 18.
Jer. 17. 18. destroy with d. destruct.
1 Tim. 3. 8. deacons not d. tongued
Jas. 1. 8. d. minded man, 4. 8.
Rev. 18. 6. d. to her, fill to her d.
R. V. Job 11. 6. manifold
DOUBT, Deut. 28. 66. Gal. 4. 20.
Matt. 14. 31. of little faith, why dost d.
21. 21. have faith and d. not
Mark 11. 23. and shall not d. ¶ ш
Rom. 14. 23. he that doubteth is dam.
1 Tim. 2. 8. without wrath or doubting
Luke 12. 29. be not of doubtful mind
Rom. 14. 1. not to d. disputations
R. V. Luke 11. 20. then ; 1 Cor. 9. 10. yea ; Gal. 4. 20. perplexed ; John 10. 24. told us in suspense ; Acts 5. 24 ; 10. 17 ; 25. 20. much perplexed ; 1 Tim. 2. 8. disputing
DOUGH, Ex. 12. 34. Num. 15. 20. Neh. 10. 37. Ezek. 44. 30.
DOVE, Ps. 55. 6. & 68. 13. & 74. 19.
S. of S. 1. 15. & 2. 14. & 5. 2. & 6. 9.
Matt. 3. 16. Luke 3. 22. John 1. 32.
Isa. 38. 14. mourn as d., 59. 11.
60. 8. fly as d. to their windows
Hos. 7. 11. Ephr. is like a silly d.
Matt. 10. 16. wise as serpents, and harmless as d.

DOWN sitting, Ps. 139. 2.
Isa. 37. 31. downward, Eccl. 3. 21.
DRAGON, Ps. 91. 13. Isa. 27. 1. &
51. 9. Jer. 51. 34. Ezek. 29. 3. Rev. 12. 3-17. & 13. 2, 4, 11. & 16. 13. & 20. 2.
Deut. 32. 33. dragons, Job 30. 29.
Ps. 44. 19. & 74. 13. & 148. 7.—Isa. 13. 22. & 34. 13. & 43. 20. Jer. 9. 11. & 14. 6. Mic. 1. 8. Mal. 1. 3.
R. V. Job 30. 29 ; Ps. 44. 19 ; Isa. 13. 22 ; 14. 6 ; 49. 33 ; 51. 37 ; Mic. 1. 8 ; Mal. 1. 3. jackals
DRAUGHTS of fishes, miraculous, Luke 5. 4, 6. John 21. 6, 11.
DRAW, Gen. 24. 44. 2 Sam. 17. 13.
Job 21. 33. every man shall d.
Ps. 28. 3. d. me not away with
S. of S. 1. 4. d. me, we will run after
Isa. 5. 18. woe unto that d. iniquity
Jer. 31. 3. with loving kindness I d.
John 6. 44. except Father—d. him
12. 32. I will d. all men to me
Heb. 10. 38. if any man d. back, 39.
Ps. 73. 28. good for me to d. near to
Eccl. 12. 1. years d. nigh when say
Isa. 29. 13. d. near me with their
Heb. 7. 19. by which we d. nigh to
Jas. 4. 8. d. nigh to God, and he will d.
Ps. 18. 16. drew me out of many waters
Hos. 11. 4. I d. with cords of love
R. V. Mark 6. 53. moved ; Luke 15. 1 ; Acts 27. 27. were drawing ; Acts 19. 33. brought ; Acts 14. 19 ; 17. 6 ; 21. 30. dragged
DREAD, Ex. 15. 16. Job 13. 11, 21.
Deut. 1. 29. d. not, nor be afraid
1 Chron. 22. 13. be strong d. not
Isa. 8. 13. let him be your fear and d.
Dan. 9. 4. great and dreadful God
Gen. 28. 17. how d. is this place
Mal. 1. 14. my name is d. among
4. 5. great and d. day of the Lord
R. V. Dan. 7. 7, 19 ; Mal. 1. 14 ; 4. 5. terrible
DREAM, Gen. 37. 5. & 40. 5. & 41. 7.
Gen. 20. 3. God came to Abimelech in a d.
31. 11. angel spake to Jacob in a d.
Num. 12. 6. speak to him in a d.
1 Kings 3. 5. the Lord appeared to Solomon in a d.
Ps. 73. 20. as d. when one awaketh
Eccl. 5. 3. d. comes through multitude
Isa. 29. 7. that fight—be as a d.
Dan. 2. 3. I d. a d.
Matt. 1. 20. angel appeared in a d.
2. 12. Joseph warned of God in a d.
27. 19. suffered many things in a d.
Acts 2. 17. old men shall d. dreams, Joel 2. 28.
Job 7. 14. scarest me with d.
DRINK, Ex. 15. 24. & 32. 20.
Job 21. 20. d. of wrath of Almighty
Ps. 36. 8. d. of the river of thy pleasure
42. 20. wine of astonishment
80. 5. givest them tears to d.
Prov. 4. 17. d. the wine of violence
5. 15. d. waters out of own cistern
31. 4. it is not for kings to d. wine
7. d. and forget his poverty
S. of S. 5. 1. d. yea d. abundantly, O
Isa. 22. 13. let us eat and d., 1 Cor. 15. 32.
43. 20. to give d. to my people
Hos. 4. 18. their d. is sour, committed
Amos 2. 1. say to masters, bring, and let us d.
Matt. 10. 42. give to d. to one of these little ones
20. 22. able to d. of cup, 23.
26. 27. d. ye all of it, this is my blood
29. I will not henceforth d. of fruit
John 6. 55. my blood is d. indeed
18. 11. cup Father given, shall I not d. it

Rom. 14. 17. king. of God is not d.
1 Cor. 10. 4. drink same spiritual d.
11. 25. as often as ye d. it in rem.
12. 13. all made to d. into one spirit
Lev. 10. 9. not d. wine nor strong drink, Judg. 13. 4, 7, 14. 1 Sam. 1. 15.
Prov. 31. 6. give—to those ready to perish
Isa. 5. 11. follow—
22. mingle—
28. 7. prophet erred through—
Mic. 2. 11. prophecy to them of—
Job 15. 16. drinketh iniquity like
John 6. 54. d. my blood hath eter.
56. that d. my blood dwells in me
1 Cor. 11. 29. eateth and d. unworth.
Heb. 6. 7. earth which d. in rain
Eph. 5. 18. be not drunk with wine
Rev. 17. 2. d. with wine of fornication
Deut. 21. 20. glutton and drunkard
Prov. 23. 21. d. shall come to poverty
Isa. 24. 20. earth shall reel like a d.
1 Cor. 5. 11. with railer and d. not eat
Ps. 69. 12. drunkards, Isa. 28. 1, 3.
Joel 1. 5. Nah. 1. 10. 1 Cor. 6. 10.
Job 12. 25. stagger like a drunken man, Ps. 107. 27. Jer. 23. 9. Isa. 19. 14.
Isa. 29. 9. d. not with wine, 51. 21.
Acts 2. 15. these are not d. as ye suppose
1 Cor. 11. 21. one hungry another is d.
1 Thes. 5. 7. they that be d. are d.
Deut. 29. 19. drunkenness, Eccl. 10. 17. Jer. 13. 13. Ezek. 23. 33. Luke 21. 34. Rom. 13. 13. Gal. 5. 21.
DROP, Deut. 33. 28. Judg. 5. 4.
Deut. 32. 2. doctrine shall d. as rain
Ps. 65. 11. thy paths d. fatness, 12.
Prov. 5. 3. d. as honey-comb, S. of S. 4. 11.
Isa. 40. 15. all nations are as a d. of
S. of S. 5. 5. my hands dropped myrrh
2. locks with drops of the night
Luke 22. 44. sweat as it were great d.
DROSS, Ps. 119. 119. Isa. 1. 25.
Ezek. 22. 18.
DROUGHT, Deut. 28. 24. 1 Kings 17. Hag. 1. 11.
DROWN, S. of S. 8. 7. 1 Tim. 6. 9.
R. V. Ex. 15. 4. sunk ; Amos 8. 8 ; 9. 5. sink again ; Heb. 11. 29. swallowed up
DROWSINESS clothe, Prov. 23. 21.
DRY, Judg. 6. 37, 39. Job 13. 25.
Prov. 17. 1. Isa. 44. 3. & 56. 3. Jer. 4. 11. Ezek. 17. 24. & 37. 2, 4. Hos. 9. 14.
R. V. Lev. 2. 14 ; Isa. 5. 13. parched ; Joel 1. 12 ; Mark 11. 20. withered
DUE, Lev. 10. 13. Deut. 18. 3.
1 Chron. 15. 13. sought him not after d.
1 Chron. 16. 29. give Lord glory d. to his name, Ps. 29. 2. & 96. 8.
Prov. 3. 27. withhold not—whom it is d.
Matt. 18. 34. should pay all that was d.
Luke 23. 41. we received d. reward
Ps. 104. 27. meat in due season, 145. 15. Matt. 24. 45. Luke 12. 42.
Prov. 15. 23. a word spoken in—
Eccl. 10. 17. princes eat in—
Gal. 6. 9. in—we shall reap, if we
Deut. 32. 35. foot shall slide in due time
Rom. 5. 6. in—Christ died for the
1 Cor. 15. 8. as one born out of—
1 Tim. 2. 6. to be testified in—
Tit. 1. 3. hath in—manifested
R. V. 1 Tim. 2. 6. its own ; Tit. 1. 3. his own
DULL of hearing, Matt. 13. 15.
DUMB, Hab. 2. 18. Mark 9. 17.
Ex. 4. 11. who maketh d. or deaf
Ps. 38. 13. I was as a d. man

Ps. 39. 2. 1 was *d.* with silence, 9.
Prov. 31. 8. open thy mouth for *d.*
Isa. 35. 6. tongue of *d.* to sing
53. 7. sheep before shearers is *d.*
R. V. Lev. 1. 20, silent
DUMBNESS of Zacharias, Luke 1. 20.
DUNG of solemn feasts, Mal. 2. 3.
Phil. 3. 8. I count them but *d.* to
DURABLE riches and righteousness, Prov. 8. 18.
Isa. 23. 18. merchandise for *d.* clothing
DUST thou art, and to *d.*, Gen. 3. 19.
18. 27. who am but *d.* and ashes
Job 30. 19. I am become like *d.*
Ps. 22. 15. brought me into *d.* of
30. 9. shall the *d.* praise thee
103. 14. remembereth that we are *d.*
119. 25. soul cleaveth to the *d.*
Eccl. 12. 7. then shall *d.* retu. to *d.*
Matt. 10. 14. shake off *d.* of your feet, Luke 10. 11. Acts 13. 51.
R. V. Lev. 14. 41. mortar
DUTY of marriage, Ex. 21. 10.
2 Chron. 8. 14. as the *d.* of every day
Eccl. 12. 13. this is whole *d.* of man
Luke 17. 10. which was our *d.* to do
R. V. Rom. 15. 27. owe it to them
DWARFS not to minister, Lev. 21. 20.
DWELL in thy holy hill, Ps. 15. 1.
Ps. 23, 6. I will *d.* in the house of 84. 10. than to *d.* in the tents of wickedness
120. 5. that I *d.* in tents of Kedar
133. 1. good for brethren to *d.* together
Isa. 33. 14. who shall *d.* with devouring fire—*d.* with everlasting burnings
16. he shall *d.* on high his place
Rom. 8. 9. Spirit of God *d.* in you, 11
2 Cor. 6. 16. I will *d.* in them, Ezek. 43. 7.
Col. 1. 19. in him shall all fulness *d.*
1 John 4. 13. that we *d.* in him
Rev. 21. 3. he will *d.* with them
John 6. 56. *dwelleth* in me, and I in 14. 10. Father that *d.* in me
17. he *d.* with and shall be in you Acts 7. 48. *d.* not in temples, 17. 24.
Rom. 7. 17. sin that *d.* in me, 20.
18. in my flesh *d.* no good thing
8. 11. by his Spirit that *d.* in you
1 Cor. 3. 16. Spirit of God *d.* in you
Col. 2. 9. in him *d.* all fulness of
2 Tim. 1. 14. Holy Ghost who *d.* in
Jas. 4. 5. the Spirit which *d.* in
2 Pet. 3. 13. wherein *d.* righteous.
1 John 3. 17. how *d.* the love of God
4. 12. God *d.* in us, and his love is
16. *d.* in love, *d.* in God, and God
2 John 2. truth's sake which *d.* in
1 Tim. 6. 16. *dwelling* in light
Heb. 11. 9. *d.* in tabernacles with
2 Pet. 2. 8. righteous man *d.* among
Ps. 87. 2. more than all *d.* of Jacob
94. 17. almost *dwelt* in silence
John 1. 14. Word made flesh
Acts 13. 17. *d.* as strangers in it
2 Tim. 1. 5. faith *d.* first in grandmother
R. V. frequently in O. T., sit, sojourn

E

EAGLE stirreth up her nest, Deut. 32. 11.
Job 9. 26. as *e.* hasteth to the prey
Prov. 23. 5. fly away as *e.* towards
Jer. 49. 16. make nest as high as *e.*
Ezek. 17. 3. great *e.* with great wings
Mic. 1. 16. enlarge thy bald. as *e.*
Rev. 12. 14. to woman given wings of a great *e.*
Ex. 19. 4. bare you on *e.* wings
2 Sam. 1. 23. swifter than *eagles*

Ps. 103. 5. youth renewed like *e.*
Prov. 30. 17. young *e.* shall eat it
Isa. 40. 31. mount up with wings as *e.*
Jer. 4. 13. horses swifter than *e.*
Matt. 24. 28. there be *e.* be gathered
R. V. Lev. 11. 18; Deut. 14. 17. vulture
EAR, Num. 14. 28. Ex. 9. 31.
Ex. 21. 6. bore his *e.*, Deut. 15. 17.
2 Kings 19. 16. bow down *e.*, Ps. 31. 2.
Neh. 1. 6. let thy *e.* be attentive, 11.
Job 12. 11. *e.* try words, 34. 3.
36. 10. openeth *e.* to discipline
Ps. 10. 17. cause thine *e.* to hear
94. 9. planted the *e.* shall he not
Prov. 18. 15. *e.* of wise seek know.
20. 12. hearing *e.* and seeing eye
Eccl. 1. 8. *e.* filled with hearing
Isa. 50. 4. awaketh my *e.* to hear
59. 1. neither is *e.* heavy
Jer. 6. 10. their *e.* is uncircumcised
Matt. 10. 27. what ye hear in the *e.*
1 Cor. 2. 9. eye seen nor *e.* heard
Rev. 2. 7. he that hath an *e.* let him hear, 11. 17, 29. & 3. 6, 13, 22. & 13. 9. Matt. 11. 15. & 13. 9, 43.
Ex. 15. 26. *give ear*, Deut. 32. 1.
Judg. 5. 3. Ps. 5. 1. & 17. 1. & 39. 12. & 49. 1. & 54. 2. & 78. 1. & 86. 1. & 84. 8. & 141. 1. Isa. 1. 2, 10. & 8. 9. & 28. 23. & 32. 9. & 42. 23. Jer. 13. 15. Hos. 5. 1. Joel 1. 2. Ps. 55. 1. & 86. 6.
Ps. 17. 6. *incline ear*, 45. 10. & 71. 2. & 88. 2. & 102. 2. & 116. 2. Isa. 37. 17. Dan. 9. 18.
49. 4. — to a parable
78. 1. — to words of my mouth
Prov. 2. 2. — to wisdom
4. 20. — to my sayings
Isa. 55. 3. — and come unto me
Jer. 11. 8. *nor inclined their ear*, 17. 23. & 25. 4. & 35. 15.
Deut. 29. 4. Lord not given *ears* to
1 Sam. 3. 11. both *e.* shall tingle, 2 Kings 21. 12. Jer. 19. 3.
2 Sam. 22. 7. cry did enter in. his *e.*
Job 33. 16. open the *e.* of men
Ps. 34. 15. his *e.* are open to their cry
40. 6. my *e.* hast thou opened
44. 1. we have heard with our *e.*
Isa. 6. 10. make their *e.* heavy, lest 35. 5. *e.* of deaf shall be unstopped
Matt. 13. 15. their *e.* dull of hearing
Luke 9. 44. these sayings sink down into your *e.*
2 Tim. 4. 4. turn away their *e.* from
2 Chron. 6. 40. *thine ears* be open to
Ps. 10. 17. cause — to hear
130. 2. let — be attentive
Prov. 23. 12. apply — to words of knowledge
Isa. 30. 21. — shall hear a word
Ezek. 3. 10. hear with—, 40. 4. & 44. 5.
Gen. 45. 6. *earing*, Ex. 34. 21.
1 Sam. 8. 12. *ear his ground*, Isa. 30. 24.
Ex. 9. 31. *in the ear*, Mark 4. 28.
Job 42. 11. gave *ear-ring* of gold
Prov. 25. 12. as an *e.* of gold so is
R. V. Gen. 24. 22, 47; 35. 4; Ex. 32. 2, 3; Job 42. 11. ring, rings; Isa. 3. 20. amulets
EARLY, Gen. 19. 2. John 18. 28. & 20. 1.
Ps. 46. 5. God shall help her, and that right *e.*
57. 8. will awake right *e.*, 108. 2.
63. 1. my God, we will I seek thee
90. 14. satisfy us *e.* with mercy
Prov. 1. 28. seek me *e.* and not find
8. 17. that seek me *e.* shall find me
Isa. 26. 9. with my spir. I seek thee *e.*
Jer. 7. 13. rising up *e.*, 25. & 11. 7. & 25. 3, 4. & 26. 5. & 29. 19. & 32. 33. & 35. 14, 15. & 44. 4. 2 Chron. 36. 15.
Hos. 5. 15. in affliction will seek me *e.*
Jas. 5. 7. receive *e.* and latter rain
R. V. Judg. 7. 3; Ps. 57. 8. right early; 9. 14. in the morning; 101.

8. morning by morning; Ps. 1. 28; 8. 17. diligently; Hos. 5. 15. earnestly; Mark 16. 2. early in the morning; Acts 5. 21. about daybreak
EARNEST of Spirit given, 2 Cor. 1. 22. & 5. 5.
Eph. 1. 14. *e.* of your inheritance
Rom. 8. 19. *e.* expectation of the
2 Cor. 7. 7. told us of your *e.* desire
Heb. 2. 1. give the more *e.* heed
Job 7. 2. servant *earnestly* desireth the shadow
Jer. 11. 7. I *e.* protested to your fathers
31. 20. I do *e.* remember him still
Mic. 7. 3. do evil with both hands *e.*
Luke 22. 44. in an agony, prayed more *e.*
1 Cor. 12. 31. covet *e.* the best gifts
2 Cor. 5. 2. in this we groan *e.*
Jas. 5. 17. prayed *e.* it might not
Jude 3. *e.* contend for the faith
R. V. Mic. 7. 3. diligently; Luke 22. 56; Acts 23. 1. stedfastly; Acts 3. 12. fasten your eyes; Jas. 5. 17. fervently
EARNETH wages, Hag. 1. 6.
EARTH was corrupt, Gen. 6. 11, 12.
Gen. 6. 13. *e.* is filled with violence
11. 1. whole *e.* of one language
41. 47. *e.* brought forth by handfuls
Ex. 9. 29. *e.* is the Lord's, Deut. 10. 14. Ps. 24. 1. 1 Cor. 10. 26, 27, 28.
Num. 16. 32. *e.* opened her mouth, 26. 10. Deut. 11. 6. Ps. 106. 17.
Deut. 28. 23. *e.* under thee be iron
32. 1. O *e.* hear the words of my mouth
Judg. 5. 4. *e.* trembleth and heaven
1 Sam. 2. 8. pillars of *e.* are Lord's
2 Sam. 22. 8. *e.* shook and trembled
1 Chron. 16. 31. let *e.* rejoice, Ps. 96. 11.
Job 9. 6. shakes *e.* out of her place
24. *e.* is given into hand of wicked
11. 9. longer than *e.* broader than
16. 18. O *e.* cover not my blood
26. 7. hangeth *e.* upon nothing
28. 5. out of *e.* cometh bread and
38. 4. I laid the foundations of *e.*
Ps. 33. 5. *e.* is full of the goodness of
65. 9. visitest *e.* and waterest it
67. 6. *e.* shall yield her increase, 85. 12.
72. 19. let the whole *e.* be filled
75. 3. *e.* and inhabitants dissolved, Isa. 24. 19.
78. 69. like *e.* established for ever
97. 4. *e.* saw and trembled
104. 24. *e.* is full of thy riches, 13.
114. 7. tremble, O *e.* at presence of
115. 16. *e.* given to children of men
119. 64. *e.* is full of thy mercy
139. 15. in lowest parts of the *e.*
Prov. 25. 3. *e.* for depth is unsearchable
Isa. 6. 3. whole *e.* is full of his glory
11. 9. *e.* full of the knowledge of
24. 1. Lord maketh the *e.* empty
4. *e.* mourneth and fadeth, 33. 9.
5. *e.* is defiled under inhabitants
19. *e.* utterly broken down and
20. *e.* shall reel and stagger like a
26. 19. *e.* shall cast out her dead
Jer. 22. 29. O *e.*, *e.* hear the word
Ezek. 34. 27. the *e.* shall yield her
43. 2. the whole *e.* shined with his
Hos. 2. 22. *e.* shall hear the corn
Hab. 3. 3. *e.* was full of his praise
Matt. 13. 5. stony ground had not much *e.*
John 3. 31. that is of *e.* earthly
Heb. 6. 7. *e.* which drinketh in rain
Rev. 12. 16. *e.* opened and swallowed
Ps. 67. 2. way known *upon earth*
73. 25. none—I desire besides thee
Eccl. 5. 2. God is in heaven and thou—
7. 20. there is not a just man—

Luke 5. 24. the Son of man hath power—
Col. 3. 5. mortify your members—
Lev. 6. 28. *earthen*, Jer. 19. 1. & 32. 14. Lam. 4. 2. 2 Cor. 4. 7.
John 3. 12, 31. *earthly*, 2 Cor. 5. 1. Phil. 3. 19. Jas. 3. 15.
1 Cor. 15. 47, 48, 49. *earthy*
1 Kings 19. 11, 12. *earthquake*, Isa. 29. 6. Amos 1. 1. Zech. 14. 5. Matt. 24. 7, 27, 54. & 28. 2. Acts 16. 26.
Rev. 6. 12. a great e., 8. 5. & 11. 19. & 16. 18.
R. V. very frequently in O. T., land; John 3. 31. of the earth
EASE, Job 12. 5. & 16. 12. & 21. 23. Ps. 25. 13. & 123. 4. Deut. 28. 65. Isa. 32. 9, 11. Jer. 46. 27. & 48. 11. Ezek. 23. 42. Amos 6. 1. Zech. 1. 15.
Isa. 1. 24. I will e. me of mine adversaries
Luke 12. 19. take thine e. be merry
Matt. 11. 30. my yoke is *easy*, and burden light
Prov. 14. 6. knowledge is e. to him
1 Cor. 14. 9. words e. to be underst.
Jas. 3. 17. gentle, e. to be entreated
Matt. 9. 5. *easier*, 19. 24. Luke 16. 17.
1 Cor. 13. 5. charity is not *easily* provoked
Heb. 12. 1. sin—doth so e. beset us
R. V. Deut. 23. 13. sitteth down; 2 Chron. 10. 4, 9. make
EAST, Gen. 28. 14. & 29. 1. Matt. 2. 1, 2. Ps. 75. 6. & 103. 12.
Isa. 43. 5. bring thy seed from e.
Matt. 8. 11. many shall come from e.
Rev. 16. 12. way of kings of the e. may
Gen. 41. 6. *east wind*, Ex. 14. 21. Job 27. 21. Ps. 48. 7. Isa. 27. 8. Hos. 12. 1. & 13. 15. Hab. 1. 9.
R. V. Jer. 19. 2. Harsith; Rev. 7. 2; 16. 12. sunrising; Gen. 2. 14. in front; Num. 3. 38. toward the sunrising
EAT, Gen. 3. 5, 6, 12, 13. & 18. 8. & 19. 3.
Gen. 2. 16, 17. of every tree freely e.
3. 14. dust shalt thou e. all the
17. in sorrow thou shalt e. of it
Neh. 8. 10. e. the fat, drink the sweet
Ps. 22. 26. the meek shall e. and
53. 4. eat up my people as bread, 14. 4.
78. 25. man did e. angels' food
29. they did e. and were filled
Prov. 1. 31. e. fruit of their own way
S. of S. 5. 1. e. O friends; drink, yea
Isa. 1. 19. if obedient ye shall e.
3. 10. shall e. fruit of doings
55. 1. buy and e. yea, come buy
2. e. that which is good, and let
65. 13. my servants shall e. but ye
Dan. 4. 33. did e. grass as an ox
Hos. 4. 10. shall e. and not have enough, Hag. 1. 6. Mic. 6. 14.
Mic. 3. 3. e. flesh of my people
Matt. 6. 25. what shall we e. and
26. 26. take e. this is my body, Mark 14. 22. 1 Cor. 11. 24, 26, 28.
Luke 10. 8. e. such things as are set
15. 23. let us e. and be merry
17. 27. they did e. they drank, 28.
John 6. 26. because ye did e. of
53. except ye e. flesh of Son of man
Acts 2. 46. did e. — with gladness
1 Cor. 5. 11. with such, no, not to e.
31. whether ye e. or drink, do all
2 Thes. 3. 10. if not work neither e.
2 Tim. 2. 17. e. as doth a canker
Jas. 5. 3. e. your flesh as fire
Rev. 17. 16. shall e. her flesh, and
Ps. 69. 9. the zeal of thy house hath *eaten* me up, John 2. 17. Ps. 119. 139.
Prov. 9. 17. bread e. in secret is
S. of S. 5. 1. e. my honeycomb with
Hos. 10. 13. having e. fruit of lies
Luke 13. 26. e. and drunk in thy
Acts 12. 23. Herod was e. of worms
Judg. 14. 14. out of *eater* came meat
Isa. 55. 10. give bread to e. and seed
Nah. 3. 12. fall into mouth of e.

Eccl. 4. 5. *eateth* his own flesh
Matt. 9. 11. why e. your master with publicans and sinners, Luke 15. 2.
John 6. 54. whoso e. my flesh
57. he that e. me shall live by me
58. he that e. this bread shall live
Rom. 14. 6. he that e. e. to the Lord
20. evil for that man who e. with offence
1 Cor. 11. 29. e. and drinketh unworthily, e. and drinketh damnation, 27.
Matt. 11. 18. John came neither *eating* nor drinking, Luke 7. 33.
19. Son of man came e.
24. 38. were e. and drinking, Luke 17. 27.
Matt. 26. 26. as they were e. Jesus
1 Cor. 8. 4. concerning e. of those
EDIFY, or build up, Rom. 14. 19.
1 Thes. 5. 11. 1 Cor. 8. 1. & 10. 23. & 14. 17. Acts 9. 31.
Rom. 15. 2. please neighbor to *edification*
1 Cor. 14. 3. speak unto men to e.
1 Cor. 14. 12. excel to *edifying* of church
26. let all things be done to e.,5. 17.
2 Cor. 12. 19. we do all for your e.
Eph. 4. 29. but what is good to the use of e.
1 Tim. 1. 4. minister questions rather than e.
R. V. 1 Thes. 5. 11. build each . . up; Eph. 4. 12; 4. 16. building up; 1 Tim. 1. 4. a dispensation of God; Rom. 15. 2. unto edifying; 2 Cor. 12. 19. 13. 10. building up
EFFECT, 2 Chron. 34. 22. Ezek. 12. 23.
Isa. 32. 17. e. of righteousness quietness
Matt. 15. 6. commandment of God *of none effect*
Mark 7. 13. making work of God—
Rom. 3. 3. make faith of God—
9. 6. not as though word hath—
1 Cor. 1. 17. lest cross of Christ—
Gal. 5. 4. Christ is become—to you
1 Cor. 16. 9. door and *effectual* is opened
2 Cor. 1. 6. which is e. in enduring
Eph. 3. 7. e. working of his power
Phile. 6. faith may become e.
Jas. 5. 16. e. fervent prayer of the righteous
Gal. 2. 8. *effectually*, 1 Thes. 2. 13.
R. V. Num. 30. 8; Matt. 15. 6; Mark 7. 13; 1 Cor. 1. 17. void; Rom. 9. 6. come to nought; Gal. 5. 4. severed from Christ; Jer. 48. 30. have wrought nothing; 2 Cor. 1. 6. worketh patient; Eph. 3. 7. according to; 4. 16. working in due measure; Jas. 5. 16. supplication; Gal. 2. 8. for; 1 Thes. 2. 13 —
EFFEMINATE, 1 Cor. 6. 9.
EGG, Deut. 22. 6. Job 6. 6. & 39. 14. Isa. 10. 14. & 59. 5. Jer. 17. 11. Luke 11. 12.
ELDER, Gen. 10. 21. 2 John 1. 3 John 1.
Gen. 25. 23. e. shall serve younger, Rom. 9. 12.
1 Tim. 5. 1. rebuke not an e. but 2. entreat e. women as mothers
1 Pet. 5. 1. *elders*, I who am an e.
5. younger submit yourselves to e.
Deut. 32. 7. ask e. they will tell thee
Ezra 10. 8. according to counsel of e.
Joel 2. 16. assemble e., Ps. 107. 32.
Acts 14. 23. ordain e. in every
15. 23. e. and brethren send greeting, 6.
1 Tim. 5. 17. e. rule well, counted worthy
Tit. 1. 5. ordain e. in every church
Heb. 11. 2. e. obtained good report
Rev. 4. 4. four and twenty e. sitting, 10. & 5. 6, 8, 11, 14. & 11. 16. & 19. 4. & 7. 11, 13. & 14. 3.
R. V. Joel 1. 14; 2. 16. old men; Matt. 26. 59 —
ELECT, *chosen, choice one*

Isa. 42. 1. e. in whom my soul delighteth
45. 4. for Israel my e. I have called
65. 9. my e. shall inherit it
22. my e. shall long enjoy work
Matt. 24. 22. for e. sake the days are shortened
24. if possible deceive very e.
31. gather together his e. from the
Luke 18. 7. God avenge his own e.
Rom. 8. 33. to charge of God's e.
1 Tim. 5. 21. charge thee before the e. angels
2 Tim. 2. 10. endure all things for e.
Tit. 1. 1. according to the faith of God's e.
1 Pet. 1. 2. e. according to the fore.
2. 6. corner stone, e. precious
2 John 1. e. lady
13. e. sister
1 Pet. 5. 13. church *elected* with you
Rom. 9. 11. purpose of God according to *election*
11. 5. remnant according to the e. of grace
7. e. hath obtained it, and rest blinded
28. touching the e. they are beloved
1 Thes. 1. 4. knowing your e. of God
2 Pet. 1. 10. make calling and e. sure
R. V. Isa. 42. 1; 45. 4; 65. 9, 22. my chosen
ELEMENTS, Gal. 4. 3, 9. 2 Pet. 3. 10, 12.
R. V. Gal. 4. 3, 9. rudiments
ELOQUENT, Ex. 4. 10. Isa. 3. 3.
R. V. Isa. 3. 3. skilful; Acts 18. 24. learned
EMBALMING, of Jacob, Gen. 50. 2. of Joseph, Gen. 50. 26. of Christ, John 19. 39.
EMPTY, Gen. 31.42. & 37. 24. & 41.27.
Ex. 23. 15. none shall appear before me e., 34. 20. Deut. 16. 16.
Deut. 15. 13. not let him go away e.
Judg. 7. 16. with e. pitchers and lamps
2 Sam. 1. 22. sword of Saul returned not e.
Hos. 10. 1. Israel is an e. vine
Luke 1. 53. rich hath he sent e. away
Isa. 34. 11. stones of *emptiness*
R. V. Hos. 10. 1. luxuriant
EMULATION, Rom. 11. 14. Gal. 5. 20.
END of all flesh is come, Gen. 6. 13.
Deut. 32. 20. see what their e. shall
Ps. 37. 37. e. of that man is peace
39. 4. make me to know my e.
Prov. 5. 4. her e. is bitter as worm.
14. 12. e. thereof are ways of death
Eccl. 4. 8. no e. of all his labor
7. 2. that is the e. of all men
Isa. 9. 7. of his government shall be no e.
Jer. 5. 31. what will ye do in the e. thereof
29. 11. to give an expected e.
Lam. 4. 18. our e. is come. our e. is near, Ezek. 7. 2, 6. Amos 8. 2.
Ezek. 21. 25. when iniquity shall have an e.
Dan. 12. 8. what shall be the e. of these
13. go thy way till the e. be
Hab. 2. 3. at the e. it shall speak
Matt. 13. 39. harvest is e. of world
24. 6. but e. is not yet, Luke 21. 9.
Rom. 6. 21. e. of those things is death
10. 4. Christ is e. of law for righteousness
Rom. 14. 9. to this e. Christ both
1 Tim. 1. 5. e. of commandment is
Heb. 6. 8. whose e. is to be burned
16. oath—make an e. of all strife
13. 7. considering e. of their
Jas. 5. 11. seen the e. of the Lord
1 Pet. 1. 9. receiving the e. of your
4. 7. e. of all things is at hand
Rev. 21. 6. beginning and e., 22. 13. & 1. 8. 1 Sam. 3. 12.

Jer. 4. 27. *make a full end*, 5. 10, 18. & 30. 11. Ezek. 11. 13.
Num. 23. 10. *last end*, Jer. 12. 4. Lam. 1. 9. & 4. 18. Dan. 8. 19. & 9. 24.
Deut. 8. 16. *latter end*, 32. 29. Job 42. 12. Prov. 19. 20. 2 Pet. 2. 20.
Ps. 119. 33. *unto the end*, Dan. 6. 26. Matt. 24. 13. & 28. 20. John 13. 1. 1 Cor. 1. 8. Heb. 3. 6, 14. & 6. 11. Rev. 2. 26.
† Tim. 1. 14. *endless*, Heb. 7. 16.
Ps. 22. 27. all the *ends* of the world 65. 5. confidence of all *e.* of earth 67. 7. all *e.* of earth shall fear him
Prov. 17. 24. eyes of fool in *e.* of
Isa. 45. 22. be ye saved, all *e.* of the 52. 10. all *e.* of the earth shall see
Zech. 9. 10. his dominion to *e.* of
Acts 13. 47. for salvation to the *e.*
1 Cor. 10. 11. on whom *e.* of world
R. V. Josh. 15. 8; 18. 15; Isa. 13. 5; Acts 13. 47. uttermost part; Dan. 12. 8; Heb. 13. 7. issue; Luke 22. 37. hath fulfilment; Matt. 28. 1. now late on; 1 Pet. 1. 13. perfectly on; 2 Pet. 2. 20. last state . . become; Gen. 2. 2; Deut. 31. 30; 1 Kings 7. 51. finished; Ezek. 4. 8. accomplished; Luke 4. 2, 13; Acts 21. 27. completed; John 13. 2 ——
ENDOWED, Gen. 30. 20. 2 Chron. 2. 12, 13. Luke 24. 49. Jas. 3. 13.
ENDURE, Job 8. 15. & 31. 23.
Gen. 33. 14. as children are able to *e.*
Ps. 30. 5. weeping may *e.* for a night 132. 26. they perish, but thou shalt *e.*
Prov. 27. 24. doth crown *e.* to
Ezek. 22. 14. can thy heart *e.* or
Mark 4. 17. no root, and *e.* but for a 13. 13. that shall *e.* unto end shall
2 Tim. 2. 3. *e.* hardness as a soldier 10. *e.* all things for elect's sakes 4. 5. watch thou, *e.* afflictions, do
Heb. 12. 7. if ye *e.* chastening
Jas. 5. 11. we count happy which *e.* for ever
Rom. 9. 22. *e.* with much long suffering
2 Tim. 3. 11. what persecutions I *e.*
Heb. 6. 15. had patiently *e.* he obtained
10. 32. ye *e.* a great fight of afflic.
12. 2. *e.* cross
3. *e.* contradiction
Ps. 30. 5. his anger *endureth* but a 52. 1. the goodness of God *e.* continually
100. 5. his truth *e.* to all generations
Matt. 10. 22. that *e.* to end, shall be saved, 24. 13. Mark 13. 13.
John 6. 27. meat which *e.* unto life
1 Cor. 13. 7. charity *e.* all things
Jas. 1. 12. blessed that *e.* temptation
Ps. 9. 7. *endure for ever*, the Lord, 102. 12, 26. & 104. 31. his name, Ps. 72. 17. his seed, 89. 29, 36.
1 Chron. 16. 34, 41. *endureth for ever*, his mercy, 2 Chron. 5. 13. & 7. 3, 6. & 20. 21. Ezra 3. 11. Ps. 106. 1. & 107. 1. & 118. 1, 2. 3, 4, 29. & 136. 1-26. & 138. 8. Jer. 33. 11.
Ps. 111. 3. his righteousness—, 112. 3,9.
10. his praise —
117. 2. truth of the Lord —
119. 160. every one of thy judgments —
135. 13. thy name —
1 Pet. 1. 25. word of Lord —
Ps. 19. 9. fear of Lord *enduring* for ever
Heb. 10. 34. in heaven *e.* substance
R. V. Gen. 33. 14. according to the pace; Job 31. 23. do nothing; Ps. 9. 7. sitteth; 30. 5. tarry; John 6. 27; 1 Pet. 1. 25. abideth; Heb. 10. 34. abiding
ENEMY, Ex. 15. 6, 9. Ps. 7. 5.

Ex. 23. 22. I will be an *e.* unto thine enemies
Deut. 32. 27. I feared wrath of the *e.*
1 Sam. 24. 19. find his *e.* will he let
Job 33. 10. counteth me for his *e.*
Ps. 7. 5. let *e.* persecute my soul 8. 2. mightest still the *e.* and
Prov. 27. 6. kisses of *e.* are deceitful
Isa. 63. 10. he turned to be their *e.*
1 Cor. 15. 26. the last *e.* destroyed
Gal. 4. 16. am I become your *e.*
2 Thes. 3. 15. count him not as *e.*
Jas. 4. 4. friend of world, *e.* of God
1 Kings 21. 20. *mine enemy*, Ps. 7. 4. Mic. 7. 8, 10. Job 16. 9. Lam. 2. 22.
Ex. 23. 4. *thy enemy*, Prov. 25. 21. Rom. 12. 20. Matt. 5. 43.
Mic. 7. 6. man's *enemies* are men of
Rom. 5. 10. if when *e.* we were reconciled
1 Cor. 15. 25. put all *e.* under his feet
Phil. 3. 18. *e.* to the cross of Christ
Col. 1. 21. *e.* in your minds by wicked
Gen. 22. 17. *his enemies*, Ps. 68. 1, 21. & 112. 8. & 132. 18. Prov. 16. 7. Isa. 59. 18. & 66. 6. Heb. 10. 13.
Deut. 32. 41. *my enemies*, Ps. 18. 17. 48. & 23. 5. & 119. 98. & 139. 22. & 143. 12. Isa. 1. 24. Luke 19. 27.
Deut. 32. 31. *our enemies*, Luke 1. 71, 74.
Ex. 23. 22. *thy enemies*, Num. 10. 35. Deut. 28. 48, 53, 55, 57. & 33. 29. Judg. 5. 31. Ps. 21. 8. & 92. 9. & 110. 1. Matt. 22. 44. Heb. 1. 13.
Gen. 3. 15. I will put *enmity* between
Rom. 8. 7. carnal mind is *e.* against God
Eph. 2. 15. abolished *e.*
16. slain *e.*
R. V. Very frequently in O. T., especially in Ps., adversary
ENGAGETH his heart, Jer. 30. 21.
ENJOIN Phile. 8. Esth. 9. 31. Job 36. 23. Heb. 9. 20.
R. V. Heb. 9. 20. commanded to you ward
ENJOY, Num. 36. 8. Deut. 28. 41. Lev. 26. 34. land *e.* her sabbaths, 43.
Acts 24. 2. we *e.* great quietness
1 Tim. 6. 17. giveth richly all things to *e.*
Heb. 11. 25. *e.* pleasures of sin for
R. V. Num. 36. 8; Josh. 1. 15. possess
ENLARGE, Ex. 34. 24. Mic. 1. 16.
Gen. 9. 27. God shall *e.* Japheth
Deut. 33. 20. blessed be he that *enlargeth* Gad
2 Sam. 22. 37. *enlarged* steps, Ps. 18. 36.
Ps. 4. 1. *e.* me when in distress
25. 17. troubles of my heart are *e.*
119. 32. when thou shalt *e.* my
Isa. 5. 14. hell hath *e.* herself
54. 2. *e.* the place of thy tent
Hab. 2. 5. *e.* his desires as hell
2 Cor. 6. 11. our heart is *e.*, 13.
Esth. 4. 14. *enlargement*
R. V. Ps. 4. 1. set me at large; 2 Cor. 10. 15. magnified in
ENLIGHTEN darkness, Ps. 18. 28. Eph. 1. 18. understanding being *enlightened*
Ps. 19. 8. commandment is pure, *enlightening* the eyes
Heb. 6. 4. impossible for those once *e.*
R. V. Ps. 18. 28. lighten
ENMITY between God and man, Rom. 8. 7. Jas. 4. 4; how abolished, Eph. 2. 15. Col. 1. 20.
ENOUGH, I have, Gen. 33. 9, 11. Gen. 45. 28. it is *e.* Joseph is alive
Ex. 36. 5. bring more than *e.*
1 Kings 19. 4. it is *e.* take away
Prov. 30. 15, 16. say not, it is *e.*

Hos. 4. 10. eat, and not *e.*, Hag. 1. 6.
Matt. 10. 25. it is *e.* for disciple
Mark 14. 41. it is *e.* the hour is
Luke 15. 17. bread *e.* and to spare
R. V. Ex. 2. 19 —
ENQUIRE after iniquity, Job 10. 6.
Ps. 27. 4. to *e.* in his temple
78. 34. returned and *e.* early after God
Eccl. 7. 10. thou dost not *e.* wisely
Isa. 21. 12. if ye will *e.* ye
Ezek. 36. 37. this I will be *enquired* of by the house of Israel
Zeph. 1. 6. have not *e.* for him
Matt. 2. 7. Herod *e.* of them diligently
Judg. 20. 27. *enquired of the Lord*, 1 Sam. 23. 2, 4. & 30. 8. 2 Sam. 2. 1. & 5. 19, 23. & 21. 1. Jer. 21. 2.
Prov. 20. 25. after vows make *enquiry*
R. V. Almost always changed to inquire; Matt. 27. 7, 16. learned; 1 Pet. 1. 10. sought
ENRICHED, 1 Cor. 1. 5. 2 Cor. 9. 11.
Ps. 65. 9. thou greatly *e.* it with
ENSAMPLE, 1 Cor. 10. 11. Phil. 3. 17. 1 Thes. 1. 7. 2 Thes. 3. 9. 1 Pet. 5. 3. 2 Pet. 2. 6.
R. V. 1 Cor. 10. 11. by way of example; 2 Pet. 2. 6. example
ENSIGN, Isa. 5. 26. Zech. 9. 16.
Isa. 11. 10. stand for *e.* to people, 12.
Ps. 74. 4. set up their *e.* for signs
R. V. Zech. 9. 16. on high
ENTER, Gen. 12. 11. Num. 4. 23. Judg. 18. 9. Dan. 11. 17, 40, 41.
Job 22. 4. will he *e.* into judg.
Ps. 100. 4. *e.* into his gates with
Isa. 2. 10. *e.* into rock and hide
26. 2. open, righteous nation may *e.*
20. *e.* into thy chambers, and shut
57. 2. he shall *e.* into peace
Matt. 5. 20. in no case *e.* into the 6. 6. when thou prayest, *e.* closet 7. 13. *e.* at strait gate, Luke 13. 24. 21. shall *e.* into kingdom of heaven
18. 8. better to *e.* into life, halt
19. 23. rich man hardly *e.* into
24. than for rich man to *e.* into the kingdom of heaven, Mark 10. 25. Luke 18. 25.
25. 21. *e.* thou into joy of Lord
Mark 14. 38. watch and pray, lest ye *e.* into temptation, Luke 22. 46.
Luke 13. 24. seek to *e.* but not able
24. 26. suffered and *e.* into his glory
John 3. 4. can he *e.* the second time
5. he cannot *e.* into the kingdom
Acts 14. 22. through much tribulation *e.* kingdom of God.
Heb. 4. 3. believed, do *e.* into rest
Rev. 15. 8. no man able to *e.* into temple
21. 27. *e.* into it, any thing defileth
Rev. 22. 14. *e.* through gates into
Ps. 143. 2. *enter not into* judgment
Prov. 4. 14. *e.* not into path of
23. 10. *e.* not into the fields of th
Matt. 26. 41. that ye *e.* not into temptation
Ps. 119. 130. *entrance*, 2 Pet. 1. 11.
Luke 11. 52. ye *entered* not yourself.
John 4. 38. ye *e.* into their labors
10. 1. that *e.* not by door, but
Rom. 5. 12. sin *e.* into the world
Heb. 4. 6. *e.* not in because of unbelief
10. that is *e.* into his rest, he ceased
Matt. 23. 13. *entering*, Luke 11. 52.
Mark 4. 19. & 7. 15. 1 Thes. 1. 9. Heb. 4. 1.
R. V. Mark 5. 40; 7. 18. goeth. The same change is frequent in O. T. Ex. 35. 15. door; 2 Chron. 18. 9; 23. 13. entrance; Mark 7. 15. going; Acts 27. 2. embarking; Num. 34. 8. 1 Chron. 4. 39; 1 Thes. 2. 1. entering; 2 Chron. 12. 10. door; Ps. 119. 130. opening

ENTERTAIN strangers, Heb. 13. 2.
R. V. Show love unto
ENTICE, Ex. 20. 16. Deut. 13. 6.
2 Chron. 18. 19, 20, 21. Prov. 1. 10.
Job 31. 27. enticed, Jas. 1. 14.
1 Cor. 2. 4. enticing words, Col. 2. 4.
R. V. 1 Cor. 2. 4. persuasive; Col. 2. 4. persuasiveness of
ENVY slayeth silly one, Job 5. 2.
Prov. 3. 31. e. not the oppressor
14. 30. e. is the rottenness of bones
23. 17. let not thy heart e. sinners
Eccl. 9. 6. their e. is perished
Isa. 11. 13. e. of Ephraim shall depart, not e. Judah
Ezek. 35. 11. do according to thine e.
Matt. 27. 18. for e. they delivered
Acts 7. 9. moved with e., 17. 5.
13. 45. Jews filled with e. spake
Rom. 1. 29. full of e. murder
Phil. 1. 15. preach Christ of e.
1 Tim. 6. 4. whereof cometh e.
Jas. 4. 5. spirit in us lusteth to e.
1 Pet. 2. 1. laying aside all e.
Gen. 26. 14. Philistines envied him
30. 1. Rachel e. her sister
Ps. 106. 16. they e. Moses in camp
Eccl. 4. 4. man is e. of his neigh.
Num. 11. 29. enviest thou for my sake
1 Cor. 13. 4. charity envieth not
Rom. 13. 13. not in strife and envying
1 Cor. 3. 3. there is among you e.
2 Cor. 12. 20. debates, e. wraths
Gal. 5. 26. e. one another
Jas. 3. 14. ye have bitter e. and
Gal. 5. 21. envyings, murders
Ps. 37. 1. envious, 73. 3. Prov. 24. 1, 19.
R. V. Isa. 26. 11. see thy zeal for the people; Job 5. 2; Prov. 27. 4; Acts 7. 9; 13. 45; 17. 5. jealousy; Rom. 13. 13; 1 Cor. 3. 3; 2 Cor. 12. 20; Jas. 3. 14, 16. jealousy
EPHOD, Ex. 39. 2. Judg. 8. 27. & 17. 5. 1 Sam. 2. 18. & 21. 9. & 23. 9. & 30. 7. 2 Sam. 6. 14. Hos. 3. 4.
EPISTLE, Acts 15. 30. & 23. 33. Rom. 16. 22. 1 Cor. 5. 9. 2 Cor. 7. 8. Col. 4. 16. 1 Thes. 5. 27. 2 Thes. 2. 15. & 3. 14, 17. 2 Pet. 3. 1.
2 Cor. 3. 2. e. written in our hearts
3. ye are declared the e. of Christ
1. epistles, 2 Pet. 3. 16.
R. V. Acts 23. 33. letter
EQUAL, Job 28. 17, 19. Ps. 17. 2 & 55. 13. Prov. 26. 7. Lam. 2. 13.
Isa. 40. 25. to whom shall I be e.
46. 5. to whom will ye make me e.
Ezek. 18. 25. way of Lord is not e.
29. & 33. 17, 20. their way is not e.
Matt. 20. 12. made them e. to us
Luke 20. 36. e. to the angels
John 5. 18. making himself e. with
Rev. 21. 16. length, breadth, and height e.
Gal. 1. 14. equals, Ps. 55. 13.
2 Cor. 8. 14. equality
Ps. 99. 4. dost establish equity
Prov. 1. 3. receive instruction of e.
17. 26. to strike princes for e.
Eccl. 2. 21. whose labor is in e.
Isa. 11. 4. reprove with e. for
59. 14. truth is fallen, and e. can.
Mic. 3. 9. that pervert all e.
Mal. 2. 6. walked with me in e.
R. V. Ps. 17. 2. equity; Prov. 26. 7. hang loose; Col. 4. of mine own age
ERR, 2 Chron. 33. 9. Isa. 19. 14.
Ps. 95. 10. e. in heart, Heb. 3. 10.
119. 21. do e. from thy command.
Prov. 14. 22. do they not e. that devise ill
Isa. 3. 12. lead — cause to e., 9. 16.
63. 17. why made us to e. from thy
Jer. 23. 13. prophet caused to e. by lies, 32.
Amos 2. 4. lies caused them to e.
Mic. 3. 5. prophets make my people to e.
Matt. 22. 29. ye e. not knowing the

Jas. 1. 16. do not e. my brethren
5. 19. if any of you e. from truth
Num. 15. 22. if ye have erred
1 Sam. 26. 21. I have e. exceedingly
Job 6. 24. understand wherein I have e.
19. 4. be it that I have e., my error
Ps. 119. 110. yet I e. not from
Isa. 28. 7. have e. through wine
29. 24. they that e. in spirit
1 Tim. 6. 10. have e. from the faith
21. e. concerning faith, 2 Tim. 2. 18.
Prov. 10. 17. erreth, Ezek. 45. 20.
2 Sam. 6. 7. error, Job 19. 4. Eccl. 5. 6. & 10. 5. Dan. 6. 4.
Isa. 32. 6. will utter e. against Lord
Jer. 10. 15. vanity work of e., 51. 18.
Dan. 6. 4. neither was there any e. or fault found
Matt. 27. 64. last e. be worse than the first
Rom. 1. 27. recompense of their e.
Jas. 5. 20. sinner from e. of his
2 Pet. 2. 18. them who live in e.
1 John 4. 6. know we the spirit of e.
Jude 11. after the e. of Balaam
Ps. 19. 12. who can under. his errors
Heb. 9. 7. for the e. of the people
R. V. 1 Tim. 6. 10. been led astray; Jas. 1. 16. be not deceived; Jer. 10. 15; 51. 18. delusion
ERRAND, Judg. 3. 19. 2 Kings 9. 5.
ESCAPE, Gen. 19. 17, 22. & 32. 8.
Ezra 9. 8. leave a remnant to e.
Esth. 4. 13. think not that thou shalt e.
Job 11. 20. but the wicked shall not e.
Ps. 56. 7. shall they e. by iniquity
71. 2. deliver me and cause me toe.
141. 10. let wicked fall whilst I e.
Prov. 19. 5. he that speaks lies shall not e.
Eccl. 7. 26. pleaseth God, shall e. her
Isa. 20. 6. we flee — how shall we e.
Jer. 11. 11. evil — not be able to e.
Ezek. 17. 15. shall e. that doeth
Matt. 23. 33. how can ye e. damna.
Luke 21. 36. accounted worthy to e.
Rom. 2. 3. e. the judgment of God
1 Cor. 10. 13. with temptation make a way to e.
1 Thes. 5. 3. destruction they shall not e.
Heb. 2. 3. how shall we e. if neglect
12. 25. much more shall not we e.
Ezra 9. 15. we remain yet escaped
Job 1. 15, 16, 17, 19. I only am e. to
Ps. 124. 7. soul is e. we are e.
Isa. 45. 20. ye are e. of the nations
John 10. 39. he e. out of their hands
Heb. 12. 25. if they e. not who refused
2 Pet. 1. 4. e. corruption of the world
2. 18. those that were clean e.
20. have e. pollutions of the world
ESCHEW evil, Job 1. 8. & 2. 3.
1 Pet. 3. 11.
R. V. 1 Pet. 3. 11. turn away from
ESPECIALLY, Deut. 4. 10. Ps. 31. 11.
Gal. 6. 10. good e. to household of
1 Tim. 4. 10. e. of those that believe
5. 17. e. those that labor in word
R. V. Ps. 31. 11. exceedingly
ESPOUSALS, S. of S. 3. 11. Jer. 2. 2.
2 Cor. 11. 2. espoused to Christ
R. V. 2 Sam. 3. 14; Matt. 1. 18; Luke 1. 27. betrothed
ESPY, Josh. 14. 7. Ezek. 20. 6.
R. V. Josh. 14. 7. spy
ESTABLISH, Num. 30. 13. 1 Kings 15. 4. Deut. 28. 9. Job 36. 7.
Gen. 6. 18. e. my covenant, 9. 9. & 17. 7, 9, 21. Lev. 26. 9. Deut. 8. 18.
1 Sam. 1. 23. the Lord e. his word
2 Sam. 7. 12. I will e. his kingdom, 13.
25. e. the word for ever, and do as
2 Chron. 9. 8. God loved Israel to e.
7. 18. e. throne of kingdom

Ps. 7. 9. but e. the just, 48. 8.
89. 2. faithfulness shall e. in heav.
4. thy seed will I e. for ever
99. 4. dost e. equity, executest
119. 38. e. thy word to servant
Prov. 15. 25. he will e. border of
Isa. 9. 7. to e. with judgment and
49. 8. give thee for a covenant to e.
62. 7. no rest till he e. Jerusalem
Ezek. 16. 60. I will e. an everlast.
Rom. 3. 31. yea, we e. the law
10. 3. going about to e. their own
1 Thes. 3. 13. may e. your hearts
2 Thes. 2. 17. e. you in every good
3. 3. Lord shall e. and keep you
Jas. 5. 8. patient; e. your hearts
1 Pet. 5. 10. God of all grace e. you
Gen. 41. 32. thing is established
Ex. 6. 4. have e. my covenant with
15. 17. which thy hands have e.
Ps. 40. 2. on rock he e. my goings
78. 5. he e. a testimony in Jacob
93. 2. thy throne is e. of old
112. 8. his heart is e. trusting
119. 90. hast e. the earth, and it
148. 6. hath e. them for ever
Prov. 3. 19. Lord hath e. the heav.
4. 26. let all thy ways be e.
12. 3. man shall not be e. by wickedness
16. 12. throne is e. by righteous.
30. 4. e. all the ends of the earth
Isa. 7. 9. if believe not — not be e.
16. 5. in mercy shall throne be e.
Jer. 10. 12. e. world by wisdom, 51. 15.
Hab. 1. 12. e. them for correction
Matt. 18. 16. two or three witness. e.
2 Cor. 13. 1. word may be e.
Acts 16. 5. so were the churches e.
Rom. 1. 11. to the end you may be e.
Col. 2. 7. built up — e. in the faith
Heb. 8. 6. e. upon better promises
2 Pet. 1. 12. e. in the present truth
Lev. 25. 30. shall be established, Deut. 19. 15. Ps. 89. 21. 2 Cor. 13. 1.
2 Chron. 20. 20. believe in God so ye —
Job 22. 28. shall decree a thing and it —
Ps. 102. 28. their seed — before thee
Prov. 12. 19. lip of truth —
25. 5. his throne — in righteousness, 29. 14.
Isa. 2. 2. Lord's house —, Mic. 4. 1.
54. 14. in righteousness thou —
Jer. 30. 20. their congregation —
Prov. 29. 4. king by judgment establisheth the land
Hab. 2. 12. woe to him that e. city by
2 Cor. 1. 21. who e. us with you is God
R. V. 2 Sam. 7. 25. confirm; Isa. 49. 8. raise up; Lev. 25. 30; 2 Sam. 7. 16. made sure; Prov. 3. 28. made firm; Zech. 5. 11. prepared; Heb. 8. 6. hath been enacted; Acts 16. 5. strengthened
ESTATE, Gen. 43. 7. Esth. 1. 7, 19.
Ps. 39. 5. man at best e. is vanity
Prov. 27. 23. know e. of thy flocks
Matt. 12. 45. last e. of that man is worse than the first, Luke 11. 26.
Luke 1. 48. regarded low e. of
Rom. 12. 16. condescend to men of low e.
Phil. 4. 11. in whatsoever e. I am — content
Jude 6. angels kept not first e.
R. V. Dan. 11. 7, 20, 21, 38. place; Mark 6. 21. chief men; Rom. 12. 16. things lowly; Jude 6. own principality
ESTEEM, Job 36. 19. Isa. 29. 16, 17.
Ps. 119. 128. I e. all thy precepts
Phil. 2. 3. e. each other better than
1 Thes. 5. 13. e. them very highly in
Deut. 32. 15. lightly esteemed the
1 Sam. 2. 30. despise me, lightly e.
Isa. 29. 17. I have e. words of his
Isa. 53. 3. despised — we e. him not
4. did e. him stricken, smitten of
Luke 16. 15. is highly e. among men
Rom. 14. 5. esteemeth one day above

another, another *e.* every day alike
Rom. 14. 14. to him that *e.* it to be unclean
Heb. 11. 26. *esteeming* the reproach
R. V. Job 23. 12. treasured up; 41. 27; Isa. 27. 17. counted; Luke 16. 15. exalted; Rom. 14. 14. accounteth; Heb. 11. 26. accounting

ESTRANGED, Job 19. 13. Jer. 19. 4.
Ps. 58. 3. wicked are *e.* from womb
78. 30. not *e.* from their lusts
Ezek. 14. 5. they are all *e.* from me

ETERNAL God thy refuge, Deut. 33. 27.
Isa. 60. 15. make thee an *e.* excell.
Mark 3. 29. in danger of *e.* damna.
Rom. 1. 20. even his *e.* power and
2 Cor. 4. 17. exceeding *e.* weight of
18. things not seen which are *e.*
5. 1. have house *e.* in the heavens
Eph. 3. 11. according to *e.* purpose
1 Tim. 1. 17. unto the King *e.* be honor
2 Tim. 2. 10. salvation with *e.* glory
Heb. 5. 9. author of *e.* salvation
6. 2. baptisms, and of *e.* judgment
9. 12. obtained *e.* redemp. for us
1 Pet. 5. 10. called us to *e.* glory
Jude 7. vengeance of *e.* fire
Matt. 19. 16. that I may have *eternal life,* Mark 10. 17. Luke 10. 25.
25.46. the righteous shall go into—
Mark 10. 30. in world to come—
John 3. 15. not perish but have—
4. 36. gathereth fruit unto—
5. 39. in Scriptures ye think ye have—
6. 54. hath—and I will raise him
68. thou hast the words of—
10. 28. I give unto them—
12. 25. shall keep it unto—
17. 2. should give—to as many
3. this is—to know only true God
Acts 13. 48. ordained to—believed
Rom. 2. 7. who seek for glory and—
5. 21. grace might reign to—
6. 23. the gift of God is—through
1 Tim. 6. 12. lay hold on—, 19.
Tit. 1. 2. in hope of—which God
3. 7. heirs according to hope of—
2. 25. promise promised us, even—
3. 15. no murderer hath—
5. 13. may know that ye have—
Jude 21. for mercy unto—
R. V. Rom. 1. 20. everlasting

ETERNITY, that inhabits, Isa. 57. 15.

EUNUCH, 2 Kings 9. 32. & 20. 18.
Isa. 56. 3. let no *e.* say, I am a dry
Matt. 19. 12. some *e.* born made *e.*
Acts 8. 27. *e.* had come to Jerusa.
R. V. Jer. 52. 25. officer

EVEN balances, Job 31. 6.
Ps. 26. 12. foot stands in *e.* place
Luke 19. 44. lay thee *e.* with ground

EVEN or **EVENING,** Gen. 1. 5, 8, 31. & 19. 1. Ex. 12. 6, 18.
1 Kings 18. 29. at *e.* sacrifice, Ezra 9. 4, 5. Ps. 141. 2. Dan. 9. 21.
Hab. 1. 8. *e.* wolves, Zeph. 3. 3.
Zech. 14. 7. at *e.* time shall be light
R. V. Mark 11. 19. every evening

EVENT, Eccl. 2. 14. & 9. 2, 3.

EVER, a long time, constantly, eternally, Josh. 4. 7. & 14. 9.
Deut. 19. 9. to walk *e.* in his way
Ps. 5. 11. let them *e.* shout for joy
25. 15. my eyes *e.* toward the Lord
51. 3. my sin is *e.* before me
Luke 15. 31. son thou art *e.* with
John 8. 35. in house son abideth *e.*
1 Thes. 4. 17. we shall be *e.* with
5. 15. *e.* follow that which is good
2 Tim. 3. 7. *e.* learning, and never
Heb. 7. 24. this man continueth *e.*
25. he *e.* liveth to make interces.
Jude 25. to God be glory now and *e.*
Gen. 3. 22. eat and live *for ever*
Deut. 32. 40. I lift up hand and live—
Josh. 4. 24. fear Lord your God—
1 Kings 10. 9. Lord loved Israel—

1 Kings 11. 39. afflict the seed of David but not—
Ps. 9. 7. Lord shall endure—
12. 7. thou wilt preserve them—
22. 26. your heart shall live—
23. 6. I will dwell in the house of the Lord—
30. 12. I will give thanks to thee—
37. 18. their inheritance shall be—
28. saints are preserved—
29. in land righteous shall dwell—
49. 9. that he should still live—
52. 9. I will praise thee—
61. 4. I will abide in tabernacle—
74. 19. forget not congregation of poor—
81. 15. their time should endure—
92. 7. that they shall be destroyed—
102. 12. but thou, O Lord, shalt endure—
103. 9. the Lord will not keep his anger—
105. 8. remember his covenant—
112. 6. righteous shall not be moved—
119. 111. testimonies as heritage—
132. 14. this is my rest—I have
146. 6. who keepeth truth—
Prov. 27. 24. riches are not—crown
Eccl. 1. 4. the earth abideth—
Isa. 26. 4. trust in Lord—for in Lord
32. 17. quietness and assurance—
40. 8. word of Lord shall stand—
59. 21. my words shall not depart—
Jer. 3. 5. wilt he reserve anger—, 12.
17. 4. kindled fire shall burn—
Lam. 3. 31. Lord will not cast off—
Mic. 7. 18. retaineth not his anger—
Zech. 1. 5. prophets, do they live—
John 6. 51. eateth shall live—, 58.
Rom. 1. 25. Creator who is blessed—
9. 5. over all God blessed—
2 Cor. 9. 9. his righteousness remaineth—
Heb. 13. 8. Jesus Christ, the same yesterday, and—
1 John 2. 17. doeth will of God, abideth—
Ex. 15. 18. Lord reigns *for ever and*
1 Chron. 16. 36. blessed be God—,
29. 10. Neh. 9. 5. Dan. 2. 20.
Ps. 10. 16. the Lord is king—
45. 6. thy throne, O God, is—, Heb. 1. 8.
52. 8. I will trust in God—
111. 8. command. stand fast—
119. 44. I will keep thy law—
145. 1. I will bless thy name—, 2. 21.
Dan. 12. 3. they shine as stars—
Mic. 4. 5. walk in name of God—
Gal. 1. 5. to whom be glory—, Phil. 4. 20. 1 Tim. 1. 17. 2 Tim. 4. 18.
Heb. 13. 21. 1 Pet. 4. 11. & 5. 11.
Rev. 1. 6. & 5. 13. & 7. 12. Rom. 11. 36. & 16. 27.
Rev. 4. 9. who liveth—, 10. & 10. 6. & 15. 7. Dan. 4. 34. & 12. 7.
22. 5. they shall reign—

EVERLASTING hills, Gen. 49. 26.
Gen. 17. 8. Canaan, an *e.* possession, 48. 4.
21. 33. called on name of *e.* God
Ex. 40. 15. *e.* priesthood, Num. 25. 13.
Lev. 16. 34. this should be an *e.* statute
Deut. 33. 27. underneath are *e.* arms
Ps. 24. 7. be lifted up ye *e.* doors
41. 13. blessed be God from *e.* to *e.*
90. 2. thou art from *e.* to *e.,* 106. 48.
100. 5. his mercy is *e.*
103. 17. mercy of Lord from *e.* to *e.*
119. 142. thy righteousness is *e.*
139. 24. lead me in the way *e.*
145. 13. *e.* kingdom, Dan. 4. 3.
Prov. 10. 25. the righteous is an *e.*
Isa. 9. 6. mighty God the *e.* Father
26. 4. in Lord Jehovah is *e.* strength
33. 14. who dwell with *e.* burnings
35. 10. shall come to Zion with songs of *e.* joy, 51. 11. & 61. 7.
40. 28. *e.* God, Creator, fainteth
54. 8. with *e.* kindness will I gather

Isa. 56. 5. an *e.* name, 63. 12, 16.
60. 19. Lord shall be an *e.* light, 20.
Jer. 10. 10. true living God, *e.* King
20. 11. *e.* confusion never forgotten
23. 40. I will bring *e.* reproach
31. 3. I loved thee with an *e.* love
Dan. 4. 34. *e.* dominion, 7. 14.
9. 24. to bring in *e.* righteousness
Mic. 5. 2. goings forth of old from *e.*
Hab. 1. 12. art thou not from *e.* my God
3. 6. *e.* mountains scattered; his ways *e.*
Matt. 18. 8. cast into *e.* fire, 25. 41.
2 Thes. 1. 9. punished with *e.* destruction
2. 16. God hath given us *e.* conso.
Luke 16. 9. receive into *e.* habita.
1 Tim. 6. 16. to whom be power *e.*
2 Pet. 1. 11. *e.* kingdom of our
Jude 6. reserved in *e.* chains of darkness
Rev. 14. 6. having the *e.* Gospel to
Dan. 12. 2. awake to *everlasting life*
Matt. 19. 29. shall inherit—
Luke 18. 30. in world to come—
John 3.16. not perish but have—, 36.
4. 14. well springing up to—
5. 24. heareth my word hath—
6. 27. meat which endureth to—
47. that believeth on me hath—
Acts 13. 46. yourselves unworthy of—
Rom. 6. 22. ye have the end—
Gal. 6. 8. soweth to the Spirit, of the Spirit reap—
1 Tim. 1. 16. believe on him to—
R. V. 1 Chron. 16. 36; Ps. 100. 5; 119. 44. for ever; Hab. 3. 6; Matt. 18. 8; 19. 29; 25. 41, 46; Luke 16. 9; 18. 30; John 3. 16, 36; 5. 24; 6. 27, 40, 47; 12. 50; Acts 13. 46; Rom. 6. 22; 16. 26; Gal. 6. 8; 2 Thes. 1. 9; 2. 16; 1 Tim. 1. 16; 6. 16; Heb. 3. 20; 2 Pet. 1. 11. eternal

EVERMORE, Ps. 16. 11. & 105. 4. & 133. 3. John 6. 34. 2 Cor. 11. 31.
1 Thes. 5. 16. Rev. 1. 18.
R. V. 1 Thes. 5. 16. always

EVERY imagination evil, Gen. 6. 5.
Ps. 32. 6. for this *e.* one godly pray
119. 101. refrained feet from *e.* evil
104. I hate *e.* false way, 128.
Prov. 2. 9. understand *e.* good path
15. 3. eyes of Lord are in *e.* place
30. 5. *e.* word of God is pure
Eccl. 3. 1. a time to *e.* purpose
Isa. 45. 23. *e.* knee bow, and *e.* tongue, Rom. 14. 11. Phil. 2. 11.
1 Tim. 4. 4. *e.* creature of God is good
Tit. 3. 1. ready to *e.* good work
Heb. 12. 1. lay aside *e.* weight and
1 John 4. 1. believe not *e.* spirit

EVIDENCE, Jer. 32. 10. Heb. 11. 1.
Job 6. 28. *evidently,* Acts 10. 3. Gal. 3. 1, 11. Phil. 1. 28. Heb. 7. 14, 15.
R. V. Jer. 32. 10, 11, 12, 14, 16, 44. deed

EVIL, Gen. 2. 9, 17. & 3. 5, 22.
Deut. 29. 21. I will separate him to *e.*
30. 15. set before thee death and *e.*
Josh. 24. 15. if it seem *e.* to you
Job 2. 10. we receive good and not *e.*
5. 19. in trouble no *e.* touch thee
30. 26. looked for good *e.* came
Ps. 23. 4. I will fear no *e.* for thou
34. 21. *e.* shall slay the wicked
52. 3. lovest *e.* more than good
53. 1. no *e.* shall befall thee
97. 10. ye that love Lord, hate *e.*
Prov. 5. 14. I was almost in all *e.*
12. 21. no *e.* shall happen to just
31. 12. will do him good and not *e.*
Eccl. 2. 21. vanity and a great *e.*
5. 13. sore *e.* riches kept to hurt
9. 3. heart of men is full of *e.*
Isa. 5. 20. call *e.* good, and good *e.*
45. 7. I make peace and create *e.*
59. 7. feet run to *e.* and make haste
Jer. 17. 17. art my hope in day of *e.*
18. 11. I frame *e.* against you
44. 11. set my face against you for *e.*
27. I will watch over them for *e.*

Lam. 3. 38. proceedeth not *e.* and
good
Ezek. 7. 5. an *e.* an only *e.* is come
Dan. 9. 12. on us a great *e.*, 13. 14.
Amos 3. 6. shall there be *e.* in a city
5. 14. seek good and not *e.* that live
15. hate *e.* love good, Mic. 3. 2.
Hab. 1. 13. of purer eyes than to
behold *e.*
Matt. 5. 11. all manner of *e.* against
6. 34. sufficient to day is *e.* thereof
Rom. 2. 9. upon every soul that
doeth *e.*
7. 19. *e.* I would not that I do
12. 17. recompense no man *e.* for *e.*
16. 19. simple concerning *e.*
1 Cor. 13. 5. charity thinketh no *e.*
1 Thes. 5. 15. let no man render *e.*
for *e.*, 1 Pet. 3. 9.
22. abstain from all appearance
of *e.*
1 Tim. 6. 10. love of money is the
root of all *e.*
Tit. 3. 2. to speak *e.* of no man
Heb. 5. 14. discern both good and *e.*
Gen. 6. 5. thoughts only *e.*, 8. 21.
47. 9. few and *e.* have been the
days
Prov. 14. 19. *e.* bow before the good
15. 15. all days of afflicted are *e.*
Isa. 1. 4. a seed of *e.* doers, 14. 20.
Matt. 5. 45. sun to rise on *e.* and good
7. 11. if ye being *e.* know, Luke 11.
13.
12. 34. how can ye being *e.* speak
good
Luke 6. 35. kind to the unthankful
and *e.*
Eph. 5. 16. because the days are *e.*
3 John 11. follow not that which
is *e.*
Jude 10. speak *e.* of those things
R. V. Judg. 9. 5. wickedness; 2 Sam.
13. 16. great wrong; 1 Chron. 2. 3; 21.
17. wickedly; Ps. 40. 17. hurt; Prov.
16. 27. mischief; Jer. 24. 3, 8; 29. 17.
bad; Matt. 5. 37; 6. 13; John 17.
15; 2 Thes. 3. 3. evil one; Jas. 3.
16. vile; Jas. 4. 11; 1 Pet. 3. 16 ——;
Eph. 4. 31. railing
EXACT, Deut. 15. 2, 3. Ps. 89. 22.
Isa. 58. 3. Luke 3. 13.
Job 39. 7. *exactor,* Isa. 60. 17.
EXALT, Dan. 11. 14, 36. Obad. 4.
Ex. 15. 2. my father's God, I will *e.*
1 Sam. 2. 10. *e.* the horn of his
anointed
Ps. 34. 3. let us *e.* his name together
37. 34. *e.* thee to inherit the land
99. 5. *e.* the Lord our God for he
118. 28. my God I will *e.* thee, Isa.
25. 1.
Ezek. 21. 26. *e.* him that is low
1 Pet. 5. 6. may *e.* you in due time
Num. 24. 7. his kingdom be *exalted*
2 Sam. 22. 47. *e.* be the God of my
Neh. 9. 5. *e.* above all blessing and
Job 5. 11. *e.* to safety, 36. 7.
Ps. 89. 16. in righteousness shall be
e., 17.
Prov. 11. 11. by blessing of upright
city is *e.*
Isa. 2. 2. Lord's house *e.* above hills
11. Lord alone shall be *e.*, 17. & 5.
16. & 30. 18. & 33. 5, 10.
40. 4. every valley shall be *e.* and
52. 13. my servant shall be *e.*
Hos. 13. 1. Eph. was *e.* in Israel, 6.
Matt. 11. 23. Capernaum which art
e. to heaven, Luke 10. 15.
23. 12. humbleth himself shall be
e., Luke 14. 11. & 18. 14.
Luke 1. 52. *e.* them of low degree
Acts 2. 33. by right hand of God *e.*
5. 31. him hath God *e.* with his
2 Cor. 12. 7. I be *e.* above measure
Phil. 2. 9. God hath highly *e.* him
Jas. 1. 9. low rejoice that he is *e.*
Prov. 14. 34. righteous. *exalteth* a
Luke 14. 11. *e.* himself be abased,
18. 14.
2 Cor. 10. 5. casting down that *e.*
itself
2 Thes. 2. 4. *e.* himself above all ——

R. V. Job 36. 22. doeth loftily; Ps.
148. 14; Ezek. 31. 10. hath lifted
up; Prov. 17. 19. raiseth high;
Jas. 1. 9. his high estate
EXAMINE, Ezra 10. 16. Luke 23.
14. Acts 4. 9. & 12. 19. & 22. 24, 29.
& 28. 18. 1 Cor. 9. 3.
Ps. 26. 2. *e.* me, O Lord, prove and
1 Cor. 11. 28. let a man *e.* himself
2 Cor. 13. 5. *e.* yourselves, prove
R. V. 1 Cor. 11. 28. prove; 2 Cor.
13. 5. try your own selves
EXAMPLE, 1 Thes. 1. 7. Jas. 5. 10.
Matt. 1. 19. not make her a public *e.*
John 13. 15. I have given you an *e.*
Phil. 3. 17. ye have us for an *e.*
2 Thes. 3. 9. make ourselves an *e.*
Heb. 4. 11. fall after the same *e.* of
unbelief
8. 5. *e.* shadow of heavenly things
1 Pet. 2. 21. Christ leaving us an *e.*
5. 3. not lords but *e.* to the flock
2 Pet. 2. 6. making them an *e.*
Jude 7. Sodom—set forth for an *e.*
R. V. 1 Tim. 4. 12. example to those
that believe; Heb. 8. 5. that which
is a copy
EXCEED, Deut. 25. 3. 1 Kings 10. 7.
Matt. 5. 20. except your righteousness *e.* the righteous. of scribes
Gen. 17. 6. *exceeding* fruitful
15. 1. I am thy shield and *e.* great
reward
Num. 14. 7. land is *e.* good
1 Sam. 2. 3. why talk so *e.* proudly
1 Kings 4. 29. wisdom *e.* much
1 Chron. 22. 5. house *e.* magnifical
Ps. 43. 4. I will go to God, my *e.*
joy
Matt. 5. 12. rejoice and be *e.* glad
26. 38. my soul is *e.* sorrowful, to
Rom. 7. 13. sin might become *e.*
sinful
2 Cor. 4. 17. work a far more *e.*
weight
7. 4. I am *e.* joyful in all tribulation
Eph. 1. 19. *e.* greatness of his power
1 Tim. 1. 14. grace was *e.* abundant
1 Pet. 4. 13. rejoice, glad with *e.*
joy
2 Pet. 1. 4. *e.* great and precious
promise
Jude 24. present you with *e.* joy
Gen. 13. 13. sinners before the Lord
exceedingly, 1 Sam. 26. 21. 2 Sam.
13. 15.
Ps. 68. 3. let righteous. rejoice *e.*
1 Thes. 3. 10. praying *e.* that
R. V. Job 36. 9. behave themselves
proudly; 2 Chron. 14. 14 ——; 2 Cor.
7. 4. overflow with joy; 1 Tim. 1.
14. abounded exceedingly; Gen.
16. 10. greatly; Ps. 68. 3. with gladness; 2 Chron. 28. 6. waxed exceeding strong
EXCEL, Gen. 49. 4. 1 Kings 4. 30.
Prov. 31. 29. thou *excellest* them all
Eccl. 2. 13. wisdom *e.* folly, as far
1 Cor. 14. 12. seek that ye may *e.*
2 Cor. 3. 10. by reason of the glory
that *e.*
Gen. 49. 3. *excellency* of dignity,
and *e.*
Ex. 15. 7. in greatness of thy *e.*
Deut. 33. 26. rideth in his *e.* on sky
Job 13. 11. his *e.* make you afraid
Ps. 47. 4. *e.* of Jacob, whom he loved
Isa. 35. 2. see glory and *e.* of our
God
Amos 6. 8. I abhor the *e.* of Jacob
8. 7. the Lord hath sworn by the
e. of Jacob
1 Cor. 2. 1. not with *e.* of speech
2 Cor. 4. 7. *e.* of power may be of
God
Phil. 3. 8. count all loss for the *e.*
of Christ
Esth. 1. 4. *excellent* majesty, Job
37. 23.
Ps. 8. 1. how *e.* is thy name in the
earth, 9.
16. 3. saints, *e.* in whom all my
delight

Ps. 36. 7. how *e.* is thy lovingkind.
Prov. 12. 26. righteous is more *e.*
Isa. 12. 5. the Lord hath done *e.*
things
28. 29. wonderful in counsel, *e.* in
Dan. 5. 12. an *e.* spirit in Daniel, 6.
3.
Rom. 2. 18. approvest things more
e.
1 Cor. 12. 31. shew you a more *e.*
way
Phil. 1. 10. approve things that are
e.
Heb. 1. 4. obtained a more *e.* name
8. 6. obtained a more *e.* ministry
11. 4. offered a more *e.* sacrifice
2 Pet. 1. 17. came a voice from *e.*
R. V. 1 Chron. 15. 21. lead; Ps. 103. 20.
ye mighty; 1 Cor. 14. 12. abound
unto; Gen. 37. 4. majesty; Isa. 13.
19; Ezek. 24. 21. pride; Ps. 36. 7.
precious; 141. 5. as upon the head;
148. 13. exalted; Prov. 17. 27. cool;
12. 26. guide to
EXCESS, Matt. 23. 25. Eph. 5. 18.
1 Pet. 4. 3, 4.
R. V. Eph. 5. 18. riot; 1 Pet. 4. 3.
wine bibbings
EXCHANGE, Matt. 16. 26. Mark
8. 37.
Matt. 25. 27. *exchangers*
EXCLUDE, Rom. 3. 27. Gal. 4. 17.
EXCUSE, Luke 14. 18, 19. Rom. 1.
20. & 2. 15. 2 Cor. 12. 19.
R. V. 2 Cor. 12. 19. are excusing
EXECRATION, Jer. 42. 18. & 44. 12.
EXECUTE, Num. 5. 30. & 8. 11.
Ps. 149. 7. *e.* vengeance, Mic. 5. 15.
Rom. 13. 4. revenger to *e.* wrath
Ex. 12. 12. *execute judgment,* Deut.
10. 18. Ps. 119. 84. Isa. 16. 3. Jer.
7. 5. & 21. 12. & 22. 3. & 23. 5. Mic.
7. 9. Zech. 7. 9. & 8. 16. John 5. 27.
Jude 15.
R. V. Num. 8. 11. be to do; Jer. 5.
1. doeth; Isa. 46. 11. of; Rom. 13.
4. for
EXERCISE, Ps. 131. 1. Matt. 20. 25.
Acts 24. 16. 1 Tim. 4. 7, 8. Heb. 5.
14. & 12. 11. 2 Pet. 2. 14.
Jer. 9. 24. Lord *e.* lovingkindness
R. V. Matt. 20. 25; Mark 10. 42. lord
it; Luke 22. 25. have
EXHORT, Acts 2. 40. & 11. 23. & 15.
32. & 27. 22. 2 Cor. 9. 5. 1 Thes. 2.
11. & 4. 1. & 5. 14. 1 Tim. 2. 1.
2 Tim. 4. 2. Tit. 1. 9. & 2. 6, 9, 15.
1 Pet. 5. 1, 12. Jude 3.
2 Thes. 3. 12. we command and *e.*
by
Heb. 3. 13. *e.* one another daily
10. 25. *exhorting* one another; and
Luke 3. 18. *exhortation,* Acts 13. 15.
& 20. 2. Rom. 12. 8. 1 Cor. 14. 3.
2 Cor. 8. 17. 1 Thes. 2. 3. 1 Tim. 4.
13. Heb. 12. 5. & 13. 22.
R. V. 2 Cor. 9. 5. entreat
EXPECTATION, Luke 3. 15. Acts
12. 11.
Ps. 9. 18. *e.* of the poor shall not
perish
62. 5. for my *e.* is from him
Prov. 10. 28. *e.* of the wicked shall
11. 7. dieth, his *e.* shall perish
23. *e.* of the wicked is wrath
23. 18. *e.* shall not be cut off, 24. 14.
Isa. 20. 5. be ashamed of their *e.*, 6.
Rom. 8. 19. *e.* of creature waiteth
Phil. 1. 20. according to my earnest *e.*
Jer. 29. 11. give you an *expected* end
R. V. Prov. 23. 18; 24. 14. thy hope;
Hope in your latter
EXPEDIENT for us that one man
die for the people, John 11. 50. &
18. 14.
John 16. 7. *e.* for you that I go away
1 Cor. 6. 12. all things not *e.*, 10. 23.
2 Cor. 8. 10. this is *e.* for you
12. 1. it is not *e.* for me to glory
EXPERIENCE, Gen. 30. 27. Eccl.
1. 16. Rom. 5. 4.
2 Cor. 9. 13. by the *experiment* of
R. V. Gen. 30. 27. divined; Rom.

35

5. 4. probation : seeing that the proving of you by
EXPERT in war, 1 Chron. 12. 33, 35, 36. S. of S. 3. 8. Jer. 50. 9.
Acts 26. 3. know thee to be e. in all
EXPOUNDED, riddle, Judg. 14. 19. Mark 4. 34. Luke 24. 27. Acts 11. 4. & 18. 26. & 28. 23.
R. V. Judg. 14. 14. declare ; Luke 24. 27. interpreted
EXPRESS, Heb. 1. 3. 1 Tim. 4. 1.
R. V. 1 Sam. 20. 21 ——
EXTEND mercy, Ezra 7. 28. & 9. 9. Ps. 109. 12.
Ps. 72. my goodness e. not to thee Isa. 66. 12. I will e. peace to her like a river
EXTINCT, Job 17. 1. Isa. 43. 17.
EXTOL, Ps. 30. 1. & 66. 17. & 68. 4. & 145. 1. Isa. 52. 13. Dan. 4. 37.
R. V. Ps. 68. 4. cast up a highway for : Isa. 52. 13. lifted up
EXTORTION, Ezek. 22. 12. Matt. 23. 25. Ps. 109. 11. *extortioner*, Isa. 16. 4. Luke 18. 11. 1 Cor. 5. 10, 11. & 6. 10.
R. V. Ezek. 22. 12. oppression
EXTREME, Deut. 28. 22. Job 35. 15.
R. V. neither doth he greatly regard arrogance
EYE for e. Ex. 21. 24. Lev. 24. 20. Matt. 5. 38.
Deut. 32. 10. as the apple of his e., Ps. 17. 8.
Job 24. 15. no e. shall see me
Ps. 33. 18. e. of the Lord on them that
Prov. 20. the seeing e. Lord hath
Eccl. 1. 8. the e. not satisfied with
Isa. 64. 4. neither hath the e. seen
Matt. 6. 22. light of the body is the e., Luke 11. 34.
18. 9. if thine e. offend thee, 5. 29.
Rev. 1. 7. every e. shall see him
Prov. 23. 6. *evil eye*, 28. 22. Matt. 6. 23. & 20. 15. Mark 7. 22. Luke 11.34.
Job 16. 16. *eyelids*, 41. 18. Ps. 11. 4. & 132. 4. Prov. 4. 25. & 6. 4, 25. & 30. 13. Jer. 9. 18.
Rev. 3. 18. *eyesalve*
Eph. 6. 6. *eyeservice*, Col. 3. 22.
2 Sam. 22. 25. *eyesight*, Ps. 18. 24.
Luke 1. 2. *eye-witnesses*, 2 Pet. 1. 16.
Gen. 3. 5. your *eyes* shall be opened
Job 10. 4. hast thou e. of flesh
29. 15. I was e. to the blind
Ps. 15. 4. in whose e. a vile person
145. 15. e. of all things wait on thee
Eccl. 2. 14. wise man's e. are in his
11. 7. pleasant for e. to behold sun
Isa. 3. 16. walk with wanton e.
5. 15. the e. of the lofty shall be
29. 18. e. of the blind shall see out of obscurity
32. 3. e. of them that see shall
35. 5. e. of blind shall be opened
42. 7. to open blind e. and give
Jer. 5. 21. have e. and see not
Dan. 7. 20. horn that had e.
Hab. 1. 13. of purer e. than to beh.
Matt. 13. 16. blessed are your e. for
18. 9. having two e. to be cast into
Mark 8. 18. having e. see ye not
Luke 4. 20. e. were fastened on him
10. 23. blessed are the e. which see
John 9. 6. anointed e. of blind man
Eph. 1. 18. e. of your understand.
Heb. 4. 13. all things are opened unto e. of him
2 Pet. 2. 14. e. full of adultery
1 John 2. 16. lust of the e. and pride
Rev. 1. 14. his e. as a flame of fire
3. 18. anoint thine e.
4. 6. four beasts full of e., 8.
Deut. 13. 18. right in the *eyes of the Lord*, 1 Kings 15. 5, 11. & 22. 43.
Gen. 6. 8. Noah found grace in the—
1 Sam. 26. 24. life set by in—
2 Sam. 15. 25. find favor in—
2 Chron. 16. 9. — run to and fro
Ps. 34. 15. — are on righteous

Prov. 5. 21. ways of man are before—
15. 3. — are in every place behold.
Isa. 49. 5. I shall be glorious in—
Amos 9. 8. — are upon sinful king.
Zech. 4. 10. — which run to and fro
Ps. 25. 15. *my eyes* are ever towards
119. 123. — fail for thy salvation
141. 8. — are unto thee, O God
Isa. 1. 15. I will hide — from you
38. 14. — fail with looking upward
Jer. 9. 1. O that — were a fountain of
13. 17. — shall weep sore, because
14. 17. — run down with tears
Amos 9. 4. I will set — on them for evil
Luke 2. 30. — have seen thy salvation
Ps. 123. 2. so *our eyes* wait on the Lord
Matt. 20. 33. that — may be opened
1 John 1. 1. that we have seen with—
Deut. 12. 8. right *in his own eyes*, Judg. 17. 6. & 21. 25.
Job 32. 1. righteous—
Neh. 6. 16. cast down *in their own eyes*
Ps. 139. 16. *thine eyes* did see my
Prov. 23. 5. set — on that which is
S. of S. 6. 5. turn away — from me
Isa. 30. 20. — shall see thy teachers
Jer. 5. 3. are not — upon the truth
Ezek. 24.16. take away desire —, 25.
R.V. 1 Kings 16. 25 ; 2 Chron. 21. 6 ; 29. 6 ; Jer. 52. 2. sight ; Ruth 2. iv. thy sight

F

FABLES, 1 Tim. 1. 4. & 4. 7. 2 Tim. 4. 4. Tit. 1. 14. 2 Pet. 1. 16.
FACE, Gen. 3. 19. & 16. 8.
Lev. 19. 32. honor the f. of old man
Num. 6. 25. Lord make his f.
2 Chron. 6. 42. turn not away f., Ps. 132. 10.
Ps. 17. 15. I will behold thy f.
31. 16. make thy f. shine, 119. 135.
67. 1. cause his f. to shine on, 80. 3, 7, 19.
84. 9. behold f. of thine anointed, 132. 10.
Ezek. 1. 10. f. of a man, a lion. Rev. 4. 7.
Dan. 9. 17. cause thy f. to shine on
Hos. 5. 5. testify to his f., 7. 10.
Matt. 11. 10. my messenger before thy f., Mark 1. 2. Luke 7. 27. & 9. 52.
Acts 2. 25. set the Lord always before my f.
1 Cor. 13. 12. but then see f. to f.
2 Cor. 3. 18. with open f. beholding
Jas. 1. 23. his natural f. in a glass
R. V. Gen. 24. 47. nose ; 46. 28. way ; 1 Sam. 26. 20 ; Joel 2. 6. presence ; 1 Kings 13. 6. favor ; 20. 38, 41 ; 2 Kings 9.30 ; Jer. 4.30. eyes ; Ezek. 38. 19. nostrils ; 40. 15. forefront ; Joel 2. 20. forepart ; Deut. 14. 2 ; 2 Sam. 14. 7 ; Jer. 25. 33 ; Luke 22. 64 ——
FADE, we all, as a leaf, Isa. 64. 6.
Jas. 1. 11. rich man f. away in
1 Pet. 1. 4. inheritance that *fadeth*
5. 4. receive a crown of glory that f.
R. V. Ezek. 47. 12. wither
FAIL, Deut. 28. 32. Job. 11. 20.
Deut. 31. 6. Lord will not f. nor, 8. Josh. 1. 5. 1 Chron. 28. 20.
Ps. 12. 1. faithful f. from among
69. 3. my eyes f. while I wait for my God
Lam. 3. 22. his compassions f. not
Luke 16. 9. when ye f. they may
22. 32. prayed that thy faith f. not
Heb. 12. 15. lest any f. of the grace
S. of S. 5. 6. soul *failed* when he spake
Ps. 31. 10. my strength *faileth*, 38. 10. & 71. 9.

Ps. 40. 12. my heart f. me, 73. 26.
143. 7. hear me, my spirit f.
Luke 12. 33. lay up treasure that f. not
1 Cor. 13. 8. charity never f.
Deut. 23. 65. for *failing* of eyes
Luke 21. 26. men's hearts f. them
R. V. Judg. 11. 30. indeed ; Gen. 47. 15. was all spent ; Josh. 3. 16. wholly ; Ez. 4. 22. be slack ; Ps. 40. 26 ; 59. 15. is lacking ; Isa. 19. 3. make void ; 34. 16. be missing ; Jer. 48. 33. cease ; Luke 16. 17. fall ; 1 Cor. 13. 8. be done away ; Heb. 12. 15. that falleth short ; Luke 21. 26. fainting
FAINT, Deut. 25. 18. Judg. 8. 4, 5.
Isa. 1. 5. head sick, whole heart is f.
40. 30. youths shall f. and be weary
Luke 18. 1. to pray always and not f.
2 Cor. 4. 1. received mercy we f. not
Heb. 12. 5. nor f. when rebuked of
Ps. 27. 13. I had *fainted* unless I
Rev. 2. 3. hast labored and not f.
Ps. 84. 2. soul *fainteth* for courts of the Lord
119. 81. my soul f. for thy salvation
R. V. Isa. 13. 7. feeble ; Deut. 20. 8 ; Ezek. 21. 15. melt ; Josh. 2. 9, 24. melt away ; Isa. 13. 7. feeble ; Jer. 45. 3 ; Rev. 2. 3. weary ; Matt. 9. 36. distressed ; Isa. 7. 4. faint ; Jer. 49. 23. melted away
FAIR, Gen. 6. 2. & 24. 16.
Prov. 7. 21. f. speech, Rom. 16. 18.
S. of S. 1. 15. behold thou art f., 4. 1, 7. & 2. 10. & 6. 10. & 7. 6. Gen. 12. 11.
4. 10. how f. is thy love, better
Jer. 12. 6. they speak f. words
Acts 7. 20. Moses was exceeding f.
Ps. 45. 2. thou art *fairer* than the
Dan. 1. 15. their countenance appeared f.
R. V. Ezek. 27. 12-17. wares ; Job 37. 22. golden
FAITH, Acts 3. 16. & 13. 8.
Deut. 32. 20. children in whom is no f.
Matt. 6. 30. O ye of little f., 8. 26. & 16. 8. & 14. 31. Luke 12. 28.
8. 10. not found so great f. no
17. 20. had f. as a grain of mustard
21. 21. have f. and doubt not
Mark 4. 40. how is it that ye have no f.
11. 22. Jesus saith have f. in God
Luke 7. 9. so great f. no not in Israel
17. 5. Lord increase our f.
Acts 3. 16. the f. which is by him
6. 5. Stephen, a man full of f.
Acts 6. 7. company of priests obedient to f.
14. 9. he had f. to be healed
27. God opened door of f. to
16. 5. churches established in the f.
20. 21. f. towards our Lord Jesus
Rom. 1. 5. for obedience to the f.
3. 3. make f. of God without effect
27. but by the law of f.
4. 5. his f. is counted for righteousness
12. in the steps of that f. of Abraham, 16.
13. through the righteousness of f., 9. 30. & 10. 6.
14. if of law be heirs, f. is made
16. of f. that by grace promise sure
10. 17. f. cometh by hearing, and
12. 3. God dealt the measure of f.
6. according to the propor. of f.
14. 23. eateth not of f. is not of f. is
1 Cor. 12. 9. to another f. by the same spirit
13. 2. though I have all f. to
13. now abideth f. hope, charity
2 Cor. 4. 13. we have the same spirit of f.
Gal. 1. 23. preach the f. which once
3. 7. they which are of f., 9.
12. the law is not of f. but the man
23. before f. came, we were under
5. 6. but f. which worketh by love
22. fruit of the Spirit is f.
Eph. 4. 5. one Lord, one f. one

Eph. 4. 13. until we come in the unity of *f.*
6. 16. above all take shield of *f.*
23. love with *f.* from God the
Phil. 1. 25. I shall abide for your joy of *f.*
27. striving together for *f.* of gosp.
1 Thes. 1. 3. remem. your work of *f.*
5. 8. putting on breastplate of *f.*
2 Thes. 1. 11. fulfil work of *f.* with power
3. 2. for all men have not *f.*
1 Tim. 1. 5. charity out of *f.* unfeign.
14. exceeding abundantly with *f.*
19. holding *f.* and a good conscience; concerning *f.* have made shipwreck
4. 6. nourished up in the words of *f.*
5. 8. hath denied the *f.*
12. cast off their first *f.*
6. 10. erred from the *f.*
21. concerning the *f.*
12. fight the good fight of *f.*
2 Tim. 1. 5. unfeigned *f.* that is in
2. 18. overthrow *f.* of some
22. follow righteous. *f.* charity
3. 10. fully known my doctrine, life, *f.*
4. 7. fought a good fight, I have kept the *f.*
Tit. 1. 1. according to *f.* of God's elect
4. my son after the common *f.*
Heb. 4. 2. word did not profit, not being mixed with *f.*
10. 22. draw near in full assur. of *f.*
23. hold fast the profess. of our *f.*
11. 6. without *f.* it is impossible to
12. 2. Jesus the author and finisher of our *f.*
13. 7. whose *f.* follow, considering
Jas. 2. 1. have not *f.* of our Lord
14. say that he hath *f.* can *f.* save
17. *f.* if it hath not works, is dead, 26.
18. thou hast *f.* and I works; show *f.*—*f.* by my works
22. *f.* wrought with works
5. 15. prayer of *f.* shall save
2 Pet. 1. 1. like precious *f.* with us
1 John 5. 4. overcometh world, even our *f.*
Jude 3. contend earnestly for the *f.*
20. build up yourselves on holy *f.*
Rev. 2. 13. hast not denied my *f.*
19. I know thy works and *f.*
13. 10. here is the *f.* of the saints
14. 12. which keep the *f.* of Jesus
Hab. 2. 4. just shall live *by faith,*
Rom. 1. 17. Gal. 3. 11. Heb. 10. 38.
Acts 15. 9. purifying their hearts—
26. 18. sanctified—that is in me
Rom. 1. 12. comforted by mutual *f.*
3. 22. righteousness which is—of Christ
28. conclude a man is justified—
5. 1. being justified—we have peace
2. have access—, Eph. 3. 12.
9. 32. sought it not—but works
2 Cor. 1. 24. of your joy for—ye stand
5. 7. we walk—and not by sight
Gal. 2. 16. not justified, but—, 3.24.
20. I live—of the Son of God
3. 22. promise—might be given
26. ye are all children of God—in Christ Jesus.
5. 5. wait for hope of righteousness—
Eph. 3. 17. Christ may dwell in your hearts—
Phil. 3. 9. righteousness through *f.*
Heb. 11. 4.—Abel, 5.—Enoch, etc.
7 heir of righteousness which is—
Jas. 2. 24. justified by works, not—
Rom. 4. 19. not weak *in faith*
20. strong—giving glory to God
1 Cor. 16. 13. stand fast—quit you
2 Cor. 8. 7. ye abound—in utter.
Col. 1. 23. if ye continue—
2. 7. built up in him, established—

1 Tim. 1. 2. Timothy, my own son—
4. godly edifying which is—
2. 15. if they continue—and charity
3. 13. purchase great boldness—
4. 12. be an example—in purity
2 Tim. 1. 13. of sound words—and
Tit. 1. 13. they may be sound—2. 2.
Heb. 11. 13. all these died—not having
Jas. 1. 6. let him ask—nothing
1 Pet. 5. 9. whom resist, steadfast—
Matt. 9. 2. Jesus, seeing *their faith,*
Mark 2. 5. Luke 5. 20.
Acts 3. 16. *through faith* in his Son
Rom. 3. 25. propitiation—in his blood
31. do we make void the law—, 30.
Eph. 2. 8. by grace ye are saved—
Col. 2. 12.—of the operation of God
2 Tim. 3. 15. salvation—which is
Heb. 6. 12.—and patience inherit
11. 3.—we understand the worlds
11.—Sarah received strength to
28.—Moses kept the passover
33.—subdued kingdoms
11. 39. obtained a good report—, 2.
1 Pet. 1. 5. kept by power of God—
Matt. 9. 22. *thy faith* hath made thee whole, Luke 8. 48. & 17. 19.
15. 28. O woman, great is—be
Luke 7. 50.—hath saved thee, 18. 42.
22. 32. I have prayed that—fail not
Jas. 2. 18. show me—without thy
Luke 8. 25. where is *your faith*
Matt. 9. 29. according to—be it to
Rom. 1. 8.—is spoken of through
1 Cor. 2. 5. that—not stand in wisdom
15. 14.—is also vain, 17.
2 Cor. 1. 24. not dominion over—
Eph. 1. 15. after I heard of—, Col. 1. 4.
Phil. 2. 17. offered upon service of—
Col. 2. 5. beholding steadfast. of—
1 Thes. 1. 8.—to God-ward is spread
3. 2. establish you, comfort you, concerning—
5. I sent to know—lest the tempter
7. comforted in affliction by—
10. perfect what is lacking in—
2 Thes. 1. 3.—growth exceedingly
Jas. 1. 3. trying of—worketh patience
1 Pet. 1. 7. trial of—being precious
9. receiving end of—salvation
21. that—and hope might be in God
2 Pet. 1. 5. add to—virtue, knowledge
R. V. Acts 6. 8. grace; Rom. 3. 3;
Gal. 5. 22. faithfulness
FAITHFUL, 1 Sam. 2. 35. & 22. 14.
2 Sam. 20. 19. Neh. 13. 13. Dan. 6. 4. 1 Tim. 6. 2. 1 Pet. 5. 12.
Num. 12. 7. *f.* in all my house
Heb. 3. 2. 5. Moses *f.* in all as a ser.
Deut. 7. 9. *f.* God which keepeth
Neh. 7. 2. a *f.* man, and feared
Ps. 12. 1. the *f.* fail from among men
31. 23. Lord preserveth the *f.*
101. 6. my eyes be upon *f.* in land
119. 86. thy commandments are *f.*
138. thy testimonies are very *f.*
Prov. 11. 13. is of a *f.* spirit, concealeth
13. 17. a *f.* ambassador is health
14. 5. a *f.* witness will not lie
20. 6. a *f.* man who can find
27. 6. *f.* are wounds of a friend
28. 20. *f.* man shall abound with
Isa. 1. 21. how *f.* city became a har.
26. city of righteousness, *f.* city
8. 2. I took *f.* witness to record
49. 7. Lord is *f.* and Holy One of
Jer. 42. 5. the Lord be a true and *f.*
Hos. 11. 12. Judah is *f.* with saints

Matt. 25. 21. well done, *f.* servant, 24. 45.
23. hast been *f.* in a few, Luke 19. 17.
Luke 12. 42. who is that *f.* steward
16. 10. *f.* 'n least is *f.* also in much
Acts 16. 15. judge me *f.* to the Lord
1 Cor. 1. 9. God is *f.* by whom ye
4. 2. required in stewards. a man *f.*
17. Timothy who is *f.* in the Lord
7. 25. obtained mercy of the Lord to be *f.*
10. 13. God is *f.* and will not suffer
Eph. 1. 1. the saints and *f.* in Christ Jesus, Col. 1. 2.
6. 21. *f.* minis., Col. 1. 7. & 4. 7, 9.
1 Thes. 5. 24. *f.* is he that calleth
2 Thes. 3. 3. the Lord is *f.* and shall
1 Tim. 1. 12. he counted me *f.*
15. this is a *f.* saying and worthy, 4. 9. 2 Tim. 2. 11. Tit. 3. 8.
3. 11. wives grave, sober, *f.* in all
2 Tim. 2. 2. heard of me, commit to *f.* men
13. he abideth *f.* cannot deny
Tit. 1. 6. blame. having *f.* children
9. holding fast the *f.* word as
Heb. 2. 17. might be a *f.* high priest
10. 23. *f.* is he that promised, 11. 11.
1 Pet. 4. 19. as unto a *f.* Creator
1 John 1. 9. he is *f.* to forgive all
Rev. 1. 5. *f.* and true witness, 3. 14
2. 10. be *f.* to death
13. *f.* martyr
Rev. 21. 5. words are true and *f.,* 22. 6.
1 Sam. 26. 23. render to every man his *faithfulness*
Ps. 5. 9. no *f.* in their mouth
40. 10. declared thy *f.,* 89. 1.
89. 1. make known thy *f.* to all
2. thy *f* shalt establish in heavens
5. praise thy *f.* in the great congregation
8. who like thy *f.* round about thee
24. my *f.* shall be with him
33. I will not suffer my *f.* to fail
119. 75. in *f.* thou hast afflicted me
90. thy *f.* is to all generations
143. 1. in thy *f.* answer me, and
Isa. 11. 5. *f.* is the girdle of his reins
25. 1. thy counsels of old are *f.*
Lam. 3. 23. mercies new, great thy *f.*
Hos. 2. 20. I will betroth thee to me in *f.*
Matt. 17. 17. O *faithless* and perverse generation, Mark 9. 19. Luke 9. 41.
John 20. 27. be not *f.* but believing
R. V. 1 Tim. 6. 2. believing; Tit. 1. 6. that believe who are
FALL, Num. 11. 31. & 14. 29, 32.
Gen. 45. 24. see that ye *f.* not out
2 Sam. 24. 14. let us *f.* into the
Ps. 37. 24. though he *f.* he shall not
45. 5. whereby they *f.* under thee
82. 7. *f.* like one of the princes
141. 10. let the wicked *f.* into their
145. 14. Lord upholdeth all that *f.*
Prov. 11. 5. wicked *f.* by his own
24. 16. wicked shall *f.* into mischief
26. 27. digs a pit shall *f.* into it, Eccl. 10. 8.
28. 14. hardeneth his heart shall *f.*
Eccl. 4. 10. if they *f.* one will lift
Isa. 8. 15. many shall stumble and *f.*
Dan. 11. 35. some shall *f.* to try them
Hos. 10. 8. mountains and hills *f.* on us, Luke 23. 30. Rev. 6. 16.
Mic. 7. 8. rejoice not when I *f.*
Matt. 7. 27. great was the *f.* of it
10. 29. sparrow not *f.* on ground

Matt. 15. 14. blind both *f.* into the ditch
21. 44. upon whomsoever it *f.*, Luke 20. 18.
Luke 2. 34. set for the *f.* and rising
Rom. 11. 11. stumbled that they should *f.* through their *f.* salvation is come to the Gentiles
1 Cor. 10. 12. stands, take heed lest he *f.*
1 Tim. 3. 6. *f.* into condemnation
6. 9. rich *f.* into temptation
Heb. 4. 11. *f.* after the same exam.
10. 31. fearful thing to *f.* into the hands of God
2 Pet. 1. 10. if these ye shall never *f.*
3. 17. lest ye *f.* from your steadfastness
Luke 8. 13. in time of temptation *fall away*
Heb. 6. 6. impossible if they—to renew them
Gal. 5. 4. ye are *fallen* from grace
Ps. 16. 6. *f.* to me in pleasant places
Hos. 14. 1. hast *f.* by thine iniquity
Prov. 24. 16. just *falleth* seven times
Rom. 14. 4. to his own master he *f.*
Ps. 56. 13. thou hast delivered my feet from *falling*, 116. 8.
2 Thes. 2. 3. there come a *f.* away
Jude 24. able to keep you from *f.*
R. V. Lev. 26. 37; Ps. 64. 8; Isa. 31. 3; Jer. 6. 21; 46. 16; Ezek. 36. 15; Hos. 4. 5; 5. 5; 2 Pet. 1. 10. stumble; Acts 27. 17. cast; 27. 34. perish; Isa. 34. 4. fading; Acts 27. 41. lighting upon; Jude 24. stumbling
FALLOW, Jer. 4. 3. Hos. 10. 12.
R. V. Deut. 14. 5; 1 Kings 4. 23. roebuck
FALSE, Jer. 14. 14. & 37. 14.
Ex. 23. 1. not raise a *f.* report
7. keep thee far from a *f.* matter
Ps. 119. 104. hate every *f.* way, 128.
Prov. 11. 1. *f.* balance is abomina.
Zech. 8. 17. love no *f.* oath
Matt. 24. 24. *f.* Christs, *f.* prophets
2 Cor. 11. 13, 26. *f.* apostles, *f.* brethren, Gal. 2. 4.
2 Tim. 3. 3. *f.* accusers, Tit. 2. 3.
2 Pet. 2. 1. *f.* prophets, *f.* teachers
Ps. 119. 118. their deceit is *falsehood*
144. 8. whose right hand—of *f.*
Isa. 59. 13. from heart words of *f.*
Lev. 6. 3. sweareth *falsely*; 19. 12.
Ps. 44. 17. neither dealt *f.* in coven.
Zech. 5. 4. thief and that swears *f.*
Matt. 5. 11. evil against you *f.* for
Luke 3. 14. neither accuse any *f.*
1 Pet. 3. 16. *f.* accuse your good
Acts 13. 6. *false prophet*, Rev. 16. 13. & 19. 20. & 20. 10.
Matt. 7. 15. *false prophets*, 24. 11, 24. Luke 6. 26. 2 Pet. 2. 1. 1 John 4. 1.
Ex. 20. 16. *false witness*, Deut. 5. 20. & 19. 16. Prov. 6. 19. & 12. 17. & 14. 5. & 19. 5, 9. & 21. 28. & 25. 18. Matt. 15. 19. & 19. 18. Rom. 13. 9. 1 Cor. 15. 15.
R. V. Ps. 35. 11. unrighteous; 120. 3. deceitful; Prov. 17. 4. wicked; Jer. 14. 14; 23. 32. lying; Lam. 2. 14. vanity; Matt. 26. 60—; Luke 19. 8. wrongfully; Rom. 13. 9. covet; Tit. 2. 3. slanderers; Luke 3. 14. wrongfully; 1 Pet. 3. 16 —
FAMILIAR, Job. 19. 14. Ps. 41. 9. Lev. 19. 31. & 20. 6, 27. Isa. 8. 19.
R. V. Jer. 20. 10. familiar friends
FAMILY, Gen. 10. 5. Lev. 20. 5.
Zech. 12. 12. mourn every *f.* apart
Eph. 3. 15. whole *f.* in heaven and
Ps. 68. 6. setteth solitary in *families*
107. 41. maketh him *f.* like a flock
Amos 3. 2. known of all the *f.* of
R. V. 2 Chron. 35. 5. fathers' houses
FAMINE, Gen. 12. 10. & 41. 27.
Job 5. 20. in *f.* he shall redeem thee
Ps. 33. 19. keep them alive in *f.*

Ps. 37. 19. in the days of *f.* shall be
Ezek. 5. 16. evil arrows of *f.*, 6. 11.
Amos 8. 11. not a *f.* of bread, but
R. V. Job 5. 22. dearth
FAMISH, Gen. 41. 55. Prov. 10. 3.
Isa. 5. 13. Zeph. 2. 11.
FAN, Isa. 41. 16. Jer. 4. 11. & 51. 2.
Matt. 3. 12. Luke 3. 17.
FAR, Ex. 8. 28. Neh. 4. 19.
Ex. 23. 7. keep *f.* from false matter
Ps. 73. 27. *f.* from thee shall perish
Amos 8. 3. put *f.* away the evil day
Mark 12. 34. not *f.* from the kingd.
Phil. 1. 23. with Christ, which is *f.*
Eph. 2. 13. sometimes *f.* off, now
R. V. Job 30. 10. aloof; Judg. 9. 17; Ps. 27. 9; Isa. 19. 6; 26. 15; Ezek. 7. 20; Mark 13. 34——; Matt. 21. 33; 25. 14; Mark 12. 1. another; 2 Cor. 4. 17. more and more
FARTHING, Matt. 5. 26. & 10. 29.
FASHION, 1 Cor. 7. 31. Phil. 2. 8.
Job 10. 8. thy hands have *fashioned* me, Ps. 119. 73.
Ps. 139. 16. in continuance were *f.*
Ezek. 16. 7. thy breasts are *f.*
Phil. 3. 21. be *f.* like his glorious
Ps. 33. 15. he *fashions* their hearts
Isa. 45. 9. the clay say to him that *fashioneth* it
1 Pet. 1. 14. not *fashioning* yourselves
R. V. Acts 7. 44. figure; Phil. 3. 21. conformed to
FAST, 2 Sam. 12. 21. Esth. 4. 16.
Isa. 58. 4. ye *f.* for strife; not *f.* as
Jer. 14. 12. when they *f.* I will not
Zech. 7. 5. did ye at all *f.* unto me
Matt. 6. 16. when ye *f.* be not as
18. appear not to men to *f.*
9. 14. why do we *f.* and thy disc.
Luke 18. 12. I *f.* twice a week
1 Kings 21. 9. proclaim a *fast*, 12.
2 Chron. 20. 3. Ezra 8. 21. Isa. 58. 3, 5, 6. Jer. 36. 9. Joel 1. 14. & 2. 15.
Jonah 3. 5. Zech. 8. 19. Acts 27. 9.
Judg. 20. 26. *fasted* that day
1 Sam. 7. 6. *f.* on that day
31. 13. *f.* seven days, 1 Chron. 10. 12.
2 Sam. 1. 12. they wept and *f.* till even
1 Kings 21. 27. Ahab *f.* and lay in
Ezra 8. 23. we *f.* and besought the Lord
Isa. 58. 3. why have we *f.* and thou
Zech. 7. 5. when ye *f.* in filth and
Matt. 4. 2. when he had *f.* forty days
Acts 13. 2. ministered and *f.*
3. *f.* and prayed
Neh. 9. 1. assembled with *fasting*
Esth. 4. 3. were *f.* and weeping, 9. 31.
Ps. 35. 13. humbled soul with *f.*, 69. 10.
109. 24. my knees weak through *f.*
Jer. 36. 6. read the roll on *f.* day
Dan. 6. 18. king passed the night *f.*
9. 3. to seek by prayer with *f.*
Joel 2. 12. turn ye to me with *f.*
Matt. 15. 32. not send them away *f.*
Luke 2. 37. with *f.* and prayers
Acts 10. 30. was *f.* till this hour
14. 23. ordained elders, prayed with *f.*
1 Cor. 7. 5. give yourselves to *f.*
2 Cor. 6. 5. in *f.* often, 11. 27.
FASTENED, Job 38. 6. Eccl. 12. 11.
Isa. 22. 25. Luke 4. 20.
R. V. Ex. 28. 14. shalt put; 28. 25. put on; 40. 18. laid; Judg. 4. 21. pierced through; 1 Kings 6. 6. have hold; Matt. 17. 21; Mark 9. 29——
FAT is the Lord's, Lev. 3. 16. & 4. 8.
Prov. 11. 25. liberal shall be made *f.*
13. 4. soul of the diligent shall be made *f.*
15. 30. good report maketh bones *f.*
Isa. 25. 6. *f.* things full of marrow
11. 6. *failing*, Matt. 22. 4.
Gen. 27. 28. God give thee of *fatness* of the earth
Job 36. 16. table should be full of *f.*

Ps. 36. 8. satisfied with *f.* of house
63. 5. shall be satisfied as with *f.*
Isa. 55. 2. let your soul delight. in *f.*
Jer. 31. 14. satiate the soul with *f.*
Rom. 11. 17. root and *f.* of olive-tree
R. V. Ps. 92. 14. full of sap; Isa. 58. 11. strong; Jer. 50. 11. wanton as an; Deut. 32. 15. become sleek
FATHER, Gen. 2. 24. & 4. 20, 21.
Gen. 17. 4. be a *f.* of many nations
Job 29. 16. I was a *f.* to the poor
Ps. 68. 5. a *f.* of fatherless is God
103. 13. as a *f.* pitieth his children
Isa. 9. 6. the everlasting *F.* prince
Jer. 31. 9. I am a *F.* to Israel and
Mal. 1. 6. if I be a *F.* where is my honor
2. 10. have we not all one *F.*
John 5. 19. what he seeth the *F.* do.
20. *F.* loveth the Son, 3. 35.
22. *F.* judgeth no man but
26. *F.* hath life in himself
8. 18. *F.* beareth witness of me
44. *f.* devil is a liar and *f.* of it
16. 32. I am not alone *F.* is with
Acts 1. 4. promise of the *F.*
Rom. 4. 11. be the *f.* of all them
12. *f.* of circumcision
16. *f.* of us all
17. made thee a *f.* of many nations
1 Cor. 8. 6. the *F.* of whom are all
1 Cor. 1. 3. God and *F.* of our Lord Jesus Christ, *F.* of mer. and God of all com., Eph. 1. 3. 1 Pet. 1. 3.
6. 18. I will be a *F.* to you and
1 Tim. 5. 1. entreat him as a *f.*
Heb. 1. 5. I will be to him a *F.* and
12. 9. subjection to the *F.* of spirits
Jas. 1. 17. gift from *F.* of lights
John 5. 17. *my Father* worketh and I work
10. 30. I and my *F.* are one
14. 28. my *F.* is greater than I
Ezek. 16. 45. *your father* an Amorite
Matt. 5. 16. glorify your *F.* in heaven, 6. 1, 8, 9, 32. & 7. 11. & 45. 48.
John 8. 41. ye do deeds of your *f.*
44. ye are of your *f.* the devil
20. 17. I ascend to my *F.* and your
Ex. 15. 2. my *f.*'s God I will exalt
Neh. 9. 9, 16. *our fathers* dealt proudly
Ps. 22. 4. our *f.* trusted in thee
44. 1. our *f.* have told us, 78. 3.
Lam. 5. 7. our *f.* have sinned
Acts 15. 10. our *f.* not able to bear
Ex. 22. 22. not afflict *fatherless*
Deut. 10. 18. execute judgment of *f.*
Ps. 10. 14. thou helper of the *f.*
82. 3. defend the poor and *f.*
146. 9. Lord relieveth the *f.* and widow
Isa. 1. 17. judge *f.* plead for widow
Jas. 1. 27. visit *f.* in affliction
FAULT, Gen. 41. 9. Ex. 5. 16.
Ps. 19. 12. cleanse thou me from secret *f.*
Matt. 18. 15. if trespass, tell him his *f.*
Luke 23. 4. I find no *f.* in him, 14.
John 18. 38. & 19. 4, 6.
1 Cor. 6. 7. utterly a *f.* among you
Jas. 5. 16. confess your *f.* one to
1 Pet. 2. 20. buffeted for your *f.*
Jude 24. able to present you *faultless*
R. V. Deut. 25. 2. wickedness; Mark 7. 2—; John 18. 38; 19. 4, 6. crime; 1 Cor. 6. 7. defect; Gal. 6. 1. any trespass; Jas. 5. 16. sins; Rev. 14. 5. blemish; Jude 24. blemish in
FAVOR, Gen. 39. 21. Deut. 33. 23.
1 Sam. 2. 26. Samuel in *f.* with
Job 10. 12. granted me life and *f.*
Ps. 5. 12. with *f.* wilt thou compass
106. 4. remember me with *f.* that
Prov. 31. 30. *f.* is deceitful and
Luke 2. 52. in *f.* with God and man
Ps. 41. 11. know thou *favorest* me
R. V. Ps. 112. 5. that dealeth graciously; Prov. 14. 9. good will; S. of S. 8. 10. peace; Ps. 102. 13, 14. have pity; 41. 11. delighted in

FEAR, Gen. 9. 2. Ex. 15. 16.
Ps. 53. 5. in *f*. where no *f*. was
 119. 38. servant devoted to thy *f*.
 120. flesh trembleth for *f*. of thee
Prov. 1. 26. mock when your *f*.
 cometh
Isa. 8. 12. *f*. not their *f*. nor be
 afraid
 13. let him be your *f*., Gen. 31. 42.
Jer. 32. 40. put my *f*. in their hearts
Mal. 1. 6. if master where is my *f*.
Rom. 13. 7. render *f*. to whom *f*.
2 Tim. 1. 7. spirit of *f*. but of power
Heb. 2. 15. who through *f*. of death
 12. 28. with reverence and godly *f*.
1 Pet. 1. 17. time of sojourning here
 in *f*.
1 John 4. 18. no *f*. in love
Gen. 20. 11. *fear of God* not in this
 place
2 Sam. 23. 3. ruling in —
Neh. 5. 15. so did not I because
 of —
Ps. 36. 1. no — before his eyes,
 Rom. 3. 18.
2 Cor. 7. 1. perfecting holiness in —
Job 28. 28. *fear of the Lord*, that is
 wisdom
Ps. 19. 9. — is clean, enduring for
 ever
 34. 11. children I will teach you —
Prov. 1. 29. they did not choose —
 8. 13. — is to hate evil
 10. 27. — prolongeth days
 14. 26. in — is strong confidence
 27. — is a fountain of life
 15. 33. — is instruction of wisdom
 22. 4. by — are riches, honor, life
 23. 17. be thou in — all day long
Isa. 33. 6. — is his treasure
Acts 9. 31. walking in — and comfort
Ps. 2. 11. *with fear*, Phil. 2. 12.
Heb. 11. 7. Jude 23. save —
Deut. 4. 10. learn *to fear* me
 5. 29. such a heart that would *f*. me
 28. 58. mayest *f*. this glorious name
2 Kings 17. 39. Lord your God ye
 shall *f*.
1 Chron. 16. 30. *f*. before him all
2 Chron. 6. 31. that they may *f*.
 thee, 33.
Neh. 1. 11. servants, desire to *f*. thy
 name
Ps. 23. 4. I will *f*. no evil, for thou
 31. 19. goodness laid up for those
 that *f*.
 61. 5. heritage of those that *f*.
 86. 11. incline my heart to *f*. thy
 name
Jer. 10. 7. who would not *f*. thee
 32. 39. heart that may *f*. me for
 ever
Mal. 4. 2. to you that *f*. my name
Luke 12. 5. *f*. him who can cast,
 Matt. 10. 28.
Rom. 8. 15. not spirit of bondage
 again to *f*.
 11. 20. be not high-minded but *f*.
Heb. 4. 1. *f*. lest a promise being
 left
 12. 21. Moses said, I exceedingly *f*.
 and
Rev. 2. 10. *f*. none of these things
Gen. 42. 18. this do and live, for I
 fear God
Ex. 18. 21. such as — men of truth
Ps. 66. 16. come hear all ye that —
Eccl. 5. 7. dreams, vanities, *f*. thou
 God
 8. 12. shall go well with them
 that —
 12. 13. — and keep his commandments
Job 37. 24. therefore men do *fear
 him*
Ps. 25. 14. secret of Lord with them
 that —
 33. 18. eye of Lord upon them
 that —
 34. 9. there is no want to them
 that —
 85. 9. his salvation is nigh to them
 that —

Ps. 103. 13. as father pities, so Lord
 them that —
 111. 5. giveth meat to them that —
 145. 19. fulfil the desire of them
 that —
Matt. 10. 28. — who is able to destroy
Luke 1. 50. his mercy on them
 that —
Deut. 6. 2. mightest *fear the Lord*
 13. thou shalt — thy God, 10. 20.
 24. — our God for our good always
 10. 12. — thy God walk in his ways
 14. 23. learn to — thy God, always,
 17. 19. & 31. 12, 13.
Josh. 4. 24. that ye might — your
 24. 14. therefore — serve in sincer.
1 Sam. 12. 14. if ye will — and serve
 24. only — and serve him in truth
1 Kings 18. 12. thy servant did —,
 2 Kings 4. 1.
2 Kings 17. 28. how they should —
Ps. 15. 4. he honoreth them that —
 22. 23. ye that — trust in him, 115.
 11.
 33. 8. let all the earth —
 115. 13. he will bless them that —
 135. 20. ye that — bless the Lord
Prov. 3. 7. — and depart from evil
 24. 21. my son — and meddle not
Jer. 5. 24. let us now — that giveth
 rain
 26. 19. did not he — and besought
Hos. 3. 5. and shall — and his goodness
Jonah 1. 9. I — the God of heaven
Gen. 15. 1. *fear not*, I am thy shield
Num. 14. 9. Lord is with us —
 them
Deut. 1. 21. — neither be discour.
Ps. 56. 4. I will not *f*. what flesh
 can do, 118. 6. Heb. 13. 6.
Isa. 41. 10. — for I am with thee, I
 will help thee, 13. & 43. 5.
 43. 1. — for I have redeemed thee
Jer. 5. 22. *f*. ye not me, saith the
 Lord
 30. 10. — O my servant Jacob
Matt. 10. 28. — them that kill the
 body
Luke 12. 32 — little flock; for it is
Ex. 1. 17. midwives *feared* God, 21.
 14. 31. people *f*. Lord and be-
 lieved
1 Sam. 12. 18. all people greatly *f*.
 the Lord
1 Kings 18. 3. Obadiah *f*. the Lord
Neh. 7. 2. Hanani *f*. God above
Job 1. 1. one that *f*. God and
Ps. 76. 7. thou art to be *f*. who
 89. 7. God is greatly to be *f*. in
 96. 4. Lord is to be *f*. above all
Mal. 3. 16. they that *f*. the Lord
Acts 10. 2. one that *f*. the Lord
Heb. 5. 7. was heard in that he *f*.
Gen. 22. 12. that thou *fearest* God
Job 1. 8. that *feareth* God, 2. 3.
Ps. 25. 12. what man is he that *f*.
 128. 1. every one that *f*. the Lord
Prov. 28. 14. happy is the man that
 f. alway
Isa. 50. 10. who among you *f*. Lord
Acts 10. 22. one that *f*. God and of
 35. he that *f*. God and works righ.
 13. 26. whosoever among you *f*.
 God
Ex. 15. 11. *fearful* in praises
Matt. 8. 26. why are ye *f*., Mark
 4. 40.
Heb. 10. 27. certain *f*. looking for
 31. *f*. thing to fall into hands of
Rev. 21. 8. *f*. and unbelieving shall
Ps. 55. 5. *fearfulness* and trembling
Isa. 33. 14. *f*. hath surprised hypo-
 crites
Ps. 139. 14. I am *fearfully* and
 R. V. very often in O. T., terror;
 Luke 21. 11. terrors; Isa. 21. 4.
 horror hath; 33. 14. trembling
FEAST, Gen. 19. 3. & 21. 8.
Prov. 15. 15. merry heart has a
 continual *f*.
Eccl. 10. 9. a *f*. is made for laughter
Isa. 25. 6. Lord make to all people
 a *f*. of

1 Cor. 5. 8. let us keep *f*. but not
 R. V. Lam. 1. 4.; 2. 6.; Hos. 2. 11.
 assembly; Matt. 26. 17; Luke 23.
 17; Acts 18. 21 —
FEEBLE, Gen. 30. 42. Job 4. 4.
Ps. 105. 37. not one *f*. person
 among
Isa. 35. 3. confirm the *f*. knees
Zech. 12. 8. he that is *f*. shall be
1 Thes. 5. 14. comfort the *f*. minded
Heb. 12. 12. lift up the *f*. knees
R. V. 1 Sam. 2. 5. languisheth; Ps.
 38. 8. faint; Isa. 16. 14. of no ac-
 count; 1 Thes. 5. 14. fainthearted;
 Heb. 12. 12. palsied
FEED, *fed*, Gen. 25. 30. & 30. 36.
Ps. 28. 9. *f*. them and lift them up
 37. 3. verily thou shalt be *f*.
 49. 14. death shall *f*. on them
Prov. 10. 21. lips of righteous *f*.
Isa. 58. 14. *f*. thee with heritage of
Jer. 3. 15. pastors *f*. you with
 knowledge
Acts 20. 28. to *f*. the church of God
1 Cor. 13. 3. give all my goods to *f*.
 3. 2. I have *f*. you with milk, and
Rev. 7. 17. Lamb in the throne *f*.
1 Kings 22. 27. *f*. him with bread
Prov. 30. 8. *f*. me with food con-
 venient
S. of S. 1. 8. *f*. thy kids beside
 shepherds' tents
Mic. 7. 14. *f*. thy people with thy
 rod
John 21. 15. *f*. my lambs, *f*. my
 sheep, 16. 17.
Rom. 12. 20. if enemy hunger, *f*.
1 Pet. 5. 2. *f*. flock of God among
Isa. 44. 20. he *feedeth* on ashes
S. of S. 2. 16. he *f*. among lilies,
 6. 3.
Hos. 12. 1. Ephraim *f*. on wind —
Matt. 6. 26. heavenly Father *f*.
 them, Luke 12. 24.
1 Cor. 9. 7. who *f*. a flock and eateth not
R. V. Gen. 46. 32. keepers of; John
 21. 16; 1 Pet. 5. 2. tend; 2 Sam.
 19. 33. sustain; Ps. 49. 14; Rev.
 7. 17. be their shepherd; Rev. 12.
 6. may nourish
FEEL, *feeling*, Gen. 27. 12. Acts
 17. 27. Eph. 4. 19. Heb. 4. 15.
R. V. Job 20. 20. knew no; Eccl.
 8. 5. know
FEET, Gen. 18. 4. & 19. 2. & 49. 10.
1 Sam. 2. 9. keep *f*. of his saints
Neh. 9. 21. their *f*. swelled not
Job 12. 5. is ready to slip with his *f*.
 29. 15. eyes to the blind, and *f*.
Ps. 73. 2. my *f*. were almost gone
 116. 8. delivered my *f*. from falling
 119. 105. thy word is a lamp to my *f*.
Prov. 4. 26. ponder the path of
 thy *f*.
Isa. 59. 7. their *f*. run to evil, and
Luke 1. 79. guide our *f*. into way of
Eph. 6. 15. *f*. shod with the prep.
Heb. 12. 13. straight paths for
 your *f*.
Rev. 1. 11. they stood upon their *f*.
 R. V. Isa. 3. 18; Matt. 18. 29 —
FEIGNED, 1 Sam. 21. 13. Ps. 17. 1.
2 Pet. 2. 3. *feignedly*, Jer. 3. 10.
FELLOW, Gen. 19. 9. Ex. 2. 13.
Zech. 13. 7. man that is my *f*.
Acts 24. 5. a pestilent *f*., 22. 22.
Rom. 16. 7. my *f*. prisoner, Col.
 4. 10.
2 Cor. 8. 23. my *f*. helper, 3 John 8.
Eph. 2. 19. *f*. citizens
 3. 6. *f*. heirs
Col. 1. 7. *f*. servant, 4. 7. Rev. 6. 11.
 & 19. 10. & 22. 9.
Phil. 4. 3. *f*. laborers, 1 Thes. 3. 2.
Ps. 45. 7. oil of gladness above *f*.,
 Heb. 1. 9.
 94. 20. have *fellowship* with thee
Acts 2. 42. continued steadfastly
 in apostles' doctrine and *f*.
1 Cor. 1. 9. God by whom call. to *f*.
 10. 20. should have *f*. with devils
2 Cor. 6. 14. what *f*. hath righteous.
 8. 4. *f*. of ministering to saints

Gal. 2. 9. gave us right hand of *f.*
Eph. 5. 11. no *f.* with unfruitful
Phil. 1. 5. for your *f.* in the gospel
2. 1. if there be any *f.* of the Spi.
1 John 1. 3. *f.* with us, our *f.* with
R. V. Judg. 11. 37; Ezek. 37. 19; Dan.
2. 13. companions; 1 Sam. 29. 4;
Matt. 12. 24; 26. 61; Luke 22. 59;
23. 2; John 9. 29; Acts 18. 13. man;
Lev. 6. 2. bargain; 1 Cor. 10. 20.
communion; Eph. 3. 9. dispensation

FERVENT in spirit, Acts 18. 25.
Rom. 12. 11. *f.* in spirit serving
2 Cor. 7. 7. your *f.* mind toward me
Jas. 5. 16. *f.* prayer of righteous
2 Pet. 3. 10. melt with *f.* heat, 12.
Col. 4. 12. Epaphras always laboring *fervently* for you in prayers
1 Pet. 1. 22. love one another *f.*
R. V. 2 Cor. 7. 7. zeal for; Jas. 5.
16. much in its workings; Col.
4. 12. striving

FEVER threatened for disobedience, Deut. 28. 22.
healed: Peter's wife's mother,
Matt. 8. 14; nobleman's son, John
4. 52.

FEW, Gen. 29. 20. Ps. 105. 12.
Matt. 7. 14. way to life, *f.* find it
20. 16. many called, but *f.* chosen,
22. 14.
25. 21. been faithful in a *f.* things
Rev. 2. 14. I have a *f.* things

FIDELITY, all good, Tit. 2. 10.

FIERCENESS of anger, Deut. 13.
17. Josh. 7. 26. 2 Kings 23. 26. Job
4. 10. 4. 10. 16. & 39. 24. & 41. 10.
Ps. 85. 3. Jer. 25. 38. Hos. 11. 9.

FIERY law, Deut. 33. 2.
Num. 21. 6. *f.* serpents, 8. Deut. 8.
15.
Ps. 21. 9. make them as a *f.* oven
Eph. 6. 16. quench *f.* darts of devil
Heb. 10. 27. *f.* indignation devour
1 Pet. 4. 12. not strange the *f.* trial
R. V. Heb. 10. 27. fierceness of fire

FIGHT, 1 Sam. 17. 20. Ex. 14. 14.
Acts 5. 39. found to *f.* against God
1 Cor. 9. 26. so *f.* I not as one that
2 Tim. 4. 7. I have fought a good *f.*
Heb. 10. 32. a great *f.* of afflictions
R. V. Heb. 10. 32. conflict of suffering

FIGS, Gen. 3. 7. Isa. 34. 4. & 38. 21.
Jer. 24. 2. very good *f.* naughty *f.*,
29. 17.
Matt. 7. 16. do men gather *f.* of thistles
Jas. 3. 12. can *f.* tree bear olive
Judg. 9. 10. *fig-tree*, 1 Kings 4. 25.
Mic. 4. 4. Isa. 36. 16. Hos. 9. 10. Nah.
3. 12. Hab. 3. 17. Zech. 3. 10. Matt.
21. 19. & 24. 32. Luke 13. 6, 7. John
1. 48, 50. Rev. 6. 13.
R. V. Isa. 34. 4. fading leaf

FIGURE, Rom. 5. 14. 1 Cor. 4. 6.
Heb. 9. 9, 24. & 11. 19. 1 Pet. 3. 21.
R. V. Heb. 9. 24. like in pattern
to; 1 Pet. 3. 21. after a true likeness

FILL, Job 8. 21. & 23. 4.
Ps. 81. 10. open mouth wide, I will *f.* it
Jer. 23. 24. I *f.* heaven and earth
Rom. 15. 13. God *f.* you with all
Eph. 4. 10. ascended, might *f.* all
Col. 1. 24. I *f.* up that which is be.
Ps. 72. 19. melt with his glory
Luke 1. 53. hath *f.* hungry with
Acts 9. 17. *f.* with the Holy Ghost,
2. 4. & 4. 8, 31. & 13. 9, 52. Luke 1.
15.
Rom. 15. 14. *f.* with all knowledge
2 Cor. 7. 4. I am *f.* with comfort
Eph. 3. 19. might be *f.* with all
5. 18. not with wine but *f.* with
Phil. 1. 11. *f.* with the fruits of
Col. 1. 9. *f.* with knowledge of his
2 Tim. 1. 4. mindful of tears *f.* with
Eph. 1. 23. fulness of him that *filleth* all in all
R. V. Job 38. 39; Ezek. 32. 4. satisfy; Ps. 104. 28; Prov. 18. 20; 30.

16. satisfied, Matt. 5. 16; Mark 2.
21. should fill, Rev. 15. 1. finished;
18. 6. mingle unto; Rom. 15. 14. in
some measure I shall have been
satisfied

FILTH, Isa. 4. 4. 1 Cor. 4. 13.
Job 15. 16. more *filthy* is man
Ps. 14. 3. altogether become *f.*, 53. 3.
Isa. 64. 6. all our righteousness as *f.*
Col. 3. 8. put off *f.* communication
1 Tim. 3. 3. greedy of *f.* lucre, 8.
Tit. 1. 7, 11. 1 Pet. 5. 2.
2 Pet. 2. 7. vexed with *f.* conver.
Jude 8. *f.* dreamers defile the flesh
Rev. 22. 11. that is *f.* let him be *f.*
Jas. 1. 21. lay apart all *filthiness*
Ezek. 36. 25. from all your *f.* I
2 Cor. 7. 1. cleanse ourselves from all *f.*
R. V. Ezra 9. 11. through the uncleanness; 2 Cor. 7. 1. defilement
of; Rev. 17. 4. even the unclean
things; Job 15. 16. corrupt; Isa.
64. 6. polluted; Zeph. 3. 11. rebellious; Col. 3. 8. shameful; 1 Tim.
3. 3. money; 2 Pet. 2. 7. lascivious; Jude 8 —

FINALLY, 2 Cor. 13. 11. Eph. 6.
10. Phil. 3. 1. & 4. 8. 2 Thes. 3. 1.
1 Pet. 3. 8.

FIND, Gen. 19. 11. & 38. 22.
Num. 32. 23. your sin shall *f.* you
Job 11. 7. who by searching can *f.*
Prov. 1. 28. shall seek me and not *f.*
S. of S. 5. 6. I sought but could not *f.*
Jer. 6. 16. ye shall *f.* rest to your
29. 13. shall seek me and *f.* me
Matt. 7. 7. seek and ye shall *f.*
10. 39. *f.* life; loseth life shall *f.* it,
16. 25.
11. 29. ye shall *f.* rest to your souls
John 7. 34. seek me, and shall not *f.*
Rom. 7. 18. how to do good, I *f.* not
2 Tim. 1. 18. may *f.* mercy in that
Heb. 4. 16. may *f.* grace to help
Rev. 9. 6. seek death and shall not *f.*
Prov. 8. 35. whoso *findeth* me *f.* life
18. 22. whoso *f.* a wife, *f.* a good
Eccl. 9. 10. whatsoever thy hand *f.* to do
Matt. 7. 8. that seeketh *f.*, Luke 11.
10.
Isa. 58. 13. not *finding* thine own pl.
Rom. 11. 33. his ways past *f.* out
FINE, Job 28. 1. Isa. 3. 23. Lev. 2.
1. Ps. 81. 16. Prov. 25. 4.
R. V. Isa. 19. 9. combed; Lam. 4.
1; Dan. 10. 5. pure; Mark 15. 46.
linen cloth; Rev. 1. 15; 2. 18. burnished.
FINGER of God, Ex. 8. 19. & 31.
18. Deut. 9. 10. Luke 11. 20.
1 Kings 12. 10. my little *f.* shall
Ps. 8. 3. heaven is work of thy *f.*
144. 1. he teacheth my *f.* to fight
Prov. 6. 13. he teacheth with his *f.*
Luke 11. 46. touch not with one of your *f.*
John 20. 27. reach hither thy *f.*
FINISH transgression, Dan. 9. 24.
John 17. 4. I have *f.* work
19. 30. it is *f.*
Acts 20. 24. *f.* my course with joy
2 Cor. 8. 6. would also *f.* in you
2 Tim. 4. 7. I have *f.* my course
Jas. 1. 15. sin when it is *f.* bringeth
Heb. 12. 2. author and *finisher* of
R. V. Luke 14. 28; 2 Cor. 8. 6. complete; John 3. 34; 5. 36; 17. 4.
accomplish; Acts 20. 24. may accomplish, Jas. 1. 15. full-grown
FIRE, Ex. 3. 2. & 9. 23, 24. & 40. 38.
Gen. 19. 24. the Lord rained *f.*
Ps. 11. 6. rain *f.* and brimstone
39. 3. while musing the *f.* burned
Prov. 6. 27. can a man take *f.*
25. 22. heap coals of *f.* on his head,
Rom. 12. 20.
S. of S. 8. 6. as coals of *f.* hath vehement

Isa. 3. 18. wickedness burneth as a *f.*
10. 17. light of Israel for a *f.* for a flame
31. 9. Lord of hosts whose *f.* is in Zion
43. 2. walkest through *f.* shall not
Jer. 23. 29. is not my word like *f.*,
20. 9.
Amos 5. 6. lest Lord break out like *f.*
7. 4. Lord God called to contend by *f.*
Zech. 2. 5. I will be a wall of *f.*
3. 2. brand plucked out of *f.*, Amos
4. 11.
Mal. 3. 2. he shall be as a refiner's *f.*
Matt. 3. 10. cut down and cast into the *f.*, 7. 19.
12. burn with unquenchable *f.*,
Mark 9. 43, 44, 46, 48. Luke 3. 17.
Luke 9. 54. command *f.* to come
12. 49. I am come to send *f.* on the
1 Cor. 3. 13. revealed by *f.* — *f.* try,
15.
Heb. 12. 29. our God is consuming *f.*
Jude 23. pulling them out of the *f.*
Matt. 5. 22. *hell-fire*, 18. 9. Mark 9. 47.
Lev. 10. 1. *strange fire*, Num. 3. 4.
& 26. 61.
R. V. Matt. 5. 22; 18. 9. the hell of
fire; Mark 9. 44, 46, 47 —
FIRST, Matt. 10. 2. Esth. 1. 14.
Isa. 41. 4. the Lord the *f.* and the
last, 44. 6. & 48. 12. Rev. 1. 11, 17.
& 2. 8. & 22. 13.
Matt. 6. 33. seek *f.* the kingdom of
7. 5. *f.* cast out the beam, Luke 6.
42.
19. 30. many that be *f.* shall be last,
20. 16. Mark 10. 31.
22. 38. this is the *f.* and great
Acts 26. 23. *f.* that should rise
Rom. 11. 35. who hath *f.* given to
1 Cor. 15. 45. *f.* man Adam
47. *f.* man of the earth
2 Cor. 8. 5. *f.* gave their own selves
12. accepted, if there be *f.* willing
1 Pet. 4. 17. if judgment *f.* begin
1 John 4. 19. because he *f.* loved us
Rev. 2. 4. left thy *f.* love
5. do *f.* works
20. 5. this is the *f.* resurrection, 6.
Matt. 1. 25. *first-born*, Luke 2. 7.
Rom. 8. 29. *f.* among many breth.
Col. 1. 15. *f.* of every creature
18. *f.* from the dead
Rom. 11. 16. if *first fruit* be holy
Prov. 3. 9. honor the Lord with *f.*
Rom. 8. 23. having *first fruits*
1 Cor. 15. 20. Christ *f.* of them
Jas. 1. 18. we a kind of *f.* creatures
Rev. 14. 4. redeemed are *f.* to God
FISH, Ezek. 29. 4, 5. & 47. 9, 10.
Jer. 16. 16. *fishers*, Ezek. 47. 10.
Matt. 4. 18, 19. John 21. 7. Isa. 19. 8.
R. V. Isa. 19. 10. hire; Job 41. 1;
John 21. 7 —
FLAME, 2 Cor. 3. 2. Judg. 13. 20.
Ps. 104. 4. maketh ministers a *f.*
106. 18. *f.* burnt up wicked, Num.
16. 35.
Isa. 10. 17. the Holy One of Israel
for a *f.*
2 Thes. 1. 8. in *flaming* fire taking
R. V. Judg. 20. 38, 40. cloud; Dan.
7. 11. with fire; Isa. 13. 8. faces of
flame: Nah. 2. 3. flash in the steel
FLATTER, Ps. 78. 36. Prov. 2. 16.
& 29. 19. Job 32. 21, 22. 1 Thes. 2. 5.
R. V. Prov. 20. 19. openeth wide
FLEE, Isa. 10. 3. & 20. 6. Heb. 6. 18.
Prov. 28. 1. wicked *f.* when no
Matt. 3. 7. who warned you to *f.*
1 Cor. 6. 18. *f.* fornication
10. 14. *f.* from idolatry
1 Tim. 6. 11. man of God *f.* these
2 Tim. 2. 22. *f.* youthful lusts
Jas. 4. 7. resist the devil, he will *f.*
from you
R. V. Isa. 30. 10. stand; 30. 3. gnaw
the dry ground; Ps. 64. 8. wag the
head; Jer. 48. 9. fly; Hos. 7. 13.
wandered, Acts 16. 27. escaped

FLEECE, Gideon's, Judg. 6. 37.
FLESH, Gen. 2. 21. 1 Cor. 15. 39.
Gen. 2. 24. they shall be one f.
Matt. 19. 5. 1 Cor. 6. 16. Eph. 5. 31.
John 10. 11. clothed me with skin and f.
Ps. 56. 4. what f. can do to me
78. 39. remember that they were but f.
Jer. 17. 5. cursed that maketh f. his arm
Matt. 26. 41. spirit is willing, but f. weak
John 1. 14. the Word was made f.
6. 53. eat the f. of the Son of man, 52, 55, 56.
63. f. profiteth nothing, words are
Rom. 7. 25. serve with f. law of sin
8. 12. debtors not to the f.
9. 3. kinsmen according to the f.
5. of whom concerning f. Christ
13. 14. make not provision for f.
1 Cor. 1. 29. that no f. should glory
2 Cor. 1. 17. purpose according to f.
10. 2. walked according to the f.
Gal. 5. 17. f. lusts against the Spirit
24. Christ's have crucified f. with
Eph. 6. 5. masters according to f.
Heb. 12. 9. we had fathers of our f.
Jude 7. going after strange f.
23. hating garment spotted by f.
John 8. 15. ye judge *after the flesh*
Rom. 8. 1. walk not — but after
5. they that are—mind things of f.
13. if ye live — ye shall die, 12.
1 Cor. 1. 26. not many wise men—
10. 18. Israel—, Rom. 9. 8. Gal. 6. 13.
2 Cor. 5. 16. know no man — know Christ
10. 3. walk in f. not war—
2 Pet. 2. 10. walk — in lust of
Ps. 65. 2. to thee shall *all flesh* come
Isa. 40. 6. — is grass, 1 Pet. 1. 24.
49. 26. —shall know that I am thy
Jer. 32. 27. I am the Lord, the God of—
Joel 2. 28. I will pour my Spirit on—
Luke 3. 6. —shall see the salvation
John 17. 2. given him power over—
Rom. 7. 5. when we were *in the flesh*
8. 8. that are—cannot please God
1 Tim. 3. 16. mystery; God manifest—
1 Pet. 3. 18. he was put to death—, 4. 1.
Gen. 2. 23. *my flesh*, 29. 14. Job 19. 26.
Ps. 63. 1. & 119. 120. John 6. 51, 55, 56. Rom. 7. 18.
John 1. 13. born not of will of *the flesh*
3. 6. that which is born — is f.
Rom. 8. 5. after f. do mind things—
Gal. 5. 19. works—are manifest
6. 8. soweth to f. shall — reap cor.
Eph. 2. 3. lusts—desires—
1 Pet. 3. 21. not putting away filth—
1 John 2. 16. lust—of the eyes, pride
Matt. 16. 17. *flesh and blood* have
1 Cor. 15. 50. —cannot inherit the
Gal. 1. 16. I conferred not with—
Eph. 5. 30. members of his — and
6. 12. we wrestle not against — but
Heb. 2. 14. children are partakers of—
2 Cor. 1. 12. not with *fleshly* wisdom
1 Pet. 2. 11. abstain from f. lusts
R. V. Acts 2. 30; Rom. 8. 1; Eph. 5. 30—; 2 Cor. 3. 3. tables that are hearts of flesh
FLOCK, Gen. 32. 5. Ps. 77. 20. Isa. 40. 11. & 63. 11. Jer. 13. 17, 20.
Zech. 11. 4. feed f. of slaughter, 7.
Luke 12. 32. fear not, little f. for it
Acts 20. 28. take heed to all the f., 29.
1 Pet. 5. 2. feed the f. of God
R. V. Ezek. 34. 3, 8, 10, 15, 19, 31. sheep
FLOURISH, Isa. 17. 11. & 66. 14.
Ps. 72. 7. shall the righteous f., 16. &
92. 12, 13, 14. Prov. 11. 28. & 14. 11.
92. 7. when workers of iniquity f.
132. 18. on himself shall crown f.
R. V. Isa. 17. 11; Eccl. 12. 5. blos-

som; S. of S. 6. 11; 7. 12. budded;
Phil. 4. 10. ye have revived
FOLLOW, Gen. 44. 4. Ex. 14. 4.
Ex. 23. 2. shall not f. a multitude
Deut. 16. 20. that is just shalt thou f.
Ps. 38. 20. I f. the thing that good is
Isa. 51. 1. my people that f.
Hos. 6. 3. know if we f. on to know
Rom. 14. 19. f. things that make for
1 Cor. 14. 1. f. after charity, desire
Phil. 3. 12. but I f. after that I may
1 Thes. 5. 15. ever f. that which is
1 Tim. 6. 11. f. after righteousness
2 Tim. 2. 22. f. righteousness, faith
Heb. 12. 14. f. peace with all men
13. 7. whose faith f. considering
1 Pet. 2. 21. example should f. his
3 John 11. f. not evil, but that whi.
Rev. 14. 13. their works do f. them
Ps. 23. 6. goodness and mercy shall *follow me*, Matt. 4. 19. & 9. 9. & 19. 21. Luke 5. 27. & 9. 59. John 1. 43. & 21. 19.
Matt. 16. 24. take up cross and —
Luke 18. 22. sell all that thou hast, and—
John 12. 26. if any man serve me, let him—
Num. 14. 24. hath *followed* me fully
32. 12. wholly f. the Lord, Deut. 1. 36. Josh. 14. 8, 9, 14.
Rom. 9. 30. f. not after righteousness
31. f. law of righteousness
Ps. 63. 8. soul *followeth* hard after
Matt. 10. 38. taketh not his cross and f. me
Mark 9. 38. he f. not us, Luke 9. 49.
R. V. Ex. 14. 17. go in after; Matt. 4. 19. come ye after; 27. 62. the day after; 2 Thes. 3. 7; Heb. 13. 7; 3 John 11. imitate; Phil. 3. 12. press on
FOLLY wrought in Israel, Gen. 34. 7. Deut. 22. 21. Josh. 7. 15. Judg. 20. 6.
Job 4. 18. angels he charged with f.
Ps. 49. 13. their way is their f.
85. 8. let them not turn again to f.
Prov. 26. 4, 5. answer a fool according to his f.
2 Tim. 3. 9. their f. shall be manifest
R. V. 2 Cor. 11. 1. foolishness
FOOD, Gen. 3. 6. Deut. 10. 18.
Job 23. 12. words more than necessary f.
Ps. 78. 25. men did eat angels' f.
136. 25. who giveth f. to all flesh
146. 7. who giveth f. to the hungry
Prov. 30. 8. feed me with f. conven.
Acts 14. 17. filling our hearts with f.
2 Cor. 9. 10. ministered bread for your f.
1 Tim. 6. 8. having f. and raiment
R. V. Gen. 42. 33. corn; Lev. 22. 7; 2 Sam. 9. 10. bread; Ps. 78. 25. bread of the mighty
FOOL said in his heart, Ps. 14. 1. & 53. 1.
Jer. 17. 11. at end of days shall be f.
Matt. 5. 22. whosoever shall say to brother, thou f.
Luke 12. 20. thou f. this night thy
1 Cor. 3. 18. let him become a f. that
2 Cor. 11. 16. think me a f.
Ps. 75. 4. *fools* deal not foolishly
94. 8. ye f. when will ye be wise
107. 17. f. because of their trans.
Prov. 1. 7. f. despise wisdom
22. f. hate knowledge
13. 20. companion of f. shall be
14. 8. folly of f. is deceitful
16. 22. instruction of f. is folly
Eccl. 5. 4. he hath no pleasure in f.
Matt. 23. 17. ye f. and blind, 19.
Rom. 1. 22. professing to be wise became f.
1 Cor. 4. 10. we are f. for Christ's sake
Eph. 5. 15. walk circumspectly, not as f.
Ps. 5. 5. f. shall not stand in thy sight

Ps. 73. 22. so f. was I and ignorant
Matt. 7. 26. on sand like to a f. man
25. 2. virgins, five were wise and five f.
Rom. 1. 21. their f. heart darkened
Gal. 3. 1. O f. Galatians, who bewitched
Eph. 5. 4. filthiness, nor f. talking
Tit. 3. 3. were sometimes f. disobe.
Gen. 31. 28. done *foolishly*, Num. 12. 11. 1 Sam. 13. 13. 2 Sam. 24. 10. 1 Chron. 21. 8. 2 Chron. 16. 9. Prov. 14. 17. 2 Cor. 11. 21.
Job 1. 22. Job sinned not, nor charged God f.
2 Sam. 15. 31. turn counsel into *foolishness*
Prov. 12. 23. heart of fools proclaimeth f.
14. 24. f. of fools is folly, 15. 2, 14.
22. 15. f. is bound in heart of child
27. 22. bray a fool, yet his f. will
1 Cor. 1. 18. preaching of the cross is to them that perish, f.
23. Christ crucified, to Greeks f.
25. f. of God is wiser than men
3. 19. wisdom of world is f. with God
R. V. 2 Cor. 11. 23. one beside himself; Prov. 11. 29; 12. 15; Luke 12. 20; 1 Cor. 15. 36; 2 Cor. 11. 16; 12. 6, 11. foolish; Ps. 75. 4. arrogant; Eph. 5. 15. unwise; Ps. 5. 5; 73. 3. arrogant; 73. 12. brutish; Prov. 9. 6. ye simple ones; Rom. 1. 21. senseless; 10. 19. void of understanding; Ps. 75. 4. arrogantly; Prov. 14. 24; 15. 2, 14. folly
FOOT shall not stumble, Prov. 3. 23.
Eccl. 5. 1. keep thy f. when thou
Isa. 58. 13. turn away f. from sabbath
Matt. 18. 8. if thy f. offend thee, cut
Heb. 10. 29. trodden under f. Son of God
R. V. Ex. 31. 9; 35. 16; 38. 8; 39. 39; 41. 11; Lev. 8. 11. base; Isa. 18. 7. down; Lam. 1. 15. set at nought
FORBEAR, Ex. 23. 5. 1 Cor. 9. 6.
Rom. 2. 4. goodness and *forbearance*, 3. 25.
R. V. Neh. 9. 30. bear with; Prov. 24. 11. hold not back; Ezek. 24. 17. sigh but not aloud
FORBID, Mark 10. 14. Luke 18. 16. & 6. 29. Acts 24. 23. & 28. 31.
1 Tim. 4. 3. *forbidding* to marry
1 Thes. 2. 16. f. us to speak to the Gentiles
R. V. Matt. 3. 14. would have hindered; Luke 6. 29. withhold not; Gal. 6. 14. far be it from me; 2 Pet. 2. 16. and stayed
FORCE, Matt. 11. 12. Heb. 9. 17.
Isa. 60. 5. f. of Gentiles shall come, 11.
Job 6. 25. how *forcible* right words
R. V. Deut. 20. 19. wielding; Isa. 60. 5, 11. wealth; Ezek. 35. 5. power; Dan. 11. 38. fortresses; Obad. 11. substance
FOREFATHERS, 2 Tim. 1. 3. Jer. 11. 10.
FOREHEAD, Ex. 28. 38. Lev. 13. 41.
Jer. 3. 3. thou hast a whore's f.
Ezek. 3. 8. thy f. strong against their f.
Rev. 7. 3. sealed in their f., 9. 4.
13. 16. mark their f., 14. 9. & 20. 4.
14. 1. Father's name written in f., 22. 4.
R. V. Ezek. 16. 12. nose
FOREIGNERS, Ex. 12. 45. Deut. 15. 3. Obad. 11. Eph. 2. 19.
FOREKNOW, Rom. 8. 29. & 11. 2.
Acts 2. 23. *foreknowledge* of God, 1 Pet. 1. 2.
FOREORDAINED, 1 Pet. 1. 20.
FORERUNNER, Heb. 6. 20.
FORESEETH, Prov. 22. 3. & 27. 12.
R. V. Prov. 22. 3; 27. 12. seeth; Acts 2. 25. beheld

FOREWARN, Luke 12. 5.
R. V. Luke 12. 5. warn
FORGAT Lord, Judg. 3. 7. 1 Sam.
12. 9.
Ps. 78. 11. *f.* his works and wonders
106. 21. *f.* God their Saviour
Lam. 3. 17. I *f.* prosperity
Hos. 2. 13. *f.* me, saith the Lord
Deut. 9. 7. remember and *forget* not
Job 8. 13. paths of all that *f.* God
Ps. 45. 10. *f.* thy own people, and
103. 2. *f.* not all his benefits
119. 16. I will not *f.* thy words, 83,
93, 109, 141, 153, 176.
Prov. 3. 1. my son, *f.* not my law
Isa. 49. 15. can woman *f.* her suck-
ing child
Jer. 2. 32. can a maid *f.* her orna.
Heb. 6. 10. God is not unrighteous
to *f.* your
13. 16. to do good and to communi-
cate *f.* not
Jas. 1. 25. be not a *f.* hearer
Ps. 44. 24. thou *forgettest* our afflict.
9. 12. he *f.* not the cry of humble
Prov. 2. 17. *f.* covenant of her God
Jas. 1. 24. *f.* what manner of man
Phil. 3. 13. *forgetting* those things
Ps. 10. 11. God hath *forgotten*
42. 9. why hast thou *f.* me
77. 9. hath God *f.* to be gracious
119. 61. I have not *f.* thy law
Isa. 17. 10. hast *f.* the God of thy
Jer. 2. 32. my people have *f.* me
3. 21. have *f.* their God, Deut. 32.
18.
50. 5. covenant that shall not be *f.*
Heb. 12. 5. the exhortation
FORGAVE their iniquity, Ps. 78.
38.
Matt. 18. 27. *f.* him the debt, 32.
Luke 7. 42. frankly *f.* them both
43. love most, to whom *f.* most
2 Cor. 2. 10. *f.* any thing, I *f.* it
Col. 3. 13. as Christ *f.* you, also do
Ps. 32. 5. *forgavest* the iniquity of
99. 8. thou wast a God that *f.* them
Ex. 32. 32. now *forgive* their sin
Ps. 86. 5. thou art good and ready
to *f.*
Isa. 2. 9. therefore *f.* them not
Matt. 6. 12. *f.* us our debts as we
14. if ye *f.* men, 15. if you *f.* not
9. 6. Son of man hath power on
earth to *f.*
Luke 6. 37. *f.* and ye shall be for.
17. 3. if he repent, *f.* him, 4.
23. 34. Father *f.* them, they know
1 John 1. 9. faithful to *f.* us
Ps. 32. 1. whose transgression is
forgiven
85. 2. *f.* the iniquity of thy people
Isa. 33. 24. people shall be *f.* their
Matt. 9. 2. good cheer, thy sins be *f.*
12. 31. all manner of sin *f.* 32. not
be *f.*
Luke 7. 47. to whom little is *f.*
loveth
Rom. 4. 7. blessed whose iniquities are *f.*
Eph. 4. 32. as God hath *f.* you, Col.
3. 13.
Jas. 5. 15. if he have committed
sins, they shall be *f.*
1 John 2. 12. your sins are *f.* you
Ps. 103. 3. who *forgiveth* all thy ini.
130. 4. is there *forgiveness* with
thee
Dan. 9. 9. to the Lord belong
mercy and *f.*
Acts 5. 31. to give repent. and *f.*
26. 18. may receive *f.* of sins by
faith
Eph. 1. 7. *f.* of sins according to
the riches
Col. 1. 14. redempt., even *f.* of sin
Ex. 34. 7. *forgiving* iniquity, transgression and sin, Num. 14. 18.
Mic. 7. 18.
Eph. 4. 32. *f.* one another, Col. 3. 13.
R. V. Luke 6. 37. release ; Mark 11.
26——; Acts 5. 31. 13. 38; 26. 18.
remission
FORM, Gen. 1. 2. 1 Sam. 28. 14.

Isa. 53. 2. hath no *f.* nor comeliness
Rom. 2. 20. hast the *f.* of knowl.
6. 17. obeyed from heart that *f.*
Phil. 2. 6. who being in *f.* of God
7. took upon him the *f.* of a ser.
2 Tim. 1. 13. hold *f.* of sound words
3. 5. having the *f.* of godliness
Isa. 45. 7. I *f.* the light and create
Deut. 32. 18. hast forgotten God
that *formed* thee
Prov. 26. 10. God that *f.* all things
Isa. 27. 11. *f.* them will show no
43. 21. this people have I *f.* for
myself
Rom. 9. 20. thing *f.* say to him
Ps. 94. 9. that *formeth* the eye
Zech. 12. 1. *f.* spirit of man within
Jer. 10. 16. he is the *former* of all
things, 51. 19.
R. V. Gen. L. 2; Jer. 4. 23. waste ;
Job 4. 16. appearance ; Dan. 2. 31 ;
3. 25. aspect ; 2 Tim. 1. 13. pattern ;
Deut. 32. 18. gave birth ; Job 26. 5.
tremble ; 26. 13. pierced ; Prov.
26. 10. wounded ; Isa. 44. 10. fashioned ; Zech. 14. 8. eastern ; Mal.
3. 4. ancient ; Job 30. 3. gloom of ;
Hos. 6. 3. rain that watereth ; Rev.
21. 4. the first
FORNICATION, 2 Chron. 21. 11.
Isa. 23. 17. Ezek. 16. 15, 26, 29.
Matt. 5. 32. put away wife for
cause of *f.*
19. 9. except it be for *f.*
John 8. 41. we be not born of *f.*
Acts 15. 20. abstain from *f.*, 29. &
21. 25.
Rom. 1. 29. filled with all *f.* wickedness
1 Cor. 5. 1. there is *f.* among you
6. 13. body not for *f.*
18. flee *f.*
7. 2. to avoid *f.* every man have
his wife
2 Cor. 12. 21. not repent. of their *f.*
Gal. 5. 19. works of flesh, adult. *f.*
Eph. 5. 3. but *f.* and all uncleanness
Col. 3. 5. mortify *f.* uncleanness
1 Thes. 4. 3. should abstain from *f.*
Jude 7. giving themselves to *f.*
Rev. 2. 14. taught to commit *f.*, 20.
21. I gave her space to repent of
her *f.*
9. 21. neither repented of their *f.*
17. 4. abomination and filthiness
of her *f.*
19. 2. did corrupt earth with her *f.*
Ezek. 16. 15. *fornications*, Matt. 15.
19.
1 Cor. 5. 9. *fornicators*, 10. 11. & 6.
9. Heb. 12. 16.
R. V. 2 Chron. 21. 11. go a whor-
ing ; Isa. 23. 17. play the harlot ;
Ezek. 16. 15, 29. whoredom, Rom.
1. 29 ——
FORSAKE, Deut. 12. 19. & 31. 16.
Deut. 4. 31. Lord thy God will not
f. thee, 31. 6, 8. 1 Chron. 28. 20.
Heb. 13. 5.
Josh. 1. 5. I will not fail thee nor
f. thee, Isa. 41. 17. & 42. 16.
1 Sam. 12. 22. Lord will not *f.* his
people
1 Kings 6. 13. I will not *f.* my peo.
2 Chron. 15. 2. if ye *f.* him he will *f.*
Ps. 27. 10. father and mother *f.* me
94. 14. neither will he *f.* his inher.
Isa. 55. 7. let the wicked *f.* his way
Jer. 17. 13. they that *f.* thee shall
Jonah 2. 8. *f.* their own mercy
Ps. 71. 11. God hath *forsaken* him
22. 1. my God, why *f.* me, Matt.
27. 46.
37. 25. I have not seen the righteous *f.*
Isa. 49. 14. Lord hath *f.* my Lord
54. 7. small moment have I *f.* thee
Jer. 2. 13. *f.* me the fountain of liv.
Matt. 19. 27. we have *f.* all
29. *f.* houses or brethren or
2 Cor. 4. 9. persecuted but not *f.*
Prov. 2. 17. *forsaketh* the guide of

Prov. **28.13.** confesseth and *f.* shall
find
Heb. 10. 25. not *f.* the assembling
Deut. 32. 15. he *forsook* God which
Ps. 119. 87. I *f.* not thy precepts
Jer. 4. 16. all men *f.* me
R. V. Deut. 4. 31. fail ; Judg. 9. 11.
leave ; 6. 13 ; 2 Kings 21. 14 ; Jer.
23. 33, 39. cast off ; Job 20. 13. will
not let it go ; Jer. 15. 6. rejected ;
18. 14. dried up ; Amos 5. 2. cast
down ; Matt. 19. 27 ; 26. 56 ; Mark
14. 50 ; Luke 5. 11. left ; Luke
14. 33. renounceth
FORSAKING God, danger of
Deut. 28. 20. Judg. 10. 13. 2 Chron.
15. 2. & 24. 20. Ezra 8. 22. & 9. 10.
Isa. 1. 28. Jer. L. 16. & 5. 19. & 17.
13. Ezek. 6. 9.
FORTRESS and rock, Lord is my,
2 Sam. 22. 2. Ps. 18. 2. & 31. 3. &
71. 3. & 91. 2. & 144. 2. Jer. 16. 19.
R. V. Jer. 10. 17. siege ; 16. 19.
stronghold ; Mic. 7. 12. Egypt
FORTY DAYS, as the flood, Gen.
7. 17.
giving of the law, Ex. 24. 18.
spying Canaan, Num. 13. 25.
Goliath's defiance, 1 Sam. 17. 16.
Elijah's journey to Horeb,
1 Kings 19. 8.
Jonah's warning to Nineveh,
Jonah 3. 4.
fasting of our Lord, Matt. 4. 2.
Mark 1. 13. Luke 4. 2.
Christ's appearances during, Acts
1. 3.
FORTY STRIPES, Deut. 25. 3.
save one ; 2 Cor. 11. 24.
FORTY YEARS, manna sent, Ex.
16. 35. Num. 14. 33. Ps. 95. 10.
of peace, Judg. 3. 11. & 5. 31. & 8.
28.
FOUND, Gen. 26. 19. & 31. 37.
Eccl. 7. 27. this have I *f.* that, 29.
28. one man among a thousand
have I *f.*
So. of S. 3. 1. I *f.* him not, 4. I *f.* him
Isa. 55. 6. seek the Lord while he
may be *f.*
65. 1. I am *f.* of them that sought
Ezek. 22. 30. I sought a man but *f.*
Dan. 5. 27. weighed and *f.* wanting
Phil. 3. 9. *f.* in him, not having my
2 Pet. 3. 14. may be *f.* of him in
Matt. 7. 25. *founded* on a rock, Ps.
24. 2. Prov. 3. 19. Isa. 14. 32.
Ps. 11. 3. if the *foundations* be destroyed
Job 4. 19. whose *f.* is in the dust
Prov. 10. 25. righteous is an everlasting *f.*
Rom. 15. 20. lest I build upon another man's *f.*
1 Cor. 3. 10. laid *f.*
12. build on this *f.*
Eph. 2. 20. built on *f.* of the proph.
1 Tim. 6. 19. lay up a good *f.* for
2 Tim. 2. 19. the *f.* of God stands
Heb. 11. 10. a city which hath *f.*
Rev. 21. 14. the city hath twelve *f.*
Matt. 13. 35. *foundation of the world*,
25. 34. John 17. 24. Eph. 1. 4.
1 Pet. 1. 20. Rev. 13. 8. & 17. 8. Ps.
104. 5. Prov. 8. 29. Isa. 51. 13, 16.
R. V. Luke 6. 48. because it had
been well builded ; Isa. 16. 7.
raisin cakes ; Jer. 50. 15. bulwarks
FOUNTAIN, Gen. 7. 11. Deut. 8.
7.
Deut. 33. 28. *f.* of Jacob on a land
Ps. 36. 9. with thee is *f.* of life
Prov. 5. 18. let thy *f.* be blessed
14. 27. fear of Lord is a *f.* of life
Eccl. 12. 6. pitcher broken at the *f.*
S. of S. 4. 12. *f.* sealed
15. *f.* of gardens
Jer. 2. 13. Lord *f.* of liv. waters, **17.**
9. 1. my eyes were a *f.* of tears
Rev. 21. 6. give of *f.* of life freely,
22. 17
R. V. Num. **33. 9**; **Prov. 5. 16**
springs ; Jer. 6. 7. well

FOUR living creatures, vision of, Ezek. 1. 5. & 10. 10. Rev. 4. 6. & 5. 14. & 6. 6.
kingdoms, Nebuchadnezzar's vision of, Dan. 2. 36; Daniel's vision of, Dan. 7. 3, 16.
FOURFOLD compensation, Ex. 22. 1. 2 Sam. 12. 6. Luke 19. 8.
FOXES, Judg. 15. 4. Ps. 63. 10. S. of S. 2. 15. Lam. 5. 18. Ezek. 13. 4. Matt. 8. 20. Luke 13. 32.
FRAGMENTS, Matt. 14. 20. Mark 6. 43. & 8. 19, 20. John 6. 12, 13.
FRAIL I am, Ps. 39. 4.
FRAME, Ps. 50. 19. & 94. 20. & 103. 14. Isa. 29. 16. Jer. 18. 11. Eph. 2. 21. Heb. 11. 3.
R. V. Hos. 5. 4. their doings will not suffer them
FRAUD condemned, Lev. 19. 13. Mal. 3. 5. Mark 10. 19. 1 Cor. 6. 8. 1 Thes. 4. 6. *See* DECEIT.
FREE, Ex. 21. 2. Lev. 19. 20.
2 Chron. 29. 31. as many as were of a *f.* heart
Ps. 51. 12. uphold with thy *f.* Spirit
John 8. 32. truth shall make you *f.*
36. if Son make *f.* shall be *f.*
Rom. 5. 15. so also is *f.* gift
6. 7. *f.* from sin, 18.
20. *f.* from righteousness
7. 3. *f.* from law
8. 2. *f.* from the law of sin
1 Cor. 7. 22. the Lord's *f.* man
Gal. 3. 28. neither bond nor *f.*, Col. 3. 11.
5. 1. Christ hath made us *f.* not
1 Pet. 2. 16. as *f.* and not using lib.
Hos. 14. 4. I will love them *freely*
Matt. 10. 8. *f.* ye have received, *f.*
Rom. 3. 24. justified *f.* by his grace
8. 32. with him *f.* give us all
1 Cor. 12. things *f.* given us of
Rev. 21. 6. of fount. of life *f.*, 22. 17.
R. V. Ex. 21. 11. for nothing; 36. 3. free will; 2 Chron. 29. 31; Amos 4. 5. willing; Ps. 88. 5. cast off;
Acts 22. 28. am a Roman; Col. 3. 11. freeman; 2 Thes. 3. 1. run;
Matt. 15. 6. Mark 7. 11——; Rom. 6. 7. justified
FREEWILL offerings, Lev. 22. 18. Num. 15. 3. Deut. 16. 10. Ezra 3. 5.
FREEWOMAN and bondwoman, illustration of, Gal. 4. 22.
FRET, Ps. 37. 1, 7, 8. Prov. 24. 19.
Prov. 19. 3. his heart *f.* against the
Ezek. 16. 43. hast *fretted* me in all
FRIEND, Jer. 6. 21. Hos. 3. 1.
Ex. 33. 11. as a man to his *f.*
Deut. 13. 6. *f.* which is as his own
2 Sam. 16. 17. is this kind. to thy *f.*
Job 6. 14. pity should be showed from his *f.*
Prov. 17. 17. *f.* loveth all times
18. 24. a *f.* that sticketh closer than a brother
27. 10. own *f.* and father's *f.*
S. of S. 5. 16. my beloved and *f.*
Mic. 7. 5. trust ye not in a *f.* put
John 15. 13. lay down life for his *f.*
15. 14. ye are my *f.* if
15. called you *f.*
Jas. 4. 4. *f.* of the world is enemy of God, *friendship* of the world is enmity with God
Prov. 22. 24. make no *f.* with an
18. 24. hath *f.* must show himself *friendly*
R. V. 2 Sam. 19. 6. them that love thee; Prov. 6. 1; 17. 18. neighbor; Judg. 19. 3; Ruth 2. 13. kindly; Prov. 18. 24. doeth it to his own destruction
FROWARD, Job 5. 13. 1 Pet. 2. 18.
Deut. 32. 20. a very *f.* generation
Ps. 18. 26. will show thyself *f.*
Prov. 4. 24. *f.* mouth, 6. 12. & 8. 13.
10. 31. *f.* tongue, 11. 20. *f.* heart, 17. 20.
3. 32. the *f.* is abomination to the
Isa. 57. 17. went on *frowardly*
Prov. 6. 14. *frowardness* is in him
R. V. 2 Sam. 22. 27; Ps. 18. 26; Prov.

3. 32; 11. 20. perverse; 21. 8. him that is laden with guilt is exceeding crooked
FRUIT, Gen. 4. 3. Lev. 19. 24.
2 Kings 19. 30. bear *f.* upward, Isa. 37. 31.
Ps. 92. 14. shall bring forth *f.* in old
127. 3. *f.* of womb is his reward
Prov. 11. 30. *f.* of righteous is
S. of S. 2. 3 his *f.* was sweet
4. 13. with pleasant *f.*
6. 11. to see the *f.* of the valley
Isa. 3. 10. eat the *f.* of their doings
27. 9. all the *f.* to take away sin
57. 19. create *f.* of the lips, peace
Hos. 10. 1. empty vine brings *f.*
Mic. 6. 7. *f.* of my body for sin of
Matt. 7. 17. good tree brings forth good *f.*, 21. 19.
12. 33. *f.* good; tree known by his *f.*
26. 29. not drink of *f.* of vine till
Luke 1. 42. blessed is the *f.* of thy womb
John 4. 36. gathers *f.* to eternal life
15. 2. branch beareth not *f.* he tak.
Rom. 6. 21. what *f.* had
22. *f.* to holiness
Gal. 5. 22. *f.* of Spirit is love, joy
Eph. 5. 9. *f.* of Spirit is in all good.
Phil. 4. 17. desire *f.* that may abound
Heb. 12. 11. peaceable *f.* of righteousness
Jas. 3. 18. *f.* of righteousness is
Rev. 22. 2. yielded *f.* every month
Matt. 3. 8. bring forth *fruits* meet
7. 16. shall know them by their *f.*
2 Cor. 9. 10. increase the *f.* of right.
Phil. 1. 11. filled with the *f.* of righteousness
Jas. 3. 17. full of good *f.* without
R. V. Ex. 23. 10; Deut. 22. 9. increase; Lev. 25. 15. crops; Isa. 28. 4; S. of S. 6. 11. green plant; Mic. 7. 1. fig; Amos 7. 14. trees; Luke 12. 18. corn; Jude 12. autumn trees
FRUIT TREES saved in time of war, Deut. 20. 19.
FRUSTRATE, Isa. 44. 25. Gal. 2. 21.
R. V. Gal. 2. 21. make void
FUGITIVE servant, law of, Deut. 23. 15.
FULL, Gen. 15. 16. Ex. 16. 3, 8.
Deut. 34. 9. Joshua *f.* of the spirit
Ruth 1. 21. I went out *f.* and
1 Sam. 2. 5. that were *f.* have hired
Job 5. 26. come to grave in *f.* age
14. 1. of few days and *f.* of trouble
Ps. 17. 14. they are *f.* of children
Prov. 27. 7. *f.* soul loath the honey.
Luke 4. 1. Jesus being *f.* of the Holy Ghost
John 1. 14. of God *f.* of grace and
1 Cor. 4. 8. now ye are *f.* now ye
Col. 2. 2. riches of *f.* assurance
2 Tim. 4. 5. *f.* proof of thy ministry
10. 22. draw near in *f.* assurance
Gen. 29. 27. *fulfil*, Ex. 23. 26.
Matt. 3. 15. it becometh us to *f.* all righteousness
5. 17. not to destroy the law, but *f.*
Acts 13. 22. who shall *f.* all my will
Luke 21. 24. till times of Gentiles be *f.*
Gal. 5. 14. law is *f.* in one word
16. shall not *f.* lust of the flesh
6. 2. bear burden and so *f.* law
Eph. 2. 3. *f.* the desires of flesh and
Phil. 2. 2. *f.* ye my joy, that ye be
Col. 4. 17. ministry, in the Lord, that thou *f.* it
2 Thes. 1. 11. *f.* all the good pleas.
Jas. 2. 8. if ye *f.* the royal law
Rev. 17. 17. put in their hearts to *f.*
Job 20 22. in *fulness* of sufficiency
John 1. 16. of his *f.* have we receiv.
Rom. 11. 25. till *f.* of the Gent.
15. 29. *f.* of blessing of the Gospel
Gal. 4. 4. when *f.* of time was come
3. 19. ye may be filled with the *f.* of God

Col 1. 19. in him should all *f.* dwell
2. 9. in him dwells all the *f.* of
R. V. Lev. 2. 14; 2 Kings 4. 42. fresh; 1 Cor. 10. 28——
FURNACE, Deut. 4. 20. Jer. 11. 4.
Ps. 12. 6. Isa. 31. 9. & 48. 10. Dan. 3. 6. 11. Matt. 13. 42, 50. Rev. 1. 15.
FURNISHED, Deut. 15. 14. Prov. 9. 2.
2 Tim. 3. 17. thoroughly *f.* to all
R. V. Ps. 78. 19. prepare; Isa. 65. 11. fill up; Matt. 22. 10. filled
FURY is not in me, Isa. 27. 4.
59. 18. repay *f.* to his adversaries
Jer. 6. 11. I am full of *f.* of the
10. 25. pour out thy *f.* on heathen
Prov. 22. 24. with *furious* man not
R. V. Job 20. 23. fierceness

G

GABRIEL, Dan. 8. 16. & 9. 21. Luke 1. 19, 26.
GAIN, Prov. 3. 14. Job 22. 3.
Isa. 33. 15. despiseth the *g.* of oppre.
Phil. 1. 21. to live is Christ, to die is *g.*
3. 7. what were *g.* to me I counted
1 Tim. 6. 5. supposing *g.* is godliness
Matt. 16. 26. if he should *g.* whole
1 Cor. 9. 19. servant to all, that I might *g.*
18. 15. thou hast *gained* thy bro.
Luke 19. 16. thy pound hath *g.* ten
Tit. 1. 9. convince *gainsayers*
Acts 10. 29. *gainsaying*, Rom. 10. 21. *g.* people
Jude 11. perished in the *g.* of Core
R. V. Prov. 28. 8; Dan. 11. 39. price; Acts 19. 24. little business; 2 Cor. 12. 17, 18. take advantage; Luke 19. 16, 18. made; Acts 27. 21. gotten . . . injury
GALL, Job 16. 13. & 20. 14, 25.
Deut. 29. 18. the root bears *g.*
32. 32. their grapes are grapes of *g.*
Ps. 69. 21. gave me *g.* for drink, Matt. 27. 34.
Jer. 8. 14. given us water of *g.*, 9. 15.
Lam. 3. 19. remembering the wormwood and *g.*, 5.
Acts 8. 23. thou art in the *g.* of bit.
GAP, to stand in, Ezek. 22. 30.
GARDEN, Gen. 2. 15. & 3. 23. & 13. 10.
S. of S. 4. 12. a *g.* enclosed is my sister
16. blow on my *g.*, 5. 1. & 6. 2, 11.
Jer. 31. 12. soul as a watered *g.*, Isa. 58. 11.
GARMENT, Josh. 7. 21. Ezra 9. 3.
Job 37. 17. how thy *garments* are warm
Ps. 22. 18. parted my *g.* among
Isa. 9. 5. battle with *g.* rolled in
61. 3. *g.* of praise for the spirit
Joel 2. 13. rend your hearts and not *g.*
Matt. 21. 8. spread their *g.* in way
Acts 9. 39. showing *g.* Dorcas made
Jas. 5. 2. your *g.* are moth-eaten
Rev. 3. 4. have not defiled their *g.*
16. 15. watcheth and keepeth his *g.*
R. V. Deut. 22. 11. mingled stuff;
Judg. 14. 12, 13, 19; 1 Kings 10. 25;
2 Kings 5. 22, 23; Ps. 109. 19; Dan. 11. 9. raiment; Josh. 7. 21; Zech. 13. 4. mantle; Esth. 8. 15; Mark 16. 5. robe; 1 Sam. 18. 4; 2 Sam. 20. 8; Luke 24. 4. apparel; Mark 13. 16; Luke 22. 36. cloak; Ps. 69. 11. clothing; 104. 6. vesture; Matt.——
GATE, Gen. 19. 1. & 34. 20, 24.
Gen. 22. 17. possess *g.* of his ene.
28. 17. this is the house of God and *g.* of heaven
Job 29. 7. I went to *g.* prepared
Ps. 118. 20. this *g.* of the Lord into

Matt. 7. 13. enter strait *g.*, Luke
13. 2.
Heb. 13. 12. suffered without the *g.*
Ps. 9. 13. up from *gates* of death
24. 7. lift up your heads, O *g.*, 9
87. 2. Lord loveth *g.* of Zion
100. 4. enter his *g.* with thanks
118. 19. open for me *g.* of right.
Isa. 38. 10. to go to *g.* of the grave
Matt. 16. 18. *g.* of hell shall not
prevail
R. V. Esth. 5. 1. entrance, Ezek.
40. 6 —; Neh. 13. 19; Isa. 45. 1,
2; S. of S. 7. 13; Luke 13. 24; Acts
4. 2. door, doors

GATHER thee from all nations,
Deut. 30. 3. Neb. 1. 9. Jer. 29. 14.
Ps. 26. 9. *g.* not my soul with sin-
ners
Zeph. 3. 18. *g.* them that are sor.
Matt. 3. 12. *g.* his wheat into gar.
7. 16. do men *g.* grapes of thorns
Eph. 1. 10. to *g.* in one all things
Ex. 16. 18, 21. he that *gathered*
much
Matt. 23. 37. *g.* thy children as hen *g.*
John 4. 36. *g.* fruit unto eternal
R. V. Gen. 49. 2; Ex. 35. 1. Lev.
8. 3; Num. 8. 9; 16. 3; 19. 42; 20. 2,
8; Deut. 4. 10; 31. 12, 18; Judg. 9.
6; 20. 1; 1 Chron. 13. 5, Ezek. 38. 13;
Mic. 4. 11. assembled; Ex. 9. 19.
hasten in; Job 11. 10. call unto
judgment; Isa. 62. 9. garnered;
Jer. 6. 1. flee for safety; 51. 11.
hold firm; Joel 2. 6, Nah. 2. 10.
waxed pale; Eph. 1. 10. sum up

GAVE, Gen. 14. 20. Ex. 11. 3.
Job 1. 21. Lord *g.* and Lord taketh
Ps. 81. 12. I *g.* them up unto
Eccl. 12. 7. spirit return to God
that *g.* it
Isa. 42. 24. who *g.* Jacob for a spoil
John 1. 12. he *g.* power to become
3. 16. God *g.* his only begotten Son
1 Cor. 3. 6. God *g.* the increase, 7
2 Cor. 8. 5. first *g.* themselves to
Gal. 1. 4. who *g.* himself for our
2. 20. *g.* himself for me, Tit. 2. 14.
Eph. 4. 8. *g.* gifts unto men
11. *g.* some apostles
1 Tim. 2. 6. *g.* himself a ransom
Ps. 21. 4. asked life, thou *gavest* it
John 17. 4. work thou *g*
22. glory thou *g.* me
6. the men thou *g.* me, 12. & 18. 9.
which thou *g.* me, lost none

GENEALOGIES, 1 Tim. 1. 4. Tit.
3. 9.

GENERATION, Gen. 2. 4. & 6. 9.
Deut. 32. 5. they are a perverse
and crooked *g.*
20. a very froward *g.* in whom
Ps. 14. 5. God is in the *g.* of the
righteous
22. 30. accounted to Lord for a *g.*
24. 6. this is *g.* of them that seek
112. 2. *g.* of upright shall be
145. 4. one *g.* shall praise thy
Isa. 53. 8. who declare his *g.*, Acts
8. 33.
Matt. 3. 7. ye *g.* of vipers, 12. 34. &
23. 33.
Luke 16. 8. *g.* wiser than the child
Acts 13. 36. had served his *g.* according
1 Pet. 2. 9. chosen *g.* to show
praises
Ps. 33. 11. thoughts to all *generations*
45. 17. to be remembered in all *g.*
79. 13. show forth thy praise in
all *g.*
89. 4. build thy throne to all *g.*
90. 1. our dwelling place in all *g.*
100. 5. his truth endureth to all *g.*
119. 90. thy faithfulness to all *g.*
Col. 1. 26. the mystery hid from
ages and *g.*
R. V. Matt. 3. 7; 23. 33; 12. 34, Luke
3. 7. ye offspring. 1 Pet. 2. 9 an
elect race

GENTILES, Gen. 10. 5. Jer. 4. 7.
Isa. 11. 10. to it shall the *g.* seek

Isa. 42. 6. a light of the *g.*, 49. 6. Luke
2. 32. Acts 13. 47
60. 3. *g.* shall come to thy light
62. 2. *g.* shall see thy righteous.
Matt. 6. 32. after these things do
the *g.* seek
John 7. 35. to the dispersed among
the *g.*
Acts 13. 46. lo, we turn to the *g*
14. 27. opened door of faith unto *g.*
Rom. 2. 14. *g.* which have not law
3. 29. is he not also God of *g.* yea
15. 10. rejoice ye *g.* with his people
12. in his name shall the *g.* trust
Eph. 3. 6. *g.* be fellow heirs and
8. preach among *g.* unsearchable
1 Tim. 2. 7. a teacher of *g.*, 2 Tim.
1. 11.
3. 16. God manifest in flesh,
preached to *g.*
GENTLE among you, 1 Thes. 2. 7.
Tit. 3. 2. be *g.* showing all meek.
Jas. 3. 17. wisdom from above is *g.*
1 Pet. 2. 18. not only to the *g.* but
Ps. 18. 35. thy *gentleness* made me
2 Cor. 10. 1. beseech by the *g.* of
Gal. 5. 22. fruit of the Spirit is
love, joy, *g.*
Isa. 40. 11. *gently* lead those with
R. V. Gal. 5. 22. kindness
GIFT, 1 Cor. 1. 7. & 7. 7.
Ex. 23. 8. take no *g.* for a *g.* blind-
eth
Prov. 17. 8. *g.* is a preci. stone, 23.
18. 16. a man's *g.* maketh room for
21. 14. a *g.* in secret pacifieth
anger
Eccl. 7. 7. a *g.* destroyeth the heart
Matt. 5. 24. leave there thy *g.* and
John 4. 10. if thou knewest *g.* of
Rom. 6. 23. *g.* of God is eternal
Eph. 2. 8. through faith it is the
g. of
Phil. 4. 17. not because I desire a *g.*
1 Tim. 4. 14. neglect not the *g.* that
2 Tim. 1. 6. stir up *g.* of God
Heb. 6. 4. tasted of heavenly *g.*
Jas. 1. 17. every good and per-
fect *g.*
Ps. 68. 18. received *gifts* for men
Matt. 7. 11. give good *g.* to your
children
Rom. 11. 29. for *g* and calling of
God
Eph. 4. 8. led captivity and gave *g.*
R. V. 2 Sam. 8. 2, 6. 1 Chron. 18. 2, 6.
presents; Ezek. 22. 12. tribes;
Luke 21. 5. offerings, 2 Cor. 8. 4.
this grace
GIRD with strength, Ps. 18. 32.
Ps. 30. 11. *g.* me with gladness
Luke 12. 35. let your loins be
girded, 1 Pet. 1. 13.
Eph. 6. 14. having your loins *g.*
with
Isa. 11. 5. *girdle*, Matt. 3. 4. Rev. 1.
13. & 15. 6.
R. V. Job 12. 18. bindeth, Ex. 28.
8, 27, 28; 29 5· 39 5, 20, 21· Lev.
8. 7. band
GIRL, they have sold a *g.* for wine,
Joel 3. 3.
Zech. 8. 5. streets full of *g*
GIVE, Gen. 12. 7. & 30. 31.
1 Kings 3. 5. ask what I shall *g.*
Ps. 2. 8. I shall *g.* thee the heathen
29. 11. Lord will *g.* strength to his
37. 4. *g.* the desires of thy heart
109. 4. I *g.* myself to prayer
104. 27. mayest *g.* them their meat
Jer. 17. 10. to *g.* every man accord.
Hos. 11. 8. how shall I *g.* thee up
Luke 6. 38. *g.* and it shall be given
John 10. 28. I *g.* to them eternal
Acts 3. 6. such as I have *g.* I unto
20. 35. more blessed to *g.* than to
receive
Eph. 4. 28. that he may have to *g.*
1 Tim. 4. 15. *g.* thyself wholly to
2 Sam. 22. 50. *give thanks*, 1 Chron.
16. 8, 34, 35, 41. Neh. 12. 24. Ps. 35.
18. & 79. 13. & 92. 1 & 105. 1. & 107.
1. & 118. 1. & 136. 1
Ps. 6. 5. in grave who shall—to thee

Ps. 30. 4. — at the remembrance of
119. 62. at midnight I will rise to—
Eph. 1. 16. cease not to—, 1 Thes. 1.
2. 2 Thes. 2. 13. Col. 1. 3.
1 Thes. 5. 18. in every thing —, Phil.
4. 6.
Matt. 13. 12. to him shall be *given*
11. it is *g.* to you to know the mys.
Luke 12. 48. to whom much is *g.*
John 6. 39. of all which he hath *g.*
65. can come to me except it be *g.*
19. 11. except it were *g.* thee from
Rom. 11. 35. hath first *g.* to him
2 Cor. 9. 7 God loves the cheerful
giver
Ps. 37. 21. shows mercy and *giveth*
Prov. 28. 27. he that *g.* to poor shall
Isa. 40. 29. *g.* power to the faint
42. 5. *g.* breath to people on earth
1 Tim. 6. 17. *g.* us richly all things
Jas. 1. 5. *g.* to all men liberally
1 Pet. 4. 11. of the ability that God *g.*
GLAD, my heart is, Ps. 16. 9.
Ps. 31. 7. I will be *g.* and rejoice in
64. 10. righteous shall be *g.* in Lord
104. 34. I will be *g.* in the Lord
122. 1. I was *g.* when they said
Luke 1. 19. *glad tidings*, & 8. 1.
Mark 6. 20. heard him *gladly*, 12. 37.
Luke 8. 40. people *g.* received him
Acts 2. 41. that *g.* received his word
2 Cor. 12. 15. I will very *g.* spend
Ps. 4. 7. put *gladness* in my heart
30. 11. hast girded me with *g.*
51. 8. make me to hear joy and *g.*
97. 11. *g.* sown for the upright
100. 2. serve the Lord with *g.*
Isa. 35. 10. shall obtain joy and *g.*
51. 3. joy and *g.* shall be found
Acts 2. 46. eat their meat with *g.*
R. V. Ps. 48. 11; 104. 34; Acts 2. 26;
1 Cor. 16. 17; 9 Cor. 13. 9; 1 Pet. 4.
13; Rev. 19. 7. rejoice; Luke 1. 19;
8. 1; Acts 13. 32. good; Luke 8. 40;
Acts 2. 41 — ; Ps. 105. 43. singing;
2 Sam. 6. 12; Mark 4. 16; Acts 12.
14; Phil. 2. 29. joy
GLASS, we see through, 1 Cor. 13.
12.
2 Cor. 3. 18. beholding as in a *g.*
Rev. 4. 6. a sea of *g.*, 15. 2.
21. 18. the city was pure gold like
clear *g.*
R. V. Job 37. 18. mirror; Isa. 3. 23.
hand mirrors; Jas. 1. 23. mirror;
Rev. 4. 6; 15. 2. glassy sea.
GLOOMINESS, Joel 2. 2. Zeph. 1. 15.
GLORY, Gen. 31. 1. Ps. 49. 16.
1 Sam. 4. 21. *g.* is departed from
1 Chron. 29. 11. thine the power
and the *g.*, Matt. 6. 13.
Ps. 8. 5. crowned with *g.* and honor.
73. 24. afterward receive me to *g.*
145. 11. speak of the *g.* of thy king.
Prov. 3. 35. the wise shall inherit *g.*
16. 31. hoary head is a crown of *g.*
20. 29. *g.* of young men is their str.
25. 27. to search their own *g.* is
not *g.*
Isa. 4. 5. upon all the *g.* shall be
24. 16. heard songs, even *g.* to the
28. 5. Lord shall be for a crown of *g.*
Jer. 2. 11. chang. their *g.*, Ps. 106. 20.
Ezek. 20. 6. the *g.* of all lands, 15.
Hos. 4. 7. change their *g.* into shame
Hag. 2. 7. I will fill this hou. with *g.*
9. *g.* of this latter house shall be
Zech. 2. 5. be the *g.* in the midst
Matt. 6. 2. may have *g.* of men
16. 27. come in *g.* of his Father
Luke 2. 14. *g.* to God in the highest
32. light of the Gentiles, *g.* of thy
John 1. 14. his *g.* the *g.* of the only
17. 5. *glorify* me with the *g.* I had
22. *g.* which thou gavest I have
Rom. 2. 7. seek for *g.* and honor
11. 36. to whom be *g.* for ever,
1 Cor. 4. 18. Heb. 13. 21.
16. 27. in God be *g.* through Christ
1 Cor. 11. 7. man is *g.* of God, woman
is *g.* of man
15. 43. in dishonor, it is raised in
g.
2 Cor 3 18 changed from *g* to *g.*

2 Cor. 4. 17. an exceeding and eternal weight of *g.*
Eph. 1. 6. praise of *g.* of his grace
3. 21. to him be *g.* in the church
Phil. 3. 19. whose *g.* is in their shame
Col. 1. 27. Christ in you hope of *g.*
3. 4. appear with him in *g.*
1 Thes. 2. 12. hath called you to *g.*
1 Tim. 3. 16. received up into *g.*
1 Pet. 1. 8. joy unspeak., full of *g.*
4. 13. his *g.* be revealed
14. spirit of *g.*
5. 1. partaker of *g.* to be revealed
4. ye shall receive a crown of *g.*
10. called us to eternal *g.*
2 Pet. 1. 3. called us to *g.* and virtue
17. came a voice from the excellent *g.*
Rev. 4. 11. worthy to receive *q.*, 5. 12. Rom. 16. 27. 1 Tim. 1. 17. 1 Pet. 5. 11. Jude 25.
Josh. 7. 19. *give glory* to the God of Israel, 1 Sam. 6. 5. 1 Chron. 16. 29. Ps. 29. 2. & 96. 8. & 115. 1. Luke 17. 18. Rev. 14. 7.
Ps. 19. 1. *glory of God,* Prov. 25. 2. Acts 7. 55. Rom. 3. 23. & 5. 2. 1 Cor. 10. 31. & 11. 7. 2 Cor. 4. 6. Rev. 21. 11.
Ex. 16. 7. *glory of the Lord,* Num. 14. 21.
1 Kings 8. 11. Ps. 104. 31. & 138. 5. Isa. 35. 2. & 40. 5. & 60. 1. Ezek. 1. 28. & 3. 12, 23. & 43. 5. & 44. 4. Luke 2. 9. 2 Cor. 3. 18.
Ps. 29. 9. *his glory,* 49. 17. & 72. 19. & 113. 4. & 148. 13. Prov. 19. 11. Isa. 6. 3. Hab. 3. 3. Matt. 6. 29. & 19. 28. & 25. 31. John 2. 11. Rom. 9. 23. Eph. 1. 12. & 3. 16. Heb. 1. 3.
Job. 29. 20. *my glory,* Ps. 16. 9. & 30. 12. & 57. 8. & 108. 1. Isa. 42. 8. & 43. 7. & 48. 11. & 60. 7. & 66. 18. John 8. 50. & 17. 24.
Ex. 33. 18. *thy glory,* Ps. 8. 1. & 63. 2. Isa. 60. 19. & 63. 15. Jer. 13. 16.
1 Chron. 16. 10. *glory* ye in his holy
Ps. 64. 10. upright in heart shall *g.* 106. 5. I may *g.* with thy inherit.
Isa. 41. 16. shalt *g.* in Holy One of 45. 25. seed of Israel be justified, and *g.*
Jer. 9. 24. him that glorieth *g.* in this
Rom. 4. 2. hath *g.* but not bef. God
5. 3. we *g.* in tribulation
1 Cor. 1. 31. that glorieth *g.* in the
3. 21. let no man *g.* in men
2 Cor. 5. 12. to *g.* on our behalf—
11. 18. many *g.* after the flesh
12. 1. it is not exped. for me to *g.*
Gal. 6. 14. God forbid I should *g.*
Isa. 25. 5. strong people shall *glorify* thee
Matt. 5. 16. *g.* your Father in heav.
John 12. 23. Father *g.* thy name
17. 1. *g.* thy Son
21. 19. by what death he should *g.* God
1 Cor. 6. 20. *g.* God in your body
1 Pet. 2. 12. *g.* God in day of visita.
Rev. 15. 4. who shall not fear thee, and *g.* thy name
Lev. 10. 3. before all I will be *glorified*
Matt. 9. 8. they *g.* God, 15. 31.
John 7. 39. Jesus was not yet *g.*
15. 8. herein is my Father *g.*
Acts 3. 13. God of our fathers hath *g.* his
4. 21. all men *g.* God for that was
Rom. 1. 21. they *g.* him not as God
8. 30. whom he justified, them he *g.*
Gal. 1. 24. they *g.* God in me
2 Thes. 1. 10. shall come to be *g.* in
Heb. 5. 5. even Christ *g.* not him.
1 Pet. 4. 11. God in all things may be *g.*
14. on your part he is *g.*
1 Cor. 5. 6. *glorying,* 9. 15. 2 Cor. 7. 4. & 12. 11.
Ex. 15. 6. *glorious* in power
11. who is like thee, *g.* in holiness
Deut. 28. 58. fear this *g.* and fearful

1 Chron. 29. 13. praise thy *g.* name
Ps. 45. 13. king's daughter all *g.*
66. 2. make his praise *g.*
72. 19. blessed be his *g.* name
87. 3. *g.* things are spoken of
111. 3. his work is honorable and *g.*
145. 5. speak of *g.* honor of thy
12. make known his *g.* majesty
Isa. 4. 2. branch of Lord shall be *g.*
22. 23. be for a *g.* throne to his
30. 30. cause his *g.* voice to be heard
33. 21. *g.* Lord will be to us a place
49. 5. yet shall I be *g.* in eyes
60. 13. make the place of my feet *g.*
63. 1. who is this *g.* in his apparel
Jer. 17. 12. a *g.* high throne from
Rom. 8. 21. *g.* liberty of children
2 Cor. 3. 7. ministration was *g.*
4. 4. light of *g.* gospel should
Col. 1. 11. according to his *g.* power
Tit. 2. 13. looking for *g.* appearance
Ex. 15. 1. *gloriously,* Isa. 24. 23.
R. V. 1 Pet. 4. 14——; Ps. 111. 3. majesty; Isa. 49. 5. honorable; 1 Chron. 16. 27; Job 40. 10. honor; 1 Chron. 16. 35. triumph; Ps. 89. 44. brightness; Prov. 4. 9. fair; 3. beauty; Matt. 6. 13——; 2 Cor. 12. 11—

GLUTTON, Deut. 21. 20. Prov. 23. 21.
Matt. 11. 19. *gluttonous,* Luke 7. 34.
R. V. Deut. 21. 20. riotous liver

GNASH, Job 16. 9. Ps. 35. 16. & 37. 12. & 112. 10. Lam. 2. 16. Mark 9. 18.
Matt. 8. 12. *gnashing of teeth,* 13. 42. 50. & 22. 13. & 24. 51. & 25. 30. Luke 13. 28.
R. V. Mark 9. 18. grindeth

GNAT, and swallow a camel, Matt. 23. 24.

GNAW, Zeph. 3. 3. Rev. 16. 10.
R. V. Zeph. 3. 3. leave nothing

GO, Judg. 6. 14. 1 Sam. 12. 21. Matt. 8. 9. Luke 10. 37. John 6. 68.
Job 10. 21. *I go,* Ps. 39. 13. & 139. 7.
Matt. 21. 30. John 7. 33. & 8. 14, 21, 22. & 13. 33. & 16. 5.
Ex. 4. 23. *let my people go,* 5. 1.
Gen. 32. 26. *not let go,* Ex. 3. 19.
Job 27. 6. S. of S. 3. 4.
Ex. 23. 33. *shall go,* 32. 34. & 33. 14. Acts 25. 12.
1 Sam. 12. 21. *should go,* Prov. 22. 6.
Judg. 11. 35. *go back,* Ps. 80. 18.
Num. 22. 18. *go beyond,* 1 Thes. 4. 6.
Gen. 45. 1. *go out,* Ps. 60. 10. Isa. 52. 11. & 55. 12. Jer. 51. 45. Ezek. 46. 9.
Matt. 25. 6. John 10. 9. 1 Cor. 5. 10.
Deut. 4. 40. *go well* with thee, 5. 16. & 19. 13. Prov. 11. 10. & 30. 29.
Job 34. 21. seeth all his *goings*
Ps. 17. 5. hold up my *g.* in thy way
40. 2. set my feet and established my *g.*
68. 24. seen thy *g.* O God in
121. 8. Lord preserve thy *g.* out
Prov. 5. 21. he pondereth all his *g.*
Mic. 5. 2. whose *g.* are of old, from
The R. V. changes are frequent, but chiefly those relating to words before and after *go*

GOAT, Lev. 3. 12. & 16. 8, 21, 22.
Isa. 1. 11. I delight not in the blood of *goats*
Ezek. 34. 17. judge between rams and *g.*
Dan. 8. 5. he *g.*
8. rough *g.*, 21.
Matt. 25. 32, 33. set the *g.* on his
Heb. 9. 12. blood of *g.*, 13. 19. & 10. 4.

GOD, and *gods* for *men* representing God, Ex. 4. 16. & 7. 1. & 22. 28.
Ps. 82. 1, 6. John 10. 34. for *idols* which are put in God's place, Deut. 32. 21. Judg. 6. 31. and 140 other places. For devil, god of this world, 2 Cor. 4. 4. and for the true God about 3120 times
Gen. 17. 1. I am Almighty *G.*, Job 36. 5. Isa. 9. 6. & 13. 19. Jer. 32. 18.
Gen. 17. 7. to be a *G.* to thee and thy seed, Ex. 6. 7, 21, 33. everlast-

ing *G.* Ps. 90. 2. Isa. 40. 28. Rom. 16. 26.
Ex. 8. 10. none like Lord our *G.*, 1 Kings 8. 23. Ps. 35. 10. & 86. 8. & 89. 6.
18. 11. Lord is greater than all *gods*
Deut. 10. 17. *G.* of gods, Josh. 22. 22. Dan. 2. 47. Ps. 136 2.
Deut. 32. 39. there is no *g.* with me, 1 Kings 8. 23. 2 Kings 5. 15. 2 Chron. 6. 14. & 32. 15. Isa. 43. 10. & 44. 6, 8. & 45. 5, 14, 21, 22.
Job 33. 12. *G.* is greater than man, 36. 26.
Ps. 18. 31. who is *G.* save the Lord, 86. 10.
Mic. 7. 18. who is a *G.* like to thee
Matt. 6. 24. ye cannot serve *G.* and 19. 17. none good but one, that is *G.*
Mark 12. 27. not the *G.* of dead, but of the living
John 17. 3. the only true *G.*, 1 John 5. 20.
Acts 7. 2. *G.* of glory appeared to
Rom. 8. 31. if *G.* be for us, who can
9. 5. over all *G.* blessed for ever
15. 5. *G.* of patience
13. *G.* of hope
2 Cor. 1. 3. *G.* of all comfort
1 Tim. 3. 16. *G.* manifest in flesh
1 Pet. 5. 10. *G.* of all grace, when
1 John 4. 12. no man seen *G.*, John 1. 18.
Deut. 10. 17. *great God,* 2 Sam. 7. 22.
2 Chron. 2. 5. Job 36. 26. Neh. 1. 5. Prov. 26. 10. Jer. 32. 18, 19. Dan. 9. 4. Tit. 2. 13. Rev. 19. 17.
Deut. 5. 26. *living God,* Josh. 3. 10. 1 Sam. 17. 26, 36. 2 Kings 19. 4, 16. and twenty-two other places
Ex. 34. 6. *God merciful,* Deut. 4. 31. 2 Chron. 30. 9. Neh. 9. 31. Ps. 116. 5. Jonah 4. 2.
Gen. 49. 24. *mighty God,* Deut. 7. 21. & 10. 17. Neh. 9. 32. Job 36. 5. Ps. 50. 1. & 132. 2, 5. Isa. 9. 6. & 10. 21. Jer. 32. 18. Hab. 1. 12.
2 Chron. 15. 3. *true God,* Jer. 10. 10. John 17. 3. 1 Thes. 1. 9. 1 John 5. 20.
Gen. 39. 9. do this wickedness and sin *against God,* Num. 21. 5. Ps. 78. 19. Hos. 13. 16. Acts 5. 39. & 23. 9. Rom. 8. 7. & 9. 20. Rev. 13. 6. Dan. 11. 36.
Ps. 42. 2. *before God,* 56. 13. & 61. 7. & 68. 3. Eccl. 2. 26. Luke 1. 6.
Rom. 2. 13. & 3. 19. 1 Tim. 5. 21. Jas. 1. 27. Rev. 3. 2.
John 9. 16. *of God,* Acts 5. 39. Rom. 9. 16. 1 Cor. 1. 30. & 11. 12. 2 Cor. 3. 5. & 5. 18. Phil. 1. 28. 1 John 3. 10. & 4. 1, 3, 6. & 5. 19. 3 John 11.
Ex. 2. 23. *to God,* Ps. 43. 4. Eccl. 12. 7. Isa. 58. 2. Lam. 3. 41. John 13. 3. Heb. 7. 25. & 11. 6. & 12. 23. 1 Pet. 3. 18. & 4. 6. Rev. 5. 9. & 12. 5.
Gen. 5. 22. *with God,* 24. & 6. 9. & 32. 28. Ex. 19. 17. 1 Sam. 14. 45.
2 Sam. 23. 5. Job 9. 2. & 25. 4. Ps. 78. 8. Hos. 11. 12. John 5. 18. Phil. 2. 6.
Gen. 28. 21. *my God,* Ex. 15. 2. Ps. 22. 1. & 31. 14. & 91. 2. & 118. 28.
Hos. 2. 23. Zech. 13. 9. John 20. 17. 28. and about 120 other places
Ex. 5. 8. *our God,* Deut. 31. 17. & 32. 3. Josh. 24. 18. 2 Sam. 22. 32. Ps. 67. 6. and 180 other places
Ex. 20. 2. *thy God,* 5. 7, 10, 12. Ps. 50. 7. & 81. 10. and about 340 other places
Ex. 6. 7. *your God,* Lev. 11. 44. & 19. 2, 3, 4. and 140 other places
Ex. 32. 11. *his God,* Lev. 4. 22. and about sixty other places
Lev. 27. 8. *their God,* Ex. 29. 45. Jer. 24. 7. & 31. 33. & 32. 38. Ezek. 11. 20. & 34. 24. & 37. 27. Zech. 8. 8. 2 Cor. 6. 16. Rev. 21. 3. and fifty other places

2 Chron. 36. 23. *God of heaven*, Ezra
5. 11. & 6. 10. & 7. 12, 23. Neh. 1. 4.
& 2. 4. Ps. 136. 26. Dan. 2. 18, 19, 44.
Jonah 1. 9. Rev. 11. 13. & 16. 11.

Ex. 24. 10. *God of Israel*, Num. 16.
9. Josh. 7. 19. & 13. 33. & 22. 16, 24.
& 24. 23. Judg. 11. 23. Ruth 2. 12.
Isa. 41. 17. Jer. 31. 1. Ezek. 8. 4.
Matt. 15. 31.

Rom. 15. 33. *God of peace*, 16. 20.
2 Cor. 13. 11. 1 Thes. 5. 23. Heb. 13.
20.

Ps. 24. 5. *God of his salvation, of our
salvation*, 65. 5. & 68. 19, 20. & 79. 9.
& 85. 4. & 95. 1.

Acts 17. 29. Godhead, Rom. 1. 20.
Col. 2. 9.

R. V. Rom. 1. 20. divinity

GODLY, Ps. 4. 3. & 12. 1. & 32. 6.
Mal. 2. 15. 2 Pet. 2. 9. 3 John 6.
2 Cor. 1. 12. in *g.* sincerity, had our
conversation

Tit. 2. 12. live soberly, righteously,
and *g.*

1 Tim. 2. 2. quiet life in all *godliness*, 10. & 3. 16. & 6. 3, 5, 11. 2 Tim.
3. 5.

4. 8. *g.* is profitable to all things
6. 3. doctrine according to *g.*, Tit.
1. 1.

2 Tim. 3. 5. having a form of *g.* but
2 Pet. 1. 3. all that pertain to life
and *g.*

6. add to patience *g.*

7. to *g.* brotherly kindness

R. V. 2 Cor. 1. 12. sincerity ; 1 Tim.
1. 4. dispensation of God ; Heb.
12. 28. awe ; 3 John 6. worthily of
God

GOLD, Gen. 2. 11. & 13. 2. Isa. 2. 7.
Job 23. 10. I shall come forth like *g.*
31. 24. if I made *g.* my hope or
fine *g.*

Ps. 19. 10. more desired than *g.*
119. 127. love thy commandments
above *g.* yea, fine *g.*, 72.

Prov. 8. 19. my fruit is better than
g. or fine *g.*

Isa. 13. 12. man more precious than
fine *g.*

Zech. 13. 9. I will try them as *g.* is
1 Tim. 2. 9. women adorn themselves in modest apparel, not
with *g.*, 1 Pet. 3. 3.

1 Pet. 1. 7. trial of faith more precious than *g.*

Rev. 3. 18. buy of me *g.* tried in fire
GOLDEN CANDLESTICK, Ex.
25. 31.

GOOD, Deut. 6. 24. & 10. 13.
Gen. 1. 31. every thing he had
made was very *g.*

2. 18. it is not *g.* for man to be
alone

2 Kings 20. 19. *g.* is the word of the
Lord, Isa. 39 8.

Ps. 34. 8. taste and see that Lord is
g.

73. 1. truly God is *g.* to Israel
106. 5. I may see *g.* of thy chosen
119. 68. thou art *g.* and doest *g.*
145. 9. Lord is *g.* to all, 136. 1.

Lam. 3. 25. Lord is *g.* to them that
Mic. 6. 8. he hath showed thee
what is *g.*

Matt. 19. 17. why call me *g.* none
Rom. 3. 8. do evil that *g.* may come
1 Thes. 5. 15. follow that which is
g., 3 John 11.

Neh. 2. 18. hand for this *good work*
Matt. 26. 10. wrought a — on me
John 10. 33. for a — we stone thee
not

2 Cor. 9. 8. abound to every—
Phil. 1. 6. begun a — will finish
Col. 1. 10. fruitful in every—
2 Thes. 2. 17. establish you in
every—

1 Tim. 5. 10. followed every—
2 Tim. 2. 21. prepared to —, Tit. 3. 1.
Tit. 1. 16. to every — reprobate
Heb. 13. 21. perfect in every—
Matt. 5. 16. may see your *good
works*

John 10. 32. many — have I showed
you

Acts 9. 36. Dorcas was full of —
1 Tim. 2. 25. the — of some are
manifest

Tit. 3. 8. be careful to maint. —, 14.
Heb. 10. 24. provoke to love and —
1 Pet. 2. 12. may by your — which
Ex. 33. 19. make my *goodness* pass
2 Chron. 6. 41. saints rejoice in *g.*
Neh. 9. 25. delight themselves in *g.*
35. not served thee in thy great *g.*
Ps. 16. 2. my *g.* extendeth not to
23. 6. *g.* and mercy shall follow
27. 13. believed to see *g.* of Lord
31. 19. how great is thy *g.*, Zech. 9.
17.

52. 1. the *g.* of God endureth
11. crownest the year with thy *g.*
Isa. 63. 7. great *g.* bestowed on
Israel

Hos. 3. 5. fear the Lord and his *g.*
Rom. 2. 4. *g.* of God leadeth to repentance

11. 22. behold the *g.* and severity
of God

Eph. 5. 9. fruit of Spirit in all *g.*,
Gal. 5. 22.

R. V. changes are frequent, but
nearly all based on words before
or after the word *good* ; 2 Sam. 7.
28 ; 1 Chron. 17. 26. good things ;
2 Chron. 32. 32 ; 35. 26. good deeds ;
Ps. 33. 5 ; 144. 2. lovingkindness ;
Prov. 20. 6. kindness

GOSPEL, Mark 1. 1, 15. & 8. 35.
Matt. 4. 23. preaching *g.* of kingdo.
Mark 16. 15. preach the *g.* to
Acts 20. 24. *g.* of the grace of God
Rom. 1. 1. *g.* of God, 15. 16. 1 Tim.
1. 11.

1 Cor. 1. 17. but to preach the *g.*
4. 15. I have begotten you through
the *g.*

2 Cor. 4. 3. if our *g.* be hid
4. glorious *g.*
11. 4. another *g.* which ye, Gal. 1.
6.

Gal. 1. 8. preach any other *g.*, 9.
Eph. 1. 13. *g.* of salvation
6. 15. *g.* of peace
Col. 1. 5. truth of *g.*, Gal. 2. 5.
23. hope of *g.*

Phil. 1. 5. fellowship in *g.*
1 Thes. 1. 5. our *g.* came in power
Heb. 4. 2. unto us was *g.* preached
1 Pet. 4. 6. *g.* was preached to dead
Rev. 14. 6. having everlasting *g.* to
preach

R. V. Luke 4. 18 ; 7. 29 ; 1 Pet. 1. 25.
good tidings ; Rom. 10. 16. glad
tidings ; Rom. 10. 15 —

GOVERNMENT, Isa. 9. 6, 7. & 22.
21. 1 Cor. 12. 28. 2 Pet. 2. 10
R. V. 2 Pet. 2. 10. dominion

GRACE, Ezra 9. 8. Esth. 2. 17.
Ps. 84. 11. Lord will give *g.* and
glory

Prov. 3. 34. gives *g.* to the lowly
Zech. 4. 7. with shoutings, crying
g. to it.

12. 10. spirit of *g.* and supplica-
tions

John 1. 14. of Father full of *g.* and
16. of fulness we receive *g.* for *g.*
17. *g.* and truth came by Jesus
Christ

Acts 18. 27. helped them believe
through *g.*

Rom. 3. 24. justified freely by his *g.*
5. 20. *g.* did much more abound
6. 14. not under law, but under *g.*
11. 5. according to the election of
g.

2 Cor. 12. 9. my *g.* is sufficient for
Eph. 2. 5. by *g.* are saved, 8.
7. show exceed. riches of his *g.*, 1. 7.
4. 29. minister *g.* to hearers
Tit. 3. 7. justified by his *g.*
Heb. 4. 16. come boldly to the
throne of *g.*

13. 9. heart be established with *g.*
1 Pet. 3. 7. heirs of the *g.* of life
5. 5. and giveth *g.* to the humble

---

2 Pet. 3. 18. grow in *g.* and in
knowledge

Rom. 1. 7. *grace and peace* to you,
1 Cor. 1. 3. 2 Cor. 1. 2. Gal. 1. 3.
Eph. 1. 2. Phil. 1. 2. Col. 1. 2.
1 Thes. 1. 1. 2 Thes. 1. 2. Phile. 3.
1 Pet. 1. 2. 2 Pet. 1. 2. Jude 2.
Rev. 1. 4.

Luke 2. 40. *grace of God*, Acts 11.
23. & 13. 43. & 14. 3, 26. & 15. 40. &
20. 24, 32. Rom. 5. 15. 1 Cor. 1. 4. &
3. 10. & 15. 10. Eph. 3. 2, 7. Heb. 2.
9. & 12. 15.

2 Cor. 1. 12. by — we have had our
conversation

6. 1. receive not — in vain
8. 1. of — bestowed on churches
9. 14. for the exceeding — in you
Gal. 2. 21. I do not frustrate—
Col. 1. 6. knew — in truth
1 Pet. 4. 10. stewards of manifold—

Jude 4. turning — into lascivious.
Acts 15. 11. *grace of our Lord Jesus
Christ*, Rom. 16. 20, 24. 1 Cor. 16.
23. 2 Cor. 8. 9. & 13. 14. Gal. 6. 18.
Phil. 4. 23. 1 Thes. 5. 28. 2 Thes. 3.
18. Phile. 25.

Rev. 22. 21. — be with you all
Gen. 43. 29. God be *gracious* to
thee

Ex. 22. 27. I will hear for I am *g.*
33. 19. I will be *g.* to whom I will
34. 6. Lord God merciful and *g.*
2 Chron. 30. 9. Neh. 9. 17, 31. Ps.
103. 8. & 116. 5. & 145. 8. Joel 2. 13.
Num. 6. 25. the Lord be *g.* to thee
Job 33. 24. then he is *g.* to him
Ps. 77. 9. hath God forgotten to
be *g.*

86. 15. full of compassion and *g.*
Isa. 30. 18. the Lord wait that he
may be *g.*

Amos 5. 15. may be, the Lord will
be *g.*

Jonah 4. 2. knew that thou art a *g.*
God

Mal. 1. 9. beseech God to be *g.*, Isa.
33. 2.

Gen. 33. 5. *graciously*, 11. Ps. 119. 29.
Hos. 14. 2. receive us *g.*
R. V. 2 Sam. 16. 4. favor ; Rom. 11.
6 ; 16. 24 —, Jer. 22. 23. to be
pitied ; Hos. 14. 2. accept . . . good
GRAFTED, Rom. 11. 17, 19, 23, 24
GRANT, Job 10. 12. Ps. 140. 8.
Prov. 10. 24. Rom. 15. 5. Eph. 3. 16.
2 Tim. 1. 18. Rev. 3. 21.
R. V. 1 Chron. 21. 22 ; Rev. 3. 21. give ;
Matt. 20. 21. command ; Rev. 19.
8. given unto

GRAPES, of gall, Deut. 32. 32.
S. of S. 2. 13. the tender *g.*, 15.
7. 7. clusters of *g.*
Isa. 5. 4. wild *g.*
Ezek. 18. 2. sour *g.*
Mic. 7. 1. soul desireth first ripe *g.*
R. V. Lev. 19. 10. fallen fruit ; S.
of S. 2. 13 ; 7. 12. in blossom
GRASS, Ps. 37. 2. & 90. 5. & 92. 7.
& 102. 4, 11. Isa. 44. 4. & 51. 12.
Ps. 103. 15. man's days are like *g.*
Isa. 40. 6. all flesh is *g.*, 7. 8. 1 Pet.
1. 24. Jas. 1. 10, 11.

Matt. 6. 30. if God so clothe the *g.*
Rev. 8. 7. green *g.*
9. 4. not hurt *g.*
R. V. Isa. 15. 6. hay ; Jer. 14. 6.
herbage ; Jer. 50. 11. treadeth out
the corn

GRAVE, 1 Kings 2. 9. & 14. 13.
1 Sam. 2. 6. Lord brings down to *g.*
Job 5. 26. come to thy *g.* in full
14. 13. hide me in the *g.*, 17. 1, 13.
Ps. 6. 5. in *g.* who shall give thanks
Prov. 1. 12. swallow them up alive,
as the *g.*

Isa. 38. 18. *g.* cannot praise thee
Hos. 13. 14. the power of the *g.* O
g. I will be thy destruction
1 Cor. 15. 55. O *g.* where is thy vic.
Zech. 3. 9. I will *engrave* the grav-
ing

Job 19. 24. *graven* with an iron pen
Isa. 49. 16. I have *g.* thee upon
Jer. 17. 1. sin *g.* upon table of their
1 Tim. 3. 4, 8, 11. *grave*, Tit. 2. 2, 7.
R. V. Job 33. 22. pit; Matt. 27. 52;
Luke 11. 44; John 5. 28; 11. 17, 31;
Rev. 11. 9. tombs; 1 Cor. 15. 55.
death; Isa. 14. 19. sepulchre; Job
30. 24. ruinous heap; Job 7. 9; 17.
13; Ps. 6. 5; 30. 3; 31. 17; 49. 14, 15;
88. 3; 89. 48; Prov. 1. 12; Hos.
13. 14. Sheol
GRAY, Ps. 71.18. Prov. 20.29. Hos.
7. 9.
R. V. Prov. 20. 29. hoary
GREAT, Gen. 12. 2. & 30. 8.
Deut. 29. 24. *g.* anger, 2 Chron. 34.
21,
1 Sam. 6. 9. *great evil*, Neh. 13. 27.
Eccl. 2. 21. Jer. 44. 7. Dan. 9. 12
Ps. 47. 2. *great king*, 48. 2. & 95. 3.
Mal. 1. 14. Matt. 5. 35.
Job 32. 9. *great men*, Jer. 5. 5.
Ex. 32. 11. *great power*, Neh. 1. 10.
Job 23. 6. Ps. 147. 5. Nah. 1. 3. Acts
4. 33. & 8. 10. Rev. 11. 17.
Ex. 32. 21. so *great*, Deut. 4. 7, 8,
1 Kings 3. 9. Ps. 77. 13. & 103. 11.
Matt. 8. 10. & 15. 28. 2 Cor. 1. 10.
Heb. 2. 3. & 12. 1. Rev. 16. 18. &
18. 17.
Job 5. 9. *great things*, Job 9. 10. & 37. 5.
Jer. 45. 5. Hos. 8. 12. Luke 1. 49.
Gen. 6. 5. *great wickedness*, 39. 9.
Job 22. 5. Joel 3. 13. 2 Chron. 28.
13.
Job 33. 12. God is *greater* than man
Matt. 12. 42. *g.* than Solomon is
here
John 1. 50. see *g.* things than these
4. 12. art thou *g.* than, 8. 53.
14. 28. my Father is *g.* than I
1 Cor. 14. 5. *g.* is he that prophe-
1 John 4. 4. *g.* is he that is in you,
3. 20.
5. 9. witness of God is *g.*
1 Sam. 30. 6. David was *greatly*
distressed
2 Sam. 24. 10. I have sinned *g.* in
1 Kings 3. 3. Obadiah feared the
Lord *g.*
1 Chron. 16. 25. great is the Lord
and *g.* to be praised, Ps. 48. 1. &
96. 4. & 145. 3.
2 Chron. 33. 12. humbled himself
g. before God
Job 3. 25. thing I *g.* feared is come
Ps. 28. 7. my heart *g.* rejoiceth
47. 9. God is *g.* exalted
Dan. 9. 23. O man *g.* beloved, 10.
11, 19.
Mark 12. 27. ye do *g.* err
Ex. 15. 7. *greatness* of thy excellency
Num. 14. 19. pardon according
to *g.*
Deut. 32. 3. ascribe ye *g.* to our
God
1 Chron. 29. 11. thine is the *g.*
Neh. 13. 22. spare according to the
g. of thy mercy
Ps. 66. 3. *g.* of thy power, 79. 11.
Eph. 1. 19.
145. 3. his *g.* is unsearchable, 6.
Isa. 63. 1. travelling in the *g.* of
his strength
The R. V. changes, which are
frequent, mostly turn on antece-
dent and consequent words
GREEDY of gain, Prov. 1. 19. &
15. 27.
Isa. 56. 11. they are *g.* dogs, never
Eph. 4. 19. work uncleanness with
greediness
GRIEF, Isa. 53. 3, 4, 10. Heb. 13.
17.
Gen. 6. 6. *grieved* him at his heart
Judg. 10. 16. his soul was *g.* for
Ps. 95. 10. forty years long was
I *g.*
Isa. 54. 6. woman forsaken and *g.*
Jer. 5. 5. hast stricken them, they
have not *g.*
Lam. 3. 33. nor *g.* children of men

Amos 6. 6. not *g.* for the affliction
of Joseph
Mark 3. 5. being *g.* for hardness
of heart
10. 22. went away *g.* for he had
Rom. 11. 15. if brother be *g.* at thy
meat
Ps. 10. 5. his ways are always
grievous
Matt. 23. 4. burdens *g.* to be borne
Acts 20. 29. shall *g.* wolves enter
Matt. 8. 6. *grievously* tormented,
15. 22.
R. V. 1 Sam. 1. 16. provocation;
2 Chron. 6. 29; Ps. 31.10; 69. 29; Jer.
45. 3; 2 Cor. 2. 5. sorrow; Job 6, 2.
vexation; Jer. 6. 7. sickness;
Jonah 4. 6. evil case; 1 Sam. 15. 11.
was wroth; 1 Chron. 4. 10. not to
my sorrow; Prov. 26.15. wearieth;
Isa. 57. 10. faint; Mark 10. 22. sorrowful; Acts 4. 2; 16. 18. sore
troubled; 2 Cor. 2. 4. made sorry;
2. 5. caused sorrow; Heb. 3. 10,
17. displeased; Gen. 12. 10. sore;
Ps. 10. 5. firm; 31. 18. insolently;
Isa. 15. 4. trembleth within; Jer.
23. 19. whirling; Phil. 3. 1. perilous; Isa. 9. 1. hath made it glorious; Jer. 23. 19. burst; Ezek. 14.
13. committing a trespass
GRIND the faces of the poor, Isa.
3. 15.
Matt. 21. 44. it will *g.* him to powder
Eccl. 12. 3. *grinders* cease because
few, 4.
R. V. Lam. 5. 13. young men bare
the mill; Matt. 21. 44; Luke 20.
18. scatter
GROAN earnestly, 2 Cor. 5. 2, 4.
John 11. 33. Jesus *groaned* in spirit
Rom. 8. 22. whole creation *groan-
eth*
Ps. 6. 6. weary with my *groaning*
Rom. 8. 26. *g.* that cannot be ut-
tered
GROUNDED, or *correcting* staff,
Isa. 30. 32.
Eph. 3. 17. rooted and *g.* in love
Col. 1. 23. if continue in the faith *g.*
R. V. Isa. 30. 32. appointed
GROW, Gen. 48. 16. 2 Sam. 23. 5.
Ps. 92. 12. *g.* like cedar in Lebanon
Hos. 14. 5. shall *g.* as a lily
7. *g.* as the vine
Mal. 4. 2. shall *g.* up as calves of
Eph. 2. 21. *g.* unto a holy temple
1 Pet. 2. 2. sincere milk that ye
may *g.*
2 Pet. 3. 18. *g.* in grace and knowl.
R. V. Lev. 13. 39. hath broken out;
Job 14. 19. overflowings; 18. 18.
spring; 38. 38. runneth; Isa. 11. 1.
bear fruit; Hos. 14. 5, 7. blossom;
Mal. 4. 2. gambol; Matt. 21. 19. no
fruit from
GRUDGE, Lev. 19. 18. Jas. 5. 9.
1 Pet. 4. 9. *grudging*, 2 Cor. 9. 7.
R. V. Ps. 59. 15. tarry all night;
Jas. 5. 9; 1 Pet. 4. 9. murmur
GUIDE unto death, Ps. 48. 14.
Ps. 73. 24. shall *g.* me with thy
counsel
Prov. 2. 17. forsaketh the *g.* of her
youth
Isa. 58. 11. Lord shall *g.* thee con.
Jer. 3. 4. my Father thou art *g.* of
Luke 1. 79. *g.* our feet into way
John 16. 13. *g.* you into all truth
1 Tim. 5. 14. bear children, *g.*
house
R. V. Ps. 55. 13. companion; Prov.
2. 17. friend; 6. 7. chief; Ps. 32.
8. counsel; 112. 5. shall maintain;
1 Tim. 5. 14. rule
GUILE, Ex. 21.14. Ps. 55.11. 2 Cor.
12. 16. 1 Thes. 2. 3.
Ps. 32. 2. in whose spirit is no *g.*
34.13. keep thy lips from *g.*, 1 Pet.
3. 10.
John 1. 47. Israelite in whom there
is no *g.*
22. neither was *g.* found in mouth
R. V. Rev. 14. 5. lie

GUILTY, Lev. 4. 13. & 22. 27.
Ex. 34.7. by no means clear the *g.*
Num. 14. 18. Gen. 42. 21.
Rom. 3. 19. all world *g.* before
1 Cor. 11. 27. *g.* of body and blood
of Lord
Jas. 2. 10. offend in one point, is
g. of all
Ex. 20. 7. not hold him *guiltless*
R. V. Num. 5. 31. free; Matt. 23.
18. debtor; 26. 66; Mark 14. 64.
worthy; Rom. 3. 19. brought un-
der judgment of
GULF, fixed, Luke 16. 26.

H

HABITABLE part, Prov. 8. 31.
HABITATION, 2 Chron. 6. 2. &
29. 6.
Deut. 26. 15. look down from thy
holy *h.*, Ps. 68. 5. Jer. 25. 30. Zech.
2. 13.
Ps. 26. 8. have loved the *h.* of thy
74. 20. earth full of *h.* of cruelty
89. 14. are *h.* of thy throne, 97. 2.
91. 9. hast made Most High thy *h.*
Prov. 3. 33. he blesseth *h.* of the
just
Isa. 33. 20. see Jerusalem a quiet *h.*
Jer. 31. 23. the Lord bless thee, O
h. of justice
Luke 16. 9. receive you into everlasting *h.*
Jude 6. angels which left their
own *h.*
Rev. 18. 2. Babylon is become *h.* of
R. V. Gen. 49. 5. their swords; Ex.
15. 2. praise him; Lev. 13. 46.
dwelling; 1 Chron. 4. 41. Meunim
(Mehunim); Job 5. 24; Jer. 25.
30, 37. fold; 41. 17. Geruth; Ps.
89. 14; 97. 2. foundation; Jer. 9.
10; 50.19; Amos 1.2.pasture; Luke
9. 2. eternal tabernacles
HAIL, Isa. 28. 2, 17. Rev. 8. 7. &
16. 21.
HAIR, Job 4. 15. S. of S. 4. 1.
Ps. 40. 12. more than the *h.* of my
head, 69. 4.
Hos. 7. 9. gray *h.* are here and
there
Matt. 5. 36. make one *h.* white or
10. 30. *h.* of your head are numbered, Luke 12. 7.
1 Cor. 11. 14. if man have long *h.*
1 Pet. 3. 3. not of plaiting the *h.*
HALT, between two, 1 Kings 18. 21.
Mic. 4. 6. will I assemble her that
halteth
Jer. 20. 10. watched for thy *halting*
R. V. Luke 14. 21. lame
HAND, Gen. 3. 22. & 16. 12.
Deut. 33. 3. all his saints are in
thy *h.*
Ezra 7. 9. the good *h.* of his God is
upon him
8. 22. *h.* of our God is upon them
Job 12. 6. into whose *h.* God bring.
Prov. 10. 4. *h.* of diligent maketh
11. 21. though *h.* join in *h.*, 16. 5.
Isa. 1. 12. who required this at
your *h.*
Matt. 22. 13. bind him *h.* and foot
John 13. 3. given all things into
his *h.*
1 Pet. 5. 6. humble yourselves
under the mighty *h.* of God
Num. 11. 23. *Lord's hand* waxed
2 Sam. 24. 14. let us fall into—not
man
Job 2. 10. received good at—and
not evil
12. 9.—hath wrought all this, Isa.
41. 20.
Isa. 40. 2. received of the—double
59. 1.—is not shortened that cannot save
Ps. 16. 8. he is at my *right hand*, I
shall not
11. at thy—are pleasures for ever
18. 35. thy—hath holden me up

Ps. 73. 23. hast holden me by my —
137. 5. let my — forget her cunning
139. 10. thy *h.* lead and thy — hold
Prov. 3. 16. length of days is in
her —
Eccl. 10. 2. wise man's heart is at
his —
9. 1. wise and their works are in
the *h.* of God
S. of S. 2. 6. his — doth embrace
me, 8. 3.
Matt. 5. 30. if thy — offend thee,
cut it off
6. 3. left *h.* know what thy — doeth
20. 21. one on the — and the other
on the left
25. 33. sheep on his — goats on the
left, 34. 41.
Mark 14. 62. sitting on — of power
16. 19. sat on — of God, Rom. 8. 34.
Col. 3. 1. Heb. 1. 3. & 8. 1. & 10. 12.
1 Pet. 3. 22. Acts 2. 33. & 7. 55, 56.
Ps. 31. 5. into *thy hand* I commit
Prov. 30. 32. lay — upon thy mouth
Eccl. 9. 10. whatsoever — findeth to
Isa. 26. 11. when — is lifted up, they
Matt. 18. 8. if — or thy foot offend
Gen. 27. 22. *hands* are the *h.* of Esau
Ex. 17. 12. Moses' *h.* were heavy
Job 17. 9. hath clean *h.* shall be
stronger
Ps. 24. 4. hath clean *h.* and a pure
76. 5. men of might found their *h.*
Prov. 31. 20. reacheth forth *h.* to
the needy
31. give her of the fruit of her *h.*
Isa. 1. 15. spread forth your *h.* I
will hide
Mic. 7. 3. do evil with both *h.* earn.
Matt. 18. 8. having two *h.* or feet
Luke 1. 74. delivered out of the *h.*
9. 44. delivered into *h.* of men
John 13. 9. but also my *h.* and head
2 Cor. 5. 1. house not made with *h.*
Eph. 4. 28. working with his *h.*
1 Tim. 2. 8. every where lifting up
holy *h.*
Heb. 9. 11. tabernacle, not made
with *h.*
10. 31. fearful thing to fall into the
h. of the living God
Jas. 4. 8. cleanse your *h.* ye sinners
Col. 2. 14. *handwriting* of ordi-
nances
HANDLE me and see, Luke 24. 39.
Col. 2. 21. touch not, taste not, *h.*
2 Cor. 4. 2. not *h.* the word of God
HANDMAID, Ps. 86. 16. & 116. 16.
Prov. 30. 23. Luke 1. 38, 48.
R. V. 1 Sam. 1. 18; 25. 27; 2 Sam.
14. 15. servant
HANG, Ps. 137. 2. Josh. 8. 29.
Deut. 21. 33. *h.* is accursed of God,
Gal. 3. 13.
Job 26. 7. he *h.* the earth on nothing
Matt. 18. 6. millstone *h.* about neck
22. 40. on these *h.* all the law and
Heb. 12. 12. hands which *h.* down
HAPPEN, Jer. 44. 23. Rom. 11. 25.
Prov. 12. 21. no evil shall *h.* to just,
1 Pet. 4. 12.
Eccl. 2. 14. one event *h.* to them all
8. 14. *h.* according to work of
1 Cor. 10. 11. these *h.* for ensam-
ples
R. V. Rom. 11. 25. hath befallen
HAPPY am I, for the daughters,
Gen. 30. 13.
Deut. 33. 29. *h.* art thou, O Israel
1 Kings 10. 8. *h.* are thy men, *h.*
these
Job 5. 17. *h.* is the man whom God
correcteth
Ps. 127. 5. *h.* is the man who hath
his quiver full
137. 8. *h.* that rewards thee, 9.
144. 15. *h.* that people whose God
is the Lord
Jer. 12. 1. why are they *h.* that deal
treacherously
Prov. 3. 13. *h.* is the man that findeth wisdom, 18.
14. 21. he that hath mercy on poor,
h. is

Prov. 16. 20. whoso trusteth in the
Lord *h.* is he
29. 18. he that keepeth the law, *h.*
is he
Mal. 3. 15. we call the proud *h.* that
John 13. 17. *h.* are ye, if ye do them
Rom. 14. 22. *h.* he that conde. not
Jas. 5. 11. count them *h.* which
endure
1 Pet. 3. 14. suffer for righteousness' sake, *h.* are ye
4. 14. *happier* if she so abide
R. V. Jer. 12. 1. at ease; John 13.
17; Jas. 5. 11; 1 Pet. 3. 14; 4. 14.
blessed
HARD, Gen. 35. 16, 17. Ex. 1. 14. &
18. 26. 2 Sam. 13. 2. Ps. 88. 7.
Gen. 18. 14. is any thing too *h.* for
the Lord
2 Sam. 3. 39. sons of Zeruiah be too
h. for me
2 Kings 2. 10. thou askest a *h.* thing
Ps. 60. 3. hast showed thy people *h.*
things
Prov. 13. 15. the way of transgressors is *h.*
Matt. 25. 24. that thou art a *h.* man
Mark 10. 24. how *h.* is it for them
John 6. 60. this is a *h.* saying; who
Acts 9. 5. *h.* for thee to kick, 26. 14.
Jude 15. of all their *h.* speeches
R. V. Job 41. 24. firm; Ps. 94. 4.
arrogantly; Prov. 13. 15. rugged;
Acts 9. 5. —
HARDEN, Ex. 4. 21. Deut. 15. 7.
Josh. 11. 20. Job 6. 10. & 39. 16.
Heb. 3. 8. *h.* not your hearts as in
the provocation, 15. & 4. 7. Ps. 95. 8.
Prov. 21. 29. *h.* his face
28. 14. *h.* his heart
29. 1. *h.* his neck shall be destroyed
Job 9. 4. hath *hardened* himself
against
Isa. 63. 17. *h.* our heart from thy
fear
Mark 6. 52. their heart was *h.*, 3. 5.
Rom. 9. 18. whom he will, he
hardeneth
Prov. 18. 19. a brother offended is
harder
Jer. 5. 3. made faces *h.* than a rock
Ezek. 3. 9. *h.* than a flint thy fore.
Matt. 19. 8. because of *hardness* of
your hearts
Mark 3. 5. grieved for the *h.* of their
2 Tim. 2. 3. endure *h.* as a good
soldier
R. V. Job 6. 10. exult; Ex. 7. 14;
9. 7. stubborn; Jer. 7. 26; 19. 15.
made stiff
HARLOT, Gen. 34. 31. Josh. 2. 1.
Judg. 11. 1. Prov. 7. 10. Isa. 1. 21.
& 23. 15.
Jer. 2. 20. play the *h.*, 3. 1, 6, 8. Ezek.
16. 15, 16, 41. Hos. 2. 5. & 4. 15.
Matt. 21. 31. *h.* go into the kingdom
1 Cor. 6. 16. joined to *h.* is one body
Jas. 2. 25. was not Rahab the *h.*
justified
Rev. 17. 5. mother of *h.* and abomi-
nations
HARM, Gen. 31. 52. Acts 28. 5.
1 Chron. 16. 22. do my prophets no *h.*,
Ps. 105. 15. Prov. 3. 30. Jer. 39. 12.
1 Pet. 3. 13. who is he that will *h.*
Matt. 10. 16. *harmless,* Phil. 2. 15.
Heb. 7. 26. holy, *h.* undefiled
R. V. Acts 27. 21. injury; 28. 6. no-
thing amiss; Heb. 7. 26. guileless
HARVEST, Gen. 8. 22. & 30. 14.
Ex. 34. 21. in *h.* thou shalt rest
Isa. 9. 3. joy before thee according
to joy of *h.*
Jer. 5. 24. reserved appointed
weeks of *h.*
8. 20. the *h.* is past, the summer
51. 33. time of *h.* shall come, Joel
3. 13.
Matt. 9. 37. *h.* plenteous
38. pray ye the Lord of the *h.*
Rev. 14. 15. *h.* of earth is ripe, Joel
3. 13.
HASTE, Ex. 12. 11, 33. Isa. 52. 12.
Ps. 31. 22. I said in my *h.*, 116. 11.

Ps. 38. 22. make *h.* help me, 40. 13,
& 70. 1, 5. & 71. 12. & 141. 1.
119. 60. I made *h.* and delayed not
S. of S. 8. 14. make *h.* my beloved
Isa. 28. 16. believ. shall not make *h.*
49. 17. thy children shall make *h.*
Ps. 16. 4. *hasten* after another god
Isa. 5. 19. let him *h.* his work that
60. 22. I the Lord will *h.* it in his
time
Jer. 1. 12. I will *h.* my word to
Prov. 14. 29. *hasty* of spirit, Eccl.
7. 9.
20. 21. inheritance gotten *hastily*
R. V. Job 9. 26. swoopeth; 40. 23.
trembleth; John 11. 31. quickly;
Isa. 28. 4. first ripe; Dan. 2. 15.
urgent
HATE, Gen. 24. 60. Deut. 21. 15.
Lev. 19. 17. shall not *h.* thy brother
Deut. 7. 10. repayeth them that *h.*
1 Kings 22. 8. I *h.* him for he doth
not
Ps. 68. 1. let them that *h.* him flee
97. 10. ye that love Lord, *h.* evil
139. 21. do not I *h.* them that *h.*
Prov. 8. 13. fear of Lord is to *h.* evil
36. all they that *h.* me love death
Jer. 44. 4. abominable thing that I
h.
Amos 5. 10. they *h.* him that rebuk
eth
15. *h.* the evil, and love the good
Mic. 3. 2. who *h.* the good and love
Luke 14. 26. and *h.* not his father
John 7. 7. world cannot *h.* you, but
15. 18. if the world *h.* you it hated
Prov. 7. 15. what I *h.* that do I
1 John 3. 13. marvel not if world *h.*
Rev. 2. 6. hatest the deeds, which
I also *h.*, 15.
17. 16. these shall *h.* the whore
Prov. 1. 29. for that they *hated*
knowledge
5. 12. and say how have I *h.* in-
struction
Isa. 66. 5. your brother that *h.* you
Mal. 1. 3. I *h.* Esau, Rom. 9. 13.
Matt. 10. 22. shall be *h.* of all men,
Mark 13. 13. Luke 21. 17.
Luke 19. 14. his citizens *h.* him
John 15. 24. *h.* me and my father, 18.
Eph. 5. 29. no man ever *h.* his own
Rom. 1. 30. backbiters, *haters* of
God
2 Sam. 19. 6. *hatest* friends and
lovest thine enemies
Ps. 5. 5. *h.* all workers of iniquity
Ex. 23. 5. ask of him that *hateth* thee
Prov. 13. 24. spareth rod, *h.* his
son
John 12. 25. *h.* his life in this world
Ex. 18. 21. men of truth *hating* cov-
etousness
Tit. 3. 3. *hateful* and *h.* one another
Jude 23. *h.* garment spotted by
flesh
R. V. Gen. 49. 23; Ps. 55. 3. perse-
cute; Matt. 5. 44 —
HAUGHTY, my heart is not, Ps.
131. 1.
Prov. 16. 18. *h.* spirit before fall,
18. 12.
21. 24. proud and *h.* scorner dealeth
Zeph. 3. 11. no more be *h.* because
Isa. 2. 11. *haughtiness,* 17. & 13. 11.
& 16. 6.
R. V. Isa. 16. 6. arrogancy; Isa. 10.
33; 24. 4. lofty
HEAD, Gen. 2. 10. & 40. 13.
Gen. 3. 15. it shall bruise thy *h.*
49. 26. blessings on *h.* of him
Ezra 9. 6. iniquity increased over
our *h.*
Prov. 16. 31. hoary *h.* a crown of
20. 29. beauty of old men is gray *h.*
Eccl. 2. 14. wise men's eyes are in *h.*
Ps. 38. 4. iniquity gone over my *h.*
S. of S. 2. my *h.* is filled with
Isa. 1. 5. whole *h.* is sick and heart
6. from sole of foot even unto *h.*
Ezek. 9. 10. their way on *h.*, 16. 4.
Dan. 2. 28. visions of thy *h.* on

48

Zech. 4. 7. bring forth *h.* stone thereof
Matt. 8. 20. not where to lay his *h.*
14. 8. give me *h.* of John Baptist
Rom. 12. 20. coals of fire on his *h.*, Prov. 25. 22.
1 Cor. 11. 3. *h.* of man is Christ, *h.* of woman is man, *h.* of Christ is God
Eph. 1. 22. gave him to be *h.* over
Col. 1. 18. he is *h.* of the body, 2. 19.
Rev. 19. 12. on his *h.* many crowns
Ps. 24. 7. lift up your *heads*, O ye gates, 9.
Isa. 35. 10. everlasting joy on their *h.*, 51. 11.
Luke 21. 28. lift up your *h.* for a
Rev. 13. 1. seven *h.* and ten horns
Job 5. 13. *headlong*, Luke 4. 29. Acts 1. 18.
2 Tim. 3. 4. *heady*, high-minded
HEAL her now, O God, Num. 12. 13.
Deut. 32. 39. I wound, I *h.* and I
2 Chron. 7. 14. I will *h.* their land
Ps. 6. 2. *h.* me, for my bones are
60. 2. *h.* breaches for land shaketh
Isa. 57. 18. I have seen his way and will *h.* him
Jer. 3. 22. I will *h.* your backsliding, Hos. 14. 4.
17. 14. *h.* me, and I shall be *h.*
Hos. 6. 1. hath torn and he will *h.*
Luke 4. 18. *h.* the broken-hearted
John 12. 40. convert. and I should *h.*
2 Chron. 30. 20. Lord *healed* the
Ps. 30. 2. I cried and thou hast *h.*
Isa. 6. 10. convert and be *h.*, Acts 28. 27.
53. 5. with his stripes we are *h.*, 1 Pet. 2. 24.
Jer. 6. 14. *h.* the hurt of the daughter of, 8. 11.
Hos. 7. 1. when I would have *h.* Israel
Matt. 4. 24. he *h.* them all, 12. 15. & 14. 14.
Heb. 12. 13. let it rather be *h.*
Jas. 5. 16. pray that ye may be *h.*
Rev. 13. 3. his deadly wound was *h.*
Ex. 15. 26. I am the Lord that *healeth* thee
Ps. 103. 3. who *h.* all thy diseases
147. 3. he *h.* the broken in heart
Isa. 30. 26. Lord *h.* stroke of their
Jer. 14. 19. looked for time of *healing*
30. 13. thou hast no *h.* medicine
Mal. 4. 2. with *h.* in his wings
Matt. 4. 23. *h.* all manner of sick.
1 Cor. 12. 9. to another the gifts of *h.*
Rev. 22. 2. leaves were for *h.* nations
Ps. 42. 11. *health* of my countenance, 43. 5.
Prov. 3. 8. shall be *h.* to thy navel
Jer. 8. 15. looked for a time of *h.*
30. 17. I will restore *h.* and heal
R. V. Mark 5. 23 ; Luke 8. 36 ; Acts 14. 9. made whole ; 28. 9. cured ; Nah. 3. 19. assuaging ; 2 Sam. 20. 9. Is it well with thee
HEAP coals, Prov. 25. 22. Rom. 12. 20.
Deut. 32. 23. I will *h.* mischiefs
Job 36. 13. hypocrites in heart *h.*
2 Tim. 4. 3. *h.* to themselves teach.
Ps. 39. 6. he *heapeth* up riches, and
Jas. 5. 3. ye have *heaped* treasures
Judg. 15. 16. *heaps* upon *h.* with the
R. V. Isa. 17. 11. fleeth away ; Jer. 31. 21. guide posts
HEAR, Gen. 21. 6. & 23. 6.
Deut. 30. 17. if heart turn away, so that thou wilt not *h.*
1 Kings 8. 30. *h.* thou in heaven thy dwelling place
2 Kings 19. 16. bow down thine ear, and *h.*
2 Chron. 6. 21. *h.* from thy dwelling
Job 5. 27. *h.* it and know it for
Ps. 4. 1. *h.* my prayer, 39. 12. & 54. 2. & 51. 8. & 84. 8. & 102. 1. & 143. 1.
Dan. 9. 17, 19.

Ps. 4. 3. Lord will *h.*, 17. 6. & 145. 19. Zech. 10. 6.
51. 8. make me to *h.* joy and
59. 7. who, say they, doth *h.*, 10.
66. 16. come and *h.* all ye that
115. 6. they have ears, but *h.* not
Prov. 19. 27. cease to *h.* instruction
Eccl. 5. 1. be more ready to *h.* than S. of S. 2. 14. let me *h.* thy voice, 8. 13.
Isa. 1. 2. *h.* O heavens, and give
6. 10. lest they *h.* with ears, Deut. 29. 4.
Matt. 10. 27. what ye *h.* in the ear
13. 17. to *h.* those things ye *h.*
17. 5. this is my beloved Son, *h.* ye
Mark 4. 24. take heed what ye *h.*
33. spake the word as they were able to *h.* it
Luke 8. 18. take heed how ye *h.*
16. 29. Moses and the prophets, let them *h.* them
John 5. 25. they that *h.* shall live
Acts 10. 33. to *h.* all things that
Jas. 1. 19. every man be swift to *h.*
Rev. 2. 7. let him *h.* what the Spirit saith to the churches, 3. 6, 13, 22. & 11. 17, 29.
3. 20. if any *h.* my voice, and open
Ex. 2. 24. God *heard* their groaning
Ps. 6. 9. Lord hath *h.* my supplica.
10. 17. hast *h.* desire of humble, 34. 6.
34. 4. I sought the Lord, and he *h.*
61. 5. thou hast *h.* my vows, 116. 1.
120. 1. I cried to Lord and he *h.*
Isa. 40. 28. hast thou not *h.* that God
64. 4. from beginning men have not *h.*
Jer. 8. 6. I hearkened and *h.* but
Jonah 2. 2. I cried to Lord and he *h.*
Mal. 3. 16. Lord hearkened and *h.*
Matt. 6. 7. be *h.* for much speaking
Luke 1. 13. thy prayer is *h.* and thy
John 3. 32. what he hath seen and *h.*
Rom. 10. 14. of whom they have not *h.*
1 Cor. 2. 9. eye hath not seen nor ear *h.*
Phil. 4. 9. what *h.* and seen in me
Heb. 4. 2. with faith in them that *h.*
Jas. 5. 11. ye have *h.* of patience of Job
Ex. 3. 7. *I have heard* their cry
6. 5. — the groaning, Acts 7. 34.
16. 12. — the murmurings, Num. 14. 27.
1 Kings 9. 3. — thy prayer and supplication, 2 Kings 19. 20. & 20. 5. & 22. 19.
Job 42. 5. — of thee by the hearing
Isa. 49. 8. in an acceptable time —
Ps. 65. 2. thou that *hearest* prayer
John 11. 42. I knew thou *h.* me
1 Sam. 3. 9. speak, Lord, thy servant *heareth*
Prov. 8. 34. blessed is man that *h.*
Matt. 7. 24. whoso *h.* these sayings
Luke 10. 16. he that *h.* you *h.* me
John 9. 31. God *h.* not sinners, but
Rev. 22. 17. let him that *h.* say come
Rom. 2. 13. not *hearers* but doers
Eph. 4. 29. minister grace to the *h.*
Jas. 1. 22. be doers of the word and not *h.*
Job 42. 5. of thee by *hearing* of ear
Prov. 20. 12. the *h.* ear, and seeing
28. 9. turneth away his ear from *h.*
Matt. 13. 14. *h.* they hear not, Acts 28. 27.
Rom. 10. 17. faith cometh by *h.* and *h.* by
Heb. 5. 11. seeing ye are dull of *h.*
2 Pet. 2. 8. in seeing and *h.* vexed his
R. V. The O. T. changes, which are numerous, are chiefly to *answer*
HEARKEN unto the voice of, Deut. 28. 15.
Deut. 28. 1. if thou *h.* diligently, 30. 10.

1 Sam. 15. 22. to *h.* better than the fat of rams
Ps. 103. 20. angels *h.* to voice of
Isa. 46. 12. *h.* unto me, ye stout
HEART, Ex. 28. 30. & 35. 5.
1 Sam. 1. 13. she spake in her *h.* only
16. 7. but Lord looketh on *h.*
24. 5. David's *h.* smote him after
1 Chron. 16. 10. let the *h.* of them rejoice that seek the Lord, Ps. 105. 3.
22. 19. set your *h.* to seek the Lord your God
2 Chron. 17. 6. his *h.* was lifted up
30. 19. prepareth his *h.* to seek God
Ps. 22. 26. your *h.* shall live for ever, 69. 32.
37. 31. law of his God is in his *h.*
51. 17. a broken and a contrite *h.*, Isa. 66. 2.
64. 6. inward thought, and *h.* is
Prov. 4. 23. keep thy *h.* with dili.
10. 20. *h.* of wicked is little worth
16. 9. a man's *h.* deviseth his way
27. 19. of man answereth to man
Eccl. 7. 4. *h.* of wise is in house
10. 2. wise man's *h.* is at his right hand, but a fool's *h.* is at his left
S. of S. 3. 11. in the day of gladness of his *h.*
Isa. 6. 10. make *h.* of this people fat
Jer. 11. 20. triest the reins and the *h.*, 17. 10.
12. 11. no man layeth it to *h.*, Isa. 42. 25.
17. 9. *h.* is deceitful above all
24. 7. I will give them a *h.* to know
32. 39. I will give them one *h.*, Ezra 11. 19.
Lam. 3. 41. lift up our *h.* with our
Ezek. 11. 19. take stony *h.* give *h.* of flesh
36. 26. new *h.* take stony *h.* give *h.*
Joel 2. 13. rend your *h.* not your
Mal. 4. 6. turn *h.* of fathers to
Matt. 6. 21. there will your *h.* be
12. 34. out of abundance of the *h.* the mouth speaketh
Luke 2. 19. pondered them in her *h.*, 51.
24. 25. O fools, and slow of *h.* to
32. did not our *h.* burn within us
John 14. 1. let not your *h.* be troubled, 27.
Acts 5. 33. were cut to the *h.*, 7. 54.
11. 23. with purpose of *h.* cleave to the Lord
13. 22. found man after mine own *h.*
Rom. 10. 10. with *h.* man believeth
1 Cor. 2. 9. nor entered into *h.* of man
2 Cor. 3. 3. in fleshly tables of the *h.*
1 Pet. 3. 4. in the hidden man of the *h.*
1 John 3. 20. if *h.* condemn us, God
Deut. 11. 13. serve him *with all heart*, Josh. 22. 5. 1 Sam. 12. 20.
13. 8. love Lord your God —, 30. 6.
Matt. 22. 37. Mark 12. 30, 33. Luke 10. 27.
Deut. 26. 16. keep and do them —
30. 2. turn to the Lord — and soul, 10. 2 Kings 23. 25. Joel 2. 12.
1 Kings 2. 4. walk before me in truth —
8. 23, 48. return to thee —, 2 Chron. 6. 38.
2 Chron. 15. 12. seek the God of their fathers —
15. sworn —
Prov. 3. 5. trust in Lord — and be
Jer. 29. 13. search for me —
Zeph. 3. 14. sing, be glad, rejoice —
Acts 8. 37. if thou believest —
Ps. 86. 12. I will praise thee *with all my heart*
45. 1. *my heart* is inditing a
57. 7. — is fixed, O God, — is fixed
61. 2. what time — is overwhelmed
84. 2. my flesh and — crieth for

49

Ps. 109. 22. — is wounded within me
131. 1. Lord — is not haughty
S. of S. 5. 2. I sleep, but — waketh
Hos. 11. 8. — is turned within me
1 Kings 8. 61. *heart perfect* with the
   Lord, 11. 4. & 15. 3, 14. 2 Chron.
   15. 17.
2 Kings 20. 3. and with —, 2 Chron.
   19. 9.
1 Chron. 28. 9. serve him with —,
   29. 9.
2 Chron. 16. 9. in behalf of them
   whose —
Ps. 101. 2. I will walk within my
   house with a —
   24. 4. clean hands and *pure heart*
Matt. 5. 8. blessed are the pure
   in *h.*
1 Tim. 1. 5. charity out of a —
2 Tim. 2. 22. call on Lord out of —
1 Pet. 1. 22. love with — fervently
Ps. 9. 1. praise him *with my whole
   heart*
   119. 2. seek him —
Jer. 3. 10. not turned with her
   whole *h.*
Col. 3. 23. do it *heartily* as to Lord
R. V. 2 Sam. 3. 21; Ezek. 25. 15;
   27. 31; Lam. 3. 51. soul; Job 38.
   36; Jer. 7. 31. mind
HEATH, Jer. 17. 16. & 48. 6.
HEATHEN, Lev. 25. 44. & 26. 45.
Ps. 2. 1. why do the *h.* rage
   2. 8. give them the *h.* for
Matt. 18. 17. let him be as a *h.* man
Gal. 3. 8. justify the *h.* through
   faith
HEAVEN of *h.* cannot contain,
   1 Kings 8. 27. 2 Chron. 2. 6. & 6. 18.
Ps. 103. 11. as *h.* is high above the
Prov. 25. 3. *h.* for height, and earth
Isa. 66. 1. *h.* is my throne, Acts 7.
   49.
Jer. 31. 37. if *h.* above can be
Hag. 1. 10. *h.* over you is stayed
Matt. 5. 18. till *h.* and earth pass
Luke 15. 18. sinned against *h.*, 21.
John 1. 51. see *h.* open and angels
Ps. 73. 25. whom have I *in heaven*
Eccl. 5. 2. God is — and thou upon
Heb. 10. 34. have — a better sub.
1 Pet. 1. 4. inheritance reserved —
   for you
Ps. 8. 3. consider *the heavens*, the
   19. 1. — declare the glory of God
   89. 11. — are thine, and earth also
Isa. 65. 17. I create new *h.* and
   Acts 3. 21. *h.* must receive him till
2 Cor. 5. 1. house eternal in the *h.*
Eph. 4. 10. ascend far above all *h.*
Matt. 6. 14. *heavenly* Father, 26. 32.
   & 15. 13. & 18. 35. Luke 11. 13.
John 3. 12. if I tell you of *h.* things
1 Cor. 15. 48. as is *h.* such are the *h.*
Eph. 1. 3. in *h.* places, 20. & 2. 6.
2 Tim. 4. 18. unto his *h.* kingdom
Heb. 3. 1. partak. of the *h.* calling
R.V. March 11. 26; Luke 11. 2; Heb.
   10. 34; 1 John 5. 7; Rev. 16. 17 —
HEAVE OFFERING, Ex. 29. 27.
   Num. 15. 19. & 18. 8, 28, 29.
HEAVY, Num. 11. 14. Job 33. 7.
Ps. 38. 4. as a *h.* burden too *h.* for
Prov. 31. 6. wine to those of *h.*
   hearts
Isa. 6. 10. make their ears *h.* lest
   58. 6. to undo the *h.* burden
Matt. 11. 28. labor and are *h.* laden
   23. 4. bind *h.* burdens and griev.
Ps. 69. 20. I am full of *heaviness*
   119. 28. my soul melteth for *h.*
Prov. 12. 25. *h.* in the heart
   14. 13. the end of that mirth is *h.*
Rom. 9. 2. I have great *h.* and
1 Pet. 1. 6. in *h.* through
R. V. Ezra 9. 5. humiliation; Job
   9. 27. sad countenance; Isa. 29. 2.
   mourning; 2 Cor. 2. 1. with sorrow; Phil. 2. 26. sore troubled;
   1 Pet. 1. 6. have **been** put to grief;
   Prov. 31. 6. bitter; Isa. 30. 27. rising smoke; 46. 1. made a load;
   58. 6. bands of the yoke; Matt. 26.
   37; Mark 14. 33. troubled

HEDGE, Job 1. 10. Prov. 15. 19.
   Isa. 5. 5. Hos. 2. 6. Job 3. 23. Lam.
   3. 7.
R. V. 1 Chron. 4. 23. Gederah; Ps. 80.
   12; Eccl. 10. 8; Jer. 49. 3. fences;
   Lam. 3. 7. fenced; Matt. 21. 33.
   set a hedge about
HEED, 2 Sam. 20. 10. 2 Kings 10. 31.
Deut. 2. 4. take good *h.* to yoursel.
Josh. 22. 5. take diligent *h.* to do
Ps. 119. 9. by taking *h.* thereto
Eccl. 12. 9. he gave good *h.* sought
Jer. 18. 18. not give *h.* to any of his
R. V. Deut. 27. 9. silence; 2 Chron.
   19. 6. consider; 33. 8. observe;
   Eccl. 12. 9. pondered; Matt. 18.
   10. see; Luke 11. 35. look; Acts
   8. 11. regard; 22. 26; Rom. 11.
   21
HEEL, his, thou shalt bruise
Ps. 41. 9. lifted up his *h.* against
Hos. 12. 3. he took his brother by
   h.
HEIFER, Num. 19. 2. Jer. 46. 20.
   & 48. 34. Hos. 4. 16. & 10. 11. Heb.
   9. 13.
HEIR, Gen. 15. 4. & 21. 10.
Prov. 30. 23. handmaid *h.* to her
Jer. 49. 1. hath Israel no sons,
   hath he no *h.*
Matt. 21. 38. this is the *h.* let us
Rom. 4. 13. Abraham should be *h.*
   8. 17. if children, *h.* of God, joint
   h. with Christ
Gal. 3. 29. children *h.* according
   4. 7. if a son, then an *h.* of God
Eph. 3. 6. Gentiles should be fel-
   low *h.*
Heb. 1. 2. God hath appointed *h.* of
   6. 17. might show to *h.* of promise
   21. 7. became *h.* of righteousness
1 Pet. 3. 7. *h.* together of grace of
R. V. Jer. 49. 2; Mic. 1. 15. possess; Gal. 4. 30. inherit
HELD, Ps. 94. 18. S. of S. 3. 4.
HELL, Matt. 18. 9. Mark 9. 43, 45.
Deut. 32. 22. shall burn to lowest *h.*
2 Sam. 22. 6. the sorrows of *h.*
Job 11. 8. it is deeper than *h.*
   26. 6. *h.* is naked before him and
Ps. 9. 17. wicked be turned into *h.*
   16. 10. not leave my soul in *h.*
   116. 3. pains of *h.* gat hold on me
139. 8. make my bed in *h.* thou
   art
Prov. 5. 5. her steps take hold of *h.*
   7. 27. her house is the way to *h.*
   9. 18. her guests are in depths
   of *h.*
   15. 11. *h.* and destruction are
   24. that he may depart from *h.*
   23. 14. shalt deliver his soul from
   h.
   27. 20. *h.* and destruction are
Isa. 5. 14. *h.* hath enlarged herself
   14. 9. *h.* from beneath is moved
   to
   28. 15. with *h.* are we at agree.
   57. 9. debase thyself even to *h.*,
   Ezek. 31. 16, 17. & 32. 21, 27.
Amos 9. 2. though they dig into *h.*
Jonah 2. 2. out of belly of *h.* cried I
Hab. 2. 5. enlarged his desire as *h.*
Matt. 5. 22. be in danger of *h.* fire
   29. body be cast into *h.*, 30. & 18.9.
Mark 9. 43, 45, 47.
   10. 28. destroy both soul and
   body in *h.*
   11. 23. brought down to *h.*, Luke
   10. 15.
   16. 18. the gates of *h.* shall not
   23. 15. twofold more the child of
   h.
Luke 12. 5. power to cast into *h.*
   16. 23. in *h.* he lifted up his eyes
Acts 2. 31. his soul not left in *h.*, 27.
Jas. 3. 6. tongue set on fire of *h.*
2 Pet. 2. 4. cast them down to *h.*
Rev. 1. 18. having keys of *h.* and
   6. 8. death and *h.* followed with
   20. 13. death and *h.* delivered up
   14. death and *h.* were cast into
R. V. 2 Sam. 22. 6; Job 11. 8; 26.
   6; Ps. 16. 10; 18. 5; 116. 3; 139. 8;

Prov. 5. 5; 7. 27; 9. 18; 15. 11, 24;
   23. 14; 27. 30. Sheol; Matt. 11. 23;
   16. 18; Luke 10. 15; 16. 23; Acts 2.
   27, 31; Rev. 1. 18; 6. 8; 20. 13, 14.
   Hades; Matt. 5. 22; 18. 9. hell of
   fire
HELMET, 1 Sam. 17. 5. 2 Chron.
   26. 14.
Isa. 59. 17. a *h.* of salvation on head
Eph. 6. 17. take the *h.* of salvation
1 Thes. 5. 8. for a *h.* the hope of sal.
HELP meet for him, Gen. 2. 18.
Deut. 33. 29. Lord shield of thy *h.*
Judg. 5. 23. came not to the *h.* of
Ps. 27. 9. thou hast been my *h.*
   33. 20. he is our *h.* and shield
   40. 17. my *h.* and deliverer, 70. 5.
   46. 1. God is a very present *h.* in
   trouble
   60. 11. vain is *h.* of man, 108. 12.
   71. 12. O my God, make haste for
   my *h.*
   89. 19. laid *h.* upon one that is
   115. 9. Lord is their *h.* and shield,
   10, 11.
   124. 8. our *h.* is in name of Lord
Hos. 13. 9. but in me is thy *h.*
Acts 26. 22. having obtained *h.* of
   God
1 Cor. 12. 28. *helps*, governments
2 Chron. 14. 11. nothing with thee
   to *h.*
Ps. 40. 13. make haste to *h.* me,
   70. 1.
Isa. 41. 10. I will *h.* thee
   63. 5. there was none to *h.*
Acts 16. 9. come unto Macedonia,
   and *h.* us
Heb. 4. 16. find grace to *h.* in time
1 Sam. 7. 12. hitherto hath the
   Lord *helped* us
Ps. 118. 13. I might fall; but Lord
   h. me
Isa. 49. 8. in day of salvation I *h.*
Zech. 1. 15. they *h.* forward af-
   flicted
Acts 18. 27. *h.* them much who had
Rev. 12. 16. the earth *h.* the woman
Rom. 8. 26. Spirit *helpeth* our in-
   firmities
Ps. 10. 14. thou art the *helper*
   54. 4. God is my *h.*, Heb. 13. 6.
Job 9. 13. proud *helpers* do stoop
2 Cor. 1. 24. we are *h.* of your joy
3 John 8. fellow *h.* to the truth
R. V. 1 Sam. 11. 9. deliverance;
   1 Chron. 18. 5. succor; 2 Chron.
   20. 9. save; Job 8. 20. uphold; Ps.
   116. 6. saved; Eccl. 4. 10. lift
HEM, Matt. 9. 20. & 14. 36.
R. V. Ex. 28. 33, 34; 39. 24, 25, 26.
   skirts; Matt. 9. 20; 14. 36. border
HEN, Matt. 23. 37. Luke 13. 34.
HERESY, Acts 24. 14. 1 Cor. 11.
   19. Gal. 5. 20. 2 Pet. 2. 1.
Tit. 3. 10. a man that is a *heretic*
R. V. Acts 24. 14. a sect
HERITAGE appointed by God,
   Job 20. 29.
Ps. 16. 5. I have a goodly *h.*
   61. 5. given me the *h.* of those
   127. 3. lo, children are a *h.* of Lord
Isa. 54. 17. this is *h.* of servants
Jer. 3. 19. goodly *h.* of the host
Joel 2. 17. give not thy *h.* to rep.
1 Pet. 5. 3. not as lords over
   God's *h.*
R. V. 1 Pet. 5. 3. charge allotted
HEW tables of stone, Ex. 34. 1.
   Deut. 12. 3.
Jer. 2. 13. *hewed* them out cisterns
Hos. 6. 5. therefore have I *h.* them
Matt. 3. 10. *hewn* down, 7. 19.
R. V. 1 Kings 5. 18. fashion; 1 Sam.
   11. 7. cut
HID themselves, Adam and wife,
   Gen. 3. 8.
Ps. 119. 11. word have I *h.* in heart
Zeph. 2. 3. it may be, ye shall be *h.*
Matt. 10. 26. nor *h.* that shall not
   be
   11. 25. *h.* these things from wise
2 Cor. 4. 3. if Gospel be *h.* it is *h.*

Col. 2. 3. in whom are *h.* all treas.
3. 3. your life is *h.* with Christ
Ps. 83. 3. and consulted against thy *hidden* ones
1 Cor. 4. 5. bring to light *h.* things of
1 Pet. 3. 4. the *h.* man of heart
Rev. 2. 17. give to eat the *h.* manna
Gen. 18. 17. shall I *hide* from Abra.
Job 33. 17. may he *hide* from man
Ps. 17. 8. *h.* me under the shadow
27. 5. in time of trouble he shall *h.*
30. 7. didst *h.* thy face and I
31. 20. shalt *h.* them in secret
Ps. 51. 9. *h.* thy face from my sin
143. 9. I flee to thee to *h.* me, 7.
Isa. 26. 20. *h.* thyself for a moment
Jas. 5. 20. *h.* a multitude of sins
Rev. 6. 16. *h.* us from the face of
Job 13. 24. why *hidest* thou thy face,
Ps. 30. 7. & 44. 24. & 88. 14. & 143. 7.
Isa. 45. 15. thou art a God that *h.*
Job 34. 29. when he *hideth* his face
42. 3. who is he that *h.* counsel
Ps. 139. 12. darkness *h.* not from
Isa. 8. 17. I will wait on Lord that *h.*
Hab. 3. 4. *hiding* of his power
Ps. 32. 7. *h.* place, 119. 114.
R. V. Deut. 30. 11. too hard for;
Job 15. 20; 20. 26; 24. 1; Prov. 2. 1.
laid up; Prov. 19. 24; 26. 15. buri-
eth; 21. 16. restraineth; Jer. 16. 17;
Luke 9. 45. concealed; Luke 8. 17.
secret; 2 Cor. 4. 3, 13. is veiled;
Jas. 5. 20. cover

HID TREASURE, parable, Matt. 13. 44.

HIGH, Deut. 3. 5, 12. & 28. 43.
Deut. 26. 19. make thee *h.* above all
1 Kings 9. 8. house which is *h.*
1 Chron. 17. 17. man of *h.* degree
Job 11. 8. as *h.* as heaven, what
Ps. 49. 2. both low and *h.* rich and
89. 13. strong arm, and *h.* is right
97. 9. thou Lord art *h.* above all
103. 11. as heaven is *h.* above earth
131. 1. not in things too *h.* for me
Prov. 21. 4. a *h.* look and proud
Eccl. 12. 5. afraid of that which is *h.*
Isa. 57. 15. I dwell in the *h.* and
Ezek. 21. 26. abase him that is *h.*
Rom. 12. 16. mind not *h.* things
2 Cor. 10. 5. every *h.* thing that
Phil. 3. 14. for the prize of the *h.* calling of God
Num. 24. 16. *Most High,* Deut. 32. 8.
2 Sam. 22. 14. Ps. 7. 17. & 9. 2. & 21. 7. & 46. 4. & 50. 14. & 56. 2.
Ps. 47. 2. the Lord — is terrible
83. 18. Jehovah art — over all earth
92. 8. thou art — for evermore
Isa. 14. 14. I will ascend and be like the —
Acts 7. 48. — dwelleth not in temples
Job 5. 11. set up on *high* those that
Ps. 107. 41. setteth the poor — from
113. 5. like our God who dwell-
eth —
Isa. 26. 5. bring down those that dwell —
Luke 24. 49. be endued with power from —
Eccl. 5. 8. there be *higher* than they
Isa. 55. 9. heaven *h.* than earth
Heb. 7. 26. made *h.* than the heavens
Ps. 18. 13. *Highest* gave his voice
87. 5. *H.* himself shall establish
Eccl. 5. 8. he that is higher than *h.*
Luke 1. 35. power of the *H.* shall
2. 14. glory to God in the *h.*, 19. 38.
6. 35. children of the *H.*
14. 8. sit not down in the *h.* room
1. 28. thou that art *highly* favored
16. 15. which is *h.* esteemed
Rom. 12. 3. not think of himself more *h.*
1 Thes. 5. 13. esteem them very *h.*
2 Tim. 3. 4. heady, *high-minded*
Rom. 11. 20. be not — but fear
1 Tim. 6. 17. rich, that they be not —
Job 22. 12. *height,* Rom. 8. 39. Eph. 3. 18.
R. V. 2 Tim. 3. 4. puffed up

HILL, Ex. 24. 4. Ps. 68. 15, 16.
Ps. 2. 6. set my King on holy *h.* of Zion, 3. 4. & 15. 1. & 43. 3. & 68. 15. & 99. 9.
Gen. 7. 19. all high *h.* under heaven
Num. 23. 9. from the *h.* I behold
Ps. 65. 12. little *h.* rejoice on every
68. 16. why leap ye, high *h.*
98. 8. let *h.* be joyful together
Hos. 10. 8. to the *h.* fall on us, Luke 23. 30.
Hab. 3. 6. the perpetual *h.* did bow
R. V. Ex. 24. 4; 1 Kings 11. 7. mount; Gen. 7. 19; Num. 14. 44, 45; Deut. 1. 41, 43; Josh. 15. 9; 18. 13, 14; 24. 30; Judg. 2. 9; 16. 3; 1 Sam. 25. 20; 26. 13; 2 Sam. 21. 9; 1 Kings 22. 17; Ps. 18. 7; 68. 15, 16; 80. 10; 95. 4; 97. 5; 104. 10, 13, 18, 32; 121. 1; Luke 9. 37. mountain, or mountains; Deut. 1. 7; Josh. 9. 1; 11. 16; 17. 6. hill country; 1 Sam. 9. 11; 2 Sam. 16. 1. ascent; Acts 17. 22. the Areopagus

HIND, 2 Sam. 22. 34. Ps. 29. 9. Prov. 5. 19. S. of S. 2. 7. & 3. 5. Hab. 3. 19.

HIRE, Deut. 24. 15. Isa. 23. 18. Mic. 1. 7. & 3. 11. Luke 10. 7. Jas. 5. 4.
Job 7. 1. a *hireling,* John 10. 12, 13.
R. V. Gen. 31. 8. wages

HITHERTO Lord helped us, 1 Sam. 7. 12.
Job 38. 11. *h.* shalt thou come, but
John 16. 24. *h.* ye asked nothing
1 Cor. 3. 2. *h.* ye were not able to
R. V. 1 Sam. 7. 18; 1 Chron. 17. 16. thus far; 2 Sam. 15. 34. in time past; Isa. 18. 2, 7. onward; Dan. 7. 28. here; John 5. 17. even until now; 1 Cor. 3. 2. yet

HOLD, Gen. 21. 18. Ex. 9. 2. & 20. 7.
Judg. 9. 46. a *h.* of the house
Job 17. 9. righteous shall *h.* on way
Isa. 41. 13. God will *h.* thy right
62. 1. for Zion's sake will I not *h.*
Jer. 2. 13. cisterns that can *h.* no
Matt. 6. 24. *h.* to one and despise the
Rom. 1. 18. *h.* truth in unrighteous.
Phil. 2. 29. *h.* such in reputation
Heb. 3. 14. if we *h.* beginning of
1 Thes. 5. 21. prove all, *hold fast* that which is good
2 Tim. 1. 13. — form of sound words
Heb. 3. 6. if we — the confidence of hope
Heb. 4. 14. let us — our profession
Rev. 2. 25. what ye have — till I
3. 11. — that thou hast that no man
Ps. 77. 4. *holdest* my eyes waking
Rev. 2. 13. *h.* fast my name and
Job 2. 3. still he *holdeth* fast
Ps. 66. 9. which *h.* our soul in life
Prov. 17. 28. a fool, when he *h.*
Jer. 6. 11. I am weary with *holding*
Phil. 2. 16. *h.* forth the word of life
Col. 2. 19. not *h.* the head, from
1 Tim. 1. 19. *h.* faith and a good
3. 9. *h.* mystery of faith in
Tit. 1. 9. *h.* fast the faithful word
R. V. Jer. 51. 30. strongholds; Dan. 11. 39; Nah. 3. 12, 14. fortresses; Acts. 4. 3. ward
The R. V. changes are based on words before and after *hold*

HOLY ground, Ex. 3. 5.
Ex. 16. 23. *h.* sabbath, & 31. 14, 15.
19. 6. *h.* nation, 1 Pet. 2. 9.
29. 6. *h.* crown; 30. 25. *h.* ointment
Lev. 16. 33. *h.* sanctuary
27. 14. house to be *h.*; 30. *h.* tithes
Num. 5. 17. *h.* water; 31. 6. *h.* in-struments
Lev. 11. 45. be ye *h.* for I am *h.*, 20. 7.
1 Sam. 2. 2. there is none *h.* as Lord
21. 5. vessels of young men are *h.*
Ps. 22. 3. thou art *h.* that inhabitest
98. 5. worship at his footstool, for he is *h.*
145. 17. Lord is *h.* in all his works
Prov. 20. 25. a snare to devour that which is *h.*
Isa. 6. 3. *h. h. h.* Lord God of hosts
Ezek. 22. 26. difference between *h.*
Matt. 7. 6. give not that which is *h.*

Luke 1. 35. *h.* thing which shall be
Acts 4. 27. thy *h.* child Jesus, 30.
Rom. 7. 12. law *h.* commandment *h.*
12. 1. sacrifice *h.* acceptable to God
1 Cor. 7. 14. children unclean, but now *h.*
Eph. 1. 4. be *h.* and without blame
2 Tim. 1. 9. called us with *h.* calling
3. 15. hast known the *h.* Scriptures
Tit. 1. 8. sober, just, *h.*, temperate
1 Pet. 1. 15. be ye *h.* in all manner
2. 5. a *h.* priesthood, 9. *h.* nation
2 Pet. 1. 21. *h.* men of God spake as
3. 11. *h.* in all conversation and
Rev. 3. 7. saith he that is *h.* and
4. 8. *h. h. h.* Lord God Almighty
15. 4. fear thee for thou only art *h.*
20. 6. blessed and *h.* is he that hath
22. 11. he that is *h.* let him be *h.*
Ex. 26. 33. *most holy place,* 34. & 29. 37. & 40. 10. 1 Kings 6. 16. & 7. 50. & 8. 6. Ezek. 44. 13. & 45. 3.
Lev. 6. 25. *most holy offering,* 7. 1, 6. & 10. 17. & 14. 13. Num. 18. 9, 10. Ezek. 48. 12.
21. 22. bread of his God most *h.*
27. 28. *most holy things,* Num. 4. 4, 19. 1 Chron. 6. 49. & 23. 13. 2 Chron. 31. 14.
Ezek. 43. 12. the whole limit shall be most *h.*
Jude 20. building up on your most *h.* faith
Ps. 42. 4. with multitude that kept *holy day,* Isa. 58. 13. Col. 2. 16. Ex. 25. 2.
Matt. 1. 18. with child of *Holy Ghost*
20. that is conceived in her is of —
3. 11. baptize you —, Mark 1. 8.
John 1. 33. Acts 1. 5. & 11. 16.
12. 31. blasphemy against —, 32.
Mark 3. 29.
Luke 12. 36. David said by —, Acts 1. 16.
13. 11. not ye that speak, but the —
Luke 1. 35. — shall come upon thee
2. 15. — was upon him
3. 22. — descended in bodily shape
12. 12. — shall teach you in that same
John 7. 39. for — was not yet given
14. 26. Comforter which is — whom
20. 22. receive ye the —
Acts 1. 2. though — had given
8. after that the — is come upon
2. 33. receive promise of the —
38. receive gift of —, 10. 45.
7. 51. ye do always resist the —
8. 15. receive —, 19.
18. — given
9. 31. walking in the fear of Lord and in the comfort of the —
10. 38. anointed Jesus with the —
44. — fell on all them, 11. 15.
47. received the —, 8. 17.
19. 2. be any —, 6.
13. 2. the — said, separate me Saul
4. they being sent forth by the —
15. 28. it seemed good to — and us
16. 6. forbidden of — to preach in
20. 23. save that — witnesseth
21. 11. thus saith — so shall the Jews
28. 25. well spake the — by Esaias
Rom. 5. 5. love of God shed abroad by —
14. 17. righteousness, peace, and joy in —
15. 13. abound in hope through power of —
16. offering of Gentiles sanctified by —
1 Cor. 2. 13. in words which the — teacheth
6. 19. temple of — which is in you
12. 3. can say Jesus is Lord but by the —
2 Cor. 6. 6. by — by love unfeigned
13. 14. communion of — be with you
1 Thes. 1. 5. in — much assurance
2 Tim. 1. 14. keep by — which dwell
Tit. 3. 5. not by works, but by the renewing of —
Heb. 2. 4. miracles and gifts of —

Heb. 3. 7. wherefore, as — saith
6. 4. made partakers of —
9. 8.—this signifying that the way
10. 15. whereof — is a witness to
1 Pet. 1. 12. preach unto you—sent
2 Pet. 1. 21. holy men of God moved
by—
1 John 5. 7. Father, Word, and —
are
Jude 20. building up . . praying
in—
Luke 1. 15. *filled with,* or *full of the Holy Ghost,* 41. 67. Acts 2. 4. & 4. 8. & 6. 3, 5. & 9. 17. & 11. 24. & 13. 9, 52.
Ps. 51. 11. take not thy *Holy Spirit* from me
Isa. 63. 10. rebell. and vexed his —
Luke 11. 13. give — to them that
Eph. 1. 13. ye were sealed with—
of promise
4. 30. grieve not the — of God
Ps. 87. 1. *holy mountain,* Isa. 11. 9. & 56. 6. & 57. 13. & 65. 11, 25. & 66. 20. Dan. 9. 16. & 11. 45. Joel 2. 1. & 3. 17. Obad. 16. Zeph. 3. 11. Zech. 8. 3.
Lev. 20. 3. *holy name,* & 22. 2, 33. 1 Chron. 16. 10, 35. Ps. 33. 21. & 103. 1. & 111. 9. & 145. 21. Isa. 57. 15. Ezek. 36. 20, 21.
Deut. 33. 8. *Holy One,* Job 6. 10. Ps. 16. 10. & 89. 19. Isa. 10. 17. & 29. 23. & 40. 25. & 43. 15. & 49. 7. Hab. 1. 12. & 3. 3. Mark 1. 24. Acts 3. 14. & 4. 27, 30. 1 John 2. 20.
2 Kings 19. 22. *Holy One of Israel,* Ps. 71. 22. & 78. 41. & 89. 18. Isa. 1. 4. & 5. 19, 24. & 10. 20. & 12. 6. & 17. 7. & 29. 19. & 30. 11, 12. & 31. 1. & 41. 14. & 45. 11. & 47. 4. & 49. 7. & 55. 5. & 60. 9, 14. Jer. 50. 29. & 51. 5.
Deut. 7. 6. *holy people,* 14. 2, 21. & 26. 19. & 28. 9. Isa. 62. 12. Dan. 8. 24. & 12. 7.
Ex. 28. 29. *holy place,* Lev. 6. 16. & 10. 17. Eccl. 8. 10. and about thirty other texts
Ps. 5. 7. *holy temple,* 11. 4. & 65. 4. & 79. 1. & 138. 2. Jonah 2. 4, 7. Mic. 1. 2. Hab. 2. 20. Eph. 2. 21.
Isa. 65. 5. I am *holier* than thou
Heb. 9. 3. the *holiest* of all. 8.
1 Thes. 3. 10. how *holily* and justly
Ex. 15. 11. glorious in *holiness*
28. 36. to Lord, 39. 30. Isa. 23. 18. 1 Chron. 16. 29. in beauty of *h.,* Ps. 29. 2. & 96. 9. & 110. 3. 2 Chron. 20. 21. 2 Chron. 31. 18. sanctified themselves in *h.*
Ps. 30. 4. at remembrance of his *h.*
47. 8. God sits on throne of his *h.*
48. 1. in mountain of his *h.*
89. 35. I have sworn by my *h.*
93. 5. *h.* becometh thy house
Isa. 23. 18. her hire shall be *h.* to
35. 8. it shall be called the way of *h.*
63. 15. habitation of thy *h.*
18. people of *h.*
Jer. 2. 3. Israel was *h.* to the Lord
Amos 4. 2. Lord hath sworn by his *h.*
Obad. 17. on mount Zion there shall be *h.*
Zech. 14. 20. on horse bells, *h.* to
Mal. 2. 11. Judah hath profaned *h.*
Luke 1. 75. in *h.* and righteousness
Acts 3. 12. as though by our own *h.*
Rom. 1. 4. Son of God according to the Spirit of *h.*
6. 19. yield members servants to righteousness unto *h.*
22. fruit unto *h.* and end everlast.
2 Cor. 7. 1. perfecting *h.* in the fear
Eph. 4. 24. created in righteousness and true *h.*
1 Thes. 3. 13. unblameable in *h.*
4. 7. called not to uncleanness but to *h.*
1 Tim. 2. 15. in faith, love, *h.*
Tit. 2. 3. in behavi. as becometh *h.*
Heb. 12. 10. partakers of his *h.*
14. *h.* without which no man shall

R. V. Ex. 38. 24; Lev. 10. 17, 18; 14. 13; Ps. 68. 17; Ezek. 21. 2. sanctuary; Matt. 12. 31, 32; Mark 3. 29; Luke 2. 25, 26; John 1. 33; 7. 39; Acts 2. 4; 6. 5; 1 Cor. 2. 13. Holy Spirit
HOME, Gen. 39. 16. & 43. 16.
Ps. 68. 12. that tarried at *h.* divided
Eccl. 12. 5. man goeth to his long *h.*
2 Cor. 5. 6. while we are at *h.* in
Tit. 2. 5. obedient, keepers at *h.*
R. V. Gen. 43. 16; Josh. 2. 18; 1 Sam. 10. 26; Matt. 8. 6; Mark 5. 19. house; Luke 9. 61—; 1 Tim. 5. 4. family
HONEST and good heart, Luke 8. 15.
Acts 6. 3. men of *h.* report, full of
Rom. 12. 17. provide things *h.* in
2 Cor. 8. 21. providing for *h.* things
Phil. 4. 8. whatsoever things are *h.*
1 Pet. 2. 12. have your conversation *h.*
Rom. 13. 13. walk *honestly* as in day
1 Thes. 4. 12. walk *h.* towards them
Heb. 13. 18. in all things willing to live *h.*
1 Tim. 2. 2 in all godliness and *honesty*
R. V. Acts 6. 3. good; Rom. 12. 17; 1 Cor. 8. 21; 2 Cor. 13. 7; Phil. 4. 8. honorable; 1 Pet. 2. 12. behavior seemly
HONEY, Gen. 43. 11. Lev. 2. 11.
Judg. 14. 8, 18. 1 Sam. 14. 26, 29.
Ps. 19. 10. sweeter than *h.* and
Prov. 25. 27. it is not good to eat much *h.*
S. of S. 4. 11. *h.* and milk are under
Isa. 7. 15. butter and *h.* shall he eat
Matt. 3. 4. his meat was locusts and wild *h.*
Rev. 10. 9. in mouth sweet as *h.,* 10.
1 Sam. 14. 27. dipt in *honeycomb,*
Prov. 5. 3, 16, 24. & 24. 13. & 27. 7.
S. of S. 4. 11. & 5. 1. Luke 24. 42.
HONOR, be not thou united
1 Chron. 29. 12. both riches and *h.*
Ps. 7. 5. lay mine *h.* in the dust
8. 5. crown. him with glory and *h.*
26. 8. place where thine *h.* dwell.
49. 12. man being in *h.* abideth not
20. man that is in *h.* and under.
Prov. 4. 16. in her left hand riches and *h.*
15. 33. before *h.* is humility
26. 1. *h.* is not seemly for a fool
29. 23. *h.* shall uphold the humble
Mal. 1. 6. if I be a father where is mine *h.*
Matt. 13. 57. prophet is not without *h.*
John 5. 41. I receive not *h.* from men
Rom. 2. 7. seek for glory and *h.* and immortality
12. 10. in *h.* preferring one another
13. 7. give *h.* to whom *h.* is due
2 Cor. 6. 8. by *h.* and dishonor
2 Tim. 2. 20. some to *h.* and some to
Heb. 5. 4. taketh this *h.* to himself
1 Pet. 1. 7. be found unto praise and *h.*
Ex. 20. 12. *h.* thy father and mother
1 Sam. 2. 30. that *h.* me I will *h.*
Prov. 3. 9. *h.* Lord with substance
Isa. 29. 13. with their lips do *h.* me
John 5. 23. should *h.* the Son as *h.*
12. 26. if any man serve me him will my Father *h.*
1 Pet. 2. 17. *h.* all men, love
Ps. 15. 4. he *honoreth* them that
Mal. 1. 6. a son *h.* his father
Matt. 15. 8. *h.* me with their lips
Heb. 13. 4. marriage is *honorable* in
R. V. Gen. 49. 6; Ps. 7. 5; 26. 8; 66. 2; Prov. 14. 28; 25. 2; Dan. 4. 30; John. 5. 41, 44; 8. 54; 2 Cor. 6. 8. glory; Ps. 31. 25. dignity; Dan. 4. 36. majesty; Rev. 19. 1; 21. 24—; John 8. 54. glorify
HOOF, Ex. 10. 26. Lev. 11. 3-7.
HOOK, Ex. 26. 32. Ezek. 29. 4. & 38. 4.

Isa. 2. 4. *pruning hooks,* 18. 5. Mic. 4. 3.
R. V. Job 41. 1. fishhook; 2. rope
HOPE in Israel concerning this, Ezra 10. 2.
Job 8. 13. hypocrite's *h.* shall perish
27. 8. what is the *h.* of hypocrite
Ps. 78. 7. might set their *h.* in God
146. 5. whose *h.* is in Lord his God
Prov. 10. 28. *h.* of righteous shall
11. 7. the *h.* of unjust men perishes.
14. 32. righteous hath *h.* in death
19. 18. chasten thy son while there is *h.*
Isa. 57. 10. saidst thou there is no *h.,*
Jer. 2. 25. & 18. 12. Ezek. 37. 11.
Jer. 14. 8. O the *h.* of Israel, 17. 13. & 50. 7.
17. 7. blessed is the man that trusteth in the Lord, and whose *h.* the Lord is
Lam. 3. 29. if so be there may be *h.*
Hos. 2. 15 valley of Achor for door of *h.*
Joel 3. 16. Lord will be the *h.* of
Zech. 9. 12. turn to the strong hold ye prisoners of *h.*
Acts 24. 15. have *h.* towards God
Rom. 5. 4. experience *h.*
5. *h.* maketh not ashamed
8. 24. we are saved by *h.* but *h.* that is seen is not *h.*
15. 4. comfort of Scriptures, might have *h.*
1 Cor. 9. 10. husbandman partaker of his *h.*
13. 13. now abideth faith, *h.* and
15. 19. if in this life only, *h.*
Gal. 5. 5. wait for *h.* of righteous.
Eph. 2. 12. having no *h.* and with.
Col. 1. 23. not moved away from *h.*
1 Thes. 4. 13. sorrow not as others that have no *h.*
5. 8. for a helmet, the *h.* of salva.
1 Tim. 1. 1. Jesus Christ who is our *h.*
Tit. 2. 13. looking for that blessed *h.*
3. 7. according to the *h.* of eternal
Heb. 6. 11. to the full assurance of *h.*
19. which *h.* we have as an anchor
1 Pet. 1. 3. begotten us again to a lively *h.*
21. that your faith and *h.* might be
3. 15. asketh a reason of *h.* in you
1 John 3. 3. man that has his *h.* in
Ps. 16. 9. my flesh also shall rest *in hope*
Rom. 4. 18. against *h.* believed —
5. 2. rejoice — of glory of God, 12. 12.
Tit. 1. 2. — eternal life of which
Ps. 39. 7. *my* hope is in thee
71. 5. thou art —, Jer. 17. 17.
22. 9. didst make me *hope* when I
42. 5. *h.* thou in God, for, 11.
119. 49. thou hast caused me to *h.*
81. 1 *h.* in thy word, 114.
130. 7. let Israel *h.* in the Lord
147. 11. those that *h.* in his mercy
Lam. 3. 26. good that man should *h.*
Rom. 8. 25. if we *h.* for that we see
1 Pet. 1. 13. be sober and *h.* to end
Ps. 119. 43. I have *hoped* in thy
74. I have *h.* in thy word, 147.
166. I have *h.* in thy salvation
Heb. 11. 1. faith is the substance of things *h.* for
1 Cor. 13. 7. charity *hopeth* all
Luke 6. 35. lend, *hoping* for nothing
R. V. Job 8. 14. confidence; Ps. 16. 9. safety; Jer. 17. 17. refuge; Lam. 3. 18. expectation; Jer. 3. 23. look.
HORN of my salvation, Ps. 18. 2.
Ps. 75. 4. lift not up the *h.,* 5, 10.
92. 10. my *h.* shalt thou exalt as the *h.* of the unicorn
148. 14. he exalted the *h.* of his
Luke 1. 69. raised up *h.* of salva.
Mic. 4. 13. I will make thy *h.* iron
Dan. 8. 20. having two *horns*
Hab. 3. 4. *h.* coming out of his hand
Rev. 13. 1. beast having ten *h.*

Rev. 13. 11. had two *h.* like a lamb
  5. 6. lamb having seven *h.*
R. V Ex. 21. 29 —— ; Hab. 3. 4. rays
HORRIBLE, Ps. 11. 6. & 40. 2. Jer.
  5. 30. & 18. 13. & 23. 14. Hos. 6. 10.
  Jer. 2. 12. Ezek. 32. 10.
  R. V. Ps. 11. 6. burning
HORROR, Gen. 15. 12. Job 18. 20.
  Ps. 55. 5. & 119. 53. Ezek. 7. 18.
  R. V. Ps. 119. 53. hot indignation
HORSE and rider thrown, Ex.
  15. 21.
  Ps. 32. 9. be ye not as *h.* or mule
  33. 17. *h.* is a vain thing for safety
  Prov. 21. 31. *h.* is prepared for the
  Eccl. 10. 7. I have seen serv. on *h.*
  Jer. 8. 6. as *h.* rusheth into battle
  12. 5. canst thou contend with *h.*
  Hos. 14. 3. we will not ride upon *h.*
  Zech. 1. 8. & 6. 2, 3, 6. *h.* red, white,
  black, Rev. 6. 2, 4, 5, 8. & 9. 17.
  Rev. 6. 2. and behold a white *h.*
HOSPITALITY, Rom. 12. 13.
  1 Tim. 3. 2. Tit. 1. 8. 1 Pet. 4. 9.
HOST, Luke 10. 35. Rom. 16. 23.
  Ps. 27. 3. & 33. 16. & 103. 21. & 108.
  11. & 148. 2. Isa. 40. 26. Luke 2. 13.
  Ps. 103. 21. Jer. 3. 19.
  R. V. Ex. 16. 13; Deut. 2. 14, 15;
  Josh. 1. 11; 3. 2; 18. 9; Judg. 7.
  8, 10, 13, 15; 1 Sam. 11. 11; 14. 15,
  19; 1 Chron. 9. 19. camp; 2 Kings
  18. 17; 25. 1; 2 Chron. 14. 9; 24.
  23: 26. 11. army
HOT, Ps. 38. 1. & 39. 3. Prov. 6. 28.
  Hos. 7. 7. 1 Tim. 4. 2. Rev. 3. 15.
  R. V. Judg. 2. 14; 3. 8; 6. 39; 10. 7.
  kindled
HOUR, Dan. 3. 6, 15. & 4. 33.
  Matt. 10. 19. shall be given you in
  the same *h.*
  24. 36. of that day and *h.* knoweth
  25. 13. ye know neither day nor *h.*
  Luke 12. 12. Holy Ghost shall teach
  you that same *h.*
  22. 53. this is your *h.* and power
  of darkness
  John 2. 4. my *h.* is not yet come
  4. 23. the *h.* cometh and now is
  12. 27. save me from this *h.*
  Rev. 3. 3. not know what *h.* I come
  10. will keep thee from the *h.* of
  17. 12. power as kings one *h.* with
  18. 10. in one *h.* is thy judgment
  R. V. Matt. 24. 42. on what day;
  1 Cor. 8. 7. until now
HOUSE, Ex. 20. 17. Lev. 14. 36.
  Ex. 12. 30. not a *h.* where not one
  Job 21. 28. where is the *h.* of prince
  30. 23. *h.* appointed for all living
  Prov. 3. 33. curse of the Lord is in
  h.
  12. 7. *h.* of righteous shall stand
  19. 14. *h.* and riches are inherit.
  Eccl. 7. 2. go to the *h.* of mourn.
  12. 3. when keepers of *h.* tremble
  ble
  S. of S. 2. 4. brought me to the
  banqueting *h.*
  Isa. 5. 8. woe to them that join *h.*
  to *h.*
  60. 7. I will glorify the *h.* of my
  64. 11. our holy and beautiful *h.*
  Matt. 10. 13. *h.* worthy
  23. 38. *h.* left desolate, Luke
  11. 17.
  Luke 12. 3. proclaimed on *h.* tops
  John 14. 2. in my father's *h.* are
  Rom. 16. 5. church in their *h.*,
  1 Cor. 16. 19. Col. 4. 15. Phile. 2.
  2 Cor. 5. 1. earthly *h.* . . *h.* of God
  not made with hands
  2 Tim. 1. 16. give mercy to the *h.*
  Heb. 3. 3. built *h.* hath more honor
  than the *h.*
  2 John 10. receive him not into *h.*
  Ps. 105. 21. made him Lord of all
  his *house*
  112. 3. wealth and riches shall be
  in —
  Acts 10. 2. feared God with all —
  16. 34. believed in God with all—
  Heb. 3. 2. faithful in all —, 5. 6.
  John 4. 53. his *whole house* believed

1 Tim. 5. 8. especially for those of
  his own *h.*
Josh. 24. 15. as for me and *my*
  house
2 Sam. 23. 5. though — be not so
  Ps. 101. 2. will walk within — with
  Isa. 56. 7. joyful in — of prayer,
  Matt. 21. 13. Mark 11. 7. Luke 19.
  46.
  Matt. 12. 44. will return to —, Luke
  11. 24.
  Acts 16. 15. judged me faithful,
  come into —
  Deut. 6. 7. when sittest in *thy*
  house
  Ps. 26. 8. I loved habitation of —
  Isa. 38. 1. set — in order, for thou
  Acts 11. 14. thou and all — saved,
  16. 31.
  Gen. 28. 17. *house of God* or Lord,
  Ps. 42. 4. & 55. 14. & 23. 6. & 27. 4.
  Eccl. 5. 1. Isa. 2. 3. Mic. 4. 2.
  1 Tim. 3. 15. 1 Pet. 4. 17. Ex. 23.
  John 6. 24. and about one hun-
  dred other places
  Job 4. 19. dwell in *houses* of clay
  Ps. 49. 11. *h.* shall continue for
  Matt. 11. 8. in soft linen sit in
  kings' *h.*
  19. 29. forsaken *h.* or lands
  23. 14. devour widows' *h.*
  Luke 16. 4. may receive me into *h.*
  1 Cor. 11. 22. have ye not *h.* to eat
  12. 12. ruling their own *h.*
  2 Tim. 3. 6. creep into *h.* and lead
  Tit. 1. 11. subvert whole *h.* teach.
  Acts 16. 15. baptized and her whole
  household
  Gal. 6. 10. *h.* of faith
  Eph. 2. 19. *h.* of God
  Matt. 13. 52. like *householder*, 20. 1.
  R. V. Ex. 12. 3; 2 Kings 7. 11; 10.
  5, 12; 15. 5; Isa. 36. 3; 1 Cor. 1. 11;
  1 Tim. 5. 14. household; 2 Cor.
  5. 2. habitation; Deut. 6. 22;
  1 Sam. 25. 17; 2 Sam. 6. 11; 17. 23;
  1 Kings 11. 20; 2 Tim. 4. 19. house
HOW long, Ps. 6. 3. & 13. 1. & 74. 9.
  & 79. 5. & 80. 4. & 89. 46. Isa. 6. 11.
  Jer. 4. 14. Dan. 8. 13. & 12. 6. Matt.
  17. 17. Luke 9. 41. Rev. 6. 10.
  Job 15. 16. *how much more*, Prov.
  21. 27. Matt. 7. 11. Luke 12. 24, 28.
  Heb. 9. 14.
  Matt. 18. 21. & 23. 37. *how oft*, Luke
  13. 34. Job 21. 17. Ps. 78. 40.
HOWL, Isa. 13. 6. & 14. 31. Jer. 4.
  8. Joel 1. 5, 11, 13. Jas. 5. 1. Hos.
  7. 14. Deut. 32. 10. Amos 8. 3.
HUMBLE person shall save, Job
  22. 29.
  Ps. 9. 12. forgett. not the cry of *h.*
  10. 12. forget not the *h.*
  17. desire of the *h.*
  34. 2. *h.* shall hear of it, and be
  69. 32. *h.* shall see this, and be
  Prov. 16. 19. to be of an *h.* spirit
  29. 23. honor shall uphold *h.* in
  Isa. 57. 15. of contrite and *h.* spirit
  Jas. 4. 6. giveth grace to the *h.*
  Ex. 10. 3. thou refuse to *h.* thyself
  Deut. 8. 2. to *h.* thee, and to prove
  2 Chron. 7. 14. shall *h.* themselves
  34. 27. because didst *h.* thyself
  Prov. 6. 3. ,, thyself, and make
  Jer. 13. 18. *h.* yourselves, sit down
  Matt. 18. 4. whoso *h.* himself shall
  2 Cor. 12. 21. my God will *h.* me
  Jas. 4. 10. *h.* yourselves in sight
  1 Pet. 5. 6. *h.* yourselves therefore
  Lev. 26. 41. if uncircumcised
  hearts be *humbled*
  2 Kings 22. 19. hast *h.* thyself
  2 Chron. 12. 6. princes and kings
  h. themselves
  33. 12, 23. *h.* not himself before
  the Lord, 36. 12.
  Ps. 35. 13. I *h.* my soul with fasting
  113. 6. Lord who *h.* himself to
  Isa. 2. 11. lofty looks shall be *h.*
  10. 33. high and haughty shall be *h.*
  Jer. 44. 10. are not *h.* unto this day
  Lam. 3. 20. my soul is *h.* in me
  Dan. 5. 22. hast not *h.* thy heart

Phil. 2. 8. *h.* himself and became
Deut. 21. 14. *humbled her*, 22. 24, 29.
  Ezek. 22. 10, 11.
Col. 3. 12. put on *humbleness* of
Mic. 6. 8. walk *humbly* with thy
  God
Prov. 22. 4. by *humility* are riches
Acts 20. 19. serv. Lord with all *h.*
Col. 2. 18. in a voluntary *h.*, 23.
1 Pet. 5. 5. be clothed with *h.*
  R. V. Ps. 9. 12; 10. 12. poor; Ps.
  10. 17; 34. 2; 69. 32; Prov. 16. 19;
  29. 23. lowly; Ps. 35. 13. afflicted;
  Isa. 2. 11; 10. 33. brought low;
  Lam. 3. 20. brought down ; 2 Sam.
  16. 4. do ; Acts 20. 19. lowliness
HUNGER, Ex. 16. 3. Deut. 28. 48.
  Ps. 34. 10. young lions suffer *h.*
  Prov. 19. 15. idle soul shall suffer *h.*
  Lam. 4. 9. no war nor have *h.* of
  with *h.*
  Deut. 8. 3. suffered thee to *h.*
  Isa. 49. 10. shall not *h.* nor thirst
  Matt. 5. 6. blessed are they that *h.*
  Luke 6. 21. blessed are ye that *h.*
  John 6. 35. that cometh to me shall
  never *h.*
  Rom. 12. 20. if thine enemy *h.* feed
  1 Cor. 4. 11. we both *h.* and thirst
  11. 34. if any man *h.* let him eat
  Ps. 107. 9. fill the *hungry* with
  goodness
  146. 7. God giveth food to the *h.*
  Prov. 25. 21. if enemy be *h.* give
  27. 7. to the *h.* every bitter thing
  Isa. 58. 7. is it not to deal thy
  bread to the *h.*
  10. if thou draw out thy soul to *h.*
  Ezek. 13. shall eat; but ye shall be *h.*
  Ezek. 18. 7. hath given his bread
  to the *h.*, 16.
  Luke 1. 53. filled the *h.* with good
  Phil. 4. 12. how to be full and to
  be *h.*
  R. V. Jer. 38. 9; Ezek. 34. 29; Rev.
  6. 8. famine
HUNT, 1 Sam. 26. 20. Job 38. 39.
  Ps. 140. 11. evil doth *h.* the violent
  Prov. 6. 26. adulteress will *h.* for
  precious
  Ezek. 13. 18. ye *h.* the souls of my
  people
  Job 10. 16. thou *huntest* me as
HURT, Gen. 4. 23. & 26. 29.
  Josh. 24. 20. will turn and do you
  h.
  Ps. 15. 4. sweareth to his *h.* and
  Eccl. 5. 13. riches kept for owners
  to their *h.*
  Jer. 6. 14. healed *h.* of the daugh.
  Rev. 2. 11. shall not be *h.* of
  6. 6. *h.* not the oil and wine
  Ezra 4. 15. *hurtful*, Ps. 144. 10.
  1 Tim. 6. 9. fall into foolish and *h.*
  R. V. Josh. 24. 20. evil; Acts 27. 10.
  injury; Acts 18. 10. harm
HUSBAND, Gen. 3. 6, 16. & 29. 32.
  Ex. 4. 25. bloody *h.* art thou to me
  Isa. 54. 5. thy Maker is thy *h.* Lord
  Jer. 31. 32. though I was a *h.* to
  Mark 10. 12. if a woman put away
  her *h.*
  John 4. 17. I have no *h.*
  1 Cor. 7. 14. unbelieving *h.* is sanc.
  34. careth how she may please *h.*
  14. 35. let them ask *h.* at home
  2 Cor. 11. 2. espoused you to one *h.*
  Eph. 5. 22. wives submit to your *h.*
  23. the *h.* is the head of wife, 24.
  25. *h.* love your wives, as Christ
  Eph. 5. 33. the wife see that she
  reverence her *h.*
  Col. 3. 18. wives submit to your *h.*
  1 Pet. 3. 1. subject to their own *h.*
  7. ye *h.* dwell with them, accord.
  R. V. 1 Cor. 7. 14. brother
HUSBANDMAN, thy Father is.
  John 15. 1.
  1 Tim. 2. 6. *h.* that labors must be
  Jas. 5. 7. *h.* waiteth for precious
  1 Cor. 3. 9. ye are God's *husbandry*
HYMN, Matt. 26. 30. Eph. 5. 19
  Col. 3. 16.

HYPOCRISY, Isa. 32. 6. Matt. 23.
28. Mark 12.15. Luke 12.1. 1 Tim.
4. 2. Jas. 3. 17. 1 Pet. 2. 1.
Matt. 7. 5. *hypocrite*, Luke 6. 42. &
13. 15.
Matt. 24. 51. appoint him portion
with *h.*
Job 20. 5. joy of *h.* is but for a moment
27. 8. what is the hope of the *h.*
36. 13. *h.* in heart heap up wrath
Isa. 9. 17. every one is a *h.* and evil
33. 14. fearful. hath surprised *h.*
Matt. 6. 2. *hypocrites*, 6. 16. & 15. 7. &
16. 3. & 23. 13, 14, 15, 23.
Job 8. 13. the *h.* hope shall perish
15. 34. congregation of *h.* shall
R. V. Isa. 32. 6. profaneness ; Job
8. 13 ; 13. 16 ; 17. 8 ; 20. 5 ; 27. 8 ; 34.
30 ; 36. 13 ; Prov. 11. 9 ; Isa. 33. 14.
godless ; Isa. 9. 17. profane ; Matt.
16. 3 ; 23. 14 ; Luke 11. 44——

I

IDLE, they be, Ex. 5. 8, 17.
Prov. 19. 15. an *i.* soul shall suffer
Matt. 12. 36. every *i.* word give
20. 3. standing *i.*
6. why stand ye *i.*
Luke 24. 11. words seemed as *i.* tales
1 Tim. 5. 13. they learn to be *i.*
Prov. 31. 27. *idleness*, Eccl. 10. 18.
Ezek. 16. 49.
R. V. Matt. 20. 6——; Ezek. 16. 49.
ease
IDOL, 2 Chron. 15. 16. & 33. 7.
Isa. 66. 3. as if he blessed an *i.*
Zech. 11. 17. who to the *i.* shepherd
1 Cor. 8. 4. an *i.* is nothing in world
Ps. 96. 5. gods of nations are *idols*
Isa. 2. 8. land is full of *i.* they wor.
Jer. 50. 38. they are mad upon *i.*
Hos. 4. 17. Ephraim is joined to *i.*
Acts 15. 20. abstain from pollu. of *i.*
Rom. 2. 22. thou that abhorrest *i.*
1 Cor. 8. 1. touch. things offered to *i.*
2 Cor. 6. 16. temple of God with *i.*
1 John 5. 21. keep yourselves from *i.*
Rev. 2. 14. eat things sacrificed to *i.*
9. 20. worship devils and *i.* of gold
1 Cor. 5. 10, 11. *idolater*, 6. 9. & 10. 7.
Eph. 5. 5. Rev. 21. 8. & 22. 15.
1 Sam. 15. 23. stubbornness as iniquity and *idolatry*
Acts 17. 16. city wholly given to *i.*
1 Cor. 10. 14. dearly beloved, flee *i.*
Gal. 5. 20. *i.* witchcraft, hatred
Col. 3. 5. covetousness, which is *i.*
1 Pet. 4. 3. walked in abominable
idolatries
R. V. 1 Kings 15. 13 ; 2 Chron. 15. 16 ;
Jer. 50. 2. image, and images ;
2 Chron. 15. 18. abominations ; Isa.
57. 5. among oaks ; Jer. 22. 28. vessel ; Zech. 2. 10. teraphim ; 11. 17.
worthless ; 1 Cor. 12. 28——; 1 Sam.
15. 23. teraphim ; Acts 17. 16. full
of idols
2 Chron. 34. 7. hewed down all the
sun-images throughout all the
land of Israel
IGNORANCE, sin through, Lev.
4. 2, 13, 22, 27. Num. 15. 24, 25. Acts
3. 15.
Acts 17. 30. the times of this *i.*
Eph. 4. 18. alienated through *i.* in
Ps. 73. 22. so foolish was I and
ignorant
Isa. 63. 16. though Abraham be *i.*
of
Rom. 10. 3. being *i.* of God's righteousness
1 Cor. 14. 38. if any man be *i.* let
Heb. 5. 2. who can have compassion
on *i.*
Acts 17. 23. *ignorantly*, 1 Tim. 1. 13.
R. V. Lev. 4. 2, 22, 27 ; 5. 18 ; Num.
15. 24, 26, 27, 28, 29. unwittingly ;
Lev. 4. 13. shall err ; Num. 15. 25.
was an error ; Isa. 56. 10. without
knowledge ; 63. 16. knoweth not ;

Num. 15. 28. erreth ; Deut. 19. 4.
unawares
ILLUMINATED, Heb. 10. 32.
IMAGE, Lev. 26. 1. Dan. 2. 31.
Gen. 1. 26. let us make man in our
own *i.*, 27. & 5. 1. & 9. 6. Col. 3. 10.
Gen. 5. 3. Adam begat a son after
his *i.*
Ps. 73. 20. Lord, thou shalt despise
their *i.*
Matt. 22. 20. whose *i.* is this, Luke
20. 24.
Rom. 8. 29. conformed to *i.* of Son
1 Cor. 15. 49. have borne the *i.* of
the earthly we shall also bear *i.*
of the heavenly
4. 4. Christ who is the *i.* of God
2 Cor. 3. 18. into same *i.* from glory
Heb. 1. 3. express *i.* of his person
Rev. 13. 14. make an *i.* to the beast
Ex. 23. 24. break down *images*, 34. 13.
R. V. Lev. 26. 1. figured stones ;
Ex. 23. 24 ; 34. 13 ; Lev. 26. 1 ; Deut.
7. 5 ; 16. 22 ; 1 Kings 14. 23 ; 2 Kings
17. 10 ; 18. 4 ; 23. 14 ; 2 Chron. 14. 3 ;
31. 1 ; Jer. 43. 13 ; Hos. 1. 2 ; Mic. 5.
13. pillar, and pillars ; Job 4. 16.
form ; Rom. 11. 4——
IMAGINE, Ps. 2. 1. Nah. 1. 9. Zech.
7. 10. & 8. 17. Acts 4. 25.
Gen. 6. 5. every *imagination* of the
thoughts was evil, 8. 21. Prov. 6.
18. Lam. 3. 60, 61. Rom. 1. 21. 2 Cor.
10. 5.
R. V. Lam. 3. 60, 61. devices ; Rom.
1. 21. reasonings ; Gen. 11. 6. purpose
IMMEDIATELY, Mark 4. 15. Acts
12. 23.
IMMORTAL, invisible, 1 Tim. 1.
17.
Rom. 2. 7. seek for *immortality*
1 Cor. 15. 53. this mortal must put
on *i.*
1 Tim. 6. 16. who only hath *i.* in
2 Tim. 1. 10. brought *i.* to light
R. V. *incorruption*
Rom. 2. 7. seek for glory . , and *i.*
IMMUTABLE, Heb. 6. 17, 18.
IMPART, Luke 3. 11. Rom. 1. 11.
1 Thes. 2. 8.
IMPENITENT heart, Rom. 2. 5.
IMPERIOUS whorish woman,
Ezek. 16. 30.
IMPLACABLE, unmerciful,
Rom. 1. 31.
R. V. Rom. 1. 31——
IMPORTUNITY, Luke 11. 8.
IMPOSSIBLE, Matt. 17. 20. & 19. 26.
Luke 1. 37. with God nothing is *i.*
17. 1. it is *i.* but offences will come
Heb. 6. 4. it is *i.* for those once
18. in two things it is *i.* for God to
11. 6. without faith it is *i.* to please
R. V. Luke 1. 37. void of power ;
Heb. 6. 4. as touching
IMPUDENT, Prov. 7. 13. Ezek. 2. 4.
R. V. Ezek. 3. 7. of hard forehead
IMPUTE, 1 Sam. 22. 15. Lev. 7. 18.
& 3. 7.
Ps. 32. 2. to whom Lord *i.* not iniq.
Rom. 4. 6. *i.* righteousness without
8. blessed to whom Lord will not *i.*
22. *i.* to him for righteousness
2 Cor. 5. 19. not *i.* their trespasses
Jas. 2. 23. *i.* to him for righteous.
R. V. Hab. 1. 11. even ; Rom. 4. 6, 8,
11, 22, 23, 24. reckon ; 2 Cor. 5. 19.
reckoning ; Jas. 2. 23. reckoned
IN Christ, Acts 24. 24. Rom. 12. 5.
1 Cor. 1. 2, 30. & 3. 1. & 15. 18, 22,
2 Cor. 1. 21. & 2. 14. & 5. 17. & 5. 17,
19. & 12. 2. Gal. 1. 22. Eph. 1. 1, 3,
10, 12, 20. & 2. 6, 10, 13. Phil. 1. 1, 13.
& 2. 1, 5. & 3. 14. Col. 1. 2, 4.
1 Thes. 1. 1. *in* God, 4. 16. John 3.
21. Col. 3. 3.
Gen. 15. 16. *in the Lord*, Ps. 4. 5. &
31. 24. & 34. 2. & 35. 9. & 37. 4, 7. Isa.
45. 17, 24, 25. Jer. 3. 23. Zech. 12. 5.
1 Cor. 1. 31. & 4. 17. & 7. 22, 39. Eph.
2. 21. & 6. 10. Phil. 4. 2, 4. Col. 3. 18.
& 4. 7, 17. 1 Thes. 5. 12. Phile. 16,
20. Rev. 14. 13.

INCEST condemned, Lev. 18. & 20.
17. Deut. 22. 30. & 27. 20. Ezek. 22.
11. Amos 2. 7. cases of, Gen. 19.
33. & 35. 22. & 38. 18. 2 Sam. 13. &
16. 21. Mark 6. 17. 1 Cor. 5. 1.
INCHANTMENT, Lev. 19. 26.
Num. 23. 23. Eccl. 10. 11. Isa. 47. 9.
INCLINE heart, Josh. 24. 23. Judg.
9. 3. 1 Kings 8. 58. Ps. 119. 36, 112. &
141. 4.
Ps. 78. 1. *incline*, 40. 1. & 116. 2. Prov.
2. 2. & 5. 13. Jer. 7. 24, 26. & 11. 8.
& 17. 23. & 25. 4. & 34. 14. & 35. 15.
& 44. 5. Isa. 55. 3.
R. V. Ps. 71. 2. bow down
INCLOSED, Ps. 17. 10. & 22. 16.
S. of S. 4. 12. & 8. 9. Lam. 3. 9.
R. V. S. of S. 4. 12. shut up ; Lam.
3. 9. fenced up
INCONTINENT, 1 Cor. 7. 5. 2 Tim.
3. 3.
INCORRUPTIBLE God, Rom. 1.
23.
1 Cor. 9. 25. to obtain an *i.* crown
15. 52. dead shall be raised *i.*
1 Pet. 1. 4. begotten to inherit
ance *i.*
23. born not of corruptible seed,
but of *i.*
1 Cor. 15. 42, 50, 53, 54. *incorruption*
INCREASE, Lev. 19. 25. & 25. 7.
Lev. 25. 36. take no usury nor *i.*, 37.
Deut. 16. 15. bless thee in all thine *i.*
Ps. 67. 6. earth yield her *i.*, 85. 12.
Prov. 3. 9. with first fruits of all *i.*
1 Cor. 3. 6. I planted ; but God gave
the *i.*, 7.
Col. 2. 19. increaseth with *i.* of God
Ps. 62. 10. if riches *i.* set not heart
Prov. 1. 5. wise man will *i.* learn.
Isa. 29. 19. meek shall *i.* their joy
Luke 17. 5. Lord, *i.* our faith
John 3. 30. he must *i.* but I decrease
1 Thes. 3. 12. Lord make you to *i.* in
2 Tim. 2. 16. will *i.* to more ungod.
Ezra 9. 6. iniquities are *increased*
Isa. 9. 3. multi. nation, not *i.* joy
Luke 2. 52. Jesus *i.* in wisdom and
Acts 6. 7. the word of God *i.* and
the
Rev. 3. 17. am rich and *i.* with goods
Eccl. 1. 18. *increaseth* knowledge
Isa. 40. 29. have no might, he *i.*
Col. 2. 19. whole body *i.* with the
1 Chron. 11. 9. David went on in *in-
creasing*
Col. 1. 10. *i.* in knowledge of God
R. V. Gen. 47. 34. ingathering ; Job
10. 16. exalteth ; Prov. 28. 8. aug
menteth ; Ps. 7. 23. ascendeth ;
Isa. 52. 1. made many ; Lam. 2. 5.
multiplied ; Luke 2. 52. advanced ;
2 Cor. 2. 15. groweth ; Rev. 3. 17.
have gotten
INCREDIBLE thing, Acts 26. 8.
INCURABLE wound, Job 34. 6.
Jer. 15. 18.
Mic. 1. 9. *i.* bruise, Jer. 30. 12, 15.
INDEED, 1 Kings 8. 27. 1 Chron. 4.
10. Matt. 3. 11. Luke 4. 24. John 1.
47. 4. 42. & 6. 55. & 8. 31, 36.
1 Tim. 5. 3, 5. 1 Pet. 2. 4.
INDIGNATION, Neh. 4. 1. Esth.
5. 9. Ps. 69. 24. & 78. 49. & 102. 10.
Isa. 10. 5. staff in their hand is my *i.*
26. 20. hide thee until *i.* be over.
Mic. 7. 9. I will bear the *i.* of Lord
Nah. 1. 6. who can stand before
his *i.*
Matt. 20. 24. moved with *i.*
Rom. 2. 8. *i.* and wrath, tribulation
2 Cor. 7. 11. yea, what *i.* yea, what
Heb. 10. 27. fiery *i.* which shall
Rev. 14. 10. poured into cup of his *i.*
R. V. 2 Kings 3. 27 ; Esth. 5. 9.
wrath ; Acts 5. 17. jealousy ; Isa.
10. 27. fierceness of fire ; Rev. 14.
10. anger
INDITING a good matter, Ps. 45. 1.
INDUSTRY, Gen. 2. 15. & 3. 23. Prov.
6. 6, 8. & 10. 4. & 12. 24. & 13. 4. & 21. 5.
& 22. 29. & 27. 23. Eph. 4. 28. 1 Thes.

4. 11. 2 Thes. 3. 12. Tit. 3. 14; re-
warded, Prov. 13. 11. & 31. 13.
INEXCUSABLE, O man, Rom.
2. 1.
INFALLIBLE proofs, many, Acts
1. 3.
INFANT, 1 Sam. 15. 3. Job 3. 16.
Isa. 65. 20. Hos. 13. 16. Luke 18. 15.
R. V. Luke 18. 15. their babes
INFIDEL, 2 Cor. 6. 15. 1 Tim. 5. 8.
INFINITE iniquities, Job 22. 5.
Ps. 147. 5. his understanding is i.
Nah. 3. 9. her strength, and it was i.
R. V. Job 22. 5. end
INFIRMITY, this is my i., Ps. 77. 10.
Prov. 18. 14. the spirit of a man
will sustain his i.
Matt. 8. 17. himself took our in-
firmities
Rom. 8. 26. the Spirit also helpeth
our i.
15. 1. strong ought to bear the i.
2 Cor. 12. 9. glory in my i.
10. pleasure in i.
1 Tim. 5. 23. drink wine for thine
often i.
Heb. 4. 15. with the feeling of our i.
R. V. Lev. 12. 2. her sickness;
Luke 7. 21; 2 Cor. 12. 5, 9, 10. weak-
nesses
INFLAME them, wine, Isa. 5. 11.
& 57. 5.
INFLICTED punishment, 2 Cor.
2. 6.
INFLUENCES of Pleiades, Job
38. 31.
INGATHERING, feast of, Ex. 23.
16. & 34. 22.
INGRAFTED word, receive, Jas.
1. 21.
INGRATITUDE to God, Rom. 1.
21.
INHABIT, Prov. 10. 30. Isa. 65. 21,
22.
Vs. 22. 3. thou that *inhabitest* the
praises of Israel
Isa. 57. 15. lofty One that *inhabiteth*
R. V. Prov. 10. 30; Jer. 48. 18. dwell
in; Lev. 16. 22. solitary land;
1 Chron. 5. 9; Zech. 12. 6; 14. 10,
11. dwell
INHERIT, Gen. 15. 8. Ps. 82. 8.
1 Sam. 2. 8. to make them i. throne
Ps. 25. 13. his seed shall i. earth
27. 11. the meek shall i. the earth,
Matt. 5. 5.
Ps. 37. 29. the righteous shall i. the
land, Isa. 60. 21.
Prov. 3. 35. wise shall i. glory; but
Matt. 19. 29. hath forsaken, shall i.
everlasting life
25. 34. i. king. prepared for you
Mark 10. 17. what shall I do that I
may i. eternal life, Luke 10. 25. &
18. 18.
1 Cor. 6. 9. unrighteous not i. the
kingdom of God, 10.
Gal. 5. 21. do such things not i. the
kingdom of God
Heb. 6. 12. through faith i. prom.
1 Pet. 3. 9. that ye should i. bless.
Rev. 21. 7. overcometh shall i. all
Num. 18. 20. I the Lord am thy in-
heritance, Deut. 10. 9. & 18. 2.
Ezek. 44. 28.
Deut. 4. 20. a people of i., 9, 20, 29.
& 32. 9. 1 Kings 8. 5. Ps. 28. 9. & 33.
12. & 68. 9. & 74. 2. & 78. 62, 71. & 79.
1. & 94. 14. & 106. 5, 40. Isa. 19. 25.
Jer. 10. 16. & 51. 19.
Ps. 16. 5. Lord is portion of mine i.
Prov. 19. 14. riches are i. of fathers
Eccl. 7. 11. wisdom is good with
an i.
Acts 20. 32. i. among the sanctified
Eph. 1. 11. among whom he ob-
tained an i.
14. earnest of our i. and purchased
5. 5. hath an i. in the kingdom
Col. 1. 12. partakers of i. of saints
3. 24. shall receive the reward of i.
Heb. 9. 15. receive the promise of
eternal i.
1 Pet. 1. 4. to an i. incorruptible

R. V. Isa. 54. 3; Jer. 8. 10; 49. 1.
possess; Josh. 13. 15, 24, 32 ——;
Job 31. 2; Eph. 1. 11. heritage;
Ezek. 22. 16. be profaned
INIQUITY, Gen. 15. 16. & 19. 15.
Ex. 20. 5. visiting i. of the fathers
34. 7. forgiving i. transgression
Lev. 26. 41. accept the punishment
of their i., 43.
Num. 23. 21. hath not beheld i.
Deut. 32. 4. a God of truth, without i.
Job 4. 8. they that plough i. reap
11. 6. less than thine i. deserveth
15. 16. man drinketh in i. like
22. 23. put away i. far from thee
34. 32. if I have done i. I will do
Ps. 32. 5. mine i. have I not hid
39. 11. with rebukes correct man
for i.
51. 5. behold I was shapen in i.
66. 18. if I regard i. in my heart
119. 3. they also do not i. they walk
Prov. 22. 8. that soweth i. shall
Eccl. 3. 16. place of righteousness.
i. was there
Isa. 1. 4. a people laden with i.
5. 18. woe to them that draw i.
27. 9. by this shall i. of Jacob
33. 24. people shall be forgiven
their i.
53. 6. Lord laid on him the i. of us
57. 17. for i. of his covetousness
59. 3. defiled your fingers with i.
Jer. 2. 5. what i. have your
3. 13. only acknowledge thine i.
31. 30. every one shall die for i.
50. 20. i. of Israel be sought for
Ezek. 3. 18. he shall die in his i.
18. 30. so i. shall not be your ruin
Dan. 9. 24. makes reconcilia. for i.
Hos. 14. 2. take away all i. and
Mic. 7. 18. a God like thee, that
pardoneth i.
Hab. 1. 13. Holy One canst not look
on i.
Matt. 7. 23. depart from me ye that
work i.
Acts 8. 23. in gall of bitterness and
bond of i.
Rom. 6. 19. servants to uncleanness
and to i. unto i.
1 Cor. 13. 6. charity rejoic. not in i.
2 Thes. 2. 7. mystery of i. already
2 Tim. 2. 19. that nameth Christ
depart from i.
Tit. 2. 14. he might redeem us from
all i.
Jas. 3. 6. tongue is a fire, a world
of i.
Ps. 18. 23. *my iniquity,* 25. 11. & 32.
5. & 38. 18. & 51. 2.
Job 34. 22. *workers of iniquity,* Ps.
5. 5. & 6. 8. & 14. 4. & 92. 7. Prov.
10. 29. & 21. 15. Luke 13. 27.
Lev. 16. 21. confess over him all
iniquities
26. 39. pine in their i. and i. of
Ezra 9. 6. our i. are increased
Neh. 9. 2. confessed the i. of
Job 13. 26. to possess i. of my youth
Ps. 38. 4. mine i. are gone over my
40. 12. mine i. have taken hold
51. 9. hide from my sins, blot out
my i.
79. 8. remember not against us
former i.
90. 8. thou hast set our i. before
103. 3. who forgiveth all thine i.
10. not rewarded us accord. to i.
130. 3. if thou, Lord, shouldest
mark i.
8. he shall redeem Israel from
all i.
Prov. 5. 22. his own i. shall take
Isa. 43. 24. hast wearied me with i.
53. 5. he was wounded, bruised
for i.
Jer. 14. 7. though our i. testify
Dan. 4. 27. break off thy i. by show.
Mic. 7. 19. he will subdue our i.
Acts 3. 26. bless you in turning
from i.
Rom. 4. 7. blessed are they whose i.

Rev. 18. 5. God hath remem. her i.
Isa. 53. 11. he shall bear *their iniquities*
Jer. 33. 8. I will cleanse them from
all — and I will pardon all —
Ezek. 43. 10. may be ashamed of —
Heb. 8. 12. their sins, and — will I
Num. 14. 34. shall ye bear *your iniquities*
Isa. 50. 1. for — have ye sold
59. 2. — have separated between
you and God
Jer. 5. 25. — turned away these
things
Ezek. 24. 23. ye shall pine away
for —
36. 31. loathe yourselves . . for —
33. I shall have cleansed you
from all —
Amos 3. 2. I will punish you for
all —
R. V. 1 Sam. 15. 23. idolatry; Job 6.
29, 30. injustice; Job 22. 23; 36. 23;
Ps. 37. 1; 119. 13; Jer. 2. 5; Ezek. 28.
15, 18; Mal. 2. 6; 1 Cor. 13. 6; 2 Tim.
2. 19. unrighteousness; Ps. 94. 20;
Eccl. 3. 16. wickedness; Dan. 9. 5.
perversely; Hab. 1. 13. perverse-
ness; 2 Thes. 2. 7. lawlessness;
Heb. 8. 12 ——; 2 Pet. 2. 16. transgression
INJURED me, ye have not, Gal.
4. 12.
1 Tim. 1. 13. was a persecutor and
injurious
INJUSTICE, Ex. 22. 21. & 23. 6.
Lev. 19. 15. Deut. 16. 19. & 24. 17.
Job 31. 13. Ps. 82. 2. Prov. 22. 16.
& 29. 7. Jer. 22. 3. Luke 16. 10.
results of, Prov. 11. 7. & 28. 8. Mic.
6. 10. Amos 5. 11. & 8. 5. 1 Thes. 4.
6. 2 Pet. 2. 9.
INK, 2 John 12. 3 John 13.
INNER, 1 Kings 6. 27. Eph. 3. 16.
R. V. Eph. 3. 16. inward
INNOCENT, Ps. 19. 13. Prov. 28.
20.
Gen. 20. 5. in *innocency* of hands
Ps. 6. 6. wash my hands in i., 73. 13.
Dan. 6. 22. before him i. was
Hos. 8. 5. how long ere they at. i.
R. V. Ps. 19. 3. clear; Prov. 6. 29;
28. 20. unpunished
INNUMERABLE, Job 21. 33. Ps.
40. 12. Luke 12. 1. Heb. 11. 12. & 12.
22.
INORDINATE, Ezek. 23. 11. Col.
3. 5.
R. V. *passion;* Col. 3. 5. unclean-
ness, i. affection
INQUISITION, Deut. 19. 18. Ps.
9. 12.
INSCRIPTION to unknown God,
Acts 17. 23.
INSPIRATION, Job 32. 8. 2 Tim.
3. 16.
R. V. Job 32. 8. breath; 2 Tim. 3.
16. inspired
INSTANT, Isa. 29. 5. & 30. 13. Jer.
18. 7. Rom. 12. 12. 2 Tim. 4. 2. Acts
12. 5.
Luke 7. 4. besought him *instantly*
Acts 26. 7. i. serving God day and
R. V. Luke 2. 38. very hour; Rom.
12. 12. earnestly
INSTRUCT, Deut. 4. 36. & 32. 10.
Neh. 9. 20. thy good Spirit to i. them
Job 40. 2. contendeth with the Al-
mighty i.
16. 7. my reins i. me in the night
32. 8. I will i. thee, and teach
S. of S. 8. 2. moth. who would i. me
Isa. 28. 26. his God doth i. him
Dan. 11. 33. that under. shall i.
1 Cor. 2. 16. Lord that he may i. him
Ps. 2. 10. be i. ye judges of earth
Matt. 13. 52. every scribe, i. unto
Phil. 4. 12. in all things I am i. both
2 Tim. 2. 25. in meekness i. those
Rom. 2. 20. an *instructor* of foolish
1 Cor. 4. 15. have ten thousand i.
Job 33. 16. sealeth their *instruction*
Ps. 50. 17. hatest i. and castest my

Prov. 4. 13. take fast hold of *i*. keep
5. 12. how have I hated *i*.
19. 27. cease to hear *i*. that causeth
23. 12. apply thy heart to *i*. and
2 Tim. 3. 16. profitable for *i*. in
R. V. Deut. 32. 10. cared for;
2 Chron. 3. 3. laid; Job 40. 2. contend with Almighty; Matt. 13. 52. hath been made a disciple; 14. 8. put forward by; Phil.4. 12.learned the secret; 2 Tim. 2. 25. correcting; Prov. 10. 17; 12. 1; 13. 18; 15, 32; 16. 22; Zeph. 3. 7. correction

INSTRUMENTS of cruelty, Gen. 49. 5.
Ps. 7. 13. prepared for him *i*. of
Rom. 6. 13. neither yield members *i*. of unrighteousness; but *i*. of righteousness to God
Isa. 32. 7. the *i*. of the churl are
R. V. Gen. 49. 5; Isa. 54. 16. weapon; Ex. 25. 9; Num. 3. 8; 7. 1; 2 Sam. 24. 22. furniture; Num. 4. 12; 31. 6; 1 Chron. 9. 20; 28. 14; 2 Chron. 4. 16; 5. 1. vessels; Ps. 68. 25. minstrels; 87. 7. that dance; 33. 2; 144. 9 ——

INTANGLE, Matt. 22. 15. Gal. 5. 1.
2 Tim. 2. 4. 2 Pet. 2. 20.

INTEGRITY of my heart, Gen. 20. 5.
Job 2. 3. still he holdeth fast his *i*.
27. 5. I will not remove mine *i*.
Ps. 7. 8. according to my *i*. that is
25. 21. let *i*. and uprightness
26. 1. I have walked in mine *i*.
Prov. 11. 3. *i*. of upright shall guide

INTERCESSION, Jer. 7. 16. & 27. 18.
Isa. 53. 12. made *i*. for transgressors.
Rom. 8. 26. Spirit maketh *i*. for us, 27.
34. who also maketh *i*. for
11. 2. Elias maketh *i*. to God
1 Tim. 2. 1. prayers and *i*. be made
Heb. 7. 25. he ever liveth to make *i*.
Isa. 59. 16. wondered there was no *intercessor*
R. V. Rom. 11. 2. pleadeth with

INTERMEDDLE, Prov. 14. 10. & 18. 1.
R. V. Prov. 18. 1. rageth against

INTERPRETATION, Gen. 40. 5. & 41. 11. Judg. 7. 15. Dan. 2. 4, 7, 36. 1 Cor. 12. 10. & 14. 26. 2 Pet. 1. 20.
Job 33. 23. *interpreter* one among
R. V. 1. 6. a figure

INTREAT, Gen. 12. 16. & 23. 8. Ex. 8. 8. & 9. 28. & 10. 17. Jer. 15. 11.
1 Sam. 2. 25. man sin, who shall *i*.
1 Cor. 4. 13. we suffer; being defamed we *i*.
1 Tim. 5. 1. but *i*. him as a father
Jas. 3. 17. gentle and easy to be *intreated*
Prov. 18. 23. the poor useth *intreaties*
2 Cor. 8. 4. praying us with much *i*.
R. V. Job 19. 17. my supplication;
Phil. 4. 3. beseech; 1 Tim. 5. 1. exhort

INTRUDING into those things, Col. 2. 18.

INVENT, Amos 6. 5. Rom. 1. 30.
Ps. 99. 8. tookest vengeance of their *inventions*
106. 28. provoked him with their *i*.
Prov. 8. 12. find out knowledge of witty *i*.
Eccl. 7. 29. men have sought many *i*.
R. V. Ps. 99. 8; 106. 29, 39. doings;
Prov. 8. 12. and discretion

INVISIBLE, Rom. 1. 20. Col. 1. 15, 16. 1 Tim. 1. 17. Heb. 11. 27.

INWARD friends abhorred me, Job 19. 19.
Ps. 5. 9. *inward part*, 51. 6. Prov. 20. 27. Jer. 31. 33. Luke 11. 39.
Rom. 7. 22. *inward man*, 2 Cor. 4. 16.
2 Cor. 7. 15. *inward affection* is
Ps. 62. 4. curse *inwardly*

Matt. 7. 15. *i*. wolves
Rom. 2. 29. he is a Jew that is one *i*.

IRON sharpeneth iron, Prov. 27. 17.
Eccl. 10. 10. if the *i*. be blunt, put
Isa. 48. 4. neck is an *i*. sinew, and
Jer. 15. 12. shall *i*. break northern *i*.
Dan. 2. 33. legs of *i*. his feet *i*. and
4. 23. even with a band of *i*. and
1 Tim. 4. 2. conscience seared with hot *i*.

ISSUES from death, Ps. 68. 20.
Prov. 4. 23. out of the heart are the *i*. of life
R. V. Lev. 12. 7. fountain; Matt. 22. 23. seed

ITCHING ears, 2 Tim. 4. 3.

IVORY, 1 Kings 10. 18. & 22. 39.
Ps.45. 8. S. of S. 5.14. & 7.4. Ezek. 27. 6. Amos 3. 15. & 6. 4. Rev. 18. 12.

J

JAW-BONE of an ass, Samson uses, Judg. 15. 15; water flows from, 15. 19.

JEALOUS God, I am a, Ex. 20. 5. & 34. 14. Deut. 5. 9. & 6. 15. Josh. 24. 19.
1 Kings 19. 10. I have been very *j*.
Ezek. 39. 25. be *j*. for my holy
Joel 2. 18. will Lord be *j*. for land
Nah. 1. 2. God is *j*. and the Lord
Zech. 1. 14. I am *j*. for Jerusalem
2 Cor. 11. 2. *j*. over you with godly *jealousy*
Deut. 29. 20. Lord's *j*. shall smoke
Ps. 79. 5. shall thy *j*. burn like fire
Prov. 6. 34. *j*. is the rage of a man
S. of S. 8. 6. *j*. is cruel as the grave
Rom. 10. 19. provoke you to *j*.
1 Cor. 10. 22. do we provoke Lord to *j*.

JEHOVAH, Ex. 6. 3. Ps. 83. 18. Isa. 12. 2. & 26. 4. Gen. 22. 14. Ex. 17. 15.
Judg. 6. 24. it is about 2000 times translated Lord, in capitals

JERUSALEM, for the church, Isa. 24. 23. & 62. 1. & 65. 18. Jer. 3. 17. Joel 2. 32. & 3. 16, 17. Zech. 12. 10. & 8. 22. Gal. 4. 25, 26. Heb. 12. 22. Rev. 3. 12. & 21. 2.

JESHURUN, i. e. Israel, Deut. 32. 15. & 33. 5, 26. Isa. 44. 2.

JESTING, evil, censured, Eph. 5. 4.

JESUS, or Joshua, Acts 7. 45. Heb. 4. 8.

JESUS the Saviour of men, Matt. 1. 21. & 2. 1. & 8. 29. & 14. 1. & 27. 37. 1 Cor. 12. 3. 2 Cor. 4. 5. Eph. 4. 21. Heb. 2. 9. & 12. 2. Rev. 22. 16. and in about 650 other places

JEWELS, I make up my, Mal. 3. 17.
R. V. 2 Chron. 32. 27. vessels; S. of S. 1. 10. hair; Ezek. 16. 12. ring

JEWS first, and also Greeks, Rom. 1. 16. & 2. 9, 10, 28. not a *J*. which is one outwardly, but is a *J*. which is one inwardly, 29.
Rom. 10. 12. no difference between *J*. and Greek
1 Cor. 9. 20. to *J*. I became as a *J*. to gain *J*.
Gal. 3. 28. neither *J*. nor Greek
Rev. 2. 9. say they are *J*. and are

JOIN, Ex. 1. 10. Ezra 9. 14.
Prov. 11. 21. though hand *j*. in
Isa. 5. 8. woe to them that *j*. house
Jer. 50. 5. let us *j*. ourselves to Lord
Acts 5. 13. of the rest durst no man *j*. himself
9. 26. assayed to *j*. himself to the
Hos. 4. 17. Ephraim is *joined* to idols
Num. 25. 3. Israel *j*. himself to Ba.
Eccl. 9. 4. *j*. to all living there is
Zech. 2. 11. many nat. shall be *j*.
Matt. 19.6. what God hath *j*. let not

---

1 Cor. 1. 10. be perfectly *j*. together
6. 17. he that is *j*. to the Lord is
Eph. 5. 31. shall be *j*. to his wife
Col. 2. 19. all the body by *joints* and bands
Heb. 4. 12. dividing asunder of *j*.
R. V. Ex. 4. 12. repaired; Isa. 9. 11. stir up; Gen. 14. 8. set in array;
Ezra 4. 12. repaired; Job 3. 6. rejoice; Ezek. 46. 22. inclosed; 1 Cor. 1. 10. perfected; Eph. 4. 16. framed; 5. 31. cleave to; Gen. 32. 25. strained

JOURNEY, Num. 9. 13. Rom. 1. 10.
R. V. Num. 33. 12; Deut. 10. 6. journeyed; Mark 13. 34. sojourning in another country; Rom. 1. 10 ——

JOY, 1 Chron. 12. 40. 2 Chron. 20. 27.
Neh. 8. 10. *j*. of Lord is your strength
Esth. 8. 17. the Jews had *j*. and
Job 20. 5. *j*. of the hypocrite is
Ps. 16. 11. in thy presence is fulness of *j*.
30. 5. but *j*. cometh in the morn.
51. 8. make me hear *j*. and glad.
12. restore to me *j*. of thy salva.
126. 5. who sow in tears shall reap in *j*.
Eccl. 9. 7. eat thy bread with *j*.
Isa. 9. 3. hast not increased the *j*.
12. 3. with *j*. shall draw water out
35. 10. with songs and everlast. *j*.
61. 3. give them the oil of *j*. for
7. everlasting *j*. shall be to them
66. 5. shall appear to your *j*.
Zeph. 3. 17. the Lord will *j*. over
Matt. 2. 10. rejoiced with exceeding great *j*.
13. 20. hear the word and with *j*.
25. 21. enter into *j*. of thy Lord
Luke 1. 44. babe leaped in my womb for *j*.
15. 7. *j*. shall be in heaven over
24. 41. while they believe not for *j*.
John 15. 11. that your *j*. might be
16. 20. your sorrow be turn. into *j*.
22. your *j*. no man taketh from
Acts 20. 24. finish my course with *j*.
Rom. 14. 17. righteousness and peace and *j*. in the Holy Ghost
2 Cor. 1. 24. we are help. of your *j*.
Gal. 5. 22. fruit of the Spirit is love, *j*.
Phil. 4. 1. brethren, my *j*. and crown
1 Thes. 1. 6. receive word with *j*. of
Heb. 12. 12. who for the *j*. set be.
Jas. 1. 2. count it all *j*. when ye
1 Pet. 1. 8. rejoice with *j*. unspeak.
4. 13. rejoice, be glad with exceeding *j*.
1 John 1. 4. we write that your *j*.
Col. 2. 5. *joying* and beholding
Heb. 12. 11. no chastening is *joyous*
Ezra 6. 22. the Lord hath made them *joyful*
Ps. 35. 9. my soul shall be *j*. in Lord
63. 5. I will praise thee with *j*. lips
89. 15. blessed they that know *j*.
Eccl. 7. 14. in day of prosper. be *j*.
Isa. 56. 7. make them *j*. in my
61. 10. my soul shall be *j*. in God
2 Cor. 7. 4. exceeding *j*. in all our tribulations
Deut. 28. 47. servedst not the Lord with *joyfulness*
Col. 1. 11. patience and long-suffering with *j*.
Eccl. 9 9. live *joyfully* with the wife
R. V. Job 41. 22. terror danceth:
Jer. 48. 27. the head; Acts 2. 28. gladness; Rom. 5. 11. rejoice; Ps. 96. 12; 149. 5. exult; 98. 8. sing for;
Col. 1. 11. joy

JUDGE, Deut. 17. 9. & 25. 2.
Gen. 18. 25. shall not the *J*. of earth
Ex. 2. 14. who made thee a *j*.
Judg. 11. 27. Lord the *J*. be *j*. this

1 Sam. 2. 25. the *j.* shall *j.* him;
Isa. 33. 22. Lord is our *j.* and our
Ps. 68. 5. father of fatherless and *j.*
75. 7. God is the *j.* he putteth
Luke 12. 14. who made me a *j.* over
Acts 10. 42. to be the *J.* of quick
2 Tim. 4. 8. Lord the righteous *J.*
Heb. 12. 23. are come to God the *J.*
Jas. 5. 9. the *J.* standeth before
Gen. 16. 5. Lord *j.* between me and
Deut. 32. 36. the Lord shall *j.* his
  people, Ps. 135. 14. Heb. 10. 30.
Ps. 7. 8. Lord shall *j.* the people
9. 8. the Lord shall *j.* the world in
  righteous. 96. 13. & 98. 9. Acts 17. 31.
Mic. 3. 11. heads thereof *j.* for re.
Matt. 7. 1. *j.* not that ye be not jud.
John 5. 30. as I hear I *j.* and my
12. 47. I came not to *j.* the world
Acts 23. 3. sittest thou to *j.* me
Rom. 2. 16. when God shall *j.* the
  3. 6. then how shall God *j.* the
  world
14. 10. why dost thou *j.* thy brother
1 Cor. 4. 3. I *j.* not mine own self
5. *j.* nothing before the time, until
11. 31. if we would *j.* ourselves, we
14. 29. let the prophets speak, and
  others *j.*
Col. 2. 16. let no man *j.* you in meat
2 Tim. 4. 1. who shall *j.* the quick
Jas. 4. 11. if ye *j.* the law
Ps. 51. 4. *judgest,* Rom. 14. 4. Jas.
  4. 12.
7. 11. God *judgeth* the righteous
John 5. 22. the Father *j.* no man
1 Cor. 2. 15. he that is spiritual *j.*
Matt. 19. 28. *judging* twelve tribes
Deut. 1. 17. the *judgment* is God's
32. 4. all his ways are *j.* a God of
Ps. 1. 5. the ungodly shall not stand
  in the *j.*
9. 16. the Lord is known by the *j.*
101. 1. I will sing of mercy and *j.*
119. 66. teach me good *j.* for
143. 2. enter not into *j.* with thy
Prov. 21. 15. it is joy to just to do *j.*
29. 26. every man's *j.* cometh from
Eccl. 11. 9. God will bring into *j.*
Isa. 1. 27. Zion shall be redeemed
  with *j.*
28. 17. *j.* also will I lay to the line
30. 18. Lord is a God of *j.*
42. 1. shall bring forth *j.* to the
53. 8. was taken from prison and *j.*
61. 8. I the Lord love *j.* and hate
Jer. 5. 1. if there be any that exe-
  cuteth *j.*
8. 7. they know not the *j.* of Lord
Dan. 4. 37. all whose ways are *j.*
7. 22. *j.* was given to the saints
Hos. 12. 6. keep mercy and *j.* wait
Amos 5. 7. who turn *j.* to worm.
24. let. *j.* run down as waters, and
Matt. 5. 21. be in danger of the *j.*
12. 20. till he send forth *j.* unto
  victory
John 5. 22. Father committed all *j.*
27. given him author. to execute *j.*
9. 39. for *j.* I am come into the
16. 8. he will reprove the world of
  sin and *j.*
Acts 24. 25. he reasoned of *j.* to
  come
Rom. 5. 18. *j.* came on all men to
14. 10. must all stand before *j.* seat
Heb. 9. 27. all men once to die, but
  after this the *j.*
1 Pet. 4. 17. *j.* must begin at house
Jude 15. to execute *j.* upon all
Rev. 17. 1. show thee *j.* of great
Ps. 19. 9. *judgments* of Lord are
36. 6. thy *j.* are a great deep
119. 75. I know that thy *j.* are
108. O Lord, teach me thy *j.*
Isa. 26. 8. in the way of thy *j.* we
9. when thy *j.* are in the earth
Jer. 12. 1. let me talk with thee of *j.*
Rom. 11. 33. how unsearchable are
  his *j.*
R. V. 1 Sam. 2. 25. God; Job 9. 15.
  mine adversary; 1 Sam. 24. 15.
  give sentence; Jer. 5. 28. plead;
  Ezek. 24. 23. fall; 1 Cor. 6. 5. decide;

11. 31; 14. 29. discern; Heb. 11. 11.
  counted; Acts 24. 6; Jas. 4. 12——;
  Job 29. 14. justice; Ps. 76. 8; Acts
  25. 15; 2 Pet. 2. 3. sentence; Judg.
  5. 10. on rich carpets; Phil. 1. 9.
  discernment; Mark 6. 11——
JUST man was Noah, Gen. 6. 9.
Lev. 19. 36. *j.* balance, *j.* weights
Deut. 16. 20. that which is *j.* shalt
32. 4. a God of truth, *j.* and right
2 Sam. 23. 3. ruleth over men must
  be *j.*
Neh. 9. 33. *j.* in all that is brought
Job 4. 17. shall man be more *j.* than
9. 2. how should man be *j.* with
Prov. 4. 18. path of *j.* is as shining
10. 6. blessings are on head of *j.*
11. 1. but a *j.* weight is his delight
12. 21. no evil shall happen to *j.*
17. 26. to punish the *j.* is not good
20. 7. a *j.* man walketh in integrity
21. 15. it is joy to *j.* to do judgment
24. 16. *j.* man falleth seven times
Eccl. 7. 15. *j.* man that perisheth in
20. there is not a *j.* man on earth
Isa. 26. 7. way of the *j.* is upright.
45. 21. none beside me; a *j.* God
Hab. 2. 4. *j.* shall live by his faith
Zeph. 3. 5. the *j.* Lord is in the
Zech. 9. 9. he is *j.* and having sal.
Matt. 1. 19. Joseph being a *j.* man
5. 45. sendeth rain on the *j.* and
Luke 15. 7. more than over ninety-
  nine *j.* persons
John 5. 30. my judgment is *j.*
Acts 7. 52. showed coming of *j.* one
24. 15. resurrection both of *j.* and
Rom. 2. 13. not the hearers of the
  law are *j.*
3. 26. he might be *j.* and justifier
7. 12. commandment holy, *j.* and
Phil. 4. 8. whatsoever things are
  true, *j.* pure
Col. 4. 1. give that which is *j.* and
Heb. 2. 2. received a *j.* recompense
12. 23. the spirits of *j.* men made
1 John 1. 9. he is faithful and *j.* to
Rev. 15. 3. *j.* and true are thy ways
Mic. 6. 8. to do *justly,* and love
Luke 23. 41. we indeed *j.* for we
1 Thes. 2. 10. how *j.* we behaved
Gen. 18. 19. to do *justice* and
Ps. 89. 14. *j.* and judgment are the
Prov. 8. 15. by me princes decree *j.*
Jer. 31. 23. O habitation of *j.*
Ezek. 45. 9. execute judg. and *j.*
R. V. For most part, righteous;
  Ps. 89. 14; Isa. 9. 7; 56. 1; 59. 9, 14.
  righteousness; 1 Thes. 2. 10. right-
  eously
JUSTIFY not the wicked, Ex. 23. 7.
Deut. 25. 1. they shall *j.* righteous
Job 9. 20. if I *j.* myself, my mouth
27. 5. God forbid that I should *j.*
33. 32. speak, for I desire to *j.* thee
Isa. 5. 23. woe to them that *j.* the
Luke 10. 29. he, willing to *j.* himself
16. 15. ye are they which *j.* your.
Rom. 3. 30. God shall *j.* circumci.
Gal. 3. 8. God would *j.* heathen
Job 11. 2. should a man full of talk
  be *justified*
13. 18. I know I shall be *j.*
25. 4. can a man be *j.* with God
Ps. 51. 4. mightest be *j.* when thou
143. 2. in thy sight shall no man
  living be *j.*
Isa. 43. 9. that they may be *j.*, 26.
Jer. 3. 11. hath *j.* herself more
Ezek. 16. 51. *j.* thy sisters in all
Matt. 11. 19. wisdom is *j.* of child.
12. 37. by thy words thou shalt be *j.*
Luke 7. 29. *j.* God, being baptized
18. 14. went away *j.* rather than
Acts 13. 39. are *j.* from all things
Rom. 2. 13. doers of law shall be *j.*
3. 4. might be *j.* in thy sayings
20. there shall no flesh be *j.* in his
24. being *j.* freely by his grace
28. man is *j.* by faith without
4. 2. if Abraham were *j.* by works
5. 1. being *j.* by faith, we have
9. being *j.* by his blood, be saved

Rom. 8. 30. whom he *j.* them he also
1 Cor. 4. 4. yet am I not hereby *j.*
6. 11. ye are *j.* in name of the Lord
Gal. 2. 16. not *j.* by works of the law
3. 11. no man is *j.* by the law
24. that we might be *j.* by faith
1 Tim. 3. 16. God manifest in flesh,
  j. in Spirit
Tit. 3. 7. that being *j.* by his grace
Jas. 2. 21. was not Abraham *j.* by
24. by works a man is *j.* not faith
25. was not Rahab *j.* by works
Prov. 17. 15. he that *justifieth* the
  wicked
Isa. 50. 8. he is near, that *j.* me
Rom. 4. 5. God that *j.* the ungodly
8. 33. it is God that *j.* who is he
3. 26. the *justifier* of him that
1 Kings 8. 32. condemning the
  wicked and *justifying* the righteous, 2 Chron. 6. 23.
Rom. 4. 25. raised for our *justifica-
  tion*
5. 16. gift is of many offences
  unto *j.*
18. free gift came on all men, to *j.*
R. V. Job 13. 18. am righteous; 25.
  4. just; Job 9. 20; 13. 18. righteous

K

KEEP, Gen. 2. 15. & 33. 9.
Gen. 18. 19. they shall *k.* the way
28. 15. I am with thee and will *k.*
Ex. 23. 7. *k.* thee far from a false
20. I send an angel to *k.* thee in
Num. 6. 24. the Lord bless thee,
  and *k.* thee
Deut. 23. 9. *k.* thee from every
29. 9. *k.* words of this covenant
1 Sam. 2. 9. he will *k.* the feet of
1 Chron. 4. 10. thou wouldst *k.* me
Ps. 17. 8. *k.* me as the apple of the
  eye
25. 10. to such as *k.* his covenant
20. *k.* my soul
89. 28. my mercy will I *k.* for
91. 11. angels to *k.* thee in all
103. 9. not chide nor *k.* his anger
119. 2. *k.* his testimonies, 33, 129,
  146; *k.* thy precepts, 4, 63, 69, 100; *k.*
  his statutes, 119. 33; *k.* his word
  and law, 17, 34, 57, 106, 136.
127. 1. except the Lord *k.* the city
140. 4. *k.* me, O Lord, from the
141. 3. *k.* the door of my lips
Eccl. 5. 1. *k.* thy foot when thou
Isa. 26. 3. Lord will *k.* him in per.
27. 3. I the Lord *k.* it; I will *k.* it
Jer. 3. 12. I will not *k.* anger for
Hos. 12. 6. *k.* mercy and judgmen.
Mic. 7. 5. *k.* the door of thy mouth
Mal. 2. 7. priest's lips *k.* knowledge
Luke 11. 28. hear the word of God
  and *k.* it
John 12. 25. he that hateth his life
  shall *k.* it
14. 23. if man love me, will *k.* my
17. 11. holy Father, *k.* through
15. thou shouldest *k.* them from
1 Cor. 5. 8. let us *k.* the feast, not
11. not to *k.* company with such
9. 27. I *k.* under my body, and
Phil. 4. 7. peace of God shall *k.*
1 Tim. 5. 22. *k.* thyself pure
6. 20. *k.* that is committed to thy
2 Tim. 1. 12. able to *k.* that which
  is
Jas. 1. 27. *k.* himself unspotted
Jude 21. *k.* yoursel. in love of God
24. who is able to *k.* you from
Rev. 1. 3. blessed are they that
  hear and *k.*
3. 10. I will *k.* thee from the hour
22. 9. thy brethren which *k.* say.
Lev. 26. 3. if ye *keep* my command
  ments
Deut. 6. 7. diligently—always
13. 4. — his — and obey his voice
Ps. 119. 60. I delayed not to—thy—
Prov. 4. 4.— my —and live, 7. 2.
Eccl. 12. 13. fear God and—his—

Matt. 19. 17. **if** ye will enter into
life – the –
John 14. 15. if ye love me – my –
1 John 2. 3. we know him, if we –
his –
5. 3. this is tne love of God that
we – his –
Rev. 14. 12. here are they that –
the –
Judg. 3. 19. *keep silence*, Ps. 35. 22.
& 50. 3, 21. & 83. 1. Eccl. 3. 7. Isa.
41. 1. & 62. 6. & 65. 6. Lam. 2. 10.
Amos 5. 13. Hab. 2. 20. 1 Cor. 14.
28, 34.
1 Kings 8. 23. who *keepest* covenant
and nier., 2 Chron. 6.14. Neh. 9. 32.
Deut. 7. 9. which *keepeth* covenant
Ps. 121. 3. he that *k.* thee will not
146. 6. which *k.* truth for ever
Prov. 13. 3. he that *k.* his mouth *k.*
29. 18. he that *k.* the law, happy
1 John 5. 18. that is of God *k.* him.
Rev. 16. 15. blessed is he that *k.*
22. 7. blessed is he that *k.* his
Ex. 34. 7. *keeping* mercy for thous.
Ps. 19. 11. in *k.* of them there is
Dan. 9. 4. *k.* thecovenantand mercy
1 Pet. 4. 19. commit the *k.* of their
Ps. 121. 5. the Lord is thy *keeper*
Eccl. 12. 3. when *k.* of house shall
S. of S. 1. 6. made me *k.* of vine.
5. 7. *k.* took away my veil from
me
Tit. 2. 5. chaste, *k.* at home, good
Deut. 32. 10. *k.* them as the apple
33. 9. they *kept* thy-covenant
Josh. 14. 10. Lord hath *k.* me alive
2 Sam. 22. 22. *k.* ways of the Lord
23. *k.* myself from mine iniquity
Job 23. 11. his ways have I *k.* and
Ps. 17. 4. *k.* me from paths of the
30. 3. *k.* me alive, that I go not
S. of S. 1. 6. mine own vineyard
have I not *k.*
Matt. 19. 20. these have I *k.* from
Luke 2. 19. Mary *k.* all these things
John 15. 20. if they have *k.* my say.
17. 6. they have *k.* thy word
12. all thou gavest me, I have *k.*
Rom. 16. 25. *k.* secret since the
world
2 Tim. 4. 7. I have *k.* the faith
1 Pet. 1. 5. *k.* by the power of God
Rev. 3. 8. hast *k.* my word, and not
R. V. Deut. 5. 1, 12; 23. 23; 1 Chron.
28. 8; Ps. 105. 45; 119. 5, 8, 44, 57, 60,
63, 88. observe; Acts 12. 4; Phil. 4.
7; 2 Thes. 3. 3; 1 Tim. 6. 20; 2 Tim.
1. 12; 1 John 5. 21; Jude 24. guard;
Matt. 28. 4. watchers; Acts 12. 6;
12. 19. guards; 16. 27. jailor; Tit. 2.
5. workers
KERCHIEFS, woe respecting,
Ezek. 13. 18.
KEY of house of David, Isa. 22.
22. Rev. 3. 7.
Matt. 16. 19. *k.* of the kingdom of
Luke 11. 52. taken away the *k.* of
Rev. 1. 18. I have *k.* of hell
9. 1. *k.* of the bottomless pit
KICK, Deut. 32. 15. 1 Sam. 2. 29.
Acts 9. 5. & 26. 14.
KID, Isa. 11. 6. Luke 15. 29.
8. of S. 1. 8. feed *k.* beside sheph.
R. V. In Gen. Lev. Num. and Ezek.
mostly he-goat, or goat
KIDNEYS, for sacrifices, burnt,
Ex. 29. 13. Lev. 3. 4.
– of wheat, fat of, Deut. 32. 14.
KILL, thou shalt not, Ex. 20. 13.
Deut. 32. 39. I *k.* and I make alive
2 Kings 5. 7. I am God to *k.* and
Eccl. 3. 8. time to *k.* and to heal
Matt. 10. 28. fear not them which *k.*
the body, but are not able to *k.*
Mark 3. 4. lawful to save life, or *k.*
Acts 10. 13. rise, Peter, *k.* and eat
1 Kings 21. 19. hast thou *killed* and
Ps. 44. 22. we are *k.* all day long
Luke 12. 5. after he hath *k.* hath
Acts 3. 15. t. the Prince of Life
2 Cor. 6. 9. we are chast. and not *k.*
1 Thes. 2. 15. both *k.* the Lord
Rev. 13. 10. that *k.* with the sword

Matt. 23. 37. thou that *killest* the
prophets, Luke 13. 34.
1 Sam. 2. 6. the Lord *killeth*, and
John 16. 2. who *k.* you will think
2 Cor. 3. 6. letter *k.* but spirit
R. V. Ex. 20. 13; Deut. 5. 17; Matt.
19. 18. do no murder; Num. 35. 27;
1 Sam. 19. 1; 2 Kings 11. 15; Acts
23. 15; Rev. 6. 4. slay; Mark 14. 12;
Luke 22. 7. sacrificed
KIND, Gen. 1. 11. 1 Chron. 16. 7.
Luke 6. 35. he is *k.* to unthankful
1 Cor. 13. 4. charity suff. long . is *k.*
Eph. 4. 32. be *k.* to one another
1 Sam. 20. 14. show me the *kindness*
2 Sam. 9. 3. may show the *k.* of God
16. 17. is this thy *k.* to thy friend
Neh. 9. 17. a God slow to anger and
of great *k.*
Ps. 117. 2. his merciful *k.* is great
Prov. 19. 22. the des. of man is his *k.*
31. 26. in her tongue is law of *k.*
Isa. 54. 8. with everlasting *k.* will
10. my *k.* shall not depart from
Jer. 2. 2. I remember thee, the *k.*
Joel 2. 13. God is of great *k.*
Col. 3. 12. put on bowels of mer., *k.*
2 Pet. 1. 7. to godliness, brother. *k.*
Ps. 25. 6. remember thy *loving
kindness*
36. 7. how excellent is thy –
63. 3. thy – is better than life
103. 4. who crowneth thee with –
Isa. 63. 7. I will mention the – of
Jer. 9. 24. I am the Lord which
exercise –
32. 18. thou showest – to thous.
Hos. 2. 19. I will betroth thee in –
R. V. Matt. 11. 21 –
KINDLE, Prov. 26. 21. Isa. 10. 16.
Isa. 30. 33. breath of Lord doth *k.*
it
Hos.11.8. my repentings are *kindled*
2 Sam. 22. 9. coals *k.* by it, Ps. 18. 8.
Ps. 2. 12. when his wrath is *k.* but a
Isa. 50. 11. walk in light of sparks
ye have *k.*
Luke 12. 49. fire on earth, what if
it be already *k.*
R. V. Prov. 26. 21. inflame; Jer. 33.
18. burn; Jas. 3. 5. much wood is
kindled by how small a fire
KING, Gen. 14. 18. & 36. 31.
Job 18. 14. bring him to *k.* of ter.
34. 18. is it fit to say to a *k.* thou
Ps. 10. 16. Lord is *K.* for ever and
24. 7. the *K.* of glory shall come
33. 16. no *k.* saved by multitude
47. 7. God is *K.* of all the earth
74. 12. God is my *k.*, 5. 2. & 44. 4.
Prov. 30. 31. a *k.* against whom is
Eccl. 5. 9. *k.* himself is served by
8. 4. where word of *k.* is there
S. of S. 1. 4. the *k.* brought me into
12. while the *k.* sitteth at his table
7. 5. the *k.* is held in the galleries
Isa. 32. 1. a *k.* shall reign in
33. 22. the Lord is our lawgiver
and our *k.*
43. 15. Creator of Israel, your *K.*
Jer. 10. 10. Lord is true God, and
everlasting *K.*
23. 5. a *K.* shall reign and prosper
46. 18. saith the *K.* whose name
Hos. 3. 5. seek the Lord and David
their *k.*
7. 5. in day of our *k.* the princes
13. 11. I gave them a *k.* in anger
Matt. 25. 34. then shall the *K.* say
Luke 23. 2. he himself is Christ, a *k.*
John 6. 15. come by force to make
him *k.*
19. 14. behold your *k.*
15. no *k.* but Cæsar
1 Tim. 1. 17. to the *K.* eternal
6. 15. *K.* of kings, and Lord of
lords, Rev. 16. 16. & 17. 14.
1 Pet. 2. 17. fear God, honor *k.*, 16.
Rev. 15. 3. just and true, thou *K.*
Ps. 76. 12. terrible to *kings* of the
earth, 72. 11.
102. 15. *k.* of the earth see thy glory
144. 10. that giveth salva. to *k.*
149. 8. to bind their *k.* with fetters

Prov. 8. 15. by me *k.* reign, and
Hos. 8. 4. they set up *k.* but not by
Matt. 11. 8. soft clothing are in *k.*
houses
Luke 22. 25. *k.* of Gentiles exercise
1 Cor. 4. 8. reigned as *k.* without us
1 Tim. 2. 2. give thanks for *k.* and
Rev. 1. 6. made us *k.* and priests
16. 12. that way of *k.* of the east
Ex. 19. 6. be a *kingdom* of priests
1 Sam. 10. 25. Samuel told man. of *k.*
1 Chron. 29. 11. thine is the *k.* O
Lord, Matt. 6. 13.
Ps. 22. 28. for the *k.* is the Lord's
Dan. 2. 44. in last days shall God
set up a *k.*
7. 27. whose *k.* is everlasting *k.*, 14.
Matt. 12. 25. every *k.* divided
38. good seed are the children of *k.*
25. 34. inherit *k.* prepared for you
Mark 11. 10. blessed be the *k.* of
Luke 12. 32. Father's pleasure to
give you the *k.*
19. 12. to receive for himself a *k.*
John 18. 36. *k.* is not of this world
1 Cor. 15. 24. shall have delivered
up the *k.*
Col. 1. 13. translated us into the *k.*
2 Tim. 4. 18. preserve me to his
heavenly *k.*
Heb. 12. 28. we receiving a *k.* not to
Jas. 2. 5. rich in faith, heirs of *k.*
2 Pet. 1. 11. into everlasting *k.* of
Rev. 1. 9. in *k.* and patience of
11. 15. the *k.* of this world are *k.*
17. 17. to give their *k.* to the beast
Matt. 6. 33. *kingdom of God*, 12. 28.
& 21. 43. Mark 1. 15. & 10. 14, 15. &
12. 34. & 15. 43. Luke 4. 43. & 6. 20.
& 9. 62. & 10. 9, 11. & 13. 29. & 17. 20,
21. & 18. 16, 17, 29. & 21. 16.
John 3. 3. except born again, cannot see –, 5.
Rom. 14. 17. – is not meat and drink
1 Cor. 4. 20. – is not in word, but
6. 9. unright. shall not inherit –
15. 50. flesh and blood cannot in.
herit –
Eph. 5. 5. hath any inheritance in –
2 Thes. 1. 5. be counted worthy of –
Rev. 12. 10. now is come – and
power
Matt. 3. 2. *kingdom of heaven*, 4. 17.
& 10. 7. & 5. 3, 10, 19, 20. & 7. 21. &
8. 11. & 11. 11, 12. & 13. 11, 24, 31, 52.
& 16. 19. & 18. 1, 3, 23. & 20. 1. & 22.
2. & 23. 13. & 25. 1, 14.
KISS the Son, lest he be angry,
Ps. 2. 12.
S. of S. 1. 2. let him *k.* me with the *k.*
Rom. 16. 16. salute with a holy *k.*
1 Pet. 5. 14. greet with *k.* of charity
Ps. 85. 10. righteousness and peace
have *kissed*
Luke 7. 38. *k.* his feet and anointed
Prov. 27. 6. *kisses* from an enemy
KNEELING in prayer, 2 Chron. 6.
13. Ezra 9. 5. Ps. 95. 6. Dan. 6. 10.
Acts 7. 60. & 9. 40. & 21. 5. Eph. 3. 14.
KNEES, Gen. 30. 3. & 41. 43.
Job 4. 4. feeble *k.*, Isa. 35. 3. Heb.
12. 12.
Isa. 45. 23. to God every *k.* shall
bow, Rom. 14. 11. Phil. 2. 10. Matt.
27. 29. Eph. 3. 14.
Nah. 2. 10. the *k.* smite together
KNIFE, Prov. 23. 2. & 30. 14.
R. V. Ezek. 5. 1, 2. sword
KNIT, 1 Sam. 18. 1. Col. 2. 2, 19.
KNEW, Gen. 3. 7. & 4. 1. & 42. 7.
Gen. 28. 16. God is in this place, I
k. it not
Deut. 34. 10. whom Lord *k.* face to
Jer. 1. 5. before I formed thee, I *k.*
Matt. 7. 23. depart ye, I never *k.*
John 4. 10. if you *k.* the gift of God
Rom. 1. 21. when they *k.* God, they
2 Cor. 5. 21. made him to be sin
who *k.* no sin
Deut. 8. 2. to *know* what was in thy
Josh. 22. 22. God knoweth, and
Israel he shall *k.*
1 Sam. 3. 7. Samuel did not yet *k.*
1 Kings 8. 38. man shall *k.* plague

1 Chron. 28. 9. *k.* thou the God of
Job. 5. 27. *k.* thou it for thy good
13. 23. make me to *k.* my trans.
22. 13. how doth God *k.*, Ps. 73. 11.
Ps. 4. 3. *k.* the Lord hath set apart
9. 10. that *k.* thy name will trust in
46. 10. be still, and *k.* that I am God
51. 6. God shall make me to *k.*
139. 23. *k.* my heart; and *k.* my
Eccl. 11. 9. *k.* that for all these
Isa. 58. 2. they seek and delight to *k.*
Jer. 17. 9. heart is dece. who can *k.*
22. 16. was not this to *k.* me
24. 7. I will give them a heart to *k.*
31. 34. saying, *k.* the Lord
Ezek. 2. 5. shall *k.* that a prophet
hath, 33. 33.
Hos. 2. 20. in faithfulness thou
shalt *k.* the Lord
Mic. 3. 1. is it not for you to *k.*
Matt. 6. 3. let not left hand *k.* what
7. 11. *k.* how to give good gifts
13. 11. given you to *k.* mystery
John 4. 42. we *k.* this is indeed
7. 17. he shall *k.* of the doctrine
10. 4. sheep follow him, for they *k.*
14. I *k.* my sheep and am known
13. 7. *k.* not now, but shalt *k.*
17. if ye *k.* these things, happy are
35. by this men *k.* ye are my
Acts 1. 7. it is not for you to *k.* the
Rom. 10. 19. did not Israel *k.* yes
1 Cor. 2. 14. neither can ye *k.* them
4. 19. I will *k.* not the speech
8. 2. *k.* any thing, *k.* nothing as he
Eph. 3. 19. to *k.* love of Christ
1 Thes. 5. 12. to *k.* them who labor
Tit. 1. 16. they profess that they *k.*
Ex. 4. 14. *I know*, Job 9. 2, 28.
Gen. 18. 19. — him that he will
22. 12. now — that thou fearest God
2 Kings 19. 27. — thy abode and thy
Job 19. 25. — that my Redeemer
liveth
Ps. 41. 11. by this — that thou fav.
Jer. 16. 23. — that the way of man
Matt. 25. 12. — you not, Luke 13. 25.
John 13. 18. — whom I have chosen
Acts 26. 27. — that thou believest
Rom. 7. 18. — that in me
1 Cor. 4. 4. though — nothing by
13. 12. now — in part; but then
Phil. 4. 12. — how to be abased
2 Tim. 1. 12.—whom I have believed
1 John 2. 4. he that saith — him, is
Rev. 2. 2. — thy works, 9. 13, 19. & 3.
1, 3, 15.
Hos. 6. 3. *we know*, 8. 2. John 4. 22.
1 Cor. 2. 12. 1 John 2. 3, 5.
John 16. 30. *thou knowest* all things
21. 17. — all things — that I love
thee
Ps. 1. 6. Lord *knoweth* the way of
94. 11. Lord *k.* thoughts of man
103. 14. he *k.* our frame, that we
139. 14. my soul *k.* right well
Eccl. 9. 1. no man *k.* either love or
Isa. 1. 3. ox *k.* his owner, and ass
Jer. 8. 7. stork *k.* appointed times
9. 24. understandeth and *k.* me to
Zeph. 3. 5. the unjust *k.* no shame
Matt. 6. 8. *k.* what things ye have
24. 36. of that day and hour *k.* no
1 Cor. 8. 2. *k.* any thing, he *k.* nothing yet
2 Tim. 2. 19. the Lord *k.* them that
Jas. 4. 17. that *k.* to do good doeth
2 Pet. 2. 9. Lord *k.* how to deliver
Rev. 2. 17. a name which no man *k.*
Ps. 9. 16. Lord is *known* by the
31. 7. hast *k.* my soul in adversity
67. 2. thy way may be *k.* on earth
Isa. 45. 4. thou hast not *k.* me, 5.
Amos 3. 2. you only have I *k.* of all
Matt. 10. 26. there is nothing hid
that shall not be *k.*, Luke 8. 17. &
12. 2.
Luke 19. 42. if thou hadst *k.* in this
Acts 15. 18. *k.* unto God are all his
Rom. 1. 19. that which may be *k.*
7. 7. I had not *k.* sin but by the
1 Cor. 8. 3. the same is *k.* of him
Gal. 4. 9. *k.* God, or rather are *k.* of
Rev. 2. 24. have not *k.* the depths of

Gen. 2. 17. *knowledge* of good and
1 Sam. 2. 3. the Lord is a God of *k.*
Ps. 19. 2. night unto night show. *k.*
73. 11. is there *k.* in the Most High
94. 10. he that teacheth men *k.*
139. 6. such *k.* is too wonderful
Prov. 8. 12. I find out *k.* of witty
14. 6. *k.* is easy to him that understandeth
19. 2. the soul be without *k.* is not
30. 3. I have not the *k.* of the holy
Eccl. 9. 10. there is no device nor *k.*
Isa. 28. 9. whom shall he teach *k.*
Jer. 3. 15. pastors shall feed you
with *k.*
Dan. 12. 4. run to and fro, and *k.* be
Hos. 4. 6. are destroy. for lack of *k.*
Hab. 2. 14. earth filled with *k.* of the
Lord, Isa. 11. 9.
Mal. 2. 7. priest's lips should keep
k.
Rom. 2. 20. a teacher hast form of *k.*
3. 20. for by the law is *k.* of sin
10. 2. zeal for God not accord. to *k.*
1 Cor. 8. 1. all have *k. k.* puffeth up
Eph. 3. 19. the love of Christ which
passeth *k.*
Phil. 3. 8. loss for excellency of
the *k.*
Col. 2. 3. are hid treasures of wisdom and *k.*
3. 10. renewed in *k.* after image of
1 Pet. 3. 7. dwell with them according to *k.*
2 Pet. 1. 5. add to virtue *k.* and to *k.*
3. 18. grow in grace and in the *k.*
of Jesus Christ
R. V. Many changes to, perceive,
understand, learn, discern, etc.,
but none affecting general meaning. Prov. 2. 3. discernment; Eph.
3. 4. understanding
KNOCK, Matt. 7. 7. Rev. 3. 20.

L

LABOR, Gen. 31. 42. & 35. 16.
Ps. 90. 10. yet is their strength *l.*
104. 23. man goeth to his *l.* until eve
128. 2. thou shalt eat the *l.* of thine
Prov. 14. 23. in all *l.* there is profit
Eccl. 1. 8. all things are full of *l.*
4. 8. yet is there no end of all his *l.*
Isa. 55. 2. ye spend your *l.* for that
Hab. 3. 17. though *l.* of the olive
1 Cor. 15. 58. your *l.* is not in vain
1 Thes. 1. 3. work of faith, and *l.*
Heb. 6. 10. God will not forget
your *l.* of
Rev. 14. 13. dead may rest from *l.*
Prov. 23. 4. *l.* not to be rich; cease
Matt. 11. 28. come all ye that *l.* and
John 6. 27. *l.* not for the meat
1 Thes. 5. 12. know them which *l.*
1 Tim. 5. 17. honor those who *l.*
Heb. 4. 11. let us *l.* to enter into
Isa. 49. 4. I have *labored* in vain
John 4. 38. other men *l.* and ye
1 Cor. 15. 10. I *l.* more abundantly
Phil. 2. 16. not run, nor *l.* in vain
Prov. 16. 26. he that *laboreth*, *l.*
Eccl. 5. 12. sleep of the *laboring*
man is sweet
Col. 4. 12. Epaphras *l.* fervently
Luke 10. 7. the *laborer* is worthy
Matt. 9. 37. but *laborers* are few,
Luke 10. 2.
1 Cor. 3. 9. we are *l.* toge. with God
R. V. Deut. 26. 7; Rev. 2. 2. toil;
Eccl. 1. 8. weariness; Phil. 1. 22.
work; Josh. 7. 3; 1 Cor. 4. 12. toil;
Neh. 4. 21. wrought; Lam. 5. 5.
are weary; 2 Cor. 5. 9. make it
our aim; Col. 4. 12. striving;
1 Thes. 2. 9. working; Heb. 4. 11.
give diligence; Rev. 2. 3 —
LACK, Hos. 4. 6. Matt. 19. 20, 21.
2 Cor. 11. 9. 1 Thes. 3. 10. Jas.1.5.
R. V. 1 Thes. 4. 12. need
LADEN with iniquity, Isa. 1. 4.
Matt. 11. 28. labor and heavy *l.*
2 Tim. 3. 6. silly women, *l.* with

LADDER, Jacob's, Gen. 28. 12.
LADY of kingdoms, Isa. 47. 5.
Isa. 47. 7. I shall be a *l.* for ever
2 John 1. unto the elect *l.*
Esth. 1. 18. *ladies* of Persia
Judg. 5. 29. her wise *l.* answered
R. V. Esth. 1. 18. princesses
LAMB, Gen. 22. 7, 8. Ex. 12. 3.
2 Sam. 12. 3. man had nothing save
one ewe *l.*
Isa. 11. 6. wolf shall dwell with *l.*
53. 7. he is brought as a *l.* to the
John 1. 29. behold the L. of God
1 Pet. 1. 19. as a *l.* without blem.
Rev. 5. 12. worthy is the L. that
6. 16. fall on us and hide us from
the face of the L.
7. 14. robes made white in blood
of the L., 12. 11.
17. L. in the midst of the throne
shall feed them
13. 8. L. slain from the foundation of the world
R. V. In Num., he-lamb
LAME, Lev. 21. 18. Mal. 1. 8, 13.
Job 29. 15. eyes to the blind and
feet to the *l.*
Prov. 26. 7. legs of the *l.* are not
Isa. 35. 6. the *l.* man shall leap
Heb. 12. 13. lest the *l.* be turned
LAMP, Gen. 15. 17. Ex. 27. 20.
1 Kings 15. 4. Matt. 25. 1, 3, 4, 7, 8.
2 Sam. 22. 29. thou art my *l.* O Lord
Ps. 119. 105. thy word a *l.* to my
132. 17. I have ordained a *l.* for
Prov. 6. 23. the command. is a *l.*
13. 9. *l.* of wicked shall be put out
Isa. 62. 1. salvation as a *l.* that
Ex. 25. 37. *seven lamps*, 37. 23. Num.
8. 2. Zech. 4. 2. Rev. 4. 5.
R. V. Gen. 15. 17; Rev. 8. 10. torch;
Judg. 7. 16, 20; Job 41. 19; Ezek.
1. 13. torches
LAND, Eccl. 10. 16, 17. Isa. 5. 30.
Deut. 19. 14. remove *landmark*, 27.
17. Job 24. 2. Prov. 22. 28. & 23. 10.
R. V. Many changes in O. T. to
earth, ground, country, etc.
LANGUAGE, Gen. 11.1. Neh.13.24.
Ps. 81. 5. Isa. 19. 18. Zeph. 3. 9.
LANGUISH, Isa. 24. 4. Ps. 41. 3.
LASCIVIOUSNESS, Mark 7. 22.
2 Cor. 12. 21. Gal. 5. 19. Eph. 4. 19.
1 Pet. 4. 3.
Jude 4. turning grace of God
into *l.*
LAST end be like his, Num. 23.
10.
Lam. 1. 9. she remembered not
her *l.* end
Luke 11. 26. *l.* state is worse than
1 Pet. 1. 5. *last time*, 20. 1 John 2.
18.
Jude 18. should be mockers in
the—
R. V. Gen. 49. 1; Isa. 2. 2; Jer. 12.
4; Lam. 1. 9; Dan. 8. 19; Mic. 4. 1.
latter; Matt. 21. 37; Luke 20. 32.
afterward
LATTER day, Job 19. 25; *l.* end,
Prov. 19. 20; *l.* house, Hag. 2. 9; *l.*
time, 1 Tim. 4. 1. 2 Tim. 3. 1.
LAUGH, Gen. 17. 17. & 18. 12, 15.
2 Chron. 30. 10. but they *l.* them
Job 5. 22. at destruction and fam
ine thou shalt *l.*
Ps. 2. 4. he that sitteth in the heavens shall *l.*
37. 13. the Lord shall *l.* at him
52. 6. righteous. shall see and *l.*
59. 8. thou, O Lord, shall *l.* at
Prov. 1. 26. I will *l.* at your calam.
Luke 6. 21. blessed that weep, for
ye shall *l.*
Job 8. 21. he fill thy mouth with
laughing
Ps. 126. 2. our mouth was filled
with *laughter*
Prov. 14. 13. even in *l.* heart is sor.
Eccl. 7. 3. sorrow is better than *l.*
Jas. 4. 9. let your *l.* be turned
LAW, Gen. 47. 26. Prov. 28. 4.
Deut. 33. 2. from his right hand
went a fiery *l.*

Neh. 8. 7. caused people to under-
stand the *l.*
10. 28. separated from people to *l.*
Ps. 1. 2. his delight is in the *l.*
19. 7. *l.* of the Lord is perfect
37. 31. *l.* of his God is in his heart
119. 72. *l.* of thy mouth is better
Prov. 6. 23. *l.* is light
7. 2. keep my *l.* as apple of eye
28. 9. turns away from hearing *l.*
28. 18. keepeth the *l.* happy is he
Isa. 2. 2. shall go forth the *l.*
8. 16. seal the *l.* among my dis.
20. to the *l.* and the testimony
42. 21. magnify the *l.* and make
51. 7. peo. in whose heart is my *l.*
Jer. 18. 18. *l.* shall not perish from
31. 33. I will put my *l.* in inward
Ezek. 7. 26. *l.* shall perish from
Hos. 8. 12. writ. great things of my *l.*
Mal. 2. 7. people seek *l.* at his
Luke 16. 16. *l.* and prophets till
John 1. 17. *l.* was given by Moses
19. 7. we have a *l.* and by our *l.*
Acts 13. 39. not justified by the *l.*
Rom. 2. 12. sinned without *l.*
13. not hearers of *l.* but doers of *l.*
3. 20. by deeds of *l.* shall no flesh
27. boasting by what *l.* by *l.* of
31. do we make void the *l.*
5. 13. sin is not imput. where no *l.*
7. 7. had not known sin but by *l.*
8. for without the *l.* sin was dead
12. the *l.* is holy, just, and good
14. *l.* is spiritual, but I am carnal
22. I delight in the *l.* of God
23. *l.* in my members against *l.*
8. 2. *l.* of Spirit made free from *l.*
10. 4. Christ is end of the *l.* for
5. righteousness of *l.*, 9. 31, 32.
1 Cor. 6. 1. dare any of you go to *l.*
Gal. 2. 16. man not justified by
works of the *l.*
3. 10. of works of the *l.* are under
12. the *l.* is not of faith, but the
13. Christ redeemed us from the
curse of the *l.*
5. 23. love, faith, against such
there is no *l.*
1 Tim. 1. 8. the *l.* is good if we use
9. that *l.* is not made for right.
Heb. 7. 19. *l.* made nothing perfect
Jas. 1. 25. whoso looketh into the
perfect *l.*
1 John 3. 4. sin transgresseth the *l.*
sin is transgression of *l.*
Neh. 9. 26. cast *thy law* behind
their backs
Ps. 40. 8. — is within my heart
94. 12. whom thou teach. out of —
119. 70. I delight in —, 77. 92, 174.
18. wondrous things out of —
97. how I love —, 113. 163.
Ezek. 18. 5. do that which is *lawful* and right, 33. 14, 19.
1 Cor. 6. 12. all things are *l.* to
Isa. 33. 22. Lord is *lawgiver*
R. V. Gen. 47. 26 ; 1 Chron. 16. 17 ; Ps.
94. 20 ; 105. 10. statute ; Acts 15. 24 ;
24. 6 ; Rom. 9. 32 ; 1 Cor. 7. 39 ; 9.
20 — ; Acts 19. 39. regular ; Gen.
49. 10. ruler's staff ; Num. 21. 18 ;
Ps. 60. 7 ; 108. 8. sceptre
LAY, Gen. 19. 33, 35. Job 29. 19.
Eccl. 7. 2. the living will *l.* it to
Isa. 28. 16. I *l.* in Zion a tried
Mal. 2. 2. I cursed, ye do not *l.*
Matt. 8. 20. hath not where to *l.*
Acts 7. 60. *l.* not this sin to their
15. 28. *l.* on you no greater bur.
Heb. 12. 1. *l.* aside every weight
Jas. 1. 21. *l.* apart all filthiness
John 10. 15. *lay down life,* 13. 37. &
15. 13.
1 Tim. 5. 22. *lay hands,* Heb. 6. 2.
6. 12. *lay hold* on eternal life
Heb. 6. 18. — on hope set before us
Matt. 6. 20. *lay up* for yourselves
Ps. 62. 9. to be *laid* in the balance
89. 19. I *l.* help on one that is
Isa. 53. 6. Lord *l.* on him iniquities
Matt. 3. 10. axe *l.* to root of trees
1 Cor. 3. 10. I have *l.* foundation
Heb. 6. 1. not *l.* again foundation

1 Sam. 21. 12. David *laid up* these
Ps. 31. 19. thy goodness — for them
Luke 1. 66. — in their hearts
Col. 1. 5. hope which is — for you
2 Tim. 4. 8. — for me a crown of
Job 21. 19. God *layeth* up his iniq.
24. 12. yet God *l.* not folly to them
Prov. 2. 7. *l.* up wisdom
26. A. 1. up deceit
Isa. 56. 2. blessed is the man that
l. hold on
57. 1. no man *l.* to heart, 42. 25.
R. V. The frequent changes do
not modify general meaning.
See also the *v. i.* Lie, lay, lain.
LEAD, Ex. 15. 10. Job 19. 24. Zech.
5. 7, 8. Gen. 33. 14. Ex. 13. 21.
Ps. 5. 8. *lead me* in thy righteous.
25. 5. — in thy truth
27. 11. — in a plain path
61. 2. — to rock higher than I
24. — in the way everlasting
Isa. 11. 6. a little child shall *l.* them
40. 11. gently *l.* those with young
Matt. 15. 14. if blind *l.* the blind,
Luke 6. 39.
1 Tim. 2. 2. may *l.* a quiet and
Rev. 7. 17. Lamb shall *l.* them to
Ps. 23. 2. *leadeth* me beside still
48. 17. God which *l.* thee by way
Matt. 7. 13. gate *l.* to destruction
John 10. 3. calleth sheep and *l.*
Rom. 2. 4. goodness of God *l.*
Gen. 24. 27. *Lord led,* 48. Ex. 13. 18.
& 15. 13. Deut. 8. 2. & 29. 5. & 32.
10, 12. Neh. 9. 12. Ps. 77. 20. & 80.
1. & 78. 14, 53. & 106. 9. & 136. 16. &
107. 7.
Isa. 48. 2. & 63. 13, 14. Jer. 26. 17.
Rom. 8. 14. *led by Spirit,* Gal. 5. 18.
Isa. 55. 4. *leader* to people, 9. 16.
R. V. Ps. 25. 5 ; Matt. 15. 14 ; Luke
6. 39 : Rev. 7. 17. guide
LEAF, Job 13. 25. Ezek. 47. 12. Rev.
22. 2.
LEAGUE with stones of field, Job
5. 23.
R. V. Josh. 9. 6, 7, 11, 15, 16 ; Judg.
2. 2 ; 2 Sam. 3. 21 ; 5. 3. covenant
LEAN not to own understanding,
Prov. 3. 5.
Job 8. 15. he shall *l.* upon his
S. of S. 8. 5. that *l.* on her beloved
Mic. 3. 11. yet will they *l.* on Lord
John 13. 23. *l.* on Jesus' bosom
R. V. John 13. 23. reclining
LEANNESS, Job 16. 8. Ps. 106. 15.
Isa. 10. 16. & 24. 16. my *l.* my *l.*
R. V. Isa. 24. 16. I pine away
LEAP, S. of S. 2. 8. Isa. 35. 6. Zeph.
1. 9.
Luke 1. 41. & 6. 23. rejoice and *l.* for
LEARN to fear me, Deut. 4. 10. &
5. 1. & 14. 23. & 31. 12, 13.
Ps. 119. 71. might *l.* thy statutes
Prov. 22. 25. lest thou *l.* his ways
Isa. 1. 17. *l.* to do well, seek
26. 10. yet will he not *l.* righteous.
Jer. 10. 2. *l.* not way of the heathen
Matt. 9. 13. *l.* what that means
11. 29. *l.* of me, for I am meek
1 Tim. 2. 11. let woman *l.* in silence
Tit. 3. 14. let ours *l.* to maintain
Rev. 14. 3. no man could *l.* that
Ps. 106. 35. *learned* their works
Isa. 50. 4. Lord God hath given me
the tongue of the *l.*
John 6. 45. hath *l.* of Father cometh
Acts 7. 22. Moses was *l.* in all wis.
Eph. 4. 20. ye have not so *l.* Christ
Phil. 4. 11. I have *l.* in whatsoever
Heb. 5. 8. though a son, yet *l.* he
Prov. 1. 5. wise will incre. *learning*
Acts 26. 24. much *l.* doth make
Rom. 15. 4. was written for our *l.*
2 Tim. 3. 7. ever *l.* never come
R. V. Isa. 50. 4. are taught ; Acts 7.
22. instructed
LEAST of thy mercies, Gen. 32. 10.
Jer. 31. 34. shall know me from *l.* to
Matt. 11. 11. *l.* in kingdom of God
Luke 16. 10. faithful in *l.* is faithful
1 Cor. 4. 4. judge who are *l.* es-
teemed

1 Cor. 15. 9. I am *l.* of all the apostles
Eph. 3. 8. less than the *l.* of all
R. V. 1 Sam. 21. 4. only ; Matt. 13.
22. less than ; 11. 11 ; Luke 7. 28.
but little ; Luke 16. 10. a very
little ; 1 Cor. 6. 4. of no account
LEAVE father and mother and
cleave to his wife, Gen. 2. 24.
Matt. 15. 9. Eph. 5. 31.
1 Kings 8. 57. let him not *l.* us, nor
Ps. 16. 10. not *l.* my soul in hell
27. 9. *l.* me not, neither forsake me
Matt. 5. 24. *l.* there thy gift before
23. 23. and not to *l.* other undone
John 14. 18. I will not *l.* you com.
27. peace I *l.* with you, my peace
Heb. 13. 5. I will never *l.* nor
Acts 14. 17. *left,* Rom. 9. 29. Heb. 4.
1. Jude 6. Rev. 2. 4.
R. V. Changes frequent, but usu*al*
meanings retained
LEAVEN, Ex. 12. 15. Lev. 2. 11.
Matt. 13. 33. the kingdom of hea-
ven is like *l.*
16. 6. beware of *l.* of Pharisees
1 Cor. 5. 7. purge out the old *l.*
6. a little *l.* leaveneth lump
LEES, Isa. 25. 6. Jer. 48. 11. Zeph.
1. 12.
LEFT-HANDED slingers, Judg.
20. 16.
LEGS, Ps. 147. 10. Prov. 26. 7.
R. V. Isa. 47. 2. train
LEND, Ex. 22. 25. Deut. 23. 19, 20.
Jer. 15. 10. neither *l.* on usury
Luke 6. 35. do good and *l.* hoping
Ps. 37. 26. ever merci. and *lendeth*
Prov. 19. 17. giveth to the poor *l.*
22. 7. borrower is servant to *lender*
1 Sam. 1. 28. I have *lent* him to Lord
R. V. Lev. 25. 37. give ; 1 Sam. 1.
28. granted
LEOPARD, S. of S. 4. 8. Isa. 11. 6.
Jer. 5. 6. & 13. 23. Hos. 13. 7. Hab.
1. 8.
LEPROSY, in a house, Lev. 14. 33 ;
of Miriam, Num. 12. 10 ; of Naaman
and Gehazi, 2 Kings 5 ; of Uzziah,
2 Chron. 26. 19 ; symptoms of, Lev.
13 ; observances on healing, Lev.
14. & 22. 4. Deut. 24. 8 ; cured by
Christ, Matt. 8. 3. Mark 1. 41. Luke
5. 12. & 17. 12.
LESS, Ezra 9. 13. Job 11. 6. Isa. 40.
17. Heb. 7. 9. Eph. 3. 8. Gen. 32. 10.
LETTER, Rom. 7. 2. 2 Cor. 3. 6.
R. V. 2 Cor. 7. 8 ; 2 Thes. 2. 2. epis-
tle ; Luke 23. 38 ; 2 Cor. 3. 1 ; Heb.
13. 22—
LETTEST, Luke 2. 29. 2 Thes. 2. 7.
LEVIATHAN, Job 41. 1. Ps. 74. 14.
LIBERAL, Prov. 11. 25. Isa. 32. 5,
8. 2 Cor. 9. 13.
1 Cor. 16. 3. *liberality,* 2 Cor. 8. 2.
Jas. 1. 5. God giveth to all men
liberally
R. V. 1 Cor. 16. 3. bounty
LIBERTINES, the, Acts 6. 9.
LIBERTY, Lev. 25. 10. Jer. 34. 8.
Ps. 119. 45. I will walk at *l.* for I
Isa. 61. 1. anoint. me to proclaim *l*
Luke 4. 18. sent me to set at *l.*
Rom. 8. 21. into glorious *l.* of the
2 Cor. 3. 17. where Spirit of Lord is
there is *l.*
Gal. 5. 1. stand fast in *l.*
13. use not *l.* for an occasion to
Jas. 1. 25. whoso looketh into the
law of *l.*
2. 12. be judged by the law of *l.*
1 Pet. 2. 16. not using your *l.*
R. V. Acts 27. 3. leave ; 1 Cor. 7. 39.
free ; Gal. 5. 13. freedom
LIE, Lev. 6. 3. & 19. 11. Job 11. 3.
Ps. 58. 3. wicked go astray speak
ing *l.*
62. 9. men of high degree are a *l.*
101. 7. that telleth a *l.* shall not
Hos. 11. 12. compasseth me about
with *l.*
2 Thes. 2. 11. that they should believe a *l.*
1 Tim. 4. 2. speaking *l.* in hypocrisy
Rev. 22. 15. loveth and maketh a *l*

Num. 23. 19. God is not a man, that he should *l.*
Isa. 63. 8. children that will not *l.*
Hab. 2. 3. at the end it shall speak and not *l.*
Col. 3. 9. *l.* not one to another
Tit. 1. 2. God that cannot *l.* hath
Heb. 6. 18. impossible for God to *l.*
Ps. 116. 11. I said, all men are *liars*
Tit. 1. 12. the Cretians are always *l.*
Rev. 2. 2. hast tried and found them *l.*
21. 8. all *l.* shall have their part
John 8. 44. he is a *liar* and the
Rom. 3. 4. God be true, and every man a *l.*
1 John 1. 10. we make him a *l.*
2. 4. keepeth not the commandments is a *l.*
Ps. 119. 29. remove from me the way of *lying*
163. I abhor *l.* but love thy law
Prov. 12. 19. *l.* tongue but for a
Jer. 7. 4. trust not in *l.* words
Hos. 4. 2. by stealing and *l.* the,
Jonah 2. 8. observe *l.* vanities
R. V. Job 11. 3; Jer. 48. 30. boastings; Ezek. 24. 12. toil; Ps. 101. 7; Prov. 29. 12; Jer. 9. 3; Hos. 11. 12. falsehood; Gen. 4. 7; 49. 25. coucheth

LIFE, Gen. 2. 7, 9. & 42. 15. & 44. 30.
Deut. 30. 15. set before you *l.* and
1 Sam. 25. 29. bound in bundle of *l.*
Ps. 16. 11. thou wilt show me the path of *l.*
21. 4. asked *l.* of thee and thou gavest
36. 9. with thee is the fountain of *l.*
63. 3. loving-kind. better than *l.*
66. 9. God holdeth our soul in *l.*
Prov. 8. 35. whoso findeth me findeth *l.*
15. 24. way of *l.* is above to wise
18. 21. death and *l.* are in power
Isa. 57. 10. hast found *l.* of thy
Matt. 6. 25. take no thought for *l.*
Luke 12. 15. man's *l.* consists not in
John 1. 4. in him was *l.* and the *l.*
3. 36. believ. on Son hath ever. *l.*
5. 40. not come, that ye might have *l.*
6. 35. I am the bread of *l.*, 48. 40, 47, 54.
51. my flesh I give for *l.* of world
63. words I speak are spirit and *l.*
8. 12. followeth me shall have light of *l.*
10. 10. I am come that they might have *l.*
11. 25. I am the resurrection and *l.*
14. 6. I am the way, truth, and *l.*
Rom. 5. 17. reign in *l.* by Jesus
8. 2. law of Spirit of *l.* in Christ Jesus
6. to be spiritually minded is *l.*
2 Cor. 2. 16. the savor of *l.* unto *l.*
3. 6. the letter killeth, but the spirit giveth *l.*
4. 11. *l.* of Jesus might be mani.
Gal. 2. 20. the *l.* I now live in flesh
Eph. 4. 18. being alienated from *l.*
Col. 3. 3. your *l.* is hid with Christ
1 Tim. 2. 2. lead a peaceful *l.*
4. 8. having promise of the *l.* that
2 Tim. 1. 10. brought *l.* and immor.
2 Pet. 1. 3. that pertain to *l.* and
1 John 5. 12. he that hath the Son hath *l.* he that hath not the Son hath not *l.*
Job 2. 4. all that a man will he give for *his life*
Prov. 13. 3. keepeth his mouth, keepeth —
Matt. 20. 28. Son of man gave—a ransom
Rom. 5. 10. much more saved by—
1 Kings 19. 4. to take away *my life*
Ps. 26. 9. gather not—with bloody men
27. 1. the Lord is strength of
Jonah 2. 6. brought up—from cor.
John 10. 15. I lay down—for sheep
Acts 20. 24. neither count I—dear

Ps. 17. 14. *this life*, Luke 8. 14. & 21. 34. Acts 5. 20. 1 Cor. 15. 19. & 6. 3.
Deut. 30. 23. he is *thy life*, and
Ps. 103. 4. redeem — from destruc.
Jer. 39. 18.—shall be for a prey, 45. 5.
Prov. 10. 16. tends to *life*, 11. 19. & 19. 23. Matt. 7. 14. John 5. 24. Acts 11. 18. Rom. 7. 10. Heb. 11. 35. 1 John 3. 14.
LIFT *up* his countenance on thee, Num. 6. 26.
1 Sam. 2. 7. Lord brings low—again
2 Kings 19. 4. — prayer for remnant
2 Chron. 17. 6. heart — in ways of
Ps. 4. 6. Lord—light of thy counte.
7. 6. Lord — thyself because
24. 7. --ye gates, — ye doors, and
25. 1. to thee I — my soul, 86. 4.
75. 4. — not the horn, 5.
83. 2. — the head
102. 10. thou — me and castest me
121. 1. — mine eyes, 123. 1.
147. 6. Lord — the meek, but casts
Prov. 2. 3. — thy voice for under.
Eccl. 4. 10. one will — his fellow
Isa. 26. 11. Lord when thy hand is —
33. 10. I will be exalted; now I — myself
42. 2. he shall not cry, nor — voice
Jer. 7. 16. nor — a prayer for them
Lam. 3. 14. let us—our hearts with
Hab. 2. 4. his soul which is—is
Luke 21. 28. — your heads for day of redemption
John 3. 14. so must the Son of man be—, 12. 34.
8. 28. when ye have — Son of man
12. 32. if I be — I will draw all men
Heb. 12. 12. — hands which hang
Jas. 4. 10. the Lord shall *l.* you up
Ps. 3. 3. my glory and *lifter up* of
141. 2. *lifting* up of hands, 1 Tim. 2. 8.
R. V. Ps. 30. 1; Mark 1. 31; 9. 27; Acts 3. 7; 9. 41. raised
LIGHT, Num. 21. 5. Deut. 27. 16.
Judg. 9. 4. 1 Kings 16. 31. Ezek. 8. 17. & 22. 7.
Isa. 49. 6. it is a *l.* thing to be my
Zeph. 3. 4. her prophets *l.* and
Matt. 11. 30. my yoke is easy and my burden *l.*
2 Cor. 4. 17. *l.* affliction endureth
Ps. 62. 9. man is *lighter* than vanity
Jer. 3. 9. *lightness* of whoredoms
Gen. 1. 3. let there be *light*, 4, 5, 16. & 44. 3.
Job 18. 5. *l.* of wicked men shall
33. 30. enlightened with *l.* of living
Ps. 4. 6. lift up *l.* of thy countenance
36. 9. in thy *l.* shall we see *l.*
43. 3. O send out thy *l.* and truth
90. 8. set secret sins in the *l.* of
97. 11. *l.* is sown for the righteous
104. 2. coverest thyself with *l.*
112. 4. to the upright ariseth *l.* in
119. 105. thy word is *l.* to my path
139. 12. darkness and *l.* are both
Prov. 4. 18. path of the just is as the shining *l.*
6. 23. law is *l.* and reproofs are way
13. 9. *l.* of the righteous rejoiceth
15. 30. *l.* of the eyes rejoiceth the
Eccl. 11. 7. *l.* is sweet and a pleasant
Isa. 5. 20. darkness for *l.* and *l.* for
8. 20. because there is no *l.* in them
9. 2. walked in darkness, have seen a great *l.*
30. 26. *l.* of moon as *l.* of sun
42. 6. keep thee, and give thee for a *l.* of the Gentiles
50. 10. walketh in darkness and hath no *l.*
11. walk ye in the *l.* of your fire
58. 8. shall thy *l.* break forth as
60. 1. arise, shine; for thy *l.* is
Zech. 14. 6. *l.* shall not be clear nor
7. evening time it shall be *l.*
Matt. 5. 14. ye are the *l.* of the world
16. let your *l.* so shine before men
6. 22. the *l.* of the body is the eye
Luke 2. 32. a *l.* to lighten Gentiles
John 1. 4. the life was the *l.* of men

John 1. 7. John came to bear witness of *l.*
9. true *l.* that lighteth every man
3. 19. men loved darkness rather than *l.*
20. cometh not to the *l.*
21. cometh to the *l.*
5. 35. John burn. and a shining *l.*
8. 12. I am the *l.* of the world
12. 35, 36. walk while ye have the *l.*
Acts 13. 47. I have set thee for a *l.*
26. 18. turn them from dark. to *l.*
Rom. 13. 12. put on the armor of *l.*
1 Cor. 4. 5. bring to *l.* hidden
2 Cor. 4. 4. lest the *l.* of the Gospel
6. 14. what communion hath *l.* with
Eph. 5. 8. walk as children of *l.*
14. awake, and Christ shall give thee *l.*
1 Thes. 5. 5. ye are the children of *l.*
1 Pet. 2. 9. called to his marvell. *l.*
1 John 1. 5. God is *l.* and in him is
Rev. 21. 23. the Lamb is the *l.* thereof
Ps. 136. 7. *lights*, Ezek. 32. 8. Luke 12. 35. Phil. 2. 15. Jas. 1. 17.
2 Sam. 22. 29. *lighten*, Ezra 9. 8. Ps. 13. 3. & 35. 5. Rev. 21. 23.
Ex. 19. 16. *lightning*, Ps. 18. 14. Matt. 28. 3. & 24. 27. Luke 10. 18.
R. V. Jer. 23. 32. vain boasting; 2 Cor. 1. 17. fickleness; 2 Sam. 21. 17; 1 Kings 11. 36; 2 Kings 8. 19; 2 Chron. 21. 7; Matt. 6. 22; Luke 11. 34. lamp
LIKE men, quit you, 1 Cor. 16. 13.
Heb. 2. 17. to be made *l.* his breth.
1 John 3. 2. he appears we shall be *l.*
Phil. 2. 2. *like-minded*
20. no man—
Gen. 1. 26. after our *likeness*
5. 3. Adam begat a son in his own *l.*
Ps. 17. 15. I shall be sat. with thy *l.*
Rom. 6. 5. been planted in *l.* of his
8. 3. in *l.* of sinful flesh, Phil. 2. 7.
R. V. Rom. 1. 28. refused. Frequent changes to, as
LILY, S. of S. 2. 1, 2. 16. & 4. 5. & 5. 13. & 6. 2, 3. & 7. 2. Hos. 14. 5. Matt. 6. 28.
LINE upon *l. l.* upon *l.* Isa. 28. 10, 13.
28. 17. judgment will I lay to the *l.*
34. 11. stretch on it *l.* of confusion
2 Cor. 10. 16. not boast in another man's *l.*
Ps. 16. 6. *l.* are fallen in pleasant
R. V. Isa. 44. 13. pencil; 2 Cor. 10. 16. province
LINGER, Gen. 19. 16. 2 Pet. 2. 3.
LION, Gen. 49. 9. Judg. 14. 5, 18. Job 4. 10, 11. & 10. 16. & 28. 8. Ps. 7. 2. & 17. 12. & 10. 9. & 22. 13. Isa. 38. 13.
Prov. 22. 13. there is a *l.* without, 26. 13.
28. 1. righteous are bold as a *l.*
Eccl. 9. 4. living dog is better than a dead *l.*
Isa. 11. 6. calf and young *l.*
35. 9. no *l.* shall be there, nor
Ezek. 1. 10. face as of a *l.*, 10. 14.
Hos. 5. 14. be as a young *l.*
Mic. 5. 8. rem. of Jacob be as a *l.*
2 Tim. 4. 17. delivered out of mouth of the *l.*
1 Pet. 5. 8. the devil as a roaring *l.*
Rev. 5. 5. *L.* of the tribe of Juda
R. V. Gen. 49. 9; Num. 23. 24; 24. 9; Deut. 33. 20; Job 38. 39. lioness
LIPS, Ex. 6. 12, 30. Prov. 16. 10.
Ps. 12. 3. all flattering *l.*
17. 1. not feigned *l.*
31. 18. lying *l.*, 120. 2. Prov. 10. 18. & 12. 22. & 17. 4, 7. Isa. 59. 3.
Ps. 63. 5. I will praise thee with joyful *l.*
Prov. 10. 21. the *l.* of the righteous
26. 23. burning *l.* and wicked heart
S. of S. 7. 9. *l.* of those that are asleep
Isa. 6. 5. man of unclean *l.* people
57. 19. create the fruit of the *l.*
Hos. 14. 2. render calves of our *l.*
Mal. 2. 7. priest's *l.* should keep
Ps. 51. 15. open thou *my lips*; and
63. 3. —shall praise thee, 71. 23.

Ps. 141. 3. keep the door of —
17. 4. *thy lips*, 34. 13. & 45. 2.
LITTLE, Ezra 9. 8. Neh. 9. 32.
Ps. 2. 12. when his wrath is kindled
but a *l.*
8. 5. a *l.* lower than the angels
37. 16. a *l.* that a righteous man
Prov. 6. 10. a *l.* sleep, a *l.* slumber
10. 20. heart of wicked is *l.* worth
15. 16. better is *l.* with fear of the
Isa. 28. 10. here a *l.* and there a *l.*
54. 8. in a *l.* wrath I hid my face
Ezek. 11. 16. I will be as a *l.* sanc.
Zech. 1. 15. I was but a *l.* displeased
Matt. 6. 30. of *l.* faith, 8. 26. & 14. 31.
Luke 12. 32. fear not *l.* flock, it is
19. 17. thou hast been faithful in
a very *l.*
1 Tim. 4. 8. bod. exercise profit. *l.*
Rev. 3. 8. hast *l.* strength, and kept
LIVE, Gen. 3. 22. & 17. 18.
Lev. 18. 5. if a man do, he shall *l.*,
Neh. 9. 29. Ezek. 3. 21. & 18. 9. &
33. 13, 15, 16, 19. Rom. 10. 5. Gal. 3.
12.
Deut. 32. 40. *live for ever*, 1 Kings
1. 31. Neh. 2. 3. Ps. 22. 26. & 49. 9.
Dan. 2. 4. & 3. 9. & 5. 10. & 6. 21.
Zech. 1. 5. John 6. 51, 58. Rev. 4. 9.
& 5. 14. & 10. 6. & 15. 7.
Job 14. 14. if a man die, shall he *l.*
Ps. 55, 23. bloody men not *l.* out
118. 17. I shall not die, but *l.* and
Isa. 38. 16. by these men *l.* and
55. 3. hear, and your soul shall *l.*
Ezek. 16. 6. said, when thou wast
in thy blood, *l.*
18. 32. turn yourselves and *l.*
Hab. 2. 4. just shall *l.* by faith
Matt. 4. 4. man not *l.* by bread
John 14. 19. because I *l.*, ye shall *l.*
Acts 17. 28. in him we *l.* and move
Rom. 8. 13. if *l.* after the flesh, ye
41. whether we *l.* we *l.* to Lord
2 Cor. 5. 15. who *l.* should not *l.* to
6. 9. as dying, and behold we *l.*
13. 11. be of one mind, *l.* in peace
Gal. 12. 20. I *l.* yet not I, but Christ
5. 25. if we *l.* in Spirit, walk in
Phil. 1. 21. to *l.* is Christ, 22.
2 Tim. 3. 12. all that will *l.* godly in
Tit. 2. 12. *l.* soberly, righteously
Heb. 13. 18. willing to *l.* honestly
1 Pet. 2. 24. should *l.* to righteous.
1 John 4. 9. that we might *l.*
Acts 23. 1. I *lived* in all good con.
Jas. 5. 5. ye have *l.* in pleasure
Rev. 18. 9. *l.* deliciously
20. 4. they *l.* and reigned with
Job 19. 25. I know that my Redeemer *liveth*
Rom. 6. 10. in that he *l.* he *l.* to God
14. 7. none *l.* to himself or dieth
1 Tim. 5. 6. *l.* in pleasure, dead
Heb. 7. 25. *l.* to make intercession
Rev. 1. 18. I am he that *l.* and was
3. 1. I know that thou *l.* and art
Acts 7. 38. received *lively* oracles
1 Pet. 1. 3. bego. again to a *l.* hope
2. 5. ye, as *l.* stones, are built up a
1 John 3. 16. *lives*, Rev. 12. 11.
Eccl. 7. 2. *living* will lay it to heart
Isa. 38. 19. the *l.* the *l.* shall praise
Jer. 2. 13. Lord fountain of *l.* waters
Matt. 22. 32. not the God of the
dead, but of the *l.*
Mark 12. 44. cast in all her *l.*
John 4. 10. would have given thee
l. water
7. 38. flow rivers of *l.* water
Rom. 12. 1. present your bodies a
l. sacrifice
14. 9. Lord both of dead and *l.*
1 Cor. 15. 45. the first Adam was
made a *l.* soul
Heb. 10. 20. by a new and *l.* way
1 Pet. 2. 4. coming as to a *l.* stone
Rev. 7. 17. lead them to *l.* fountains
R. V. 1 Cor. 9. 13. eat; Rev. 18. 7.
waxed
LOAD, Ps. 68. 19. Isa. 46. 1.
LOATHE themselves for evil,
Ezek. 6. 9. & 16. 5. & 20. 43. & 36. 31.
Jer. 14. 19. *loathed* Zion, Zech. 11. 8.

Num. 21. 5. soul *loatheth*, Prov. 27. 7.
Ps. 38. 7. *loathsome* disease
R. V. Job 7. 5. out afresh; Ps. 38.
7. burning
LOAVES, miraculous multiplication of, Matt. 14. 17. & 15. 32. Mark
6. 35. Luke 9. 12. John 6. 5.
LOFTY eyes, Ps. 131. 1. Prov. 30. 13.
Isa. 2. 11. *l.* looks humbled, 5. 15.
57. 15. *l.* One that inhabiteth
R. V. Isa. 2. 12. haughty; 57. 7. high
LOINS girt, Prov. 31. 17. Isa. 11. 5.
Luke 12. 35. Eph. 6. 14. 1 Pet. 1. 13.
LONG, Ps. 91. 16. Eccl. 12. 5. Matt.
23. 14. Luke 18. 7. Jas. 5. 7.
Ex. 34. 6. Lord God, *long-suffering*,
Num. 14. 18. Ps. 86. 15. Jer. 15. 15.
Rom. 2. 4. & 9. 22. 1 Tim. 1. 16.
1 Pet. 3. 20. 2 Pet. 3. 9, 15.
Gal. 5. 22. fruit of Spirit is *l.*, Eph.
4. 2. Col. 1. 11. & 3. 12. 2 Tim. 3.
10. & 4. 2.
Ps. 63. 1. my flesh *longeth* for thee
84. 2. my soul *l.* for courts of
1:9. 40. *I have longed* after thy
131. — for thy commandments
174. — for thy salvation
20. my soul breaketh for *longing*
107. 9. he satisfieth the *l.* soul
R. V. Num. 9. 19; Deut. 28. 32; Ps.
94. 4; Matt. 23. 14; Mark 16. 5;
Luke 1. 20—; Ex. 34. 6; Num.
14. 18; Ps. 86. 15. slow to anger
LOOK, Gen. 13. 14. Ex. 10. 10.
Ps. 5. 3. direct my prayer and I
will *l.* up
Isa. 8. 17. wait upon the Lord, and
l. for
45. 22. *l.* unto me and be saved
66. 2. to this man will I *l.* that is
Mic. 7. 7. I will *l.* unto the Lord
Luke 7. 19. do we *l.* for another
2 Cor. 4. 18. we *l.* at things not seen
Phil. 2. 4. *l.* not every one on own
3. 20. heaven, from whence we *l.*
Heb. 9. 28. to them that *l.* for him
1 Pet. 1. 12. angels desire to *l.* into
3. 14. seeing we *l.* for such things
Gen. 29. 32. the Lord *looked* on my
affliction, Ex. 2. 25. & 3. 7. & 4. 31.
Deut. 26. 7.
Ps. 34. 5. they *l.* to him and were
Isa. 5. 7. he *l.* for judgment, behold
22. 11. hath not *l.* to the maker
Jer. 8. 15. we *l.* for peace, but, 14.
19.
Obad. 13. not have *l.* on affliction
Hag. 1. 9. ye *l.* for much, and it
Luke 2. 38. *l.* for redemption in
22. 61. the Lord *l.* on Peter and
Heb. 11. 10. *l.* for a city whose
1 John 1. 1. which we have seen
and *l.* on
1 Sam. 16. 7. man *looketh* on the
outward appearance, but the
Lord *l.* on the heart
S. of S. 2. 9. he *l.* forth at the win.
Matt. 5. 28. *l.* on a woman to lust
24. 50. come in a day he *l.* not for
Jas. 1. 25. *l.* into perfect law of
Ps. 18. 27. thou wilt bring down
high *looks*
Isa. 38. 14. mine eyes fail with
looking upward
Luke 9. 62. no man *l.* back is fit for
Tit. 2. 13. *l.* for that blessed hope
Heb. 10. 27. a fearful *l.* of judg.
12. 2. *l.* to Jesus, the author and
15. *l.* diligently, lest any fail
2 Pet. 3. 12. *l.* for and hasting
Jude 21. *l.* for the mercy of our
R. V. The changes are chiefly
those brought about by subsequent words, and do not affect
meanings
LOOSE, Deut. 25. 9. Josh. 5. 15
Ps. 146. 7. the Lord *l.* the prisoners
102. 20. to *l.* those appointed to
Isa. 58. 6. fast chosen to *l.* bands
Eccl. 12. 6. before the silver cord
be *loosed*
Matt. 16. 19. *l.* on earth, *l.* in heav.
Acts 2. 24. having *l.* pains of death

1 Cor. 7. 27. bound to a wife, seek
not to be *l.* art thou *l.* seek not a
R. V. Judg. 15. 14. dropped; Matt.
18. 27. released; Acts 13. 13; 16. 11;
27. 21. set sail; 27. 13. weighed anchor; Rom. 7. 2. discharged
LORD, ascribed to man, Gen. 18.
12. & 23. 11. Isa. 26. 13. 1 Cor. 8. 5.
1 Pet. 5. 3. and in about fourteen
other places; and to God, Gen.
28. 16. Ex. 5. 2. 1 Cor. 12. 5. and in
about three hundred other texts
Ex. 34. 6. the *L.* the *L.* God mer.
Deut. 4. 35. *L.* is God, 39. 1 Kings
18. 39.
6. 4. *L.* our God is one *L.*, 10.
17. *L.* of *l.*, Dan. 2. 47. 1 Tim. 6. 15.
Rev. 17. 14. & 19. 16.
Neh. 9. 6. art *L.* alone, Isa. 37. 20.
Ps. 118. 27. God is the *L.*, 100. 3.
Zech. 14. 9. one *L.* and his name
Mark 2. 28. the Son of man is *L.*
of
Acts 2. 36. made him *L.* and Christ
Rom. 10. 12. same *L.* over all
14. 9. *L.* of the dead and the
1 Cor. 2. 8. *L.* of glory
15. 47. *L.* from heaven
8. 6. one God, one *L.* Jesus Christ
Eph. 4. 5. one *L.* one faith, one
Gen. 15. 6. and he believed *in the
Lord*
1 Sam. 2. 1. heart rejoiceth —, Ps.
32. 11. & 33. 1. & 35. 9. & 97. 12. &
104. 34. Isa. 41. 16. & 61. 10. Joel
2. 13. Hab. 3. 18. Zech. 10. 7. Phil.
3. 1. & 4. 4.
1 Kings 18. 5. trust —, Ps. 4. 5. & 11.
1. & 31. 6. & 32. 10. & 37. 3. & 115. 9,
10, 11. & 118. 8. & 125. 1. Prov. 3.
5. & 16. 20. & 28. 25. & 29. 25. Isa.
26. 4. Zeph. 3. 2.
Ps. 31. 24. hope —, 130. 7. & 131. 3.
34. 2. soul make her boast —
37. 4. delight thyself —, 7. rest —
Isa. 45. 17. Israel shall be saved —
24. — have I righteousness and
42. 25. — shall all the seed of Israel
Rom. 16. 12. labor —, 1 Cor. 15. 58.
Eph. 6. 10. be strong — and power
1 Thes. 5. 12. over you —, Col. 4. 7,
17.
Rev. 14. 13. blessed are the dead
which die —
LORD'S PRAYER, Matt. 6. 9.
LOSE, Eccl. 3. 6. Matt. 10. 39, 42. &
16. 26. John 6. 39. 2 John 8. Prov.
23. 8.
1 Cor. 3. 15. *loss*, Phil. 3. 7, 8.
Ps. 119. 176. astray like *lost* sheep
Ezek. 37. 11. our hope is *l.* we
Matt. 5. 13. if salt have *l.* its savor
10. 6. to the *l.* sheep of Israel
18. 11. save that was *l.*, Luke 19. 10.
Luke 15. 32. thy brother was *l.* and
John 18. 9. them thou gavest me,
I have *l.* none
2 Cor. 4. 3. the Gospel be hid it is
to them that are *l.*
R. V. Matt. 16. 26; Mark 8. 36. forfeit: John 17. 12. perished
LOT, Lev. 16. 8, 9, 10. Josh. 1. 6.
1 Sam. 14. 41. Saul said, give us a
perfect *l.*, 42.
Ps. 16. 5. thou maintainest my *l.*
125. 3. rod of wicked not rest on *l.*
Prov. 16. 33. the *l.* is cast into lap
Acts 1. 26. the *l.* fell on Matthias
8. 21. hast neither *l.* nor part in
Ps. 22. 18. on my vesture they did
cast *lots*
R. V. Matt. 27. 35 —
LOVE, Gen. 27. 4. 2 Sam. 13. 15.
2 Sam. 1. 26. passing the *l.* of wo.
Eccl. 9. 1. no man knoweth either *l.*
S. of S. 2. 5. I am sick of *l.*, 5. 8.
7. 12. there I will give thee my
loves
8. 6. *l.* is strong as death, jealous
Isa. 38. 17. thou hast in *l.* to my
Jer. 2. 2. remember the *l.* of
31. 3. loved thee with everlast. *l.*
Ezek. 16. 8. thy time was time of *l.*

Hos. 11. 4. draw them with bands of *l.*
Matt. 24. 12. the *l.* of many shall
John 15. 9. continue ye in my *l.*
13. greater *l.* hath no man than
Rom. 8. 35. who shall separate us from the *l.* of Christ, 39.
12. 9. let *l.* be without dissimula.
13. 10. *l.* is the fulfill. of the law
15. 30. for Christ's sake, and *l.*
2 Cor. 5. 14. *l.* of Christ constrain.
Gal. 5. 6. faith which worketh by *l.*
13. by *l.* serve one another
22. fruit of the Spirit is *l.* joy and
1 Thes. 1. 3. your labor of *l.*
5. 8. putting on breastplate of faith and *l.*
2 Thes. 2. 10. received not the *l.*
Heb. 13. 1. let brotherly *l.* continue
1 John 3. 1. what manner of *l.* the Father bestowed on us
4. 7. *l.* is of God
4. 9. manifest the *l.* of God
11. we ought to *l.* one another
18. perfect *l.* casteth out fear
21. who loveth God *l.* his brother
Rev. 2. 4. thou hast left thy first *l.*
Eph. 1. 4. without blame before God *in love*
4. 15. speaking truth —, 16.
5. 2. walk — as Christ hath loved
Col. 2. 2. knit together — and
1 Thes. 3. 12. abound —
5. 13. esteem —
Luke 11. 42. *love of God,* John 5. 42.
Rom. 5. 5. — is shed abroad in our
2 Cor. 3. 14. — be with you all
2 Thes. 3. 5. direct your hearts into —
1 John 2. 5. in him is — perfected
3. 16. perceive we —
17. dwelleth — in him
4. 9. in this was manifested — towards
5. 3. this is — keep his command.
Deut. 7. 7. his *love,* Zeph. 3. 17. Ps. 91. 14. Isa. 63. 9. John 15. 10. Rom. 5. 8.
Lev. 19. 18. thou shalt *l.* thy neighbor as thyself, 34. Matt. 19. 19. & 22. 39. Rom. 13. 8. Gal. 5. 14. Jas. 2. 8.
Deut. 6. 5. shalt *l.* the Lord thy God with all thy heart, Matt. 22. 37. Luke 10. 27.
Deut. 10. 12. tc fear the Lord and to *l.*
Ps. 31. 23. O *l.* the Lord, all ye his
97. 10. ye that *l.* the Lord hate
145. 20. the Lord preserveth them that *l.* him
S. of S. 1. 4. the upright *l.* thee
Mic. 6. 8. tc do justiy, and *l.* mercy
Zech. 8. 19. *l.* the truth and peace
Matt. 5. 44. *l.* your enemies, bless
John 13. 34. *l.* one another, 15. 12, 17. Rom. 13. 8. 1 John 3. 11, 23. & 4. 7, 11, 12. 1 Pet. 1. 22.
14. 23. if a man *l.* me, my Father will *l.* him
1 Cor. 16. 22. if any man *l.* not Lord
Eph. 5. 25. *l.* your wives, Col. 3. 19.
2 Tim. 4. 8. to all them that *l.* his
1 Pet. 1. 8. whom having not seen, ye *l.*
2. 17. *l.* the brotherhood, 3. 8.
1 John 2. 15. *l.* not world nor
4. 19. we *l.* him because he first *lored* us
Ps. 116. 1. *I love* the Lord because, 18. 1.
119. 97. how — thy law, 113. 119, 127, 159, 163, 167. & 26. 8. Isa. 43. 1.
John 21. 15. *lovest* thou me — thee, 16. 17.
2 John 1. whom — in the truth
Rev. 3. 19. as many as — I rebuke
Deut. 7. 8. because the Lord *lored*
1 Sam. 18. 1. *l.* David as his own
2 Sam. 12. 24. called Solomon, and Lord *l.* him
1 Kings 3. 3. Solomon *l.* the Lord
10. 3. the Lord *l.* Israel

Hos. 11. 1. Israel was a child, then I *l.* him
Mark 10. 21. Jesus beheld. him, *l.*
Luke 7. 47. sins are forgiven, she *l.*
2 Tim. 4. 10. having *l.* this present
Heb. 1. 9. hast *l.* righteousness
John 3. 16. God so *l.* the world
3. 19. men *l.* darkness rather
11. 36. behold how he *l.* him
12. 43. *l.* the praise of men more
13. 1. having *l.* his own, he *l.*
23. one of his disciples whom Jesus *l.,* 19. 26. & 20. 2. & 21. 7, 20.
14. 21. *l.* me, be *l.* of my Father
28. if ye *l.* me, ye would rejoice
15. 9. as my Father *l.* me, so have
16. 27. Father *loreth* you because
17. 23. I *l.* them as thou hast *l.* me
26. 1. wherewith thou hast *l.* them
Rom. 8. 37. conquerors through him that *l.* us
9. 13. Jacob I *l.* Esau I hated
Gal. 1. 20. Son of God, who *l.* me
Eph. 2. 4. great love where. he *l.* us
5. 2. as Christ *l.* us
25. as Christ *l.* church
2 Thes. 2. 16. God our Father *l.* us
2 Pet. 2.15. *l.* wages of unrighteous.
1 John 4. 10. not that we *l.* God but
Rev. 1. 5. that *l.* us and washed
12. 11. *l.* not their lives unto death
Ps. 11. 7. the righteous Lord *l.*
146. 8. the Lord *l.* the righteous
Prov. 3. 12. whom the Lord *l.* he
17. 17. a friend *l.* at all times
21. 17. he who *l.* pleasure, shall
S. of S. 1. 7. whom my soul *l.,* 3. 1, 4.
Matt. 10. 37. *l.* father or mother
John 3. 35. Father *l.* the Son, 15. 20.
16. 27. Father himself *l.* you
2 Cor. 9. 7. God *l.* a cheerful giver
3 John 9. *l.* to have preeminence
Rev. 22. 15. whoso *l.* and mak. a lie
2 Sam. 1. 23. *lovely,* S. of S. 5. 16.
Ezek. 32. Phile. 4. 8.
Ps. 88. 18. *lover,* Tit. 1. 8. Ps. 38. 11.
Hos. 2. 5. 2 Tim. 3. 2, 4.
R. V. Tit. 1. 8. given to
LOW, Deut. 28. 43. Ezek. 17. 24.
1 Sam. 2. 7. Lord brings *l.* and lifts
Job 40. 12. look on every one that is proud and bring him *l.*
Ps. 49. 2. both high and *l.* rich and
136. 23. remem. us in our *l.* estate
Isa. 26. 5. lofty city he layeth it *l.*
32. 19. city shall be *l.* in a *l.* place
Luke 1. 48. he regard. the *l.* estate
52. he exalted them of *l.* degree,
Job 5. 11. Ezek. 21. 26. Jas. 1. 9, 10.
Luke 3. 5. every mountain and hill be made *l.*
Rom. 12. 16. condescend to men of *l.* estate
Ps. 63. 9. *lower* parts of the earth, 139. 15. Isa. 44. 23. Eph. 4. 9.
138. 6. Lord hath respect to *lowly*
Prov. 3. 34. he giveth grace unto *l.*
11. 2. with the *l.* is wisdom
Matt. 11. 29. learn of me, for I am meek and *l.*
Eph. 4. 2. *lowliness,* Phil. 2. 3.
R. V. 2 Chron. 26. 10; 28. 18. lowland; Ps. 107. 39. bowed down; Ezek. 26. 20. nether
LUCRE, filthy, 1 Tim. 3. 3, 8. Tit. 1. 7. 1 Pet. 5. 2.
LUKEWARM, thou art, Rev.3. 16.
LUMP, Isa. 38. 21. Rom. 9. 21. & 11. 16. 1 Cor. 5. 6, 7. Gal. 5. 9.
R. V. 2 Kings 20. 7; Isa. 38. 21. cake
LUST, Ex. 15. 9. Ps. 78. 18. Jas. 4. 2.
Ps. 81. 12. gave them up to their own hearts' *l.*
Matt. 5. 28. looketh on a woman to *l.*
Rom. 7. 7. not known *l.* except law
1 Cor. 10. 6. not *l.* after evil things
Gal. 5. 16. shall not fulfil *l.* of flesh
1 Thes. 4. 5. not in the *l.* of
Jas. 1. 15. when *l.* is conceived, it
1 John 2. 16. *l.* of the flesh, and *l.*
Mark 4. 19. *lusts* of other things
John 8. 44. *l.* of your father ye will
Rom. 6. 12. should obey it in the *l.*

Rom. 13. 14. for the flesh, to fulfil the *l.*
Gal. 5. 17. flesh *l.* against Spirit
24. crucified flesh with affec. and *l.*
Eph. 2. 3. *l.* of our flesh, and mind
1 Tim. 6. 9. foolish and hurtful *l.*
2 Tim. 2. 22. flee youthful *l.* follow
3. 6. laden with sins, led away with divers *l.*
Tit. 2. 12. denying ungodliness and worldly *l.*
3. 3. divers *l.* and pleasures
Jas. 4. 3. consume it on your *l.*
1 Pet. 2. 11. abstain from fleshly *l.*
2 Pet. 3. 3. walk after their own *l.*
R. V. Ps. 81. 12. stubbornness; Rom. 7. 7. coveting; Jas. 4. 1, 3. pleasures; Deut. 14. 26. desireth; Jas. 4. 5. long

M

MAD, Deut. 28. 34. 1 Sam. 21. 13.
Eccl. 2. 2. I said of laughter it is *m.*
Jer. 50. 38. they are *m.* upon idols
Hos. 9. 7. the prophet is a fool, the spiritual man is *m.*
John 10. 20. he hath a dev. and is *m.*
Acts 26. 11. exceedingly *m.* against
24. learning doth make thee *m.*
Deut. 28. 28. madness, Eccl. 1. 17. & 2. 12. & 9. 3. & 10. 13. Zech. 12. 4.
Luke 6. 11. 2 Pet. 2. 16.
R. V. Eccl. 7. 7. foolish
MADE, Ex. 2. 14. 2 Sam. 13. 6.
Ps. 104. 24. thy works in wisdom hast thou *m.*
Prov. 16. 14. Lord *m.* all things
John 1. 3. all things were *m.* by him
Rom. 1. 3. Christ *m.* of the seed of David
1 Cor. 1. 30. Christ who of God is *m.*
9. 22. *m.* all things to all men
Gal. 4. 4. *m.* of a woman, *m.* under
Phil. 2. 7. *m.* in the likeness of men
R. V. The changes are mostly to such words as, created, wrought, become, manifested, etc.
See also MAKE.
MAGISTRATES, Ezra 7. 25 ; to be obeyed, Ex. 22. 8. Rom. 13. Tit. 3. 1. 1 Pet. 2. 14.
MAGNIFY, Josh. 3. 7. 1 Chron. 29. 25.
Job 7. 17. what is man that thou shouldst *m.* him
36. 24. remember to *m.* his work
Ps. 34. 3. *m.* the Lord with me
Isa. 42. 21. *m.* the law, and make
Luke 1. 46. my soul doth *m.* Lord
Acts 10. 46. spake with tongues and *m.* God
Gen. 19. 19. thou hast *magnified* thy
2 Sam. 7. 26. let thy name be *m.* for
Ps. 35. 27. let the Lord be *m.*
138. 2. hast *m.* thy word above
Acts 19. 17. the name of the Lord was *m.*
Phil. 1. 20. Christ shall be *m.* in
R. V. 2 Chron. 32. 23. exalted;
Rom. 11. 13. glorify my ministry
MAID, Gen. 16. 2. Deut. 22. 14.
Job 31. 1. Jer. 2. 32. Amos 2. 7.
Zech. 9. 17.
R. V. Gen. 16. 2; 29. 24; 30. 7; Ex. 2. 5. handmaid ; Matt. 9. 24. dam.
MAIMED healed by Christ, Matt. 15. 30.
animal, unfit for sacri. Lev. 22. 22.
MAINTAIN my cause, 1 Kings 8. 40, 45. Ps. 9. 4. & 140. 12. Job 13. 15.
Tit. 3. 8. care. to *m.* good works, 14.
Ps. 16. 5. thou *maintainest* my lot
R. V. 1 Chron. 26. 27. repair
MAJESTY, Dan. 4. 30, 36. & 5. 18, 19. Job 40. 10. Ps. 21. 5. & 45. 3, 4.
1 Chron. 29. 11. thine, O Lord, is *m.*
Job 37. 22. with God is terrible *m.*
Ps. 29. 4. voice of Lord is full of *m.*
93. 1. the Lord is clothed with *m.*
145. 5. glorious honor of thy *m.*
12. glorious *m.* of his kingdom

Isa. 2. 19. hide for fear of the glory of his m.
Heb. 1. 3. right hand of M. on high
8. 1. of the throne of the M.
2 Pet. 1. 16. eyewitnesses of his m.
Jude 25. to the only wise God be glory and m.
R. V. Dan. 4. 36 ; 5. 18, 19. greatness
MAKE, Gen. 1. 26. & 3. 6, 21. Deut. 32. 35. 1 Cor. 4. 15. 1 Sam. 20. 38.
Job 4. 17. shall man be purer than his *Maker*
32. 22. my M. would soon take me
35. 10. where is God my M.
36. 3. I will ascribe righ. to my M.
Ps. 95. 6. kneel before Lord our M.
Prov. 14.31. reproach. his M., 17. 5.
22. 2. Lord is the M. of them all
Isa. 17. 7. that day shall man look to his M.
51. 13. forgettest the Lord thy M.
54. 5. thy M. is thy husband ; the
Heb. 11. 10. whose builder and m.
MALE or female, Gen. 1. 27. Num. 5. 3. Mal. 1. 14. Matt. 19. 4. Gal. 3. 28.
MALEFACTORS, execution of, Deut. 21. 22.
crucified with Christ, Luke 23. 32.
MALICE, leaven of, 1 Cor. 5. 8.
1 Cor. 14. 20. in m. be children, in
Eph. 4. 31. put away with all m., Col. 3. 8. 1 Pet. 2. 1.
Tit. 3. 3. living in m. and envy
Rom. 1. 29. filled with all *malicious-ness*; full of envy, 1 Pet. 2. 1.
R. V. 1 Pet. 2. 1. wickedness
MAMMON, Matt. 6. 24. Luke 16. 9.
MAN, Gen. 1. 26, 27. 2 Kings 9. 11.
Job 4. 17. shall m. be more just
5. 7. m. is born to trouble, 14. 1.
7. 17. what is m. that thou
9. 2. how shall m. be just with God
14. 1. m. born of woman, is of
15. 14. what is m. that he should
6. m. is a worm
28. 28. unto m. he said, depart
Ps. 8. 4. what is m. that thou art
10. 18. m. of earth no more oppress
90. 3. thou turnest m. to destruc.
104. 23. m. goeth forth to his work
118. 6. not fear ; what can m. do
143. 3. what is m. that thou takest
Prov. 20. 24. m's goings are of Lord
Eccl. 6. 10. it is known that it is m.
7. 29. God made m. upright, but
12. 5. m. goeth to his long home
Isa. 2. 22. cease ye from m. whose
Jer. 17. 5. cursed be the m. that
Zech. 13. 7. awake against the m. that is my fellow
Matt. 4. 4. m. shall not live by
26. 72. I know not the m.
John 7. 46. nev. m. spake like this m.
Rom. 6. 6. old m. crucified with
1 Cor. 2. 11. what m. knoweth the things of a m. save the spirit of m. in him
14. natural m. receiveth not things
11. 8. m. not of woman, but woman of m.
15. 47. first m. is earthy ; second m.
2 Cor. 4. 16. though outward m. perish, yet inward m. is renewed
Eph. 4. 22. put off the old m. which
24. put on new m. renewed
1 Pet. 3. 4. be the hidden m. of heart
Ex. 15. 3. Lord is a *man* of war
Num. 23. 19. God is not — that he
Isa. 47. 3. I will not meet thee as — 53. 3. — of sorrows and acquainted
Jer. 15. 10. borne me — of strife
Matt. 8. 9. I am — under authority
16. 26. what shall — give in ex.
John 3. 3. except — be born again
Acts 10. 26. I myself also am —
2 Cor. 12. 2. I knew — in Christ, 3.
Phil. 2. 8. in fashion as — he hum.
1 Tim. 2. 5. one Mediator the m. Christ Jesus
Prov. 30. 2. *if any man*, Matt. 16. 24. John 6. 51. & 7. 17, 37. Rom. 8. 9. 2 Cor. 5. 17. Gal. 1. 9. Rev. 22. 19.

Ps. 39. 5. *every man*, Prov. 19. 6. Mic. 4. 4. & 7. 2. Gal. 6. 4, 5. Col. 1. 28. Heb. 2. 9.
Ps. 87. 4. *this man*, Isa. 66. 2. Mic. 5. 5. Luke 19. 14. John 7. 46. Jas. 1. 26.
Prov. 1. 5. *a wise man* will hear
9. 8. rebuke — and he will love thee
17. 10. reproof enters into — more
Eccl. 2. 14. — eyes are in his head
10. 2. — heart is at his right hand
Jer. 9. 23. let not — glory in wisdom
Jas. 3. 13. who is — among you
Deut. 33. 1. *man of God*, Judg. 13. 6, 8. 2 Kings 1. 9, 13. 1 Tim. 6. 11. 2 Tim. 3. 17.
R. V. Numerous changes in N. T. to one
MANDRAKES, Gen. 30. 14. S. of S. 7. 13.
MANIFEST, Eccl. 3. 18. 1 Cor. 15. 27.
Mark 4. 22. nothing hid which shall not be m.
John 14. 21. I will m. myself
2. 11. m. forth his glory to dis.
17. 6. I have m. thy name unto
1 Cor. 4. 5. make m. counsels
Gal. 5. 19. works of the flesh are m.
2 Thes. 1. 5. a m. token of right.
1 Tim. 3. 16. God was m. in the flesh
Heb. 4. 13. any creature not m. in
1 John 3. 5. he was m. to take
10. in this children of God are m.
4. 9. in this was m. the love of God
Luke 8. 17. *made manifest*, John 3. 21. 1 Cor. 3. 13. 2 Cor. 4. 10. & 5. 11. Eph. 5. 13.
Rom. 8. 19. *manifestation* of sons
1 Cor. 12. 7. m. of the Spirit is given
2 Cor. 4. 2. but by m. of the truth
R. V. 1 Cor. 15. 27 ; 1 Tim. 5. 25 ; 2 Tim. 3. 9. evident ; Rom. 8. 19. revealing
MANIFOLD mercies, Neh. 9. 19, 27.
Ps. 104. 24. how m. are thy works
Amos 5. 12. I know your m. trans.
Luke 18. 30. m. more in this pre.
Eph. 3. 10. known m. wisdom of
1 Pet. 1. 6. in heaviness through m. temptations
MANNA, Ex. 16. 15. Num. 11. 6. Deut. 8. 3, 16. Josh. 5. 12. Neh. 9. 20. Ps. 78. 24. John 6. 31, 49, 58.
Rev. 2. 17. give to eat of hidden m.
R. V. Ex. 16. 15. what is it ; John 6. 58 —
MANNER, 1 Sam. 8. 9, 11. Isa. 5. 17. Jer. 22. 21. 1 Thes. 1. 5, 9. 1 John 3. 1.
2 Kings 17. 34. *manners*, Acts 13. 18. 1 Cor. 15. 33. Lev. 20. 23. Heb. 1. 1.
R. V. Numerous changes to custom, ordinance, form, etc. ; and frequent omissions of the word
MANSIONS in my Father's house, John 14. 2.
MAN-STEALING, Ex. 21. 16. Deut. 24. 7.
MARK, set me as a, Job 7. 20. & 16. 12.
Lam. 3. 12. Gal. 6. 17. bear *marks*
Ezek. 9. 4. set a m. upon the foreheads, Rev. 13. 16, 17. & 14. 9. & 19. 20.
Phil. 3. 14. I press toward the m.
Ps. 37. 37. m. the perfect man
130. 3. if thou shouldest m. iniquity, Job 10. 14. Jer. 2. 22.
Rom. 16. 17. m. them which cause
Phil. 3. 17. m. them which walk
R. V. Gen. 4. 15. sign ; Phil. 3. 14. goal ; Rev. 15.2 — ; Job 18. 2. consider ; 22. 15. keep ; 24. 16. shut themselves up
MARRIAGE, Gen. 38. 8. Deut. 25. 5.

Matt. 22. 2. king made a m. for son
25. 10. that were ready went into the m.
Heb. 13. 4. m. is honorable in all
Rev. 19. 7. the m. of the Lamb
Jer. 3. 14. I am m. to you, saith Lord
Luke 14. 20. I have m. a wife, and
17. 27. they drank, m. and
Isa. 62. 5. as a man m. a virgin
1 Cor. 7. 9. better to m. than to burn
1 Tim. 4. 3. forbidding to m. and
5. 14. that younger women m. and
R. V. Matt. 22. 2, 4, 9 ; 25. 10. marriage feast
MARROW, to bones, Prov. 3. 8. Job 21. 24.
Ps. 63. 5. soul is satis. as with m.
Isa. 25. 6. feast of fat things full of m.
Heb. 4. 12. dividing asunder joints and m.
MARTYR, Acts 22. 20. Rev. 2. 13. & 17. 6.
MARVEL not, Eccl. 5. 8. John 5. 28. Acts 3. 12. 1 John 3. 13.
Ps. 48. 5. they *marvelled*, Matt. 8. 27. & 9. 8, 33. & 21. 20. & 22. 22.
Luke 1. 63. Acts 2. 7. & 4. 13.
Matt. 8. 10. Jesus m., Mark 6. 6.
Job 5. 9. doeth *marvellous* things
10. 16. showed thyself m. against
Ps. 17. 7. show me thy m. kind.
98. 1. done m. things, Mic. 7. 15.
118. 23. it is m. in our eyes
1 Chron. 16. 12. remember his m. works, Ps. 105. 5. & 9. 1.
Ps. 139. 14. m. are thy works, Rev. 15. 3.
R. V. Ps. 48. 5. amazed ; Matt. 9. 8. were afraid ; Rev. 17. 7. wonder ; Ps. 139. 14. wonderful ; John 9. 30. the marvel
MASTER, Isa. 24. 2. Mal. 1. 6. & 2. 12.
Matt. 23. 10. one is your M.
Mark 10. 17. good M. what shall I
John 3. 10. art thou a m. in Israel
13. 13. ye call me M. and say well
14. if I your M. have washed
Rom. 14. 4. to his own m. he stands
Eccl. 12. 11. *masters* of assemblies
Matt. 6. 24. no man can serve two m.
23. 10. neither be ye called m., Jas. 3. 1.
Col. 4. 1. m. give your servants
1 Cor. 3. 10. I as a *master builder*
R. V. 1 Sam. 24. 6 ; 26. 16 ; 29. 4, 10 ; 2 Sam. 2. 7 ; Amos 4. 1 ; Mark 13. 39 ; Rom. 14. 4 ; 2 Pet. 2. 1. lord ; Matt. 26. 25, 49 ; Mark 9. 5 ; 11. 21 ; 14. 45 ; John 4. 31 ; 9. 2 ; 11. 8. Rabbi ; Matt. 23. 8 ; John 8. 4 ; Jas. 3. 1 teacher
MATTER, Ex. 18. 22. & 23. 7. 1 Sam. 10. 16. Job 19. 28. & 32. 18. Ps. 45. 1. Dan. 7. 28. 2 Cor. 9. 5.
Acts 8. 21. part nor lot in this m.
Job 33. 13. account of any of his *matters*
Ps. 131. 1. exerc. myself in great m.
Matt. 23. 23. omitted the weight. m.
1 Pet. 4. 15. a busybody in other men's m.
R. V. Job 32. 18 ; Ps. 35. 20. words ; 1 Sam. 16. 18. speech ; Ps. 64. 5. purpose ; Dan. 4. 17. sentence ; Jas. 3. 5. much wood
MEAN, what, Ex. 12. 26. Deut. 6. 20, 24. Josh. 4. 6, 21. Ezek. 17. 12. Acts 17. 20. & 21. 13. Ezek. 37. 18. Jonah 1. 6.
Gen. 50. 20. ye thought ill ; God *meant* good
Ps. 49. 7. *by any means*, Jer. 5. 31. 1 Cor. 9. 22. Phil. 3. 11. 1 Thes. 3. 15.
R. V. Acts 21. 13. do ; 2 Cor. 8. 13. say not this ; Acts 27. 2. which was about ; Luke 15. 26. might be ; Prov. 6. 26. on account ; Luke 5

18——: 8. 36; John 9. 21. how;
Luke 10. 19; 2 Thes. 2. 3. in any
wise; Judg. 5. 22; Rev. 13. 14.
reason

MEASURE, Lev. 19. 35. Deut. 25.
15.
Job 11. 9. the *m.* is longer than
Ps. 39. 4. make me know the *m.*
Isa. 27. 8. in *m.* when it shooteth
Matt. 7. 2. with what *m.* ye mete
23. 32. fill up the *m.* of your
John 3. 34. giveth not Spirit by *m.*
Rom. 12. 3. gives to every man *m.*
2 Cor. 1. 8. were pressed out of *m.*
12. 7. I should be exalt. above *m.*
Eph. 4. 7. according to *m.* of the
13. to the *m.* of fulness of Christ
Rev. 11. 1. *m.* the temple of God
R. V. Mark 10. 26; 2 Cor. 1. 8. ex-
ceedingly; Mark 6. 51; Rev. 21.
15——; 2 Cor. 10. 14; 12. 7. over
much

MEAT, Job 6. 7. Ps. 42. 3. & 69. 21.
Ps. 104. 27. give *m.* in due season
111. 5. giveth *m.* to them that
Prov. 6. 8. provided *m.* in summer
Hos. 11. 4. I laid *m.* unto them
Hab. 1. 16. portion is fat and *m.*
3. 17. the fields shall yield no *m.*
Mal. 1. 12. that say his *m.* is con.
Matt. 6. 25. is not life more than *m.*
10. 10. workman worthy of his *m.*
John 4. 32. I have *m.* to eat ye
34. my *m.* is to do the will
6. 55. my flesh is *m.* indeed
Rom. 14. 15. destroy not him with
thy *m.*
17. kingdom of God is not *m.* and
drink
1 Cor. 6. 13. *m.* for belly, belly for
8. 8. *m.* commend. us not to God
10. 3. did all eat same spirit. *m.*
R. V. very frequent changes to
food, meal, etc.

MEDDLE, 2 Kings 14. 10. Prov.
17. 14. & 20. 3, 19. & 24. 21. & 26. 17.
R. V. Deut. 2. 5, 19. contend; Prov.
17. 4: 20. 3. quarrelling; 26. 17.
vexeth himself

MEDIATOR, is not *m.* of one,
Gal. 3. 20.
Gal. 3. 19. ordained by angels in
the hand of a *m.*
1 Tim. 2. 5. one *m.* between God
Heb. 8. 6. he is the *m.* of a better
9. 15. *m.* of New Testament
12. 24. *m.* of new covenant

MEDICINE, Prov. 17. 22. Jer. 30.
13. & 46. 11. Ezek. 47. 12.
R. V. Ezek. 47. 12. healing

MEDITATE, Isaac went to, Gen.
24. 63.
Josh. 1. 8. *m.* in thy law day and
night, Ps. 1. 2. & 119. 15, 23, 48, 78,
148.
Ps. 63. 6. *m.* on thee in the night
77. 12. I will *m.* of thy works
Isa. 33. 18. thy heart shall *m.* terror
Luke 21. 14. not *m.* before what
1 Tim. 4. 15. *m.* upon these things
Ps. 5. 1. consider my *meditation*
19. 14. let the *m.* of my heart
49. 3. *m.* of my heart shall be
104. 34. my *m.* of him shall be
sweet
119. 97. thy law is my *m.* all the
day
99. thy testimonies are my *m.*
R. V. Isa. 33. 18. muse; 1 Tim. 4.
15. be diligent in

MEEK, Moses was very, Num. 12.
3.
Ps. 22. 26. the *m.* shall eat and be
25. 9. *m.* will he guide in judg.
37. 11. *m.* shall inherit the earth
76. 9. Lord rose to save all *m.* of
147. 6. the Lord lifteth up the *m.*
149. 4. he will beautify the *m.*
Isa. 11. 4. reprove for *m.* of the
earth
29. 19. *m.* increase their joy
61. 1. preach good tidings to *m.*
Amos 2. 7. that turn aside way of
m.

Zeph. 2. 3. seek the Lord all *m.*
Matt. 5. 5. blessed are *m.* for they
11. 29. I am *m.* and lowly in heart
21. 5. thy king cometh *m.* sitting
1 Pet. 3. 4. ornament of *m.* and
Zeph. 2. 3. seek righteousness, seek
meekness
Ps. 45. 4. ride prosperously because
of *m.*
1 Cor. 4. 21. come in the spirit of
m.
2 Cor. 10. 1. I beseech you by the
m. of Christ
Gal. 5. 23. faith, *m.* against such
6. 1. restore him in spirit of *m.*
Eph. 4. 2. walk with all lowliness
and *m.*
Col. 3. 12. put on *m.* long-suffering
1 Tim. 6. 11. follow after faith,
love, *m.*
2 Tim. 2. 25. in *m.* instructing those
Tit. 3. 2. showing all *m.* to all men
Jas. 1. 21. receive with *m.*
3. 13. show his works with *m.* of
wisdom
1 Pet. 3. 15. of hope in you with *m.*

MEET, help, for him, Gen. 2. 18.
Job 34. 31. it is *m.* to be said to
God
Matt. 3. 8. fruits *m.* for repent.
1 Cor. 15. 9. not *m.* to be called
Col. 1. 12. *m.* to be partakers of the
2 Tim. 2. 21. vessel *m.* for the
master's use
Heb. 6. 7. *m.* for them by whom
Prov. 22. 2. rich and poor *m.*
Isa. 47. 3. I will not *m.* thee as a
64. 5. thou *m.* him that rejoiceth
Hos. 13. 8. I will *m.* them as a bear
Amos 4. 12. prepare to *m.* thy God
1 Thes. 4. 17. caught up to *m.* Lord
R. V. Deut. 3. 18. men of valor;
Jer. 26. 14; 27. 5; Phil. 1. 7; 2 Pet.
1. 13. right; Judg. 5. 30. on; Ezek.
15. 4. profitable; Matt. 3. 8; Acts
26. 20. worthy of; Rom. 1. 27. due;
Josh. 2. 16. light upon

MELODY in heart to the Lord,
Eph. 5. 19.

MEMBER, body not one, 1 Cor. 12.
14.
Jas. 3. 5. tongue is a little *m.*
Ps. 139. 16. and in thy book all my
members
Matt. 5. 29. one of thy *m.* perish
Rom. 6. 13. yield your *m.* as
7. 23. I see another law in my *m.*
12. 5. every one *m.* one of another
1 Cor. 6. 15. your bodies are *m.*
12. 12. the body is one, and hath
many *m.*
Eph. 4. 25. we are *m.* one of anoth.
5. 30. *m.* of his body, his flesh
Col. 3. 5. mortify your *m.* on earth
R. V. 1 Cor. 12. 23. parts

MEMORY cut off, Ps. 109. 15.
Ps. 145. 7. utter the *m.* of thy
Prov. 10. 7. *m.* of the just is blessed
Eccl. 9. 5. *m.* of them is forgotten
Isa. 26. 14. made their *m.* to per-
ish
1 Cor. 15. 2. if ye keep in *m.* what I
Ex. 3. 15. my *memorial* to all
13. 9. be for *m.* between thine eyes
17. 14. write this for a *m.* in book
Ps. 135. 13. thy *m.* through all
Hos. 12. 5. Lord of hosts; the Lord
is his *m.*
Matt. 26. 13. be told for a *m.* of her
Acts 10. 4. come up for a *m.* before

MEN, Gen. 32. 28. & 42. 11.
Ps. 9. 20. know themselves to be
but *m.*
17. 14. *m.* of thy hand; *m.* of
62. 9. *m.* of low degree are vanity
82. 7. ye shall die like *m.* and fall
Eccl. 12. 3. strong *m.* shall bow
Isa. 31. 3. Egyptians are *m.* not God
46. 8. remember this; show yourselves *m.*
Hos. 6. 7. they like *m.* transgress.
Rom. 1. 27. *m.* with *m.* working
Eph. 6. 6. *m.* pleasers, Col. 3. 22.
1 Thes. 2. 4.

MENSTRUOUS, Isa. 30. 22. Lam.
1. 17.
Ezek. 18. 6. neither come near a
m. woman
R. V. Lam. 1. 17; Isa. 30. 22. unclean
thing

MENTION, Ex. 23. 13. Job 28. 18.
Ps. 17. 16. I will make *m.* of thy
Isa. 26. 13. by thee only make *m.* of
62. 6. ye that make *m.* of the Lord
Rom. 1. 9. make *m.* of you in my
prayers, Eph. 1. 16. 1 Thes. 1. 2.
Phile. 4.
R. V. 2 Chron. 20. 34. inserted;
Ezek. 18. 22, 24; 33. 16. remember.

MERCHANT, Hos. 12. 7. Matt. 13.
45.
Isa. 23. 18. *merchandise* be holiness,
Matt. 22. 5. John 2. 16. 2 Pet. 2. 3.
R. V. Deut. 21. 14; 24. 7. deal with;
Ezek. 27. 15. mart; 28. 16. traffic;
Isa. 23. 11. concerning Canaan;
47. 15. that trafficked with thee;
Ezek. 27. 20; Hos. 12. 7. trafficker;
Ezek. 27. 13, 15, 17; 22. 23, 24. traf-
fickers

MERCY, Gen. 19. 19. & 39. 21.
Ex. 34. 7. keep *m.* for thousands,
Deut. 7. 9. 1 Kings 8. 23. Neh. 1. 5.
& 9. 32. Dan. 9. 4.
Num. 14. 18. Lord is of great *m.*
Ps. 23. 6. goodness and *m.* shall
25. 10. all paths of the Lord are *m.*
33. 18. fear him and hope in his *m.*
52. 8. I trust in the *m.* of God for
57. 3. God shall send forth his *m.*
66. 20. not turned away his *m.*
86. 5. plenteous in *m.* to all, 103. 8.
101. 1. I will sing of *m.* and
103. 11. great is his *m.* to them
17. *m.* of the Lord is from ever.
106. 1. his *m.* endureth for ever,
107. 1. & 118. 1. & 136. 1-26.
1 Chron. 16. 34, 41. 2 Chron. 5. 13.
& 7. 3, 6. & 20. 21. Ezra 3. 11. Jer.
33. 11.
Prov. 16. 6. by *m.* and truth, iniq.
20. 28. *m.* and truth preserve
Isa. 27. 11. he that made them will
not have *m.*
Hos. 6. 6. I desired *m.* and not sacrifice
10. 12. reap in *m.*
12. 6. keep *m.*
14. 3. in thee fatherless findeth *m.*
Jonah 2. 8. they for. their own *m.*
Mic. 6. 8. what doth God require,
but to love *m.*
20. *m.* to Abraham
Hab. 3. 2. in wrath remember *m.*
Luke 1. 50. his *m.* is on them that
78. through tender *m.* of our God
Rom. 9. 23. on vessels of *m.* pre.
15. *m.* on whom he will have *m.*
11. 31. through your *m.* they obtain *m.*
15. 9. may glorify God for his *m.*
2 Cor. 4. 1. as we have received *m.*
1 Tim. 1. 13. I obtained *m.* because
I did it ignorantly
2. grace, *m.* and peace, Tit. 1. 4.
2 John 3. Jude 2.
2 Tim. 1. 18. grant may find *m.* in
Tit. 3. 5. according to his *m.* saved
Jas. 2. 13. shall have judgment
without *m.* that showed no *m.*
and *m.*
Heb. 4. 16. we may obtain *m.* and
Jas. 3. 17. full of *m.* and good
5. 11. Lord is pitiful and of tend. *m.*
Jude 21. looking for the *m.* of our
Gen. 32. 10. not worthy of the least
of thy *mercies*
1 Chron. 21. 13. great are his *m.*
Ps. 69. 13. in multitude of thy *m.*
Isa. 55. 3. the sure *m.* of David
Lam. 3. 22. of Lord's *m.* we are
Dan. 9. 9. to the Lord belong *m.*
Rom. 12. 1. I beseech you by the *m.*
2 Cor. 1. 3. Father of *m.* and God of
Col. 3. 12. put on bowels of *m.*
Ps. 25. 6. *tender mercies*, 40. 11. &
51. 1. & 77. 9. & 79. 8. & 103. 4. & 119.
77, 156. & 145. 9.

Prov. 12. 10. — of wicked are cruel
Gen. 19. 19. *thy mercy*, Num. 14. 19.
 Neh. 13. 22. Ps. 5. 7. & 6. 4. & 13. 5.
 & 25. 7. & 31. 7, 16. & 33. 22. & 36. 5.
 & 44. 26. & 85. 7. & 86. 13. & 90. 14.
 & 94. 18. & 108. 4. & 57. 10. & 119.
 64. & 143. 12.
Ex. 34. 6. Lord God *merciful* and
 gracious, 2 Chron. 30. 9. Neh. 9.
 17, 31. Ps. 103. 8. Joel 2. 13. Jonah
 4. 2.
Ps. 18. 25. with *m*. show thyself *m*.
 37. 26. he is ever *m*. and lendeth
 117. 2. his *m*. kindness is great to
Prov. 11. 17. *m*. man doeth good
Isa. 57. 1. *m*. men are taken away
Jer. 3. 12. I am *m*. and will not
Matt. 5. 7. blessed are *m*. they
Luke 6. 36. be *m*. as your Father is
 m.
Heb. 2. 17. might be a *m*. high priest
 8. 12. I will be *m*. to their
R. V. Ex. 34. 6; Neh. 9. 17; Ps. 103.
 8; Joel 2. 13; Jonah 4. 2. full of
 compassion; Ps. 41. 4; 41. 10; 119.
 132. have mercy; 37. 26. dealeth
 graciously; Gen. 39. 21; 2 Sam. 22.
 51; 1 Kings 3. 6; 2 Chron. 1. 8; Ps.
 5. 7; 18. 50; 21. 7; 25. 7, 10; 36. 5; 61.
 7; 143. 12; Isa. 16. 5. kindness, or
 lovingkindness; Prov. 14. 21. pity;
 Isa. 9. 17; 14. 1; 27. 11; 49. 13; Jer.
 13. 14; 30. 18; Heb. 10. 28. compassion

MERRY, be, Luke 12. 19. & 15. 23,
 24, 29, 32.
Jas. 5. 13. is any *m*. let him sing
Prov. 15. 13. *merry-hearted*, 17. 22.
 Eccl. 9. 7. Isa. 24. 7.
R. V. Judg. 9. 27. festival; Prov.
 15. 15 ; Jas.5. 13. cheerful ; 2 Chron.
 7. 10. joyful · Eccl. 10. 19. glad in
 life
MESSAGE from God, Judg. 3. 20.
 Hag. 1. 13. 1 John 1. 5. & 3. 11.
Job 33. 23. if there be a *messenger*
Isa. 14. 32. what shall one answer
 the *m*.
 42. 19. who is blind or deaf, as *m*.
 44. 26. that performeth counsel of
 his *m*.
Mal. 2. 7. he is the *m*. of the Lord
 3. 1. I send my *m*. even the *m*. of
R. V. Luke 19. 14. ambassage; Gen.
 50. 16. message ; 1 Sam. 4. 17. that
 brought tidings ; Job 33. 23. angel ;
 Isa. 57. 9. ambassador
MESSIAH, Dan. 9. 25, 26. John 1.
 41. & 4. 25.
MICE, golden, 1 Sam. 6. 11.
MIDNIGHT, Egyptians smitten
 at, Ex. 12. 29.
 prayer at, Ps. 119. 62. Acts 16. 25.
 & 20. 7.
 bridegroom cometh at, Matt. 25. 6.
 master of house cometh at, Mark
 13. 35.
MIDST, Ps. 22. 14. & 46. 5. & 110. 2.
 Prov. 4. 21. Isa. 4. 4. & 41. 18. Ezek.
 43. 7, 9. & 6. 10. Joel 2. 27. Zeph. 3.
 5, 12, 15, 17. Phil. 2. 15. Rev. 1. 13.
 & 5. 6. & 7. 17. Lamb in *m*. of the
 throne
MIDWIVES of Egypt, Ex. 1. 16, 20.
MIGHT, Gen. 49. 3. Num. 14. 13.
 Deut. 6. 5. love Lord with all thy
 m.
 2 Kings 23. 25. turned to Lord with
 all his *m*.
 2 Chron. 20. 12. no *m*. against
 Ps. 76. 5. none of men of *m*. found
 145. 6. men speak of the *m*. of thy
 Eccl. 9. 10. findeth to do, do it
 with thy *m*.
 Isa. 40. 29. that have no *m*. he
 Zech. 4. 6. not by *m*. but by Spirit
 Eph. 3. 16. his glory, to be strengthened with *m*.
 6. 10. be strong in power of his *m*.
 Col. 1. 11. strengthened with all *m*.
 Deut. 7. 23. with *mighty* destruc.
 10. 17. a great God, a *m*. and a
 Ps. 24. 8. the Lord strong and *m*.
 the Lord *m*. in battle

Ps. 89. 10. I have laid help on one
 that is *m*.
Isa. 5. 22. *m*. to drink wine, men
 of
Jer. 32. 19. great in counsel, *m*. in
 work
1 Cor. 1. 20. not many *m*. are called
2 Cor. 10. 4. warfare not carnal
 but *m*.
Ps. 93. 4. Lord on high is *mightier*
Acts 18. 28. *mightily*, Col. 1. 29.
 19. 20. so *m*. grew word of God
R. V. changes chiefly to great,
 strong, etc.
MILK, Gen. 18. 8. & 49. 12.
Job 10. 10. hast poured me out as *m*.
S. of S. 4. 11. honey and *m*. under
Isa. 55. 1. buy wine and *m*. without
Joel 3. 18. the hills shall flow with
 m.
Heb. 5. 12. become such as have
 need of *m*.
1 Pet. 2. 2. desire sincere *m*. of
 word
MILLSTONES, Ex. 11. 5. Matt.
 24. 41. Rev. 18. 21.
MIND, Gen. 26. 35. Lev. 24. 12.
1 Chron. 28. 9. serve him with willing *m*.
Neh. 4. 6. people had a *m*. to work
Job 23. 13. he is of one *m*. who can
Isa. 26. 3. whose *m*. is stayed on
 thee
Luke 12. 29. be ye not of doubtful
 m.
Acts 17. 11. receive the word with
 readiness of *m*.
 20. 19. serving the Lord with all
 humility of *m*.
Rom. 7. 25. with the *m*. I serve law
 8. 7. carnal *m*. is enmity against
 11. 34. who hath known the *m*. of
 12. 16. be of same *m*. one
1 Cor. 1. 10. joined together in the
 same *m*.
2 Cor. 8. 12. be first a willing *m*. it
 is
 13. 11. be of one *m*. live in peace,
 Phil. 1. 27. & 2. 2. & 4. 2. 1 Pet. 3. 8.
2 Tim. 1. 7. spirit of love and of a
 sound *m*.
Tit. 1. 15. their *m*. and conscience
Rom. 8. 5. of flesh, do *m*. things of
 12. 16. *m*. not high things
Phil. 3. 16. *m*. same thing
 19. *m*. earthly things
2 Cor. 3. 14. *minds* were blinded
Phil. 4. 7. God keep your hearts
 and *m*.
Heb. 10. 16. in their *m*. I will write
1 Pet. 3. 1. stir up your pure *m*. by
Rom. 8. 6. to be carnally *minded*
 11. 20. be not high *m*. but fear
 15. 5. God of patience grant you
 to be like *m*.
Tit. 2. 6. exhort young men to be
 sober *m*.
Jas. 1. 8. a double *m*. man, 4. 8.
Ps. 111. 5. ever *mindful* of his covenant, 1 Chron. 16. 15. Ps. 105. 8.
 115. 12. Lord hath been *m*. of us
R. V. Acts 20. 13. intending
MINISTER, Josh. 1. 1. Luke 4. 20.
 Matt. 20. 26. let him be your *m*.
 Acts 26. 16. to make thee a *m*. and
 Rom. 13. 4. he is *m*. of God to thee
 15. 8. Christ was a *m*. of the
 16. I be the *m*. of Jesus Christ to
 Eph. 3. 7. was made a *m*. according
 4. 29. may *m*. grace unto hearers
Rom. 15. 25. to *m*. unto the saints
 15. 27. *m*. to them in carnal
1 Cor. 9. 13. they who *m*. about
2 Cor. 9. 10. *m*. seed to sower and
1 Pet. 4. 11. if any man *m*. let him
1 Tim. 4. 6. shall be a good *m*. of
Heb. 8. 2. *m*. of the sanctuary
Ps. 103. 21. *ministers* of his that do
 104. 4. his *m*. a flaming fire
Isa. 61. 6. men call you the *m*. of
Luke 1. 2. from beginning, *m*. of
Rom. 13. 6. they are God's *m*.
1 Cor. 3. 5. *m*. by whom ye believed
 4. 1. account of us as *m*. of Christ

2 Cor. 3. 6. made us able *m*. of
 6. 4. approved ourselves as *m*. of
 11. 23. are they *m*. of Christ, so
Matt. 4. 11. *ministered*, Luke 8. 3.
 Gal. 2. 5. Heb. 6. 10. 2 Pet. 1. 11.
Luke 1. 23. *ministration*, Acts 6. 1.
 2 Cor. 3. 7, 8. & 9. 1, 13.
Heb. 1. 14. all *ministering* spirits
Rom. 15. 16. *m*. the gospel of God
Acts6. 4. give ourselves to *ministry*
 20. 24. I might finish the *m*. I have
2 Cor. 4. 1. seeing we have this *m*.
 5. 18. given to us the *m*. of recon.
 6. 3. that the *m*. be not blamed
Col. 4. 17. take heed to *m*. that thou
1 Tim. 1. 12. putting me into the *m*.
2 Tim. 4. 5. full proof of thy *m*.
Heb. 8. 6. obtained more excell. *m*.
R. V. Ezra 7. 24. servants ; Luke 4. 24.
 attendant ; 1 Chron. 28. 1. served ;
 2 Cor. 9. 10 ; Gal. 3. 5. supplieth ;
 1 Chron. 9. 28. vessels of service ;
 Rom. 12. 7. ministry ; Acts 12. 25 ;
 2 Cor. 6. 3. ministration ; Eph. 4.
 12: 2 Tim. 4. 11. ministering ;
 1 Tim. 1. 12. his service
MIRACLE, Mark 6. 52. & 9. 39.
 Luke 23. 8. John 2. 11. & 6. 26. &
 10. 41. & 11. 47. Acts 2. 22. & 4. 16.
 & 6. 8. & 19. 11. 1 Cor. 12. 10, 28, 29.
 Gal. 3. 5. Heb. 2. 4.
R. V. Heb. 2. 4. manifold powers.
 Elsewhere, for most part,
 changed to sign or signs
MIRTH, Prov. 14. 13. Eccl. 2. 2. &
 7. 4. Isa. 24. 8, 11. Jer. 7. 34. & 16.
 9. & 25. 10. Hos. 2. 11. Ezek. 21. 10.
MISCHIEF, Gen. 42. 4. & 44. 29.
Job 15. 35. they conceive *m*. bring
Ps. 10. 14. thou beholdest *m*. and
 28. 3. *m*. is in their hearts, 10. 7.
 36. 4. he deviseth *m*. upon his bed
 94. 20. which frameth *m*. by a law
Prov. 10. 23. sport to a fool to do *m*.
 11. 27. he that seeketh *m*. it shall
 24. 16. wicked shall fall into *m*.
Acts 13. 10. full of all sub., and *m*.
R. V. Ex. 32. 12; Prov. 6. 14 ; 13. 17.
 evil ; Ps. 52. 2 ; 119. 150; Prov. 10.
 23. wickedness ; 2 Kings 7. 9. pun-
 ishment ; Ps. 36. 4. iniquity ; Prov.
 24. 16. calamity ; Acts 13. 10. villany
MISERY, Job 3. 20. Lam. 3. 19.
 Judg. 10. 16. soul grieved for *m*.
 Prov. 31. 7. drink and remember *m*.
 Eccl. 8. 6. the *m*. of man is great
 Rom. 3. 16. destruction and *m*.
Job 16. 2. *miserable* comforters are
 1 Cor. 15. 19. are of all men most *m*.
 Rev. 3. 17. knowest not thou art *m*.
R. V. 1 Cor. 15. 19. pitiable
MOCK when fear cometh
Prov. 14. 9. fools make a *m*. at sin
1 Kings 18. 27. Elijah *mocked* and
2 Chron. 36. 16. they *m*. the mes.
Prov. 17. 5. whoso *mocketh* the poor
 30. 17. eye that *m*. at his father
Isa. 28. 22. be not *mockers*, lest
Jude 18. there should be *m*. in last
R. V. Job 13. 9. deceiveth ; 12. 4.
 laughing stock ; Isa. 28. 22. scorn
 ers ; Jer. 15. 17. them that made
 merry
MODERATION known to all,
 Phil. 4. 5.
MODEST apparel, 1 Tim. 2. 9.
MOMENT, Ex. 33. 5. Isa. 27. 3.
 Num. 16. 21. consume them in a *m*.
 Job 7. 18. try him every *m*.
 20. 5. joy of hypocrite is for a *m*.
 Ps. 30. 5. his anger endureth but
 for a little *m*.
 Isa. 26. 20. hide thee, as it were,
 for a little *m*.
 54. 7. for a small *m*. have I for.
 1 Cor. 15. 52. in a *m*. in the twink.
 2 Cor. 4. 17. affliction is but for a
 m.
MONEY, Gen. 23. 9. & 31. 15.
 Eccl. 7. 12. wisdom is def. and *m*.
 10. 19. *m*. answereth all things
 Isa. 55. 1. he that hath no *m*. come
 2. wherefore spend *m*. for that

Mic. 3. 11. the prophets divine for *m.*
Acts 8. 20. thy *m.* perish with thee
1 Tim. 6. 10. love of *m.* is the root
R. V. Gen. 23. 9, 13; Ex. 21. 35. price of; Ex. 21. 30. ransom; Matt. 17. 24. half-shekel; 17. 27. shekel; Acts 7. 16. price in silver; 8. 20. silver

MORROW, Ex. 8. 23. & 16. 23.
Prov. 27. 1. boast not thy. of to *m.*
Isa. 22. 13. to *m.* we shall die
56. 12. to *m.* shall be as this day
Matt. 6. 34. take no thought for *m.*
Jas. 4. 14. know not what shall be on the *m.*

MORTAL man be just, Job 4. 17.
Rom. 6. 12. let not sin reign in *m.* body
8. 11. raised Christ, quicken *m.* body
1 Cor. 15. 53. this *m.* put on immor.
2 Cor. 5. 4. *mortality* be swallowed
Rom. 8. 13. *mortify* deeds of body
Col. 3. 5. *m.* your members on earth

MORTGAGES, Neh. 5. 3.

MOTE, Matt. 7. 3, 4, 5. Luke 6. 41.

MOTH, Job 4. 19. & 27. 18. Ps. 39. 11. Isa. 50. 9. & 51. 8. Hos. 5. 12. Matt. 6. 19, 20. Luke 12. 33.

MOTHER, Gen. 3. 20. & 21. 21. Judg. 5. 7. 2 Sam. 20. 19. 1 Kings 3. 27. Gal. 4. 26.
Job 17. 14. worm, thou art my *m.*
Ps. 27. 10. when father and *m.* for
71. 6. took me out of my *m.'s* bowels
Matt. 12. 49. behold my *m.* and my
R. V. Luke 2. 43. his parents

MOUNT to be cast against Jerusalem, Jer. 6. 6.

MOURN, Neh. 8. 9. Job 5. 11.
Isa. 61. 2. to comfort all that *m.*
Matt. 5. 4. blessed are they that *m.*
Jas. 4. 9. be afflicted and *m.* and
Matt. 11. 17. we have *mourned*
1 Cor. 5. 2. are puffed up and have not rather *m.*
Eccl. 12. 5. *mourners* go about the
Isa. 57. 18. restore comfort to him and his *m.*
Ps. 30. 11. turned *mourning* into
Isa. 22. 12. Lord did call to weeping and *m.*
61. 3. to give the oil of joy for *m.*
Jer. 9. 17. call for the *m.* women
31. 13. I will turn their *m.* into joy
Joel 2. 12. turn to me with fasting and *m.*
Jas. 4. 9. let laughter be turned into *m.*
R. V. Gen. 50. 3; Num. 20. 29. wept; 2 Sam. 11. 26. made lamentation; Job 2. 11. bemoan; Gen. 50. 10; Isa. 19. 8. lament; Ps. 35. 14. bewaileth; 55. 2. am restless; 88. 9. wasteth away; Prov. 29. 2. sigh; Ezek. 24. 23. moan; Matt. 11. 17; Luke 7. 32. wailed; Job 3. 8. leviathan; Isa. 51. 11. sighing; Mic. 1. 11. wailing

MOUTH of babes and sucklings, Ps. 8. 2.
Ps. 37. 30. *m.* of righteous speaketh
Prov. 10. 14. *m.* of fools is near
10. 31. *m.* of the just bringeth
12. 6. *m.* of upright shall deliver
14. 3. in *m.* of fools is a rod of pride
15. 2. the *m.* of fools poureth out
18. 7. a fool's *m.* is his destruction
22. 14. *m.* of strange women is a
Lam. 3. 38. out of *m.* of the Most
Matt. 12. 34. out of abundance of the heart the *m.* speaketh
Luke 21. 15. will give you a *m.* and
Rom. 10. 10. with the *m.* confession
15. 6 with one mind and *m.* glorify
Prov. 13. 3. keepeth *his mouth,* keep.
Lam. 3. 29. putteth — in dust if
Mal. 2. 7. they shall seek law at —
Ps. 17. 3. *my mouth* shall not transgress
39. 1. I will keep — with a bridle
49. 3. — shall speak of wisdom

Ps. 51. 15. — shall show forth thy
71. 15 — shall show forth thy
Eph. 6. 19. that I may open — boldly
Ps. 81. 10. open *thy mouth* wide
103. 5. who satisfieth — with good
Prov. 31. 8. open — for the dumb in
Eccl. 5. 6. suffer not — to cause flesh
R. V. Job 12. 11; 34. 3. palate; Ps. 32. 9. trappings; Isa. 19. 7. brink; Matt. 15. 8 —

MOVE, Ex. 11. 7. Judg. 13. 25.
Acts 17. 28. in him we live and *m.*
20. 24. none of these things *m.* me
Ps. 15. 5. shall never be *moved,* 21.
7. & 26. 5. & 55. 22. & 62. 2, 6. & 66. 9. & 112. 6. & 121. 3. Prov. 12. 3.
Col. 1. 23. be not *m.* away from hope
1 Thes. 3. 3. no man be *m.* by these
Heb. 12. 28. a kingdom which cannot be *m.*
2 Pet. 1. 21. spake as *m.* by the Holy Ghost
Rom. 7. 5. *motions*
Prov. 5. 6. *moveable*
R. V. Gen. 9. 2. teemeth; 2 Kings 21. 8. wander; Ps. 23. 31. goeth down smoothly; Jer. 25. 16. reel to and fro; 46. 7, 8. toss themselves; 49. 21; 50. 46. trembleth; Ezek. 47. 9. swarmeth; Mic. 7. 17. trembling; Matt. 14. 14; Mark 6. 34. he had . . on; Matt. 21. 10; Mark 15. 11. stirred; Acts 20. 24 — ; Heb. 12. 28. shaken

MULTITUDE, Gen. 16. 10. & 28. 3.
Ex. 12. 38. & 23. 2. Num. 11. 4.
Job 32. 7. *m.* of years should teach
Ps. 5. 7. *m.* of mercies
10. *m.* of transgressions
33. 16. no king saved by the *m.* of
51. 1. according unto the *m.* of thy
94. 19. in the *m.* of my thoughts
Prov. 10. 19. *m.* of words wanteth
11. 14. in the *m.* of counsellors
Eccl. 5. 3. *m.* of business, *m.* words
Jas. 5. 20. hide *m.* of sins, 1 Pet. 4. 8.
R. V. Gen. 28. 3; 48. 4; Luke 23. 1. company; Job. 39. 7; Jer. 3. 23; 10. 13; 51. 16. tumult; 46. 25. Amon; Ps. 42. 4. throng; Prov. 20. 15. abundance; Isa. 17. 12. ah, the uproar; Jer. 12. 6. aloud; Ezek. 31. 5; Matt. 12. 15. many; Mark 3. 9; Acts 21. 34. crowd; Luke 8. 37. all the people; Acts 23. 7. assembly; Job 33. 19; Acts 21. 22 —

MURDER, Rom. 1. 29. Matt. 15. 19. Gal. 5. 21. Rev. 9. 21.
Job 24. 14. *murderer* rising with light
John 8. 44. devil was a *m.* from the
Hos. 9. 13. bring forth children to *m.*
1 Pet. 4. 15. none of you suffer as a *m.*
1 John 3. 15. who hateth his brother is a *m.* and no *m.* hath eternal life
R. V. Matt. 19. 18. not kill; Gal. 5. 21 — ; Num. 35. 16, 17, 18, 21. manslayer; Hos. 9. 13. slayer; Acts 21. 38. assassins

MURMUR, Deut. 1. 27. Ps. 106. 25. Jude 16. Ex. 16. 7. Phil. 2. 14.
MUSE, Ps. 39. 3. & 143. 5.
R. V. Luke 3. 15. reasoned
MUSIC, Lam. 3. 63. Amos 6. 5.
R. V. Lam. 3. 63. song
MUSTARD seed, Matt. 13. 31. & 17. 20.
MUZZLE, Deut. 25. 4. 1 Cor. 9. 9.
MYSTERY of the kingdom, Mark 4. 11.
Rom. 11. 25. not be ignorant of *m.*
16. 25. according to revelation of the *m.*
1 Cor. 2. 7. speak the wisdom of God in a *m.*
4. 1. stewards of the *m.* of God
13. 2. prophesy and understand *m.*
14. 2. in the Spirit he speaketh *m.*
15. 51. I show you a *m.* we shall
Eph. 1. 9. made known *m.* of his
3. 4. my knowledge in *m.*
5. 32. this is a great *m.* of Christ

Eph. 6. 19. make known *m.* of gospel
Col. 1. 2. *m.* which hath been hid
1. 27. glory of this *m.* among Gen.
2. 2. acknowledg. of *m.* of God
4. 3. open a door to speak *m.* of
2 Thes. 2. 7. *m.* of iniquity doth
1 Tim. 3. 9. holding *m.* of the faith
16. great is the *m.* of godliness
Rev. 1. 20. write the *m.* of seven
10. 7. *m.* of God should be finish.
17. 5. her name, *m.* Babylon the

N

NAIL, Judg. 4. 21. & 5. 26.
Ezra 9. 8. give us a *n.* in his
Eccl. 12. 11. *n.* fastened by the masters
Isa. 22. 23. fastened as a *n.* in a sure
Zech. 10. 4. out of him came the *n.*
R. V. Judg. 4. 21, 22. tent pin
NAKED, Gen. 2. 25. & 3. 7, 11.
Ex. 32. 25. when the people were *n.*
2 Chron. 28. 19. he made Judah *n.*
Job 1. 21. *n.* came I out of
Matt. 25. 26. I was *n.* and ye cloth.
1 Cor. 4. 11. we hunger and thirst and are *n.*
2 Cor. 5. 3. clothed may not be *n.*
Heb. 4. 13. all things are *n.* and
Rev. 3. 17. misera., poor, blind, *n.*
16. 15. keepeth his garments lest he walk *n.*
R. V. Ex. 32. 25. broken loose, let them loose for derision; 2 Chron. 28. 19. dealt wantonly; Hab. 3. 9. bare

NAME, Ex. 34. 14. Lev. 18. 21.
Ps. 20. 1. the *n.* of God of Jacob
109. 13. let their *n.* be blotted
Prov. 10. 7. *n.* of the wicked shall
22. 1. good *n.* is rather to be chos.
Eccl. 7. 1. a good *n.* is better than
Isa. 55. 13. shall be to the Lord for *n.*
56. 5. a *n.* better than of sons and
62. 2. thou shalt be call. by new *n.*
Jer. 13. 11. for a people, for a *n.* and
32. 20. made thee *n.* as at this day
33. 9. shall be to me a *n.* of joy, a
Mic. 4. 5. we will walk in the *n.* of
Matt. 10. 41. receive a prophet in *n.*
Luke 6. 22. cast out your *n.* as evil
Acts 4. 12. is none other *n.*
Rom. 2. 24. *n.* of God is blasphem.
Col. 3. 17. do all in the *n.* of Lord
2 Tim. 2. 19. that nameth *n.* of Ch.
Heb. 1. 4. obtained more excell. *n.*
1 Pet. 4. 14. if ye be reproached for the *n.* of Christ
1 John 3. 23. should believe on the *n.* of his Son
5. 13. that we believe on the *n.*
Rev. 2. 17. *n.* written, which no man
3. 1. I know thy works, that thou hast a *n.*
12. write on him *n.* of my God
14. 1. Father's *n.* on their fore.
Eph. 1. 21. every *n.* that is *named,* Phil. 2. 9.
Ps. 76. 1. *his name* is great in Israel
72. 17. — shall endure for ever
106. 8. he saved them for — sake
Prov. 30. 4. what is — and what
Isa. 9. 6. — shall be called Wonder.
Zech. 14. 9. shall be one Lord and — one
John 20. 31. might have life thro.—
Rev. 3. 5. I will confess — before
13. 17. the name of the beast, or the number of —, 15. 2.
Ex. 23. 21. *my name* is in him
3. 15. this is — for ever, and my
Judg. 13. 18. askest after —, Gen. 32. 29.
Isa. 48. 9. for — sake I will defer
Ezek. 20. 9. wrought for — sake
Mal. 1. 14. —is dreadful among the
2. 2. lay it to heart to give glory to —
Matt. 10. 22. hated of all for — sake
19. 29. forsaken houses for — sake

John 14. 13. ask in —, 15. 16. & 16. 23, 26.

16. 24. asked nothing in —

Acts 9. 15. he is a chosen vessel to bear—

Rev. 2. 3. for — hast labored, and

13. holdest fast—

3. 8. hast not denied my—

2 Chron. 14. 11. in *thy name* we go

Ps. 8. 1. how excellent is — in all

9. 10. that know — will put their

48. 10. according to — so is thy

75. 1. — is near, thy works declare

138. 2. magnified thy word above all—

S. of S. 1. 3. — is as ointment pour.

Isa. 26. 8. desire of our souls is to—

64. 7. none that calleth on—

Jer. 14. 7. do it for—sake, 21. Dan. 9. 6. Josh. 7. 9. Ps. 79. 9.

Mic. 6. 9. man of wisdom shall see—

John 17. 12. I kept them in—, 26.

Ex. 23. 13. make no mention of the *names* of other gods, Deut. 12. 3. Ps. 16. 4.

Ex. 28. 12. Aaron bear their *n.*

Ps. 49. 11. call lands after their *n.*

147. 4. stars he calleth by their *n.*

Luke 10. 20. *n.* written in heaven

Rev. 3. 4. hast a few *n.* in Sardis

R. V. Mark 9. 41; 11. 10; 1 John 5. 13 —; Luke 24. 18; Acts 7. 58; 28. 7. named; Matt. 9. 9; Mark 15. 7; Luke 19. 2. called; John 11. 1 —; John 11. 49; Acts 24. 1. one; 1 Cor. 5. 1. even

NARROW, 1 Kings 6. 4. Prov. 23. 27. Isa. 28. 20. & 49. 19. Matt. 7. 14.

R. V. 1 Kings 6. 4. fixed; Ezek. 40. 16; 41. 16, 26. closed; Matt. 7. 14. straitened

NATION, Gen. 15. 14. & 21. 13.

Gen. 20. 4. wilt thou slay a righteous *n.*

Num. 14. 12. make of thee a great *n.*

2 Sam. 7. 23. what *n.* is like thy

Ps. 33. 12. blessed is the *n.* whose

147. 20. not dealt so with any *n.*

Isa. 1. 4. ah sinful *n.* a people laden

2. 4. *n.* shall not lift up sword

49. 7. him whom the *n.* abhorreth

66. 8. shall a *n.* be born at once

Matt. 24. 7. *n.* shall rise against *n.*

Luke 7. 5. he loveth our *n.* and

Acts 10. 35. in every *n.* he that fear.

Rom. 10. 19. by a foolish *n.* I will

Phil. 2. 15. in midst of a crooked *n.*

1 Pet. 2. 9. ye are a holy *n.*

Rev. 5. 9. redeemed us out of every *n.*

Gen. 10. 32. nations, 17. 4, 6, 16.

Deut. 26. 19. high above all *n.*, 28. 1.

Ps. 9. 20. *n.* may know themselves

113. 4. Lord is high above all *n.*

Isa. 2. 2. all *n.* shall flow unto it

40. 17. *n.* before him are as noth.

55. 5. *n.* that knew thee not shall

Jer. 4. 2. *n.* shall bless themselves

Zech. 2. 11. many *n.* be joined

Matt. 25. 32. before him be gathered all *n.*

Acts 14. 16. suffered all *n.* to walk

Rev. 21. 24. the *n.* of them that

R. V. Gen. 14. 1, 9; Josh. 12. 23. Goiim; Lev. 18. 26. homeborn; Ex. 2. 18; Deut. 2. 25; 4. 6, 19, 27; 14. 2; 28. 37; 30. 3; 1 Chron. 16. 24; 2 Chron. 7. 20; 13. 9; Neh. 1. 8; 19. 22; Ps. 96. 5; 106. 34; Ezek. 38. 8. peoples; Isa. 37. 18. countries; Mark 7. 26. race; Gal. 1. 14. countrymen; Phil. 2. 15. generation

NATURE, Rom. 2. 27. Jas. 3. 6.

Rom. 1. 26. that which is against *n.*

2. 14. do by *n.* things contained in

11. 24. olive wild by *n.* contr. to *n.*

1 Cor. 11. 14. doth not *n.* itself teach

Gal. 2. 15. are Jews by *n.*

4. 8. served them which by *n.* are

Eph. 2. 3. were by *n.* the children

Heb. 2. 16. took not *n.* of angels

2 Pet. 1. 4. partakers of divine *n.*

Deut. 34. 7. *natural*, Rom. 1. 26, 27, 31. & 11. 21, 24. 1 Cor. 2. 14. & 15. 44, 46. 2 Tim. 3. 3. Jas. 1. 23. 2 Pet. 2. 12. Phil. 2. 20. Jude 10.

R. V. 2 Pet. 2. 12. creatures without reason

NAUGHT, it is, saith the buyer, Prov. 20. 14.

Jas. 1. 21. filthiness and superfluity of *naughtiness*

R. V. Prov. 11. 6. mischief; Jas. 1. 21. wickedness

NAVY of Solomon, 1 Kings 9. 26. 2 Chron. 8. 17.

of Jehoshaphat, 1 Kings 22. 48.

NEAR, nigh, Ps. 119. 151. & 148. 14.

Isa. 55. 6. & 57. 19. Jer. 12. 2.

R. V. frequent changes to at, nigh, ——, etc.

NECESSARY, Job 23. 12. Acts 13. 46. & 15. 28. Tit. 3. 14. Heb. 9. 23.

Rom. 12. 13. *necessity*, Acts 20. 34. 1 Cor. 9. 16. 2 Cor. 6. 4. & 9. 7. & 12. 20. Phile. 14. Heb. 9. 16.

R. V. Acts 28. 10. we needed; Luke 23. 17—; Heb. 8. 3. necessary; Phil. 4. 16. need

NECK, S. of S. 1. 10. Isa. 48. 4. Rom. 16. 4.

Acts 15. 10. put a yoke on *n.* of

2 Kings 17. 14. hardened their *necks*, Neh. 9. 16, 17, 29. Jer. 7. 26. & 19. 15.

NEED of all these things, Matt. 6. 32.

Matt. 9. 12. they that are whole *n.*

Luke 15. 7. the righteous *n.* no

Heb. 4. 16. find grace to help in time of *n.*

1 John 2. 27. *n.* not that any

Rev. 3. 17. rich, and have *n.* of

21. 23. no *n.* of sun

22. 5. *n.* no candle

Eph. 4. 28. give to him that *needeth*

2 Tim. 2. 15. *n.* not be ashamed of

Luke 10. 42. one thing is *needful*

Ps. 9. 18. *needy* not always be for.

72. 12. he shall deliver the *n.* and

82. 3. do justice to afflicted and *n.*

Isa. 14. 30. *n.* shall lie down in saf.

Jer. 22. 16. he judgeth cause of *n.*

R. V. Jude 3. was constrained

NEGLECT to hear, Matt. 18. 17.

1 Tim. 4. 14. *n.* not the gift that is

Heb. 2. 3. if we *n.* so great salva.

R. V. Matt. 18. 17. refuse; Col. 2. 23. severity of

NEIGH, Jer. 5. 8. & 8. 16. & 13. 27.

NEIGHBOR, Ex. 3. 22. & 11. 2.

Ex. 20. 16. not bear false witness against thy *n.*

Lev. 19. 13. thou shalt not defr. *n.*

17. thou shalt rebuke thy *n.*

18. thou shalt love thy *n.* as thyself, Matt. 19. 19. & 22. 39. Rom. 13. 9. Gal. 5. 14. Jas. 2. 8. Matt. 7. 12. Heb. 13. 3.

Ps. 15. 3. nor doeth evil to his *n.*

Prov. 27. 10. better is a *n.* near

Jer. 22. 13. useth *n.*'s servant

31. 24. teach no more his *n.*

Luke 10. 29. who is my *n.*, 36.

Rom. 13. 10. love worketh no il to his *n.*

15. 2. let every one please his *n.*

R. V. 1 Kings 20. 35. fellow; Ps. 15. 3; Prov. 19. 4. friend; Heb. 8. 11. fellow-citizen

NEST, Job 29. 18. Ps. 84. 3. Prov. 27. 8. Isa. 10. 14. Hab. 2. 9. Matt. 8. 20.

NET, Job 18. 8. & 19. 6. Ps. 9. 15. & 25. 15. & 31. 4. & 35. 7, 8. & 57. 6. & 66. 11. Isa. 51. 20. Hab. 1. 15, 16. Matt. 13. 47. Ps. 141. 10. Eccl. 7. 20.

NEW, Lord make a *n.* thing, Num. 16. 30.

Judg. 5. 8. they chose *n.* gods, Deut. 32. 17.

Eccl. 1. 9. no *n.* thing under sun, 10.

Isa. 65. 17. *n.* heavens and a *n.* earth, 66. 22. 2 Pet. 3. 13. Rev. 21. 1.

Jer. 31. 22. created a *n.* thing in earth

Lam. 3. 23. his mercies are *n.*

Ezek. 11. 19. I will put a *n.* spirit

18. 31. make you a *n.* heart and *n.* spirit

36. 26. *n.* heart I will give, and a *n.* spirit

Matt. 9. 16. putteth *n.* cloth on old

17. neither put *n.* wine in old bot.

13. 52. bringeth forth things *n.*

Mark 1. 27. what *n.* doctrine is this, Acts 17. 19.

John 13. 34. a *n.* commandment I give unto you, 1 John 2. 7, 8.

Acts 17. 21. to tell or hear some *n.* thing

1 Cor. 5. 7. that ye may be a *n.*

2 Cor. 5. 17. if any man be in Christ, he is a *n.* creature

Gal. 6. 15. neither circumcision nor uncircumcision, but a *n.* creature

Eph. 4. 24. that ye put on *n.* man

1 Pet. 2. 2. as *n.* born babes desire

Rev. 2. 17. a *n.* name written

5. 9. sung a *n.* song, 14. 3.

Rom. 6. 4. should walk in *newness*

7. 6. we should serve in *n.* of spirit

R. V. Joel 1. 5; 3. 18. sweet; Matt. 9. 16; Mark 2. 21; Luke 5. 38. fresh; Matt. 9. 16; Mark 2. 21. undressed; Neh. 10. 39; Matt. 26. 28; Mark 2. 22; 14. 24 —

NIGH, Lev. 25. 49. Num. 24. 17

Deut. 4. 7. who hath God so *n.*

Ps. 34. 18. Lord is *n.* them of brok.

85. 9. salvation is *n.* them that

145. 18. Lord is *n.* them that call

Matt. 15. 8. draweth *n.* with mouth

Eph. 2. 13. made *n.* by blood of

R. V. Gen. 47. 29; Ex. 24. 2; Lev. 21. 3; Luke 7. 12. near; Luke 21. 20; John 6. 4; Jas. 5. 8. at hand; Matt. 15. 8. honoreth

NIGHT, Gen. 1. 5, 14. & 26. 24.

Ex. 12. 42. this is that *n.* of Lord

Ps. 19. 2. *n.* unto *n.* showeth know.

30. 5. weeping may endure for a *n.*

Isa. 21. 11. what of the *n.*

Jer. 14. 8. as wayfaring man to tarry for a *n.*

Luke 6. 12. continued all *n.* in pray.

12. 20. this *n.* shall thy soul be

John 9. 4. *n.* cometh when no man

Rom. 13. 12. *n.* is far spent: day is

1 Thes. 5. 5. children not of *n.* nor

Rev. 21. 25. shall be no *n.* there

Ps. 134. 1. *by night*, S. of S. 3. 1. John 3. 2. & 7. 50. & 19. 39.

Job 35. 10. who giveth songs *in the night*

Ps. 16. 7. instruct me — seasons

42. 8. — his song shall be with me

77. 6. I call to remembrance my song—

119. 55. I have remem. thy name—

Isa. 26. 9. my soul desired thee —

59. 10. stumble at noon day as —

John 11. 10. if a man walk — he

1 Thes. 5. 7. sleep— and are drunk—

Ps. 63. 6. *night watches*, 119. 148.

R. V. Lev. 6. 20. evening; Isa. 21. 4; 59. 10. twi.; Judg. 19. 13; Matt. 26. 47; Mark 14. 27; 2 Pet. 3. 10 —

NOBLE, Esth. 6. 9. Jer. 2. 21. Luke 19. 12. Acts 17. 11. Ex. 24. 11. Num. 21. 12.

1 Cor. 1. 26. not many *n.* are called

Col. 3. 5. *nobles* put not their necks

13. 17. I contended with the *n.* of

Ps. 149. 8. bind their *n.* with fetters

Prov. 8. 16. by me princes rule, and *n.*

Eccl. 13. 17. when thy king is the son of *n.*

R. V. Isa. 43. 14. as fugitives; Jer. 30. 21. prince; Nah. 3. 18. worthless; Acts 24. 3; 26. 25. excellent

NOISOME, Ps. 91. 3. Rev. 16. 2.

NOSE, Prov. 30. 33. Isa. 65. 5.

Isa. 2. 22. breath in *nostrils*, Lam. 4. 20.

R. V. S. of S. 7. 8. breath; Ezek. 39. 11. them that pass through; Job 4. 9. anger; 39. 20. snorting

NOTHING, Gen. 11. 6. Ex. 9. 4. &

12. 10. Num. 6. 4. & 16. 26. Josh.
11. 15.
2 Sam. 24. 24. offer that which costs
me *n.*
1 Kings 8. 9. *n.* in ark save the two
Neh. 8. 10. send to them from whom
n. is prepared
Job 6. 21. ye are *n.*
8. 9. of yesterday, and know *n.*
26. 7. hangeth earth on *n.*
34. 9. it profiteth *n.*
Ps. 17. 3. thou hast tried me and
shalt find *n.*
39. 5. my age is as *n.* before thee
49. 17. when he dieth, shall carry *n.*
119. 165. *n.* shall offend them
Prov. 13. 4. the sluggard desireth
and hath *n.*
7. that make. him.rich, yet hath *n.*
Isa. 40. 17. all nations before him
are as *n.*
Jer. 10. 24. lest thou bring me to *n.*
Lam. 1. 12. is it *n.* to you, all ye
Hag. 2. 3. is it not in your eyes in
comparison of it as *n.*
Luke 1. 37. with God *n.* shall be
John 8. 28. I do *n.* of myself
14. 30. prince of this world hath
n. in me
15. 5. without me ye can do *n.*
1 Cor. 1. 19. bring to *n.* the under.
13. 2. I am *n.*
2 Cor. 12. 11. having *n.*, yet possess-
ing all, 2 Cor. 6. 10.
1 Tim. 6. 7. we brought *n.* into
world
NOUGHT, Gen. 29. 15. Deut. 13. 17.
Isa. 41. 12. shall be as a thing of *n.*
49. 4. I have spent my strength
for *n.*
52. 3. sold yourselves for *n.*
Amos 6. 13. rejoice in a thing of *n.*
Luke 23. 11. Herod and men set
him at *n.*
Acts 19. 27. Diana in danger to be
set at *n.*
Rom. 14. 10. why set at *n.* brother
NOVICE, not a, lest, 1 Tim. 3. 6.
NUMBER our days, teach us to,
Ps. 90. 12.
Isa. 65. 12. I will *n.* you to the sword
Rev. 7. 9. multitude which no man
could *n.*
Isa. 53. 12. was *numbered* with
transgressors
Dan. 5. 26. God hath *n.* thy kingdom
Job 14. 16. thou *numberest* my steps
Ps. 71. 15. I know not the *numbers*
Rev. 13. 17. the *n.* of his name, 18.
R. V. Mark 10. 46: Acts 1. 15. mul-
titude; 2 Sam. 24. 2. sum; Josh.
8. 10; 1 Kings 20. 15, 26, 27; 2 Kings
3. 6. mustered; 1 Tim. 5. 9. enrolled
NUMBERING of the people, by
Moses, Num. 1. 26; by David,
2 Sam. 24. 1 Chron. 21, of the
Levites, Num. 3. 14. & 4. 34.
NURSE, 1 Thes. 2. 7. Isa. 49. 23.

○

OATH, Gen. 24. 8. & 26. 3, 28.
1 Sam. 14. 26. people feared the *o.*
2 Sam. 21. 7. Lord's *o.* was between
2 Chron. 15. 15. Israel rejoiced at *o.*
Eccl. 8. 2. keep in regard of *o.* of
God
9. 2. that feareth and sweareth an
o.
Ezek. 16. 59. despised the *o.*
Luke 1. 73. *o.* which he sware to
Heb. 6. 16. *o.* for confirmat. is end
Jas. 5. 12. swear not by heaven
neither by any other *o.*
OBEY, Gen. 27. 8. Ex. 5. 2.
Deut. 11. 27. a blessing if ye *o.*
13. 4. walk after the Lord and *o.*
Josh. 24. 24. his voice will we *o.*
1 Sam. 12. 14. fear the Lord and *o.*
15. 22. to *o.* is better than sacrifice
Jer. 7. 23. *o.* my voice and I will
26. 13. amend your ways, and *o.*

Acts 5. 29. ought to *o.* God rather
Rom. 2. 8. contenti., and do not *o.*
6. 16. his servants ye are to whom
ye *o.*
Eph. 6. 1. children *o.* your parents
Col. 3. 22. servants *o.* in all things
2 Thes. 1. 8. that *o.* not the Gospel
3. 14. if any man *o.* not your word
Tit. 3. 1. put them in mind to *o.*
Heb. 5. 9. salvation to all who *o.*
13. 17. *o.* them that have rule over
1 Pet. 3. 1. if any *o.* not the word
Rom. 6. 17. *obeyed* from heart that
1 Pet. 3. 6. Sarah *o.* Abraham
4. 17. the end of them that *o.* not
Isa. 50. 10. *obeyeth* voice, Jer. 11. 3.
1 Pet. 1. 22. purified in *obeying*
truth
Rom. 1. 5. received grace for *obedience*
15. 19. by the *o.* of one many
6. 16. yield *o.* unto righteousness
16. 19. your *o.* is come abroad
26. made known for *o.* of faith
1 Cor. 14. 34. women to be under *o.*
2 Cor. 7. 15. remember the *o.* of you
10. 5. every thought to *o.* of Christ
Heb. 5. 8. learned he *o.* by things
1 Pet. 1. 2. sanctifi. of Spirit unto *o.*
Ex. 24. 7. will we do and be *obedient*
Num. 27. 20. children of Israel
may be *o.*
Deut. 3. 30. turn and be *o.* to voice
8. 20. perish because not *o.* to Lord
2 Sam. 22. 45. strangers shall be *o.*
Isa. 1. 19. if ye be *o.* ye shall eat
42. 24. they were not *o.* to his law
Acts 6. 7. priests were *o.* to the faith
Rom. 15. 18. Gentiles *o.* by word
2 Cor. 2. 9. whether ye be *o.* in all
Eph. 6. 5. servants be *o.* to masters
Phil. 2. 8. he became *o.* unto death
Tit. 2. 5. discreet, *o.* to your hus.
1 Pet. 1. 14. as *o.* children, not
R. V. Ex. 5. 2; 23. 21, 22; Deut. 11.
27, 28; 28. 62; Josh. 24. 24; 1 Sam.
8. 19; 12. 14, 15; Job 36. 11, 12; Jer.
7. 23; Rom. 10. 16. hearken; Josh.
5. 6; 22. 2; Judg. 2. 2; 6. 10; 1 Sam.
28, 21; Jer. 17. 23, 28; 2 Chron. 11.
4. hearkened; Jer. 11. 3; 12. 17.
hear; Gal. 3. 1 —— ; 1 Cor. 14. 34.
subjection; Deut. 8. 20; Dan. 4.
30. hearken; Num. 27. 20; 2 Sam.
22. 45. obey; Tit. 2. 5, 9. subjection;
1 Pet. 1. 22. obedience
OBSCURITY, Isa. 29. 18. & 58. 10.
R. V. 58. 10; 59. 9. darkness
OBSERVE, Ex. 12. 17. & 34. 11.
Ps. 107. 43. who is wise and will *o.*
119. 34. *o.* it with my whole heart
Prov. 23. 26. let thine eyes *o.* my
Jonah 2. 8. that *o.* lying vanities
Matt. 28. 20. teaching them to *o.*
Gal. 4. 10. ye *o.* days months and
Gen. 37. 11. his father *observed* the
Ex. 12. 42. a night to be much *o.*
Mark 6. 20. Herod fear. John and *o.*
10. 20. all these have I *o.* from my
Luke 17. 20. cometh not with *ob-
servation*
R. V. Lev. 19. 26; 2 Kings 21. 6;
2 Chron. 33. 6. practise; Deut. 16.
13; 2 Chron. 7. 17; Neh. 1. 5; Ps.
105. 45. keep; Prov. 23. 26. delight
in; Hos. 14. 8; John 2. 8. regard;
Gen. 37. 11; Mark 6. 20. kept; Ps.
107. 43. give heed; Hos. 13. 7.
watch; Matt. 23. 3; Acts 21. 25 ——
OBSTINATE, Deut. 2. 30. Isa. 48. 4.
OBTAIN favor of Lord, Prov. 8. 35.
Isa. 35. 10. shall *o.* joy and gladness
Luke 20. 35. worthy to *o.* that world
1 Cor. 9. 24. so run, that ye may *o.*
Heb. 4. 16. may *o.* mercy and find
11. 35. might *o.* better resurrection
Hos. 2. 23. her that had not *obtained*
mercy
Acts 26. 22. having *o.* help of God
Rom. 11. 7. the election hath *o.* it
Eph. 1. 11. in whom we have *o.* an
1 Tim. 1. 13. I *o.* mercy, because
Heb. 1. 4. *o.* a more excellent
6. 15. endured, he *o.* the promises

Heb. 9. 12. *o.* eternal redemption
for us
R. V. Luke 20. 35; 1 Cor. 9. 24. attain; 1 Cor. 9. 25; Heb. 4. 16; Acts
1. 17. receive; Neh. 13. 6. asked
OCCASION, Gen. 43. 18. Judg. 14. 4.
2 Sam. 12. 14. given *o.* to enemies
Job 33. 10. he findeth *o.* against me
Jer. 2. 24. in her *o.* who can turn
Dan. 6. 4. could find none *o.*, 5.
Rom. 7. 8. sin taking *o.* by the
14. 13. *o.* to fall in brother's way
2 Cor. 11. 12. cut off *o.* from the
Gal. 5. 13. use not for *o.* to the flesh
1 Tim. 5. 14. give none *o.* to adver.
1 John 2. 10. none *o.* of stumbling
OCCUPY, Luke 19. 13. Heb. 13. 9.
R. V. Ex. 38. 24. used; Ezek. 27.
16, 19, 22. Luke 19. 13. trade, or
traded; 1 Cor. 14. 16. filleth
ODOR, Phil. 4. 18. Rev. 5. 8.
R. V. Jer. 34. 5. make burning;
Rev. 5. 8; 18. 13. incense
OFFENCE, 1 Sam. 25. 31. Isa. 8. 14.
Eccl. 10. 4. yield. pacifieth great *o.*
Hos. 5. 15. acknowledge their *o.*
Acts 24. 16. conscience void of *o.*
Rom. 4. 25. delivered for our *o.* and
Matt. 16. 23. thou art an *o.* unto me
18. 7. woe to the world because of
o. for *o.* must come
Rom. 5. 15. not as *o.* so is free gift
16. the free gift is of many *o.*
17. by one man's *o.* death came
9. 33. rock of *o.*, 1 Pet. 2. 8. Isa. 8. 14.
14. 20. is evil for him that eateth
with *o.*
16. 17. cause divisions and *o.*
1 Cor. 10. 32. give none *o.* neither
2 Cor. 6. 3. giving no *o.* in any
11. 7. committed an *o.* in abasing
Gal. 5. 11. then is the *o.* of the
Phil. 1. 10. without *o.* till day of
Christ
R. V. Matt. 16. 23; Gal. 5. 11. stumbling block; Matt. 18. 7. occasion;
Rom. 4. 25; 5. 15–18. trespass;
Matt. 18. 7; Luke 17. 1; Rom. 16.
17; 2 Cor. 6. 3. occasion for stum.
OFFEND, I will not any more,
Job 34. 31.
Ps. 73. 15. *o.* against generation
119. 165. nothing shall *o.* them
Jer. 2. 3. all that devour him
shall *o.*
50. 7. we *o.* not because we have
Matt. 5. 29. if thy right eye *o.*
thee
13. 41. gather out of his kingdom
all that *o.*
17. 27. yet lest we should *o.* go
18. 6. whoso shall *o.* one of these
1 Cor. 8. 13. if meat make thy brother to *o.*
Jas. 2. 10. *o.* in one point is guilty
3. 2. in many things we *o.* all
Prov. 18. 19. brother *offended* is
harder to be won
Matt. 11. 6. blessed who is not *o.*
26. 33. though all be *o.* I will
Mark 4. 17. immediate. they are *o.*
Rom. 14. 21. *o.* or is made weak
2 Cor. 11. 29. who is *o.* and I burn
Isa. 29. 21. make a man *offender*
for
R. V. Gen. 20. 9; Jer. 37. 18; Acts
25. 8. sinned; Jer. 2. 3; Hab. 1. 11.
guilty; Rom. 14. 21 ——. In most
of the above references under
the head of *Stumble*, the word
stumble, stumbling or stumbleth
has been introduced in R. V.
text; Acts 21. 11. wrong doer
OFFER, Gen. 31. 54. Lev. 1. 3.
Matt. 5. 24. then come and *o.* thy
gift
Heb. 13. 15. let us *o.* the sacrifice
Rev. 8. 3. *o.* it with prayers of
Mal. 1. 11. incense *offered* to my
Phil. 2. 17. *o.* upon sacrifice and
service
2 Tim. 4. 6. I am now ready to be *o.*
Heb. 9. 14. *o.* himself without spot
28. Christ was once *o.* to bear

Heb. 11. 4. by faith Abel o. to God a
17. Abraham o. up Isaac
Ps. 50. 14. o. to God thanksgiving
23. whoso *offereth* praise glori.
Eph. 5. 2. *offering* a sacrifice to God
Heb. 10. 5. sacrifice and o. thou
14. by one o. hath perfected for
R. V. Frequent changes to sacrifice, present, bring or brought, especially in O. T. Frequent changes in Lev. and Num. to oblation

OFFSCOURING, Lam. 3. 45. 1 Cor. 4. 16.

OFFSPRING, Acts 17. 28. Rev. 22. 16.
R. V. Job 31. 8. produce

OFTEN reproved hardeneth, Prov. 29. 1.
Mal. 3. 16. spake o. one to another
Matt. 23. 37. how o. would I have
1 Cor. 11. 26. o. as ye eat this
Phil. 3. 18. of whom I have told you o.
Heb. 9. 25. needed not offer himself o.

OIL, Gen. 28. 18. Ex. 25. 6.
Ps. 45. 7. with o. of gladness
89. 20. with my holy o. I have
92. 10. be anointed with fresh o.
104. 15. o. to make his face shine
141. 5. o. which shall not break
Isa. 61. 3. o. of joy for mourning
Matt. 25. 3. took no o. in lamps
8. give us of your o. for our lamps
Luke 10. 34. pouring in wine and o.

OINTMENT, Ps. 133. 2. Prov. 27. 9, 16. Eccl. 7. 1. & 10. 1. S. of S. 1. 3. Isa. 1. 6. Amos 6. 6. Matt. 26. 7. Luke 7. 37.
R. V. Ex. 30. 25. perfume; 2 Kings 20. 13; Ps. 123. 2; Isa. 1. 6; 39. 2. oil

OLD, Gen. 5. 32. & 18. 12, 13.
Ps. 37. 25. been young, and now am o.
71. 18. when I am o. and gray.
Prov. 22. 6. when he is o. he will
Jer. 6. 16. ask for the o. paths and
Acts 21. 16. Mnason an o. disciple
1 Cor. 5. 7. purge out the o. leaven
2 Cor. 5. 17. o. things are passed
2 Pet. 1. 9. purged from his o. sins
Gen. 25. 8. *old age*, Judg. 8. 32. Job 30. 2. Ps. 71. 9. & 92. 14. Isa. 46. 4. Rom. 6. 6. *old man*, Eph. 4. 22. Col. 3. 9.
Prov. 17. 6. of *old men*, 20. 29.

OLD PROPHET, the, 1 Kings 13. 11.

OMEGA, Alpha and, **Rev. 1. 8, 11.** & 21. 6. & 22. 13.
R. V. Rev. 1. 11 ——

ONE, Gen. 2. 24. Matt. 19. 5.
Jer. 3. 14. o. of a city, and two of
Zech. 14. 9. shall be o. Lord and
Matt. 19. 17. none good but o.
1 Cor. 8. 4. none other God but o.
10. 17. we being many are o. bread
Gal. 3. 20. mediator not of o. but
1 John 5. 7. these three are o.
Josh. 23. 14. not *one thing* hath failed
Ps. 27. 4. — have I desired of Lord
Mark 10. 21. — thou lackest, go sell
Luke 10. 42. but — is needful
Phil. 3. 13. this — I do, forgetting

OPEN thou my lips, Ps. 51. 15.
Ps. 81. 10. o. thy mouth wide
119. 18. o. thou mine eyes, that I
Prov. 31. 8. o. thy mouth for dumb
S. of S. 5. 2. o. to me, my sister, my
Isa. 22. 22. shall o. and none shall
42. 7. to o. blind eyes, Ps. 146. 8.
Ezek. 16. 63. never o. thy mouth
Matt. 25. 11. Lord o. to us
Acts 26. 18. to o. their eyes, and
Col. 4. 3. o. to us door of utterance
Rev. 5. 2. who is worthy to o.
Gen. 3. 7. eyes of them both were *opened*

Isa. 35. 5. eyes of the blind shall be o.
53. 7. he o. not his mouth
Matt. 7. 7. knock and it shall be o.
Luke 24. 45. then o. he their
Acts 14. 27. o. the door of faith
16. 14. Lydia whose heart Lord o.
1 Cor. 16. 9. a great door and effectual is o.
2 Cor. 2. 12. a door was o. to me of
Heb. 4. 13. naked and o. to eyes of
Ps. 104. 28. *openest* thy hand, 145. 16.
R. V. Gen. 38. 14. gate of Enaim; 2 Cor. 3. 18. unveiled; 1 Tim. 5. 24. evident; Job 38. 17; Jer. 20. 12. revealed; Mark 1. 10. rent asunder

OPERATION, Ps. 28. 5. Isa. 5. 12. Col. 3. 12. 1 Cor. 12. 6.
R. V. 1 Cor. 12. 6. workings; Col. 2. 12. in the working

OPINION, Job 33. 6, 10. 1 Kings 18. 21.

OPPORTUNITY, Matt. 26. 16. Gal. 6. 10. Phil. 4. 10. Heb. 11. 15.

OPPOSE, 2 Tim. 2. 25. 2 Thes. 2. 4.
R. V. Job 30. 21. persecutest

OPPRESS, Ex. 3. 9. Judg. 10. 12.
Ex. 22. 21. o. not a stranger, 23. 9.
Lev. 25. 14. o. not one another, 17.
Deut. 24. 14. shall not o. a hired
Ps. 10. 18. that man may no more o.
Prov. 22. 22. neither o. afflicted in
Zech. 7. 10. o. not the widow or
Mal. 3. 5. a witness against those that o.
Jas. 2. 6. do not rich men o. you
Ps. 9. 9. the Lord will be a refuge for the *oppressed*
10. 18. judge the fatherless and o.
Eccl. 4. 1. tears of such as were o.
Isa. 1. 17. relieve the o., 58. 6.
38. 14. I am o. undertake for me
53. 7. he was o. and afflicted
Ezek. 18. 7. hath not o. any
Acts 10. 38. Jesus healed all o. of
Prov. 22. 16. *oppresseth,* 14. 31. & 28. 3.
Deut. 27. 7. Lord looked on our *oppression*
2 Kings 13. 4. the Lord saw the o.
Ps. 12. 5. for o. of poor and sighing
62. 10. trust not in o. and become
Eccl. 7. 7. o. maketh a wise man
Isa. 5. 7. looked for judgment but behold o.
33. 15. he that despiseth gain of o.
Ps. 72. 4. *oppressor,* 54. 3. & 119. 121.
Prov. 3. 31. & 28. 16. Eccl. 4. 1. Isa. 3. 12. & 14. 4. & 51. 13.
R. V. Lev. 25. 14, 17. wrong; Job 35. 9. cry out; Ezek. 18. 7, 12, 16. wronged; Ps. 12. 5. spoiling; Eccl. 7. 7. extortion; Ezek. 46. 18 ——; Job 3. 18. taskmaster; Ps. 54. 3. violent man; Zech. 10. 4. exactor

ORACLES of God, Acts 7. 38. Rom. 3. 2. Heb. 5. 12. 1 Pet. 4. 11.

ORDAIN, Isa. 26. 12. Tit. 1. 5.
Ps. 8. 2. hast *ordained* strength
132. 17. o. a lamp for mine anoint.
Isa. 30. 33. Tophet is o. of old, for
Jer. 1. 5. o. thee a prophet
Hab. 1. 12. thou hast o. them
Acts 13. 48. as were o. to eternal
14. 23. o. elders in every church
17. 31. judge that man whom he hath o.
Rom. 7. 10. commandment which was o.
1 Cor. 9. 14. Lord o. that they
Gal. 3. 19. o. by angels in hand
Eph. 2. 10. God before o. we
1 Tim. 2. 7. o. a preacher and an
Heb. 5. 1. o. for men in things
Jude 4. o. to this condemnation
R. V. 1 Chron. 17. 9; Tit. 1. 5. appoint; Ps. 8. 2. established; 7. 13. maketh; Isa. 30. 33; Eph. 2. 10; Heb. 9. 6. prepared; 1 Cor. 2. 7. foreordained; 2 Chron. 11. 15; Ps.

81. 5; Jer. 1. 5; Dan. 2. 24; Mark 3. 14; John 15. 16; Acts 14. 23; 1 Tim. 2. 7; Heb. 5. 1; 8. 3. appointed

ORDER, Gen. 22. 9. Job 33. 5.
Job 23. 4. o. my cause before
Ps. 40. 5. be reckoned up in o.
50. 21. sins set them in o. before
119. 133. o. my steps in thy word
1 Cor. 14. 40. all things be done decently and in o.
Col. 2. 5. joying and beholding your o.
Tit. 1. 5. set in o. things wanting
2 Sam. 23. 5. everlasting covenant, *ordered* in all things
Ps. 37. 23. steps of a good man are o. by the Lord
50. 23. that *ordereth* his conversation aright
R. V. Ex. 40. 4; Luke 1. 1; Heb. 7. 21 —— ; Ex. 26. 17. joined; 1 Chron. 15. 13; 23. 31; 2 Chron. 8. 14. ordinance; 1 Kings 20. 14. begin; Ps. 37. 23; Isa. 9. 7. establish

ORDINANCE of God, Isa. 58. 2. Rom. 13. 2.
1 Pet. 2. 13. submit to every o. of man
Neh. 10. 32. make *ordinances* for us
Isa. 58. 2. ask of me the o. of justice
Jer. 31. 35. o. of the moon and of
Ezek. 11. 20. keep mine o. and do them, Lev. 18. 4, 30, & 22. 9. 1 Cor. 11. 2.
Luke 1. 6. walking in all o. of Lord
Eph. 2. 15. law contained in o.
Col. 2. 14. handwriting of o. against
20. why are ye subject to o.
Heb. 9. 1. had o. of divine service
R. V. Lev. 18. 30; 22. 9; Mal. 3. 14. charge; Ex. 18. 20; Lev. 18. 3, 4, 30; 22. 9; Num. 9. 12, 14; 10. 8; 15. 15 : 19. 2; 31. 21; Ps. 99. 7. statute, or statutes; Ezra 3. 10. order; Ezek. 45. 14. portion; 1 Cor. 11. 2. traditions

ORNAMENTS, Ex. 33. 5. Prov. 1. 9. & 25. 12. Isa. 49. 18. & 61. 10. Jer. 2. 32. Ezek. 16. 7, 11. 1 Pet. 3. 4.
R. V. Judg. 8. 21, 26. crescents; Prov. 1. 9; 4. 3. chaplet; Isa. 30. 22. plating; 61. 10. garland; 3. 20. ankle chains; 3. 18. anklets; 1 Pet. 3. 4. apparel

OSTENTATION condemned, Prov. 25. 14; 27. 2; Matt. 6. 1.

OUGHT ye to do, Matt. 23. 23. Jas. 3. 10.

OURS, Gen. 26. 20. Num. 32. 32.
Mark 12. 7. inheritance shall be o., Luke 20. 14.
1 Cor. 1. 2. Christ our Lord both theirs and o.
Tit. 3. 14. let o. learn to maintain good works

OUTCASTS of Israel, Ps. 147. 2. Isa. 11. 12. & 16. 3. & 56. 8.
Isa. 16. 14. let mine o. dwell

OUTER, Ezek. 46. 21. & 47. 2. Matt. 8. 12. & 22. 13. & 25. 30.

OUTGOINGS, Josh. 17. 9. Ps. 65. 8.
R. V. In Josh. goings out

OUTRAGEOUS, Prov. 27. 4.

OUTSIDE, Ezek. 40. 5. Matt. 23. 25.

OUTSTRETCHED arm, Deut. 26. 8. Jer. 21. 5. & 27. 5.

OUTWARD, 1 Sam. 16. 7. Rom. 2. 28. 2 Cor. 4. 16. & 10. 7. 1 Pet. 3. 3.
Matt. 23. 28. *outwardly*, Rom. 2. 28.

OVEN, Ps. 21. 9. Hos. 7. 4. Mal. 4. 1.
R. V. Ps. 21. 9; Mal. 4. 1. furnace

OVERCHARGE, Luke 21. 31. 2 Cor. 2. 5.

OVERCOME, Gen. 49. 19. Num. 13. 30.
S. of S. 6. 5. thine eyes have o. me
John 16. 33. I have o. the world
Rom. 12. 21. be not o. of evil

1 John 2. 13. ye have *o.* the wick.
4. 4. ye are of God, and have *o.*
Rev. 17. 14. Lamb shall *o.* them
1 John 5. 4. born of God *overcometh*
Rev. 2. 7. to him that *o.* I will give
26. he that *o.* will I give power
3. 5. he that *o.* shall be clothed
12. him that *o.* will I make a pillar
21. him that *o.* will I grant to sit
21. 7. he that *o.* shall inherit all
R. V. Acts 19. 16. mastered
OVERMUCH, Eccl. 7. 16, 17. 2 Cor. 2. 7.
OVERPAST, Ps. 57. 1. Isa. 26. 20. Jer. 5. 28.
OVERSEER, Prov. 6. 7. Acts 20. 28.
R. V. Acts 20. 28. bishops
OVERSIGHT, Gen. 43. 12. 1 Pet. 5. 2.
R. V. Num. 4. 16. charge; Neh. 13. 4. who was appointed
OVERTAKE, Ex. 15. 9. Amos 9. 13. Hos. 2. 7. Gal. 6. 1. 1 Thes. 5. 4.
OVERTHROW, Deut. 12. 3. & 29. 23. Job 12. 19. Ps. 140. 4, 11. Prov. 13. 6. & 21. 12. Amos 4. 11. Acts 5. 39. 2 Tim. 2. 18.
R. V. Deut. 12. 3. break down; Ps. 140. 4. thrust aside; Prov. 18. 5. turn aside; 2 Sam. 17. 9. fallen; Job 19. 6. subverted
OVERTURN, Ezek. 21. 27. Job 9. 5, & 12. 15. & 28. 9. & 34. 25.
OVERWHELMED, Ps. 55. 5. & 61. 2. & 77. 3. & 124. 4. & 142. 3. & 143. 4.
R. V. Job 6. 27. cast lots upon
OVERWISE, neither make self, Eccl. 7. 16.
OWE, Rom. 13. 8. Matt. 18. 24, 28.
OWL, Job 30. 29. Ps. 102. 6. Isa. 13. 21. & 34. 11, 15. & 43. 20. Mic. 1. 8.
R. V. Lev. 11. 16; Deut. 14. 15; Job 30. 29; Isa. 13. 21; 34. 13; 43. 20; Jer. 50. 39; Mic. 1. 8. ostrich, or ostriches; Isa. 34.14. night-monster; 34. 15. arrowsnake
OWN, Deut. 24. 16. Judg. 7. 2.
John 1. 11. his *o.* and his *o.* receiv.
1 Cor. 6. 19. ye are not your *o.*
10. 24. let no man seek his *o.*
Phil. 2. 4. look not on his *o.* things
21. all seek their *o.* not of Jesus
R. V. In very many instances, the word is omitted.
OX knoweth his owner, Isa. 1. 3. & 11. 7. Ps. 7. 22. & 14. 4. & 15. 17.
Ps. 144. 14, *oxen*, Isa. 22. 13. Matt. 22. 4. Luke 14. 19. John 2. 14. 1 Cor. 9. 9.
R. V. Gen. 34. 28; Ex. 9. 3. herds; Num. 23. 1. bullocks; Deut. 14. 5. antelope; 1 Sam. 14. 14. half furrow's length; Jer. 11. 19 ——

P

PACIFY, Esth. 7. 10. Prov. 16. 14.
Ezek. 16. 63. when I am *pacified*
Prov. 21. 14. gift in secret *pacifieth* anger
Eccl. 10. 4. yield. *p.* great offences
R. V. Eccl. 10. 4. allayeth; Ezek. 16. 63. have forgiven
PAIN, Isa. 21. 3. & 26. 18. & 66. 7. Jer. 6. 24. Mic. 4. 10. Rev. 21. 4.
Ps. 116. 3. *pains* of hell gat hold
Acts 2. 24. loosed the *p.* of death
Ps. 55. 4. my heart is sore *pained*, Isa. 23. 5. Jer. 4. 19. Joel 2. 6.
Rev. 12. 2. travail. in birth and *p.*
Ps. 73. 16. *painful*, 2 Cor. 11. 27.
R. V. Nah. 2. 10. anguish; Acts 2. 24. pangs; Joel 2. 6. anguish
PAINTED, 2 Kings 9. 30. Jer. 4. 30. & 22. 14. Ezek. 23. 40.
PALACE, 1 Chron. 29. 19. Ps. 45. 8, 15. S. of S. 8. 9. Isa. 25. 2. Phil. 1. 13.
R. V. 1 Kings 16. 18; 2 Kings 15. 25; Neh. 2. 8; 7. 2; Hos. 8. 14. castle;

Ps. 78. 69. heights; 2 Chron. 9. 11. house; S. of S. 8. 9. turret; Amos 4. 3. Harmon; Matt. 26. 3, 29, 58; Mark 14. 54, 66; Luke 18. 21; John 18. 15. court; John 18. 28. judgment hall; Phil. 1. 13. prætorian guard; Ezek. 25. 14. encampments
PALM tree, Ps. 92. 12. S. of S. 7. 7.
PANT, Amos 2. 7. Ps. 38. 10. & 42. 1. & 119. 131. Isa. 21. 4.
R. V. Ps. 38. 10. throbbeth
PAPER REEDS of Egypt, Isa. 19. 7.
PARABLE, Ps. 49. 4. & 78. 2. Prov. 26. 7, 9. Ezek. 20. 49. Mic. 2. 4. Matt. 13. 3. Luke 5. 36. & 13. 6. & 21. 29.
PARADISE, Gen. 2. 15. Luke 23. 43. 2 Cor. 12. 4. Rev. 2. 7.
PARCHMENTS, 2 Tim. 4. 13.
PARDON our iniquity, Ex. 34. 9.
Ex. 23. 21. he will not *p.* your
Num. 14. 19. *p.* iniquity of people
1 Sam. 15. 25. *p.* my sin, 2 Kings 5. 18.
2 Kings 24. 4. which the Lord would not *p.*
2 Chron. 30. 18. the good Lord *p.*
Neh. 9. 17. a God ready to *p.*
Job 7. 21. why dost not *p.* my
Ps. 25. 11. for name's sake *p.*
Isa. 55. 7. our God, he will abundantly *p.*
Jer. 5. 7. how shall I *p.* thee for
33. 8. I will *p.* all their iniquities
Isa. 40. 2. cry that her iniquity is *pardoned*
Lam. 3. 42. we transgressed thou hast not *p.*
Mic. 7. 18. a God like thee that *p.*
PARENTS, Luke 2. 27. & 8. 56.
Matt. 10. 21. children rise up against their *p.*
Luke 18. 29. no man hath left house or *p.*
John 9. 2. who did sin, this man or his *p.*
Rom. 1. 30. disobedient to *p.*
2 Cor. 12. 14. children ought not to lay up for *p.* but *p.* for children
1 Tim. 5. 4. learn to requite their *p.*
PART, it shall be thy, Ex. 29. 26.
Num. 18. 20. I am thy *p.* and
Ps. 5. 9. their inward *p.* is very
51. 6. in hidden *p.* make me know
Luke 10. 42. hath chos. that good *p.*
John 13. 8. if I wash thee not, thou hast no *p.*
Acts 8. 21. neither *p.* nor lot in this
1 Cor. 13. 9. know in *p.* and proph.
10. that which is in *p.* shall be done
R. V. Frequent changes to portion; and many omissions of word. Also many changes due to preceding word
PARTAKER with adulterers, Ps. 50. 18.
Rom. 15. 27. *p.* of their spiritual
1 Cor. 9. 10. *p.* of this hope
13. *p.* with altar
10. 17. *p.* of one bread
21. *p.* of Lord's table
30. if I by grace be a *p.* why am
1 Pet. 5. 1. a *p.* of the glory reveal.
2 John 11. is *p.* of his evil deeds
Eph. 5. 7. be not *partakers* with
1 Tim. 5. 22. be not *p.* of other
Heb. 3. 14. *p.* of Christ
6. 4. *p.* of the Holy Ghost
12. 10. might be *p.* of his holiness
R. V. 1 Cor. 9. 14. have their portion; Heb. 2. 14. sharers in
PARTIAL, Mal. 2. 9. Jas. 2. 4.
1 Tim. 5. 21. *partiality*, Jas. 3. 17.
R. V. *divided in own mind*; Jas. 2. 4. are ye not *p.* in yourselves; Jas. 3. 17. variance
PASS, Ex. 33. 19. Ezek. 20. 37. Zeph. 2. 2. Zech. 3. 4. 2 Pet. 3. 10.
Mark 14. 35. the hour might *p.* from
Luke 16. 17. easier for heaven and earth to *p.*
1 Pet. 1. 17. *p.* the time of sojourn.

John 5. 24. is *passed* from death to
Isa. 43. 2. when thou *passest* throu.
Mic. 7. 18. *passeth* by transgression
1 Cor. 7. 31. fashion of this world *p.*
Eph. 3. 19. love of Christ which *p.*
Phil. 4. 7. peace of God which *p.*
1 John 2. 17. world *p.* away and lusts
PASSION, Acts 1. 3. & 14. 15.
PASSOVER, Ex. 12. 11. Deut. 16. 2. Josh. 5. 11. 2 Chron. 30. 15. & 35. 1, 11. Heb. 11. 28.
1 Cor. 5. 7. Christ our *p.* is sacri.
PASTORS, Jer. 3. 15. & 17. 16. Eph. 4. 11.
Ps. 74. 1. sheep of thy *pasture*, 79. 13. & 95. 7. & 23. 2. & 100. 3. Isa. 30. 23. & 49. 9. Ezek. 34. 14, 18. John 10. 9.
R. V. Jer. 2. 8. rulers; 3. 15; 10. 21; 12. 10; 17. 16; 22. 22; 23. 1, 2. shepherds: Isa. 49. 9. all bare heights
PASTURE, spiritual, Ps. 23. 2. & 74. 1. & 79. 13. & 95. 7. & 100. Ezek. 34. 14. John 10. 9.
PATH, Num. 22. 24. Job 28. 7.
Ps. 16. 11. wilt show me *p.* of life
27. 11. lead me in a plain *p.*
119. 35. go in *p.* of thy
Prov. 4. 18. *p.* of the just is as
26. ponder the *p.* of thy feet
5. 6. lest thou ponder the *p.* of life
Isa. 26. 7. thou dost weigh *p.* of just
Ps. 17. 4. keep me from *paths of*
25. 4. show thy ways; teach me *p.*
10. all *p.* of the Lord are mercy
Prov. 3. 17. all her *p.* are peace
Isa. 59. 7. destruc. are in their *p.*
8. they have made them crook. *p.*
Jer. 6. 16. ask for old *p.* the good
Hos. 2. 6. shall not find her *p.*
Matt. 3. 3. make his *p.* straight
Heb. 12. 13. make straight *p.* for
R. V. Num. 22. 34. hollow way; Ps. 17. 4. ways; Jer. 18. 15. by paths
PATIENCE with me, Matt. 18. 26, 29.
Luke 8. 15. bring forth fruit with *p.*
21. 19. in your *p.* possess your souls
Rom. 5. 3. tribulation worketh *p.*
15. 4. that we through *p.* might have hope
2 Cor. 6. 4. as minist. of God, in *p.*
Col. 1. 11. strengthened unto all *p.*
1 Thes. 1. 3. of hope in our Lord
2 Thes. 1. 4. for your *p.* and faith
1 Tim. 6. 11. follow after *p.* meek.
2 Tim. 3. 10. my doctr., charity, *p.*
Tit. 2. 2. sound in faith, charity, *p.*
Heb. 6. 12. through *p.* inherit the
10. 36. have need of *p.* that after
12. 1. run with *p.* race set bef. us
Jas. 1. 3. trying of your faith worketh *p.*
4. let *p.* have her perfect work
5. 7. long *p.* for it till he receive
10. prophets for an example of *p.*
11. ye have heard of the *p.* of Job
2 Pet. 1. 6. to temperance *p.* to *p.*
Rev. 1. 9. brother in the *p.* of Jesus
2. 2. I know thy *p.*, 19.
Eccl. 7. 8. the *patient* in spirit
Rom. 2. 7. by *p.* continuance in
12. 12. *p.* in tribulation, instant in
1 Thes. 5. 14. be *p.* towards all men
2 Thes. 3. 5. *p.* waiting for Christ
1 Tim. 3. 3. not gree. of lucre but *p.*
2 Tim. 2. 24. gentle, apt to teach, *p.*
Jas. 5. 7. *p.* unto coming of Lord
8. be ye also *p.* establish your
Ps. 37. 7. wait *patiently* for the Lord
Heb. 6. 15. after he had *p.* endured
1 Pet. 2. 20. ye be buffeted for your faults take it *p.*
R. V. 1 Thes. 5. 14. long suffering; 1 Tim. 3. 3. gentle; 2 Tim. 2. 24. forbearing
PATRIARCH, Acts 2. 29. & 7. 8. Heb. 7. 4.
PATRIMONY, his, Deut. 18. 8.
PATTERN, 1 Tim. 1. 16. Tit. 2. 7. Ezek. 43. 10. Heb. 8. 5. & 9. 23.

R. V. 1 Tim. 1. 16; Tit. 2. 7. ensample; Heb. 9. 23. copies
PAVILION, Ps. 27. 5. & 31. 20. &
18. 11. 1 Kings 20. 12, 16. Jer. 43.
10.
PAY, Matt. 18. 28. Ps. 37. 21.
R. V. Num. 20. 19. give price;
2 Chron. 27. 5. render
PEACE, Lev. 26. 6. Num. 6. 26.
Job 22. 21. acquaint thyself with
God, and be at *p.*
Ps. 34. 14. seek *p.* and pursue it
37. 37. the end of that man is *p.*
85. 10. righteousness and *p.* kissed
119. 165. great *p.* have they that
122. 6. pray for *p.* of Jerusalem
125. 5. *p.* shall be upon Israel
Prov. 16. 7. his enemies to be at *p.*
Isa. 9. 6. everl. Father, Prince of *p.*
26. 3. keep him in perfect *p.*
27. 5. that he may make *p.* with me
45. 7. I make *p.* and create evil
48. 18. had thy *p.* been as a river
22. there is no *p.* to the wicked
57. 2. enter into *p.* shall rest in
19. *p. p.* to him that is far off
59. 8. way of *p.* they know not
63. 17. will make thy officers *p.*
66. 12. I will extend *p.* to her
Jer. 6. 14. saying, *p.* when there
is no *p.*, 8. 11. Ezek. 13. 10. 2 Kings
9. 18, 22.
Jer. 8. 15. looked for *p.* but no
29. 7. seek *p.* of the city, for in
11. thoughts of *p.* and not of evil
Mic. 5. 5. this man shall be the *p.*
Zech. 8. 19. love the truth and *p.*
Matt. 10. 34. I came not to send *p.*
Mark 9. 50. have *p.* one with another
Luke 1. 79. guide our feet into the
way of *p.*
2. 14. on earth *p.* good will towards
29. lettest thy servant depart in *p.*
John 14. 27. *p.* I leave; my *p.* I give
16. 33. in me ye might have *p.*
Rom. 5. 1. we have *p.* with God
8. 6. spiritual. minded is life and *p.*
15. 13. fill you with all *p.* and joy
1 Cor. 7. 15. God hath call. us to *p.*
2 Cor. 13. 11. live in *p.* and the God
of *p.* shall
Gal. 5. 22. fruit of Spirit is love, *p.*
Eph. 2. 14. he is our *p.*
15. making *p.*
Phil. 4. 7. the *p.* of God, Col. 3. 15.
1 Thes. 5. 13. at *p.* among your.
Heb. 12. 14. follow *p.* with all men
Jas. 3. 18. sown in *p.* of them
1 Pet. 3. 11. let him seek *p.* and
2 Pet. 3. 14. found of him in *p.*
1 Tim. 2. 2. lead a *peaceable* life in
Heb. 12. 11. yielding *p.* fruit of
Jas. 3. 17. is first pure, then *p.*
Rom. 12. 18. live *peaceably* with all
Matt. 5. 9. blessed are the *peace-
makers*
R. V. 1 Cor. 14. 30. silence; Rom.
10. 15 — ; Dan. 11. 21, 24. time of
security; Rom. 12. 18. at peace
PEACE OFFERINGS, laws per-
taining to, Ex. 20. 24. & 24. 5. Lev.
3. 6. & 7. 11. & 19. 5.
PEARL of great price, Matt. 13. 46.
Matt. 7. 6. cast not *pearls* before
1 Tim. 2. 9. gold, or *p.* or costly
array
Rev. 21. 21. gates were twelve *p*
R. V. Job 28. 18. crystal
PECULIAR treasure, Ex. 19. 5.
Ps. 135. 4.
Eccl. 2. 8. *p.* treasure of provinces
Deut. 14. 2. *p.* people, 26. 18. Tit. 2.
14. 1 Pet. 2. 9.
PEN of iron, Job 19. 24. Jer. 17. 1.
Ps. 45. 1. tongue is as the *p.* of a
ready writer
R. V. Tit. 2. 14 ; 1 Pet. 2. 9. own
possession
PENURY, Prov. 14. 23. Luke 21. 4.
R. V. Luke 21. 4. want
PEOPLE, Gen. 27. 29. Ex. 6. 7.
Ps. 144. 15. happy is the *p.* whose
148. 14. Israel is a *p.* near unto him

Isa. 1. 4. sinful nation, a *p.* laden
10. 6. against the *p.* of my wrath
34. 5. upon the *p.* of my curse
Hos. 4. 9. like *p.* like priest
1 Pet. 2. 10. in time past were not *p.*
Ps. 73. 10. *his people* return hither
100. 3. we are — and sheep of his
Matt. 1. 21. Jesus shall save — from
Rom. 11. 2. God hath not cast
away —
Ps. 50. 7. hear, O *my people*, and I
will speak
81. 11. — would not hearken, 8. 13.
Isa. 19. 25. blessed be Egypt — and
63. 8. surely they are — that will
Jer. 30. 22. ye shall be — and I will
be your God, 31. 33. & 24. 7. & 32.
38. Ezek. 11. 20. & 36. 38. & 37. 27.
Zech. 2. 11. & 8. 8. & 13. 9. 2 Cor. 6.
16.
Hos. 1. 9. ye are not —
10. say to them which were not —
thou art —
Heb. 11. 25. *p.* of God, 1 Pet. 2. 10.
R. V. Very frequent changes to
peoples, multitude, multitudes,
etc.
PERCEIVE, Deut. 29. 4. 1 John 3.
16.
R. V. Deut. 29. 4; Josh. 22. 31;
1 Sam. 12. 17; 1 John 3. 16. know;
Judg. 6. 22; 1 Kings 22. 33; 2 Chron.
18. 32; Eccl. 3. 22; Luke 9. 27. saw;
Neh. 6. 12; Prov. 1. 2. discern;
Acts 8. 23; 14. 9; 2 Cor. 7. 8. see
and seeing; Luke 6. 41. considereth; Mark 12. 28. knowing; John
12. 19. behold; Acts 23. 29. found
PERDITION, John 17. 12. Phil. 1.
28. 2 Thes. 2. 3. 1 Tim. 6. 9. Heb.
10. 39. 2 Pet. 3. 7. Rev. 17. 3, 11.
R. V. 2 Pet. 3. 7. destruction
PERFECT, Deut. 25. 15. Ps. 18. 32.
Gen. 6. 9. Noah was a just man
and *p.*
17. 1. walk before me, and be *p.*
Deut. 18. 13. shalt be *p.* with God
32. 4. this work is *p.*, just, and right
2 Sam. 22. 31. his way is *p.*
Job 1. 1. man was *p.* and upright
Ps. 19. 7. law of the Lord is *p.* con.
37. 37. mark the *p.* man and
Ezek. 16. 14. it was *p.* through my
Matt. 5. 48. *p.* as your Father is *p.*
19. 21. if thou wilt be *p.* go and
1 Cor. 2. 6. wisdom among them
that are *p.*
2 Cor. 12. 9. strength is made *p.* in
13. 11. be *p.* be of good comfort
Eph. 4. 13. to a *p.* man unto the
Phil. 3. 12. not as though I were
already *p.*
15. as many as be *p.* thus minded
Col. 1. 28. present every man *p.*
4. 12. may stand *p.* and complete
2 Tim. 3. 17. man of God may be *p.*
Heb. 2. 10. captain of salvation *p.*
12. 23. spirits of just men made *p.*
13. 21. make you *p.* in every good
Jas. 1. 4. be *p.* and entire
17. *p.* gift
1 Pet. 5. 10. make you *p.* establish
1 John 4. 18. *p.* love casteth out fear
Rev. 3. 2. not found thy works *p.*
2 Cor. 7. 1. *perfecting* holiness in
Eph. 4. 12. for the *p.* of the saints
Job 11. 7. find out the Almighty
perfection
Ps. 119. 96. have seen end of all *p*
Luke 8. 14. bring no fruit to *p.*
2 Cor. 13. 9. we wish, even your *p.*
Heb. 6. 1. let us go on unto *p.*
Col. 3. 14. charity the bond of *per-
fectness*
R. V. Isa. 42. 16. at peace; Acts 22.
3. strict; 24. 22. exact; Eph. 4. 13.
full grown; 2 Tim. 3. 17. complete;
Job 28. 3. furtherest bound; Isa.
47. 9. full measure
PERFORM, Gen. 26. 3. Ruth 3. 13.
Job 5. 12. hands cannot *p.* their
Ps. 119. 106. I have sworn and I
will *p.* it
112. inclined my heart to *p.* thy

Isa. 9. 7. zeal of Lord of hosts will
p.
44. 28. shall *p.* all my pleasure
Rom. 4. 21. promis., was able to *p.*
7. 18. how to *p.* that which is good
Phil. 1. 6. he will *p.* it unto day of
1 Kings 8. 20. Lord hath *performed*
Neh. 9. 8. hast *p.* thy words
Isa. 10. 12. Lord hath *p.* his whole
Jer. 51. 29. every purpose of Lord
shall be *p.*
Ps. 57. 2. God that *performeth* all
things
Isa. 44. 26. *p.* counsel of messengers
R. V. Gen. 26. 3; Deut. 9. 5; 1 Kings
6. 12; 8. 20; 12. 15; 2 Chron. 10. 15;
Jer. 11. 5. establish, or estab-
lished; Num. 4. 23. wait upon
Deut. 23. 23; Esth. 1. 15; Rom. 7.
18. do or done; 2 Kings 23. 3, 4;
Ps. 119. 106. confirm; Num. 15. 38;
Luke 2. 39; Rom. 15. 28. accom-
plish; 2 Cor. 8. 11. complete; Phil.
1. 6. perfect
PERILOUS times, 2 Tim. 3. 1.
PERISH, Gen. 41. 36. Lev. 26. 38.
Num. 17. 12. we die, we *p.* we all *p.*
Esth. 4. 16. I will go in, if I *p.* 1 *p.*
Ps. 2. 12. *p.* from the way, when
119. 92. have *p.* in my affliction
Prov. 29. 18. where no vision is,
the people *p.*
Matt. 8. 25. Lord save us, or we *p.*
John 3. 15. believeth should not *p.*
10. 28. I give eternal life, they
shall never *p.*
1 Cor. 8. 11. through thy knowledge
the weak *p.*
2 Pet. 3. 9. not willing that any *p.*
R. V. Num. 17. 12; Jer. 48. 46. un-
done; 2 Cor. 4. 16. is decaying
PERJURY condemned, Ex. 20. 16.
Lev. 6. 3. & 19. 12. Deut. 5. 20. Ezek.
17. 16. Zech. 5. 4. & 8. 17. 1 Tim. 1. 10.
PERMIT, if Lord, 1 Cor. 16. 7.
Heb. 6. 3.
1 Cor. 7. 6. by *permission*, not of
commandment
PERNICIOUS ways, 2 Pet. 2. 2.
PERPETUAL, Jer. 50. 5. & 51. 39,
57.
R. V. Ps. 9. 6. forever; Jer. 50. 5;
Hab. 3. 6. everlasting
PERPLEXED, 2 Cor. 4. 8. Isa. 22. 5.
PERSECUTE me, Ps. 7. 1. & 31. 15.
Job 19. 22. why *p.* me as God, 28.
Ps. 10. 2. wicked doth *p.* the poor
35. 6. let angel of the Lord *p.* them
71. 11. *p.* and take him ; is none
83. 15. *p.* them with thy tempest
Lam. 3. 66. *p.* and destroy them in
Matt. 5. 11. blessed are ye when
men *p.* you
44. pray for them that *p.* you
Rom. 12. 14. bless them which *p.*
Ps. 109. 16. *persecuted* the poor and
119. 161. princes *p.* me without
143. 3. the enemy hath *p.* my soul
John 15. 20. if they *p.* me they
Acts 9. 4. why *p.* thou me, 22. 7.
22. 4. I *p.* this way to death, 7. 8.
26. 11. I *p.* them to strange cities
1 Cor. 4. 12. being *p.* we suffer it
15. 9. because I *p.* the church of
2 Cor. 4. 9. *p.* but not forsaken, cast
Gal. 1. 13. beyond measure I *p.* the
4. 29. *p.* him born after the Spirit
1 Thes. 2. 15. have *p.* us and please
1 Tim. 1. 13. who was before a
persecutor
2 Tim. 3. 12. live godly, shall suffer
persecution
R. V. Ps. 7. 1, 5, 13; 3. 6; 71. 11;
83. 15; Jer. 29. 18; Lam. 3. 43, 66;
2 Cor. 4. 9. pursue, or pursued;
1 Thes. 2. 15. drave out; Acts 11. 19.
tribulation; Neh. 9. 11; Lam. 4.
19. pursuers; Ps. 7. 13. fiery shafts
PERSEVERANCE, watching,
Eph. 6. 18.
PERSON, Lev. 19. 15.
Mal. 1. 8. will he accept thy *p.*
Matt. 22. 16. regardest not *p.* of
Acts 10. 34. God is no respecter of

p., Deut. 19. 16. Gal. 2. 6. Eph. 6. 9.
Col. 3. 25. 1 Pet. 3. 17.
Heb. 1. 3. express image of his *p.*
12. 16. fornicator or profane *p.* as
2 Pet. 3. 11. what manner of *p.*
Jude 16. men's *p.* in admiration
R. V. Gen. 36. 6; Num. 5. 6. soul;
Deut. 15. 22; Ps. 49. 10 ——; Judg.
9. 4. fellows; Jer. 52. 25. face;
Matt. 27. 24. man; Heb. 1. 3. substance

PERSUADE we men, 2 Cor. 5. 11.
Gal. 1. 10. do I *p.* men, or God
Acts 13. 43. *persuaded* them to
21. 14. when we would not be *p.*
Rom. 8. 38. I am *p.* that neither
death
Heb. 6. 9. we are *p.* better things
11. 13. having seen them, were *p.*
Acts 26. 28. almost thou *persuadest*
me to be a Christian
Gal. 5. 8. this *persuasion* cometh
R. V. 1 Kings 22. 20, 21, 22. entice;
2 Chron. 18. 2. moved; Acts 13. 43.
urged; Rom. 4. 21; 14. 5. assumed;
Heb. 11. 13. greeted

PERTAIN, Lev. 7. 29. 1 Cor. 6. 3,
4. Rom. 9. 4. Heb. 2. 17. & **5.** 1. &
9. 9. 2 Pet. 1. 3.
Acts 1. 3. *pertaining*
R. V. Num. 4. 16. shall be; 31. 43.
congregation's half; Josh. 24. 33;
1 Chron. 11. 31. of; 2 Sam. 2. 15.
and for; 1 Kings 7. 48. were in;
Acts 1. 3. concerning; Rom. 4. 1.
according; 9. 4. whose is; Heb. 7.
13. belongeth; 9. 9. touching

PERVERSE, Num. 22. 32. Deut.
32. 5. Job 6. 30. Prov. 4. 24. & 12. 8.
& 14. 2. & 17. 20. Isa. 19. 14. Matt.
17. 17. Acts 20. 30. Phil. 2. 15. 1 Tim.
6. 5.
R. V. Job 6. 30. mischievous; Prov.
23. 33. froward; 1 Tim. 6. 5. wranglings

PERVERT judgment, Deut. 24. 17.
& 16. 19. 1 Sam. 8. 3. Job 8. 3. & 34.
12. Prov. 17. 23. & 31. 5. Mic. 3. 9.
Acts 13. 10. not cease to *p.* right
Gal. 1. 7. would *p.* Gospel of Christ
Job 33. 27. *perverted* that which
Jer. 3. 21. they have *p.* their way
Prov. 19. 3. foolishness of man *p.*
Luke 23. 2. this fellow *p.* the nation
R. V. Deut. 24. 17; 27. 19. wrest;
Prov. 19. 3. subverteth; Eccl. 5. 8.
taking away

PESTILENCE, 2 Sam. 24. 15.
1 Kings 8. 37. Ps. 78. 50. & 91. 3.
Jer. 14. 12. Ezek. 5. 12. Amos 4. 10.
Hab. 3. 5. Matt. 24. 7.
Acts 24. 5. found this man a *pestilent* fellow
R. V. Matt. 24. 7 ——

PETITION, 2 Sam. 1. 17. Esth. 5. 6.
Ps. 20. 5. *petitions*, 1 John 5. 15.

PHILOSOPHY, Col. 2. 8.

PHYLACTERIES, Matt. 23. 5.

PHYSICIAN of no value, Job 13. 4.
Jer. 8. 22. is there no *p.* there
Matt. 9. 12. that be whole need not
p.
Luke 4. 23. say to me, *p.* heal thyself
Col. 4. 14. Luke the beloved *p.*

PIECE of bread. Prov. 6. 26. & 28.
21.
Matt. 9. 16. no man putteth a *p.*
Luke 14. 18. bought a *p.* of ground

PIERCE, Num. 24. 8. 2 Kings 18. 21.
Luke 2. 35. sword shall *p.*
Ps. 22. 16. they *pierced* my hands
Zech. 12. 10. on me whom they *p.*
1 Tim. 6. 10. *p.* themselves through
Rev. 1. 7. they also which *p.* him
Heb. 4. 12. *piercing* even to divid.
R. V. Num. 24. 8. smite; Isa. 27. 1.
swift

PIETY at home, 1 Tim. 5. 4.

PILGRIMS, Heb. 11. 13. 1 Pet. 2.
11.
Gen. 47. 9. *pilgrimage*, Ex. 6. 4. Ps.
119. 54.
R. V. Ex. 6. 4. sojournings

PILLAR of salt, Gen. 19. 26.
Ex. 13. 21. by day in *p.* of cloud;
and by night in a *p.* of fire, Num.
12. 5. & 14. 14. Deut. 31. 15. Neh. 9.
12. Ps. 99. 7.
Isa. 19. 19. a *p.* at the border
Jer. 1. 18. I have made thee iron *p.*
1 Tim. 3. 15. *p.* and ground of truth
Rev. 3. 12. in temple I will make
him a *p.*
Job 9. 6. *pillars* thereof tremble
26. 11. the *p.* of heaven tremble
Ps. 75. 3. I bear up the *p.* of it
Prov. 9. 1. hewn out her seven *p.*
S. of S. 3. 6. *p.* of smoke
5. 15. *p.* of marble
3. 10. *p.* of silver
Rev. 10. 1. *p.* of fire

PILLOW, Gen. 28. 11. Ezek. 13. 18.
R. V. Gen. 28. 11, 18. under his
head; Mark 4. 38. cushion

PINE, Lev. 26. 39. Ezek. 24. 23.

PINE TREE, Isa. 41. 19. & 60. 13.

PIPE, Zech. 4. 2, 12. Matt. 11. 17.
R. V. Zech. 4. 12. spouts

PIT, Gen. 14. 10. & 37. 20.
Ex. 21. 33. if a man dig a *p.*, 34.
Num. 16. 30. they go down quick
into the *p.*
Job 33. 24. deliver him from going
to the *p.*
Ps. 9. 15. sunk in *p.* they had made
28. 1. go down to the *p.*, 30. 3. &
88. 4. & 143. 7. Prov. 1. 12. Isa. 38.
18.
Ps. 40. 2. horrible *p.*
119. 85. proud digged a *p.* for me
Prov. 22. 14. strange wom. a deep *p.*
28. 10. fall into his own *p.*, Eccl.
10. 8.
Isa. 38. 17. delivered it from the *p.*
51. 1. hole of *p.* whence he digged
Jer. 14. 13. come to *p.* and found
Zech. 9. 11. sent prison. out of *p.*
Rev. 9. 1. key of bottomless *p.*, 20.
1.
R. V. Job 6. 27. make merchandise; 17. 16. Sheol; Isa. 30. 4.
abyss; Luke 14. 5. well; Rev. 9.
1, 2, 11; 11. 7; 17. 8; 20. 1, 3. abyss

PITY, Deut. 7. 16. & 13. 8. & 19. 13.
Job 6. 14. to the afflicted *p.* should
19. 21. have *p.* on me, have *p.*
Prov. 19. 17. hath *p.* on poor, lend.
Isa. 63. 9. in his *p.* he redeemed
Ezek. 36. 21. I had *p.* for my
Matt. 18. 33. even as I had *p.* on
Ps. 103. 13. as father *pitieth* his
children, so the Lord *p.* them
Jas. 5. 11. *pitiful*, 1 Pet. 3. 8.
R. V. 1 Pet. 3. 8. tenderhearted;
Job 6. 14. kindness; Matt. 18. 33.
mercy

PLACE, Ex. 3. 5. Deut. 12. 5, 14.
Ps. 26. 8. *p.* where thine honor
32. 7. art my hiding *p.*, 119. 114.
90. 1. hast been our dwelling *p.*
Prov. 15. 3. eyes of the Lord are in
every *p.*
Isa. 66. 1. where is the *p.* of my
Num. 5. 15. go and return to my *p.*
John 8. 37. my word hath no *p.* in
Rom. 12. 19. aven. not, but give *p.*
1 Cor. 4. 11. no certain dwelling *p.*
Eph. 4. 27. neither give *p.* to
devil
2 Pet. 1. 19. a light that shineth in
a dark *p.*
Rev. 12. 6. hath *p.* prepared of God
Job 7. 10. neither shall *his place*
Ps. 37. 10. diligently consider ——
Isa. 26. 21. Lord cometh out of ——
Acts 1. 25. that he might go to ——
Ps. 16. 6. lines fallen in pleasant
places
Isa. 40. 4. rough *p.* shall be made
Eph. 1. 3. in *heavenly p.*, 20. & 2. 6.
& 3. 10.
6. 12. *high p.*, Hab. 3. 19. Amos 4.
13. Hos. 10. 8. Prov. 8. 2. & 9. 14.
R. V. Frequent changes, mostly
dependent on antecedent and
consequent words

PLAGUE, 1 Kings 8. 37, 38. Ps. 89.
23. Hos. 13. 14. *plagues*, Rev. 16. 9.
& 18. 4, 8. & 22. 28.
R. V. Ex. 32. 35. smote; Ps. 89. 23.
smite

PLAIN man, Jacob was a, Gen.
25. 27.
Ps. 27. 11. lead me in a *p.* path
Prov. 8. 9. words are all *p.* to him
Zech. 4. 7. before Zerubbabel thou
shalt become *p.*
John 16. 29. now speakest *plainly*
2 Cor. 3. 12. we use great *plainness*
R. V. Gen. 12. 6; 13. 18; 14. 13;
Judg. 4. 11; 9. 6; 1 Sam. 10. 3. oak,
or oaks; Obad. 19; Zech. 7. 7.
lowland; 2 Sam. 15. 28. fords;
Luke 6. 17. level place; 1 Sam.
2. 27. reveal; Heb. 11. 14. make
manifest

PLAISTER, Lev. 14. 42. Isa. 38. 21.

PLAIT, Matt. 27. 29. 1 Pet. 3. 3.

PLANT, Gen. 2. 5. Job 14. 9.
Isa. 53. 2. will grow up as a tend. *p.*
Jer. 2. 21. turned into degener. *p.*
24. 6. *p.* them, and not pluck
Ezek. 34. 29. raise for them a *p.*
Ps. 128. 3. children like olive *plants*
1. 3. like a tree *planted* by river
92. 13. *p.* in the house of the Lord
94. 9. that *p.* ear, shall he not hear
Isa. 40. 24. yea, they shall not be *p.*
Jer. 2. 21. I *p.* thee a noble vine
17. 8. as a tree *p.* by the waters
Matt. 15. 13. my Father hath not *p.*
21. 33. *p.* a vine, and let it out
Rom. 6. 5. *p.* together in likeness
1 Cor. 3. 6. I have *p.* Apollos
9. 7. who *planteth* a vineyard
Isa. 60. 21. my *planting*
61. 3. *p.* of the Lord

PLAY, Ex. 32. 6. 2 Sam. 2. 14. & 10.
12. Ezek. 33. 32. 1 Cor. 10. 7.
R. V. S. of S. 4. 13. shoots; Jer. 48.
32. branches; Ezek. 31. 4; 34. 29.
plantation; 1 Chron. 4. 23. inhabitants of Netaim

PLEAD for Baal, Judg. 6. 31.
Job 13. 19. who will *p.* with me
16. 21. might *p.* for me with God
23. 6. will he *p.* against me with
Isa. 1. 17. *p.* for the widow
43. 26. let us *p.*
66. 16. by fire and sword will Lord
p.
Jer. 2. 9. I will *p.* with you and
29. wherefore will ye *p.* with me
25. 31. he will *p.* with all flesh
Hos. 2. 2. *p.* with your mother, *p.*
Joel 3. 2. I will *p.* with them for
R. V. Job 16. 21. maintain right;
23. 6. contend with; Ps. 35. 1.
strive; Prov. 31. 9. minister judg.

PLEADING of God with Israel
Isa. 1. & 3. 13. & 43. 26. & Jer. 2. 6. &
13. Ezek. 17. 20. & 20. 36. & 22. Hos.
2. &c. Joel 3. 2. Micah 2; of Job
with God, Job 9. 19. & 16. 21.

PLEASE, 2 Sam. 7. 29. Job 6. 9.
Ps. 69. 31. this also shall *p.* Lord
Prov. 16. 7. when a man's ways *p.*
Isa. 55. 11. accomp. that which I *p.*
56. 4. choose the things that *p.* me
Rom. 8. 8. that in flesh cannot *p.*
God
15. 1. bear with weak and not *p.*
2. let every one *p.* his neighbor
1 Cor. 7. 32. how *p.* the Lord
33. *p.* his wife
10. 33. I *p.* men, in all things
Gal. 1. 10. do I seek to *p.* men
1 Thes. 4. 1. walk, and to *p.* God
Heb. 11. 6. without faith impossible to *p.* God
Ps. 51. 19. thou be *pleased* with
sacrifices
115. 3. hath done whatsoever he *p.*
Isa. 42. 21. Lord is well *p.* for his
53. 10. it *p.* the Lord to bruise him
Mic. 6. 7. will the Lord be *p.*
Matt. 3. 17. beloved Son, in whom
he is well *p.*, 17. 5.
Rom. 15. 3. Christ *p.* not himself
Col. 1. 19. *p.* the Father that in him

Heb. 13. 16. with such sacrifices God is well *p.*
Eccl. 7. 26. *p.* God, shall escape
8. 3. he doeth whatever *p.* him
Phil. 4. 18. a sacrifice well *pleasing*
Col. 1. 10. worth. of Lord unto all *p.*
3. 20. obey parents is well *p.* to
1 Thes. 2. 4. not as *p.* men, Eph. 6. 6. Col. 3. 22.
Heb. 13. 21. working in you, that is well *p.*
1 John 3. 22. do things *p.* in his
Gen. 2. 9. *pleasant,* 3. 6. Mic. 2. 9
2 Sam. 1. 23. Saul and Jonathan were *p.*
Ps. 16. 6. lines fallen to me in *p.*
133. 1. how *p.* for brethren to
Prov. 2. 10. knowledge is *p.* to soul
9. 17. bread eaten in secret is *p.*
Eccl. 11. 7. for eyes to behold
S. of S. 1. 16. thou art fair, yea, *p.*
4. 13. *p.* fruits, 16. & 7. 13.
7. 6. how *p.* art thou, O love
Isa. 5. 7. men of Judah, his *p.* plant
Jer. 31. 20. Ephraim, is he a *p.* child
Dan. 8. 9. *p.* land, Jer. 3. 19. Zech. 7. 14.
Prov. 3. 17. her ways are ways of *pleasantness*
Gen. 18. 12. shall I have *pleasure*
1 Chron. 29. 17. *p.* in uprightness
Ps. 5. 4. not a God that hath *p.* in
35. 27. hath *p.* in prosperity of
51. 18. do good in good *p.* to Zion
102. 14. servants take *p.* in stones
103. 21. ministers that do his *p.*
147. 11. Lord taketh *p.* in them
Prov. 21. 17. he that loveth *p.* shall
Eccl. 5. 4. he hath no *p.* in fools
12. 1. say, I have no *p.* in them
Isa. 44. 28. shall perform all my *p.*
53. 10. *p.* of Lord shall prosper in
58. 13. not finding thy own *p.*
Jer. 22. 28. vessel wherein is no *p.*
Ezek. 18. 32. have no *p.* in death
Mal. 1. 10. I have no *p.* in you
Luke 12. 32. fear not, it is your Father's good *p.*
2 Cor. 12. 10. I take *p.* in infirmi.
Eph. 1. 5. according to the good *p.*
Phil. 2. 13. and to do of his good *p.*
2 Thes. 1. 11. fulfil all good *p.* of
Heb. 10. 38. soul shall have no *p.*
12. 10. chastened us after their *p.*
Rev. 4. 11. for thy *p.* they are cre.
Ps. 16. 11. at thy right hand are *pleasures* evermore
36. 8. drink of the river of thy *p.*
2 Tim. 3. 4. lovers of *p.* more than
Tit. 3. 3. serv. divers lusts and *p.*
Heb. 11. 25. than to enjoy *p.* of sin
R. V. Gen. 3. 6. a delight; S. of S. 4. 13; 7. 13. precious; Dan. 8. 9. glorious; Jer. 23. 10. pastures; Gen. 16. 6. good in eyes; 2 Chron. 3. 4. right in eyes; Ps. 51. 19. delight in; Rom. 15. 26, 27; 1 Cor. 1. 21; Gal. 1. 15; Col. 1. 19. good pleasure; Gal. 1. 10: Heb. 11. 5. pleasing; 1 Cor. 7. 12. content; Acts 15. 32. seemed good; Acts 15. 34——; Job 21. 25. good; Jer. 2. 24; 2 Thes. 1. 11. desire; Acts 24. 27; 25. 9. gain favor; Jas. 5. 5. delicately
PLEDGE. Ex. 22. 26. Deut. 24. 6.
PLEIADES, Job 9. 9. & 38. 31.
PLENTY, Job 37. 23. Prov. 3. 10.
Ps. 86. 5. *plenteous* in mercy, 103. 8.
130. 7. with him is *p.* redemption
Matt. 9. 37. harvest is *p.* but
R. V. Lev. 1. 36. gathering; Job 22. 25. precious; 37. 23. plenteous
PLOUGH, Deut. 22. 10. Prov. 20. 4.
Job 4. 8. they that *p.* iniquity, and
Isa. 28. 24. doth ploughman *p.* all
Luke 9. 62. hav. put his hand to *p.*
Judg. 14. 18. if ye had not *ploughed*
Ps. 129. 3. ploughers *p.* on my back
Jer. 26. 18. Zion shall be *p.* as a
Hos. 10. 13. ye have *p.* wickedness

Prov. 21. 4. *ploughing* of wicked is
1 Cor. 9. 10. *plougheth* should *p.*
Amos 9. 13. *ploughman,* Isa. 61. 5.
Isa. 2. 4. *ploughshares,* Joel 3. 10. Mic. 4. 3.
PLUCK out, Ps. 25. 15. & 52. 5. & 74. 11. Amos 4. 11. Zech. 3. 2.
Matt. 5. 29. & 18. 9. John 10. 28, 29. Gal. 4. 15.
2 Chron. 7. 20. *pluck up,* Jer. 12. 17. & 18. 7. & 31. 28, 40. Dan. 11. 4. Jude 12.
Ezra 9. 3. *pluck off,* Job 29. 17. Isa. 50. 6. Ezra 23. 34. Mic. 3. 2.
R. V. Ex. 4. 7. took; Lev. 1. 16. take; Num. 33. 52. demolish; Ruth 4. 7. drew; Ezek. 23. 34. tear; Luke 17. 6. root up; Mark 5. 4. rent; 9. 7. cast; John 10. 28, 29. snatch
PLUMBLINE and plummet, 2 Kings 21. 13. Isa. 28. 17. Amos 7. 8. Zech. 4. 10.
POISON, Deut. 32. 24, 33. Job 6. 4. & 20. 16. Ps. 58. 4. & 140. 3. Rom. 3. 13. Jas. 3. 8.
POLLUTE, Num. 18. 32. Ezek. 7. 21. Mic. 2. 10. Zeph. 3. 1. Mal. 1. 7, 12.
Acts 15. 20. *pollutions,* 2 Pet. 2. 20.
R. V. Jer. 7. 30. defile; Num. 18. 23; Ezek. 7. 21, 22; 13. 19; 20. 39; 39. 7; 44. 7; Dan. 11. 31. profane, or profaned; Isa. 47. 6; 48. 11; Jer. 34. 16; Lam. 2. 2; Ezek. 20. 9, 13, 14, 16, 21, 22, 24. profaned; Ezek. 16. 6, 22. weltering; 2 Kings 23. 16; Jer. 2. 23; Ezek. 14. 11; 36. 18; Acts 21. 28. defiled; Hos. 6. 8. stained; Amos 7. 17. unclean; Mic. 2. 10. uncleanness; 2 Pet. 2. 20. defilements
PONDER path of thy feet, Prov. 4. 26.
Luke 2. 19. *pondered* them in heart
Prov. 5. 21. *pondereth* all his goings
21. 2. Lord *p.* the hearts, 24. 12.
R. V. Prov. 4. 26; 5. 6; 5. 21. level, and make level; 21. 2; 24. 12. weigheth
POOR may eat, Ex. 23. 11.
Ex. 30. 15. the *p.* shall not give less
Lev. 19. 15. not respect person of *p.*
Deut. 15. 4. there shall be no *p.*
1 Sam. 2. 7. Lord maketh *p.* and
8. raiseth *p.* out of dust, Ps. 113. 7.
Job 5. 16. the *p.* hath hope
36. 15. delivereth *p.* in affliction
Ps. 10. 14. *p.* committeth himself
69. 33. the Lord heareth the *p.* and
72. 2. he shall judge thy *p.,* 4. 13.
132. 15. satisfy her *p.* with bread
Prov. 13. 7. there is that maketh himself *p.*
14. 20. *p.* is hated of his neighbor
31. oppresseth *p.* reproacheth
19. 4. the *p.* is separated from
7. all brethren of the *p.* do hate
22. 2. rich and the *p.* meet together
22. rob not the *p.* because he is *p.*
30. 9. lest I be *p.* and steal
Isa. 14. 32. *p.* of his people shall
29. 19. among men shall rejoice
41. 17. when the *p.* and needy
58. 7. bring *p.* that are cast into
66. 2. that is *p.* and of a contrite
Jer. 5. 4. surely these are *p.* they
Amos 2. 6. sold *p.* for a pair of
Zeph. 3. 12. an afflicted and *p.* peo.
Zech. 11. 11. *p.* of flock waited on
Matt. 5. 3. blessed are the *p.* in spi.
11. 5. *p.* have Gospel preached to
11. have *p.* with you, John 12. 8.
Luke 6. 20. blessed be ye *p.* for
14. 13. call the *p.* maimed and the
2 Cor. 6. 10. as *p.* yet making rich
8. 9. for your sakes he became *p.*
9. 9. he hath given to *p.,* Ps. 112. 9.
Gal. 2. 10. that we should remember the *p.*
Jas. 2. 5. God hath chosen *p.* of
Rev. 3. 17. knowest not that thou art *p.*

R. V. In O. T., frequent changes to needy
PORTION, Deut. 21. 17. & 33. 21.
Deut. 32. 9. Lord's *p.* is his people
2 Kings 2. 9. double *p.* of thy spir.
Job 20. 29. the *p.* of a wicked man
26. 14. how little a *p.* is heard
31. 2. what *p.* of God is there
Ps. 16. 5. the Lord is the *p.* of my
17. 14. have their *p.* in this life
63. 10. shall be a *p.* for foxes
3. 26. God is my *p.* for ever, 119. 57.
142. 5. art my *p.* in land of living
Eccl. 11. 2. give *p.* to seven and to
Isa. 53. 12. divide him a *p.* with the
61. 7. they shall rejoice in their *p.*
Jer. 10. 16. the *p.* of Jacob not
Lam. 3. 24. Lord is my *p.* saith my
Hab. 1. 16. by them their *p.* is fat
Zech. 2. 12. the Lord shall inherit Judah his *p.*
Matt. 24. 51. appoint him his *p.*
Neh. 8. 10. send *portions,* Esth. 9. 19, 22.
R. V. Josh. 17. 14; 19. 9. part; Job 26. 14. whisper; Prov. 31. 15. task; Hos. 5. 7. fields; Ezek. 45. 7; 48. 18——
POSSESS, Gen. 22. 17. Judg. 11. 24.
Job 7. 3. I am made to *p.* months
13. 26. makest *p.* iniquities of
Luke 21. 9. in patience *p.* your souls
1 Thes. 4. 4. know how to *p.* vessel
Ps. 139. 13. hast *possessed* my reins
Prov. 8. 22. Lord *p.* me in beginning
Isa. 63. 18. people of thy holiness *p.*
Dan. 7. 22. saints *p.* kingdom, 18.
1 Cor. 7. 30. as though they *p.* not
2 Cor. 6. 10. having nothing yet *p.* all things
Eph. 1. 14. redemption of purchased *possession*
Gen. 14. 9. God *possessor* of heaven
R. V. Job 13. 26; Zeph. 2. 9; Zech. 8. 12. inherit; Num. 26. 56; Josh. 22. 7. inheritance
POSSIBLE, all things with God, Matt. 19. 26.
Matt. 24. 24. if *p.* shall deceive elect
Mark 9. 23. all things *p.* to him
14. 36. Father, all things are *p.* to
Luke 18. 27. impossible with men, *p.* with God
Rom. 12. 18. if *p.* much as in you
Heb. 10. 4. not *p.* that blood of bulls
POSTERITY, Gen. 45. 7. Ps. 49. 13.
Jer. 1. 13. Zech. 14. 21.
Job 2. 8. *potsherd,* Ps. 22. 15. Prov. 26. 23. Isa. 45. 9. Rev. 2. 27.
Isa. 29. 16. *potter,* 64. 8. Jer. 18. 6. Lam. 4. 2. Rom. 9. 21.
R. V. Lev. 6. 28. vessel; Job 41. 31; Mark 7. 8——; Ps. 68. 13. sheepfolds; 81. 6. basket; Jer. 1. 13. caldron; 35. 5. bowls; Prov. 26. 23. earthen vessel
POTENTATE, blessed, 1 Tim. 6. 15.
POUND, Luke 19. 13. John 19. 39.
POUR, Job 36. 27. Lev. 14. 18, 41.
Ps. 62. 8. *p.* out your heart
79. 6. *p.* out thy wrath on the heathen, 69. 24. Jer. 10. 25. Zeph. 3. 8.
Prov. 1. 23. I will *p.* out my Spirit
Isa. 44. 3. *p.* water on the thirsty; *p.* my Spirit
Joel 2. 28. *p.* my Spirit on all flesh
Job 10. 10. *poured* me out as milk
12. 21. *p.* contempt on princes
16. 20. mine eye *p.* out tears to
30. 16. my soul *p.* out in me
Ps. 45. 2. grace is *p.* into thy lips
S. of S. 1. 3. name is as ointment *p.*
Isa. 26. 16. in trouble *p.* out a pray.
53. 12. *p.* out his soul unto death
Jer. 7. 20. my fury shall be *p.* out, 42. 18. & 44. 6. Isa. 42. 25. Ezek. 7. 8. & 14. 19. & 20. 8, 13, 21. & 30. 15.
Rev. 16. 1-17. *p.* out vials of God's wrath

POVERTY, Gen. 45. 11. Prov. 11. 24.
Prov. 6. 11. so shall thy *p.* come, 24. 34.
10. 15. destruction of the poor is *p.*
20. 13. love not sleep lest thou come to *p.*
23. 21. drunkard and glutton shall come to *p.*
30. 8. give me neither *p.* nor rich.
2 Cor. 8. 2. their deep *p.* abounded
9. ye through his *p.* might be rich
Rev. 2. 9. I know thy works and *p.*
R. V. Prov. 11. 24; 28. 22. want

POWDER, Ex. 32. 20. Deut. 28. 24.
2 Kings 23. 15. S. of S. 3. 6. Matt. 21. 44.
R. V. Matt. 21. 44; Luke 20. 18. dust

POWER, with God as a prince, Gen. 32. 28.
Gen. 49. 3. excell. of dignity and *p.*
Lev. 26. 19. I will break the pride of your *p.*
Deut. 8. 18. giveth *p.* to get wealth
2 Sam. 22. 33. God is my strength and *p.*
1 Chron. 29. 11. thine is the *p.* and
Ezra 8. 22. *p.* and wrath is against
Job 26. 2. him that is without *p.*
14. thunder of his *p.* who can
Ps. 62. 11. *p.* belongeth unto God
90. 11. knoweth *p.* of thy anger
Prov. 3. 27. when it is in the *p.* of
18. 21. death and life are in *p.*
Isa. 40. 29. he giveth *p.* to the faint
Eccl. 8. 4. where word of king is there is *p.*
Jer. 10. 12. made the earth by his *p.*
Hos. 12. 3. by his strength had *p.*
Mic. 3. 8. I am full of *p.* by the
Hab. 1. 11. imputing his *p.* to God
Zech. 4. 6. not by might, nor by *p.*
Matt. 9. 6. *p.* on earth to forgive
8. glorified God who had given *p.*
22. 29. not knowing the *p.* of God
28. 18. *p.* is given to me in heaven
Mark 9. 1. kingdom of God come with *p.*
Luke 1. 35. *p.* of the Highest
4. 32. astonished, for his word was with *p.*
5. 17. *p.* of the Lord to heal them
22. 53. this is your hour and *p.* of
24. 49. till ye be endued with *p.*
John 1. 12. gave he *p.* to become
10. 18. *p.* to lay it down and *p.*
17. 2. given him *p.* over all flesh
19. 10. *p.* to crucify, *p.* to release
Acts 26. 18. turn them from the *p.*
Rom. 1. 16. Gospel is *p.* of God to
20. his eternal *p.* and Godhead, 4.
9. 22. to make his *p.* known
13. 1. there is no *p.* but of God
1 Cor. 1. 24. Christ, the *p.* of God, 18.
2. 4. demonstra. of Spirit and *p.*
4. 19. speech of them, but the *p.*
5. 4. gathered together with the *p.*
9. 4. have we not *p.* to eat and
2 Cor. 4. 7. excellency of *p.* may be
13. 10. according to *p.* Lord
Eph. 1. 19. exceed. greatness of *p.*
2. 2. prince of the *p.* of the air
6. 12. principalities and *p.*, 1. 21.
Phil. 3. 10. know *p.* of his resur.
Col. 1. 11. according to his glorious
13. delivered from *p.* of darkness
1 Thes. 1. 5. Gospel not in word, but in *p.*
2 Thes. 1. 9. the glory of his *p.*
11. fulfil the work of faith with *p.*
2 Tim. 1. 7. Spirit of *p.* and of love
3. 5. form of godliness, deny. *p.*
Heb. 1. 3. upholding all things by word of his *p.*
6. 5. tasted word of God and *p.* of
1 Pet. 1. 5. *p.* of God through faith
2 Pet. 1. 3. his divine *p.* hath given
Rev. 2. 26. to him will I give *p.*
4. 11. worthy to receive *p.*, 5. 13. &
7. 12. & 19. 1. 1 Tim. 6. 16. Jude 25.
Rev. 11. 3. *p.* to my two witnesses
17. taken to thee thy great *p.*
12. 10. now is come *p.* of his Chri.

Rev. 16. 9. had *p.* over these plagues
Ex. 15. 6. *in power*, Job 37. 23. Nah. 1. 3. 1 Cor. 4. 20. & 15. 43. Eph. 6. 10.
Ps. 63. 2. *thy power*, 110. 3. & 145. 11.
29. 4. *powerful*, Heb. 4. 12.
R. V. 1 Sam. 9. 1. valor; Esth. 9. 1. rule; Job 41. 12; Ps. 59. 16; Dan. 11. 6; 2 Cor. 12. 9; Eph. 6. 10. strength; Ps. 66. 7; 71. 8; 2 Thes. 1. 19. might; Hab. 2. 9. hand; Matt. 10. 1; 28. 18; Mark 3. 15; 6. 7; Luke 4. 6, 32; 10. 19; John 17. 2; Acts 1. 7; 1 Cor. 11. 10; 2 Cor. 13. 10; Eph. 1. 21; Rev. 2. 26; 6. 8; 8. 1; 12. 10; 13. 4, 7, 12, 15; 17. 12. authority; Luke 9. 43. majesty; Rom. 9. 21; 1 Cor. 9. 4, 5, 6, 12; 2 Thes. 3. 9. a right; Rev. 5. 13. dominion; Matt. 6. 13; Rev. 11. 3——; 2 Cor. 10. 10. strong; Heb. 4. 12. active

PRAISE, Judg. 5. 3. Ps. 7. 17.
Deut. 10. 21. he is thy *p.* and thy
Neh. 9. 5. above all blessing and *p.*
Ps. 22. 25. my *p.* shall be of thee
33. 1. *p.* is comely for upright
34. 1. his *p.* is continually in
50. 23. who offers *p.* glorifies me
65. 1. *p.* waiteth for thee, O God
109. 1. hold not thy peace, God of my *p.*
Isa. 60. 18. walls Salvation, gates *P.*
62. 7. Jerusalem a *p.* in the earth
Jer. 13. 11. for a *p.* and for a glory
17. 14. art my *p.*
26. sacrifice of *p.*
Hab. 3. 3. earth was full of his *p.*
John 12. 43. loved the *p.* of men
Rom. 2. 29. whose *p.* is not of men
2 Cor. 8. 18. whose *p.* is in Gospel
Eph. 1. 6. *p.* of glory of his grace
Phil. 4. 8. if there be any *p.* think
Heb. 13. 15. offer sacrifice of *p.*
1 Pet. 2. 14. *p.* of them that do well
Ex. 15. 11. *praises*, Ps. 22. 3. & 78. 4. & 149. 6. Isa. 60. 6. & 63. 7. 1 Pet. 2. 9.
Ps. 30. 9. shall dust *praise* thee
42. 5. I shall *p.* him for help
63. 3. my lips shall *p.* thee
88. 10. shall the dead arise and *p.*
119. 164. seven times a day will I *p.*
Prov. 27. 2. let another *p.* thee, not
31. 31. let her own works *p.* her
Isa. 38. 18. the grave cannot *p.* thee
19. the living shall *p.* thee as I do
Dan. 2. 23. I thank thee, and *p.* thee
Joel 2. 26. eat in plenty, and *p.* Lord
Ps. 9. 1. *I will praise thee*, 111. 1. & 138. 1. & 35. 18. & 52. 9. & 56. 4. & 118. 21. & 119. 7. & 139. 14. Isa. 12. 1.
2 Sam. 22. 4. worthy to be *praised*
1 Chron. 16. 25. greatly to be *p.*, Ps. 48. 1. & 96. 4. & 145. 3. & 72. 15.
2 Chron. 5. 13. *praising*, Ezra 3. 11.
Ps. 34. 4. Luke 2. 13, 20. Acts 2. 46.
R. V. A few changes to thanksgiving. Many changes, especially in Ps., to give thanks

PRATING, Prov. 10. 8, 10. 3 John 10.

PRAY for thee and shalt live, Gen. 20. 7.
1 Sam. 7. 5. I will *p.* for you to
2 Sam. 7. 27. found in heart to *p.*
Job 21. 15. profit have we if we *p.*
42. 8. my servant Job shall *p.* for
Ps. 5. 2. my God, to thee will I *p.*
55. 17. evening and morning and noon I will *p.*
Jer. 7. 16. *p.* not for this people, 11. 14. & 14. 11.
Zech. 8. 22. seek Lord and *p.* before
Matt. 5. 44. *p.* for them that desp.
26. 41. watch and *p.* that ye enter
Mark 11. 24. things ye desire when ye *p.*
13. 33. watch and *p.* ye know not
Luke 11. 1. teach us to *p.* as John
18. 1. men ought always to *p.*
21. 36. watch ye and *p.* always
John 16. 26. I will *p.* the Father for
20. neither *p.* I for these alone
Acts 8. 22. *p.* God, if perhaps the

Acts 8. 24. *p.* ye to the Lord for me
10. 9. Peter went on housetop to *p.*
Rom. 8. 26. we know not what we should *p.* for
1 Cor. 14. 15. I will *p.* with Spirit
2 Cor. 5. 20. *p.* you in Christ's stead
Col. 1. 9. do not cease to *p.* for you
1 Thes. 5. 17. *p.* without ceasing
25. *p.* for us, 2 Thes. 3. 1. Heb. 13. 18.
Jas. 5. 13. any afflicted let him *p.*
16. *p.* for one another, Eph. 6. 18.
Luke 22. 32. I have *prayed* for thee
Acts 10. 2. gave a'ms and *p.* to God
20. 36. Paul *p.* with them all
Jas. 5. 17. he *p.* earnestly that it
Acts 9. 11. behold he *prayeth*
Dan. 9. 20. *praying*, 1 Cor. 11. 4.
1 Thes. 3. 10. night and day *p.* ex.
Jude 20. building up faith, *p.* in
1 Kings 8. 45. hear in heaven their *prayer*
2 Sam. 7. 27. found in his heart to pray this *p.*
1 Kings 8. 28. respect to *p.* of serv.
38. what *p.* and supplication
2 Chron. 30. 27. *p.* came up to God
Neh. 1. 6. mayest hear *p.* of servant
4. 9. we made our *p.* to our God
Job 15. 4. restrainest *p.* before God
Ps. 65. 2. thou that hearest *p.* to
102. 17. he will regard the *p.* of
109. 4. I give myself to *p.*
Prov. 15. 8. *p.* of the upright is his
29. Lord heareth *p.* of righteous
Isa. 26. 16. poured out a *p.* when
56. 7. an house of *p.* for all people
Jer. 7. 16. lift up cry, nor *p.* for
Lam. 3. 44. our *p.* should not pass
Dan. 9. 3. by *p.* and supplication
Matt. 17. 21. not come out but by *p.*
Acts 3. 1. to temple at hour of *p.*
6. 4. give ourselves continu. to *p.*
12. 5. *p.* was made without ceasing
1 Cor. 7. 5. give yourselves to fasting and *p.*
2 Cor. 1. 11. helping together by *p.*
Eph. 6. 18. *praying* alw. with all *p.*
Phil. 4. 6. in every thing by *p.* and
1 Tim. 4. 5. sanctifi. by word and *p.*
Jas. 5. 15. *p.* of faith shall save
16. effectual fervent *p.* of right.
1 Pet. 4. 7. watch unto *p.*, Col. 4. 2.
Luke 6. 12. continued *in prayer*, Acts 1. 14. Rom. 12. 12. Col. 4. 2.
Job 16. 17. *my prayer*, Ps. 5. 3. & 6. 9. & 17. 1. & 35. 13. & 66. 20. & 88. 2.
Lam. 3. 8. Jonah 2. 7.
Job 22. 27. *thy prayer*, Isa. 37. 4.
Luke 1. 13. Acts 10. 31.
Ps. 72. 20. *prayers* of David ended
Isa. 1. 15. when ye make many *p.*
Matt. 23. 14. make long *p.*
Acts 10. 4. thy *p.* and thine alms
1 Tim. 2. 1. first of all that *p.* and
1 Pet. 3. 7. your *p.* be not hindered
12. his ears are open to their *p.*
Rev. 5. 8. which are *p.* of saints
R. V. But few changes, and mostly to beseech, intreat. Job 15. 4. devotion; Ps. 64. 1. complaint.
Luke 1. 13; 2. 37; 5. 33; Rom. 10. 1; 2 Cor. 1. 11; 9. 14; Phil. 1. 4, 19; 2 Tim. 1. 3; Jas. 5. 16; 1 Pet. 3. 12. supplication; Matt. 17. 21; 23. 14——

PREACH at Jerusalem, Neh. 6. 7.
Isa. 61. 1. anointed to *p.* good
Jonah 3. 2. *p.* to it preaching I bid
Matt. 4. 17. Jesus began to *p.*
10. 27. what ye hear in ear, *p.* on
Mark 1. 4. *p.* baptism of repent.
Luke 4. 18. *p.* liberty to captives
9. 60. go and *p.* kingdom of God
Acts 10. 42. commanded to *p.* to
Rom. 10. 8. word of faith we *p.*
15. how shall they *p.* except they
1 Cor. 1. 23. we *p.* Christ crucified
15. 11. so we *p.* and so ye believed
2 Cor. 4. 5. we *p.* not ourselves but
Phil. 1. 15. some *p.* Christ of envy
Col. 1. 28. whom we *p.* warning
2 Tim. 4. 2. *p.* the word; be instant
Ps. 40. 9. I *preached* righteousness

Mark 2. 2. he *p.* the word unto them
6. 12. he *p.* that men should rep.
16. 20. *p.* every where, the Lord
Luke 4. 44. he *p.* in the synagogues
24. 47. remission of sins be *p.* in
Acts 8. 5. Philip *p.* Christ, 40.
9. 20. Saul *p.* Christ in synagogues
1 Cor. 9. 27. when I have *p.* to
15. 7. Gospel which I *p.* unto you
2. keep in memory what I *p.*
12. if Christ be *p.* that he rose
2 Cor. 11. 4. *p.* another Jesus whom
Gal. 1. 23. *p.* faith he once destroyed
Eph. 2. 17. *p.* peace to you, which
Col. 1. 23. which was *p.* to every
Heb. 4. 2. the word *p.* did not profit
1 Pet. 3. 19. *p.* to the spirits in
Eccl. 1. 1. *preacher*, 2. 12. & 12. 8, 9.
Rom. 10. 14. how shall they hear
    without a *p.*
1 Tim. 2. 7. I am ordained a *p.*
2 Pet. 2. 5. saved Noah a *p.* of
Acts 10. 36. *preaching* peace, by
11. 19. *p.* word to none but Jews
1 Cor. 1. 18. *p.* of the cross to them
21. by foolishness of *p.* to save
2. 4. my *p.* was not with enticing
15. 14. then is our *p.* vain, and faith
R. V. Ps. 40. 9; Luke 6. 90. *published*; Matt. 10. 27; Luke 4. 18,
19; Acts 4. 2; 8. 5; 9. 20; 13. 5, 38;
15. 36; 17. 13; 1 Cor. 9. 14; Phil. 1.
16, 18; Col. 1. 28. *proclaim*, or *proclaimed*; Mark 2. 2; Acts 20. 7. *discoursed*; Acts 11. 19. *speaking*;
1 Cor. 1. 18. *word*; Tit. 1. 3; 2 Tim.
4. 17. *message*; 2 Cor. 5. 20.
PRECEPTS, Neh. 9. 14. Jer. 35. 18.
Ps. 119. 4. commanded us to keep *p.*
15. I will meditate in thy *p.*, 78.
40. long after thy *p.*
56. I kept thy *p.*, 63, 69, 100, 134.
110. I erred not from thy *p.*
141. I do not forget thy *p.*, 93.
159. I love thy *p.*
173. chosen thy *p.*
Isa. 28. 10. *p.* upon *p.*, *p.* upon *p.*
29. 14. fear is taught by *p.* of men
R. V. Isa. 29. 13; Neh. 9. 14; Mark
10. 5; Heb. 9. 19. commandment
PRECIOUS things, Deut. 33. 13-16.
1 Sam. 3. 1. word of the Lord *p.* in
26. 21. my soul was *p.* in thine eyes
Ps. 49. 8. redemption of soul is *p.*
72. 14. *p.* shall their blood be in
116. 16. *p.* in sight of the Lord
126. 6. goeth forth, bearing *p.* seed
139. 17. how *p.* are thy thoughts
Eccl. 7. 1. good name is better than
    p. ointment
Isa. 13. 12. a man more *p.* than
28. 16. foundation *p.* corner stone
Jer. 15. 19. if thou take forth *p.*
Lam. 4. 2. *p.* sons of Zion are as
Jas. 5. 7. husbandman waiteth for
    p. fruit
1 Pet. 1. 7. tri. of your faith more *p.*
19. redeemed with *p.* blood of
2. 4. stone chosen of God and *p.*, 6.
7. unto them who believe he is *p.*
2 Pet. 1. 1. obtained the like *p.*
    faith
4. exceeding great and *p.* promis.
R. V. Ps. 49. 8; Mark 14. 3; 1 Cor.
3. 12. costly; Isa. 13. 12. rare; Dan.
11. 8. goodly
PREDESTINATE, Rom. 8. 29, 30.
Eph. 1. 5. *predestinated*, 11.
PREEMINENCE, man hath no,
Eccl. 3. 19. Col. 1. 18. 3 John 9.
PREFER, Ps. 137. 6. John 1. 15, 27, 30.
Rom. 12. 10. *preferring*, 1 Tim. 5. 21.
R. V. Esth. 2. 9. removed; Dan. 6.
3. distinguished; John 1. 15, 30.
become; 1 Tim. 5. 21. prejudice
PREMEDITATE not, Mark 13. 11.
PREPARE, Ex. 15. 2. & 16. 5.
1 Sam. 7. 3. *p.* your hearts to Lord
1 Chron. 29. 18. *p.* hearts unto thee
2 Chron. 35. 6. *p.* your brethren

Job 11. 13. if thou *p.* thy heart and
Ps. 10. 17. thou wilt *p.* their heart
Prov. 24. 27. *p.* thy work without
Isa. 40. 3. *p.* ye the way of the Lord
Amos 4. 12. *p.* to meet thy God, O
Mic. 3. 5. they *p.* war against him
Matt. 11. 10. shall *p.* thy way
John 14. 2. I go to *p.* a place for you
2 Chron. 19. 3. hast *prepared* heart
27. 6. *p.* his ways before the Lord
30. 19. every one that *p.*
Ezra 7. 10. Ezra had *p.* his heart to
Neh. 8. 10. for whom nothing is *p.*
Ps. 23. 5. thou hast *p.* a table before
68. 10. *p.* goodness
147. 8. who *p.* rain for the earth
Isa. 64. 4. what God *p.* for, 1 Cor.
    2. 9.
Hos. 6. 3. his going forth is *p.*
Matt. 20. 23. given to them for
    whom it is *p.*
22. 4. I have *p.* my dinner; my
25. 34. inherit the kingdom *p.* for
Luke 1. 17. ready people *p.* for Lord
12. 47. knew Lord's will, and *p.*
Rom. 9. 23. vessels of mercy *p.* to
2 Tim. 2. 21. *p.* to every good work
Heb. 10. 5. a body hast thou *p.* me
11. 7. *p.* ark to save his house
16. God hath *p.* for them a city
Rev. 12. 6. into the wilderness, a
    place *p.* of God
21. 2. new Jerusalem *p.* as a bride
Prov. 16. 1. *preparations* of heart
Mark 15. 42. it was the *p.* the day
Eph. 6. 15. shod with *p.* of Gospel
R. V. Many changes to make
    ready, establish, etc.
PRESBYTERY, 1 Tim. 4. 14.
PRESENT help in troub., Ps. 46. 1.
Acts 10. 33. all here *p.* before God
Rom. 7. 18. to will is *p.*
8. 38. nor things *p.* nor, 1 Cor. 3. 22.
1 Cor. 5. 3. absent in body, *p.* in
2 Cor. 5. 8. to be *p.* with the Lord
9. whether *p.* or absent, we may
2 Tim. 4. 10. having loved *p.* world
Heb. 12. 11. chastening for the *p.*
2 Pet. 1. 12. established in *p.* truth
Rom. 12. 1. *p.* your bodies a living
2 Cor. 11. 2. *p.* you as a chaste
Col. 1. 22. to *p.* you holy and
28. *p.* every man perfect in Christ
Jude 24. *p.* you faultless before
Gen. 3. 8. hide themselves from
    the *presence* of the Lord
4. 16. Cain went from *p.* of Lord
Job 1. 12. *p.* of the Lord, 2. 7. Jer. 4.
26. Jonah 1. 3, 10. Zech. 1. 7. Jude
24.
Job 23. 15. I am troubled at his *p.*
Ps. 16. 11. in thy *p.* is fulness
31. 20. hide them in secret of thy *p.*
100. 2. before his *p.* with singing
114. 7. tremble, earth, at *p.* of Lord
139. 7. whither shall I flee from *p.*
140. 13. upright shall dwell in thy
    p.
Isa. 63. 9. angel of his *p.* saved
Jer. 5. 22. will ye not tremble at
    my *p.*
Luke 13. 26. eaten and drunk. in *p.*
Acts 3. 19. blotted out from *p.* of
    Lord
1 Cor. 1. 29. no flesh glory in his *p.*
2 Cor. 10. 1. in *p.* am base among
2 Thes. 1. 9. punished from *p.* of
Rev. 14. 10. *p.* of holy angels
R. V. Few changes to before;
Matt. 21. 19. immediately; 26. 53.
even now; Phil. 2. 23. forthwith
PRESERVE, Gen. 45. 7. Ps. 12. 7.
Ps. 16. 1. *p.* me, O God, for I trust
25. 21. let integrity and truth *p.*,
32. 7. thou shalt *p.* me from
61. 7. mercy and truth *p.* him
64. 1. *p.* life from fear of enemies
86. 2. *p.* my soul, for I am holy
121. 7. Lord shall *p.* thee from evil
140. 1. *p.* me from the violent man
Prov. 2. 11. discretion shall *p.* thee
Luke 17. 33. will lose his life, *p.* it
2 Tim. 4. 18. will *p.* to his heaven.
Josh. 24. 17. *preserved* us in all the

---

2 Sam. 8. 6. Lord *p.* David
Job 10. 12. thy visitation *p.* my
1 Thes. 5. 23. soul and body be *p.*
Jude 1. *p.* in Christ Jesus, and
Ps. 36. 6. Lord thou *preservest* man
29. 10. he *preserveth* the souls of
116. 6. Lord *p.* the simple
145. 20. Lord *p.* all that love him
Prov. 2. 8. he *p.* way of his saints
Job 7. 20. O thou *Preserver* of men
R. V. 2 Sam. 8. 6, 14; 1 Chron. 18. 6,
13. gave victory; 29. 12; Prov.
2. 11. watch over; Ps. 121. 7. keep;
2 Tim. 4. 18. save; Jude 1. kept;
Luke 5. 38 ——
PRESS, Gen. 40. 11. Judg. 16. 16.
Phil. 3. 14. 1 *p.* towards the mark
Ps. 38. 2. thy hand *presseth* me sore
Luke 16. 16. kingdom of God every
    man *p.* unto
Amos 2. 13. *pressed* as a cart is *p.*
Luke 6. 38. good measure, *p.* down
Acts 18. 5. Paul was *p.* in spirit
R. V. Joel 3. 13. winepress; Mark
2. 4; 5. 27, 30; Luke 8. 19; 19. 3.
crowd; 8. 45. crush; Gen. 19. 3.
urged; Acts 18. 5. constrained;
2 Cor. 1. 8. weighed down; Luke
16. 16. entereth violently
PRESUMPTION of Israelites,
Num. 14. 44. Deut. 1. 43; prophets,
Deut. 18. 20; builders of Babel,
Gen. 11; Korah, &c., Num. 16;
Beth-shemites, 1 Sam. 6. 19; Hiel,
the Bethelite, 1 Kings 16. 34; Uzzah, 2 Sam. 6. 6; Uzziah, 2 Chron.
26. 16; Jewish exorcists, Acts 19.
13; Diotrephes, 3 John 9.
PRESUMPTUOUS, Ps. 19. 13.
2 Pet. 2. 10. Num. 15. 30. Deut. 17.
12, 13.
R. V. 2 Pet. 2. 10. daring
PRETENCE, Matt. 23. 14. Phil. 1.
18.
R. V. Matt. 23. 14 ——
PREVAIL, Gen. 7. 20. Judg. 16. 5.
1 Sam. 2. 9. by strength, shall no
    man *p.*
Ps. 9. 19. O Lord, let not man *p.*
65. 3. iniquities *p.* against me
Eccl. 4. 12. if one *p.* against him
Matt. 16. 18. gates of hell not *p.*
Gen. 32. 28. power with God and
    hast *prevailed*
Ex. 17. 11. Moses held up hand,
    Israel *p.*
Hos. 12. 4. pow. over angels, and *p.*
Acts 19. 20. word of God grew, and
    p.
Job 14. 20. thou *prevailest* for ever
R. V. Gen. 47. 20; 2 Kings 25. 3. was
sore upon; Job 18. 9. lay hold on;
Isa. 42. 13. do mightily; Rev. 5. 5.
overcome
PREVENT, Job 3. 12. Ps. 59. 10. &
79. 8. & 88. 13. & 119. 148. Amos 9.
10. 1 Thes. 4. 15.
2 Sam. 22. 6. *prevented*, 19. Job 30.
27. & 41. 11. Ps. 18. 5, 18. & 21. 3. &
119. 147. Isa. 21. 14. Matt. 17. 25.
R. V. Job 3. 12. receive; Ps. 88. 13.
come before; 2 Sam. 22. 6, 19; Job
30. 27; Ps. 18. 5, 18. came upon;
Matt. 17. 25. spake first to
PREY, Gen. 49. 9, 27. Esth. 9. 15, 16.
Isa. 49. 24. *p.* be taken from mighty
Jer. 21. 9. life for a *p.*, 38. 2 & 39. 18.
& 45. 5.
Ps. 124. 6. not given us a *p.* to their
R. V. Judg. 5. 30; 8. 24, 25, Esth. 9.
15, 16; Isa. 10. 2; Jer. 50. 10. spoil;
Job 24. 5. meat; Prov. 23. 28. robber
PRICE, Lev. 25. 16. Deut. 23. 18.
Job 28. 13. man knoweth not the *p.*
Ps. 44. 12. not increase wealth, by
    their *p.*
Prov. 17. 16. a *p.* in the hand of
Isa. 55. 1. wine and milk without *p.*
Matt. 13. 46. pearl of great *p.*
Acts 5. 2. kept back part of the *p.*
1 Cor. 6. 20. bought with a *p.*, 7. 23.
1 Pet. 3. 4. sight of God of great *p.*
R. V. Deut. 23. 18. wages; Zech.
11. 12. hire

PRICKS, kick against, Acts 9. 5. & 26. 14.

Ps. 73. 21. *pricked*, Acts 2. 37.

R. V. Acts 9. 5——; 26. 14. goad

PRIDE of heart, 2 Chron. 32. 26.
Ps. 10. 4.

Job 33. 17. he may hide *p.* from

Ps. 10. 2. wicked in *p.* doth per.
31. 20. hide them from *p.* of man

73. 6. *p.* compasseth them about

Prov. 8. 13. *p.* and arrogance I hate
13. 10. by *p.* cometh contention

16. 18. *p.* goeth before destruction

Isa. 23. 9. Lord purposed it, to stain *p.*

Jer. 13. 17. weep in secr. for your *p.*

Ezek. 7. 10. rod hath blossomed, *p.*
16. 49. iniquity of Sodom, *p.* and

Dan. 4. 37. those that walk in *p.*

Hos. 5. 5. *p.* of Israel testify

Obad. 3. *p.* of thy heart deceived

Mark 7. 22. blasphemy, *p.* foolish.

1 Tim. 3. 6. lifted up with *p.* he fall

1 John 2. 16. lust of eyes, *p.* of life

R. V. Ps. 31. 20. plottings; 1 John 2. 16. vainglory. A few other changes due to the context

PRIEST, Gen. 14. 18. Ex. 2. 16.

Lev. 6. 20, 26, & 5. 6. & 6. 7. & 12. 8.

Isa. 24. 2. with peop., so with the *p.*
28. 7. *p.* and prophet have erred

Jer. 23. 11. prophet and *p.* profane

Ezek. 7. 26. law shall perish from *p.*

Hos. 4. 4. those that strive with *p.*
9. like people, like *p.*

Mal. 2. 7. *p.* lips should keep

Heb. 5. 6. a *p.* for ever, 7. 17, 21.

Lev. 21. 10. high priest, Heb. 2. 17. & 3. 1. & 4. 14, 15. & 5. 1, 10. & 6. 20. & 7. 26. & 8. 1, 3. & 9. 11. & 10. 21.

Ps. 132. 9. let thy *priests* be clothed
16. clothe her *p.* with salvation

Isa. 61. 6. ye be named *p.* of

Jer. 5. 31. *p.* bear rule by their
31. 14. satisfy soul of *p.* with

Ezek. 22. 26. *p.* have violated my

Joel 1. 9. *p.* Lord's ministers, 2. 17.

Mic. 3. 11. the *p.* teach for hire

Matt. 12. 5. *p.* in the temple

Acts 6. 7. company of *p.* obedient

Rev. 1. 6. kings and *p.* to God

Ex. 40. 15. everlasting *priesthood*

Heb. 7. 24. an unchangeable *p.*

1 Pet. 2. 5. ye are a holy *p.*

PRINCE, Gen. 23. 6. & 34. 2.

Gen. 32. 28. as a *p.* hast power with

Ex. 2. 14. who made thee a *p.* over

2 Sam. 3. 38. *p.* and great man

Job 31. 47. as a *p.* would I go

Isa. 9. 6. everlasting Fath-r, *p.* of

Ezek. 34. 24. my servant David, a *p.* among them, 37. 24, 25. & 44. 3. & 45. 7. & 46. 10, 16. Dan. 9. 25.

Dan. 10. 21. Michael your *p.*

Hos. 3. 4. many days without a *p.*

John 12. 31. now shall *p.* of world
14. 30. *p.* of world cometh and
16. 11. *p.* of this world judged

Acts 3. 15. ye killed the *p.* of life
5. 31. to be a *P.* and a Saviour

Eph. 2. 2. *p.* of the power of air

Rev. 1. 5. Jesus *p.* of kings of earth

Job 12. 19. leads *princes* away
21. pours contem. on *p.*, Ps. 107. 40.

Job 34. 18. is it fit to say to *p.*

Ps. 45. 16. thou makest *p.* in earth
82. 7. shall fall like one of the *p.*
118. 9. than to put confidence in *p.*
161. *p.* persecuted me without
146. 3. put not trust in *p.* nor man

Prov. 8. 15. by me *p.* decree jus.
17. 26. not good to strike *p.* for
31. 4. not for *p.* to drink strong

Eccl. 10. 7. seen *p.* walk on earth

Isa. 3. 4. give children to be their *p.*

Hos. 7. 5. *p.* made the king sick

Matt. 20. 25. *p.* of Gentiles exer.

1 Cor. 2. 6. wisdom of *p.* of world
8. none of *p.* of this world knew

Prov. 4. 7. wisdom is the *principal*

Eph. 1. 21. *principality* and power,
Col. 2, 10. Jer. 13. 18. Rom. 8. 38.

Eph. 6. 12. Col. 2. 15. Tit. 3. 1.

Heb. 5. 12. *principles*, 6. 1.

R. V. Frequent changes in Kings and Chron. to captains; in Dan. to satraps; in N. T. to rulers; Ex. 30. 23; Neh. 11. 17. chief; 2 Kings 25. 19; Jer. 52. 25. captain Jer. 13. 18. headtires; Eph. 1. 21. rule; Tit. 3. 1. rulers

PRISON, Gen. 39. 20. Eccl. 4. 14.

Isa. 42. 7. bring out prison. from *p.*
58. 8. he was taken from *p.* and
61. 1. opening of the *p.* to them

Matt. 5. 25. and thou be cast into *p.*
18. 30. cast into *p.* till he should
25. 36. I was in *p.* and ye came

1 Pet. 3. 19. preach. to spirits in *p.*

Rev. 2. 10. devil cast some into *p.*

Luke 21. 12. *prisons*, 2 Cor. 11. 23.

Ps. 79. 11. sighing of *prisoner* come
102. 20. to hear the groaning of *p.*

Eph. 4. 1. I the *p.* of the Lord

Job 3. 18. there the *prisoners* rest

Ps. 69. 33. Lord despiseth not his *p.*
146. 7. the Lord looseth the *p.*

Zech. 9. 11. sent forth thy *p.* out

R. V. Gen. 42. 16. bound; Neh. 3. 25; Jer. 32. 2, 8, 12; 33. 1; 37. 21; 38. 6, 13, 28; 39. 14, 15. guard; Isa. 42. 7. dungeon; Acts 12. 7. cell; Num. 21. 1. Isa. 20. 4. captive; Acts 28. 16——

PRIVATE, 2 Pet. 1. 20. Gal. 2. 2.

PRIVY, Deut. 23. 1. Acts 5. 2.

Ps. 10. 8. *privily*, 11. 2. & 101. 5. Acts 16. 37. Gal. 2. 4. 2 Pet. 2. 1.

R. V. Ezek. 21. 14——; Judg. 9. 31. craftily; Ps. 11. 2. darkness

PRIZE, 1 Cor. 9. 24. Phil. 3. 14.

PROCEED, 2 Sam. 7. 12. Jer. 30. 21.

Job 40. 5. twice spoken; I will *p.*

Isa. 29. 14. I will *p.* to do a marvel.
51. 4. a law shall *p.* from me

Jer. 9. 3. they *p.* from evil to evil.

Matt. 15. 19. out of heart *p.* evil

Eph. 4. 29. no corrupt communication *p.* out of your mouth

2 Tim. 3. 9. they shall *p.* no further

Luke 4. 22. the gracious words that *proceeded* out of his mouth

John 8. 42. I *p.* and came from God

Gen. 24. 50. thing *proceedeth* from

Deut. 8. 3. by every word that *p.*

1 Sam. 24. 13. wickedness *p.* from

Lam. 3. 38. out of the mouth of the Lord *p.* not evil

John 15. 26. Spirit of tru. which *p.*

Jas. 3. 10. out of the same mouth *p.* blessing

Rev. 11. 5. fire *p.* out of their mouth

PROCLAIM, Lev. 23. 2. Deut. 20. 10.

Ex. 33. 19. I will *p.* the name of the Lord, 34. 6.

Prov. 20. 6. most men will *p.* their

Isa. 61. 1. *p.* liberty to the captives
2. to *p.* the acceptable year of Lord

Prov. 12. 23. the heart of fools *proclaimeth* foolishness

PROCURED, Jer. 2. 17. & 4. 18.

R. V. Prov. 11. 27. seeketh; Jer. 26. 19. commit

PRODIGAL son, parable of, Luke 15. 11.

PROFANE not the name of Lord, Lev. 18. 21. & 19. 12. & 20. 3. & 21. 6. & 22. 9, 15.

Neh. 13. 17. *p.* sabbath, Matt. 12. 5.

Ezek. 22. 26. put no difference between holy and *p.*

Amos 2. 7. to *p.* my holy name

1 Tim. 1. 9. law is for unholy and *p.*
4. 7. refuse *p.* and old wives' fa.

Heb. 12. 16. fornicator or *p.* person

Ps. 89. 39. hast *profaned* his crown

Ezek. 22. 8. hast *p.* my sabb.

Mal. 1. 11. Judah hath *p.* the holi.
2. 10. by *profaning* the covenant

R. V. Ezek. 21. 25. deadly wounded; 22. 26; 44. 23. common

PROFESS, Deut. 26. 3. Tit. 1. 16.

1 Tim. 6. 12. *profession*, 13. Heb. 3. 1. & 4. 14. & 19. 23.

R. V. 1 Tim. 6. 12. confess; Heb. 3. 1; 4. 14; 10. 23. confession

PROFIT, Prov. 14. 23. Eccl. 7. 11.

Jer. 16. 19. 2 Tim. 2. 14. Heb. 12. 10.

1 Sam. 12. 21. *not profit*, Job 33. 27. & 34. 9. Prov. 10. 2. & 11. 4. Isa. 30. 5. & 44. 9, 10. & 57. 12. Jer. 2. 8, 11. & 7. 8. & 23. 32. John 6. 63. 1 Cor. 13. 3. Gal. 5. 2. Heb. 4. 2. Jas. 2. 14.

Job 22. 2. *profitable*, Eccl. 10. 10.

Acts 20. 20. 1 Tim. 4. 8. 2 Tim. 3. 16. Tit. 3. 8. Phile. 11.

1 Tim. 4. 15. thy *profiting* appear

PROLONG thy days, Deut. 4. 26, 40. & 5. 16, 33. & 6. 2. & 11. 9. & 17. 20. & 22. 7. & 30. 18. & 32. 47. Prov. 10. 27. & 28. 16. Eccl. 8. 13. Isa. 53. 10.

R. V. Job 6. 11. be patient; Ezek. 12. 25, 28. deferred

PROMISE, Num. 14. 34. Neh. 5. 12

Ps. 77. 8. doth his *p.* fail for ever
105. 42. he remember. his holy *p.*

Luke 24. 49. the *p.* of my Father

Acts 1. 4. wait for *p.* of the Father
2. 39. *p.* is to you, and your child.

Rom. 4. 16. *p.* might be sure to all
9. 8. children of *p.*, 9. Gal. 4. 28.

Eph. 1. 13. holy Spirit of *p.*
2. 12. covenant of *p.* having no
6. 2. commandment with *p.*

1 Tim. 4. 8. *p.* of the life, 2 Tim. 1. 1.

Heb. 4. 1. lest a *p.* being left us of
6. 17. heirs of his *p.*, 11. 9.
9. 15. receive *p.* of eternal life

2 Pet. 3. 4. where is the *p.* of com.

1 John 2. 25. *p.* he *promised* eternal life, Luke 1. 72. Rom. 1. 2. & 4. 21.

Tit. 1. 2. Heb. 10. 23. & 11. 11. & 12. 26.

Rom. 9. 4. pertain the *promises*
15. 8. confirm *p.* made to fathers

2 Cor. 1. 20. all *p.* of God are yea
7. 1. having these *p.* let us

Gal. 3. 21. is the law against the *p.*

Heb. 6. 12. patience inherit *p.*
11. 17. he that had received *p.*

2 Pet. 1. 4. great and precious *p.*

R. V. Deut. 10. 9; Josh. 9. 21; 22. 4; 23. 5, 10, 15. spake unto; Luke 1. 72. shew mercy; 22. 6. consented

PROMOTION, Ps. 75. 6. Prov. 3. 35.

PROOF, Acts 1. 3. 2 Cor. 2. 9. & 8. 24.

PROPER, 1 Chron. 29. 3. Heb. 11. 23.

R. V. 1 Cor. 7. 7. own gift from

PROPHECY, 1 Cor. 12. 10. 1 Tim. 4. 14. & 1. 18. 2 Pet. 1. 19, 20. Rev. 1. 3. & 11. 6. & 19. 10. & 22. 7, 10, 18, 19.

1 Kings 22. 8. not *prophesy* good, 18.

Isa. 30. 10. speak smooth things, *p.* deceits

Jer. 14. 14. prophets *p.* lies in my

Joel 2. 28. your sons and your daughters shall *p.*

Amos 2. 12. *p.* not

1 Cor. 13. 9. we *p.* in part
14. 1. but rather that ye may *p.*
39. covet to *p.* and forbid not to

Rev. 10. 11. thou must *p.* again

Num. 11. 25. they *prophesied*

Jer. 23. 21. not spoken yet they *p.*

Matt. 7. 22. we have *p.* in thy
11. 13. the prophets *p.* until John

John 11. 51. *p.* that Jesus should

1 Pet. 1. 10. prophets *p.* of the grace

Jude 14. Enoch also *p.* of these

Ezra 6. 14. *prophesying*, 1 Cor. 11. 4. & 14. 6, 22. 1 Thes. 5. 20.

Gen. 20. 7. he is a *prophet*, and

Ex. 7. 1. Aaron thy brother shall be thy *p.*

Deut. 18. 15. raise up un. thee a *p.*

1 Kings 5. 13. if the *p.* had bid
Ps. 74. 9. there is no more any *p.*
Ezek. 33. 33. then shall they know
that a *p.* hath been among them
Hos. 9. 7. *p.* is a fool, spiritual man
12. 13. by a *p.* was he preserved
Amos 7. 14. no *p.* neither a *p.'s* son
Matt. 10. 41. he that receiveth a *p.*
11. 9. see a *p.* and more than a *p.*
13. 57. a *p.* is not without honor
Luke 7. 28. there is not a greater *p.*
24. 19. *p.* mighty in deed and
John 7. 40. this is the *p.*, 1. 21. & 6. 14.
52. out of Galilee ariseth no *p.*
Acts 3. 22. a *p.* shall the Lord raise
23. will not hear that *p.* shall
Tit. 1. 12. a *p.* of their own, said
1 Pet. 2. 16. madness of the *p.*
Num. 11. 29. all the Lord's people *prophets*
1 Sam. 10. 12. is Saul among the *p.*
Ps. 105. 15. do my *p.* no harm
Jer. 5. 13. the *p.* shall become
23. 26. are *p.* of the deceit of
Lam. 2. 14. *p.* have seen vain
Hos. 6. 5. I hewed them by the *p.*
Zeph. 3. 4. her *p.* are treacherous
Zech. 1. 5. *p.* do they live for ever
Matt. 5. 17. not come to destroy law, or the *p.*
7. 12. this is the law and the *p.*
13. 17. many *p.* have desired
22. 40. on these hang all the law and the *p.*
23. 34. I send you *p.* and wise men
Luke 1. 70. spake by mouth of holy *p.*, 2 Pet. 1. 20.
6. 23. so did their fathers to *p.*
16. 29. they have Moses and the *p.*
31. if they hear not Moses and *p.*
24. 25. to believe all that *p.*
John 8. 52. Abraham is dead, and *p.*
Acts 3. 25. ye are children of the *p.*
10. 43. to him give all the *p.*
13. 27. knew not voices of the *p.*
26. 27. believest thou the *p.*
22. things which the *p.* and Moses
Rom. 1. 2. which he had promised afore by his *p.* in Holy Scriptures
1 Cor. 12. 28. God hath set some in the church, first apostles; secondarily *p.*
Eph. 2. 20. are built upon the foundation of the apostles and *p.*
1 Cor. 14. 32. spirit of *p.* sub. to *p.*
1 Thes. 2. 15. who kill. their own *p.*
Heb. 1. 1. God spake to fath. by *p.*
Jas. 5. 10. take *p.* for example
1 Pet. 1. 10. of which salva. the *p.*
Rev. 18. 20. rejoice over her, ye apostles and *p.*
22. 6. Lord God of holy *p.* sent his 9. and of the brethren the *p.*
R. V. Prov. 30. 1. oracle

PROPHETESSES, Anna, Luke 2. 36; Deborah, Judg. 4. 4; Huldah, 2 Kings, 22. 14; Miriam, Ex. 15. 20; Noadiah, Neh. 6. 14.
PROPITIATION, Rom. 3. 25. 1 John 2. 2. & 4. 10.
PROPORTION of faith. Rom. 12. 6.
R. V. 1 Kings 7. 36. space
PROSELYTE, Matt. 23. 15. Acts 2. 10. & 6. 5. & 13. 43.
PROSPER, Gen. 24. 40. Neh. 1. 11.
Gen. 39. 3. Lord made all to *p.*
Deut. 29. 9. may *p.* in all ye do
2 Chron. 20. 20. believe prophets, so shall ye *p.*
Job 12. 6. tabernacles of robbers *p.*
Ps. 1. 3. whatsoever he doeth, it shall *p.*
122. 6. they shall *p.* that love thee
Isa. 53. 10. pleasure of Lord shall *p.*
54. 17. no weapon formed against thee shall *p.*
55. 11. shall *p.* in the thing whereto
Jer. 12. 1. wherefore doth the way of the wicked *p.*
1 Cor. 16. 2. God hath *prospered* him

3 John 2. *p.* as thy soul *prospereth*
Job 36. 11. spend their days in *prosperity*
1 Kings 10. 7. thy wisdom and *p.* exceedeth
Ps. 30. 6. in my *p.* I shall never
73. 3. when I saw *p.* of the wicked
122. 7. be within thy palaces
Prov. 1. 32. *p.* of fools shall destroy
Eccl. 7. 14. in day of *p.* be joyful
Jer. 22. 21. I spake to thee in thy *p.*
Gen. 24. 21. journey *prosperous*,
Josh. 1. 8. Ps. 45. 4. Rom. 1. 10.
R. V. Ps. 73. 12. being at ease; Jer. 20. 11; 23. 5. deal wisely; Jer. 33. 9. peace
PROTEST, Gen. 43. 3. 1 Sam. 8. 9. Jer. 11. 7; Zech. 3. 6. 1 Cor. 15. 31.
PROUD, Job 9. 13. & 26. 12. & 38. 11. & 40. 11, 12. Ps. 12. 3.
Ps. 40. 4. respecteth not the *p.* nor
101. 5. a *p.* heart I will not suffer
Prov. 6. 17. *p.* look and lying tongue
21. 4. high look and *p.* heart
Eccl. 7. 8. patient is better than *p.*
Mal. 3. 15. we call the *p.* happy
Luke 1. 51. the *p.* in imagination
1 Tim. 6. 4. is *p.* knowing nothing
Jas. 4. 6. God resisteth *p.*, 1 Pet. 5. 5.
Ex. 18. 11. wherein dealt *proudly*
1 Sam. 2. 3. no more so exceeding *p.*
Neh. 9. 10. knowest they dealt *p.*, 16.
Ps. 17. 10. they spake *p.*, 31. 18.
Isa. 3. 5. child shall behave *p.* against
R. V. Job 26. 12. Rahab; Ps. 12. 3; Ps. 138. 6; Prov. 6. 17; Hab. 2. 5; Rom. 1. 30; 2 Tim. 3. 2. haughty; 1 Tim. 6. 4. puffed up
PROVE them, Ex. 16. 4. Deut. 8. 16. Ex. 20. 20. God is come up to *p.* you
Deut. 13. 3. the Lord *p.* you
33. 8. Holy One thou didst *p.* at
1 Kings 10. 1. she came to *p.* him
Job 9. 20. mouth shall *p.* me
Ps. 26. 2. examine me, O Lord, *p.*
Rom. 12. 2. *p.* what is will of God
2 Cor. 8. 8. to *p.* the sincerity of
13. 5. *p.* your own selves, know
Gal. 6. 4. let every man *p.* his work
1 Thes. 5. 21. *p.* all things; hold fast
Ps. 17. 3. thou hast *proved* my heart
66. 10. thou, O God, hast *p.* us as
Acts 9. 22. *proving*, Eph. 5. 10.
PROVERB and a by-word, Deut. 28. 37. 1 Kings 9. 7. Jer. 24. 9. Ezek. 14. 8.
Ps. 69. 11. I became a *p.* to them
Eccl. 12. 9. he set in order many *p.*, 1 Kings 4. 32. Prov. 1. 1. & 10. 1. & 25. 1.
Isa. 14. 4. thou shalt take up this *p.* against, Luke 4. 23.
John 16. 25. I have spoken in *p.*
2 Pet. 2. 22. according to true *p.*
R. V. Isa. 14. 4; Luke 4. 23. parable
PROVIDE, Ex. 18. 21. Acts 23. 24. Gen. 22. 8. God will *p.* himself a
Ps. 78. 20. can he *p.* flesh for people
Matt. 10. 9. *p.* neither gold nor
Rom. 12. 17. *p.* things honest in
Job 38. 41. *provideth* raven his food
Prov. 6. 8. *p.* her meat in summer
1 Tim. 5. 8. if any *p.* not for his
Ps. 132. 15. *provision*, Rom. 13. 14.
R. V. Ps. 65. 9. prepared; Matt. 10. 9. get you no; Luke 12. 33. make for; Rom. 12. 17; 2 Cor. 8. 21. take thought for
PROVIDENCE of God, Gen. 8. 22. Josh. 7. 14. 1 Sam. 6. 7. Ps. 36. 6. 104. & 136. & 145. & 147. Prov.16. & 19. & 20. & 33. Matt. 6. 26. & 10. 29, 30. Luke 21. 18. Acts 1. 26. & 17. 26.
PROVOKE him not, Ex. 23. 21. Num. 14. 11. how long will ye *p.*
Deut. 31. 20. *p.* me, and break my
Job 12. 6. that *p.* God are secure
Ps. 78. 40. how oft did they *p.* him
Isa. 3. 8. to *p.* the eyes of his glory

Jer. 7. 19. do they *p.* me to anger
14. 8. ye *p.* me to wrath with your
Luke 11. 53. to *p.* him to speak of
Rom. 10. 19. *p.* you to jealousy
1 Cor. 10. 22. do we *p.* the Lord to
Eph. 6. 4. fathers *p.* not children
Heb. 3. 16. when they heard did *p.*
10. 24. to *p.* unto love and good
Num. 16. 30. these have *provoked*
14. 23. neither any which *p.* me
Deut. 9. 8. ye *p.* Lord to wrath
1 Sam. 1. 6. adversary *p.* her sore
1 Kings 14. 22. *p.* him to jealousy
2 Kings 23. 26. because Manasseh *p.*
1 Chron. 21. 1. Satan *p.* David to
Ezra 5. 12. our fathers had *p.* God
Ps. 78. 56. and *p.* the Most High
106. 7. *p.* him at the Red sea
Zech. 8. 14. when your fathers *p.*
1 Cor. 13. 5. not easily *p.* thinketh
2 Cor. 9. 2. your zeal hath *p.* many
Deut. 32. 19. *provoking*, 1 Kings 14. 15. & 16. 7. Ps. 78. 17. Gal. 5. 26.
R. V. Num. 14. 11, 23; 16. 30; Deut. 31. 20; Isa. 1. 4. despise; Deut. 32. 16; 1 Chron. 22. 1. moved; Ps. 78. 40, 56. rebel against; Ps. 106. 7, 33, 43. were rebellious; 2 Cor. 9. 2. stirred up
PRUDENT in matters, 1 Sam. 16. 18.
Prov. 12. 16. a *p.* man covereth
23. *p.* man concealeth knowledge
13. 16. every *p.* man dealeth with
14. 8. wisdom of the *p.* is to
15. the *p.* man looketh well to his
15. 5. he that regard. reproof is *p.*
16. 21. wise in heart shall be call. *p.*
18. 15. heart of *p.* getteth knowl.
22. 3. a *p.* man foreseeth the evil
Isa. 5. 21. woe to them that are *p.* in
Jer. 49. 7. is counsel perish. from *p.*
Hos. 14. 9. who is *p.* and he shall
Amos 5. 13. *p.* shall keep silent in
Matt. 11. 25. hid these things from the wise and *p.*
1 Cor. 1. 19. I will bring to nothing the understanding of the *p.*
Isa. 52. 13. my servant shall deal *prudently*
2 Chron. 2. 12. endued with *prudence* and understanding, Prov. 8. 12. Eph. 1. 8.
R. V. 2 Chron. 2. 12. discretion; Prov. 8. 12. subtlety; Isa. 3. 2. diviner; Matt. 11. 25; Luke 10. 21; Acts 13. 7. understanding
PSALM, 1 Chron. 16. 7. Ps. 81. 2. & 98. 5. Acts 13. 33. 1 Cor. 14. 26.
1 Chron. 16. 9. sing *psalms* unto him, Ps. 105. 2.
Ps. 95. 2. a joyful noise with *p.*
Eph. 5. 19. speaking to your. in *p.*
Col. 3. 16. admon. one another in *p.*
Jas. 5. 13. merry, let him sing *p.*
R. V. 1 Chron. 16. 9; Ps. 105. 2; Jas. 5. 13. praises
PSALMODY, singing, service of song, Jewish, Ex. 15. 1. 1 Chron. 6. 31. & 13. 8. 2 Chron. 5. 13. & 20. 22. & 29. 30. Neh. 12. 27; Christian, Matt. 26. 30. Mark 14. 26. Jas. 5. 13; spiritual songs, Eph. 5. 19. Col. 3. 16.
PUBLICAN, Matt. 18. 17; Luke 18. 13.
Matt. 5. 46. even the *p.* the same, 47
11. 19. a friend of *p.* and sinners
Luke 3. 12. came also *publicans* to
7. 29. the *p.* justified God
R. V. Matt. 5. 47. Gentiles
PUBLISH name of the Lord, Deut. 32. 3.
2 Sam. 1. 20. *p.* it not in the streets
Ps. 26. 7. *p.* with voice of thanks.
Isa. 52. 7. feet of him that *publisheth* peace
Jer. 4. 15. a voice *p.* affliction
Mark 13. 10. the Gospel must first be *published*
Acts 13. 49. word of the Lord was *p.*
R. V. Deut. 32. 3. proclaim; 1 Sam. 31. 9. carry tidings; Ps. 26. 7. make to be heard; Mark 13. 10.

preached; Acts 13. 49. spread abroad

PUFFED up, 1 Cor. 4. 6, 19. & 5. 2. & 8. 1. & 13. 4. Col. 2. 18.

PULL out, Ps. 31. 4. Jer. 12. 3. Matt. 7. 4. Luke 14. 5. Jude 23.

Isa. 22. 19. *pull down*, Jer. 1. 10. & 18. 7. & 24. 6. & 42. 10. Luke 12. 18. 2 Cor. 10. 4.

Lam. 3. 11. *pull in pieces*, Acts 23. 10.

Ezek. 17. 9. *pull up*, Amos 9. 15.

Zech. 7. 11. they *pulled* away the R. V. Gen. 8. 9; 19. 10. brought; 1 Kings 31. 4. 5. draw; Ps. 31. 4; Amos 9. 15. pluck; Jer. 1. 10; 18. 7. break; Mic. 2. 8. strip; Matt. 7. 4; Luke 6. 42. cast; Acts 23. 10. torn; 2 Cor. 10. 4. casting, Jude 23. snatching.

PULPIT of wood, Neh. 8. 4.

PUNISH, seven times, Lev. 26. 18. Prov. 17. 26. to *p.* the just is not Isa. 10. 12. *p.* fruit of the stout 13. 11. I will *p.* the world for their Jer. 9. 25. *p.* all circumcised with Hos. 4. 14. I will not *p.* daughters Ezra 9. 13. *p.* us less than we 2 Thes. 1. 9. be *p.* with destruction

2 Pet. 2. 9. reserve unjust to be *p.* Gen. 4. 13. my *punishment* is great. Lev. 26. 41. accept *p.* of their iniq. Job. 31. 3. a strange *p.* to workers Lam. 3. 39. complain for *p.* of sins Amos 1. 3. not turn away the *p.* Matt. 25. 46. go into everlasting *p.* 2 Cor. 2. 6. suffi. to such is this *p.* Heb. 10. 29. of how much sorer *p.* 1 Pet. 2. 14. sent by him, for the *p.* R. V. Ex. 21. 22. fined; Lev. 26. 18. chastise; 26. 24. smite; Prov. 22. 3; 27. 12. suffer for it; Jer. 41. 44. do judgment; Amos 3. 2. visit upon you; Zech. 8. 14. do evil unto; Prov. 19. 19. penalty; Lam. 4. 6; Ezek. 14. 10——; Ezek. 14. 10. iniquity; Job 31. 3. disaster; 1 Pet. 2. 14. vengeance

PURCHASED, Ps. 74. 2. Acts 8. 20. & 20. 28. Eph. 1. 14. 1 Tim. 3. 13. R. V. Lev. 25. 33. redeem; Acts 1. 18; 8. 20. obtain

PURCHASES, Gen. 23. Ruth 4. Jer. 32. 6.

PURE, Ex. 27. 20. & 30. 23, 34.

2 Sam. 22. 27. with the *p.* thou wilt Job 4. 17. can man be more *p.* than 25. 5. stars are not *p.* in his sight Ps. 12. 6. words of the Lord are *p.* 19. 8. commandment of Lord is *p.* 24. 4. clean hands and a *p.* heart Prov. 15. 26. words of *p.* are pleas. 30. 5. every word of God is *p.* 12. a generation *p.* in Zeph. 3. 9. turn to the people a *p.* Acts 20. 26. I am *p.* from blood of Rom. 14. 20. all things indeed are *p.* Phil. 4. 8. whatsoever things are *p.* 1 Tim. 3. 9. mystery of faith in a *p.* conscience 5. 22. of other men's sins keep thyself *p.* Tit. 1. 15. to the *p.* all things are *p.* Heb. 10. 22. washed with *p.* water Jas. 1. 27. *p.* religion and undefiled 3. 17. wis. from above is first *p.* 2 Pet. 3. 1. stir up your *p.* minds Isa. 1. 25. *purely* purge away dross Job 22. 30. by *pureness*, 2 Cor. 6. 6. 1 Tim. 4. 12. *purity*, 5. 2. Hab. 1. 13. of *purer* eyes than to R. V. Ex. 30. 23. flowing; Ps. 21. 3. fine; Prov. 30. 5. tried; Rom. 14. 20. clean; 2 Pet. 3. 1. sincere; Rev. 22. 1——

PURGE me with hyssop, Ps. 51. 7. Ps. 65. 3. our transgressions, thou shalt *p.* them away 79. 9. *p.* away our sins for thy Mal. 3. 3. purify and *p.* them as Matt. 3. 12. thoroughly *p.* his floor 1 Cor. 5. 7. *p.* the old leaven 2 Tim. 2. 21. if a man *p.* himself Heb. 9. 14. *p.* your conscience from

Prov. 16. 6. by mercy iniquity is *purged*

Isa. 6. 7. iniqu. is taken, and sin *p.* Ezek. 24. 13. because I *p.* thee Heb. 1. 3. had by himself *p.* our 2 Pet. 1. 9. he was *p.* from sins John 15. 2. he *purgeth* that it may R. V. Ezek. 43. 20. make atonement; Dan. 11. 35. purify, Matt. 3. 12; Mark 7. 19; Luke 3. 17; John 15. 2; Heb. 9. 14, 22; 10. 2; 2 Pet. 1. 9. cleanse, cleansed, clean

PURIFY sons of Levi, Mal. 3. 3. Jas. 4. 8. *p.* your hearts, ye double Ps. 12. 6. silver *purified* seven Dan. 12. 10. many shall be *p.* 1 Pet. 1. 22. *p.* your souls in obey. Mal. 3. 3. sit as *purifier* of silver 1 John 3. 3. *purifieth* himself as he Acts 15. 9. *purifying* their hearts Tit. 2. 14. *p.* to himself a peculiar Heb. 9. 13. sanctifieth to *p.* of flesh R. V. Job. 41. 25. are beside; Heb. 9. 23. cleansed; Num. 8. 7. expiation, Acts 15. 9. cleansing

PURPOSE, Jer. 6. 20. & 49. 30. Job 33. 17. withdraw man from *p.* Prov. 20. 18. every *p.* is established Eccl. 3. 17. a time to every *p.*, 8. 6. Isa. 14. 26. the *p.* that is purposed Jer. 51. 29. *p.* of Lord shall stand Acts 11. 23. with *p.* of heart cleave Rom. 8. 28. according to his *p.* Eph. 1. 11. according to *p.* of him 3. 11. the eternal *p.* which he *p.* 2 Tim. 1. 9. according to his own *p.* 1 John 3. 8. for this *p.* he was R. V. Acts 26. 18; 1 John 3. 8. to this end. Acts 20. 3. determined

PURSE, Prov. 1. 14. Matt. 10. 9.

PURSUE, Gen. 35. 5. Deut. 28. 22. Ex. 15. 9. the enemy said, I will *p.* Job 13. 25. wilt thou *p.* dry stubble Ps. 34. 14. seek peace and *p.* it Prov. 11. 19. that *pursueth* evil, *p.* it 28. 1. wicked flee when none *p.* R. V. Judg. 20. 45. followed; Job 30. 15; Lam. 4. 19. chase

PUT, Gen. 2. 8. & 3. 15, 22. Neh. 2. 12. what God *p.* in my heart, 7. 5. Ezra 7. 27. Rev. 17. 17. Neh. 3. 5. nobles *p.* not their necks Job 4. 18. he *p.* no trust in servants 38. 36. hath *p.* wisdom in inward Ps. 4. 7. hast *p.* gladness in heart 8. 6. *p.* all things under his feet Eccl. 10. 10. *p.* to more strength S. of S. 5. 3. *p.* off my coat, how shall Isa. 5. 20. woe to them that *p.* dark. 42. 1. I will *p.* my Spirit upon 53. 10. Lord hath *p.* him to grief 63. 11. who *p.* his Holy Spirit in Jer. 31. 33. *p.* law in inward parts 32. 40. I will *p.* my fear in hearts Ezek. 11. 19. *p.* a new spirit within 36. 27. I will *p.* my Spirit within Mic. 7. 5. *p.* not confidence in guide Matt. 5. 15. *p.* it under a bushel 19. 6. what God joined, let no man *p.* asunder Luke 1. 52. *p.* down mighty from Acts 1. 7. which Father *p.* in his 13. 46. seeing you *p.* the Gospel 15. 9. *p.* no difference between us Eph. 4. 22. *p.* off the old man 2 Pet. 1. 14. I must *p.* off this Gen. 28. 20. God will give raiment to *put on* Job 29. 14. I——righteousness and it Isa. 51. 9. awake, arm of Lord,—— strength 59. 15. for he——righteousness as a breastplate Matt. 6. 25. nor for body what ye—— Rom. 13. 12.——armor of light 14.——Lord Jesus Christ Gal. 3. 27. baptized into Christ have——Christ Eph. 4. 24.——the new man, Col. 3. 10. 6. 11.——whole armor of God Col. 3. 12.——bowels of mercies 1 Chron. 5. 20. *put trust* in, Ps. 4. 5. & 7. 1. & 9. 10. & 56. 4. & 146. 3.

Prov. 28. 25. & 29. 25. Isa. 57. 13. Jer. 39. 18. Hab. 2. 13.

Num. 22. 38. word that God *putteth* Job 15. 15. he *p.* no trust in saints Ps. 15. 5. that *p.* not out money 75. 7. God *p.* down one, and set. S. of S. 2. 13. *p.* forth green figs Lam. 3. 29. he *p.* his mouth in Mic. 3. 5. that *p.* not into their Mal. 2. 16. he hateth *putting* away Eph. 4. 25. *p.* away lying, speak Col. 2. 11 in *p.* off the body of sins 1 Thes. 5. 8. *p.* on the breastplate 2 Tim. 1. 6. gift given thee by *p.* 1 Pet. 3. 3. wearing of gold or *p.* on R. V. Many changes, but chiefly due to context

Q

QUAILS, Ex. 16. 13. Num. 11. 31.

QUAKE, Ex. 19. 18. Matt. 27. 51. Ezek. 12. 18. *quaking*, Dan. 10. 7.

QUARREL, Lev. 26. 25. Col. 3. 13. R. V. Lev. 26. 25. execute vengeance, Mark 6. 19. set herself; Col. 3. 13. complain

QUEEN, 1 Kings 10. 1. & 15. 13. Ps. 45. 9. S. of S. 6. 8. Jer. 44. 17, 24. Rev. 18. 7. Matt. 12. 42. *q.* of the south rise Isa. 49. 23. *q.* their nursing moth. R. V. Jer. 13. 18; 29. 12. queenmother

QUENCH my coal, 2 Sam. 14. 7. 2 Sam. 21. 17. that thou *q.* not S. of S. 8. 7. waters cannot *q.* love Isa. 42. 3. flax he will not *q.* Eph. 6. 15. to *q.* fiery darts of dev. 1 Thes. 5. 19. *q.* not the Spirit Mark 9. 43. fire that never shall be *quenched*, 44. 46, 48. R. V. Num. 11. 2. abated; Mark 9. 44, 45, 46——

QUESTION, Mark 12. 34. 1 Cor. 10. 25. 1 Kings 10. 1. *questions*, Luke 2. 46. 1 Tim. 1. 4. & 6. 4. 2 Tim. 2. 23. R. V. 1 Tim. 1. 4; 6. 4; 2 Tim. 2. 23; Tit. 3. 9. questionings

QUICK, Num. 16. 30. Ps. 55. 15. Ps. 124. 3. had swallowed us up *q.* Isa. 11. 3. of *q.* understanding Acts 10. 42. Judge of *q.* and dead 2 Tim. 4. 1. who shall judge the *q.* Ps. 71. 20. *quicken* me again and 80. 18. *q.* us and we will call 119. 25. *q.* me according to word 40. *q.* me in thy righteousness 149. *q.* me according to judgment Rom. 8. 11. *q.* your mortal bodies Eph. 2. 5. *q.* us together with Ps. 119. 50. for thy word hath *quickened* me Eph. 2. 1. you he *q.* who were 1 Pet. 3. 18. but *q.* by the Spirit John 5. 21. Son *quickeneth* whom he 1 Cor. 15. 45. last Adam be made a *quickening* Spirit R. V. Num. 16. 30; Ps. 55. 15; 124. 3. alive; Isa. 11. 3. his delight shall be; Heb. 4. 12. living; 1 Cor. 15. 45. become a life giving

QUICKLY, Ex. 32. 8. Deut. 11. 17. Eccl. 4. 12. cord is not *q.* broken Matt. 5. 25. agree with adversary *q.* Rev. 3. 11. behold I come *q.*, 22. 7. R. V. Mark 16. 8; Rev. 2. 5——

QUIET, Judg. 18. 27. Job 3. 13, 26. Eccl. 9. 17. the words of the wise are heard in *q.* Isa. 7. 4. take heed and be *q.* fear 33. 20. shall see Jerusalem a *q.* 1 Thes. 4. 11. study to be *q.* and to 1 Tim. 2. 2. lead a *q.* and peaceable 1 Pet. 3. 4. ornament of a meek and *q.* spirit 1 Chron. 22. 9. *quietness*, Job 20. 20. Job 34. 29. when he giveth *q.* who Prov. 17. 1. better is dry morsel and *q.* Eccl. 4. 6. better is a hand. with *q.*

Isa. 30. 15. in *q.* shall be strength
32. 17. the effect of righteousness shall be *q.*
2 Thes. 3. 12. exhort with *q.* they
R. V. Nah. 1. 12. in full strength;
Judg. 8. 28. had rest; Acts 24. 2. much peace
QUIT you like men, 1 Sam. 4. 9. 1 Cor. 16. 13.
R. V. Josh. 2. 20. guiltless
QUIVER full of them, Ps. 127. 5.
Isa. 49. 2. in his *q.* hath he hid me
Jer. 5. 16. *q.* is an open sepulchre

R

RABBI, Matt. 23. 7, 8. John 20. 16.
R. V. Matt. 23. 7 ——
RACE, Ps. 19. 5. Eccl. 9. 11. 1 Cor. 9. 24. Heb. 12. 1.
R. V. Ps. 19. 5. course
RAGE, 2 Kings 5. 12. 2 Chron. 16. 10.
2 Chron. 28. 9. ye have slain them in a *r.*
Ps. 2. 1. why do the heathen *r.*
Prov. 6. 34. jealousy is *r.* of a man
29. 9. whether he *r.* or laugh is no
Ps. 46. 6. the heathen *raged*
Prov. 14. 16. the fool *rageth*
Ps. 89. 9. rulest the *raging* of sea
Prov. 20. 1. wine is a mocker, strong drink is *r.*
Jude 13. *r.* waves of sea, foaming
R. V. Job 40. 11. overflowings;
Prov. 29. 9. be angry; 14. 16. beareth himself insolently; Prov. 20. 1. a brawler
RAGS, Prov. 23. 21. Isa. 64. 6.
RAILER, or drunkard, 1 Cor. 5. 11.
1 Tim. 6. 4. *railing*, 1 Pet. 3. 9.
2 Pet. 2. 11. *r.* accusation, Jude 9.
R. V. 1 Pet. 3. 9. reviling
RAIMENT to put on, Gen. 28. 20.
Ex. 21. 10. food and *r.* not dimin.
Deut. 8. 4. thy *r.* waxed not old
Zech. 3. 4. clothe thee with change of *r.*
Matt. 6. 28. body more than *r.*, 28.
11. 8. man clothed in soft *r.*
17. 2. his *r.* was white as the light
1 Tim. 6. 8. having food and *r.* let
Rev. 3. 5. clothed in white *r.*, 18.
R. V. Ex. 22. 26, 27; Deut. 22. 3; 24. 13; Num. 31. 20; Matt. 17. 2; 27. 31; Mark 9. 3; Luke 23. 34; John 19. 24; Acts 22. 20; Rev. 3. 5, 18; 4. 4. garment or garments; Ps. 45. 14. broidered work; Zech. 3. 4. apparel; 1 Tim. 6. 8. covering; Jas. 2. 2. clothing; Luke 10. 30 ——
RAIN in due season, Lev. 26. 4. Deut. 11. 14. & 28. 12.
Deut. 32. 2. my doctrine drop as *r.*
2 Sam. 23. 4. clear shining after *r.*
1 Kings 8. 35. no *r.* because sinned
2 Chron. 7. 13. that there be no *r.*
Job 5. 10. giveth *r.* on the earth
38. 28. hath the *r.* a father
Ps. 68. 9. didst send a plentiful *r.*
72. 6. he shall come down like *r.*
147. 8. who prepareth *r.* for earth
Prov. 16. 15. king's favor is like the latter *r.*
Eccl. 12. 2. nor clouds ret. after *r.*
S. of S. 2. 11. winter is past; *r.* is over
Isa. 4. 6. covert from storm and *r.*
30. 23. shall give the *r.* of thy
55. 10. as *r.* cometh down from
Jer. 5. 24. fear Lord who giveth *r.*
14. 22. vanities of the Gentiles that can *r.*
Amos 4. 7. withholden *r.* from you
Zech. 10. 1. ask of the Lord *r.* in
14. 17. upon them shall be no *r.*
Matt. 5. 45. sendeth *r.* on the just
Heb. 6. 7. earth which drink. in *r.*
Jas. 5. 18. he prayed, and heaven gave *r.*
Job 38. 26. cause it to *r.* on the earth

Ps. 11. 6. on the wicked he shall *r.*
Hos. 10. 12. till he *r.* righteousness
Ps. 78. 27. had *rained* upon them
Ezek. 22. 24. land not cleansed nor *r.* upon
Prov. 27. 15. continual dropping in a *rainy* day
RAISE, Deut. 18. 15, 18. 2 Sam. 12. 11.
Isa. 44. 26. *r.* up decayed places
58. 12. *r.* up foundations of
Hos. 6. 2. third day he will *r.* us
Amos 9. 11. I will *r.* up tabernacle
Luke 1. 69. *r.* up a horn of salva.
John 6. 40. I will *r.* him up at
Ex. 9. 16. I *raised* thee up to show
Matt. 11. 5. deaf hear, dead are *r.*
Rom. 4. 25. *r.* again for justifica.
6. 4. as Christ was *r.* by glory of
1 Cor. 6. 14. God hath *r.* up the
2 Cor. 4. 14. he that *r.* up the
Eph. 2. 6. hath *r.* us up together
1 Sam. 2. 8. he *raiseth* up the poor
Ps. 113. 7. he *r.* up poor out of
145. 14. *r.* up those that be
R. V. Job 3. 8; 14. 12. roused; S. of S. 8. 5. awakened; Job 50. 9; Ezek. 1. 5; Jer. 6. 22; 50. 41; Joel 3. 7; Zech. 9. 13; Acts 13. 50. stir or stirred
RANSOM of life, Ex. 21. 30.
Ex. 30. 12. give every man a *r.* for
Job 33. 24. deliver him, I have found *r.*
36. 18. great *r.* cannot deliver
Ps. 49. 7. nor give to God a *r.* for
Prov. 6. 35. will not regard any *r.*
13. 8. *r.* of man's life are his
21. 18. wicked ar *a r.* for right.
Isa. 43. 3. I gave Egypt for thy *r.*
Hos. 13. 14. *r.* them from power
Matt. 20. 28. to give his life a *r.* for
1 Tim. 2. 6. gave himself a *r.* for
Isa. 35. 10. *ransomed*, 51. 10. Jer. 31. 11.
R. V. Ex. 21. 30. redemption; Isa. 51. 10. redeemed
RASH, Eccl. 5. 2. Isa. 32. 4.
RAVISHED, Prov. 5. 19. S. of S. 4. 9.
REACH, Gen. 11. 4. John 20. 27.
Ps. 36. 5. faithfulness *reacheth* to
Phil. 3. 13. *reaching* forth to those
R. V. Ex. 26. 28. pass through;
Phil. 3. 13. stretching forward
READ in audience, Ex. 24. 7.
Deut. 17. 19. *r.* therein all his life
Neh. 13. 1. *r.* in the book of Moses
Luke 4. 16. as his custom was, stood up to *r.*
Acts 15. 21. *r.* in synagogue
2 Cor. 3. 2. known and *r.* of all
Acts 8. 30. understandest thou what thou *readest*
Rev. 1. 3. blessed is he that *readeth*
Neh. 8. 8. *reading*, 1 Tim. 4. 13.
READY to pardon, God, Neh. 9. 17.
Ps. 45. 1. tongue is as a pen of a *r.* writer
86. 5. thou, Lord, art good, and *r.* to forgive
Eccl. 5. 1. more *r.* to hear, than
Matt. 24. 44. be ye also *r.*
Mark 14. 38. spirit is *r.* but the
Acts 21. 13. *r.* not to be bound
1 Tim. 6. 18. do good *r.* to distrib.
2 Tim. 4. 6. now *r.* to be offered
Tit. 3. 1. *r.* to every good work
1 Pet. 5. 2. willingly of a *r.* mind
Rev. 3. 2. strengthen things *r.* to
Acts 17. 11. *readiness*, 2 Cor. 10. 6.
R. V. 2 Chron. 35. 14; 2 Cor. 9. 2, 3. prepared; 1 Chron. 12. 23, 24. armed for; Mark 14. 38. willing; Acts 20. 7. intending; Heb. 8. 13. nigh; Rev. 12. 4. about
REAP, Lev. 19. 9.
Hos. 10. 12. *r.* in mercy
1 Cor. 9. 11. a great thing if we *r.*
Gal. 6. 9. shall *r.* if we faint not
Hos. 10. 13. ploughed wickedness, ye have *reaped* iniquity
Rev. 14. 16. the earth was *r.*, 15.
Matt. 13. 39. *reapers* are angels, 30.

John 4. 36. he that *reapeth* receiv.
R. V. Lev. 23. 22 ——; Jas. 5. 4. mowed
REASON, Prov. 26. 16. Dan. 4. 36.
Isa. 41. 21. bring forth your strong *r.*
1 Pet. 3. 15. asketh a *r.* of the hope
Acts 24. 25. as he *reasoned* of
Rom. 12. 1. your *reasonable* service
REBEL not against Lord, Num. 14. 9. Josh. 22. 19.
Job 24. 13. of those that *r.* against
Neh. 9. 26. they *rebelled* against thee
Isa. 63. 10. they *r.* and vexed his
1 Sam. 15. 23. *rebellion*, the sin
Num. 20. 10. hear now, ye *rebels*
Ezek. 20. 38. purge out the *r.* from
Deut. 9. 7. been *rebellious* against
Ps. 68. 18. received gifts for men, for the *r.* also
Isa. 30. 9. this a *r.* people, lying
50. 5. I was not *r.* nor turned
Jer. 4. 17. hath been *r.*
Ezek. 2. 3, 5, 8. *r.* house, 3. 9, 26. & 12. 2, 3. & 17. 12. & 24. 3. & 44. 6.
REBUKE thy neighbor, Lev. 19. 17.
2 Kings 19. 3. a day of *r.*
Ps. 6. 1. *r.* me not in anger, nor
Prov. 9. 8. *r.* a wise man, he will
27. 5. open *r.* is better than secret
Zech. 3. 2. the Lord said to Satan, the Lord *r.* thee
Matt. 16. 22. Peter began to *r.* him
Luke 17. 3. if thy brother trespass, *r.* him
Phil. 2. 15. sons of God without *r.*
1 Tim. 5. 1. *r.* not an elder, entreat
20. them that sin *r.* before all
Tit. 1. 13. *r.* them sharply, that
3. 15. exhort and *r.* with author.
Heb. 12. 5. not faint, when *rebuked*
Prov. 28. 23. he that *rebuked*, shall
Amos 5. 10. hate him that *r.* in
R. V. Phil. 2. 15. blemish; Jer. 15. 15. reproach; Prov. 9. 7, 8; Amos 5. 10; 1 Tim. 5. 20; Tit. 2. 15; Rev. 3. 19. reprove or reproveth
RECEIVE good and not evil, Job 2. 10.
Job 22. 22. *r.* the law from his
Ps. 6. 9. the Lord will *r.* my prayer
73. 24. guide me and afterwards *r.*
75. 2. when I shall *r.* congregation
Hos. 14. 2. take away iniqu., *r.* us
Matt. 10. 41. *r.* a prophet's reward
18. 5. *r.* little child in my name
19. 11. all men cannot *r.* this
21. 22. ask, believing, ye shall *r.*
Mark 4. 16. hear the word, and *r.*
11. 24. believe that ye *r.* and ye
Luke 16. 9. may *r.* into everlast.
John 3. 27. man can *r.* nothing
5. 44. which *r.* honor one of
Acts 2. 38. shall *r.* gift of Holy Ghost
7. 59. Lord Jesus *r.* my spirit
13. 43. he that believeth shall *r.*
20. 35. more bless. to give than *r.*
26. 18. may *r.* forgiveness of sins
Rom. 14. 1. that is weak in faith *r.*
1 Cor. 3. 8. every man *r.* his reward
2 Cor. 5. 10. may *r.* things done
6. 1. *r.* not grace of God in vain
Gal. 3. 14. *r.* promise of the
4. 5. might *r.* the adoption of
Eph. 6. 8. same shall he *r.* of
Col. 3. 24. *r.* reward of inheritance
Jas. 1. 21. *r.* with meekness
3. 1. *r.* greater condemnation
1 Pet. 5. 4. shall *r.* a crown of glory
1 John 3. 22. whatso. we ask, we *r.*
2 John 8. look that we *r.* a full
Job 4. 12. mine ear *received* a little
Ps. 68. 18. thou hast *r.* gifts for
Jer. 2. 30. *r.* no correction
Matt. 10. 8. freely ye have *r.* freely
Luke 6. 24. have *r.* your consola.
16. 25. hast *r.* thy good things
John 1. 11. own *r.* him not
16. of his fulness have we all *r.*
Acts 8. 17. they *r.* the Holy Ghost
17. 11. *r.* the word

Acts 20. 24. which I *r.* of Lord
Rom. 5. 11. Christ by whom we
have *r.* atonement
14. 3. judge him not, for God hath
r. him
15. 7. *r.* one anoth. as Christ *r.* us
1 Tim. 3. 16. *r.* up into glory
4. 3. to be *r.* with thanksgiving
Heb. 11. 13. not having *r.* promises
Jer. 7. 28. nor *receiveth* correction
Matt. 7. 8. every one that asketh *r.*
10. 40. he that *r.* you, *r.* me
13. 20. hears the word, and anon *r.*
John 3. 32. no man *r.* his testimony
12. 48. rejecteth me, *r.* not my
1 Cor. 2. 14. natural man *r.* not
Phil. 4. 15. in giving and *receiving*
Heb. 12. 28. we *r.* à kingdom
1 Pet. 1. 9. *r.* the end of your faith
R. V. Ex. 29. 25; 1 Sam. 12. 3; 2
Kings 12. 7, 8; John 16. 14; Heb.
7. 6. take; Hos. 14. 2; Mark 4. 20;
1 Thes. 2. 13. accept; Luke 9. 11;
3 John 8. welcome; many other
changes due to context
RECKONED, Ps. 40. 5. Isa. 38. 13.
Luke 22. 37. Rom. 4. 4, 9, 10. & 6. 11.
& 8. 18.
RECOMPENSE, Prov. 12. 14. Isa.
35. 4.
Deut. 32. 35. to me belongeth *r.*
Job 15. 31. vanity shall be his *r.*
Prov. 20. 22. say not thou I will *r.*
evil
Jer. 25. 14. I will *r.* your iniquities
Luke 14. 14. they cannot *r.* thee
Rom. 12. 17. *r.* to no man evil for
Isa. 34. 8. it is the year of *r.* for
66. 6. render *r.* to his enemies
Jer. 51. 56. the Lord God of *r.*
Hos. 9. 7. the days of *r.* are come
Luke 14. 12. lest a *r.* be made thee
Heb. 2. 2. received just *r.* of re-
ward
11. 26. he had respect unto *r.* of
Num. 5. 8. trespass be *recom-
pensed*
2 Sam. 22. 21. according to right-
eousness he *r.* me
Prov. 11. 31. righteous shall be *r.*
Jer. 18. 20. shall evil be *r.* for good
Rom. 11. 35. it shall be *r.* to him
R. V. Num. 5. 7, 8. restitution;
Ezek. 7. 3, 4, 9; 11. 21; 16. 34; 17.
19; 22. 31; 2 Chron. 6. 23; bring
or brought; Rom. 12. 17. render
RECONCILE with blood, Lev. 6.
30.
Eph. 2. 16. *r.* both to God into one
Col. 1. 20. to *r.* all things to him.
2 Cor. 5. 19. God in Christ *reconciling* the world
Matt. 5. 24. be *reconciled* to brother
Rom. 5. 10. when enemies we
were *r.*
2 Cor. 5. 18. he hath *r.* us to
20. be ye *r.* to God
Lev. 8. 15. to make *reconciliation,*
2 Chron. 29. 24. Ezek. 45. 15, 17.
Dan. 8. 24. Heb. 2. 17.
2 Cor. 5. 18. given to us ministry
of *r.*
19. committ. to us the word of *r.*
R. V. Lev. 6. 30; Ezek. 45. 20. make
atonement; Lev. 8. 15; 16. 20;
Ezek. 45. 15, 17. atonement;
2 Chron. 29. 24. sin offering; Heb.
2. 17. propitiation
RECORD my name, Ex. 20. 24.
Deut. 30. 19. I call heaven and
earth to *r.* against, 31. 28.
Job 16. 19. my witness and my *r.*
John 1. 32. bare *r.*, 8. 13, 14. & 12. 17.
& 19. 35. Rom. 10. 2. Gal. 4. 15.
2 Cor. 1. 23. I call God for a *r.*
1 John 5. 7. three bear *r.* in heaven
11. this is the *r.* God hath given
Rev. 1. 2. bare *r.* of the word of
R. V. Very general change to witness; Deut. 30. 19. witness;
1 Chron. 16. 4. celebrate; Acts 20.
26. testify

RECOVER strength, Ps. 39. 13.
Hos. 2. 9. I will *r.* my wool and
2 Tim. 2. 26. may *r.* themselves
Jer. 8. 22. is not health of my peo-
ple *recovered*
Luke 4. 18. *recovering* of sight to
R. V. 1 Sam. 30. 19. brought back;
Hos. 2. 9. pluck away
RED, Ps. 75. 8. Isa. 1. 18. & 27. 2. &
63. 2. Zech. 1. 8. & 6. 2. Rev. 6. 4. &
12. 3.
R. V. Ps. 75. 8. foameth
RED DRAGON, Rev. 12. 3.
RED HORSE, vision of, Zech. 1.
8. & 6. 2. Rev. 6. 4.
REDEEM with outstretched arm,
Ex. 6. 6.
2 Sam. 7. 23. Israel whom God
went to *r.*
Job 5. 20. in famine he shall *r.*
thee
Ps. 44. 26. *r.* us for thy mercies'
sake
130. 8. shall *r.* Israel from
Hos. 13. 14. I will *r.* them from
Tit. 2. 14. might *r.* us from iniquity
Gen. 48. 16. angel which *redeemed*
2 Sam. 4. 9. hath *r.* my soul out
Ps. 136. 24. hath *r.* us from our
Isa. 1. 27. Zion shall be *r.* with
51. 11. *r.* of the Lord shall return
52. 3. shall be *r.* without money
63. 9. in his love and pity he *r.*
Luke 1. 68. visited and *r.* his peo.
24. 21. he that should have *r.*
Gal. 3. 13. Christ hath *r.* us from
1 Pet. 1. 18. not *r.* with corrupti.
Rev. 5. 9. hast *r.* us to God, by
14. 4. these were *r.* from among
Ps. 34. 22. Lord *redeemeth* the soul
103. 4. who *r.* thy life from de.
Eph. 5. 16. *redeeming* the time
Job 19. 25. I know that my *Re-
deemer* liveth
Ps. 19. 14. my strength and my *R.*
Prov. 23. 11. their *R.* is mighty
Isa. 63. 16. our Father and *R.*
Jer. 50. 34. their *R.* is strong
Lev. 25. 34. *redemption,* Num. 3. 49.
Ps. 49. 8. *r.* of their soul is pre.
130. 7. with him is plenteous *r.*
Luke 2. 38. looked for *r.* in Jeru-
salem
21. 28. your *r.* draweth nigh
Rom. 3. 24. through *r.* in Christ
8. 23. waiting for the *r.* of our
body
1 Cor. 1. 30. made unto us wisdom,
and righteousness, and *r.*
Eph. 1. 7. in whom we have *r.*
14. until *r.* of the purchased
4. 30. sealed unto the day of *r.*
Heb. 9. 12. obtain. eternal *r.* for us
R. V. Lev. 25. 29; 27. 27; Isa. 5. 1;
Jer. 31. 11. ransom; Lev. 25. 29;
Num. 3. 51; Ruth 4. 6. redemption; Ps. 136. 24. delivered; Rev.
5. 9; 14. 3, 4. purchased
REFINE, Isa. 25. 6. & 48. 10. Zech.
13. 9. Mal. 3. 2, 3.
REFORMATION, Heb. 9. 10.
REFRAIN, Prov. 1. 15. 1 Pet. 3. 10.
Prov. 10. 29. he that *refraineth* his
lips is wise
REFRESHING, Isa. 28. 12. Acts
3. 19.
REFUGE, Num. 35. 13. Josh. 20. 3.
Deut. 33. 27. eternal God is thy *r.*
Ps. 9. 9. the Lord also will be a *r.*
for the oppressed, 14. 6. Isa. 4. 6.
& 25. 4.
Ps. 57. 1. God is my *r.* and, 59. 16.
& 62. 7. & 71. 7. & 142. 5. Jer. 16. 19.
Ps. 46. 1. God is our *r.*, 7. 11. & 62.
8.
Isa. 28. 15. have made lies our *r.*
Heb. 6. 18. fled for *r.* to lay hold
on
R. V. Deut. 33. 27. dwelling place;
Ps. 9. 9. high tower
REFUSE, Lam. 3. 45. Amos 8. 6.
Neh. 9. 17. *refused* to obey, neither
Ps. 77. 2. my soul *r.* to be comforted
118. 22. the stone which builders *r.*

Prov. 1. 24. I have called, and ye *r.*
Jer. 31. 15. Rachel *r.* to be com.
Hos. 11. 5. because they *r.* to return
1 Tim. 4. 4. good and noth. to be *r.*
Jer. 3. 3. *refusedst* to be ashamed
15. 18. *refuseth* to be healed
Heb. 12. 25. *r.* not him that speak.
R. V. 1 Sam. 8. 7; Ps. 118. 22;
Ezek. 5. 6; 1 Tim. 4. 4. reject or
rejected; Prov. 10. 17. forsaketh;
Isa. 54. 6. cast off
REGARD not works of the Lord,
Ps. 28. 5.
Ps. 66. 18. if I *r.* iniquity in heart
102. 17. will *r.* prayer of destitute
Isa. 5. 12. that *r.* not work of Lord
Prov. 1. 24. no man *regarded*
Ps. 106. 44. he *r.* their affliction
Luke 1. 48. *r.* low estate of his
Heb. 8. 9. not in my covenant I *r.*
them not
Deut. 10. 17. God *regardeth* not
Job 34. 19. nor *r.* rich more than
Prov. 12. 10. righteous *r.* life of
15. 5. he that *r.* reproof is pru-
dent
Eccl. 5. 8. he that is higher than
the highest *r.*
Rom. 14. 6. he that *r.* the day, *r.* it
Matt. 22. 16. *regardest* not person
R. V. *gave heed*; 2 Sam. 13. 20. take
thing to heart; Job 39. 7. heareth;
Ps. 94. 7. consider; Prov. 5. 2. pre-
serve; Mal. 1. 9. accept; Luke 1.
48. looked upon; Acts 8. 11. gave
heed; Phil. 2. 30. hazarding; Rom.
14. 6; Gal. 6. 4 ——
REGENERATION, Matt. 19. 28.
Tit. 3. 5.
REIGN, Gen. 37. 8. Lev. 26. 17.
Ex. 15. 18. Lord shall *r.* for ever,
Ps. 146. 10.
Prov. 8. 15. by me kings *r.* and
Isa. 32. 1. a king shall *r.* in right.
Jer. 23. 5. a king shall *r.* and pros.
Luke 19. 14. not have this man to *r.*
Rom. 5. 17. shall *r.* in life by one
1 Cor. 4. 8. would to God ye did *r.*
2 Tim. 2. 12. if we suffer, we shall *r.*
Rev. 5. 10. we shall *r.* on the earth
22. 5. they shall *r.* for ever and
Rom. 5. 14. death *reigned* from
21. that as sin *r.* unto death so
Rev. 20. 4. they lived and *r.* with
1 Chron. 20. 12. thou *reignest* over
Ps. 93. 1. Lord *reigneth,* 97. 1. & 99. 1.
Isa. 52. 7. saith unto Zion, thy God
r.
Rev. 19. 6. Alleluia, Lord God
omnipotent *r.*
R. V. Lev. 26. 17; Deut. 15. 6; Josh.
12. 5; Judg. 9. 2; 1 Kings 4. 21;
Rom. 15. 12. rule or ruled
REINS, Job 16. 13. & 19. 27.
Ps. 7. 9. God trieth hearts and *r.*,
Jer. 17. 10. & 20. 12. Rev. 2. 23.
Ps. 16. 7. my *r.* instruct me in
73. 21. I was pricked in my *r.*
139. 13. thou hast possessed my *r.*
Prov. 23. 16. my *r.* shall rejoice
Jer. 12. 2. thou art far from their *r.*
REJECT, Mark 6. 26. Gal. 4. 14.
Mark 7. 9. ye *r.* command. of God
Tit. 3. 10. after first and second
admonition *r.*
1 Sam. 8. 7. have not *rejected* thee
Isa. 53. 3. is despised and *r.* of men
Jer. 2. 37. Lord hath *r.* confidences
6. 30. Lord *r.* them, 7. 29. & 14. 19.
2 Kings 17. 20. Lam. 5. 22.
Jer. 8. 9. *r.* word of the Lord
Hos. 4. 6. hast *r.* knowledge
Luke 7. 30. *r.* the counsel of God
Heb. 12. 17. was *r.* for he found no
John 12. 48. he that *rejecteth* me
REJOICE, Ex. 18. 9. Deut. 12. 7.
Deut. 28. 63. Lord will *r.* over you
1 Sam. 2. 1. because I *r.* in thy
2 Chron. 6. 41. let thy saints *r.* in
20. 27. the Lord made them to *r.*
Neh. 12. 43. God made them *r.* with
Ps. 2. 11. serve God and *r.* with
5. 11. let those that trust in thee *r.*
9. 14. I will *r.* in thy salvation

Ps. 58. 10. righteous will *r.* when he
63. 7. in the shadow of thy wings
I will *r.*
65. 8. thou makest the morning
and the evening to *r.*
68. 3. let righteous *r.* before God
86. 4. *r.* the soul of thy servant
104. 31. Lord shall *r.* in his works
119. 162. I *r.* at thy word as one
Prov. 5. 18. *r.* with wife of thy
24. 17. *r.* not when enemy falleth
Eccl. 11. 9. *r.* O young man, in thy
Isa. 29. 19. poor among men shall *r.*
62. 5. thy God shall *r.* over thee
Jer. 32. 41. I will *r.* over them to do
Zeph. 3. 17. *r.* over thee with joy
Luke 6. 23. *r.* ye in that day; leap
10. 20. rather *r.* that your names
John 5. 35. willing to *r.* in his light
14. 28. if ye loved me ye would *r.*
Rom. 5. 2. *r.* in hope of glory of God
12. 15. *r.* with them that do *r.*
1 Cor. 7. 30. that *r.* as though *r.* not
Phil. 3. 3. worship God and *r.* in
Col. 1. 24. *r.* in my sufferings for
1 Thes. 5. 16. *r.* evermore
Jas. 1. 9. brother of low degree *r.*
1 Pet. 1. 8. *r.* with joy unspeakable
Ps. 33. 1. rejoice *in the Lord,* 97. 12.
Isa. 41. 16. & 61. 10. Joel 2. 23. Hab.
3. 18. Zech. 10. 7. Phil. 3. 1. & 4. 4.
Ps. 119. 14. I have *rejoiced* in thy
Luke 1. 47. my spirit *r.* in God my
10. 21. Jesus *r.* in spirit and said
John 8. 56. Abraham *r.* to see my
1 Cor. 7. 30. as though they *r.* not
Ps. 16. 9. my heart is glad, my
glory *rejoiceth*
28. 7. Lord my heart greatly *r.*
Prov. 13. 9. the light of righteous *r.*
Isa. 62. 5. bridegroom *r.* over bride
64. 5. thou meetest him that *r.*
1 Cor. 13. 6. *r.* not in iniquity
Jas. 2. 13. mercy *r.* against
Ps. 19. 8. the statutes of the Lord
rejoicing the heart
119. 111. are the *r.* of my heart
Prov. 8. 31. *r.* in the habitable
Isa. 65. 18. I create Jerusalem a *r.*
Jer. 13. 15. 16. thy word was the *r.*
Acts 5. 41. *r.* that they were
counted
8. 39. eunuch went on his way *r.*
Rom. 12. 12. *r.* in hope, 5. 2. 3.
2 Cor. 1. 12. our *r.* is the testimony
Gal. 6. 4. he shall have *r.* in him.
Heb. 3. 6. *r.* of hope, firm to the
R. V. 1 Sam. 2. 1; 1 Chron. 16. 32;
Ps. 9. 2; 60. 6; 68. 3. 4; 108. 7; Isa.
13. 3. exult; Ps. 20. 5; Prov. 28. 12.
triumph; Ps. 96. 12; 98. 4. sing for
joy; Ps. 96. 11; 107. 42; Prov. 23.
15; Zech. 10. 7: Acts 2. 26. be glad;
Prov. 31. 25. laugheth; Phil. 2. 16;
3. 3; Jas. 1. 9; 2. 13; 4. 16. glory;
Job 8. 21. shouting; Ps. 107. 22.
singing; 126. 6. joy; 1 Cor. 15. 31;
2 Cor. 1. 12, 14; Gal. 6. 4; Phil. 1.
26; 1 Thes. 2. 19; Heb. 3. 6; Jas. 4.
16. glorying

RELEASE, year of, Ex. 21. 2.
Deut. 15. 1. & 31. 10. Jer. 34. 14.
RELIEVE. Lev. 25. 35. Isa. 1. 17.
Ps. 146. 9. Acts 11. 29. 1 Tim. 5. 16.
R. V. Lev. 25. 35: Ps. 146. 9. uphold;
Lam. 1. 11, 16, 19. refresh
RELIGION, Acts 26. 5. Gal. 1. 13,
14. Jas. 1. 26, 27.
Acts 13. 43. *religious,* Jas. 1. 26.
REMAINDER, 1 Thes. 4. 13. Rev.
3. 2. Eccl. 2. 9. Lam. 5. 19. John 1.
33.
John 9. 41. your sin *remaineth*
2 Cor. 9. 9. righteousness *r.* for
Heb. 4. 9. *r.* a rest for people of God
10. 26. there *r.* no more sacrifice
1 John 3. 9. his seed *r.* in him
Ps. 76. 10. *remainder* of wrath
R. V. Several changes, chiefly to
abide, or to a sense of settling,
rest ; Lev. 6. 16. is left ; Ps. 76. 10.
residue
REMEDY, 2 Chron. 36. 16. Prov. 6.
15. &. 29. 1.

REMEMBER, Gen. 40. 23. Neh. 1.
8.
Gen. 9. 16. look upon it that I may *r.*
Ex. 13. 3. *r.* this day ye came out
Deut. 5. 15. *r.* thou wast a servant
8. 8. thou shalt *r.* Lord thy God
9. 7. *r.* and forget not how
32. 7. *r.* days of old, consider
2 Kings 20. 3. *r.* how I walked
Ps. 20. 7. we will *r.* name of Lord
74. 2. *r.* thy congregation, 18.
79. 8. *r.* not against us former, Isa.
64. 9. Jer. 14. 10. Hos. 8. 13.
89. 47. *r.* how short my time is
132. 1. *r.* David and his afflictions
Eccl. 12. 1. *r.* thy Creator in days
S. of S. 1. 4. we will *r.* thy love
Isa. 43. 25. I will not *r.* thy sins
46. 8. *r.* this, show yourselves
Jer. 31. 20. I do earnestly *r.* him
Ezek. 16. 61. shall *r.* thy ways
63. mayest *r.* and be confounded
36. 31. shall *r.* your own evil
Mic. 6. 5. *r.* what Balak consulted
Hab. 3. 2. in wrath *r.* mercy
Luke 1. 72. to *r.* his holy covenant
17. 32. *r.* Lot's wife, Gen. 19. 26.
Gal. 2. 10. that we should *r.* the
Col. 4. 18. *r.* my bonds
Heb. 8. 12. iniquity I will *r.* no
13. 3. *r.* them that are in bonds
Neh. 13. 14. *r.* me, 22. 31. Ps. 25. 7.
& 106. 4. Luke 23. 43.
Ps. 63. 6. *I remember,* 143. 5.
Jer. 2. 2. for—kindness of thy
Lev. 26. 43. *I will remember* my
covenant, 45. Ezek. 16. 60.
Ps. 79. 11—the works of the Lord
Jer. 31. 34.—their sin no more
Gen. 8. 1. God *remembered* Noah
30. 22. God *r.* Rachel, 1 Sam. 1. 19.
Ex. 2. 24. God *r.* his covenant
Num. 10. 9. shall be *r.* before Lord
Ps. 77. 3. I *r.* God and was troubled
78. 39. he *r.* they were but flesh
98. 3. hath *r.* his mercy and truth
119. 52. I *r.* thy judgments of old
136. 23. who *r.* us in our low estate
137. 1. we wept when we *r.* Zion
Matt. 26. 35. Peter *r.* words of
Luke 24. 8. they *r.* his words, and
John 2. 17. his disciples *r.* that it
Rev. 18. 5. God hath *r.* her iniqui.
Ps. 103. 14. he *r.* we are but dust
Lam. 1. 9. she *r.* not her last end
3. 19. *remembering,* 1 Thes. 1. 3.
1 Kings 17. 18. call my sin to *re-
membrance*
Ps. 6. 5. in death there is no *r.* of
Isa. 26. 8. *r.* of thee
Lam. 3. 20. my soul hath them in *r.*
Mal. 3. 16. in a book of *r.* was
Luke 1. 54. he hath holpen Israel
in *r.* of his mercy
22. 19. this do in *r.* of me
John 14. 26. bring all things to
your *r.*
Acts 10. 31. thy alms are had in *r.*
2 Tim. 1. 6. put in *r.,* 2. 14. 2 Pet. 1.
12. & 3. 1. Jude 5.
Rev. 16. 19. Babylon came in *r.*
R. V. Ps. 20. 7; 77. 11; S. of S. 1. 4;
Hos. 2. 17. mention; Job 32. 12.
memorable sayings; Isa. 57. 8.
memorial; 1 Tim. 4. 6. mind
REMIT sins, they shall, John 20. 23.
Matt. 26. 28. *remission of sins,* Mark
1. 4. Luke 1. 77. & 3. 3. & 24. 47.
Acts 2. 38. & 10. 43. Rom. 3. 25. Heb.
9. 22. & 10. 18.
REMNANT, Lev. 2. 3. Deut. 3. 11.
2 Kings 19. 4. lift up thy prayer
for *r.*
Ezra 9. 8. leave us a *r.* to escape
Isa. 1. 9. Lord left us a small *r.*
10. 21. a *r.* shall return, 22.
Jer. 15. 11. it shall be well with thy
r.
23. 3. I will gather *r.* of my flock
Ezek. 6. 8. yet will I leave a *r.*
Rom. 9. 27. a *r.* shall be saved, 11. 5.
R. V. Lev. 2. 3. which is left ; Ex.
2. 12. overhanging part; 2 Kings
25. 11 ; Jer. 39. 9 ; Ezek. 23. 25 ; Mic.

5. 3. residue; Lev. 14. 18; 1 Kings
12. 23; 1 Chron. 6. 70; Ezra 3. 8;
Matt. 22. 6; Rev. 11. 13; 12. 17; 19.
21. rest
REMOVE thy stroke from me, Ps.
39. 10.
Ps. 119. 22. *r.* from me reproach
29. *r.* from me the way of lying
Prov. 4. 27. *r.* thy foot from evil
30. 8. *r.* far from me vanity
Eccl. 11. 10. *r.* sorrow from thy
Matt. 17. 20. *r.* hence, and it shall *r.*
Luke 22. 42. if willing *r.* this cup
Rev. 2. 5. I will *r.* thy candlestick
Ps. 103. 12. so far he *removed* our
Prov. 10. 30. the righteous shall
never be *r.*
Isa. 30. 20. teachers not be *r.*
Ezek. 36. 17. as uncleanness of a *r.*
woman
Gal. 1. 6. so soon *r.* for him that
R. V. Gen. 13. 18; Ps. 104. 5; 125. 1;
Isa. 24. 20. moved; Ex. 20. 18.
trembled; Num. (in all places)
journeyed; 2 Sam. 20. 12; 2 Kings
17. 26; 1 Chron. 8. 6, 7; Isa. 38. 12.
carried; 1 Kings 15. 14; 2 Kings
15. 4, 35. taken away; Job 19. 10;
Isa. 33. 20. plucked up; Isa. 10. 31.
fugitive; Lam. 1. 8; Ezek. 7. 19.
unclean; Deut. 28. 25; Jer. 15. 4;
24. 9; 29. 18; 34. 17; Ezek. 23. 46.
tossed to and fro; Matt. 21. 21;
Mark 11. 23. taken up; other
changes of minor moment
REND heav. and come, Isa. 64. 1.
Joel 2. 13. *r.* hearts and not gar.
Jer. 4. 30. though thou *rendest* face
R. V. Gen. 37. 33 ; Mark 9. 26. torn ;
Jer. 4. 30. enlargest
RENDER vengeance, Deut. 32.
41, 43.
2 Chron. 6. 30. *r.* to every man
Job 33. 26. he will *r.* to man his
34. 11. work of a man shall he *r.* to
Ps. 116. 12. what shall I *r.* to Lord
Prov. 26. 16. men that can *r.* a
Hos. 14. 2. *r.* the calves of our lips
Matt. 22. 21. *r.* to Cesar the things
Rom. 13. 7. *r.* to all their dues
1 Thes. 5. 15. that none *r.* evil, 3. 9.
2 Chron. 30. 25. Hezekiah *rendered*
R. V. Judg. 9. 56, 57. requite; Job
33. 26. restoreth
RENDING the clothes, Gen. 37.
34. 2 Sam. 13. 19. 2 Chron. 34. 27.
Ezra 9. 5. Job 1. 20. & 2. 12. Joel 2.
13; by the high priest, Matt. 26.
65. Mark 14. 63.
RENEW right spirit within me,
Ps. 51. 10.
Isa. 40. 31. wait on Lord shall *r.*
Heb. 6. 6. *r.* them again to repent.
Ps. 103. 5. thy youth is *renewed* like
2 Cor. 4. 16. inward man is *r.* day
Eph. 4. 23. be *r.* in spirit of mind
Col. 3. 10. *r.* in knowledge, image
Ps. 104. 30. *renewest* face of earth
Rom. 12. 2. *renewing,* Tit. 3. 5.
RENOUNCED hidden things of,
1 Cor. 4. 2.
RENOWN, Ezek. 34. 29. & 39. 13.
Isa. 14. 20. *renowned,* Ezek. 23. 23.
R. V. Num. 1. 16. called; Isa. 14.
20. named
REPAIRER of breach., Isa. 58. 12.
R. V. 2 Chron. 24. 27. rebuilding
REPAY, Job 21. 31. & 41. 11.
Deut. 7. 10. he will *r.* him to his
Isa. 59. 18. according to deeds he *r.*
Rom. 12. 19. vengeance is mine, I
will *r.*
Prov. 13. 21. to the righteous good
be *repaid*
R. V. Prov. 13. 21; Rom. 12. 19.
recompense
REPENT of this evil, Ex. 32. 12.
Num. 23. 19. not the son of man
that he should *r.*
Deut. 32. 36. Lord shall *r.* himself
1 Sam. 15. 29. not man that he
should *r.*
1 Kings 8. 47. *r.* and make suppli.
Job 42. 6. I abhor and *r.* in dust

Ps. 90. 13. let it *r*. thee concerning
135. 14. will *r*. himself concerning
Jer. 18. 8. I will *r*. of evil I
Ezek. 14. 6. *r*. and return, 18. 30.
Joel 2. 14. if he will *r*. and
Jonah 3. 9. can tell if God will turn and *r*.
Matt. 3. 2. *r*. for kingdom of
Mark 1. 15. *r*. and believe Gospel
6. 12. preached that men should *r*.
Luke 13. 3. except ye *r*. ye shall
17. 3. if he *r*. forgive him, 4.
Acts 2. 38. *r*. and be baptized
3. 19. *r*. and be converted, that
17. 30. commandeth all men to *r*.
26. 30. should *r*. and turn to God
Rev. 2. 5. rem. whence fall. and *r*.
16. *r*. or I will come unto thee
21. I gave her space to *r*. of her
3. 19. be zealous and *r*.
Gen. 6. 6. *repented* the Lord, Ex.
32. 14. Judg. 2. 18. 2 Sam. 24. 16.
Joel 2. 13.
Jer. 8. 6. no man *r*. of his wicked.
Matt. 21. 29. afterward *r*. and went
27. 3. Judas *r*. himself, and
Luke 15. 7. one sin. that *repenteth*
Jer. 15. 6. *repenting*, Hos. 11. 8.
Hos. 13. 14. *repentance* hid from
Matt. 3. 8. fruits meet for *r*.
11. baptize. you with water unto *r*.
9. 13. not righte. but sinners to *r*.
Mark 1. 4. baptism of *r*., Luke 3. 3.
Luke 15. 7. just persons need no *r*.
24. 47. that *r*. and remission be
Acts 5. 31. give *r*. to Israel and
11. 18. God to Gentiles granted *r*.
20. 21. testifying *r*. towards God
Rom. 2. 4. goodness of God leadeth thee to *r*.
2 Cor. 7. 19. sorrow worketh *r*.
Heb. 6. 1. not laying foundation of *r*.
12. 17. found no place of *r*.
2 Pet. 3. 9. all should come to *r*.
R. V. 1 Kings 8. 47. turn again;
Ezek. 14. 6; 18. 30. return ye; 2 Cor.
7. 8. regret; Matt. 9. 13; Mark 2.
17 —— ; *compassions*; Hos. 11. 8. my
c. are kindled together

REPETITIONS, vain, Matt. 6. 7.

REPLIEST against God, Rom. 9. 20.

REPORT, evil, Gen. 37. 2. Num.
13. 32. & 14. 37. Neh. 6. 13.
Ex. 23. 1. should not raise a false *r*.
Prov. 15. 30. good *r*. maketh bones
Isa. 53. 1. who hath believed our *r*.,
John 12. 38. Rom. 10. 16.
2 Cor. 6. 8. by evil *r*. and good *r*.
1 Tim. 3. 7. a good *r*. of them who
Heb. 11. 2. obtained a good *r*.
R. V. Isa. 28. 19. message; Jer. 50.
43. fame; Prov. 15. 30. good tidings; 1 Tim. 3. 7. testimony; Heb.
11. 2, 39; 3 John 12. witness; Neh.
6. 19. spake of; 1 Pet. 1. 12. announced; Matt. 28. 15. spread abroad

REPROACH, Josh. 5. 9. Neh. 1. 3.
Ps. 69. 7. Prov. 18. 3. Isa. 54. 4. Jer.
31. 19. Heb. 13. 13. Gen. 30. 23. Luke
1. 25.
Job 27. 6. my heart shall not *r*. me
Ps. 15. 3. up a *r*. against neighbor
20. *r*. hath broken my heart
Prov. 14. 34. sin is a *r*. to any peo.
Isa. 51. 7. fear ye not the *r*. of men
Zeph. 3. 18. to whom *r*. of it
Heb. 11. 26. esteeming the *r*. of Christ
Ps. 69. 9. *r*. of them that *reproached*
2 Cor. 12. 10. I take pleasure in *reproaches*
Prov. 14. 31. *reproacheth* his Maker
1 Pet. 4. 14. if *reproached* for name
R. V. Prov. 22. 10. ignominy; Job
20. 3. reproof; 2 Cor. 11. 21. disparagement; 12. 10. injuries; Isa.
43. 28. a reviling; Num. 15. 30. blasphemeth

REPROBATE, Jer. 6. 30. Rom. 1.
28. 1 Cor. 13. 5, 6, 7. 2 Tim. 3. 8.
Tit. 1. 16.
R. V. Jer. 6. 30. **refuse**

REPROOF, astonished at, Job 26. 11.
Prov. 1. 23. turn ye at my *r*. I will
10. 17. he that refuseth *r*. erreth
13. 18. he that regardeth *r*. shall be honored
15. 5. he that regardeth *r*. is
10. he that hateth *r*. shall die
31. heareth *r*. abideth among wise
17. 10. *r*. entereth more into a wise
29. 15. the rod and *r*. give wisdom
2 Tim. 3. 16. Scripture profitable for *r*.
Ps. 38. 14. *reproofs*, Prov. 6. 23.
Ps. 50. 21. I will *reprove* thee, and
Prov. 9. 8. *r*. not a scorner, lest he
Hos. 4. 4. let no man strive nor *r*.
John 16. 8. *r*. world of sin
Eph. 5. 11. works of dark. but *r*.
Ps. 105. 14. he *reproved* kings
Prov. 29. 1. he that being often *r*.
John 3. 20. deeds should be *r*.
Isa. 29. 21. snare from him that *reproveth* in the gate
Prov. 9. 7. that a *r*. a scorner, getteth
15. 12. loveth not one that *r*. him
25. 12. *reprover*, Ezek. 3. 26.
R. V. Job 26. 11; Prov. 17. 10. rebuke; 2 Kings 19. 4; Isa. 37. 4;
Jer. 29. 27. rebuke; John 16. 8. convict

REPUTATION, Eccl. 10. 1. Acts
5. 34. Gal. 2. 2. Phil. 2. 7, 29.
R. V. Eccl. 10. 1. outweigh; Acts 5.
34. honor of; Gal. 2. 2. repute;
Phil. 2. 7. emptied himself

REQUEST, Ps. 106. 15. Phil. 4. 6.
R. V. Phil. 1. 4. supplication

REQUIRE, Gen. 9. 5. & 42. 22.
Ezek. 3. 18, 20. & 33. 8.
Deut. 10. 12. what doth the Lord *r*.
18. 19. speak in my name, I will *r*.
1 Kings 8. 59. maintain as matter shall *r*.
Prov. 30. 7. two things I *required*
Isa. 1. 12. who *r*. this at your
Luke 12. 20. shall thy soul be *r*.
48. of him shall much be *r*.
1 Cor. 4. 2. it is *r*. of stewards to be
R. V. Neh. 5. 18. demanded; Ex.
12. 36; Prov. 30. 7; Luke 23. 23, 25.
ask; Ruth 3. 11. sayest, Eccl. 3.
15. seeketh again

REQUITE, Gen. 50. 15. 2 Sam. 16. 12.
Deut. 32. 6. do ye thus *r*. the Lord
1 Tim. 5. 4. learn to *r*. their parents
2 Chron. 6. 23. by *requiting* wicked
R. V. 1 Sam. 25. 21. returned; Ps.
10. 14. take

RERE-WARD, Isa. 52. 12. & 58. 8.

RESERVE, Jer. 50. 20. 2 Pet. 2. 9.
Jer. 3. 5. will he *r*. his anger for ever
Job 21. 30. wicked is *reserved* to
1 Pet. 1. 4. inheritance *r*. in heav.
Jude 6. *r*. in everlasting chains
Jer. 5. 24. he *reserveth* the appoin.
Nah. 1. 2. *r*. wrath for his enemies
R. V. Deut. 33. 21. seated; Judg.
21. 22. took; Ruth 2. 18; Rom. 11.
4. left; Acts 25. 21; Jude 6. kept

RESIDE, Zeph. 2. 9. Matt. 1. 15.

RESIST not evil, Matt. 5. 39.
Zech. 3. 1. Satan at his right hand to *r*. him
Acts 7. 51. ye do always *r*. the Holy
2 Tim. 3. 8. so do these *r*. the truth
Jas. 4. 7. *r*. the devil and he
5. 6. *r*. you; 9. *r*. stedfast in
Rom. 9. 19. who *r*. his will
Heb. 12. 4. have not yet *r*. to blood
Rom. 13. 2. that *resisteth* shall
Jas. 4. 6. God *r*. proud, 1 Pet. 5. 5.
R. V. Luke 21. 15; Acts 6. 10; Rom.
9. 19; 13. 2; 2 Tim. 3. 8; 1 Pet. 5. 9.
withstand; Zech. 3. 11. be adversary

RESPECT to Abel, Lord had,
Gen. 4. 4. Ex. 2. 25. Lev. 26. 9.
2 Kings 13. 23.
Deut. 1. 17. ye shall not *r*. persons

2 Chron. 19. 7. nor *r*. of persons,
Rom. 2. 11. Eph. 6. 9. Col. 3. 25.
Acts 10. 34. Job 37. 24. 1 Pet. 1. 17.
Ps. 40. 4. *r*. not the proud
119. 6. *r*. to all thy commandments
138. 6. *r*. the lowly
Prov. 24. 23. not good to have *r*. of persons, 28. 21. Lev. 19. 15. Jas. 2. 1, 3, 9.
Heb. 11. 26. he had *r*. to recom.
R. V. Ex. 2. 25. took knowledge;
Heb. 11. 26. looked; Jas. 2. 3. regard; Job 37. 24. regardeth

REST, Ex. 16. 23. & 33. 14. Deut. 12. 9.
Ps. 95. 11. not enter into my *r*.
116. 7. return to thy *r*. O my soul
132. 14. this is my *r*. here I will
Isa. 11. 10. his *r*. shall be glorious
28. 12. this is the *r*. and refreshing
62. 7. him no *r*. till he establish
Jer. 6. 16. shall find *r*. for your
Mic. 2. 10. this is not your *r*. it is
Matt. 11. 28, 29. I will give *r*. to
Acts 9. 31. had the churches *r*.
2 Thes. 1. 7. who are troubled *r*.
Heb. 4. 9. *r*. for the people of God
10. enter into his *r*.
11. enter into that *r*. lest any
Rev. 14. 11. they have no *r*. day nor
Ps. 16. 9. my flesh shall *r*. in hope
37. 7. *r*. in the Lord and wait
Isa. 57. 2. in peace *r*. on their beds
20. wicked are like the troubled sea when it cannot *r*.
Hab. 3. 16. I might *r*. in the
Zeph. 3. 17. he will *r*. in his love
Rev. 14. 13. dead in the Lord, *r*.
Rom. 2. 17. art a Jew, and *restest*
Prov. 14. 33. wisdom *resteth*
Eccl. 7. 9. anger *r*. in bosom
1 Pet. 4. 14. Spirit of God *r*. upon
Num. 10. 33. *resting place,* 2 Chron.
6. 41. Prov. 24. 15. Isa. 32. 18. Jer.
56. 6.
R. V. Several changes, but none of moment

RESTORE, Ps. 51. 12. & 23. 3. & 69.
4. Isa. 58. 12. Luke 19. 8. Gal. 6. 1.
Ex. 22. 3. *restitution,* Acts 3. 21.
R. V. Job 20. 18. hath gotten; Acts
3. 21. restoration; Ex. 22. 1. pay;
Lev. 24. 21. make good; 25. 28. get
it back; 2 Chron. 8. 2. given

RESTRAIN, 1 Sam. 3. 13. Job 15.
4. Ps. 76. 10. Isa. 63. 15.
R. V. Gen. 11. 6. withholden

RESURRECTION, Matt. 22. 23,
28, 30. Acts 23. 8. 1 Cor. 15. 12.
Heb. 6. 2.
Luke 20. 36. children of God being children of the *r*.
John 5. 29. done good to *r*. of life
11. 25. I am the *r*. and the life
Acts 17. 18. preached Jesus and *r*.
Rom. 6. 5. in likeness of his *r*.
Phil. 3. 10. power of *r*.
11. attain unto the *r*. of the dead
1 Tim. 2. 18. erred, say. that *r*. is
Heb. 11. 35 might obtain better *r*.
Rev. 20. 5. this is the first *r*., 6.

RETAIN, Job 2. 9. John 20. 23,
Prov. 3. 18. & 11. 16. Eccl. 8. 8.
Rom. 1. 28.
Mic. 7. 18. *retaineth* not his anger
R. V. Job 2. 9. hold fast; Rom. 1
28. have; Phile. 13. fain have kept

RETURN to the ground, Gen. 3
19. *r*. to dust
1 Kings 8. 48. *r*. to thee with all
Job 1. 21. naked shall I *r*. thither
Ps. 73. 10. his people *r*. hither
116. 7. *r*. unto thy rest, O my soul
Eccl. 12. 7. dust shall *r*. to the
S. of S. 6. 13. *r*. *r*. O Shulamite
Isa. 10. 21. remnant shall *r*. to
35. 10. the ransomed of the Lord shall *r*., 51. 11.
55. 11. my word shall not *r*. void
Jer. 3. 12. *r*. backsliding Israel
4. 1. if thou wilt *r*. unto me
Hos. 2. 7. *r*. to my first husband
5. 15. I will go and *r*. to my place
7. 16. they *r*. but not to Most High
11. 9. not *r*. to destroy Ephraim

Mal. 3. 7. *r.* to me, and I will *r.* to
Ps. 35. 13. my prayer *returned*
78. 34. they *r.* and inquired early
Amos 4. 6. ye *r.* not to me, 8-11.
1 Pet. 2. 25. are *r.* unto Shepherd
Isa. 30. 15. in *returning* and rest
Jer. 5. 3. they refused to *return*
Deut. 30. 2. *return to the Lord,*
1 Sam. 7. 3. Isa. 55. 7. Hos. 6. 1. &
3. 5. & 7. 10. & 14. 1, 7.

R.   V.   Several unimportant
changes, chiefly to sense of
turned, came, or bring back
REVEAL, Prov. 11. 13. Dan. 2. 19.
Job 20. 27. heaven shall *r.* his ini.
Gal. 1. 16. pleased God to *r.* his
Phil. 3. 15. God shall *r.* even this
Deut. 29. 29. those things which
are *revealed*
Isa. 22. 14. it was *r.* in mine ears
53. 1. to whom is arm of Lord *r.*
Matt. 10. 26. covered that shall
not be *r.*
11. 25. hid from wise, and *r.*
16. 17. flesh and blood hath not *r.*
Rom. 1. 17. righteous. of God *r.*
1 Cor. 2. 10. God hath *r.* them to
us
2 Thes. 1. 7. when the Lord Jesus
shall be *r.*
2. 3. fall. away, man of sin be *r.*
Prov. 20. 19. a tale-bearer *revealeth*
Amos 3. 7. *r.* his secret to servants
Rom. 2. 5. *revelation,* 16. 25. Gal.
1. 12. Eph. 1. 17. & 3. 3. 1 Pet. 1. 13.
2 Cor. 12. 1. Rev. 1. 1.
R. V. 1 Cor. 14. 30; 2 Thes. 1. 7;
1 Pet. 4. 13. revelation
REVELLINGS, Gal. 5. 21. 1 Pet.
4. 3.
REVENGE, Jer. 15. 15. 2 Cor. 7.
11. & 10. 6. Nah. 1. 2.
Ps. 79. 10. by *revenging* blood
Num. 35. 19. *revenger,* Rom. 13. 4.
R. V. Deut. 32. 42. leaders; 2 Cor.
7. 11. avenging; Jer. 15. 15; 2 Cor.
10. 6. avenge
REVERENCE my sanctuary, Lev.
19. 30.
Ps. 89. 7. to be had in *r.* of all
Eph. 5. 33. see that she *r.* her
Heb. 12. 28. serve God acceptably
with *r.*
Ps. 111. 9. and *reverend* is his name
R. V. 2 Sam. 9. 6; 1 Kings 1. 31.
obeisance; Ps.89.7.feared above;
Eph. 5. 33. fear
REVILE, Ex. 22. 28. Matt. 5. 11.
1 Cor. 4. 12. being *reviled* we bless
1 Pet. 2. 23. when he was *r. r.* not
1 Cor. 6. 10. nor *revilers* inherit
Isa. 51. 7. *revilings,* Zeph. 2. 8.
R. V. Matt. 27. 39. railed on; Mark
15. 32. reproached
REVIVE us again, Ps. 85. 6.
Isa. 57. 15. to *r.* the spirit of the
Hos. 6. 2. after two days will *r.* us
14. 7. they shall *r.* as the corn
Hab. 3. 2. *r.* thy work in midst of
Rom. 7. 9. sin *revived* and I died
14. 9. Christ died, and rose, and *r.*
Ezra 9. 8. give us a little *reviving*
R. V. Ps. 85. 6. quicken; Rom. 14.
9. lived again
REVOLT more and more, Isa. 1.
5.
Isa. 31. 6. children of Israel have
deeply *revolted*
Jer. 5. 23. this people hath a *revolting* heart
6. 28. *revolters,* Hos. 5. 2. & 9. 5.
REWARD, exceeding great, Gen.
15. 1.
Deut. 10. 17. God taketh not *r.*
Ps. 19. 11. keeping them is great *r.*
58. 11. there is a *r.* for righteous
Prov. 11. 18. that soweth right-
eousness sure *r.*
Isa. 3. 11. the *r.* of his hands
5. 23. who justify wicked for a *r.*
Mic. 7. 3. the judge asketh for a *r.*
Matt. 5. 12. great is your *r.* in
6. 2. verily they have their *r.*
10. 41. shall receive a prophet's *r.*

Rom. 4. 4. *r.* is not reckoned of
1 Cor. 3. 8. shall receive his own *r.*
Col. 2. 18. man beguile you of *r.*
1 Tim. 5. 18. labor. is worthy of *r.*
Heb. 2. 2. just recompense of *r.*
2 John 8. we may receive a full *r.*
Matt. 6. 4. Father shall *r.* openly
2 Tim. 4. 14. Lord *r.* him accord.
Rev. 22. 12. I come and my *r.* is
with
18. 6. *r.* her as she *rewarded* you
Ps. 103. 10. nor *r.* us according
Isa. 3. 9. *r.* evil unto themselves
Ps. 31. 23. plentifully *rewardeth*
Heb. 11. 6. *rewarder* of them that
R. V. Job 6. 22; Prov. 21. 14; Jer.
40. 5. present; Job 7. 2. wages; Ps.
40. 15; 70. 3. by reason; 94. 2. desert; Ezek. 16. 34; Hos. 2. 12;
9. 1; 1 Tim. 5. 18; 2 Pet. 2. 13;
Jude 11. hire; Obad. 15. dealing;
Col. 2. 18. prize by; 3. 24. recompense; 1 Sam. 24. 17; Matt. 16. 27;
2 Tim. 4. 14; Rev. 18. 6. render;
Deut. 32. 41; Matt. 6. 4, 6, 18. recompense; Ps. 54. 5. requite
RICH, Gen. 13. 2. & 14. 23. Ex. 30.15.
Prov. 10. 4. hand of diligent maketh *r.*
22. bless. of the Lord maketh *r.*
13. 7. maketh himself *r.* yet
14. 20. *r.* man hath many friends
18. 11. *r.* man's wealth is
23. the *r.* answereth roughly
22. 2. *r.* and poor meet together
23. 4. labor not to be *r.*
28. 11. *r.* man is wise in his
Eccl. 5. 12. abundance of the *r.*
10. 20. curse not the *r.* in thy
Jer. 9. 23. let not *r.* man glory in
Matt. 19. 23. *r.* man hardly enter
Luke 1. 53. *r.* he sent empty away
6. 24. woe unto you that are *r.*
12. 21. layeth up, and is not *r.*
16. 1. certain *r.* man which had
18. 23. sorrow. for he was very *r.*
2 Cor. 6. 10. yet making many *r.*
8. 9. Jesus, though he was *r.*
Eph. 2. 4. God who is *r.* in mercy
1 Tim. 6. 9. they that will be *r.*
18. they that be *r.* in good works
Jas. 2. 5. poor of this world, *r.*
Rev. 2. 9. I know thy poverty, but
thou art *r.*
3. 17. sayest, I am *r.*
18. mayest be *r.*
1 Chron. 29. 12. *riches* and honor
Ps. 39. 6. he heapeth up *r.* and
52. 7. trust. in abundance of his *r.*
62. 10. if *r.* increase, set not
104. 24. the earth is full of thy *r.*
112. 3. wealth and *r.* shall be
119. 14. rejoic. as much as in all *r.*
Prov. 3. 16. in her left hand *r.*
11. 4. *r.* profit not in day of
13. 8. ransom of man's life are
his *r.*
23. 5. *r.* make themselves wings
27. 24. *r.* are not for ever, nor the
30. 8. give me neither pover. nor *r.*
Jer. 17. 11. so he that getteth *r.*
Matt. 13. 22. deceitfulness of *r.*
Luke 16. 11. your trust the true *r.*
Rom. 2. 4. despisest thou *r.* of his
9. 23. known the *r.* of his glory
2 Cor. 8. 2. abounded unto *r.* of
Eph. 1. 7. according to the *r.* of
2. 7. show exceeding *r.* of grace
Phil. 4. 19. according to his *r.* in
Col. 2. 2. unto all *r.* of the full
1 Tim. 6. 17. trust in uncertain *r.*
Heb. 11. 26. the reproach of Christ
greater *r.*
Jas. 5. 2. your *r.* are corrupted
Col. 3. 16. word of God dwell *richly*
1 Tim. 6. 17. giveth us *r.* all things
R. V. Gen. 36. 7; Dan. 11. 13, 24, 28.
substance; Josh. 22. 8; Isa. 61. 6.
wealth; Ps. 37. 16; Jer. 48. 36.
abundance; Prov. 22. 16. gain
RIDE, Ps. 45. 4. & 66. 12. Hab. 3. 8.
Deut. 33. 26. *rideth,* Ps. 68. 4, 33. Isa.
19. 1.
RIGHT, Num. 27. 7. Deut. 21. 17.

Gen. 18. 25. shall not the Judge of
the earth do *r.*
Ezra 8. 21. seek of him a *r.* way for
Job 34. 23. lay on man more than *r.*
Ps. 19. 8. statu. of the Lord are *r.*
51. 10. renew a *r.* spirit within
119. 128. I esteem all thy precepts
to be *r.*
Prov. 4. 11. I have led thee in *r.*
paths
8. 9. all *r.* to them that find
12. 5. thoughts of righteous are *r.*
14. 12. a way which seemeth *r.* to
21. 2. way of man is *r.* in own
Isa. 30. 10. prophesy not unto us *r.*
15. 10. be just and do lawful
and *r.*
Hos. 14. 9. ways of the Lord are *r.*
Amos 3. 10. know not to do *r.*
Mark 5. 15. and in his *r.* mind
Luke 12. 57. jud. ye not what is *r.*
Acts 4. 19. whether it be *r.* in sight
8. 21. thy heart is not *r.* in sight
13. 10. not cease to pervert *r.*
ways
Eph. 6. 1. children obey your
parents; this is *r.*
2 Pet. 2. 15. forsaken the *r.* way
Rev. 22. 14. have *r.* to tree
2 Tim. 2. 15. *rightly* dividing word
Gen. 7. 1. seen thee *righteous* be.
18. 23. wilt thou destroy *r.*
Num. 23. 10. let me die death of *r.*
Deut. 25. 1. justify *r.* and condemn
1 Kings 8. 32. justifying the *r.* to
Job 4. 7. where were the *r.* cut off
17. 9. the *r.* shall hold on his way
Ps. 1. 6. Lord knoweth way of *r.*
5. 12. wilt bless the *r.* with favor
7. 11. God judgeth the *r.*
11. 5. Lord trieth *r.* but wicked
32. 11. rejoice in the Lord ye *r.*
34. 17. *r.* cry, and Lord heareth
37. 17. the Lord upholdeth the *r.*
25. I have not seen the *r.* forsaken
29. the *r.* shall inherit the land
55. 22. shall never suffer the *r.*
58. 11. there is a reward for the *r.*
64. 10. *r.* shall be glad in the Lord
68. 3. let the *r.* be glad and rejoice
92. 12. the *r.* shall flourish like
97. 11. light is sown for the *r.*
112. 6. the *r.* shall be in everlast.
141. 5. let *r.* smite me; it shall be
Ps. 145. 17. Lord is *r.,* Lam. 1. 18.
Dan. 9. 14.
146. 8. the Lord loveth the *r.*
Prov. 3. 22. his secret is with the *r.*
10. 3. will not suffer the soul of *r.*
16. labor of the *r.* tendeth to life
21. the lips of the *r.* feed many
24. desire of the *r.* shall be grant.
25. *r.* is an everlasting foundation
28. the hope of *r.* shall be glad.
30. the *r.* shall never be removed
32. the lips of the *r.* know what
11. 8. *r.* is delivered out of
21. seed of *r.* shall be delivered
28. the *r.* shall flourish as a
30. fruit of the *r.* is a tree of life
12. 3. root of *r.* shall not be
5. the thoughts of the *r.* are *r.*
7. the house of the *r.* shall
12. root of *r.* man regardeth life of
12. root of *r.* yieldeth fruit
13. 9. the light of the *r.* rejoiceth
25. *r.* eateth to satisfying of soul
14. 32. *r.* hath hope in his death
15. 6. in house of *r.* is much
29. Lord heareth the prayer of *r.*
18. 10. *r.* runneth into it and is
28. 1. the *r.* are bold as a lion
Eccl. 7. 16. be not *r.* overmuch, nor
Isa. 3. 10. say to *r.* it shall be well
41. 2. raised up *r.* man from east
74. the perisheth and are
60. 21. thy people also shall be *r.*
Ezek. 3. 20. when a *r.* man turneth
Mal. 3. 18. discern between *r.* and
Matt. 9. 13. not come to call *r.* but
10. 41. shall receive *r.* man's rew.
25. 46. *r.* shall go into life eternal
Luke 1. 6. were both *r.* before God
18. 9. trusted that they were *r.*

Rom. 3. 10. there is none *r.* no not
5. 7. scarcely for a *r.* man will one
19. by the ob. of one many made *r.*
2 Thes. 1. 5. a manifest token of *r.*
   judgment
1 Tim. 1. 9. law is not made for a *r.*
Jas. 5. 16. fervent prayer of *r.* man
1 Pet. 4. 18. the *r.* scarcely be saved
1 John 3. 7. he that doeth righteousness is *r.* even as he is *r.*
Rev. 22. 11. he that is *r.* let him be *r.*
Tit. 2. 12. live soberly, *righteously*
Deut. 6. 25. it shall be our *right-*
   eousness
33. 19. offer sacrifice of *r.*
Job 29. 14. I put on *r.* and it cloth.
36. 3. I will ascribe *r.* to my Maker
   's.,11. 7. righteous Lord loveth *r.*
15. 2. walk upright. and work. *r.*
97. 2. *r.* and judgment are habita.
106. 3. he that doeth *r.* at all
Prov. 10. 2. *r.* delivereth from
11. 5. *r.* of perfect shall direct way
6. *r.* of upright shall deliver them
18. to him that soweth *r.* a sure
19. *r.* tendeth to life; so evil to
12. 28. in the way of *r.* is life
13. 6. *r.* keepeth the upright in
14. 34. *r.* exalteth a nation, but sin
15. 9. he loveth him that followeth after *r.*
16. 8. better is a little with *r.* than
12. his throne is established by *r.*
Isa. 11. 5. *r.* shall be girdle of his
26. 9. inhabitants of the world will
   learn *r.*
28. 17. judgment to line and *r.* to
32. 17. work of *r.* shall be peace
45. 24. in the Lord have I *r.* and
46. 12. far from *r.*
13. I bring near my *r.*
54. 17. their *r.* is of me, saitn Lord
61. 3. trees of *r.* planting of Lord
10. covered me with robes of *r.*
62. 1. till the *r.* thereof go forth
64. 5. that rejoiceth and work. *r.*
Jer. 23. 6. be called Lord our *r.*
Dan. 4. 27. break off thy sins by *r.*
9. 7. O Lord *r.* belongeth unto thee
12. 3. that turn many to *r.* shine
Zeph. 2. 3. seek *r.* seek meekness
Mal. 4. 2. Sun of *r.* arise with
Matt. 3. 15. it becom. to fulfil all *r.*
5. 6. hunger and thirst after *r.*
20. except your *r.* exceed the *r.* of
21. 32. John came in the way of *r.*
Luke 1. 75. in holiness and *r.* before
John 16. 8. reprove world of sin, *r.*
Acts 10. 35. he that worketh *r.* is
13. 10. thou enemy of all *r.*
24. 25. as he reasoned of *r.*
Rom. 1. 17. therein is the *r.* of God
3. 22. even *r.* of God by faith
4. 6. man to whom God imput. *r.*
11. a seal of the *r.* of faith
5. 18. by *r.* of one free gift came
21. grace reign through *r.* unto
6. 13. membe. as instruments of *r.*
18. servants of *r.* to holiness, 19.
8. 4. that the *r.* of the law might
9. 30. Gentiles who followed not
   after *r.* have attained to *r.* even
   r. of faith, 31.
10. 3. ignorant of *r.* of God, establish their own *r.* have not submitted to *r.* of God
5. *r.* of law
6. *r.* which is of faith
9, 10. with the heart man beli. to *r.*
14. 17. kingdom of God is *r.* peace
1 Cor. 1. 30. made unto us wisdom
   and *r.*
15. 34. awake to *r.* and sin not
2 Cor. 5. 21. the *r.* of God in him
6. 7. armor of *r.*
14. what fellowship hath *r.*
9. 10. increase the fruits of your *r.*
11. 15. ministers as ministers of *r.*
Gal. 2. 21. if *r.* come by the law
Eph. 6. 14. having on the breastplate of *r.*
Phil. 1. 11. being filled with fruits
   of *r.*
3. 6. touching *r.* of law blameless

1 Tim. 6. 11. follow *r.*, 2 Tim. 2. 22.
Tit. 3. 5. not by works of *r.* we
Heb. 12. 11. peaceable fruits of *r.*
Jas. 1. 20. man worketh not the *r.*
   of God
3. 18. fruit of *r.* is sown in peace
1 Pet. 3. 14. if ye suffer for *r.* happy
2 Pet. 1. 1. through the *r.* of God
2. 5. Noah a preacher of *r.*
3. 13. wherein dwelleth *r.*
1 John 2. 29. that doeth *r.* is born
3. 7. he that doeth *r.* is righteous
Rev. 19. 8. fine linen is the *r.* of
   saints
Gen. 15. 6. counted to him for
   righteousness, Ps. 106. 31. Rom. 4.
   3, 5, 9, 22. Gal. 3. 6.
1 Kings 8. 32. *his righteousness*, Job
   33. 26. Ps. 50. 6. Ezek. 3. 20. Matt.
   6. 33. Rom. 3. 25. 2 Cor. 9. 9.
Ps. 17. 15. *in righteousness*, Hos. 10.
   12. Acts 17. 31. Ps. 96. 13. & 98. 9.
   Eph. 4. 24. Rev. 19. 11.
Deut. 9. 5. *thy righteousness*, Job
   35. 8. Ps. 35. 28. & 40. 10, & 51. 14. &
   89. 16. & 119. 142. Isa. 57. 12. & 58. 8.
   & 62. 2.
Isa. 64. 6. *all our righteousness*,
   Ezek. 33. 13. Dan. 9. 18.
R. V. Many changes, chiefly due
   to context. Many changes in Job,
   Ps., and Prov. to upright; Ps.
   67. 4; 96. 10. with equity; Rom.
   2. 26; 5. 4. ordinance; Rom. 9.
   28; 10. 3.
RIGOR, Ex. 1. 13. Lev. 25. 43, 53.
RIOT, Tit. 1. 6. 1 Pet. 4. 4.
2 Pet. 2. 13. *rioting*, Rom. 13. 13.
Prov. 23. 20. *riotous*, 28. 7. Luke 15.
   13.
R. V. Rom. 13. 13. revelling; 2 Pet.
   2. 13. revel; Prov. 23. 20; 28. 7.
   gluttonous
RIPE fruit, Ex. 22. 29. Num. 18. 13.
   Mic. 7. 1. Jer. 24. 2; *r.* figs, Hos. 9.
   10. Nah. 3. 12.
Gen. 40. 10. *ripe grapes*, Num. 13. 20.
Joel 3. 13. harvest is *r.*, Rev. 14. 15.
RISE, S. of 2. 12. Isa. 14. 21. & 24.
   20. & 26. 14. & 33. 10. & 43. 17. & 54.
   17. & 58. 10. 1 Thes. 4. 16.
Prov. 30. 31. *rising*, Luke 2. 34.
R. V. Many changes to arise; oth.
   frequent but suiting context
RIVER, Ex. 1. 22. & 4. 9. Job 40. 23.
   Ps. 36. 8. & 46. 4. & 65. 9. Isa. 48. 18.
   & 66. 12. Rev. 22. 1, 2.
Job 20. 17. *rivers*, 29. 9. Ps. 119. 136.
   Prov. 5. 16; & 21. 1. Isa. 32. 2. & 33.
   21. Mic. 6. 7. John 7. 38.
R. V. Num. 34. 5; Deut. 10. 7; Josh.
   15. 4, 47; 16. 8; 17. 9; 19. 11; 1 Kings
   8. 65; 2 Kings 24. 7; 2 Chron. 7. 8;
   S. of 5. 12; Ezek. 47. 19; Amos
   6. 14; Joel 3. 18. brook or brooks;
   Ezek. 6. 3; 31. 12; 32. 6; 34. 13; 35.
   8; 36. 4, 6; Prov. 21. 1. water
   courses; Deut. 2. 24, 36; 3. 8, 12;
   4. 48; Josh. 12. 1, 2; 13. 9, 16; 2 Sam.
   24. 5; 2 Kings 10. 33. valley; Ex. 8.
   5; Ps. 1. 3. streams; Isa. 23. 3, 10;
   Zech. 10. 11. Nile; Job 28. 10;
   Ezek. 31. 4. channels
ROAR, Isa. 42. 13. Jer. 25. 30. Hos.
   11. 10. Joel 3. 16. Amos 1. 2.
R. V. Isa. 42. 13. shout aloud
ROB, Lev. 19. 13. Prov. 22. 22.
Mal. 3. 8. will a man *r.* God
Isa. 42. 22. a people *robbed* and
2 Cor. 11. 8. I *r.* other churches
Job 5. 5. the *robber* swalloweth up
John 10. 1. that climbeth up is a
   thief and a *r.*
Ps. 62. 10. *robbery*, Prov. 21. 7. Isa.
   61. 8. Amos 3. 10. Phil. 2. 6.
R. V. Ps. 119. 61. wrapped me
   round; Job 5. 5; 18. 9. snare; Dan.
   11. 14. children of the violent;
   Prov. 21. 7. violence; Nah. 3. 1.
   rapine
ROBE, Isa. 61. 10. Rev. 7. 9, 13, 14.
R. V. Luke 23. 11. apparel; John
   19. 2. garment; Rev. 22. 14. do his
   commandments

ROCK, Ex. 17. 6. Num. 20. **8, 11.**
   Deut. 32. 4, 13, 15, 18, 30, 31.
Ps. 18. 2. Lord is my *r.* and, 92. **15.**
31. 3. thou art my *r.* and fortress
61. 2. lead me to the *r.* higher
62. 2. he only is my *r.* and, 6.
71. 3. thou art my *r.* and fortress
89. 26. my Father and *r.* of my
94. 22. God is the *r.* of my refuge
Matt. 7. 24. wise man built his
   house on a *r.*
16. 18. on this *r.* will I build
1 Cor. 10. 4. that *r.* was Christ
Rev. 6. 16. said to *rocks*, fall on us
R. V. Judg. 6. 26. stronghold; 1 Sam.
   14. 4. crag; Isa. 42. 11. Sela; Luke
   6. 48. well builded; Acts 27. 29.
   rocky ground
ROD, Ex. 4. 4, 20. Num. 17. 2, 8.
Ps. 23. 4. thy *r.* and staff comfort
125. 3. *r.* of wicked shall not rest
Prov. 13. 24. spareth *r.* hateth his
22. 15. *r.* of correction shall drive
29. 15. *r.* and reproof give wisdom
Isa. 10. 5. *r.* of my anger, staff of
Ezek. 20. 37. cause to pass under *r.*
Mic. 6. 9. hear the *r.*
Rev. 12. 5. rule with *r.* of iron, 19.
R. V. Ps. 125. 3. sceptre; Isa. 11. 1.
   shoot; Jer. 10. 16; 51. 19. tribe
ROOM, Prov. 18. 6. Luke 14. 22.
R. V. 2 Kings 15. 25; 1 Chron. 4. 41.
   stead; Ps. 31. 8; Luke 14. 9, 10; 20.
   46; 1 Cor. 14. 16. place; Matt. 23. 6;
   Mark 12. 39. chief place; Luke 14.
   7. 8. chief seat; Acts 1. 13. chamber
ROOT, Job 5. 3. & 31. 12. Ps. 52. 5.
   Deut. 29. 18. a *r.* that beareth gall
Job 19. 28. seeing *r.* of the matter
Prov. 12. 3. *r.* of the righteous
Isa. 11. 10. there shall be *r.*
Matt. 3. 10. axe is laid to *r.* of tree
   13. 6. because it had no *r.* it
Rom. 11. 16. if *r.* be holy, so are
1 Tim. 6. 10. love of money is *r.* of
Heb. 12. 15. lest *r.* of bitterness
Matt. 15. 13. plant Father hath not
   planted shall be *rooted* up
Eph. 3. 17. being *r.* and grounded
Col. 2. 7. *r.* and built up in him
ROSE, S. of S. 2. 1. Isa. 35. 1.
ROYAL diadem in hand of God,
   Isa. 62. 3.
Jas. 2. 8. if ye fulfil *r.* law
1 Pet. 2. 9. ye are a *r.* priesthood
RUBIES, price of wisdom is
   above, Job 28. 18. Prov. 3. 15. & 8.
   11. & 31. 10.
RUDDY, S. of S. 5. 10. Lam. 4. 7.
RUDIMENTS, Col. 2. 8, 20.
RULE, Esth. 9. 1. Prov. 17. 2.
Prov. 25. 28. no *r.* over own spirit
Gal. 6. 16. walk according to this *r.*
Phil. 3. 16. let us walk by same *r.*
Heb. 13. 7. which have *r.* over you
Col. 3. 15. let the peace of God *r.*
1 Tim. 3. 5. how to *r.* his own house
5. 17. let the elders that *r.*
Rev. 12. 5. man child was to *r.* all
2 Sam. 23. 3. *ruleth* over men
Ps. 103. 19. his kingdom *r.* over all
Prov. 16. 32. he that *r.* his spirit
Hos. 11. 12. Judah yet *r.* with God
Mic. 5. 2. is to be *ruler* in Israel
Matt. 25. 21. make thee *r.* over
Acts 23. 5. not speak evil of *r.*
Rom. 13. 3. *rulers* are not a terror
Eph. 6. 12. *r.* of darkness of world
R. V. 1 Kings 22. 31. command;
   Prov. 25. 26. restraint; Isa. 44. 13.
   line; 2 Cor. 10. 13, 15. province;
   Ezek. 22. 33. be king; Matt. 2. 6.
   be shepherd; Ruth 1. 1. judged;
   Gen. 43. 16. steward; Num. 13. 2;
   1 Sam. 25. 30; 2 Sam. 6. 21; 7. 8;
   1 Kings 1. 35; 1 Chron. 2. 12; 5. 2; 11.
   2; 17. 7; 28. 4; 2 Chron. 6. 5; 11. 22;
   29. 20; Ezra 10. 14; Neh. 11. 1; Esth.
   3. 12; 8. 9, 3. prince or princes;
   1 Kings 11. 28; Neh. 7. 2. charge;
   2 Kings 25. 22; Mark 13. 9; Luke
   21. 12. governor; 2 Chron. 26. 11.
   officer; 2 Sam. 8. 18; 20. 26. priest;
   Gen. 41. 43; Matt. 24. 45, 47; 25. 21.

23. set; Deut. 1. 13; Isa. 29. 10.
heads; 1 Chron. 26. 32. overseers;
Jer. 51. 23, 28, 57. deputies

RUN, Gen. 49. 22. Lev. 15. 3. 1 Sam.
8. 11. Ps. 19. 5. Eccl. 1. 7. Heb. 6. 20.
2 Chron. 16. 9. eyes of the Lord *r*.
Ps. 119. 32. I will *r*. in way
S. of S. 1. 4. draw me, we will *r*.
Isa. 40. 31. shall *r*. and not be
Dan. 12. 4. many shall *r*. to and
1 Cor. 9. 24. *r*. so that we may
Gal. 2. 2. *r*. in vain
5. 7. did *r*. well
Heb. 12. 1. *r*. with patience the
race
1 Pet. 4. 4. *r*. not to same excess of
Ps. 23. 5. my cup *runneth* over
Prov. 18. 10. righteous *r*. into it
Rom. 9. 16. it is not of him that *r*.
R. V. Judg. 18. 25. fall; 1 Sam. 17.
17. carry quickly; Amos 5. 24.
roll; Joel 2. 9. leap upon; Matt.
9. 17. is spilled

S

SABBATH holy, Ex. 16. 23, 29. &
20. 8–11. & 31. 14. Acts 13. 42. & 18.
4.
Lev. 23. 3. seventh day is *s*. of rest
Neh. 9. 14. madest known thy *s*.
13. 18. bring wrath by profan. *s*.
Isa. 56. 2. keepeth *s*. from pollut.
58. 13. call *s*. a delight, holy
Matt. 12. 5. priests profane *s*. and
28. 1. end of *s*. as it began to
dawn
Lev. 19. 3. *my sabbaths*, 30. & 26. 2.
Isa. 56. 4. Ezek. 20. 12, 13. & 22. 8,
26. & 23. 38. & 44. 24. & 46. 3.
Deut. 5. 12. *sabbath day*, Neh. 13.
22. Jer. 17. 21. Acts 15. 21. Col. 2.
16.
R. V. Lev. 23. 24, 39. solemn rest;
Lam. 1. 7. desolations

SACKCLOTH, Gen. 37. 34. Job 16.
15. Ps. 30. 11. & 35. 13. Isa. 22. 12.
Rev. 11. 3.

SACRIFICE, Gen. 31. 54. Ex. 8.
25.
1 Sam. 2. 29. wherefore kick ye at
my *s*.
3. 14. Eli's house not purg. with *s*.
15. 22. to obey is better than *s*.
Ps. 4. 5. offer *s*. of righteousness
40. 6. *s*. and offering thou
51. 16. desirest not *s*. else I would
17. *s*. of God are a broken spirit
107. 22. *s*. the *s*. of thanksgiving
141. 2. lifting up hands as even. *s*.
Prov. 15. 8. *s*. of wicked is abomination
21. 3. to do justice more acceptable than *s*.
Eccl. 5. 1. than to give *s*. of fools
Dan. 8. 11. daily *s*. was taken
away
9. 27. cause *s*. and oblation to
cease
11. 31. take away daily *s*., 12. 11.
Hos. 6. 6. mercy and not *s*.
Mark 9. 49. every *s*. be salted
Rom. 12. 1. present bodies a liv. *s*.
1 Cor. 5. 7. Christ our passover is *s*.
Eph. 5. 2. *s*. to God for a sweet
Phil. 2. 17. offered on *s*. of your
4. 18. a *s*. acceptable to God
Heb. 9. 26. put away sin by *s*. of
13. 15. *s*. of praise
1 Pet. 2. 5. priesthood to offer spiritual *s*.
R. V. In O. T. frequent changes
to offering, oblation

SACRILEGE, commit, Rom. 2.
22.

SAD, 1 Sam. 1. 18. Ezek. 13. 22.
Mark 10. 22.
Eccl. 7. 3. by *sadness* the heart is
R. V. Ezek. 13. 22. grieved; Mark
10. 22. countenance fell

SAFE, Ps. 119. 117. Prov. 18. 10. &
29. 25.

Job 5. 4. *safety*, 11. Ps. 4. 8. & 12. 5.
& 33. 17. Prov. 11. 14. & 21. 31.
R. V. Ezek. 34. 27. secure; 2 Sam.
18. 29, 32. well with; Job 3. 26.
ease; 24. 23. security; Prov. 21.
31. victory

SAINTS, Ps. 52. 9. & 79. 2. & 89. 5.
Deut. 33. 2. came with ten thousands of *s*., Jude 14.
Deut. 33. 3. all his *s*. are in thy
1 Sam. 2. 9. keep feet of his *s*.
2 Chron. 6. 41. let thy *s*. rejoice
Job 15. 15. he putteth no trust
in *s*.
Ps. 16. 3. goodness extendeth to *s*.
37. 28. Lord forsaketh not his *s*.
50. 5. gather my *s*. together
97. 10. Lord preserveth souls of *s*.
106. 16. envied Aaron *s*. of Lord
116. 15. precious in the sight of
the Lord is death of *s*.
149. 9. this honor have all his *s*.
Prov. 2. 8. preserv. way of his *s*.
Hos. 11. 12. Judah is faith. with *s*.
Zech. 14. 5. shall come and all *s*.
Rom. 1. 7. called to be *s*., 1 Cor. 1.
2. 2 Cor. 1. 1. Eph. 1. 1. Col. 1. 2,
4, 12, 26.
Rom. 8. 27. intercession for *s*.
12. 13. necessity of *s*.
15. 25. minister to *s*., 26. 31. 1 Cor.
16. 1. 2 Cor. 8. 4. & 9. 1. Heb. 6. 10.
1 Cor. 6. 2. *s*. shall judge the world
Eph. 3. 8. less than the least of all
s.
4. 12. for perfecting the *s*. for
1 Thes. 3. 13. coming of Jesus with
all his *s*.
2 Thes. 1. 10. come to be glorified
in his *s*.
Rev. 5. 8. prayers of the *s*., 8. 3, 4.
11. 18. reward of *s*.
14. 11. patience of *s*.
15. 3. King of *s*.
16. 16. blood of *s*., 17. 6. & 18. 24.
19. 8. righteousness of *s*.
R. V. Deut. 33. 2; 1 Sam. 2. 9; Job
5. 11; 15. 15; Ps. 89. 5, 7; Dan. 8.
13; Hos. 11. 12; Zech. 14. 5; Jude
14. holy one, or ones; Rev. 15. 3.
ages

SALT, Gen. 19. 26. Lev. 2. 13. Matt.
5. 13. Mark 9. 49, 50. Col. 4. 6.
R. V. Mark 9. 49 —

SALVATION, Ps. 14. 7. & 53. 6.
Ex. 14. 13. stand still and see the *s*.
Ps. 3. 8. *s*. belongeth only to Lord
50. 23. I will show him the *s*. of
68. 20. God is the God of *s*., 65. 5.
85. 9. his *s*. is nigh them that
98. 2. made known his *s*.
119. 155. *s*. is far from the wicked
149. 4. Lord will beautify the
meek with *s*.
Isa. 25. 9. we will rejoice in his *s*.
26. 1. *s*. will God appoint for walls
33. 2. our *s*. also in the
46. 13. I will place *s*. in Zion for
52. 7. him that publisneth *s*.
59. 16. arm brought *s*. unto me
17. for a helmet of *s*., Eph. 6. 17.
Ps. 60. 18. call thy walls *s*. thy
62. 1. : . as a lamp
Jer. 3. 23. in vain is *s*. hoped for
Lam. 3. 26. quietly wait for *s*.
Jonah 2. 9. *s*. is of the Lord
Hab. 3. 8. ride on thy char. of *s*.
Zech. 9. 9. king cometh having *s*.
Luke 19. 9. *s*. is come to thy house
John 4. 22. *s*. is of the Jews
Acts 4. 12. neither is there *s*. in
13. 26. word of *s*. sent
Rom. 1. 16. Gospel is the power of
God to *s*.
11. 11. through their fall *s*. is
come
2 Cor. 1. 6. for your *s*.
Eph. 1. 13. the Gospel of your *s*.
Phil. 2. 12. work out your own *s*.
1 Thes. 5. 8. hope of *s*.
2 Thes. 2. 13. hath chosen you to *s*.
2 Tim. 2. 10. to obtain *s*. with eter.
3. 15. scriptures able to make
wise unto *s*.

Tit. 2. 11. grace of God bringeth *s*.
Heb. 1. 14. who shall be heirs of *s*.
2. 3. how escape if we neglect so
great *s*.
10. make Captain of our *s*. perfect
6. 9. things that accompany *s*.
9. 28. appear without sin unto *s*.
1 Pet. 1. 5. kept through faith to *s*.
Jude 3. write unto you of com. *s*.
Rev. 7. 10. *s*. to our God, 12. 10. &
19. 1.
Ex. 15. 2. God is become *my salvation*, Job 13. 16. Ps. 18. 2. & 25. 5. &
27. 1. & 38. 22. & 51. 14. & 62. 7. &
88. 1. & 118. 14. Isa. 12. 2. Mic. 7. 7.
Hab. 3. 18.
Ps. 89. 26. rock of —
140. 7. strength of —
2 Sam. 23. 5. thy covenant is all —
Isa. 46. 13. — shall not tarry, 49. 6.
& 51. 5, 6, 8. & 56. 1.
Gen. 49. 18. *thy salvation*, 1 Sam.
2. 1. Ps. 9. 14. & 13. 5. & 20. 5. & 18. 35.
& 21. 1, 5. & 35. 3. & 40. 10, 16. & 51.
12. & 69. 13, 29. & 70. 4. & 71. 15. &
85. 7. & 106. 4. & 119. 41, 81, 123, 166,
174. Isa. 17. 10. & 62. 11. Luke 2.
30.
R. V. 1 Sam. 11. 13; 2 Sam. 22. 51;
Ps. 68. 20. deliverance; 1 Sam.
19. 5. victory; Jer. 3. 23. help;
2 Cor. 1. 6 —

SAME, Ps. 102. 27. Heb. 13. 8. Rom.
10. 2. 1 Cor. 12. 4, 5, 6. Eph. 4. 10.

SANCTIFY, Ex. 13. 2. & 19. 10.
Ex. 31. 13. I am Lord that doth *s*.
Lev. 20. 7. *s*. yourselves and be
holy
Num. 20. 12. believed me not, to *s*.
Isa. 8. 13. *s*. the Lord of hosts
Ezek. 28. 23. I will *s*. myself
Joel 1. 14. *s*. a fast
John 17. 17. *s*. them through truth
19. for their sakes I *s*. myself
Eph. 5. 26. might *s*. and cleanse it
1 Thes. 5. 23. God of peace *s*. you
Heb. 13. 12. that he might *s*. peo-
ple
1 Pet. 3. 15. *s*. the Lord God in
Gen. 2. 3. blessed the seventh day
and *sanctified* it
Lev. 10. 3. I will be *s*. in them
Deut. 32. 51. ye *s*. me not in midst
Job 1. 5. Job sent and *s*. them
Isa. 5. 16. God that is holy shall
be *s*.
13. 3. commanded my *s*. ones
Jer. 1. 5. before thou camest I *s*.
Ezek. 20. 41. be *s*. in you before the
heathen, 28. 22, 25. & 38. 16. & 39.
27.
John 10. 36. whom Father hath *s*.
Acts 20. 32. inheritance among all
them which are *s*., 26. 18.
Rom. 15. 16. offering of Gent. *s*.
1 Cor. 1. 2. *s*. in Christ Jesus
7. 14. unbelieving husband is *s*.
1 Tim. 4. 5. *s*. by word and
2 Tim. 2. 21. *s*. and meet for mas.
Heb. 2. 11. they who are *s*. all
Matt. 23. 17. temple that *sanctifieth*
1 Cor. 1. 30. *sanctification*, 1 Thes.
4. 3, 4. 2 Thes. 2. 13. 1 Pet. 1. 2.
R. V. Gen. 2. 3; 2 Chron. 7. 16, 20.
hallowed; Deut. 5. 12. keep it
holy; 1 Sam. 21. 5. be holy; Isa.
13. 3. consecrated; Jude 1. beloved

SANCTUARY, Ps. 63. 2. & 73. 17.
Isa. 8. 14 Ezek. 11. 16. Dan. 9. 17.
Heb. 9. 2.
R. V. Ezek. 45. 2; Heb. 9. 2; 13. 11.
holy place

SAND, Gen. 22. 17. & 32. 12. Job 6.
3. & 29. 18. Isa. 10. 22. Matt. 7. 26.

SATAN provoked David, 1 Chron
21. 1.
Job 1. 6. *s*. came also among
Ps. 109. 6. let *s*. stand at his right
Matt. 4. 10. get thee hence *s*.
Luke 10. 18. I beheld *s*. as light.
22. 31. *s*. hath desired to

Acts 26. 18. turn from power of *s*.
Rom. 16. 20. God shall bruise *s*.
1 Cor. 5. 5. deliver such a one to *s*.
 7. 5. that *s*. tempt you not for
2 Cor. 2. 11. let *s*. get advantage
 11. 14. *s*. is transformed into
 angel
 12. 7. messenger of *s*. to
1 Tim. 1. 20. I have delivered to *s*.
Rev. 2. 9. synagogue of *s*.
 24. depth of *s*.
SATIATE, Jer. 31. 14, 25. & 46. 10.
SATISFY, Job 38. 27. Prov. 6. 30.
Ps. 90. 14. O *s*. us early with mercy
 91. 16. with long life I will *s*. him
 103. 5. who *s*. thy mouth with
 107. 9. he *s*. the longing soul
 132. 15. will *s*. her poor with
Prov. 5. 19. breasts *s*. thee at all
Isa. 55. 2. that which *s*. not
Ps. 17. 15. *satisfied* with thy like.
 22. 26. meek shall eat and be *s*.
 63. 5. soul shall be *s*. as with
 65. 4. *s*. with goodness of house
Prov. 14. 14. good man *s*. from
 27. 20. eyes of man are never *s*.
 30. 15. are three things never *s*.
Eccl. 5. 10. that loveth silver shall
 not be *s*.
Isa. 9. 20. shall eat and not be *s*.
 66. 11. be *s*. with breasts of her
Jer. 31. 14. my people be *s*. with
Ezek. 16. 28. couldest not be *s*.
Amos 4. 8. they were not *s*.
Hab. 2. 5. his desire cannot be *s*.
Num. 35. 31. shall take no *satisfaction*, 32.
R. V. Prov. 12. 11. have plenty;
 18. 20. filled
SAVE your lives, preserve and,
 Gen. 45. 7.
Gen. 50. 20. for good to *s*. much
Job 22. 29. he shall *s*. the humble
Ps. 18. 27. wilt *s*. afflicted people
 28. 9. *s*. thy people and lift them
 69. 35. God will *s*. Zion
 72. 4. *s*. children of needy
 13. *s*. souls of needy
 86. 2. *s*. thy servant
 109. 31. poor to *s*. him
 118. 25. *s*. now; send prosperity
Prov. 20. 22. he shall *s*. thee
Isa. 35. 4. God will come and *s*.
 45. 25. cannot *s*., 59. 1. Jer. 9. 14.
Isa. 49. 25. I will *s*. thy children
Ezek. 18. 27. shall *s*. his soul
 36. 29. I will *s*. from all unclean.
Hos. 1. 7. I will *s*. them by Lord
Zeph. 3. 17. he will *s*.
 19. *s*. her that halteth
Zech. 8. 7. I will *s*. my people
Matt. 1. 21. *s*. his people from sins
 16. 25. who will *s*. his life shall
 8. 11. Son of man is come to *s*.
 that which was lost, Luke 19. 10.
Mark 3. 4. is it lawful to *s*. life or
John 12. 47. not to judge but to *s*.
Acts 2. 40. *s*. yourselves from this
1 Cor. 1. 21. by foolishness of
 preaching to *s*.
 9. 22. became all, that I might *s*.
1 Tim. 1. 15. to *s*. sinners, of whom
Heb. 7. 25. able to *s*. to the utter.
Jas. 1. 21. word able to *s*.
 2. 14. faith *s*.
 5. 15. faith shall *s*. sick
 20. converts a sinner shall *s*. soul
Jude 23. others *s*. with fear
Ps. 6. 4. *save me*, 55. 16. & 57. 3. &
 119. 94. Jer. 17. 14. John 12. 27.
Isa. 25. 9. *save us*, 33. 22. & 37. 20.
Hos. 14. 3. Matt. 8. 25. 1 Pet. 3. 21.
Ps. 44. 7. thou hast *saved* us from
 106. 8. *s*. them for his name's sake
Isa. 45. 22. look . . and be ye *s*.
Jer. 4. 14. mayest be *s*.
 8. 20. we are not *s*.
Matt. 19. 25. who then can be *s*.,
 Luke 18. 26.
Luke 1. 71. be *s*. from our enemies
 7. 50. thy faith hath *s*. thee
 13. 23. are few *s*.
 23. 35. he *s*. others
John 3. 17. through him be *s*.

Acts 2. 47. added to church such
 as should be *s*.
 4. 12. name whereby be *s*.
 16. 30. what must I do to be *s*.
Rom. 8. 24. we are *s*. by hope
 10. 1. prayer for Israel that they
 may be *s*.
1 Cor. 1. 18. to us who are *s*. it is
Eph. 2. 5. by grace ye are *s*., 8.
1 Tim. 2. 4. all men to be *s*.
Tit. 3. 5. according to his mercy *s*.
1 Pet. 4. 18. righteous scarcely be *s*.
Rev. 21. 24. nations which are *s*.
Ps. 80. 3. *shall be saved*, 7. 19. Isa. 45.
 17. & 64. 5. Jer. 23. 6. & 30. 7. Matt.
 10. 22. & 24. 13. Mark 16. 16. Acts
 16. 31. Rom. 5. 10, 11, 26. 1 Tim. 2.
 15.
2 Sam. 22. 3. God my refuge and
 my *Saviour*
2 Kings 13. 5. Lord gave Israel a *S*.
Ps. 106. 21. forgat God their *S*.
Isa. 43. 3. I am thy *S*., 49. 26.
 11. besides me is no *S*., Hos. 13. 4.
 45. 15. of Israel, the *S*., Jer. 14. 8.
Obad. 21. *S*. shall come up on
Luke 1. 47. rejoiced in God my *S*.
 2. 11. to you is born a *S*. which is
Acts 5. 31. him hath God exalted
 to be a *S*.
Eph. 5. 23. Christ is head and *S*.
1 Tim. 4. 10. who is the *S*. of all
 men, 1. 1; God our *S*., Tit. 1. 4. &
 2. 10, 13. & 3. 4, 6. 2 Pet. 1. 1, 11.
 Jude 25.
2 Pet. 2. 20. knowledge of our *S*.
SAVOR, sweet, Gen. 8. 21. Ex. 29.
 18. Lev. 1. 9. & 2. 9. & 3. 16.
S. of S. 1. 3. of *s*. of thy good oint.
2 Cor. 2. 14. the *s*. of his knowledge
 15. are to God a sweet *s*. of Christ
 16. to one *s*. of death
Eph. 5. 2. sacrifice to God of sweet
 smelling *s*.
Matt. 16. 23. *savorest* not things of
 God
SAY, Matt. 3. 9. & 5. 22, 28, 32, 34, 39,
 44. & 7. 22. & 23. 3. 1 Cor. 12. 3.
R. V. Frequent changes to speak,
 tell, etc.
SCAB, Lev. 13. 1; Deut. 28. 27; Isa.
 3. 17.
SCARCELY, Rom. 5. 7. 1 Pet. 4. 18.
SCATTER them in Israel, Gen.
 49. 7.
Num. 10. 35. let thine enemies be
 scattered
Matt. 9. 36. *s*. abroad as sheep
Luke 1. 51. *s*. proud in imagination
Prov. 11. 21. that *scattereth* and yet
SCEPTRE not depart from Judah,
 Gen. 49. 10.
Num. 24. 17. a *s*. shall rise out of
Ps. 45. 6. the *s*. of thy kingdom is
Zech. 10. 11. *s*. of Egypt shall de.
R. V. 2 Sam. 18. 8; Job 37. 1.
 spread; Ps. 60. 1. broken down;
 Prov. 20. 26. winnoweth; Isa. 18.
 2. tall; 30. 30. a blast; Dan. 12. 7.
 breaking in pieces; Ezek. 12. 15;
 Acts 5. 36. disperse; Jas. 1. 1;
 1 Pet. 1. 1. the Dispersion
SCHISM, 1 Cor. 1. 10. & 12. 25.
SCHOLAR, 1 Chron. 25. 8. Mal. 2.
 12.
Gal. 3. 24. the law was our *school-
 master*
R. V. Mal. 2. 12. that answereth
SCOFFERS, Hab. 1. 10. 2 Pet. 3. 3.
R. V. Mal. 2. 12. that answereth
SCORN, Job 16. 20. Ps. 44. 13.
Prov. 9. 8. reprove not a *scorner*
 14. 6. a *s*. seeketh wisdom and
 1. 22. *scorners* delight in scorning
 3. 34. he *scorneth* the *s*. but giveth
 9. 12. if thou *scornest* thou
Ps. 1. 1. *scornful*, Prov. 29. 8. Isa.
 28. 14.
R. V. Job 12. 4. laughing-stock;
 Hab. 1. 10. derision; Prov. 19. 28.
 mocketh at
SCORPIONS, 2 Chron. 10. 11. Ezek.
 2. 6.
SCOURGE of the tongue, Job 5. 21.

Isa. 28. 15. overflowing *s*., 18.
Heb. 12. 6. Lord *scourgeth* every
R. V. Lev. 19. 20. punished
SCRIPTURE of truth, Dan. 10. 21.
Matt. 22. 29. err, not knowing *s*.
John 5. 39. search *s*., Acts 17. 11. &
 18. 24.
Rom. 15. 4. through comfort of *s*.
2 Tim. 3. 15. from a child known *s*.
 16. all *s*. is given by inspiration
2 Pet. 1. 20. no prophecy of *s*. is of
 private interpretation
R. V. Dan. 10. 21. writing; 2 Tim
 3. 15. holy writing; Mark 15.
 28 ——
SCROLL, the heavens compared
 to, Isa. 34. 4; Rev. 6. 14.
SEA, Ps. 35. 7. & 72. 8. Prov. 8 29.
Isa. 48. 18. & 57. 20. Zech. 9. 10.
Rev. 4. 6. & 10. 2. & 15. 2. & 21. 1.
SEAL upon thine heart, S. of S. 8. 6.
John 3. 33. set to his *s*. that God is
Rom. 4. 11. *s*. of the righteousness
1 Cor. 9. 2. *s*. of my apostleship
2 Tim. 2. 19. having *s*. Lord know.
Rev. 7. 2. angel having *s*. of living
Deut. 32. 34. *sealed* up among
Job 14. 17. my transgression is *s*.
S. of S. 4. 12. spring shut up, foun-
 tain *s*.
John 6. 27. hath God the Father *s*.
2 Cor. 1. 22. who hath *s*. us and
Eph. 1. 13. ye were *s*. with the
Rev. 5. 1. a book *s*. with seven
 7. 3. *s*. the servants of our God
 4. were *s*. a hundred and forty
R. V. Rev. 7. 5-8 ——
SEARCH out resting place, Num.
 10. 33.
Ps. 139. 23. *s*. me, O God, and
Prov. 25. 27. men to *s*. own glory
Jer. 17. 10. I the Lord *s*. the heart
 29. 13. when ye shall *s*. with me
Lam. 3. 40. *s*. and try our ways
Zeph. 1. 12. *s*. Jerusalem with
Acts 17. 11. *s*. Scriptures, John 5. 39.
1 Chron. 28. 9. the Lord *searcheth*
 all hearts
1 Cor. 2. 10. Spirit *s*. deep things
Rev. 2. 23. I am he that *s*. the
Job 10. 6. that *searchest* after my
Prov. 2. 4. *s*. for her as for hidden
Judg. 5. 16. great *searchings* of
R. V. Job 38. 16. recesses; Gen. 31.
 34, 37. felt about; Num. 10. 33;
 Deut. 1. 33. seek; Num. 13. 2, 21,
 32; 14. 6, 7, 34, 36, 38; Deut. 1. 24.
 spy or spied out; Acts 17. 11. ex-
 amining; Num. 13. 25. spying out
SEARED, with hot iron, 1 Tim.
 4. 2.
SEASON, Gen. 40. 4. Ex. 13. 10.
Ps. 1. 3. bring. forth fruit in his *s*.
Eccl. 3. 1. to . . thing there is a *s*.
Isa. 50. 4. to speak a word in *s*.
Luke 4. 13. depart. from him for *s*.
John 5. 35. willing for a *s*. to re.
Acts 1. 7. know the times and *s*.
 14. 17. gave us rain and fruitful *s*.
1 Thes. 5. 1. of times and *s*. ye
2 Tim. 4. 2. instant in *s*. and out
Heb. 11. 25. pleasures of sin for a *s*.
1 Pet. 1. 6. for a *s*. ye are in heav.
Col. 4. 6. let speech be *seasoned*
R. V. Josh. 24. 7. days; 1 Chron. 21.
 29; Luke 23. 8; Acts 20. 18; Rev. 6.
 11; 20. 3. time; Acts 19. 22; 1 Pet.
 1. 6. while; John 5. 4 ——
SECOND COMING, Christ's, Acts
 1. 11.
SECOND DEATH, Rev. 20. 14.
SECRET, Gen. 49. 6. Job 40. 13.
Job 11. 6. show thee *s*. of wisdom
 29. 4. *s*. of God on my tabernacle
Ps. 25. 14. *s*. of Lord is with them
 31. 20. hide them in *s*. presence
Prov. 3. 32. his *s*. is with righteous
 9. 17. bread eaten in *s*. is pleasant
 11. 13. talebearer revealeth *s*.
 25. 9. discover not *s*. to another
Dan. 2. 28. a God that revealeth *s*.
Amos 3. 7. revealeth his *s*. unto
Matt. 6. 4. alms in *s*. Father seeth
 in *s*.

John 18. 20. in s. have I said no.
19. 38. *secretly* for fear of Jews
Rom. 2. 16. when God shall judge *secrets* of men
R. V. Gen. 49. 6. council; Judg. 13. 18. wonderful; Job 40. 13; Ps. 19. 12; Prov. 27. 5; Eccl. 12. 14; Matt. 13. 35. hidden; Ps. 10. 8; 27. 5; 31. 20; S. of S. 2. 14. covert; Ps. 18. 11. hiding; Job 20. 26. treasures; Matt. 24. 26. inner; Luke 11. 33. cellar; 1 Sam. 23. 9——; Ps. 10. 9. the covert
SECT. Acts 24. 5. & 26. 5. & 28. 22.
SEDITION, Gal. 5. 20; 2 Pet. 2. 19.
SEDUCE, Ezek. 13. 10. Mark 13. 22.
2 Tim. 3. 13. *seducers*, 1 Tim. 4. 1.
R. V. Isa. 19. 13; Mark 13. 22; 1 John 2. 26. go or lead astray
SEE, Ps. 34. 8. Matt. 5. 8. John 16. 22. 1 John 3. 2. Rev. 1. 7. & 22. 4.
Matt. 6. 1. before men to be *seen* of
13. 17. to see and have not s.
23. 5. their works to be s.
John 1. 18. no man hath s. God
14. 9. he that hath s. me hath s. the Father
20. 29. thou hast s. and believed
2 Cor. 4. 18. look not at things s.
1 Tim. 6. 16. no man hath s.
Heb. 11. 1. evidence of things not s.
1 Pet. 1. 8. having not s. ye love
1 John 1. 1. that which we have s.
12. no man hath s. God at any
Job 10. 4. seest thou as man *seeth*
John 12. 17. because it s. him not
12. 45. he that s. me, s. him that
SEED, Gen. 1. 11. & 17. 7. & 38. 9. Ps. 126. 6 bearing precious s.
Eccl. 11. in morning sow thy s
Isa. 55. 10. give s. to the sower
Matt. 13. 38. goo 1 s. are children
Luke 8. 11. good s. is word of God
1 Pet. 1. 23. born again not of corruptible s.
1 John 3. 9. his s. remaineth in
Ps. 37. 28. s. of wicked shall be
69. 36. s. of his servants
Prov. 11. 21. s. of righteous
Isa. 1. 4. sinful nation s. of evil
14. 20. the s. of evil doers
45. 5. all s. of Israel be justified
Mal. 2. 15. might seek a godly s.
Rom. 9. 8. children are count. for s.
Gal. 3. 16. not to *seeds* but to thy s.
SEEK, Ezra 8. 21. Job 5. 8. Ps. 19. 15.
Deut. 4. 29. if thou s. him with all the heart, 1 Chron. 28. 9. 2 Chron. 15. 2. Jer. 29. 13.
2 Chron. 19. 3. prepare heart to s. God, 30. 19.
Ezra 8. 22. them for good that s.
Ps. 9. 10. forsake them that s.
63. 1. God, early will I s. thee
69. 32. heart . live that s. God
119. 2. bless. are they that s. him
Prov. 8. 17. that s. me early
S. of S. 3. 2. s. him whom soul lov.
Isa. 26. 9. my spirit will I s. thee
45. 19. I said not s. me in vain
Jer. 29. 13. he shall s. me and
Amos 5. 4. s. me and ye shall live
Zeph. 2. 3. s. Lord, s. righteous.
Mal. 2. 7. s. the law
Matt. 6. 33. s. first kingdom of God
7. 7. s. and ye shall find
Luke 13. 24. many will s. to enter
19. 10. to s. and to save that which is lost, Matt. 18. 11.
John 8. 21. shall s. me and not
Rom. 2. 7. s. for glory, honor
1 Cor. 10. 24. let no man s. own
13. 5. charity s. not her own
Phil. 2. 21. all s. their own, not
Col. 3. 1. s. things which are above
1 Pet. 3. 11. s. peace and ensue it
Lam. 3. 25. to soul that *seeketh*
John 4. 23. the Father s. such
1 Pet. 5. 8. *seeking* whom he may
SEEM, Gen. 27. 12. Deut. 25. 3.
1 Cor. 11. 16. if any man s. conten.
Heb. 4. 1. lest any s. to come short
Jas. 1. 26. if any s. to be religious

Luke 8. 18. taken that he *seemeth*
1 Cor. 3. 18. if any man s. wise
Heb. 12. 11. no chastening s. joyous
SELF-DENIAL, Prov. 23. 2. Jer. 35. Luke 3. 11. & 14. 33. . Acts 2. 45.
Rom. 6. 12. & 8. 13. & 14. 20. & 15. 1.
1 Cor. 10. 23. & 13. 5. & 24. 33. Gal. 5. 24. Phil. 2. 4. Tit. 2. 12. 1 Pet. 2. 11.
Christ an example of, Matt. 4. 8. & 8. 20. Rom. 15. 3. Phil. 2. 6.
incumbent on His followers, Matt. 10. 38. & 16. 24. Mark 8. 34. Luke 9. 23.
SELF-EXAMINATION enjoined, Lam. 3. 40. Ps. 4. 4. 1 Cor. 11. 28. 2 Cor. 13. 5.
SELFISHNESS, Isa. 56. 11. Rom. 15. 1. 1 Cor. 10. 24. 2 Cor. 5. 15. Phil. 2. 4, 21. 2 Tim. 3. 2. Jas. 2. 8.
SELF-WILL, Ps. 75. 5. Tit. 1. 7. 2 Pet. 2. 10.
SELL me thy birthright, Gen. 25. 31.
Prov. 23. 23. buy truth and s. it
Matt. 19. 21. go s. that thou hast
25. 9. go to them that s. and buy
13. 44. he *selleth* all and buyeth
R. V. Jas. 4. 13. trade
SENATORS, Ps. 105. 22.
SEND help from the sanctuary, Ps. 20. 2.
Ps. 43. 3. O s. out thy light and
57. 3. he shall s. from heaven
Matt. 9. 38. s. forth laborers into
John 14. 26. the Father will s.
16. 7. if I depart I will s. him
2 Thes. 2. 11. s. them strong delus.
R. V. Gen. 12. 20. brought; Judg. 5. 15. rushed forth; other changes of slight moment, and chiefly dependent on antecedent or consequent word
SENSE, Neh. 8. 8. Heb. 5. 14.
Jas. 3. 15. *sensual*, Jude 19.
SENTENCE, Deut. 17. 9. Dan 12.
Prov. 16. 10. a divine s. is in lips
2 Cor. 1. 9. we had s. of death in
R. V. Jer. 4. 12; Acts 15. 19. judgment
SEPARATE, Gen. 13. 9. Ex. 33. 16.
Gen. 49. 6. head of him that was s. from his brethren, Deut. 33. 16.
Deut. 29. 21. Lord shall s. him
Isa. 59. 2. iniquities have *separated*
Acts 13. 2. me Saul and Barna.
19. 9. departed and s. the disciples
Rom. 8. 35. who s. us from Christ
2 Cor. 6. 17. come out, be ye s.
Gal. 1. 15. who s. me from moth.
Heb. 7. 26. holy, harmless, s. from
R. V. Num. 6. 2. make special; Jer. 37. 12. receive his portion; Hos. 4. 14. go apart; 9. 10. consecrated
SERAPHIMS, Isa. 6. 2, 6.
SERMON on the mount, Matt. 5-7. Luke 6. 20. *See* CHRIST.
SERPENT, Gen. 3. 1, 13. & 49. 17.
Num. 21. 6. Lord sent fiery s., 8, 9.
Prov. 23. 32. it biteth like a s.
Eccl. 10. 11. s. will bite without
Matt. 7. 10. will he give him a s.
10. 16. be wise as s. harmless as
John 3. 14. as Moses lifted up s.
2 Cor. 11. 3. as the s. beguiled Eve
Rev. 12. 9. that old s. called devil
R. V. Deut. 32. 24. crawling things; Jas. 3. 7. creeping things
SERVE the Lord with all thy heart, Deut. 10. 12, 20. & 11. 13. Josh. 22. 5. 1 Sam. 12. 20.
Deut. 13. 4. shall s. him, and cleave
Josh. 24. 14. fear the Lord, s. him
15. choose this day whom ye will s. . . me and my house, we will s. the Lord
1 Sam. 12. 24. fear the Lord, s. him
Job 21. 15. what is the Almighty that we should s. him
Ps. 2. 11. s. Lord with fear, rejoice
Isa. 43. 24. made me to s. with sins
Matt. 6. 24. no man can s. two masters; ye cannot s. God and mam.

Luke 1. 74. s. him in holiness
12. 37. will come forth and s.
John 12. 26. if any man s. me let
Acts 6. 2. leave word of God and s. tables
27. 23. whose I am, and whom I s.
Rom. 1. 9. whom I s. with my spirit
6. 6. henceforth should not s. sin
7. 25. s. law of God
Col. 3. 24. s. Lord Jesus Christ
Gal. 5. 13. by love s. one another
1 Thes. 1. 9. to s. living God
Heb. 12. 28. may s. God accept.
Rev. 7. 15. s. him day and night
Prov. 29. 19. a *servant* will not be
Isa. 24. 2. with s. so with his mas.
42. 1. behold my s., 49. 3. & 52. 13.
Matt. 20. 27. be chief, let him be s.
25. 21. well done, good and faithful s., 23.
John 8. 34. committeth sin is s.
15. 16. s. is not greater than his
1 Cor. 7. 21. called, being a s.
9. 19. I made myself s. to
Gal. 1. 10. pleased men, not s.
Phil. 2. 7. took on him form of a s.
2 Tim. 2. 24. s. of Lord must not
Ezra 5. 11. *servants* of the God of heaven, Dan. 3. 26. Acts 16. 17.
1 Pet. 2. 16. Rev. 7. 3.
Rom. 6. 16. yield yourselves s. to obey, his s. ye are, whom ye obey
19. members s. to uncleanness
1 Cor. 7. 23. ye the s. of men
Phil. 1. 1. s. of Christ
2 Pet. 2. 19. s. of corruption
Rev. 22. 3. his s. shall serve him
Rom. 12. 1. reasonable *service*
Luke 10. 40. cumbered about much *serving*
Acts 20. 19. s. Lord with all humil.
26. 7. tribes instantly s. God
Rom. 12. 11. fervent in spirit s. Lord
Tit. 3. 3. s. divers lusts and pleas.
R. V. Gen. 26. 14. household; 44. 10, 16, 17. bondmen; Gen. 14. 14. 1 Sam. 24. 7. men; 1 Sam. 16. 18; 25. 19; 2 Sam. 21. 2. young men; Ex. 33. 11; Num. 11. 28; Mark 9. 35. minister; Deut. 15. 18. hireling; 2 Kings 10. 19. worshippers; Ezra 2. 65; Eccl. 2. 7. menservants; Matt. 26. 58; Mark 14. 54. officers; John 8. 34, 35; 1 Cor. 7. 21, 22, 23; Gal. 4. 1, 7; 1 Pet. 2. 16; 2 Pet. 2. 19. bondservant; Gen. 39. 4; 40. 4; 2 Chron. 29. 11; Esth. 1. 10; Ps. 101. 6, Isa. 56. 6. minister; 19. 23. worship; Jer. 40. 10; 52. 12. stand before; Ezek. 48. 18, 19. labor in; Ex. 35. 19; 39. 1, 41; 1 Chron. 9. 28. ministering; Num. 4. 47, & 24. work; Rom. 15. 31. ministration; Gal. 4. 8. bondage; Rev. 2. 19. ministry; 2 Cor. 11. 8. minister unto
SERVILE work forbidden on holy days, Lev. 23. 7. Num. 28. 18 & 29. 1.
SET, Ps. 2. 6. & 4. 3. & 12. 5. & 16. 8. & 54. 8. & 75. 7. & 113. 8. Prov. 1. 25. S. of S. 8. 6. Rom. 3. 25. Col. 3. 2
R. V. Frequent changes, chiefly due to antecedent and consequent words
SETTLE, Luke 21. 14. 1 Pet. 5. 10.
Col. 1. 23. if ye continue in faith, *settled*
R. V. Ezek. 36. 11. cause to be inhabited; 1 Pet. 5. 10——
SEVENTY elders, the, Ex. 18. 25. Num. 11. 16.
years' captivity foretold, Jer. 25. 11.
weeks, Daniel's prophecy concerning, Dan. 9. 24.
disciples, Christ's charge to, Luke 10.
SEVERITY, goodness and, Rom. 11. 22.
SHADE, Lord is thy, Ps. 121. 5.

SHADOW, our days are as a,
1 Chron. 29. 15. Eccl. 8. 13. & 6. 12.
Job 8. 9. Ps. 107. 11. & 109. 23. &
144. 4.
Ps. 17. 8. hide me under the s. of
thy wings, 36. 7. & 57. 1. & 63. 7.
S. of S. 2. 3. I sat under his s.
Isa. 4. 6. for a s. from heat
49. 2. in s. of his hand hath he
Jer. 6. 4. s. of evening are stretch.
Acts 5. 15. s. of Peter might
Col. 2. 17. s. of things to come
Jas. 1. 17. no variableness nor s.
SHAKE heaven and earth, Hag.
2. 6, 21.
Hag. 2. 7. I will s. all nations
Matt. 10. 14. s. off the dust of feet
11. 7. a reed *shaken* with the wind
Luke 6. 38. good measure s. toget.
2 Thes. 2. 2. be not soon s. in mind
Ps. 44. 14. *shaking,* Isa. 17. 6. & 24.
13. & 30. 32. Ezek. 37. 7. & 38. 19.
R. V. Lev. 26. 36. driven; Job 16.
12. dashed; Isa. 13. 13; Heb. 12. 26.
make tremble; Matt. 28. 4. quake;
Job 41. 29. rushing; Ezek. 37. 7. an
earthquake
SHAME, 1 Sam. 20. 34. 2 Sam. 13.
13.
Ps. 119. 31. put me not to s., 69. 7.
Prov. 3. 35. s. shall be the promo-
tion of fools, 9. 7. & 10. 5. & 11. 2.
& 13. 5, 18. & 14. 35. & 17. 2. & 18.
13. & 19. 26. & 25. 8. & 29. 15. Isa.
22. 18.
Isa. 50. 6. hid not my face from s.
Dan. 12. 2. some to life, some to s.
Hos. 4. 7. change glory into s.
Zeph. 3. 5. unjust knoweth no s.
Acts 5. 41. worthy to suffer s. for
Phil. 3. 19. glory is in their s.
Heb. 12. 2. endured the cross, de-
spising the s.
Rev. 3. 18. s. of thy nakedness
1 Tim. 2. 9. *shamefacedness*
R. V. Ex. 32. 25. derision; Ps. 4. 2;
35. 4; 40. 14; 44. 9; 109. 29; Acts 5.
41; 1 Cor. 11. 14. dishonor; Ps. 83.
16. confusion; 83. 17. confounded;
Prov. 25. 10. revile; Jer. 3. 24;
Hos. 9. 10; 1 Cor. 14. 35. shameful;
Mic. 2. 6. reproaches
SHAPE, Luke 3. 22. John 5. 37.
Ps. 51. 5.
R. V. Luke 3. 22; John 5. 37. form
SHARP, Isa. 41. 15. & 49. 2. Rev. 1.
16.
Job 16. 9. *sharpeneth,* Prov. 27. 17.
Mic. 7. 14. *sharper* than, Heb. 4. 12.
Judg. 8. 1. *sharply,* Tit. 1. 13.
2 Cor. 13. 10. should use *sharpness*
R. V. Josh. 5. 2, 3. flint; 1 Sam. 14.
4. rocky; Job 41. 30. threshing
wain; Ex. 4. 25——; Mic. 7. 4.
worse
SHEARING sheep, rejoicing at,
1 Sam. 25, 4. 2 Sam. 13. 23.
SHEAVES of corn, Joseph's
dream, Gen. 37. 7.
sheaf of the firstfruits of harvest,
Lev. 23. 10-12.
forgotten, to be left in the field,
Deut. 24. 19. Job 24. 10.
typical, Ps. 126. 6. Mic. 4. 12. Matt.
13. 30.
SHED for many, for remission,
Matt. 26. 28.
Rom. 5. 5. love of God is s. abroad
Tit. 3. 6. Holy Ghost he s. on us
R. V. Ex. 22. 2, 3; 1 Sam. 25. 26, 33.
bloodguiltiness; Ezek. 35. 5. given
over to; Ezek. 36. 18; Luke 22. 20;
Acts 2. 33; Tit. 3. 6; Rev. 16. 6.
poured out
SHEEP, Ps. 49. 14. & 74. 1. & 78. 52.
Ps. 44. 22, 23. s. for the slaughter
79. 13. s. of thy pasture, 100. 3.
119. 176. gone astray like lost s.
Isa. 53. 6. like s. have gone astray
Ezek. 34. 12. s. that are scattered
Matt. 9. 36. as s. having no shep.
10. 6. to lost s. of house of
18. 12. hundred s. and one of
25. 32. divideth the s. from goats

John 10. 2-7. the s.
27. my s.
21. 15-17. feed lambs, feed my s.
1 Pet. 2. 25. were as s. going astray
R. V. Gen. 34. 28; Ex. 9. 3; Lev.
22. 21; Num. 31. 28; Deut. 7. 13;
15. 19; 28. 4, 18, 51; 1 Sam. 8. 17;
Ps. 49. 17. flock or flocks; S. of S.
4. 2; 6. 6. ewes; John 10. 4. his
own; 14. mine own
SHEPHERD, Gen. 46. 34. & 49. 24.
Ex. 2. 17, 19.
Num. 17. 17. sheep that have no s.,
1 Kings 22. 17. Mark 6. 34.
Ps. 23. 1. the Lord is my s.
S. of S. 1. 8. feed thy kids before
the s. tents
Ezek. 34. 2. prophesy against s.,
woe to the s.
5. scattered because no s.
12. s. seeketh ou t his flock
23. set up one s. even David
37. 24. all shall have one s.
Mic. 5. 5. against him seven s.
John 10. 11. I am the good s.
16. one fold and one s., Eccl. 12. 11.
Heb. 13. 20. Jesus, that great s.
1 Pet. 2. 25. returned to s. of souls
5. 4. when the chief s. shall ap.
SHIELD and great reward, Gen.
15. 1.
Deut. 33. 29. Lord the s. of thy
help
Ps. 3. 3. Lord is a s. for me, 28. 7.
33. 20. Lord our s., 59. 11. & 84. 9.
84. 11. God is a sun and a s.
115. 9. their help and their s.
Prov. 30. 5. a s. unto them that
Eph. 6. 16. taking the s. of faith
SHINE, Job 22. 28. & 36. 32. & 37.
15.
Num. 6. 25. make his face to s.
Job 10. 3. on counsel of wicked
Ps. 31. 16. thy face to s. on thy
Eccl. 8. 1. man's wisdom maketh
his face s.
Dan. 12. 3. wise shall s. as firma.
Matt. 5. 16. let your light so s.
13. 43. righteous s. forth as the
2 Cor. 4. 6. commanded light to s.
Phil. 2. 15. among whom ye s. as
R. V. Matt. 24. 27. is seen; Job 25.
25. no brightness
SHIPWRECK, 1 Tim. 1. 19.
SHORT, is the Lord's hand waxed,
Num. 11. 23.
Ps. 89. 47. remember how s. time
Rom. 3. 23. and come s. of glory
Ps. 102. 23. he *shortened* my days
Isa. 50. 2. is my hand s., 59. 1.
Matt. 24. 22. except the days be s.
Ps. 47. 5. God is gone up with a s.
1 Thes. 4. 16. the Lord shall de-
scend with a s.
SHOW, Ps. 39. 6. Luke 20. 47. Col.
2. 23.
Ps. 4. 6. who will s. us any good
16. 11. wilt s. me path of life
91. 16. I will s. him my salvation
1 Cor. 11. 26. s. forth Lord's death
Tit. 2. 7. s. thyself a pattern
1 Pet. 2. 9. s. forth the praise
Rev. 22. 6. sent his angel to s.
John 5. 20. loved Son, and *showeth*
R. V. frequent changes, chiefly to
tell, declare, manifest, etc.
SHRINES, Acts 19. 24.
SHUT up or left, Deut. 32. 36.
Matt. 23. 13. ye s. up the kingdom
Gal. 3. 23. s. up to the faith which
Rev. 3. 7. that openeth, and no
man *shutteth,* Isa. 22. 22.
R. V. Deut. 32. 30. delivered
SICK of love, S. of S. 2. 5. & 5. 8.
Isa. 1. 5. whole head is s. and
John 11. 3. a certain man was s.
Jas. 5. 14. is any s. call the
15. faith shall save the s.
1 Cor. 11. 30. are weak and *sickly*
Ps. 41. 3. make his bed in *sickness*
Ex. 23. 25. I will take s. away

Matt. 8. 17. bare our *sicknesses*
R. V. Prov. 23. 35. hurt; Mic. 6. 13.
wound; Luke 7. 10 ——; 5. 24;
Acts 9. 33. palsied; Matt. 8. 17.
diseases; Mark 3. 15 ——
SIFT, Isa. 30. 28. Amos 9. 9. Luke
22. 31.
SIGHT, Ex. 3. 3. 2 Cor. 5. 7.
R. V. Many changes to eyes,
presence, appearance, etc.
SIGN, Gen. 9. 12, 13. & 17. 11. Ex.
4. 17. Isa. 8. 18. Rom. 15. 19.
Rom. 4. 11. received the s. of cir.
Jer. 22. 24. *signet,* Hag. 2. 23.
SILENT in darkness, 1 Sam. 2. 9.
Ps. 21. 1. be not s. to me, 30. 12.
Zech. 2. 13. be s. O all flesh before
Ps. 31. 18. *silence,* 32. 3. & 35. 22. &
50. 3. 21. & 83. 1. & 94. 17. Jer. 8. 11.
Amos 5. 13. & 8. 3. 1 Cor. 14. 34,
1 Tim. 2. 11, 12. 1 Pet. 2. 15. Rev.
8. 1.
R. V. Ps. 31. 18. dumb; Isa. 15. 1.
nought; 62. 6. take no rest; Acts
22. 2. quiet; 1 Tim. 2. 11, 12. quiet-
ness; Ps. 28. 1. deaf unto
SILLY, Job 5. 2. 2 Tim. 3. 6.
SIMPLE, Prov. 1. 4, 22, 32. & 7. 7 &
8. 5. & 9. 4, 13. & 19. 25. & 21. 11.
Ps. 19. 7. testimony sure, making
wise the s.
116. 16. Lord preserveth the s.
119. 130. understanding to the s.
Prov. 14. 15. the s. believeth
22. 3. s. pass on and are punished
Rom. 16. 19. but s. concerning evil
R. V. Rom. 16. 18. innocent
SIN lieth at the door, Gen. 4. 7.
Job 10. 6. searchest after my s.
Ps. 4. 4. stand in awe and s. not
32. 1. blessed is he whose s. is
covered
38. 18. I will be sorry for my s.
51. 3. my s. is ever before me
119. 11. that I might not s. against
Prov. 14. 34. s. is a reproach to
Isa. 30. 1. counsel to add s. to s.
53. 10. offering for s.
John 1. 29. take. away s. of world
5. 14. s. no more lest a worse
Rom. 5. 12. by one s. entered
6. 14. s. shall not have dominion
7. 13. s. might appear s.
17. s. that dwelleth in me
8. 2. free from the law of s.
1 Cor. 15. 34. awake to righteous.
ness and s. not
2 Cor. 5. 21. made s. for us, who
Eph. 4. 26. be angry, and s. not
Jas. 1. 15. lust bringeth forth s.
and s. death
1 Pet. 2. 22. who did no s. neither
1 John 1. 8. say we have no s.
2. 1. ye s. not; if any man s. we
have an advocate
5. 16. there is a s. unto death
Ps. 19. 13. keep me from presumptuous *sins*
Isa. 43. 25. not remember s.
Ezek. 33. 16. none of his s. shall
Dan. 9. 24. transgression, make
end of s.
1 Tim. 5. 22. partaker of other
men's s.
2 Tim. 3. 6. women laden with s.
1 John 2. 2. propitiation for s. of
Ps. 69. 5. my sins, 51. 9. Isa. 38. 17.
79. 9. our sins, 90. 8. & 103. 10,
Isa. 59. 12. Dan. 9. 16. Gal. 1. 4.
1 Cor. 15. 3. Heb. 1. 3. 1 Pet. 2. 24.
Rev. 1. 5.
Matt. 1. 21. their sins, Rom. 11. 27.
Heb. 8. 12. & 10. 17. Num. 16. 26.
Isa. 59. 2. your sins, Jer. 5. 25. John
8. 21. 1 Cor. 15. 17. Josh. 24. 19.
Ex. 32. 33. who hath *sinned,* I
Job 1. 22. in all this Job s. not
Lam. 1. 8. Jerusalem grievously s.
Rom. 2. 12. many as s. without
3. 23. all have s. and come short
1 John 1. 10. say we have not s.
Ex. 9. 27. *I have sinned,* Num 22.
34. Josh. 7. 20. 1 Sam. 15. 24, 30.
Sam. 12. 13. & 24. 10. Job 7. 20. &

33. 27. Ps. 41. 4. & 51. 4. Mic. 7. 9.
Matt. 27. 4. Luke 15. 18, 21.
Judg. 10. 10. *we have sinned*, 1 Sam.
7. 6 Ps. 106. 6. Isa. 42. 24. & 64. 5.
Jer. 3. 25. & 8. 14. & 14. 7, 20. Lam.
5. 16. Dan. 9. 5, 8, 11, 15.
1 Kings 8. 46. man that *sinneth*
Prov. 8. 36. *s.* against me wrong
Eccl. 7. 20. doeth good, and *s.* not
Ezek. 18. 4. soul that *s.* it shall die
1 John 5. 18. is born of God *s.* not
Eccl. 7. 20. the *sinner* shall be
9. 18. *s.* destroyeth much good
Isa. 65. 20. *s.* a hundred years
Luke 15. 7. joy over one *s.* that re-
penteth
18. 13. be merciful to me a *s.*
Jas. 5. 20. convert a *s.* from
1 Pet. 4. 18. where shall *s.* appear
Gen. 18. 13. *sinners* before the
Ps. 1. 1. standeth in way of *s.*
51. 13. *s.* shall be converted to
thee
Isa. 33. 14. *s.* in Zion are afraid
Matt. 9. 13. call *s.* to repentance
John 9. 31. God heareth not *s.*
Rom. 5. 8. that while we were yet
s. Christ died for us
19. by disobedi. many made *s.*
Gal. 2. 15. are Jews and not *s.*
1 Tim. 1. 15. Jesus came to save *s.*
Heb. 7. 26. holy, separate from *s.*
Jude 15. ungodly *s.* have spoken
Num. 32. 14. *sinful*, Isa. 1. 4. Luke
5. 8. Rom. 7. 13. & 8. 3.
R. V. Prov. 10. 12, 19; 28. 13. transgression; 14. 9. Jer. 51. 5. guilt; 2
Chron. 28. 10; Eph. 1. 7; 2. 5; Col.
1. 13. trespasses: Col. 2. 11; 1 John
2. 2 —; Lev. 4. 13. err
SINCERE, Phil. 1. 10, 16. 1 Pet. 2.
2.
Josh. 24. 14. serve him in *sincerity*
1 Cor. 5. 8. unleavened bread of *s.*
2 Cor. 1. 12. in godly *s.* we have
2. 17. as of *s.* in the sight of God
8. 8. prove the *s.* of your love
Eph. 6. 24. love Jesus Christ in *s.*
Tit. 2. 7. showing gravity, *s.*
R. V. 1 Pet. 2. 2. spiritual; Eph.
6. 24. uncorruptness; Tit. 2. 7 —
SINEW, Isa. 48. 4. Job 10. 11.
R. V. Job 30. 17. gnaw
SING to the Lord, Ex. 15. 21. 1
Chron. 16. 23. Ps. 30. 4. & 68. 32. &
81. 1. & 95. 1. & 96. 1, 2. & 98. 1. &
147. 7. & 149. 1. Isa. 12. 5. & 52. 9.
Eph. 5. 19.
Ex. 15. 1. I will *s.*, Judg. 5. 3. Ps. 13.
6. & 57. 7, 9. & 59. 16, 17. & 101. 1. &
104. 33. & 144. 9. Isa. 5. 1. 1 Cor. 14.
15.
Job 29. 13. *s.* for joy, Isa. 65. 14.
Ps. 9. 11. *s.* praise, 18. 49. & 27. 6. &
30. 12. & 47. 6, 7. & 68. 4. & 75. 9. &
92. 1. & 108. 1, 3. & 135. 3. & 146. 2.
& 147. 1. & 149. 3.
Ps. 145. 7. *s.* of thy righteousness
Prov. 29. 6. righteous doth *s.*
Isa. 35. 6. shall tongue of dumb *s.*
1 Cor. 14. 15. I will *s.* with the
spirit
R. V. Ps. 30. 4; 33. 2; 57. 9; 71. 22,
23; 98. 5; 101. 1. sing praises; Isa.
24. 14. shout; Hos. 2. 15. make
answer
SINGLE eye, Matt. 6. 22. Luke 11.
34.
Acts 2. 46. *singleness* of heart, Eph.
6. 5. Col. 3. 22.
SINK, Ps. 69. 2, 14. Luke 9. 44.
SISTER, Son of S. 4. 9. & 5. 1. & 8. 8.
R. V. 1 Chron. 7. 15; 1 Cor. 9. 15.
wife; Col. 4. 10. cousin
SITUATION, 2 Kings 2. 19. Ps. 48.
2.
R. V. Ps. 48. 2. elevation
SKIN for skin, Job 2. 4. & 10. 11. &
19. 26. Jer. 13. 23. Heb. 11. 37.
R. V. Ex. 16. 10; 36. 19; Num. 4.
6, 8, 10, 11, 12, 14, 25; Ezek. 16. 10.
sealskin; Job 18. 13. body; Ps.
102. 5. flesh; Mark 1. 6. leathern
girdle

SKIP, Ps. 29. 6. & 114. 4. S. of S. 2.
8.
R. V. Jer. 48. 27. waggest the head
SLACK, Deut. 7. 10. Prov. 10. 4.
Hab. 1. 4. Zeph. 3. 16. 2 Pet. 3. 9.
SLANDER, Ex. 23. 1; Ps. 15. 3;
31. 13; 34. 13. (1 Pet. 3. 10.); 50. 20;
64. 3; 101. 5; Prov. 10. 18; Jer. 6.
28; 9. 4; Eph. 4. 31; Tit. 3. 2.
effects of, and conduct under,
Prov. 16. 28; 17. 9; 18. 8; 26. 20, 22;
Jer. 38. 4; Ezek. 22. 9; Matt. 5.
11; 26. 59; Acts 6. 11; 17. 7; 24. 5;
1 Cor. 4. 13.
SLANDEROUSLY reported,
Rom. 3. 8.
SLAY, Job 13. 15. Ps. 139. 19. Lev.
14. 13.
Eph. 2. 16. having *slain* the enmi.
Rev. 5. 9. wast *s.* and hast redeem.
6. 9. were *s.* for word of God
13. 8. Lamb *s.* from foundation
R. V. Lev. 26. 17; Deut. 1. 1. smit-
ten. Many changes to kill, smote,
put to death, etc.
SLAYING unpremeditatedly,
Num. 35. 11. Deut. 4. 42. & 19. 3.
Josh. 20. 3.
SLEEP, deep, Gen. 2. 21. & 15. 12.
1 Sam. 26. 12. Job 4. 13. Ps. 76. 6.
Prov. 19. 15. Isa. 29. 10.
Ps. 90. 5. as a *s.* in morning
127. 2. he giveth his beloved *s.*
Prov. 3. 24. thy *s.* shall be sweet
6. 10. a little *s.* a little slumber
20. 13. love not *s.* lest thou
Eccl. 5. 12. *s.* of a laboring man
Jer. 31. 26. my *s.* was sweet to me
Luke 9. 32. were heavy with *s.*
Rom. 13. 11. time to wake out of *s.*
Esth. 6. 1. night king could not *s.*
Eccl. 5. 12. the abundance of the
rich will not suffer him to *s.*
S. of S. 5. 2. I *s.* but my heart wak.
1 Cor. 11. 30. for this cause many *s.*
15. 51. we shall not all *s.* but
1 Thes. 4. 14. them which *s.* in
Jesus
5. 6. let us not *s.* as others; but
Ps. 3. 5. laid me down and *slept*
76. 5. they have *s.* their sleep
1 Cor. 15. 20. the firstfruits of them
that *s.*
Eph. 5. 14. awake, thou that *sleep-
est*
R. V. Isa. 56. 10. dreaming
SLIDE, Deut. 32. 35. Ps. 26. 1. & 37.
31. Jer. 8. 5. Hos. 4. 16.
R. V. Ps. 26. 1. without waver-
ing; Hos. 4. 16. behaved stub-
bornly
SLIGHTLY, Jer. 6. 14. & 8. 11.
SLING, 1 Sam. 25. 29. Jer. 10. 18.
SLIP, Ps. 17. 5. & 18. 36. & 38. 16. &
94. 18. Heb. 2. 1.
Ps. 26. 6. *slippery*, 73. 18. Jer. 23. 12.
R. V Heb. 2. 1. drift away
SLOTHFUL are under tribute,
Prov. 12. 24.
Prov. 12. 27. *s.* roasteth not which
18. 9. *s.* is brother to great waster
19. 24. *s.* hideth hand in bosom
24. 30. by the field of the *s.*
26. 14. door on hinges so doth *s.*
Rom. 12. 11. not *s.* in business
Heb. 6. 12. be not *s.* but followers
Prov. 19. 15. *slothfulness* casteth in
a deep sleep
R. V. Prov. 15. 19; 19. 24; 22. 13; 26.
13, 14, 15. sluggard; 18. 9. slack;
Heb. 6. 12. sluggish
SLOW to anger, Neh. 9. 17.
Luke 24. 25. fools, *s.* of heart to
Jas. 1. 19. *s.* to speak, *s.* to wrath,
Prov. 14. 29.
R. V. Tit. 1. 12. idle
SLUGGARD, go to ant, Prov. 6. 6.
Prov. 6. 9. how long wilt sleep, O *s.*
20. 4. *s.* will not plough by reason
26. 16. *s.* is wiser in his own con-
ceit
SLUMBER, Ps. 132. 4. Rom. 11. 8.
Ps. 121. 3. he that keepeth thee will
not *s.*, 4.

Matt. 25. 5. they all *slumbered* and
2 Pet. 3. 10. their damnation *slum-
bereth* not
R. V. Rom. 11. 8. stupor
SMITE, Lord shall, Deut. 28. 22.
Ps. 141. 5. let the righteous *s.* me
Zech. 13. 7. *s.* the shepherd
Matt. 5. 39. *s.* thee on thy right
John 18. 23. why *smitest* thou me
Isa. 53. 4. him *smitten* of God
Hos. 6. 1. hath *s.* and he will bind
R. V. 1 Sam. 23. 5. slew · 2 Sam. 10.
15, 19. put to the worse; 2 Chron.
22. 5. wounded; Matt. 24. 49; Luke
12. 63. beat; Matt. 26. 51; Luke 22.
64 · John 18. 10; 19. 3. struck
SMOKE, Gen. 19. 28. Ex. 19. 18.
Deut. 29. 20. anger of Lord shall *s.*
Ps. 74. 1. why doth thy anger *s.*
102. 3. as *s.*, Prov. 10. 26. Isa. 65. 5.
Rev. 14. 11. *s.* of torment ascend.
Isa. 42. 3. *smoking* flax, Matt. 12.
20.
SMOOTH, Gen. 27. 11, 16. Isa. 30.
10.
Ps. 55. 21. *smoother*, Prov. 5. 3.
SNARE, Ex. 23. 33. Judg. 2. 3.
Ps. 69. 22. table become a *s.*
91. 3. deliver thee from the *s.*
119. 110. wicked laid a *s.* for me
Prov. 29. 25. fear of man bringeth
a *s.*
1 Tim. 6. 9. they that will be rich
fall into a *s.*
2 Tim. 2. 26. out of the *s.* of devil
Ps. 11. 6. on the wicked he will
rain *snares*
Prov. 13. 14. depart from *s.* of dea.
Ps. 9. 16. *snared*, Prov. 6. 2. & 12.
13. Eccl. 9. 12. Isa. 8. 15. & 28. 13.
& 47. 29.
R. V. Job 18. 8. toils; 18. 10. noose;
Prov. 29. 8. flame; Lam. 3. 47. pit;
Jer. 5. 26. lie in wait
SNOW, as, Ps. 51. 7. & 68. 14. Isa.
1. 18. Dan. 7. 9. Matt. 28. 3. Rev. 1.
14.
SNUFFED, Mal. 1. 13. Jer. 2. 24.
SOAP, Jer. 2. 22. Mal. 3. 2.
SOBER for your cause, 2 Cor. 5. 13.
1 Thes. 5. 6. watch and be *s.*
1 Tim. 3. 2. bishop must be vigilant, *s.*
11. wives not slanderers, *s.*
Tit. 1. 8. *s.* just, holy, temperate
2. 4. teach young women to be *s.*
1 Pet. 1. 13. gird up your loins, be *s.*
4. 7. be *s.* and watch unto prayer
5. 8. be *s.* be vigilant, for your
Rom. 12. 3. not to think highly,
but *soberly*
Tit. 2. 12. teaching us to live *s.*
Acts 26. 25. words of *soberness*
1 Tim. 2. 9. *sobriety*, 15.
R. V. 2 Cor. 5. 13; 2 Tim. 3. 2; Tit.
1. 8. soberminded; 1 Tim. 3. 11;
Tit. 2. 2. temperate; 1 Pet. 4. 7. of
sound mind; Tit. 2. 4 —
SOFT, God maketh my heart, Job
23. 16.
Prov. 15. 1. *s.* answer turneth
25. 15. *s.* tongue breaketh the
Matt. 11. 8. man clothed in *s.* rai.
R. V. Job 23. 16. faint
SOJOURN, Gen. 12. 10. Ps. 120. 5.
Lev. 25. 23. *sojourners* with me,
1 Chron. 29. 15. Ps. 39. 12.
Ex. 12. 40. *sojourning*, 1 Pet. 1. 17.
SOLD thyself to work evil, 1 Kings
21. 20.
Rom. 7. 14. I am carnal, *s.* under
sin
SOLDIER of Jesus Christ, 2 Tim.
2. 3, 4.
R. V. 1 Chron. 7. 4. host; 2 Chron.
25. 13; Isa. 15. 4. men; 1 Chron. 7.
11; Mat. 27. 27 —
SON, 2 Sam. 18. 33. & 19. 4.
Ps. 2. 12. kiss the *S.* lest he be
Prov. 10. 1. a wise *s.* maketh a glad
father, 15. 20.
Mal. 3. 17. as a man spareth his *s.*
Matt. 11. 27. no man know. the *S.*
17. 5. this is my beloved *S.* 3. 17.

Luke 10. 6. if *s.* of peace be there
John 1. 18. only begotten *S.*, 3. 16.
 5. 21. *S.* quickeneth whom he will
 8. 35. *S.* abideth ever
 36. the *S.* maketh free
Rom. 8. 3. sent his own *S.* in the
Gal. 4. 7. if *s.* then an heir of God
2 Thes. 2. 3. man of sin, *s.* of per.
Heb. 5. 8. though a *S.* yet learned
1 John 2. 22. denieth the *S.* denieth
 5. 12. that hath *S.* hath life
Matt. 21. 37. *his son*, Acts 3. 13. Rom.
 1. 3, 9. & 5. 10. & 8. 29, 32. 1 Cor. 1. 9.
 Gal. 1. 16. & 4. 4, 6. 1 Thes. 1. 10.
 Heb. 1. 2. 1 John 1. 7. & 2. 23. & 3.
 23. & 4. 9, 10, 14. & 5. 9, 10, 11, 20.
Luke 15. 19. *thy son*, John 17. 1. & 19.
 26.
Dan. 3. 25. *the son of God*, Matt. 4. 3.
 & 16. 16. and forty-one other
 places
Num. 23. 19. *Son of man*, Job 25. 6.
 Ps. 8. 4. & 80. 17. & 144. 3. Dan. 7. 13.
 Ezekiel is so called about ninety
 and Christ about eighty-four
 times
Ps. 144. 12. that our *sons* may be as
 S. of S. 2. 3. is my beloved among *s.*
 Isa. 60. 10. *s.* of strangers, 61. 5. &
 62. 8.
Mal. 3. 3. purify *s.* of Levi
Mark 3. 17. Boanerges, *s.* of thun.
1 Cor. 4. 14. as my beloved *s.* I
Gal. 4. 6. because ye are *s.* God
 sent forth the Spirit of his Son
Heb. 2. 10. bring many *s.* to glory
 12. 7. God dealeth with you as *s.*
Gen. 6. 2. *sons of God*, Job 1. 6. &
 2. 1. & 38. 7. Hos. 1. 10. John 1. 12.
 Rom. 8. 14, 19. Phil. 2. 15. 1 John
 3. 1, 2.
R. V. Gen. 23. 3, 16, 20; 25. 10; 32.
 22; Num. 2. 14, 18, 22; Deut. 4. 1;
 2 Chron. 21. 7; Mark 13. 12; John
 1. 12; 1 Cor. 4. 14, 17; Col. 3. 6;
 Phil. 2. 15, 22; 1 Tim. 1. 18; 2 Tim.
 1. 2; 2. 1; Tit. 1. 4; Phile. 10 ; 1 John
 3. 1, 2. child or children; Num. 1.
 20 ; 26. 5. firstborn; 2 Sam. 23. 6.
 ungodly; Acts 3. 13, 26. Servant;
 Col. 4. 10. cousin; Gen. 36. 15; Isa.
 56. 3, 6; Matt. 18. 11; 24. 36; 25. 13;
 Luke 9. 56; John 12. 4; Acts 8. 37;
 1 John 5. 13——
SONG to the Lord, Ex. 15. 1. Num.
 21. 17.
 Ex. 15. 2. Lord is my *s.*, Ps. 118. 14.
 Isa. 12. 2.
Job 30. 9. I am their *s.*, Ps. 69. 12.
 35. 10. giveth *s.* in the night, Ps.
 42. 8. & 77. 6. Isa. 30. 29.
Ps. 32. 7. compass with *s.* of deliv.
 119. 54. *s.* in house of pilgrimage
Ezek. 33. 32. as a very lovely *s.*
Eph. 5. 19. speak to yourselves in
 spiritual *s.*
Rev. 14. 3. could learn that *s.*
 15. 3. sing *s.* of Moses and of Lamb
Ps. 33. 3. sing a *new song*, 40. 3. &
 96. 1. & 144. 9. & 149. 1. Isa. 42. 10.
 Rev. 5. 9.
R. V. 1 Chron. 25. 7; Isa. 35. 10.
 singing
SOON as they be born, Ps. 58. 3.
 Ps. 106. 13. *s.* forget his works
Prov. 14. 17. *s.* angry dealeth fool.
Gal. 1. 6. *s.* removed to another
R. V. Ps. 68. 31. haste to; Matt. 21.
 20. immediately; Gal. 1. 6; 2 Thes.
 2. 2. quickly; Josh. 3. 13; 2 Sam.
 6. 18; Mark 14. 45; Luke 1. 44; 15.
 30; 23. 7; John 16. 21; Acts 10. 29;
 Rev. 10. 10; 12. 4. when
SORCERER, Acts 13. 6, 8. & 8. 9, 11.
 Jer. 27. 9. *sorcerers*, Mal. 3. 5. Rev.
 21. 8.
SORE, 2 Chron. 6. 28. Job 5. 18.
 Heb. 10. 29. much *sorer* punish.
 Isa. 1. 6. and putrefying *sores*
R. V. Lev. 13. 42, 43; 2 Chron. 6. 28,
 29 ; Ps. 38. 11. plague
SORRY, Ps. 38. 18. 2 Cor. 2. 2. & 7. 8.
 Ps. 90. 10. labor and *sorrow*
 Prov. 15. 13. by *s.* of heart the

Eccl. 1. 18. knowledge increaseth *s.*
 7. 3. *s.* is better than laughter
Isa. 35. 10. *s.* and sighing flee, 51. 11.
Lam. 1. 12. be any *s.* like unto my
John 16. 6. *s.* hath filled your
 20. *s.* shall be turned into joy
2 Cor. 7. 10. godly *s.* worketh repentance to salvation, but *s.* of
 world, 9.
Phil. 2. 27. should have *s.* upon *s.*
 1 Thes. 4. 13. *s.* not as others
Rev. 21. 4. no more death, neither *s.*
 Ps. 18. 5. the *s.* of hell
 116. 3. the *s.* of death
Isa. 53. 3. man of *s.*
 4. carried our *s.*
Matt. 24. 8. beginning of *sorrows*
1 Tim. 6. 10. pierced through with
 many *s.*
2 Cor. 7. 9. *sorrowed*, Jer. 31. 12.
1 Sam. 1. 15. woman of *sorrowful*
 spirit
Prov. 14. 13. in laughter heart is *s.*
Jer. 31. 25. replenished *s.* soul
Matt. 19. 22. man went away *s.*
 26. 22, 38. my soul is exceeding *s.*
2 Cor. 6. 10. *s.* yet always rejoicing
Luke 2. 48. *sorrowing*, Acts 20. 38.
R. V. Gen. 3. 17; Ps. 127. 2. toil;
 Ex. 15. 14. pangs; Deut. 28. 65.
 pining; Job 3. 10. trouble; 41. 22.
 terror; Job 6. 10; Jer. 30. 15; 45. 3;
 51. 29; Rom. 9. 2. pain; 2 Sam. 22.
 6; Ps. 18. 4, 5; 116. 3. cords; Ps. 55.
 10. mischief; Isa. 5. 30. distress;
 Isa. 29. 2. lamentation; Matt. 24.
 8; Mark 13. 8. travail; Rev. 18. 7;
 21. 4. mourning; Neh. 8. 10; Matt.
 14. 9. grieved; Isa. 51. 19. be-
 moaned
SORT, 2 Cor. 7. 11. 3 John 6.
R. V. Deut. 22. 11. mingled stuff;
 Ps. 78. 45; 105. 31. swarms; Dan.
 1. 10. own age; Acts 17. 5. rabble;
 Rom. 11. 15. measure
SOUGHT the Lord, Ex. 33. 7.
 2 Chron. 14. 7.
 Ps. 34. 4. I *s.* Lord, and he heard
 119. 10. with my whole heart I *s.*
Eccl. 7. 29. *s.* out many inventions
Isa. 62. 12. be called *s.* out, a city
 65. 1. found of them that *s.* me
Rom. 9. 32. *s.* it not by faith, but
 Heb. 12. 17. though he *s.* it care.
2 Chron. 16. 12. *s.* not Lord
1 Chron. 15. 13. *sought him*, 2 Chron.
 14. 7. & 15. 4. Ps. 78. 34. S. of S. 3.
 1, 2. & 5. 6. Jer. 8. 2. & 26. 21.
SOUL abhor my judgments, Lev.
 26. 15, 43.
 Gen. 2. 7. man became a living *s.*
Deut. 11. 13. serve him with all *s.*
 13. 3. love the Lord with all thy
 s., Josh. 22. 5. 1 Kings 2. 4. Mark
 12. 33.
1 Sam. 18. 1. *s.* of Jonathan knit
1 Kings 8. 48. with all their *s.*
 1 Chron. 22. 19. set your *s.* to seek
Job 16. 4. if your *s.* were in my *s.*'s
 stead
 Ps. 19. 7. law is perfect, convert. *s.*
 49. 8. redemption of *s.* is precious
 107. 9. filleth the hungry *s.* with
Prov. 10. 3. not suffer *s.* of right.
 18. 2. *s.* be without knowledge
 27. 17. full *s.* loatheth honey-comb
Isa. 55. 2. let your *s.* delight
 58. 10. I will satisfy the afflicted *s.*
Jer. 31. 25. have satiated weary *s.*
 38. 16. the Lord made us this *s.*
Ezek. 18. 4. *s.* that sinneth, it
Matt. 10. 28. not able to kill *s.*
Rom. 13. 1. let every *s.* be subject
 1 Thes. 5. 23. spirit, *s.* and body
Heb. 4. 12. piercing to divid. of *s.*
 10. 39. believe to saving of the *s.*
Ex. 30. 12. ransom for *his soul*
Judg. 10. 16. — was grieved for
2 Kings 23. 25. turned to Lord with
 all—
Job 27. 8. God taketh away —
Hab. 2. 4. — lifted up, is not
Matt. 16. 26. lose—; what in ex-
 change for—

Ps. 16. 10. not leave *my soul* in
 23. 3. say to — I am thy salvation
 42. 5, 11. why cast down, O —
 62. 1. — waiteth upon God, 5.
 63. 1.— thirsteth for thee, my flesh
Isa. 26. 9. with — have I desired
 thee, 8.
 61. 10. shall be joyful in my God
Luke 1. 46. — doth magnify the
John 12. 27. now is — troubled,
 Matt. 26. 38.
Ps. 33. 20. *our soul*, 44. 25. & 66. 9. &
 123. 4. & 124. 4. Isa. 26. 8.
Deut. 13. 6. *own soul*, 1 Sam. 18. 1. &
 20. 17. Ps. 22. 29. Prov. 8. 36. & 11.
 17. & 15. 32. & 19. 8, 16. & 6. 32. & 20.
 2. & 29. 24. Mark 8. 36. Luke 2. 35.
Deut. 4. 9. *with all thy soul*, 6. 5. &
 10. 12. & 30. 6. Matt. 22. 37.
Ezek. 3. 19. deliver *thy soul*, 21. &
 33. 9.
Luke 12. 20. this night — shall be
 required of thee
3 John 2. prosper — as prospereth
Ps. 72. 13. save *souls* of the
Prov. 11. 30. winneth *s.* is wise
Isa. 57. 16. spirit fail, and *s.*
Ezek. 14. 14. should but deliver *s.*
 1 Pet. 3. 20. few, i. e. eight *s.* saved
2 Pet. 2. 14. beguiling unstable *s.*
Rev. 6. 9. *s.* of slain and behead.
Luke 21. 19. *your souls*, Josh. 23. 14.
 Jer. 6. 16. & 26. 19. Matt. 11. 29.
 Heb. 13. 17. 1 Pet. 1. 9, 22. & 2. 25.
R. V. Lev. 17. 11; Num. 16. 38;
 1 Sam. 26. 21; Job 31. 30; Prov. 22.
 23; Matt. 16. 26; Mark 8. 36, 37. life
 or lives; Lev. 4. 2; 5. 1, 2, 4, 15, 17
 6. 2; 7. 21. any one; Num. 15. 27.
 one person; Job 30. 15. honor;
 Prov. 19. 18. heart; Hos. 9. 4. appetite; Ps. 16. 2; Jer. 5. 41; Mark
 12. 23——
SOUND, dreadful, Job 15. 21.
 Ps. 47. 5. God is gone up with *s.*
 119. 80. let my heart be *s.*
 Prov. 2. 7. *s.* wisdom, 3. 21.
Eccl. 12. 4. *s.* of the grinding is
Amos 6. 5. that chant to *s.* of viol
Rom. 10. 18. *s.* went into all the
 1 Tim. 1. 10. contrary to *s.* doc.
2 Tim. 1. 7. *s.* mind
 13. of *s.* words
Tit. 1. 9. *s.* doctrine, *s.* in faith
 2. 8. *s.* speech that cannot
Isa. 63. 15. *sounding* of bowels, 16.
 11.
Ps. 38. 3, 7. no *soundness*, Isa. 1. 6.
R. V. Job 39. 24; John 3. 8; 1 Cor.
 14. 7, 8; Rev. 1. 15; 18. 22. voice;
 Ps. 119. 80. perfect; 2 Tim. 1. 7.
 discipline; Isa. 63. 15. yearning;
 Ezek. 7. 7. joyful shouting
SOUR GRAPES, proverb con-
 cerning, Jer. 31. 29. Ezek. 18. 2.
SOUTH, the king of, Dan. 11.
 — queen of, Matt. 12. 42.
SOW that was washed, 2 Pet. 2. 22.
SOW wickedness reap the same,
 Job 4. 8.
 Ps. 126. 5. *s.* in tears, reap in joy
Isa. 32. 20. blessed that *s.* beside
Jer. 4. 3. *s.* not among thorns
Hos. 10. 12. *s.* in righteousness
Mic. 6. 15. thou shalt *s.* and not
Matt. 13. 3. sower went out to *s.*
Luke 12. 24. the ravens neither *s.*
Ps. 97. 11. light is *sown* for right.
Hos. 8. 7. *s.* wind, reap whirlwind
 10. 12. *s.* in righteousness spiritual
 15. 42. it is *s.* in corruption
2 Cor. 9. 10. multiply your seed *s.*
Jas. 3. 18. fruit of righteousness is
 s. in peace
Prov. 11. 18. that *soweth* righteous
 22. 8. *s.* iniquity, shall reap van.
John 4. 37. one *s.* another reapeth
2 Cor. 9. 6. *s.* sparingly, *s.* bounti.
Gal. 6. 7. what a man *s.* that shall
Isa. 55. 10. seed to *sower*, 2 Cor. 9.
 10.
R. V. Prov. 16. 28. scattereth
SPARE all the place, Gen. 18. 16.
Neh. 13. 22. *s.* me according to

Ps. 39. 13. *s.* me that I may
Prov. 19. 18. let not thy soul *s.* for
Joel 2. 17. *s.* thy people and give
Mal. 3. 17. I will *s.* them, as
Rom. 8. 32. *spared* not his own Son
  11. 21. if God *s.* not the natural
2 Pet. 2. 4. God *s.* not angels that
Prov. 13. 24. he that *spareth* rod
R. V. Ps. 72. 13; Jonah 4. 11. have
  pity on; Prov. 21. 26. withholdeth
SPARKS, Job 5. 7. Isa. 50. 11.
R. V. Isa. 50. 11. firebrands
SPARROW, Ps. 102. 7. Matt. 10. 29.
SPEAK against Moses, Num. 12. 8.
Gen. 18. 27. taken on me to *s.*
Ex. 4. 14. Aaron thy brother can *s.*
  34. 35. went in to *s.* to the Lord
1 Sam. 3. 9. *s.* Lord, thy servant
Ps. 85. 8. Lord will *s.* peace to peo.
Isa. 8. 20. if *s.* not according to
Jer. 18. 7. at what instant I *s.*, 9.
Hab. 2. 3. at end it shall *s.* and
Matt. 10. 19. what ye shall *s.*
Luke 6. 26. when all men *s.* well
John 3. 11. we *s.* that we do know
Acts 4. 20. cannot but *s.* things
1 Cor. 1. 10. ye all *s.* the same
Tit. 3. 2. to *s.* evil of no man
Jas. 1. 19. swift to hear, slow to *s.*
2 Pet. 2. 10. *s.* evil of dignities
Jude 10. *s.* evil of things which
Matt. 12. 32. *speaketh* against Son
  34. out of the abundance of the
  heart the mouth *s.*
Heb. 11. 4. he being dead yet *s.*
  12. 24. *s.* better things than
1 Pet. 2. 12. *s.* against you as evil
Isa. 45. 19. *I speak,* 63. 1. John 4.
  26. & 7. 17. & 8. 26, 28, 38. & 12. 50.
  Rom. 3. 5. & 6. 19. 1 Tim. 2. 7.
Isa. 58. 13. nor *speaking* own
  65. 24. while they are *s.* I will
Dan. 9. 20. while I was *s.* and
Matt. 6. 7. heard for much *s.*
Eph. 4. 15. *s.* the truth in love
  31. evil *s.* be put away
  5. 19. *s.* to yourselves in psalms
1 Tim. 4. 2. *s.* lies in hypocrisy
Rev. 13. 5. a mouth *s.* great
Gen. 11. 1. earth was of one *speech*
Deut. 32. 2. my *s.* shall distil
Matt. 26. 73. thy *s.* bewrayeth
1 Cor. 2. 1. with excellency of *s.*
2 Cor. 3. 12. great plainness of *s.*
Col. 4. 6. let your *s.* be with grace
Tit. 2. 8. sound *s.* that cannot
Jude 15. all their hard *speeches*
Rom. 16. 18. by fair *s.* deceive
Matt. 22. 12. he was *speechless*
R. V. Many changes, chiefly to
  say, said, answered, spoken, ut-
  ter; 2 Sam. 14. 20. matter; 2 Chron.
  32. 18. language; S. of S. 4. 3.
  mouth; Ezek. 1. 24. tumult; Hab.
  3. 2. report; 1 Cor. 4. 19. word;
  Jude 15. things; Luke 1. 22. dumb
SPECTACLE to angels, 1 Cor. 4.
  9.
SPEED, Gen. 24. 12. 2 John 10. 11.
Ezra 7. 21. *speedily,* 26. Ps. 31. 2. &
  79. 8. Ex. 8. 11. Luke 18. 8.
R. V. Ezek. 6. 12. all diligence;
  2 John 10. 11. greeting; Gen. 44.
  11. hasted; 2 Sam. 17. 16. in any
  wise; 2 Chron. 35. 13. quickly;
  Ezek. 6. 13; 7. 17, 21, 26. with diligence; Ps. 143. 7. make haste
SPEND their days in wealth, Job
  21. 13.
Ps. 90. 9. *s.* our years as a tale
Isa. 55. 2. *s.* money for that is
  49. 4. have *spent* my strength
Rom. 13. 12. night is far *s.* day
2 Cor. 12. 15. spend and be *s.*
R. V. Ps. 90. 9. bring to an end;
  Prov. 21. 20. swalloweth; 29. 3.
  wasteth
SPICES, S. of S. 4. 10, 14, 16. & 8.
  14.
R. V. Gen. 43. 11. spicery; 1 Kings
  10. 15 ——; Ezek. 24. 10. make thick
  the broth
SPIDER, Prov. 30. 28. Job 8. 14.
  Isa. 59. 5.

Prov. 30. 28. *s.* take hold with hands
R. V. *lizard*
SPIES sent into Canaan by Moses,
  Num. 13. 3, 17, 26. & 14. 36. Deut.
  1. 22. Heb. 3. 17.
  sent to Jericho by Joshua, Josh.
  2. 1, 4, 17, 23. & 6. 17, 23.
SPIKENARD, S. of S. 1. 12. & 4.
  13, 14.
SPIRIT made willing, Ex. 35. 21.
Num. 11. 17. take of *s.* which is
2 Kings 2. 9. portion of thy *s.*
Ezra 1. 5. whose *s.* God raised
Neh. 9. 20. gavest good *s.* to instr.
Job 26. 13. by his *s.* he garnished
Ps. 31. 5. into thy hand I commit *s.*
  32. 2. in whose *s.* there is no guile
  51. 10. renew a right *s.* within me
  12. uphold me with thy free *s.*
  17. a broken *s.* and contrite, 34. 18.
Prov. 15. 13. & 17. 22. Isa. 57. 15. &
  66. 2.
Ps. 76. 12. will cut off *s.* of princes
  104. 30. sendest forth thy *s.*
  139. 7. whither should I go from *s.*
  142. 3. my *s.* was overwhelmed
  143. 7. *s.* faileth
  10. thy *s.* is good
Prov. 14. 29. hasty of *s.* exalteth
  15. 13. sorrow of heart the *s.*
  16. 18. a haughty *s.* before a fall
  18. 14. a wounded *s.* who can bear
Eccl. 3. 21. who knoweth *s.* of man
  8. 8. no power over *s.* to retain *s.*
  12. 7. the *s.* shall return to God
Isa. 32. 15. until *s.* be poured on us
Mic. 2. 11. walking in *s.* and false.
Zech. 10. 1. formeth *s.* of man
  within
Mal. 2. 15. take heed to your *s.*
Matt. 22. 43. doth David in *s.* call
  26. 41. *s.* is willing, but flesh
Luke 1. 80. John waxed strong in *s.*
  8. 55. *s.* came again and she arose
  9. 55. what kind of *s.* ye are
  24. 39. *s.* hath not flesh and
John 3. 5. born of water and of *s.*
  34. God giveth not *s.* by measure
  4. 24. God is a *s.* worship him
  6. 63. it is the *s.* that quickeneth
Acts 6. 10. not able to resist the *s.*
  16. 7. the *s.* suffered them not
  17. 16. Paul's *s.* was stirred in
Rom. 8. 1. not after flesh, but *s.*
  2. *s.* of life in Christ Jesus made
  9. if any have not *s.* of Christ
  13. if ye through *s.* mortify
  26. the *s.* helpeth our infirmi.
1 Cor. 2. 10. *s.* searcheth all things
  5. 3. present in *s.*
  5. *s.* may be saved
  6. 17. joined unto the Lord is one
  s., 12. 13.
2 Cor. 3. 3. written with *s.* of liv.
  17. *s.* of Lord is, there is liberty
Gal. 3. 3. begun in *s.* are now per.
  4. 6. sent forth *s.* of Son into
  5. 16. walk in the *s.*
  18. if led by *s.* are not under law
  22. fruit of *s.* is love, joy, peace
  25. if we live in the *s.* let us walk
  6. 18. grace be with your *s.*
Eph. 1. 13. with holy *s.* of promise
  4. 4. one body and one *s.*
  23. renewed in *s.* of your mind
  5. 9. fruit of *s.* is in all godliness
Col. 2. 5. I am with you in the *s.*
1 Thes. 5. 23. whole *s.* soul and
Heb. 4. 12. dividing asunder of
  soul and *s.*
  9. 14. through eternal *s.* offered
Jas. 4. 5. *s.* that dwelleth in us
1 Pet. 3. 4. ornament of a meek and
  quiet *s.*
  4. 6. live according to God in the *s.*
1 John 4. 1. believe not every *s.* but
  try *s.*
Rev. 1. 10. I was in *s.* on Lord's
  11. 11. *s.* of life from God entered
  14. 13. yea, saith the *s.* that they
Gen. 6. 3. my *spirit,* Job 10. 12. Ps.
  31. 5. & 77. 6. Isa. 38. 16. Ezek. 36.
  27. Zech. 4. 6. Luke 1. 47. & 23. 46.
  Acts 7. 59. Rom. 1. 9. 1 Cor. 14. 14.

Gen. 1. 2. *Spirit of God,* Ex. 31. 3.
  2 Chron. 15. 1. Job 33. 4. Ezek. 11.
  34. Matt. 3. 16. & 12. 28. Rom. 8. 9,
  14. & 15. 19. 1 Cor. 2. 11, 14. & 3. 16.
  & 6. 11. & 12. 3. 2 Cor. 3. 3. Eph. 4.
  30. 1 Pet. 4. 14. 1 John 4. 2.
Isa. 11. 2. *s.* of wisdom, Eph. 1, 17.
Zech. 12. 1. unclean *s.,* Matt. 12.
  43.
Ps. 104. 4. maketh angels *spirits*
Prov. 16. 2. Lord weigheth the *s.*
Matt. 10. 1. *unclean spirits,* Acts 5.
  16. & 8. 7. Rev. 16. 13, 14.
Luke 10. 20. the *s.* are subject
1 Cor. 14. 32. *s.* of the prophets
Heb. 12. 23. to *s.* of just men made
1 Pet. 3. 19. preached to *s.* in prison
1 John 4. 1. try *s.* whether they be
Hos. 9. 7. the *spiritual* man is mad
Rom. 1. 11. impart some *s.* gift
  7. 14. law is *s.* but I am carnal
  15. 27. partakers of their *s.* things
1 Cor. 2. 13. comparing *s.* things
  15. he that is *s.* judgeth all things
  9. 11. sown to you *s.* things
  10. 3. eat *s.* meat
  15. 44. it is raised a *s.* body
Gal. 6. 1. ye which are *s.* restore
Eph. 1. 3. blessed us with *s.* bless.
  5. 19. speaking in *s.* songs
  6. 12. wrestle against *s.* wicked.
Col. 1. 9. filled with *s.* understand.
1 Pet. 2. 5. built us *s.* house; offer
Rom. 8. 6. to be *spiritually* minded
1 Cor. 2. 14. because *s.* discerned
Rev. 11. 8. *s.* is called Sodom and
R. V. Ps. 104. 4; Eccl. 1. 14, 17; 2.
  11, 17, 26; 4. 4, 6, 16; 6. 9; 11. 5;
  Zech. 6. 5; Heb. 1. 7. wind or
  winds; Isa. 40. 7; 59. 19; 2 Thes.
  2. 8; Rev. 11. 1. breath; Matt. 14.
  26; Mark 6. 49. apparition; Acts
  18. 5. by word; Eph. 5. 9. light;
  Luke 2. 40; 9. 55; Rom. 8. 1; 1 Cor.
  6. 20; 1 Tim. 4. 12; 1 Pet. 1. 22 ——
SPITE, Ps. 10. 14. Matt. 22. 6.
SPITTING, Isa. 50. 6. Luke 18. 32.
SPITTING, Isa. 50. 6. Luke 18. 32.
SPOIL, Gen. 49. 27. Ps. 68. 12.
Ps. 119. 162. that finds great *s.*
Matt. 12. 29. he will *s.* his house
Col. 2. 8. lest any *s.* you through
Ex. 12. 36. *spoiled* the Egyptians
Col. 2. 15. having *s.* principalities
Heb. 10. 34. took joyfully *spoiling*
R. V. Num. 31. 53; 2 Chron. 14. 13.
  booty; Job 29. 17. prey; Prov. 31.
  11. gain; Isa. 25. 11. craft; Hab. 2.
  17. destruction; Ps. 35. 12. bereav-
  ing
SPOT, without, Num. 19. 2. & 28. 3.
  9. Job 11. 19. 2 Tim. 6. 14. Heb. 9.
  14. 1 Pet. 1. 19. 2 Pet. 3. 14.
S. of S. 4. 7. there is no *s.* in thee
Eph. 5. 27. not having *s.* or wrinkle
Jer. 13. 33. *spots,* Jude 12, 23.
R. V. Num. 28. 3, 9, 11; 29. 17, 26;
  Deut. 32. 5; Heb. 9. 14. blemish;
  Lev. 13. 39. tetter; Jude 12. hidden
  rocks
SPREAD, Job 9. 8. Isa. 25. 11. &
  37. 14. Jer. 4. 3. Lam. 1. 17. Ezek.
  16. 8.
R. V. 2 Sam. 17. 19. strewed;
  1 Chron. 14. 9. made raid; Job 9.
  8. stretcheth; Mark 1. 28. went
  out; 6. 14. become known; 1 Thes.
  1. 8. gone forth
SPRING, Ps. 85. 11. Matt. 13. 5, 7.
Ps. 65. 10. *springing,* John 4. 14.
  Heb. 12. 15.
Ps. 87. 7. all my *springs* are in thee
R. V. Deut. 4. 49; Josh. 10. 40; 12.
  8. slopes; Ps. 87. 7; Jer. 51. 36.
  fountains; Lev. 13. 42. breaking
  out; Matt. 13. 7; Luke 8. 6, 7, 8.
  grew; Mark 4. 8. growing
SPRINKLE, Lev. 14. 7. & 16. 14.
Isa. 52. 15. he shall *s.* many nations
Ezek. 36. 25. I will *s.* clean water
Heb. 10. 22. having hearts *sprinkled*
  from an evil conscience
  12. 24. to blood of *sprinkling*
1 Pet. 1. 2. through *s.* of the blood
SPUE thee out of my mouth, Rev.

S. 16. Hab. 2. 16. Lev. 18. 28. Jer. 25. 27.
R. V. Lev. 18. 28; 20. 22. vomit
SPY, Num. 13. 16. Josh. 2. 1. Gal. 2. 4.
STABILITY of times, Isa. 33. 6.
STAFF, Gen. 32. 10. Zech. 11. 10.
Ps. 23. 4. thy rod and *s.* comfort
Isa. 3. 1. stay and *s.* of bread
10. 5. *s.* in their hand is my
STAGGER, Ps. 107. 27. Rom. 4. 20.
STAIN, Isa. 23. 9. & 63. 3.
R. V. Job 3. 5. claim it
STAKES, Isa. 33. 20. & 54. 2.
STAMMER, Isa. 28. 11. & 33. 19. & 32. 4.
STAND, Ezek. 29. 7. Ex. 9. 11.
Job 19. 25. *s.* at latter day on earth
Ps. 76. 7. who may *s.* in thy sight
130. 3. if Lord mark iniquities who shall *s.*
Isa. 46. 10. my counsel shall *s.*
Mal. 3. 2. who shall *s.* when he
Matt. 12. 25. house divided against itself shall not *s.*
Rom. 5. 2. this grace wherein we *s.*
14. 4. God is able to make him *s.*
2 Cor. 1. 24. by faith ye *s.*
Eph. 6. 13. having done all to *s.*
1 Pet. 5. 12. grace of God wherein ye *s.*
Rev. 3. 20. 1 *s.* at the door and
Nah. 1. 6. *stand before*, 1 Sam. 6. 20. Luke 21. 36. Rom. 14. 10. Rev. 20. 12.
1 Cor. 16. 13. *stand fast* in the faith
Gal. 5. 1. — in the liberty where.
Phil. 1. 27.— in one spirit
4. 1.— in the Lord
1 Thes. 3. 8. live, if ye— in Lord
2 Thes. 2. 15.— and hold traditions
Ps. 1. 5. *stand in*, 4. 4. & 24. 3.
Ex. 14. 13. *stand still*, see salvation, 2 Chron. 20. 17. Josh. 10. 12. Zech. 11. 16.
Ps. 1. 1. *standeth*, 26. 12. & 33. 11. Prov. 8. 2. S. of S. 2. 9. Isa. 3. 13.
Ps. 119. 16]. my heart *s.* in awe of
1 Cor. 10. 12. thinketh he *s.* take
2 Tim. 2. 19. foundation of God *s.*
Jas. 5. 9. the Judge *s.* at the door
R. V. Several changes, but chiefly due to words before and after
STAR, Num. 24. 17. Matt. 2. 2.
Judg. 5. 20. *stars* in their courses
Job 25. 5. *s.* are not pure in his
Dan. 12. 3. shall shine as *s.* for
Jude 13. wandering *s.* to whom 1s
Rev. 12. 1. a crown of twelve *s.*
R. V. Amos 5. 8. Pleiades
STATURE, Matt. 6. 27. Eph. 4. 13.
STATUTES and laws, Neh. 9. 14.
Ps. 19. 8. *s.* of the Lord are right
Ezek. 20. 25. *s.* not good
Ex. 15. 26. *his statutes*, Deut. 6. 17.
2 Kings 17. 15. Ps. 18. 22. & 105. 45.
1 Chron. 29. 19. *thy statutes*, Ps. 119. 12, 16, 23, 26, 33, 54, 64, 68, 71, 117.
STAVES for the tabernacle, Ex. 25. 13. & 37. 15. & 40. 20. Num. 4. 6.
STAY, Ps. 18. 18. S. of S. 2. 5. Isa. 10. 20. & 26. 3. & 27. 8. & 48. 2. & 50. 10.
R. V. 1 Sam. 24. 7. checked; Job 38. 37. pour out
STEAD, Gen. 4. 25. & 22. 13.
Job 16. 4. if your soul were in my soul's *s.*
2 Cor. 5. 20. pray you in Christ's *s.*
R. V. Phile. 13. behalf
STEADFAST, Job 11. 15. Dan. 6. 26.
Ps. 78. 8. spirit not *s.* with God
Acts 2. 42. continued *s.* in apos.
1 Cor. 15. 58. be ye *s.*, immovable
Heb. 3. 14. hold confidence *s.* to
Col. 2. 5. *steadfastness*, 2 Pet. 3. 17.
R. V. Ps. 78. 37. faithful; Heb. 3. 14. firm
STEAL, Ex. 20. 15. Lev. 19. 11.
Prov. 6. 30. if he *s.* to satisfy his
30. 9. lest I be poor and *s.* and.
Matt. 6. 19. thieves break through and *s.*

Matt. 27. 64. disciples come by night and *s.* him away
Eph. 4. 28. that *stole*, steal no more
Prov. 9. 17. *stolen* waters are sweet
STEALING, Ex. 20. 15. & 21. 16. Lev. 19. 11. Deut. 5. 19. & 24. 7. Ps. 50. 18. Zech. 5. 4. Matt. 19. 18. Rom. 13. 9. Eph. 4. 28. 1 Pet. 4. 15.
restoration inculcated, Ex. 22. 1.
Lev. 6. 4. Prov. 6. 30, 31.
STEPS, Ex. 20. 26. Ps. 18. 36.
Ps. 37. 23. *s.* of good men ordered
44. 18. neither our *s.* declined
Prov. 16. 9. Lord directeth his *s.*
Jer. 10. 23. man to direct his *s.*
Rom. 4. 12. walk in *s.* of that faith
1 Pet. 2. 21. should follow his *s.*
R. V. Ps. 27. 23. goings; 85. 13. foot-steps
STEWARD, Luke 12. 42. & 16. 2.
1 Cor. 4. 1. Tit. 1. 7. 1 Pet. 4. 10.
R. V. 1 Chron. 28. 1. rulers
STIFF neck, Deut. 31. 27. Jer. 17. 23.
Ex. 32. 9. *stiff-necked* people, 33. 3, 5. & 34. 9. Deut. 9. 6, 13. & 10. 16.
Acts 7. 51.— ye do always resist
2 Chron. 36. 13. he *stiffened* his neck
STILL, Ex. 15. 16. Ps. 8. 2. & 139. 18.
Ps. 4. 4. be *s.*, Jer. 47. 6. Mark 4. 39.
46. 10. be *s.* and know that I am
Isa. 30. 7. their strength is to sit *s.*
Rev. 22. 11. unjust *s.* filthy *s.*
Ps. 65. 7. *stilleth* noise of the sea, 89. 9.
STING, 1 Cor. 15. 55, 56. Rev. 9. 10.
Prov. 23. 32. it *stings* like an adder
STINK, Ps. 38. 5. Isa. 3. 24.
R. V. Isa. 3. 24. rottenness
STIR up, Num. 24. 9. Job 17. 8.
Ps. 35. 23. *s.* up thyself, awake
78. 38. did not *s.* up all his wrath
S. of S. 2. 7. that ye *s.* not up
2 Tim. 1. 6. *s.* up gift of God that
2 Pet. 1. 13. think it meet to *s.* you
R. V. Isa. 22. 2. shoutings; Num. 24. 9. rouse; 1 Kings 11. 14, 23. raised; Dan. 11. 10. war; Acts 13. 50. urged on; 17. 16. provoked
STONE of Israel, Gen. 49. 24.
Ps. 118. 22. *s.* which the builders refused
Isa. 8. 14. a *s.* of stumbling
28. 16. a tried *s.* a precious cor. *s.*
Hab. 2. 11. *s.* shall cry out of wall
Matt. 3. 9. of *s.* to raise up children unto Abraham
7. 9. bread, will he give him *s.*
1 Pet. 2. 4. as unto a living *s.*
6. lay in Sion a chief corner *s.*
Ezek. 11. 19. *stony*, Matt. 13. 5.
R. V. Ex. 4. 25. flint; Job 40. 17. thighs; Ps. 137. 9. rock; Isa. 34. 11. plummet; Mark 12. 4.——;
John 1. 42. Peter; Matt. 13. 5, 20; Mark 4. 5, 16. rocky
STOOP, Job 9. 13. Prov. 12. 25. Mark 1. 7.
R. V. 1 Sam. 24. 8; 28. 14. bowed
STORE, 1 Cor. 16. 2. 1 Tim. 6. 19.
Luke 12. 24. *storehouse*, Ps. 33. 7.
R. V. Deut. 28. 5, 17. kneading-trough
STORM, Ps. 55. 8. & 83. 15.
Ps. 107. 29. maketh the *s.* a calm
Isa. 4. 6. covert from the *s.*
Mark 4. 37. a great *s.*, Luke 8. 23.
Ps. 148. 8. *stormy* wind fulfilling
R. V. Isa. 29. 6. whirlwind
STOUT hearted, Ps. 76. 5. Isa. 46. 12.
Isa. 10. 12. punish fruit of *s.* heart
Mal. 3. 13. words have been *s.*
Isa. 9. 9. say to pride and *stout-ness*
STRAIGHT, Josh. 6. 5. Jer. 31. 9.
Ps. 5. 8. thy way *s.* before my
Isa. 40. 3. make *s.* a highway
4. crooked he made *s.*, 45. 16. Luke 3. 5.
Luke 3. 4. way of the Lord, make his paths *s.*
Heb. 12. 13. make *s.* paths for feet
R. V. Isa. 45. 2. plain
STRAIN at a gnat, Matt. 23. 24.

STRAIT, 2 Sam. 24. 14. Job 20. 22. & 36. 16. Isa. 49. 20. Phil. 1. 23.
Matt. 7. 13. enter in at the *s.* gate
Job 18. 7. steps *straitened*
Mic. 2. 7. spirit of the Lord *s.*
Luke 12. 50. how am I *s.* till it be
2 Cor. 6. 12. not *s.* in us, *s.* in your
R. V. Job 36. 16. distress; Matt. 7. 13, 14; Luke 13. 24. narrow
STRANGE, Ex. 21. 8. & 30. 9. Lev. 10. 1. Ps. 81. 9. Jer. 2. 21. Luke 5. 26. Heb. 11. 9. 1 Pet. 4. 12. Jude 7.
Job 31. 3. is not a *s.* punishment
Isa. 28. 21. do his *s.* work bring
Hos. 8. 12. counted as a *s.* thing
Zeph. 1. 8. clothed with *s.* apparel
Heb. 13. 9. about with *s.* doctrines
Judg. 11. 2. *strange* women, Prov. 2. 16. & 5. 3, 20. & 6. 24. & 20. 16. & 23. 27. & 27. 13. Ezra 10. 2, 11.
Gen. 23. 4. *stranger* and sojourner, Ps. 39. 12. & 119. 19. 1 Chron. 29. 15.
Prov. 14. 10. a *s.* doth not meddle
Jer. 14. 8. should. thou be as a *s.*
Matt. 25. 35. I was a *s.* and ye
Luke 17. 18. to give God glory save this *s.*
John 10. 5. a *s.* will they not follow
Ps. 105. 12. very few and *strangers*
146. 9. Lord preserveth the *s.*
Eph. 2. 12. *s.* from the covenant
Heb. 11. 13. confessed they were *s.*
13. 2. not forgetful to entertain *s.*
1 Pet. 2. 11. beseech you as *s.*
R. V. Job 31. 3. disaster; 19. 13. hardly with; Prov. 21. 8. crooked; Judg. 11. 2. another; Zeph. 1. 8; Acts 26. 11. foreign; Heb. 11. 9. not his own; Gen. 17. 8; 28. 4; 36. 7; 37. 1. sojournings; Ex. 12. 43; Prov. 5. 10; Ezek. 44. 7, 9. alien; Ex. 2. 22; 18. 3; 19. 1. sojourn; Lev. 25. 47; 1 Chron. 16. 19; Ps. 105. 12; 119. 19; Jer. 14. 8; Acts 2. 10; 7. 29; 1 Pet. 2. 11. sojourner; Deut. 17. 15; 23. 20; 29. 22. foreigner; Isa. 5. 17. wanderers; 29. 5. foes; Obad. 12. of his disaster
STRANGLED, Acts 15. 20, 29. & 21. 25.
Job 7. 15. soul chooseth *strangling*
STREAM, Isa. 30. 33. & 66. 12. Dan. 7. 10. Amos 5. 24. Luke 6. 48.
Ps. 46. 4. *streams*, 126. 4. S. of S. 4. 15. Isa. 30. 25. & 33. 21. & 35. 6.
R. V. Ex. 7. 19; 8. 5. rivers; Num. 21. 15. slope; Job 6. 15. channel; Isa. 27. 12. brook; 57. 6. valley
STREET, Rev. 11. 8. & 21. 21. & 22. 2.
Prov. 1. 20. *streets*, S. of S. 3. 2. Luke 14. 21.
R. V. 2 Chron. 29. 4; 32. 6; Ezra 10. 9; Neh. 8. 1, 3, 16; Esth. 4. 6; Prov. 1. 20; 7. 12; Isa. 15. 3; Amos 5. 16. broad place or way; Ps. 144. 13. fields; Mark 6. 56. market place
STRENGTH, Gen. 49. 24. Ex. 13. 3.
Ex. 15. 2. the Lord is my *s.* and my song, Ps. 18. 2. & 28. 7. & 118. 14. Isa. 12. 2.
Judg. 5. 21. soul thou hast trodden down *s.*
1 Sam. 2. 9. by *s.* shall no man
Job 9. 19. if I speak of *s.* lo, he
Ps. 18. 32. girded me with *s.*, 39.
27. 1. the Lord is the *s.* of my life
29. 11. Lord will give *s.* to his
33. 16. mighty not delivered by *s.*
39. 13. spare me that I recover *s.*
46. 1. God is our refuge and *s.*
73. 26. God is *s.* of my heart
84. 5. blessed whose *s.* is in thee
93. 1. the Lord is clothed with *s.*
96. 6. *s.* and beauty are in his
140. 7. Lord, the *s.* of my salvation
Prov. 10. 29. Lord is *s.* to the up.
Eccl. 9. 16. wisd. is better than *s.*
Isa. 25. 4. *s.* to poor and *s.* to needy
26. 4. in Jehovah is everlasting *s.*
Joel 3. 16. Lord is the *s.* of child.
Luke 1. 51. shewed *s.* with his

Rom. 5. 6. we were without *s*.
1 Cor. 15. 56. *s*. of sin is the law
Rev. 3. 8. thou hast a little *s*. and
   5. 12. worthy is the Lamb to receive *s*.
  17. 13. give their *s*. to beast
1 Chron. 16. 11. *his strength*, Ps. 33.
  17. Isa. 61. 1. Hos. 7. 9. & 12. 3.
Gen. 49. 24. *in strength*, Job 9. 4. &
  36. 5. Ps. 71. 16. & 103. 20. & 147. 10.
  Isa. 33. 6.
Gen. 49. 3. *my strength*, Ex. 15. 2.
2 Sam. 22. 33. Job 6. 12. Ps. 8. 1, 2.
  & 19. 14. & 28. 7. & 38. 10. & 43. 2.
  & 59. 17. & 62. 7. & 71. 9. & 99. 4. &
  102. 23. & 118. 14. & 144. 1. Isa. 12.
  2. & 27. 5. & 49. 4, 5. Jer. 16. 19.
  Hab. 3. 19. 2 Cor. 12. 9.
Ps. 37. 39. *their strength*, 89. 17. Prov.
  20. 29. Isa. 30. 7. & 40. 31.
Ps. 8. 2. *thy strength*, 86. 16. & 110. 2.
  Prov. 24. 10. & 31. 3. Isa. 17. 10. &
  63. 15. Mark 14. 32. Deut. 33. 25.
Neh. 8. 10. *your strength*, Isa. 23.
  14. & 30. 15. Ezek. 24. 21. Lev. 26.
  20.
Ps. 20. 2. Lord *strengthen* thee
  27. 14. the Lord, he shall *s*. your
  31. 24. he shall *s*. your heart
  41. 3. *s*. him on bed of languish.
Isa. 35. 3. *s*. ye the weak hands
Dan. 11. 1. stood to confirm and *s*.
Zech. 10. 12. I will *s*. them in Lord
Luke 22. 32. when converted *s*. thy
  brethren
Rev. 3. 2. *s*. the things that rema.
1 Sam. 23. 16. *strengthened* his
  hand in God
Ezek. 34. 4. diseased have ye not *s*.
Eph. 3. 16. *s*. with might, Col. 1. 11.
2 Tim. 4. 17. the Lord stood with
  me and *s*. me
Ps. 138. 3. *s*. me with *s*. in my soul
  104. 15. bread which *strengtheneth*
Phil. 4. 13. Christ who *s*. me
R. V. Job 12. 13; 39. 19; Ps. 80. 2;
  Prov. 8. 14; 24. 5; Rev. 5. 12.
  might; Ps. 18. 2; 144. 1; Isa. 26. 4.
  rock; Ps. 60. 7; 108. 8. defence;
  Ps. 31. 4; 37. 39; Prov. 10. 29; Isa.
  23. 4, 14; 25. 4; Ezek. 30. 15; Nah.
  3. 11. strong hold; Ps. 33. 17;
  Ezek. 24. 21; 30. 18; 33. 28; 1 Cor.
  15. 56; 2 Cor. 12. 9; Heb. 11. 11;
  Rev. 3. 8; 12. 10. power; Ps. 41. 3.
  support; Ezek. 30. 25. hold up;
  Luke 22. 32; Acts 18. 23; Rev. 3. 2.
  stablish
STRETCH thy hands, Job 11. 13.
Amos 6. 4. *s*. themselves on couch.
Matt. 12. 13. *s*. forth thy hand
John 21. 18. thou shalt *s*. forth
Gen. 22. 10. *stretched* forth his
  1 Kings 17. 21. *s*. himself upon
1 Chron. 21. 16. drawn sword *s*.
Isa. 5. 25. hand is *s*. out still
Job 15. 25. he *stretcheth* out hand
Prov. 31. 20. she *s*. out hand to
Isa. 40. 22. *s*. out the heavens as a
  curtain, 42. 5. & 44. 24. & 45. 12. &
  51. 13. Jer. 10. 12. & 51. 15. Zech.
  12. 1.
R. V. Ex. 3. 20; 9. 15; 1 Sam. 24.
  6; 26. 9, 11, 23; 2 Sam. 1. 14; Job
  30. 24; Acts 12. 1. put; Ex. 25. 20;
  Ps. 44. 20; 88. 9; 143. 6; Prov.
  31. 20; Isa. 16. 8; Rom. 10.
  21. spread, or spread forth
STRIFE between me, Gen. 13. 8.
Ps. 80. 6. us a *s*. to our neighbors
Prov. 10. 12. hatred stirreth up *s*.
  16. 28. froward man soweth *s*.
  20. 3. an honor to cease from *s*.
  28. 25. proud heart stirreth up *s*.
Isa. 58. 4. ye fast for *s*. and debate
Luke 22. 24. was a *s*. among them
Rom. 13. 13. not in *s*. and envying
Gal. 5. 20. wrath, *s*., sedition
Phil. 1. 15. preach Christ of *s*. and
2 Tim. 2. 23. genders., 2 Cor. 12. 20.
Jas. 3. 14. bitter envying and *s*.
  16.
R. V. Ps. 106. 32. Meribah; Prov.
  15. 18; 26. 20; Luke 22. 24. con-

tention; 2 Cor. 12. 20; Gal. 5. 20;
  Phil. 2. 3; Jas. 3. 14, 16. faction;
  1 Tim. 6. 4. disputes
STRIKE hands, Job 17. 3. Prov.
  6. 1.
Prov. 17. 26. *s*. princes for equity
Isa. 1. 5. why be *stricken* any more
  53. 4. esteem him *s*. of God
1 Tim. 3. 3. a bishop, no *striker*
R. V. Ex. 12. 7. put; Deut. 21. 4.
  break; 2 Kings 5. 11. wave; Hab.
  3. 14. pierce; Mark 14. 65. received
  blows; 2 Chron. 13. 20; Matt. 26.
  51. smote; Luke 22. 64 ——
STRIPES, Isa. 53. 5. 1 Pet. 2. 24.
Prov. 17. 10. & 20. 30. Luke 12. 47,
  48.
R. V. Prov. 20. 30. strokes
STRIVE, Ex. 21. 18, 22. Job 33. 13.
Gen. 6. 3. Spirit shall not alw. *s*.
Prov. 8. 30. *s*. not without cause
Hos. 4. 4. let no man *s*. nor reprove
Matt. 12. 19. he shall not *s*. nor
Luke 13. 24. *s*. to enter in at strait
Isa. 45. 9. that *striveth* with Maker
Phil. 1. 27. *striving* together for
Heb. 12. 4. resisted unto blood *s*.
R. V. Ex. 21. 18; 2 Tim. 2. 5. con-
  tend; Rom. 15. 20. making it my
  aim
STRONG this day, Josh. 14. 11.
Ps. 24. 8. Lord is *s*. and mighty
  30. 7. made mountain to stand *s*.
  31. 2. be thou my *s*. rock
  71. 7. thou art my *s*. refuge, 3.
Prov. 10. 15. rich man's wealth is
  his *s*. city
  18. 10. name of Lord is a *s*. tower
  24. 5. a wise man is *s*. and
  Eccl. 9. 11. battle is not to the *s*.
S. of S. 8. 6. love is *s*. as death
Isa. 1. 31. *s*. shall be as tow and
  35. 4. be *s*. fear not, behold your
  53. 12. divide the spoil with *s*.
Jer. 50. 34. their Redeemer is *s*.
Joel 3. 10. the weak say I am *s*.
Luke 11. 21. *s*. man armed keepeth
Rom. 4. 20. *s*. in faith, giving glory
  15. 1. we that are *s*. ought to bear
  the infirmities of the weak
Heb. 11. 34. weakness made *s*.
1 John 2. 14. because ye are *s*.
Isa. 35. 4. *be strong*, Hag. 2. 4. 1 Cor.
  16. 13. Eph. 6. 10. 2 Tim. 2. 1.
1 Cor. 1. 25. *stronger* than men
Job 17. 9. clean hands shall be *s*.
Jer. 20. 7. thou art *s*. than I
R. V. Few changes to mighty, val-
  iant, etc.
STUBBLE, Job 13. 25. & 21. 18. Ps.
  83. 13. Isa. 33. 11. Mal. 4. 1. 1 Cor.
  3. 12.
STUBBORN, Deut. 21. 18. Ps. 78.
  8.
1 Sam. 15. 23. *stubbornness*, Deut.
  9. 27.
R. V. Prov. 7. 11. wilful
STUDY, Eccl. 12. 12. 1 Thes. 4. 11.
2 Tim. 2. 15. Prov. 15. 28. & 24. 2.
R. V. 2 Tim. 2. 15. give diligence
STUMBLE, foot shall not, Prov.
  3. 23.
Prov. 4. 12. runnest, shalt not *s*.
Isa. 5. 27. shall be weary nor *s*.
  8. 15. many shall *s*. and fall
Mal. 2. 8. cause many to *s*. at law
1 Pet. 2. 8. which *s*. at the word
Rom. 9. 32. they *stumbled* at that
John 11. 9. day he *stumbleth* not
Rom. 14. 21. whereby thy brother
  s.
Isa. 8. 14. *stumbling*, 1 John 2. 10.
Lev. 19. 14. *stumbling-block*, Isa. 8.
  14. & 57. 14. Jer. 6. 21. Ezek. 3. 20.
  & 7. 19. & 14. 3, 4, 7. Rom. 9. 32, 33.
  & 11. 9. & 14. 13. 1 Cor. 1. 23. & 8. 9.
  Rev. 2. 14.
R. V. Prov. 24. 17. is overthrown
SUBDUE our iniquities, Mic. 7. 19.
Ps. 81. 14. soon *s*. their enemies
Phil. 3. 21. able to *s*. all things
Heb. 11. 33. through faith *subdued*
R. V. Deut. 20. 20. fall; Dan. 7. 24.
  put down; Mic. 7. 19. tread under

foot; Zech. 9. 15. tread down;
  1 Cor. 15. 28; Phil. 3. 21. subject
SUBJECT, devils are, Luke 10. 17,
  20.
Rom. 8. 7. not *s*. to law of God
  13. 1. every soul be *s*. to higher
1 Cor. 14. 32. spirit of prophets *s*.
  15. 28. Son shall be *s*. to him that
Eph. 5. 24. as church is *s*. to Christ
Tit. 3. 1. to be *s*. to principalities
Heb. 2. 15. all lifetime *s*. to bond.
Jas. 5. 17. Elias, a man *s*. to
1 Pet. 2. 18. servants be *s*. to mas.
  3. 22. angels and powers made *s*.
  5. 5. all ye be *s*. one to another
1 Cor. 9. 27. *subjection*, 1 Tim. 2. 11.
  & 3. 4. Heb. 2. 5, 8. & 12. 9. 1 Pet.
  3. 1, 5.
R. V. Rom. 13. 5; Tit. 3. 1; 1 Pet. 2.
  18. in subjection; 1 Cor. 9. 27.
  bondage; 2 Cor. 9. 13. obedience
SUBMIT, Gen. 16. 9. Ps. 18. 44. &
  66. 3. & 68. 30. & 81. 15.
1 Cor. 16. 16. *submit yourselves*,
  Eph. 5. 21, 22. Col. 3. 18. Heb. 13.
  17. Jas. 4. 7. 1 Pet. 2. 13. & 5. 5.
Rom. 10. 3. have not *submitted* to
  righteousness
R. V. Rom. 10. 3; Eph. 5. 21, 22;
  1 Cor. 16. 16; Col. 3. 18; Jas. 4. 7;
  1 Pet. 2. 13; 5. 5. be subject or sub-
  jection
SUBSCRIBE, Isa. 44. 5. Jer. 32. 44.
SUBSTANCE, Gen. 7. 4. & 15. 14.
Deut. 33. 11. bless Lord, his *s*.
Job 30. 22. thou dissolvest my *s*.
Ps. 139. 15. my *s*. was not hid
Prov. 3. 9. honor Lord with thy *s*.
Hos. 12. 8. I have found me out *s*.
Luke 8. 3. ministered to him of *s*.
Heb. 10. 34. a more enduring *s*.
  11. 1. faith is *s*. of things hoped
R. V. Gen. 7. 4. thing; Deut. 11. 6.
  living thing; Gen. 36. 6; Heb. 10.
  34. possession; Ps. 139. 15. frame;
  Prov. 10. 3. desire; Isa. 6. 13.
  stock; Hos. 12. 8. wealth; Heb. 11.
  1. assurance
SUBTIL, Gen. 3. 1. Prov. 7. 10.
Acts 13. 10. *subtilty*, 2 Cor. 11. 3.
  Prov. 1. 4.
R. V. Prov. 7. 10. wily
SUBVERT, Lam. 3. 36. Tit. 1. 11.
  & 3. 11.
Acts 13. 24. *subverting* souls, 2 Tim.
  2. 14.
R. V. Tit. 1. 11. overthrow; 3. 11.
  perverted
SUCK, Gen. 21. 7. Deut. 32. 13. &
  33. 19.
Job 20. 16. *s*. poison of asps and
Isa. 60. 16. *s*. milk of Gentiles
  66. 11. *s*. and be satisfied, 12.
Matt. 24. 19. to them that give *s*.
Luke 23. 29. blessed are paps which
  never gave *s*.
  11. 27. blessed are paps thou hast
  sucked
Isa. 11. 8. *sucking* child, 49. 15.
Ps. 8. 2. *suckling*, Lam. 2. 11. & 4. 4.
R. V. Ezek. 23. 34. drain
SUDDEN, Prov. 3. 25. 1 Thes. 5. 3.
SUFFER, Ex. 12. 23. Lev. 19. 17.
Ps. 55. 22. never *s*. righteous
  89. 33. nor *s*. my faithfulness
  121. 3. *s*. thy foot to be moved
Prov. 10. 3. *s*. soul of righteous
Matt. 16. 21. must *s*. many things
  17. 17. how long shall I *s*. you
  19. 14. *s*. little children to come
1 Cor. 4. 12. being persecuted, we *s*.
Phil. 1. 29. also to *s*. for his sake
2 Tim. 2. 12. if we *s*. we shall reign
Heb. 11. 25. rather to *s*. affliction
  13. 3. them who *s*. adversity
1 Pet. 4. 15. none *s*. as a murderer
Ps. 105. 14. he *suffered* no man
Acts 14. 16. *s*. all to walk in his
  16. 7. the Spirit *s*. them not
Phil. 3. 8. for whom I *s*. loss of all
Heb. 5. 8. learned obedience by
  the things he *s*.
1 Pet. 2. 21. *s*. for us leaving us
  3. 18. Christ hath *s*. once for sins

Matt. 11. 12. *suffereth*, 1 Cor. 13. 4.
Rom. 8. 18. *sufferings*, 2 Cor. 1. 5,
  6. Phil. 3. 10. Col. 1. 24. Heb. 2.
  10. 1 Pet. 1. 11. & 4. 13. & 5. 1.
R. V. Lev. 22. 16. cause; Lev. 19.
  17; Prov. 19. 19; Matt. 17. 17; Mark
  9. 19; Luke 4; 1 Cor. 9. 12;
  2 Cor. 11. 19, 20; Heb. 13. 22. bear,
  or bear with; Luke 8. 32. give
  leave; 12. 39. left; 1 Cor. 4. 12;
  2 Tim. 2. 12. endure; 1 Tim. 2. 12.
  permit; 4. 10. strive
SUFFICE, 1 Pet. 4. 3. John 14. 8.
Matt. 6. 34. *sufficient* to-day is evil
2 Cor. 2. 16. who is *s*. for these
  3. 5. we are not *s*. of ourselves
12. 9. my grace is *s*. for thee
Job 20. 22. *sufficiency*, 2 Cor. 3. 5. &
  9. 8.
SUM, Ps. 139. 17. Ezek. 28. 12. Heb.
  8. 1.
R. V. Ex. 21. 30. ransom; Acts 7.
  16. price; Heb. 8. 1. chief point
SUMMER and winter not cease,
  Gen. 8. 22.
Ps. 74. 17. hast made *s*. and winter
Prov. 6. 8. provideth her meat in *s*.
10. 5. gathereth in *s*. is a wise
Isa. 18. 6. fowls shall *s*. and winter
Jer. 8. 20. harvest past and *s*. ended
Zech. 14. 3. living waters in *s*.
SUMPTUOUSLY, fared, Luke 16.
  19.
SUN, stand thou still, Josh. 10. 12.
Ps. 19. 4. he set a tabernacle for *s*.
  104. 19. *s*. knoweth his going
  121. 6. *s*. not smite thee by day
  136. 8. *s*. to rule day, Gen. 1. 16.
Eccl. 12. 2. while *s*. or stars be not
  darkened
S. of S. 1. 6. because the *s*. hath
Isa. 30. 26. light of the *s*. shall
  66. 19. *s*. no more thy light by
Jer. 31. 35. giveth *s*. for a light by
Mal. 4. 2. *S*. of righteousness arise
Matt. 5. 45. his *s*. to rise on evil
  13. 43. shine as *s*. in the kingdom
1 Cor. 15. 41. there is one glory of
  s.
Eph. 4. 26. let not *s*. go down on
Rev. 7. 16. neither *s*. light on them
  10. 1. his face as *s*., 1. 16.
  21. 23. city had no need of the *s*.,
  22. 5.
SUP, Luke 17. 8. Rev. 3. 20. Hab. 1.
  9.
Luke 14. 16. certain man made a
  great *supper*
1 Cor. 11. 20. to eat Lord's *s*., Luke
  22. 20.
Rev. 19. 9. to marriage *s*.
R. V. Hab. 1. 9. set eagerly
SUPERFLUITY of naughtiness,
  Jas. 1. 21.
SUPERSTITION, Acts 25. 19. &
  17. 22.
SUPPLICATION, 1 Kings 8. 28. &
  9. 3. Job 8. 5. & 9. 15. Ps. 6. 9. & 30.
  8. & 55. 1. & 142. 1. & 119. 170. Dan.
  6. 11. & 9. 20. Hos. 12. 4. Zech. 12.
  10. Eph. 6. 18. Phil. 4. 6. 1 Tim. 2.
  1. & 5. 5. Heb. 5. 7.
SUPPLY spirit of Jesus Christ,
  Phil. 1. 19.
Phil. 4. 19. God shall *s*. all need
2 Cor. 9. 12. *supplieth*, Eph. 4. 16.
R. V. 2 Cor. 9. 12. filleth measure
SUPPORT the weak, Acts 20. 35.
  1 Thes. 5. 14.
R. V. Acts 20. 35. help
SUPREME, 1 Pet. 2. 13.
SURE, Gen. 23. 17. 1 Sam. 25. 28.
Neh. 9. 38. we make a *s*. covenant
Ps. 19. 7. testimo. of the Lord is *s*.
  111. 7. his commandments are *s*.
Prov. 11. 15. hateth suretiship is *s*.
  18. righteous. shall be *s*. reward
Isa. 22. 23, 25. *s*. place
  28. 16. *s*. foundation
  55. 3. *s*. mercies of David
John 6. 69. we believe and are *s*.
Rom. 4. 16. promise might be *s*.
2 Tim. 2. 19. the foundation of God
  standeth *s*.

2 Pet. 1. 10. calling and election *s*.
R. V. Prov. 6. 3. importune; Ex. 3.
  19; 1 Sam. 20. 7; Luke 10. 11; John
  6. 69; 16. 30; Rom. 2. 2; 15. 29.
  know; 2 Tim. 2. 19. firm
SURETY for servant, Ps. 119. 122.
Heb. 7. 22. Jesus made *s*. of better
R. V. Acts 12. 11. truth
SURETYSHIP, evils of, Prov. 6.
  1. & 11. 15. & 17. 18. & 20. 16. & 22.
  26. & 27. 13.
SURFEITING and drunkenness,
  Luke 21. 34.
SURPRISED hypocrites, Isa. 33.
  14.
SUSTAIN, Ps. 55. 22. Prov. 18. 14.
Ps. 3. 5. *sustained*, Isa. 59. 16.
R. V. Isa. 59. 16. upheld
SWALLOW, Ps. 84. 3. Jer. 8. 7.
Isa. 25. 8. will *s*. up death in vic.
Matt. 23. 24. gnat, and *s*. a camel
Ex. 15. 12. earth *swallowed* them
Ps. 124. 3. they had *s*. us up quick
2 Cor. 2. 7. be *s*. up with overmuch
  sorrow
  5. 4. mortality be *s*. up of life
R. V. Job 5. 5. gapeth for; Hab. 1.
  13. devoureth
SWEAR, Num. 30. 2. Deut. 6. 13.
Isa. 45. 23. every tongue shall *s*.
  65. 16. shall *s*. by the God of truth
Jer. 4. 2. shalt *s*. Lord liveth in
Zeph. 1. 5. *s*. by Lord, and *s*.
Matt. 5. 34. *s*. not at all
Ps. 15. 4. *sweareth* to his own hurt
Eccl. 9. 2. *s*. as he that feareth
Zech. 5. 3. every one that *s*. shall
Jer. 23. 10. because of *swearing*
Hos. 4. 2. by *s*. and lying they
  10. 4. *s*. falsely in making a cov.
Mal. 3. 5. I will be a witness
  against false *s*.
R. V. Ex. 6. 8. lifted up my hand;
  Lev. 5. 1. adjuration
SWEAT, Gen. 3. 19. Luke 22. 44.
SWEET, Job 20. 12. Ps. 55. 14.
Ps. 104. 34. meditation of him be *s*.
  119. 103. how *s*. thy words to my
Prov. 3. 24. thy sleep shall be *s*.
  9. 17. stolen waters are *s*.
  27. 7. to hungry bitter thing is *s*.
Eccl. 5. 12. sleep of labor. man *s*.
S. of S. 2. 8. his fruit was *s*. to my
  14. *s*. is thy voice and thy counte.
Isa. 5. 20. put bitter for *s*. and *s*.
Phil. 4. 18. odor of a *s*. smell
Rev. 10. 9. in thy mouth *s*. as hon.
Ps. 19. 10. *sweeter* than honey
Judg. 14. 14. *sweetness*, Prov. 16. 21,
  & 27. 9.
R. V. Jer. 6. 20. pleasing; Mark 16.
  1 ——
SWELLING, Jer. 12. 5. 2 Pet. 2. 18.
R. V. Jer. 12. 5; 49. 19; 50. 44. pride
SWIFT, Deut. 28. 49. Job 9. 26.
Eccl. 9. 11. race is not to the *s*.
Rom. 3. 15. feet are *s*. to shed
Jas. 1. 19. *s*. to hear, slow to
2 Pet. 2. 1. bring on themselves *s*.
  destruction
Job 7. 6. days *swifter* than a shut.
Ps. 147. 15. *swiftly*, Joel 3. 4.
SWIM, 2 Kings 6. 6. Ps. 6. 6. Ezek.
  47. 5.
SWORD, Ex. 32. 27. Lev. 26. 24.
Deut. 32. 29. *s*. of thy excellency
Judg. 7. 20. *s*. of Lord and Gideon
2 Sam. 12. 10. *s*. shall never depart
Ps. 17. 13. wicked which is thy *s*.
  149. 6. two-edged *s*. in their hands
S. of S. 3. 8. man hath his *s*. on
Jer. 9. 16. send a *s*. after them
Ezek. 21. 13. if *s*. contemn rod
Zech. 11. 17. *s*. shall be upon his
  13. 7. awake, O *s*., against shep.
Matt. 10. 34. not send peace, but *s*.
Luke 2. 35. a *s*. shall pierce through
Rom. 13. 4. beareth not *s*. in vain
Eph. 6. 17. *s*. of the Spirit, which
Heb. 4. 12. word is sharper than
  any two-edged *s*.
Rev. 1. 16. a sharp two-edged *s*.
Ps. 55. 21. *swords*, 59. 7. Prov. 30. 14.
Isa. 2. 4. Ezek. 32. 27. Joel 3. 10.

R. V. Job 2. 25. point; Joel 2. 8.
  weapons
SWORN by myself, Gen. 22. 16.
Ps. 24. 4. that hath not *s*. deceit.
  119. 106. I have *s*. and will per.
SYNAGOGUE, Ps. 74. 8. Matt. 6.
  5. & 23. 6. Luke 7. 5. John 9. 22. &
  18. 20. Acts 15. 21. Rev. 2. 9. & 3. 9.
R. V. Acts 13. 42 ——

T

TABERNACLE, Ex. 26. 1. & 29. 43.
Job 5. 24. thy *t*. shall be in peace
Ps. 15. 1. who shall abide in thy *t*.
  27. 5. in secret of his *t*. shall hide
Prov. 14. 11. *t*. of the upright shall
Isa. 33. 20. a *t*. shall not be taken
Amos 9. 11. raise up *t*. of David
2 Cor. 5. 1. earthly house of this *t*.
Heb. 8. 2. minister of the true *t*.
2 Pet. 1. 13. I am in this *t*.
Rev. 21. 3. *t*. of God is with men
Job 12. 6. *tabernacles* of robbers
Ps. 84. 1. how amiable are thy *t*.
  118. 15. salvation is in the *t*. of the
Heb. 11. 9. dwell in *t*. with Isaac
R. V. In O. T. nearly always tent
  or tents; Luke 16. 9; Acts 7. 46.
  habitation
TABLE, Ex. 25. 23. Job 36. 16.
Ps. 23. 5. prepared a *t*. before me
  69. 22. let their *t*. become a snare
Prov. 3. 3. write them on *t*. of heart
S. of S. 1. 12. king sitteth at his *t*.
Mal. 1. 7. *t*. of Lord is contempt.
Matt. 15. 27. crumbs from mast. *t*.
1 Cor. 10. 21. partakers of Lord's *t*.
Deut. 10. 4. *tables*, 5. Heb. 9. 4.
  2 Chron. 4. 8, 19. Isa. 28. 8. Ezek.
  40. 41.
Hab. 2. 2. make it plain upon *t*.
Acts 6. 2. leave . . God and serve *t*.
2 Cor. 3. 3. not in *t*. of stone, but
R. V. Isa. 30. 8; Luke 1. 63. tablet;
  Mark 7. 4 ——; John 12. 2. meat
TAKE you for a people, Ex. 6. 7
Ex. 20. 7. not *t*. name of the Lord
  34. 9. *t*. us for thine inheritance
Ps. 27. 12. the Lord will *t*. me up
  116. 12. I will *t*. cup of salvation
  119. 43. *t*. not the word of truth
Hos. 14. 2. *t*. with you words; say *t*.
Matt. 16. 24. *t*. up his cross and
  18. 16. *t*. with thee one or two
  20. 14. *t*. that thine is, and go thy
  26. 26. said *t*. eat, this is my body,
  1 Cor. 11. 24.
Luke 12. 19. *t*. thine ease, eat
Eph. 6. 13. *t*. the whole armor of
Rev. 3. 11. no man *t*. thy crown
Ex. 23. 25. *take away*, Josh. 7. 13.
  2 Sam. 24. 10. 1 Chron. 17. 13. Job
  7. 21. & 32. 22. & 36. 1. Ps. 58. 9. Isa.
  58. 9. Jer. 15. 15. Hos. 1. 6. & 4. 11.
  & 14. 2. Amos 4. 2. Mal. 2. 3. Luke
  17. 31. John 1. 29. 1 John 3. 5. Rev.
  22. 19.
Deut. 4. 9. *take heed*, 11. 16. & 27. 9.
  2 Chron. 19. 6. Ps. 39. 1. Isa. 7. 4.
Mal. 2. 15. Matt. 6. 1. & 16. 6. & 18.
  10. & 24. 4. Mark 4. 24. & 13. 33.
  Luke 8. 18. & 12. 15. 1 Cor. 10. 12.
Col. 4. 17. Heb. 3. 12. 2 Pet. 1. 19.
Deut. 32. 41. *take hold*, Ps. 69. 24.
  Isa. 27. 5. & 56. 4. & 64. 7. Zech. 1. 6.
Ps. 83. 3. *taken* crafty counsel
  119. 111. testimony have I *t*.
Isa. 53. 8. he was *t*. from prison
Lam. 4. 20. the anointed was *t*. in
Matt. 21. 43. kingdom of God *t*.
  24. 40. one shall be *t*. the other
Mark 4. 25. be *t*. that which he hath
Acts 1. 9. *t*. up into heaven
2 Tim. 2. 26. *t*. captive by him
Isa. 6. 7. thy iniquity is *taken away*
  57. 1. merciful men are ——
Luke 10. 42. good part not be—from
2 Cor. 3. 16. return to Lord, veil ——
Ps. 40. 12. my iniquities *taken hold*
Prov. 1. 19. *taketh away*, John 1. 29
  & 10. 18. & 15. 2; *taketh from*. 16. 22

Ps. 119. 9. by *taking* heed thereto
Matt. 6. 27. who by *t.* thought can
Rom. 7. 8. sin *t.* occasion deceived
Eph. 6. 16. above all *t.* shield of
R. V. The frequent changes are mostly due to context; as, Matt. 6. 25. take no thought, becomes, be not anxious, etc.
TALE, Ps. 90. 9. Ezek. 22. 29. Luke 24. 11.
Lev. 19. 16. *tale-bearer*, Prov. 11. 13. & 18. 8. & 20. 19. & 26. 20, 22.
R. V. Luke 24. 11. talk
TALENTS, Matt. 18. 24. & 25. 15, 25.
TALK of them when thou sittest, Deut. 6. 7.
1 Sam. 2. 3. *t.* no more so proudly
Job. 13. 7. and *t.* deceitfully for
Ps. 71. 24. my tongue shall *t.*
77. 12. I will *t.* of thy doings
105. 2. *t.* ye of his wondrous works
145. 11. speak of glory and *t.* of
Jer. 12. 1. *t.* with thee of judgment
John 14. 30. I will not *t.* much
Ps. 37. 30. his tongue *talketh* of
Eph. 5. 4. nor foolish *talking*
Tit. 1. 10. unruly and vain *talkers*
R. V. Several changes and nearly all to speak or spake; 1 Kings 18. 27. musing
TAME, Mark 5. 4. Jas. 3. 7, 8.
TARRY, 1 Chron. 19. 5. 2 Kings 14. 10.
Prov. 23. 30. that *t.* long at wine
Isa. 46. 13. my salvation shall not *t.*
Hab. 2. 3. though it *t.* wait for it
Matt. 26. 38. *t.* ye here and watch
John 21. 22. that he *t.* till I come
1 Cor. 11. 33. come to eat *t.* for one
Ps. 68. 12. she that *tarried* at home
Matt. 25. 5. the bridegroom *t.* all
Luke 2. 43. child Jesus *t.* behind in
Acts 22. 16. why *tarriest* thou
Ps. 40. 17. make no *tarrying*, 70. 5.
R. V. Lev. 14. 8. dwell; 1 Sam. 14. 2; 2 Sam. 15. 29; 2 Kings 14. 10; Matt. 26. 38; Mark 14. 34; Luke 24. 29; John 4. 40; Acts 9. 43; 18. 20. abide or abode; Ps. 101. 7. be established; Hab. 2. 3. delay; Acts 20. 5; 27. 33; 1 Cor. 11. 38. wait or waiting, Acts 15. 33. spent time; Acts 20. 15 ——
TASKMASTERS, Ex. 1. 11. & 5. 6.
TASTE, Ex. 16. 31. 1 Sam. 14. 43.
Job 6. 6. *t.* in white of an egg
Ps. 34. 8. *t.* and see Lord is good
119. 103. sweet are thy words to *t.*
S. of S. 2. 3. fruit was sweet to *t.*
Jer. 48. 11. *t.* remained in him
Matt. 16. 28. not *t.* of death
Luke 14. 24. *t.* of my supper
John 8. 52. keep my saying, never *t.* death
Col. 2. 21. touch not, *t.* not, handle
Heb. 2. 9. *t.* death for every man
6. 4. *t.* heavenly gift
5. *t.* good word of God
1 Pet. 2. 3. if ye have *tasted* that
TATTLERS, 1 Tim. 5. 13.
TAXATION of all the world, under Cæsar Augustus, Luke 2. 1.
TEACH, Ex. 4. 12. Lev. 10. 11.
Deut. 4. 9. *t.* them thy sons, 6. 7.
33. 10. shall *t.* Jacob thy judg.
1 Sam. 12. 23. *t.* good way
2 Chron. 17. 7. to *t.* in cities of
Job 21. 22. shall any *t.* God
Ps. 25. 8. *t.* sinners in the way
34. 11. *t.* you fear of Lord
51. 13. *t.* transgressors thy way
90. 12. *t.* us to number our days
Isa. 2. 3. he will *t.* us of his ways
Jer. 31. 34. *t.* no more every man
Matt. 28. 19. go and *t.* all nations
John 9. 34. dost thou *t.* us
14. 26. Holy Ghost shall *t.* you all
1 Cor. 4. 17. as I *t.* in every church
1 Tim. 3. 2. given to hospitality, apt to *t.*
2 Tim. 2. 2. faithful men able to *t.*
Heb. 5. 12. need that one *t.* you
Job 34. 32. what I see not, *teach me*
Ps. 25. 4. —— thy paths, 5. & 27. 11. ——

thy way, 86. 11. & 119. 12. —— thy statutes, 26. 64, 66, 68, 124, 135. —— good judgment, 108. —— thy judgments, 143. 10. —— to do thy will
2 Chron. 32. 22. *taught* good knowl.
Ps. 71. 17. hast *t.* me from my
119. 171. hast *t.* me thy statutes
Eccl. 12. 9. he *t.* people knowledge
Isa. 29. 13. *t.* by precepts of men
John 6. 45. shall be all *t.* of God
Acts 20. 20. *t.* you publicly and
Gal. 6. 6. let him that is *t.* in word
1 Thes. 4. 9. yourselves are *t.* of God
Ps. 94. 12. *teachest* him out of law
Matt. 22. 16. *t.* way of God in
Rom. 2. 21. *t.* another, *t.* not thy.
Job 36. 22. who *teacheth* like him
Ps. 18. 34. *t.* my hands to war
94. 10. he that *t.* man knowledge
Isa. 48. 17. Lord thy God *t.* thee to
1 Cor. 2. 13. words which man's wisdom *t.* but which the Holy Ghost *t.*
1 John 2. 27. anointing *t.* you
Hab. 2. 18. *teacher*, John 3. 2. Rom. 2. 20. 1 Tim. 2. 7. 2 Tim. 1. 11.
Ps. 119. 99. *teachers*, Isa. 30. 20.
2 Tim. 4. 3. heap to themselves *t.*
Tit. 2. 3. be *t.* of good things
Heb. 5. 12. ought to be *t.* ye have
2 Chron. 15. 3. a *teaching* priest
Matt. 15. 9. *t.* for doctrines the
28. 20. *t.* them to observe all things
Col. 1. 28. *t.* every man in all wis.
Tit. 2. 12. *t.* us that denying
R. V. 1 Sam. 12. 23; Ps. 25. 8, 12; Acts 22. 3; 1 Cor. 14. 19. instruct; Jer. 28. 16; 29. 32. spoken; Matt. 28. 19. make disciples; Acts 16. 21. set forth; Tit. 2. 4. train; Isa. 43. 27. interpreters
TEAR, Ps. 50. 22. Hos. 5. 14. Job 16. 9.
R. V. 2 Sam. 13. 31. rent; Jer. 16. 17. break bread; Mark 9. 18. dasheth down; Isa. 5. 25. refuse; Mal. 1. 13. taken by violence
TEARS, Job 16. 20. Ps. 6. 6. Isa. 38. 5.
Ps. 56. 8. put *t.* in thy bottle
126. 5. they that sow in *t.* shall
Isa. 25. 8. wipe away all *t.* from off
Jer. 9. 1. eyes were a fountain of *t.*
Luke 7. 38. to wash his feet with *t.*
Acts 20. 19. *t.* and temptations, 31.
2 Cor. 2. 4. wrote with many *t.*
2 Tim. 1. 4. being mindful of thy *t.*
Heb. 5. 7. with strong crying and *t.*
Rev. 7. 17. wipe all *t.* from their
R. V. Mark 9. 24 ——
TEATS, Isa. 32. 12. Ezek. 23. 3, 21.
TEETH white as milk, Gen. 49. 12.
Job 4. 10. *t.* broken, Ps. 3. 7. & 58. 6.
S. of S. 4. 2. *t.* are like a flock of
Jer. 31. 29. children's *t.* set on
Amos 4. 6. cleanness of *t.* in all
Matt. 8. 12. weeping and gnashing of *t.*, 22. 13. & 24. 51. & 25. 30. Ps. 112. 10.
TEKEL, Dan. 5. 25.
TELL it not in Gath, 2 Sam. 1. 20.
Ps. 48. 13. *t.* it to the generation
Prov. 30. 4. name, if thou canst *t.*
Matt. 8. 4. see thou *t.* no man
18. 15. *t.* him his fault
John 3. 8. not *t.* whence it cometh
4. 25. he is come he will *t.*
8. 14. ye cannot *t.* whence I come
2 Cor. 12. 2. out of body I cannot *t.*
Gal. 4. 16. I *t.* you the truth
Phil. 3. 18. *t.* you even weeping
Ps. 56. 8. *tellest* all my wanderings
R. V. Frequent changes to speak, say, shew, etc.
TEMPERANCE, Acts 24. 25. Gal. 5. 23. 2 Pet. 1. 6.
1 Cor. 9. 25. *temperate*, Tit. 1. 8. & 2. 2.
TEMPLE, 1 Sam. 1. 9. 1 Kings 6. 5.
Ps. 29.9. in *t.* doth every one speak
Jer. 7. 4. *t.* of the Lord, *t.* of Lord
Mal. 3. 1. suddenly come to his *t.*
Matt. 12. 6. greater than the *t.* is
John 2. 19. destroy this *t.* and in
21. he spake of the *t.* of his body

1 Cor. 3. 16. ye are the *t.* of God
6. 19. body is *t.* of Holy Ghost
2 Cor. 6. 16. what agreement hath the *t.* of God with idols, for ye are the *t.* of the living God
Rev. 7. 15. serve him in his *t.*
11. 19. *t.* of God was opened in
S. of S. 4. 3. thy *temples*, 6. 7.
Acts 7. 48. Most High dwel. not in *t.*
R. V. 1 Kings 11. 10, 11, 13; 1 Chron. 6. 10; 10. 10; 2 Chron. 23. 10; Acts 7. 48. house or houses; Hos. 8. 14. palaces; Matt. 23. 35; 27. 5; Luke 11. 51. sanctuary
TEMPORAL, 2 Cor. 4. 18.
TEMPT Abraham, God did, Gen. 22. 1.
Ex. 17. 2. wherefore do ye *t.* Lord
Deut. 6. 16. shall not *t.* the Lord
Isa. 7. 12. ask, nor will I *t.* Lord
Matt. 4. 7. shalt not *t.* the Lord
22. 18. why *t.* ye me, show
Acts 5. 9. agreed together to *t.*
1 Cor. 7. 5. that Satan *t.* you not
Ex. 17. 7. they *tempted* Lord
Num. 14. 22. *t.* me now ten times
Ps. 78. 18. *t.* God in their heart
95. 9. when your fathers *t.* me
Matt. 4. 1. wilderness, to be *t.*
Luke 4. 2. lawyer *t.* him, saying
1 Cor. 10. 13. suffer you to be *t.*
Gal. 6. 1. lest thou also be *t.*
Heb. 2. 18. he is able to succor them that are *t.*
4. 15. in all points *t.* as we are
Jas. 1. 13. I am *t.* of God
14. every man is *t.* when drawn
Matt. 16. 1. *tempting* him, 19. 3. & 22. 35. Luke 11. 16. John 8. 6.
Ps. 95. 8. as in day of *temptation*
Matt. 6. 13. lead us not into *t.*
Luke 4. 13. devil had ended all *t.*
8. 13. in time of *t.* fall away
1 Cor. 10. 13. no *t.* taken you
Gal. 4. 14. my *t.* in flesh despised
1 Tim. 6. 9. rich fall into *t.* and
Heb. 3. 8. in day of *t.* in wilderness
Jas. 1. 12. blessed is he that endureth *t.*
Deut. 4. 34. *temptations*, 7. 19.
Luke 22. 28. Acts 20. 19. Jas. 1. 2.
1 Pet. 1. 6. 2 Pet. 2. 9.
Matt. 4. 3. *tempter*, 1 Thes. 3. 5.
R. V. Luke 20. 23 ——; Ps. 95. 8. Massah; Acts 20. 19; Rev. 3. 10. trial
TENDER, thy heart was, 2 Kings 22. 19. Eph. 4. 32.
Luke 1. 78. *t.* mercy, Jas. 5. 11.
R. V. S. of S. 2. 13, 15; 7. 12. in blossom; Dan. 1. 9. compassion; Jas. 5. 11. merciful
TENDETH, Prov. 10. 16. & 11. 19. & 19. 23. & 11. 24. & 14. 23. & 21. 5.
TENTS of Shem, dwell in, Gen. 9. 27.
1 Kings 12. 16. to your *t.* O Israel, 2 Sam. 20. 1.
Ps. 84. 10. dwell in *t.* of wickedness
S. of S. 1. 8. kids besi. shepherds' *t.*
R. V. Gen. 26. 17; 33. 18; Num. 9. 17, 18, 20-23; Ezra 8. 15. encamped; Num. 25. 8. pavilion; Num. 13. 19; 1 Sam. 17. 53; 2 Kings 7. 16; 2 Chron. 31. 2. camp or camps; 2 Sam. 11. 11. booths
TERRESTRIAL, 1 Cor. 15. 40.
TERRIBLE, Ex. 34. 10. Deut. 1. 19.
Deut. 7. 21. a mighty God and *t.*, 10. 17. Neh. 1. 5. & 4. 14. & 9. 32. Jer. 20. 11.
Deut. 10. 21. done *t.* things
Job 37. 22. with God is *t.* majesty
Ps. 45. 4. hand shall teach *t.*
47. 2. Lord most high is *t.*
65. 5. *t.* things wilt thou answer
66. 3. how *t.* art thou in thy
76. 12. he is *t.* to kings of the
99. 3. praise thy great and *t.*
S. of S. 6. 4. *t.* as army with ban.
Isa. 64. 3. *t.* things we looked not
Joel 2. 11. day of the Lord is *t.*
Zeph. 2. 11.
Heb. 12. 21. so *t.* was the sight

1 Chron. 17. 21. *terribleness,* Jer. 49. 16.
Job 7. 14. *terrifiest,* Phil. 1. 28.
R. V. Lam. 5. 10. burning; Dan. 7. 7. powerful; Heb. 12. 21. fearful
TERROR, Gen. 35. 5. Deut. 32. 25.
Job 31. 23. destr. from God was a *t.*
Isa. 33. 18. heart shall meditate *t.*
Jer. 17. 17. be not a *t.* unto me
20. 4. a *t.* to thyself, and all
Rom. 13. 3. rulers are not a *t.* to
2 Cor. 5. 11. know. *t.* of the Lord
1 Pet. 3. 14. be not afraid of their *t.*
Job 6. 4. *terrors,* 18. 11, 14. & 27. 20.
Ps. 55. 4. & 73. 19. & 88. 15, 16.
R. V. 2 Cor. 5, 11; 1 Pet. 3. 14. fear
TESTAMENT, Matt. 26. 28. Luke 22. 20. 1 Cor. 11. 25. 2 Cor. 3. 6, 14.
Gal. 3. 15. Heb. 7. 22. & 9. 15, 16, 17, 18. Rev. 11. 19.
Heb. 9. 16. death of the *testator*
TESTIFY, Deut. 8. 19. & 32. 46.
Neh. 9. 26, 34. Ps. 50. 7. & 81. 8.
Num. 35. 30. witness shall not *t.*
Isa. 59. 12. our sins *t.* against us
Hos. 5. 5. pride of Israel *t.* to his
John 3. 11. *t.* that we have seen
5. 39. search the Scriptures, they *t.* of me, 15. 26.
Acts 20. 24. *t.* the Gospel of grace
1 John 4. 14. *t.* that the Father
2 Chron. 24. 19. *testified,* Neh. 13. 15.
Acts 23. 11. 1 Tim. 2. 6. 1 John 5. 9.
Heb. 11. 4. *testifying,* 1 Pet. 5. 12.
2 Kings 11. 12. gave him the *testimony*
Ps. 78. 5. established a *t.* in Jacob
Isa. 8. 16. bind up the *t.,* seal the law
Matt. 10. 18. for a *t.* against them
John 3. 32. no man receiveth his *t.*
Acts 14. 3. *t.* to word of his grace
2 Cor. 1. 12. the *t.* of our conscience
Rev. 1. 9. *t.* of Jesus Christ
11. 7. have finished their *t.*
Ps. 25. 10. keep his *testimonies,* 93. 5; *thy testimonies,* 119. 14, 24, 31, 46, 59, 95, 111, 129, 144.
R. V. John 2. 25; 3. 11, 39; 5. 39; 15. 26; 21. 24; Heb. 11. 14; 1 John 4. bear witness; 1 Cor. 15. 15; Heb. 7. 17. witnessed; Ruth 4. 7. attestation; John 3. 32, 33; 8. 17; 21. 24. witness; Acts 13. 22; 14. 3; Heb. 11. 5. bear witness; 1 Cor. 2. 1. mystery
THANK, 1 Chron. 16. 4. & 29. 13.
Matt. 11. 25, 26. Luke 6. 32, 33. & 17. 9. & 18. 11. John 11. 41. Rom. 1. 8. & 7. 25. 1 Cor. 1. 4. 2 Thes. 2. 13.
1 Tim. 1. 12.
Ps. 100. 4. be *thankful,* Acts 24. 3.
Rom. 1. 21. Col. 3. 15.
1 Pet. 2. 19. this is *thankworthy*
Dan. 6. 10. gave *thanks,* Matt. 26. 27. Mark 8. 6. Luke 22. 17. Rom. 14. 6.
2 Cor. 9. 15. *t,* to God for his unspeakable gift, 2. 14. & 8. 16. 1 Cor. 15. 57.
Eph. 5. 4. *giving of thanks,* 20. 1.
Tit. 2. 1. Heb. 13. 15.
1 Thes. 3. 9. what *t.* can we render
Lev. 7. 12. *thanksgiving,* Neh. 11. 17.
Ps. 26. 7. & 50. 14. & 100. 4. & 107. 22. & 116. 17. Isa. 51. 3. Phil. 4. 6.
1 Tim. 4. 3. Rev. 7. 12.
R. V. Heb. 13. 15. confession; Ps. 100. 4; Rom. 1. 21. give thanks
THEATRE, Acts 19. 29.
THINE is the day and night, Ps. 74. 16.
Ps. 119. 94. I am *t.,* save me
Isa. 63. 19. we are *t.* thou never
Matt. 20. 14. take that *t.* is and go
John 17. 6. *t.* they were, and thou
10. all mine are *t.* and *t.* are mine
R. V. Many changes to thy
THINGS devoted, Lev. 27. Num. 18. 14. Ezek. 44. 29: not to be redeemed, Lev. 27. 33; abuse of (Corban), Matt. 15. 5. Mark 7. 11.
THINK on me for good, Neh. 5. 19.
Job 31. 1. should I *t.* on a maid

Jer. 29. 11. I know that I *t.* toward
Rom. 12. 3. not to *t.* more highly
1 Cor. 8. 2. if any *t.* that he know.
Gal. 6. 3. *t.* himself to be some.
Eph. 3. 20. above all we ask or *t.*
Phil. 4. 8. *t.* on these things
Gen. 50. 20. *thought* evil against
Ps. 48. 9. we have *t.* of thy loving
119. 59. I *t.* on my ways and
Matt. 3. 16. that *t.* on his name
Mark 14. 72. he *t.* thereon wept
1 Cor. 13. 11. I *t.* as a child, spake
Phil. 2. 6. *t.* it not robbery to be
Ps. 139. 2. understandest my *t.*
Prov. 24. 9. the *t.* of foolishness
Eccl. 10. 20. curse not king in thy *t.*
Matt. 6. 25. take no *t.* for life
6. 34. take no *t.* for the morrow
Mark 13. 11. take no *t.* beforehand
10. 6. every *t.* into captivity
Ps. 50. 21. thou *thoughtest* I was
Gen. 6. 5. imagination of *thoughts*
Judg. 5. 15. were great *t.* of heart
Ps. 10. 4. God is not in all his *t.*
33. 11. the *t.* of his heart to all
94. 11. Lord know. the *t.* of man
19. in multitude of my *t.* within
119. 113. hate vain *t.* but thy law
139. 17. how precious are thy *t.*
139. 23. try me and know my *t.*
Prov. 12. 5. *t.* of righte. are right
15. 26. the *t.* of the wicked are
16. 3. thy *t.* shall be established
Isa. 55. 7. let the unrighteous man forsake his *t.*
8. my *t.* are not your *t.*
Jer. 4. 14. how long shall vain *t.*
29. 11. *t.* I think toward you are *t.*
Mic. 4. 12. know not *t.* of the Lord
Matt. 15. 19. out of the heart proceed evil *t.*
Luke 2. 35. the *t.* of many hearts
24. 38. do *t.* arise in your hearts
Rom. 2. 15. their *t.* accusing, or
1 Cor. 3. 20. Lord knoweth the *t.*
Heb. 4. 12. a discerner of the *t.*
Jas. 2. 4. become judges of evil *t.*
R. V. Gen. 50. 10. meant; Ex. 32. 14; Esth. 6. 6. said; 2 Sam. 14. 13; Ezek. 38. 10. devise; 2 Chron. 11. 32. was minded; Neh. 5. 19. remember; Job 31. 1. look; 42. 2. purpose; Ezek. 38. 10. device; Luke 9. 47; 12. 7. reasoned; Luke 19. 11; Acts 13. 25. suppose; Acts 26. 8; Heb. 10. 29. judged; Rom. 2. 3. reckon; 2 Cor. 3. 5; 12. 16. account; 10. 7. consider; 10. 11. reckon
THIRST, Deut. 28. 48. & 29. 19.
Isa. 49. 10. shall not hunger nor *t.*
Matt. 5. 6. blessed are they which hunger and *t.* after righteousness
John 4. 14. shall never *t.,* 6. 35.
7. 37. if any *t.* let him come
Rom. 12. 20. if he *t.* give him drink
Rev. 7. 16. hunger nor *t.* any more
Ps. 42. 2. my soul *thirsteth* for God
Isa. 55. 1. ho, every one that *t.*
THORNS in your sides, Num. 33. 55. Judg. 2. 3. Gen. 3. 18.
Josh. 23. 13. be *t.* in your eyes
2 Sam. 23. 6. as *t.* thrust away
Jer. 4. 3. sow not among *t.*
Hos. 2. 6. hedge up thy way with *t.*
Matt. 7. 16. gather grapes of *t.*
13. 7. some fell among *t.,* 22.
Heb. 6. 8. that which beareth *t.*
R. V. 2 Chron. 33. 11. in chains; Job 41. 2. hook
THREATENING, Eph. 6. 9. Acts 4. 29. & 9. 1. 1 Pet. 2. 23.
THREE, 2 Sam. 24. 12. Prov. 30. 15, 18, 21, 29. Amos 1. 3, 13. & 2. 1. 1 Cor. 14. 27. 1 John 5. 7, 8. Rev. 16. 13.
THRESH, Isa. 21. 10. & 41. 15. Jer. 51. 33. Mic. 4. 13. Hab. 3. 12. 1 Cor. 9. 10.
Lev. 26. 5. and your *threshing* shall reach unto the vintage
2 Sam. 24. 18. *threshing-floor,* 21. 24.
R. V. Judg. 6. 11. beating out; Jer. 51. 33. trodden

THROAT is an open sepulchre, Ps. 5. 9.
Ps. 69. 3. weary of crying, my *t.*
Prov. 23. 2. put a knife to thy *t.*
THRONE, Lord is in heaven, Ps. 11. 4.
Ps. 94. 20. *t.* of iniquity have fel.
Prov. 25. 5. *t.* is established by
Isa. 66. 1. heaven is my *t.*
Jer. 14. 21. not disgrace *t.* of glory
Lam. 5. 19. *t.* from generation to
Dan. 7. 9. *t.* was like fiery flame
Matt. 19. 28. sit in *t.* of his glory, ye shall sit on twelve *thrones*
Col. 1. 16. whether they be *t.* or
Heb. 4. 16. boldly to the *t.* of grace
Rev. 3. 21. sit on my *t.* with my Father on his *t.*
22. 3. *t.* of God and Lamb shall be
Job 26. 9. *his throne,* Ps. 89. 14, 29, 44. & 97. 2. & 103. 19. Prov. 20. 28. & 25. 5. Dan. 7. 9. Zech. 6. 13.
Ps. 45. 6. *thy throne,* 99. 4. Heb. 1. 8.
Isa. 22. 33. *glorious throne,* Jer. 17. 12.
THRUST, Ex. 11. 1. Job 32. 13. Luke 13. 28. John 20. 25. Acts 16. 37.
R. V. Deut. 13. 5, 10. draw; Judg. 6. 38. pressed; 9. 41; 11. 2. drave; Job 32. 13. vanquished; 1 Sam. 11. 2; Luke 5. 3; John 20. 25, 27. put; Luke 4. 29; Acts 16. 24, 37; Rev. 14. 19. cast; Luke 10. 15. brought; Acts 27. 39. drive; Heb. 12. 20——; Rev. 14. 15, 18. send forth
THUNDER, Job 26. 14. & 40. 9. Ps. 29. 3. & 81. 7. Mark 3. 17.
Rev. 4. 5. *thunderings,* 8. 5. & 10. 3. & 11. 19. & 16. 18. & 19. 6.
R. V. Job 39. 19. quivering mane
TIDINGS, evil, Ex. 33. 4. Ps. 112. 7.
Luke 1. 19. show the glad *t.,* 8. 1.
Acts 13. 32. Rom. 10. 15.
R. V. 1 Sam. 11. 4, 5, 6. word; Acts 11. 22 report
TIME when thou mayest be found, Ps. 32. 6.
Ps. 37. 19. evil *t.*
41. 1. *t.* of trouble
69. 13. acceptable *t.,* Isa. 49. 8. 2 Cor. 6. 2.
Ps. 89. 47. how short my *t.*
Eccl. 3. 1–8. *a time* to every purpose
——to be born—to die—to plant—to pluck up—to love—to hate—of war—of peace
9. 11. *t.* and chance happen.
Ezek. 16. 8. *t.* was the *t.* of love
Dan. 7. 25. till a *t.* and times, div.
Amos 5. 13. evil *t.,* Mic. 2. 3.
Luke 19. 44. knew. not *t.* of thy
John 7. 6. my *t.* is not yet come
Acts 17. 21. spent *t.* in nothing
Rom. 13. 11. high *t.* to awake out
1 Cor. 7. 29. the *t.* is short, it rem.
2 Cor. 6. 2. accepted *t.* the day of
Eph. 5. 16. redeeming the *t.*
Tit. 1. 17. past *t.* of your sojourn.
Rev. 10. 6. *t.* shall be no longer
Ps. 31. 15. my *times* are in thy
Luke 21. 24. till *t.* of the Gentiles
Acts 1. 7. for you to know the *t.*
17. 26. determined the *t.* before
1 Tim. 4. 1. in latter *t.* some shall
2 Tim. 3. 1. in last days perilous *t.*
Ps. 34. 1. bless the Lord *at all times*
106. 3. blessed is he that doeth righteousness
Prov. 5. 19. her breasts satisfy—
17. 17. a friend loveth—
R. V. Many changes to day, season, hour. So, many to suit context, as Matt. 4. 6. at any time to haply
TIN, Num. 31. 22. Isa. 1. 25. Ezek. 22. 18.
TITHES, Gen. 14. 20. Mal. 3. 8.
Amos 4. 4. Matt. 23. 23. Luke 18. 12.
TITTLE or jot pass from the law, Matt. 5. 18.
2 Kings 23. 17. monument
TOGETHER, Ps. 2. 2. Prov. 22. 2.
Rom. 8. 28. all things work *t.* for
1 Cor. 3. 9. laborers *t.* with God

2 Cor. 6. 1. as workers *t.* with him
Eph. 2. 5. quickened us *t.* with
  6. raised us up *t.* made us sit *t.*
TOKEN of covenant, Gen. 9. 12, 13.
  & 17. 11.
Ps. 86. 17. show me a *t.* for good
Phil. 1. 28. evident a *t.* of perdition
2 Thes. 1. 5. manifest *t.* of right.
Job 21. 29. not know their *tokens*
Ps. 65. 8. they are afraid at thy *t.*
  135. 9. who sent *t.* and wonders
Isa. 44. 25. frustrated the *t.* of liars
R. V. Ex. 13. 16; Ps. 135. 9. sign
TONGUE, Ex. 11. 7. Josh. 10. 21.
Job 5. 21. hid from scourge of *t.*
Ps. 34. 13. keep thy *t.* from evil
Prov. 10. 20. *t.* of the just is as
  12. 18. *t.* of wise is health
  15. 4. wholesome *t.* is a tree of
  21. 6. get. treasure by a lying *t.*
  25. 15. soft *t.* breaketh the bone
Isa. 30. 27. *t.* as a devouring fire
Jer. 9. 5. taught their *t.* to speak
  18. 18. smite him with the *t.*
Jas. 1. 26. be religious and bri-
  dleth not his *t.*
  3. 8. the *t.* can no man tame, 5.
1 Pet. 3. 10. refrain his *t.* from evil
1 John 3. 18. love in *t.* but deed
Ps. 35. 28. *my tongue*, 39. 1. & 45. 1.
  & 51. 14. & 71. 24. & 119. 172. & 137.
  6. & 139. 4. Acts 2. 26.
Ps. 31. 26. *tongues*, 55. 9. Mark 16. 17.
Acts 19. 6. 1 Cor. 12. 10, 28. & 14. 23.
TOOK out of the womb, Ps. 22. 9.
Phil. 2. 7. *t.* on him form of ser.
Heb. 10. 34. *t.* joyfully the spoiling
R. V. Ezra 4. 17; Esth. 7. 4; Job 6.
  24; 13. 19; Amos 6. 10. peace;
  Acts 2. 8; 21. 40; 22. 2; 26. 14. lan-
  guage; Rev. 9. 11; 16. 16 —
TOPHET, Isa. 30. 33. Jer. 7. 31, 32.
TORCH, Zech. 12. 6. Nah. 2. 3, 4.
R. V. Nah. 2. 3. flash with steel
TORMENT us before the time,
  Matt. 8. 29.
Luke 16. 28. to this place of *t.*
Rev. 18. 7. so much *t.* and sorrow
Luke 16. 24. am *tormented* in this
  25. he is comforted, thou art *t.*
Heb. 11. 37. destitute, afflicted, *t.*
R. V. 1 John 4. 18. punishment;
  Luke 16. 24, 25. in anguish; Heb.
  11. 37. evil entreated
TORN, Hos. 6. 1. Mal. 1. 13. Mark
  1. 26.
TOSS, Isa. 22. 18. Jer. 5. 22. Jas. 1. 6.
Ps. 109. 23. I am *tossed* up and
Isa. 54. 11. *t.* with a tempest
Eph. 4. 14. children *t.* to and fro
R. V. Prov. 21. 6. driven; Matt. 14.
  24. distressed; Acts 27. 18. la-
  bored
TOUCH not mine anointed, Ps.
  105. 15.
Job 5. 19. in seven shall no evil *t.*
Isa. 52. 11. *t.* no unclean thing
Matt. 9. 21. but *t.* his garment
  14. 36. only *t.* hem of his garment
Mark 10. 13. chil. that he should *t.*
Luke 11. 46. *t.* not the burdens
John 20. 17. *t.* me not, for I am
2 Cor. 6. 17. *t.* not the unclean
Col. 2. 21. *t.* not, taste not, handle
1 Sam. 10. 26. whose heart God
  had *touched*
Job 19. 21. hand of God hath *t.*
Luke 8. 45. who *t.* me
Zech. 2. 8. *toucheth* you, *t.* apple
1 John 5. 18. wicked one *t.* him
TOWER, God is a high, Ps. 18. 2.
  & 144. 2.
Ps. 61. 3. strong *t.*, Prov. 18. 10.
S. of S. 4. 4. *t.* of David
  7. 4. *t.* of ivory; *t.* of Lebanon
Isa. 5. 2. built a *t.*, Matt. 21. 33.
R. V. 2 Kings 5. 24. hill; Zeph. 1.
  16; 3. 6. battlements
TRADERS in Tyre, Ezek. 27.
TRADITION, Matt. 15. 3. Gal. 1.
  14. Col. 2. 8. 2 Thes. 2. 15. & 3. 6.
1 Pet. 1. 18.
R. V. 1 Pet. 1. 18. handed down
TRAIN. Prov. 22. 6. Isa. 6. 1.

TRAITOR, Luke 6. 16. 2 Tim. 3. 4.
TRAMPLE, Isa. 63. 3. Matt. 7. 6.
TRANCE, Num. 24. 4. Acts 10. 10.
  & 11. 5. & 22. 17.
R. V. Num. 24. 4, 16. down
TRANQUILLITY, Dan. 4. 27.
TRANSFIGURED, Matt. 17. 2.
  Mark 9. 2.
TRANSFORMED, Rom. 12. 2.
  2 Cor. 11. 14, 15.
R. V. 2 Cor. 11. 13, 14, 15. fashion
TRANSGRESS the command-
  ment of the Lord, Num. 14. 41.
1 Sam. 2. 24. ye make the Lord's
  people to *t.*
2 Chron. 24. 20. why *t.* ye the
Neh. 1. 8. if ye *t.* I will scatter
Ps. 17. 3. mouth shall not *t.*
  25. 3. ashamed that *t.* without
Prov. 28. 21. for piece of bread
  man will *t.*
Amos 4. 4. come to Bethel and *t.*
Matt. 15. 2. why do thy disciples *t.*
  3. why do ye *t.* the command.
Rom. 2. 27. by circumcision dost *t.*
Deut. 26. 13. not *transgressed* thy
Josh. 7. 11. have *t.* my covenant
Isa. 43. 27. teachers have *t.* against
Jer. 2. 8. pastors also *t.* against
Lam. 3. 42. have *t.* and rebelled
Ezek. 2. 3. and their fathers *t.*
Dan. 9. 11. all Israel have *t.* thy
Hos. 6. 7. men have *t.* the covenant
Hab. 2. 5. *transgresseth* by wine
1 John 3. 4. committeth sin, *t.*
Ex. 34. 7. forgiving iniquity,
  transgression, and sin, Num. 14.
  18.
1 Chron. 10. 13. Saul died for his *t.*
Ezra 10. 6. mourned because of *t.*
Job 13. 23. make me to know my *t.*
Ps. 32. 1. blessed is he whose *t.* is
  forgiven
  89. 32. visit their *t.* with rod
Prov. 17. 9. he that covereth *t.* seek.
Isa. 53. 8. for *t.* of my people
  58. 1. show my people their *t.*
Dan. 9. 24. to finish *t.* and make
Amos 4. 4. at Gilgal multiply *t.*
Mic. 3. 8. declare to Jacob his *t.*
Rom. 4. 15. no law is, there is no
  t.
1 John 3. 4. sin is the *t.* of the
Ex. 23. 21. pardon *transgressions*
Lev. 16. 21. all their *t.* in all their
Josh. 24. 19. not forgive your *t.*
Job 31. 33. covered my *t.* as Adam
Ps. 25. 7. remember not my *t.*
  39. 8. deliver me from all my *t.*
  51. 1. blot out my *t.*
  65. 3. our *t.* thou shalt purge
  103. 12. so far removed our *t.*
Isa. 43. 25. he that blotteth out *t.*
  44. 22. out as a thick cloud, thy *t.*
  53. 5. he was wounded for our *t.*
Ezek. 18. 31. cast away all your *t.*
Heb. 9. 15. the redemption of *t.*
Isa. 48. 8. wast a *transgressor* from
Jas. 2. 11. if thou kill, thou art be-
  come a *t.* of the law
Ps. 51. 13. teach *transgressors* thy
  59. 5. be not merciful to wicked *t.*
  119. 158. I beheld the *t.* and
Prov. 13. 15. the way of *t.* is hard
Isa. 53. 12. was numbered with *t.*
  and make intercession for *t.*,
  Mark 15. 28.
Hos. 14. 9. the *t.* shall fall therein
R. V. 1 Chron. 2. 7; 5. 25; 2 Chron.
  12. 2; 26. 16; 28. 19; 36. 14; Ezra 10.
  10; Neh. 1. 8; 13. 27; Hos. 7. 13.
  trespass; 1 Sam. 14. 33; Ps. 25. 3;
  Hab. 2. 5. deal treacherously;
  Jer. 2. 20. serve; 1 John 3. 4. doeth
  lawlessness; 2 John 9. goeth onward; Josh. 22. 22; 1 Chron. 10. 13;
  Ezra 9. 14; 10. 6; 2 Chron. 29. 19.
  trespass; 1 John 3. 4. lawlessness;
  Prov. 2. 22; 11. 3, 6; 13. 2, 15; 21.
  18; 22. 23; 28. 28. treacherous;
  26. 10. that pass by
TRANSLATION, of Enoch, Gen.
  5. 24. Heb. 11. 5; of Elijah, 2 Kings
  2

TRAVAIL, Isa. 53. 11. Gal. 4. 19, 27.
Job 15. 20. the wicked *travaileth*
Ps. 7. 14. he *t.* with iniquity
Isa. 66. 7. before she *travailed*, 8.
  42. 14. *travailing* woman, Hos. 13.
  13. Isa. 13. 8. & 21. 3. Jer. 31. 18.
  Rev. 12. 2.
R. V. Eccl. 4. 4. labor; 5. 14. ad-
  venture
TRAVEL, Eccl. 1. 13. & 2. 23, 26.
  & 4. 4, 6, 8. & 5. 14. 2 Thes. 3. 8.
Job 15. 20. *travelleth*, Prov. 6. 11. &
  24. 34.
Isa. 21. 13. *travelling*, 63. 1.
R. V. Prov. 6. 11; 24. 34. a robber;
  Isa. 63. 1. marching; Matt. 25. 14.
  going
TREACHEROUS, Isa. 21. 2. & 24.
  16.
Jer. 9. 2. an assembly of *t.* men
Isa. 21. 2. *treacherously*, 24. 16. &
  33. 1.
  48. 8. knew thou wouldst deal *t.*
Jer. 3. 20. as a wife *t.* departeth
  12. 1. all happy that deal *t.*
Hos. 5. 7. dealt *t.* against Lord
Mal. 2. 15. none deal *t.* against
TREACHERY, instances of, Gen.
  34. 13. Judg. 9. 1 Sam. 21. 7. & 22.
  9. (Ps. 52.) 2 Sam. 3. 27. & 11. 14. & 16.
  & 20. 9. 1 Kings 21. 5. 2 Kings 10. 18.
  Esth. 3. Matt. 26. 47. Mark 14. 43.
  Luke 22. 47. John 18. 3.
TREAD down wicked in place,
  Job 40. 12.
Ps. 7. 5. let him *t.* down my life
Isa. 1. 12. required this to *t.* my
  63. 3. *t.* them in mine anger, 6.
Hos. 10. 11. Ephraim loveth to *t.*
Rev. 11. 2. city shall be *t.* under
Deut. 25. 4. not muzzle the ox that
  treadeth out the corn, 1 Cor. 9. 9.
  1 Tim. 5. 18.
Isa. 22. 5. *treading*, Amos 5. 11.
R. V. Isa. 1. 12; Amos 5. 11. tram-
  ple
TREASON, instances, 2 Sam. 15-
  18. & 20. 1 Kings 1. & 16. 10. 2 Kings
  11. & 15. 10. 2 Chron. 22. 10. Esth. 2.
  21.
TREASURE, Prov. 15. 6, 16. & 21.
  20.
Ex. 19. 5. peculiar *t.*, Ps. 135. 4.
Isa. 33. 6. fear of the Lord is his *t.*
Matt. 6. 21. where your *t.* is there
  12. 35. good man out of good *t.*
  13. 52. bringeth forth out of his *t.*
  19. 21. shalt have *t.* in heaven
Luke 12. 21. layeth up *t.* for him,
2 Cor. 4. 7. this *t.* in earthen ves.
Deut. 32. 34. sealed up among my
  treasures
Ps. 17. 14. fillest with thy hid *t.*
Prov. 2. 4. search. for her as hid *t.*
  10. 2. *t.* of wickedness profit no.
Matt. 6. 19. lay not up *t.* on earth
  20. lay up for yourselves *t.* in
Col. 2. 3. in *treasure* hid all the
  t. of wisdom
Rom. 2. 5. *treasurest* up unto thy.
R. V. 1 Chron. 26. 20, 22, 24, 26; 27. 25;
  Job 38. 22; Prov. 8. 21; Jer. 10. 3;
  51. 16. treasuries; Jer. 41. 8. stores
  hidden
TREE, Gen. 2. 16, 17. & 3. 22.
Ps. 1. 3. like a *t.* planted by rivers
  52. 8. I am like a green olive *t.*
Prov. 3. 18. she is a *t.* of life to
  11. 30. fruit of righteous. is *t.* of
Isa. 6. 13. be eaten as a teil *t.*
  56. 3. eunuch say, I am a dry *t.*
Jer. 17. 8. a *t.* planted by the wat.
Matt. 3. 10. *t.* that bringeth not
  7. 17. good *t.* bringeth forth
  12. 33. make the *t.* good; or else
1 Pet. 2. 24. in his own body on the *t.*
Rev. 2. 7. give to eat of *t.* of life
  22. 2. midst of city was *t.* of life
  14. have right to the *t.* of life
Ps. 104. 16. the *trees* of the Lord
Isa. 61. 3. called *t.* of righteous.
Ezek. 47. 12. grow all *t.* for meat
Mark 8. 24. I see men as *t.* walk.
Jude 12. *t.* whose fruit withereth

TREMBLE at the commandment of our God, Ezra 10. 3.
Ps. 99. 1. Lord reign., let people *t.*
Isa. 66. 5. ye that *t.* at his word
Jer. 5. 22. not *t.* at my presence
10. 10. at his wrath earth shall *t.*
Dan. 6. 26. men *t.* before the God
Jas. 2. 19. devils believe and *t.*
1 Sam. 4. 13. heart *trembled* for ark
Ezra 9. 4. every one that *t.* at
Acts 24. 25. he reasoned, Felix *t.*
Job 37. 1. *trembleth*, Ps. 119. 120.
Isa. 66. 2.
1 Sam. 13. 7. followed *trembling*
Deut. 28. 65. give thee a *t.* heart
Ezra 10. 9. people sat *t.* because
Ps. 2. 11. serve God and rejoice *t.*
Ezek. 12. 18. drink thy water with
t., 26. 16.
Hos. 13. 1. Ephraim spake *t.*
1 Cor. 2. 3. fear and in much *t.*
Eph. 6. 5. fear and *t.* in singleness
Phil. 2. 12. work out your sal. with *t.*
R. V. Hab. 3. 10. were afraid; Acts
24. 25. was terrified; Job 21. 6.
horror; Isa. 51. 17, 22. staggering;
Zech. 12. 2. reeling

TRESPASS, Lev. 26. 40. Ezra 9. 6.
1 Kings 8. 31. Matt. 18. 15. Luke
17. 3.
Ezra 9. 15. *trespasses*, Ezek. 39. 26.
Ps. 68. 21. goeth on still in his *t.*
Matt. 6. 14. forgive men their *t.*
18. 35. if ye forgive not every one
his brother their *t.*
Eph. 2. 1. dead in *t.* and sins
Col. 2. 13. forgiven you all *t.*
R. V. Gen. 50. 17. transgression;
Num. 5. 7, 8; Lev. 6. 5; 22. 16;
1 Chron. 21. 3; 2 Chron. 19. 10;
Ezra 9. 7, 13; 10. 10, 19. guilt or
guilty; 2 Chron. 24. 18; Ezra 6.
15. 9. 6, 15; Ps. 68. 21. guilti-
ness; Matt. 8.35; Mark 11. 26 ——;
2 Chron. 19. 10. be guilty; 1 Kings
8. 31; Matt. 18. 5; Luke 17. 3, 4.
sin

TRIAL, Job 9. 23. Ezek. 21. 13.
2 Cor. 8. 2. Heb. 11. 36. 1 Pet. 1. 7.
& 4. 12.
R. V. 2 Cor. 8. 2; 1 Pet. 1. 7. proof

TRIBES, Num. 24. 2.
Ps. 105. 37. one feeble among *t.*
122. 4. whither *t.* go up, *t.* of
Matt. 24. 30. all the *t.* of earth
Acts 26. 7. promise our twelve *t.*

TRIBULATION, art in, Deut. 4. 30.
Judg. 10. 14. deliver you in *t.*
Matt. 13. 21. when *t.* or persecu.
24. 21. then shall be great *t.* such
29. immediately after the *t.*
John 16. 33. ye shall have *t.*
Acts 14. 22. through much *t.*
Rom. 2. 9. *t.* and anguish on every
5. 3. knowing *t.* worketh patience
12. 12. in hope, patient in *t.*
2 Cor. 1. 4. comfort. us in all our *t.*
1 Thes. 3. 4. we should suffer *t.*
2 Thes. 1. 6. to recompense *t.* to
Rev. 1. 9. and companion in *t.*
2. 9. I know thy works and *t.*
22. cast into great *t.* except
7. 14. have come out of great *t.*
Rom. 5. 3. glory in *tribulations*
1 Sam. 10. 19. save. you out of all *t.*
Eph. 3. 13. faint not at my *t.* for
2 Thes. 1. 4. patience in all *t.*
R. V. Judg. 10. 14; 1 Sam. 10. 19.
distress; 2 Cor. 1. 4; 7. 4; 1 Thes.
1. 4; 3. 4; 2 Thes. 1. 6. affliction

TRIBUTE, Gen. 49. 15. Num. 31. 28.
Matt. 17. 24. doth not your Master
pay *t.*
22. 17. is it lawful to give *t.* to
Cæsar
Rom. 13. 7. *t.* to whom *t.* is due
R. V. Gen. 49. 15; Josh. 16. 10;
17. 13; Judg. 1. 28; Prov. 12. 24.
task work; 1 Kings 4. 6; 9. 21; 12.
18; 2 Chron. 10. 18. levy; 2 Chron.
8. 8. bond servants; Matt. 17. 24.
half shekel

TRIMMED, Jer. 2. 33. Matt. 25. 7.
TRIUMPH, 2 Sam. 1. 20. Ps. 25. 2.
Ps. 92. 4. *t.* in works of thy hands
2 Cor. 2. 14. always cause. us to *t.*
Ex. 15. 1. *triumphed* gloriously
Job 20. 5. *triumphing*, Col. 2. 15.
R. V. Ps. 60. 8; 108. 9. shout

TRODDEN down strength, Judg. 5. 21.
Ps. 119. 118. *t.* down all them
Isa. 63. 3. have *t.* winepress alone
Luke 21. 24. Jerusalem shall be *t.*
Heb. 10. 29. *t.* under foot Son of

TROUBLE, 2 Chron. 15. 4. Neh. 9. 32.
Job 5. 6. neither doth *t.* spring
14. 1. man is of few days and full
of *t.*
Ps. 9. 9. refuge in times of *t.*
22. 11. *t.* is near; there is none
27. 5. in time of *t.* he shall hide
46. 1. God is a present help in *t.*
91. 15. I will be with him in *t.*
143. 11. bring my soul out of *t.*
Prov. 11. 8. the righteous is delivered out of *t.*
Isa. 26. 16. Lord. in *t.* have they
33. 2. our salvation in time of *t.*
Jer. 8. 15. looked for health, and
behold *t.*
14. 8. and Saviour in time of *t.*
Dan. 12. 1. shall be a time of *t.*
Cor. 7. 28. have *t.* in the flesh
Ps. 25. 17. the *troubles* of my heart
34. 17. deliver them out of all *t.*
88. 3. my soul is full of *t.*
Ex. 14. 24. Lord *troubled* the host
Ps. 30. 7. and I was *t.*
Isa. 57. 20. wic. are like the *t.* sea
John 12. 27. now is my soul *t.*
14. 1. let not your hearts be *t.*
2 Cor. 4. 8. *t.* on every side, 7. 5.
2 Thes. 1. 7. to you who are *t.* rest
Job 23. 16. Almighty *troubleth* me
1 Kings 18. 17. he that *t.* Israel
Prov. 11. 17. cruel *t.* his own flesh
29. he that *t.* his own house
Luke 18. 5. because this widow *t.*
Gal. 5. 10. he that *t.* you shall
Job 3. 17. *troubling*, Ps. 5. 4.
R. V. 1 Chron. 22. 14; Ps. 9. 13;
31. 7, 9; 2 Cor. 1. 4, 8. affliction;
2 Chron. 15.4; Job 15. 24; Ps. 59. 16;
66. 14, 17; 102. 2; Isa. 8. 22. distress; 2 Chron. 29. 8. tossed to and
fro; Neh. 9. 32. travail; Job 34.
29. condemn; Ps. 41. 1. evil; Ps.
78. 33; Isa. 17. 14. terror; Ps. 3. 1;
13. 4; 60. 11. adversaries; Isa. 22.
5. discomfiture; 65. 23. calamity;
Jer. 8. 15; 14. 19. dismay; Ezek.
7. 7. tumult; Acts 20. 10. make no
ado; 1 Cor. 7. 28. tribulation;
2 Tim. 2. 9. hardship; Mark 13. 8
——; Ex. 14. 24. discomfited; Job
34. 20. shaken; Ps. 38. 5. pained;
77. 3. disquieted; 77. 16. trembled;
48. 5; 83. 17; Ezek. 26. 18. dis-
mayed; Zech. 10. 2; 2 Thes. 1. 7.
afflicted; John 5. 4 ——

TRUCE breakers, 2 Tim. 3. 3.
TRUE, Gen. 42. 11. 2 Sam. 7. 28.
Ps. 19. 9. judgments of Lord are *t.*
119. 160. thy word is *t.*
Prov. 14. 25. *t.* witness delivereth
Jer. 42. 5. be *t.* and faithful wit.
Ezek. 18. 8. *t.* judgment, Zech. 7. 9.
Matt. 22. 16. we know thou art *t.*
Luke 16. 11. *t.* riches
John 1. 9. *t.* light
4. 23. *t.* worshippers
6. 32. *t.* bread from heaven
15. 1. I am the *t.* vine
2 Cor. 1. 18. as God is *t.* our word
6. 8. as deceivers and yet *t.*
Phil. 4. 8. what. things are *t.*
1 John 5. 20. know him that is *t.*
Rev. 3. 7. saith he that is *t.*
19. 11. was called faithful and *t.*
R. V. 2 Cor. 1. 18; 1 Tim. 3. 1. faithful

TRUMP, 1 Cor. 15. 52. 1 Thes. 16. 4.
TRUMPET, Ex. 19. 16. Ps. 81. 3.
Isa. 27. 13. great *t.* shall be blown

Isa. 58. 1. lift up thy voice like a *t.*
Matt. 6. 2. not sound a *t.* before
Num. 10. 2. *trumpets*, Josh. 6. 4.
Ps. 98. 6. Rev. 8. 9.

TRUST in him, 1 Chron. 5. 20.
Job 4. 10. put no *t.* in servants
8. 14. his *t.* is a spider's web
Ps. 4. 5. put your *t.* in the Lord
40. 4. maketh the Lord his *t.*
71. 5. art my *t.* from my youth
Prov. 22. 19. thy *t.* may be in Lord
Job 13. 15. though he slay me I will *t.*
Ps. 37. 3. *t.* in Lord, and do good
5. *t.* in him; he will bring it to
55. 23. I will *t.* in thee
62. 8. *t.* in him at all times, ye
115. 8, 9, 10, 11. *t.* in the Lord
118. 8. it is better to *t.* in Lord, 9.
119. 42. for I *t.* in thy word
Prov. 3. 5. *t.* in the Lord with all
Isa. 36. 4. *t.* ye in the Lord for ever
Jer. 7. 4. *t.* not in lying words
9. 4. *t.* not in any brother
Mic. 7. 5. *t.* ye not in a friend
Mark 10. 24. them that *t.* in riches
2 Cor. 1. 9. not *t.* in ourselves
Phil. 3. 4. whereof to *t.* in flesh
1 Tim. 6. 20. committed to thy *t.*
Ps. 22. 4. our fathers *trusted* in
52. 7. *t.* in abundance of his
Luke 18. 9. *t.* in themselves
Eph. 1. 12. who first *t.* in Christ
Ps. 32. 10. *trusteth* in Lord's
34. 8. blessed is man that *t.* in
86. 2. save servant that *t.* in thee
Jer. 17. 5. cursed be the man that *t.* in
1 Tim. 5. 5. desolate *t.* in God
Ps. 112. 7. heart is fixed *trusting*
R. V. Ruth 2. 12; Ps. 36. 7; 37. 40;
61. 4; 91. 4; Isa. 14. 32. take refuge; Matt. 12. 21; Luke 24. 21;
Rom. 15. 12, 24; 1 Cor. 16. 7;
2 Cor. 1. 10, 13; 5. 11; 13. 6; Eph. 1.
12; Phil. 2. 19; 1 Tim. 4. 10; 6. 17;
Phile. 22; 2 John 12; 3 John 14.
hope or hoped; 2 Cor. 3. 4; Phil.
3. 4. confidence; Heb. 13. 18. persuaded

TRUTH, Gen. 24. 27. Ex. 18. 21.
Deut. 34. 4. a God of *t.* and with.
Ps. 15. 2. speaketh *t.* in his heart
25. 10. the paths of the Lord are
mercy and *t.*
91. 4. his *t.* shall be thy shield
117. 2. his *t.* endureth for ever
119. 30. chosen the way of *t.*
Prov. 12. 19. lip of *t.* shall be
16. 6. by mercy and *t.* iniquity
23. 23. buy the *t.* and sell it not
Isa. 59. 14. *t.* is fallen in the streets
Jer. 4. 2. swear Lord liveth in *t.*
Dan. 4. 37. all whose ways are *t.*
Zech. 8. 16. speak every man *t.* to
his neighbor
Mal. 2. 6. law of *t.* was in his mouth
John 1. 14. full of grace and *t.*
8. 32. know the *t.* and the *t.* shall
make you free
14. 6. the way, the *t.* and life
17. 17. sanctify them through *t.*
18. 37. bear witness to *t.*
Acts 26. 25. words of *t.* and sober.
Rom. 1. 18. hold *t.* in unrighteous.
2. 2. judg. of God is accord. to *t.*
1 Cor. 5. 8. the unleavened bread
of sincerity and *t.*
2 Cor. 13. 8. do nothing against *t.*
Gal. 3. 1. should not obey the *t.*
Eph. 4. 15. speaking *t.* in love
5. 9. fruit of the Spirit is in all *t.*
6. 14. loins girt about with *t.*
2 Thes. 2. 10. receiv. not love of *t.*
1 Tim. 3. 15. pillar and ground of *t.*
6. 5. corrupt, destitute of the *t.*
2 Tim. 2. 18. who concerning the *t.*
25. acknowledging of the *t.*
3. 7. come to the knowl. of the *t.*
4. 4. turn away their ears from *t.*
Jas. 3. 14. nor lie against *t.*
2 Pet. 1. 12. establish. in present *t.*
1 John 1. 8. *t.* is not in us
5. 6. Spirit is *t.*

Josh. 24. 14. *in truth*, 1 Sam. 12. 24.
Ps. 145. 18. Jer. 4. 2. John 4. 24.
1 Thes. 2. 13. 1 John 3. 18. 2 John 4.
Ps. 25. 5. *thy truth*, 26. 3. & 43. 3. & 108. 4. John 17. 17.
R. V. Deut. 32. 4; Ps. 33. 4; 89. 49; 98. 3; 119. 30. faithfulness
TRY, Judg. 7. 4. Job 12. 11. Jer. 6. 27.
2 Chron. 32. 31. God left him to *t*.
Job 7. 18. visit him and *t*. him
Ps. 11. 4. eyelids *t*. the children
26. 2. *t*. my reins and my heart
Jer. 9. 7. melt them, and *t*. them
Lam. 3. 40. search and *t*. our ways
Dan. 11. 35. shall fall to *t*. them
Zech. 13. 9. *t*. them as gold is tried
1 Cor. 3. 13. fire shall *t*. every
1 Pet. 4. 12. fiery trial which is to *t*.
1 John 4. 1. *t*. the spirits whether
Rev. 3. 10. to *t*. them that dwell
3 Sam. 22. 31. word of Lord is *tried*, Ps. 18. 30.
Ps. 12. 6. word is pure as silver *t*. 66. 10. *t*. us as silver is *t*.
105. 19. word of the Lord *t*. him
Jer. 12. 3. *t*. mine heart towards
Dan. 12. 10. be purified and *t*.
Jas. 1. 12. when he is *t*. he shall receive the crown of life
Rev. 2. 2. hast *t*. them and found
3. 18. buy of me gold, *t*. in the
1 Chron. 29. 17. I know thou *triest*
Jer. 11. 20. that *t*. the reins and
20. 12. thou that *t*. the righteous
Ps. 7. 9. the righteous God *trieth*
11. 5. the Lord *t*. the righteous
1 Thes. 2. 4. pleasing God, who *t*.
Jas. 1. 3. *trying* of your faith
R. V. Dan. 11. 35. refine ; 1 Cor. 3. 13 ; 1 Pet. 4. 12 ; 1 John 4. 1. prove
TUMULT, Ps. 65. 7. 2 Cor. 12. 20.
R. V. 2 Kings 19. 28 ; Isa. 37. 29. arrogancy ; Acts 21. 34. uproar
TURN, from their sin, 1 Kings 8. 35.
2 Kings 17. 13. *t*. from your evil
Job 23. 13. who can *t*. him
Prov. 1. 23. *t*. you at my reproof
S. of S. 2. 17. *t*. my belov., be thou
Isa. 31. 6. *t*. ye unto him, from
Jer. 18. 8. if *t*. from their evil ; I
31. 18. *t*. thou me and I shall
Lam. 5. 21. *t*. us unto thee, O Lord
Ezek. 3. 19. *t*. not from his wicked.
18. 30. *t*. yourselves from your
32. *t*. yourselves and live, 33. 9.
Hos. 12. 6. Joel 2. 12. Zech. 9. 12.
Zech. 1. 3. *t*. to me, and I will *t*.
Mal. 4. 6. *t*. hearts of fathers to
Acts 26. 18. *t*. them from darkness
20. should repent, and *t*. to God
2 Pet. 2. 21. to *t*. from holy com.
2 Chron. 30. 6. *turn again*, Ps. 60. 1. & 80. 3, 7, 19. & 85. 8. Lam. 3. 40.
Mic. 7. 19. Zech. 10. 9. Gal. 4. 9.
1 Sam. 12. 20. *turn aside*, Ps. 40. 4.
Isa. 30. 11. Lam. 3. 35. Amos 2. 7. & 5. 12.
Ps. 119. 37. *turn away*, 39. S. of S. 6. 5. Isa. 58. 13. 1 Tim. 3. 5. Heb. 12. 25.
Deut. 4. 20. *turn to the Lord*, 30. 10. 2 Chron. 15. 4. Ps. 4. 22, 27. Lam. 3. 40. Hos. 14. 2. Joel 2. 13. Luke 1. 16. 2 Cor. 3. 16.
Ps. 9. 17. wicked shall be *turned*
30. 11. *t*. my mourning into danc.
119. 5. *t*. my feet to thy testimo.
Isa. 53. 6. *t*. every one to own
63. 10. was *t*. to be their enemy
Jer. 2. 27. *t*. their back to me
8. 6. every one *t*. to his own
Hos. 7. 8. Ephraim is a cake not *t*.
John 6. 20. sorrow shall be *t*. to
1 Thes. 1. 9. *t*. to God from idols
Jas. 4. 9. laughter be *t*. to mourn.
2 Pet. 2. 22. dog is *t*. to his vomit
Deut. 9. 12. *turned aside*, Ps. 78. 57.
Isa. 44. 20. 2 Tim. 1. 6. & 5 15.
1 Kings 11. 3. *turned away*, Ps. 66. 20. & 78. 38. Isa. 5. 25. & 9. 12. & 10. 4. Jer. 5. 25.

Ps. 44. 18. *turned back*, 78. 9, 41. Isa. 42. 17. Jer. 4. 8. Zeph. 1. 6.
Job 15. 13. *turnest*, Ps. 90. 3.
Ps. 146. 9. wicked he *turneth*
Prov. 15. 1. soft answer *t*. away
21. 1. he *t*. it whithersoever he
Isa. 9. 13. the people *t*. not unto
Jer. 14. 8. *t*. aside to tarry for a
Jas. 1. 17. no shadow of *turning*
Jude 4. *t*. grace of God into
R. V. Changes are chiefly to return, change, and other words dependent on context
TURTLE, Lev. 1. 14. & 5. 7, 11. & 12. 6. Ps. 74. 19. S. of S. 2. 12. Jer. 8. 7.
TUTORS, Gal. 4. 2.
TWAIN, Matt. 5. 41. & 19. 5. Eph. 2. 15.
TWELVE, the, ordained, Mark 3. 14.
TWICE, Gen. 41. 32. Ex. 16. 22. Num. 20. 11. 1 Kings 11. 9. Job 33. 14. & 40. 5. Ps. 62. 11. Mark 14. 30. Luke 18. 12. *t*. dead, Jude 12.
TWINKLING, 1 Cor. 15. 52.
TYPES of Christ. *See* CHRIST
TYRANNY, instances of, Ex. 1. & 5. 1 Sam. 22. 9. 1 Kings 12. 4. & 21. Jer. 26. 20. Matt. 2. Acts 12.

U

UNACCUSTOMED, Jer. 31. 18.
UNADVISEDLY, Ps. 106. 33.
UNAWARES, Deut. 4. 42. Ps. 35. 8. Luke 21. 34. Heb. 13. 2. Jude 4.
R. V. Num. 35. 11, 15 ; Josh. 20. 3, 9. unwittingly ; Luke 21. 34. suddenly ; Gal. 2. 4 ; Jude 4. privily
UNBELIEF, did not many mighty works there bec. of, Matt. 13. 58.
Mark 6. 6. marvelled because of *u*. 9. 24. help thou mine *u*.
Rom. 4. 20. stagger. not through *u*. 11. 20. because of *u*. were broken
1 Tim. 1. 13. ignorantly in *u*.
Heb. 3. 12. an evil heart of *u*. 19. not enter in because of *u*.
R. V. Matt. 17. 20. little faith ; Rom. 11. 30, 32 ; Heb. 4. 6, 11. disobedience ; Rom. 3. 3. want of faith
UNBELIEVERS, Luke 12. 46. 2 Cor. 6. 14.
R. V. Luke 12. 46. unfaithful
UNBELIEVING, Acts 14. 2. 1 Cor. 7. 14, 15. Tit. 1. 15. Rev. 21. 8.
R. V. Acts 14. 2. disobedient
UNBLAMABLE, Col. 1. 22. 1 Thes. 3. 13.
1 Thes. 2. 10. *unblamably* behaving
R. V. Col. 1. 22. without blemish
UNCERTAIN, 1 Cor. 14. 8. 1 Tim. 6. 17.
UNCIRCUMCISED, Ex. 6. 12, 30. Jer. 6. 10. & 9. 25, 26. Acts 7. 51.
UNCIRCUMCISION, Rom. 2. 25, 26, 27. & 3. 30. & 4. 10. 1 Cor. 7. 18, 19. Gal. 2. 7. & 5. 6. & 6. 15. Col. 2. 13. & 3. 11.
UNCLEAN, Lev. 5. 11, 13, 15. Num. 19. 19.
Lev. 10. 10. difference between *u*.
Isa. 6. 5. I am a man of *u*. lips
Lam. 4. 15. depart ye ; it is *u*.
Ezek. 44. 23. discern between *u*.
Hag. 2. 13. if one *u*. touch
Acts 10. 28. not call any man common or *u*., 14.
Rom. 14. 14. is nothing *u*. of itself
1 Cor. 7. 14. else were children *u*.
Eph. 5. 5. nor *u*. person hath any
Num. 5. 19. *uncleanness*, Ezra 9. 11.
Zech. 13. 1. fountain for sin and *u*.
Matt. 23. 27. are with. full of all *u*.
Eph. 4. 19. all *u*. with greediness
5. 3. all *u*. let it not once be
1 Thes. 4. 7. not called us to *u*.
Ezek. 36. 29. save you from all *u*.
R. V. 2 Pet. 2. 10. defilement

UNCLEAN SPIRITS, Matt. 10. 1. & 12. 43, 45. Acts 5. 16. Rev. 16. 13. —animals, Lev. 11. & 20. 25. Deut. 14. 3.
UNCLOTHED, 2 Cor. 5. 4.
UNCOMELY, 1 Cor. 7. 36. & 12. 23.
UNCONDEMNED, Acts 16. 37. & 22. 25.
UNCORRUPTNESS, Tit. 2. 7.
UNCOVER, Lev. 18. 18. 1 Cor. 5. 13.
R. V. Lev. 21. 6, 10 ; Num. 5. 18. let hair go loose ; Isa. 47. 2. remove ; Hab. 2. 16. circumcised ; Zeph. 2. 14. laid bare ; 1 Cor. 11. 5, 13. unveiled
UNCTION, 1 John 2. 20, 27.
UNDEFILED in way, Ps. 119. 1. S. of S. 5. 2. my dove, my *u*., 6. 9. Heb. 7. 26. holy, harmless, *u*.
Jas. 1. 27. pure religion and *u*.
R. V. Ps. 119. 1. perfect
UNDER their God, Hos. 4. 12.
Rom. 3. 9. all *u*. sin, 7. 14. Gal. 3. 22 ; *u*. law, Rom. 6. 15. 1 Cor. 9. 20. Gal. 3. 23. & 4. 4.
1 Cor. 9. 27. I keep *u*. my body
UNDERSTAND not, one another's speech, Gen. 11. 7.
Neh. 8. 7. caused people to *u*.
Ps. 19. 12. who can *u*. his errors
107. 43. shalt *u*. loving kindness
119. 100. I *u*. more than ancients
Prov. 2. 5. shalt thou *u*. fear of
8. 5. *u*. wisdom
19. 25. *u*. knowledge
Isa. 32. 4. heart of the rash shall *u*.
1 Cor. 13. 2. to *u*. all mysteries
Ps. 139. 2. thou *understandest* my thoughts
Acts 8. 30. *u*. thou what thou
1 Chron. 28. 9. *understandeth* all the imaginations
Ps. 49. 20. man that *u*. not, is like
Prov. 8. 9. plain to him that *u*.
Jer. 9. 24. glory in this, that he *u*.
Matt. 13. 19. hear. word and *u*. not
Ex. 31. 3. wis. and *understanding*
Deut. 4. 6. is your wisdom and *u*.
1 Kings 3. 11. asked for thyself *u*.
4. 29. Solomon wisdom and *u*.
7. 14. filled with wisdom and *u*.
1 Chron. 12. 32. men that had *u*. of
Job 12. 13. he hath counsel and *u*.
17. 4. hid their heart from *u*.
28. 12. where is the place of *u*.
28. to depart from evil is *u*.
38. 36. who hath given *u*. to heart
Ps. 47. 7. sing ye praise with *u*.
49. 3. the meditations of my heart shall be of *u*.
119. 34. give me *u*. and I shall keep
130. giveth *u*. unto the simple
147. 5. his *u*. is infinite
Prov. 2. 2. apply thine heart to *u*.
11. *u*. shall keep thee ; to deliver
8. 5. lean not to thine own *u*.
13. the man that getteth *u*.
8. 1. doth not *u*. cry
9. 6. go in the way of *u*.
14. 29. slow to wrath is of great *u*.
19. 8. keepeth *u*. shall find good
21. 30. no *u*. nor counsel against
23. 23. buy truth, wisdom and *u*.
30. 2. I have not the *u*. of a man
Eccl. 9. 11. nor riches to men of *u*.
Isa. 11. 2. spirit of wisdom and *u*.
3. make him of quick *u*. in the
27. 11. it is a people of no *u*.
Jer. 51. 15. stretched out heaven by his *u*.
Matt. 15. 16. also without *u*.
Mark 12. 33. love him with all the heart and with all the *u*.
Luke 2. 47. astonished at his *u*.
Rom. 1. 31. without *u*. unthankful
1 Cor. 1. 19. bring to nothing the *u*. of the prudent
14. 14. my *u*. unfruitful
15. pray with the *u*. also
Eph. 1. 18. eyes of *u*. enlightened
4. 18. having the *u*. darkened
Phil. 4. 7. the peace of God, which passeth all *u*.

Col. 1. 9. filled with all spiritual *u.*
2 Tim. 2. 7. give thee *u.* in all
1 John 5. 20. given us *u.* to know
Ps. 111. 10. *good understanding,*
   Prov. 3. 4. & 13. 15.
Prov. 1. 5. *a man of understanding,*
   10. 23. & 11. 12. & 15. 21. & 17. 27.
Deut. 32. 29. O that they *understood*
Ps. 73. 17. then *u.* I their end
Dan. 9. 2. *u.* by books number
Matt. 13. 51. have ye *u.* all these
John 12. 16. these things *u.* not
1 Cor. 13. 11. when a child I *u.*
2 Pet. 3. 16. things hard to be *u.*
R. V. Gen. 41. 15. hearest; Deut. 9.
   3, 6. know; Neb. 8. 13. give attention; Ps. 19. 12; Dan. 9. 25.
   discern; 11. 33. be wise; Ps. 73.
   17; 94. 8; 107 43; Isa. 44. 18. consider; Ps. 81. 5; 1 Cor. 13. 2; Phil.
   1. 12. know or knew; Matt. 15. 17;
   26. 10; John 8. 27; 12. 40; Rom. 1.
   20; Eph. 3. 14. perceive; Acts 23.
   27. learned; 1 Cor. 13. 11. felt;
   Ezra 8. 16. teachers; 8. 18. discretion; Prov. 17. 28. prudent; 10. 13.
   discernment; Dan. 11. 35. wise;
   Luke 1. 3. accurately; 24. 45;
   1 Cor. 14. 20. mind; Eph. 1. 18.
   heart
UNDERTAKE for me, Isa. 38. 14.
R. V. Isa. 38. 14. be surety
UNDONE, Isa. 6. 5. Matt. 23. 23.
UNEQUAL, your ways are, Ezek.
   18. 25.
2 Cor. 6. 14. not *unequally* yoked
UNFAITHFUL, Prov. 25. 19. Ps.
   78. 57.
R. V. Ps. 78. 57. treacherously
UNFEIGNED, 2 Cor. 6. 6. 1 Tim.
   1. 5. 2 Tim. 1. 5. 1 Pet. 1. 22.
UNFRUITFUL, Matt. 13. 22.
   1 Cor. 14. 14. Eph. 5. 11. Tit. 3. 14.
   2 Pet. 1. 8.
UNGODLY men, 2 Sam. 22. 5.
2 Chron. 19. 2. should. help the *u.*
Job 16. 11. delivered me to the *u.*
   34. 18. say to princes *ye are u.*
Ps. 1. 1. walketh not in counsel
   of *u.*
   6. way of *u.* men shall perish
   3. 7. hast broken the teeth of *u.*
   73. 12. these are *u.* that prosper
Prov. 16. 27. *u.* man diggeth up
   19. 28. an *u.* witness scorneth
Rom. 4. 5. God that justifi. the *u.*
   5. 6. in due time Christ died for *u.*
1 Tim. 1. 9. law not for righteous,
   but for the *u.*
1 Pet. 4. 18. where shall *u.* appear
2 Pet. 2. 5. bring a flood on world
   of the *u.*
   3. 7. day of perdition of *u.* men
Jude 4. 4. men turning grace
   15. convince all that are *u.* of
   18. mockers walk after *u.* lusts
Rom. 1. 18. wrath revealed against
   ungodliness
2 Tim. 2. 16. increase to more *u.*
Tit. 2. 12. denying *u.* and worldly
R. V. Prov. 16. 27; 19. 28. worthless;
   2 Chron. 19. 2; Job 34. 18; Ps. 1. 1,
   4, 5, 6; 3. 7; 78. 12. wicked
UNHOLY, Lev. 10. 10. 1 Tim. 1. 9.
   2 Tim. 3. 2. Heb. 10. 29.
R. V. Lev. 10. 10. the common
UNION in worship and prayer, Ps.
   34. 3. & 55. & 14. & 122. Rom. 15. 30.
   2 Cor. 1. 11. Eph. 6. 18. Col. 1. 3. &
   3. 16. Heb. . 4. 25.
UNITE, Ps. 86. 11. Gen. 49. 6.
Ps. 133. 1. brethren to dwell together in *unity*
Eph. 4. 3. keep the *u.* of the Spirit
   13. till we all come in *u.* of faith
UNJUST, deliver from, Ps. 43 1.
Prov. 11. 7. hope of the *u.* perish.
   29. 27. *u.* man is abomination
Zeph. 3. 5. the *u.* knoweth no
Matt. 5. 45. rain on the just and *u.*
Luke 16. 8. Lord commended the
   u. steward
   10. he that is *u.* in least, is
   18. 6. hear what the *u.* judge

Acts 24. 15. resurrection both of
   just and *u.*
1 Cor. 6. 1. go to law before the *u.*
1 Pet. 3. 18. suffered, just for *u.*
2 Pet. 2. 9. reserve the *u.* to day
Rev. 22. 11. that is *u.* let him be *u.*
Ps. 82. 2. will ye judge *unjustly*
Isa. 26. 10. will he deal *u.*
R. V. Prov. 28. 8——; 11. 7. iniquity; Luke 16. 8, 10; 18. 6; 1 Cor.
   6. 1; 1 Pet. 3. 18; 2 Pet. 2. 9; Rev.
   22. 11. unrighteous
UNKNOWN God, Acts 17. 23. Gal.
   1. 22.
1 Cor. 14. 2. speak in an *u.* tongue,
   2 Cor. 6. 9. as *u.* and yet well
UNLAWFUL, Acts 10. 28. 2 Pet.
   2. 8.
R. V. 2 Pet. 2. 8. lawless
UNLEARNED, Acts 4. 13. 1 Cor.
   14. 16, 23, 24. 2 Tim. 2. 23. 2 Pet. 3. 16.
R. V. 2 Tim. 2. 23; 2 Pet. 3. 16. ig-
   norant
UNLEAVENED, Ex. 12. 39. 1 Cor.
   5. 7.
UNMARRIED (virgins), Paul's
   exhortation to, 1 Cor. 7. 8, 11, 25,
   32.
UNMERCIFUL, Rom. 1. 31.
UNMINDFUL, Deut. 32. 8.
UNMOVABLE, 1 Cor. 15. 58.
UNPERFECT, Ps. 139. 16.
UNPREPARED, 2 Cor. 9. 4.
UNPROFITABLE talk, Job 15.
   3.
Matt. 25. 30. cast the *u.* servant
Luke 17. 10. are all *u.* servants
Rom. 3. 12. altogether become *u.*
Tit. 3. 9. they are *u.* and vain
Phile. 11. was to thee *u.* but
Heb. 13. 17. for that is *u.* for you
UNPUNISHED, Prov. 11. 21. &
   16. 5. & 17. 5. & 19. 5, 9. Jer. 25. 29.
   & 30. 11. & 46. 28. & 49. 12.
UNQUENCHABLE, Matt. 3. 12.
   Luke 3. 17.
UNREASONABLE, Acts 25. 27.
   2 Thes. 3. 2.
UNREBUKABLE, 1 Tim. 6. 14.
UNREPROVABLE, Col. 1. 22.
UNRIGHTEOUS decrees, Isa.
   10. 1.
Isa. 55. 7. *u.* man forsake his
Rom. 3. 5. is God *u.* who taketh
1 Cor. 6. 9. *u.* shall not inherit
Heb. 6. 10. God is not *u.* to forget
Lev. 19. 15. do no *unrighteousness*
Ps. 92. 15. there is no *u.* in him
Luke 16. 9. mammon of *u.*
John 7. 18. true, and no *u.* in him
Rom. 1. 18. hold the truth in *u.*
   6. 13. members instruments of *u.*
   9. 14. is there *u.* with God? God
2 Cor. 6. 14. fellowship hath right-
   eousness with *u.*
2 Thes. 2. 10. all deceivable. of *u.*
Heb. 8. 12. be merciful to their *u.*
1 John 1. 9. cleanse us from all *u.*
   5. 17. all *u.* is sin
R. V. 2 Cor. 6. 14; Heb. 8. 12. in-
   iquity; 2 Pet. 2. 13. wrong do-
   ing
UNRULY, 1 Thes. 5. 14. Tit. 1. 6,
   10. Jas. 3. 8.
R. V. 1 Thes. 5. 14. disorderly; Jas.
   3. 8. restless
UNSAVORY, Job 6. 6. Jer. 23. 13.
UNSEARCHABLE things, Job
   5. 9.
Ps. 145. 3. his greatness is *u.*
Prov. 25. 3. heart of kings is *u.*
Rom. 11. 33. *u.* are his judgments
Eph. 3. 8. preach *u.* riches of
UNSEEMLY, Rom. 1. 27. 1 Cor.
   13. 5.
UNSKILFUL in word, Heb. 5. 13.
UNSPEAKABLE, 2 Cor. 9. 15. &
   12. 4. 1 Pet. 1. 8.
UNSPOTTED, Jas. 1. 27.
UNSTABLE, Gen. 49. 4. Jas. 1. 8.
   2 Pet. 2. 14. *u.* souls
   3. 16. unlearned and *u.*
R. V. 2 Pet. 2. 14; 3. 16. unstedfast

UNTHANKFUL, Luke 6. 35,
   2 Tim. 3. 2.
UNTOWARD, Acts 2. 40.
UNWASHEN, Matt. 15. 20. Mark
   7. 2, 5.
R. V. Mark 7. 5. defiled
UNWISE, Deut. 32. 6. Hos. 13. 13.
   Rom. 1. 14. Eph. 5. 17.
R. V. Rom. 1. 14. Eph. 5. 17. foolish
UNWORTHY, Acts 13. 46. 1 Cor
   6. 2.
1 Cor. 11. 27. drinketh *unworthily*
UPBRAID, Judg. 18. 15. Matt. 11.
   20. Mark 16. 14. Jas. 1. 5.
UPHOLD me with thy Spirit, Ps.
   51. 12.
Ps. 119. 116. *u.* me according to
Prov. 29. 23. honor shall *u.* humble
Isa. 41. 10. I will *u.* thee with the
   right hand of my righteousness
   42. 1. my servant whom I *u.*
   63. 5. my fury it *upheld* me
   57. 17. Lord *upholdeth* righteous
   145. 14. Lord *u.* all that fall
   41. 12. thou *upholdest* me in
Heb. 1. 3. *upholding* all by word
UPRIGHT in heart, Ps. 7. 10.
Ps. 11. 7. his countenance doth behold the *u.*
   18. 23. I was also *u.* before him
   25. with *u.* wilt show thyself *u.*
   25. 8. good and *u.* is the Lord
   37. 37. mark the perfect man and
   behold the *u.*
   64. 10. all *u.* in heart shall glory
   112. 4. to *u.* light ariseth in dark.
   140. 13. the *u.* shall dwell in
Prov. 2. 21. *u.* shall dwell in the
   11. 3. integrity of *u.* shall guide
   20. *u.* in their way, are his de.
   12. 6. mouth of *u.* shall deliver
   13. 6. righteous. keepeth the *u.*
   15. 8. prayer of *u.* is his delight
   21. 18. the transgressor for the *u.*
   28. 10. *u.* shall have good things
Eccl. 7. 29. God hath made man *u.*
S. of S. 1. 4. the *u.* love *thee
Hab. 2. 4. his soul is not *u.* in him
Ps. 15. 2. that walketh *uprightly*,
   84. 11. Prov. 2. 7. & 10. 9. & 15. 21.
   & 29. 18. Mic. 2. 7. Gal. 2. 14.
Ps. 58. 1. do ye judge *u.*, 75. 2.
Isa. 33. 15. he that speaketh *u.*
Deut. 9. 5. not for the *uprightness*
   of thy heart
Job 33. 23. to show unto man
   his *u.*
Ps. 25. 21. let integrity and *u.* pre-
   serve me
Isa. 26. 7. way of the just is *u.*
   10. land of *u.* will he deal unjustly
R. V. 2 Sam. 22. 24, 26; Job 12. 4;
   Ps. 18. 23, 25; 19. 13; 37. 18; Prov.
   11. 20; 28. 10; 29. 10. perfect; Prov.
   2. 7; Job 4. 6; Prov. 28. 6. integrity
URIM and Thummin, Ex. 28. 30.
   Lev. 88. Num. 27. 21. 1 Sam. 28. 6.
   Ezra 2. 63. Neh. 7. 65.
US, Gen. 1. 26. & 3. 22. & 11. 7. Isa.
   6. 8. & 9. 6. Rom. 4. 24. 2 Cor. 5.
   21. Gal. 3. 13. 1 Thes. 5. 10. Heb.
   6. 29. 1 Pet. 2. 21. & 4. 1. 1 John
   5. 11.
USE, Rom. 1. 26. Eph. 4. 29. Heb.
   5. 14.
1 Cor. 7. 31. *u.* world as not abus.
Gal. 5. 13. *u.* not liberty for occa.
1 Tim. 1. 8. law is good if a man *u.*
1 Cor. 9. 15. I have *used* none of
Jer. 22. 13. *useth* his neighbor's
Tit. 3. 14. learn good works for
   necessary *uses*
Ps. 119. 132. as thou *usest* to do to
Col. 2. 22. *using*, 1 Pet. 2. 16.
R. V. 2 Sam. 1. 18. song
USURP, 1 Tim. 2. 12.
USURY, Ex. 22. 25. Lev. 25. 36, 37.
   Deut. 23. 19, 20. Neh. 5. 7, 10. Ps.
   15. 5. Prov. 28. 8. Isa. 24. 2. Jer. 15.
   10. Ezek. 18. 8, 13, 17. & 22. 12.
   Matt. 25. 27. Luke 19. 23.
R. V. Matt. 25. 27; Luke 19. 23. in-
   terest
UTTER, Ps. 78. 2. & 94. 4.

Ps. 106. 2. who can *u.* mighty acts
2 Cor. 12. 4. lawful for a man to *u.*
Rom. 8. 26. groanings that cannot be *uttered*
Heb. 5. 11. things hard to be *u.*
Ps. 19. 2. day unto day *uttereth*
Acts 2. 4. as the spirit gave them *utterance*
Eph. 6. 19. that *u.* may be given
Deut. 7. 2. *utterly*, Ps. 89. 33. & 119. 8, 43. S. of S. 8. 7. Jer. 14. 9.
1 Thes. 2. 16. *uttermost*, Heb. 7. 25.
R. V. *outer*, Ezek. 40. 31. arches were toward *u.* court; 42. 1; 44. 19; 46. 20; 47. 2; Ex. 26. 4; 36. 11, 17; 2 Kings 7. 5, 8. outmost; Deut. 11. 24. hinder; Josh. 15. 5. end; Matt. 5. 26. last

V

VAIL (of women), Gen. 24. 65.
Ruth 3. 15. 1 Cor. 11. 10.
of Moses, Ex. 34. 33. 2 Cor. 3. 13.
of the tabernacle and temple, Ex. 26. 31. & 36. 35. 2 Cor. 3. 14. *See* Heb. 6. 19. & 9. 3. & 10. 20.
of temple rent at crucifixion, Matt. 27. 51. Mark 15. 38. Luke 23. 45.

VAIN, Ex. 5. 9. & 20, 7.
Deut. 32. 47. it is not a *v.* thing
1 Sam. 12. 21. turn not after *v.*
Ps. 39. 6. every man walketh in a *v.* shew, and they are disquiet. in *v.*
Job 11. 12. *v.* man would be wise
Ps. 60. 11. *v.* is help of man
119. 113. I hate *v.* thoughts, but
Jer. 4. 14. long shall *v.* thoughts
Mal. 3. 14. it is *v.* to serve God
Matt. 6. 7. use not *v.* repetitions
Rom. 1. 21. they glorified not God, but became *v.* in their imagina.
1 Cor. 3. 20. thoughts of wise are *v.*
Eph. 5. 6. deceive you with *v.*
Col. 2. 8. through *v.* philosophy
1 Pet. 1. 18. from *v.* conversation
Ps. 73. 13. cleansed my heart *in vain*
89. 47. why hast thou made all men —
127. 1. labor —; walketh —·
Isa. 45. 19. seek ye me —
Jer. 3. 23 — is salvation hoped
Matt. 15. 9.— do they worship me
Rom. 13. 4. bear not the sword —
1 Cor. 15. 58. your labor is not —
2 Cor. 6. 1. receive not grace of God —
Phil. 2. 16. not run — nor labored —
2 Kings 17. 15. followed *vanity*
Job 7. 3. possess months of *v.*
16. let me alone; my days are *v.*
Ps. 12. 2. speak *v.* every one
24. 4. nor lifted up his soul to *v.*
11. surely every man is *v.*
62. 9. men of low degree are *v.*
119. 37. turn mine eyes from beholding *v.*
Prov. 22. 8. that soweth iniquity shall reap *v.*
Eccl. 1. 2. *v.* of vanities, all is *v.*, 14. & 3. 19. & 2. 1. & 4. 8. & 12. 8.
Isa. 5. 18. iniquity with cords of *v.*
40. 17. less than nothing and *v.*
Hab. 2. 13. weary themselves for *v.*
Rom. 8. 20. the creature was made subject to *v.*
Eph. 4. 17. walk in *v.* of their
2 Pet. 2. 18. swelling words of *v.*
Ps. 31. 6. I hate them that regard lying *vanities*
Jer. 10. 8. a doctrine of *v.*
Jonah 2. 8. that observe lying *v.*
Acts 14. 15. turn from these *v.*
R. V. Ex. 5. 9. lying; Job 35. 16; Ps. 89. 47; Isa. 49. 4; Jer. 10. 3; 23. 15; 51. 58; Lam. 2. 14; Isa. 49. 4. vanity; Jer. 4. 14. evil; Isa. 45. 18. waste; Eph. 5. 6. empty; Gal.

2. 21. nought; 1 Tim. 6. 20; 2 Tim. 2. 16 ——

VALIANT, S. of S. 3. 7. Isa. 10. 13.
Jer. 9. 3. not *v.* for the truth
Heb. 11. 34. faith waxed *v.*
Ps. 60. 12. *valiantly*, 108. 13. & 118. 15, 16. Num. 24. 18.
R. V. 1 Kings 1. 42; 1 Chron. 7. 2, 5; 11. 26; 28. 1; S. of S. 3. 7; Heb. 11. 34. mighty; Jer. 46. 15. strong

VALUE, Job 13. 4. Matt. 10. 31.

VAPOR, Jer. 10. 13. Jas. 4. 14.

VARIABLENESS, Jas. 1. 17.

VARIANCE, Matt. 10. 35. Gal. 5. 29.
R. V. Gal. 5. 20. strife

VAUNT, Judg. 7. 2. 1 Cor. 13. 4.

VEHEMENT, S. of S. 8. 6. 2 Cor. 7. 11.
R. V. 2 Cor. 7. 11 ——

VEIL, Gen. 24. 65. S. of S. 5. 7.
Isa. 25. 7. destroy the *v.* spread
Matt. 27. 51. *v.* was rent from top
2 Cor. 3. 13. Moses put a *v.* over
15. *v.* is upon their heart
Heb. 6. 19. into that within *v.*

VENGEANCE taken, Gen 4. 15.
Deut. 32. 35. to me belongeth *v.*,
Ps. 94. 1. Rom. 12. 19. Heb. 10. 30.
Ps. 58. 10. rejoice when he seeth *v.*
99. 8. tookest *v.* of their inven.
Isa. 34. 8. day of the Lord's *v.*
Jer. 11. 20. let me see thy *v.*
51. 6. time of the Lord's *v.*, 11.
Luke 21. 22. these be days of *v.*
2 Thes. 1. 8. fire taking *v.*
Jude 7. suffering *v.* of eternal fire
R. V. Acts 28. 4. justice; Jude 7. punishment

VENISON, Gen. 25. 28. & 27. 3.

VERILY, Gen. 42. 21. Jer. 15. 11.
It is often used by Christ, as well as *verily, verily*, John 1. 51. & 3. 3, 5, 11. & 5. 19, 24, 25. & 6. 26.

VERITY, Ps. 111. 7. 1 Tim. 2. 7.

VERY, Prov. 17. 9. Matt. 24. 24.
John 7. 26. & 14. 11. 1 Thes. 5. 23.

VESSEL, Ps. 2. 9. & 31. 12. Jer. 18. 4.
Jer. 22. 28. *v.* wherein is no pleas.
48. 11. emptied from *v.* to *v.*
Acts 9. 15. he is a chosen *v.* unto
Rom. 9. 21. one *v.* to honor and
1 Thes. 4. 4. possess his *v.* in sanc.
2 Tim. 2. 21. be a *v.* unto honor
1 Pet. 3. 7. honor to wife as the weaker *v.*
Rom. 9. 21. *vessels* of wrath fitted
2 Cor. 4. 7. treasure in earthen *v.*
R. V. Ex. 27. 19; 39. 40; Num. 3. 36. instruments; Ex. 40. 9; Num. 1. 50; 4. 15, 16; 1 Chron. 9. 29. furniture

VESTURE, lots cast for Christ's, Matt. 27. 35; John 19. 24. *See* Ps. 22. 18. Rev. 19. 13.

VEXED, Job 27. 2. Ps. 6. 2, 3, 10.
Isa. 63. 10. and *v.* his Holy Spirit
2 Pet. 2. 7. Lot *v.* with filthy con.
R. V. Neh. 9. 27; 2 Pet. 2. 7. distressed; Isa. 63. 10. grieved; Ezek. 22. 7. wronged; Luke 6. 18. troubled

VIAL, Rev. 5. 8. & 16. 1. & 21. 9.
R. V. In Rev. bowl or bowls

VICTORY is thine, O Lord, 1 Chron. 29. 11.
Ps. 98. 1. hand and arm gotten him the *v.*
Isa. 25. 8. swallow up death in *v.*
Matt. 20. 12. judgment unto *v.*
1 Cor. 15. 54. death is swallowed up in *v.*
55. O grave, where is thy *v.*
57. God who giveth us *v.*
1 John 5. 4. *v.* that overcometh

VIGILANT, 1 Tim. 3. 2. 1 Pet. 5. 8.
R. V. 1 Tim. 3. 2. temperate; 1 Pet. 5. 8. watchful

VILE, thy brother seem, Deut. 25. 3.
1 Sam. 3. 13. made themselves *v.*
2 Sam. 6. 22. I will yet be more *v.*
Job 40. 4. I am *v.*; what shall I an.

Ps. 15. 4. whose eyes a *v.* person
Isa. 32. 6. *v.* person will speak vill.
Rom. 1. 26. up to *v.* affections
Phil. 3. 21. change our *v.* body
R. V. Judg. 19. 24. folly; Job 18. 3. unclean; 40. 4. small account; Ps. 15. 4. reprobate; Dan. 11. 21. contemptible; Phil. 3. 21. humiliation

VINE, 1 Kings 4. 25. Mic. 4. 4.
Deut. 32. 32. *v.* is the *v.* of Sodom
Ps. 128. 3. thy wife shall be as a fruitful *v.*
Jer. 2. 21. planted thee a noble *v.*
Hos. 10. 1. Israel is an empty *v.*
14. 7. they shall grow as the *v.*
Matt. 26. 29. drink of fruit of *v.*
John 15. 1. I am the true *v.* and my Father is the husbandman
5. I am the *v.* ye are the branch.
Ps. 80. 15. *vineyard*, Prov. 24. 30.
S of S. 1. 6. Isa. 5. 1, 7. Matt. 20. 1. & 21. 33. Luke 13. 6. 1 Cor. 9. 7. S. of S. 8. 11, 12.
R. V. Rev. 14. 19. vintage

VIOLENCE, Lev. 6. 2. 2 Sam. 22. 3.
Gen. 6. 11. earth was filled with *v.*
Hab. 1. 2. cry out unto thee of *v.*
Matt. 11. 12. the kingdom of heaven suffereth *v.*
Luke 3. 14. do *v.* to no man, and
Heb. 11. 34. quenched the *v.* of
R. V. Lev. 6. 2. robbery; Mic. 2. 2. seize; Acts 24. 7 ——; Heb. 11. 34. power; Rev. 18. 21. mighty fall

VIRGIN, Isa. 7. 14. 2 Cor. 11. 2.
S. of S. 1. 3. *virgins*, Rev. 14. 4.

VIRTUE, Mark 5. 30. Luke 6. 19.
2 Pet. 1. 3. call. us to glory and *v.*
5. to faith *v.* and to *v.* knowledge
Phil. 4. 8. if there be any *v.* think
Prov. 12. 4. *virtuous* woman, 31. 10.
R. V. Mark 5. 30; Luke 6. 19; 8. 46. power

VISAGE, Isa. 52. 14. Lam. 4. 8.

VISIBLE and invisible, Col. 1. 16.

VISION, 1 Sam. 3. 1. Ps. 89. 19.
Matt. 17. 9. Acts 10. 19. & 16. 9.
Hab. 2. 2. write the *v.*
3. the *v.* is for a time
Ezek. 13. 16. see *visions* of peace
Hos. 12. 10. I have multiplied *v.*
Joel 2. 28. young men shall see *v.*
2 Cor. 12. 1. I will come to *v.* and
R. V. Ezek. 8. 4. appearance; Acts 9. 12 ——

VISIT you, Gen. 50. 24, 25. Ex. 13. 19.
Job 7. 18. shouldest *v.* him every
Ps. 106. 4. *v.* me with thy salvation
Jer. 5. 9. shall I not *v.* you for
Lam. 4. 22. *v.* iniquity, Jer. 14. 10. & 23. 2. Hos. 2. 13. & 8. 13.
Acts 7. 23. *v.* his brethren, 15. 36.
15. 14. God did *v.* the Gentiles
Jas. 1. 27. to *v.* the fatherless
Ps. 8. 4. *visitest*, 65. 9. Heb. 2. 6.
Ex. 20. 5. *visiting* the iniquity of the fathers upon the children, 34. 7.

VOCATION, worthy of, Eph. 4. 1.

VOICE is *v.* of Jacob, Gen. 27. 22
Gen. 4. 10. *v.* of brother's blood
Ex. 5. 2. who is the Lord that I should obey his *v.*
Ps. 5. 3. my *v.* shalt thou hear
18. 13. the Highest gave his *v.*
95. 7. to-day, if ye will hear his *v.*,
Eccl. 12. 4. rise up at the *v.* of
S. of S. 2. 14. let me hear thy *v.*
Isa. 30. 19. gracious at *v.* of thy
Ezek. 33. 32. hath a pleasant *v.*
John 5. 25. dead shall hear the *v.*,
10. 3. sheep hear his *v.*, 4, 16, 27.
Gal. 4. 20. I desire to change my *v.*
1 Thes. 4. 16. with *v.* of archangel
Rev. 3. 20. if any man hear my *v.*
Acts 13. 27. *voices*, Rev. 4. 5. & 11. 19.

VOID of counsel, Deut. 32. 28.
Ps. 30. 39. made *v.* the covenant
Isa. 55. 11. shall not return *v.*
Acts 24. 16. conscience *v.* of offence
Rom. 3. 31. do we make *v.* the law
1 Cor. 9. 15. make my glorying *v.*
VOLUME, Ps. 40. 15. Prov. 23. 8. &
26. 11. Isa. 19. 14. 2 Pet. 2. 22.
VOMIT, Job 20. 15. Prov. 23. 8. &
26. 11. Isa. 19. 14. 2 Pet. 2. 22.
VOW, Jacob vowed a, Gen. 28. 20.
& 31. 13. Num. 6. 2. & 21. 2. & 30.
1 Sam. 1. 11. 2 Sam. 15. 7, 8.
Ps. 65. 1. to thee shall the *v.* be
76. 11. *v.* and pay unto the
Eccl. 5. 4. a *v.* defer not to pay, 5.
Isa. 19. 21. shall a *v.* to the Lord
Jonah 2. 9. pay that I have *vowed*
Job 22. 27. shall pay thy *vows*
Ps. 22. 25. I will pay my *v.* before
56. 12. thy *v.* O God are upon
61. 5. heard my *v.*
Prov. 20. 25. after *v.* to make enqu.
31. 2. son of my *v.,* 1 Sam. 1. 11.
Jonah 1. 16. offer. sacri. and made *v.*
VOYAGE, Paul's, Acts 27. & 28.

W

WAGES, Lev. 19. 13. Ezek. 29. 18.
Jer. 22. 13. neighbor's service
without *w.*
Hag. 1. 6. earneth *w.* to put it
Mal. 3. 5. oppress hirel. in his *w.*
Luke 3. 14. be conte. with your *w.*
Rom. 6. 23. the *w.* of sin is death
R. V. 2 Pet. 2. 15. hire
WAIT till my change come, Job
14. 14.
Ps. 25. 5. on thee do I *w.* all the day
27. 14. *v.* on the Lord; *w.* I say
37. 34. *w.* on the Lord and keep
62. 5. *w.* thou only upon God
130. 5. I *w.* for the Lord, my
145. 15. eyes of all *w.* upon thee
Prov. 20. 22. *w.* on the Lord and
Isa. 8. 17. I will *w.* upon the Lord
30. 18. will the Lord *w.* blessed
40. 31. that *w.* on the Lord shall
renew their strength
Lam. 3. 25. good to them that *w.*
26. quietly *w.* for salvation of
Hos. 12. 6. *w.* on thy God contin.
Mic. 7. 7. I will *w.* for God of my
Hab. 2. 3. *w.* for it, it will surely
Zeph. 3. 8. *w.* ye on me, I will rise
Luke 12. 36. men that *w.* for their
Gal. 5. 5. through the Spirit *w.*
1 Thes. 1. 10. *w.* for his Son from
Gen. 49. 18. *waited* for thy salva.
Ps. 40. 1. I *w.* patiently for the
Isa. 25. 9. our God, we have *w.* for
Zech. 11. 11. poor of flock that *w.*
Mark 15. 43. *w.* for kingdom of God
1 Pet. 3. 20. long suffering of God *w.*
Ps. 33. 20. our soul *waiteth* for
65. 1. praise *w.* for thee, in Zion
130. 6. my soul *w.* for Lord more
Isa. 64. 4. prepared for him that
w.
Prov. 8. 34. *waiting* at the posts
Luke 2. 25. *w.* for the consolation
Rom. 8. 23. *w.* for the adoption
1 Cor. 1. *t. w.* for coming of Lord
2 Thes. 3. 5. to a patient *w.* for
R. V. Job 17. 13; Isa. 59. 9; Ps.
128. 2; Luke 12. 36. look; Ps. 71.
10; Jer. 5. 26. watch; Judg. 9. 35.
ambush
WAKETH, Ps. 127. 1. S. of S. 2. 2.
Ps. 77. 4. holdest my eyes *waking*
Isa. 50. 4. *wakeneth,* Joel 3. 12.
WALK in my law, Ex. 16. 4.
Gen. 17. 1. *w.* before me and be per.
24. 40. before whom I *w.*
Lev. 26. 12. I will *w.* among
24. will I *w.* contrary unto you
Deut. 5. 33. *w.* in the ways of the
Lord, 8. 6. & 10. 12. & 11. 22. & 13.
5. & 28. 9.
13. 4. shall *w.* after the Lord
Ps. 23. 4. though I *w.* through valley
of death

Ps. 84. 11. no good thing from
them that *w.* uprightly
Eccl. 11. 9. *w.* in way of thy heart
Isa. 2. 3. will *w.* in his paths
30. 21. this is the way, *w.* ye in
40. 31. shall *w.* and not faint
Dan. 4. 37. that *w.* in pride he is
Hos. 14. 9. just shall *w.* in them
Mic. 6. 8. *w.* humbly with thy
Amos 3. 3. how can two *w.* to.
Zech. 10. 12. *w.* up and down in
Luke 13. 33. I must *w.* to-day and
John 8. 12. followeth me, not *w.*
11. 9. *w.* in day, he stumbleth not
Rom. 4. 12. *w.* in steps of that faith
8. 1. *w.* not after the flesh, 4.
2 Cor. 5. 7. we *w.* by faith, not
10. 3. though *w.* in the flesh, we
Gal. 5. 16. as many as *w.* accord.
Eph. 2. 10. ordained that we *w.*
5. 15. *w.* circumspectly, not as
Phil. 3. 17. mark them who *w.* so
Col. 1. 10. that ye might *w.* worthy
1 Thes. 2. 12. ye would *w.* worthy
4. 1. how ought ye to *w.* and
1 John 1. 7. if we *w.* in the light
2. 6. ought so to *w.* as he walked
Rev. 3. 4. *w.* with me in white
16. 15. lest he *w.* naked and see
21. 24. nations shall *w.* in light
John 12. 35. *w.* in light while ye
Rom. 13. 13. let us *w.* honestly as
Gal. 5. 16. *w.* in Spirit, and not ful.
25. if we live in Spirit, let us *w.*
Eph. 5. 2. *w.* in love as Christ
8. *w.* as children of light
Phil. 3. 16. let us *w.* by the same
Gen. 6. 9. Noah *walked* with God
5. 22. Enoch *w.* with God, 24.
Ps. 55. 14. we *w.* unto the house
81. 12. *w.* in their own counsels
Isa. 9. 2. people that *w.* in dark-
ness
2 Cor. 10. 2. as if we *w.* accord.
12. 18. *w.* we not in same spirit
Gal. 2. 14. they *w.* not uprightly
Eph. 2. 2. in time past we *w.*
1 Pet. 4. 3. we *w.* in lasciviousness
Isa. 43. 2. when thou *walkest*
through the fire
Rom. 14. 15. *w.* thou not charitably
Ps. 15. 2. he that *walketh* uprightly
39. 6. every man *w.* in a vain
Prov. 10. 9. he that *w.* uprightly
13. 20. *w.* with wise men shall
Isa. 50. 10. *w.* in darkness, and
Jer. 10. 23. not in man that *w.* to
direct his steps
Mic. 2. 7. him that *w.* uprightly
2 Thes. 3. 6. from brother that *w.*
disorderly
1 Pet. 5. 8. *w.* about seeking
Rev. 2. 1. *w.* in midst of the
Gen. 3. 8. voice of Lord *walking* in
Isa. 57. 2. *w.* in his own upright.
Jer. 6. 28. revolters *w.* with sland.
Mic. 2. 11. if man *w.* in falsehood
Luke 1. 6. *w.* in all command.
Acts 9. 31. *w.* in the fear of the
2 Cor. 4. 2. not *w.* in craftiness
2 Pet. 3. 3. *w.* after their own
2 John 4. thy children *w.* in truth
WALL, Ps. 62. 3. Prov. 18. 11. S.
of S. 2. 9. & 8. 9, 10. Isa. 26. 1. &
60. 18.
R. V. Gen. 49. 6. ox; Num. 13. 28;
22. 24; Deut. 1. 28; Isa. 5. 5; Hos.
2. 6. fence or fenced; 1 Kings 21.
23. rampart
WANDER, Num. 14. 33. Ps. 119.
10.
Lam. 4. 14. *wandered,* Heb. 11. 37.
Prov. 21. 16. *wandereth,* 27. 8.
1 Tim. 5. 13. *wandering,* Jude 13.
Ps. 56. 8. tellest my *wanderings*
WANT, Deut. 28. 48. Job 31. 19.
Ps. 23. 1. the Lord is my shepherd,
I shall not *w.*
34. 9. no *w.* to them that fear
Prov. 6. 11. thy *w.* come as an
2 Cor. 8. 14. a supply for your *w.*
Phil. 4. 11. speak in respect of *w.*
Jas. 1. 4. perfect and entire, *want-
ing*

R. V. Prov. 10. 21. lack; Phil. 2. 25
need; Prov. 28. 16; Eccl. 6. 2; Jas.
1. 4. lack or lacking
WANTONNESS, Rom. 13. 13.
2 Pet. 2. 18.
R. V. 2 Pet. 2. 18. lasciviousness
WAR, Ex. 13. 17. & 17. 16. Ps. 27.
3.
Job 10. 17. changes and *w.* are
Ps. 18. 34. teacheth my hands to *w.*
120. 7. I am for peace, they for *w.*
Prov. 20. 18. good advice make *w.*
Eccl. 8. 8. discharge in that *w.*
Isa. 2. 4. not learn *w.* any more
Mic. 3. 5. prepare *w.* against him
2 Cor. 10. 3. do not *w.* after flesh
1 Tim. 1. 18. mightest *w.* a good
warfare
Rev. 11. 7. beast shall make *w.*
12. 7. there was *w.* in heaven
Num. 21. 14. in the book of the
wars of the Lord
Ps. 46. 9. he maketh *w.* to cease
Matt. 24. 6. hear of *w.* and ru-
mors of *w.*
Jas. 4. 1. whence come *w.* and
2 Tim. 2. 4. no man that *warreth*
Isa. 37. 8. *warring,* Rom. 7. 23.
R. V. Deut. 21. 10; Judg. 21. 22;
2 Chron. 6. 34; Jer. 6. 23. battle
WARFARE, Isa. 40. 2. 1 Cor. 9. 7.
2 Cor. 10. 4. 1 Tim. 1. 18.
WARN, 2 Chron. 19. 10. Acts 10. 22.
Ezek. 3. 19. if thou *w.* the wicked
33. 3. blow the trumpet and *w.*
Acts 20. 31. I ceased not to *w.* every
one night and day
1 Cor. 4. 14. my beloved sons I *w.*
1 Thes. 5. 14. *w.* them that are un.
Ps. 19. 11. by them is thy servant
warned
Matt. 3. 7. who hath *w.* you to flee
Heb. 11. 7. Noah being *w.* of God
Jer. 6. 10. to whom I give *warning*
Col. 1. 28. teaching every man, *w.*
R. V. Acts 20. 31; 1 Cor. 4. 14;
1 Thes. 5. 14. admonish
WASH, Lev. 6. 27. & 14. 15, 16.
Job 9. 30. if I *w.* myself in snow
Ps. 26. 6. *w.* my hands in innocen.
51. 7. *w.* me and I shall be whiter
58. 10. shall *w.* his feet in blood
Isa. 1. 16. *w.* you, make you clean
Jer. 2. 22. *w.* thee with nitre
Luke 7. 8. *w.* his feet with tears
John 13. 5. *w.* disciples' feet
8. I *w.* thee not, thou hast no
14. *w.* one another's feet
Acts 22. 16. baptized and *w.* away
Job 29. 6. I *washed* my steps
S. of S. 5. 3. I have *w.* my feet
Isa. 4. 4. *w.* away the filth
Ezek. 16. 4. neither wast thou *w.*
16. 9. I thoroughly *w.* away blood
1 Cor. 6. 11. we are *w.* justified
Heb. 10. 22. *w.* with pure water
Rev. 1. 5. *w.* us from sins in his
7. 14. *w.* robes, and made white
in
Eph. 5. 26. *washing,* Tit. 3. 5.
R. V. Ex. 2. 5; Lev. 14. 8, 9; 15. 16
16. 4, 24; 22. 6; Deut. 23. 11; 2 Sam.
11, 8; John 13. 10. bathe; Luke 7.
38, 44. wet; Rev. 1. 5. loosed
WASTE, Ps. 80. 13. Matt. 26. 8.
Luke 15. 11. *wasted,* 36. 1. Gal. 1. 13.
Job 14. 10. *wasteth,* Prov. 19. 26.
Prov. 18. 9. *waster,* Isa. 54. 16.
Isa. 59. 7. *wasting* and destruction,
60. 18.
R. V. Prov. 18. 9. destroyer
WATCH, Neh. 4. 9. Job 7. 12.
Job 14. 15. dost thou not *w.* over
Ps. 102. 7. I *w.* and am as a sparrow
141. 3. set a *w.* before my mouth
Jer. 44. 27. *w.* over them for evil
Matt. 24. 42. *w.* for ye know not
26. 41. *w.* and pray that ye enter
Mark 13. 33. take heed, *w.* and
1 Cor. 16. 13. *w.* ye, stand fast in
1 Thes. 5. 6. let us *w.* and be sober
2 Tim. 4. 5. *w.* thou in all things
Heb. 13. 17. they *w.* for your souls
1 Pet. 4. 7. be sober, *w.* unto prayer

Jer. 31. 28. like as I *watched* over
Matt. 24. 43. he would have *w.*
Ps. 37. 32. the wicked *watcheth*
Ezek. 7. 6. the end is come ; it *w.*
Rev. 16. 15. blessed is he that *w.*
Dan. 4. 13. a *watcher* and holy
Ps. 63. 6. *watches,* 119. 148. Lam. 2. 19.
Rev. 3. 2. be *watchful*
Prov. 8. 34. *watching* daily at gates
Luke 12. 37. blessed whom the Lord shall find *w.*
2 Cor. 6. 5. in *watchings,* 11. 27.
Isa. 21. 11. *watchman,* Ezek. 3. 17. & 33. 7.
S. of S. 3. 3. *watchmen,* 5. 7. Isa. 52. 8. & 56. 10. & 62. 6. Jer. 31. 6.
WATER, Gen. 49. 4. Ex. 12. 9. & 17. 6.
2 Sam. 14. 14. we are as *w.* spilt
Job 15. 16. drink. iniquity like *w.*
Ps. 22. 14. I am poured out like *w.*
Isa. 12. 3. draw *w.* out of the wells of salvation
30. 20. give you *w.* of affliction
58. 11. shalt be like a spring of *w.*
Lam. 1. 16. mine eye runneth down with *w.,* 3. 48.
Ezek. 36. 25. sprinkle clean *w.* on
Amos 8. 11. nor a thirst for *w.*
Matt. 3. 11. I baptize you with *w.*
10. 42. cup of cold *w.* in name of
Luke 16. 24. tip of his finger in *w.*
John 3. 5. man be born of *w.*
4. 14. shall be in him a well of *w.*
7. 38. flow rivers of living *w.*
19. 34. there out blood and *w.*
Acts 8. 38. went down into the *w.*
Eph. 5. 26. cleanse it with the washing of *w.*
1 John 5. 6. he that came by *w.*
8. three bear witness, Spirit, *w.*
Jude 12. clouds they are without *w.*
Rev. 7. 17. lead them to living fountains of *w.*
21. 6. fountain of *w.* of life
22. 17. take the *w.* of life freely
Ps. 23. 2. leadeth me beside the still *waters*
Prov. 5. 15. drink *w.* out of thine
9. 17. stolen *w.* are sweet
Eccl. 11. 1. cast thy bread upon *w.*
S. of S. 4. 15. a well of living *w.*
Isa. 32. 20. blessed are ye that sow beside all *w.*
35. 6. in wilderness shall *w.* break
55. 1. come ye to *w.* buy and eat
58. 11. whose *w.* fail not
Jer 2. 13. fountain of living *w.*
9. 1. O that my head were *w.*
Hab. 2. 14. as *w.* cover the sea
Zech. 14. 8. living *w.* shall go out
Rev. 1. 15. his voice as the sound of many *w.,* 14. 2. & 19. 6.
Prov. 11. 25. he that *watereth* shall be *watered*
Isa. 58. 11. be like a *w.* garden
1 Cor. 3. 6. I planted, Apollos *w.*
Ps. 42. 7. noise of thy *waterspouts*
WAVERING, Heb. 10. 23. Jas. 1. 6.
R. V. Jas. 1. 6. doubteth
WAX, Ex. 32. 10, 11, 22. Ps. 22. 14. & 68. 2. & 97. 5. Matt. 24. 12. Luke 12. 33. 1 Tim. 5. 11. 2 Tim. 3. 13.
R. V. Gen. 41. 56; Josh. 23. 1. was; Acts 13. 46. spake out
WAY, Ex. 13. 21. & 23. 20. & 32. 8.
1 Sam. 12. 23. teach you good and right *w.*
1 Kings 2. 2. *w.* of all the earth
Ezra 8. 21. seek of him a right *w.*
Ps. 1. 6. the Lord knoweth the *w.* of the righteous
49. 13. their *w.* is their folly
67. 2. thy *w.* may be known
119. 30. chosen *w.* of truth
104. I hate every false *w.*
Prov. 2. 8. Lord preserveth the *w.* of his saints
10. 29. *w.* of the Lord is strength
14. 12. a *w.* that seemeth right
Eccl. 11. 5. thou knowest not what is the *w.* of the spirit

Isa. 26. 7. *w.* of just is upright.
30. 21. this is the *w.* walk ye in
35. 8. a high *w.* and a *w.* called
40. 3. prepare the *w.* of the
43. 19. a *w.* in the wilderness
59. 8. *w.* of peace they know not
Jer. 6. 16. where is a good *w.* and
21. 8. set before you the *w.* of life
32. 39. give them one heart and *w.*
Amos 2. 7. turn aside *w.* of the
Mal. 3. 1. prepare the *w.* before
Matt. 7. 13. broad is *w.* to destruc.
14. narrow is *w.* that leadeth to
22. 16. teacheth *w.* of God in
John 1. 23. straight the *w.* of Lord
14. 4. *w.* ye know
6. I am the *w.*
Acts 16. 17. which show unto us the *w.* of salvation
1 Cor. 10. 13. make a *w.* to escape
12. 31. show you more excellent *w.*
2 Pet. 2. 2. the *w.* of truth be evil
1 Kings 8. 32. bring *his way* on his head
Job 17. 9. right. shall hold on —
Ps. 18. 30. as for God — is perfect
37. 23. delight in —
34. and keep —
119. 9. young man cleanse —
Prov. 14. 8. prudent to understand —
Isa. 55. 7. let the wicked forsake —
Ps. 25. 8. teach sinners *in the way*
119. 14. I rejoiced — of testimo.
139. 24. lead me — everlasting
Isa. 26. 8. — of thy judgments we
Matt. 5. 25. agree with adversary —
21. 32. John came — of righteous.
Luke 1. 79. guide your feet —
Job 40. 19. he is chief of *ways* of
Ps. 84. 5. in whose heart are *w.*
Prov. 3. 17. *w.* are *w.* of pleasant.
5. 21. *w.* of man are before Lord
16. 7. a man's *w.* please
Jer. 7. 3. amend your *w.* and doings
Lam. 1. 4. the *w.* of Zion do mourn
Deut. 32. 4. *his ways,* Ps. 145. 17.
Isa. 2. 3. Mic. 4. 2, Rom. 11. 33.
Ps. 119. 5. *my ways,* 15, 26, 59, 168, & 139. 3. & 39. 1. Prov. 23. 26. Isa. 55. 8. & 49. 11.
Prov. 14. 14. *own ways,* Isa. 53. 6 & 58. 13. & 66. 3. Ezek. 36, 31, 32.
Job 21. 14. *thy ways,* Ps. 25. 4. & 91. 11. Prov. 3. 6. & 4. 26. Isa. 63. 17. Ezek. 16. 61. Dan. 5. 23. Rev. 15. 3. Isa. 35. 8. *wayfaring,* Jer. 14. 8.
WEAK, 2 Chron. 15. 7. Job 4. 3. Ps. 6. 2.
Isa. 35. 3. strengthen ye *w.* hands
Ezek. 16. 30. how *w.* is thy heart
Matt. 26. 41. spirit is willing but the flesh is *w.*
Rom. 4. 19. not *w.* in faith
14. 1. him that is *w.* in faith receive
1 Cor. 4. 10. we are *w.* but ye
2 Cor. 11. 29. who is *w.* and I not *w.*
12. 10. I am *w.* then am I strong
1 Thes. 5. 13. support the *w.* be
Isa. 14. 12. *weaken* Ps. 102. 23. Job 12. 21.
2 Sam. 3. 1. *weaker,* 1 Pet. 3. 7.
1 Cor. 1. 25. *weakness,* 2. 3. & 15. 43.
2 Cor. 12. 9. & 13. 4. Heb. 11. 34.
R. V. Job 12. 21. looseth; Isa. 14. 12. lay low
WEALTH, Gen. 34. 29. Deut. 8. 17.
Deut. 8. 18. give. power to get *w.*
Job. 21. 13. spend their days in *w.*
Ps. 49. 6. that trust in their *w.*
112. 3. *w.* and riches are in his
Prov. 10. 15. the rich man's *w.* is
13. 11. *w.* gotten by vanity
22. *w.* of sinners is laid up for
19. 4. *w.* maketh many friends
1 Cor. 10. 24. seek another's *w.*
R. V. Ezra 9. 12; Job 21. 13. prosperity; Esth. 10. 3 ; 1 Cor. 10. 24. good; Prov. 5. 10. strength
WEANED, Ps. 131. 2. Isa. 11. 8. & 28. 9.
WEAPON, Isa. 13. 5. & 54. 17. 2 Cor. 10. 4.

WEAR, Deut. 22. 5, 11. Dan. 7. 25.
Matt. 11. 8. Jas. 3. 3. 1 Pet. 3. 3.
WEARY of my life, Gen. 27. 46.
Job 3. 17. there the *w.* be at rest
10. 1. soul is *w.* of life, Jer. 4. 31.
Prov. 3. 11. neither be *w.* of his
Isa. 7. 13. *w.* men, but will ye *w.*
40. 31. shall run and not be *w.*
43. 22. hast been *w.* of me, O
Jer. 6. 11. *w.* with holding in
9. 5. *w.* themselves to commit
15. 6. I am *w.* with repenting
Gal. 6. 9. *w.* in well doing
Isa. 43. 24. *wearied,* 57. 10. Jer. 12. 5.
Ezek. 24. 12. Mic. 6. 3. Mal. 2. 17.
John 4. 7. Heb. 12. 3.
Eccl. 12. 12. *weariness,* Mal. 1. 13.
Job 7. 3. *wearisome* nights
R. V. Job 37. 11. ladeth
WEB, Job 8. 14. Isa. 59. 5, 6.
WEDDING, Matt. 22. 3, 8, 11. Luke 14. 8.
WEEK, Dan. 9. 27. Matt. 28. 1. Luke 18. 12. Acts 20. 7. 1 Cor. 16. 2. Jer. 5. 24. *weeks,* Dan. 9. 24-26. & 10. 2.
WEEP, Job 30. 25. Isa. 30. 19. & 33. 7. Jer. 9. 1. & 13. 17. Joel 2. 17.
Luke 6. 21. blessed are ye that *w.*
Acts 21. 13. what mean ye to *w.*
Rom. 12. 15. *w.* with them that *w.*
1 Cor. 7. 30. that *w.* as though *wept*
Jas. 5. 1. rich men *w.* and howl
Ps. 126. 6. *weepeth,* Lam. 1. 2.
1 Sam. 1. 8. why *weepest,* John 20, 13, 15.
Ps. 30. 5. *weeping* may endure for
Isa. 22. 12. Lord call to *w.* and
Jer. 31. 9. they shall come with *w.*
Joel 2. 12. turn to me with *w.*
Matt. 8. 12. *w.* and gnashing of teeth, 22. 13. & 24. 51. & 25. 30.
WEIGH the paths of the just, Isa. 26. 7.
Prov. 16. 2. Lord *weigheth* spirits
Job 31. 6. me be *weighed* in balances
Dan. 5. 27. art *w.* in the balances
Prov. 11. 1. just *weight* is his de.
2 Cor. 4. 17. eternal *w.* of glory
Heb. 12. 1. laying aside every *w.*
Lev. 19. 36. just *weights*
Deut. 25. 13. divers *w.,* Prov. 20. 10, 23.
Matt. 23. 23. omit *weightier* matters
WELL, Ps. 84. 6. Prov. 5. 15. & 10. 11. S. of S. 4. 15. Isa. 12. 3. John 4. 14. 2 Pet. 2. 17.
Gen. 4. 7. if thou doest *well,* shalt
Ex. 1. 20. God dealt *w.* with mid.
Ps. 119. 65. hast dealt *w.* with thy
Eccl. 8. 12. it shall be *w.* with them
Isa. 3. 10. shall be *w.* with him
Rom. 2. 7. *well doing,* Gal. 6. 9.
2 Thes. 3. 13. 1 Pet. 2. 15. & 3. 17. & 4. 19.
R. V. Gen. 24. 13, 16, 29, 30, 42, 43; 49. 22; Josh. 18. 15; 2 Kings 3. 19, 25; Prov. 10. 11. fountain or fountains; Ex. 15. 27; Judg. 7. 1; Ps. 84. 6; 2 Pet. 2. 17. spring or springs; Deut. 6. 11; 2 Kings 26. 10; Neh. 9. 25. cisterns
WENT, Ps. 42. 4. & 119. 67. Matt. 21. 30.
WEPT, Neh. 1. 4. Ps. 69. 10. Hos. 12. 4. Matt. 26. 75. Luke 19. 41. John 11. 35.
WHEAT, Ps. 81. 16. Prov. 27. 22. S. of S. 7. 2.
Jer. 12. 13. have sown *w.* but reap
23. 28. what is the chaff to the *w.*
Matt. 3. 12. gather his *w.* into the
Luke 22. 31. may sift you as *w.*
John 12. 24. except a corn of *w.* fall
R. V. Num. 18. 12. corn; Prov. 27. 28. bruised corn
WHEEL, Ps. 83. 13. Prov. 20. 26.
Ezek. 1. 16. a *w.* in the midst of a *w.*
Ex. 14. 25. *wheels,* Judg. 5. 28. Dan. 7. 9. Nah. 3. 2.
R. V. Ps. 83. 13. whirling dust; Ezek. 23. 24 ; 26. 10. wagons
WHELPS (lions'), parable of Ezek. 19. Nah. 2. 12.

WHET, Deut. 32. 41. Ps. 7. 12. & 64. 3.

WHISPERER, Prov. 16. 28.

WHIT, John 7. 23. & 12. 10. 2 Cor. 11. 5.

WHITE, Lev. 13. 3, 4. Num. 12. 10.
Job 6. 6. in the *w.* of an egg
Ps. 68. 14. *w.* as snow. Dan. 7. 9.
Eccl. 9. 8. garments be always *w.*
S. of S. 5. 10. my beloved is *w.* and
Isa. 1. 18. sins shall be *w.* as snow
Dan. 11. 35. fall . . to make them *w.*
Matt. 17. 2. his raiment was *w.*
Rev. 2. 17. gave him a *w.* stone
3. 4. walk with me in *w.* raiment,
5. 18. & 4. 4. & 7. 9, 13. & 15. 16. & 19. 8, 14.
Matt. 23. 27. *whited,* Acts 23. 3.
Ps. 51. 7. *whiter* than snow

WHITE HORSE, Rev. 6. 2. & 19. 11 ; cloud, Rev. 14. 14.

WHITE THRONE, Rev. 20. 11.

WHOLE, Ps. 9. 1. & 119. 10. Isa. 54. 5. Mic. 4. 13. Zech. 4. 14. Matt. 6. 26. Eph. 6. 11. 1 John 2. 2. & 5. 19.
Job 5. 18. his hands make *w.*
Matt. 9. 12. those that are *w.* need not a physician, Luke 5. 31.
Mark 5. 34. faith hath made thee *w.,* 10. 52. Luke 8. 48. & 17. 19.
John 5. 4. *w.* of whatsoever dis.
Acts 9. 34. Christ maketh thee *w.*
Jer. 46. 28. *wholly,* 1 Thes. 5. 23.
1 Tim. 4. 15.
Prov. 15. 4. *wholesome,* 1 Tim. 6. 3.

WHORE, Lev. 19. 29. & 21. 7, 9.
Deut. 22. 21. & 23. 17, 18. Prov. 23. 27. Ezek. 16. 28. Rev. 17. 1, 16.
Jer. 3. 9. *whoredom,* Ezek. 16. Hos. 2. 2, 4. & 4. 11, 12. & 5. 3, 4.
Eph. 5. 5. *whoremonger,* 1 Tim. 1. 10. Heb. 13. 4. Rev. 21. 8. & 22. 15.
R. V. Lev. 19. 29 ; 21. 7, 9 ; Deut. 22. 21 ; 23. 17 ; Judg. 19. 2 ; Ezek. 16. 28, 33 ; Rev. 17. 1, 15, 16 ; 19. 2. harlot

WICKED, Ex. 23. 7. Deut. 15. 9. & 25. 1.
Gen. 18. 25. destroy right. with *w.*
1 Sam. 2. 9. *w.* shall be silent
Job 21. 30. *w.* is reserved till the 34. 18. Is it fit to say to king thou art *w.*
Ps. 7. 11. God is angry with the *w.*
9. 17. *w.* shall be turned into
11. 6. on *w.* he will rain snares
119. 155. salvation is far from *w.*
145. 20. all the *w.* shall he destroy
Prov. 11. 5. *w.* shall fall by his
21. *w.* shall not be unpunished
21. 12. God overthroweth the *w.*
28. 1. the *w.* flee when no man
Eccl. 7. 17. be not overmuch *w.*
Isa. 55. 7. let the *w.* forsake his
57. 20. *w.* are like the troubled
Jer. 17. 9. heart is desperately *w.*
Ezek. 3. 18. warn the *w.,* 33. 8, 9.
Dan. 12. 10. *w.* shall do *wickedly*
Gen. 19. 7. do not so *w.,* Neh. 9. 33.
1 Sam. 12. 25. if ye shall do *w.*
Job 13. 7. will ye speak *w.* for God
Ps. 18. 21. have not *w.* departed
Gen. 6. 5. God saw that *wickedness*
39. 9. how can I do this great *w.*
1 Sam. 24. 13. *w.* proceedeth from
Job 4. 8. that sow *w.* shall reap
Ps. 7. 9. *w.* of wicked come to end
Prov. 8. 7. *w.* is abomination to
13. 6. *w.* overthroweth sinners
Eccl. 3. 8. neither shall *w.* deliver
Isa. 9. 18. *w.* burneth as the fire
Jer. 2. 19. thine own *w.* shall cor.
14. 20. we acknowledge our *w.*
Hos. 10. 13. ye have ploughed *w.*
Acts 8. 22. repent of this thy *w.*
1 John 5. 19. world lieth in *w.*
R. V. Frequent changes to evil, unrighteous, etc.

WIDE, Deut. 15. 8, 11. Ps. 35. 2. & 81. 10. Prov. 13. 3. Matt. 7. 13.

WIDOW, Mark 12. 42. 1 Tim. 5. 5.
Deut. 10. 18. Ps. 146. 9. Luke 18. 3, 5.
Ps. 68. 5. *widows,* Jer. 49. 11. Matt. 23. 14. 1 Tim. 5. 3. Jas. 1. 27.

WIFE, Ex. 20. 17. Lev. 21. 13.
Prov. 5. 18. rejoice with *w.* of
18. 22. findeth a *w.* findeth a good
Eccl. 9. 9. live joyfully with thy *w.*
Hos. 12. 12. Israel served for a *w.*
Mal. 2. 15. against *w.* of thy youth
Luke 17. 32. remember Lot's *w.*
Eph. 5. 33. every man love his *w.*
Rev. 19. 7. his *w.* made herself
21. 9. the bride, the Lamb's *w.*
1 Cor. 7. 29. *wives,* Eph. 5. 25, 28, 33.
Col. 3. 18, 19. 1 Tim. 3. 11. 1 Pet. 3. 1, 7.
R. V. Ex. 19. 15 ; Lev. 21. 7 ; Judg. 21. 14 ; Ezra 10. 2, 10, 11, 14, 17, 18 ; Neh. 12. 43 ; 13. 23, 27 ; 1 Tim. 3. 11 ; 1 Pet. 3. 7. woman or women ; Matt. 19. 29 ; 22. 25 ; Mark 10. 29 ; Luke 17. 27 ; 20. 30 —

WILDERNESS, Deut. 32. 10.
Prov. 21. 19. S. of S. 3. 6. & 8. 5.
Isa. 35. 1, 6. & 41. 18, 19. & 42. 11. & 43. 19, 20. Rev. 12. 6.
R. V. Job 30. 3. dry ground ; Ps. 107. 40. waste ; Amos 6. 14. Arabah ; Ps. 78. 17 ; Prov. 21. 19 ; Isa. 33. 9 ; Jer. 51. 43 ; Matt. 15. 43 ; Mark 8. 14 ; Luke 5. 16 ; 8. 29. desert, or desert place

WILES, Num. 25. 18. Eph. 6. 11.

WILL, Lev. 1. 3. & 19. 5. & 22. 19.
Deut. 33. 16. the good *w.* of him that dwelt in the bush
Matt. 7. 21. doeth *w.* of my Father
Luke 2. 14. good *w.* towards men
John 1. 13. *w.* of flesh, nor
3. 34. my meat is to do *w.* of him
6. 40. this is the *w.* of him that
Acts 21. 14. *w.* of the Lord be done
Eph. 5. 17. understandeth what the *w.* of the Lord is
Acts 22. 14. his *will,* John 7. 17.
Rom. 2. 18. Eph. 1. 5, 9. Col. 1. 9.
2 Tim. 2. 26. Heb. 13. 21. 1 John 5. 14. Rev. 17. 17.
Luke 22. 42. my *will,* Acts 13. 22.
John 5. 30. own *will,* 6. 38. Eph. 1. 11. Heb. 2. 4. Jas. 1. 18.
Ps. 40. 8. thy *will,* 143. 10. Matt. 6. 10. & 26. 42. Heb. 10. 7, 9.
Ezra 7. 18. *will of God,* Mark 3. 35.
Rom. 1. 10. & 8. 27. & 12. 2. 1 Cor. 1. 1. 2 Cor. 8. 5. Gal. 1. 4. Eph. 1. 1. & 6. 6. Col. 1. 1. & 4. 12. 1 Thes. 4. 3. Heb. 10. 36. 1 Pet. 4. 2, 19. 1 John 2. 17.
Matt. 26. 39. not as *I will,* but as
John 15. 7. ask what ye *w.* and it
17. 24. I *w.* that those thou hast
Rom. 7. 18. to *w.* is present with
Phil. 2. 13. worketh to *w.* and to
Rev. 22. 17. whosoever let him
Rom. 9. 16. of him that *willeth*
Heb. 10. 26. if we sin *wilfully*
Ex. 35. 5. whoso is of a *willing* heart
1 Chron. 28. 9. with a perfect heart and *w.* mind
Ps. 110. 3. people shall be *w.* in the
Isa. 1. 19. be *w.* and obedient
Matt. 26. 41. Spirit is *w.* but the
Luke 22. 42. if thou be *w.* remove
John 5. 35. *w.* for a season to rej.
2 Cor. 5. 8. *w.* rather to be absent
1 Tim. 6. 18. be *w.* to communicate
Heb. 13. 18. *w.* in all things to
2 Pet. 3. 9. not *w.* any should per.
Judg. 5. 2. *willingly* offered them.
1 Chron. 29. 9. heart offered *w.*
Lam. 3. 33. Lord doth not afflict *w.*
Hos. 5. 11. he *w.* walked after the
Col. 2. 23. wisdom in *will worship*
R. V. Changes of the pure auxiliary are to would, should, shall, etc. Ex. 35. 29. free will ; 39. 9. content ; Mark 15. 15 ; 2 Pet. 3. 9. wishing ; Luke 10. 29 ; 23. 20 ; Acts 24. 27 ; 25. 9 ; 27. 43 ; Heb. 13. 18. desiring ; 1 Thes. 2. 8. well pleased ; Heb. 6. 17. being minded

WILLOWS, Lev. 23. 40. Isa. 44. 4.

WIN, Phil. 3. 8.
Prov. 11. 30. *winneth*
R. V. Phil. 3. 8. gain

WIND, Job 7. 7. & 36. 15. Ps. 103. 16.
Prov. 11. 29. inherit *w.*
30. 4. gathereth the *w.*
Eccl. 11. 4. that observeth the *w.*
Isa. 26. 18. have brought forth *w.*
Jer. 5. 13. prophets shall become *w.*
10. 13. bring *w.* out of his treas.
Hos. 8. 7. sown *w.*
John 3. 8. *w.* bloweth where it
Eph. 4. 14. about with every *w.*
2 Kings 2. 11. *whirlwind,* Prov. 1. 27. & 10. 25. Isa. 66. 15. Hos. 8. 7. & 13. 3. Nah. 1. 3. Hab. 3. 14.
Zech. 7. 14. & 9. 14.
Ezek. 37. 9. *winds,* Matt. 8. 26.
Luke 8. 25.
R. V. Isa. 27. 8. blast ; Jer. 14. 6. air ; Hos. 13. 15. breath ; Ezek. 41. 7. encompass

WINDOWS, Gen. 7. 11. Eccl. 12. 3. S. of S. 2. 9. Isa. 60. 8. Jer. 9. 21.
R. V. Gen. 6. 16. light ; 1 Kings 7. 4, 5. prospects ; Isa. 54. 12. pinnacles

WINE maketh glad the heart, Ps. 104. 15.
Prov. 20. 1. *w.* is a mocker
21. 17. loveth *w.* and oil shall
23. 30. that tarry long at *w.* that
31. look not upon *w.* when it is
S. of S. 1. 2. love is better than *w.*
Isa. 5. 11. till *w.* inflame them
25. 6. *w.* on the lees well refined
55. 1. buy *w.* and milk
Hos. 2. 9. take away my *w.* in
4. 11. *w.* take away the heart
Hab. 2. 5. transgresseth by *w.*
Eph. 5. 18. not drunk with *w.*
1 Tim. 3. 3. not given to *w.,* 8.
5. 23. a little *w.* for stomach's
Prov. 23. 20. *wine-bibber,* Matt. 11. 19.
R. V. Num. 18. 12 ; Mic. 6. 15. vintage ; Num. 28. 7. drink ; 2 Sam. 6. 19 ; 1 Chron. 16. 3 ; Hos. 3. 1. raisins

WINGS of the God of Israel, Ruth 2. 12.
Ps. 17. 8. hide under s...adow of *w.,*
36. 7. & 57. 1. & 61. 4. & 91. 4.
18. 10. on *w.* of the wind, 2 Sam. 22. 11.
Prov. 23. 5. riches make themselves *w.* and fly away
Isa. 6. 2. seraphims ; each had six *w.*
Mal. 4. 2. with healing in his *w.*
R. V. Deut. 32. 11. pinions

WINK, Job 15. 12. Ps. 35. 19. Prov. 6. 13. & 10. 10. Acts 17. 30.
R. V. *overlook,* Acts 17. 30. ignorance God *w.* at

WINTER, S. of S. 2. 11. Zech. 14. 8.

WIPE, 2 Kings 21. 13. Neh. 13. 14.
Prov. 6. 33. Isa. 25. 8. Rev. 7. 17. & 21. 4.

WISE, Gen. 41. 39. Ex. 23. 8. Deut. 16. 19.
Deut. 4. 6. this great nation is a *w.* people
Job 5. 13. taketh the *w.* in their
11. 12. vain man would be *w.*
32. 9. great men are not always *w.*
Ps. 2. 10. be *w.* O kings, be taught
29. 7. making the simple *w.*
Prov. 3. 7. be not *w.* in own eyes
35. the *w.* shall inherit glory
26. 12. a man *w.* in his own conceit
Eccl. 7. 4. heart of *w.* in house
9. 1. the *w.* are in the hand of God
Isa. 5. 21. are *w.* in their own eyes
Jer. 4. 22. they are *w.* to do evil
Dan. 12. 3. *w.* shall shine as stars
Hos. 14. 9. who is *w.* and he shall
Matt. 10. 16. be ye *w.* as serpents
Rom. 1. 22. professing themselves to be *w.*
16. 19. be *w.* to that which is good
1 Cor. 3. 18. seem. *w.* in this world
4. 10. but ye are *w.* in Christ
Eph. 5. 15. not as fools but as *w.*
2 Tim. 3. 15. is able to make thee *w.*

Matt. 10. 42. *in no wise* lose his
Luke 18. 17. shall — enter therein
John 6. 37. cometh, I will—cast out
Rev. 21. 27. shall — enter into it
Deut. 4. 6. this is your *wisdom*
1 Kings 4. 29. God gave Solomon
  w. 5. 12
Job 28. 28. fear of Lord, that is *w.*
Prov. 4. 5. get *w.* get understand.
  7. *w.* is the principal thing, 8.
16. 16. better to get *w.* than gold
19. 8. he that getteth *w.* loveth his
  own soul
Eccl. 1. 18. in much *w.* is much grief
8. 1. a man's *w.* maketh his face
Matt. 11. 19. *w.* is justified of her
1 Cor. 1. 30. who of God is made
  unto us *w.*
2. 6. we speak *w.* among perfect
3. 19. *w.* of this world is foolish.
2 Cor. 1. 12. not with fleshly *w.*
Col. 1. 9. might be filled with all *w,*
4. 5. walk in *w.* towards them that
Jas. 1. 5. if any lack *w.* ask it of
3. 17. *w.* from above is pure
Rev. 5. 12. worthy is the Lamb to
  receive *w.*
13. 18. here is *w.* let him that hath,
17. 9.
Ps. 111. 10. *of wisdom,* Prov. 9. 10. &
10. 21. Mic. 6. 9. Col. 2. 3. Jas. 3. 13.
64. 9. *wisely,* 101. 2. Eccl. 7. 10.
1 Kings 4. 31. *wiser,* Job 35. 11. Ps.
119. 98. Luke 16. 8. 1 Cor. 1. 25.
R. V. 1 Chron. 26. 14. discreet;
  Prov. 1. 5. sound; 1 Tim. 1. 17;
Jude 25——; Lev. 19. 17; Deut.
21. 23. surely; Rom. 10. 6. thus;
1 Chron. 22. 12. discretion; Job
36. 5; Ps. 136. 5; Prov. 10. 21; Eccl.
10. 3. understanding; Prov. 1. 3
  wise dealing; 8. 5. subtilty; 8. 14.
  knowledge; Dan. 2. 14. prudence
WITCH, Ex. 22. 18. Deut. 18. 10.
1 Sam. 15. 23. *witchcraft,* Gal. 5. 20.
WITHDRAW, Job 9. 13. & 33. 17.
Prov. 25. 17. S. of S. 5. 6. 2 Thes.
3. 6. 1 Tim. 6. 5.
WITHERED hand of Jeroboam
  healed, 1 Kings 13.
——hand healed by Christ, Matt.
  12. 10. Mark 3. Luke 6. 6.
WITHHOLD not thy mercies, Ps.
  40. 11.
Ps. 84. 11. no good thing will he *w.*
Prov. 3. 27. *w.* not good from them
23. 13. *w.* not correction from child
Gen. 20. 6. *withheld,* 22. 12. Job 31. 16.
Job 42. 2. *withholden,* Jer. 5. 25.
Prov. 11. 24. *withholdeth,* 2 Thes.
2. 6.
R. V. Job 42. 2; 2 Thes. 2. 6. restrain
WITHIN, Ps. 40. 8. & 45. 13. Matt.
3. 9. & 23. 26. Mark 7. 21. 2 Cor. 7. 5.
Rev. 5. 1.
WITHOUT, Prov. 1. 20. & 24. 27.
1 Cor. 5. 12. 2 Cor. 7. 5. Col. 4. 5.
Rev. 22. 15.
WITHSTAND, Eccl. 4. 12. Eph. 6.
  13.
Acts 11. 17. what was I, that I could
  w. God
Gal. 2. 11. *withstood,* 2 Tim. 4. 15.
WITNESS, Gen. 31. 44, 48. Lev. 5. 1.
Num. 35. 30. one *w.* shall not testify
  against him, Deut. 17. 6. & 19. 15.
2 Cor. 13. 1.
Judg. 11. 10. Lord be *w.*, 1 Sam. 12.
5. Jer. 42. 5. & 29. 23. Mic. 1. 2.
Ps. 89. 37. as a faithful *w.* in heaven
Prov. 14. 5. a faithful *w.* will not lie
Isa. 55. 4. him for a *w.* to the people
Mal. 3. 5. I will be a swift *w.* again.
John 3. 11. ye receive not our *w.*
Acts 14. 17. left not himself with-
  out *w.*
1 John 5. 10. believeth him hath *w.*
Rev. 1. 5. is the faithful *w.*, 3. 14.
20. 4. beheaded for *w.* of Jesus
Deut. 17. 6. two or three *witnesses,*
19. 15. 2 Cor. 13. 1. Matt. 18. 16.
Heb. 10. 28. 1 Tim. 5. 19. Num. 35.
30.
Josh. 24. 22. ye are *w.* against

Isa. 43. 10. ye are my *w.* saith the
  Lord, 12. & 44. 8.
1 Thes. 2. 10. ye are *w.* and God
6. 12. before many *w.*
Heb. 12. 1. so great a cloud of *w.*
Rev. 11. 3. power unto my two *w.*
WIVES, their duties to husbands,
  Gen. 3. 16. Ex. 20. 14. Rom. 7. 2.
1 Cor. 7. 3. & 14. 34. Eph. 5. 22, 33.
Tit. 2. 4. 1 Pet. 3. 1.
  good, Prov. 12. 4. & 18. 22. & 19. 14. &
  31. 10.
Levitical laws concerning, Ex. 21.
3, 22. & 22. 16. Num. 5. 12. & 30. Deut.
21. 10, 15. & 24. 1. Jer. 3. 1. Matt.
19. 3.
the wife a type of the church,
  Eph. 5. 23. Rev. 19. 7. & 21. 9.
WIZARDS, Lev. 19. 31. & 20. 6. Isa.
  8. 19.
WOES against wickedness, etc.,
  Isa. 5. 8. & 10. 1. & 29. 15. & 31. 1. &
45. 9. Jer. 22. 13. Amos 6. 1. Mic.
2. 1. Hab. 2. 6. Zeph. 3. 1. Zech. 11.
17. Matt. 26. 24. Luke 6. 24. Jude 11.
Rev. 8. 13. & 9. 12. & 11. 14.
  against unbelief, Matt. 11. 21. & 23.
13. Luke 10. 13. & 11. 42.
WOLF, Isa. 11. 6. & 65. 25. Jer. 5. 6.
Ezek. 22. 27. *wolves,* Hab. 1. 8. Zeph.
3. 3. Matt. 7. 15. & 10. 16. Acts 20.
29.
WOMAN, Gen. 2. 23. & 3. 15. Lev.
18. 22, 23. & 20. 13. Num. 30. 3.
Prov. 11. 16. gracious *w.* retaineth
  honor
Ps. 48. 6. pain as of a *w.* in travail
Prov. 12. 4. a virtuous *w.* is a crown
14. 1. every wise *w.* buildeth her
31. 10. a virtuous *w.* who can find
30. *w.* that feareth the Lord shall
Eccl. 7. 26. *w.* whose heart is snares
28. *w.* among all I have not found
Isa. 49. 15. can a *w.* forget her suckl-
54. 6. called thee as a *w.* forsaken
Jer. 31. 22. *w.* shall compass a man
Matt. 5. 28. looketh on a *w.* to lust
15. 28. O *w.* great is thy faith
John 2. 4. *w.* what have I to do with
8. 3. brought *w.* taken in adultery
19. 26. *w.* behold thy son
Rom. 1. 27. the natural use of *w.*
1 Cor. 11. 7. *w.* is the glory of man
Gal. 4. 4. sent his Son made of a *w.*
1 Tim. 2. 12. I suffer not *w.* to teach
14. *w.* being deceived was in the
Rev. 12. 1. *w.* clothed with the sun,
6. 16.
17. 18. *w.* thou sawest is that city
Judg. 5. 24. blessed above *women*
  shall Jael be
Prov. 31. 3. give not thy strength
  to *w.*
S. of S. 1. 8. fairest among *w.*, 5. 9.
  & 6. 1.
Jer. 9. 17. call for the mourning *w.*
Lam. 4. 10. *w.* had sodden children
Matt. 11. 11. among them born of *w.*
Luke 1. 28. blessed art thou among
  w.
Rom. 1. 26. *w.* did change their
1 Cor. 14. 34. let *w.* keep silence
1 Tim. 2. 9. let *w.* adorn themselves
11. let *w.* learn in silence with
5. 14. that the younger *w.* marry
1 Pet. 3. 5. after this manner holy
  w.
Rev. 14. 4. are not defiled with *w.*
WOMB, Gen. 25. 23. & 29. 31.
Gen. 49. 25. blessings of the *w.* and
1 Sam. 1. 5. Lord hath shut her *w.*
Ps. 22. 9. took me out of the *w.*
10. I was cast upon thee from *w.*
139. 13. covered me in mother's *w.*
Eccl. 11. 5. how bones grow in *w.*
Isa. 44. 2. the Lord that formed
  thee from the *w.*
Hos. 9. 14. give them miscarrying
  w.
Luke 1. 42. blessed is fruit of thy
  w.
11. 27. blessed is *w.* that bare thee
23. 29. blessed are *w.* that never
R. V. Deut. 7. 13. body

WONDER, Deut. 13. 1. & 28. 46.
Ps. 71. 7. Isa. 29. 14. Rev. 12. 1.
Acts 13. 41. *w.* and perish, Hab. 1. 5.
Ex. 3. 20. *wonders,* 7. 3. & 15. 11.
1 Chron. 16. 12. remember his *w.,*
  Ps. 105. 5.
Job 9. 10. God doeth *w.,* Ps. 77. 11, 14.
Ps. 88. 11. wilt thou show *w.* to the
  dead
Dan. 12. 6. how long to the end of
  these *w.*
John 4. 48. except they see signs
  and *w.*
Acts 2. 43. many *w.* were done, 6. 8.
Rom. 15. 19. mighty signs and *w.*
2 Thes. 2. 9. and signs and lying *w.*
Rev. 13. 13. he doeth great *w.*
Zech. 3. 8. they are men *wondered*
Isa. 59. 16. *w.* there was no inter.
Luke 4. 22. *w.* at the gracious words
Rev. 13. 3. all the world *w.* after
17. 6. I *w.* with great admiration
Job 37. 14. *wondrous* works, Ps. 26.
7. & 75. 1. & 105. 2. & 119. 27. & 145.
5. & 71. 17. & 78. 32. & 106. 22.
Ps. 72. 18. *w.* things, 86. 10. & 119. 18.
Judg. 13. 19. *wondrously,* Joel 2. 26.
Deut. 28. 59. thy plagues *wonderful*
Ps. 119. 129. thy testimonies are *w.*
Prov. 30. 18. three things too *w.* for
Isa. 9. 6. his name shall be called
  W.
Jer. 5. 30. a *w.* thing is committed
Ps. 139. 14. *wonderfully,* Lam. 1. 9.
R. V. Rev. 12. 1, 3. sign; Gen. 24.
21. looked stedfastly; Mark 6. 51.
——; Luke 8. 25; 11. 14. marvelled;
Acts 8. 13. amazed; Ps. 78. 4. won-
drous; Matt. 7. 22; Acts 2. 21.
mighty; 1 Chron. 16. 9; Ps. 105. 2.
marvellous
WOOD, hay, stubble, 1 Cor. 3. 12.
2 Tim. 2. 20. also vessels of *w.* and
R. V. Deut. 19. 5; Josh. 17. 18;
1 Sam. 14. 25, 26; Ps. 83. 14; Eccl.
2. 6; Isa. 7. 2; Mic. 7. 14. forest;
1 Chron. 22. 4. trees; Ex. 26. 32, 37;
36. 36; Ps. 141. 7——
WORD, Num. 23. 5. Deut. 4. 2.
Deut. 8. 3. every *w.* of God, Matt.
  4. 4.
30. 14. *w.* is very nigh, Rom. 10. 8.
Ps. 68. 11. the Lord gave the *w.*
Prov. 15. 23. *w.* spoken in due season
25. 11. a *w.* fitly spoken is like
  apples of gold
Isa. 29. 21. man an offender for a *w.*
50. 4. how to speak a *w.* in season
Jer. 5. 13. the *w.* is not in them
Matt. 8. 8. speak the *w.* only and
  my servant shall be healed
12. 36. every idle *w.* that men
Luke 4. 36. what a *w.* is this
John 1. 1. in the beginning was the
  W. and the *W.* was with God
14. the *W.* was made flesh
15. 3. ye are clean through the *w.*
Acts 13. 15. any *w.* of exhortation
26. to you is *w.* of salvation sent
17. 11. the *w.* with all readiness
20. 32. and to the *w.* of his grace
1 Cor. 4. 20. kingdom of God is not
  in *w.*
Gal. 6. 6. taught in *w.* communicate
Eph. 5. 26. washing of water by *w.*
Col. 3. 16. let *w.* of Christ dwell in
17. whatsoever ye do in *w.* or deed
1 Thes. 1. 5. Gospel came not in *w.*
2 Thes. 2. 17. stablish you in every
  good *w.*
3. 14. if any obey not our *w.* note
1 Tim. 5. 17. labor in *w.* and
2 Tim. 4. 2. preach *w.* be instant in
Tit. 1. 9. holding fast the faithful
  w.
Heb. 4. 2. the *w.* preached did not
5. 13. is unskilful in *w.* of right.
13. 22. suffer the *w.* of exhortation
Jas. 1. 21. receive the engrafted *w,*
22. be doers of the *w.*
3. 2. offend not in *w.*
1 Pet. 3. 1. if any obey not the *w.*
2 Pet. 1. 19. sure *w.* of prophecy
1 John 1. 1. hands handled of the *w.*

1 John 5. 7. Father, *W.* and Holy Ghost

Rev. 3. 10. kept *w.* of my patience

12. 11. overcame by *w.* of their testimony

Ps. 130. 5. in *his word* do I hope, 119. 81.

Jer. 20. 9.—was in my heart as fire

John 5. 38. have not—abiding in you

Acts 2. 41. that gladly received— were baptized

John 8. 37. *my word,* 43. Rev. 3. 8.

Isa. 8. 20. *this word,* Rom. 9. 9.

Ps. 119. 11. *thy word* have I hid in mine heart

105.—is a lamp unto my feet

140.—is very pure

160.—is true from the beginning

Jer. 15. 16.—was unto me joy and John 17. 6. I kept—

17.—is truth

Prov. 30. 5. *word of God,* Isa. 40. 8.

Mark 7. 13. Rom 10. 17. 1 Thes. 2. 13. Heb. 4. 12. & 6. 5. 1 Pet. 1. 23. Rev. 19. 13.

2 Kings 20. 19. *word of the Lord,* Ps. 18. 30. & 33⁴ 4. 2 Thes. 3. 1. 1 Pet. 1. 25.

Ps. 119. 43. *word of truth,* 2 Cor. 6. 7. Eph. 1. 13. Col. 1. 5. 2 Tim. 2. 15. Jas. 1. 18.

Job 23. 12. esteemed *words* of

Prov. 15. 26. *w.* of pure are pleas. 22. 17. bow down thine ear, hear *w.*

Eccl. 10. 12. the *w.* of a wise man

11. *w.* of the wise are as goads

Jer. 7. 4. trust ye not in lying *w.*

Dan. 7. 25. speak great *w.* against

Hos. 6. 5. slain by *w.* of my mouth

Zech. 1. 13. good *w.* comfortable *w.*

Matt. 26. 44. prayed, saying same *w.*

Luke 4. 22. the gracious *w.* that

John 6. 63. *w.* I speak are Spirit and 68. thou hast the *w.* of eternal life

17. 8. given unto them *w.* which

Acts 7. 22. Moses mighty in *w.* and 15. 24. troubled you with *w.,* 18. 15. 20. 35. remember the *w.* of Lord 26. 25. speak the *w.* of truth and

1 Cor. 2. 4. not with enticing *w.* of

2 Tim. 1. 13. hold fast the form of sound *w.*

2. 14. strive not about *w.* to no

Rev. 1. 3. hear *w.* of this prophecy, 22. 18.

Ps. 50. 17. *my words,* Isa. 51. 16. & 59. 21. Jer. 5. 14. Mic. 2. 7. Mark 8. 38. & 13. 31. John 5. 47. & 15. 7.

1 Thes. 4. 18. *these words,* Rev. 21. 5.

Ps. 119. 103. *thy words,* 130. & 139.

Prov. 23. 8. Eccl. 5. 2. Ezek. 33. 31. Matt. 12. 37.

R. V. Num. 4. 45; Josh. 19. 50; 22. 9. commandment; Deut. 8. 3; 2 Kings 23. 16; John 7. 9; 8. 30; 9. 22, 40; 17. 1. thing; 2 Sam. 19. 14; 1 Kings 2. 42; Luke 20. 26; John 12. 47, 48. saying; 1 Kings 13. 26. mouth; 1 Chron. 21. 12. answer; Jonah 3. 6. tidings; Matt. 2. 13. tell; Luke 4. 4; Acts 28. 29; 1 John 5. 7 —

WORK, Gen. 2. 3. Ex. 20. 10. & 31. 14.

Deut. 33. 11. accept *w.* of his hands

Job 1. 10. thou hast blessed the *w.*

10. 3. despise the *w.* of thy hands

36. 9. he showeth them their *w.*

Ps. 19. 1. the firmament sheweth his handy-*w.*

101. 3. I hate the *w.* of them that

143. 5. muse on *w.* of thy hands

Eccl. 8. 14. according to *w.* of wicked

17. I beheld all the *w.* of God

12. 14. God shall bring every *w.* into judgment

Isa. 16. 12. performed his whole *w.*

64. 8. we are called *w.* of thy hands

Jer. 10. 15. vanity and *w.* of error

18. 3. potter wrought a *w.* on the

Hab. 1. 5. a *w.* in your days, Acts 13. 41.

Mark 6. 5. could do no mighty *w.*

John 17. 4. finished *w.* thou gavest

Acts 5. 38. if this *w.* be of men

13. 2. for the *w.* whereto I called

Rom. 2. 15. show *w.* of law written

11. 6. otherwise *w.* is no more *w.*

1 Cor. 3. 13. every man's *w.* made

9. 1. are not ye my *w.* in the Lord

Eph. 4. 12. for *w.* of the ministry

2 Thes. 1. 11. *w.* of faith with pow.

2. 17. stablish you in every good *w.*

2 Tim. 4. 5. do *w.* of an evangelist

Jas. 1. 4. let patience have perfect *w.*

25. doer of the *w.* shall be blessed

1 Pet. 1. 17. judgeth every man's *w.*

Ps. 104. 23. *his work,* 62. 12. & 111. 3.

Prov. 24. 29. Isa. 40. 10. Job 36. 24.

Ps. 90. 16. *thy work,* 92. 4. Prov. 24. 27. Jer. 31. 16. Hab. 3. 2.

Ex. 32. 16. *work of God,* Ps. 64. 9.

Eccl. 7. 13. & 8. 17. John 6. 29. Rom. 14. 20.

Ps. 28. 5. *work of the Lord,* Isa. 5. 12. Jer. 48. 10. 1 Cor. 15. 58. & 16. 10.

Ps. 17. 4. concerning *works* of men

92. 4. triumph in *w.* of thy hands

138. 8. forsake not *w.* of thy hands

Prov. 31. 31. let her own *w.* praise

Isa. 26. 12. wrought all our *w.* in us

Dan. 4. 37. all whose *w.* are truth

John 5. 20. show him greater *w.*

10. 32. of those *w.* do ye stone me

38. believe the *w.* that I do

Acts 26. 20. *w.* meet for repent.

Rom. 3. 27. by what law? of *w.*

4. 6. God imputeth righteousness without *w.*

9. 32. sought it as by *w.* of the law

11. 6. then it is no more of *w.*

13. 12. us cast off *w.* of darkness

Gal. 2. 16. by *w.* of law no flesh be

3. 2. received ye spirit by *w.* of law

10. as many as are *w.* of the law

5. 19. *w.* of the flesh are manifest

Eph. 2. 9. not of *w.*

10. to good *w.* which God

5. 11. unfruitful *w.* of darkness

Col. 1. 21. enemies in mind by wicked *w.*

1 Thes. 5. 13. love them for their *w.*

2 Tim. 1. 9. not according to our *w.*

Tit. 1. 16. in *w.* they deny him

3. 5. not by *w.* of righteousness

Heb. 6. 1. repentance from dead *w.*

9. 14. conscience from dead *w.*

Jas. 2. 14. and have not *w.* can

20. faith without *w.* is dead, 17. 26.

21. justified by *w.,* 24. 25.

22. by *w.* was faith made perfect

1 John 3. 8. he might destroy *w.* of

Rev. 9. 20. repented not of the *w.* of

18. 6. according to her *w.,* 20. 12, 13.

Ps. 33. 4. *his works,* 78. 11. & 103. 22. 104. 31. & 106. 13. & 107. 22. & 145. 9. 17. Dan. 9. 14. Acts 15. 18. Heb. 4. 10.

Ps. 106. 35. *their works,* Isa. 66. 18.

Jonah 3. 10. Matt. 23. 3, 5. 2 Cor. 11. 15. Rev. 14. 13. & 20. 12, 13.

Deut. 15. 10. *thy works,* Ps. 66. 3. & 73. 28. & 92. 5. & 104. 24. & 143. 5.

Prov. 16. 3. Eccl. 9. 7. Rev. 2. 3.

Ps. 40. 5. *wonderful works,* 78. 4. & 107. 8. & 111. 4. Matt. 7. 22. Acts 2. 11.

Job 37. 14. *works of God,* Ps. 66. 5. & 78. 7. Eccl. 11. 5. John 6. 28. & 9. 3.

Ps. 46. 8. of the Lord, 111. 2.

1 Sam. 14. 6. may be the Lord will *work* for us

Isa. 43. 13. I will *w.* and who

Matt. 7. 23. depart from me ye that *w.* iniquity

John 6. 28. might *w.* works of God

9. 4. I must *w.* the works of him

Phil. 2. 12. *w.* out your salvation

2 Thes. 2. 7. iniquity doth already *w.*

3. 10. if any *w.* not, neither should

Prov. 11. 18. the wicked *worketh* a deceitful

Isa. 64. 5. meet. him that *w.* right.

John 5. 17. my Father *w.* and I *w.*

Acts 10. 35. that *w.* righteousness is accepted

2 Cor. 4. 17. *w.* for us a far more

Gal. 5. 6. faith which *w.* by love

Phil. 2. 13. it is God that *w.* in you

1 Thes. 2. 13. effectually *w.* in you

Mark 16. 20. the Lord *w.* with them

Rom. 7. 13. sin *w.* death in me

Eph. 1. 10. accord. to *w.* of mighty

3. 7. by effectual *w.* of his power

4. 28. *w.* with his hands the thing

Phil. 3. 21. accord. to *w.* whereby

2 Thes. 3. 11. *w.* not at all, but are

Heb. 13. 21. *w.* in you that which

2 Cor. 6. 1. *workers,* 11. 13. Phil. 3. 2.

Job 31. 3. *workers of iniquity,* 34. 8, 22. Ps. 5. 5. & 6. 8. & 28. 3. & 125. 5. & 141. 9. Prov. 10. 29. & 21. 15.

Matt. 10. 10. *workman,* 2 Tim. 2. 15.

Ex. 31. 3. *workmanship,* Eph. 2. 10.

R. V. Ex. 35. 33, 35. workmanship; Prov. 11. 18. wages; Isa. 40. 10; 49, 4; 61. 8; 62. 11. recompense; Ps. 77. 11; 141. 4; Matt. 16. 27. deeds; Rom. 11. 6. grace; Heb. 13. 21. thing

WORLD, 1 Sam. 2. 8. 1 Chron. 16. 30.

Ps. 17. 14. from men of the *w.*

24. 1. *w.* is the Lord's, 9. 8. Nah. 1. 5.

Ps. 50. 12. *w.* is mine and the ful.

Eccl. 3. 11. hath set *w.* in his heart

Isa. 26. 9. the inhabitants of the *w.* learn righteousness

Jer. 10. 12. established the *w.* by his wisdom, 51. 15. Ps. 93. 1. & 96. 10.

Matt. 16. 26. what is a man profited if he shall gain the whole *w.* and lose his own soul, Mark 8. 36.

18. 7. woe to the *w.* because

Mark 16. 15. go into all the *w.* and

Luke 20. 35. worthy to obtain that *w.*

John 1. 10. *w.* was made by him, and *w.* knew him not

29. Lamb of God taketh away sin of the *w.*

3. 16. God so loved the *w.* he gave

17. *w.* through him might be saved

7. 7. the *w.* cannot hate you, but

14. 17. whom *w.* cannot receive

19. *w.* seeth me no more; but ye

15. 18. if the *w.* hate you

19. chosen you out of the *w.* there- fore the *w.* hateth you

17. 9. I pray not for the *w.*

11. I am no more in the *w.*

16. not of *w.* even as I am not of *w*

23. *w.* may know thou hast sent

Rom. 3. 19. all the *w.* become guilty

1 Cor. 1. 21. *w.* by wisdom knew not

Gal. 6. 14. *w.* is crucified unto me

Col. 1. 6. as in all *w.* and bringeth

Tit. 1. 2. promised before *w.* began

Heb. 2. 5. *w.* to come, 6. 5.

11. 38. the *w.* was not worthy

1 John 2. 2. a propitiation for sins of the whole *w.*

2. 15. love not the *w.* nor things in the *w.*

16. all that is in the *w.* is of the *w.*

3. 1. the *w.* knoweth us not

4. 5. they are of the *w.* they speak of the *w.* and the *w.* heareth them

Rev. 3. 10. temptation come on all *w.*

13. 3. all *w.* wondered after beast

Matt. 12. 32. *this world,* John 8. 32. & 13. 36. Rom. 12. 2. 1 Tim. 6. 7.

Heb. 1. 2. he made the *worlds*

11. 3. the *w.* were framed by him

R. V. Ps. 22. 27; Isa. 62. 11; Rev. 13. 13. earth; 1 Cor. 10. 11; Eph. 3. 9; Heb. 6. 5; 9. 26. age or ages; Isa. 60. 4. of old; Matt. 12. 32. that which is; Rom. 16. 25; 2 Tim. 1. 9; Tit. 1. 2. time eternal; John 17. 12—

WORM, Ex. 16. 20. Isa. 51. 8.
Job 25. 6. man that is a w.
Isa. 41. 14. fear not, thou w. Jacob
66. 24. their w. shall not die, Mark 9. 44, 48.
Job 19. 26. worms destroy my body, Acts 12. 23.
Deut. 29. 18. wormwood, Prov. 5. 4. Lam. 3. 15, 19. Amos 5. 7. Rev. 8. 11.
R. V. Mic. 7. 17. crawling thing; Job 19. 26; Mark 9. 44, 46—

WORSE, Matt. 12. 45. John 5. 14. 1 Cor. 8. 8. & 11. 17. 2 Tim. 3. 13. 2 Pet. 2. 20.

WORSHIP the Lord in beauty of holiness, 1 Chron. 16. 29. Ps. 29. 2. & 66. 4. & 96. 9. & 45. 11. & 95. 6. & 99. 5. Matt. 4. 10.
Matt. 15. 9. in vain do they w. me
John 4. 24. w. him must in truth
Acts 17. 23. whom ye ignorantly w.
24. 14. so w. I the God of my
Rev. 3. 9. w. before thy feet
19. 10. to w. God, 22. 9.
Ex. 4. 31. worshipped, 32. 8. Jer. 1. 16. 1 Chron. 29. 20. Rom. 1. 25. 2 Thes. 2. 4. Rev. 5. 14. & 7. 11. & 11. 16. & 13. 4.
R. V. 2 Kings 17. 36. bow; Luke 14. 10. glory; Acts 7. 42; 17. 25; 24. 14. serve

WORTH, Job 24. 25. Prov. 10. 20. Gen. 32. 10. I am not worthy of least
Matt. 8. 8. I am not w. thou shouldest
10. 10. workman is w. of his meat
13. if house be w. let your peace
22. 8. that were bidden were not w.
Luke 3. 8. fruits w. of repentance
7. 4. w. for whom he should do this
10. 7. laborer is w. of his hire
15. 19. no more w. to be called
Acts 5. 41. counted w. to suffer
Rom. 8. 18. not w. to be compared
Eph. 4. 1. walk w. of the vocation
Col. 1. 10. walk w. of the Lord being
1 Thes. 2. 12. walk w. of God who
2 Thes. 1. 5. be counted w. of the
11. God count you w. of this calling
1 Tim. 1. 15. w. of all acceptation, 4. 9.
5. 17. elders w. of double honor
18. laborer is w. of reward
6. 1. counted masters w. of honor
Heb. 11. 38. of whom world was not w.
Rev. 3. 4. walk in white, they are w.
5. 12. w. is the Lamb that was slain
16. 6. blood to drink; for they are w.

WOULD God, Ex. 16. 3. Num. 11. 29. Acts 26. 29. 1 Cor. 4. 8. 2 Cor. 11. 1.
Neh. 9. 30. would not, Isa. 30. 15. Matt. 18. 30. & 23. 30, 37. Rom. 11. 25.
Prov. 1. 25. w. none of my reproof
30. they w. none of my counsel
Matt. 7. 12. whatsoever ye w. that men should do unto you
Rev. 3. 15. I w. thou wert cold or hot
R. V. Many changes to did, could, may, should, might, etc.

WOUND, Rev. 21. 25. Prov. 6. 33. Jer. 10. 19. & 15. 18. & 30. 12, 14. Mic. 1. 9.

Prov. 27. 6. wounds, Isa. 1. 6. Jer. 30. 17.
Deut. 32. 39. I wound and I heal
1 Cor. 8. 12. w. their weak conscience
Rev. 13. 3. his deadly w. was healed, 14.
Ps. 69. 26. wounded, 109. 22. S. of S. 5. 7.
Prov. 18. 14. a w. spirit who can bear
Isa. 53. 5. w. for our transgressions
Job 5. 18. he woundeth and his hands
R. V. Prov. 18. 8; 26. 22. dainty morsels; Obad. 7. snare; Rev. 13. 3, 12. death stroke; 2 Sam. 22. 39; Ps. 18. 38; 32. 39; 110. 6; Rev. 13. 13. smite or smitten through; 1 Sam. 31. 3; 1 Chron. 10. 3. distressed; Isa. 51. 9. pierced; Luke 10. 30. beat

WRATH, Gen. 49. 7. Ex. 32. 10, 11. Num. 16. 46. w. gone out from
Deut. 32. 27. feared w. of the enemy
Neh. 13. 18. bring more w. on Israel
Job 5. 2. w. killeth the foolish man
Prov. 16. 14. w. of a king as mes.
Isa. 54. 8. in a little w. I hid my face
Matt. 3. 7. flee from w. to come
Rom. 2. 5. treasure up w. against
5. 9. saved from w. through him
12. 19. give place unto w.
Eph. 2. 3. by nature children of w.
4. 26. let not the sun go down on your w.
1 Thes. 1. 10. delivered from the w.
2. 16. w. is come on them to the
1 Tim. 2. 8. holy hands without w.
Heb. 11. 27. not fearing w. of king
Jas. 1. 19. slow to speak, slow to w.
20. w. of man worketh not right.
Rev. 6. 16. from w. of the Lamb
12. 12. having great w. because
14. 8. wine of w. of her fornication, 18. 3.
Ezra 8. 22. his wrath, Ps. 2. 5, 12. & 78. 38. Jer. 7. 29. & 10. 10. Rev. 6. 17.
Num. 25. 11. my wrath, Ps. 95. 11. Isa. 10. 6. & 60. 10. Ezek. 7. 14. Hos. 5. 10.
Ps. 38. 1. thy wrath, 85. 3. & 88. 7, 16. & 9. 46. & 90. 9, 11. & 102. 10.
89. 38. wroth, Isa. 54. 9. & 57. 17.
R. V. Num. 11. 33; Deut. 11. 17; 2 Chron. 29. 10; 30. 8; Job 36. 13; 40. 11; Ps. 55. 3; 78. 31; Prov. 14. 29; Jer. 44. 8. anger; Deut. 32. 27. provocation; Job 5. 2; Prov. 12. 16; 27. 3. vexation; Ps. 58. 9. burning

WREST, Ex. 23. 2. 2 Pet. 3. 16.
WRESTLE, Gen. 32. 24, 25. Eph. 6. 12.
WRETCHED, Rom. 7. 24. Rev. 3. 17.
WRINKLE, Job 16. 8. Eph. 5. 27.
WRITE, Ex. 34. 1, 27. Deut. 27. 3. Isa. 3. 8. Jer. 30. 2. Hab. 2. 2.
Deut. 6. 9. w. them upon the posts
Prov. 3. 3. w. them on the table of thine heart, 7. 3.
Jer. 31. 33. I will w. it in their hearts
Ps. 102. 18. be written for the generation
Prov. 22. 20. have not I w. to thee
Eccl. 12. 10. that which was w.
Dan. 12. 1. shall be found w. in book
1 Cor. 10. 11. w. for our admonition
2 Cor. 3. 3. ministered by us, w. not with ink, but with the Spirit
Heb. 12. 23. are w. in heaven, Luke 10. 20.
R. V. Few changes, and chiefly to wrote

WRONG, Ps. 105. 14. Jer. 22. 3, 13.
Matt. 20. 13. I do thee no w. didst
1 Cor. 6. 7. why not rather take w., 8.
Col. 3. 25. that doeth w. shall receive
2 Cor. 7. 2. wronged, Phile. 18.
Prov. 8. 36. wrongeth his own soul
R. V. Jer. 22. 13. injustice; Hab. 1. 4. perverted

WROUGHT, 1 Sam. 6. 6. & 14. 45. Ps. 139. 15. curiously w. in lowest
Ezek. 29. 9. I w. for my name's sake, 22.
John 3. 21. his works are w. in God
2 Cor. 5. 5. that hath w. us for the selfsame thing is God
Eph. 1. 20. which he w. in Christ
1 Pet. 4. 3. have w. will of Gentiles
R. V. Ex. 26. 36; 27. 16; 36. 1. work; Deut. 17. 2. doeth; 1 Kings 16. 25; 2 Kings 3. 2; 2 Chron. 21, 6; 34. 13. did; 2 Sam. 18. 13. dealt; Jonah 1. 11. grow; Ps. 78. 43. set; Matt. 20. 12. spent; 2 Thes. 3. 8. working

Y

YARN, Solomon brought out of East, 1 Kings 10. 28.
2 Chron. 1. 16. merchants received linen y.
R. V. 1 Kings 10. 28; 2 Chron. 1. 16. droves
YE, wherefore look so sadly, Gen. 40. 7.
Matt. 5. 13. y. are the salt of earth
YEA, yea, nay, nay, Matt. 5. 37.
2 Cor. 1. 18. y. and nay
20. y. and amen
YEAR, Gen. 1. 14. & 47. 9.
Ex. 7. 7. Moses was fourscore y. old
Lev. 12. 6. sh. bring lamb of first y.
Num. 1. 3. from twenty y. old and upward
Deut. 8. 2. God led thee forty y. in
Josh. 5. 6. chil. of Is. walk. forty y.
Judg. 3. 11. land had rest forty y.
Ruth 1. 1. dwelt there about ten y.
1 Sam. 1. 7. he did so y. by y. when
2 Sam. 14. 28. A. dw. two y. in Jer.
1 Kings 5. 11. Solomon gave to Hiram y. by y.
2 Kings 1. 17. in second y. of Jehoram
1 Chron. 21. 12. either three y. famine, or
2 Chron. 8. 13. three times in y.; or
Ezra 1. 1. in first y. of Cyrus of Persia
Neh. 1. 1. twent y., I was in Shus.
Esth. 1. 3. third y. he ma. a decree
Job 10. 5. are thy y. as man's days
Ps. 90. 4. thousand y. in thy sight are but as yesterday
10. our y. are threescore and
Prov. 10. 27. y. of the wicked shall be shortened
Eccl. 6. 3. so that his y. be many
Isa. 6. 1. In y. Uz. died I saw Lord
Jer. 17. 8. not care. in y. of drought
Ezek. 1. 2. fifth y. of King Jehoiac.
Dan. 1. 5. so nourish. them three y.
Joel 2. 2. ev. to y. of many genera.
Amos 1. 1. two y. before the earth.
Mic. 6. 6. come with calves of a y. old?
Hab. 3. 2. thy work in midst of y.
Hag. 1. 1. in second y. of Da. came
Zech. 14. 16. go up y. to y. to wor.
Mal. 3. 4. offerings, as in former y.
Matt. 9. 20. an issue of bl. twenty y.
Mark 5. 42. she was age of twelve y.
Luke 4. 19. to preach accep. y. of Lord
John 2. 20. forty and six y. was the temple in building
Acts 4. 22. the man was ab. fort. y
Rom. 15. 23. hav. gr. desire many y.
2 Cor. 8. 10. but to be forward a y.
Gal. 1. 18. aft. three y. went to Jer.
1 Tim. 5. 9. to num. und. threesc. y.

Heb. 1. 12. and thy *y*. shall not fail
2 Pet. 3. 8. and thous. *y*. as one day
Rev. 20. 2. Sa., bound him thous. *y*.
YESTERDAY, Job 8. 9. Hab. 13. 8.
YIELD, fruit after his kind, Gen.
1. 11.
Lev. 25. 19. land shall *y*. her fr., and
Num. 17. 8. rod of Aa. *y*. almonds
Deut. 11. 17. land *y*. not her fruit
2 Chron. 30. 8. *y*. yourselves unto
Lord
Neh. 9. 37. it *y*. increase to kings
Ps. 67. 6. shall earth *y*. her increase
Prov. 12. 12. root of right. *y*. fruit
Eccl. 10. 4. *y*. pacifi. great offences
Isa. 5. 10. ten acres sh. *y*. one bath
Jer. 17. 8. nei. shall cease fr. *y*. fruit
Ezek. 34. 27. earth sh. *y*. her incre.
Hos. 8. 7. the bud shall *y*. no meal
Joel 2. 22. fig tree and vi. *y*. stren.
Hab. 3. 17. altho. fields *y*. no meat
Matt. 27. 50. Jesus *y*. up the ghost
Mark 4. 7. choked it, it *y*. no fruit
Acts 23. 21. do not thou *y*. to them
Rom. 6. 13. but *y*. yourselves unto
God
Heb. 12. 11. it *y*. peaceable fruit
Jas. 3. 12. no fount. bo. *y*. salt wat.
Rev. 22. 2. tree of life *y*. her fruit
R. V. Num. 17. 8. bare ; Acts 5. 10.
gave ; Rom. 16. 19. presented
YOKE, break from thy neck, Gen.
27. 40.
Lev. 26. 13. brok. bands of your *y*.
Num. 19. 2. on which nev. came *y*.
Deut. 28. 48. put *y*. of iron on thy n.
1 Sam. 11. 7. they took a *y*. of oxen
14. 14. a *y*. of oxen might plow
1 Kings 12. 4. thy father made our
y. grievous

2 Chron. 10. 11. 1 will put more to
your *y*.
Job 1. 3. J. had fiv. hun. *y*. of oxen
Isa. 9. 4. hast brok. *y*. of his burd.
Jer. 2. 20. of old I ha. broken thy *y*.
Lam. 1. 14. *y*. of my trans. is bound
Ezek. 30. 18. break there *y*. of Egy.
Hos. 11. 4. as they had taken off *y*.
Nah. 1. 13. now will I break his *y*.
Matt. 11. 30. for my *y*. is easy, and
Luke 14. 19. I bought five *y*. of oxen
Acts 15. 10. put *y*. on disciples' neck
Gal. 5. 1. be not entangled with *y*.
1 Tim. 6. 1. as many as under *y*.
R. V. Jer. 27. 2 ; 28. 10, 12, 13. bar or
bars ; 1 Sam. 14. 14 ——
YOU only have I known, Amos 3.
2.
Luke 10. 16. heareth *y*. heareth me
13. 28. and *y*. yourselves thrust
out
2 Cor. 12. 14. I seek not *yours* but *y*.
Eph. 2. 1. *y*. hath he quickened
Col. 1. 21. *y*. that were sometime
Luke 6. 20. *y*. is the kingdom of
God
1 Cor. 3. 22. all are *y*. and ye are
Christ's, 23.
YOUNG, I have been, Ps. 37. 25.
Isa. 40. 11. gently lead those with *y*.
1 Tim. 5. 1. entreat the *younger*
14. I will that *y*. women marry
1 Pet. 5. 5. ye *y*. submit to elder
Gen. 8. 21. the imagination of man
is evil from his *youth*
1 Kings 18. 12. the Lord from my *y*.
Job 13. 26. possess iniquities of
my *y*.
Ps. 25. 7. sins of my *y*.
103. 5. thy *y*. is renewed as eagle's

Eccl. 11. 9. O young man, in thy *y*.
10. childhood and *y*. are vanity
Jer. 2. 2. the kindness of thy *y*.
1 Tim. 4. 12. man despise thy *y*.
Prov. 7. 7. *youths*, Isa. 40. 30.
2 Tim. 2. 22. flee *youthful* lusts
R. V. 1 Sam. 20. 22. boy ; Mark 7.
25 ; 10. 13. little ; Acts 20. 12. lad ;
Job 29. 4. ripeness ; 30. 12. rabble

Z

ZEAL for Lord, 2 Kings 10. 16.
Ps. 69. 9. the *z*. of thine house hath
119. 139. my *z*. hath consumed me
Isa. 9. 7. *z*. of the Lord will perform
59. 17. I was clad with *z*. as a
cloak
63. 15. where is thy *z*. and stren.
Rom. 10. 2. they have a *z*. for God
2 Cor. 7. 11. *z*. yea, what revenge
Phil. 3. 6. concerning *z*. persecut.
Num. 25. 13. was *zealous* for his
God
Acts 22. 3. I was *z*. towards God as
Tit. 2. 14. people *z*. of good works
Rev. 3. 19. therefore be *z*. and re-
pent
Gal. 4. 18. good to be *zealously* affected in a good thing
R. V. Num. 25. 11, 13. jealous
ZION, 2 Sam. 5. 7. 1 Kings 8. 1. for
Jerusalem, temple, or church,
2 Kings 19. 31. Ps. 2. 6. & 9. 11. &
14. 7. & 48. 2, 11, 12. & 146. 10. & 147.
12. Isa. 1. 27. & 2. 3. & 60. 14. & 62.
1. and in about seventy other
places

CURIOUS FACTS AND INTERESTING INFORMATION
ABOUT THE BIBLE

The 66 Books or sub-divisions }   1,189 Chapters,
comprising the Old and New }   31,093 Verses,
Testaments contain: }   773,692 Words,
   3,586,489 Letters.

The Shortest Verse in the Bible is the 35th in the
11th Chapter of St. John.
The Longest Verse in the Bible is the 9th in the
9th Chapter of Esther.
The Middle Verse in the Bible is the 8th in the
118th Chapter of Psalms.

The 21st Verse of the 7th Chapter of Ezra con-
tains all the letters of the Alphabet except " j."
The 8th, 15th, 21st, and 31st Verses of the 107th
Psalm are alike.

Every Verse in the 136th Psalm has the same end-
ing.
The Longest Chapter is the 119th Psalm.
The Shortest Chapter is the 117th Psalm.

The word "Lord" occurs 7736 times in the Old
and New Testaments.
The word "God" occurs 4370 times in the Old
and New Testaments.
The words "Boy" and "Boys" are mentioned 3
times as follows: Gen. 25. 27 ; Joel 3. 3 ; Zech. 8. 5.
The words "Girl" and "Girls" are mentioned 2
times as follows: Joel 3. 3 ; Zech. 8. 5.
The name of "God" is not mentioned in the
Book of Esther, or in the Song of Solomon (A. V.).
The 19th Chapter of II. Kings and the 37th Chap-
ter of Isaiah are practically alike.

OLD TESTAMENT CHRONOLOGY.

I. FROM "THE BEGINNING" TO THE DELUGE.

SUBJECTS.	EVENTS.	USSHER'S DATES.
CREATION and **EARLIEST MAN.**	The Creation of the world. The formation of lands and seas. The Creation of plants and animals. The Creation of Man.	B.C. 4004
MAN in his **EARLIEST HOME.**	The Garden of Eden, in the region of the Tigris and the Euphrates; ancient Mesopotamia and Babylonia. The first sin. Expulsion of Adam and Eve from Eden.	4004
CAIN and **ABEL.**	Cain born, perhaps in . . . . Abel born, perhaps in . . . . Cultivation of the soil, and keeping of flocks begun. Abel murdered by his brother Cain	4002 4001 3875
From the **DEATH** of **ABEL** to the **DELUGE.**	Seth born, Adam being 130 years old . . . . Enoch born . . . . Methuselah born . . . . Adam dies, being 930 years old . . . . Enoch translated, being 365 years old . . . . Seth dies, aged 912 years . . . . Noah born . . . . Methuselah dies, aged 969 years	3874 3382 3317 3074 3017 2962 2948 2348
THE DELUGE.	Noah enters into the ark, being 600 years old . . . . Noah leaves the ark, after dry land appears . . . . . Traditions of the Deluge are found among all races. The Babylonian story of the Deluge was found, written on clay tablets, in the ruins of Nineveh. It differs little in its main points from that in the Bible.	2348 2347
THE NEW START.	The Covenant with Noah, immediately following the Deluge	2347

NOTE: There is great uncertainty among Bible scholars as to the dates in this period. The dates we have given here are those found in the margins of many of our Bibles. They were calculated by Archbishop Ussher, of Armagh, in A.D. 1650–1654, and first put into the Bible in 1701. While they are based on the statements in the Bible they are not a part of the inspired word.

II. FROM THE DELUGE TO THE EXODUS.

EVENTS IN SCRIPTURE HISTORY.	PLACES.	DATES. Beecher.	Ussher.	Others.	OTHER HISTORICAL EVENTS.
			B.C.		
THE DELUGE	....	?	2348	or	Seventh ruler of China died 2257.
The confusion of tongues	Babylonia	....	2247	long	
Death of Noah	Arabia	....	1998	before	Nineveh built 2218 (?).
Abram, Birth of, at Ur	Chaldea	(2003)	1996	....	Zoroaster 2115 (?).
Abram moves from Ur to Haran	Mesopotamia	....	1926	....	Celts in Europe about 2000.
The call of Abram	"	**1928**	1921	2250	
Abram and Lot move to Canaan	Canaan	**1928**	1921	to	Hyksos in Egypt in time of Abraham, probably. Dates vary from 2100-1675.
Abram and Lot separate	"	**1924**	1918	1906	
Lot captured by Chedorlaomer	Sodom	**1921**	1913		
The Covenant with Abraham	Hebron	**1920**	1912		
Birth of Ishmael	"	**1917**	1910		Sesostris I, Egypt, 1980-1935 (?).
Renewal of Covenant. Change of Abram's name to Abraham	"	**1904**	1897		Hammurabi (Amraphel of Gen. 14:1), and his code, contemporary with Abraham. The dates vary from 2300 B.C. to 1900. His Monument discovered at Susa, (Shushan) of Persia (in A.D. 1901, 2) contains the earliest known writing on stone, with laws something like those in Leviticus.
Destruction of *Sodom*	Sodom	**1904**	1897		
Isaac, Birth of	Moab	**1903**	1896		
Ishmael sent away	....	**1901**(?)	1892		
Covenant with Abimelech	....	**1900**(?)	1891		
Moab and Ammon born	....	**1899**(?)	1897		
Ishmael marries an Egyptian	....	**1895**(?)	....		
Sacrifice of Isaac	Moriah	**1879**	1871		
Death of Sarah	Hebron	**1866**	1860		
Abraham marries Keturah	....	**1865**(?)	....		
Marriage of Isaac and Rebekah	Lahai-roi	**1864**	1857		
Jacob and Esau, Birth of	Beersheba	**1844**	1837		
Death of Abraham	"	**1828**(?)	1822		
Esau sells his birthright	Lahai-roi	**1827**(?)	1804		
Isaac forbidden to enter Egypt goes to	Gerar	**1826**(?)	1804		
Esau marries Hittite wives	....	**1805**	1796		
Jacob obtains birthright blessing	Beersheba	**1784**(?)	1760	These dates are all only approximate.	
Jacob goes to Padan-aram. His vision at Bethel	....	**1784**(?)	1760		
Esau's Ishmaelite marriages	....	**1783**(?)	1760		Tel-el-Amarna letters, 15th century or earlier, 300 letters inscribed on clay tablets 2 by 3 inches, and sent between Palestine and Amarna in Egypt showing a general prevalence of dissatisfaction with the rule of Egypt.
Death of Ishmael	....	**1781**(?)	1773		
Jacob marries Leah and Rachel	Padan-aram	**1776**(?)	1753		
Birth of Jacob's children (except Benjamin)	"	**1775-1752**	1752-1739		
Joseph, Birth of	"	**1752**	1739		
Jacob returns to Canaan	....	**1747**	....		
Jacob wrestles with the angel	Peniel	**1747**	1739		
Birth of Benjamin and death of Rachel	Bethlehem	**1747**	1729		
Joseph sold into Egypt from	Dothan	**1736**	1718		
Joseph put in prison	Egypt	**1725**	1718		
Death of Isaac	Hebron	**1724**	1716		
Joseph interprets Pharaoh's dream	Egypt	**1723**	1716		
Joseph made prime minister	"	**1723**	1716		
The seven years of plenty begin	....	....	1716		
Birth of Manasseh and Ephraim	Egypt	....	....		
The seven years of famine begin	....	....	1709		The Israelites were shepherds in the fertile land of Goshen for 116 years, 1715-1599. Then they were slaves of the Egyptians for 100 years, 1599-1498.
Jacob and his family move to	Goshen in Egypt	**1715**	1706		
Death of Jacob	"	**1698**	1689	1300	
Death of Joseph	"	**1643**	1635	to	
Beginning of oppression of Israel	"	**1599**(?)	1573	1208	
Moses, Birth of	"	**1578**	1571		Others make the slavery in Egypt to continue much longer and the date of the Exodus to be between 1300 and 1200 B.C.
Exile of Moses begins	Arabia	**1539**	1531		
Call of Moses. Burning bush	"	**1499**	1492		
Plagues of Egypt	Egypt	**1499-8**	1492-1		
The first Passover	"	**1498**	1491		
THE EXODUS in April	....	**1498**	1491		

NOTE. The dates in this period are still more or less uncertain. The *New Encyc. Britannica* calls its dates only approximate. For instance, the 19th dynasty in which this period ends, begins in 1490, or 1320 according to different authorities.

The date of the Exodus depends partly on whether the Pharaoh of the Oppression was Thotmes III, or Rameses II. Most modern authorities incline to Rameses II, and a date for the Exodus about 200 years later. Beecher, in his *Dated Events* reconciles the history by giving Rameses the earlier date, but still making him the "Pharaoh of the Oppression." He puts an interrogation point after all these dates.

On the whole there is not better authority than Beecher in this book. He does not differ much from Ussher. We give other authorities in another column.

III. FROM EGYPT TO PALESTINE. — *40 years.*

PERSONS.	EVENTS.	PLACES.	Beecher.	Ussher.	Others.
	The Exodus, in April				1300 or 1200
	The Pillar of fire	Arabia	1498	1491	
	The giving of the manna	"	1498	1491	
MOSES.	The giving of the law	Mt. Sinai	1498	1491	
	The golden calf	"	1498	1491	
	The Tabernacle set up	"	1497	1490	
AARON.	The ceremonial law given	"	1497	1490	
	Nadab and Abihu	Wilderness of Arabia			Most scholars incline to these later dates and Rameses II as the Pharaoh of the Oppression.
CALEB.	Wandering for 40 years in Wilderness.	Between branches of Red Sea	1498–1459	1491–1451	
	New start for Canaan from	Kadesh			
JOSHUA.	Waters from the rock	Meribah	1459	1452	
	Death of Aaron on	Mt. Hor	1459	1452	
	Brazen serpent	The Arabah	1459	1452	
	Balaam's blessing	Moab	1459	1452	
	Death of Moses	Nebo-Pisgah	1459	1451	

IV. THE CONQUEST OF PALESTINE.

PERSONS.	EVENTS.	PLACES.	Beecher.	Ussher.	Others.
	Passing over Jordan opposite	Jericho	1458	1451	
	The Fall of Jericho	"	1458	1451	
JOSHUA.	Defeat at Ai	Near Jericho	1458	1451	
	Law read from Ebal and Gerizim	Shechem	1458	1451	
CALEB.	Conquest of Canaan		1458–1449	1451–1443	See above.
	Cities of Refuge appointed		1453	1444	
	Joshua renews the covenant	Shechem	1451 (?)	1427	
	Death of Joshua	Timnath-serah	1450 (?)	1427	

V. THE PERIOD OF THE JUDGES. *See Notes below.*

JUDGES AND EVENTS.	PLACES.	Years of Oppression.	Years of Peace.	YEARS B. C. FROM BEECHER.
Oppression of Chushan-Rishathaim, from Mesopotamia (during the last years of Joshua).	Palestine	8		1441–1434
I. OTHNIEL, Son-in-law of Caleb, Deliverer. Judge 14 years	Near Hebron			1434
Peace and Prosperity			37	1434–1397
Oppression by Eglon of Moab	So. Palestine	18		1397–1380
II. EHUD of Benjamin	Near Jericho			1380
Peace and Prosperity			10	1380–1370
Oppression by Jabin of Canaan	Northern tribes	20		1370–1351
Oppression by the Philistines, during the last 3 years of Jabin's oppression.	Southern tribes			1353–1351
III. DEBORAH of Ephraim IV. BALAK of Naphtali } deliverers from Jabin	No. Palestine			1351
V. SHAMGAR of Judah, delivers from Philistines	S. W. Palestine			1351
Peace and Prosperity			22	1351–1329
Oppression by Midianites	So. Galilee	7		1329–1323
VI. GIDEON of Manasseh, Deliverer and Judge	So. Galilee			1323
Peace and Prosperity			24	1323–1299
VII. ABIMELECH, Prince of Israel for 3 years	Shechem		3	1298–1296
VIII. TOLA of hill country of	Ephraim		23	1295–1273
Oppression by Philistines begun	S. W. Israel			1283
IX. JAIR was a judge of Israel E. of Jordan.	Gilead		22	1272–1251
X. SAMSON — exploits as judge	S. W. Israel		20	1250–1231
Oppression by Ammonites beyond Jordan	East Israel	18		1230–1213
XI. JEPHTHAH, judge 6 years beyond Jordan	Gilead		6	1212–1207
XII. IBZAN, judge from Bethlehem 7m. N. W. of Nazareth	Galilee		7	1206–1200
XIII. ELON of Zebulun, a part of	Galilee		10	1199–1190
XIV. ABDON, a judge for 8 years in	Ephraim		8	1189–1182
Oppression by Philistines began again	W. Israel			1182
XV. ELI, the high priest acts as judge. Shiloh	Benjamin		40	1182–1142
XVI. SAMUEL called to be prophet	Shiloh			1160?
Judge of Israel, or chief citizen	Israel			1141–1065?

NOTE I. The dates given here are from Prof. Willis J. Beecher's *Dated Events of the Old Testament*, and for the most part do not vary very largely from those given by Ussher in many of our Bibles. The tendency of scholars is to shorten this period, and to make the earlier dates much later than those given above. No definite and certain chronology is possible.

NOTE II. It is entirely probable that many of the Oppressions and Deliverances were not successive, but took place at the same time in different parts of the country. Prof. Moore in *Int. Crit. Com.* is right when he says " They were, in fact, without exception, local struggles; and it is not only conceivable, but highly probable, that while one part of the land was enjoying security under its judge, other tribes were groaning under the foreign yoke." Hence the mere adding together of the figures given in the book would not give the correct length of the period.

VI. THE UNITED KINGDOM.

Period 120 years $\begin{cases} 1103 & 983 \\ 1057 & 937 \end{cases}$ or

EVENTS IN SCRIPTURE HISTORY.	PLACES.	DATES.			OTHER EVENTS.
		Beecher.	Ussher.	Revised from Assyrian Records.	
Saul's Kingdom.					
Israel asks for a king...............	....	1103(?)	1095	......	Chow dynasty in
SAUL chosen and made king........	Gilgal	1102	1095	1057	China brings us to
Saul's victory over Ammon.........	....	1102	1095	......	historic ground,
Birth of David................	Bethlehem	1092	1085	1047	1123–255.
Saul's final rejection and break with Samuel.................	....	1078(?)	1079	......	
Private anointing of David..........	Bethlehem	1077(?)	1065	......	
David becomes Saul's minstrel.....	....	1074(?)	1063	......	
David and Goliath	Ephes-dammim	1073(?)	1063	......	
David's marriage to Michal	....	1071(?)	1062	......	
David's outlaw life, 7 years.........	....	1068–1063	1062–1055	......	
David spares Saul's life (skirt)	Engedi.........	1066(?)	1060	......	
Death of Samuel.....................	Ramah.........	1065(?)	1060	......	
David and Nabal.....................	Carmel	1065(?)	1059	......	
The spear and the cruse incident....	....	1065(?)	1058	......	
David among the Philistines	Ziklag........	1064	1057	......	
Death of Saul and Jonathan.........	Gilboa..........	1063	1056	......	
David's Kingdom.					
DAVID becomes king in Judah	Hebron..........	1063	1056	1017	Hiram, King of
War between David and *Ish-bosheth*.	....	1063–1056	1056–1048	......	Tyre, contempo-
David king over all Israel...........	....	1055	1048	......	rary of David and
Jerusalem becomes capital.					Solomon.
Period of war	....	1055–1043	1048–1042	......	
Ark brought to Jerusalem...........	....	1042(?)	1042	1003	
The great promise to David..........	Jerusalem......	1041(?)	1042	......	Homer thought by
Birth of Solomon	"	1041(?)	1033	......	some to be con-
Preparation for building the temple.	"	....	....	......	temporary with
Absalom's rebellion..................	....	1023	1023	......	David.
Solomon anointed and proclaimed..	Jerusalem......	1022	1015	......	
Death of David	"	1022	1015	977	
Solomon's Kingdom.					
SOLOMON becomes real king.........	Jerusalem......	1022	1015	977	Homer, 1000(?)
Temple foundations laid.............	"	1019	1012	......	Zoroaster, 1000(?)
Temple dedicated.....................	"	1011	1004	966	
Visit of Queen of Sheba to Solomon.	"	995(?)	995	......	Shishak in Egypt,
Jeroboam flees to Shishak in Egypt.	....	986(?)	980	.....	who invades Is-
Death of Solomon....................	Jerusalem......	983	975	937	rael.

NOTE ON THE DIVIDED KINGDOM.

The dates are given according to Prof. Willis J. Beecher in his *Dated Events of the Old Testament History*, the most thorough and scholarly study of the subject including the Assyrian Canon. There are also given the dates of Arbp. Ussher, as in many Bibles ; and of Hastings' and other Bible Dictionaries, as they interpret the Assyrian Canon, and make the division of the kingdom to begin at various dates from 939 to 931.

THE MOVEMENT OF THE HISTORY. FIVE GREAT PERIODS.

I. **The United Kingdom.** Three kings. 120 years, 1102–982.

II. **The Divided Kingdom.** $\begin{cases} \text{JUDAH.} \text{ One dynasty. 11 kings. 1 queen} \\ \text{ISRAEL.} \text{ Nine dynasties. 19 kings.} \end{cases}$ 260 years to 720.

III. **Judah. Alone.** 8 kings, David's dynasty 136 years, 722–586.

IV. **The Exile.** 70 years, 605–536.

V. **The Return. The New Nation.** 536–400 and on.

VII. THE DIVIDED KINGDOMS OF JUDAH AND ISRAEL.

JUDAH. One dynasty (David's). 11 kings and one queen.

ISRAEL. 9 Dynasties. 19 kings.

Periods: Judah nearly 400 years. Israel about 260 years. Judah alone 136 years.

JUDAH — PROPHETS	JUDAH — KINGS AND EVENTS	YEARS OF REIGN	Beecher	Hastings B.D.	Usher	Assyr. Eponym.	YEARS OF REIGN	ISRAEL — KINGS AND EVENTS	ISRAEL — PROPHETS	CONTEMPORARY HISTORY
	Rehoboam, 17 years......... Influx of Levites, etc., from Israel. Rehoboam forsakes Jehovah. Invasion by Shishak......	1, 3, 5, 17	982, 980, 978, 965	939, 936, 934, 922	975, 957, 955	931, 930, 927, 914	1	Jeroboam I, 22 years. Semi-idolatry established.	Ahijah.	Shishak monument.
	Abijam, 3 years.........	1, 3	962, 961	919, 918	954	911, 910	3, 5, 18	Exodus of religious people to Judah.		
	Asa, 41 years............ Land at rest 10 years. Invasion by Zerah the Ethiopian......... Great revival and reformation. War with Israel.........	3, 14, 15, 16, 26, 27	960, 949, 948, 947, 937, 936	917, 894, 893	953, 941, 930, 929	909, 898, 897, 886, 885	21, 22, 1, 2, 12, 13, 14, 24	Nadab, parts of 2 years. Baasha, 24 years. Civil war with Judah. Elah. Parts of 2 years. Zimri, 7 days. Omri, 12 years. Great enlargement of kingdom.		Moabite stone naming Omri.
	Decline.	38	925	882	918	874	1	Ahab, 22 years.		Shalmanezer II, Assyria.
	Jehoshaphat, 25 years......... Wide extended revival. Outward prosperity. Decline through alliance with Jezebel.	41, 16, 17	921, 905, 904	878, 862, 861	917, 854, 853	870, 854, 853	12, 21, 22	Marries Jezebel. Idolatry introduced. Religious persecution. Ahaziah. Co-regnant, 2 years. Jehoram, 12 years.	Elijah.	Battle of Karkar, 854, Assyr.
	Jehoram, Co-regnant, 4 years. Alone, 4 years.......	22, 25, 1, 4	900, 897	857, 854	893	849, 846	2, 5, 8	Mesha or Moab revolts.		
	Ahaziah. Part of one year..	5, 8, 1	893	850	885	842	12	Jehu, 28 years. Zealous reformer. Destroys house of Ahab.	Elisha.	Black Obelisk, with name of Jehu.
	Athaliah, 6 years......... Murder of seed-royal. Baal worship. Temple desecrated.	1, 2	892	849	884	841				907 (?) Homer, Hesiod. 884 Lycurgus.
(son of Jehoiada.)	Joash, 40 years..........	6	886	843	878	835	7	Tributary to Assyria.		878 (?) } Carthage founded. 858 (?) }

Prophets (left margin, bottom to top): **Zechariah.** | **Amos.** | **Isaiah.** | **Micah.**

Prophets (center, spanning): **Jonah.** | **Hosea.** | **Amos.**

Judah — events	Judah yrs	(date)	(date)	(date)	(date)	Israel yrs	Israel — events	World events
Temple and its worship restored.	23 / 37	864 / 850	821 / 807	856 / 842	813 / 799	28 — 1 · 15 · 17	**Jehoahaz**, 17 years. *Jehoash.* Co-regnant, 3 years. Hazael's expedition. **Jehoash**, sole ruler 16 years. Death of Elisha.	Sheshonk III, Egypt. 820 (?) Lycurgus, Sparta. 814 Macedonia founded.
Amaziah......	40	847						
Defeat of Edom......		846	803	840	795	1		814 (?) Carthage founded.
Conquest by Jehoash of Israel. Nominal ruler under suzerainty of Israel.	14 / 15	833 / 832	804	825	782	16 — 1 · 15	Victories over Damascus. Conquest of Judah. **Jeroboam II**, 41 years.	797. Damascus taken by Assyrians.
Death of Amaziah...... INTERREGNUM for 11 years..	29	818		811	767	27	Suzerain of all peoples from Mediterranean to Euphrates.	
Uzziah, 52 years ...... Also called Azariah.	11 / 1	806 / 792	801		741	I — 41	Death of Jeroboam. INTERREGNUM, 22 years.	Blank in Assyrian history. Confusion in Egyptian. First Olympiad, 776 B. C.
Succeeds Jeroboam as suzerain of region......	15	791 / 769	763 / 763	773 / 772	741	22 — 1	Zechariah, 6 months. Shallum, 1 month. Menahem, 10 years.	The Jewish Cyclopedia gives 2 reigns of Jeroboam II, 825–799 and 788–773; Israel being under Syria 799 to 788. Rome founded 753. Draco.
Leprosy of Uzziah (?)...... *Jotham* regent 23 years......	16 / 38, 39 / 40	768 / 767	762	772	741			
Eclipse of sun by which Assyrian dates are determined. June 15, 763 B. C.	1							
	44 / 49	763 / 758	763 / 752	761	738 / 737	5 / 10 — 1 · 2	Pekahiah, 2 years.	Expedition of Pul or Tiglath-pileser of Damascus, captures Damascus and Samaria. 733 (?)
Jotham sole king 16 years	52	755	750	759	736	1 / 2	Pekah, 20 years.	
Invasion by Israel and Rezin of Damascus...... Ahaz, 16 years......	23 / 1, 15 / 16	754	749	742	735	16 / 17	Invasion of Judah.	The Jewish Cycl. gives 2 reigns for Pekah, 759–744, and 735–730. Time between Israel under Menahem II, under Assyria.
Tributary to Assyria......	3	740 / 730	741	742	734	18	Deportation by Tiglath-pileser. Death of Pekah.	
	13 / 16	738 / 736	730 / 727	730 / 726	734	20	*Hoshea*, governor.	
Hezekiah, 29 years...... Great Passover......	1 / 2	726 / 723 / 722				1 · 4 — 5	Hoshea, king 9 years.	*Taylor Cylinder.*

VII. THE DIVIDED KINGDOMS OF JUDAH AND ISRAEL (Continued).

JUDAH					DATES			ISRAEL			CONTEMPORARY
PROPHETS.	KINGS AND EVENTS.	YEARS OF REIGN.	Beecher.	Hastings B.D.	Ussher.	Assyr. Eponym.	YEARS OF REIGN.	KINGS AND EVENTS.	PRO-PHETS.	HISTORY.
Isaiah	First invasion of Sennacherib.	4	720	....	....	....	7	First siege and capture of Samaria.		Year in Rome begun with January, 713. Sargon I, Assyria, 722. Sennacherib, Assyria, 705.
	Hezekiah's sickness. Second invasion of Sennacherib.	6	718	722 } 721 }	....	722	9	{ Final FALL of SAMARIA. { End of Kingdom of Israel.		First Mikado in Japan, 660–585.
	First invasion of Sennacherib.	14	710	....	697	....				Esarhaddon, Assyria, 681.
	Manasseh, 55 years.	23 29	701 684	....	....	....				Second Messenian war, 685–668.
	Death of Isaiah (?). Manasseh carried to Babylon (?).	16 47	679 648	....	....	....				Byzantium founded, 659.
	Manasseh's return and reformation.	48 55	647	....	....	....				Scythian invasion.
	Amon, 2 years.	1 2	639	....	642	....				Median Empire independent, 640. Draco's legislation, 624 [621?].
Jeremiah	Josiah, 31 years.	1	638	....	640	....				"Buddha," India, 623–543. Public beginning, July, 594.
	Josiah begins reforms.	12 13	627 626	....	....	....				Expedition of Pharaoh Necho, 608.
	Josiah's great reformation } Reformation passover }	17	622	....	....	....				Destruction of Nineveh, 606.
	Jehoahaz, 3 months.	31	608	....	609	609				Nebuchadnezzar, 604.
	Jehoiakim, 11 years. *First captivity begins.*	1	607	....	609	609				Carchemish, 603. Daniel in exile, 605. Expounds king's dream, 603.
Daniel	First deportation. Second deportation.	3 10 11	605 598 597	....	606	606				
Ezekiel	Jehoiachin, 3 months.			....	598	598				Phœnicians circumnavigate Africa, 604.
Joel	The great deportation. Zedekiah, 11 years.	1 1 9	597	....	598	598				Solon's legislation, 594. Seven wise men in Greece, 593.
Zephaniah	Siege of Jerusalem. Destruction of Jerusalem and the Temple. Beginning of great captivity	11 11	588 586 586	....	588 586 586	....				Pythian games begin, 588.
Nahum										
Habakkuk										

Authorities are practically agreed on these dates.

116

VIII. THE CAPTIVITY TO THE END OF THE OLD TESTAMENT.
Period about 200 years.

PROPHETS.	JEWISH EVENTS.	DATES.			CONTEMPORARY HISTORY.
		Beecher.	Hastings.	Usher.	
Jeremiah. Obadiah. Ezekiel. Daniel.	*First* captivity......................	605	......	606	
	Second captivity....................	597	......	....	
	Final captivity.....................	586	586	586	Nebuchadnezzar besieges Tyre,585. Æsop.
	Last of Ezekiel's prophecies.........	......	......	571	Evil Merodach, Babylon, 562.
	Jehoiachin released..................	561	......	....	Temple of Diana, Ephesus, 552. Public library at Athens, 544. Babylon taken by Cyrus, 539.
	Belshazzar's feast....................	539	......	538	First year of Cyrus, 538.
	Daniel in den of lions................	538	......	538	Pythagoras, 540–510.
	The decree for the return............	538	538	536	
	End of first reckoning of 70 years...				Pisistratus, Athens, 560–527.
Haggai. Zechariah.	**First return.** 50,000 under ZERUBBABEL.	538	538–7	....	Nabonidus, Babylon, 556.
	Foundation of Temple laid..........	537–6	536	....	Darius in Babylon, 521.
	Long delay	....	....	....	
	Building of Temple resumed........	520	520	....	Beginning of Roman republic, 510.
	TEMPLE DEDICATED	516	516	516	Marathon, 490.
	End of second reckoning of 70 years	......	......	....	Xerxes (Ahasuerus), 489.
	No knowledge of events until.......	......	......	....	Invasion of Greece, 480.
	Feast of Ahasuerus (Xerxes)........	483	......	....	Herodotus, Socrates.
Malachi.	Esther becomes queen................	479	......	....	Xenophon, Plato.
	Haman's plot........................	474	......	....	First decemvirate, Rome, 451.
	Second return under Ezra....	458	458	....	Pericles, Athens, 444.
	Return under NEHEMIAH	......	......	....	Parthenon, Athens, 443–438.
	Wall of Jerusalem rebuilt	444	445	....	First Peloponnesian war,431.
	Reforms.............................	......	......	...	Xenophon's retreat, 401.
	Death of Nehemiah. After........	391	....|....		

NOTE. It will perhaps be easier to understand the double reckoning of the 70 years' captivity by the following diagram showing how it is reckoned as beginning at different points, and closing at equi-different points.

70 Years.

First Captivity began 605
Second Captivity began 597
Third Captivity and
    Temple Destroyed, 586

The Seventy Years of Exile foretold by Jeremiah.

537,6   First Return.

516 { Second Temple Completed.

IX. PERIOD BETWEEN THE TESTAMENTS.

B.C.	JEWISH HISTORY.	CONTEMPORARY HISTORY.	B.C.	JEWISH HISTORY (continued).	CONTEMPORARY HISTORY.
350	Jaddua, High Priest	Egypt a Persian Province.	149	....	Third Punic War: Rome.
359	....	Philip II of Macedon.	146	....	Greece a Roman Province.
336	....	Darius Codomannus, king of Persia.	141	Deliverance of Judea complete.	
		Alexander the Great.	109	Pharisees and Sadducees first mentioned.	
332	Alexander visits Jerusalem.	Alexandria in Egypt founded.	107	Aristobulus "king."	
331	Jews settle in Alexandria.	Battle of Arbela.	63	Pompey captures Jerusalem.	Judea annexed to Rome. Conspiracy of Catiline.
330	Onias I, High Priest.	End of Persian Empire.	58	Herod in Palestine.	Cæsar in Gaul.
320	Ptolemy takes Jerusalem.	Ptolemy I, Soter.	54	Crassus plunders Temple.	
312	Seleucidæ in Syria.	Seleucus I, Nicator.	48	....	Battle of Pharsalia.
301	Palestine under Egypt.	Battle of Ipsus.	47	Antipater procurator. Herod governor of Galilee.	Cæsar dictator at Rome.
284	Septuagint.				
264	....	First Punic War: Rome.	44	....	Cæsar assassinated.
261	....	Manetho, in Egypt.	40	Herod king of Judea.	
219	Beginning of War of Antiochus and Ptolemy.	Second Punic War: Rome.	37	Herod takes Jerusalem.	
			31	Earthquake in Judea.	BATTLE OF ACTIUM.
198	Antiochus the Great master of Palestine.		30	....	Egypt a Roman Province.
170	Tyranny of Antiochus Epiphanes.		29	....	Temple of Janus closed.
167	Revolt of Maccabees.		27	....	Augustus made Emperor.
166	Judas Maccabeus.		19	Herod begins rebuilding the Temple.	
165	Rededication of Temple.		4	Herod dies at Jericho.	

DATE OF THE BIRTH OF CHRIST.

Many people are greatly perplexed by the statement that Jesus was born four years before the time from which we count his birth, or on December 25, B.C. 5. The reason is that no one began to reckon dates generally from the birth of Christ till centuries had passed. The general method was from the founding of Rome (A.U.C.) and not till after Rome ceased to be the mistress of the world would people begin to think seriously of a change. Finally, in A.D. 526, a monk, Dionysius Exiguus, made the calculations, but made an error of four years. He placed the birth of Christ in the year of Rome 754. But Herod the Great, who slew the innocents of Bethlehem, died in April of the year of Rome 750, so that Jesus must have been born several months before. The date, December 25th, is generally accepted, but we cannot be sure of that. Since it is manifestly impossible to rectify the dates in all books and records throughout the world, we simply apply the true dates to the life of Christ, and say he was five years old at the close of A.D. 1. The following table may aid in making the matter clear.

Year of Rome (*Anno Urbis Conditæ* = A.U.C.)	749	750	751	752	753	754	755	756
Year of Our Lord (*Anno Domini* = A.D.)	B.C. 5	B.C. 4	B.C. 3	B.C. 2	B.C. 1	A.D. 1	A.D. 2	A.D. 3
Age of Jesus	birth	1st year	2d year	3d year	4th year	5th year	6th year	7th year

HARMONY OF THE LIFE OF CHRIST.

EVENTS.	PLACES.	DATES.	MATT.	MARK.	LUKE.	JOHN.
Pre-existence						1: 1-14
Genealogies			1:1-17		3: 23-28	
Birth of John the Baptist foretold	Jerusalem	Sept., B.C. 6			1: 5-23	
Annunciation to Mary	Nazareth	Mar., B.C. 5			1: 24-38	
Birth of John the Baptist	Judea	June, B.C. 5			1: 57-80	
Birth of Jesus	Bethlehem	Dec. 25, B.C. 5	1: 18-25		2: 1-20	
Presentation in the Temple at	Jerusalem	Feb. 2, B.C. 4			2: 22-39	
Visit of the Magi	Bethlehem	Early Feb., B.C. 4	2: 1-12			
Flight into Egypt		Feb., B.C. 4	2:13-23			
Childhood and youth	Nazareth	B.C. 2–A.D. 26	2:23		2: 39-52	
First passover he attended	Jerusalem	April, A.D. 8			2: 41-50	
Ministry of John the Baptist	Wilderness of Judea	Summer A.D. 26 to Mar. A.D. 28	3: 1-12	1: 1-8	3: 1-18	1: 19-28
Baptism of Jesus	Jordan	Jan. A.D. 27	3:13-17	1: 9-11	3: 21-23	1: 20-34
Temptation of Jesus	Wilderness of Judea	Jan.–Feb.	4: 1-11	1:12,13	4: 1-13	
		A.D. 27.				
First disciples won	Bethabara	February				1: 35-51
First miracle: Wedding at Cana	Cana	"				2: 1-12
First cleansing of the Temple	Jerusalem	April 11-17				2: 13-25
First recorded discourse: Nicodemus	"	"				3: 1-21
First ministry in Judea begun	Judea	Summer				3:22-36
First convers in Samaria: Jacob's Well	Sychar	December "				4: 1-42
Healing of the nobleman's son	Capernaum	"				4: 43-54

JOHN THE BAPTIST: Birth. Early Life. A.D. 26.

MINISTRY OF JESUS — Divisions / Years: Birth B.C. 4. Youth B.C. 4 to A.D. 26. Training for his work. A.D. 26-30 years—B.C. 4. Special Preparations A.D. 26. First Year A.D. 27. Year of Beginnings. Judean Ministry. Public Ministry.

The Great Galilean Ministry. — One Year and Nine Months.

Marginal bands (read vertically, left side):
- John's Public Ministry. March A.D. 28.
- JOHN THE BAPTIST IN PRISON. — AT MACHAERUS (one year). — Martyred March A.D. 29.

Section bands:
- ❋ SECOND YEAR A.D. 28. — YEAR OF FUNDAMENTAL PRINCIPLES.
- ❋ THIRD YEAR A.D. 29. — YEAR OF DEVELOPMENT. — GREAT DEEDS AMID GREAT OPPOSITION.

Event	Place	Date	Matthew	Mark	Luke	John
		A.D. 28.				
Passover	Macherus	March or April.				5: 1
Imprisonment of John the Baptist	Galilee	March	14: 3-5	6:17-18	3:19-20	
Beginning of Great Galilean Ministry	Nazareth	April.	4:12	1:14,15	4:14,15	
[First (?) rejection at Nazareth	Nazareth	"			4:16-30]	
Takes up residence at Capernaum.	Capernaum.		4:13-17		4:31	
Calls first disciples to follow him.	"		4:18-22	1:16-20	5: 1-11	
Cure of demoniac in Synagogue.	"	April, May		1:21-28	4:31-37	
Many miracles of healing	Capernaum and	April and	4:23-25; 8:14-17	1:29-39	4:38-44	
Cure of a leper	Galilee.	May		1:40-45	5:12-16	
Healing a paralytic.	Galilee.	May, June	9: 2-8	2: 1-12	5:17-26	
Call of Matthew: His feast.	Capernaum.		9: 9-17	2:13-22	5:27-39	
Healing at Pool of Bethesda.	Jerusalem.					5: 2-47
Man with withered hand.	Capernaum.	Midsummer	12: 1-14	2:23-3:6	6: 1-11	
Appointing of the twelve Apostles	Horns of Hattin.	"	10: 2-4	3:13-19	6:12-19	
The Sermon on the Mount.	"		Chs. 5-7		6:20-49	
Healing of the Centurion's servant.	Capernaum.		8: 5-13		7: 1-10	
Raising of the widow's son.	Nain.				7:11-17	
John the Baptist sends messengers to Jesus.	Galilee.		11: 2-19		7:18-35	
Warnings and Invitations (later?).	"		11:20-30			
Anointing of Jesus by the penitent woman.	"				7:36-50	
Another tour of Galilee.	Galilee.	Autumn			8: 1-3	
Blind and dumb demoniac.	Capernaum.	"	12:22-45			
Visit of his mother and brethren.	"	"	12:46-50	3:31-35	8:19-21	
Eight parables by the seaside	"	"	13: 1-53	4: 1-34	8: 4-18	
Stilling of the tempest.	Sea of Galilee.	"	8:18-27	4:35-41	8:22-25	
Restoration of the demoniac.	Gergesa.	"	8:28-34	5: 1-20	8:26-39	
Jairus' daughter raised: Woman cured.	Capernaum.	"	9:18-26	5:21-43	8:40-56	
Cure of two blind and one dumb.	"	"	9:27-34			
		A.D. 29.				
Second (?) rejection at Nazareth.	Nazareth.	Winter.	13:53-58	6: 1-6	(4:16-30)	
The twelve sent out to preach.	Galilee.		9:35-11:1	6: 6-13	9: 1-6	
Death of John the Baptist.	Macherus.	March.	14: 1-12	6:14-29	9: 7-9	
Feeding of the 5,000.	Bethsaida.	April.	14:13-21	6:30-46	9:10-17	6: 1-15
Jesus walks on the water.	Sea of Galilee.	"	14:22-33			6:16-21
Heals many sick	Gennesaret.		14:34,35	6:53-56		
Discourse on the Bread of Life	Capernaum.					6:22-71
Eating, with unwashed hands.	"		15: 1-20	7: 1-23		
Heals daughter of Syrophenician woman	Phœnicia.	Summer.	15:21-28	7:24-30		
Miracles of healing in Decapolis.	Decapolis.	"	15:29-31	7:31-37		
Feeding the 4,000.	Capernaum.	"	15:32-39	8: 1-10		
Demand for a sign from heaven.	Bethsaida.	"	16: 1-12	8:11-21		
Blind man healed.	Bethsaida.	"		8:22-26		
Peter's great confession of faith.	Near Cesarea-Philippi.	"	16:13-20	8:27-30	9:18-21	
Jesus for the first time foretells his death.	"	"	16:21-28	8:31-9:1	9:22-27	
The Transfiguration.	"	"	17: 1-13	9: 2-13	9:28-36	
Healing of the demoniac boy.	Galilee.	"	17:14-21	9:14-29	9:37-43	
Jesus again foretells his death.	"	"	17:22,23	9:30-32	9:43-45	
Jesus and the children.	Capernaum.	"	18: 1-14	9:33-50	9:46-50	
Unmerciful servant.	"	"	18:15-35			

HARMONY OF THE LIFE OF CHRIST (*Continued*).

DIVISIONS.	YEARS.	EVENTS.	PLACE.	DATE.	MATT.	MARK.	LUKE.	JOHN.
	THIRD YEAR. A.D. 29. YEAR OF DEVELOPMENT. GREAT DEEDS AMID GREAT OPPOSITION.	At the Feast of Tabernacles	Jerusalem	*A.D. 29.* Autumn				7:1-10:21
		The water of Life	"	Oct. 11-18				7:37-39
		Officers sent to arrest him	"	"				7:44-53
		Discourse on light and freedom	"	"				8:12-59
		Healing of man born blind	"	"				9: 1-39
		The Good Shepherd; final departure	"					10: 1-21
		Returns to Galilee	Samaria	Nov.–Dec.			9:51	
		Repulse by the Samaritans	Perea	"			9:51-62	
		The mission of the Seventy	"	"			10: 1-24	
		Parable of the Good Samaritan	"	"			10:25-37	
		Discourse on prayer	"	"			11: 1-13	
		Answers attack of Pharisees	"	"			11:14-54	
		The Rich Fool; the Watchful Servant, etc.	"	"			12: 1-59	
		Discourses: Galileans slain by Pilate; Healing on Sabbath; Parables of mustard seed and leaven; the strait gate; lament over Jerusalem	"	"			13: 1-35	
		Jesus the guest of Mary and Martha	Bethany	Dec. 20-27			10:38-42	
		Feast of Dedication. Discourses	Jerusalem	"				10:22-39
	A.D. 30. THREE MONTHS. CULMINATION OF MIRACLES AND TEACHING.	Jesus retires beyond Jordan into	Perea	*A.D. 30.* January	19:1	10:1		10:40-42
		Dines with a Pharisee	"	"			14: 1-14	
		Parable of the Great Supper	"	"			14:15-24	
		Counting the cost of discipleship	"	"			14:25-35	
		Parables of lost sheep and lost coin	"	"			15: 1-10	
		Parable of prodigal son	"	"			15:11-32	
		Parable of the unjust steward	"	"			16: 1-13	
		Parable of the rich man and Lazarus	"	"			16:14-31	
		Teachings on forgiveness	"	"			17: 1-10	
		Raising of Lazarus	Bethany	February				11: 1-46
		Retreat to Ephraim	Ephraim	Feb, March				11:47-57
		The healing of the ten lepers	Samaria	March			17:11-19	
		On the coming of the kingdom	Perea	"			17:20-37	
		Parable of the importunate widow	"	"			18: 1-8	
		Parable of the Pharisee and publican	"	"			18: 9-14	
		Discourse about divorce	"	"	19: 2-12	10: 2-12		
		Christ blesses little children	"	"	19:13-15	10:13-16	18:15-17	
		The rich young man	"	"	19:16-30	10:17-31	18:18-30	
		The laborers in the vineyard	"	"	20: 1-16			
		Jesus again predicts his death	"	"	20:17-19	10:32-34	18:31-34	
		Ambitious request of James and John	"	"	20:20-28	10:35-45		
		Healing two blind men (one being Bartimeus)	Jericho		20:29-34	10:46-52	18:35-43	
		Visit to Zaccheus the publican	"				19: 1-10	
		Parable of the pounds (Minæ)	"				19:11-28	

Close of the Galilean Ministry. Dec. A.D. 29.

PEREAN MINISTRY (Four or five months). A.D. 30. March.

A. D. 30.

THE LAST WEEK. March 31 to April 7.

Day	Event	Place	Date (A.D. 30)	Matt.	Mark	Luke	John
FRI. MAR. 31.	Jesus arrives at Bethany	Bethany	Friday, Mar. 31				12: 1
SAT. APR. 1.	Anointing by Mary	Bethany	Sat. Apr. 1	26: 6-13	14: 3-9		12: 2-11
SUN. APR. 2.	Triumphal Entry. Visit to Temple. Return to Bethany.	Jerusalem	Sun. Apr. 2	21: 1-11	11: 1-11	19:29-44	12:12-19
MON. APR. 3.	Cursing of barren fig-tree	Mt. of Olives	Mon. Apr. 3	21:18-19	11:12-14		
MON. APR. 3.	Cleansing of the temple and return to Bethany	Jerusalem	"	21:12-17	11:15-19	19:45-48; 21:37,38	
TUES. APR. 4.	The fig-tree withered. Lesson on faith	Mt. of Olives	Tues. Apr. 4	21:20-22	11:20-26		
	Christ's authority challenged	The Temple	"	21:23-27	11:27-33	20: 1-8	
	Three parables of warning:						
	The Two Sons	"	"	21:28-32			
	The Wicked Husbandman	"	"	21:33-46	12: 1-12	20: 9-19	
	Marriage of the king's son	"	"	22: 1-14			
	Three Questions by Jewish rulers	"	"	22:15-40	12:13-34	20:20-40	
	Christ's unanswerable question	"	"	22:41-46	12:35-37	20:41-44	
	Woes against Scribes and Pharisees	"	"	23: 1-36	12:38-40	20:45-47	
	Lamentation over Jerusalem	"	"	23:37-39			
	The Widow's two mites	"	"		12:41-44	21: 1-4	
	Greeks seeking Jesus	"	"				12:20-36
THE LAST DAY OF PUBLIC TEACHING.	Prophecy of the end of the age	Mt. of Olives	"	24: 1-51	13: 1-37	21: 5-36	
	Parable of the ten virgins	"	"	25: 1-13			
	Parable of the talents	"	"	25:14-30			
	The last judgment	"	"	25:31-46			
	Conspiracy between the rulers and Judas	Jerusalem	"	26: 1-5, 14-16	14: 1, 2, 10-11	22: 1-6	
WED. APR. 5.	Jesus in retirement	Bethany	Wed. Apr. 5				
THURS. APR. 6.	Preparation for the Passover	Jerusalem	Thurs. Apr. 6	26:17-20	14:12-17	22: 7-14	
	Strife for precedence	"	"			22:24-30	
	Jesus washes the disciples' feet	"	"			22:15-18	13: 1-20
	The last supper	"	"				
	Jesus declares the betrayer. Judas goes out	"	"	26:21-25	14:18-21	22:21-23	13:21-35 (1Cor.11)
THE LAST DAY WITH HIS DISCIPLES.	Institution of the Lord's Supper	"	"	26:26-30	14:22-25	22:19, 20	13:36-38
	Jesus foretells the fall of Peter	"	"			22:31-38	Chs. 14-
	Christ's farewell Discourses	"	"				17: 1-2
	Prayer of Jesus for the disciples	"	"			22:39	18: 1-3
	Jesus goes forth. Peter's confidence	"	"	26:30-35	14:26-31		
	The Agony in the Garden of Gethsemane	Mt. of Olives	"	26:36-46	14:32-42	22:40-46	

121

HOURS.		EVENTS.	PLACE.	DATE.	MATT.	MARK.	LUKE.	JOHN.
	THE LAST DAY / **FRIDAY, APR. 7.**			**Friday, April 7**				
1–5 A.M.	THE ARREST.	Betrayal by Judas....	....	Midnight....	26:47-50	14:43-45	22:47,48	18: 4-9
		The arrest....	....		26:50-56	14:46-52	22:49-53	18:10-12
5–6 A.M.	THE JEWISH TRIAL.	The trial before Annas	Jerusalem....	1–5 A.M.	....	....	....	18:13-15
		Before Caiaphas	"	"	26:57,58	14:53,54	22:54,55	18:19-24
		Before the Sanhedrin	"	"	26:59-66	14:55-64	....	18:15-18, 25-27
		Denials by Peter....	"		26:69-75	14:66-72	22:56-62	....
		Mockery by enemies....	"	5–6 A.M.	26:67,68	14:65	22:63-65	....
		Legal meeting of Sanhedrin; Jesus condemned for blasphemy....	"		27: 1,2	15:1	22:66-71; 23:1	....
		Death of Judas....	"		27: 3-10	....	(Acts 1: 18, 19)	....
6–9 A.M.	THE ROMAN TRIAL.	Jesus before Pilate....	"	6–9 A.M.	27:11-14	15: 2-5	23: 2-5	18:28-38
		Jesus sent to Herod....	"	"	....	....	23: 6-12	....
		Pilate seeks to release Jesus; people demand Barabbas....	"	"	27:15-23	15: 6-14	23:13-23	18:38-40
		Jesus condemned, scourged and mocked....	"	"	27:26-30	15:15-19	23:24,25	19: 1-3
		"Ecce Homo." Other attempts by Pilate to release Jesus....	"	"	27:24,25	....	....	19: 4-16
9 A.M. to 3 P.M.	THE CRUCIFIXION.	Jesus led away to be crucified....	"	9 A.M.	27:31-34, 38	15:20,23, 27, 28	23:26-32	19:16-18
		The superscription....	"	"	27:37	15:26	23:38	19:19-22
		First word from the cross: "*Father, forgive them,*" etc....	"	"	....	....	23:33,34	....
		Soldiers cast lots for garments....	"	"	27:35,36	15:24	23:34	19:23,24
		Jews mock at Jesus on the cross....	"	"	27:39-44	15:29-32	23:35-37	....
		Second word from the cross: to the penitent thief....	"	"	....	....	23:39-43	....
		Third word: "*Woman, behold thy son.*"....	"	12 M.	....	....	....	19:25-27
		Darkness covers the land....	"	"	27:45	15:33	23:44,45	....
		Fourth word: cry of distress to God....	"	"	27:46,47	15:34,35	....	....
		Fifth word: "*I thirst*"....	"	"	27:48,49	15:36	....	19:28,29
		Sixth word: "*It is finished.*"....	"	3 P.M.	....	....	....	19:30
		Seventh word: "*Into thy hands,*" etc....	"	"	....	....	23:46	....
		Jesus dies. Veil rent. Earthquake....	"	"	27:50-56	15:37-41	23:45-49	....
		Jesus is pierced in the side....	"		....	....	....	19:31-37
3–6 P.M.	THE BURIAL.	The burial....	....	3–6 P.M.	27:57-61	15:42-47	23:50-56	19:38-42

RESURRECTION DAYS A.D. 30.

Period	Event	Place	Date	(Matt.)	(Mark)	(Luke)	(John)
THREE DAYS IN THE TOMB. Parts of April 7, 8, 9.	The watch at the tomb	Jerusalem	Sat., April 8	27:62-66			
	The morning of the resurrection	"	Sunday, April 9	28: 2-4		24: 1,2	20:1
	Women come to the tomb	"	"	28:1	16: 1-4		20:2
	Mary Magdalene calls Peter and John	"	"				20:2
	The women at the tomb	"	"	28: 5-8	16: 5-8	24: 3-8	
	Peter and John at the tomb	"	"			24:12	20: 3-10
	Jesus appears to Mary Magdalene	"	"		16: 9-11		20:11-18
	Jesus appears to the women	"	"	28: 9,10		24: 9-11	
	The guards report to the priests	"	"	28:11-15			
40 RESURRECTION DAYS. April 9 to May 18.	The walk to Emmaus	Emmaus	"		16:12,13	24:13-35	
	Jesus appears to Peter	Jerusalem	"	(1 Cor. 15:5)		24:34	
	Jesus appears to the Apostles except Thomas	"	"	(1 Cor. 15:5)	16:14	24:36-48	20:19-23
	Jesus appears to all the Apostles, including Thomas	"	......				20:24-29
	Jesus appears to seven in Galilee	Sea of Galilee	April				21: 1-23
	Appears to over 500 at once	"	April, May	28:16-20	16:15-18	(1 Cor. 15:6)	
	Jesus appears to James	"	"			(1 Cor. 15:7)	
	Jesus appears to the apostles	Jerusalem	"			24:49	Acts 1:1-18
THE ASCENSION. May 18.	Jesus ascends to heaven	Bethany, Mt. of Olives	Thurs., May 18		16:19	24:50-53	Acts 1:9-12
	The conclusions of Mark and John	......	......		16:20		20:30,31; 21:24,25
BIRTH OF THE CHURCH. May 28.	Holy Spirit given at Pentecost	Jerusalem	......			Acts 2:1-11	
CONTINUED LIFE OF JESUS.	Jesus appears to Paul	Damascus	A.D. 36			(Acts 22:6-16)	
	Jesus appears to John	Patmos	A.D. 68 or 96				(Rev. 1:9-20)

CHART OF THE LIFE OF JESUS CHRIST.

Life of Jesus

ANCESTRY. On one side God himself. On the other every phase of character, every human tendency represented in his genealogy.

PREPARATIONS FOR HIS COMING.

1. Universal peace.
2. One empire.
3. One language generally known.
4. The Jews with the Scriptures in all lands.
5. A general awakening.

Birth of Jesus about December, B.C. 5.

CHILDHOOD AND YOUTH.

1. Home training.
2. Bible study.
3. Schooling.
4. Different languages.
5. Travel to Jerusalem.
6. Great religious meetings.
7. Village life.
8. Work at a trade.
9. Knowledge of his country's history and hopes.
10. A perfect and beautiful character.

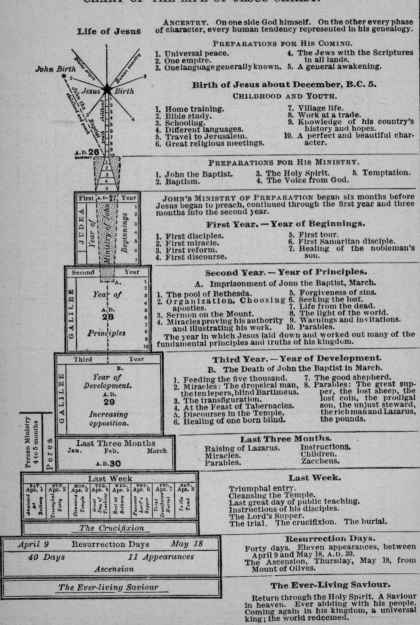

PREPARATIONS FOR HIS MINISTRY.

1. John the Baptist.
2. Baptism.
3. The Holy Spirit.
4. The Voice from God.
5. Temptation.

First A.D. 27 Year — JUDEA — Year of Ministry of John — Beginnings

JOHN'S MINISTRY OF PREPARATION began six months before Jesus began to preach, continued through the first year and three months into the second year.

First Year. — Year of Beginnings.

1. First disciples.
2. First miracle.
3. First reform.
4. First discourse.
5. First tour.
6. First Samaritan disciple.
7. Healing of the nobleman's son.

Second Year — GALILEE — Year of — A.D. 28 — Principles

Second Year. — Year of Principles.

A. Imprisonment of John the Baptist, March.

1. The pool of Bethesda.
2. Organization. Choosing apostles.
3. Sermon on the Mount.
4. Miracles proving his authority and illustrating his work.
5. Forgiveness of sins.
6. Seeking the lost.
7. Life from the dead.
8. The light of the world.
9. Warnings and invitations.
10. Parables.

The year in which Jesus laid down and worked out many of the fundamental principles and truths of his kingdom.

Third Year — GALILEE — Year of Development. — A.D. 29 — Increasing opposition.

Third Year. — Year of Development.

B. The Death of John the Baptist in March.

1. Feeding the five thousand.
2. Miracles: The dropsical man, the ten lepers, blind Bartimeus.
3. The transfiguration.
4. At the Feast of Tabernacles.
5. Discourses in the Temple.
6. Healing of one born blind.
7. The good shepherd.
8. Parables: The great supper, the lost sheep, the lost coin, the prodigal son, the unjust steward, the rich man and Lazarus, the pounds.

Perean Ministry 4 to 5 months — Perea

Last Three Months — Jan. Feb. March — A.D. 30

Last Three Months.

Raising of Lazarus. — Instructions.
Miracles. — Children.
Parables. — Zaccheus.

Last Week — SAT. Apr. 1 Anointed at Bethany | SUN. Apr. 2 Triumphal Entry | MON. Apr. 3 Cleansing Temple | TUE. Apr. 4 Great Day of Teaching | WED. Apr. 5 Rest at Bethany | THU. Apr. 6 Passover Lord's Supper | FRI. Apr. 7 Trial Crucifixion Burial | SAT. Apr. 8 In the Tomb

The Crucifixion

Last Week.

Triumphal entry.
Cleansing the Temple.
Last great day of public teaching.
Instructions of his disciples.
The Lord's Supper.
The trial. The crucifixion. The burial.

April 9 Resurrection Days May 18 — 40 Days — 11 Appearances — Ascension

Resurrection Days.

Forty days. Eleven appearances, between April 9 and May 18, A.D. 30.
The Ascension, Thursday, May 18, from Mount of Olives.

The Ever-living Saviour

The Ever-Living Saviour.

Return through the Holy Spirit. A Saviour in heaven. Ever abiding with his people. Coming again in his kingdom, a universal king; the world redeemed.

THE APOSTLES AND THEIR HISTORY.

	NAME.	SURNAME.	PARENTS.	HOME.	BUSINESS.	WRITINGS.	WORK.	DEATH.
1	Simon.	Peter } = Rock. Cephas }	Jonah.	Early Life: Bethsaida. Later: Capernaum.	Fisherman.	1 Peter, 2 Peter. (Mark?).	A missionary among the Jews, as far as Babylon, 1 Pet. 5:13. Probably = Rome.	Trad.: Crucified head downward, at Rome.
2	Andrew.		Jonah.	Early Life: Bethsaida. Later: Capernaum.	Fisherman.		Tradition. Preached in Scythia, Greece, and Asia Minor.	Trad.: Crucified on St. Andrew's cross (X).
3	James the greater or elder.	Boanerges, or Sons of Thunder.	Zebedee and Salome.	Bethsaida and afterward in Jerusalem.	Fisherman.		Preached in Jerusalem and Judea.	Beheaded by Herod, A.D. 44, at Jerusalem.
4	John, the beloved disciple.				Fisherman.	Gospel. 3 Epistles. Revelation.	Labored among the churches of Asia Minor, especially Ephesus.	Banished to Patmos, A.D. 95. Recalled. Died a natural death. Trad.
5	James the less or younger.		Alpheus or Cleophas and Mary.	Galilee.		(Epistle of James?).	Preached in Palestine and Egypt. Bishop of Jerusalem(?).	Trad.: Crucified in Egypt; or thrown from a pinnacle.
6	Jude.	Same as Thaddeus and Lebbeus.		Galilee.		Epistle	Preached in Assyria and Persia. Trad.	Martyred in Persia. Trad.
7	Philip.			Bethsaida.			Preached in Phrygia.	Died martyr at Hierapolis in Phrygia. Trad.
8	Bartholomew.	Nathaniel.		Cana of Galilee.				Flayed to death. Trad.
9	Matthew.	Levi.	Alpheus.	Capernaum.	Tax collector.	Gospel.		Trad.: Died a martyr in Ethiopia.
10	Thomas.	Didymus.		Galilee.			Claimed by the Syrian Christians as the founder of their church; perhaps also in Persia and India.	Trad.: Shot by arrows while at prayer.
11	Simon.	The Cananaean, or Zelotes.		Galilee.				Trad.: Crucified.
12	Judas.	Iscariot.		Kerioth of Judea.				Suicide.

Acts.	Events.	Place.	Date A.D.*	Contemporary History.
1: 1–3	Resurrection days................	Galilee...........	30. April, May	Tiberius, emperor, 14–37 A.D.
1: 4–12	Commission to Apostles and Ascension....................	Bethany........	30. May 18	Pontius Pilate, procurator, 26–36.
1: 13, 14	Waiting for the promise of the Father..........................	Jerusalem, in an upper room.	30	PAUL enters public life, A.D. 29, aged 30.
1: 15–26	Election of Matthias to take the place of Judas...............	" ...	....	
2: 1–13	Pentecost: the Gift of Tongues..	Jerusalem......	....	Seneca. 4 B.C.–65 A.D.
2: 14–36	Peter's address.................	"	....	Essays and Tragedies.
2: 37–41	The first converts: 3000.........	"	....	
2: 42–47	The early church................	"	....	
3: 1–10	The lame man healed............	Temple courts..	....	Gamaliel. 30–40 A.D.
3: 11–26	Second address by Peter	"	....	
4: 1–22	The first persecution: Peter and John imprisoned...........	Jerusalem......	....	Philo Judæus. 20 B.C.— after 40 A.D.
4: 23–37	A fresh baptism of the Spirit....	"	....	
5: 1–11	Ananias and Sapphira...........	"	30	
5: 12–16	Spread of Gospel in Jerusalem..	"	to	
5: 17–42	Second persecution: Sanhedrin.	"	34	
6: 1–7	Appointment of deacons........	"	35	
6: 8–15	Preaching of Stephen...........	"	35 to 36	Deposition of Pontius Pilate. 36.
7: 1–60	Martyrdom of Stephen..........	"	36	
8: 1–4	General persecution............			Sent to Rome for trial.
8: 5–25	Philip the Evangelist in.........	Samaria.........	....	Vitellius takes his place as governor.
8: 26–40	Philip and the Ethiopian........	Road to Gaza..	....	
9: 1–22 (Gal. 1: 17)	Conversion of Saul of Tarsus.... Saul in Arabia...............	Near Damascus.	....	PAUL, aged 37. Death of Tiberius, 16 March, 37.
9: 23–27	St. Paul persecuted; escapes....	Damascus......	38	Accession of Caligula.
9: 28–29	St. Paul preaches in Jerusalem..	Jerusalem......	....	Release of Herod Agrippa I.
9: 30	St. Paul goes to Cilicia.........	Tarsus, etc.....	38–40	
9: 31–35	St. Peter cures Æneas..........	Lydda..........	....	Banishment of Antipas, 39.
9: 36–42	Dorcas restored to life..........	Joppa..........	....	
10: 1–48	Cornelius the Centurion converted.....................	Cæsarea......	41	Caligula orders his statue to be set up at Jerusalem.
11: 1–18	The question of admitting the Gentiles	Jerusalem......	....	Claudius Emperor, Jan. 24, 41, to Oct. 13, 54.
11: 19–21	First Gentile church............	Antioch........	38–41	Seneca in exile, 41–49.
	Herod Agrippa I, King of Judea.		41	
11: 22, 23	Barnabas at Antioch...........	Antioch........	42, 43	
11: 25, 26	Paul called from Tarsus to Antioch	"	42, 43	Romans in Britain, 43.
12: 1, 2	Martyrdom of St. James.........	Jerusalem.....	44. Spring	
12: 3–18	Imprisonment and deliverance of St. Peter................	"	44. Spring	Death of Herod Agrippa I, 44.
12: 19–23	Death of Herod Agrippa I.......	Cæsarea........	44. Early Summer	London founded, 47.
11: 27–30	Famine. Relief sent to Jerusalem by Barnabas and Saul....		44–46	
12: 24, 25	Return of Saul and Barnabas with John Mark to...........	Antioch........	46	Expulsion of Jews from Rome, 48 (?)
13: 1–14: 28	**First Missionary Journey** by Saul and Barnabas.	Asia Minor.....	March 47 to 49	
13: 1–3	Ordained as missionaries.......	Antioch........	....	
13: 4–52	In Cyprus and Antioch of Pisidia.	Asia Minor.....	....	
14: 1–20	In Iconium, Lystra, Derbe......	"	....	
14: 21–25	Revisiting the churches........	"	49	
14: 26–28	Report to home church..........	Antioch........	49	Caractacus defeated in Britain.
15: 1–35	Council at Jerusalem...........	Jerusalem......	50	
15: 40–18: 22	**Second Missionary Journey** by St. Paul and Silas	Asia Minor and Greece........	50–52	
16: 1–5	Revisiting the churches	Asia Minor.....	50–52	
16: 6–11	St. Paul enters Europe.........	Macedonia.....	50–52	
16: 12–40	St. Paul at Philippi; Lydia; conversion of jailer...........	Philippi........	50–52	
17: 1–14	St. Paul in Thessalonica and Berea.	Macedonia.....	....	Gallio pro-consul at Corinth.
17: 15–34	St. Paul at Athens............. .	Greece..........	51–52	

NOTE I. The dates in this column are the prevalent ones, and are sufficiently accurate for understanding the course of the history. Almost every writer on Acts differs slightly from them, but only slightly.

CHRONOLOGY OF THE ACTS (*Continued*).

ACTS.	EVENTS.	PLACE.	DATE A.D.	CONTEMPORARY HISTORY.
18: 1–18	St. Paul at Corinth. Crispus....	Greece..........	51–52	
	1 and 2 Thessalonians...........			
18:18–22	Returns home via Ephesus and Cæsarea to....	Antioch..........	51–52	Felix, procurator, 52–59.
18: 22	Brief visit to Jerusalem........	Jerusalem......	....	
18: 22,23	St. Paul in Antioch.............	Syria............	52	Nero, emperor, 54–68.
	Galatians...................			
18: 23–21: 16	**Third Missionary Journey** by Paul.	Asia Minor and Greece........	53–57	Birth of Tacitus, 55.
18: 24–28	Apollos at Ephesus.............	Asia Minor......	....	St. Peter at Corinth, 55 or 56.
19: 1–11	St. Paul nearly three years at...	Ephesus......	53–56	
	1 Corinthians.................	"	56	
19:12–20	Sceva the Exorcist.............	"		
19: 21–41	Riot at Ephesus. Diana........	"		
20: 1–5	St. Paul revisits Macedonia....	Macedonia.....	57	
	2 Corinthians	"		
	St. Paul three months at Corinth.	Greece..........		
	Romans.....................			
20: 6–12	St. Paul at Troas. Eutychus....	Troas..........		
20: 13–16	Sails to Miletus...............			
20:17–38	Address to Ephesian elders at...	Miletus........	57	
21: 1–16	Journey by Tyre and Cæsarea to	Jerusalem......		
21: 17–20	St. Paul's reception by church..	Jerusalem......		
21: 21–40	St. Paul's arrest in Temple.....	"		
22: 1–23: 11	St. Paul a prisoner in Castle of Antonia.................	"		
23:12–22	The conspiracy against Paul's life.	"		
23: 23–35	St. Paul sent secretly to........	Cæsarea........		
24: 1–22	St. Paul's trial before Felix....	"		
24: 23–27	St. Paul in prison two years at..	"	57	Festus, procurator, 59–63.
25: 1–12	St. Paul accused to Festus. He appeals to Cæsar..........	"	59	*St. Luke's Gospel* probably written.
25: 13–26: 32	St. Paul before Festus and Agrippa...................	"		
27: 1–44	St. Paul's voyage and shipwreck.	Mediterranean.	Sept. 59	
28: 1–10	St. Paul on the Island of Malta..	"	60	Nero murders Agrippina.
28: 11–29	St. Paul at Rome: Conference with the Jews................	Rome..........		
28: 30, 31	Paul a prisoner in his own hired house at.............	"	61, 62	
	Colossians, Philemon, Ephesians....................	"		Rebellion of Boadicea in Britain.
	Philippians.................	"		Boadicea defeated by Suetonius about 62.
	Close of the history in the *Acts*..	....		
	*Probable composition of *Acts*..	Rome..........	62–68	
	First trial. Release............	"	63	Great earthquake at Pompeii.
	James		62 or earlier	
	Hebrews (?).................			
	Goes to Asia by way of Macedonia.			
	Sails with Titus to Crete and returns to Ephesus.......			Great Fire of Rome, ascribed by Nero to the Christians, July 19, 64.
	Leaving Timothy goes by Philippi to Corinth.............			
	1, 2, Peter..................		58–64	
	1 Timothy. Titus...........			
	Journey to Spain (?)...........			
	Winters at Nicopolis...........			
	Journey to Dalmatia (?) and through Macedonia to Troas...	....		
	Martyrdom of St. Peter........	....	65	
	St. Paul's second arrest. Sent to Rome................		66	
	Trial before Emperor..........			Jewish war begins.
	2 Timothy................	Rome..........		Massacre by Florus at Jerusalem.
	Martyrdom of St. Paul.........	"	66 or 67	Repulse of Cestius Gallus.
	Destruction of Jerusalem.......		Aug. 70	
	Jude. 1, 2, 3, John...........			

NOTE II. What follows in this column is based chiefly on tradition and probability. But authorities vary both as to dates and fact. The events after this point refer to St. Paul's life when not definitely connected with another.

ENGLISH VERSIONS OF THE BIBLE.

Translations of the Psalter, Gospels and other portions of the Scriptures were made into Anglo-Saxon as early as the eighth century, and into English of the thirteenth century. These translations had no traceable effect on the English Bible.

WYCLIF'S VERSION (1380). — Wyclif, with some of his followers, translated the entire Bible into English from the Latin Vulgate. Being accomplished before the days of printing, it existed only in MS. form up until 1848 or 1850, when it was published in type.

TINDALE'S NEW TESTAMENT (1525). — William Tindale began the publication of his translation of the New Testament in Cologne in 1525. Being compelled to flee, he finished the publication in Worms. Three thousand copies of quarto size were printed. These Testaments began to reach England in 1526, and were burned by order of the bishops, who bought the whole edition for that purpose. Tindale used this money to print his new edition in 1534.

TINDALE'S PENTATEUCH (1530). — This was published in Mardeburg, Hesse.

TINDALE'S NEW TESTAMENT (1534). — Tindale's New Testament, carefully revised throughout by the translator, was printed at Antwerp and paid for with the money paid for the older edition.

COVERDALE'S BIBLE (1535). — This was the first version of the entire Bible published in English.

MATTHEW'S BIBLE (1537). — This was made up of Tindale's Pentateuch and New Testament, and completed from Coverdale for the rest of the Old Testament and Apocrypha, the whole edited by John Rogers. It was probably printed at Antwerp, but was published in London with the license of King Henry VIII, thus becoming the first "authorized version."

TAVERNER'S BIBLE (1539). — An edition of Matthew's Bible, edited by Taverner.

THE GREAT BIBLE (1539). — This was a new edition of Matthew's Bible, revised and compared with the Hebrew by Coverdale, and published in England under the sanction of Thomas Cromwell in 1539.

THE GENEVA BIBLE (1560). — Two years after the accession of Elizabeth an entirely new edition of the Bible was printed at Geneva. Three men out of a company of English refugees and reformers at Geneva began this work, in January, 1558, and finished it in April, 1560. This was the most scholarly English Bible that had yet appeared. It was of handy size and clear Roman type. It became for a period of seventy-five years *the* Bible of the English people. Because of the rendering in Gen. 3. 7, it became known as the "Breeches" Bible.

THE BISHOPS' BIBLE (1568). — The rapid popularity of the Geneva Bible was not acceptable to Elizabeth and her bishops, who did not sympathize with Genevan church views and polity. Therefore, a revision of the Great Bible was made, at the suggestion of Archbishop Parker, by fifteen theologians, eight of whom were bishops. A second edition of the Bishops' Bible appeared in 1572.

REIMS NEW TESTAMENT (1582). — This translation was made from the Latin Vulgate, and was published in 1583 at Reims. At the same time and place the New Testament portion of the Douay, or Roman Catholic, version appeared.

AUTHORIZED VERSION (1611). — There is no evidence that this version was authorized in any special way. It won its place, under royal and ecclesiastical patronage, by its merits. The work had its inception at Hampton Court Conference in 1604, and was promoted by James I, who approved a list of fifty-four scholars to be assigned to the undertaking. Of these but forty-seven appear to have taken part.

The central thought was "not to make a new translation, nor yet to make of a bad one a good one, but to make a good one better." The A. V. was, therefore, not a new translation, but a thorough and scholarly revision of an already good version.

THE REVISED VERSION (1881-85). — The King James or Authorized Version stood practically untouched for 270 years. True, many small changes had been introduced into the text by successive printers, but no authoritative revision had taken place. It began to be felt that revision was needed.

Accordingly, in 1870, the English Houses of Convocation appointed two bodies of revisers, consisting of twenty-five for the Old Testament and twenty-five for the New. Among other rules adopted for their guidance, they were to introduce as few changes as possible into the A. V. text; adopt no text except the evidence in favor of it greatly preponderated; make or retain no change in the text on final revision except two-thirds of those present approved.

Two similar companies of American scholars co-operated in the work. The Revised New Testament was issued in 1881, and the Revised Bible in 1885. The work as completed was a decidedly forward step in English Biblical scholarship.

THE AMERICAN STANDARD VERSION of 1901. — The American Committee of the Revisers of the 1881 Revision dissented from some of the decisions of their English associates, a partial list of which was placed in the Appendix. But the American company retained their organization, and for 20 years worked upon a new Revision which was issued in 1901 by the Nelsons of Edinburgh. "In details it shows but slight and infrequent deviations from its predecessor." But it retains largely the solid paragraphing which made the 1881 Revision so difficult to use by ordinary readers. Still in many details it is superior to the former Revision.

Yet with all the aid afforded by the Revised Version to the Bible reader and student, the Authorized Version still retains its wonted place in the popular heart.

THE DATE OF EASTER.

EASTER is the first Sunday after the full moon that occurs on or next after March 21; and if the full moon fall on Sunday, Easter is the next Sunday. Of course, if the date were the same each year, the day would be Sunday only once in six years. Some of the early Christians did fix the date in this way, while others used the present way. But in the year 325 the matter was brought by Constantine before the Council of Nice, and it was evidently thought best that the anniversary of the event which they thought changed the Sabbath from the seventh day of the week to the first day, should always fall upon the first day; for they, deciding between the two ways then in use, selected for the whole church the method which would bring Easter always on Sunday.

Since that decision, Easter cannot fall earlier than March 22, nor later than April 25, in any year. These dates are called the "Easter Limits."

The most of the other holy days of the church depend for their dates upon the date of Easter.

LENT begins 46 days before Easter, with *Ash Wednesday*. Sundays being always feast days, not fast days, this gives 40 days of fasting.

Palm Sunday is the Sunday before Easter.

Good Friday is the Friday before Easter.

Passion Week is the week ending with Palm Sunday.

Holy Week is the week ending with Easter.

WHITSUNDAY or *Pentecost* is 7 weeks after Easter.